Mac OS® X Tiger™

UNLEASHED

John Ray and William Ray

SAMS 800 East 96th Street, Indianapolis, Indiana 46240

Mac OS X Tiger Unleashed

International Standard Book Number: 0-672-32746-5

Library of Congress Catalog Card Number: 2004097472

Printed in the United States of America

First Printing: July 2005

08 07 06 05 4 3 2 1

Trademarks

All terms mentioned in this book that are known to be trademarks or service marks have been appropriately capitalized. Sams Publishing cannot attest to the accuracy of this information. Use of a term in this book should not be regarded as affecting the validity of any trademark or service mark.

Warning and Disclaimer

Every effort has been made to make this book as complete and as accurate as possible, but no warranty or fitness is implied. The information provided is on an "as is" basis.

Bulk Sales

Sams Publishing offers excellent discounts on this book when ordered in quantity for bulk purchases or special sales. For more information, please contact

U.S. Corporate and Government Sales
1-800-382-3419
corpsales@pearsontechgroup.com

For sales outside of the U.S., please contact

International Sales
international@pearsoned.com

Acquisitions Editor
Betsy Brown

Development Editor
Damon Jordan

Managing Editor
Charlotte Clapp

Project Editor
George E. Nedeff

Copy Editor
Mike Henry

Indexer
Larry Sweazy

Technical Editor
Terry Talbot

Publishing Coordinator
Vanessa Evans

Book Designer
Gary Adair

Page Layout
Eric S. Miller

Contents at a Glance

Table of Contents

Part II Hardware Setup and Configuration

About the Lead Authors

John Ray is the Senior Systems Engineer for The Ohio State University Extension and College of Food, Agricultural and Environmental Sciences. He is responsible for managing computer services for the OSU CFAES campus and Extension offices throughout the state. John also provides custom network, security, and programming solutions for clients across the country, including the National Regulatory Research Institute and the Brevard Metropolitan Planning Organization in Florida. A Macintosh owner and programmer since 1984, John has written/contributed to numerous titles including *Maximum Mac OS X Security*, *Sams Teach Yourself Macromedia Studio MX 2004 All in One*, *Sams Teach Yourself Mac OS X*, and *Tiger All In One*.

William Ray is a mathematician turned computer scientist turned biophysicist who has gravitated to the field of bioinformatics for its interesting synergy of logic, hard science, and human-computer-interface issues. A longtime Macintosh and Unix enthusiast, Will has owned Macs since 1985 and has worked with Unix since 1987. Prior to switching his professional focus to the biological sciences, Will spent five years as a Unix programmer developing experimental interfaces to online database systems. Shortly after migrating to biophysics, Will developed a Macintosh and Unix-based computational biology/graphics laboratory and training center for The Ohio State University's College of Biological Sciences. At the facility, which he managed for five years, Will introduced hundreds of students and faculty to Unix, and provided training and assistance in the development of productive computing skills on the paired Macintosh and Unix platforms. Will is currently a Professor of Pediatrics at the Columbus Children's Research Institute Children's Hospital in Columbus, Ohio, and the Department of Pediatrics, The Ohio State University, where he is investigating tools that work at the interface between humans, computers, and information, and working to build a core computational research and training facility for his institute.

Contributing Author

Joan Ray (Contributing Author) is a Unix system administrator and webmaster for the College of Biological Sciences at The Ohio State University. Joan has a degree in French from OSU and is working toward additional degrees in Japanese and geology.

When not helping with this or other books, Joan is administering a cluster of SGI and Sun Unix workstations and servers; helping and providing training for users with Unix, Classic Mac OS, and Mac OS X questions; and serving as college webmaster.

Dedication

This book is dedicated too.—John

For Sage, whose appreciation of this book and Mac OS X grows with each release, and for Will, who is just starting to compute.—Will

Acknowledgments

As always, many thanks to Betsy Brown for managing this behemoth project, *Terence Talbot* for finding the errors that have an annoying tendency to creep in, and Damon Jordan, George Nedeff, and Mike Henry for making "sentences" that we type at 2 a.m. actually turn into something coherent.

We Want to Hear from You!

As the reader of this book, *you* are our most important critic and commentator. We value your opinion and want to know what we're doing right, what we could do better, what areas you'd like to see us publish in, and any other words of wisdom you're willing to pass our way.

You can email or write me directly to let me know what you did or didn't like about this book—as well as what we can do to make our books stronger.

Please note that I cannot help you with technical problems related to the topic of this book, and that due to the high volume of mail I receive, I might not be able to reply to every message.

When you write, please be sure to include this book's title and author as well as your name and phone or email address. I will carefully review your comments and share them with the author and editors who worked on the book.

Email: consumer@samspublishing.com

Mail: Mark Taber
Associate Publisher
Sams Publishing
800 East 96th Street
Indianapolis, IN 46240 USA

Reader Services

For more information about this book or another Sams Publishing title, visit our website at www.samspublishing.com. Type the ISBN (excluding hyphens) or the title of a book in the Search field to find the page you're looking for.

Introduction

Welcome to Tiger

When Mac OS X 10.0 (or the "second" public beta, as some referred to it) was released in 2000, how many of us really thought that we'd still be in love with it five years later? As much as I adore Apple and the products it produces, I had my own trepidations as to whether we'd all give up and be living on Windows (or, more realistically, Linux) in 2005.

Thankfully, Mac OS X has been a great success and has generated a steady stream of accolades from enterprise computing publications. Just today (early January 2005), InfoWorld released its "Technology of the Year" awards for 2004, including "Best Operating System: Mac OS X 10.3 Panther" and "Best Server Hardware: Apple Xserve G5."

Things will only get better with Tiger.

What's New Pussycat?

The first step in writing a book about Tiger is using the operating system. We've been running it for several months now, picking at the pieces, experimenting with the applications, and so on. Inevitably one of us has to end up writing the "what's new" section of the book—and it's usually close to the last piece that gets typed up. By then, however, we're faced with two problems: First, there are so many new things that we could list, picking only a few seems inherently wrong; second, many of the features are so well integrated that they seem to have always been a part of Mac OS X—at least until we sit down in front of an old Panther installation.

So, what *do* we consider the most outstanding new features? Let's take a quick look at what you can expect. Don't be surprised if your favorite new feature isn't listed here. This is our personal take on what will be the most influential new features in your Tiger experience.

- Spotlight—The Spotlight search, combined with the new Tiger file-system metadata, enables information searches that have never before been possible. These features are integrated into the Finder, Open/Save dialogs, and can be added to third-party applications. The days of organizing information into discrete folders are coming to an end.

- Dashboard—The Classic Mac OS provided near instant access to tiny, unobtrusive applications called *Desk Accessories*. Desk Accessories went away with the first release of Mac OS X, but have been reborn in the form of the Dashboard. This "instant-on" overlay of useful (and fun!) programs brings an entirely new dynamic to the traditional operating system desktop.

- Automator—AppleScript is great, but it requires its user to have at least basic programming skills. With the release of Automator in Tiger, Apple brings the power of application scripting to a purely visual environment. Automator enables even the most technically challenged individuals to author linear application workflows in seconds.

- Darwin/HFS+ Compatibility—Ever make a mistake and `cp` or `tar` a Mac file with a resource fork? In Tiger, you'll have no problem. Apple provides cross-platform support in the Darwin core for managing Tiger's special metadata, resource forks, and so forth. Common BSD utilities can now properly cope with Mac-specific data.
- Sync Services—Your premium-priced .Mac account is finally going to get a workout! Apple has recently expanded iDisk storage and introduced expanded .Mac Sync features in Tiger. You can now replicate your most important account settings between machines by way of .Mac syncing.
- `launchd`—Not satisfied with the transition from `inetd` to `xinetd`, Apple has *again* decided to change how processes are started. We have some thoughts on this, and we won't hesitate to share them with you.
- Filesystem/Userland Synchronization—When a file is updated, it is almost instantly reindexed for inclusion in Spotlight. The integration of file system and user interface doesn't end there. For the first time *ever* in Mac OS X, when you create a file at the command line or otherwise, it will immediately be displayed in the Finder. No more wondering when and where a file will appear. If it exists, you can see it.
- Enhanced Internet Experience—Safari, Mail, and iChat have all seen significant updates. Mail sports a new interface and *finally* updates IMAP mailboxes quickly and correctly. Safari supports RSS feeds and serves as an easy-to-use aggregator. Finally, iChat connects to Jabber servers and can host multiperson video and audio conferencing.
- Access Control Lists—Access Control Lists *(ACLs)* provide extremely granular control over file permissions—beyond what is easily accomplished by basic owner and group settings. Tiger's support for ACLs will go a long way toward helping its adoption into the workplace.
- VoiceOver—After years of going without, Mac OS X now provides a high-quality screen reader feature for the visually impaired. Because VoiceOver is integrated with the operating system, it can work with any application and give an audible play-by-play of onscreen actions.
- Parental Controls—Tiger provides much more strict controls over what a user account can do and what Internet features it can access. For those sharing a machine with children, this is a much-needed addition.

Again, these are just what we consider to be the most notable of what's new in Tiger. As you work with the operating system, you'll discover just how many tweaks and changes have been made. Apple certainly hasn't been sitting still in the last 18 months.

Mac OS X Tiger Unleashed

By its very design, Mac OS X accomplishes two seemingly contradictory goals. It creates an easy-to-use system that is crash-resistant and resilient to user error. First-time users can sit down in front of the system, find the tools they need, and immediately start working. At the same time, advanced users have complete access to an underlying Unix subsystem, advanced networking capabilities, and a wealth of Open Source technologies including the Apache web server, Perl, Postfix, and many other powerful applications.

We've now been working on this book for almost five years, and with each revision of the operating system, we try to evaluate what you, the reader, will find most useful. We must balance the ever-increasing feature set of the operating system with the finite space of this book. For example: Gone from this edition is the no-longer-free iLife suite. We still provide everything you need to use the core Tiger software effectively, but dedicating 300 pages to applications that were designed to be used without needing an instruction manual (and don't come with the operating system) wasn't a good use of space.

At the same time iLife was removed, we beefed up other areas of the text, such as writing a chapter on setting up QuickTime Streaming Server and QuickTime Broadcaster, including spam and virus filtering in the Postfix mail server chapter, adding a how-to for creating dynamic Safari-compatible RSS feeds, and much more. The content itself has also been reorganized and topic headings rewritten to provide quicker and easier access to the information you need.

Reading through the book, you might be surprised to find that we question how a number of operating system features have been implemented, and are sometimes vocally critical of Apple's design decisions. Although there are many things we love about the operating system, there are still plenty of headache-inducing "gotchas" that crop up from time to time, and we'll do what we can to steer you clear of them.

Mac OS X will grow and update frequently as Apple continues its efforts to provide an optimal user and server platform. As we work to create this resource, we will make every attempt to present the latest and most accurate Mac OS X information available. Be aware that to get this book on the shelves before the *next* version of Mac OS X ships, we often have to work with software that is beta quality. In addition, Apple provides periodic updates to Mac OS X throughout the year. If you find an example that no longer works as you'd expect, drop us a note and we'll try to find an answer for you.

Comments, suggestions, and questions, are always welcomed.

Sincerely,

John Ray (`jray@macosxunleashed.com`)

William Ray (`wray@macosxunleashed.com`)

PART I

Using Mac OS X

IN THIS PART

CHAPTER 1

Managing the Tiger Workspace

IN THIS CHAPTER

- Getting Started
- Using the Tiger Finder
- Using the Dock
- Accessing Common Functions Through Menu Extras
- Force Quitting Applications
- Managing Windows with Exposé
- Using the Dashboard
- Using Fast User Switching
- Help Viewer

Before you can actually sit down and be productive with a computer, you must master the basics of using it. How do you navigate the drive? How do you find and manipulate files? And, most importantly, how can you change the desktop background to a picture of your (or your neighbors') kids? This chapter covers the components of Tiger that help you customize your workspace and the files, applications, and plethora of windows you're bound to have covering your screen.

Getting Started

What? Introductory material? You've got to be kidding me! Don't worry, we won't trouble you with an entire chapter of how to click your mouse, but you *will* need to know a handful of things to successfully use your computer:

- Apple menu—The menu on the upper-left side of the menu bar contains the functions you need to log out and shut down your system. You'll also find a few shortcuts to commonly used features here.
- Application menus—Each running application has a menu titled with the application name. This is called the *Application menu* and typically contains application preference settings.
- System preferences—The System Preferences application contains all the various esoteric settings for Tiger. You can access it from the Apple menu or from the switch icon with the big gray apple on it in the Dock at the bottom of your screen.

- Action menus—You'll see these scattered around the place. The action pop-up menu is denoted by a gear icon and contains additional options that can be accessed—usually affecting whatever is currently selected in the window with the menu.
- Contextual menu—The Mac has contextual menus that can be accessed by Control-clicking on *many* objects in the operating system. Tiger even recognizes most two-button and scroll mice and will automatically map the second button to a control-click and the scroll wheel to window scrollbars.
- Window controls—Windows are controlled by the three buttons in the top-left corner (red, yellow/orange, and green). These buttons close, minimize, and expand windows.

See? That wasn't so bad. Let's get started with the reason why you're here: using Tiger.

Using the Tiger Finder

Simply put, Finder is the application that Tiger uses to launch and manipulate files and applications. Finder handles all common tasks such as creating, deleting, moving, and copying files and folders. It is, in effect, the portal to the underlying operating system.

Unlike other tools and utilities, Finder is always active and is automatically launched immediately after logging in to the system. Much of the Macintosh's legendary ease of use is attributed to Finder and its intuitive interface to the filesystem.

Understanding the Finder Window Components

Finder offers many ways to navigate through your data using windows, menus, and the keyboard. All navigation takes place inside a Finder window. To open a new Finder window, double-click a folder or disk icon that is on your desktop, use the New Finder Window selection from the Finder's File menu (Command-N). If there are no open Finder windows, clicking the Mac "smiley face" icon in your Dock will also open a window.

Three elements of the Finder window that are not related to file browsing help organize, navigate, and provide information about your workspace: the Sidebar, Toolbar, and Status bar.

The Sidebar

The Finder Sidebar puts all your commonly used folders and volumes in a single place: the pane found at the left side of the Finder window, as shown in Figure 1.1. You can shrink and expand the width of the Sidebar using the vertical gray bar separating the Sidebar and content panes. Double-clicking the vertical line closes the pane entirely; double-clicking again restores it.

Viewing Storage Volumes The top portion of the Sidebar pane displays the available volumes mounted on your system. As disks are inserted or network shares mounted, the Sidebar refreshes to show the new volumes. Removable media can be ejected by clicking the Eject icon that appears to the right of their entry in the list.

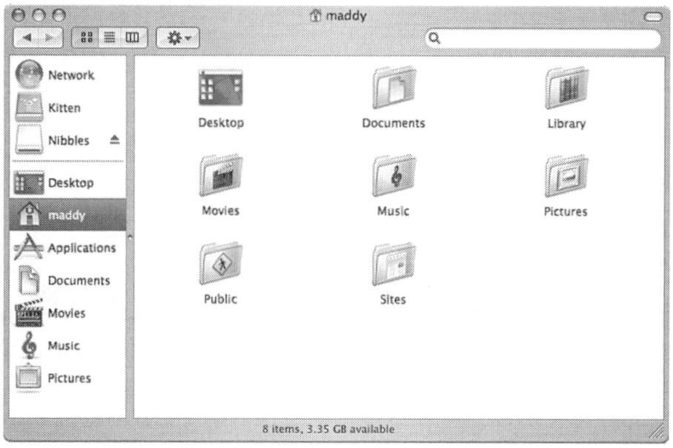

FIGURE 1.1 The Sidebar provides access to different areas of the filesystem.

NOTE

You cannot use the Sidebar to unmount partitions that aren't recognized as removable media. To unmount any partition or drive that isn't your startup disk, drag it to the trash can in the Dock.

Clicking an entry in the list refreshes the right side of the Finder window with the contents of the chosen item. For disks, this is obviously the contents of the disk. However, three additional storage elements behave a bit differently than a normal disk: Computer, iDisk, and Network.

- Computer—A top-level view of your computer and attached storage devices. When viewing the computer, you will see all accessible drives, mounted servers, and so on.
- iDisk—Your Internet-based personal storage that comes with your $100/year .Mac subscription. For more information on iDisk and .Mac, see Chapter 3, "Using the Tiger Internet Application Suite."
- Network—A convenient means of browsing network NFS/AppleTalk/CIFS volumes within the familiar comfort of the Finder interface. We'll discuss network browsing and connections further in this chapter and throughout the book.

By default, Tiger doesn't display the Computer or iDisk icons unless .Mac has been configured in the .Mac System Preference pane (see Chapter 3 for details) or you've turned these elements on in the Sidebar defaults, which will be discussed shortly.

Adding User-Defined Elements The bottom portion of the Sidebar comes with a few predefined shortcuts to your home directory, along with the Applications folder and your personal Desktop, Documents, Movies, Music, and Pictures folders.

Again, clicking an entry in the list of user-defined elements also refreshes the right portion of the window to display the contents. You can drag additional folders, files, or applications to the list. As you drag, a horizontal bar is displayed in the list to show where the new item will be inserted. If you drag directly on top of an existing folder or application you've added to the Sidebar, the list entry highlights to accept the element you're dragging. You can use this to put items in folders, or drag documents onto applications to launch them.

To remove an item from the Sidebar, click and drag its label or icon out of the pane (it will disappear in a poof) or open a contextual menu for the item and choose Remove.

> **TIP**
>
> Elements added to the Finder Sidebar automatically show up in the sidebar of Open/Save dialog boxes.

Changing Sidebar Defaults To change the default items displayed in the Finder Sidebar, choose Finder, Preferences; then click the Sidebar icon to open the Sidebar preferences pane, shown in Figure 1.2.

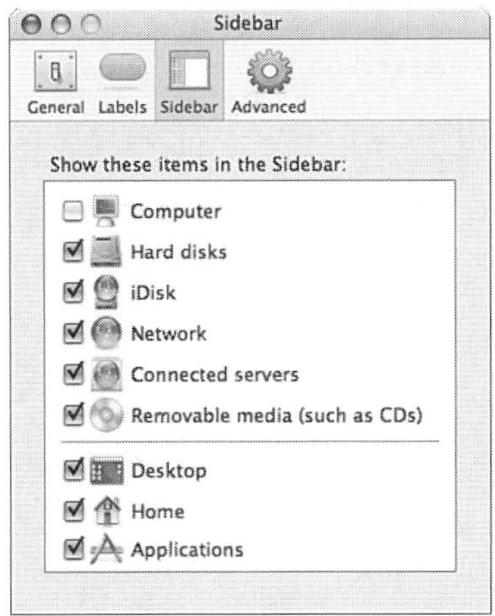

FIGURE 1.2 Choose the default items for your Sidebar.

Use the check boxes to enable or disable the default storage devices and personal folders automatically added to the Sidebar. Close the preferences window to save and enable your changes.

The Toolbar

The Finder toolbar holds useful functions that you might want to access from wherever you are in the Finder. Like the Sidebar, the Finder toolbar can hold shortcuts to files, but it can also be used to carry out actions on files, folders, and the navigation process itself.

There are two ways to customize the toolbar: by using the supplied buttons (shortcuts) and by adding your own applications and folders.

Using Predefined Toolbar Shortcuts By default, Finder comes with four active sets of toolbar components, as shown in Figure 1.3:

- Backward/Forward—Move back to the previously visited folder, or forward again. These buttons work just like the controls of a web browser.
- View—Set a viewing style for Finder's file listings. We'll cover the views shortly.
- Action—Perform an action on the selected files or folders, such as opening, moving to the trash, and so on.
- Search—Search for a file or folder using Spotlight (which will be covered later in this chapter).

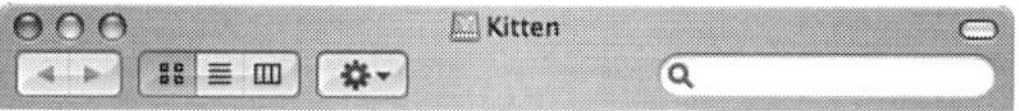

FIGURE 1.3 The default Toolbar components help you navigate and control your Finder views.

To customize your Finder windows with additional Apple-defined options, choose View, Customize Toolbar from Finder's menu or hold Command-Option and click the elongated toolbar button in the upper right corner of the window. A display of all the available shortcuts appears, as shown in Figure 1.4.

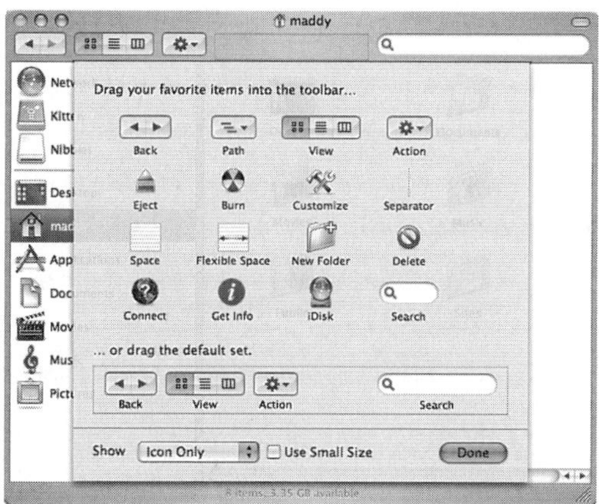

FIGURE 1.4 Finder buttons give single-click access to applications, folders, and special features.

To add one of these buttons to the toolbar, drag it from the window to wherever you want it to appear in the toolbar. If the number of shortcuts in the toolbar exceeds the size of the window, the shortcuts that can't be displayed appear in a pop-up menu (look for the >> icon) at the right side of the toolbar. These are the available toolbar buttons:

- Back/Forward—Navigates through previously visited folders. This is part of the default toolbar set.

- Path—Adds a pop-up menu to the toolbar that contains all the folders in the current path. Choose an item from the menu to jump to that folder. This is virtually identical to holding down the Command key while clicking on the title of a Finder window but doesn't require a modifier key.
- View—Quickly toggles between the three available Finder views. This is part of the default Finder toolbar.
- Action—Performs an action on the selected item. Actions are, for the most part, the same things you can find under the File menu or by Control-clicking on an icon.
- Eject—Ejects drive media (CDs, DVDs, and so on). If you have a modern Apple keyboard, you already have an Eject key, so this added button really won't be necessary. This is the same as pressing Command-E or dragging a disk icon to the Dock's trash can.
- Burn—Burn the currently active CD, if available. CD burning will be covered later in this chapter.
- Customize—The Customize shortcut opens the customize window directly.
- Separator—Serves to separate icons in the Finder's toolbar, but does not have an active function.
- Space—A fixed-size blank space. This button does not perform an action.
- Flexible Space—A flexible-sized blank space that grows and shrinks with the width of the window; does not perform an action.
- New Folder—Creates a new folder within the current Finder window. This is the same as pressing Shift-Command-N.
- Delete—Moves the currently selected Window item (or items) to the trash. This command does not empty the trash.
- Connect—Opens the file server connection window. This is the same as choosing Go, Connect To Server (Command-K).
- Get Info—Gets information about the selected file or folder (Command-I).
- iDisk—If you've set up a .Mac account and given the system your username and password (either during installation or in the Internet System Preferences pane), this shortcut automatically mounts your Apple iDisk.
- Search—Adds a search field for quick file searches using Spotlight. This is part of the default Finder toolbar.
- Default Set—Replaces the existing toolbar icons with the defaults.

At the bottom of the toolbar customization pane, you can choose how you want the toolbar displayed using the Show pop-up menu. You can pick Icon Only, Text Only, or Icon & Text if you prefer both. The default selection is Icon & Text. You can also shrink the size of the toolbar icons by checking the Use Small Size box.

TIP

In most applications, including the Finder, you can toggle through each of the different toolbar states by holding down Command and clicking the toolbar button in the window's title bar.

You can also Control-click in any toolbar to access a contextual menu and change the toolbar options.

As you are editing your toolbar, you might want to reorder the existing icons or remove them entirely. Just drag the toolbar elements into the order you want—they will automatically move to adjust to the new ordering. To remove an element, drag it outside the current toolbar and it disappears. Click Done when you're satisfied with the results.

NOTE

The toolbar buttons can be rearranged at any time by holding down the Command key and dragging them.

Adding User-Defined Toolbar Shortcuts In addition to the many predefined customizations, the toolbar also supports user-defined shortcuts, just like the Sidebar. Users can drag common applications, documents, or folders to any place in the toolbar.

When folders and applications are added to the toolbar, a single click on the icon opens or launches the respective object. Users can also drag documents onto toolbar application and folder icons to open the file using the application or to move the file into a particular folder. Toolbar shortcuts can be removed by holding down Command and dragging them off the toolbar or by opening a contextual menu for the item and choosing Remove.

Toolbar and Sidebar customization is done on a per-Finder, per-user account basis. When you modify your toolbar, it is modified for all Finder windows in your workspace, not just the currently open folder. Because these changes happen on a per-user basis, customizations you make to your Finder do *not* affect other users.

Switching to Classic Mac OS Navigation/Toolbarless Mode By default, when you double-click a folder, it refreshes your existing window to display the contents. This, along with all the bells and whistles of the Sidebar and toolbar, can be confusing for some users. To revert to a traditional form of navigation and simplified Aqua windows, switch to the Icon or List views, and then click the toolbar button in the upper-right corner of the Finder window, or choose View, Hide Toolbar (Option-Command-T).

In this mode, the Finder works as it did in pre–Mac OS X versions of the operating system: Double-clicking a folder always opens a new window, and the Sidebar and toolbar are not visible.

The Status Bar

The status bar, located at the bottom of a Finder window, has long supplied Mac users with important information about their systems. Finder's status bar shows the number of items contained in a folder and the amount of space available on the drive (this can be seen in Figure 1.1).

In addition to the storage usage information, the status bar may also contain one of three icons in the left corner of the bar:

- Grid pattern—If a small grid pattern appears, the view is set to snap to grid, allowing minimal flexibility in the movement of icons.
- Arranged icons—If you've chosen to keep the icons automatically arranged, you'll see four tiny folders.
- Slash pencil—A pencil with a line through it means that you can read the items in the directory but not store files within it (in other words, the directory is read only).

CAUTION

Even if you add up the sizes of all the folders that you use, you're probably going to come up short. Many hidden Unix directories are also counted when calculating the amount of available space. Unfortunately, to an end user, it's going to appear as if he's lost several hundred megabytes on his hard drive.

When Finder is operating in the toolbar-less mode, the status bar shifts to the top of the window and is initially hidden. It can be displayed by choosing View, Show Status Bar. It is *never* hidden when the Sidebar and toolbar are active.

Managing Finder Navigation Views

Although the Sidebar and toolbar aid in navigation, they aren't the meat of Finder. The content pane of Finder displays all the files and folders in your current location. Depending on the View mode of the content pane, you can browse your files in a traditional icon-style mode, columns, or a hierarchical list. To switch among these modes, use the three-button View control in the Finder toolbar (icons, list, columns, respectively), or choose your poison from the View menu.

Using the Icon View

The first time you log in, Finder will be using the Icon view. If you have already been using Finder and are no longer in Icon view, you can quickly switch to Icon view by choosing View, Icons (Command-1) or by clicking the first icon in the View area of the toolbar. Figure 1.5 shows a Finder window in Icon view.

Within the Icon view, you can navigate through the folders on your drive by double-clicking them. If you prefer to use the keyboard, you can move between the icons in the frontmost Finder window by pressing the arrow keys or by typing the first few letters that start the name of the folder or file you want to select. To open a selected item, choose File, Open, or press Command-O on the keyboard.

By default, moving from folder to folder refreshes the current window. You can switch to a multiwindow view by clicking the toolbar button in the upper-right corner of the Finder window or by using the Finder Preferences. Alternatively, to momentarily switch to a multiwindow mode, hold down Command when double-clicking a folder. This opens the folder in a new window.

FIGURE 1.5 The default view mode is the Icon view.

> **TIP**
>
> To toggle between open Finder windows, press Command-`. Note that the desktop itself is considered a Finder window.

Another method of navigating your drive is to Command-click the icon or text in the center of the Finder window's title bar. You will then see a pop-up menu that displays a bottom-to-top hierarchy of the folder path required to reach the current directory. You can choose any of the folders in the list to quickly jump to that location.

> **WHY ARE ALL MY FILENAMES CUT OFF?**
>
> Tiger supports long filenames, but Finder displays only two lines of each name, abbreviating the middle with an ellipsis (...).
>
> Thankfully, there is a way to view more of the name of the file. Select the icon and leave your mouse cursor over an abbreviated title, or hold down Option while moving your mouse over the title. Without the Option key, a ToolTip with the full name of the file will be displayed under the icon in three or four seconds. If you hold down the Option key, the expanded name is shown instantly.

Icon View Options The most basic form of customization in Icon view is to drag the icons around to suit your tastes. To add more dramatic effects to a window in Icon view, choose View, Show View Options from the menu, or press Command-J. Figure 1.6 shows the View Options window for the Icon view.

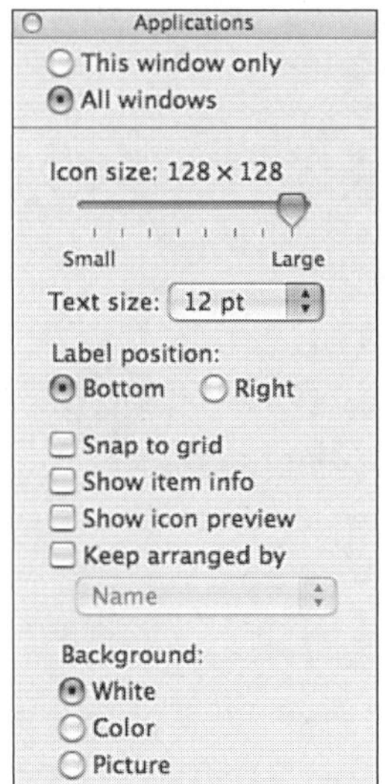

FIGURE 1.6 The Icon view options let you create a different look for the Finder window.

Global Settings The first decision you must make when adjusting view options is whether to inherit global settings, or apply the changes to the current window. At the top of the View Options window are two choices: This Window Only and All Windows. Choosing the first setting tells Tiger that the changes you make to the view are specific to that window—no other windows will be changed. For example, using This Window Only, you can set your home directory and each of the directories within it to their own style independently of one another. On the other hand, picking All Windows indicates that any changes made to the view options will affect *all* other windows set to inherit the global settings. This is a great way to create a common look and feel across multiple folders without having to maintain separate settings for each.

Icon and Text Options There are three primary settings for the Icon view, the first being icon size. Mac OS X supports icon sizes from 16×16 pixels all the way up to 128×128 (the standard Mac size was previously 32×32). The large icons are impressive and detailed, but take up quite a bit of window/desktop real estate. You can scale the icons from their smallest size to the largest size by dragging the Icon Size slider from the left to the right.

You can control the size of the icon title font with the Text Size pop-up menu. Apple allows a selection between 10 and 16 points but does *not* provide a means of changing the title font. The positioning of the icon's title can be changed from on the bottom to the right using the Label Position setting—this can maximize window space when using small icons.

TIP

If you find the antialiased fonts difficult to read, use the Appearance System Preferences pane to set the smallest font size that Tiger will antialias and the style of antialiasing used.

If you're still displeased with the settings, you can manually set the antialiasing threshold to anything you want using the Terminal application and the command:

```
defaults write .GlobalPreferences AppleAntiAliasingThreshold <fontsize>
```

You'll find out more about the Terminal starting in Chapter 9, "Accessing the BSD Subsystem."

Icon Arrangement The next group of settings control icon arrangement, which determines how the icons are displayed and laid out on the screen.

To keep your icons straight and neat all the time, choose Snap to Grid. Tiger maintains an invisible grid within Finder windows that is used to keep icons evenly aligned with one another. Unfortunately, there are no provisions for changing the spacing on the grid. As a result, the icons that are aligned to the grid might seem more loosely spaced than you want.

NOTE

If you take advantage of the Icon view with no preset arrangement, you might find that your icons get a bit messy after a while. To quickly align your icons to the Finder's grid, choose View, Clean Up from the menu.

You can also choose to display additional information in the icon and its label. The Show Icon Preview setting displays thumbnails of recognized image formats—even PDF files! Show Item Info, on the other hand, adds a count of the number of files contained within each folder directly under each folder's icon and displays information about media files (resolution, duration, and so on).

A final form of icon arrangement is to keep the icons arranged by attributes of the files that they represent. Click the Keep Arranged By check box and then choose from the list of available options:

- Name—Sorts the icons by the alphabetical order of their names.
- Date Modified—Sorts the icons by the day and time they were last modified. Newly modified files and folders appear at the bottom of the list.
- Date Created—Sorts the icons by the date and time they were created. The first time a file is saved, the created and modified times are identical.
- Size—Sorts by the size of the files or the size of the files contained within folders.
- Kind—Sorts the files by their type (that is, folders, applications, images, and so on).
- Label—Sort the files by a user-defined color label. We'll look at the label features shortly.

TIP

To quickly arrange icons in a Finder window, choose View, Arrange. This allows you to arrange your icons by any of the aforementioned attributes. It's a quick way to add some order to your life without opening View Options.

Note that if you have an arrangement set for a given window, the Arrange menu will be dimmed and cannot override your View Option settings.

Window Background The Background options allow you to choose a background color or picture on a per-folder basis. This enables you to create a visually impressive system and can also provide quick cues for your current location within the operating system.

The default folder background is white. To choose an alternative color, just click the Color radio button. A small square appears to the right of the button. Click this square to launch the Color Picker.

An even more impressive effect is to use a background picture for the window rather than just a color. Background images can be based on any of the QuickTime-supported formats (GIF, JPEG, TIFF, and so on). Click the Picture radio button and then click the Select button that appears. You are prompted to open an image file from the system.

After you've chosen a picture, the Finder window refreshes with the chosen image in the background. Currently, in Tiger, pictures cannot be scaled to match the size of a window. Instead, Finder background pictures are tiled, much like a repeating background on a web page.

NOTE

The Icon view is presently the only view that supports background colors and images.

Using the List View

Any easier way to view a large number of files is through the Finder's List view. You can switch to List view by clicking the middle icon in the Finder toolbar's View area, or, if the toolbar isn't present, by choosing View, As List from the Finder's menu. Demonstrated in Figure 1.7, the List view is a straightforward means of displaying all available information about a file or folder on a multicolumn screen.

The columns in the List view represent the attributes of each file. You can contract or expand the columns by placing the mouse cursor at the edge of the column and click-dragging to the left or right. Clicking a column highlights it and sorts the file listing based on that column's values. By default, the column values are listed in descending order. Clicking a column again toggles the sorting order. An arrow pointing up or down at the right of each column represents the current sort order.

You can reposition the columns by clicking and dragging them into the order you want. However, the first column, Name, cannot be repositioned.

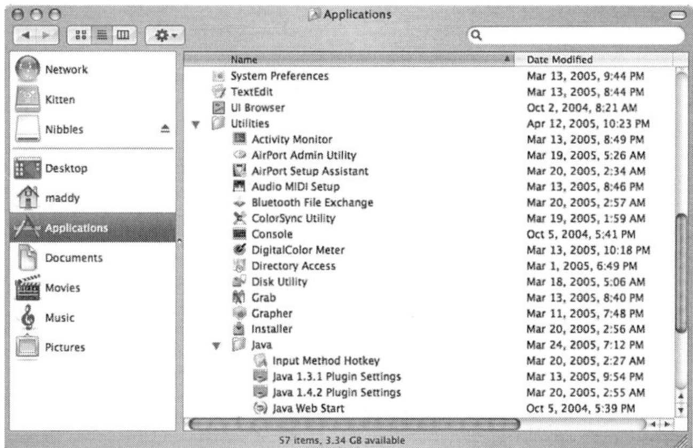

FIGURE 1.7 List view packs a lot of information into a small amount of space.

When a folder appears in the file listing, a small disclosure arrow precedes its name. Clicking the arrow reveals the hierarchy within that folder. You can drill down even further if you want, revealing multiple levels of files. Figure 1.7 shows three levels of files displayed simultaneously. Windows users might find a level of comfort in this view because it is similar to the Windows Explorer.

As with the Icon view, double-clicking a folder anywhere within this view either opens a new window (toolbarless mode) or refreshes the contents of the existing window with the new location.

If keyboard navigation is your thing, the same rules apply as in the Icon view. You can navigate up and down through the listing using the up-arrow key and the down-arrow key. In addition, you can use the left-arrow key and right-arrow key to move in and out of folders in the hierarchy. Holding down Command-Option along with the right-arrow key or left-arrow key expands or collapses all folders inside the currently selected folder. Typing the first few characters of an object's name highlights that object in the listing. You can then use Command-O to open it.

Finally, Command-clicking on the title of the window reveals the same pop-up list of folders as the Icon view. Choose one of the items in the list to jump to it.

List View Options As with the Icon view, there are a number of options that you can use to customize the appearance and functionality of the List view. To alter the options for a window, make sure that it is the frontmost Finder window and then choose View, Show View Options (Command-J). Figure 1.8 shows the List View Option window.

Icon and Text Options The Icon Size option offers a choice of two icon sizes: small or large. To change the size of the icon that precedes every line in the list, click the radio button below the size that you want. Unlike the Icon view icons, the List view icons cannot be scaled beyond the two presets. Text size for the list can also be chosen from 10 to 16 points.

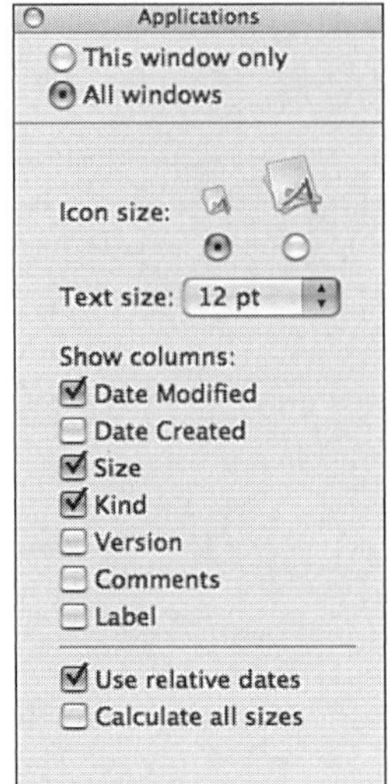

FIGURE 1.8 The List view also can be customized.

Column Display Options To change what information is visible in the List view, use the Show Columns options. By checking or unchecking the box in front of each option, you can add or remove the corresponding column in the List view.

- Date Modified—Shows the date that a file or folder was last changed.
- Date Created—Shows the date that a file or folder was created.
- Size—Shows the size of a file on the system.
- Kind—Shows an abstract representation of a file (image, application, and so on).
- Version—Displays the version of an application. Not always available.
- Comments—Shows any comments set for the file or folder. Comments are set from the Get Info (Command-I) window.
- Label—Shows the color label (if any) assigned to the file or folder.

TIP

To determine a file's type from the command line, try `file <filename>`:

```
% file jeans1024x768.jpg
jeans1024x768.jpg: JPEG image data, JFIF standard
```

For more information about the command line, see Chapter 9.

Two additional settings at the bottom of the options window affect the column display:

- Use Relative Dates—Relative dates are a way of representing dates relative to the current day. For example, items modified during the current day are listed as *Today*, whereas files modified a day earlier are listed as *Yesterday*. Clicking the Use Relative Dates check box displays the Created and Modified columns using these conventions.
- Calculate All Sizes—By default, folder sizes are not calculated and displayed in the file listing. Checking this box enables folder sizes to be displayed in the file listing.

CAUTION

Calculating folder sizes might seem like a good idea, but it can bog down your system tremendously. If you have multiple file listing windows open, and each is calculating folder sizes, it can slow down Finder operations and application responsiveness.

A quick way to display the usage of each directory in kilobytes is the `du -sk` command from the command line:

```
% du -sk *
40   Addresses
0    Assistants
0    Audio
4096 Caches
0    ColorPickers
8    Documentation
16   Favorites
2520 Fire
```

Using the Column View

The final type of window view is the Column view. This will be recognized by NeXT-heads as virtually identical to the original File Browser used on the NeXT operating system. There are two primary advantages of this view: ease of navigation and file identification. You can switch to the Column view style by choosing View, As Columns from the menu, or by clicking the third icon in the View area of the toolbar. Figure 1.9 shows a Finder window in Column view.

The key feature of the Column view is its navigation. Unlike the other views, which can either overwhelm you with information or require multiple windows to move easily from point to point, the Column view is designed with one thing in mind: ease of navigation.

The concept is simple: Click an item in the first column and its contents will be shown in the next column. You can continue to drill down further into the filesystem by choosing a folder that was within your original folder. The display will then do one of two things: If your window is open wide enough, it will display the contents of the second folder in yet another column. If no other columns are available, the columns will slide to the left, and a scrollbar will appear at the bottom of the window. Using this scrollbar, you can quickly trace the steps you've taken to reach a file.

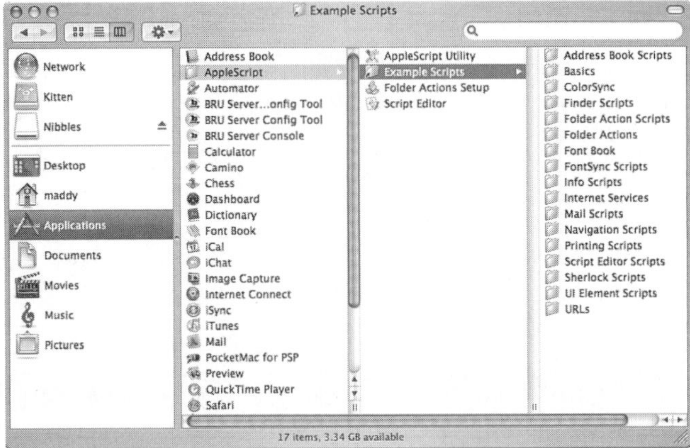

FIGURE 1.9 The Column view uses...columns.

TIP

If you use the horizontal scrollbar to move back along a path, the folders you've chosen remain highlighted in the columns. You can, at any time, choose a different folder from any of the columns. This refreshes the column to the right of your choice. There is no need to start from the beginning every time you want to change your location.

TIP

When you use one of the shortcut pane items to jump to a location on your system, *that* location becomes the top level of the filesystem display. You will not be shown any directories preceding that point.

If you want to adjust the width of the columns, hold down Option, grab the handle (represented by two vertical lines) and drag it—all the columns resize accordingly. To resize only the columns to the left or right of the divider line, drag without using Option.

TIP

Option-Double-clicking the handle at the right side of a column auto-resizes that column so that the column fits the largest icon name string. Double-clicking without the Option key resizes *all* columns to the smallest size needed to fit the largest icon name string.

As with the other views, Command-clicking on the title of the window reveals the same pop-up list of folders as the Icon view. Choose one of the items in the list to jump to it.

There is one other big bonus of using the Column view: the ability to instantly see the contents of a file without opening it. If you drill down to an individual file, a preview or description of the selected item will appear in the column to the right. This is demonstrated in Figure 1.10, where the front page of a PDF file is displayed.

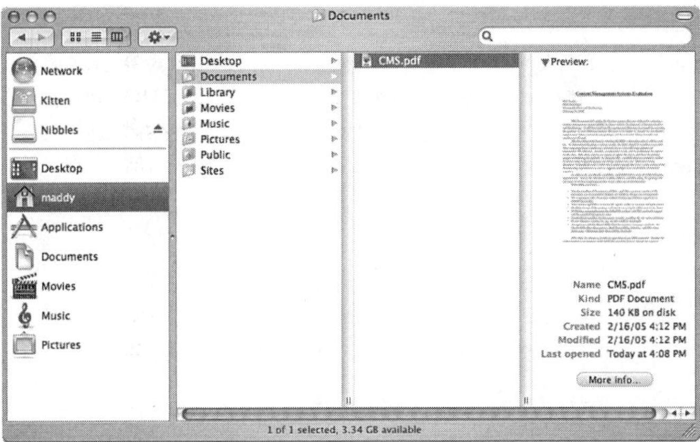

FIGURE 1.10 When a file is selected, a preview is shown in the rightmost column.

This is a convenient way of viewing pictures, listening to MP3s, and even watching QuickTime movies. When an application or a file that cannot be previewed is chosen, information about the file is displayed, such as the creation/modification dates, size, and version.

Column View Options The Column view options, shown in Figure 1.11, are sparse. The text size is adjustable, and you can also choose to show the small icons in each column, and whether the far right column is used for a preview or will just act as a file list. There are no global view options for the Column view mode.

FIGURE 1.11 Choose whether to display icons in each column and whether a preview is displayed.

Navigating Using the Go Menu

If you want to navigate quickly from any view, use the folder shortcuts contained in the Go menu. The top three options, Back (Command-[), Forward (Command-]), and Enclosing Folder (Command-Up-arrow) can be used to move around based on your current Finder location.

This menu also enables one to jump to one of several predefined locations:

- Computer—Jump to the Computer level of the file hierarchy. At the Computer level, you can browse connected storage devices and network volumes (Shift-Command-C).
- Home—Go to your home directory (Shift-Command-H).
- Network—Open the network browser (Shift-Command-K).
- iDisk—Choose to open your, or another user's, iDisk or iDisk public folder (if you have .Mac). For more information, see Chapter 5, "Configuring Tiger Hardware Support and Preferences."
- Applications—Jump to the system-level Applications folder (Shift-Command-A).
- Utilities—Open the Utilities folder, found in `/Applications/Utilities`. Many tools for managing and monitoring your system are found here (Shift-Command-U).
- Recent Folders—The Recent Folders submenu contains a system-managed list of the last folders you visited. The number of items maintained can be configured in the Appearance System Preference pane.

The second-to-last quick-navigation option is Go to the Folder (Shift-Command-G). From here you can manually enter a pathname and open it within Finder. Figure 1.12 shows the Go to the Folder dialog box.

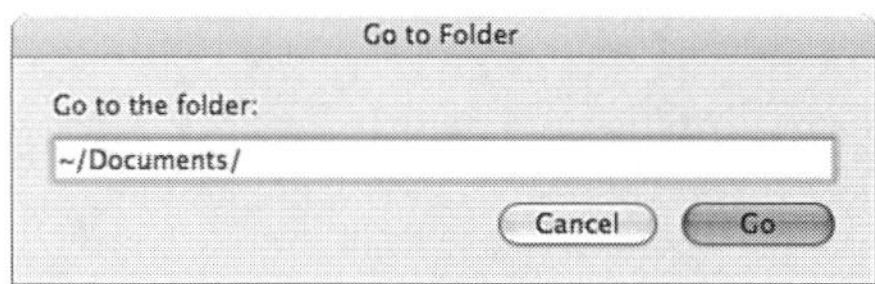

FIGURE 1.12 Go to Folder lets you enter your destination by hand.

Type any folder pathname into the Go to the Folder field. Folder names are separated by the / character. Table 1.1 shows a few shortcuts you can use to navigate your drive.

TABLE 1.1 Shortcuts to Help You Navigate Your System

Path	Purpose
/	The root (top) level of your hard drive.
~/	Your home directory.
~*<username>*	Replace *<username>* with the name of another user to jump to that user's home directory.

TABLE 1.1 Continued

Path	Purpose
`/<directory>`	Move to a directory relative to the root of the filesystem.
`<directory>`	Move to a directory relative to the directory you're currently in.

As you type, Tiger watches what you're typing and attempts to auto-complete the name of the directory; press Tab to accept an auto-completed pathname.

Click Go or press Return when you've finished typing the directory you want to visit.

NOTE

This feature can be used to jump to the hidden Unix directories on your system, such as `/etc`, `/usr`, and so on.

TIP

The Mac and Unix systems make strange bedfellows. The Mac has traditionally used a colon (`:`) to separate folder names in a path; therefore, it didn't allow colons within filenames. Unix, on the other hand, doesn't allow a slash (`/`) within filenames, but it does allow colons.

In Finder, the `:` character still isn't allowed (it is replaced with a hyphen [`-`] if you try to use it in a file or directory name), but `/` can be used in a name. Unfortunately, the Go to the Folder dialog box cannot deal with directories that include the `/` because it is thinking in terms of Unix directories. The moral of the story is, "Don't name your directories with a `/` and expect to be able to navigate to them using the Go to the Folder dialog box."

The final Go menu option, Connect to Server, will be discussed in the next section, "Connecting to Network Resources."

Connecting to Network Resources

Tiger makes it extremely easy to work in a cross-platform environment by enabling users to connect to a number of different types of file shares, specifically—AppleShare over AppleTalk, AppleShare over TCP/IP, NFS, SMB (Windows), FTP, and WebDAV. By adopting a common interface to all of these different protocols, interacting with a remote server is as simple as browsing a local drive on your computer.

Browsing and Mounting Network Resources

To look for available servers, click the Network icon in the Finder Sidebar. After several seconds, your screen refreshes with any results that it found, as shown in Figure 1.13.

AppleTalk Zones and Windows Workgroups are represented by folders, whereas machines registered through Rendezvous can be found under the My Network folder. Double-clicking the icon of a shared resource attempts to connect and mount that device, as shown in Figure 1.14.

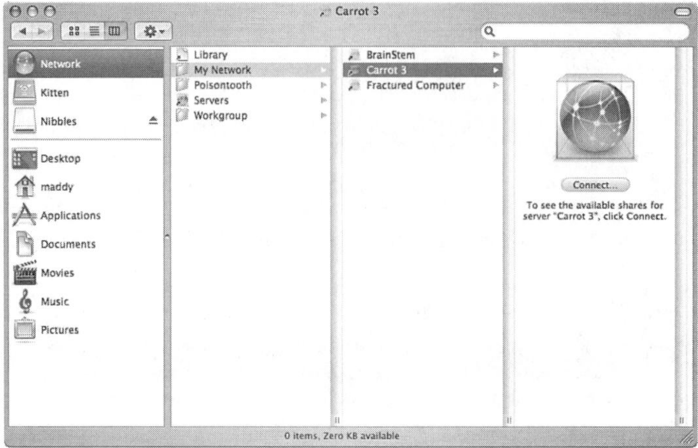

FIGURE 1.13 Browse network volumes directly in Finder.

FIGURE 1.14 Browse and connect to remote devices.

TIP

You will *not* see legacy AppleTalk devices in your Network listing until you enable AppleTalk in the Network System Preferences pane. See Chapter 7, "Configuring Network Connectivity," for details.

Because Tiger allows you to connect to quite a few different types of file services, the server connection dialog varies depending on the server type. We'll look at Windows and WebDAV connections in Chapters 27 and 23, respectively. For now, assume that we're connecting from Tiger to Tiger.

Logging In to a Server As shown in Figure 1.14, when connecting, you can choose to authenticate as a Guest or Registered user. Tiger Personal File Sharing automatically allows Guest connections with write access to the path `~Public/Dropbox` in your home directory. Registered users can access their entire home directory and, if they are administrative users, all storage volumes attached to a machine.

After entering a username and password, you can click Remember Password in Keychain to automatically authenticate with the server in the future.

TIP

A Mac OS X file server will recognize both your full name and shortname when logging in.

Configuring Connection Security To help maintain sharing security, the Action menu (the gear icon) provides direct access to changing your password on the remote server and to additional security options. Choosing Options from the Action menu will display the dialog box shown in Figure 1.15.

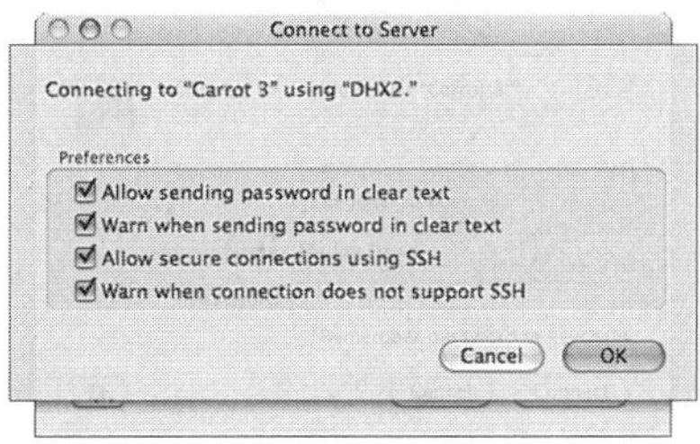

FIGURE 1.15 Configure the security of your connection.

Here you can choose whether your password will be sent over the network in clear text—that is, a human-readable (and interceptable) form—and whether you should be warned if the password is transmitted in this manner. Although it might seem like a good idea to *never* allow this feature, some servers might not allow secure connections and will deny access without clear text passwords.

The best security is achieved by clicking the Allow Secure Connections Using SSH check box. This uses SSH (Secure Shell) to create an encrypted link between the client and the server and virtually eliminates the risk of password or information interception. For more information on SSH, see Chapter 21, "Accessing and Controlling Tiger Remotely."

Choosing Volumes to Mount After entering your username and password and configuring your security options, click the Connect button. Assuming that you have a successful login, you will be presented with a list of volumes that are available to your account. Highlight one or more in the list, and then click OK. The selected volumes will be mounted in the Finder and accessible from the Finder window or your desktop (if configured within the Finder preferences).

Connecting to a Network Volume via URI

If you already know the IP address or hostname of the computer you want to connect to, or a resource doesn't allow browsing (WebDAV/FTP/NFS), you can also connect by choosing Go, Connect to Server. The Connect To Server dialog is displayed in Figure 1.16.

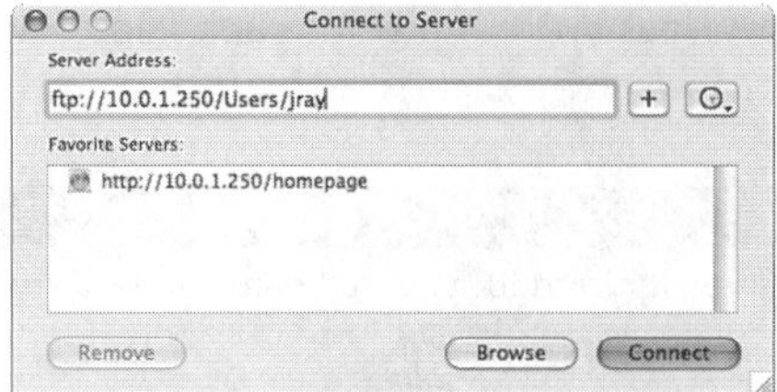

FIGURE 1.16 Connect to and store commonly used server URLs here.

To connect to a networked resource, type the resource URI using the following formats:

- **`afp:`*`<machine IP/hostname>`*`[/`*`<volume>`*`]`**—Standard AppleShare IP or Mac OS X Server shares.
- **`http://`*`<WebDAV URL>`***—WebDAV shares. See Chapter 23, "Creating a Web Server," for details.
- **`cifs://`*`<machine IP/hostname>`*`[/`*`<volume>`*`]`**—Or `smb://`; see Chapter 27, "Working with Windows-Based Systems," for details.
- **`ftp://`*`<machine IP/hostname>`*`[/`*`<volume>`*`]`**—See Chapter 22, "Creating an FTP Server," for details on FTP.
- **`nfs://`*`<machine IP/hostname>`*`[/`*`<volume>`*`]`**—See Chapter 20, "Configuring Advanced System Features via NetInfo," for details.

After entering a URL, click Connect to connect to the network resource. You can also choose + to add a URL to the list of favorite servers (where subsequently it can simply be clicked to access). Use the Remove button to remove a URL from the Favorite Servers list. Recently used URLs are available via the clock icon drop-down menu to the right of the +.

Finder File Operations

Because you're reading an *Unleashed* title, you probably already know the basics of most graphical operating systems: Click and drag files to move them; double-click applications to launch them. Tiger doesn't break any new ground in the handling of files. Everyone who has used Windows, KDE/GNOME, or an earlier version of Mac OS will be able to carry their existing knowledge over to the new operating system. To be thorough, this portion of the chapter serves as a quick reference to standard file and application operations.

Assigning Labels

Labels are a color code that you can assign to an arbitrary file or group of files. Your important work files, for example, might be labeled with the color red, whereas personal files might be labeled green. Rather than having to separate the files into different folders, you can simply apply different labels. The Finder highlights the name of each icon with the color of the chosen labels so that you can easily pick them out. In addition, you can use the View Options in List mode to sort by assigned labels or even use the new Spotlight search feature to search by label. (Searching is discussed later in this chapter in the section "Finding and Organizing Information with Spotlight.")

To assign a label to an icon or group of icons, select the object(s) and then use File, Color Label; the Toolbar Action button; or the contextual (Control-click) menu to choose one of the seven different color options, shown in Figure 1.17. The meaning is entirely up to the user—labels have no effect on how the operating system manages the files.

FIGURE 1.17 Choose one of seven different color labels to apply to the file(s).

When setting a label using any of the available methods, you might notice that directly to the left of the color options is an X icon. Choosing the X removes any existing label from the selected item(s).

Each label has an associated word (the label *name*) displayed along with the highlight color in the Finder List view. To change the names (defaulted to the color names) associated with each label, choose Finder, Preferences; click the Labels icon to open the Label Name preferences pane.

Use the fields beside each color to change the label names, as shown in Figure 1.18. Close the preferences window to save and activate your changes.

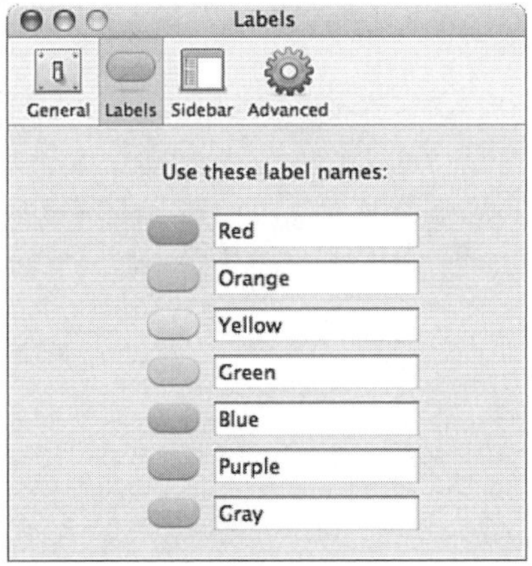

FIGURE 1.18 Assign names to each of the color labels.

Zipping and Unzipping Files

Tiger can compress and decompress files directly from the Action toolbar button or contextual menus. To zip (compress), choose the files or folders to include in the archive and then use the Action button or Control-click and choose Archive.

To unzip (decompress), select a Zip file and choose Unarchive from the Action button or contextual menu. The file will be unarchived in the current location.

Zipping and unzipping does not affect the original files or the archive file; they are left untouched.

Moving Files and Folders

Moving a file changes its location, but does not alter the contents of the file or its creation and modification dates. To move a file in Tiger, drag its icon to the folder or location where you want it to reside. If you are dragging within a Finder window, the window automatically scrolls as your cursor reaches the border, allowing you to move around within the view without having to drop the icon and manually scroll the window.

If you attempt to move a file from one device (such as a disk) to another, the cursor changes to include a + sign, and the file is *copied* rather than moved. The original file stays in its current location, and a new version is created on the other storage media. You must delete the original copy of the file if you do not want to keep multiple versions of the file.

TIP

Finder (and some application) windows include a proxy icon in the title bar. If you click and hold this miniature icon for a few seconds, it becomes draggable. The icon, called a *proxy*, represents the currently open folder or document and can be used just like dragging the item's icon within the Finder window.

Copying Files and Folders

Copying a file creates an exact duplicate of an original file. The new file sports a new creation and modification date, although the contents are identical to the original. There are a number of ways to create a copy:

- Drag a file to a different disk—Dragging a file to a disk other than the one it is currently stored on results in a copy of the file being created at the destination. The copy has the same name as the original.
- Drag a file while holding down Option—If you drag a file to a folder on the same disk it is currently located on while holding down the Option key, a duplicate of that file is created in the new location. If the Option key is not held down, the file is simply moved. The copy has the same name as the original.
- Choose Duplicate from contextual/Finder menu—If you want to create an exact duplicate of a file within the same folder, highlight the file to copy and then choose File, Duplicate (Command-D). Or, alternatively, Control-click the icon and choose Duplicate from the pop-up contextual menu. A new file is created with the word *copy* appended to the filename.

- Use the Finder contextual menus—Control-click on a Finder icon (or selection of multiple icons); then choose Copy. Next, locate where you want to copy the files to and then choose Edit, Paste from the menu. You can also use the toolbar's Action menu to perform a copy-and-paste action. Windows users will recognize this immediately.

As a file is copied, Finder displays the progress of the operation. If multiple copies take place at the same time, the status of each operation is shown stacked on one another in the copy status window. In Figure 1.19, two copies are taking place.

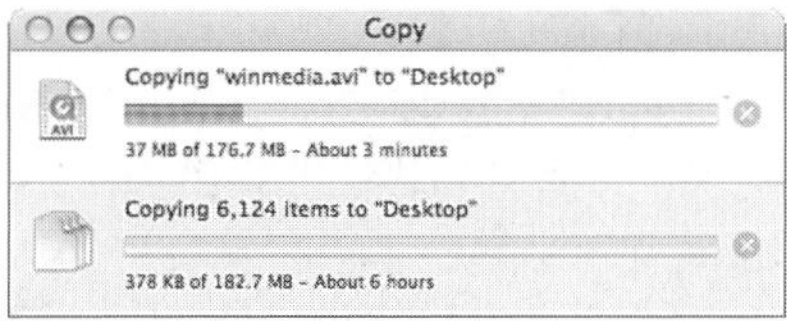

FIGURE 1.19 A single window contains all the status information for multiple copy operations.

When attempting to copy over existing files, the Finder prompts you whether you want to replace them and displays an Apply to All check box to apply your decision to any other conflicting files it finds during the copy.

Remember that under Tiger, you cannot alter certain system files and directories or another user's files. If you attempt to replace existing files to which you do not have access, the copy operation will fail.

Dragging with Spring-Loaded Folders and Windows

Using the spring-loaded folder feature of Tiger, you can drag items onto closed folders, and after a few seconds, those folders spring open, allowing you to continue the drag operation. To force the spring action to occur immediately, press the spacebar while hovering over the folder you want to open.

Tiger also includes *spring-loaded windows*. Spring-loaded windows spring onto the screen when an icon is dragged over them. To demonstrate this effect, drag a Finder window to the bottom of your screen until only the title bar is showing. Next, drag an icon over the title bar—the window springs up from the bottom of the screen and then disappears when you release the item or move your mouse off the window. You can force a window to spring immediately by pressing the spacebar.

TIP

The amount of time it takes a folder to spring open is controlled through the General Finder preferences, discussed later.

Deleting Files and Folders

Deleting files and folders permanently removes them from your system. Although Finder has an Undo menu, it cannot undo the effects of erasing a file from your system. As with copying a file, there are a number of ways to delete one:

- Drag to Dock trash—Dragging an icon from a Finder window into the Dock's trash can is one of the most obvious and easy ways to get rid of a file.
- Move to Trash contextual/Action/Finder menu—You can move a selected item to the trash by Control-clicking the icon and choosing Move to Trash from the contextual menu, or choosing the option of the same name from the Finder's File menu or Action toolbar button.
- Toolbar—A Delete shortcut can be added to the Finder's toolbar. Any items selected can be quickly moved to the trash by clicking the Delete shortcut.

Moving an item to the trash does not delete it permanently from your drive. Instead, it places the item inside an invisible folder called `.Trash` in your home directory—you cannot see or access this folder directly from the GUI. The trash can icon in the Dock fills with crumpled paper when it contains items waiting to be deleted.

Although Tiger doesn't give you a true representation of the `.Trash` folder, it does let you view the contents of the trash by clicking the trash can icon in the Dock. The Trash window works identically to other Finder windows. If you want to rescue a file you've accidentally sent to the trash, you can drag the file's icon out of the trash.

To completely remove a file from your system, choose Empty Trash from the Finder's application menu or press Shift-Command-Delete. Alternatively, you can Control-click or click and hold on the trash can, and choose Empty Trash from the resulting pop-up menu. Holding down Option when emptying the trash (including via the keyboard shortcut) bypasses Finder's warning messages.

If you are deleting a large number of files, Finder might bring up a dialog box similar to the Copy dialog box. You can click Stop to cancel the trash operation, sparing the files that haven't yet been erased.

Securely Erasing Files By default, emptying the trash removes only pointers to the files from the filesystem. The data itself remains on the drive and can be recovered by a number of available disk forensics tools. If you work for the NSA or any other organization that requires high level security, this poses a security threat in that even if you've deleted sensitive information from your computer, *someone* can recover it.

Tiger provides a Secure Empty Trash feature, also available under the Finder's Application menu. Using the Secure Empty Trash option overwrites files several times to ensure that they cannot be recovered.

ISN'T ONCE ENOUGH?

Magnetic media is an analog storage medium. If you've ever erased a cassette tape with a tape eraser, you might have noticed that you can hear a very faint version of the original recording. The same holds true for magnetic computer media. To be absolutely certain that no data can be recovered, multiple passes must be made to eliminate any trace of the original data.

For an excellent discussion of the topic, read "Secure Deletion of Data from Magnetic and Solid-State Memory" by Peter Gutmann (`http://www.cs.auckland.ac.nz/~pgut001/pubs/secure_del.html`).

Creating Aliases

An *alias* is a representation of a file that, for all intents and purposes, appears to be the file. Windows users will recognize it as being similar to a shortcut.

Suppose that you have a document called `My Diary` buried deep in your drive, but you want to leave a copy of the icon on your desktop. Instead of duplicating the file and maintaining two copies, you can create an alias of the original file and then place the alias wherever you want. Accessing the alias is the same as accessing the real file. Finder uses aliases for recent folders. Rather than having to move the real directories, it can just create aliases of them. You can tell an alias from the original by the arrow in the lower-left corner of the icon. Figure 1.20 shows several aliases to other files.

There are two ways to create aliases:

- Drag a file while holding down Option-Command—If you drag a file to a folder while holding down the Option-Command keys, an alias of that file is created in the new location.
- Choose Make Alias from contextual/Finder/Action menu—If you want to create an alias of a file within the same folder, highlight the file to alias and then choose File, Make Alias (Command-L), Control-click the icon and choose Make Alias from the pop-up contextual menu, or use the Make Alias option under the Action toolbar button. A new file is created with the word *alias* appended to the filename.

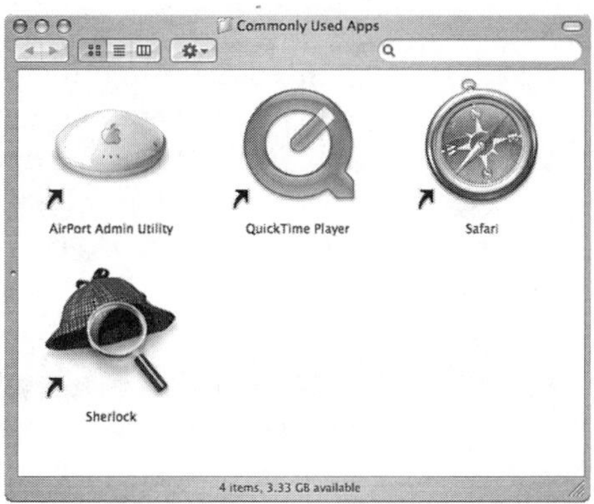

FIGURE 1.20 Aliases represent real files on your system.

Although aliases can be used to represent the original file, throwing them away does not delete the original file. Alternatively, deleting the original file doesn't delete the alias. If the original file is erased, the alias becomes broken. Double-clicking a broken alias displays a dialog box similar to the one in Figure 1.21.

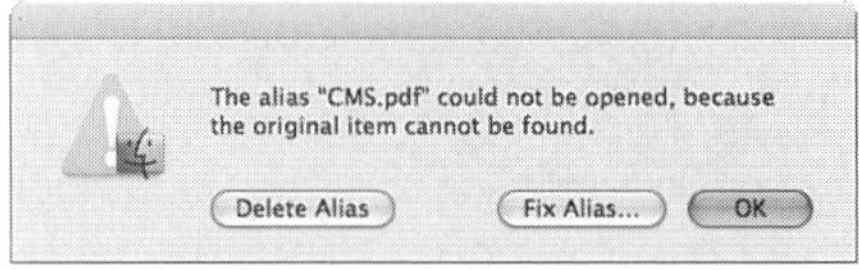

FIGURE 1.21 Broken aliases can be deleted or fixed.

If you just want to get rid of a broken alias, click the Delete Alias button. If you want to point the alias to a different file, choose Fix Alias and locate the file you want to use, and the alias will be reattached. To leave things the way they are, click OK.

NOTE

Aliases aren't quite the same as symbolic links in Linux/Unix. The Mac filesystem assigns a unique identifier to each file. Aliases reference that identifier and can be used to locate a file wherever it is on your drive. If the original is moved, the ID does not change, and the alias continues to work. Aliases do not translate to the BSD subsystem in any form and *cannot* be substituted for `ln -s`.

Finding an Alias's Original To locate the file to which an alias points, select the alias and choose Show Original (Command-R) from the Finder's File menu, from the icon's contextual menu, or use the toolbar's Action button. The original file is highlighted in Finder.

Launching Applications and Opening Documents

Launching an application or loading a document is a matter of double-clicking its icon or dragging a document on top of the application's icon. In the latter case, the application starts and loads or processes the document that was dropped on it.

You can also launch an application by selecting it and then choosing File, Open; by choosing Open in the icon's contextual menu; or by using the toolbar Action button. If you're opening a document and want it to load into an application other than the default application, use File, Open With; or choose Open With in the item's contextual menu; or use the toolbar Action button. To set a file to always open with an alternative application, hold down Option when the Open With menu selection is visible onscreen, and it will change to Always Open With.

NOTE

If you use a contextual menu or the Action button to open applications and documents, you might notice a Show Package Contents selection in the menu as well. Only available in certain cases, this effectively opens the file as if it were a folder, showing the various resources (images, sounds, and so on) that the application uses.

While an application is launching, its icon will bounce in the Dock.

Dealing with Unrecognized Files If you attempt to double-click a document that the system does not recognize, Tiger warns you that there is no application available to open the document you've tried to access, as demonstrated in Figure 1.22. If you're sure that a program on your system is capable of viewing the file, select the Choose Application button. You are prompted to choose the application that will open the file. If the system does not allow you to pick the appropriate application, change the selection in the Show pop-up menu to read All Applications rather than Recommended Applications. By default, the system tries to guess the best application for the job—sometimes it fails miserably.

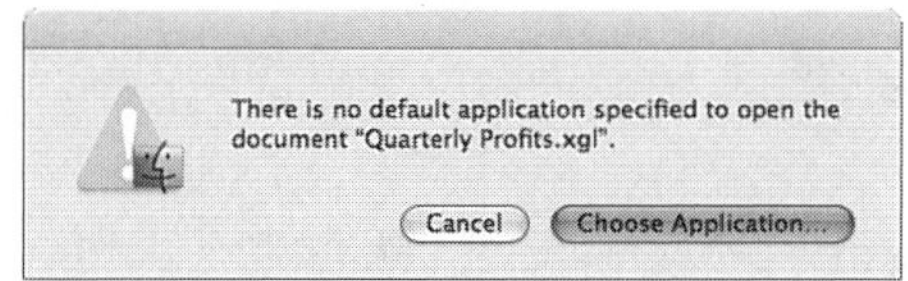

There is no default application specified to open the document "Quarterly Profits.xgl".
Cancel
Choose Application...

FIGURE 1.22 If a file can't be opened, you can choose an application to open it with.

You can also fix unrecognized files by setting the application to open them through the Get Info Finder command, discussed later in this chapter.

Renaming Files

To rename a file in the Finder, click on the file's icon label. The filename becomes editable in a few seconds. If you're the impatient sort, just press the Return key after you've selected an icon; you'll immediately find yourself in Edit mode. Alternatively, you can use File, Get Info in the Finder menu to edit the name in a larger field.

A shortcut in the Sidebar (and the object it represents) can be renamed by choosing Rename from that item's contextual menu.

Viewing File Information and Metadata

The Mac OS has always returned a wealth of information about a file via the Get Info option from the Finder's File menu. In Tiger this capability has been significantly expanded by the new metadata-aware file system. Instead of just recognizing a file's type, size, and other typical information, Tiger maintains an index of information *about* information—that is, metadata. For digital photographs, this is everything from image resolution to the aperture used when taking a picture. To access this and other information, select a file, and then choose File, Get Info (Command-I); or, if you're using the Column view, click the More Info button when a file is selected.

Let's take a look at each part of the Get Info display, the information it contains, and what it means to you.

TIP

By default, the Get Info window opens a separate window for each item you request information about. To display a single inspector-style window that switches as you move between items, use the Show Inspector option that appears in the File menu when you hold down the Option key. You can also show a summary of information for all selected items by holding down Control, and then choosing File, Get Summary Info.

Spotlight Comments

As you'll learn shortly, *Spotlight* is the name of Tiger's new metadata search system. Because the types of metadata stored with files are predefined, Tiger provides a field for you to enter your own comments, information, and so forth.

General

The General Information pane provides basic details about a file's type, size, and creation/modification dates, as shown in Figure 1.23.

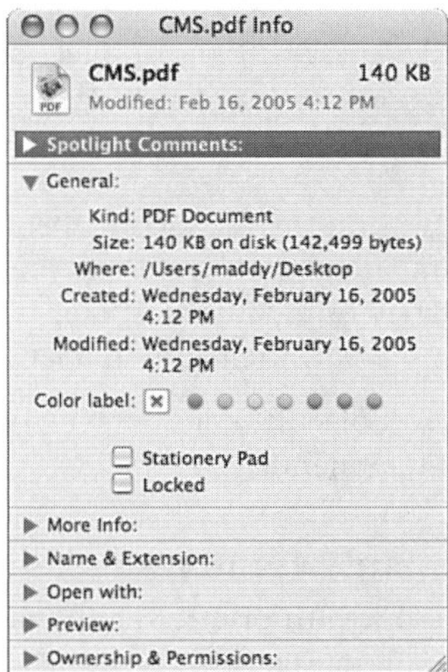

FIGURE 1.23 The General Information pane provides basic size, location, and type information about a file.

Specifically, you can use this view to get and set the following file and folder attributes:

- Kind—The type of file being examined (application, movie, and so on).
- Size—The size of the file or folder.
- Where—The full path to the selected resource.
- Created—The day and time the item was created.
- Modified—The day and time the item was last modified.

- Version—The version (revision) of the selected object, typically only available for applications.
- Color Label—Set or unset the label for the item by clicking a color or the X, respectively.
- Stationery Pad—Available for document files only. If the Stationery Pad check box is checked, the file can be used to create new files but cannot be modified itself. This is used to create template files for common documents.
- Locked—If this option is checked, the file cannot be modified or deleted until it is unlocked. For Linux/Unix users, this is equivalent to setting the immutable flag for the file.

If the file you are viewing is an alias file, the General Information pane also shows the location of the original file along with a Select New Original button that lets you pick a new file to attach the alias to.

Changing an Icon If you're unhappy with the icon of the resource you're examining, you can click the object's icon within the General Information pane, and then use the Copy and Paste options in the Edit menu to move icons or images from other files onto the selected item. The Cut option can be used to remove a custom icon from a file and restore the default.

TIP

An excellent source for high-quality icons is Iconfactory at `http://www.iconfactory.com` or Xicons, located at `http://www.xicons.com`.

More Info

New to Tiger's Get Info dialog is More Info. Here you can find the metadata available for the selected item, and, as mentioned previously, this can be quite an extensive list of values. Applications and documents might present copyright and version information. Digital photograph files display color space, resolution, and the attributes of the device that took the picture, as demonstrated in Figure 1.24.

Music and other media files might provide bit rate, length, and genre data...the list goes on and on. The easiest way to get a sense of everything that could be displayed is to view the Spotlight search attributes, which you'll do later in the chapter.

Even if a file has no native metadata for its file type, Tiger will begin tracking the last time the object was opened and, if nothing else, this value will be visible.

TIP

If you view the metadata for a file (such as an image) that should be showing something but isn't, try creating a copy of the file. When the file is duplicated, Tiger will index the metadata and it will become available. These problems should occur only with files that weren't created on Tiger, such as those being accessed on from an external or network storage device.

FIGURE 1.24 More Info displays the metadata for known file types.

Name & Extension

Tiger shares something with Windows: file extensions. Although it is still possible for files to have the traditional Macintosh file types and creators, it is no longer the norm. To shield users from the shock of seeing extensions to the names of their files, Apple added the option to hide file extensions within the Get Info Name & Extension view.

To edit the filename (including the extension), make modifications within the Name & Extension field. Turn on (or off) file extensions by clicking the Hide Extension check box.

Open With

If you have selected a document icon (not an application or a folder), you should be able to access the Open With pane within the Get Info window. This is used to configure the applications that open certain types of documents on the system. Unlike previous versions of Mac OS, which relied on a hidden creator and file type, Tiger can also use file extensions or creator/file type resources. If you download a file from a non-Mac system, your computer might not realize what it needs to do to open the file. The Open With pane, shown in Figure 1.25, lets you configure how the system reacts.

The default application name is shown at the top of a pop-up menu containing alternative application choices. If the application you want to use isn't in the menu, choose Other, and then use the standard file dialog box to browse to the application you want to use.

If you have a group of files that you want to open with a given application, you can select the entire group and use the Open With settings to adjust them all simultaneously. Alternatively, click the Change All button to set the default application for all files of that type on your system. This beats selecting each file and making the setting individually.

Preview

Preview provides a quick look at the contents of a wide variety of media files including MP3s, CD audio tracks (AIFF), JPEGs, GIFs, TIFFs, PDFs, and other QuickTime-recognized formats.

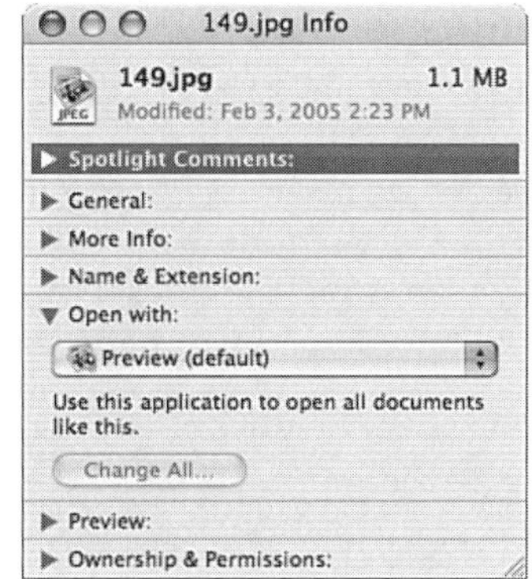

FIGURE 1.25 The Open With option allows you to choose what application will read a particular file or type of file.

If you are previewing a video or audio track, the QuickTime player controls will appear and enable you to play the contents of the file. This is a great way to play your CDs or listen to MP3s without starting up a copy of iTunes.

Languages

If you have an application selected, you might be able to choose Languages within the Get Info window. Applications can have multiple internal resources that change the application to the appropriate system conditions—the Languages pane allows you to add or remove the language resources within an application.

NOTE

Tiger bundles languages and other resources within a structure called a *package*. A package is nothing more than a directory hierarchy that appears to the user to be a single file. Most applications, in fact, are actually folders, not the single file they appear. You can open an application package by Control-clicking its icon and choosing Show Package Contents.

Ownership & Permissions

Because Tiger is a multiuser system, it provides a means of setting and maintaining ownership and a set of permissions for files. A file's owner has full control over a file; the owner can read it, edit it, run it (if appropriate), and delete it. Owners can also provide some or all of these rights to other users. The Ownership & Permissions settings provide a straightforward graphical means of managing these file attributes with the exception of the "execute" (run) permission.

Because there can be serious implications to incorrectly setting permissions and proper use of this feature is essential in administering a machine with multiple login accounts, we've devoted a chapter to the topic: Chapter 11, "Using File Permissions and Access Control Lists."

Finding and Organizing Information with Spotlight

In addition to organizing and providing information about your files, the Tiger Finder enables you to locate files—even email messages—based on dozens of attributes, including the file's contents. This new feature, called *Spotlight*, provides systemwide searches for content without any of the penalties of pre-indexing. When a file is updated on Tiger, it is immediately indexed and fully searchable. Previous versions of the operating system forced users to explicitly set up content indexing for volumes and folders and would only re-index on a set schedule.

Using the Spotlight Menu

Located in the upper-right corner of the menu bar is the Spotlight looking glass (or magnifying glass) icon. Clicking the icon or pressing Command-space displays a search field, as shown in Figure 1.26.

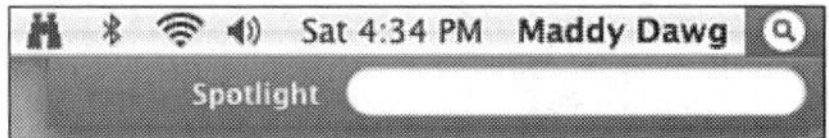

FIGURE 1.26 Enter a search term in the Spotlight search field.

As you type in the search field, the top matches are immediately displayed in a category-sorted list below the field. Clicking one of the results will open the appropriate document and, when appropriate, highlight the search term.

> **NOTE**
>
> If you notice the Spotlight menu icon pulsing, it is in the process of creating the initial index of your drive or a recently attached volume. Wait until it stops and Spotlight will be ready to go.

Because Spotlight has full access to the Tiger metadata, the search results can be a bit surprising. System Preference panels, for example, contain metadata describing their function in the system. If I received a brand new DSL modem and the instructions said I needed to configure PPPoE on my machine, entering that string in the Spotlight field would identify the Network System Preference panel and allow me to open it instantly.

Similarly, files that you wouldn't expect to have any searchable information can be targeted by Spotlight. Image files, for example, have a wide range of metadata that can be stored. Typing `Canon Powershot G5` locates images that were taken using my Powershot camera. Entering `640x480` identifies the photos that are stored at 640×480 resolution. I could go on and on, but the best way to see what Spotlight can do is to try it for yourself.

Expanding Spotlight Results

When a Spotlight search is finished, it's very possible to have located more items than can comfortably be displayed in the menu. As such, Spotlight provides the top matches to your query, much as Google doesn't overwhelm you with several million pages all at once. If you don't see what you're looking for within a set of search results or want more information about a particular item, choose Show All at the top of the Spotlight results list. This will create a free-floating window, as shown in Figure 1.27, that provides some additional control over the results.

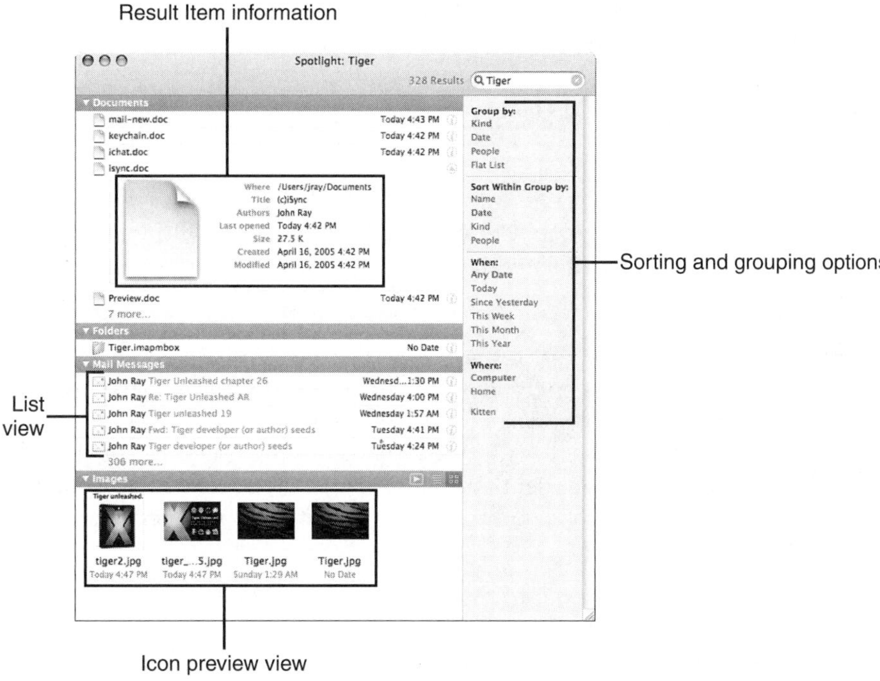

FIGURE 1.27 The Spotlight window gives greater control over the Spotlight search results.

> **TIP**
>
> If you'd prefer to start Spotlight in the full window mode, press Command-Option-Space at any time and the window will appear.

The pane on the right side of the window provides grouping and sorting controls. A unique element in the list is the ability to group and sort by People. This is an attribute available in many files that identifies a file's author. Another grouping option, Flat Lists, removes groups altogether and presents a single list including all the files. Other options, such as Kind, Name, Date, and so on, should be self-explanatory.

In the Spotlight window's content pane are the search results themselves, grouped as determined by the settings on the right. You can expand and collapse a group by using the disclosure arrows in front of the group name. Entries in the list can be double-clicked to open them, or can be dragged out of the window to move or copy them (the standard Finder key modifiers apply). Opening a contextual menu for a Spotlight result will also allow you to send the item as an email attachment, view it in a slideshow (if it is an image), create an Automator workflow that starts with that item, or reveal its location within the Finder.

Depending on the items within a group, you might see several small icons to the right of the group name; these can be used to change how the search results are displayed. Typically, results are displayed in a list. If an icon of four small squares is displayed, clicking it will display the results in an icon preview mode that shows icon representations of the contents of media files (images, PDFs, QuickTime movies). This feature can be seen in Figure 1.27.

To the right of each result entry is a lowercase i button. Clicking the button will display information, including a preview of the content with full playback controls for movies and sound files.

If all the search results don't file within the Spotlight results window, a More link will appear at bottom of each group. Clicking the link will show all the files in the group. You can shorten the listing by clicking the Show Top link, which will subsequently appear next to the group name.

Configuring Spotlight Categories and Privacy Features

By default, Spotlight lists every type of file that it can find. This makes for an impressive show, but most of us really won't need to identify preference panels on a daily basis. In addition, there are probably files that we'd prefer Spotlight ignored—temporary files, working directories, and confidential data, to name a few. To configure file types used in search results and private folders, open the Spotlight System Preference panel (path: `/Applications/System Preferences`).

There are two setting categories in the Spotlight pane. The first, "Search Results", shown in Figure 1.28, can be used to turn result categories on and off by clicking the check box in front of their names. You also can reorder the results by dragging categories with the list. Use the keyboard shortcut settings to change the keys used to invoke the Spotlight menu and window from the keyboard.

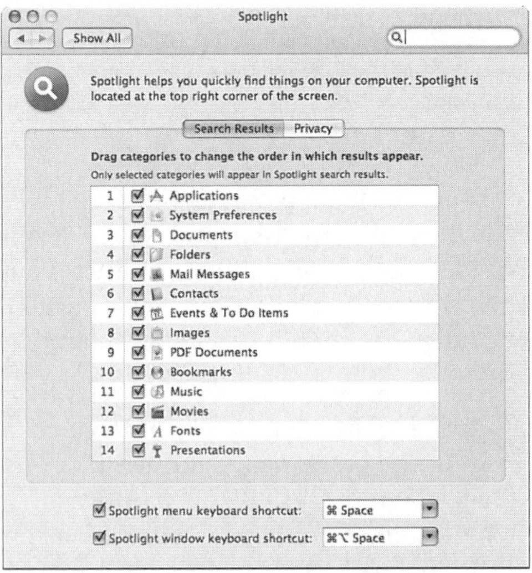

FIGURE 1.28 Choose the categories displayed in the Spotlight results.

The second set of options, "Privacy", restrict a location from the Spotlight indexing engine. Within the Privacy settings, either drag folders into the exclusion list or use the + button at the bottom of the window to browse to the location that will be restricted. After a path has been entered, it will not show up in the Spotlight results. To remove a restriction, select the path in the list and click the - button.

Working with Smart Folders and Finder Finds

Although Spotlight provides an excellent systemwide search, it returns very generalized results. In many cases, you might want to limit your searches by a specific file attribute rather than displaying everything that happens to match the search terms. To do this, Apple has reworked Finder's Find feature to integrate Spotlight functionality and has also introduced the notion of *Smart Folders*.

The Smart Folders in the Tiger Finder are a logical extension of Apple's Smart Folders within iTunes and other applications. A Smart Folder is a folder whose contents always match a stored set of search criteria. It isn't actually a folder in a traditional sense—you can't access it from the command line and you can't move files *into* it—but for other GUI operations (file browsing, opening/copying files), a Smart Folder behaves just like any other folder.

In the Tiger Finder, there are three ways to perform a search and use that search as the basis for a Smart Folder: by choosing File, Find (Command-F); or File, New Smart Folder (Option-Command-N); or by typing directly into the Find field within a window's toolbar. Even though these might seem quite different, they all have the same result—they start a new Spotlight-based search within Finder. If the search is saved, it becomes a Smart Folder. Not even choosing New Smart Folder actually *creates* the virtual folder until the search is saved. The only real difference between how a search or Smart Folder starts is the title shown at the top of the Finder window—for that reason, we will combine these two topics. If you're interested in searching but not in creating a Smart Folder, all you have to do is follow these instructions and *not* click Save.

Creating a Smart Folder

In previous versions of Mac OS X, you've had the ability to save a search so that you could run it in the future. In Tiger, a saved search *is* a Smart Folder. For example, to perform a search and create a Smart Folder from it, you would follow these steps:

1. Start a New Search with File, Find (Command-F).
2. Using the first line of buttons beneath the Finder toolbar, set the search scope to the entire computer, the home directory, or the folder being browsed when the search started. If you can't get to what you want from the default options, you can drag other folders or volumes from the Finder into this area and they will be added.
3. Next, choose the criteria and values to search for using the pop-up menus in the lines below the search scope. Each line contains file attributes that can be matched. If you run out of lines for search criteria, more can be added by clicking the + button on the last attribute line. Extra search criteria can be removed by clicking the - button.

4. If there is specific metadata you want to search for, choose Other from the attribute pop-up menu. A full list of available metadata items will be displayed, as seen in Figure 1.29.

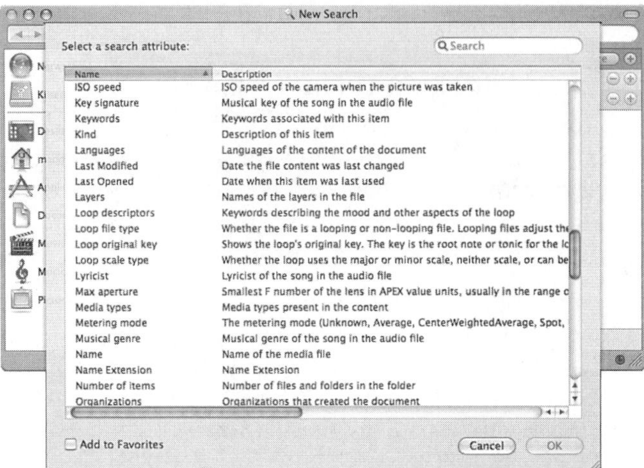

FIGURE 1.29 Choose search criteria from the full metadata list.

5. Select the metadata item from the list. If you plan to use this metadata item frequently, click the Add to Favorites check box. This will add the search criteria to the pop-up list of available attributes for future ease of access. Selecting Clear All Favorites from the attribute pop-up menu will clear any stored favorites.

6. If you are creating a search and want to search across *any* attribute (file name, metadata, and so forth), use the Find field in the Finder toolbar to supplement your search criteria.

7. As you enter your search criteria lines, a list of results will build below them. This list should look and act very similar to the Spotlight search list you saw earlier. If your goal was to simply perform a search, you're done.

8. To save the search as Smart Folder, click the Save button within the search scope line. You will be prompted for a location to save the file and whether you want the folder added to your Sidebar. Pick your poison and click Save. The Smart Folder will appear on your desktop, as shown in Figure 1.30.

After a Smart Folder has been created, you can open it and immediately see the search results. You can also alter the search criteria and resave the folder simply by changing the search lines at the top of the window and clicking Save. A small circular arrow icon at the bottom-right of the folder will rerun the search manually, if, for example, additional files have become available since the folder was opened.

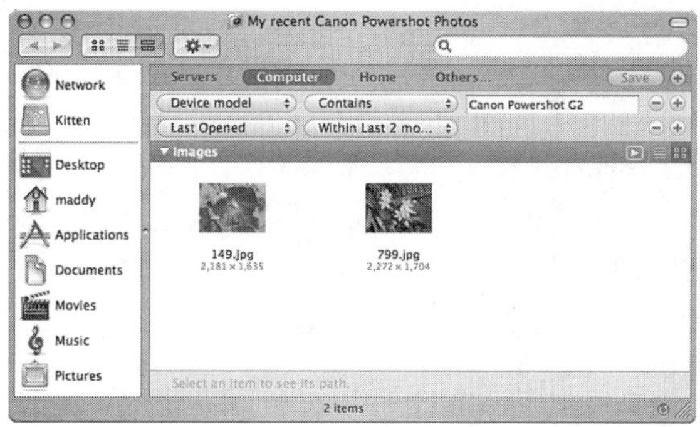

FIGURE 1.30 A Smart Folder is really just an instantly accessible saved search.

> **TIP**
>
> If you're attempting to find a file to open it, you'll be happy to learn that Tiger supports Spotlight within the File Open dialog boxes. A miniature of the same interface you use in Finder is accessible each time you go to open a file.

Changing Smart Folder Views

A Smart Folder, as we've said, works very similar to a traditional folder but doesn't allow files to be added to the folder (except by creating files that match the search criteria, of course). Files can be opened, moved, and copied to other locations. Since you have no immediate means of knowing where a result is located, a small bar across the bottom of the window reveals the full path to any selected file. Unfortunately, this bar, coupled with the criteria themselves, can become a bit distracting.

If you've used more than one or two search criteria, a Smart Folder's window real estate can suffer. One of the benefits of the Smart Folder approach is that it integrates visually with other Finder windows. The more search criteria and clutter, the less this holds true. To alleviate the problem, use the Action menu to hide the search criteria, or the View menu to choose a List, Icon, or Group (the default) style view for the search results. You can even open the View, Show View Options dialog (Command-J) to select the same visual settings as a normal Finder window, or grouping and sorting options while in the Group view.

The goal of Spotlight and the associated Smart Folder technology is to eliminate the dependence on the file system for providing organization. Rather than having to place each file in its own appropriate folder, Smart Folders break this dependence and allow groups of related files to fall anywhere on the file system.

Burning CDs and DVDs

Burning CD-Rs, CD-RWs, or DVDs within the Tiger Finder is similar to working with any other storage device. To make the process as transparent as possible, Tiger creates a hidden CD/DVD-sized temporary storage area on your hard drive. Applications, files, and folders that are added to a CD/DVD are actually copied to this location until the user tells the system to burn the CD/DVD. Only after the burn has started are files actually transferred to the CD/DVD media.

Drag and Drop Burning

To write your own CD/DVD, first insert media into the writer. The Tiger Finder prompts you to choose how you want to use the disc, as shown in Figure 1.31. Again, this doesn't actually write anything to the media just yet, but it tells the computer what your intentions are for the disc.

Enter a name for the disc you are writing—it will appear with this name on the desktop. Next, choose an action. Four are provided:

- Open Finder—An HFS+/ISO 9660 disk image for storing Macintosh data and files is mounted in the Finder.
- Open iTunes—Opens iTunes so that the CD can be used for burning MP3s. A CD image is not mounted.
- Open Other Application—Open another application to work with the CD (such as the popular Toast burning software).
- Run Script—Run an AppleScript.

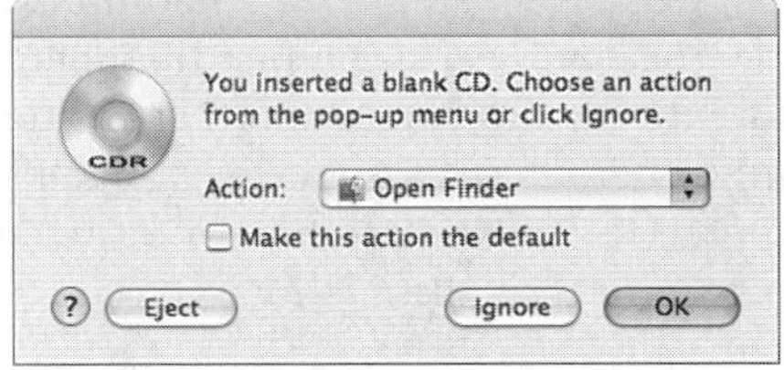

FIGURE 1.31 Before you can start using a CD, you must tell Tiger what type of CD it will be.

If you want to leave the CD in the drive but not prepare it, click Ignore. You can also choose to make the current settings the default with the Make This Action the Default check box. Because this chapter focuses on the Finder, choose Open Finder and then click OK.

After a few seconds, an icon representing the CD will appear on the desktop. You can interact with this virtual volume as you would any other under Tiger—copy files to it, delete files, and so on.

When you've created the CD layout that you like, you can start the burn process by choosing File, Burn Disc. In addition, dragging the CD to the trash also prompts for burning to begin. However you start it, Tiger will respond by displaying the dialog box shown in Figure 1.32.

> **NOTE**
>
> To choose File, Burn Disc from the menu, the frontmost Finder window must be the CD's window. If the CD is not the active window, the menu item will be disabled.

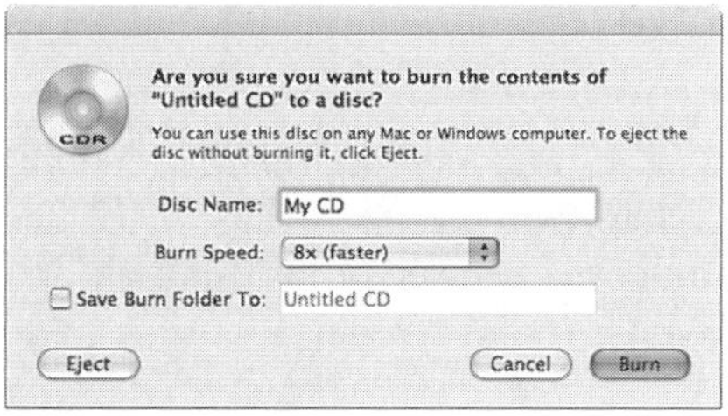

FIGURE 1.32 Choose Burn to write the CD.

Choose your burn speed and click the Burn button to start the process of writing the CD. This will take a few minutes and will be tracked by the Finder much like a normal copy operation. If you've decided against writing the CD, click Eject to remove the media and erase the CD layout you've created. You'll also notice that you can save a Burn Folder—this new Tiger feature makes creating CDs from commonly burned files and folders much simpler.

Creating Burn Folders

If you work on sets of files and frequently want to burn to CD or DVD, creating a Burn Folder gives you a convenient way to quickly burn the latest contents of multiple files and folders without having to drag them to a CD as described in the process just described.

To create a new Burn Folder, choose File, New Burn Folder. A folder with the yellow and black Burn symbol will appear, as shown in Figure 1.33.

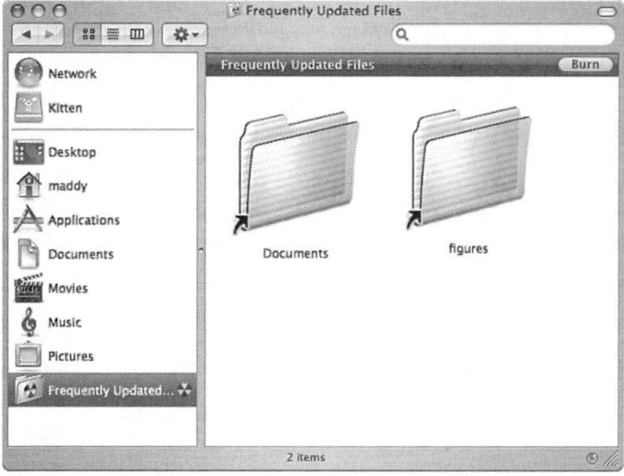

FIGURE 1.33 A Burn Folder enables you to group frequently updated files so that they can be burned at a moment's notice.

A Burn Folder acts like any other folder, but, when you drag an item into it, only an alias to that item is added. In addition, an extra line appears above the folder contents with a Burn button in it, and the folder is also displayed in the Sidebar with a Burn button. Whenever you want to burn the current contents to a CD, insert your optical media, and then click either of these buttons—the burning process will begin.

Customizing the Desktop

The desktop is, for all intents and purposes, a global Finder window that sits behind all the other windows on the system. You can copy files to the desktop, create aliases on the desktop, and so on. The primary difference is that the desktop is available only in the Icon View mode.

TIP

The contents of the desktop are also accessible from the Desktop folder contained within your home directory (path: `~/Desktop`).

Like other Finder windows, the desktop layout is controlled by the View Options located in the View menu. Use the Icon Size slider and arrangement settings exactly as you would adjust any other window within Icon View mode.

Changing Backgrounds and Screensavers

A more visually exciting change that you can perform on your Finder desktop is changing the background image. To do this, you can access the Desktop & Screen Saver panel within the System Preferences application.

Desktop Backgrounds After launching, make sure that the Desktop button is selected. Figure 1.34 shows the Desktop portion of the Desktop & Screen Saver Preferences pane.

TIP

To quickly enter the Desktop Preferences, Control-click on the Desktop background and choose Change Desktop Background from the contextual menu that appears.

To change the current background, drag an image file from the Finder into the image well within the pane. Alternatively, you can browse collections of images by choosing from the Collection list and then using the scrollbar to move through the available options. A collection is nothing more than a folder of images. There are six preset collections: Apple backgrounds, Nature, Abstract, Solid Colors, Pictures, and Desktop Pictures. The Pictures option selects your personal `~/Pictures` folder. To browse an arbitrary folder, choose the Choose Folder item, and then select the folder you want to use. (If you've created albums in iPhoto, these will also be displayed in the collection list.)

To have your desktop picture change automatically, click the Change Picture check box and then pick the change interval from the pop-up menu.

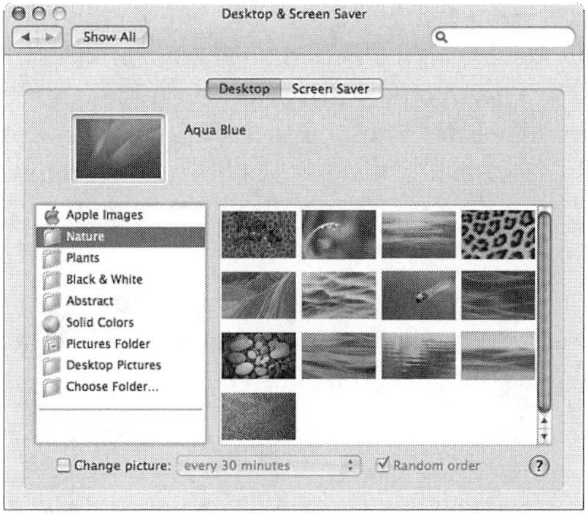

FIGURE 1.34 Set your background image using the Desktop Preferences pane.

> **NOTE**
>
> The Apple image collections are located within `/Library/Desktop Pictures` and can be added to or modified by any administrative user on the system.

Screensavers Screensavers are like desktop backgrounds for when you're lazy. Screensavers were traditionally invoked to save monitors from suffering burn-in. Today, screensavers are largely for show only and in reality serve only to shorten the lifespan of your LCD's backlight. Even so, they're fun to look at and, in Mac OS X, a screensaver engine is built-in.

To access the screensaver functions of the Desktop & Screen Saver pane, click the Screen Saver button within the preferences pane. Your display should resemble Figure 1.35.

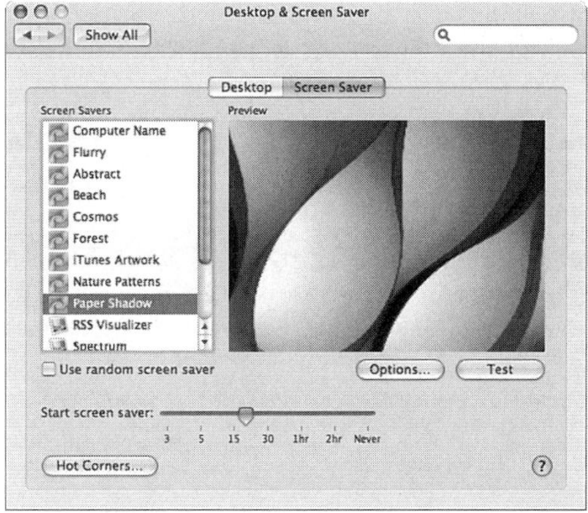

FIGURE 1.35 Set your computer to display pretty pictures when you're not working.

From the list on the left, choose a screensaver that sounds interesting. The Pictures Folder saver uses images in your Pictures directory to create an onscreen slideshow, and the Choose Folder saver allows you to choose an arbitrary folder to use for a slideshow. The .Mac option is discussed in Chapter 3. If you've created albums in iPhoto, these will also be displayed in the screensaver list. After you've chosen a screensaver, a preview will appear in the pane on the right. If you want a random screensaver to display each time it starts, click the Use Random Screen Saver check box.

Many screensavers offer configuration for fine-tuning their graphics and performance. Click the Options button to display a dialog containing advanced configuration for the selected screensaver. The Test button can be used to test the full-screen screensaver.

To set up when the screensaver will be displayed, use the Start Screen Saver slider to choose when (if ever) the screensaver should start. Because a screensaver doesn't actually turn off your display, this is largely meaningless; it is simply how long you have to wait until you see pretty pictures.

NOTE

Use the Energy Saver preferences pane to completely turn off your monitor after a set period of time.

Finally, to enable and choose corners where you can place your cursor to immediately (or never) start a screensaver, click the Hot Corners button. A dialog appears, allowing you to choose a screen corner to disable or start the screensaver as well as what corners activate the Exposé and Dashboard effects discussed shortly. Positioning your mouse in the chosen corner will have the selected effect.

TIP

Screensavers are plentiful (visit `http://www.versiontracker.com` or `http://www.macupdate.com` and search for *screen saver*).

To install a new screensaver, manually copy the `.saver` file to `/Library/Screen Savers` or `~/Library/Screen Savers` for use by all users on the system or for personal use, respectively. Or, take advantage of Tiger's capability to install it for you by double-clicking the file and then following the onscreen instructions.

TIP

To run the screensaver (discussed in the next section) as your desktop background, use the command `/System/Library/Frameworks/ScreenSaver.framework/Resources/_ScreenSaverEngine.app/Contents/MacOS/ScreenSaverEngine -background` or use a utility such as Xback (`http://www.gideonsoftworks.com/xback.html`).

Fine-tuning Finder Preferences

A few more Finder Preferences can be used to adjust even more settings that control how you will interact with your desktop and icons. Open the General preferences by choosing Finder, Preferences. Figure 1.36 shows the General pane.

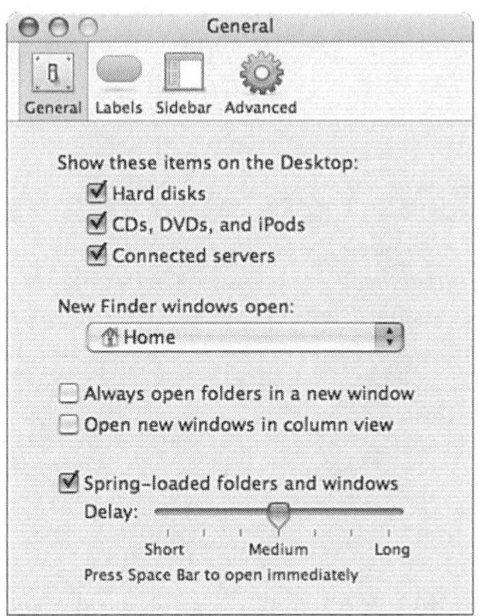

FIGURE 1.36 Finder Preferences control file extensions, trash warnings, and more.

Use the General Finder Preferences to configure these elements:

- Show These Items on the Desktop—Choose whether different storage devices will be automatically shown on the desktop. Use the "Hard Disks," "CDs, DVDs, and iPods," and "Connected Servers" check boxes to display the associated devices on the desktop. If an item is not on the desktop, it will be accessible by moving to the computer level of the filesystem hierarchy.
- New Finder windows Open—Determine what location a new Finder window opens in. Choose from common predefined locations or Other to pick an arbitrary path.
- Always Open Folders in a New Window—Clicking this option forces a new window to open each time a folder is double-clicked. This is the only way to make the toolbar-mode Finder windows behave like the traditional Finder.
- Open New Windows in Column View—Force all Finder windows being opened into the Column view.
- Spring-Loaded Folders and Windows—Choose the length of time a folder or window waits before springing open while your mouse hovers over it. Refer to the "Moving Files and Folders" section earlier in this chapter.

The Advanced pane provides a few more choices that ordinarily you won't need to change:

- Show All File Extensions—Turn on this setting to force all file extensions to be shown in the Finder and other windows. Most Mac users won't want to do this.
- Show Warning Before Emptying the Trash—When emptying the trash can, the system displays a warning message. To bypass this dialog, deselect this check box. Alternatively, hold down Option when choosing Empty Trash to temporarily bypass the warning.

A SIMPLER FINDER?

I'd like to introduce my child (husband, wife, mother, father) to Tiger, but she's not ready for Finder; what can I do? A Simple Finder mode can be activated on a per-user basis within the Accounts System Preferences pane. The Simple Finder removes much of the complexity (and feature set) of the standard Finder but makes operating the computer much easier for those who just want to launch applications. See Chapter 8, "Customizing User and System Settings," for information about user accounts.

Using the Dock

The Dock is constant within the interface. No matter what application you're in, the Dock is either present on your screen or a mouse motion away. The Dock supplements Finder operations by enabling you to launch applications, open documents, and delete items without having to dig through (or under) dozens of windows. Figure 1.37 shows the Dock.

FIGURE 1.37 The Dock acts as application launcher, switcher, and more.

Adding and Launching Application Shortcuts

To use the Dock as an application launcher, commonly used applications can be added to the Dock, much like a Finder toolbar, by dragging them to the position you want on the left side (or top in vertical mode) of the Dock divider bar. This half of the bar contains all docked and currently running applications.

If you have placed an application on the Dock, you can launch it by single-clicking the icon. The application icon begins bouncing and continues to do so until the software is ready for user interaction. A running application is denoted by a small triangle under its icon.

TIP

To add an application currently running to a permanent spot in the Dock, just click and hold (or Control-click) the icon, and then choose Keep in Dock from the pop-up menu.

Switching Active Applications

To switch between active applications, just click the icon of the application that you want to bring to the front. Holding down the Option key as you click on an application brings the application to the front and hides the previously active process. Simultaneously holding down both the Option and Command keys while clicking brings the clicked application to the front and hides all other applications.

To switch between open programs from the keyboard, use Command-Tab—this should seem familiar to Windows users. This displays a list of active icons, shown in Figure 1.38, that you can cycle through with the Tab key or via the arrow keys (as long as the Command key is held down).

FIGURE 1.38 Switch between active applications with Command-Tab.

TIP

To hide the currently selected application in the Command-Tab switcher, continue holding Command and press the H key. Similarly, to quit the application, keep Command held down and press the Q key.

Interacting with Running Applications

Common functions, such as quitting an application, hiding it, or jumping to one of its open windows, can be accessed by clicking and holding a running application's Dock icon or by Control-clicking on the icon. Some applications, such as iTunes, allow basic controls (playback controls, in the case of iTunes) to be accessed through the Dock pop-up menu. After the menu has appeared, you can press the Option key to reveal hidden menu options; this particular key/mouse combination changes a Dock icon's Quit selection to Force Quit when used.

Application icons also serve as proxy drop points for documents. You can drag documents on top of an application's Dock icon to open them in that application.

TIP

Dragging a document to a running application or to the trash is a bit of a pain. In an effort to accommodate the icon you're dragging with the assumption that you're adding it to the Dock, the other icons move out of its way. For a user, this means that the icon she's headed for might not hold still long enough for a traditional drag-and-drop operation. To keep the Dock icons from sliding, hold down the Command key during the drag.

TIP

To force a docked application to accept a dropped document that it doesn't recognize, hold down Command-Option when holding the document over the application icon. The icon immediately highlights, allowing you to perform your drag-and-drop action.

Creating File and Folder Shortcuts

Shortcuts to files and folders that are used frequently can be stored to the right (or bottom in vertical mode) of the Dock separator bar. When a folder is added to the Dock, it can be single-clicked to open a Finder window containing the contents of that folder. Clicking and holding (or Control-clicking) a folder in the Dock creates a pop-up hierarchical menu that displays the contents of the folder. Any elements added to the folder will be immediately visible in the pop-up menu.

TIP

Moving an icon to the Dock does not change the location of the original file or folder. The icon within the Dock is just an alias to the real file.

To locate an application, file, or folder that you've dragged to the Dock, hold down Command and click the Dock icon, or choose Show in Finder while Control-clicking or click-holding the icon. The Finder opens a window and highlights the original file or folder.

Using the Predefined Dock Shortcuts and Behaviors

The Dock, although a useful launching utility, also plays a critical role in some of the basic features of Tiger. Several predefined functions are resident as a permanent part of the Dock; these handy shortcuts can help you navigate, operate, and organize.

The Finder

The first icon on the left side (default orientation) of the Dock is the Finder icon. You can use the Finder icon to quickly jump to the Finder application or bring any active Finder window to the top.

Dashboard

The Dashboard icon, located directly to the left of the Finder icon, invokes Tiger's new mini-apps Dashboard. The Dashboard is a next generation desk accessory engine that enables you to run small utility applications and have them ready for use at any time. We'll talk more about the Dashboard in the "Using the Dashboard" section later in this chapter.

The Trash Can

The Mac OS trash can lives on the right side of the Dock. You can drag files and folders directly from the Finder into the Dock's trash can. If you want to remove an item from the trash, click the trash can icon, and a window appears containing all the items waiting to be deleted. You can drag files from this window just as you can in any other Finder window.

To empty the trash, use the Finder's application menu and choose Empty Trash (Shift-Command-Delete); or click-and-hold or Control-click the trash can icon, and choose Empty Trash from the pop-up menu. Holding down Option while emptying the trash bypasses any system warning messages. The Finder preferences can permanently disable the Empty Trash warning.

TIP

If you don't like Apple's new trash icons, you can replace them (along with several other built-in Dock icons) by opening `/System/Library/CoreServices/Dock.app/Contents/Resources` and editing the assorted `.png` image files located there. The `trashempty.png` and `trashfull.png` icons define the two states of the trash can.

Even easier, use CandyBar, by Panic Software (`http://www.panic.com`) to swap icon sets for your computer.

NOTE

Although not available from the Dock trash can's Empty Trash pop-up menu—keep in mind that the Secure Empty Trash option is available from Finder's application menu.

Ejecting Media

There are a number of ways to eject disks under Tiger. Control-clicking on a mounted volume opens a contextual menu with an Eject option. Alternatively, you can highlight the resource to remove and choose File, Eject (Command-E) from the Finder's menu; press the Eject key on most Apple keyboards; or use the Eject icon beside each removable resource in the Finder's shortcut pane.

The final method of ejecting a disk might seem a bit unusual to some users, but it has been a standard on the Macintosh for many years. Disks can be safely unmounted and ejected by dragging them to the trash can. To get around the obvious "Hey, isn't that going to erase my disk?" reaction that many have, the system conveniently changes the trash can icon into an eject symbol during a drag operation that includes a storage volume.

Windows

Minimized windows are placed in a thumbnail view beside the trash can. Depending on the application, these iconified windows might continue to update as their respective applications attempt to display new information. The QuickTime player, for example, can continue to play miniaturized movies in the Dock.

Customizing the Dock Appearance

After the initial "gee whiz, that's pretty" reaction to the Dock has worn off, you'll probably want to customize the Dock to better suit your Finder settings. Depending on your screen size, you might be looking at a Dock that, by default, eats up about one-third of the available desktop space on your machine. Don't worry; there are ways to rectify the situation.

For fine-tuning the Dock, turn to the System Preferences application. The Dock has a settings pane within System Preferences that you can use to adjust its size, adjust its icon magnification, and make it disappear when not in use. Users of Apple's widescreen PowerBooks or cinema-aspect displays, will be pleased to find that the Dock can even move into a vertical mode, occupying space along the sides of the screen.

Open System Preferences and then click the Dock icon, or choose Dock, Dock Preferences from the Apple menu. Your screen should now resemble Figure 1.39.

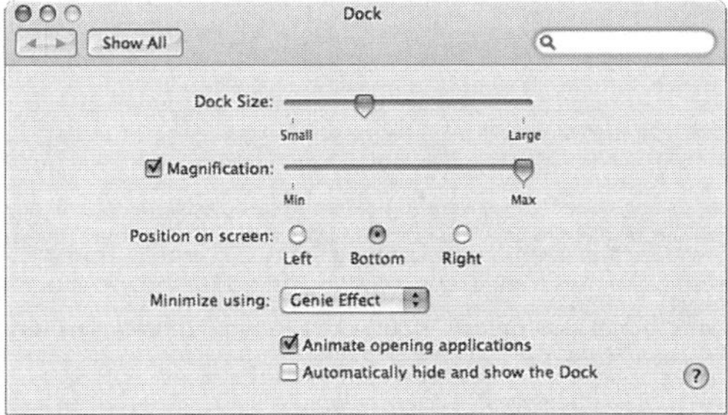

FIGURE 1.39 Customize the Dock's appearance from the Dock pane within the System Preferences application.

Within this pane, you can choose how you want the Dock to look and act on your computer. There are six settings:

- Dock Size—This sets the size of the Dock icons. Moving this slider from left to right increases the size of the default Dock icon. Keep in mind that the Dock does not expand beyond the edges of the screen and shrinks automatically to make room for additional icons.
- Magnification—If you activate Dock magnification by clicking the check box, the Dock icons automatically scale as you move your cursor over them. You can use the magnification slider to adjust the maximum size that a magnified icon will take. Although this is useful if you have an extremely small Dock, its main purpose seems

to be eye candy. If you haven't seen this effect demonstrated, turn it on—you're in for a treat.

- Position on Screen—Use these radio buttons (Left, Bottom, Right) to control where the Dock appears on your desktop. The default position is at the bottom of the screen, but many users may find that a vertical orientation (left or right) is more useful and appealing.
- Minimize Using—Audiences were wowed when they first saw the Dock's Genie effect for minimizing windows. Although nifty, it isn't exactly the fastest thing on the planet. Starting in Mac OS X 10.1, Apple includes a second minimization effect: Scale. This effect is much less dramatic but also much faster. Use the Minimize Using pop-up menu to choose your minimization style.
- Animate Opening Applications—By default, when an application is starting, the Dock bounces the application's icon up and down. This provides visual feedback that the system hasn't stalled. Shutting off this feature might result in a small speed increase but is likely to be a bit frustrating when you can no longer tell whether the system is starting the application you selected.
- Automatically Hide and Show the Dock—If this check box is set, the Dock automatically disappears when you move your mouse out of it. To make the Dock reappear, just move your cursor to the bottom of the screen—it will grow back into the original position. You can toggle this at any time from the Finder by pressing Option-Command-D.

Easy access to several of the Dock's configuration options is also available through the Dock submenu in the Apple menu or by Control-clicking the dock right/left separator line to show a Dock contextual menu.

HOW CAN I CONFIGURE DOCK SOUNDS?

What you're hearing when the Dock makes a "poof" are the interface sounds, which can be turned on from the Sound Preferences pane. The individual sound files are located at `/System/Library/Components/CoreAudio.component/Contents/Resources/SystemSounds` and can be replaced (at your own risk) with customized sound files.

TIP

The easiest and fastest way to resize the Dock is to click and hold on the divider line that separates the right and left sides of the Dock. With your mouse held down, drag up and down. The Dock dynamically resizes as you move your mouse. Let go of the mouse button when the Dock reaches the size you want.

After you've played with different Dock sizes, you might notice that some sizes look better than others. This is because Tiger must interpolate between several different native icon graphics to scale the images. To choose only native icon sizes, hold down the Option key while using the separator bar to resize.

TIP

There are three built-in minimizing effects for Mac OS X, two of which (Genie and Scale) are accessible in the Dock Preferences pane. You can manually switch to a third effect (Suck) by using the following command within the Terminal window:

```
defaults write com.apple.Dock mineffect suck
```

Accessing Common Functions Through Menu Extras

Opposite the Dock at the top of your screen lives (and I hope that you know this) the menu bar. Another workspace customization is the addition of Menu Extras to the menu bar. These are GUI elements that appear in the right side of the menu bar to the left of Spotlight. These handy additions provide quick access to common system settings or functions. Figure 1.40 shows a number of Menu Extras.

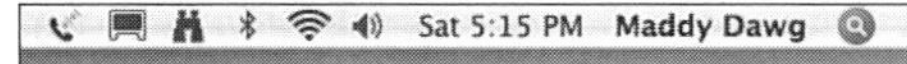

FIGURE 1.40 Menu Extras provide quick access to system settings.

Each Menu Extra is added to the menu bar through System Preferences panes that correspond to the item's function. A few of the Menu Extras provided in Tiger include

- Displays—Adjusts the resolution and color depth from the menu bar.
- Volume—Changes the sound volume.
- AirPort—Monitors AirPort signal strength and quickly adjusts network settings.
- iChat—Controls your connection to the AIM (AOL Instant Messenger) network. Provides quick access to online buddies and an easy way to change your AIM status.
- Date and Time—Displays date and time graphically as a miniature clock or using the standard text format.
- Battery—Keeps track of battery usage and recharge time.
- Modem Status—Displays modem connect time as well as options for initiating/terminating connections.

Clicking a Menu Extra opens a pop-down menu that displays additional information and settings. Items such as Battery and Date and Time can be modified to show textual information rather than a simple icon status representation.

You can alter the position of *some* Menu Extras by holding down the Command key and dragging the icons to the desired position. Menu Extras can be removed entirely by Command-dragging them off the menu bar.

Force Quitting Applications

For a long time, the Macintosh didn't have an effective and reliable method of quitting a hung application. Windows users are accustomed to pressing Control-Alt-Del to force an application to exit, but Mac users were stuck pressing Option-Command-Escape and hoping for the best. If a force quit worked without completely crashing Mac OS, it usually made the system unstable and forced a reboot within minutes.

The Option-Command-Escape keystroke still works, but now it brings up a small process manager with a list of running applications, as shown in Figure 1.41. Applications that your Mac has identified as crashed are highlighted in red.

FIGURE 1.41 Choose an application to kill and then click Force Quit.

To force an application to exit, just choose it from the list and click Force Quit. This terminates the application without reducing your system stability. If Finder seems to be misbehaving, you can choose it from the application list, and the Force Quit button becomes Relaunch—allowing you to quit and restart Finder without logging out.

You can also access the Force Quit feature from the Apple menu, or by opening the pop-up Dock menu for a running application and then pressing the Option key to toggle the standard Quit selection to Force Quit.

CAUTION

Forcing an application to quit does not save any open documents. Be sure that the application is truly stalled, not just busy, before you use this feature.

TIP

For more extensive information about process control within Tiger, see Chapter 12, "Managing Processes."

Managing Windows with Exposé

As you use Tiger, you'll find that way too often you've buried yourself in windows. Although you can minimize and maximize windows to find what you want, this is not an efficient way to deal with the clutter.

Apple recognized this and introduced a feature in 10.3 called *Exposé*. Rather than rearrange your workspace to find a specific window, Exposé temporarily rearranges all your windows so that you can see them simultaneously and find what you want. After you've located the window you want, you can select it by positioning your mouse over the top of it and clicking, shown in Figure 1.42. All the onscreen windows return to their original positions with the chosen window on top.

What makes Exposé unique is that it does not change your working environment (your windows stay exactly where they are), and it allows you to choose a window based on its content as well as its title (minimized windows are often too small to recognize the content).

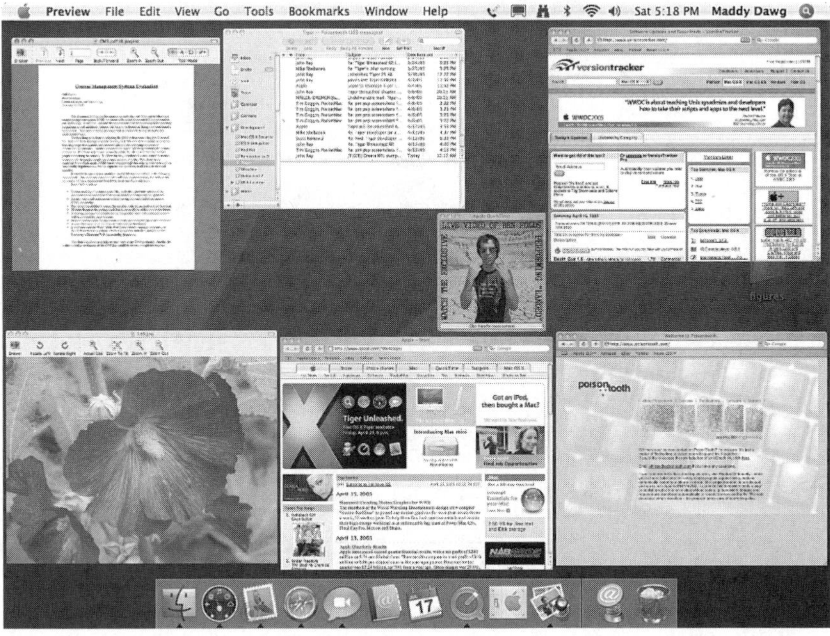

FIGURE 1.42 Itty-bitty windows, everywhere….

In addition to quickly locating windows, Exposé can be used to hide all active windows so that you can see your desktop, and then make them instantly reappear. This is useful for dragging and dropping icons that would normally be obscured from the desktop into your active applications.

To configure Exposé, open the Dashboard & Exposé & System Preferences pane shown in Figure 1.43.

FIGURE 1.43 Use Exposé to manage your window clutter.

At the top of the Exposé pane, choose whether the Exposé effect will be activated by moving the mouse into any of the four screen corners. Moving the mouse into a corner starts Exposé; moving back into the corner returns the windows to normal. There are three separate Exposé effects from which to choose:

- All Windows—Shrinks all onscreen windows to locate a specific one.
- Application Windows—Shrinks all the current application's windows to find a window within your chosen program.
- Desktop—Moves all windows temporarily off screen to access the desktop.

Setting a screen corner to - removes any action previously attached to that corner.

NOTE

Because Exposé, the Tiger Dashboard, and Screensavers can be activated by placing your mouse in a screen corner, you'll notice that you can configure screensaver and Dashboard corners in Exposé.

At the bottom of the Exposé pane, you can choose keyboard shortcuts for each of the Exposé modes and Dashboard, eliminating the need to mouse across the screen. Holding down Shift, Control, Option, or Command when choosing a keyboard shortcut sets a modifier key that must also be held down to activate the Exposé mode.

TIP

When using Exposé in All Windows or Application Windows modes, pressing the Tab key cycles through each active application's windows. This is an *extremely* useful feature if you have dozens of open windows and working through them all in the All Windows mode proves to be a bit overwhelming.

Using the Dashboard

Since the first demonstrations of Dashboard, Apple has been referring to it as "Exposé for Widgets!" and has even gone so far as to include Dashboard preferences within the Exposé panel. Considering that we had Hide All before Exposé, I can only wonder if Apple would have been calling it an equally meaningless "Hide All for Widgets!" if it were introduced a few years ago.

What does Exposé have to do with Dashboard? Nothing, other than they both turn your screen slightly dark and won't let you interact with any active applications.

What Is Dashboard?

Dashboard is a modern implementation of "lite" applications—Desk Accessories as they were called in 1984. These miniature applications are now called *widgets* and run on a layer that is normally not visible on your desktop. By pressing a button (F12, by default), the Dashboard zooms into view and you can use the various widget tools to quickly look up addresses in your address book, play simple games, and interact with various Internet information sources. When you're finished using dashboard, you just press F12 again and it zooms out of view.

What makes Dashboard more useful than just running standard Tiger applications to access the same functionality is that it is *always* available and maintains a static configuration. You can start a calculator widget, game widget, and a dozen other widgets, arrange them on your screen and, even after reboots, they'll appear just where you left them by starting the Dashboard.

Activating and Deactivating the Dashboard

To activate the Dashboard, click the Dashboard icon in the Dock or press the F12 key. You can also set up a hot corner for starting Dashboard using the Exposé & Dashboard System Preference panel discussed in the previous section, "Managing Windows with Exposé."

Your screen will change to a dark gray color and further clicks will not be transferred to your running applications. You are now within the Dashboard layer. There should be a few widgets active by default, as shown in Figure 1.44. After a few seconds, you can start interacting with the widgets—clicking, typing, and so on.

To deactivate the Dashboard, just click outside of one of the active widgets, press the F12 key, or use the chosen hot-corner again and your screen will go back to normal.

TIP

Some widgets might offer features that require you to drag content into them from other applications or the Finder. The Tile Game widget, for example, allows you to customize the background picture by dragging in a new picture. To do this seemingly impossible task, just start dragging the file/content, activate Dashboard, and then finish dragging.

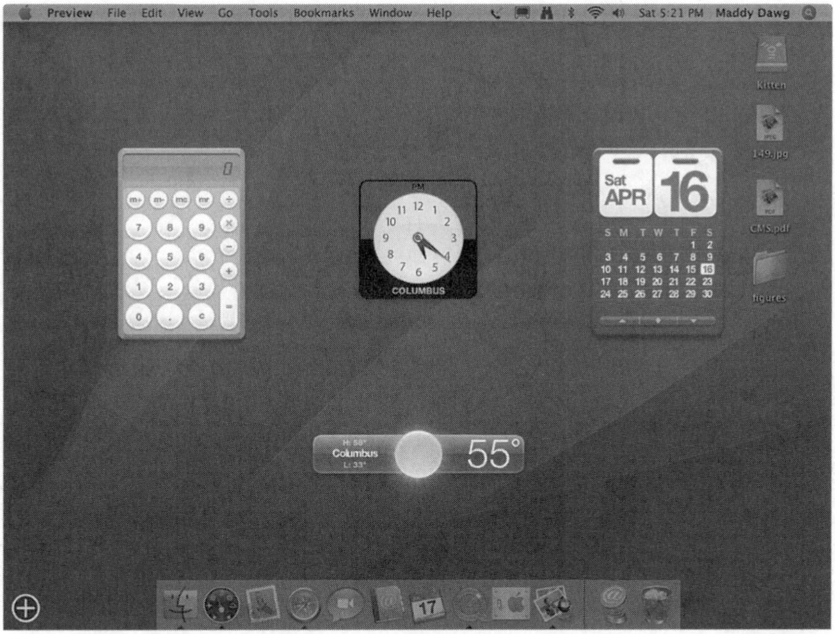

FIGURE 1.44 The Dashboard starts and displays any active widgets.

Managing Widgets

Obviously, the key to doing anything productive with the Dashboard is finding and adding the right widgets to the screen. To access the Dashboard widget library, click the + icon located in the bottom-left corner of the screen. A horizontal scrolling list of widgets will appear. You can click and drag from this widget repository to anywhere on your screen and the widget will launch and appear at that location, as seen in Figure 1.45. For some widgets, you can add multiple instances to the screen. Stickies, for example, would hardly be useful if you could have only one onscreen at a time.

The first time a third-party widget is launched, you might see a warning asking whether you should trust the file. If you have downloaded it from a reputable source, click OK; if not, you probably shouldn't be running it.

While the widget library is open, you can close any active widgets by clicking the X icon in their upper-left corners.

To close the widget library itself, click the + icon again.

Widget preferences are usually accessed by clicking a small "i" on the face of the widget. This will spin the widget around (a nifty graphical effect borrowed from Sun's Project Looking-glass) to reveal additional settings and features on the "back" of the widget's window. Widget settings can be accessed regardless of the state of the widget library.

FIGURE 1.45 Add new widgets to your screen using the widget library.

Adding Widgets to the Widget Library

Adding new widgets to your widget library is simple. To download widgets directly from Apple, click the More Widgets link in the widget library and then follow the onscreen instructions. To install a third-party widget that isn't included in this list, download the widget to your desktop (outside of Dashboard) and place it in either `/Library/Widgets` or `~/Library/Widgets` for systemwide or personal use, respectively. Or just double-click the widget file and it will be installed for you automatically.

Using Fast User Switching

To ease access to a computer by multiple people, Tiger includes *fast user switching*. By default, if you've added multiple user accounts to your computer (see Chapter 8 for information), you have to close your applications and then choose Log Out from the Apple menu to allow another user to access the system. In Tiger, fast user switching can preserve your current desktop, let another user log in and use his account, and then return you to where you left off.

To enable fast user switching, open the Accounts system preferences pane, authenticate by clicking the lock icon in the lower-left corner, and then click the Login Options button. Your screen should resemble Figure 1.46.

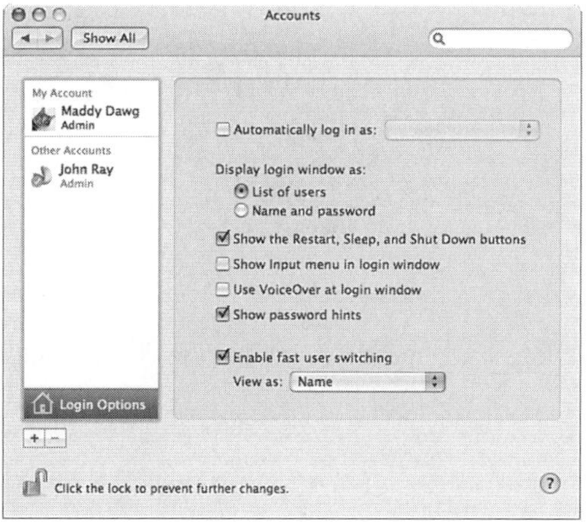

FIGURE 1.46 Enable fast user switching.

Click the Enable Fast User Switching check box and choose how you would like to the switching menu to appear in the menu bar (as the current user's name, short name, or just an icon).

A menu item will appear in the upper-right corner of the menu bar—the switching menu, directly to the left of Spotlight. Clicking the menu reveals a list of local user accounts with login enabled along with a Login Window option. Choosing a user's name prompts for that user's login information and then switches to the user's desktop. Choosing the Login Window selection leaves your applications running but displays the login window, allowing other users to log in without disrupting your workspace.

TIP

If you want to be able to switch to another user account without entering that user's password, the user *must* have a blank password. See Chapter 8 for more information on setting up user accounts.

User accounts that are active (that is, have running applications) are denoted with an orange check mark in front of their name in the switching menu and the login screen, as shown in Figure 1.47. Switching to an active account is almost instantaneous.

CAUTION

Users should log out (Shift-Command-Q) completely when finished using the computer. Shutting down or restarting your computer while there are active sessions could result in lost data for users who are still logged in.

FIGURE 1.47 Active sessions are denoted by an orange check mark in the switching menu and login screen.

Help Viewer

Finishing up our look at the Tiger workspace is the Help Viewer. The Help Viewer provides a simple browserlike interface to help files for many OS Apple and third-party applications. For example, Figure 1.48 shows the basic Tiger help screen.

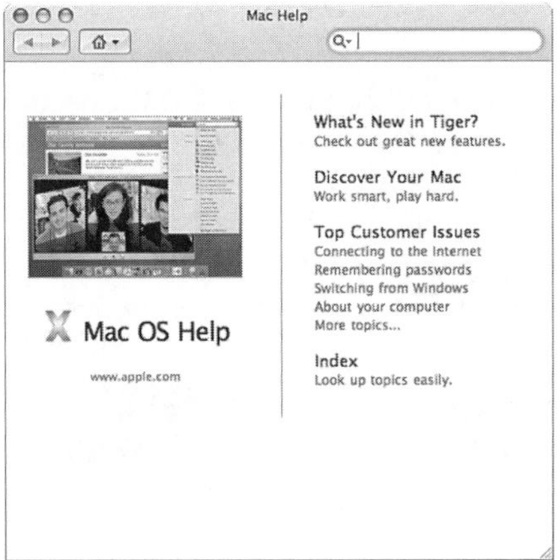

FIGURE 1.48 The help system works exactly like a web browser.

You can click through the browser information just as you would a web browser. Put your mouse over something of interest (it should underline or already be underlined if it is clickable) and then click.

The Tiger help is divided into guides that are automatically installed with your applications. To browse a guide for a particular program, choose it from the Library menu or click and hold the Home button in the toolbar. You can return to the top of the guide you are browsing by single-clicking the home button. The arrows in the window's toolbar move you forward and backward through the pages you've viewed.

To locate specific information, type a few keywords in the Search field, such as `open PDFs`, and then press the Return key. A few seconds later, the Help Viewer application displays all matching documents that it found, along with a relevance rating and the guide that it was located in. Choose an item in the list and then click Show at the bottom of the viewer to open the corresponding documents.

TIP

The guide index is generated by aliases to individual applications' HTML help folders placed in `~/Library/Documentation/Help`. You can copy these aliases to the systemwide `/Library/Documentation/Help` directory to make them available to all users, or delete them if you don't want the help guide to appear in the list.

To improve the timeliness of information delivered by Help Viewer, below the initial help results Apple also includes online support documents (denoted by a red + icon to the left of each document's title). This information is often related to solving specific problems with a certain technology or feature and is an excellent resource for troubleshooting something that just isn't working as documented.

Summary

In Tiger, Finder continues to evolve with new features and capabilities. Spotlight and Smart Folders open up new possibilities in filesystem navigation and organization, whereas Exposé and Dashboard provide a means of managing the ever-growing problem of window clutter. With each release of Mac OS X, Apple continues to improve the Macintosh user experience and add features never before seen on *any* operating system.

CHAPTER 2

Useful Tiger Applications and Utilities

IN THIS CHAPTER

- Storing Contact Information: Address Book
- Creating Calendars, Events, and To Do Lists: iCal
- Basic Image and PDF Manipulation: Preview
- Multimedia Playback: QuickTime 7
- Storing and Managing Sensitive Information: Keychain Access
- Synchronizing Information Between Devices: iSync
- Running Legacy Mac OS Applications: Classic
- Other Tools and Utilities

Tiger comes with dozens of utilities and applications—many of which can be easily cataloged, such as the Internet and scripting tools discussed in the upcoming chapters. Many applications, however, can't easily be assigned a category. This chapter covers the Tiger applications and utilities that you're likely to use *regularly*. If you're a big fan of Stickies, sorry; it gets an honorable mention, but we have to draw the line somewhere!

Storing Contact Information: Address Book

The Tiger Address Book (path: `/Applications/Address Book`) is more than a simple contact manager or a mailing label printer. It is a systemwide database that stores all your contact information and is accessible from other applications that require you to "contact people." So, you, ask, what are these other applications; email is the only place where it could be useful, right? Wrong. Address Book data is available in Safari, Mail, Sherlock, iCal, Fax, iChat AV, Dashboard, and more! A properly maintained Address Book can organize your data and streamline how you use your computer.

Understanding the Address Book Standards

With the LDAP protocol *(Lightweight Directory Access Protocol)* and vCard 3.0 Personal Data Interchange format, the Address Book is based entirely on open standards and can be used in a cross-platform environment.

vCards

The most common way to send contact information with an email is by adding a signature. Unfortunately, there is no standard for signatures, so picking up contact information from one is an exercise in futility. The vCard (`.vcf`) format attempts to change this by defining a simple cross-platform MIME standard for an electronic business card. vCards can be used on PDAs such as the Palm Pilot, and then copied to your system and used directly within the Address Book application.

Tiger uses version 3.0 of the vCard standard, developed by the Internet Mail Consortium and documented in RFC2426 (`http://www.ietf.org/rfc/rfc2426.txt`). A sample vCard, generated by Michael Heydasch's vCard CGI (`http://www.vicintl.com/vcf/`) is shown here.

```
BEGIN:VCARD
  FN:Mr. John P. Smith, Jr.
  TITLE:General Manager
  ORG:XYZ Corp.;North American Division;Manufacturing
  ADR;POSTAL;WORK:;;P.O. Box 10010;AnyCity;AnyState;00000;U.S.A.
  LABEL;POSTAL;WORK;ENCODING=QUOTED-PRINTABLE:P.O. Box 10010=0D=0A=
  Anywhere, TN 37849=0D=0A=
  U.S.A.
  ADR;PARCEL;WORK:;133 Anywhere St.;Suite 360;AnyCity;AnyState;00000;U.S.A.
  LABEL;POSTAL;WORK;ENCODING=QUOTED-PRINTABLE:133 Anywhere St.=0D=0A=
  Anywhere, TN 37849=0D=0A=
  U.S.A.
  TEL;Work;VOICE;MESG;PREF:+1-234-456-7891 x56473
  TEL;Home:+1-234-456-7891
  TEL;Pager:+1-234-456-7891
  TEL;Cell:+1-234-456-7891
  TEL;Modem;FAX:+1-234-456-7891,,*3
  EMAIL;Internet:webmaster@anywhere.com
  URL:http://www.anywhere.com/mrh.vcf
  UID:http://www.anywhere.com/mrh.vcf
  TZ:-0500
  BDAY:1997-11-29
  REV:20010510T104344
  VERSION:2.1
END:VCARD
```

The vCard defines a person object based on X.520 and X.521 directory services standards—implemented on a large scale in enterprise directory systems. Even encoded images can be included in vCards!

After a vCard has been generated, it can be attached to email messages for easy importing into remote address books. In Tiger, you can drag the vCard from an Email message window into the Address Book, and it will be added to your contact list. To attach your own vCard, you can drag from the Address Book into a message Compose window.

LDAP

The Lightweight Directory Access Protocol defines a means of querying remote directory systems that contain personnel data. Linux, Windows, and Mac OS X computers all have the capability to poll LDAP servers for account information, such as login and password.

The Address Book uses LDAP server connectivity to retrieve contact information from network servers. You can add your own LDAP server to the mix as long as you know the name or IP address of the server, and the search base.

The *search base* defines a starting point in the LDAP hierarchy to begin looking for information. Companies might have their LDAP directories built based on a per-department schema or other arrangement. Unless you are the LDAP administrator, it is impossible to guess the appropriate search base. Your best bet is not to use a search base, or to contact your network administrator for the correct value. Bases are specified in the following format:

```
<key name>=<base string>
```

My internal search base for my small `poisontooth.com` domain is just `cn=poisontooth.com`—but the complexity varies from server to server.

Finding Your Way Around the Address Book

The main Address Book window, shown in Figure 2.1, has two viewing styles: Card and Column view and Card Only view. To toggle between them, use the View buttons at the upper left. You will do most of your work with Address Book in Card and Column view. The Card view displays only a single contact at a time, making its usefulness questionable, although you *can* use the arrows at the bottom right to move between cards.

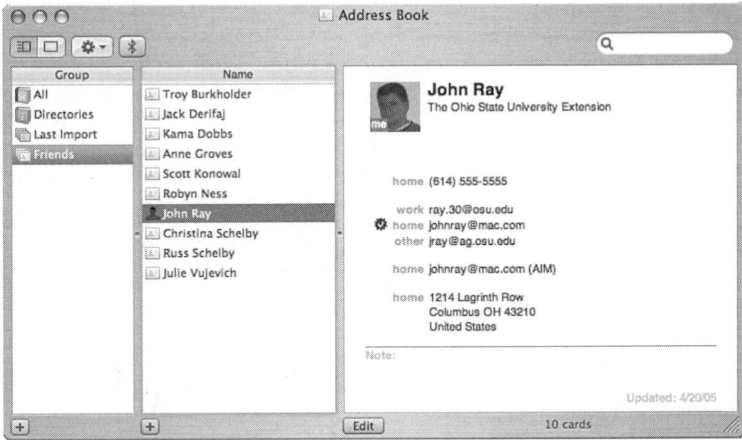

FIGURE 2.1 The Address Book, shown here in Card and Column view, keeps track of your contact information with a simple uncluttered interface.

The Card and Column view displays a three-column view with these elements:

- Group—A list of all the groups of contacts on your system. The three predefined groups are All, which shows the contents of all your group, Directories (LDAP Servers), and Last Import, which contains the last card/cards you imported via LDAP or from an external source.
- Name/Directory—The contacts (or available directory servers) within the selected group.
- Contact Card—A business card view of the currently selected contact.

At the bottom of the Group and Name columns are + buttons that add new Groups and Contacts to the system. Under the Contact Card pane is an Edit button that switches the current contact to Edit mode.

You can browse through your contacts much like using the Finder's column view. Choose a group and then a contact within the group, and view that contact's information in the Contact pane. The Search field at the top of the Address Book window searches the currently selected group for a string of your choice.

Working with Address Book Cards

Because Address Book maintains contact information, the base unit of information is a single person stored in an Address Book card. Address cards can store multiple addresses, phone numbers, and contact information for an individual, making it unnecessary to maintain multiple cards for a single person.

Adding and Editing Contacts

To add a card, select a group that should contain the contact. If this is your first time using Address Book, you'll have only the All group—this is fine, you can organize your contacts into groups at any time. Next, click the + button under the Name column; this opens a blank card in the right column where you can type the information you want to save.

There are fields for name, work and mobile phone, email address, names of friends/assistants, AIM handle, and address as well as a space at the bottom for notes. You can Tab between fields or click into the ones you want to insert. You can add as much or as little information as you want, but an email address is required if you plan to use the card with Mail, and an AIM handle is required for iChat AV.

> **NOTE**
>
> vCards are a standard across multiple platforms and are often included in email messages. You can drag vCard attachments (resembling a little Rolodex card) from within the Mail application into Address Book to add them.

If the label to the left of the field doesn't match the information you want to add, you can adjust it by clicking the up/down arrow icon. This opens a pop-up menu with several common labels as well as an option to customize. In some cases, such as adding a phone number, you may want (or need) to add multiple values. When you're editing a field that supports multiple entries, plus and minus buttons appear to the left of the field. Clicking the plus button adds a new field of the same type; minus removes the field. To add completely *new* fields, choose Card, Add Field; then pick from any of the available fields.

TIP

The default template for creating new cards can be changed in the Address Book application preferences, or by choosing Card, Add Field, Edit Template.

In the upper-left corner of the Card column is the card image well (a drop point for images). If you want to add a custom picture, you can paste it into the well, double-click the picture well, or select Card, Choose Custom Image from the menu to open a window where you can drag an image file and zoom/crop the image, or even take a video snapshot. This process is *identical* to setting your Buddy icon in iChat, which is covered in detail in Chapter 3, "Using the Tiger Internet Application Suite." To clear a custom image, select Card, Clear Custom Image.

When you've finished adding information, click the Edit button again to deselect it, and the unfilled fields disappear.

To edit a card you've already created, select the name of the individual from the Name column and click the Edit button below the Card column, or choose Edit, Edit Card (Command-L) from the menu.

To delete a card, select it and press the Delete key on your keyboard or choose Edit, Delete Card. You are asked to confirm the action before it is carried out.

Setting Your Owner Card

Besides contact information for *other* people, Address Book also holds your personal address card. By telling the system who and where you are, it can simplifying processes in other applications—such as drawing a map to an address or finding movies that are nearby (Sherlock). When you create a Tiger account, it automatically adds a card for you, the owner. This card, unlike others, is represented with a "head" icon in the Address Book listings.

In the event you enter a new card for yourself, you can tell Address Book which card it is by selecting the card, and then choose Card, Make This My Card from the menus. You can jump to your own card at any time by choosing Card, Go to My Card.

Choosing Name and Company Information Ordering

When storing information about a company, it is often desirable to display the card with a company name first, followed by a personal contact within the company. Address Book can accommodate this preference by choosing Card, This Is a Company (Command+\) from the menu bar, or by clicking the Company check box when in edit mode. The card icon will also change to three small buildings.

Another common display preference is to view cards as lastname, firstname rather than the more casual firstname lastname default ordering. To make this change, choose Card, Swap First/Last Name. To reset to the default ordering, choose Card, Reset First/Last Name to Default.

NOTE

The card "name swap" changes affect only the currently selected card(s). To change the default name ordering (first/last, last/first) use the General pane of the application preferences.

Setting Custom Telephone Formats

To create and choose custom phone layouts and activate/deactivate automatic formatting of phone numbers, open the Phone application preferences, shown in Figure 2.2. Note that auto-formatting must be enabled for you to use the custom defined layouts.

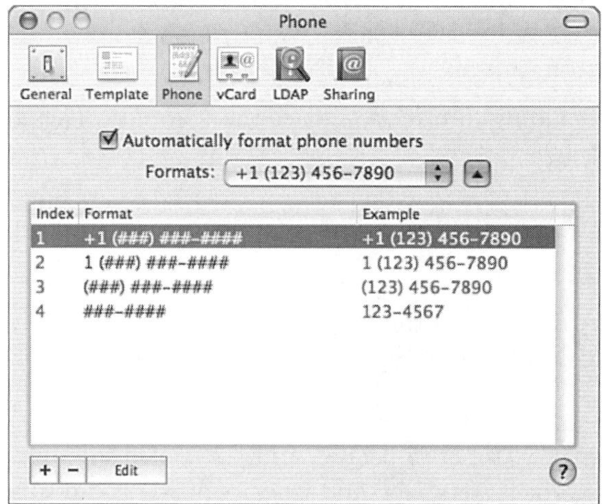

FIGURE 2.2 Create custom phone number formats.

Use the Formats menu to choose from one of the predefined formats, or click the disclosure button to display the format editor. To use the format editor, click the + button to add a new format and type the number format as you want it to appear, substituting the pound (#) sign for the actual phone number digits.

Creating Custom Address Card Templates

If you find that the default Address Card format doesn't suit your needs, you can create an entirely new default template with the Template application preferences pane. Using the same controls available when creating a card entry, you can create your own custom template, as shown in Figure 2.3.

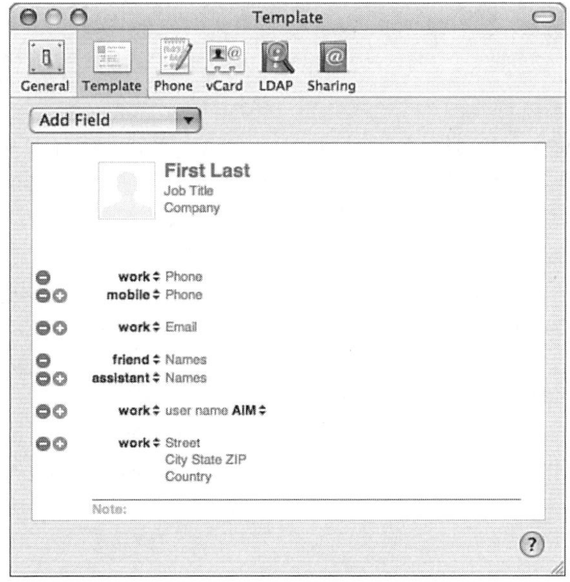

FIGURE 2.3 Create your own custom Address Book templates.

Use the Add Field pop-up menu to add additional fields to the template. After closing the preference pane, the new template will be active.

Merging Duplicate Cards

As you use applications like Mail and iChat AV, you're likely to end up with duplicates of many of your contacts. You might have friends with multiple AIM accounts and so forth that are added twice.

Address Book's Merge Selected Cards function (Command+I) found under the Card menu can take multiple contact cards and merge them into a single card—removing any redundant data in the process.

Tiger also adds a duplicate card "finder" that will automatically locate duplicates and merge them, if desired. To use this feature, choose Cards, Look for Duplicate Entries Address Book will scan your contacts and, if duplicates are found, prompt to merge them.

Viewing Cards

When a card is not in Edit mode, the Action button (Gear icon) and many of the card labels provide links to useful functions. Clicking a friend/relation name, for example, displays the option to jump to that person's contact card, if it exists.

Another unique feature is the capability to display a web-based map of any street address in your address book. Click the label to the right of any address field and choose Map Of from the pop-up menu. Your web browser opens to a map of the location. You can also choose to copy the URL of the map, or copy an address-label form of the address to the Clipboard.

NOTE

The action button actually provides fewer options than clicking directly on the labels. Go figure.

If you have the Apple Bluetooth adapter, you can click the button in the Address Book to locate paired Bluetooth phones within range. You can then click a phone number within an address card and choose Dial from the pop-up menu to dial your phone.

In addition, Bluetooth-paired phones automatically trigger Address Book to display the Address card (if available) for incoming calls, and provide the capability to answer the call or send the call to voicemail.

Organizing Contacts into Groups

You can arrange your cards into your own custom groups, which, in addition to creating organization, can be used to send email to a collection of people—for example, a simple mailing list.

Creating Groups

To create a group, click the + button under the Group column and type a name for it (Shift+Command+N). You can add contacts to the group by selecting another contact group (such as All or a Directory group) and dragging the contact card icons from the Name column to the new group. Hold down the Command key to select more than one addressee at a time.

If you already know who is going to be in a new group, you can create a group based on an initial selection of contacts. To do this, first select all the contacts you want in the group, and then choose File, New Group from Selection.

Setting Up Distribution Groups

An Address Book group can be used with Mail to send messages to a group of people simultaneously by dragging the group into the Address field in Mail, or by Control-clicking the group name and choosing Mail To.

When used in this manner, the group is considered a *distribution group*. All Address Book groups can be used as distribution groups, but before using them, you might want to choose which email address each contact in the group uses when the message is sent. Because many people have multiple addresses, it is likely that some addresses are more appropriate to use than others.

To choose the addresses for a distribution list, highlight your group in Address Book; then choose Edit, Edit Distribution List. A window similar to that shown in Figure 2.4 appears.

Use the pop-up menu in the upper right-left of the Distribution List window to switch all contacts in the group to their work, home, or other addresses. To switch on a person-by-person basis, click the correct contact address in the list to highlight it.

When all the correct addresses are selected, click OK. You can now use your Address Book group as a mailing distribution list.

FIGURE 2.4 Choose the address to use if a group is used to send email.

Creating Smart Groups

After using Tiger for awhile, you'll begin to wonder if your previous versions of the operating system were, well, stupid. Smart Folders in the Finder, Smart Mailboxes in Mail, and now, Smart Group in Address Book—Tiger is very, *very smart*. A Smart Group is a virtual address book group whose members are based on search criteria rather than specific cards. For example, you might create a smart group for Columbus, OH based on phone numbers beginning with 614 (or a city of Columbus and state of Ohio). The Smart Group doesn't require that you rearrange any of your existing groups; if a contact matches, it is included—it's as simple as that.

To add a Smart Group, choose File, New Smart Group (Option+Command+N). The Smart Group creation dialog is displayed, as seen in Figure 2.5.

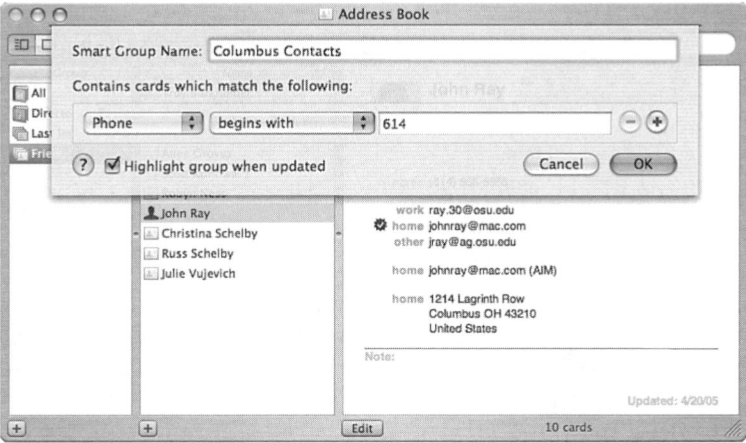

FIGURE 2.5 Choose the criteria for your Smart Address Book Group.

Provide a name for the group, and then use the pop-up menus and search fields to create the search criteria. Click the + button to add additional search fields, or the - button to remove unneeded criteria.

Because you won't manually be adding anything to the Smart Groups, Address Book will automatically highlight Smart Groups when a new contact has matched their criteria. If you find this distracting, uncheck the Highlight Group When Updated check box.

Click OK to create your new Smart Group. To edit the group, select it and then use the Edit menu or Control-Click the group name and choose Edit Smart Group.

Sending Owner Card Updates

If you happen to update your personal contact information frequently (or infrequently, for that matter), you can configure Address Book to automatically notify an Address Book group of the changes.

Open the General application preference pane and click the Notify People When My Card Changes check box. When you change any piece of information in your card, you are prompted whether you want to email the update to your contacts. You can choose the groups to send email to, and type a brief message to them, as shown in Figure 2.6.

FIGURE 2.6 Provide a brief message notifying your friends/family/coworkers of your contact changes.

To force a notification to go out manually, choose File, Send Updates from the menu.

Setting Up Directory Servers

Many companies and organizations maintain their personnel information on certain directory servers. LDAP, as discussed earlier, is a common method for retrieving information from a directory server. To set up Address Book for LDAP queries, open the LDAP pane in the application preferences. The LDAP pane allows you to configure multiple LDAP servers to query. The + button opens a sheet for configuring your server, as shown in Figure 2.7.

Add a name for the server that will be displayed in the Address Book, along with the necessary information for querying the directory.

Click Save to save the LDAP server. You can use the +, -, and Edit buttons in the LDAP tab to manage your LDAP servers.

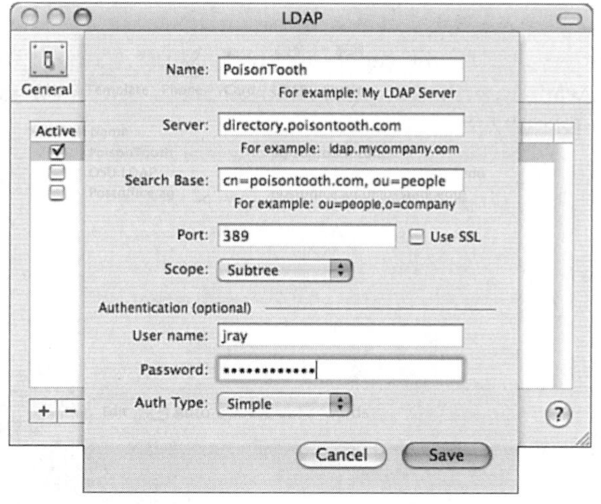

FIGURE 2.7 Set up your LDAP server in the LDAP preferences pane.

To automatically inherit changes to contact information made on the central server, be sure the Auto-Update LDAP Cards check box is selected.

Searching an LDAP Server

After adding an LDAP server, you can choose the Directories group in the Address Book window and then select the directory server you added. Finally, type a query string in the Search field and press the Return key. The results are displayed in a list, as shown in Figure 2.8.

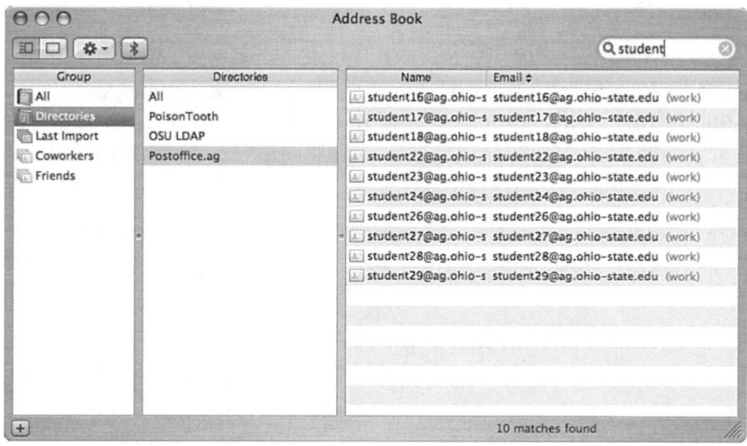

FIGURE 2.8 Search an LDAP directory for contact information.

You can drag any entry in the result list to the All group or one of your personally defined groups. It will be added and can be edited like any other address card.

Printing Envelopes, Mailing Lists, and Labels

Built into Tiger's Address Book is the capability to easily print labels. To print labels, first select the group you want to print and then Choose File, Print. Address Book displays the dialog box shown in Figure 2.9.

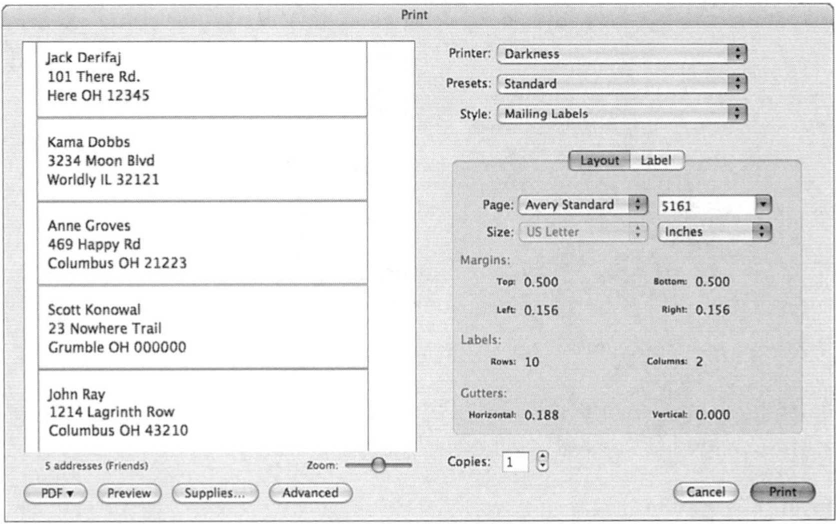

FIGURE 2.9 Print lists, labels, and envelopes with ease.

Use the Style pop-up menu to choose between envelopes, a mailing label layout, a "cute" pocket mailing list, and a simple list of names. When printing lists, you are given the option of choosing which attributes are printed in the list and what font to use.

Mailing labels (the style chosen in Figure 2.9) provide settings for controlling your paper layout under the Layout button bar option and include several label standards, such as Avery. The Label button displays settings for choosing between which Address Book addresses are printed (Home or Work), sorting, font options, and an image that can be printed beside each address.

Make your setting choices and view the results in the preview on the left side of the window; then click Print to start printing.

Importing and Exporting vCard Data

The easiest way to import or export cards from the Address Book is to drag the contacts in and out of the application. You can also export and import vCards and groups directly from the File, Import and Export menus.

Use the vCard application preference pane, shown in Figure 2.10, to choose the default format of your address card exports (2.1 or 3.0).

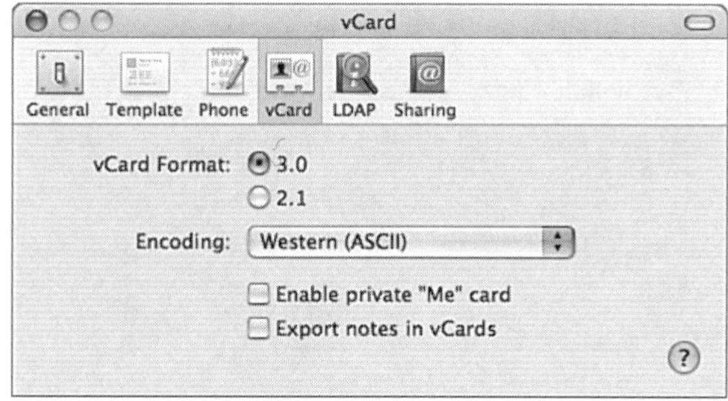

FIGURE 2.10 Choose your vCard export options.

You can also ensure the privacy of your personal card by enabling the Enable Private 'Me' Card option. This keeps everything but your *work* contact data from being exported with your card. By default, the Notes field is not included in any export—to *include* notes, check the Export Notes check box.

NOTE

Many applications, including Address Book, have a Scripts menu that provides access to many prebuilt AppleScripts. Address Book includes scripts for importing addresses from other applications.

TIP

To back up *all* Address Book data in a nonportable format for your own use, choose File, Backup Address Book. You can restore any previous backup with File, Revert to Address Book Backup.

Sharing and Synchronizing Contacts Through .Mac

Address Book provides two additional features for .Mac users—the ability to synchronize contact information between computers and share address books with other .Mac members. To turn on Contact synchronization, open the General application preference pane and choose Synchronize My Contacts with Other Computers Using .Mac, as shown in Figure 2.11.

When they're active, all computers registered with your .Mac account will automatically sync their contact information; changes on one machine will be reflected on another. To learn more about managing your .Mac synchronization, refer to Chapter 3.

NOTE

Exchange users will be happy to know that Address Book now supports Exchange synchronization. This is discussed in Chapter 27, "Working with Windows-Based Systems."

FIGURE 2.11 Activate Contact syncing with .Mac.

The second .Mac feature is the ability to publish contact information through .Mac and subscribe to other .Mac users' data. To share your information, open the Sharing pane in the application preferences, as shown in Figure 2.12.

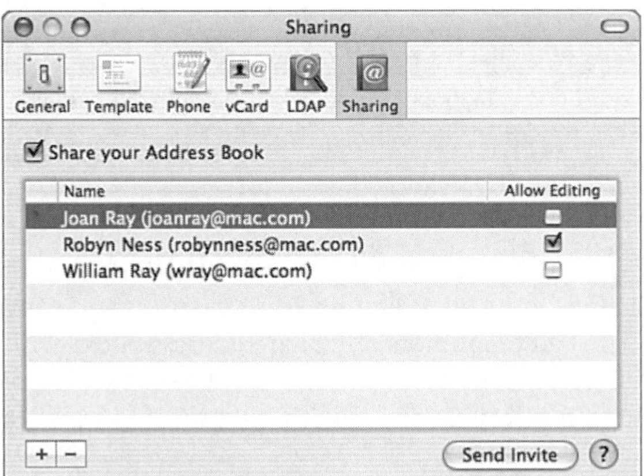

FIGURE 2.12 Configure who can subscribe to and (if desired) edit your contacts.

Click the Share Your Address Book check box to enable sharing. Next, use the + button to add a user that can access your shared information. Address Book with display a list of contacts. Choose one or more .Mac members, and then click OK to add them to your access list. If you want to permit a user to edit your contacts, click the Allow Editing check box beside that user's name. After setting up users and permissions, click Send Invite to invite the members to subscribe to your shared address book.

To subscribe to a shared address book, choose File, Subscribe to Address Book and provide the full .Mac address of the published address book owner when prompted. After a few seconds, a new Address Book group labeled with the publisher's name will be added to the bottom of the contact group listings. You can interact with this group as you would any other—even editing entries if the publisher granted you permission.

Creating Calendars, Events, and To Do Lists: iCal

The iCal calendaring solution is Apple's first in-house calendar for the Macintosh and one of the only available standards-based scheduling applications for the Macintosh. iCal supports network calendar publishing and subscribing, event notifications and invitations, and, of course, a lovely Aqua interface.

Understanding the iCal/vCal Standard

iCal gets its name from both Apple's i marketing department and the calendar standard it supports—iCalendar. The iCalendar standard is defined in RFC 2445: `http://www.ietf.org/rfc/rfc2445.txt`. For a change, we can blame someone else for adding the i in front of an otherwise perfectly usable title. The iCalendar format is an object-oriented description language that can define a series of event objects within a calendar object, and a series of alarms within each event.

For example, a single one-calendar, one-event, one-alarm iCal file looks like this:

```
BEGIN:VCALENDAR
CALSCALE:GREGORIAN
X-WR-TIMEZONE;VALUE=TEXT:US/Pacific
VERSION:2.0
BEGIN:VEVENT
SEQUENCE:1
UID:1380303474
DTSTAMP:20050910
SUMMARY:MS PACMAN Auction
DESCRIPTION: A Classic Ms. Pacman Arcade Game. Mint Condition
DTSTART;TZID=US/Pacific:20050917T121631
DURATION:PT1H00M
BEGIN:VALARM
TRIGGER;VALUE=DURATION:-PT15M
ACTION:DISPLAY
DESCRIPTION:Event reminder
END:VALARM
END:VEVENT
END:VCALENDAR
```

The `BEGIN` and `END` statements mark the start and end of an iCal object definition. In this example, a calendar object in the Pacific time zone is created; then an event is defined for a Ms. Pac-Man arcade game auction that starts on 09/17/2005 at 12:16:31AM and lasts for

1 hour and 00 minutes. Within that event, an alarm is defined that displays a warning when the current time is equal to the auction time minus 15 minutes.

By basing iCal on a standard, Apple has opened up the door to integration with enterprise calendaring solutions (including MS Exchange) and the exchange of information to and from a wide variety of platforms such as the Windows Outlook client.

Managing Calendars and Calendar Views

iCal's strength is in its simplicity. If you can use a personal organizer, you can use iCal. Almost all iCal activities take place in a single window, shown in Figure 2.13.

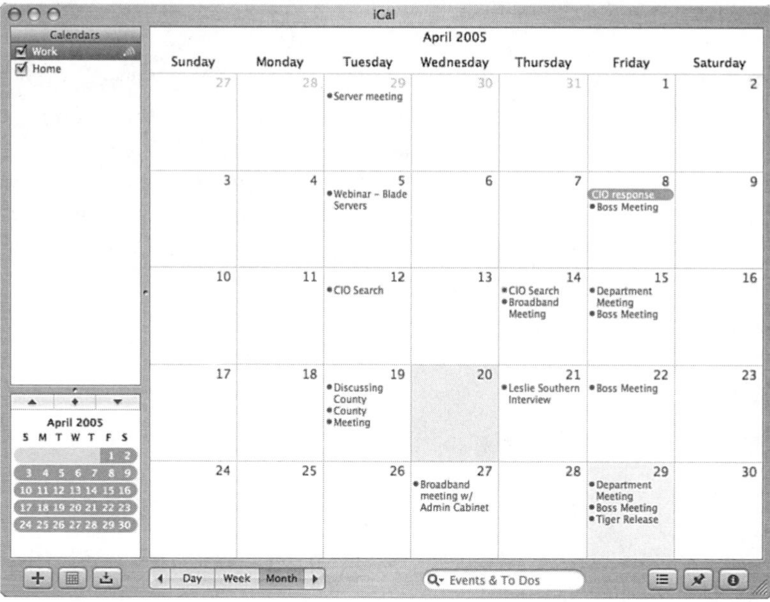

FIGURE 2.13 The iCal workspace gives you complete control over your schedule.

Adding and Removing Calendars

The upper-left corner of the iCal workspace is the Calendars list. Each calendar that you've added or subscribed to is displayed here. By default, iCal comes with two Calendars—Home and Work. These can be used or deleted; it's up to you.

> **TIP**
>
> A special virtual Birthdays calendar also exists in iCal, but is disabled by default. This calendar automatically uses Address Book information to display all the birthdays of your contacts. To enable the birthday calendar, choose Show Birthdays Calendar in the General application preference pane.

To add a calendar, click the + button under the Calendar pane, or by choose File, New Calendar (Option-Command-N). Calendars can be deleted by highlighting them in the list and pressing the Delete key, or by choosing Edit, Delete from the menu. To reorder calendars, simply drag them up and down within the list.

Navigating Calendar Views

To the right of the calendar list is the calendar viewing area. Calendars with the check box in front of them selected are active and are displayed in the main calendar view to the right of the Calendars list. Multiple active calendars are superimposed over one another to allow them to be viewed simultaneously.

The Day, Week, and Month buttons beneath the viewing area determine the style of the main calendar—whether you're looking at a single day, week, or month. The arrows to either side of these buttons move forward and back to the next appropriate calendar unit (day, week, or month).

A Month calendar view looks like a traditional wall or desk calendar. The Day and Week views divide each day up by hours, enabling you to see event start and stop times easily, as shown in Figure 2.14.

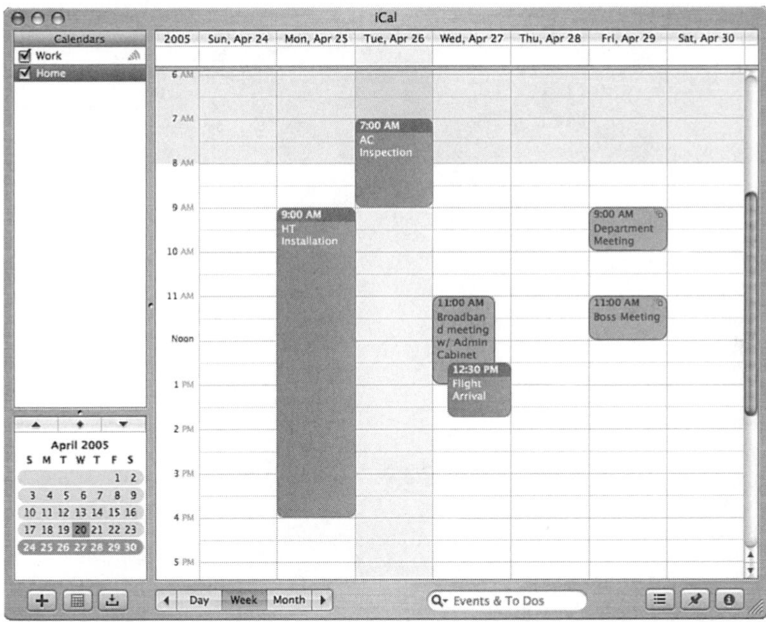

FIGURE 2.14 Day and Week views show your workdays broken up by hour.

> **TIP**
>
> The General application preference pane can be used to change display attributes for the calendar views—such as setting the week start day, choosing the typical working hours, displaying times on the monthly calendar, and so on.

When using the day or week views, a separate All Day area is displayed at the top of the calendar—events that fall within this division do not have a specific start or stop time; instead, they occur "that day." You might, for example, enter in birthdays or anniversaries as all-day events. We'll cover adding events shortly.

Directly beneath the Calendars list is a mini-month view. Move through the months using the three icons (up arrow, diamond, and down arrow) to move back, to the current day in the calendar view, or to the next month, respectively. Clicking a date within one of the mini-months jumps the main calendar view to that day. You can shrink this view dragging the divider line between the Calendars list and the by-month view, or click the small calendar icon below the Calendar list.

Setting Calendar Notes and Colors

The Color of the check box beside a calendar is the color used to display events in the viewing area. You can choose the color of your calendar as well as enter notes for it using the Information pane. iCal's Information pane, accessed by clicking the i button in the lower-right corner of the window, opens a window drawer that provides customization of a selected object. When a calendar in the calendar list is highlighted, the information drawer gives you access color and notes for the calendar, as shown in Figure 2.15.

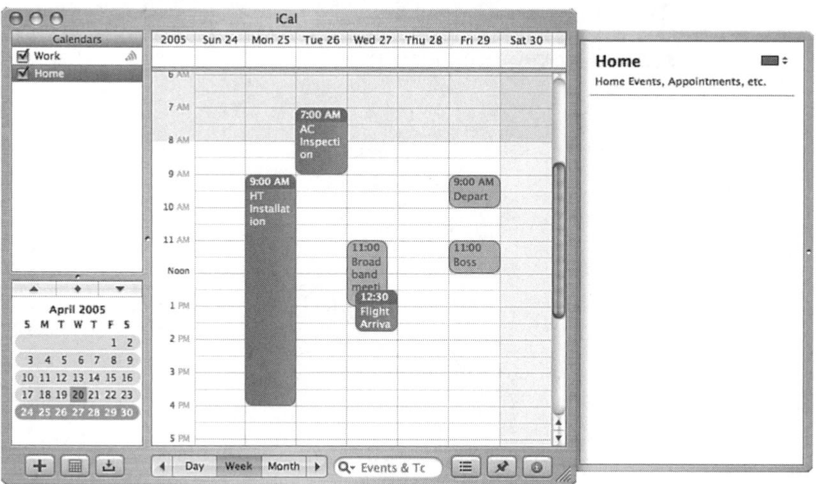

FIGURE 2.15 Enter colors and notes for your calendar.

> **NOTE**
>
> The Information drawer can be detached into a separate window by choosing Window, Detach Info from the menu.

Grouping Calendars

New to Tiger's iCal are calendar groups. You might, for example, want to maintain a personal calendar, but also want to divide your person entries into doctor appointments, family gatherings, and such. With calendar groups, this is as simple as creating separate calendars for each of these event types, and then organizing them all under a Personal group—similar to putting files in a folder.

To create a group, choose File, New Calendar Group (Command+Shift+N). A hierarchical group will be added to the calendar list. You can name the group just as you would a calendar, and then drag existing calendars onto the name to file them within the group. The group can be expanded by using the disclosure arrow in front of the name. You can use the group's check box to turn on and off all the contained calendars, or expand the group and use the check boxes for each individual calendar for more granular control.

Like calendars, you can select a calendar group and open the Information panel. The only available settings, however, are the calendar name and a brief description field.

Managing Events

When you understand how to navigate calendars, your next step will be creating events. Events are the content of your calendar. At the most simplistic level, they are defined by a title and a time. More complex event scenarios including repeating events, attendees, and event invitations can also be handled by iCal.

Adding and Editing Events

Adding an event is easiest within the Day and Week calendar views. Highlight the calendar that should hold the event, navigate in the calendar view to the day where you want to create an event, and then click and drag from the start time to the end time. As you drag, the event end time will be displayed near your cursor.

A New Event box is drawn that covers the selected time, and, when you release the mouse button, the subject (title) is highlighted. Start typing immediately to enter a new subject (title), or double-click the event subject to edit it after it has been deselected. Figure 2.16 shows a day view with a new event (Meeting with Annican) added.

After an event has been added, it can be dragged between different time slots or days. The event duration can be changed by putting the cursor at the bottom edge or top edge of the event block and dragging it to resize the box.

You can also add new events using File, New Event (Command-N). This creates a new one-hour event starting one hour after the *current* time but on the selected day. Use the editing techniques discussed previously to position and change its duration.

NOTE

Although events on the same calendar cannot be drawn over the same time slot, you can make two events at the same time with the same duration by creating them in separate time slots and then dragging them to the same slot.

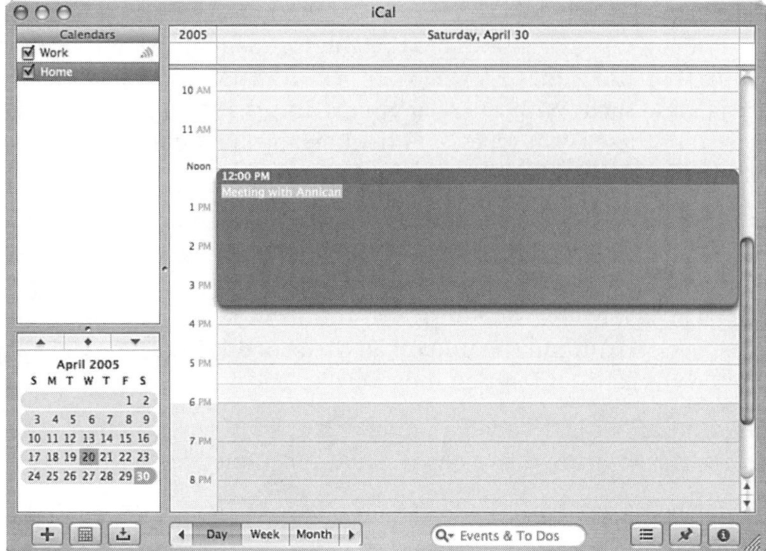

FIGURE 2.16 Add new events by clicking and dragging to cover the desired time span.

If you prefer working within the Month view, you can add new events in this view by double-clicking on the calendar cell of a given day. This creates a new event and extends the Information drawer, which provides convenient access to the time/duration values for the event.

TIP

If you'd prefer to edit the event duration by dragging, you can quickly jump to the Day view by double-clicking the date (number) in the Month view.

To remove any event, highlight it in any of the three calendar views; then press your Delete key, or choose Edit, Delete.

TIP

To automatically remove events that have passed, choose the Delete Events XX Days After They Have Passed option in the Advanced application preference pane.

Setting Event Alarms, Locations, and Other Attributes

Events can store quite a bit more information than just a start and end time. To access the additional fields, highlight an event and click the information button in the lower right corner of the iCal window.

Information can be entered in any or all of the following fields:

- Event Title—The name of the event being edited.
- Event Location—An arbitrary value, presumably where the event is taking place.

- All-Day—Whether it is an all-day event (not scheduled for a specific time). All-day events are shown above the hourly events in Day and Week views.
- From/To—The date/time/duration of the event.
- Repeat—If an event occurs over several days, weeks, months, or years, use the Repeat field to set how often it appears on your calendar. You can also choose when the recurrences will end, if ever.
- Attendees—Individuals who will be attending or at least invited to an event. This will be discussed shortly.
- Alarm—Choose to display a message, send an email, play a sound, open a file, or run a script. After choosing an action, a second field appears allowing you to set the number of minutes, hours, or days before an event starts that the action will take place. iCal does *not* need to be open for an alarm to be triggered.
- Calendar—The calendar the event is stored on. Use this field to easily move an event between calendars.
- URL—A URL pertinent to the given event.
- Notes—General notes and other information you might want to store about an event.

TIP

If you want to store time zone information with events, you can add a Time Zone field to the Event Information display using the Advanced pane of the iCal application preferences.

NOTE

iCal does not need to be active for alarms to go off. If you'd prefer to only sound alarms when the application *is* open, choose Turn Off Alarms When iCal Is Not Open from the Advanced application preference pane.

Working with Event Attendees and Invitations

Events don't usually happen in a vacuum. If you're planning a party and no one else is invited, you might have a problem. iCal supports the notion of event invitations and acceptance. After creating an event, you can invite other people listed in your address book to the event, and they, in turn, can accept or decline. All without having to type a thing or interpret someone's cryptic response.

Adding Event Attendees

To add attendees to an event, switch to the Day or Week calendar view so that the event is visible. Next, open the Information drawer. You should see a field called Attendees. Here, start typing email addresses or names. If they are recognized as an Address Book entry, they will be automatically completed. Press the Return key between multiple addresses. After an address is added and recognized, it becomes an object in iCal. You can use the small pull-down menu attached to each attendee to choose between multiple email addresses stored for them, or to remove them or manually edit their email addresses.

An easier method of adding attendees is to invite people directly from your Address Book. Open the Address Panel window by selected Window, Address Panel from the menu (Option-Command-A). The Address Panel is just a "lite" interface to Address Book. To add an attendee or attendees, dragging their vCard or a group vCard onto the Attendees field or even the event itself. An icon of a person appears in the upper-right corner of the event in Day or Week view mode.

Sending Event Invitations

After you've added attendees to an event, you've officially told iCal that you want to invite the listed people, but you haven't yet sent invitations. To do this, click the Send button at the bottom of the Information drawer for the event.

When you click the Send Invitations button, iCal works with Mail to send an invitation file to the people on the list. You'll also notice the attendees are displayed with an arrow icon in front of their names. This indicates that they have not yet responded to an event invitation. Confirmed attendees are displayed with a check mark, whereas declined attendees show an X and tentative attendees are shown with a ?.

If an event changes, or you alter any of the information within an event, you can send the updated event data to all the attendees by clicking the Send button in the information drawer again.

Receiving Responses and Notifications

When an attendee responds to an invitation, you will receive the response as an iCal email attachment. Tiger's Mail application recognizes and automatically adds the response information to iCal and also triggers an iCal notification that describes the response. Notifications are stored in the Notifications box, which can be made visible by clicking the inbox icon—third from the left—at the bottom-left side of the iCal window. This is demonstrated in Figure 2.17.

The status of an event's invitations and status is reflected by icons in the upper right corners of the event boxes (in Day or Week views). Events with a crossed circle in the corner have been canceled, those with an ellipsis (...) have received mixed responses from the attendees (some have declined, whereas others accepted), and, finally, an exclamation point indicates that the event has changed and needs updating.

A count of active notifications is also added as a count overlaid on the iCal dock icon, letting you know whether there are either responses or incoming event invitations that you need to deal with.

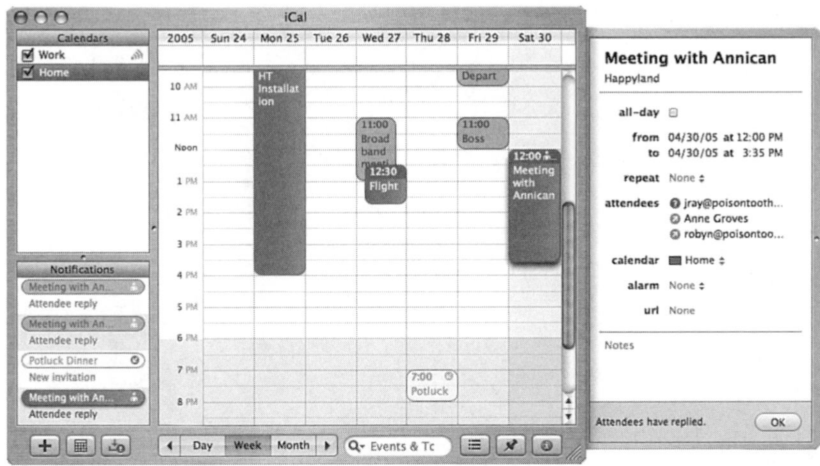

FIGURE 2.17 The Notifications area displays information about event responses and invitations.

Responding to Event Invitations

The recipient of an invitation, assuming that he has iCal installed, will automatically have the event added to iCal when it arrives in his Mail Inbox.

> **NOTE**
>
> To disable the automatic addition of events and responses through Tiger Mail, deselect Automatically Retrieve Invitations from Mail in the Advanced pane of the iCal application preferences. (This is also found in the Add Invitations to iCal setting in the General application preferences pane of Mail.)
>
> After it has been deactivated, you must manually click iCal email attachments to import responses and invitations.

Even though event invitations are automatically added to iCal, they are not stored in any active calendar. Instead, they appear within the Notifications pane and are overlaid in gray on the calendar so you can better visualize how the event fits your schedule.

To view event details and send a response, either double-click the notification or the gray event within your calendar. iCal opens the Information drawer for the invitation as seen in Figure 2.18.

Here you can choose to accept, tentatively accept, or decline the invite, what calendar to add it to, and whether an alarm should be set for the event.

To send a response, choose your status settings, and then click the Reply button. Another automatically generated message is sent back to the event creator, which will update *their* calendar with your response.

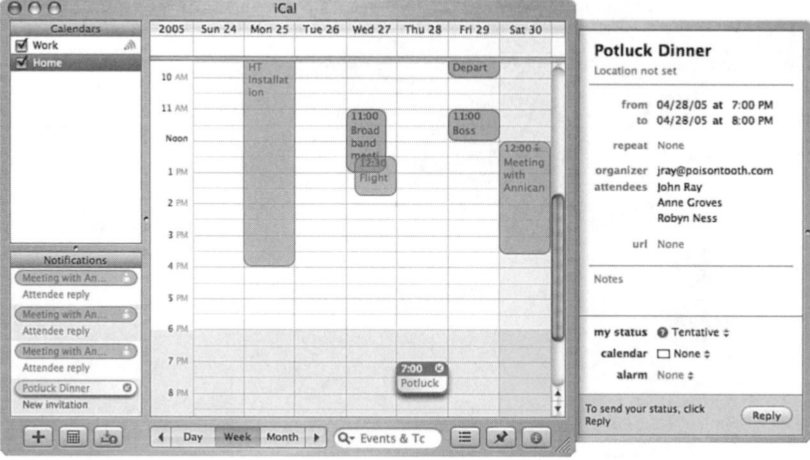

FIGURE 2.18 An invitation is in progress.

> **CAUTION**
>
> Mail's ability to automatically add iCal responses and invitations to a calendar only extends to your account inboxes. If you have server-side rules that sort your mail into other folders, invitations in those folders will *not* be recognized, even if they are flagged as new mail.

Creating To Do Lists

A To Do item differs from an event in that it doesn't take place at a certain time but often must be completed by a given date. iCal can track your To Do items using the To Do List. Click the pushpin icon in the lower-right corner of the iCal window to display the To Do List, shown in Figure 2.19.

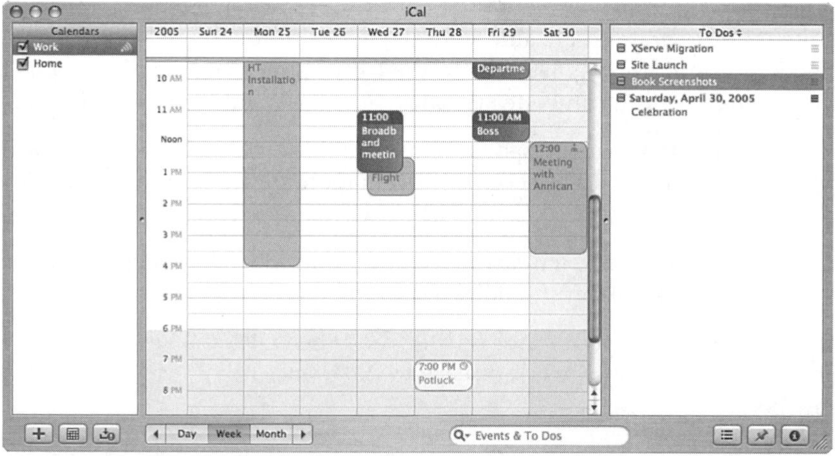

FIGURE 2.19 The To Do List contains a list of things to do.

To add a new item to the list, highlight the calendar that should contain the To Do, and then double-click within the To Do List pane, or choose File, New To Do (Command-K). A new item is added to the list. By default, new To Dos have no deadline; they can be flagged as "finished" by clicking the check boxes in front of them. To the right of each To Do is a small three-line icon. Click and hold on the icon to choose a priority for the item.

If, after you've entered a To Do, you decide that it is better suited to be an event, just drag the item from the To Do list to the calendar and it will become an event. This same transformation can also work in the other direction—moving events to To Dos.

Setting Additional To Do Attributes

To add additional notes about a To Do entry and set a deadline, highlight the item in the To Do List and then open the Information Window drawer.

The To Do Info window allows you to enter extended text information about the item, choose whether it has been completed, pick a due date, assign it a priority, activate an alarm, pick the calendar it should be a part of, and assign an appropriate URL for extended information.

TIP

To Do lists can become very cluttered because they aren't organized by a date or time. To create a bit of order, use the Advanced application preference pane to automatically hide To Do items with due dates outside of your calendar view, hide To Dos that have been completed, and even delete To Dos a certain number of days after their due date.

Searching for Calendars

Apple's new search technology allows you to locate events and To Do items from anywhere in the system using the Spotlight menu (refer to Chapter 1, "Managing the Tiger Workspace," for details). iCal also has built-in searching capabilities accessed through the search field at the bottom of the iCal window. Before starting a search, click and hold the magnifying glass icon in the search field and choose the target of your search—To Dos, Events, Attendees, and so on.

Next, just start typing. As you type in the field, iCal's display changes to provide a list of entries that match the string you've entered. Figure 2.20 shows a calendar search in progress.

Click an item in the search results and it will be highlighted in the calendar viewing area or To Do list. Open the Information drawer to display all of the available information about the result.

To hide the search results, click the search list icon (three horizontal lines) directly to the right of the search field.

TIP

To quickly display a list of upcoming events in chronological order, click the search list icon *without entering anything* in the search field.

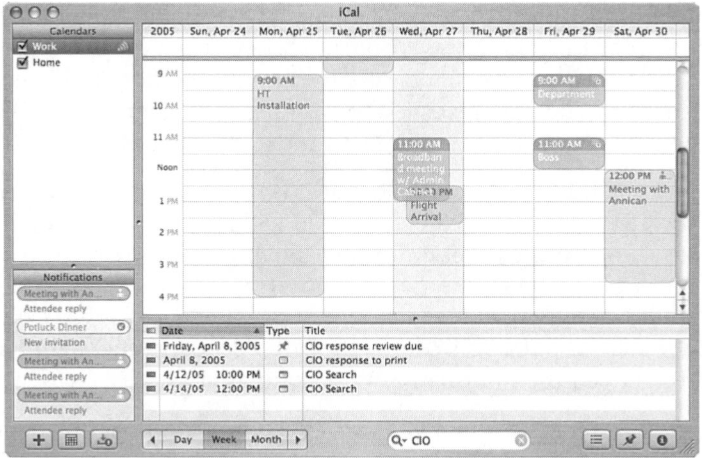

FIGURE 2.20 Search across all of your calendars to find events, to dos, locations, and more.

Sharing Calendar Information

One of the most useful features of iCal is the capability to publish calendars to a .Mac account or WebDAV share (see Chapter 23, "Creating a Web Server," for information about setting up WebDAV on your computer) and for others to subscribe to your calendar.

Publishing to .Mac and WebDAV Servers

To publish an existing calendar to the Internet, highlight the calendar within your calendar list and then choose Calendar, Publish from the menu. The dialog box shown in Figure 2.21 appears.

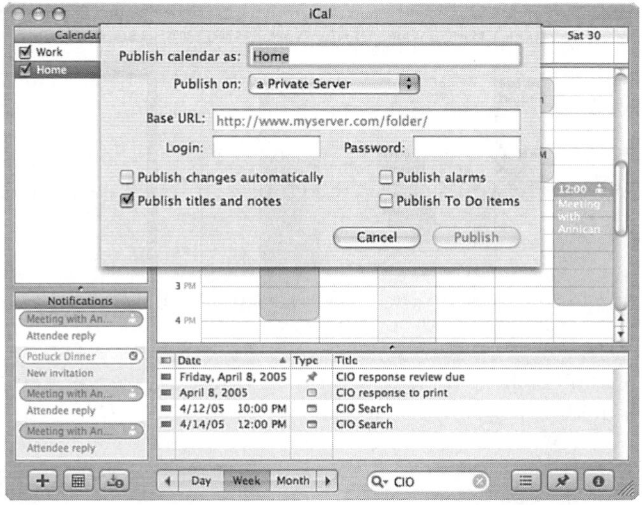

FIGURE 2.21 Publish your calendar to a .Mac account or WebDAV share.

First, choose whether you're using a .Mac account or a Private Server (WebDAV). If you're using .Mac, iCal automatically uses the account information contained in the .Mac System Preferences pane. Otherwise, it prompts for the WebDAV Base URL, login, and password.

Next, choose the information you want to be published:

- Publish Name—The name that the subscribers see when viewing your calendar.
- Publish Changes Automatically—Automatically update your published calendar when you make local changes in iCal.
- Publish Titles and Notes—Publish the title and note fields for events.
- Publish Alarms—Publish alarm information (alarm type, time, and so on) along with your events.
- Publish To Do Items—Include any To Do items in the calendar as part of the publication.

TIP

You can change any of these attributes later by highlighting the calendar in the calendar list and opening the Information drawer.

Click the Publish button to send your calendar to the remote server. Published calendars are denoted by a transmission icon appearing after their name in the Calendar list.

After publishing, you are prompted with the option to Send Mail with your calendar information to those who might be interested in subscribing. You can also choose Visit Page to see a web view of your Calendar. The Visit Page option is available only to .Mac subscribers for the purpose of publishing and provides a fully interactive Web view of your calendar; users who are not Mac.com members can still visit the web page just to see the calendar but cannot update it.

TIP

If you have your own web server and want to publish calendars online, visit `http://sourceforge.net/projects/iwebcal/` for a free open source solution.

To update a published calendar with the latest local changes choose Calendar, Refresh (Command-R) or Calendar, Refresh All (Shift-Command-R) to refresh *all* published calendars. To completely remove a Published calendar, use Calendar, Unpublish.

TIP

If you start publishing your calendars to a .Mac server and then want to move to a WebDAV server or vice versa, you can easily move your published calendars using the Calendar, Change location menu option.

Subscribing to a Calendar

To manually enter a subscription, choose Calendar, Subscribe (Option-Command-S) from the menu. The subscription dialog appears, as shown in Figure 2.22.

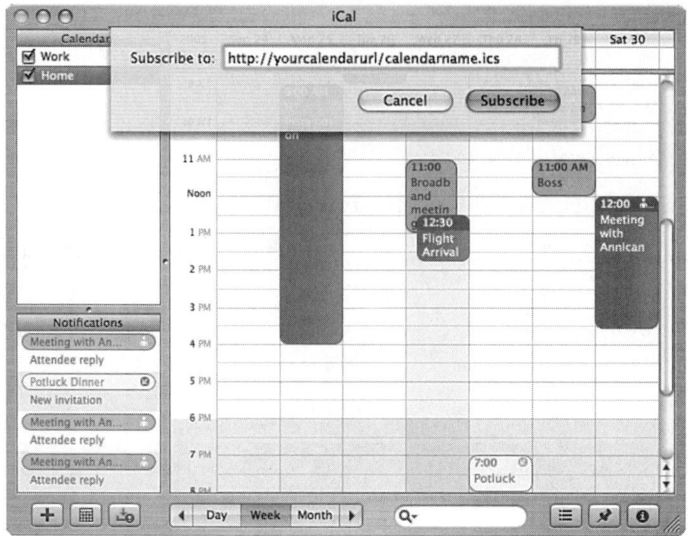

FIGURE 2.22 Enter a URL to subscribe to a calendar.

Enter the URL of an appropriately prepared iCal source and then click Subscribe.

If the calendar is protected, you will be prompted for a username and password. Enter your information, and then click OK. Next, iCal will all you to choose how often the calendar should automatically refresh, and choose whether to remove the creator's alarms and To Do items from the calendar. (You can change these settings at any time in the Information drawer.)

Configure the subscription to suit your needs, and then click Subscribe. After a few seconds, the subscribed calendar appears in your calendar list (differentiated from local calendars by the shortcut arrow following its name).

To refresh a subscribed calendar, use the Calendar, Refresh (Command-R) or Calendar, Refresh All (Shift-Command-R) menu selections.

TIP

To browse a library of public online event, holiday, and special-interest calendars, choose Calendar, Find Shared Calendars from the menu bar.

Syncing Calendars Through .Mac

Publishing and subscribing to your own calendars is a somewhat effective means of taking your event information wherever you go. An even better approach is to use .Mac to automatically synchronize your calendars wherever you go. This means you'll see the same calendars at each machine you sit down at, and you can add and edit events that will automatically be synced across all of your machines.

To use this feature, you'll need a .Mac account, of course. Open the General application preference pane and click Synchronize My Calendars with Other Computers Using .Mac. Any other computers that are registered with your .Mac account will automatically be kept up to date. See Chapter 3 for more information about .Mac.

Importing, Exporting, and Backing Up Event Data

iCal, being the friendly plays-nice-with-others application it is, can easily import existing calendars from vCal, iCal, or Entourage data files as well as export entire calendars in the iCal format.

To import calendar data, select an existing calendar that will hold the incoming information, and then choose File, Import, from the menu. iCal will prompt for one of the three supported calendar types and allow you to choose the import file. Within a few seconds, the events will be imported and added to your calendar. An even easier way to import calendar data in `.ics` files is to drag the file from the desktop into the calendar list or the viewing area. These actions will create a new calendar with the stored events or add the events to the existing active calendar, respectively.

To reverse the process and export an iCal file, first choose the calendar you wish to export, and then select File, Export from the menu bar. Enter a filename and click Export; your iCal file will be created. Alternatively, to export an event to an `.ics` file, drag it to the desktop.

A final method getting data into and out of iCal is via an iCal backup. The purpose of the backup is to protect you in the event of data loss, or to completely move all of your iCal data from one machine to another. To create a full backup file, choose File, Backup Database and provide a filename when prompted. To restore from a backup database, use File, Revert to Backup Database.

Printing Calendars

The iCal application that ships with Tiger introduces a whole new range of calendar printing options. Calendars can now be output in any of the standard iCal views (reformatted for printing, of course) along with a new List view that provides a quick reference to upcoming events and deadlines.

To print a calendar, choose File, Print. The iCal print dialog is demonstrated in Figure 2.23.

Use the View pop-up menu to choose between the four available layouts, set a time range to be printed, select the calendars to include, pick the additional elements to include in the printout, and, finally, click Print. You can even change the settings and use the preview and zoom control to make sure that what you see is what you want.

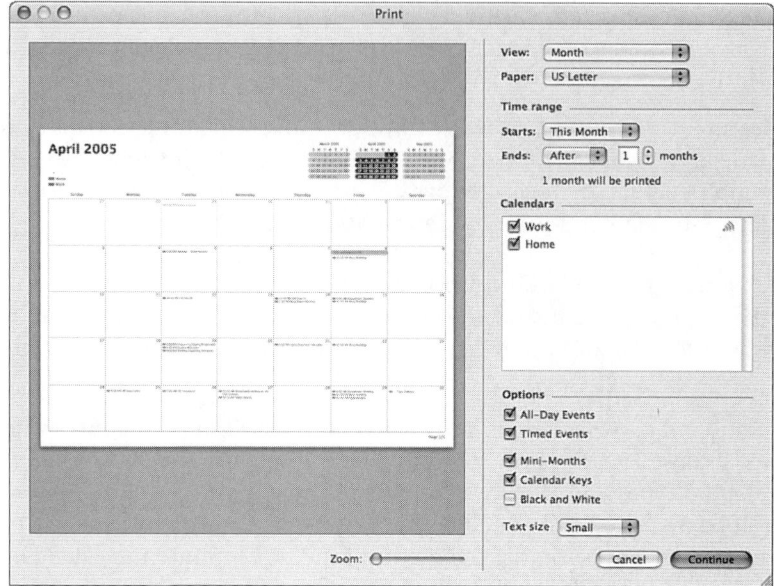

FIGURE 2.23 Print your calendars any way you'd like.

Basic Image and PDF Manipulation: Preview

For viewing PDF files and images of all sorts, Tiger comes with the Preview application (path: `/Applications/Preview`).

Preview can be launched by either double-clicking a supported file, or by selecting a group of files and then dragging them onto the Preview icon. Preview is also integrated into the printing system; clicking Preview in any Print dialog box opens it.

Using the Viewer

When you open an image or PDF document in Preview, it is automatically resized to fit the available window space and displayed in Preview viewer.

Almost everything you'll want to do to control the viewing area or manipulate the document can be performed in the viewer toolbar. The first button, Drawer, (Shift-Command-D) is common to both image and PDF viewing. This button opens and closes a window drawer with thumbnail images of the pages or files open in the active Preview window, as shown in Figure 2.24. To change the thumbnail size and background of the viewing area, use the General application preferences pane.

Clicking a thumbnail displays the full image in the main viewing area. The rest of the toolbar functions change depending on whether you are viewing a PDF or an image file.

FIGURE 2.24 The Preview drawer displays thumbnails of each page or image loaded.

TIP

To disable automatic resizing of the viewing area contents, uncheck the View, Automatic Resize menu item (Shift-Command-R). You can also use the Image and PDF application preference panes to set default scaling for each.

Viewing and Editing PDFs

When viewing a PDF, Preview will automatically open the window drawer to display the PDF Table of Contents if one is available. Toggle between the TOC and thumbnail views using the icons at the top left corner of the window drawer. If the PDF does not contain a table of contents, you can still click the Drawer toolbar icon to display thumbnails of all the pages. Clicking an item in the drawer will jump you to the appropriate page in the PDF.

TIP

If you want a PDF's thumbnails to display regardless of whether a TOC is present in the file, use the PDF application preference to uncheck Open Drawer only for Table of Contents.

The PDF toolbar provides features best suited for moving through a multi-page document (see Figure 3.26 as an example). Use the following icons to navigate your PDF files:

- Previous (Command-left arrow) and Next (Command-right arrow)—If you're viewing a multipage file, you can move through the pages sequentially using the Previous and Next arrows.
- Page Number—When you're viewing a multipage TIFF, PDF file, or multiple files in a single window, Page Number enables you to enter a page number to jump directly to that page.
- Back and Forward—If you've viewed several pages in a multipage file out of sequence, you can page back through in the order you visited using the Back/Forward arrows.
- Zoom In (Command-+) and Zoom Out (Command--)—These two options enable you to view a larger or smaller version of the selected image or PDF. If the image is larger than the Preview window, scrollbars appear.
- Scroll Tool (Tool Mode, Command-1)—The Scroll tool can be used to grab the image and move it around the page. Just click, hold, and drag.
- Text Mode (Tool Mode, Command-2)—The Text Mode tool is used with PDFs to select the text within a PDF for copying and pasting.
- Selection Tool (Tool Mode, Command-3)—The Selection tool can be used with images to select a portion of an image for copying, pasting, or cropping (Command-K).
- Annotate Tool (Tool Mode, Command-4)—Use the Annotate tool to add nondestructive notes and markings to PDF files.

Cropping and Scaling functions also can be added to the Toolbar by choosing View, Customize Toolbar.

Several additional PDF viewing features can be found under the View, PDF Display menu, including the ability to display two pages simultaneously and view the entire PDF as a continuous scrolling document rather than jumping from page to page. Functions to rotate pages to the left or right (if oriented incorrectly in the PDF, for example), can be found under the Tools menu.

Increasing PDF Viewer Speed

If you find that viewing a PDF is a bit slower than you'd like, the PDF application preferences contain a few settings to help speed things up. First, the Greeking Threshold sets a minimum size at which Preview will render the text in a PDF. If a page is shrunk smaller than the size, it will be *greeked*—that is, displayed as meaningless blocks. You can also turn off anti-aliasing. Anti-aliasing cleans up text and graphics by removing the jaggies along their edges, but at a cost of significantly slower display speed.

Searching PDFs

Preview can search through the PDF text much like you would search through a word processor document. To search, first open the Preview window drawer. Type a text string into the Search field and then press the Return key. The results are returned in the drawer.

Each page is listed, along with each instance found on the page. Click on a search result line to highlight that line in your document. To clear the search results, click the X icon at the end of the Search field.

Adding Bookmarks

If you've ever found yourself browsing a several hundred page PDF document and wishing you could stick a post-it in to mark your place, you'll be pleased with Tiger's new Bookmark feature. To bookmark any page, choose Bookmarks, Add Bookmark from the menu. Preview will prompt you to enter a label for the bookmark, and then will add it to the Bookmark menu.

Bookmark management is simple—you can delete them. To delete a bookmark, open the Bookmarks application preferences pane, as shown in Figure 2.25. Find the bookmark you want to remove, highlight it, and then click the Remove button.

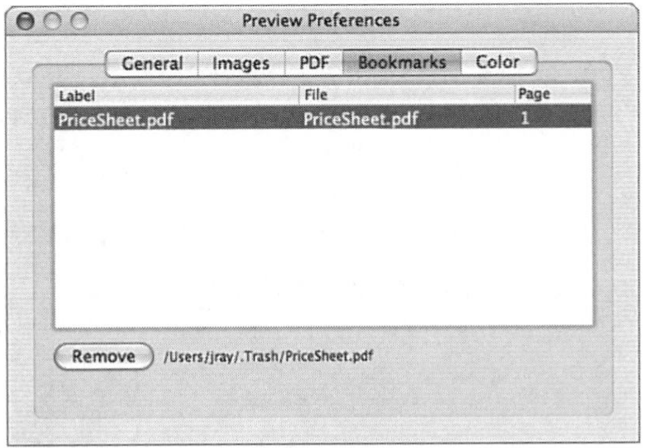

FIGURE 2.25 Your options for bookmark management are Remove and, well, that's it.

Copying Content from PDFs

If you find content that you would like to "lift" from a PDF, you can copy and paste styled text using the Text tool (the A icon near the upper right corner of the viewer window). After the Text tool has been selected, just copy and paste as you would from any other program. Keep in mind that you should always have permission to use content that is not your own and you should always cite your sources. In fact, some PDFs might be protected to disable copying of text altogether.

Opening and Saving Password-Protected PDFs

PDFs can be password protected to provide control over viewing, printing, and copying of content. If you attempt to open a PDF that is "viewing" protected, Preview will display a password prompt before rendering any of the pages.

In some cases, a PDF might allow viewing but require a password for advanced functions such as copying text or printing—in these cases, Preview will *not* force you to enter a password. Instead, choose File, Password to open a password dialog box and unlock the additional functions.

To set a password on your own PDFs, first create the PDF file (see Chapter 6, "Automating Native Applications with Automator and AppleScript," for information on printing directly to a PDF), open it in Preview, and then choose File, Save As. In the Save dialog, click the Encrypt check box. Preview will prompt for a password, and then create a new protected version of your file.

> **NOTE**
>
> Preview does not provide any means of choosing *what* features you want to password protect—*everything*, including viewing, is locked until the password is entered.

Annotating PDFs

The ability to annotate documents can be helpful when content needs to be passed between several individuals for approval. Each person can add her own markup without changing the original contents of the document.

Preview supports two types of PDF annotations: ovals and text. You can draw ovals around content or type text into a small rectangular note. Both types can be seen in Figure 2.26.

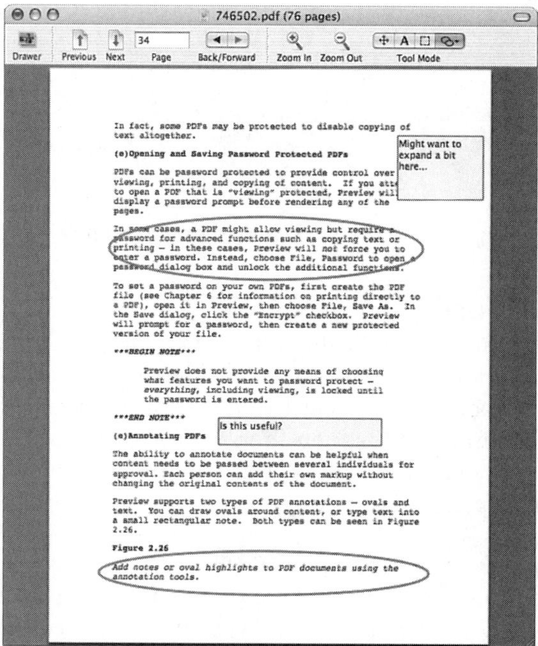

FIGURE 2.26 Add notes or oval highlights to PDF documents using the annotation tools.

To create an annotation, click and hold on the annotation tool icon (by default, a pencil for text) at the far right of the Preview toolbar. Choose the pencil to create a text note, or the oval to draw an oval-shaped highlight.

After the tool has been selected, click and drag where you want the oval or text to appear. The Oval tool will, obviously, draw an oval. The Text tool, on the other hand, will draw a yellow box (think Post-It) that will contain your comments. Double-click the yellow box to begin typing.

Viewing and Editing images

When you open images one at a time in Preview, they will each open in a separate window. To open images together in a single window, select them and use the Finder File, Open menu item, or drag them onto the Preview icon. You can use the Images pane within the application preferences to adjust this behavior.

Just as with PDF viewing, image viewing has its own special toolbar with functions more appropriate to images. The default controls are

- Rotate Left (Command-L)—Rotate the image to the left.
- Rotate Right (Command-R)—Rotate the image to the right.
- Actual Size (Command-0)—View the image at its actual size, not zoomed in or out.
- Zoom to Fit—Zoom the image to fit the size of the Preview window.
- Zoom In (Command-+)—Zoom in (enlarge) the image in the viewing area.
- Zoom Out (Command--)—Zoom out of the image in the viewing area.

Images can also be viewing in a slideshow format, the same as the Spotlight slideshow discussed in the previous chapter. To start a slideshow, choose View, Slideshow (Shift+Command+F).

In addition, horizontal and vertical image flips can be selected in the Tools menu. Basic image cropping can be accomplished by clicking and dragging anywhere in the image to draw a crop rectangle, and then choosing Tools, Crop (Command+K).

Image Color Correction

Preview in Tiger now offers simple color correction capabilities for any open image. To use the image correction feature, choose Tools, Image Correction (Option+Command+C); a floating window will appear, as seen in Figure 2.27.

Use the sliders to change the appearance of the image—the changes you make are immediately visible in the viewing area. To undo any changes you've made, click Reset All. Even if you close the window after making adjustments, the changes are not permanent until you save the image. You can always reopen the Image Correction window and reset the sliders.

Assigning ColorSync Profiles and Color Models

If you have an image that you would like to force into a specific color model (such as RGB to CMYK), you can use the Tools, Match to Profile function. The Match to Profile dialog is seen in Figure 2.28.

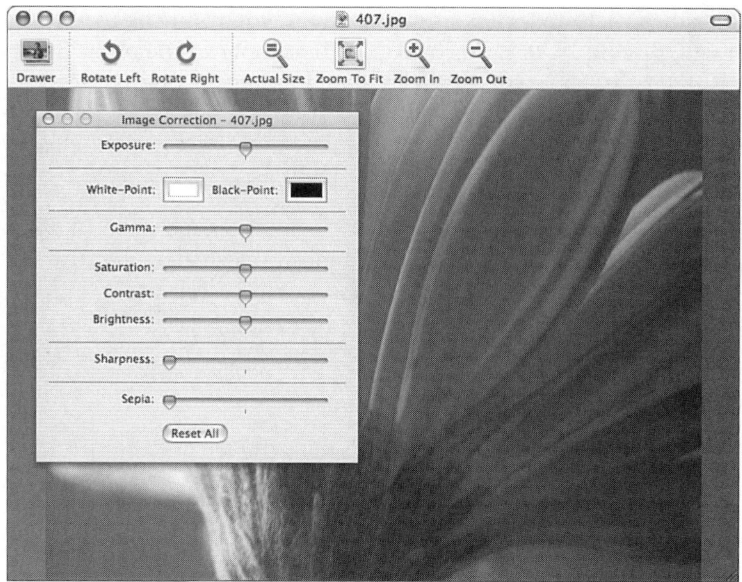

FIGURE 2.27 Use Preview to make basic color adjustments to an image.

FIGURE 2.28 Choose a color model and ColorSync profile for your image.

Changing the color model will alter the image—potentially losing color information, but will make it conform to the model chosen. Use the pop-up menus to choose the color model and a ColorSync profile to assign to the image to ensure proper color reproduction throughout your workflow.

If you just want to assign a ColorSync profile without changing the color model, use Tools, Assign Profile instead. You'll learn more about ColorSync in Chapter 5, "Printer, Fax, and Font Management."

Taking Screenshots

To take a screenshot directly within Preview, choose File, Grab, and then select the type of screenshot you'd like. Preview can capture the entire screen, individual windows, or take picture of the screen after a short (roughly eight second) pause. After taking the picture, the image will be opened in a new Preview window.

> **TIP**
>
> Screenshots can be taken at any time in Tiger by pressing Shift+Command+3 for fullscreen, Shift+Command+4 to select an area using crosshairs, or Shift+Command+4 and then the spacebar to choose and capture individual windows. The resulting files (PNGs) will be labeled Picture 1, Picture 2, and so on, and saved on the Desktop.
>
> To copy to the Clipboard rather than a file, modify these screenshot shortcuts to include the Control key along with Shift+Command.

Saving Images in Other Formats

One of the most useful features of Preview is its ability to save in over ten different image formats—even PDF documents can be saved as images. To save an image in a new format, choose File, Save As from the menu bar. Use the Format menu to choose your output format, enter a filename, and then click Save.

Viewing and Setting Image and PDF Metadata

As you know, Spotlight helps you locate files on your system based on attributes (metadata) that have been recorded as part of the file (such as the camera that took an image), or added to the file manually—such as keywords. Preview can display the detailed metadata for any file that you are viewing. In addition, Preview can set keywords in PDFs and Images that may help them be found by future Spotlight searches.

To view information about a file, choose Tools, Get Info (Command+I) when the file is active in the Viewing area. The Get Info window appears, as shown in Figure 2.29.

Use the buttons at the top of the window to view summarized or detailed information about the file. To enter keywords, click the Keywords button, and then use the Add and Remove buttons that appear to add and delete keywords from the file's metadata.

> **TIP**
>
> Because Spotlight cannot identify the subject of a photograph or other attributes of an image's composition, adding keywords provides the additional information that will make locating and the file easier in the future. Searching for "Dog" and "Maddy" (my dog's name, by the way) is much easier than using a color depth or resolution to try to find my dog photos.

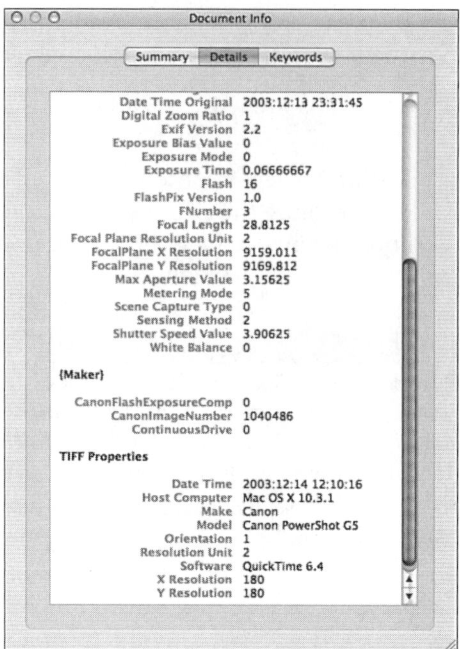

FIGURE 2.29 Get and set file metadata in Preview.

Multimedia Playback: QuickTime 7

QuickTime is Apple's digital media engine that processes everything from MIDI to movies and still images. If you've viewed streaming media online or downloaded and viewed movie files on your computer, chances are you've used QuickTime. Tiger introduces QuickTime 7, including advanced payment-required Pro features, the H.264 codec for improved video quality with higher compression rates, and a new streamlined interface.

Setting Up QuickTime

There are two places you're most likely to run into QuickTime media—through the QuickTime player and via a web browser. Before you can use either, you should first configure QuickTime through its System Preferences pane. Failing to do this might cause your system to display the lowest-quality video streams. Open System Preferences click the QuickTime icon to configure your QuickTime settings.

There are five settings panes: Register, Browser, Update, Streaming, and Advanced. Let's review those now.

> **NOTE**
>
> QuickTime settings are made on a per-user basis. This includes registration. Each user of the system needs to license QuickTime Pro separately if he wants to access its advanced features.

Registering QuickTime Pro

To register QuickTime and gain access to the Pro features (we'll review these a little bit later), click the Register button. The pane will refresh with the appropriate registration fields.

If you've already purchased QuickTime Pro, enter your registration information, if not, click Buy QuickTime Pro to launch Safari and begin the purchase process.

Setting Browser Preferences

The QuickTime Browser plug-in is used when movies are viewed in your web browser. To change how it functions, click the Browser button in the QuickTime System Preferences pane. There are options: Play Movies Automatically, Save Movies in Disk Cache, Cache Size, and Empty Download Cache.

If you've checked Play Movies Automatically, QuickTime starts playing a movie after enough of it has been buffered. This applies to nonstreamed movies. If this option is not selected, you must click the Play button to start viewing a movie. If you want to save movies that have played in your browser, click the Save Movies in Disk Cache check box. This speeds up commonly accessed movies and is great for those days when you repeatedly keep pulling up the one funny video clip to show your coworkers. You can adjust the amount of drive space reserved for movie caching using the Movie Download Cache Size slider, or empty the cache by clicking Empty Download Cache.

Updating QuickTime Components

QuickTime supports automatic updating in much the same way as the operating system itself. Unlike Tiger, however, QuickTime checks for updates outside the normal system updater context. Click the Update button to open the QuickTime update settings.

To activate automatic updates, click the Check for Updates Automatically check box. After that check box has been selected, the software will occasionally scan for updates and additions that can be downloaded. To manually force the system to look for updates, click the Update button.

The QuickTime Update pane can also be used to add third-party software, such as new codecs, to the system. Click the Install button to launch Safari and load the QuickTime components page.

Configuring Streaming Options

Use the Streaming pane to configure the type of network access QuickTime can expect your computer to have.

Choose your network speed from the Streaming Speed pop-up menu. This is not the speed you *wish* you had, but rather the actual speed of your line. This choice helps QuickTime choose the appropriate type of media to display depending on how fast it can be received. By default, QuickTime attempts to automatically determine your connection speed. In some cases, it might be right; in others, it might assume too high or too low. Manually setting this option is the only way to be certain.

Click the Instant-On button to enable the QuickTime 7 Instant On feature, which starts displaying QuickTime movie virtually immediately after it has been accessed. Use the Play slider to choose how long QuickTime should wait for (and buffer) information before it starts playing.

Advanced QuickTime Settings

The final configurable QuickTime options are found in the Advanced pane. This is a rather esoteric collection of settings that, chances are, an average user won't need to change.

First is the QuickTime Synthesizer. QuickTime supports multiple plug-in synthesizers when playing MIDI music. By default, it uses the QuickTime Music Synthesizer.

If you install software that offers another synthesizer plug-in, you can select it from the list in this preferences pane. Highlight the item you want to use by default and click Make Default. This sets it as the default synthesizer used by any application playing QuickTime MIDI files.

Next, the Transport Setup button to choose the protocol used for streaming. By default, QuickTime attempts to choose the best transport based on your network topology. It's best not to change these settings unless you know your network supports them. Users behind a firewall can choose the ports used for either HTTP or UDP transports. It's best to talk to your network administrator before changing anything.

Users interested in using QuickTime in kiosks can limit the end user's access to QuickTime controls by clicking the Enable Kiosk Mode check box. This isn't needed for normal use.

> **NOTE**
>
> If your computer is connected directly to the Internet via a DSL/cable modem or you are on a network without a firewall, either of the transports should work fine for you. Try each to see which displays faster and cleaner streams on your system.

The MIME Settings button opens a list of all the MIME types that QuickTime can handle and everything it is currently configured to display. Some items are intentionally disabled (such as Flash) because they are better handled by other software (like the official Flash plug-in).

Finally, Media Access; some media files can be secured with an access key. The Media Keys button opens a dialog to enter keys directly into the QuickTime preferences, enabling the files to be accessed transparently at any time. Use the Delete, Edit, and Add buttons within the dialog box to modify your access keys.

Using the QuickTime Browser Plug-in

Many QuickTime movies play from within your browser window. This is probably the most common place you'll view streaming media, so let's take a look at the controls of the QuickTime browser plug-in. Figure 2.30 shows a QuickTime movie playing in the Safari browser.

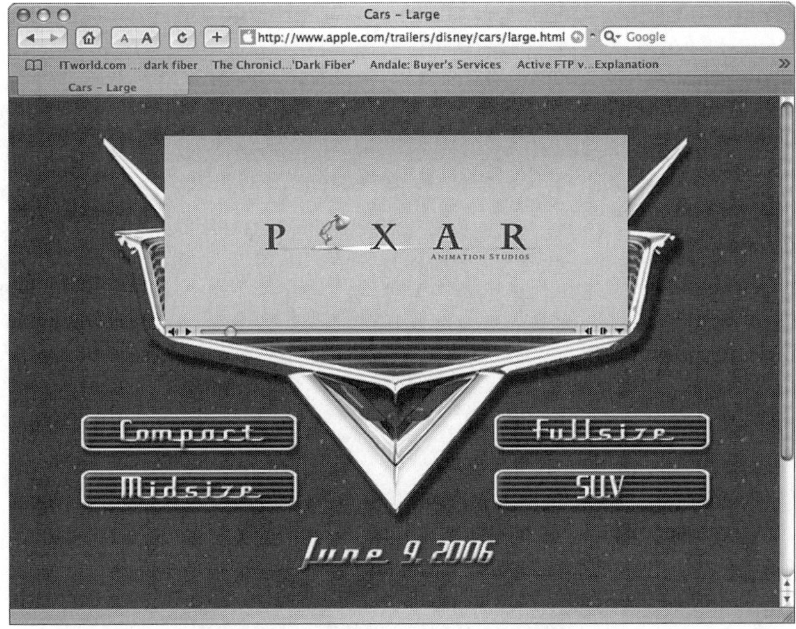

FIGURE 2.30 Most users experience QuickTime through their browser.

The movie controls are located across the bottom of the video. If you've used a VCR or other media player, you've certainly seen these before. There are, however, a few shortcuts you might want to know. The volume control, for example, can be instantly muted by Option-clicking the speaker icon. You can also control the volume level using the up arrow and down arrow keys on the keyboard. To increase the volume beyond its normal limit, hold down the Shift key while dragging the control.

Playback can be activated from the keyboard, negating the need to mouse around on your screen. To toggle between playing and pausing, press the spacebar. To rewind or fast forward, use the left arrow and right arrow keys, respectively.

At the lower right of the control bar area is the QuickTime menu. This provides quick access to QuickTime settings. QuickTime Pro users can use this menu to save movies to their hard drive. (Note: Saving a streaming movie saves a reference to the movie, not the actual contents of the movie.)

If the movie being played is streaming from the remote server, some of these controls might not be available. For example, live streams can't be fast-forwarded or rewound, but streamed files can be. The available controls depend entirely on the movie you're viewing.

Using the Standalone QuickTime Player

The QuickTime Player application (path: `/Applications/QuickTime Player`) provides another means of viewing movies and streams. In fact, many users might be surprised to find that they can use the Player application to tune in a variety of interesting streams—ranging from news to entertainment—without the need for a web browser.

Playing QuickTime Content from the Online Content Guide

To start using the QuickTime Player, open it from its default home in the Dock or from the System Applications folder. The QuickTime window should open directly to a featured Content Guide item—something Apple thinks you should be interested in, but you probably aren't.

Clicking in the guide window launches Safari and takes you to the advertised content piece. Clicking the Click Here for More Content button also opens Safari but takes you to Apple's online content guide. Choose from whatever interests you, and the content will stream back either in the browser or within the QuickTime Player, as shown in Figure 2.31.

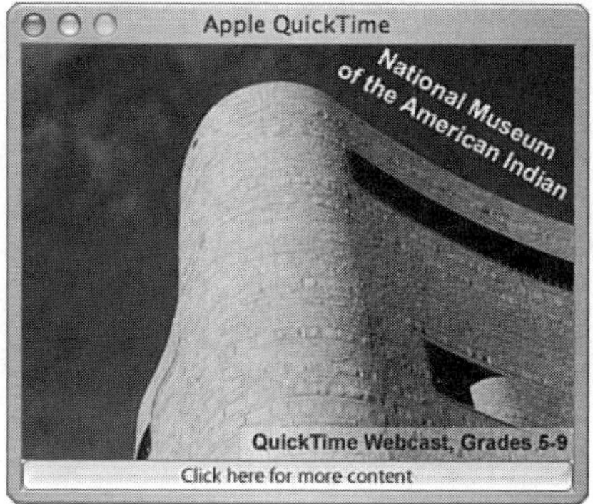

FIGURE 2.31 The Content Guide can help you find free online QuickTime media.

> **NOTE**
>
> If you find that you don't really use the Content Guide, you can shut it off in the QuickTime application preferences.

When QuickTime starts to load a streaming video clip, it goes through four steps before displaying the video:

- Connecting—Connection is made to the streaming server.
- Requesting data—Waits for acknowledgement from remote server.
- Getting info—Retrieves information about the QuickTime movie.
- Buffering—QuickTime buffers several seconds of video to eliminate stuttering from the playback.

If the player stalls during any of these steps, there might be a problem with the remote server or your transport setting. Try another streaming source, and if it still fails, use the QuickTime Preferences pane to select an alternative transport.

Choosing Other QuickTime Sources

You can use the QuickTime Player to play information from other sources in addition to the Apple-linked content. You can open local movie files by choosing File, Open File (Command-O) or by dragging a movie file onto the QuickTime Dock icon. If you have a streaming server URL, you can select File, Open URL in New Player (Command-U) to directly open the stream.

QuickTime refers to *any* media type as a *movie*. For example, you can open and play CD audio tracks and MP3s using the Open Movie command. Even though there aren't any visuals, these media types are still referred to as *movies* in QuickTime's vocabulary.

By default, QuickTime will open new movies in a new window rather than reusing your existing QuickTime windows. You can change this behavior within the QuickTime application preferences. You can also use the preferences to automatically enable playback as soon as a movie is opened.

TIP

An interesting example of QuickTime streaming in action is the Race Rocks website. Race Rocks is an inside view of an ecological preserve being transmitted 24 hours a day using Macintosh and AirPort technology: `http://www.racerocks.com/`.

Controlling QuickTime Playback

The QuickTime Player, shown in Figure 2.32, works much like a VCR. The top of the window holds the video pane. Directly below the video is a status bar to display the progress of the player and any feedback it needs to provide to the user.

FIGURE 2.32 If you've used a VCR, you can control the QuickTime Player.

The status bar has four components: the elapsed time, the playback progress, a scene pop-up menu, and a miniature equalizer. Dragging the triangle above the progress bar quickly moves the current position in the movie (except in the cases of live streams, for reasons that should be obvious).

TIP

QuickTime Pro users might notice that directly below the progress bar are two selection triangles. Use these triangles to select start and end points for the video clip. The selection can then be copied or pasted into other movies.

The scene pop-up menu, if available, can be used to jump between scenes in the movie, if they have been set.

NOTE

To disable the mostly useless equalizer, use the QuickTime player application preferences.

Below the status bar are the main playback controls that provide the basic control over movie playback: volume, skip to start, rewind, play/pause, fast forward, and skip to end, respectively.

Because many video clips are small, the QuickTime Player window can be resized by using the window resize handle in the lower-right corner. By default, QuickTime Player resizes the window to maintain the same aspect ratio. To squeeze or stretch the window, hold down Shift while resizing. To switch between common sizes, use the Movie menu to select from Half Size (Command-0), Normal Size (Command-1), Double Size (Command-2), and Full Screen (Command-3).

Minimizing a QuickTime Player movie while it is playing adds a live icon to the Dock. The movie (with sound) continues to play in the minimized Dock icon.

NOTE

QuickTime Pro users have an additional View menu option to present the movie on the screen. This clears all other information from the monitor and plays the full-screen video (Command-F).

Controlling Video and Audio Output

New to Tiger is a single control window for changing your audio and video settings—from bass and treble on your sound to tint and contrast on video. To access the settings, choose Window, A/V Controls (Command+K). The window shown in Figure 2.33 will appear.

Use the audio and video sliders to adjust the sound and picture quality, respectively. The sliders at the bottom of the window can be user to scrub forward and backward through the video (Jog Shuttle) and to change the playback speed to anywhere from one-half to three times the regular playback speed.

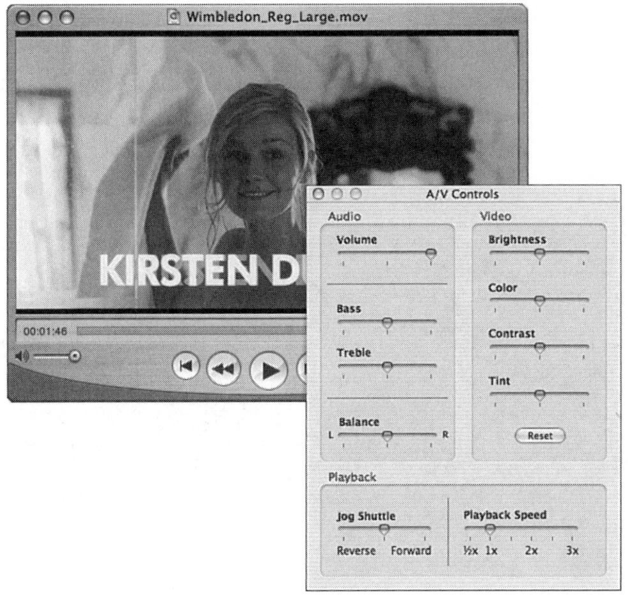

FIGURE 2.33 Control the appearance and sound of QuickTime movie playback.

The QuickTime application preferences also have a few settings for audio and video—including a High Quality video setting that provides better playback at a cost of significantly higher processor usage. The preferences also have the ability to enable or disable simultaneous audio output from multiple QuickTime player windows and sound playback in background windows.

Bookmarking QuickTime Favorites

To keep track of your favorite movies (either local files or streaming), you can use the QuickTime Favorites menu, which works just like a lame version of your favorite browser's bookmark menu.

When viewing a movie that you want to bookmark as a favorite, choose Window, Favorites, Add Movie as Favorite (Command-D). You can now select the movie from the Favorites menu itself.

To remove a favorite item, choose Window, Favorites, Show Favorites. A window with a list of all the favorite movies appears. Highlight the item to remove and press your Backspace key. If you'd rather organize than delete, dragging the items in the Favorites window reorders them.

TIP

The File, Open Recent menu gives you a quick and easy way to access your commonly used movies without creating favorites. You can choose how many movies are maintained in this list through the application preferences.

Getting Movie Information

To display information about a movie, choose Window, Show Movie Info (Command-I). QuickTime will display a window with the codecs used in the file, FPS, duration, and other useful tidbits, as shown in Figure 2.34.

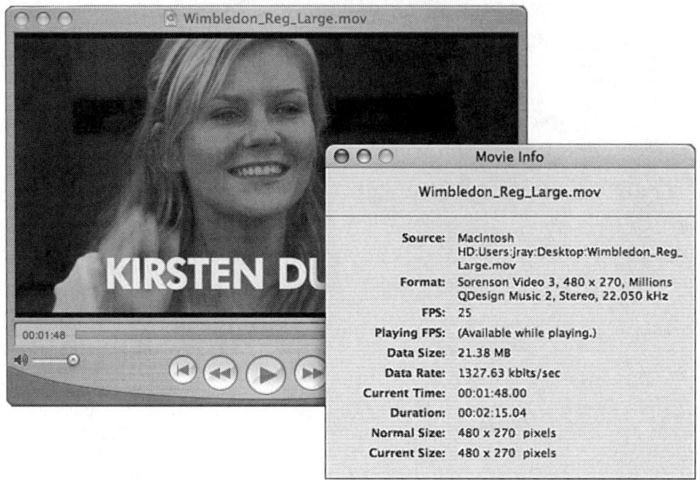

FIGURE 2.34 The expanded Movie Info window contains summary data on the currently playing file.

The type of information shown depends on the type of movie being played. Streaming video, for example, includes network data such as bit rate and quality.

> **NOTE**
>
> QuickTime Pro users can access and *change* movie information such as its color palette, graphics mode, mask, and track settings using the Window, Show Movie Properties feature.

Adding Codecs and Playing the Unplayable

As much as we all like QuickTime, there are, frankly, a large number of files that it simply can't handle—such as most Divx, Xvid, and most Windows media files. In the event that QuickTime encounters a file that it doesn't have the codec for, it will ask to check online to see if it can find the necessary component. Unless you're extremely lucky, it won't find a thing.

Thankfully, you can easily add to the QuickTime codecs by dropping new codecs in the `/Library/QuickTime` directory (or your `~/Library/QuickTime` folder for personal playback only). There are a number of free codec add-ons any playback engines available at `http://www.pure-mac.com/video.html`.

One of the easiest solutions for media incompatibility is to change players entirely. The Video LAN Client player, pictured in Figure 2.35, supports a huge number of video and audio formats and often plays files back more smoothly than even the properly codec-enabled QuickTime player. You can download VLC for free from `http://www.videolan.org/vlc/download-macosx.html`.

FIGURE 2.35 VLC can play what QuickTime can't, won't, or struggles to display.

QuickTime Pro Features

For most users, the standard version of QuickTime is probably more than enough to handle their media needs. If you're interested in creating or editing digital movies, you can upgrade to QuickTime Pro and gain access to some interesting new features. There isn't anything additional to install, just a registration code to enter, so it's easy to get up and running with QuickTime Pro.

Upgrading gives you access to a number of video editing functions, such as copying and pasting portions of video tracks, applying effects filters, altering video codecs, and working with the Internet standard MPEG 4. Users can extract and convert audio and video tracks—even export video tracks as image sequences.

Probably the best new capability of QuickTime Pro is audio and video recording. Apple provides no other built-in means of recording media in Tiger, so, if you're willing to pay ($30) about half the cost of the iLife suite (which obviously also features video and audio input), you can get almost 1/10th of the features!

Storing and Managing Sensitive Information: Keychain Access

Using a computer is a never-ending struggle to keep track of passwords for email servers, file servers, websites, and other private information. The Keychain Access software (path: `/Applications/Utilities/Keychain Access`) automatically stores passwords from

Keychain-aware applications such as Mail and Safari. Users can also manually add their own passwords to the keychain. Later, the keychain can be unlocked to reveal the original cleartext password. Keychain also manages digital certificates—virtual documents that are used to authoritatively identify servers and individuals.

Understanding Keychains and Keychain Scope

By default, all users have their own keychain named `login`. This is called the *User* keychain. Additional User keychains can be created to store specific information, such as credit card numbers, PINs, and so on. Think of the keychain as a database of your most sensitive information, all accessible through your account password.

The User keychain is automatically unlocked by your account password when you log in. Sensitive information is best placed in a secondary keychain with a different password; otherwise, a single compromise of your account unlocks access to all your secure information. Read how to add new keychains in the "Managing Keychains" section later in the chapter.

In addition to User keychains, *Global* keychains are accessible by all users on the system. A Global keychain can be created by an administrator and shared to the other users on the system. An example of the usefulness of this feature is creating a keychain with corporate login data for intranet file servers that should be available to everyone. There can also be *System Global* keychains—these global keychains are also for use throughout the system, but should be maintained by the operating system, not the end user.

By default, there are two Global keychains that your account inherits: `System` and `X509Anchors`. The `System` keychain is initially empty, but can be used by the administrator to add new global entries for all users. The second Global keychain, `X509Anchors`, is a System Global keychain that contains all the Tiger-recognized certificate authorities. These certificates are used by applications such as Safari to validate websites that present a certificate purportedly signed by one of these authorities. (that is, these certificates enable websites to positively identify themselves for the sake of secure online transactions).

User keychains are stored in `~/Library/Keychains`, whereas Global and System Global keychains are located in `/Library/Keychains` and `/System/Library/Keychains`, respectively.

Understanding Keychain and Application Interaction

Launching Keychain Access displays the contents of your default keychain: `login`. For an account that has been using the keychain to store file server passwords, HTTP authentication information, and so on, the Keychain Access window should look similar to that shown in Figure 2.36. Don't worry about the interface just yet, right now we just want to figure out how these items got here.

When an application wants to store something in the keychain, you'll typically be given the option of storing it. For example, when accessing a site that requires HTTP authentication, some web browsers present a dialog box requesting a username and password, and offering to remember it or "add to keychain." Choosing these options automatically adds the entered password to the default keychain. Over time, your keychain could become populated with hundreds of items and you might not ever know it!

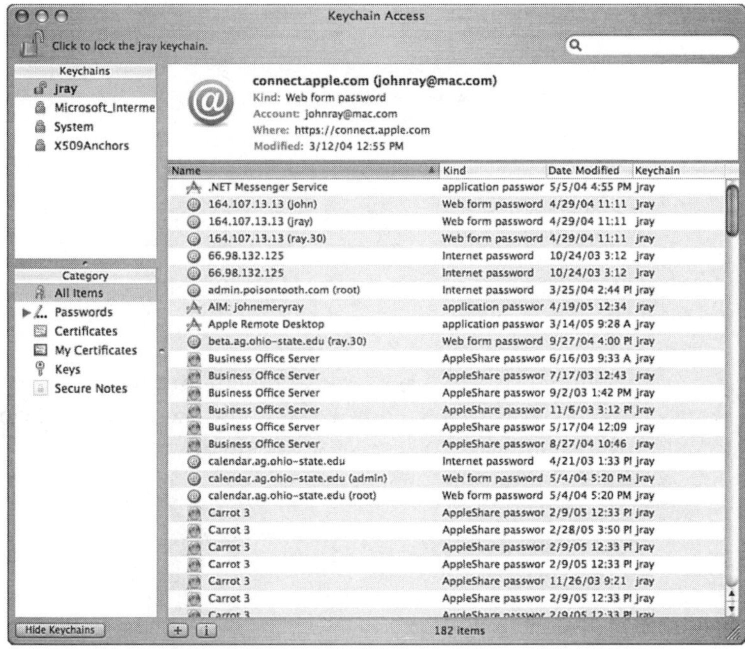

FIGURE 2.36 The Keychain Access window displays a list of stored passwords and other information.

When an application wants to access information from your keychain, it must first make sure that the keychain is *unlocked*. Your `login` keychain is automatically unlocked when you log in to your account, making its passwords accessible to the applications that stored them.

To manually lock or unlock a keychain, click the Lock button at the top of the Keychain Access window. The Keychain Access window, along with its Dock icon, changes to reflect its security status.

If an application attempts to access information on a locked keychain, it displays a dialog box, as shown in Figure 2.37. Entering the correct password (your account password for the `login` keychain) unlocks the keychain. Clicking the Details disclosure pushbutton displays what keychain is being unlocked and the application making the keychain request.

Even after a keychain has been unlocked, an application might require a bit more help before it can retrieve the information it needs from the keychain. Each stored piece of information can be controlled in a way that makes it accessible to only specific applications. Mail passwords, for example, are accessible only by the Mail application. If a program you just downloaded off the Internet attempts to unlock your web or email passwords, you'll know something nefarious is afoot.

FIGURE 2.37 If an application attempts to access data in a locked keychain, you are prompted for the keychain's password.

When the keychain notices an unauthorized application attempting to access a piece of information, it prompts the user with a window to deny the access, allow it only once (Allow Once), or allow the application to access the information whenever it wants (Always Allow), demonstrated in Figure 2.38.

FIGURE 2.38 Each application must be authorized to access a specific piece of information.

Before making a choice, always click the Details disclosure pushbutton to view which keychain is being accessed and which application wants the data. If you don't recognize the application, click Deny to disallow access.

Creating and Managing Passwords and Notes

Users who want to access stored data, or manually add new information to a keychain, can do so through the Keychain Access program. Keychain Access has a simple interface—categories of secure information in the column on the left:

- All Items—All items stored in the keychain.
- Passwords—Any application, AppleShare, or Internet (website) passwords that have been stored.
- Certificates—All digital certificates stored in the keychain.

- My Certificates—Digital certificates specifically for your identities that are stored in the keychain.
- Keys—The public and private keys from all stored certificates.
- Secure Notes—Secure text notes you've entered.

Selecting a category displays the entries on the right, with a summary of the selected item's details directly above it, as shown in Figure 2.39.

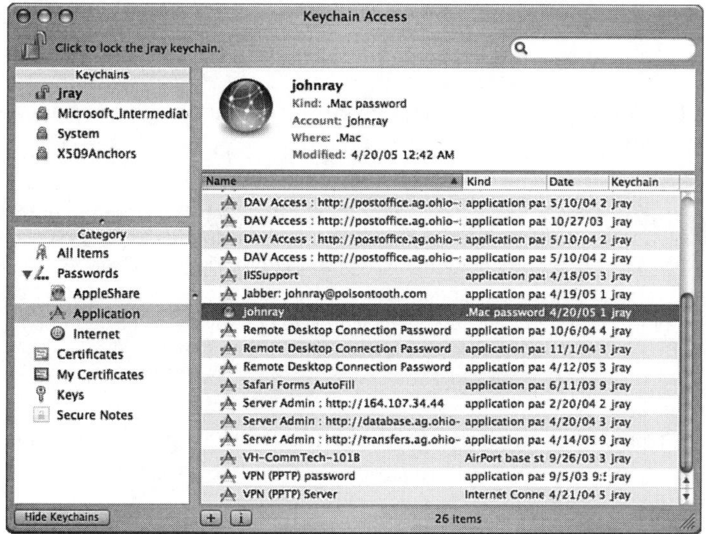

FIGURE 2.39 The Keychain Access interface is easy to navigate and follows the interface model of most Tiger applications.

The list of keychain items can be sorted using the column headings or the View menu, or for extremely long lists, the search field can be used to locate items by name.

Directly below the keychain item list are two buttons: + and i. The + button is used to manually add a new Keychain item to the active keychain. The i button displays and allows editing of item attributes and access controls.

Viewing and Editing Attributes

To view an item's attributes, double-click its list entry, or select it and click the i button at bottom of the window.

The Attributes pane provides basic information about the stored information. For example, Figure 2.40 shows the attributes for an IMAP password in my default keychain.

The Kind field identifies the type of information, Where shows the resource that stored the information, and Account displays the creating user account. Additional comments can be added by typing in the Comments field. Click the Show Password button to display the password in cleartext.

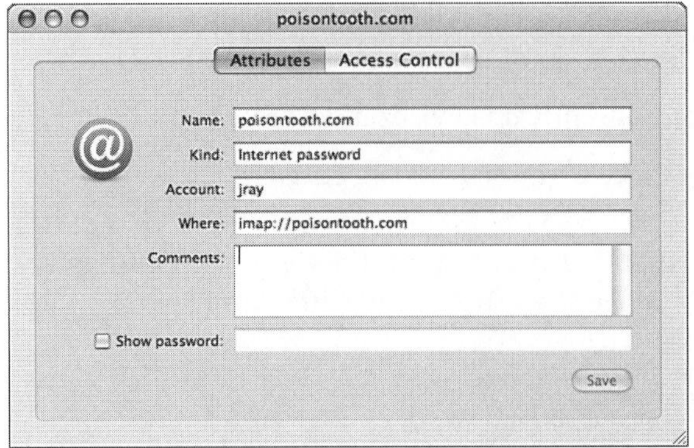

FIGURE 2.40 The Attributes pane displays what type of data is stored and when it was added to the keychain.

> **NOTE**
>
> When you click Show Password, you often are prompted to allow Keychain Access to retrieve the data. Although this might seem strange, it is because Keychain Access itself must obey the same rules as the rest of the system. Because Keychain Access isn't listed as having unlimited access to stored items, it asks each time it needs to retrieve the information.

You can edit any of the item attributes within the Attributes pane. Click the Save button in the lower-right corner to save any modifications you've made.

Setting Access Controls

To control what applications can access a piece of information and when, first open the item attribute view, and then click the Access Control button to switch panes. Shown in Figure 2.41, the controls of this pane are straightforward. Click Allow All Applications to Access This Item to transparently provide access to the resource with no user interaction.

You can specify individual applications by clicking the Confirm Before Allowing Access radio button; then use the + and - buttons to add and remove applications from the list. Leave the application list blank to always force a confirmation. Finally, check the Ask for Keychain Password check box to force the user to enter a password each time access is confirmed.

Adding and Removing Items

New passwords and notes can be added to the keychain by clicking the + button in the main Keychain window, or choosing File, New Password Item or File, New Secure Note Item from the menu, or clicking the Password or Note buttons in the toolbar.

Keychain Access opens a window for entering the attributes for the new item, as demonstrated in Figure 2.42.

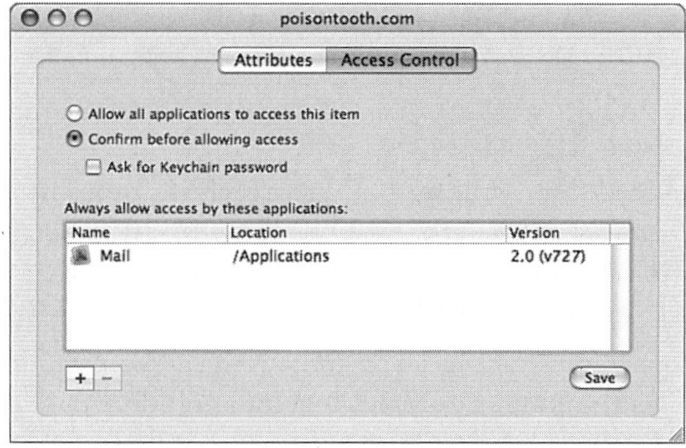

FIGURE 2.41 The Access Control pane provides control over what applications can access a piece of data.

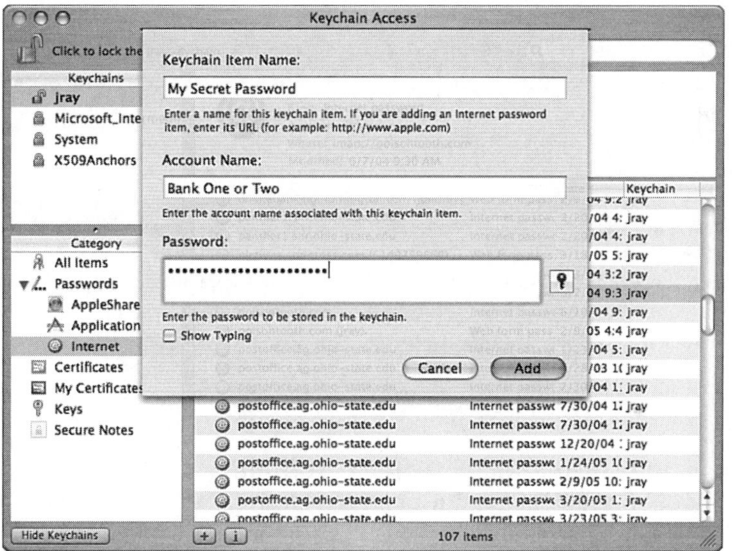

FIGURE 2.42 Enter the information to store in the keychain.

Enter the name or URL of the stored item in the Name field, the account name associated with the data in the Account field, and, finally, the sensitive data in the Password field. By default, the password is hidden as you type. To display the password as it is typed, click the Show Typing check box. Click Add when you've finished.

NOTE

When creating a Secure Note, only name and note fields are displayed.

To remove any item from the keychain (either automatically or manually entered), select its name in the list and then Edit, Delete or press the Backspace key.

Managing Digital Certificates

Digital certificates are used to provide authoritative identification information for people and services online. Secure websites use certificates to prove that they are legitimate for online transactions, whereas email certificates are used to send and receive encrypted email. Tiger supports secure mail services to and from clients using the S/MIME standard.

Unlike passwords or other keychain items, digital certificates are more than just an encrypted password. They contain information about an individual or service and are subject to a number of policies and verifications to ensure that they are properly used and contain accurate information. Certificates are signed by a Certificate Authority *(CA)*—a recognized and trusted third party that vouches for an entity. Consider it the digital equivalent of visiting a notary public.

To properly use a certificate, your system must verify both the certificate of the service/individual you are trying to use *and* the signature of the CA that signed it. Luckily, there is a limited set of CAs and Tiger includes certificates for dozens of popular authorities already. The assumption is that if the CA is trusted, the individual or service that obtained a certificate through them can also be trusted.

NOTE

If you use the Internet to make purchases, you are using CA certificates already. As you go through the checkout process, the remote site presents its certificate for verification. In almost all cases, this certificate is signed by one of the CAs that Tiger already aware of and the process happens transparently. If your web browser was unable to verify the CA that signed the site's certificate, it would display an error message warning you that the site's authenticity is in question.

Requesting and Adding an S/MIME Digital Certificate

To support encryption in mail, you must add an X.509 digital certificate containing a private and public key. The public key is used to *sign* outgoing messages so that other users can encrypt mail to you, which, subsequently is decrypted with your private key. Other users who sign their outgoing messages with their public key (using the S/MIME standard) can send you mail, and the Tiger Mail application *automatically* saves a certificate with their public key to your keychain. This, in turn, allows you to send encrypted messages to that person.

To obtain a certificate for signing mail, contact a Certificate Authority (CA), such as `http://www.thawte.com/email/index.html` and step through the application process (it varies from CA to CA). The Thawte Freemail certificates take only a few minutes to request and works wonderfully with Mail. When requesting the certificate, you will be prompted for the application you want to use it in—sadly, Mac OS X is rarely (never?) given as an option. That said, choosing Netscape Communicator works just fine. In fact, the certificate, which is downloaded through your web browser, is *automatically* recognized by Safari and Keychain Access and added to your `login` keychain, as shown in Figure 2.43.

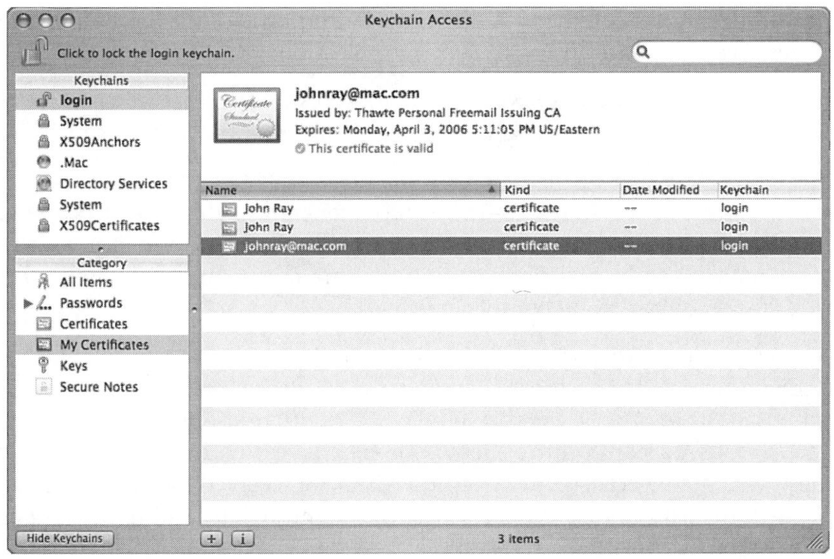

FIGURE 2.43 After a simple application process, the certificate is downloaded and added to my `login` keychain—automatically.

> **NOTE**
>
> Certificates are attached to a *single* identity, which can have, of course, multiple email addresses. When creating a certificate request, you will be prompted for your email addresses. The issued certificate can *only* be used with those addresses!

After an S/MIME certificate has been added, encryption features appear in Mail, as described in the next chapter.

Importing and Exporting Certificate Files

If a certificate downloads as a file without being imported, choose File, Import to manually import the certificate or just double-click the certificate file. Keychain Access supports certificates with the extensions `.cer`, `.crt`, `.p12`, `.pfx`, `.p7r`, `.p7b`, `.p7m`, `.p7c`, and `.p7s`. You will be given the option of viewing the certificate details and choosing the Keychain to hold the certificate before it is imported.

To export a certificate, select it in the Items list, and then choose File, Export from the menu. You will be prompted for a certificate name and format. You quickly export a file by dragging the certificate icon from the detailed summary pane to a Finder window.

Generating Your Own Certificates: Certificate Assistant

Hidden within Tiger's new Keychain Access application is a new utility that makes it possible to become a CA and issue your own digital certificates or create a new self-signed certificate. Obviously no one out in the real world will have your CA root certificate stored on their system or trust a self-signed certificate, but within a controlled LAN environment, you can import your CA certificate into the `X509Anchors` chain and become a one-stop certificate shop for inter-office communications.

To start the Certificate Assistant, choose Keychain Access, Certificate Assistant from the menu bar. The Certificate Assistant will launch and walk you through one of five different processes:

- Create a Certificate for Yourself—This option generates a digital certificate file that is self-signed. Being self-signed, it does not have any means of proving that the identity it contains is valid. Self-signed certificates are most commonly used for testing services that require a valid certificate.
- Create a Certificate Authority—In creating a certificate authority, you will become your own root CA. This process generates a CA certificate and can also send certificate invitations to other users through email. The invitations can be opened to start the Certificate Assistant on the client computers, creating new certificate signing requests *(CSRs)* for each client. When the CSRs are received by you, the CA, you can click them to again invoke the Certificate Assistant, finish signing the requests, and send the final certificate to the client.
- Use Your CA to Create a Certificate for Someone Else—If you have an incoming certificate signing request in your mailbox, you can drag the `.certSigningRequest` file to the CSR pane displayed in the Certificate Assistant to sign and return the certificate.
- Request a Certificate from an Existing CA—Creates a certificate signing request that is sent to, presumably, another Tiger account that is configured to be a CA. This action is usually carried out from any client machines that didn't initially receive a certificate invitation from the CA but need a certificate generated nonetheless.
- View and Evaluate Certificates—This feature allows you to review the information stored for a certificate file, including the chain of trust between certificate and CAs. You can also use this feature to retrieve and review certificates from secure web servers. Certificates can be imported directly by dragging their icons from the information display to the Keychain Access utility.

When working in the Certificate Assistant, you will need to have a good grasp of how to configure certificate capabilities for your specific needs. This can be quite complex, and a dedicated reference is wise investment for large-scale deployment. *Digital Certificates: Applied Internet Security* by Jalal Feghhi, Peter Williams (Addison-Wesley Professional, ISBN: 0201309807) is an excellent reference for everything related to digital certificates.

Viewing and Setting Certificate Information and Trust

To view all available information about a certificate, select the certificate in the Keychain items list, and then click the i button at the bottom of the window to display full details, as demonstrated in Figure 2.44.

FIGURE 2.44 View the full details of a certificate including issuer, expiration, and so on.

At the bottom of the information window are trust settings. A trust setting is used by the system to determine how, when, and if a certificate should be used. By default, Tiger makes some assumptions that you can overrule, if need be.

To change the trust policies for the certificate you are viewing, click the disclosure triangle in front of the Trust Settings label; pop-up menus appear for each potential certificate. Use the pop-ups to force the certificate to always be trusted, have the system prompt before using it, or to never be trusted.

Note that not all certificates can be used for all functions, so changing many of the trust settings would probably not have an effect.

Setting Certificate Revocation Preferences

A feature of digital certificates is that they are not valid indefinitely and can be revoked at any time. Invalid certificates are displayed with a red error message when viewed in Keychain Access and will not be used by the system. Mail, in fact, will display a large banner noting that it cannot verify an invalid digital signature.

Tiger has two means of detecting invalid certificates—the Online Certificate Status Protocol *(OCSP)* and the Certificate Revocation List *(CRL)*. To choose which of these methods is used to validate signatures, use the Certificates application preference pane. Use the pop-up menus to enable or disable each method and also pick which is the higher priority service (if any). A useful option for both OCSP and CRL is Best Attempt. When Best Attempt is selected, the certificate will be assumed valid unless it gets an explicit negative response from the remote server.

Managing Keychains

Each user account can have as many keychains as needed, including systemwide Global keychains. Click the Keychains button at the bottom of the window to manage the available keychains for your user account; the Keychains pane appears in the upper-left corner of the window, as seen in Figure 2.45. (Note: This has been visible in the screenshots preceding this point.)

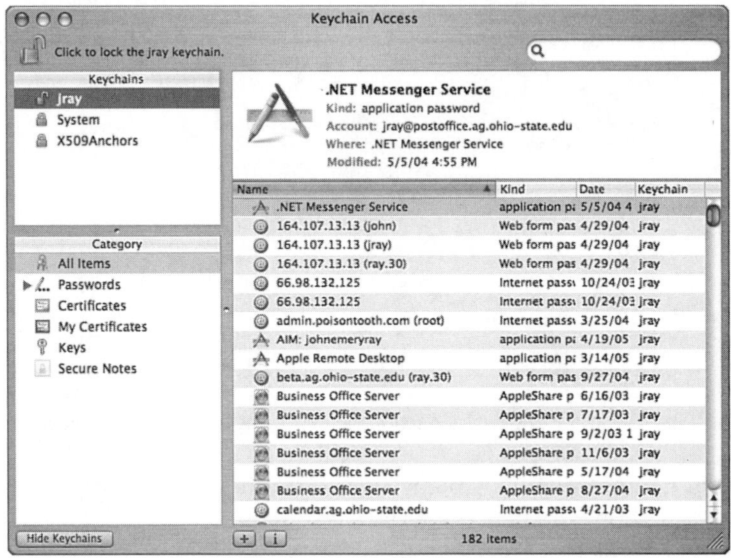

FIGURE 2.45 Use the Keychain list to manage your available keychains.

As mentioned earlier, a default keychain is generated for each user account named `login`. Also included is a default Global keychain named `System`, which is shared throughout all user accounts, and the System Global keychain `X509Anchors`, which contains root certificates for dozens of CAs.

> **NOTE**
>
> To use keychains stored on your .Mac account or directory servers, use the Search .Mac and Search Directory Servers options in the General application preferences pane.

Adding and Removing Keychains

To create a new keychain, choose File, New Keychain. You are prompted for a name and a save location for the keychain. The default for a User keychain is `~/Library/Keychains`; Global keychains should be stored in `/Library/Keychains`.

Next, you need to enter a passphrase that unlocks the new keychain. It's best to choose something different from your account password to prevent people who might gain access to your account from seeing your most sensitive information. Click OK and your keychain is unlocked and added to the Keychain list.

To add an existing keychain file (perhaps from your account on another Tiger machine), just double-click the keychain file and it will be imported into Keychain Access.

To work with your new keychain, you can switch to it by clicking its name in the Keychain list.

To remove a keychain from the system, highlight its name in the list and then choose File, Delete Keychain. You will be given the option of deleting just the reference to the keychain (removing it from the Keychain list, but leaving the actual data), or removing the reference *and* file associated with the keychain.

Creating Shared Keychains

Shared keychains are just like any other keychain, but have a flag toggled to make them immediately available to all users—the Shared flag (surprise). You can convert any keychain to or from Shared keychain status by using the Keychain List (Edit, Keychain List; Command-Option-L). The Keychain List is shown in Figure 2.46.

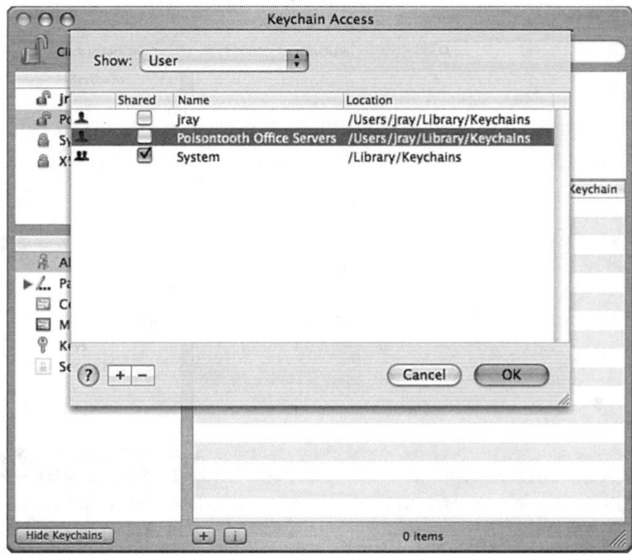

FIGURE 2.46 Manage Shared keychains.

The pop-up menu at the top of the list enables you to choose between User (your keychains) and System keychains. System keychains are stored at the system (`/Library/Keychains`, `/System/Library/Keychains`) level but are *not* necessarily Shared keychains. If installing a keychain for everyone on the system, it should be stored as a System keychain and should *also* be set as a Shared keychain.

To add additional keychains to the list, click the + button at the bottom of the window; to remove keychains, click the -button. This action also adds or removes the reference to the keychain in the main Keychain Access window, but does not change the actual keychain data files.

To convert a keychain to or from shared status, highlight it in the Keychain List; then use the Shared check box to change its status. Shared keychains automatically show up in other users' Keychain Lists.

Common Keychain Functions

After you've established your keychains, you can use the following functions to configure them to your heart's content—from replacing the default `login` keychain to resetting your keychain passwords and settings:

- Setting the Default Keychain—To make a keychain your default keychain (displacing `login`), choose File, Make Keychain Default.
- Moving Keychain Items—To move entries from one keychain to another, select the items you want to move and then drag them to the appropriate keychain in the Keychain List.
- Unlock/Lock Keychains—To lock or unlock a keychain, use the Lock icon in the Keychain Access Toolbar.
- Lock All Keychains—To lock all of your active keychains, choose File, Lock All Keychains.
- Changing Keychain Passwords—To change the password for a keychain, select it in the Keychain list, and then choose Edit, Change Password for Keychain.

NOTE

If you change the password on your default keychain to something other than your account password, it will not be automatically unlocked when you first log in.

The Keychain First Aid process (discussed shortly) will detect this problem and fix it if applied.

TIP

You can add a Keychain menu extra to your menu bar by choosing Show Status in the menu bar from the General application preference pane. The Keychain Access menu extra can instantly lock or unlock (with a password, of course) any of your keychains.

Configuring Keychain Security and .Mac Sync Settings

Each keychain in Keychain Access can be configured with additional security settings and included in .Mac syncing (see Chapter 3 for more information about .Mac). To open the settings, highlight the appropriate keychain from the Keychains List and then choose Edit, Change Settings for Keychain. You should see a new window, much like the one shown in Figure 2.47.

Within the Settings window, you can use the Lock After XX Minutes of Inactivity setting to force the system to lock a keychain if it isn't used for a certain length of time. Clicking Lock When Sleeping causes the keychain to be locked if the computer goes to sleep.

FIGURE 2.47 Set your keychains to lock after a certain length of time.

Finally, if you have a .Mac account and would like the keychain to automatically be synchronized between all of your .Mac registered computers, check the Synchronize This Keychain Using .Mac button. Click Save to put your changes into effect.

Repairing Keychain Problems

As you work with keychains, a variety of problems can occur, such as passwords getting out of sync, improper keychains being set as the default, or invalid data being stored or duplicated within entries. The Keychain First Aid tool can repair some of these common problems for any user account on the system.

To access Keychain First Aid, choose Keychain Access, Keychain First Aid (Option-Command-A). The First Aid window, shown in Figure 2.48, appears.

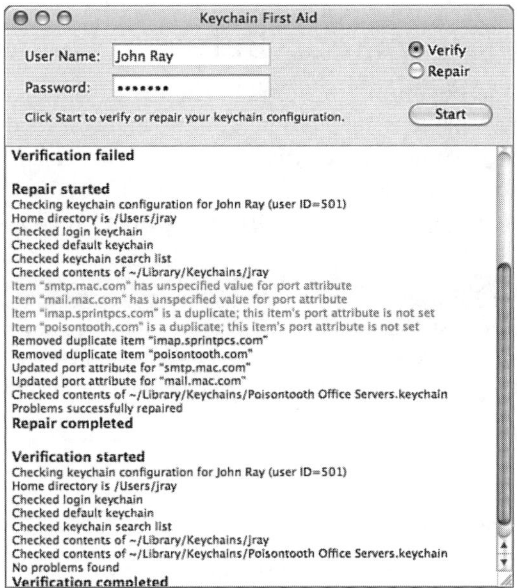

FIGURE 2.48 Keychain First Aid can repair common keychain problems.

To verify a user's keychain, click the Verify radio button, enter the username and password, and click the Start button. If problems are found, switch to Repair mode and then click Start again.

To change what repairs will be made by Keychain First Aid, use the First Aid pane of the application preferences. Choose whether to force the `login` keychain to always be the default, to synchronize the `login` keychain password and the actual Tiger *login* password, and to force `login` to always remain unlocked.

The First Aid features are primarily useful for fixing problems for users who have accidentally messed up their default `login` keychain. It does not fix a keychain that has suffered serious data corruption or recover information that has otherwise been lost. It is a tool to help you, as an administrator, handle keychain problems for your users without logging in to their accounts.

For most, the default First Aid preferences will be the behavior they expect. Advanced security conscience folks might decide to set up their keychains differently, so be sure that any repairs you perform actually are repairing a problem.

NOTE

To start fresh with a completely new factory-default keychain, open the General application preference pane and click Reset My Keychain. A new default keychain will be created in your account. Your old keychain will not be deleted, but will be dereferenced in the keychain list.

Synchronizing Information Between Devices: iSync

Most people's lives extend beyond their home to their workplace (or vice versa). Information should be available wherever you go, on whatever device you use. To this end, Apple has created the iSync software. iSync supports dozens of mobile phones, Palm devices, your iPod, iCal, Safari, Address Book, and more. If you have a .Mac account, no matter what Macintosh you're using, your critical information is only a "sync" away.

NOTE

Although an iCal Calendar subscription might seem like the perfect way to share information between your home and work computers, you can't edit a subscribed calendar. iSync allows you to have local calendar files that are synchronized automatically between your different workstations.

Managing iSync Devices

The iSync window, shown in Figure 2.49, provides the control over what you're syncing and when you're syncing it.

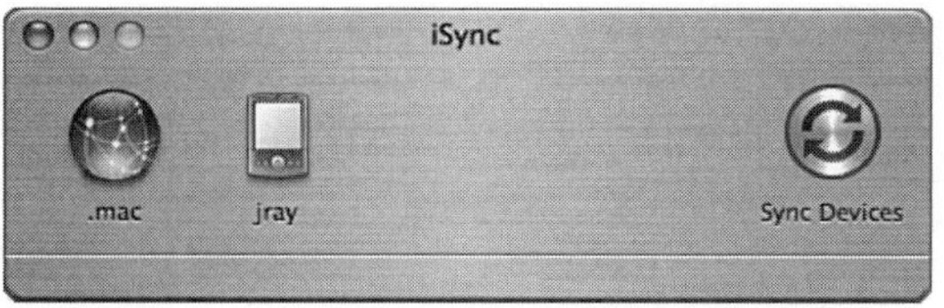

FIGURE 2.49 Devices to sync and a big shiny button.

On the left side of the window are the devices (data sources) that have been registered with iSync, and on the right is the Sync Devices button to start the synchronization process. Clicking a device icon in the iSync window opens a pane with all available synchronization settings for that device.

Setting Up .Mac Synchronization

By default, only one item is available for synchronizing: your .Mac account. This is a special device in that it provides a holding area for multiple computers to send and then retrieve information. If you have a .Mac account, it can be used with each of your Macintosh workstations to synchronize Bookmarks and other data.

Starting with Tiger, .Mac sync setup is performed within the .Mac system preference panel, discussed in Chapter 3. You can quickly jump to the .Mac sync preferences by selecting the .mac icon in iSync, and then clicking the Open .Mac Preferences.

Adding and Removing Devices

To add other devices to iSync, first make sure that the device is connected and turned on; if you are using Bluetooth, be sure to pair your device before trying to sync (see Chapter 5 for information about connecting Bluetooth devices).

In many cases, your device will automatically be recognized by iSync. If it isn't, choose Devices, Add Device from the menu. Click Scan if nothing is initially detected. iSync scans for iPods, PDAs, and Bluetooth-paired devices within the range of your computer, as shown in Figure 2.50.

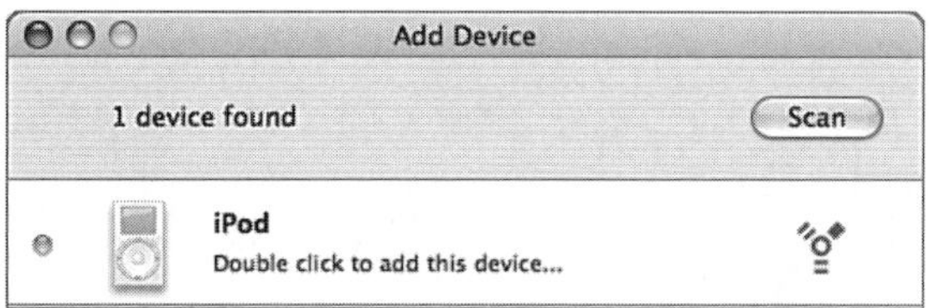

FIGURE 2.50 Scan for other iSync-capable devices.

Double-click the found devices to add them to the iSync window and register them with the iSync process.

Unfortunately, iSync doesn't and won't recognize all devices natively. To sync many popular handheld devices, you'll need some additional third-party software.

If you're a Palm user, you *must* have the iSync-Palm conduit and the Sync Manager from the Palm Desktop installed for iSync to work. The conduit is available from `http://www.apple.com/isync/download/`. After installing the pre-requisite components, choose Devices, Enable Palm OS syncing.

For a wider range of syncing options for everything from Palm and Pocket PC to the BlackBerry and Sony PSP, visit `http://www.markspace.com/` and `http://www.pocketmac.net/`. If it's a popular handheld device, one of these vendors will have a sync solution.

To remove a registered device, select it in the iSync window, and then choose Devices, Remove. .Mac registered computers can remove their registrations within the Advanced settings of the .Mac system preference pane. Devices can be re-added by repeating the same steps you used to originally add them.

Setting Device Options

Choosing a registered device in the iSync window displays the synchronization options specific to that device. For example, Figure 2.51 shows the synchronization options for my iPod.

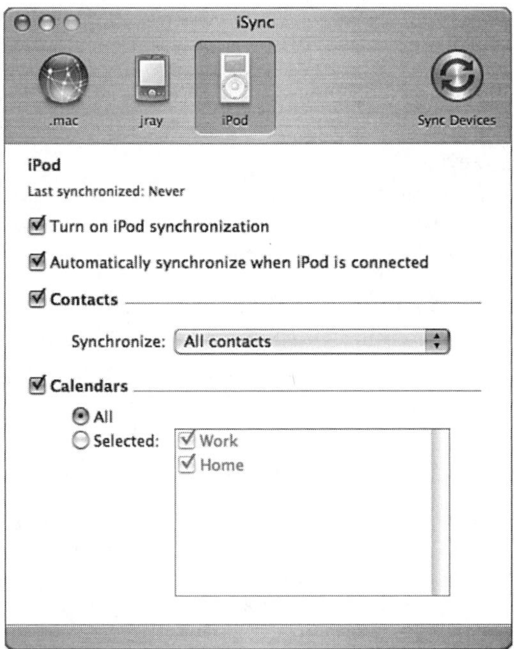

FIGURE 2.51 Synchronization options are unique for each device.

For the iPod, you can choose to automatically synchronize each time your iPod is connected as well as what contacts and calendars should be synchronized. The options for your devices are likely *will* vary from what you see here. It depends on the type of device you have and the features it supports.

Synchronizing

After setting the sync options for each of the devices you want to use, click the Sync Devices button, or choose Devices, Sync Devices (Command-T) from the menu. Normally the sync process is silent and requires no additional user interaction. Figure 2.52 demonstrates a typical synchronization process.

FIGURE 2.52 iSync gathers information from your devices and software and then synchronizes it.

In some cases, the first time a device is synchronized iSync may prompt to either merge the data on the device with your computer's sync data or replace it. Unless the device has been synchronized before, iSync has no way of knowing whether your computer or your device has the most accurate/current information, so this is its way of finding out.

After a few seconds, all your devices will have a copy of the latest calendars and contacts.

In the event that iSync determines that a significant number of changes are about to be made, it displays a confirmation message with the updates, allowing you to stop or apply the modifications. This simple safety feature can be disabled or adjusted using the Show Data Change Alert option in the application preferences.

TIP

To completely disable iSync, uncheck Enable Syncing on This Computer in the application preferences. To disable syncing of an individual device, select it in the iSync window and look for a Turn On Synchronization check box.

Adding the iSync Menu Extra

iSync will automatically run and synchronize your devices when changes are detected or a device is plugged in. You can force a sync by using the Sync Devices button, or by adding the iSync menu extra to your menu bar.

To add the iSync menu, open the application preferences and check Show Status in Menu Bar. The iSync menu (two chasing arrows) gives you an indication of your sync status as well as the option to force a sync at any time or open the .Mac sync preferences, as shown in Figure 2.53.

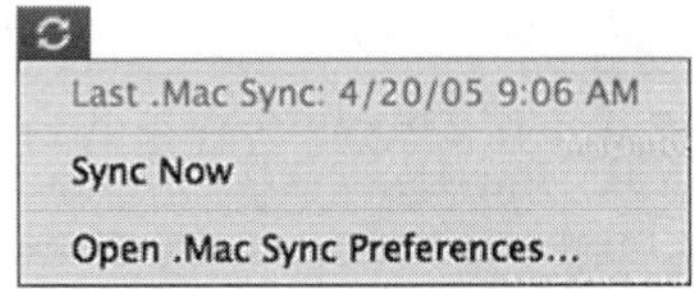

FIGURE 2.53 The iSync menu extra makes manual syncing convenient.

Resetting Device Synchronization States

iSync does what it can to keep your devices up to date, but things can happen. Suppose that you tried a new piece of software on your Palm that bungled up all of your event information, or your nephew managed to enter in new phone numbers for all of your contacts. In these cases, you might find yourself wanting to reset the synchronization state of the device.

When a device is reset, iSync treats it as a new device. The next time it is synced, you will be given the option of replacing all of the information on the device with your local sync database—which is presumably still intact.

To reset a device, select it in the iSync window and choose Device, Reset Device from the menu. To reset *all* devices, choose Device, Reset All Devices.

Because your computer is also a device and could potentially be corrupted, iSync provides a method of resetting the computer sync data as well. To do this, open the application preferences and choose Reset Sync History. At the next sync, you will be given the option to merge the information stored on your devices with your computer—effectively re-creating your sync information using what is stored on your devices.

Examining the iSync Log

To view a log of what iSync has done, when it was done, and the result, choose Window, Sync Log. Figure 2.54 shows the log window.

iSync Log
2:47:54 AM "iPod" engine processing complete
2:47:54 AM Applying changes to "iPod"
2:47:56 AM "iPod" applying changes complete
2:47:56 AM Device "iPod" synchronization complete
2:48:17 AM Warning Device "jray" synchronization cancelled
2:48:17 AM Warning Device "iPod" synchronization cancelled
Friday, April 22, 2005 2:48:18 AM EDT
Friday, April 22, 2005 2:48:36 AM EDT
Friday, April 22, 2005 2:49:47 AM EDT
Friday, April 22, 2005 2:50:02 AM EDT
Friday, April 22, 2005 2:52:13 AM EDT
Friday, April 22, 2005 2:52:56 AM EDT
2:52:57 AM Connecting to jray
2:52:57 AM Device "jray" connected
2:52:57 AM Connecting to iPod
2:52:57 AM Device "iPod" connected
2:52:58 AM Receiving changes from "iPod".
Friday, April 22, 2005 2:52:56 AM EDT
Clear Log

FIGURE 2.54 iSync logs each synchronization.

Use the disclosure arrows in front of each log line to expand or collapse details about each entry.

Running Legacy Mac OS Applications: Classic

We all know what happened with New Coke—and most of us (Coke drinkers at least) are probably pretty happy that we're still drinking Coke Classic. Unfortunately, the same can't be said for the Classic Mac OS. As we head toward the sixth year of Mac OS X's release, we still haven't closed the book on the original Mac OS operating system—now called Classic.

The Classic environment is a complete implementation of Mac OS 9.x on top of Tiger. To Tiger, Classic is nothing but another application; to a user, however, Classic is a gateway to older Mac software programs.

> **TIP**
>
> You must have at least 128MB of memory to use Classic, an installed copy of Mac OS 9.x, and a 400MHz G3 (or faster) is recommended. Because Mac OS 9.x does not come with Tiger, you must order it from Apple.

When using the Classic environment, the 9.x operating system must access all hardware through the Tiger kernel. This means that software that accesses hardware directly will likely fail. Users of 3Dfx video cards, hardware DVD playback, video capture cards, and such are out of luck.

On a positive note, Classic brings the benefit of Tiger's virtual memory underpinnings to legacy applications. Each Mac OS 9.x application can be configured for a much larger memory partition than was possible previously. To the Classic environment, the virtual memory appears to be real memory. Programs have much more breathing room in which to function.

> **NOTE**
>
> Classic does not gain all the stability features of Tiger, such as protected memory. If an application crashes in Classic, it can bring down all applications running in Classic. The overall system will be unaffected, but you might need to manually restart the Classic environment.

Working within the Classic environment is a somewhat unusual experience. Depending on the application running, there can be graphic anomalies and confusing filesystem navigation. It isn't perfect, but if you're a user who absolutely positively *must* run an old app, it'll do the trick.

Classic is typically launched once during a Tiger login session—either manually or automatically. After it is running, Classic remains active until you log out or otherwise force it to shut down.

There are two ways to launch Classic: by double-clicking a Classic application or through the Classic System Preferences pane.

Configuring Classic Applications

Classic applications are automatically recognized by Tiger and treated slightly differently by the operating system. When using Get Info, the information panes change slight to display extended information and settings not required for native Mac OS X applications.

Identifying Classic Applications

In the Finder, Classic applications appear just like any other application. To verify that a piece of software is indeed a Classic application, you can select the icon and choose File, Get Info or choose Get Info from the contextual or action menus. Figure 2.55 shows the General Get Info pane for Key Caps, a Classic application.

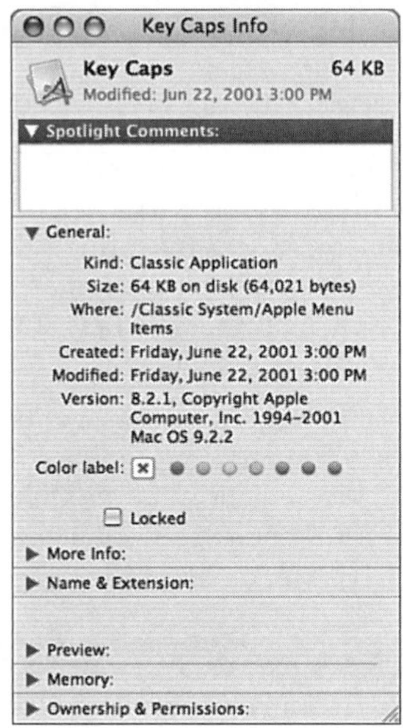

FIGURE 2.55 The General Get Info pane identifies Classic applications.

Adjusting Memory Settings

Classic applications, because they still use the Mac OS 9.x Memory Manager, require a preferred and minimum memory size to be set. Because you have no direct access to the 9.x Finder under Mac OS X, Classic applications have an additional Get Info pane called Memory, as shown in Figure 2.56.

Two limits can be set:

- Minimum Size—The minimum amount of memory that an application must have to run. The Mac OS 9.x environment prohibits the application from launching unless the minimum memory size can be met.

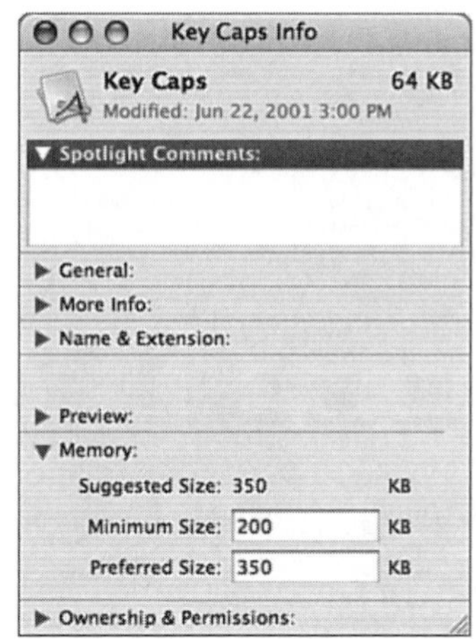

FIGURE 2.56 Classic applications allow memory limits to be set.

- Preferred Size—The amount of memory that you want the application to have. This is the upper limit of the memory partition that will be requested from Mac OS 9.x.

To take advantage of the new Tiger memory architecture, set these values higher than you would in older versions of the Mac OS.

Forcing Carbon Applications into Classic

Carbon applications are a special case of Mac OS X application. They are capable of running natively on Tiger *and* on Mac OS 9.x through the use of CarbonLib. If you want to use the Classic environment to launch a Carbon application, a setting within the General pane of the Get Info pane can force a Carbon-compliant package to launch through Classic.

To launch a Carbon application in Classic, check the Open in the Classic Environment check box and then close the info pane. Subsequent launches will occur in Classic.

Controlling the Classic Environment

The operation and setup of the Classic environment is performed in the Classic system preference pane. The Start/Stop settings control how and when Classic boots, as demonstrated in Figure 2.57.

- Select a Startup Volume for Classic—Tiger can start the Classic environment by booting any available Mac OS 9.x system. Use this list to choose between any detected Classic-compatible systems.
- Start Classic When You Log In—If you want Classic to start up immediately after you log in to your computer (or immediately at startup, if you're using Tiger as a single-user system), click this button. Be warned: The Classic environment takes a few minutes to start, and your system performance will be degraded during this time.

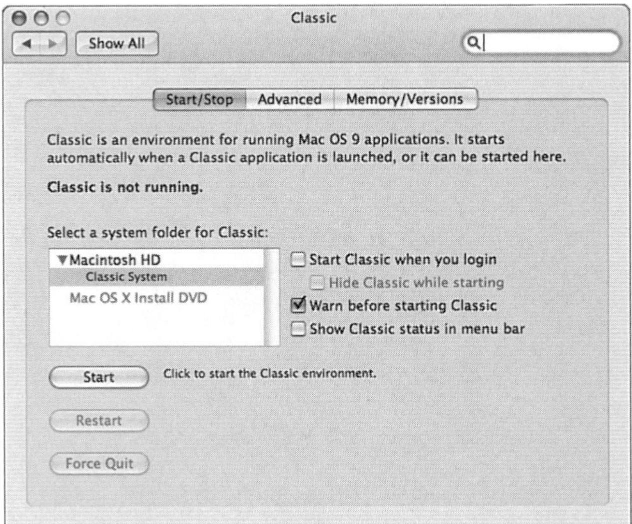

FIGURE 2.57 The Classic System Preferences pane configures the startup volume and allows manual startup and shutdown.

- Hide Classic While Starting—The Classic startup window will be hidden while the Classic environment boots.
- Warn Before Starting Classic—Use this option to force Tiger to prompt you each time it launches the Classic environment. If you find yourself accidentally starting Classic by double-clicking legacy files, and so on, this can be helpful.
- Show Classic Status in Menu Bar—Adds a menu extra that can start and stop Classic and provides access to the Classic Apple menu items.
- Start/Stop—Click the Start button to launch Classic manually or Stop to shut it down.
- Restart—Equivalent to choosing Restart from the Mac OS 9.x Finder. Open applications prompt you to save open documents and then exit. The Classic environment will reboot.
- Force Quit—If Classic becomes unresponsive (that is, it crashes), the only option is to force it to quit. Open documents are lost, exactly as if Mac OS 9.x crashed (as it tends to do from time to time). You can also use the Control-Option-Escape keystroke to force it to quit.

Setting Advanced Startup Options

Use the Advanced settings pane to provide additional control over the boot sequence and basic Classic functions. You can make several modifications to the startup process and overall operation:

- Turn Off Extensions—Turning off the extensions is the equivalent of pressing Shift while booting into Mac OS 8 or 9. This prohibits additional control panels and extensions—beyond those needed by the 9.x operating system—from loading.
- Open Extensions Manager—This opens the Mac OS 9.x Extensions Manager control panel during the boot process, allowing you to disable extensions that appear to be causing system instability.
- Use Key Combination—This unusual option enables the user to choose up to five keys that will be kept in pressed state while Classic boots. Some extensions can be individually disabled by certain keystrokes; this feature lets you target those processes.
- Use Mac OS 9 Preferences from Your Home—If selected, Classic maintains a separate set of preferences for your account. If unchecked, a systemwide preferences location is used.
- Put Classic to Sleep When It Is Inactive For—When Classic is running, it is using your system resources. The Classic environment continues to use CPU time even if you aren't running a Classic application. This is because Mac OS 9.x must keep up the basic system maintenance and monitoring processes that happen behind the scenes. If you choose to put Classic to sleep, it stops using these resources after the length of time you choose.
- Rebuild Desktop—Rebuilding the Mac OS 9.x desktop can help solve "generic icon" problems (files that should have custom icons show up as generic white icons in the Finder), as well as issues with documents that can't find the appropriate Classic application to open them. If your Classic environment starts to act in unusual ways, rebuilding the desktop is a good place to start.

NOTE

The first time you boot Classic, the advanced options will not be available. Subsequent executions will enable all the advanced features.

Viewing Memory Usage and Application Information

With Classic running, the Memory/Versions pane displays the processes that are active and how much memory they are consuming, as shown in Figure 2.58.

To display information about background Classic processes, click the Show Background Processes check box. Information about the version of Classic and its supporting software is displayed at the bottom of the pane.

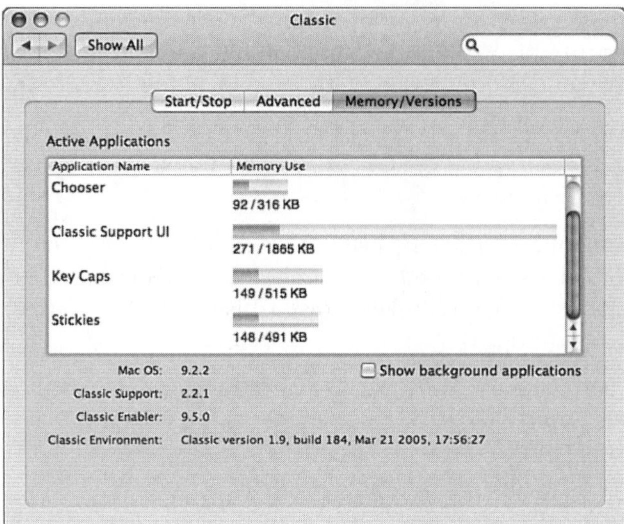

FIGURE 2.58 The Memory/Versions pane gives feedback on active Classic processes.

Other Tools and Utilities

Tiger includes a number of other tools and toys that you might be interested in using. These aren't covered in detail because of the nature of the tools; if you've used a computer, you'll be familiar enough with these applications that you'll be right at home.

- Address Book (Dashboard)—The Address Book dashboard widget gives you instant access to stored contacts without opening the Address Book application.
- Calculator (path: `/Applications/Calculator` and Dashboard)—The calculator application has simple and scientific modes, a paper-tape display, and numerous conversion features, including a currency converter that updates exchange rates via the Internet. The Dashboard variant provides only simple calculations.
- Calendar (Dashboard)—The Calendar widget acts as a simple desktop calendar, displaying the current day and date, or an overview of any month of the year.
- Chess (path: `/Applications/Chess`)—The 3D Chess application is an intellectually stimulating gaming experience on your Mac. When your Windows friends are playing Solitaire, show them a real game. Although based on GNUChess, Apple provides a beautiful 3D interface to the classic Unix game.
- Dictionary (path: `/Application/Dictionary` and Dashboard)—Tiger includes the entire Oxford American Dictionary and Thesaurus. The Dictionary application can be used to instantly look up words of your choice. You can even set parental controls for Dictionary (see the Accounts system preference panel) to prevent user accounts from looking up "dirty" words.

TIP

Dictionary is integrated into contextual menus such that you can highlight and Control-click a word virtually anywhere in Tiger and choose Look Up in Dictionary. By default, this will launch the Dictionary application and display the results for the work.

To create an even better integration, open Dictionary and use the application preference to choose Open Dictionary Panel. When selected, looking up a work will open only a small floating panel, as shown in Figure 2.59, without requiring the Dictionary application to open. For the ultimate trick, hold down Control-Command-D and Tiger will instantly look up any word over which you hold your cursor, in almost any application.

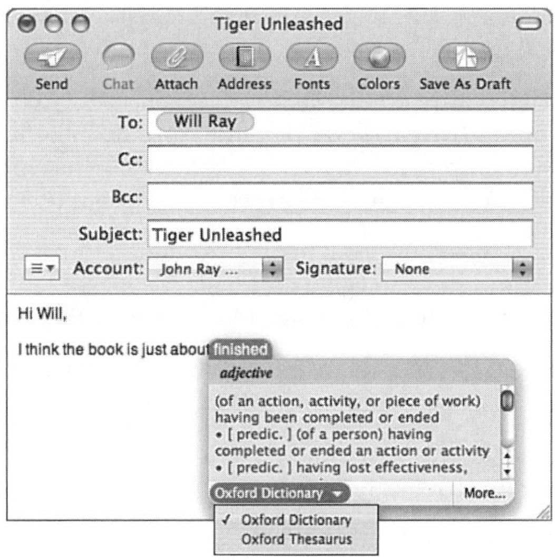

FIGURE 2.59 Dictionary integrates cleanly into almost all Tiger applications.

- DigitalColor Meter (path: `/Applications/Utilities/DigitalColor Meter`)—The DigitalColor Meter utility allows you to sample onscreen colors and display their representation in a variety of color spaces, including HTML-ready hex RGB.
- DVD Player (path: `/Applications/DVD Player`)—The Tiger DVD player has been updated with new image controls and *finally* (after five years!) has the capability to playback video in the Dock icon on Quartz Extreme-enabled machines.
- Flight Tracker (Dashboard)—Use the Flight Tracker widget to check the status of any flight and view the plane's current location on a map (if the data is available).
- Grapher (path: `/Applications/Utilities/Grapher`)—New to Tiger is a 2D/3D graphing calculator. Grapher is an *extremely* full-featured application with numeric differentiation and integration capabilities built-in.
- iTunes (Dashboard)—A simple widget for controlling the iTunes application. Why you wouldn't just use iTunes itself (it must to be running in order to use this tool) is beyond me...but it looks cool.

- Migration Assistant (path: `/Applications/Utilities/Migration Assistant`)—Although its unlikely you'll be using this on anything but a fresh Tiger install, the Migration Assistant can be used to copy user accounts and applications from an existing computer running in Target Disk mode to a Tiger machine.
- Phone Book (Dashboard)—The Phone Book widget is a virtual Yellow Pages. Look up businesses by name or choose a business type to display everything nearby that matches (based on your Address Book "Me" location).
- Stickies (path: `/Applications/Stickies` and Dashboard)—The classic Stickies application allows you to jot down brief notes and attach them to your screen.
- Stocks (Dashboard)—Use the Stocks widget to view stock and overall market activity, including historical graphs.
- TextEdit (path: `/Applications/TextEdit`)—TextEdit is a styled text editor capable of opening, editing, and saving RTF, HTML, and Word documents. TextEdit can save HTML and XHTML compliant documents—complete with embedded style sheets. Best of all, if you can use a basic word processor, you can use TextEdit.
- Tile Game (Dashboard)—The classic tile puzzle game returns in Tiger To use your own picture, select and start dragging an image file in the Finder, invoke Dashboard using the keyboard, then drop the image file onto an active copy of the Tile Game.
- Translation (Dashboard)—As if by magic, this dashboard widget translates text between different languages *as it is entered!*
- Unit Converter (Dashboard)—Provides instant conversion between units of measure and currency (similar to the features found in the Calculator application).
- Weather (Dashboard)—The Weather widget displays current weather conditions and extended forecasts for any location in an attractive graphic format.
- World Clock (Dashboard)—Add as many world clocks to your Dashboard as you'd like. Each instance of the World Clock can be set to display the time in any time zone of your choice.

Summary

This chapter covered the applications and utilities in Tiger that, although useful, are difficult to catalog into a specific category and probably too small to warrant a chapter of their own. There's quite a bit you can do in the operating system without resorting to third-party products. The applications discussed here should get you started—and there's plenty more to come.

CHAPTER 3

Internet Applications

IN THIS CHAPTER

- Browsing the Web: Safari
- Accessing Email: Apple Mail
- Video and Audio Conferencing: iChat AV
- Searching the Internet: Sherlock
- The Enigma That Is .Mac

The Mac OS has long been the leader in network connectivity among desktop operating systems. The Macintosh was using MacTCP and Open Transport while Windows 3.1 struggled to get online using third-party TCP stacks and DOS-based network card drivers. Although the playing field has mostly leveled, it's little surprise that Tiger includes a wide variety of Internet-related tools. Users who are interested in getting online, finding old friends, chatting with others, sending email, and surfing the Internet will be happy to find many applications to get them online in a matter of minutes.

This chapter covers the applications that work specifically with the Internet to gather information, send and receive messages, and make your online life easier:

- Safari (path: `/Applications/Safari`)—Apple's web and RSS/Atom browser based on open source technologies.
- Mail (path: `/Applications/Mail`)—Apple's application features IMAP/POP3 support, HTML/RTF email, dynamic filtering, Smart Folders, spam protection, and a somewhat non-Mac OS X-like interface.
- iChat AV (path: `/Applications/iChat`)—A chat program compatible with AOL Instant Messenger (AIM), provides Audio and Video conferences with multiple people, and integrates with .Mac, Mail, and Address Book.
- Sherlock (path: `/Applications/Sherlock`)—Sherlock performs multiple search engine queries on popular e-commerce, news, and entertainment sites and returns results without the need for a web browser.
- .Mac—Apple's pay-for Internet service for bringing Tiger with you, wherever you might be.

As with the previous chapters, the applications discussed here are presented with basic use information, followed by configuration and menu options. The goal is to provide information for beginners as well as useful reference for advanced users.

TIP

The assumption is that you already have a working network connection configured at installation or in your previous version of Mac OS X. For information on setting up an Internet connection, see Chapter 7, "Configuring Network Connectivity."

Browsing the Web: Safari

Many people purchase computers just to access information over the Internet. The iMac, in fact, was introduced as the "Internet" Mac. Unfortunately, Apple's "Internet Experience" has been tied to Internet Explorer for the last few years. Although a capable browser, IE was *not* fast, lacked many features of other browsers, and, let's face it, was a Microsoft product.

With Tiger, Apple has official phased out Internet Explorer in favor of Safari—the modern and *fast* browser for Tiger. Safari is based on the `khtml` engine—part of the popular KDE (usually associated with Linux) project. Safari provides excellent web browsing features including pop-up blocking, complete bookmark management, and RSS/Atom syndication support.

Understanding the Basic Browsing Controls

Figure 3.1 shows the Safari interface, with all available interface options on (this is *not* the default state). Most interface elements are turned on and off directly from the View menu or by choosing Customize Address Bar from the View menu—with the exception of Tabs, a popular feature that allows multiple web pages to be viewed in single window. If you've used a web browser before, you might want to skip this section because it will likely be review. We've had many readers ask for a more tutorial approach for novices, however, so the information is included for their benefit.

Address Bar

The top row of controls in the Safari window is the address bar. It contains the controls you use to navigate websites.

- The Back and Forward buttons work together. Use the Back button to return to the web page you viewed previously. After you've gone back, you can use the Forward button to move ahead to where you were. If you haven't gone back through any pages you've already viewed, the Forward button is grayed out to show that it is not an active option at the current time.

TIP

Clicking and holding on a forward or backward arrow shows a list of pages that you've visited either in front of (since) or behind (before) your current page.

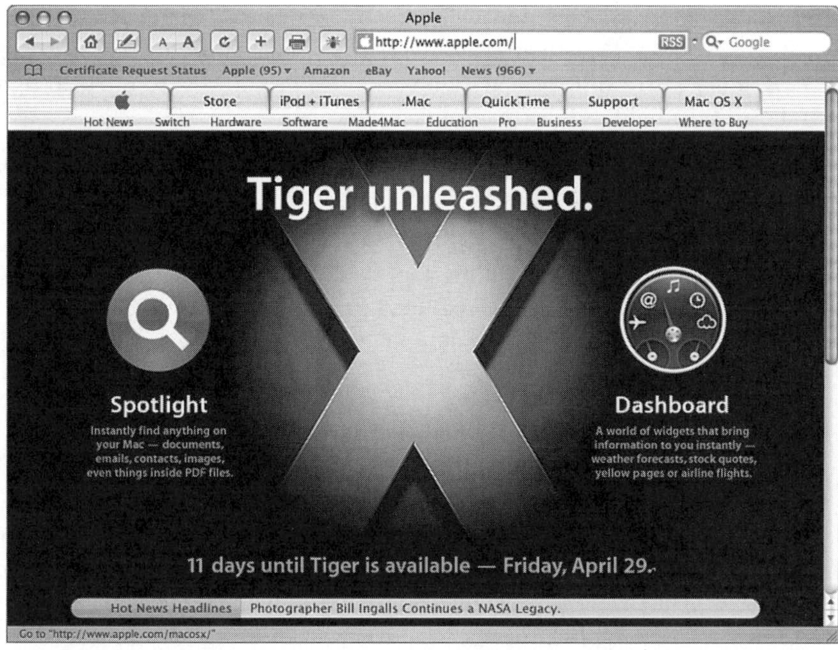

FIGURE 3.1 Apple's Safari web browser with a full set of interface options.

- The Home button returns you to the page set as your default startup page. Think of it as a shortcut for connecting to the site you visit most frequently.

NOTE

To change the page that comes up automatically when Safari is launched, use the General pane of the Application preferences.

- The Autofill button attempts to fill in form information based on your Address Book entries and forms that you've completed previously in Safari.
- The Text Size button allows you to easily increase or decrease the font size in the current page.
- The Stop/Reload button changes depending on whether the current page identified in the address field has been loaded, or is loading. If a page has been loaded, you see the Reload button, which allows you to refresh the page. The Stop button appears as a page is loading to allow you to stop retrieving the current page.
- Clicking the Add Bookmark button, which looks like a +, adds the current page to your bookmark list so that you can easily visit it again without writing down the address. We'll discuss Bookmarks more later in this section.
- The Print button, as expected, prints the contents of the current page.

- The Address field is where you provide the URL of the site you want to browse. Safari also uses the address field as a status bar to indicate how much of a page has loaded. As a page is read into Safari, a blue-shaded bar moves from left to right across the address field as information is received.
- The Google Search field allows you to type a word or phrase of interest and search the Google search engine for relevant sites. The results listing appears in your browser window. This is just a shortcut for visiting `http://www.google.com/`.
- The Bug button was included to allow people to report any problems they experience in viewing pages. If a page fails to load in Safari, clicking this button allows you to submit an error report to Apple.

Bookmarks Bar

The Bookmarks bar holds shortcuts to websites and news feeds that you want to keep close at hand—think of it as a Dock for bookmarks.

You can add sites to the Bookmarks bar by dragging the icon in front of the URL in the address field into the Bookmarks bar. A dialog appears, allowing you to enter a more intelligible name than *eBay item #442231*. Remove Bookmarks bar shortcuts by Command-dragging (or Click, Hold, and Drag) them outside the Safari window. If you drag within the Bookmarks bar area, you can rearrange them.

As the Bookmarks bar grows beyond the size of the Safari window (trust me, it will) or the window is resized so that your existing bookmarks don't fit, Safari adds the >> icon to the end of the Bookmarks bar (just like the Finder and other applications). Clicking and holding on this icon displays the hidden shortcuts in a list.

A special permanent and nonmovable shortcut called Show All Bookmarks within the Bookmarks bar resembles a book. This icon opens the Bookmark Manager, which provides *extensive* control over your Safari bookmarks.

> **TIP**
>
> In some of the Apple-supplied default Bookmarks bar shortcuts you might notice entries with a down arrow after their name. These are called collections and can only be added to the Bookmarks bar through the Bookmarks Library. You can add Bookmarks to a collection on the bar, however, by dragging the bookmark to the collection.

Tab Bar

Tabs are an option in Safari that allows you to have several web pages open at one time without all the clutter of extra browser windows. After a page has been loaded into a tab, it can be switched to by clicking the appropriate tab in the bar—just as you use tabs to navigate between different screens in a popular applications.

Tabs have become a popular feature largely through the development of the Mozilla and Opera browsers. Safari borrows a page from both of these popular alternative browser platforms. Tabs must be activated through the Tabs pane of the application preferences.

Status Bar

The status bar, located at the bottom of the Safari window, displays information about a page as it loads—whether it has contacted the remote host, how many elements (such as images) of the page have been retrieved, and so on.

The status bar also provides information about hyperlinked elements on a page as you move your mouse cursor across them. For example, if you run your mouse across a text link or a linked image, the address of the link appears.

Browsing the Web in Safari

To visit a website for which you know the address, type the address in the address field in the Address bar and press the Return key on your keyboard. You see a blue-shaded bar move across the address field as the page loads and, if you've chosen to view the Status Bar, a countdown of the page elements that are loading.

NOTE

Web pages aren't a single object. Typically, they are composed of a page file and separate image files. (In some cases, there might be additional supporting files containing page content or formatting information as well.) The countdown in the status bar as a page loads tells you just how many files it requires!

When a page has loaded, you can click text links or linked images or buttons to move to other pages. To cycle through form and navigation elements from the keyboard press Option-Tab.

TIP

Websites don't always work. If you try to visit a site and receive a Server Not Found message, the problem is not likely to be Safari. Such a message occurs when there are technical difficulties for the computer hosting the website or when a site is no longer available. Safari provides a "help" button that you can click to help diagnose problems.

Beyond that, your best option is to double-check the address you've entered. If the address is correct, you might need to wait before trying the site again, in case there's some kind of temporary site outage. If the site doesn't return, you might want to try a Google search on the name of the site to see whether a cached version of the content is still available.

If you're looking for a site that you know was available at *some* time but appears to have vanished off the face of the earth, you might want to try the WayBack Machine at `http://www.archive.org` to retrieve an archived copy.

Using Address Autocompletion

If you begin to type in an address you've visited recently, Safari tries to autocomplete it. A drop-down menu of addresses for pages you've been to that match what you've typed so far appears; Safari's best guess of which address you're typing is highlighted. If the page you want to view is listed in the drop-down menu, use your arrow keys or mouse cursor to select it. If it isn't listed, continue to type the rest of the address.

Completing Forms with AutoFill

As you enter data in forms within Safari, you're creating a database that can be used to automatically fill in the contents of similar forms, hopefully saving you some typing.

By default, Safari completes a form if it is recognized. To control Form AutoFill for unknown forms, enable the AutoFill button in the address bar. Clicking the AutoFill button (Shift-Command-A) forces Safari to fill in a form to the best of its ability. You'll also notice that much like address autocompletion, Safari attempts to fill in individual form fields as you type.

If you resubmit a form that Safari has already stored, Safari might prompt you whether to keep the old values or replace them with the new entries—or do nothing at all.

To control where Safari pulls the data for Form AutoFill, open the application preferences and click the AutoFill icon to open the AutoFill preferences pane, shown in Figure 3.2.

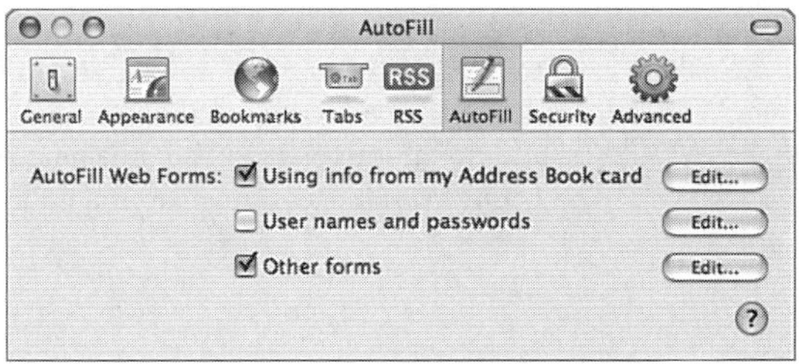

FIGURE 3.2 Choose where Safari AutoFill data comes from.

There are three sources for AutoFill data: Address Book (addresses, phone numbers, and such), usernames and passwords (names and passwords you've used to log in to websites), and other forms (any form you've filled in on a website).

Beside each of these options is an Edit button. Clicking Edit opens a window to display what username and passwords have been stored and what web domains have forms saved (or, in the case of the Address Book, it opens the Address Book). You can select elements in these lists and remove them if they contain elements that you'd rather not use for AutoFill or that contain inaccurate data.

Returning to Pages with SnapBack

As you use Safari, you might notice an icon displaying a return arrow in an orange circle at the far-right side of the address field and Google field. Apple has dubbed this the SnapBack button. It appears in any page you navigate to through links within other web pages. If clicked (or Option-Command-P is pressed), the SnapBack button takes you back to the last address you physically typed in the address field.

You can also manually set a page to be the one to which Snap-Back returns. Choose History, Mark Page for SnapBack from the menu (Option-Command-K). This is a convenient way to mark a specific page while you continue to following links.

> **NOTE**
>
> Google searches executed using the Google field in Safari automatically enable SnapBack. Just click the Snap-Back icon at the right end of the Google field or press (Option-Command-S)

Using the Browsing History

Although the SnapBack feature is great for a single browsing session, it can't take you back to where you were earlier in the day, yesterday, or last week. To do this, you'll want to use the History menu.

As you browse, Safari keeps track of where you've been. The History menu displays a list of addresses you've visited in the current session, along with submenus for pages visited in the past week. To clear your history (you aren't ashamed of where you've been browsing, are you?) choose History, Clear History.

Using Tabbed Browsing

Tabs allow you to have several web pages open at one time without the clutter of extra browser windows.

If you want to use tabs, open the Safari application preferences and then choose the Tabs pane (shown in Figure 3.3). Check the box for Enable Tabbed Browsing. You can also choose whether tabs containing freshly loaded pages are automatically selected (brought to the front) or whether they wait for you to click them. Finally, you can choose whether to show the Tab bar even when only one tab exists.

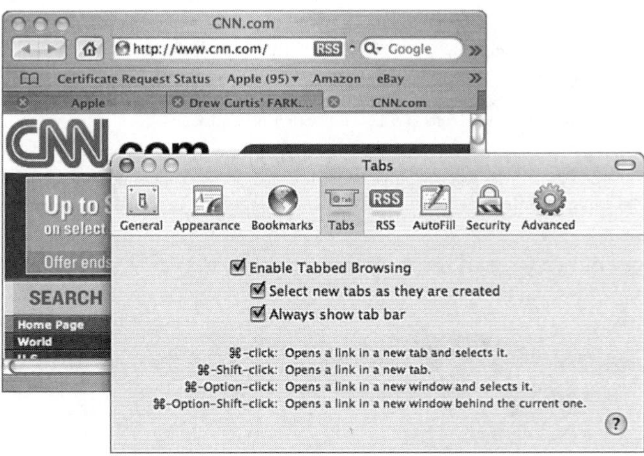

FIGURE 3.3 The Tabs preferences pane contains a few options as well as a list of keyboard shortcuts.

Tabs are easy to use. When you want one, choose File, New Tab from the menu (Command-T). You then see a row of boxlike buttons, or *tabs* just below the Address bar. Each Tab is labeled with the name of the web page it contains, as shown in Figure 3.4, so you can easily click between them. If you want to close a tab, click the close icon on its far-left side.

CAUTION

If tabbed browsing isn't enabled in the Safari preferences, you will not see the option to open a tab under the File menu!

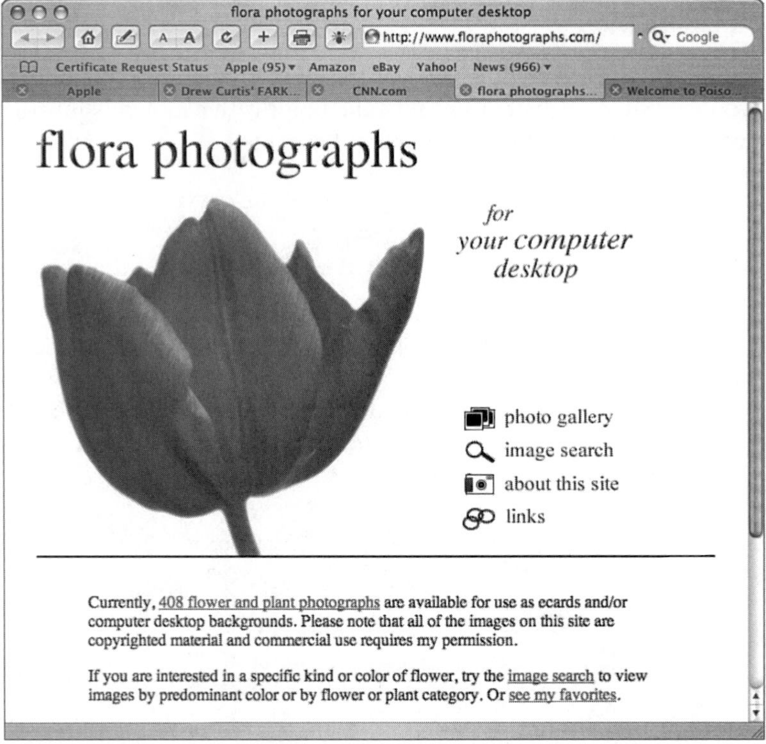

FIGURE 3.4 A row of tabs—each representing a web page ready for viewing.

TIP

If you want to open a link in a new tab, hold down the Command key while clicking the link.

A unique feature of Apple's tab implementation is the ability to open any bookmark collection in tabs—all at once. When tabs are active, an extra option, Open in Tabs, appears within the submenu of any collection shown in the Bookmark menu. Choosing this loads all the pages in the collection in your current window—one in each tab. We'll look at how to create collections with the Bookmarks Library shortly.

TIP

If you want links clicked in external applications (such as Mail) to automatically open in a new tab, use the General application preferences pane to choose Open Links from Applications in a new tab in the Current Window. You will *not* lose the page you were currently viewing.

Downloading Files

In addition to viewing web pages with Safari, you can also use it to download files linked from web pages.

NOTE

Safari only handles `http` protocol downloads. FTP downloads are handed off to the Finder. So, if you click an FTP link and Safari appears to do nothing, check the Finder.

When you click a link for a downloadable document, Safari automatically opens a Downloads window. Depending on your preference settings, this window might list other files you've downloaded as well as show status of the current download. You can clear the download list by clicking the Clear button.

TIP

If Safari does not recognize the document as something to download and instead starts to display it on the screen, you can force a link to download by holding down Option when clicking it.

Incidentally, this is not usually a failing of Safari, but a mistake in the MIME-type mapping of the remote server.

By default, Safari stores downloaded files on your desktop and attempts to post-process safe files by decompressing archives and opening common file formats such as QuickTime media. Safari will warn you if the file you are downloading might contain something harmful and will prompt to make sure you want to open it.

These settings can be adjusted through the General pane of the application preferences.

NOTE

Apple recently introduced Internet-enabled Disk Images that copy the software they contain to your desktop and then remove themselves without a trace. Be aware that if you're downloading a `.dmg` file, you might not see the image on your desktop after downloading. If it is an Internet-enabled disk image, and processing of safe files is turned on in Safari (the default), you will be left with only the files the image contained. For more information, see `http://developer.apple.com/documentation/DeveloperTools/Conceptual/SoftwareDistribution/Concepts/sd_disk_images.html`.

Viewing PDFs Online

Starting with Tiger, Safari can now directly view PDFs linked from websites without needing to launch an external helper like Preview. The PDF viewer, shown in Figure 3.5 provides basic controls over the image by Control-clicking on a PDF page. The corresponding contextual menu is also shown in Figure 3.5.

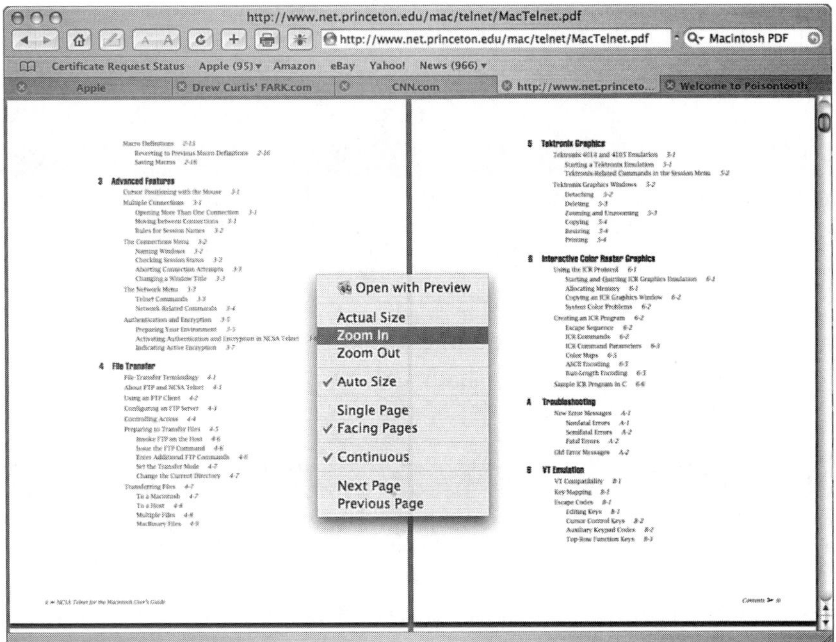

FIGURE 3.5 Use the contextual menu to control the appearance of PDFs in Safari.

The menu can be used to zoom in and out of the PDF image, auto-size it, move between pages, and switch to a side-by-side (facing) page view mode.

While it is admirable that Apple has included inline PDF viewing in Safari, the implementation leaves a bit to be desired. For greater control, try the PDF Browser Plugin from Shubert-it (`http://www.schubert-it.com/pluginpdf`). This third-party plug-in has much greater control over the PDF output and includes a toolbar for easily manipulating the PDF in the browser.

Maintaining Your Security and Privacy Online

Protecting your identity online and your browsing experience in general is key to the Safari experience. Safari offers several options to control cookies, pop-up windows, and more.

Limiting Web Content

To access the security features, open the Security pane of the Safari preferences pane, shown in Figure 3.6.

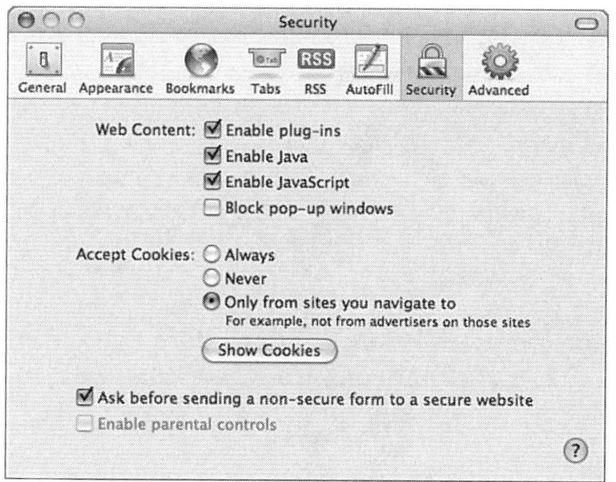

FIGURE 3.6 Protect yourself online.

The Web Content options choose what Safari allows on a web page:

- Enable Plug-ins—Additional software components that allow the display of alternative media—such as QuickTime movies, Flash animation, and so on.
- Enable Java—Enables Java applications (used by products such as TurboTax Online) to run within your browser.
- Enable JavaScript—A scripting language that enables your browser to perform basic computing functions on a web page. Often used to verify form field contents before submitting them back to a server or to create rollover image effects on web pages.
- Block Pop-up Windows—You know what they are. You hate them. Now block them!

TIP

Block Pop-up Windows can also be toggled on and off from the Safari application menu (Command-K).

Additionally, you can set when your browser will accept cookies from websites. Choose Always to allow *any* cookie to be set, Never to never allow any cookies, or Only from Sites You Navigate To to block cookies from advertisers and others not directly associated with the sites you are browsing.

Clicking the Show Cookies button displays a list of cookies stored on your machine and gives you the option to remove those you don't want stored.

NOTE

Cookies are a valuable tool for web developers and are used extensively on major consumer sites. Disabling cookies completely is likely to result in sites that can no longer successfully be navigated.

It's important to note that much of the "controversy" surrounding cookies is purely hype. Cookies are sent to your browser by a remote site. They cannot be retrieved by any arbitrary website. In fact, cookies are not retrieved at all; they are sent voluntarily by the Safari browser on returning to a site that stored a cookie.

Finally, if you want to be prompted before sending information over the Internet in an insecure manner, click the Ask Before Sending a Non-Secure Form to a Secure Website check box.

Resetting the Safari Cache and Configuration

As you browse, Safari automatically stores portions of websites so they can be quickly accessed in the future. Unfortunately, this can leave a very traceable track of where you've been online.

Safari makes it simple to dump any content that it might have cached while browsing, or even reset it to the default configuration—including removing bookmarks. Under the application menu, choose Safari, Empty Cache (Option-Command-E) to remove the contents of the Safari cache. To reset Safari to its default configuration, choose Safari, Reset Safari. This removes *everything*—your tracks will be wiped clean. No one will ever know you spend your entire workday browsing the PowerPuff Girls website.

Private Browsing

A new feature of Tiger's Safari browser is a Private Browsing mode activated by choosing Safari, Private Browsing from the menu. In Private Browsing mode, sites are not added to the history, form data isn't cached for auto-completion, and files are automatically removed from the downloads list. If you have a family computer and decide to shop online for holiday or birthday gifts, using this mode will ensure that your family members aren't given any inadvertent clues as to what they might be receiving.

Private Browsing stays in effect until you choose it again from the Safari menu, or you quit the browser. Since its state is not maintained between different executions of Safari, you must remember to reactivate it if necessary.

Parental Controls

If you would like to limit the sites that your youngster (that is, your spouse) has access to through Safari, this is easily accomplished by opening the Accounts System Preference Pane, selecting the user to restrict, and then clicking the Parental Controls button.

A list of all the controllable applications will be displayed, as shown in Figure 3.7. Be sure the check box in front of Safari is selected. For more information on the Accounts preference pane (including managing user accounts) see Chapter 8, "Customizing User and System Settings."

FIGURE 3.7 Use parental controls to restrict what children (of any age) can view.

When parental controls are active, the user will only be allowed to access existing bookmarks within Safari. Obviously, it is up to you to add what you consider to be appropriate bookmarks to the account before you turn your kids loose.

To do this, you will need to log in to the user's account, start Safari, and then use either the bookmark manager to directly add new bookmarks (discussed shortly), or attempt to visit the websites that the account should be able to access. In either case, you will be prompted for an administrator username and password before the sites can be added or viewed. After the bookmarks have been made, the user will be able to visit those sites without restrictions.

Reading News (RSS/Atom) Feeds in Safari

At the advent of the Internet (before we had a chance of finding things with Google), there was much talk of eventually having intelligent agents scouring the Internet to retrieve news stories and other information automatically for our perusal. The problem with this vision is that web pages are not required to follow any standards for information organization. Trying to consistently determine what is news through pattern matching or other automated approaches is virtually impossible.

Enter the feed.

Over the past few years, the popularity of XML (extensible Markup Language) has resulted in the creation of information exchange standards. Sites that previously only presented information visually are now capable of making that information available in a way that other programs can interpret and work with. Two popular formats for syndicating news and other timely information are RSS (Really Simple Summary/Really Simple Syndication/Rich Site Summary/RDF Site Summary—take your pick) and Atom. With very little work, a site can publish a feed in one of these formats that can be published by other sites, or aggregated by desktop applications—in this case, Safari.

So, what does this all mean to you? In short, Safari's ability to work with RSS and Atom feeds means that you can subscribe to *hundreds* of potential news and information feeds that will delivery summaries of the latest information to you—rather than you having to go get it. Safari lets you combine feeds from any number of sources simultaneously, limit the news displayed based on keywords, or even choose how much of the summary you see and what range of dates is displayed.

Viewing a News Feed

To view a feed, first you must know where it is. In some cases this might be a URL which you enter into Safari using the syntax `feed://<feed location>` (for example, `feed://www.apple.com/main/rss/hotnews/hotnews.rss`). In other cases, it will be a link you click on from a feed portal such as `http://www.syndic8.com` or `http://www.feedster.com`. In still others, Safari will automatically recognize that a website offers a feed and will add an RSS graphic to the end of the Address field, as shown in Figure 3.8. Clicking the RSS graphic will open the feed associated with the site.

FIGURE 3.8 In some cases, Safari will automatically identify feeds by placing a graphic in the Address Field.

Whatever your means of arriving at a feed, the resulting view should be the same. Figure 3.9 demonstrates Safari viewing an RSS feed. Because the purpose of feeds is to present content, not promote a visual style, all feeds are displayed using the same style.

Each news or information article summary is listed along with a link that will open the article itself. The right column of the page provides simple search and sorting features. You can also use the Article Length slider to limit the size of the article summaries, if desired.

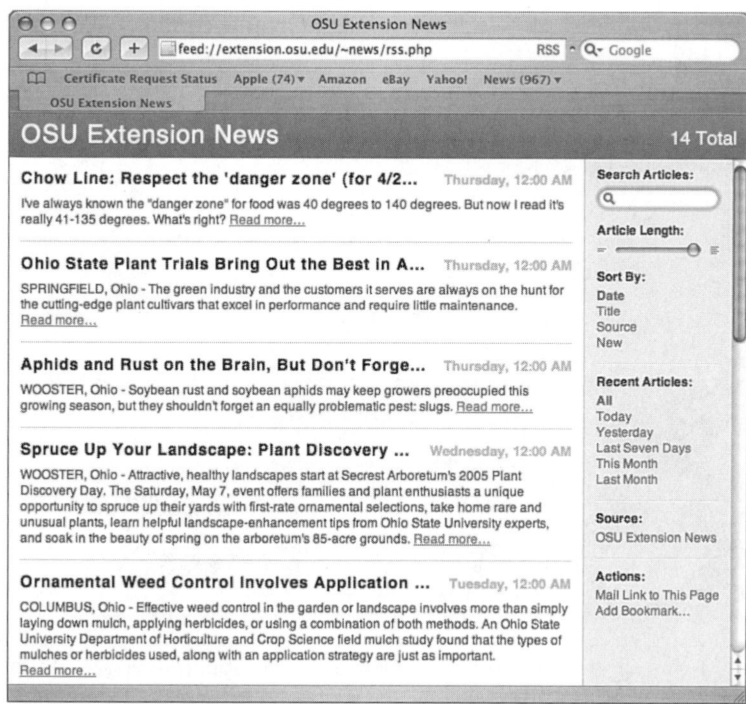

FIGURE 3.9 News feeds are displayed in the same style, regardless of where they are from.

Feeds can been bookmarked like any other URL. Use the + (Add Bookmark) button in the toolbar, the Add Bookmark link in the lower right corner of the feed view, or drag it to the bookmark bar. Feeds that are added to the bookmark bar will automatically add a number in parenthesis after their entry—this represents the number of new stories on the site since the feed was last viewed.

TIP

RSS feeds can be viewed in the new RSS Visualizer Tiger screensaver. This screensaver will render feed headlines in a swirling 3D view. Any bookmarked RSS feeds can be used as the source material.

Use the Desktop and Screen Saver system preference pane to activate the RSS Visualizer.

Aggregating Multiple Feeds

The true power of feeds becomes apparent when you start to view multiple feeds together. Instead of needing to visit ten different sites for your Apple news, all you need is to simultaneously all the feeds for the sites, and all the news you want is presented on the same page together—sortable and searchable as if it were coming from a single location.

To open multiple RSS/Atom feeds, you must build them into collections within the bookmark management interface. Apple includes several prebuilt feed collections already in your browser bookmark bar. The News and Apple selections contain multiple RSS feeds ready for your use.

For example, to aggregate all the news feeds into a single page click and hold on the News element in the bookmark bar. When the pop-up menu appears, choose View All RSS Articles, as shown in Figure 3.10.

FIGURE 3.10 Use a collection and the View All RSS Articles option to aggregate multiple feeds.

Obviously, the power of having the latest news whenever you want without needing to open multiple websites is great, but you can take it even further. Using the search and sorting functions on the right side of the viewing area, you can customize the news display. What is truly unique, however, is that after you've customized the display for *exactly* what you're interested in, you can then *bookmark* your feed view. This bookmark will open the feeds with the search criteria you specified—allowing you to create your own instant news pages tailored to your personal interests.

TIP

Command-Clicking a bookmark bar collection will open all the RSS feeds *and* any URLs within that collection.

Changing Feed Settings

The RSS pane of the Safari preferences provides additional controls over how feeds are handled in Tiger. The settings are shown in Figure 3.11.

If you prefer to let a third-party utility such as NetNewsWire (`http://ranchero.com/netnewswire/`) handle your feeds, use the default RSS Reader setting to choose the default application for opening `feed://` URLs.

The other available settings control how articles and updates are handled in Safari. Use the Automatically Update Articles check boxes to choose whether Safari will check for new articles and display the unread count in the Bookmarks bar and/or menu. You can also choose the frequency at which updates are retrieved, a color to highlight new articles, and when existing articles should be removed.

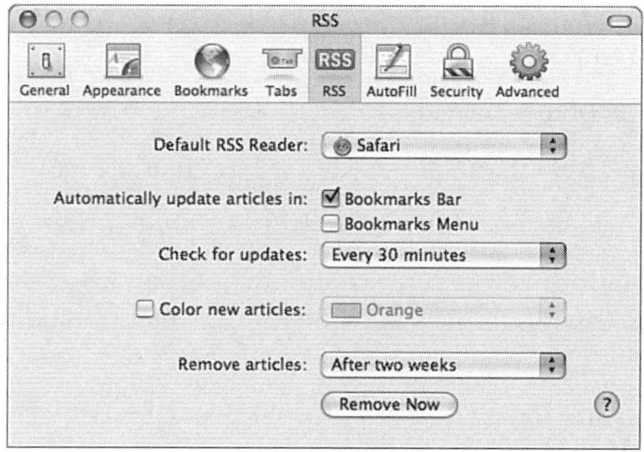

FIGURE 3.11 The Safari Feed settings are used to configure the default RSS reader for your system amongst other things.

Bookmark Management

Earlier, you learned to drag a web or feed address from the address field into the Bookmarks bar to quickly store it for later reference. As useful as that feature is, there's limited space for all the pages you want to keep. However, there is plenty of room in the Bookmarks window, shown in Figure 3.12, which you can open by clicking the Show All Bookmarks button at the far left of the Bookmarks bar.

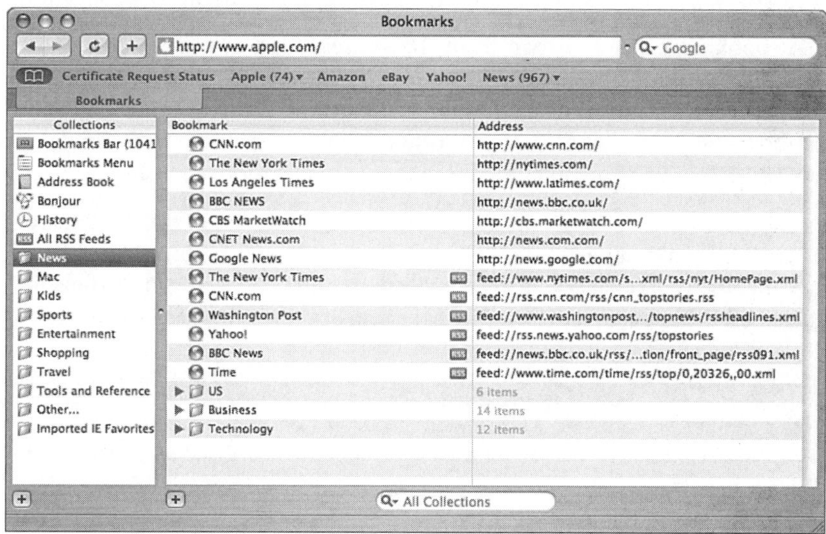

FIGURE 3.12 A special window to view and organize lists of your favorite websites. (When opened, it displays the last collection you visited.)

Understanding Collections

The Bookmarks Library offers a simple view of your URLs. Along the left side of the window is a list of collections—these are categories that you define (except for a few built-in collections) to help better organize bookmarks. There are five special categories, and the rest are entirely up to you:

- Bookmarks Bar—Bookmarks stored in the Bookmarks bar.
- Bookmarks Menu—Bookmarks stored in the Bookmarks menu.
- Address Book—URLs found within your Address Book entries.
- Bonjour—Websites located on your local network that are advertised via Bonjour. (See Chapter 23, "Creating a Web Server," for information about advertising websites via Bonjour.)
- History—A list of websites that you've visited over the past week. These are also accessible through the History menu.
- All RSS Feeds—All the RSS feeds that have been bookmarked—regardless of the collection they are directly stored in.

To view the contents of a collection, select it in the left-hand collection list. The content area to the right of the collections refreshes to display the bookmarks of sites stored in that collection.

Working with Bookmarks and Collections

Drag URLs in the Bookmark listing up or down to change their ordering (this makes a difference if you display the collections in the Bookmarks menu, which we'll discuss shortly) or drag them to one of the folders in the collection listing to add them to a collection.

To add a new bookmark, drag its icon from the address field to the Bookmark listing (just as you did to add to the Bookmarks bar). To delete a bookmark, drag it to the trash or select it and press Delete. If you want to edit a bookmark name or URL, Control-click on the entry and choose Edit Name or Edit Address. Double-clicking on the fields opens the URL; it does not allow you to edit the field values, as you might expect.

To add new collections, click the + button below the collection list in the Bookmark Manager. A new untitled folder icon appears. Type a name for the new collection, or double-click its label at any time to edit it. Like bookmarks, collections can be rearranged by dragging within the list or deleted by dragging to the trash or selecting and pressing the Delete button

NOTE

If you had another web browser, such as Internet Explorer, on your computer at the time that Safari was installed, Safari might have created a folder of the bookmarks saved for its use.

You can add folders to a collection (think of it as a collection within a collection) by using the + button under the Bookmark listing. This adds a new folder to the Bookmark list (not the collection list). Drag bookmark entries into these folders to further refine your collection.

Both Collection folders and subfolders can be dragged from the Bookmarks Library into the Bookmarks bar to add a drop-down collection menu to the Bookmarks bar.

TIP

When adding folders of bookmarks to the Bookmarks bar collection, you are also given an extra item called Open in Tabs if Tabbed Browsing is active. This will open all the bookmarks in the collection or folder within tabs simultaneously. If RSS feeds are also bookmarked in the folder, a second entry, View All RSS Feeds, will be present. Choosing this option will display an aggregation of all the feeds within that folder.

NOTE

Control-clicking on a bookmark in the library provides an option for opening that bookmark in a tab. Control-clicking on a subfolder within a collection shows an option for opening *all* bookmarks in that subfolder within tabs.

Adding Bookmarks with the Add Bookmark Button

Although the Bookmarks Library is great for arranging your URL shortcuts, opening it each time you want to add a site isn't necessarily efficient. Thankfully, Safari provides a quick solution. Clicking the Add Bookmark button in the address bar when you are viewing a page you want to add displays a dialog, shown in Figure 3.13, where you can name your bookmark and select a collection in which to store it.

FIGURE 3.13 Name and categorize the site.

Bookmark Display and .Mac Synchronization Options

Safari gives you several options on how you access bookmark collections. Obviously, you can always open the Bookmark Manager and see everything. Likewise, the Bookmarks Bar and Bookmark Menu collections are easy to find. However, it would be convenient if you could access *all* your collections through a single menu?

Furthermore, it would be great to access all your bookmarks on *all* of your machines, or even over the World Wide Web. If you've got .Mac (discussed later in this chapter), you can!

To control what bookmarks are displayed, open the Bookmarks pane of the application preferences pane, shown in Figure 3.14.

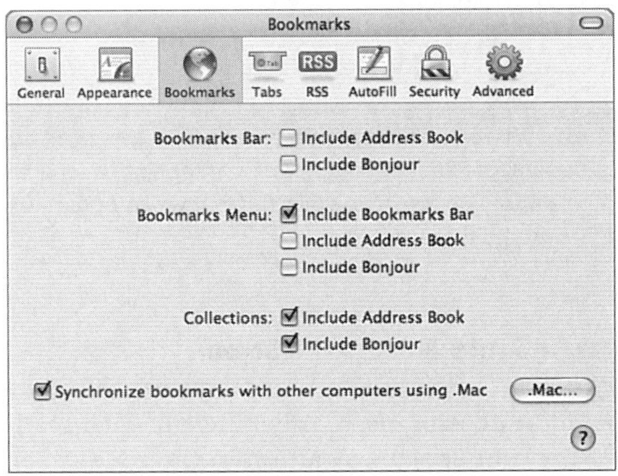

FIGURE 3.14 Fine-tune your bookmark settings.

Here you can choose whether the Bookmarks bar should display Address Book URLs and Bonjour entries (as drop-down collections) and, likewise, which of these entries should be shown in the Bookmark menu.

You can also click the Synchronize Bookmarks with Other Computers Using .Mac check box to create a central .Mac library of bookmarks that all your computers can use *and* an online Bookmark Manager that enables you to view your bookmarks from anywhere. Clicking the Configure button launches the .Mac System Preference panel, which controls the .Mac bookmark synchronization.

Additional Safari Preferences

Although we've already covered the Bookmarks, Tabs, AutoFill, RSS, and Security application preferences within the discussion of Safari, there are several more esoteric settings that you might want to change to suit your browsing needs. Let's take a look at the remaining panes: General, Appearance, and Advanced.

General

Options under the General pane, shown in Figure 3.15, include settings related to how a Safari window is opened and how pages and files are accessed.

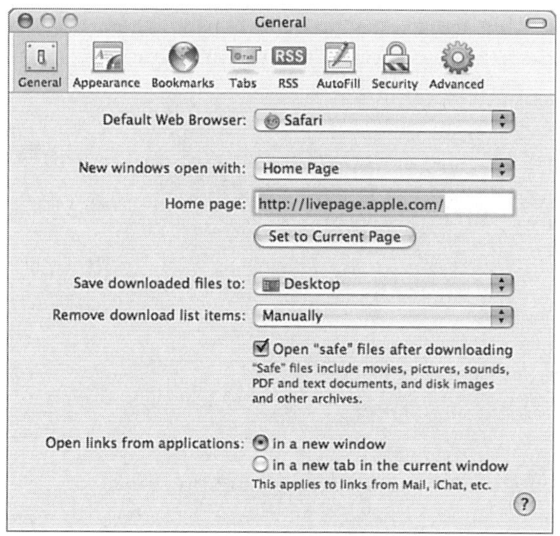

FIGURE 3.15 Choose your default web browser and default home page in the General preferences pane.

The first option is the choice of your default web browser (the web browser that automatically launches whenever you click a link received in email or through another program). The drop-down menu lists any application recognized as a web browser by your system.

You also have the option of choosing whether new windows that open come up with a specific home page that you've chosen, as an empty page, with any page that's currently open, or in Bookmarks mode.

The next three options pertain to downloading files. You have the option to save downloaded files to the desktop or to choose another location using the standard file browser. You can also decide how items will be removed from your download list: manually, when Safari quits, or upon successful download. If you like to keep a record of what you've downloaded, set it at Manual; if you prefer a clean slate, choose one of the other options.

The third download-related preference is a check box to Open "Safe" Files After Downloading. Safe files, by Safari's definition, are files unlikely to cause harm to your system, including media files, such as images and sounds, PDF or text files, and disk images. If this option is checked, any safe files are processed automatically when they are downloaded; otherwise, you need to double-click downloaded files to launch or to uncompress them.

The final setting relates back to how Safari reacts to links you open from other applications. Decide whether to open links in a new window or in the current window. When using tabs, opening a link in the current window creates a new tab; it doesn't replace the contents of the existing tab.

Appearance

The Appearance pane, shown in Figure 3.16, contains the web page display settings over which the viewer can have some input. You can choose any font on the system to be used on web pages where another font is not specified. You can also choose a *fixed-width* font, a font for which all letters take up the same width in a line of text, to be used when the specified font needs to align in a specific way.

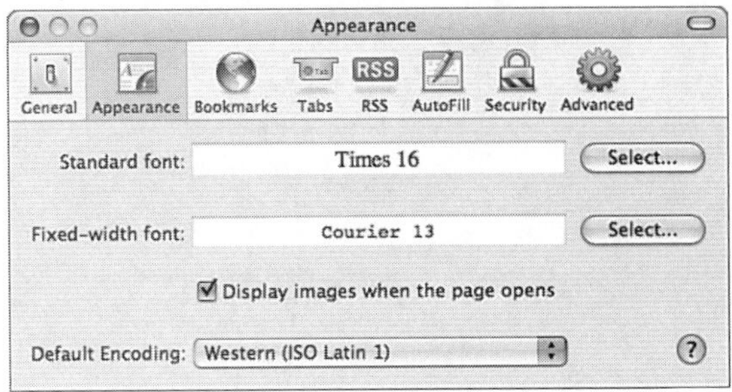

FIGURE 3.16 Choose fonts and character encoding preferences.

You can also decide whether to load images in a web page, in cases where bandwidth is an issue, you might want to turn this off.

Finally, you can set a default character encoding, which tells your browser how to interpret characters in a web page. For example, if you regularly read Japanese websites, you would only be able to see the correct characters if your character encoding and the web page used the same setting.

Advanced

The Advanced preferences pane allows you to set the smallest size font that will be displayed in Safari, or, for more customization—your own Style Sheet (Cascading Style Sheet or CSS).

Style sheets are specially formatted description of how text on a page should be displayed. With a carefully written style sheet, for example, you could have text in a web page that is coded as a heading appear in extremely large type or change its color, or you could reset the background of a page to another color to increase or reduce contrast. (Although this feature can be useful, writing style sheets is outside the scope of this book. You might want to visit `http://www.blooberry.com/` for reference to the style sheet syntax.)

In addition, if you need to set a Proxy server for your web connection, click the Change Settings button. This launches the System Preferences Network pane, which is where *all* proxy settings are configured.

Finally, to aid keyboard navigation of a page, you can enable the ability to use Tab to cycle through and highlight each element on a web page. By default. Option-Tab performs this action.

Accessing Email: Apple Mail

The Mac OS X Mail application started as a reasonably straightforward port of NeXT Computer's Mail.app for NeXTStep/OpenStep. It had sloppy HTML rendering, and was really, (really) slow. Since its first incarnation on Mac OS X, a few features have been added, but the application has largely remained the same.

In Tiger, Apple has given Mail an overhaul—both visually and internally. It is better looking (in my opinion), faster, and integrates Spotlight searching for near instantaneous access to messages regardless of where they reside.

Setting Up Mail

During the Tiger installation procedure the Setup Assistant will prompt for email account information. If this setup was sufficient for your email, and then you're in good shape and can skip ahead. For many people, however, the first task to using Mail will be creating up a new account— and that is where we'll start.

Adding Accounts

Mail creates basic email account settings by way of an easy-to-use Setup Assistant. The Setup Assistant will automatically run the first time Mail is started in accounts that do not have *any* email configured. It will also be invoked by adding a new email account manually. Let's assume that you already have a basic account set up and need to add a new account. If this isn't the case, don't worry—we're going to start the New Account assistant, which should get us to exactly where you are now.

To create a new Mail account and open the New Account assistant, choose File, Add Account from the menu bar. Mail will now walk you through the process of setting up an account, as demonstrated in Figure 3.17.

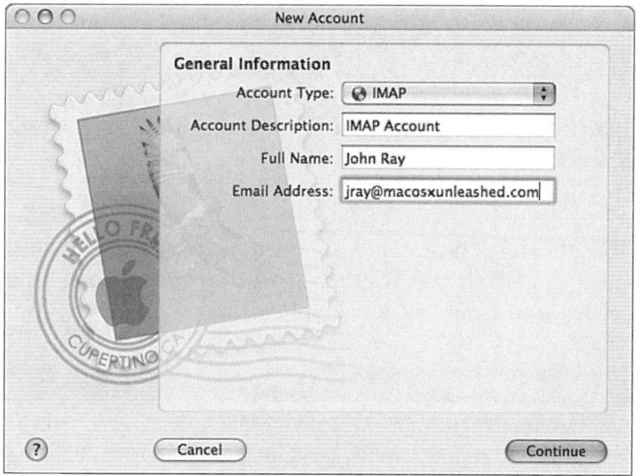

FIGURE 3.17 Provide the necessary setup information when prompted by the assistant.

There are, at most, eight pieces of information are required to create an email account (.Mac users will be required to enter just their name, password, and an Account description):

- Account Description— A name that you want to user to refer to your account ("Home email", for example).
- Full Name—That thing that people call you by.
- Email Address—Your email address (for example, `jray@mymailmachine.com`).
- Incoming Mail Server—The server that stores your email.
- Account Type—Almost all ISPs support the POP3 protocol for accessing email but IMAP offers more features. Apple's .Mac servers and MS Exchange servers use IMAP but are configured as their own account type. Read further for more information on both POP3 and IMAP and the differences between them.
- User Name—The username used to access an email account. This is the text that comes before the `@` in your email address (that is, `jray` is the username for `jray@mymailmachine.com`).
- Password—The password required to retrieve mail. Leaving this field blank prompts the user to enter the password when needed.
- Outgoing Mail Server (SMTP)—The server required to send messages and any username/password required to send mail.

If you are unsure of any of these fields, contact your ISP or network administrator. Follow through each step of the Setup Assistant, clicking Continue to move to the next screen. After each entry, Mail will attempt to verify the information you've added and will notify you if there were any problems with the server and account settings.

TIP

If you are using SSL for authentication with a remote server (for sending or receiving), you must first add the certificate to the X509 Anchors keychain (refer to Chapter 2 for more information) before Mail will "see" them.

Upon reaching the end of the setup, you will be prompted to create another account, or click Done to begin using Mail. If it is the first time you've run Mail, you'll also be given the option of importing mail from another application.

POP3 VERSUS IMAP

If your email provider supports both the POP3 and IMAP protocols, you're in luck! The POP3 protocol, although extremely popular, is not practical for people with multiple computers. I access the same email account from a number of different computers: one at work, one at home, and another while on the road. Keeping all these machines in sync is virtually impossible with POP3.

POP3 (Post Office Protocol v.3) works much as it sounds: Email is "popped" from a remote server. Incoming messages are stored on the remote server, which in turn waits for a connection from a POP3 client. The client connects only long enough to download all the messages and save them to the local hard drive. Unfortunately, after a message transfers from the server, it's gone. If you go to another computer to check your mail, it won't be there.

IMAP takes a different approach. Rather than relying on the client for message storage, IMAP servers keep everything on the server. Messages and mail folders remain on the server unless explicitly deleted by the client. When new messages arrive, the IMAP client application downloads either the message body or header from the server, but the server contents remain the same. If multiple computers are configured to access the same email account, the email appears identical between the machines—the same folders, messages, and message flags are maintained. In addition, the IMAP protocol supports shared folders between different user accounts and server-based content searches.

If your ISP does not support IMAP, you can sign up for a .Mac account. Apple's IMAP-based .Mac service provides everything you need, along with exclusive downloads and online services.

Importing Mailboxes

If this is the first time you've run Mail, you'll automatically be prompted to import mailboxes from another email client such as Entourage or Eudora. This provides a convenient way to migrate to Mail without having to launch your old mail application to read past messages. If you've already configured Mail and want to start the import assistant, just choose File, Import Mailboxes.

Mail prompts for the mail client that you will be importing from, as shown in Figure 3.18.

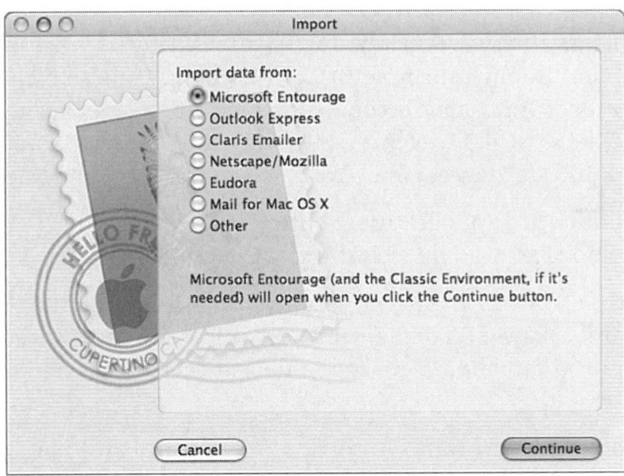

FIGURE 3.18 Choose the mail application that you want to import from.

Choose your legacy email application; then click the Continue button. If you have mail stored in the Unix `mbox` format, use the selection Other.

Next you are prompted for *what* you want to import—which mailboxes, contacts, and so on you want to bring into Mail. Mail can't necessarily import *everything* from everywhere. If you don't see your contacts listed, importing them isn't supported—it isn't an error in mail, just a shortcoming.

After choosing the items to import, click Continue. Mail will display a progress bar as it copies the information. When finished, you will be notified that the data is now available in Mail.

TIP

There are two problems with importing legacy mail with Mail.app. First, not all email clients are supported. Popular emailers such as Opera and Mulberry are nowhere to be found. If you find yourself not being able to migrate to Mail, Emailchemy—a universal email converter (`http://www.weirdkid.com/products/emailchemy/index.html`)—might be able to save the day.

The second problem with migrating to Mail is that your contacts (and filters) are not preserved (unless you're coming from an earlier version of Mail.app). Unfortunately, there is no clean way to handle this issue for every email client. If you're a Eudora user, you'll be interested in Andreas Amann's Eudora Mailbox Cleaner. EMC can completely migrate your Eudora contacts, filters, and messages to Mail and Address Book in a single pass—`http://homepage.mac.com/aamann/`.

Entourage users can drag and drop vCards (refer to Chapter 2, "Useful Tiger Widgets, Applications, and Utilities," for more information) from Entourage to Address Book to transfer contacts. Or use Paul Berkowitz's Sync Entourage-Address Book to perform the action in bulk—`http://scriptbuilders.net/category.php?search=_sync+entourage`.

You might also want to enable the Scripts menu, try the Import Addresses AppleScript. This does a decent job of importing from several popular email clients. See Chapter 4, "Managing and Configuring Hardware and Devices," for more information on AppleScript and the Scripts menu.

Modifying Accounts and Server Settings

After setting up accounts through the New Account assistant, you can configure additional options and manage all of your active accounts through the Accounts pane of the Application Preferences. Choose Mail, Preferences; then click the Accounts icon. Figure 3.19 shows the Accounts pane of the Preferences pane. Existing email accounts are listed on the left.

To add a new account to the list, click the + button—this is the same as choosing File, New Account. To remove an account, select it and click the - button.

To edit existing accounts, select them in the account list, and then use the three buttons—Account Information, Mailbox Behaviors, and Advanced—to alter and further configure the account information. Let's take a look at these three views, starting with the Account Information.

Account Information The Account Information options, displayed in Figure 3.19, contain all the settings that you initially collected and entered when adding an email account (refer to "Adding Accounts" earlier for more information). You can edit these if your server name changes or your account information is otherwise altered.

TIP

If you have multiple email return addresses and you want to be able to choose which address shows up in the From field on the final message, enter multiple addresses separated by commas in the Email Address field. This adds a pop-up menu to the message composition window where you can choose from the listed addresses.

FIGURE 3.19 Multiple email accounts can be added through the Application preferences Accounts pane.

Configuring and Managing SMTP Servers Near the bottom of the Account Information pane are options for setting your SMTP servers. Use the Outgoing Mail Server pop-up menu to add a new SMTP server, or just choose an existing server. The Server Settings button edits the currently selected SMTP server.

TIP

Apple's SMTP server management is one of the weaker areas of mail. Many people who have added and removed accounts will end up with a very large list of SMTP servers unless they manually remove servers associated with inactive accounts. To manager the servers, choose Edit Server List from the pop-up menu. This displays a list of *all* SMTP servers and shows which accounts are using which servers. Use the + and - buttons to add and remove servers from this list.

When adding or editing an SMTP server, you are prompted for the server name, port (if different from 25), and security information, as shown in Figure 3.20. If you are accessing an SSL-protected mail server (IMAPS, POPS), click the Use Secure Sockets Layer (SSL) check box. In addition, if your server uses authenticated SMTP, choose the authentication method and provide a username and password.

3

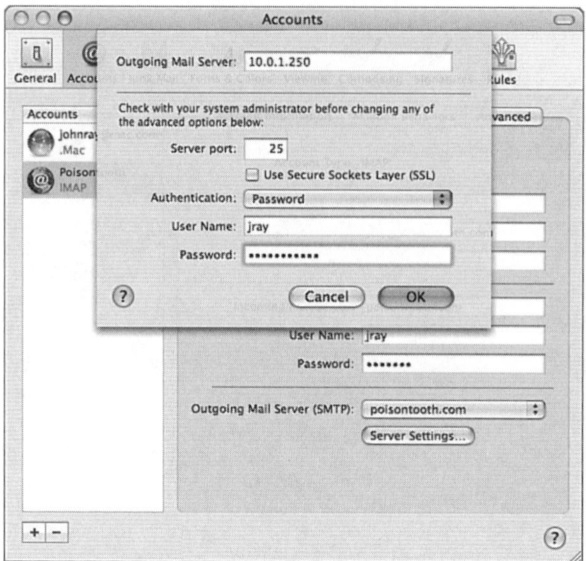

FIGURE 3.20 Enter the new email account information into this pane.

WHAT IS AUTHENTICATED SMTP?

The original SMTP protocol requires no authentication to send a message. Anyone could use any SMTP server to send any message (the origin of spam). Over time, servers developed advanced techniques to prohibit unauthorized use of the SMTP protocol, such as blocking by subnet or allowing users who have successfully checked mail to send mail from their IP address for a certain length of time.

This works, but it places some unreasonable restrictions on the user. Luckily, extensions have been made to the SMTP protocol that allow a username and password to be transmitted to the SMTP server when a connection is made. The server can then authenticate the user and allow unfettered access regardless of where or how the user is connecting.

Mailbox Behaviors The Mailboxes Behaviors view controls what Mail does with draft, sent, junk, and trash messages. When configuring an IMAP, Exchange, or .Mac account, as shown in Figure 3.21, you can choose whether these special types of mailboxes are stored on the server, and when mail should be deleted from these server-based mailboxes.

POP accounts are not given the option of storing special messages on the server. Instead, POP users can only choose when messages in any of the special mailboxes are erased or moved.

Advanced The final Advanced account settings fine-tune how Mail interacts with your email server. Depending on the account type that you've chosen, the available options will change. Figure 3.22 displays the Advanced tab for IMAP (or Mac.com) accounts.

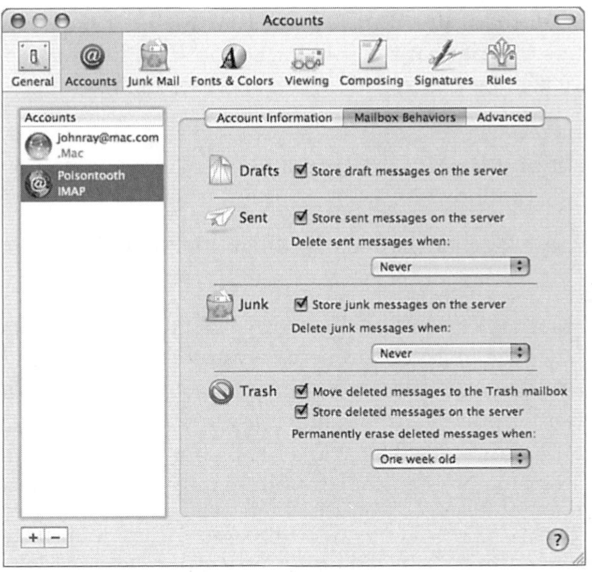

FIGURE 3.21 Special Mailboxes store drafts, junk, and other types of messages.

FIGURE 3.22 Each type of email account has different available options.

Each of the different mail account types has different available options. Choices available on the Advanced tab when using IMAP (or .Mac) include

- Enable This Account—Includes the account in the available account listing. If not enabled, it is ignored.

- Include When Automatically Checking for New Mail—If selected, the account will be polled for new messages at the interval set on the Preferences Account pane. If not, the account will be polled only when the user manually checks his mail.
- Compact Mailboxes Automatically—Cleans up the local mailbox files when exiting Mail. The benefit of using this is slight, and it can slow down the system when dealing with large mailbox files.
- Account Directory—The local directory where the Mail application stores your messages.
- Keep Copies of Messages for Offline Viewing—After a message is received on the server, the IMAP client has the option of immediately caching the text of the message on the local machine (All Messages and Their Attachments), caching read messages (Only Messages I've Read), or never caching messages on the local drive (Don't Keep Copies of Any Messages) If you want to be able to read your mail while offline, you probably want the default setting of synchronizing all messages and their attachments.
- Automatically Synchronize Changed Mailboxes—When Mail notices a change in a mailbox and this option is selected, it automatically downloads the changes instead of waiting for the mailbox to be opened or manually synchronized.
- IMAP Path Prefix—The IMAP prefix required to access your mailbox. This field is normally left blank unless a value is specified by your mail server administrator.
- Port—The default IMAP port is 143. If your server uses a different access port, enter it here.
- Use SSL—Enable SSL encryption (IMAPS) of the email traffic. This setting must be supported by the server to be used.
- Authentication—Choose how you will authenticate with the remote server. Most ISPs use a plain password; special server configurations might require Kerberos or MD5.

NOTE

The default account directories are stored in `~/Library/Mail`. POP accounts store incoming messages in a flat Unix `mbox` format, so command-line applications such as Mail can read downloaded messages. IMAP accounts, however, do not use this format and instead store each message as a separate file.

If you are using a POP account, you can control how messages are retrieved and when they are deleted from your account, among other things:

- Enable This Account—Include the account in the available account listing. If not enabled, it is ignored.
- Include This Account When Checking for New Mail—If selected, the account will be polled for new messages at the interval set on the Mail Preferences Account pane. If not, the account will be polled only when the user manually checks his mail.

- Remove Copy from Server After Retrieving a Message—Choose the length of time (if any) messages should remain on the server after downloading. By leaving the messages on the server, you can create an IMAP-like environment where multiple computers can download the same messages. This is a poor-man's IMAP and does not support multiple server-based folders, shared folders, and so on. Click Remove Now to remove downloaded messages manually.
- Prompt Me to Skip Messages over <#> KB—Automatically skips messages over a set number of kilobytes. This setting is useful for keeping attachments from being downloaded.
- Account Directory—The local directory where the Mail application stores your messages.
- Port—The default POP port is 110. If your server uses a different access port, enter it here.
- Use SSL—Enable SSL encryption (POPS) of the email traffic. This must be supported by the server to be used.
- Authentication—Choose how you will authenticate with the remote server. Most ISPs use a plain password; special server configurations might require Kerberos or MD5.

NOTE

Whenever possible, use SSL encryption for POP and IMAP traffic. By default, these protocols transmit passwords in cleartext, making them much easier to intercept.

Reading and Managing Email

Tiger changes the Mail experience dramatically from earlier versions. Gone are the sometimes-awkward window drawer and dated interface; In is a streamlined appearance and useful new features such as Smart Folders. Figure 3.23 shows the new Mail application, ready for action.

If you've used an email program such as Eudora or Outlook Express, you'll be completely comfortable with Mail's interface—mailboxes on the left and accounts on the left, messages and message content on the right.

The toolbar at the top of the window holds commonly used functions for creating, responding to, and searching for messages.

TIP

The fonts and colors used for messages and message listings in the Mail interface can be changed within the Fonts & Colors application preferences.

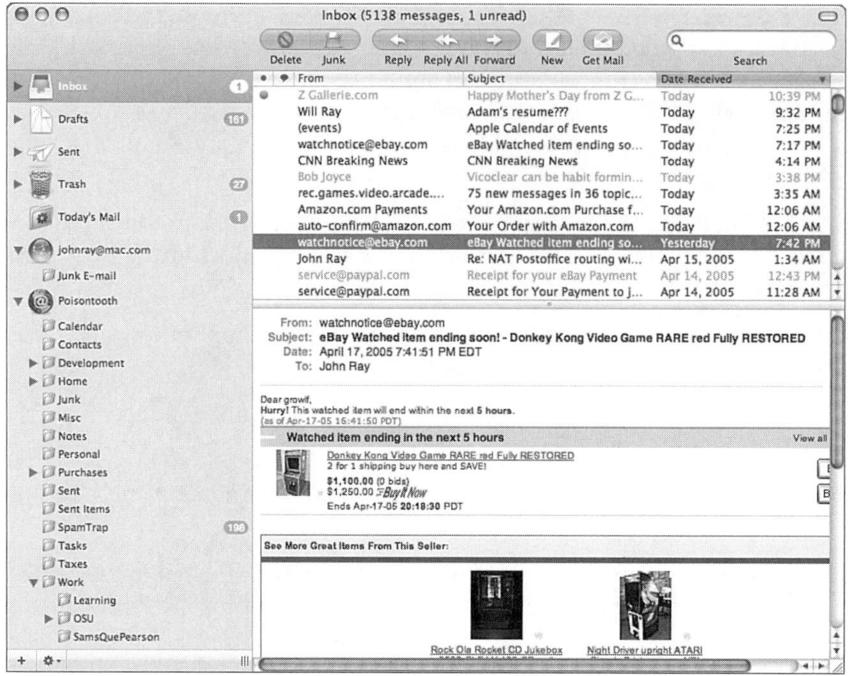

FIGURE 3.23 Tiger's new Mail has a streamlined interface and under-the-hood improvements.

Checking Mail

When you set up an account in Mail, it is automatically configured to go online and check for new messages every five minutes. To manually check your account for messages click the Get Mail toolbar icon. You can also use the menus—choose Mailbox, Get *All* New Mail to get all new message from all accounts. Or, to retrieve email from a specific account, use the Mailbox, Get New Mail, *<accountname>* menu to choose an account you want to check.

To temporarily disable an account from getting *any* email, you can take it *offline* by selecting choosing Mailbox, Mailbox Status, Take *<accountname>* offline from the menu bar. Accounts that are offline are displayed with a circular ~ icon following their name in the mailbox list. Re-enable online access by again using the Mailbox Status menu item or by clicking the ~ following their name in the mailbox listing.

TIP

You can set up how frequently Mail checks for new messages within the General pane of the application preferences.

When new messages are received, Mail automatically plays Apple's new mail sound. You can customize this sound and enable or disable sounds for other email events (such as deleting messages) also within the General application preferences.

If Mail finds new messages in your online account, they are downloaded to the main Inbox in the mailbox list. Click the Inbox to display the messages you've received.

NOTE

If you have multiple accounts, you'll notice that the Inbox can be expanded by clicking a disclosure arrow to the left of its name. Expanding the main Inbox will show all the inboxes for each of your accounts. To display a summary of all the messages in either the main inbox or a specific account inbox, click to highlight it. The message list will refresh with the contents of the selected mailbox.

This same concept applies to other special Mailboxes such as Trash, Drafts, and so on. You'll learn more about Mailbox management later in the chapter.

The Message list columns display the default columns' read/unread status, iChat status, sender, subject, and day/time sent. Additional columns can be accessed under the View, Columns submenu. As with most list views in Tiger, the columns can be sorted by clicking their headings and rearranged by clicking and dragging.

New messages appear with a small dot in front of their name (the read/unread status field). If this isn't obvious enough for you, use the Viewing application preferences to force unread messages to be displayed in bold within the listing.

TIP

You might want to enable the Message Number column under the View, Columns menu.

Sorting by the message number is the best way to keep track of new messages as they come in. If a client includes incorrect time or time zone information when sending a message, it will probably be sorted incorrectly when you use Date and Time as the sort field.

Unfortunately, Mail numbers different accounts using different numbers, so this works best on a single account, or when viewing one account at a time.

To gain a larger viewing area for the message list, you can either drag the divider bar at the bottom of the message list, or simply double-click it. This instantly drops the bar to the bottom of the Mail window filling the window with *just* the message list. Double-clicking the bar again returns it to the original position.

Reading Messages

To read a message, highlight it in the list; the lower-right of the window refreshes with the message content. Mail is capable of displaying plain-text and styled/HTML messages using the Safari rendering engine.

By default, Tiger hides some information from you—specifically, the headers that are attached to the message. Message headers can reveal the network addresses that handled a piece of email before it reached you along with other interesting information such as the mail client that transmitted the message.

If you'd like to review the full contents of a message, use View, Message to choose to view the message with the full headers, or the raw source of the message—meaning *exactly* what was sent to you, before it was processed and formatted by Mail.

TIP

For full control over the default headers shown, use the Show Header Detail option within the Viewing application preferences. You can also customize the Mail toolbar (View, Customize Toolbar) to include a Show Headers button that shows/hides mail headers.

After reading a message, you might decide that you'd rather mark the message as unread (to remind you to read it again, or perhaps so that another email program detects it as unread)—or maybe you'd just like to flag the message so it catches your attention in the future. You can do both of these by choosing the appropriate option from the Message, Mark submenu. You can also enable toggles for these options within the toolbar (View, Customize Toolbar).

If you've decided to delete the active message, use the Delete toolbar icon, press the Delete key, or choose Edit, Delete from the menu. Multiple messages can be selected at once by holding down Shift (for a range) or Command for noncontiguous blocks of messages.

Deleted messages are not immediately removed from the system; they are transferred to a Trash mailbox. What happens from there (deleting sure after a week, for example) can be configured from the Mailbox Behaviors pane of the Mail Accounts Preferences. Alternatively, one can use the Mailbox, Erase Deleted Messages menu options to erase deleted mail from all accounts or just a specific account. To view the contents of your Trash mailbox, just select it as you would the Inbox—the message list will refresh to show the contents.

Using Threaded Message Browsing

To make message reading easier, Mail provides threaded browsing of your message lists. That's nice; what is a thread? A *thread* is a conversation you've had with someone over the span of several messages. Usually these are treated like separate emails (because they are) and are scattered throughout your other spam. With Mail, you can choose to browse your email in threaded mode, making it easy to follow the course of a conversation. To enable threads, choose View, Organize by Thread. Figure 3.24 demonstrates threaded mail browsing.

Threads are identified by a blue highlight and the presence of an arrow in front of the initial message subject that started the thread and a number in the status field showing how many unread messages are in the thread, if any. Highlighting the first message subject line displays information about the thread in the message content pane, such as who started the thread, when, how many messages it contains, which contain attachments, and how many of them are unread. Clicking a line within the content pane list jumps immediately to the chosen message.

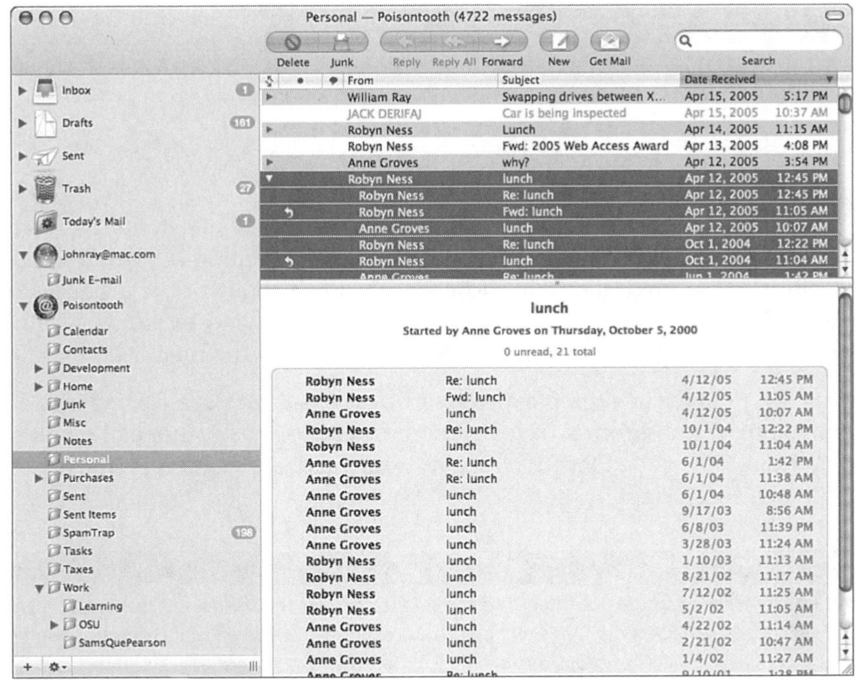

FIGURE 3.24 Organize your messages into threads.

> **NOTE**
>
> When Mail is in threaded mode, the threads are represented by a *virtual message* with the subject of the initial message. It isn't until you've opened the thread that can you choose and view the contents of the original message.

> **NOTE**
>
> Mail bases threads on a message's subject. If you have multiple messages with the same subject that *aren't* a thread, they will still be displayed as a thread.

To browse the thread within the message list, click the arrow at the front of the thread subject line. The message thread expands to show all the available emails within the thread and immediately jumps you to the first unread message. To collapse the thread, click in the first column (down and up opposing arrows) of any message within the thread or on the arrow in front of the initial thread subject line. The thread immediately collapses back to a single line.

The View menu's Expand/Collapse All Threads options can be used to quickly open and close all threads in your mailbox.

TIP

To change the color used to highlight related messages (whether viewing as threads or not) use the Highlight Related Messages Using Color option in the Viewing application preferences.

Opening, Saving, and Viewing Attachments

If the message contains an attachment and Tiger recognizes the attachment format (such as an image or PDF), it renders the attachment directly in the message. If the attachments cannot be directly displayed, they will show as icons in the body of the message. You can toggle between viewing attachments as icons and the in-line view by Control-clicking the attachment and choosing View as Icon or View in Place from the menu.

To open you can double-click the file directly in your email message or drag it to a Finder window, including the desktop, to save it. Alternatively, use the contextual menu to save the file to a default Download location (set in the General application preferences) or open the file in a specific application.

TIP

If you ever receive a message with an unreadable attachment that is labeled `winmail.dat`, `application/ms-tnef`, or `mime-attachment`, chances are you've been mailed by someone using a poorly configured Microsoft Outlook client. To open the attachment, use the Josh Jacob's excellent TNEF's Enough, available from `http://www.joshjacob.com/macdev/tnef/`.

If you have a message with *many* attachments, working with the files directly in the message body isn't very efficient—they can be scattered all over through a message. An alternative interface to the attachments is provided as an expandable list directly following the message headers. When expanded, you can drag the attachment icons to your desktop, or, alternatively, click the Save button to reveal a submenu where you can save one or all the attachments to a given location.

Tiger will default to using the folder `~/Library/Mail Downloads` for storing saved downloads. A common problem with email applications is that they store attachments in a download folder which eventually grows and grows, even after the original messages are deleted. Not so with Mail. Apple's Mail application will remove attachments automatically from the default download folder when the original attachment has not changed. It is even smart enough to *not* remove the attachment if you've opened and modified it in some way. If you prefer, you can use the General application preferences to remove attachments from the download folder each time Mail quits, or never—meaning that you'll have to clean up after yourself.

Using Image Attachments in iPhoto and Slideshows Beginning with Tiger, the Save button menu also has an Add to iPhoto option. This will take the images stored as attachments and import them directly into iPhoto. You can also click the Slideshow button located beside the Save button to instantly launch a slideshow of the image attachments in the message. Moving your mouse during the slideshow will display a control bar for moving back, pausing, moving forward, displaying a thumbnail sheet, expanding the images to fill the screen, or closing the slideshow, as shown in Figure 3.25.

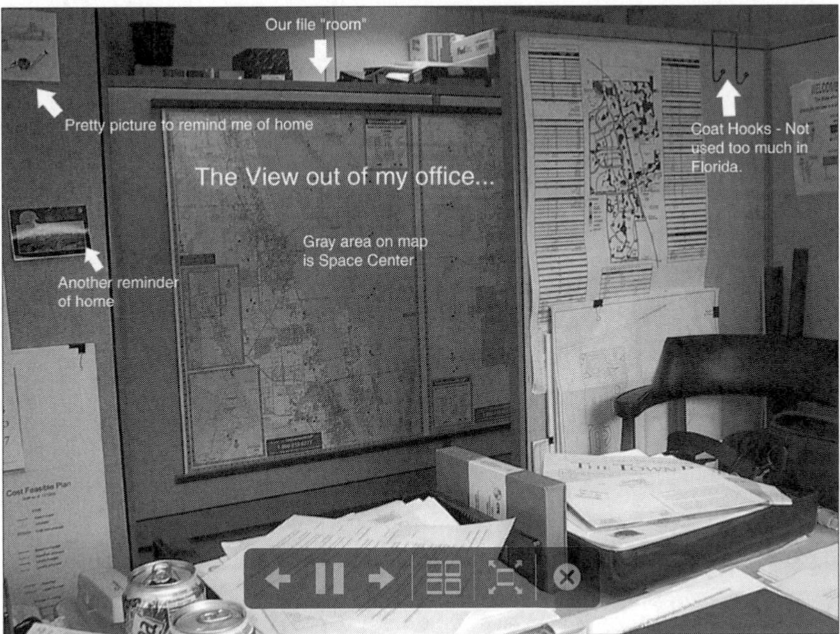

FIGURE 3.25 Control the slideshow by clicking the toolbar icons.

Searching for Messages

To search for a piece of mail, use the Search field built into the toolbar—this will conduct a Spotlight search across your mailboxes. Simply start typing and search results will begin to appear. If you want to limit your search to a specific mailbox or header field, click the appropriate heading directly under the toolbar. Figure 3.26 displays a search on my Personal mailbox using the Entire Message (any content from any message) as the target.

To reset the search results, click the X button at the end of the search field.

You might notice that a Save button appears to the right of the criteria for constraining the search. This button saves the search results to a Smart Mailbox similar to a Smart Folder in the Finder. We'll look at this in more detail in the section "Managing Mailboxes."

Reading Encrypted Messages

If you receive a message that displays a header, Security, with a lock icon and the word Encrypted, you're reading a message that has been encrypted using S/MIME (see `http://www.imc.org/ietf-smime/index.html` for details) and your public key (which can be automatically attached to messages you send).

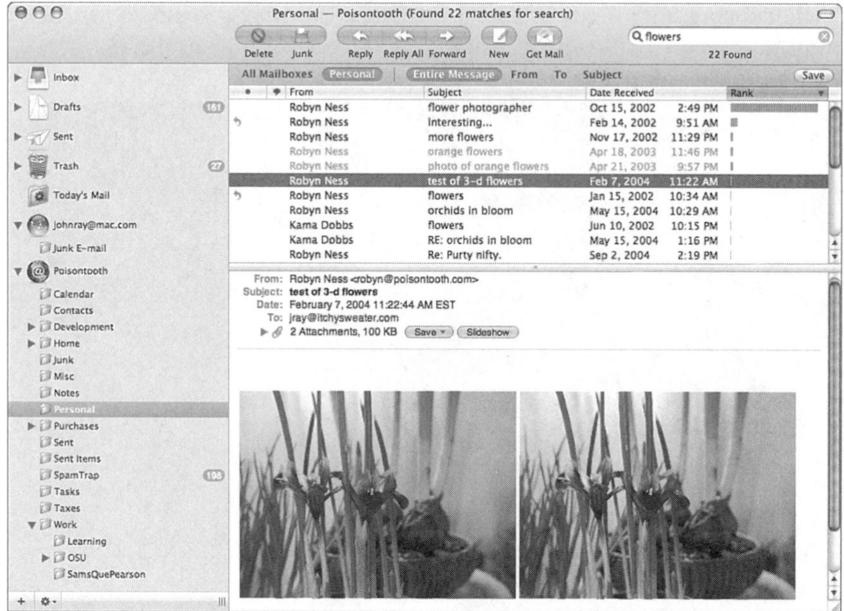

FIGURE 3.26 Use Spotlight searches on your mailboxes.

If the message is unreadable, you do not have the proper certificate installed on your system; see the message composition section for more information.

When you receive an encrypted message, it will not (for security reasons) be indexed by the Spotlight system. If you prefer to have these messages indexed, open the General application preferences and choose Index Decrypted Messages for Searching.

Saving Addresses from Messages

As you receive and read messages, you'll probably want to store some of the senders directly to your address book. Mail treats every email address it sees as an object. When viewing a message, you can click on the addresses in the header to select them. When selected, a drop-down menu can be accessed at the right side of the contact, as shown in Figure 3.27.

Depending on the context in which you display the menu, you can add the address immediately to your Address Book, create a new message to the person, perform a Spotlight search on the address, create a Smart Mailbox that will hold all the mail from that sender, or start an iChat. When an address is added to your Address Book, the email portion of the address disappears from Mail, and only the contact's full name is shown.

If an address has been used to send email but isn't in your Address Book, you might see the option to Remove from Previous Recipients List when you activate the address object's menu. Using this option removes the email address from Mail's short-term memory and keeps it from being auto-completed as you type in addresses.

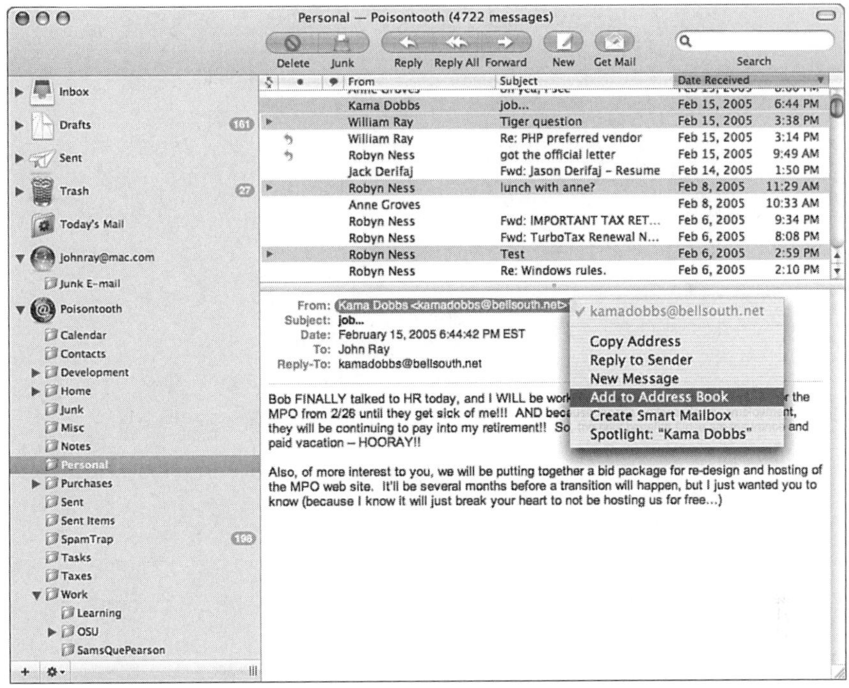

FIGURE 3.27 Addresses are recognized and can be acted on as objects.

> **NOTE**
>
> If you don't like this new form of addressing, you can shut it off by deselecting Use Smart Addresses from the Viewing application preferences.

Synchronizing Accounts for Offline Reading

When an Internet connection isn't available, you might still find yourself wanting to read your mail. This isn't a problem if an account is using POP3 (all messages are stored on your local machine), but IMAP and .Mac store messages on the server, making them inaccessible without a connection—or without synchronizing a copy of the messages with your local computer.

To synchronize IMAP/.Mac messages for offline reading, highlight a mailbox in the account you want to sync and then use the Mailbox Action button to choose Synchronize. You can also use the Mailbox, Synchronize menu to choose a specific account or Mailbox, Synchronize All Accounts to synchronize all of your active email accounts.

If mailbox synchronization is important to you, it can be set to happen automatically when mailboxes are changed (new mail comes in, is deleted, etc.). To do this, select the Automatically Synchronize Changed Mailboxes option in the Advanced area of the Accounts application preferences, as shown in Figure 3.28.

FIGURE 3.28 Use the Advanced Account preferences to control how accounts/messages are synchronized.

You can also choose to specifically keep copies of only certain messages based on the setting of the Keep Copies of Messages for Offline Viewing pop-up menu.

Dealing with Spam

Mail includes a built-in feature to help you manage the ever-increasing sea of spam that threatens to overtake your mailbox. When Mail thinks it's found a piece of spam, it highlights the item in brown in the message listing and displays a spam warning when you view the message, as shown (quite appropriately) in Figure 3.29.

Click the Not Junk button in the warning to tell Mail that it incorrectly labeled the message as spam. You can also use the Junk/Not Junk toolbar buttons to flag (or unflag) the currently selected messages(s) in the message listing as spam. The more you train Mail, the better it gets at identifying good and bad email.

The Junk Mail application preferences, shown in Figure 3.30, are used to fine-tune how Junk Mail is handled.

To help keep Mail from getting false positives, it is configured, by default to *not* mark something as spam if the sender is in your address book, is a recent recipient of an email you sent, or has addressed you using your full name. If you'd prefer not to perform these checks, they can be disabled in the Junk Mail application preferences.

When Mail has gotten to the point where it is consistently identifying spam, you can use the Junk Mail preferences to automatically move messages to a special Junk mailbox rather than leave them in your inbox, or process them using actions that you define (click Advanced in the preference pane).

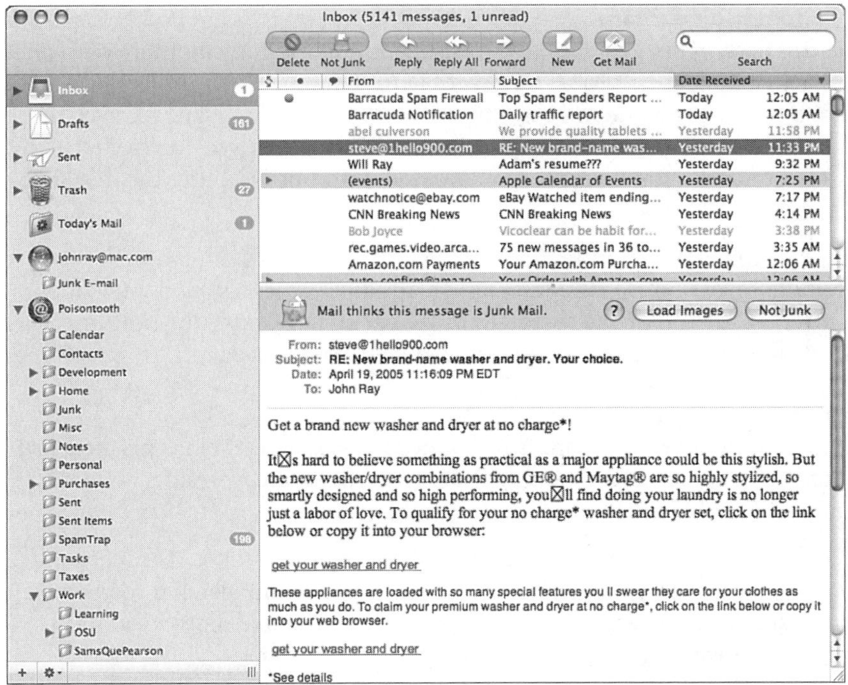

FIGURE 3.29 Mail provides built-in spam sensing heuristics.

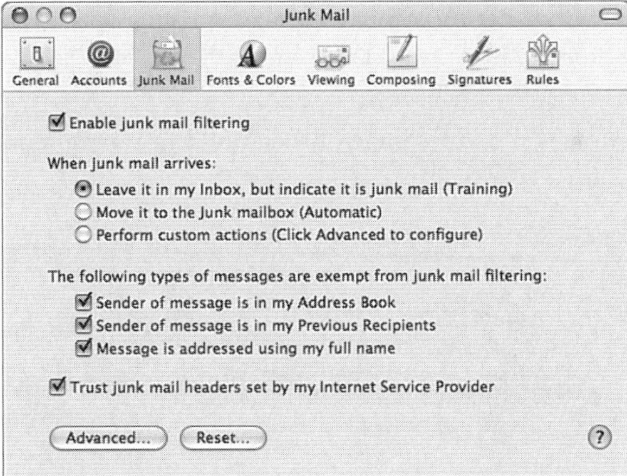

FIGURE 3.30 Help Mail determine what is/isn't spam and what it should do with it.

If you want to completely reset the junk mail system back to its defaults, click the Reset button. Mail will forget everything it has learned about what is/isn't spam on your system.

Blocking Phone-Home Images

Spammers are nasty. They use special tricks such as identifying whether your email account is active by sending HTML messages with dynamic image links to your address. If your email reader loads the images, the spammer immediately knows that the email account is active and capable of viewing HTML mail—even if you never click a link in the message! Mail understands this and provides the option of disabling the display of inline images.

Under the Viewing application preferences, you can enable or disable the option to Display remote images in HTML Messages. When images are disabled, Mail adds a Load Images button at the top of the message content area. Only after the button is clicked are images loaded—preventing the spammers from getting any feedback from your computer.

Bouncing Spam Messages

Another method of defeating spam is to bounce mail back to them. This creates the appearance that your account doesn't exist and, if you're lucky, results in having your name removed from their lists.

To bounce a message, highlight the email in your message list and then choose Message, Bounce (Shift-Command-B). Alternatively, you can add a Bounce icon to your Mail toolbar for fast access. Unfortunately, most spammers use fake reply-to addresses, which will bounce your own bounce back to you.

Applying Rules to Messages

Rules (filters) can perform actions on incoming messages, such as highlighting them in the message listing, moving them to other folders, or playing special sounds. Much like the built-in Spam features highlight and perform actions on spam messages, you can write your own rules to do the same.

Rules are managed through the Rules pane of the application preferences, shown in Figure 3.31.

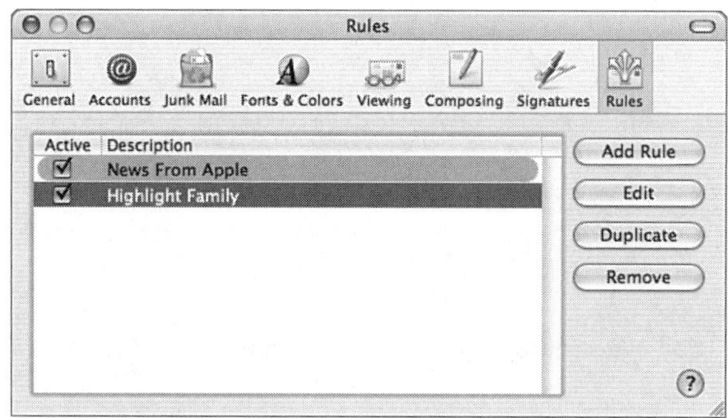

FIGURE 3.31 Rules can automate the process of going through your messages.

Each rule in the list is evaluated once per incoming message (unless the Active box is unchecked). In fact, multiple rules can act on a single message. To change the order in which the rules are applied, drag rule entries in the list to the order you want.

NOTE

Apple includes a default rule for dealing with Apple mailings. If you aren't subscribed to any Apple lists (or if you are and don't want them to be highlighted), you can delete or uncheck this rule.

There are four options for manipulating the rule list: Add Rule, Edit, Duplicate, and Remove. The function of each option is self-explanatory.

Creating a New Rule

Rule creation is simple. Each rule consists of *conditions* that look at portions of the incoming message and determine what *actions* to perform.

To create a new rule, click the Add Rule button to display the rule creation dialog, as seen in Figure 4.32. First enter a description—this is used to identify the rule in the listing. Next, decide whether the rule you're creating will require *all* of a series of conditions to be met (such as 'from `"blah@emailaddress.com"` *and* containing the subject "Lottery"') or *any* of the conditions to be matched (an *or* condition such as 'from `"blah@emailaddress.com"` or `"blah2@emailaddress.com"`'). Use the pop-up menu following If to choose "any" or "all" condition matching.

Next, compose the conditions. The Rule starts with a single condition; additional conditions can be added by clicking the + button at the end of the condition line. Conditions can be deleted with the - button. This is very similar to setting up Spotlight searches in the Finder.

In Figure 3.32, I'm matching any message where the From address contains either `jray@poisontooth.com` or `johnray@mac.com`.

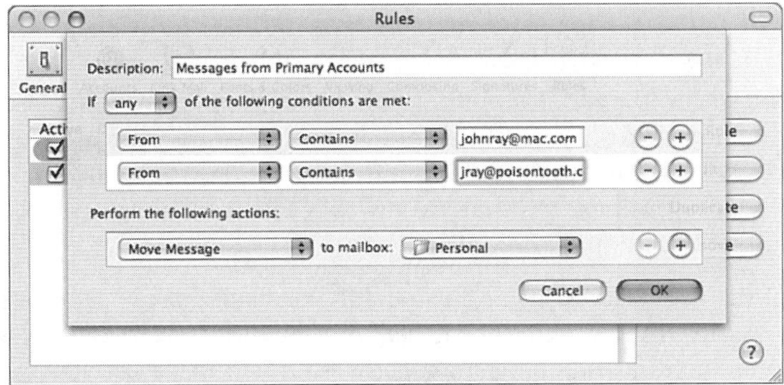

FIGURE 3.32 Unlike other email programs, Mail's rules are simple to create.

Finally, choose the actions; again using the + and - buttons to add and delete as many actions as you want. In this example, I've chosen to move any messages that match my conditions to the mailbox named Personal—you'll learn how to create new mailboxes in the next section, "Managing Email with Mailboxes."

The conditions and actions are extremely flexible and allow you to match against your Address Book entries and the message content itself. Likewise, the actions give you complete control over the message:

- Move Message—Move the message to another mailbox.
- Copy Message—Copy the message to another mailbox, leaving a copy in the default mailbox.
- Set the Color—Set the highlight color for the message.
- Play Sound—Play a system (or custom) beep sound.
- Bounce Icon in Dock—Bounce the Mail icon in the Dock.
- Forward/Redirect/Reply To—Send the message to another email address. Click the Message button to enter text that will be included with the message being sent.
- Delete the Message—Delete the message. Useful for automatically getting rid of common spam messages.
- Mark as Read—Mark the message as read.
- Mark as Flagged—Flag the message.
- Run AppleScript—Run an AppleScript for advanced processing.
- Stop Evaluating Rules—Stop processing any further rules in the filter.

Click OK to set and activate the rule; new messages will automatically be evaluated and acted on as appropriate. To manually apply new rules to existing messages, select Message, Apply Rules (Option+Command+L) from the menu bar.

Managing Email with Mailboxes

As you receive messages, they'll be stored in your inbox. If you're a casual emailer, that doesn't pose a problem—but if you rely on email for managing your life, you'll almost certainly and to start categorizing and filing messages. To do this, you can create any number of mailboxes (think *folders*) that are stored locally or, in the case of IMAP and .Mac servers, on the remote mail server itself.

Mail displays all the active accounts and the mailboxes inside those accounts in the pane on the left side of the window. Since accounts hold mailboxes and mailboxes themselves can hold more mailboxes, this pane is managed very much like a list view in the Finder. You can use the disclosure arrows to collapse and expand the hierarchy of mailboxes. The number of unread messages is displayed to the right of each mailbox.

You can grow and expand the Mailbox pane using the handle in the lower right corner of the pane. Double-clicking the handle or the separator bar will alternate between collapsing the Mailbox pane to fit the mailbox names perfectly and fitting only the mailbox icons. To hide the mailboxes entirely, choose View, Hide Mailboxes from the menu. You can also customize the toolbar (View, Customize Toolbar) to include a shortcut for hiding and showing the mailbox pane.

NOTE

The default icons in the Mailbox pane are *huge.* If you're like me and have a bunch of mailboxes created, you'll want to choose View, Use Small Mailbox Icons.

Filing Messages

To file one or more messages into a mailbox, click and drag it from the message list to the mailbox you want to use. Alternatively, you can use the Move To or Copy To options from the Message menu. Control-clicking or right-clicking a line in the message opens a contextual menu from which Transfer can also be accessed as well as most other options from the main Message menu.

Certain mailboxes, such as Inbox, Outbox, Drafts, Junk, and Trash, are special in that they contain all of a specific type of mailbox for each account and are filled automatically:

- Inbox—Contains all the inboxes for all your accounts. You can either expand the master inbox to pick a specific account's inbox, or use the top-level inbox to show all incoming messages in all your accounts, be they POP3, IMAP, or .Mac accounts.
- Outbox—Messages that are *going* to be sent but have not yet left your system. This is visible only if you have messages waiting to be sent.
- Sent—Messages that have already been sent from your computer.
- Junk—Messages that have been classified as spam by your system.
- Trash—Like the inbox, the trash is a collection of messages—in this case, all messages that have been marked for deletion but are not yet deleted.
- Drafts—Messages that you are working on but have not yet sent.

NOTE

The Mail icon displays the total number of unread messages in *all* the Inbox folders. Unfortunately, there is currently no way to change the mailboxes it monitors for the unread count.

Creating New Mailboxes

To create a new mailbox, choose Mailbox, New Mailbox from the menu or click the + button at the bottom of the Mail window drawer. You are prompted for where the Mailbox will be created, and what it should be called, as demonstrated in Figure 3.33.

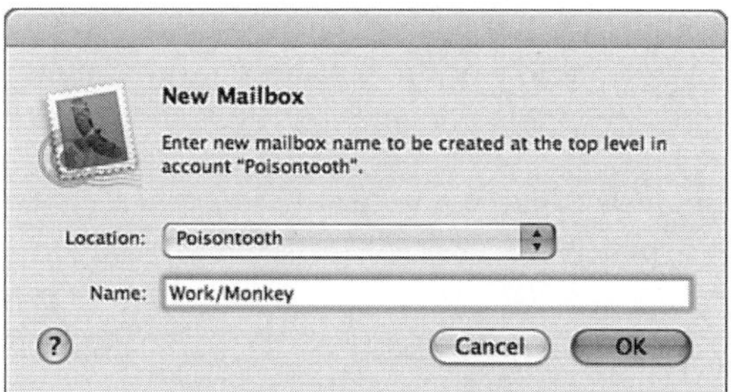

FIGURE 3.33 Choose where to create the new mailbox and what it should be called.

If you're using a POP account, your only option for the location will be On My Mac—this creates a mailbox at the top level of the Mailbox listing that is stored directly on your computer. IMAP/Mac.com users can choose an email account from the Location pop-up menu. This stores the mailbox on the remote server. To create a mailbox inside another mailbox, type the full path of the mailbox you want to create. For example, if you already have a mailbox called `Work` and you want to make the mailbox `Monkey` inside it, type **`Work/Monkey`** in the Name field. You can also select a mailbox within the hierarchy and click + and the new mailbox will be created within the selected mailbox.

Mailboxes can also be rearranged by dragging them from one location to another. You can place mailboxes inside of other mailboxes or even copy a mailbox from one IMAP/.Mac account to another.

To delete or rename a mailbox, highlight it in the mailbox list; then use Rename or Delete from the Mailbox menu.

TIP

As a shortcut for creating mailboxes within mailboxes, highlight the parent mailbox that you want to create another mailbox inside of; then click + or choose the New mailbox option.

Also, notice that, like the Finder, the mailbox pane has an action button. This button can be used to access many of the same functions as under the Mailbox menu bar.

Assigning Special Mailboxes for Sent, Trash, Draft, and Junk Email

Mail automatically creates mailboxes for storing sent items, trash, drafts, and junk mail. Unfortunately, if you use email on other platforms or you mail end up with multiple mailboxes serving the same purpose (Sent Messages and Sent Items, for example). To force Mail to use a specific mailbox for sent, trash, draft, or junk email, highlight the mailbox you want to use then, from the menu bar, choose Mailbox, Use This Mailbox For, followed by the purpose of the mailbox.

Rebuilding Corrupt Mailboxes

There might be times that Mail gets out of sync with your IMAP/.Mac mail server. The symptoms are usually missing messages or messages with the wrong content.

From my experience, this happens most often when accessing the mail server from another client and renaming/moving mailboxes. To rebuild the contents of any mailbox, choose Mailbox, Rebuild from the menu. Mail redownloads the contents of the mailbox and (hopefully) corrects the problem.

Using Smart Mailboxes

"Smart" things are everywhere in Tiger. Smart Playlists in iTunes, Smart Folders in the Finder, and now Smart Mailboxes in Mail. As with these are incarnations of smart elements, a Smart Mailbox is essentially a mail search that is attached to a virtual folder. When you open the folder, the search is performed and you see only the messages matching the search. A Smart Mailbox, for example, might be set to search for messages from a specific person and only display those messages. This eliminates the need to manually file the messages or to write rules that move the messages around—unless you want to!

Smart Mailboxes go across all of your accounts and account mailboxes. They appear as purplish geared folders the root level of your mailbox listing, as shown in Figure 3.34. Clicking the folder displays the messages that it contains—just like any other folder.

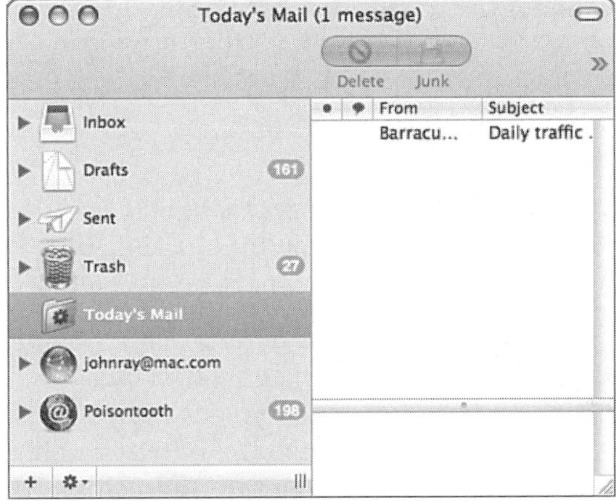

FIGURE 3.34 Smart Mailboxes appear at the top level of your mailbox hierarchy and aren't attached to a specific account.

Creating a Smart Mailbox To create a new Smart Mailbox, choose Mailbox, New Smart Mailbox from the menu bar. The Smart Mailbox creation screen will be displayed, as demonstrated in Figure 3.35.

The Smart Mailbox setup is almost identical to the rule creation we looked at earlier in the chapter. First, name the mailbox and decide whether you *any* or *all* the search conditions to apply. Next, add each of the conditions that you want to be met in order for a message to appear in the mailbox. Use the + and - buttons to add or remove conditions as needed.

3

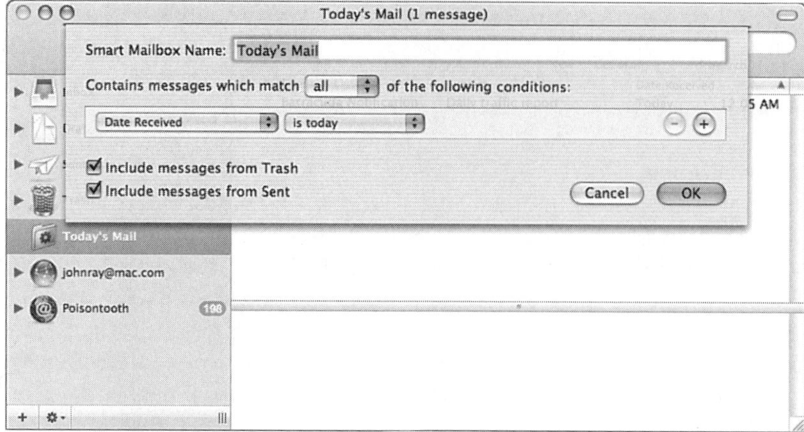

FIGURE 3.35 Create a new Smart Mailbox just as you would a mail rule.

TIP

If you have a message selected when you create a new Smart Mailbox, Mail will automatically create the first few conditions necessary to match the message. You'll need to manually click the + button for it to fill in beyond the first condition.

If you want the mailbox to also include messages that are in the Trash or your Sent mailbox, use the two check boxes at the bottom of the dialog box. When finished, click OK. Your mailbox will be added to the Mailbox pane and should be ready for use.

Editing and Arranging Smart Mailboxes Like normal mailboxes, Smart Mailboxes can be deleted by using Mailbox, Delete or renamed by double-clicking its name in the Mailbox list or using the menu item Mailbox, Rename. If you decide you want to change the Smart Mailbox search criteria, editing is just a matter of selecting it in the Mailbox list and choosing Mailbox, Edit Smart Mailbox from the Edit menu.

While at a very basic level Smart Mailboxes might seem like normal mailboxes, they aren't. You can't drag them around into and out of accounts. As a result, you might end up with dozens of Smart Mailboxes cluttering up your Mailbox pane. To help organize these virtual objects, Apple provides Smart Mailbox folders that can be used to file and organize all of your Smart Mailboxes. To create a Smart Mailbox Folder, choose Mailboxes, New Smart Mailbox Folder from the menu bar. When prompted, type the name for the folder and click OK. A new folder that looks just like a Smart Mailbox will be added to your Mailbox list.

Smart Mailbox Folders serve a single purpose—they contain Smart Mailboxes and other Smart Mailbox Folders. After a Smart Mailbox Folder has been created, you can drag your Smart Mailboxes in and out of the folder (or other Smart Mailbox Folders) and organize them as you see fit. You may *not*, however, use the folder for any other purpose or drag it into an email account.

TIP

Although Smart Mailboxes and Smart Mailbox Folders cannot be stored on your mail server, you *can* synchronize them across multiple machines using the Mail .Mac Sync feature discussed later in this chapter.

Composing and Sending Messages

If you can read messages and organize them, it stands to reason that you might also want to *write* them.

To write a new email, click the New toolbar button or choose File, New Message (Command-N). If you'd prefer to reply to an existing message, select that message in the mail list, and then click the Reply toolbar button or choose Message, Reply (Command-R). Note that you might also choose the Reply All selection from either the toolbar or menu—this will address the outgoing message to everyone who received the original message, not just the original sender.

Regardless of how you go about starting your message, the composition window will appear, as shown in Figure 3.36.

FIGURE 3.36 Mail supports styled messages and drag-and-drop attachments.

TIP

If text from the original message is selected when you choose to reply, it is included in the new message as a quote from the original message. If nothing is selected, the entire message is quoted.

Addressing Your Messages

Two fields are initially provided for addressing the message. Use the To line for single or multiple addresses that serve as the primary recipients of the message. A comma should separate multiple addresses. The Cc: line adds additional recipients who are not part of the main list. (Note that the primary recipients *can see* these addresses. To send to additional recipients without revealing them, you'll need to use the Bcc field, which can easily be enabled; see "Customizing Mail Header Fields" later in this chapter for details.) Finally, the Subject line is used to set the subject or the title of the email.

TIP

If you would like Mail to automatically Cc or Bcc your own account with every message you send, use the Automatically Cc/Bcc Myself option in the Composing application preferences.

To enter an address in a field, simply start typing the contact's name or email address. As you're typing into any of the available fields, Mail attempts to recognize the address either from your Address Book, a configured LDAP server, or from other addresses you've used recently and auto-complete the address as you type. If it gets the correct address, press Tab or click outside the area where you are typing, and the address is entered as an object. If you've entered multiple email addresses for a single contact (home and work addresses, for example), click on the object; then use the drop-down menu on the right to choose from the different addresses available for that person, as shown in Figure 3.37.

TIP

To disable address autocompletion entirely, uncheck Automatically Complete Addresses in the Composing application preferences.

From the same pop-up menu, you can also choose Edit Address to enter and edit the address manually, Remove Address to delete the address object from the field, iChat with Person (to start an iChat session if available), Open in Address book to open the Address Book application and display the appropriate record and Add to Address Book to add the address to the Tiger Address Book. Finally, you can choose to create a new Smart Mailbox that will only display messages with the highlighted address.

Managing Previous Recipients You might notice that even addresses that aren't in the Address Book are still sometimes autocompleted. If Mail doesn't recognize an address or name as being in your Address Book it will autocomplete it if it happens to be an address stored in the Previous Recipients history. The Previous Recipients list is much like a browser's page history. It is a record of addresses you've used (either through direct emails or by replying to messages) that are not part of your Address Book. You can display the stored list by choosing Window, Previous Recipients, as shown in Figure 3.38.

FIGURE 3.37 Choose which address you want to use for a given person.

FIGURE 3.38 The Previous Recipients list is a list of addresses used but not stored.

Use the buttons Remove from List to remove a selected address from the history list and Add to Address Book to move the address to your Address Book. The Search field can be used to search the list.

Accessing the Address Book To access the system Address Book, choose Window, Address Panel (Option-Command-A), and a miniature version of the Address Book application window appears. From the window, drag individual addresses, multiple addresses, or address groups, to the To/Cc/Bcc fields in the message composition window.

By default, Address Book groups that are added to a message will be expanded in the address field to display all the members. You can disable this behavior in the Composing application preferences.

Querying LDAP Servers Autocompletion of addresses uses both the entries in the address book, recent recipients, and any LDAP servers that are configured. LDAP setup is shared across Mail and the Address Book application, so if you've configured them in one, they'll work in the other.

To configure LDAP servers directly from Mail, open the Composing application preferences, and then click the Configure LDAP button. A dialog appears listing all configured servers. Click the + button to add a new server, click the - button to subtract an existing server, or click Edit to reconfigure the highlighted server. Refer to the discussion of the Address Book in Chapter 2 for more information on the Address Book LDAP server setup process.

Protecting Against Sending Accidental Email Its surprisingly easy to find yourself in a ton of trouble (or an embarrassing situation) by including the wrong addresses on a piece of mail—such as sending private corporate secrets to your gossipy arch enemy. To help guard against this, Mail can be configured so that mail addressed to domains outside a given safe domain are highlighted in red as they are entered. To activate this feature, open the Composing pane of the application preferences, and then choose Mark Addresses Not in This Domain and fill in the appropriate domain, or multiple domains separated by commas, in the accompanying field.

Customizing Mail Header Fields If you're a casual email user, the extra header fields (Cc, Bcc, and so on) might not be necessary or desired—Tiger's version of Mail makes these simple to remove. A pop-up menu at the lower left of the message header gives you quick access to adding/removing fields or customizing the entire header. For example, clicking the pop-up menu and choosing Customize will display check boxes next to each potential element of the message header, as shown in Figure 3.39.

FIGURE 3.39 Customize the header area of your messages.

Check or uncheck each element that you want to display. A few of these items might require some explanation:

The Reply-To header is used to provide an alternative address for replying. For example, if I'm sending email from my `jray@poisontooth.com` account and want replies to go to `johnray@mac.com` instead, I'd enter the Mac.com address in the Reply-To Header field.

The Accounts pop-up menu allows you to choose which account you're using to send a message (if multiple accounts are active).

The Signatures pop-up menu (second from the lower-right corner) is a simple way to quickly add a customized signature (Your name, Phone number, or witty saying) to the bottom of a message.

To the right of the Signatures menu is the message priority. This flag sets a priority (the urgency) for a message.

Adding Content and Attachments

To create the message itself, type the text into the content area of the window. The toolbar can be used to attach files or pick fonts and colors. These options are also available from the Message and Format menus.

If you add styles to the text of a message, it must be sent in a Rich Text format—Plain text messages cannot convey any styling information. As their name implies, they are *plain* text. You can toggle between Plain and Rich text messages with the Format menu. If moving from Rich to Plain, any style information you've added will be lost.

Be aware that to receive rich-text email, the remote user must have a modern email program such as Outlook Express (or, better yet, Mail!). To create a message that anyone can receive, compose the content in Plain Text mode, selectable from the Format menu. You can set this as the default Message Format within the Composing application preferences.

If you are replying to a message, you can have Mail automatically set your reply format to the format of the original message; choose Use the Same Message Format as the Original Message Again in the Composing application preferences.

To add attachments, drag images and files (and even folders!) directly into the message, or click the Attach button in the toolbar. Depending on the type of file, it is added to the message as an icon (application, archive, and so on) or shown within the body. If you frequently send to Windows recipients, you might also want to choose Edit, Attachments, Always Send Windows Friendly Attachments or use the checkbox at the bottom of the file selection window when using the "Attach" button.

When you're finished, click Send in the toolbar, or choose Message, Send (Shift-Command-D). If you want to save the message and work on it later, use File, Save as Draft (Command-S). This saves the message to your Drafts mailbox where you can open it and resume work at a later date.

TIP

When replying to a message, it is common to quote another message. As mentioned previously, you can quote a specific portion of a message by highlighting the appropriate message content before choosing Reply. Sometimes, however the quote level of the message isn't what you want—something you want to be quoted *isn't,* whereas something you don't want quoted is. To adjust the levels of quoting, select the text to change and use the menu selections Format, Quote Level, Increase or Decrease.

You can control the quoting of text and whether the quote level is automatically increased when replying within the Composing application preferences.

Forwarding and Redirecting Messages

The easiest way to write a message is to let someone else write it for you. Forwarding and redirecting messages sends the content of an existing message to a new recipient. You probably experience this frequently when your friends decide to forward you what they've determined is the funniest joke they've ever heard.

The difference between forwarding and redirecting is that a forward is the equivalent of copying and pasting the original message and basic headers into a new email and clicking send. The forward comes from you as a new message. A redirected message, on the other hand, includes the original headers and content, including the sender. A forward is most appropriate if you want to include your own comments, while a redirect is better suited for passing an original message without any modifications to another recipient.

To forward or redirect a message, select it in the message list, and then choose Redirect or Forward from the Message menu. You can also add forward/redirect buttons to the toolbar by choosing View, Customize Toolbar within the Message List window.

Spell Checking Messages

By default, Mail will automatically spell-check your messages as you type them. Words that it has identified as being incorrect will be highlighted with a red dotted line underneath them. To correct an error, Control-click the word and a list of potential corrections will be displayed, choose the corrected term and the original word is replaced in the message. You can also choose to ignore the word (and any other instances of it in the message) or learn it for future use.

TIP

Even if a word isn't spelled wrong, you can still Control-click it and choose to look it up in the Tiger dictionary, Google, or even Spotlight.

Beginning in Tiger, you can choose to have Mail perform spell checking after you click Send rather than as you type. This can be less intrusive than the underline method and ensures that you catch everything before the email goes out. To activate this feature, use the Check Spelling pop-up menu in the Composing application preferences to choose When I Click Send.

Managing and Adding Signatures

Everyone needs a signature—something to identify them as individuals or at least to tell others who you are! The Mail application handles multiple different signatures for multiple accounts with ease. Signatures are configured through the Signatures application preferences, demonstrated in Figure 3.40.

FIGURE 3.40 Create multiple signatures within the Mail application.

The Signature management interface is divided into three columns. The first displays all of your email accounts (including a generic All option). The second column shows a list of signatures for the selected account. Finally, the third column displays the actual editable signature.

To add a signature, simple choose the account you want it to be attached to (or All, for all the accounts), click the + button in the middle column to add a new signature entry, name the new signature, and then, finally, enter the signature in the column on the far right. To remove a signature, select it in the center column and click the - button.

The signature entry area is a full rich text field. As you type, you can use the same Format menu options to style the signature text. To help make things consistent, click the Always Match My Default Message Font check box to change the signature to match whatever you set for your default font in the Fonts and Colors application preferences.

After typing your signatures, you can choose which is displayed by default (if any) for each email account. Pick the email account in the left column, and then use the Choose signature pop-up menu to pick a specific signature that will be used by default for that account, or even choose to cycle sequentially through the available signatures or choose one randomly.

A final setting is the ability to place the signature above quoted text. This is useful if you typically reply to messages and quote the original text directly after your reply. Rather than pasting your signature at the very bottom of the message, it will appear above the original (quoted) text.

If you've chosen a default signature (or to randomize or sequentially choose signatures), it will automatically be inserted whenever you compose a message. If, however, you didn't set a default, you can still insert a signature using the signature pop-up menu in the lower-right corner of the message composition heading. Choose the signature you want and it will be pasted into the message.

Encrypting Messages

Tiger supports automatic encryption/decryption of email messages if you have a digital certificate for your email identity installed in your keychain (refer to Chapter 2 for details).

The S/MIME standard used within Mail is a public/private key encryption system. Messages are encrypted using the *public* key of a recipient. Only the recipient's *private* key can decrypt an encrypted message, and only the recipient should ever have access to the private key.

To use mail encryption, you must install a digital certificate that contains your private key and public key. After doing this, you can add a digital signature containing your public key to your emails. This signature is subsequently stored automatically by other popular mail applications and can be used by other people to send you encrypted messages.

Similarly, your friends/coworkers can send you *their* public keys, which are automatically added to your keychain and can be used to send *them* encrypted messages.

While all this sounds confusing, you only need to worry about two actions: signing a message with your public key and encrypting a message with another user's public key. Both of these actions are easy in Mail:

1. First, make sure that you and the people you want to communicate with have obtained and installed certificates with your private keys. This is discussed in Chapter 2.
2. Next, send each other email that is signed with your public keys. This is as easy as clicking on the stamp/check mark icon button in the lower-right corner of the addressing area of your message—this is only visible after your certificate has been added to the system (refer to Figure 3.36). If the icon is highlighted, the message automatically is signed. Exchanging signed emails adds your friend's public keys to your keychain.
3. Finally, after you've collected the public keys of your friends, you can send encrypted messages by clicking the lock icon (again refer to Figure 3.36) so that it is highlighted. The message is encrypted using the appropriate public keys before it is sent—virtually eliminating the threat of interception.

NOTE

If you do not see these icons in your window, you do not have the correct certificates installed on your system. A certificate is specific to a given email account, so you must make sure that you're using the same From address that you provided when applying for a certificate.

Replying with iChat

Mail integrates with iChat such that any email message from a contact that is also on your IM buddy list displays that person's IM status in a column within Mail. If the column isn't visible, choose View, Columns, Buddy Availability from the menu bar.

To launch an iChat AV session with an online buddy, highlight the message they've sent in your message list; then choose Message, Reply with iChat (Shift-Command-I). This feature can also be added as a toolbar customization (View, Customize Toolbar).

The same feature is also displayed when you address a message to one of your buddies. If they are shown to be online, opening the pop-up menu from their Smart Address will display an option for launching an iChat session.

You can disable this feature altogether by unchecking the Show Online Buddy Status in the Viewing application preferences.

Applying Parental Controls

If you're a parent, you might not want your child being able to email (and be emailed by) every other person on the planet. Much like Safari can restrict the URLs a user can visit, Mail can restrict the email addresses to/from which a user can send and receive messages. To active this feature, open the Accounts system preference panel, select the user you want to restrict, and then click the Parental controls button. Click the check box beside Mail, and then click Configure. The dialog shown in Figure 3.41 will prompt you for the appropriate restrictions.

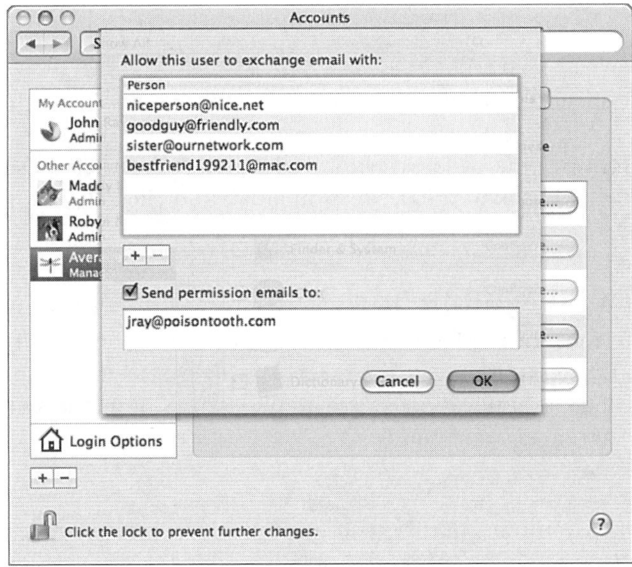

FIGURE 3.41 Enter the allowed email addresses and the person who will oversee the account.

Use the +/- buttons to add and remove addresses from the list. If you want to give the user the flexibility to request additional addresses be added to the list, check the Send Permission Emails To check box and enter a valid email address.

If the permissions feature is activated, the user will be prompted to ask for permission when they try to email an unlisted address. If you are set up to receive the permission emails, you will see the permission request message in your email with an Always Allow button at the top, as shown in Figure 3.42.

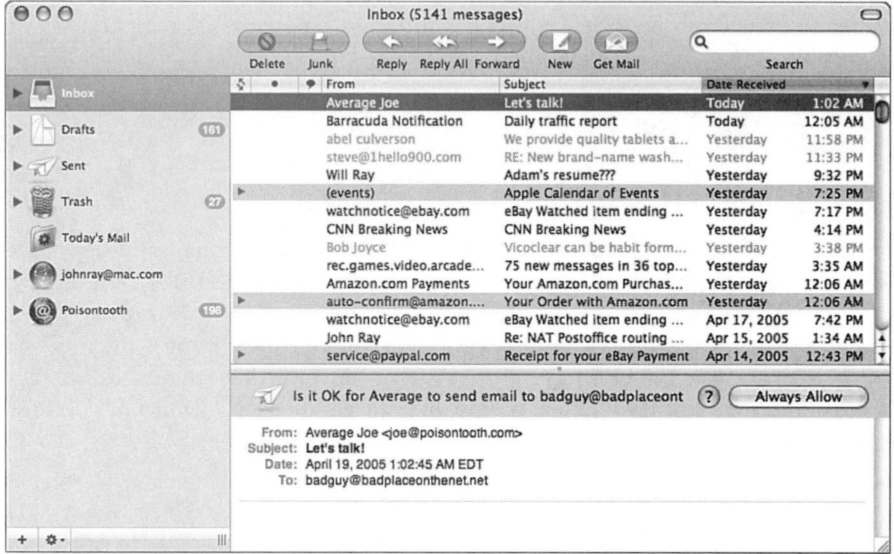

FIGURE 3.42 A restricted user can ask for permission to send email.

Click the button and the email address will be added to the restricted user's allowed list. You can, at any time, go back to the permission email and click No Longer Allow to restrict the address again.

Mail Utilities and Diagnostic Tools

To help you get the most out of Mail and figure out what in the world it is doing as the little cursor spins, Apple has included several tools within Mail that help in monitoring, diagnosing, and using the application. These aren't settings or features you'd need to access everyday, but they can be helpful.

Synchronizing Mail with .Mac

If you have multiple computers in different locations, it helps to be able to access the same information from each. To this end, Apple has added basic .Mac syncing features to Tiger mail. With a few mouse clicks you can synchronize your mail rules, signatures, Smart Mailboxes, and Accounts across multiple machines. That is, of course, if you have a .Mac account (discussed later in this chapter). Assuming you do, you can activate these features within the General application preferences or directly in the .Mac system preference pane, discussed later in this chapter.

There is no configuration for this option aside from turning it on. After it has been activated, iSync will keep your email configuration current across all registered .Mac machines.

Account Info

It isn't uncommon to have an email account with a quota but have no idea of how much space you're using. Most mail clients don't make it easy to find this information. In Tiger, Mail provides an Account Info display that quickly provides a summary of your account settings, size, and quota. To access the Account Info window, select an account within the Mailboxes pane and choose Command-I or Get Info from the Mailbox action menu. The Account Info window appears, as demonstrated in Figure 3.43.

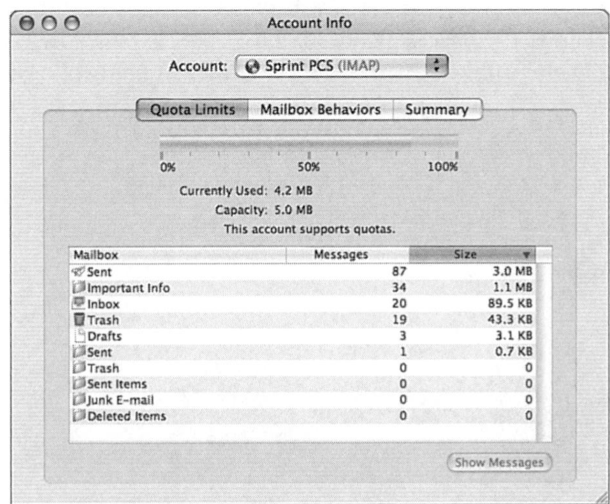

FIGURE 3.43 The Account Info window can be used to get a summary of your account usage and setup.

Use the Account pop-up menu at the top of the Window to switch between any of your accounts. Below that you can move between three different information summaries:

Quota Limits—Visible for IMAP/.Mac accounts, this shows the size of your account, the total capacity, and the sizes of each mailbox. To view the contents of a mailbox, select it in the list and click the Show Messages button; Mail will open a new viewer with that Mailbox.

Messages on Server—Available for POP users only, this displays the messages that are stored on the POP server, removed from your local account, or those that have been downloaded to your computer. Selecting a message in this list also provides the option of removing it from the server without downloading it into your mailbox—useful for extremely large attachments on a dial-in connection.

Mailbox Behaviors—Displays the settings for the Drafts, Sent, Junk, and Trash Mailboxes. This view is identical to the Mailbox Behaviors within the account settings and can be used to quickly change how your Account interacts with these default mailboxes.

Summary—Shows a simple uneditable summary of your account information.

Viewing Mail Activity

The Activity Viewer shows tasks Mail is completing, along with a description of the action that is taking place. If Mail appears to be hung, check Activity Viewer. To cancel or stop an action, click the Stop button.

Connection Doctor

New to Tiger is the Connection Doctor. This tool is an extension of the Connection Doctor idea introduced in iChat in earlier versions of Mac OS X. Rather than identifying why your chat has failed, however, it helps you locate settings that might be wrong in your email accounts. To use the Connection Doctor, choose Window, Connection Doctor from the menu bar. The window shown in Figure 3.44 will be displayed.

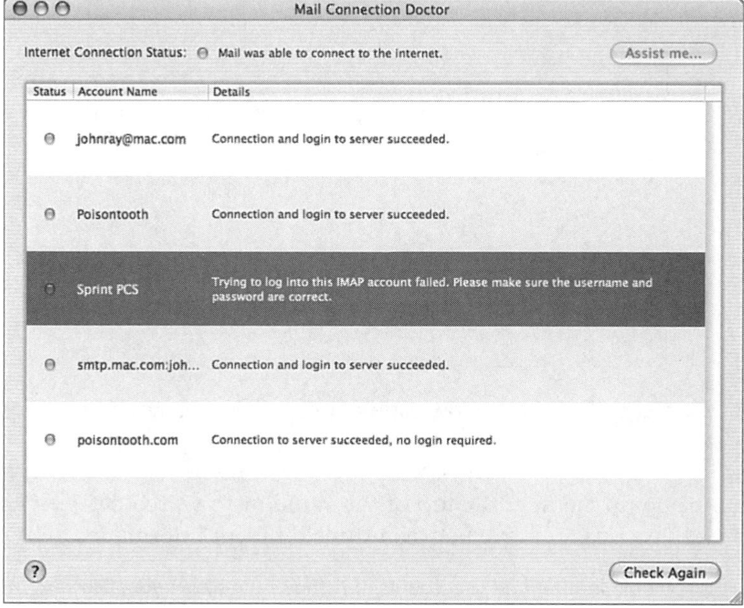

FIGURE 3.44 The Connection Doctor helps identify problems with your email account settings.

At the top of the window is your Internet status. If there is no Internet, there's no mail. If the status shows anything other than green, click the Assist Me button to launch the Network system preference panel and identify the issue.

The Connection Doctor displays a line for each email account and SMTP server configured. If connecting to the server is successful, a message to that effect is displayed next to the account/server name. If an error has occurred, the connection doctor provides a summary of the problem and an educated guess of what might be causing it.

To fix an error, double-click the error line in the Connection Doctor window and Mail will display the setting that it has determined is causing the problem. After making the necessary changes, click Check Again in the Connection Doctor window to verify that the problem is solved.

Video and Audio Conferencing: iChat AV

Computers have linked the world. The ability to carry on real-time chats—through text, audio, and video—bridges cultures and people around the globe. Unfortunately, the process of actually making a connection is often more difficult than it needs to be.

There are numerous shareware/freeware conferencing solutions—Apple's own QuickTime Broadcaster can even be coaxed into filling the niche (see Chapter 25, "Darwin Streaming Server and QuickTime Broadcaster," for details). None of these, however, approach the ease-of-use of Apple's iChat AV. iChat allows ordinary users to hold high-quality full-motion video/audio conferences with their friends and colleagues. New with Tiger's iChat AV is the ability to host and join multiparty video and audio chats. Up to 10 people (including yourself) can participate in an audio chat, and up to 4 in a video chat. Unfortunately, with the new features come lofty new system requirements.

Figure 3.45 shows an example of a video chat session in progress.

FIGURE 3.45 Videoconferencing is simple and fun with iChat AV.

iChat AV allows you to communicate in real-time with people who use `Mac.com`, have an AOL Instant Messenger (AIM) account, or a corporate Jabber server account.

Even if you have no intention of using the text messaging capabilities of iChat, you'll still need one of these accounts to establish the initial audio or video connection. You can sign up for a free AOL Instant Messenger (AIM) account at `http://www.aim.com` or an iChat-only (free) .Mac username at `http://www.mac.com`.

WHAT IS JABBER?

Jabber is a secure open source XML-based IM solution. It is widely used to set up private instant messaging servers within corporate or secure environments. Tiger Server now includes a Jabber server implementation, thus the obvious inclusion in iChat AV. For more information on Jabber, visit `http://www.jabber.org/`.

NOTE

If other users on your local network use iChat AV, you don't need to use an AIM or `Mac.com` account to chat with them. Bonjour has been incorporated into iChat so that it can automatically generate a buddy list of "nearby" users on the same network.

NOTE

Apple has chosen to use SIP (Session Initiation Protocol, RFC 2543, `http://www.zvon.org/tmRFC/RFC2543/Output/frontpage.html`) and RTP (Real Time Protocol, RFC 1889, `http://www.zvon.org/tmRFC/RFC1889/Output/index.html`) along with well-known compression codecs (H.264) for initiating and transmitting audio and video.

Unfortunately, iChat is currently incompatible with other SIP implementations of conferencing software. For cross-platform support, AIM for Windows is still the best iChat-compatible option.

Required Conferencing Hardware

iChat AV works with recognized Mac OS X video sources—FireWire camcorders, webcams, and analog A/V conversion devices, such as the Dazzle FireWire Bridge. Apple's own iSight camera (`http://www.apple.com/isight/`) is cost effective and produces high-quality images. If the $150 price tag is within range, I recommend the iSight purchase. If not, the iBot camera is available for the $30–60 range on eBay and works fine with iChat AV.

If you do not have a video camera, you can use iChat AV as an audio-conferencing solution with any system-recognized microphone and you can still participate in one-way video conferences.

On the computer side, iChat AV requires at least a 600MHz G3 for *single-party* videoconferencing. If you attempt to use video on a slower machine, it reports that video is not available on your computer.

TIP

Ecamm Network has provided a hack to get around both the 600MHz and FireWire requirements. iChatUSBCam (`http://www.ecamm.com/mac/ichatusbcam/`) enables you to use USB cameras and low-end systems to run iChat AV.

The requirements for multiparty conferencing is even higher. If you plan to use the multi-person video/audio chat features, you'll need at least a dual 1GHz G4 to host a video chat and at least a single processor 1GHz G4 or a dual-processor 800MHz G4 to join one.

Finally, no matter what high-end CPU platform or video hardware you own, you'll need network bandwidth to accommodate audio or video streams. The low-end requirements are 56kbps for audio, and 128kbps for video and 1000kbps for hosting multiparty conferences.

Realistically, 56k modem users might be able to audio conference if they have a stable and noise-free connection, but the best experience comes from a dedicated digital connection. xDSL, Cable, and LAN users should be able to carry high-quality audio/video streams easily but even these connections might not be able to host multiperson chats.

Setting Up iChat AV

Unless you entered a .Mac username during the installation of Tiger, the first time you start iChat AV it will walk you through a simple setup process. First, iChat prompts for your name and either your AIM or .Mac iChat account information, as shown in Figure 3.46. To register for a free .Mac username, click the Get an iChat Account button. Click the Continue button to move on.

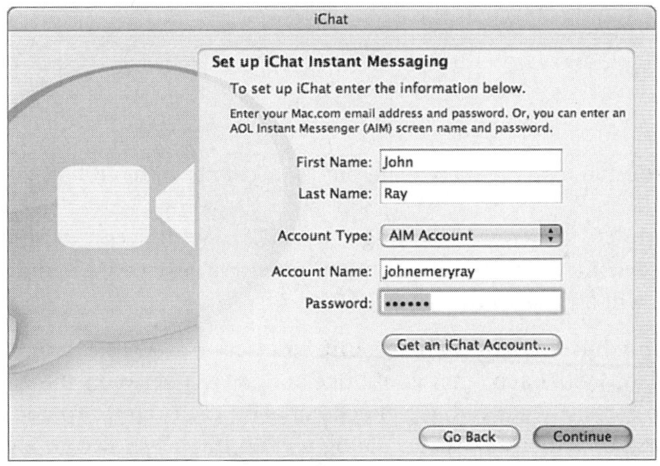

FIGURE 3.46 Enter your account information.

Next, iChat prompts to set up Jabber Instant Messaging. Unless your company or organization has a Jabber Server, you'll want to skip this configuration and click Continue. If you *do* have a Jabber server, check the Use Jabber Instant Messaging box and supply an account name and password. Click Continue to carry on setting up iChat AV.

You are now prompted to turn on Bonjour Messaging. If you have a relatively contained local network, turning on Bonjour probably isn't an issue. If you're part of a subnet with hundreds of clients, however, Bonjour is going to overwhelm your buddy list. Click Continue to move on.

Finally, iChat provides a preview of your audio and video input. Make sure that if you have a camera and a microphone attached the inputs are visible before continuing. Your setup is now complete. Click the Done button to begin using iChat AV.

Adding and Editing Additional Accounts

To edit or modify accounts after iChat AV has complete the initial setup process choose iChat, Preferences from the menu. Click the Accounts icon, to open the Account manager, as shown in Figure 3.47.

FIGURE 3.47 You can manage many different IM accounts within iChat.

Much like Mail, the iChat accounts settings are laid out with accounts on the left side of the window and account settings on the right. To edit an existing account, chose it in the list—the settings will appear to the right.

While you can only have one of each account type active at a time, you can create as many AIM, .Mac, or Jabber accounts you'd like and switch between them at will. The accounts that are currently active have checkmarks by their name. To add an account, click the + button. An account creation dialog will appear, as shown in Figure 3.48.

Use the Account Type pop-up menu to choose between AIM, .Mac, or Jabber, and then supply your account information and a description of the account in the provided fields. If you want the account to become the default active account, select the Use This Account check box. Click Add to save the account information.

Advanced Account and Server Settings

After an account is added, selecting it in the account list will display its associated properties in the pane on right side of the window. There are up to three settings views that you can switch to using the buttons at the top of the right-hand pane:

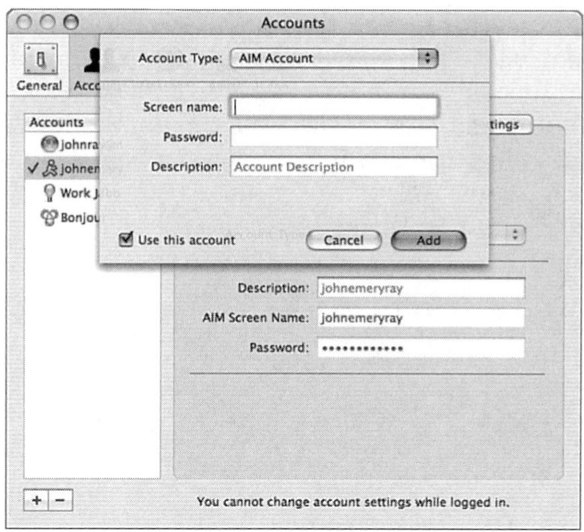

FIGURE 3.48 Enter the information for your new account.

Account Information—Basic settings for the account, username, password, and so on. These settings also determine whether an account is currently active (Use This Account) or if it will automatically be logged in to when iChat starts (When iChat Opens, Automatically Log In).

Security—Determines who can (or can't) see that you are online. We will look at the iChat security options later in this chapter.

Server Settings—The server settings can be used to configure proxy connections for your IM servers or set non-standard ports for communication. With Jabber servers, these settings also control SSL encryption of the chat session.

When you are finished adding and configuring all of your accounts and account settings, close the application preferences. You can now begin using iChat AV.

Logging In to Your IM Accounts

Unless you've configured the Account Information settings otherwise, iChat AV will automatically log in to your default accounts when it starts up and log out when you quit. To manually log in to or out of an account, use the Log In and Log Out selections under the iChat application menu. If you have multiple AIM, .Mac, or Jabber accounts, you can switch between them by choosing Switch To from the iChat menu.

TIP

There are a few system events that can be used to trigger iChat or shut it down. If you have an iSight, iChat can be set to automatically launch when the camera iris is opened (for example, when the camera is turned on).

Similarly, the Fast User switching feature will automatically log you out when you switch to another user account; this can be changed to keep you online but show you as Away. Use the Video and General application preference panes to make these adjustments, respectively.

Activating the iChat Menu Extra

While starting and stopping iChat is an effective means of logging in and out of your accounts, it also means that you have to remember to do it. If you're like many people, instant messaging is one of your primary means of communications and should be active whenever you are using your computer. To make logging in and out of iChat easier (and automatic), you can activate the iChat status menu extra by opening the General application preferences pane, as shown in Figure 3.49.

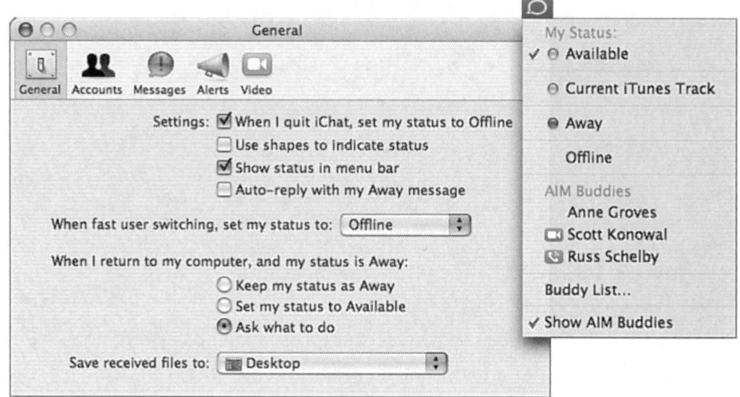

FIGURE 3.49 Add an iChat status menu to your menu bar in the General preferences.

Click the Show status in Menu Bar check box to display as a speech bubble on the right side of your menu bar. While in the General preferences, you might also want to uncheck the option When I Quit iChat, Set My Status to Offline—this will allow you to quit the iChat application but still receive messages.

When the iChat status menu is active, you do not have to have iChat AV open to set your online status, or to initiate a chat session. Simply activate the menu and choose Available to log in or Offline to log out. The last status setting you've chosen will automatically be applied when you log in to your Tiger user account.

Configuring Your Online Information

There are a number of pieces of information that other users can see when you're online—such as your account status, an AIM profile, and a picture you've chosen to represent yourself. You'll want to get a grip on how to control these settings so that you can be certain that your buddies are seeing what you expect them to.

Setting Your Account Status

When you are logged in to iChat AV, other members can see whether you are available for a chat. There are just two status states you can set your account to use: Available and Away—accessed from either the iChat Status menu extra or the drop-down menu under your name at the top of the Buddy List window. If your machine has been idle for several minutes, it automatically kicks into an idle state to show that you haven't been using your computer.

By default, your status, as well as the status of your buddies, is indicated by green (available), red (away), and orange (idle) dots next to each name (including yours) in the Buddy List window and iChat AV Status menu. If you have trouble differentiating between the colors or just want a change of pace, the availability dots can be changed to shapes using the General pane within the iChat AV application preferences.

Even though there are only two real states that your account can be set to manually, you can apply your own custom labels to these states. A custom available state called Current iTunes Track is included in Tiger. Choosing this state will show you as available and display the current iTunes track you are listening to—perhaps warning off potential chatters if they see you've spent the last two hours listening to Marilyn Manson.

To create additional states, use the two Custom selections found under the Buddy List availability menu (click directly below your iChat name in the Buddy List heading). You are allowed to type your own custom label to be displayed in your buddies' chat clients. For even greater control, choose Edit Status Menu; the dialog shown in Figure 3.50 will appear.

FIGURE 3.50 Edit the Available and Away messages for your account.

Click the + button under the appropriate column to add messages to your Available or Away pool. Use the - button to delete existing messages. If you want iChat to remember the messages you've typed between sessions, be sure the Remember Custom Messages check box is selected.

TIP

By default, if you receive a message while you're away, iChat does nothing. To configure iChat to automatically respond with your custom Away message select Auto-Reply with My Away Message in the General application preferences.

You can also use the General preferences to automatically have iChat change your Away status back to Available when you start using your machine after being Away.

Changing Your AV Capability Status

In addition to the availability status, iChat also sends your AV capability status to your buddies. This information tells the remote systems if you are capable of accepting video and/or audio chats. While presumably you *do* want to use these features (that's why you're reading about iChat AV, after all), sometimes you might want to temporarily disable them.

To disable/enable your Microphone and Camera devices, uncheck the Microphone Enabled or Camera Enabled menu items under the main Video menu (or Audio menu, if you have no video capabilities). Your AV capabilities will immediately update in your friends' buddy lists.

Updating Your Profile

Your AIM profile is nothing more than a few paragraphs of text that describe yourself, or say whatever you want. You can use the profile as a means of communicating with your friends or leaving a note larger than just a custom Away or Available message. In addition, the profile is visible even if you aren't online.

To change your profile, choose Buddies, Change My Profile from the menu bar. The profile window, shown in Figure 3.51 will appear.

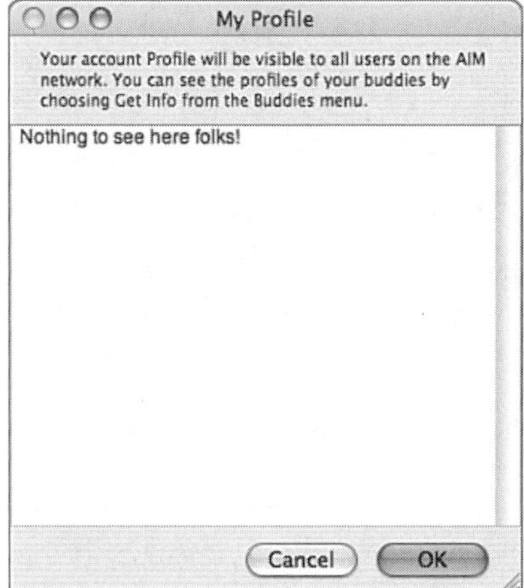

FIGURE 3.51 Set the information you want displayed when your buddies request information on your account.

Enter your text into the Profile window then choose OK to save it to the AIM servers.

Setting Your iChat AV Buddy Icon

A unique feature of the AIM service is the capability to set custom thumbnails of all your contacts and yourself—these are known as *buddy icons* (or *buddy pictures* depending on what label Apple decided to use where). Your buddy icon is automatically transmitted to your friends so that they can see whatever you've set your icon to be. Similarly, if they've set custom icons, they will automatically show up on your system.

By default your personal AIM buddy icon is the image set in the Address Book application or the icon used for your account image. To replace it with one of your choosing, drag a new image into the image well beside your name at the top of the Buddy List window or choose Buddies, Change My Picture from the menu bar to edit your existing icon.

An editing window appears to allow you to position and scale the image, as shown in Figure 3.52. Drag the image so that the section you want to use as an icon is centered in the bright square in the middle of the window; then use the zoom slider underneath the image to zoom in and out. The center square shows the icon that will be set—albeit not necessarily the same size it will be in iChat AV. When you're satisfied with the image, click Set.

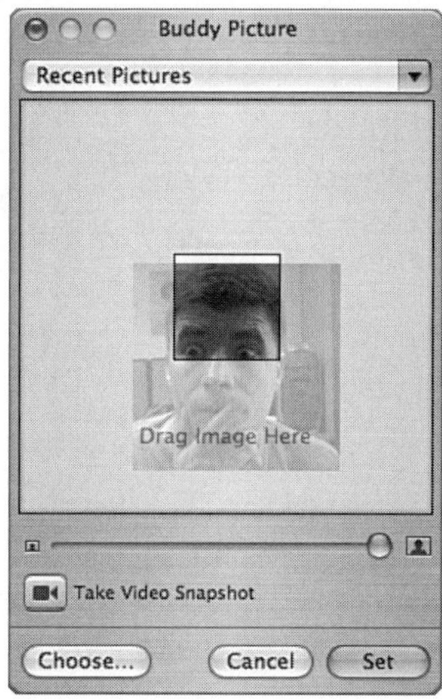

FIGURE 3.52 Position and crop your image.

If you want to choose another image from a file, click the Choose button, and you are presented with a standard file selection dialog box. Users with a camera attached will notice the Take Video Snapshot button at the bottom of their window. Clicking this button displays a live video preview, gives you roughly 3 seconds to primp and preen, and then automatically takes a snapshot that you can use as a buddy icon. This provides an easy way to create a new icon for your mood du jour.

Given that it is so easy to create and switch button icons, you'll soon end up with a library of icons. To switch to any icon you've used recently, click your thumbnail image in the Buddy List window. A palette of frequently used icons displays, enabling you to quickly switch to icons on the fly.

TIP

If you *really* want to keep your buddy icon updated, consider iChat Streaming Icon (`http://ichat.twosailors.com/`). This unique application uses your camera to capture a new buddy icon as quickly as once every half second. Best of all, *any* AIM client can see the changes making it a means of transmitting video (albeit small and jerky video) to your non-Mac friends.

Managing Your Buddy List

Virtually everything that goes on in iChat starts with the Buddy List. When you log in to AIM through iChat, the full Buddy List window appears onscreen to show which of your friends are online (not grayed out), whether they're available to chat, and what conferencing capabilities (Audio/Video) are available to them, as demonstrated in Figure 3.53.

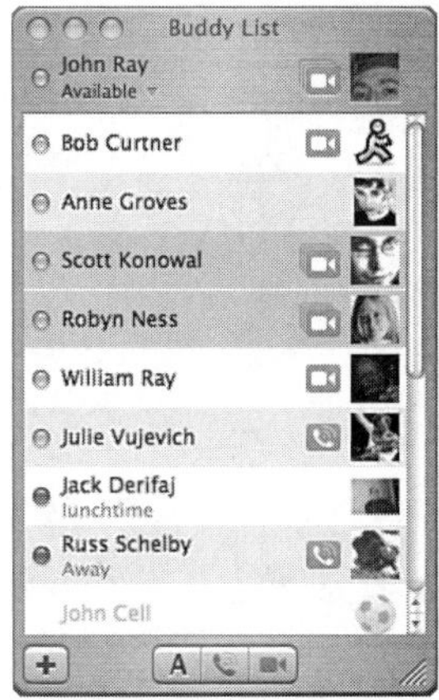

FIGURE 3.53 You can easily see who's available to chat and their capabilities using the Buddy List; the listings for people who aren't connected are dimmed.

The video camera icon shows video availability, whereas the telephone represents an audio-chat ready contact. If you see multiple stacked video/audio icons, it this indicates that your buddy can join a multiparty video or audio chat. You can customize what details are displayed in the Buddy List and sort it by different criteria using the iChat AV View menu.

Bonjour and Jabber chatting, if active, open virtually identical windows displaying the active users on your local subnet and Jabber server, respectively.

Adding Buddies

Because your buddy list is stored on the AIM servers, you must be logged in to manage the list. To add a buddy, click the + button at the bottom of the iChat Buddy List window or choose Buddies, Add Buddy.

A dialog containing your Address Book entries appears, as shown in Figure 3.54. If the person you want to add to your Buddy List has an AIM or `Mac.com` listing, highlight the person and click Select Buddy.

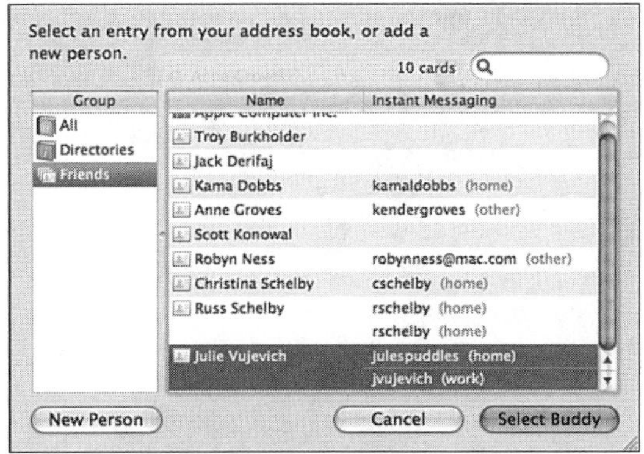

FIGURE 3.54 Add your AIM and .Mac buddies to your list.

If the person doesn't show an instant messaging name, you are prompted for the information. If the buddy-to-be isn't currently in your Address Book at all, click the New Person button to create a new entry. Enter the person's screen name, as well as his real name and email address in the window that appears. You can drag an image file (if available) into the image well to set a custom buddy icon. Click the Add button to save your new Buddy.

Address Book and iChat are integrated such that adding a new buddy to iChat automatically adds a new card in Address Book. However, because your buddy list is stored on the Instant Messenger server, you can't remove a buddy by deleting an Address Book card. Instead, you must select the buddy in the Buddy List and choose Buddies, Remove Buddy.

Also, keep in mind that deleting a buddy from the Buddy List does not remove the person's card from the Address Book.

Editing Buddy Info

To edit any information for a buddy that is already stored, select the buddy in the list; then choose Buddies, Get Info, or Control-click on the buddy herself and select Get Info. The Buddy Info, shown in Figure 3.55, provides quick access to your Address Book buddy information.

As with the initial setup, here you can set all the contact information for your buddy, as well as a custom buddy icon. If you *do* set a custom icon, you can choose to always use it in your buddy list. If this option is not set, your buddy icon can be overridden by any custom icon set on the remote system. Depending on how well you know your friends, this could lead to some embarrassment in the workplace.

Setting Buddy Actions

From the Get Info window, you can also access Buddy Actions by choosing Actions from the Show pop-up menu. A Buddy Action, displayed in Figure 3.56, is something that happens when one of your contacts becomes available or does something interesting.

FIGURE 3.55 Edit your buddies and override their ugly and/or horrifying icons.

FIGURE 3.56 Buddy actions automatically react when your contacts do something.

In this example, I've chosen to speak the text "Anne is here!" and bounce the Dock item repeatedly when my buddy becomes available. Additionally, by checking the box Perform Actions Only Next Time Event Occurs, the action automatically is removed after the first time it is used. I have something very important to say to Anne, but usually could care less whether she is online, thus the setting. (No, Anne, that isn't true, I'm just putting on airs for the reader.)

Seven possible events can be used to trigger a buddy action:

- Buddy Becomes Available—Your buddy has become available for instant messaging.
- Buddy Becomes Unavailable—Your buddy is no longer available for instant messaging.
- Message received—Your buddy has received an IM that you sent.
- Text Invitation—Your buddy has sent you a text chat invitation.
- Audio Invitation—Your buddy has sent you an audio chat invitation.
- Video Invitation—Your buddy has sent you a video chat invitation.
- Buddy Accepted A/V Invitation—Your buddy has accepted an A/V chat invitation that *you* have sent.

As you set actions for events, a megaphone icon appears beside the event that contains an action. This lets you keep track of what events trigger actions without having to select and inspect each one.

Before you ask, no, in the current release of iChat AV, there is no action for speaking the contents of the messages sent to you.

Viewing a Buddy's Capabilities and Profile

Much as you have capabilities (the ability to conduct audio chats, hold video conferences, basic ninja skills, and so on), so do your buddies. To get a summary of what IM capabilities a buddy on your list has along with a copy of their profile, select them in your buddy list, and then press Command+I to open the Get Info window. Next, use the Show menu to choose their account name, as seen in Figure 3.57.

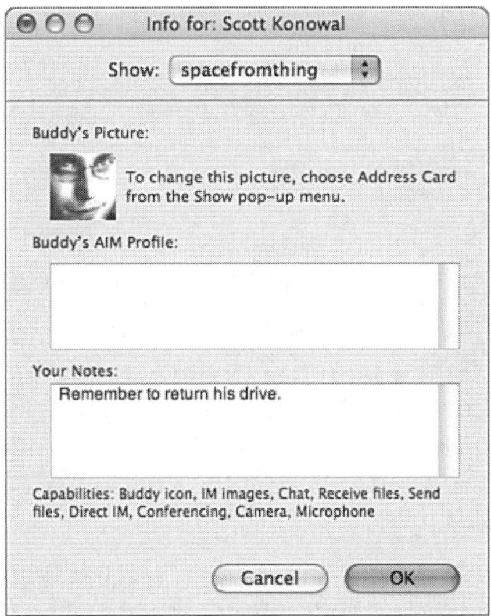

FIGURE 3.57 View the profile and capabilities of your buddies.

The profile is shown at the top of the window, following by a text area where you can type your own notes that will be stored locally. Finally, the supported IM features supported are at the bottom of the window. If you have problems communicating with one of the methods discussed in this chapter, chances are it is not an available capability.

Managing Buddy Groups

If you're the sort who actually has friends, you might find yourself with a long-scrolling list of buddies in your window. To better manage your buddy list, you can arrange them into groups such as "People I know," "People who are stalking me," and "People I am stalking." After creating the groups, you can choose which group or groups are displayed at once.

To access the groups feature of iChat AV choose View, Use Groups. Collapsible headings for each group appear in the Buddy List, as shown in Figure 3.58. Clicking the heading will toggle between hiding and showing the group members. A default group Buddies contains all your buddies.

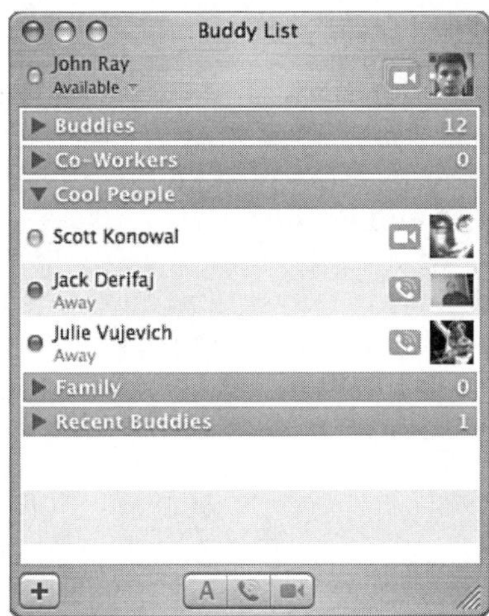

FIGURE 3.58 Arrange buddies into groups.

To add a new group, click the + button at the bottom of the Buddy List and choose Add Group. When prompted, type a name for the group and click Add. The empty group will be added to your buddy list.

To edit existing groups, click the + button again and choose Edit Groups to open a group management dialog box. Groups can be renamed by double-clicking their names in the list or selecting them and clicking Rename. Groups (and the buddies they contain) can be removed by selecting their name and clicking the - button. You can also add new groups within this view using the + button.

After adding a group, populate it with buddies by dragging their names in the Buddy List onto the group names. To remove a buddy from a group, drag the buddy back into the default Buddies group.

Blocking and Allowing Buddies

Your buddies are, presumably, actually your buddies—or at least people that you have some intention of talking to. If you're like me, however, you rarely want to talk to *everyone* all the time. iChat AV provides the ability to selectively choose who can see you are online and who can start a chat session with you. This information is configured on an account by account basis, meaning that different accounts can allow or block different people.

To configure your block/allow list, open the Accounts application preference pane, choose the account you want to configure, and then click the Security button, as shown in Figure 3.59.

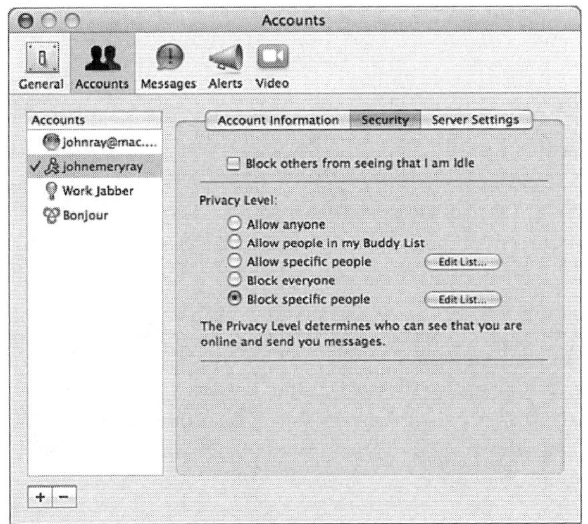

FIGURE 3.59 Set who can and can't chat with you.

By default, your IM account will allow anyone to see you are online and initiate a chat with you. Using the radio buttons, you can choose to be visible to those individuals you've added to your buddy list, or a specific list of people.

An alternative approach is to configure who is *blocked* rather than allowed. The block everyone button will prevent *anyone* from seeing you are online. The Block Specific People setting, on the other hand, will allow everyone except individuals that you choose.

To edit either the allow or block list, click the Edit List button. Use the + and - buttons in the dialog that appears to add and remove screen names from the list. Note that you *must* use the screen names in the allow/block lists, iChat will not warn you if you don't, but it will not work as expected.

Initiating IM and A/V Conferencing

In iChat AV, there are three types of messaging that you can choose to use to communicate with your friends: text, audio, and video—represented by the A, Phone, and Video camera icons at the bottom of your buddy list. To start a messaging session with one of your buddies, just select her name in the list and click the appropriate icon at the bottom of the Buddy List.

Alternatively, you can double-click your buddy's name to start a text chat, or click the telephone or video icon by her buddy picture to start an audio or video chat.

TIP

In the event you want to start a Text Chat *without* first adding the person to your buddy list, you can create a one-time chat with a nonbuddy by Choosing New Chat with Person (Shift+Command+N) from the File menu and typing the screen name of the person you want to chat with.

If your buddies' icons display multiple overlapping telephone and video camera icons, this indicates they can participate in a multiparty chat. If you are equipped to host a multiparty conference, select all the participants by Command+Clicking their buddy list entries, and then clicking the camera or phone icon at the bottom of the Buddy List. If not all the participants are available when you start the session, don't worry—you can add audio and video conference members on the fly at any time during the session.

NOTE

The iChat AV menu extra can also be used to start a chat session by choosing a buddy name from the menu. If the buddy has multiple means of communicating (besides simple text), iChat displays a window with three buttons (Text, Audio, Video) and allows you to choose your preferred chat method.

For those who want to mouse around and use their menus, the Buddies menu also allows you to initiate conferencing sessions—including two special chat types: one-way audio and one-way video. These are useful if you want to send audio or video to someone without a camera. They can type their responses to you and watch/hear your audio/video stream.

Now, let's take an in depth look at how each of the communications methods works they are initiated.

Communicating via Text Messaging

Starting a text messaging session opens an empty message window. Type your message in the field at the bottom of the window and press Return on your keyboard. If you're into sending emoticons (smiley faces) there is a convenient pull-down smiley menu on the right side of the input field. Basic formatting controls (Bold, Underline, Font, and so on) are found under the Format menu and can be used to style your text on-the-fly.

After sending your message, it appears in the upper portion of the window, along with whatever reply the other person sends. The text of a conversation can be saved by choosing File, Save a Copy As.

If you receive a message while not already engaged in a chat session with the sender, you are alerted, and a message window appears. If you click on the window, it displays an area for you to type a response (immediately accepting the invitation) or provides you the option of clicking Block to block the request and further messages from the buddy, Decline to turn down the chat with your buddy, or Accept to start chatting. Again, if you enter a response and press Return, it is assumed that you have accepted the chat.

You can add the person you're currently chatting with to your Buddy list using Buddies, Add Buddy or show their Address Book entry with Show in Address Book.

NOTE

If, during the course of a conversation, the remote party closes the connection or gets bumped offline, the chat window stays open. If they come back, a message to that effect appears in the already open window, and you can resume the conversation where you left off.

Customizing the Chat Window Appearance

If you find the conversation bubbles cute but overwhelming (or perhaps just downright annoying), you can use View, Show as Text to disable them (and Show as Balloons to turn them back on when your Windows friends are over). You can also customize the font and font and color for both your and your buddies' messages.

Further chat window View settings include the option to choose how buddies are identified in a chat (using their pictures, names, or both), the capability to set a customized picture as the chat background, and finally the option to clear the background picture after you've decided that it is way too silly a feature to enable.

Sending and Receiving Files

In addition to sending ordinary text messages, iChat allows you to send files. To send a file, drag its icon into the message area of a chat window and press Return on your keyboard. The recipient can then drag the file onto his desktop. If you send image files, they appear inside the chat window as part of the conversation. (For maximum compatibility with people using AIM programs other than iChat, it's recommended that you stick with JPEG and GIF image formats.)

NOTE

You can force a confirmation before a file is sent by choosing Confirm Before Sending Files in the Messages pane of the application preferences.

When you find yourself on the receiving end of a file transfer, the file will appear as a small icon with link in your iChat message window. Clicking the link will open a status window that displays the copy progress. By default, all downloads are made to the Desktop folder. This can be changed in the General application preference pane.

Sending and Receiving Links

Hyperlinks can also be sent as a special iChat object. To send a hyperlink, drag the bookmark from your browser, use the Edit, Add Hyperlink option to enter in a clickable URL, or just type or paste it in, and the URL will automatically be recognized.

If you receive a link in an instant message, it will appear as underlined text, just like a web browser. Click the link to open the URL in your default browser.

Direct Messages

AIM messages are not (usually) a direct line of communication between people. Instead, all IM traffic is routed through instant messaging servers, in the case of AIM—AOL's servers. Although this conveniently avoids many connection problems with firewalls and inbound traffic, it also leads to privacy concerns about who could potentially be watching your chat. In addition, the extra time required to transmit through a central server can slow file transfers between individuals. To avoid this, users can activate a direct instant messaging session where all information is passed directly between the participants' computers.

To do this, choose the buddy to send a direct IM to, and choose Buddies, Send Direct Message (Command-Option-Shift-M). If both you and the recipient are connected directly to the Internet, an IM session starts, exactly as it would through the AOL servers.

TIP

When first starting a messaging session, you can choose between direct messaging, normal IM messaging, and a multiparty Chat (discussed next), using View, Chat Options. You will be prompted for the mode that will be used for the duration of the session.

Multiparty Chat Sessions

As you've probably guessed, you can easily participate in chats with different people simultaneously, but each chat session would be in its own separate window. You can also start a chat session with multiple people where all participants can see messages and type simultaneously.

To start a group chat:

1. Highlight the buddies you want to invite to chat; then Control-click on any of the names and choose Invite To Chat, or just click the A button at the bottom of the
2. Type a message inviting the participants. When the invited buddies receive the chat request, they can choose to accept or decline. If they accept, they can send and receive messages as part of the group.

To add additional buddies to a chat, use the + button at the bottom of the participants drawer to select their name, as seen in Figure 3.60.

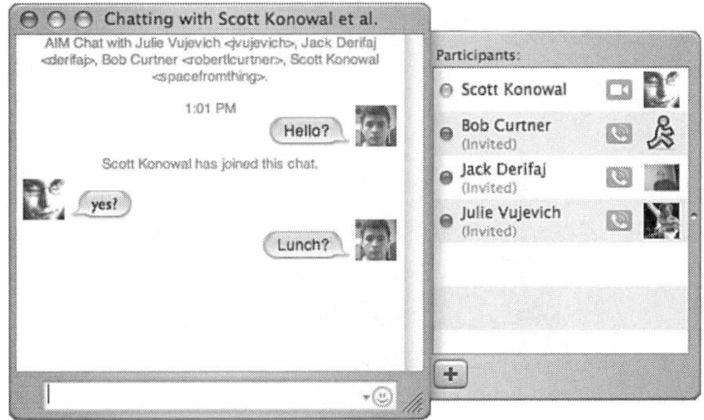

FIGURE 3.60 Start multiperson chats in iChat AV.

All multiparty chats are given a Chat Name that can be used by any AIM user to join the chat, even if they aren't on your buddy list. To choose a Chat name, select View, Chat Options and type a Chat Name in the provided field.

To join a chat given the Chat Name, choose File, Go To Chat and enter the Chat Name. Other AIM clients should offer the same feature, but how it is accessed obviously will vary.

Creating/Joining a Persistent Chat Room

The Go To Chat feature can also be used to create a persistent Chat room that other users can join. To start a persistent chat choose File, Go To Chat (Command-G). When prompted, type the name of an existing chat room (if you want to join a chat someone else has created), or make up your own name. The iChat AV chat window appears with *no* participants. Others can join your chat room using the Go To Chat feature on their copy of iChat AV.

> **NOTE**
>
> Some chat names (including those with punctuation) are unacceptable when creating a chat room. If iChat AV does not return a chat window immediately on using Go To Chat, the name you typed is invalid.

Saving Chat/Messaging Transcripts

To save the contents of a chat to a text file, choose File, Save a Copy As from the menu bar. This will create a file that you can later open and review in iChat by choosing File, Open. If you prefer, you can automatically save transcripts of all your text chats by choosing Automatically Save Chat Transcripts in the Messages pane of the application preferences.

Conversing via Audio Chats

Believe it or not, it's actually *easier* to describe the options for audio and video chats than it is for text messaging. When an audio chat has been initiated, a window containing the names and icons of each of the participants appears. Beside each conference member is a volume meter; as the person speaks, the meter flashes, making it easy to determine who is talking at any given point in time. A multiparty audio conference is shown in progress in Figure 3.61.

FIGURE 3.61 The audio chat window displays the microphone input level for each participant along with add participant, mute, and volume controls.

> **NOTE**
>
> An audio conference begins as soon as the first participant accepts the invitation. The conversation can carry on while iChat waits for other invitees to join.

At the bottom of the conference window is your own volume input meter along with controls for adding participants, muting your microphone, and controlling the output volume of your speaker.

> **NOTE**
>
> If you are only conversing with a single person, iChat will only display your input level and volume controls—presumably you can guess who is speaking on the other end. ☺

The input level meter can be used to gauge whether your microphone is positioned correctly, or whether you need to adjust the input level (gain) within the Sound System Preferences Pane. An iSight user in an average office environment should see 1/8-1/4-inch of flicker (background noise) on the left side of the bar. If background noise approaches 1/3-inch or 1/2-inch of the bar length, you might need to reduce the gain or find a quieter place to chat.

During a chat, you can adjust the volume using the chat window's volume slider, or quickly mute the conversation (so that you can swear loudly) by clicking the crossed-out microphone button.

If the volume is too high, you might experience feedback as the microphone starts to pick up the speaker sounds. You can fix this by lowering your gain, lowering the volume, or positioning the microphone farther away from your speaker.

NOTE

To change the sound input source (if more than one is available) for your machine, use the Microphone pop-up menu in the Video pane of the application preferences.

Inviting Additional Audio Chat Participants

To invite additional members to an audio chat, click the + button in the audio window and choose the audio-enabled member from the pop-up list. You can only add participants that meet the minimum requirements for an audio chat—meaning they have Tiger and at least a 1GHz G4 (or dual 800MHz G4).

If you start an audio chat with a user that doesn't support multiparty conferencing, you will not be able to add additional members.

Responding to an Audio Chat Request

If you are on the receiving end of an audio chat request, you are prompted with an incoming chat alert (similar to an incoming text message) and, after the alert window is clicked, given the option of accepting or declining the chat—or making a *text* reply. If you choose a text reply, you effectively open a new text chat with the remote party, and the audio chat is canceled.

TIP

Even if your buddy doesn't have an audio input source, you can still have a one-sided audio rant at him. Use the Buddies, Invite to One-Way Audio Chat option to start a one-way chat. It's great for setting things straight with your significant other.

Conducting Video Chats

A video chat works virtually identically to an audio chat but with the added bonus of being able to *see* as well as hear the remote participants. When a video chat is initiated, you see a preview of yourself until the chat is accepted. In the case of a single-part chat, after a connection has been established, your image shrinks to the lower-right corner of the window, and your buddy's smiling face fills the rest of the window.

You can resize your mini preview by moving your cursor over it and then dragging the resize handle that appears. You can also click and drag the mini preview to any of the four corners of the window.

Multiparty chats are a bit more interesting, as seen in Figure 3.62. When multiple individuals are invited to a chat, each person's image is displayed as a 3D panel surrounding the smaller image of yourself. The effect is similar to sitting at a table with your colleagues. You can see them and they can see you without having to search the screen for a window with their picture.

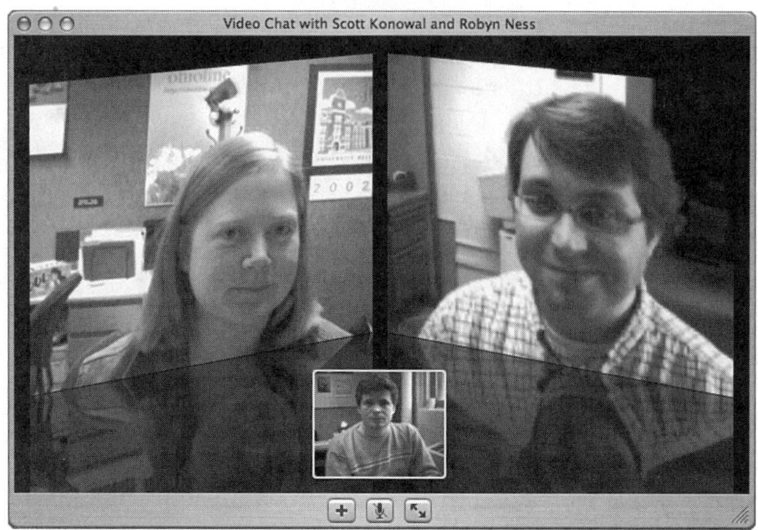

FIGURE 3.62 Video chats—be seen and heard.

> **TIP**
>
> To take a picture of a video conference, choose Video, Take Snapshot (Option+Command+S).

At the bottom of the video chat window is a microphone button for muting the audio portion of chat and a button with two opposing arrows for expanding the view to fill the whole screen (Control+Command+F). The + button is also present and active in multi-party-capable chats and can but clicked to display a menu allowing you to invite another person to the conference. Up to four (including yourself) individuals can participate in a video conference simultaneously.

> **NOTE**
>
> Apple has done an excellent job of smoothing the scaled video when in full-screen mode or when the video window is enlarged. If you haven't tried scaling the video because you're not a fan of pixelized images, give it a try anyway—it's impressive.

When in full-screen mode, moving the mouse displays several button controls above your preview image: an X to close the chat, a microphone to mute, and double arrows to shrink back to a windowed view. Again, use the drag handle that appears in the upper-left corner of the preview to resize your own image onscreen or click and drag the entire mini preview window to move it to another corner.

To pause the video display at any time, use Video, Pause Video.

Responding to a Video Chat Request

When receiving a video chat request, clicking the alert window gives you a preview of your own video feed so that you can make sure that you've dressed yourself properly before clicking the Accept button to start the chat. Like the audio chat, you can also decline a chat request or send a text reply instead of video.

Applying Parental Controls

As with Mail, if you have children, you probably want to know who they are chatting with or at least protect them from unwanted chat requests. To set parental controls for non-administrative user accounts, open the Accounts system preference panel, select the user you want to restrict, and click the Parental Controls button. Click the Configure button to create a buddy list for the account, as shown in Figure 3.63.

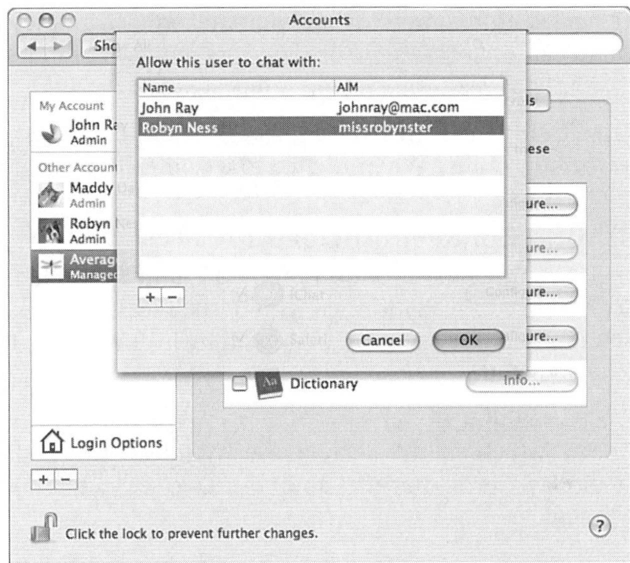

FIGURE 3.63 The iChat parental controls can protect your children from inappropriate conversations.

Use the + button to open an address book window and select an address book entry with an AIM account or create a new entry. This works identically to the process of setting up your own buddy list, discussed earlier in the chapter. To remove buddies, click the - button. When finished, click OK; the account is now restricted.

NOTE

While we appreciate the effort Apple has put into parental controls, we feel it is important that communicate *why* these restrictions are necessary with your children. It is impossible to block everything from reaching them. A solid education and understanding of the nature of the Internet will help them protect themselves.

Setting Event Alerts

iChat is a great way to converse with friends and family, especially if you have a computer that is always on. In the default iChat configuration, however, you have to pay attention to your screen to see who is logged in or what is going on—not very helpful for an always-on communications tool. To change this, Alerts can be set to notify you of events such as logins and logouts.

Under the Alerts pane of the application preferences, choose what iChat does when you or your buddies log in or out. Use the Event pop-up menu to choose an event to modify; then click the check boxes for the actions you want to apply, such as playing sounds, speaking text, and bouncing icons. This is similar to the individual Buddy Actions discussed earlier but applies to *everyone* not just a specific person.

Turning Repeated Ring On and Off

When a conference request first comes it, your computer will ring...and ring...and ring...and ring.... If you absolutely despise hearing this sound over and over, Apple provides a way to force the iChat from playing it repeatedly.

Within the Video application preference pane (great location for an alert setting, isn't it?) uncheck Play Repeated Ring Sound When Invited to a Conference.

Diagnostics with the Connection Doctor

Depending on you and your buddies' connections, video and audio chats might be a bit choppy or sporadic. As you've already learned, you need at least a 1000kbps upstream connection to host a multiparty video chat. If something isn't working, it could very well be a lack of network bandwidth.

To get an idea of the throughput of your connection, choose Video, Connection Doctor. The Connection Doctor (which doesn't really make anything better) is displayed in Figure 3.64. There are two display views—Statistics and Error Log, selected using the Show menu at the top of the window.

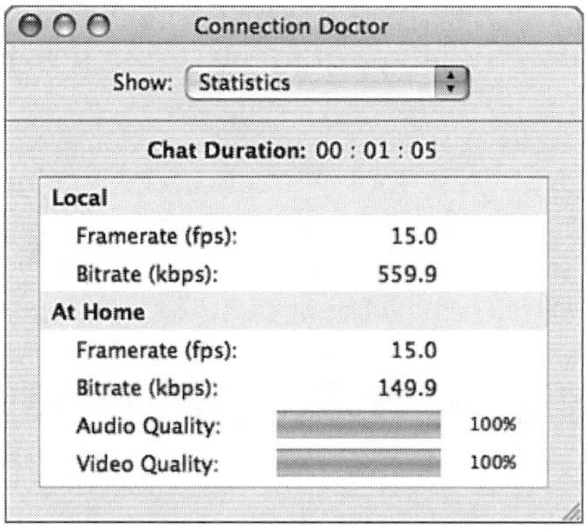

FIGURE 3.64 The Connection Doctor displays stats on your current A/V connection.

Watch the audio and video quality during the conversation. If they are not in the 90–100% range, you might have an unsatisfactory conferencing experience. The bitrate measurement will tell you exactly how much data is being sent locally and remotely.

Adjusting Bandwidth

Some choppiness problems can be rectified by limiting the amount of data being streamed to your chat partner. Usually iChat AV determines the proper streaming rate automatically, but in some cases you might want to try setting the value yourself. To do this, use the Video preferences pane within the iChat AV preferences, shown in Figure 3.65.

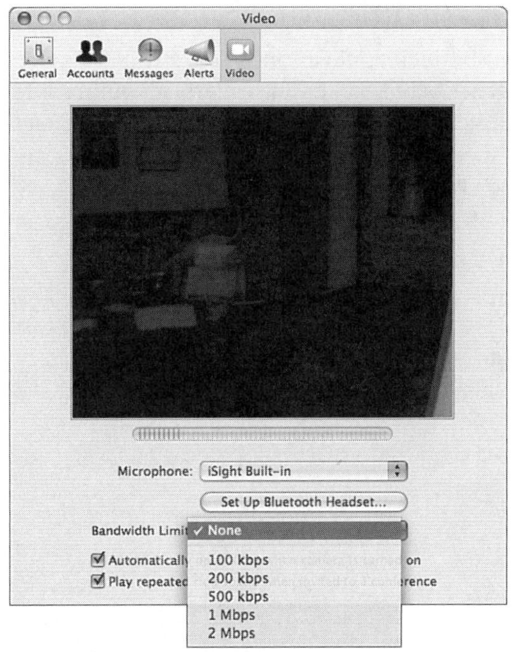

FIGURE 3.65 Adjust your iChat AV preferences.

The bandwidth limit is initially set to *none*, meaning that iChat attempts to stream data as quickly as possible to the remote site. You can limit the bandwidth to anywhere from 100kbps to 2Mbps. Low-end (ISDN) connections should restrict the bandwidth to 100kbps, whereas cable and xDSL users might be able to get away with 200kbps or possibly 500kbps. (For those saying "hey, my cable modem can max out at 3Mbps!"—that's true but is almost always the *downstream* speed. Upstream rates usually range from 192kbps to 500kbps.) Only local or high bandwidth (T1/T3/ATM) connections should attempt the upper settings.

Firewalls and Connection Errors

The Connection Doctor can also be used to view errors that occur in making the connection to remote audio and video chat partners. To view the error log, open the connection doctor and choose Error Log from the Show menu. IChat AV will display all the connections it attempted to make and what failed.

Most often, failure of a conference is due to a firewall conflict. iChat AV's audio and video features work well as long as *one side* of a connection is not behind a firewall or connection sharing device. To use video/audio conferencing behind a firewall, you must enable ports 5060 UDP (conference notifications) and 16384-16403 UDP (audio and video) to be passed through to the iChat AV computer. To read Apple's tech note on this topic, visit `http://docs.info.apple.com/article.html?artnum=93208`.

Searching the Internet: Sherlock

As its name implies, the Sherlock application is something of a detective, tracking down information on the Internet based on the information you provide. Sherlock is *not* a search engine but an application that provides a common interface to many different types of searches. With specialized categories including yellow pages and a dictionary, Sherlock can quickly become your one-stop reference tool.

Choosing a Search Channel

Sherlock packages an Internet search as an element called a *channel*. The default channels are listed in the toolbar at the top of the Sherlock window and in the Channels menu, as shown in Figure 3.66. Choosing a channel refreshes the screen to display the search options appropriate for that channel.

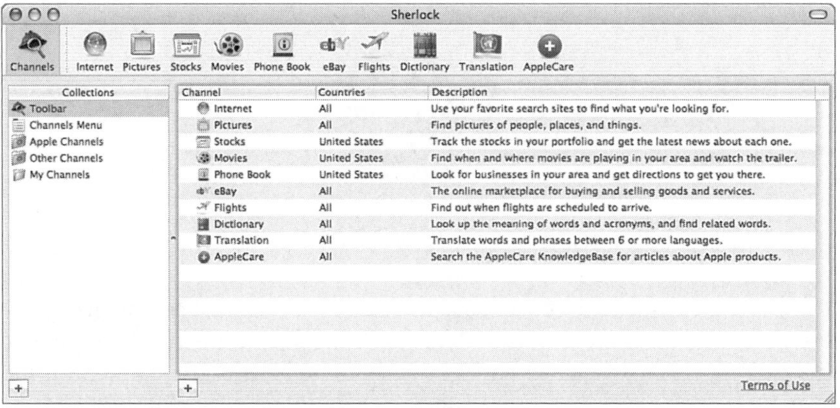

FIGURE 3.66 Choose a channel to search.

NOTE

Apple *does not* generate the information returned by Sherlock. If there are inconsistencies in the results, they are the product of the search provider, usually displayed at the bottom of each search channel pane.

Let's take a look at each of the included channel's use and special features.

Internet

The Internet channel compiles search results from popular Internet search sites, such as About and Lycos. To perform an Internet search, type your search terms into the text entry field at the top of the Internet channel pane and click the green search button or press Return. When the results listing appears, you can select an entry with a single click to see a site description if one is available. Double-clicking launches your default web browser and opens the page you requested. A sample search is shown in Figure 3.67.

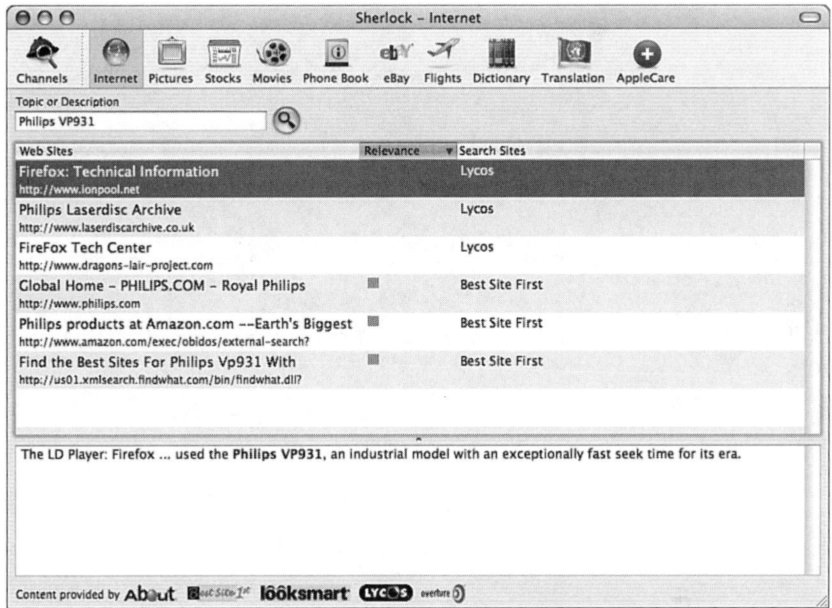

FIGURE 3.67 Quickly search a variety of information sources.

Pictures

The Pictures channel queries image databases for digital pictures based on your search terms. Thumbnail images of the results are displayed in the results pane. Double-click a thumbnail opens a web page displaying the full-sized picture.

CAUTION

The photos displayed in the Pictures channel searches might not be free for commercial use. Read the terms of service from the originating site if you have any questions about what's allowed.

Stocks

The Stocks channel, shown in Figure 3.68, provides details about the market performance of publicly traded companies. The information shown includes the stock price at last trade, price change, price range over the course of the day, and the volume of shares traded. You can also view charts of a company's performance over the past year or week or for the current day.

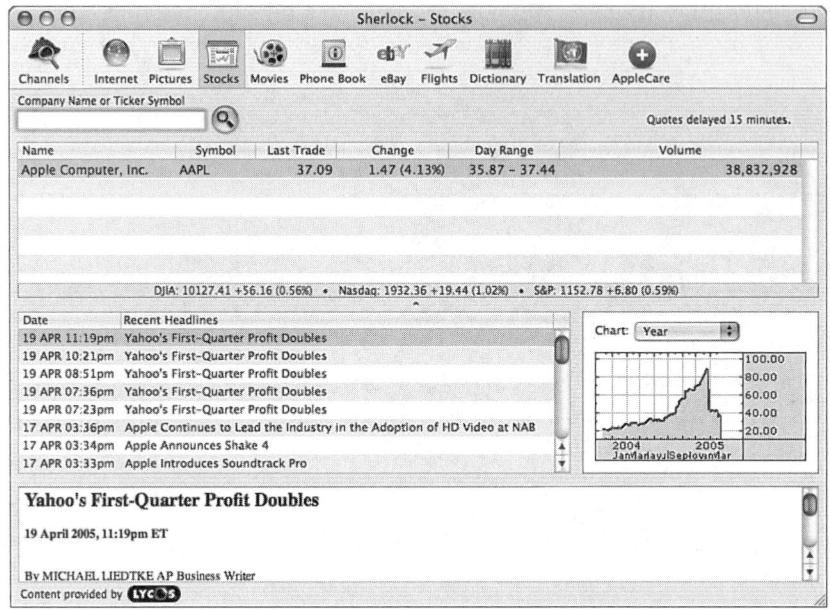

FIGURE 3.68 Enter a company's name or market symbol to see information about it, including recent news stories.

To find information about a company, enter its name or market symbol. Market symbols are unique identifiers, but many companies have similar names or several separate divisions. If you enter a name with multiple entries, Sherlock will present a sheet asking you to choose the company you're interested in. Choose the appropriate name or symbol, and then click the green search button or press the Return key.

As you view information for different companies, they are added to the list at the top of the Stocks pane so that you can quickly return to them. To remove a listing, select it and press the Delete key on your keyboard.

In addition to providing stock quotes, Sherlock also displays recent news articles pertaining to the selected company. To read a story, select its headline to the left of the chart, and the bottom pane displays the full text.

Movies

Sherlock's Movies channel pulls together all the information you need to choose a movie and a theater where you can watch it.

To use the Movies channel, enter either your city and state or your ZIP Code in the Find Near field, or just use the default Address Book entry denoted by your name. Next, choose to search either Movies or Theaters in your area. The Showtime pop-up menu allows you to choose the date of interest to you.

Choose the movie and theater listings at the top of the pane that are of interest to you, and the bottom of the window fills with theater and movie information. In addition to a text summary of the movie, you can watch a preview for the selected option in QuickTime, demonstrated in Figure 3.69.

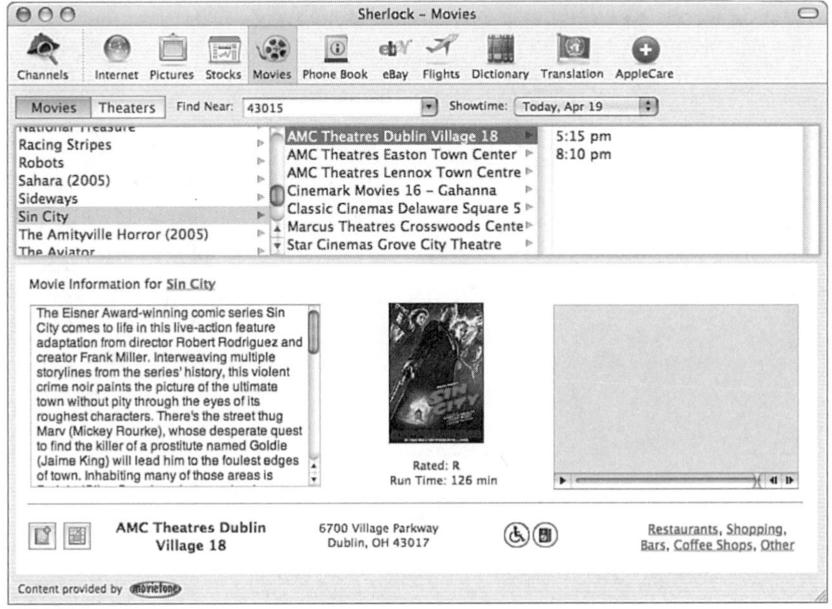

FIGURE 3.69 Choose your movie, your location, get showtimes, and watch the trailer.

> **NOTE**
>
> To play the QuickTime preview, you might be prompted to set your network connection information in QuickTime Preferences if you haven't already done so.

At the bottom left of the Movies channel you might see two additional buttons: the first adds the theater to your Address Book; the second uses the Phone Book channel (discussed next) to map the theater location.

Phone Book

The Phone Book channel has two modes: a person search (a la white pages) and a business search (a la Yellow Pages).

The person search mode, shown in Figure 3.70, allows you to find a phone number and address by entering a person's name and a general location. To perform a person search, click the information button at the upper left (the one with an i in a white circle). Enter a last name, a first name, and either the city and state or the ZIP Code of the area to search. Then click the green search button. In the middle pane, choose from among the list of potential matches to see detailed information, including a map.

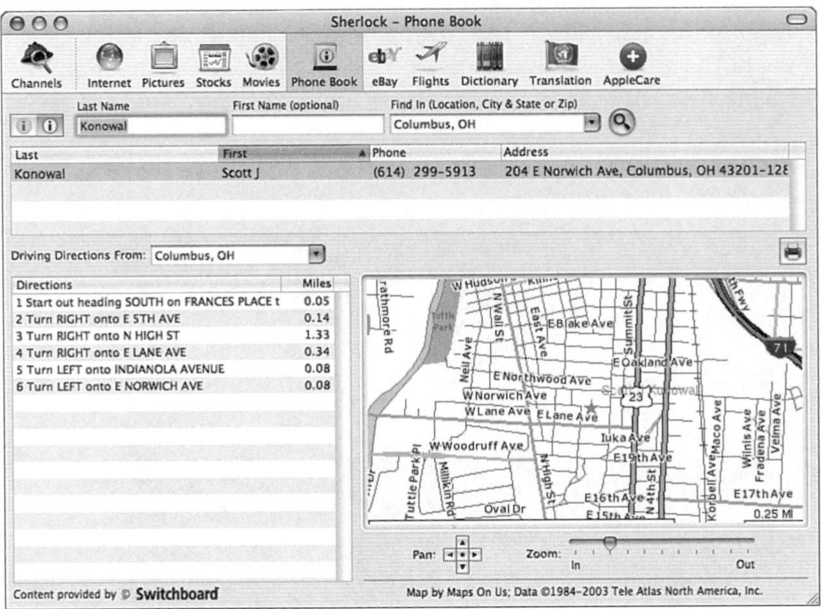

FIGURE 3.70 Locate a person by name and location.

> **NOTE**
>
> As you type in the Find Near field, Sherlock attempts to autocomplete the city, state, and ZIP Code for you.

Use the business search to obtain the phone number and address for businesses and to view a map of to their locations. Simply click the information button on the right (the one with an i in a yellow circle), enter the business name and either the city and state or the ZIP Code of the area to search, and click the green search button. In the middle pane, choose from among the list of potential matches to see detailed information.

> **NOTE**
>
> To receive driving directions to addresses retrieved in either the person or business search, you need to enter an address in text field labeled Driving Directions From, or choose your name for your Address Book address. The Directions pane fills with step-by-step instructions.

eBay

From the eBay channel, you can search active eBay auctions and track those of interest to you. To search, enter keywords in the Item Title text entry field and set your other parameters, such as product category, region, and price range, and then click the search button. When you choose a result from the search, its details are displayed in the bottom of the window, as shown in Figure 3.71.

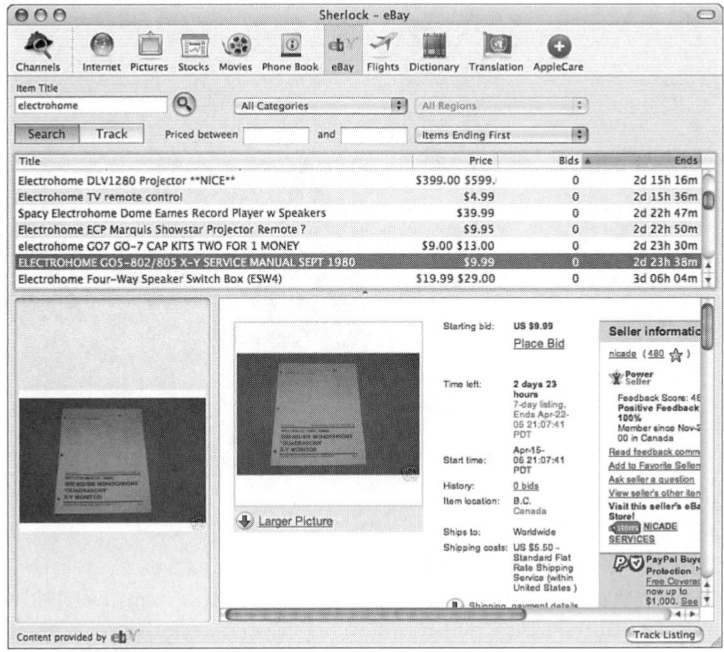

FIGURE 3.71 If you enjoy online auctions, the eBay channel will feed your addiction.

To track an item, highlight it in the results listing and click the Track Listing button at lower right. Changing to Track mode using the button just below the search field reveals a list of only those items you're tracking. To remove an item, select it and press the Delete key on your keyboard.

Flights

For information on current flights, go to the Flights channel. Here you can view flight status by route or by airline and flight number. Select a specific flight for details about the aircraft and flight. For some entries, you can also view a chart depicting the plane's position en route, as shown in the lower-right corner of Figure 3.72.

You can click the small switch-like button at the bottom right of the Flights pane to set preferences for the Flights channel. Choose airlines and airports by continent on which to focus your searches.

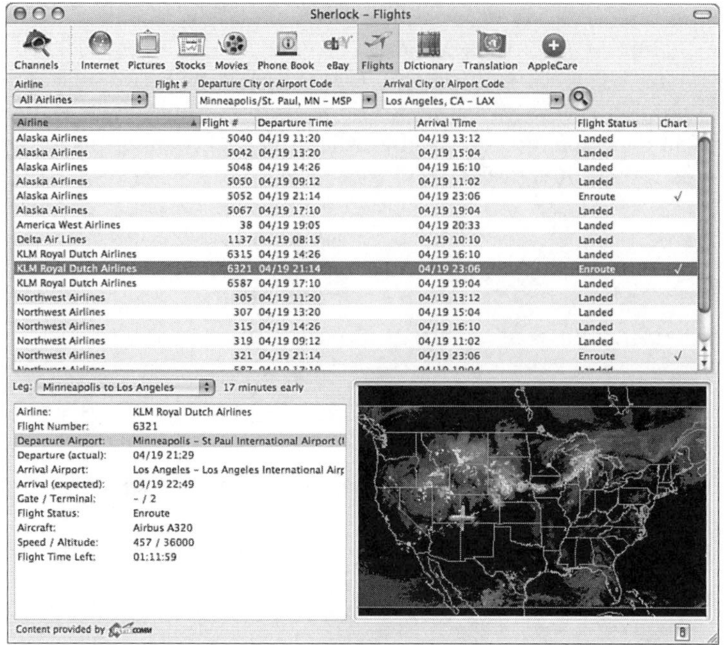

FIGURE 3.72 View the status of specific flights, including a chart of the flight path.

Dictionary

As you might expect, you look up definitions in the Dictionary channel. For some words, you also see a list of phrases in the lower half of the pane that contain that word or relate to it. Clicking the Pronunciation Key link opens Dictionary.com's pronunciation symbol key in your default browser.

Translation

The Translation channel rough translations between different languages. English speakers can translate into simplified and traditional Chinese, Dutch, French, German, Greek, Italian, Japanese, Korean, Portuguese, Russian, and Spanish, and then back to English.

To translate text, type or paste the original text into the top text field, choose an option for translating the original language into another language, and click the Translate button.

When using this service, keep in mind that computer-generated translations do not match the output of a skilled human translator.

AppleCare

If you have a specific technical question about Apple software or hardware, use the AppleCare channel to search the AppleCare Knowledge Base for reports about Apple products and issues.

> **NOTE**
>
> The functionality of several of the Sherlock tools (Dictionary, Translation, Phone Book, Flights) is now available (in flashier style) through Dashboard Widgets. Additionally, Tiger's Help Center searches the AppleCare database for relevant articles when attempting to locate help by keyword.
>
> Use the interface you're most comfortable with to access the information you need.

Expanding Search Options with Third-Party Channels

In addition to the channels you've seen so far in this chapter, which are maintained by Apple, many channels are written by others to view information on topics ranging from news to astrology and song lyrics to television listings.

To access third-party channels, click the Channels button at the upper left of the Sherlock toolbar to open the Channels Collection pane. This is *very* similar to the Bookmarks Library in Safari. Each collection contains searches. The Toolbar collection, for example, contains the default searches we just reviewed—those found in the Sherlock Toolbar.

Choose Other Channels to display the available third party offerings. As seen in Figure 3.73, a plethora of channels appears in the right-hand column along with the countries to which they apply and a brief description.

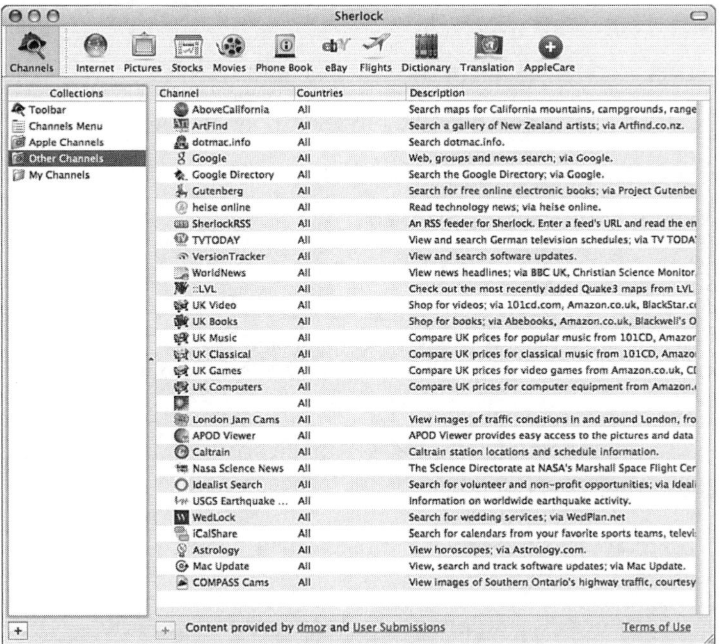

FIGURE 3.73 The list of channels created outside Apple.

To use one of these channels, simply double-click its list entry. Each channel has its own interface to support the information it displays; you have to follow the cues in the channel's interface to figure out what information is provided and how to perform a search. If you like what you see, you can add the channel to a collection in order to return to it easily. We'll look at Sherlock Channel collections now.

> **CAUTION**
>
> The quality of third-party channels varies greatly. Some are very helpful, whereas others merely frustrate. They're all free, however, so it doesn't hurt to try.
>
> Another consideration, for the security conscious, are cookies. Channels might or might not require cookies in order to operate. If you're not a "cookie" kind of person, open the Sherlock application preferences to disable cookies completely.

Managing Channel Collections

The method used in the preceding section to access the third-party channels provides a glimpse at how you can manage a collection of Sherlock channels. Clicking the Channels icon in the upper-left corner of the Sherlock window opens the Channels Collection, as seen previously.

Along the left side of the window are channel collections. Each collection contains one or more Sherlock channels, viewed by highlighting the collection name in the Collections list. There are four collections by default:

- Toolbar—Channels displayed in the Sherlock toolbar
- Channels Menu—Channels displayed in the Channels menu
- Apple Channels—Channels provided by Apple
- Other Channels—Third-party channels
- My Channels—An empty collection ready for your use

To create a new custom collection, click the + button at the bottom of the collection list. A new untitled collection folder appears. You can change the name immediately or double-click it at any time to provide a new label.

To add channels to the collection drag the channel icons from one of the channel collections (such as Other Channels) to your custom collection folder. After organizing the collection the way you want, you can even drag the collection folders themselves to the Toolbar collection to add them directly to the Sherlock toolbar, or to the Channels Menu collection to add them as a submenu of the Channels menu.

Again, like Safari, Sherlock also supports subfolders within a collection. The + button below the channel listing can be used to add a subfolder to a collection. Channels can be dragged to the subfolder to further organize your searches.

The Enigma That Is .Mac

Completing the Tiger Internet access suite is .Mac—Apple's $100 subscription-based Mac add on. Apple has had a reasonably difficult time selling .Mac as being a necessary part of Mac OS X. Apple has integrated the operating system with some of its features (as we'll see shortly) but hasn't done a good job of convincing users that they need it. In Tiger, the integration is tighter than before, but its still debatable as to whether it is a must-have product for Mac users.

Defining .Mac

Part of Apple's problem is that .Mac is not well defined. If you don't subscribe to the service, yet use a Mac on a daily basis, you're probably not feeling like there's anything missing from your operating system (except perhaps Windowshades, tabbed Finder windows, System Sounds, and so on...). Apple itself doesn't seem to know what .Mac is, other than a renewable revenue stream.

The easiest way to define .Mac is to enumerate the features it offers:

- Network storage (iDisk)—The .Mac iDisk offers 250MB of network-accessible storage. Using your iDisk, you can access your files from other machines or even share them with friends. Based on the lightweight WebDAV protocol (which runs over HTTP), iDisk is fast, cross-platform, and less susceptible to network issues such as firewalls.

> **TIP**
>
> See Chapter 23 for information on setting up Apache to act as your own WebDAV server.

- Synchronization services—.Mac, in conjunction with iSync, provides a means for all your Macs to share the same bookmarks, Contacts, Keychains, Mail accounts, and calendars. Instead of maintaining two sets of bookmarks/etc on your desktop and laptop, a single global set is maintained and synchronized through .Mac.
- Network-based Mac OS X information—A .Mac account can hold information that you normally access through applications on your computer and make it available to you through a network connection wherever you are. Calendars, Contacts, and Bookmarks are currently available with additional "access it anywhere" services in development. The .Mac screensaver (discussed shortly) even allows you to view slideshows stored on remote users' iDisks.
- .Mac email—Apple-hosted email services, including a nice web interface, are included as part of the subscription. Additional accounts with a smaller quota can be added to a .Mac account for a small fee.
- Exclusive software—Although not earth-shattering, Apple is currently offering two pieces of .Mac members only software: Virex (virus protection) and Apple's own Backup (personal document backups). These pieces of software are actually a good value if you need the functionality they offer. (See Chapter 29, "Maintaining a Healthy System," for more information on Backup.) If you were, for example,

planning to buy a Virus protection package for $50 already, that's half the cost of a .Mac subscription.

- Family-oriented Web services—The .Mac website makes it easy to create custom websites—either using files from your iDisk, or simply by exporting them from within iPhoto. Users can also send iCards created with your own or professionally photographed images.
- Training—Basic Macintosh tutorials and training materials are available online for common family/consumer activities such as using iTunes, creating web pages, and so on. These features are definitely geared toward beginners.
- Software discounts—Special software discounts are offered for select packages, such as children's games. Again, this feature of Mac.com is offered primarily for the benefit of home users. Power users expecting to find a 50% discount on DOOM 3 are going to be sorely disappointed (prove me wrong Apple, please).

TIP

Apple lists iChat as one of the .Mac features. iChat, however, is available for anyone's use. A .Mac account gets you the ability to use your .Mac email address as your buddy name; however, even if you just sign up for a demo account, you get to keep the account name and can use it with iChat indefinitely.

Because describing how to use a website (`http//www.mac.com`) is not the purpose of this book (and the information contained on the site is variable in nature), we won't attempt to document the features that you access through your web browser. Instead, we'll look at how .Mac's Tiger-integrated features are used then take a brief walkthrough of the web services so that you can make the decision of whether you want to join the .Mac club.

NOTE

If you intend to rely on .Mac for mission-critical (or life-critical) email, check around to make sure that it offers the availability and reliability that you need. Although I personally have experienced .Mac outages rarely throughout my use (which is extremely light), they do happen. Some users have experienced email outages that last for days. At present, Apple's .Mac status pages rarely reflect these problems or communicate a solution.

Setting Up .Mac Service

To set up your .Mac services, open the System Preferences application and click the .Mac pane. Your screen should resemble Figure 3.74.

Your choices are limited: Either enter your existing .Mac member name and password, or click the Sign Up button to create a new account. If signing up for the first time, your web browser is launched, and you are taken to the `http://www.mac.com` signup page. Keep in mind that you don't need to commit to a full account immediately. You can apply for a 60-day free trial and try the members-only features (except for the exclusive software) before you buy.

FIGURE 3.74 Configure or create .Mac services in the .Mac preferences pane.

If you already have a .Mac account, enter your information in the appropriate fields, and then press Enter. The system will verify your account and display a Password Valid message—assuming that it is.

Using the iDisk

The Apple iDisk is really just a WebDAV share that your system automatically knows how to connect to without additional information. If you're used to working with AppleShare, NFS, or CIFS servers and you connect to network resources regularly, there are few surprises. iDisk requires a network connection and is *barely* usable on dial-in lines. Cable or DSL should be considered the minimum tolerable network requirement for making a connection.

iDisk does have one feature that sets it apart from a normal network share—the capability to keep a local copy of its contents that are synchronized automatically when you connect to the Internet. This means that you always have an up-to-date offline copy of the files in case you don't have Internet access.

From the perspective of the end user, iDisk synchronization is entirely transparent—your iDisk appears like any other disk whether working with the contents online or using the local copy. As you make changes to the files, they are noted and automatically uploaded to the .Mac server in the background. You can also choose to manually synchronize files if you want.

iDisk Storage Space and Settings

You can customize how your iDisk works and view a quick status of how much space is available by clicking the iDisk button within the .Mac system preferences pane. The pane shown in Figure 3.75 is displayed.

FIGURE 3.75 Configure your iDisk and view the space available.

At the top of the pane is the amount of storage currently in use and the total available. You can buy additional iDisk storage space by clicking the Buy More button. Additional iDisk space is sold, like .Mac, on a subscription basis.

Here you can also turn synchronization on and off and choose where it should happen automatically or be performed manually. If you do *not* start Syncing, the iDisk will only be accessible over the Internet; You cannot work with the contents without an active network connection.

NOTE

If you ever choose to shut off synchronization after it has been running, Tiger will move the disk image file it has been using as the local iDisk copy to your desktop. You can mount it to get at the contents or throw it away if you want.

TIP

iDisk synchronization features make some big assumptions: You have a reasonably fast Internet connection, and you make small changes to the contents of your iDisk. If you find yourself replacing 100MB of files daily, synchronization is just going to eat up time and network bandwidth.

If you *always* have a fast connection and don't access your iDisk files that much anyway, not using the local iDisk option might be the most efficient options.

If synchronization takes a long time each time you use it (dial-in users), you might want to set it to Manually and only start a synchronize when you aren't going to be using your computer heavily.

Also in the iDisk pane are controls for determining how your public folder is accessed. The iDisk public folder is a special directory on the iDisk that can be read by other Mac OS X users without needing your .Mac login information. You can use the Public folder as a place to exchange files with a few people, or perhaps release a new piece of software you've written to the world.

To keep things under your control, Apple provides the option of choosing whether other users (that is, not you) have read-only or read-write access to your folder, and whether the folder should be password protected. If you choose to password protect the folder, you are prompted to set a new password; *do not* use your .Mac password. This is a password that you give out to your friends so that they can connect to your Public folder.

CAUTION

First and foremost, do not store copyrighted/pirated material in your Public folder; this should be obvious.

Second, if you enable read/write access to your Public folder, be aware that you've turned over a portion of your iDisk storage space to the public. If your public folder is filled, it counts against your 250MB iDisk total.

Accessing and Synchronizing Your iDisk

After entering the membership information needed to connect to your iDisk, you can immediately start using the service by opening a Finder window and then clicking the iDisk icon in the sidebar or by choosing Go, iDisk, My iDisk from the Finder menu (Shift-Command-I). After a few seconds, the iDisk icon (a blue orb) appears on your desktop and/or in your Finder Sidebar.

If this is the first time that you've used your iDisk (and you haven't configured it otherwise), Tiger prompts you to synchronize the entire contents of your iDisk before going any further. If you intend to keep the disk synchronized, allowing the initial synchronization is a good idea. It might take a while at first, but subsequent syncs will only need to copy the data that has changed, if any.

You can force synchronization at any time by clicking the chasing arrow (circular arrows) icon to the right of the iDisk icon in the Finder. If you've chosen to have your Mac automatically synchronize the iDisk, you can tell when the synchronization is in progress by watching the icon to the right of the iDisk in your Finder window; it spins while synchronizing.

Open the iDisk like you would any other disk. If you clicked the iDisk icon in the Finder shortcut bar, the Finder window refreshes to show its contents. If you mounted it from the Go menu, you can double-click the iDisk icon on the desktop.

An iDisk contains nine folders:

- Backup—If you've used the Apple Backup utility, this folder contains the data that has been stored. It is created and maintained automatically.
- Documents—Your personal storage space for stuff; no one has access to these files but you.
- Library—Data storage for applications such as iSync. Again, these files are maintained automatically and probably shouldn't be touched.
- Movies—A place to store your (webified) Movie files. Movies placed in this location are available for use within the .Mac HomePage website builder utility.
- Music—A place for you to store your music files. With the advent of the Apple Music Store, I'd venture a guess that Apple will be adding the capability to download song purchases to this folder in the future.
- Pictures—Like Music and Movies, Pictures provides a content-specific place for you to drop your image files. Images placed in the Pictures folder are available within HomePage and the Apple's iCard builder.
- Public—Your online folder that can be opened to the public. Files stored here can be accessed (if you choose) by friends, or anyone in the world.
- Sites—The files for your Apple-hosted mac.com website are stored in the Sites folder. Files placed here are accessible via the URL `http://homepage.mac.com/`*<mac.com username>*`/`*<filename>*.
- Software—Apple's collection of freeware and demo Mac software and music. If you need a quick software fix, this is where you can find it.

Work with iDisk as you would a hard drive or network share, but be aware that copying files to or from the iDisk takes time. If you are configured to maintain a local copy of the iDisk, transfers will be nearly instantaneous, but the actual transfer occurring in the background might take minutes or hours, depending on the quality of your connection.

Accessing Other User's iDisks

To access other Users iDisks (if you have multiple .Mac accounts, for example) choose Go, iDisk, Other User's iDisk from the Finder menu. You are prompted for the user's membership name and password, as seen in Figure 3.76

To mount another user's Public folder, choose Go, iDisk, Other User's Public Folder. In this case, you are prompted for the member name, but you do not need to supply a password unless one has been set by the owner of the remote iDisk account.

FIGURE 3.76 Mount another user's iDisk.

TIP

You can still mount the iDisk volume with Connect To Server by supplying the URL *http://idisk.apple.com/<.Mac username>*.

If you prefer the command line, `mount_webdav` *<webDAV URL>* *<mount point>* will work nicely. (For example, to mount my `johnray` account at the directory `/Users/jray/myiDisk`, I'd type **`mount_webdav http://idisk.mac.com/johnray /Users/jray/myiDisk`**.)

iDisks are the cornerstone of the .Mac service and are what make most of the other services possible. Without, for example, a central storage place to keep other sync information, there would be no means of synchronizing multiple computers on different networks.

Syncing Your Tiger Application Information

Throughout this (and other chapters), we've identified how to turn on .Mac synchronization for various pieces of information—Safari Bookmarks, Mail accounts, and so on. All of this is configured through the Sync pane within the .Mac system preference pane, as shown in Figure 3.77.

FIGURE 3.77 Choose the services you want to sync.

Obviously you'll need to have Bookmarks, Calendars, and such on one of your computers before you start syncing them. After you have them, select the Synchronize with .Mac check box and choose whether you'd like to sync automatically or manually. Finally, check off the services that you want to synchronize.

.Mac uses iSync to perform the synchronization process. If you don't already iSync added to your menu bar, click Show Status in Menu Bar to add the iSync menu extra. You can manually start a sync through the menu extra or by clicking the Sync Now button in the .Mac sync settings pane. For more information on iSync, refer to Chapter 2.

Managing Synchronized Machines and Data

As you enable .Mac syncing on your computers, they are automatically registered with .Mac. iSync keeps everything in order, but if you want to manage your machine registrations (remove computers that are no longer active, reset sync data, disable machines that should no longer sync), this can be managed through the Advanced .Mac preference pane, shown in Figure 3.78.

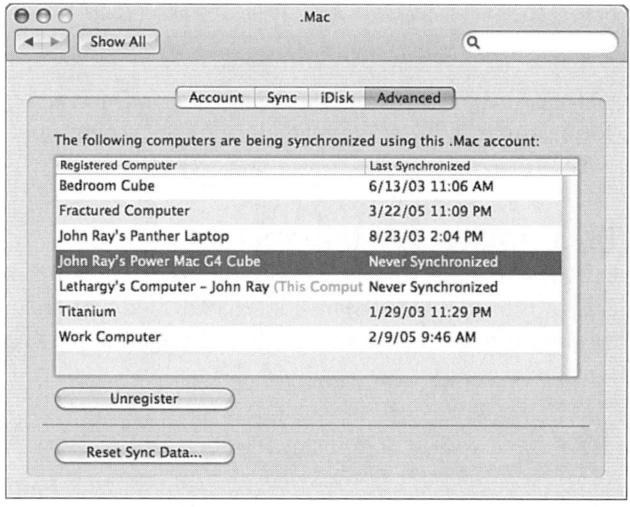

FIGURE 3.78 Control the machines registered to sync with your .Mac account.

To unregister a computer that is registered with your account, select it in the list, and then click the Unregister button.

To complete reset all synchronization information, click Reset Sync Data. This will let you choose what information (information from your local computer or .Mac account) will be used as the basis for future synchronization.

Configuring the .Mac Screensaver

Trying to fit a .Mac topic area within *Mac OS X Unleashed* is difficult. What applications should be included under .Mac, and which stand alone? In Chapter 2, we discussed iSync, iCal, and Address Book; in this chapter, we covered Safari and Mail. The determination of what falls under .Mac has boiled down to "what Tiger software wouldn't work at all if .Mac didn't exist?" iDisk is one component, and the second (perhaps unlikely) feature is a screensaver.

The .Mac screensaver enables a user to view slideshows that they (or someone else) have created and saved to their .Mac accounts.

To use the screensaver, open the Desktop and Screen Saver System Preferences pane. Choose .Mac from the list of available Screen Savers and then click the Configure button. A dialog appears, as shown in Figure 3.79, that contains all slideshows that you've subscribed to.

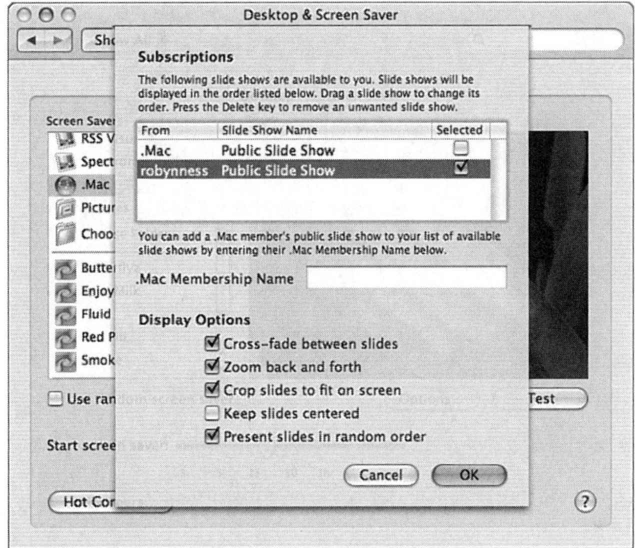

FIGURE 3.79 Create a slideshow that any Internet-connected Mac can view.

To add a new show, enter the name of the .Mac account (such as `robynness`) in the .Mac membership name field, choose the display options you want used during the presentation, and then click OK. The next time your screensaver is activated, you see the photographs you added to .Mac with iPhoto.

To remove or disable subscriptions, you must click Configure again, select the slideshow, and then press your Delete key, or use the Selected check box to simply disable it.

Using .Mac Web Services

The final .Mac features we'll look at are the web services. Accessed with a web browser through `http://www.mac.com`, these features are aimed at families and those on-the-go types who frequently have to access the Internet or send email through computers that aren't their own.

Websites

The HomePage website builder, shown in Figure 3.80, allows anyone to create web pages without any knowledge of HTML. Simply copy images and movies to your iDisk (in the appropriate folders, of course), choose a HomePage template, and then add your own narrative content.

FIGURE 3.80 Use the HomePage builder to create instant websites.

Apple provides templates for photo albums, resumes, iMovies, and more. If you're an advanced user, you can always add your own content directly to the iDisk Sites folder and create any site you want.

iCards

The Apple iCards are a collection of elegant photographs that you can add a message to and forward to your friends, demonstrated in Figure 3.81. Images that you've placed in your iDisk Pictures folder are also available for use.

Even if you aren't exactly thrilled by the idea of sending iCards, you might enjoy looking through the iCard photograph library. Apple's selection of photographs is excellent.

Access on the Go

Probably the most compelling web service for advanced users is the access to traditionally desktop information while on the go. iSync keeps everything connected so that what you see on your desktop is what you see online, and vice versa. Figure 3.82, for example, shows the Safari Bookmark browser.

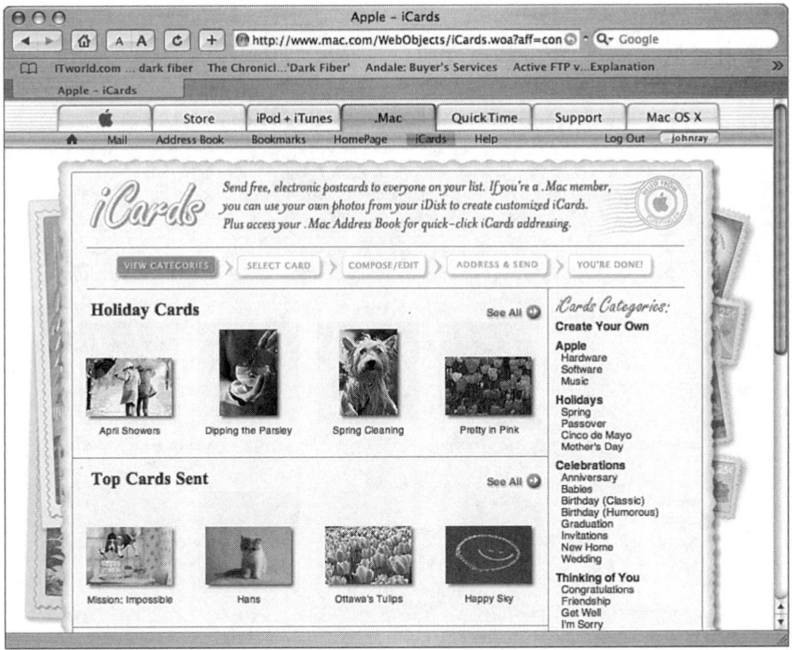

FIGURE 3.81 Create your own iCards to send to friends.

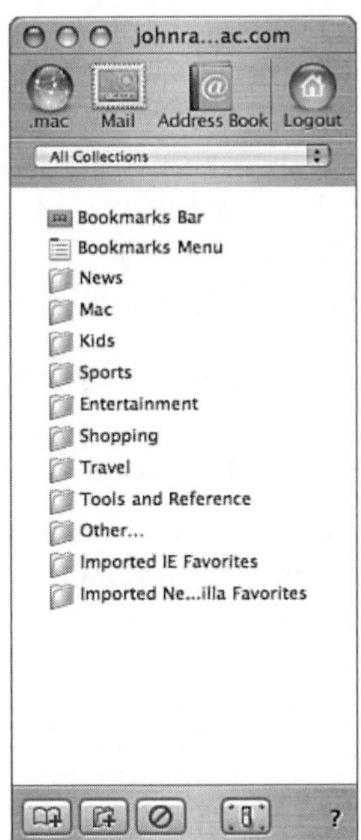

FIGURE 3.82 The Safari Bookmark browser allows you to access and update bookmarks from anywhere.

Likewise, .Mac email and Address Book entries are also accessed through a web interface and carry the feel of a native Mac application along with them. Figure 3.83 shows the .Mac web-based email.

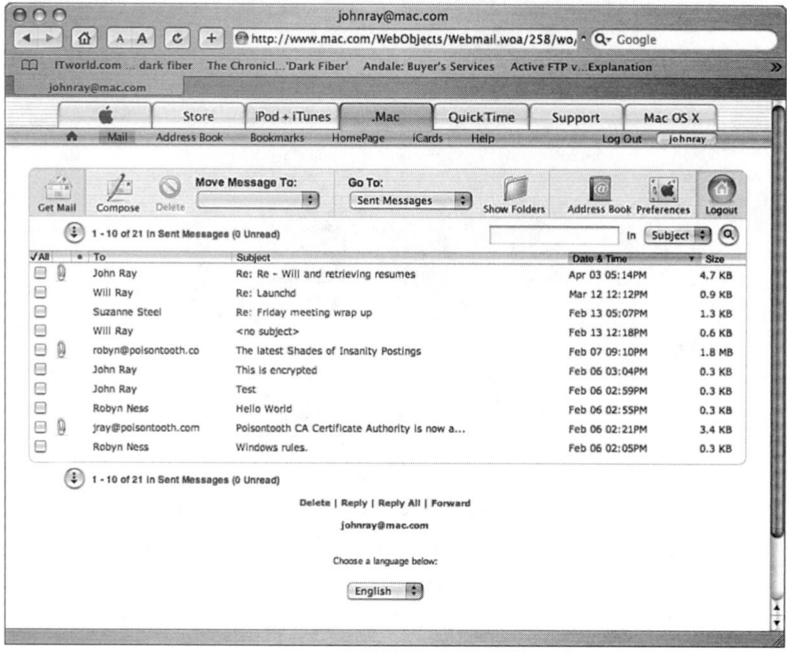

FIGURE 3.83 It's like your Tiger email application—in a web browser.

Because we've already covered the iCal web calendars earlier (refer to Chapter 2 for details), there's very little left to say.

As of the time of this writing, this *is* .Mac. The direction Apple seems to be heading in is providing ways of taking your data with you. The synchronization of desktop applications with web services is likely to continue to be the focus of future developments. As you've seen, and will continue to see throughout the book, certain applications provide support for saving information to .Mac—either through iSync, or as a direct function of the application.

If you're an enterprising user with your own server, yes, you can probably replicate many, if not all, of these services for free. The benefit of .Mac is that it is already in place, is centralized, and works (at least usually).

Summary

This chapter covered everything from searching the Internet with Sherlock and sending email to videoconferencing with iChat AV. Everything you need to communicate online. The Internet applications provided with Tiger can get anyone up and running online in a matter of minutes.

CHAPTER 4

Controlling Applications with Automator and AppleScript

IN THIS CHAPTER

- Automating Your System with Automator
- Creating Advanced Automation with AppleScript
- Understanding AppleScript Syntax
- Additional AppleScript Tools and Resources

Most of us use computers to help make our lives easier, and we choose the Macintosh because of the applications and tools it provides. Unfortunately, it's rare when we can get our work done within a single application. We usually move information back and forth between multiple programs in actions that, after awhile, seem almost automatic. Copy text from here, paste it there, repeat *ad infinitum*. Now, with Tiger, you have everything you need to make these mind-numbing tasks *truly* automatic—using AppleScript and the appropriately named Automator.

Automating Your System with Automator

For years, one of Apple's most compelling technologies within the Mac OS (even before Mac OS X) has been the AppleScript scripting language. Unfortunately AppleScript *is* a programming language. It requires at least elementary programming skills and has syntax very different from other programming languages—meaning that even experienced programmers feel like they're starting from scratch.

Starting with Tiger, everything changes. Tiger introduces Apple's new scripting environment designed for end users—Automator (path: `/Applications/Automator`). Automator enables anyone to create complex applications within minutes of starting the application. As a writer, Automator is a dream come true; it takes only a few minutes to describe and provides nearly limitless benefit to the user. It is a perfect example of Apple's legendary simplicity.

NOTE

If it sounds like I'm gushing, I am. I can't remember the last time I started up an application and became thoroughly engrossed with it almost immediately. Automator provides the right mix of useful and fun in an intuitive interface.

Understanding the Workflow Paradigm

Automator is built around the idea that Applications carry out Actions to create a Workflow. Those who have worked in publishing or design will recognize the term *workflow* immediately—it is the path that work takes as it is completed.

For example, the workflow for sending an email message might be

1. Collect the content for the email (text, files, and so forth).
2. Compress the files.
3. Start the email application.
4. Create a new message.
5. Enter the text content.
6. Add the compressed files as an attachment.
7. Send the message.

In this example, two applications of your computer are used: Finder and Mail. Each of these applications carries out actions within the workflow. Finder collects, organizes, and compresses files. Mail composes and sends the message.

In Automator, you can create workflows that automatically integrate applications and their associated actions—enabling one application to send information to another seamlessly. All that is required to build a workflow similar to (or much more complex than) the one described here is the ability to drag and drop.

Workflows are linear, meaning that you don't need to worry about branching or other traditional programming concerns. Although this does limit some of the functionality that can be implemented, you'll quickly find that Automator is still a very flexible tool.

TIP

Experienced developers can create custom Automator actions or call shell scripts and AppleScripts directly from existing Automator actions.

Actions and Data Flow

One of the most difficult tasks for a programmer is getting a handle on what the programming language is capable of, and what format (data type) information needs to be in order to be passed back and forth between functions (the programming equivalent of an action).

Automator abstracts data into very simple types. Instead of dealing with things such as character arrays, pointers, integers, floating-point numbers, and a myriad of other nastiness, Automator works with very simple data types such as folders, files, email messages, URLs, text, and so on.

Actions have clearly labeled input and output requirements that must match up with other actions' requirements. The Compress Files action, for example, takes files and folders as input, and produces a file as output. It can't be connected to an action that uses URLs, but can be connected to an action that creates a new email message that accepts files and folders and adds them as attachments to the message.

In other development environments, trying to make connections between compatible actions could very well have been a matter of trial and error. But in Automator, Apple has done a wonderful thing: All available actions are sorted based on how well they will work with the action you've currently added or selected in your workflow. Not to oversimplify things, but if you can "connect the dots," you can automate with Automator.

In the event that things do go wrong in Automator, the workflow can be debugged and corrected with just a few points and clicks.

Exploring the Automator Interface

The Automator interface, shown in Figure 4.1, is very similar to Apple's "i" applications. Along the left side of the application window are two columns—the Library, which contains Automator-aware applications, and Actions—the tasks that applications can carry out. Below the columns is a collapsible information area that provides documentation for the currently selected object. If you aren't sure what something does, selecting it will display more detailed information in this area.

The majority of your workflow composition takes place in the large pane on the right side of the window. Actions are added to this area to create an interconnected chain of applications—that is, Your workflow.

Finished workflows are executed using the Run and Stop buttons at the top of the window.

Creating a Workflow

To create a new workflow, start dragging actions into the workflow pane. As they are added to the flow, actions will appear as numbered blocks within the pane, as shown in Figure 4.2.

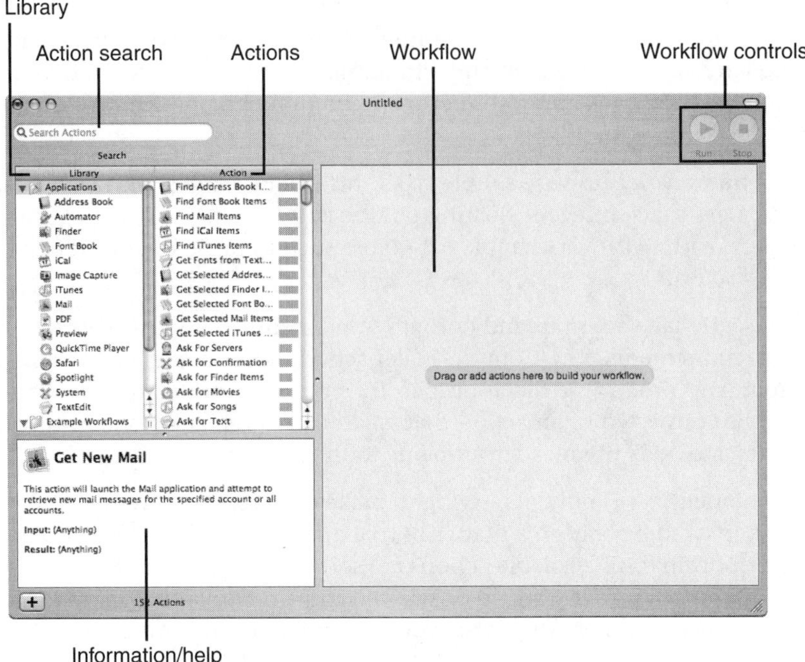

FIGURE 4.1 The Automator interface follows Apple's "i" application interface paradigm.

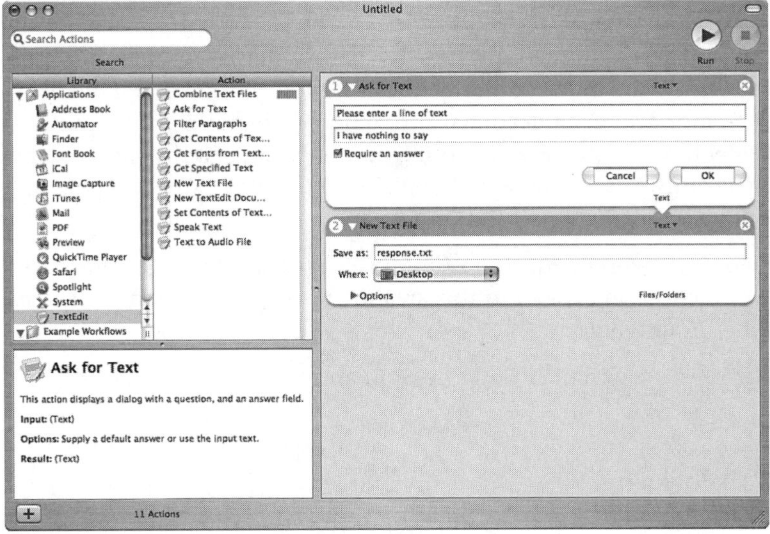

FIGURE 4.2 Drag actions into the right-hand pane to create your workflow.

TIP

Unless you know exactly what application offers a given action, you might want to have the Applications folder selected in the Library column in order to display all available actions at once.

To get you started, let's create a simple workflow that downloads the text from a URL (or URLs) that you specify, and then creates an iPod note based on the page content. This workflow consists of three actions:

1. Get Specified URLs
2. Get Text from Webpage
3. New iPod Note

Find these actions in the Library list, and then drag them, one by one, into the workflow area, as shown in Figure 4.3.

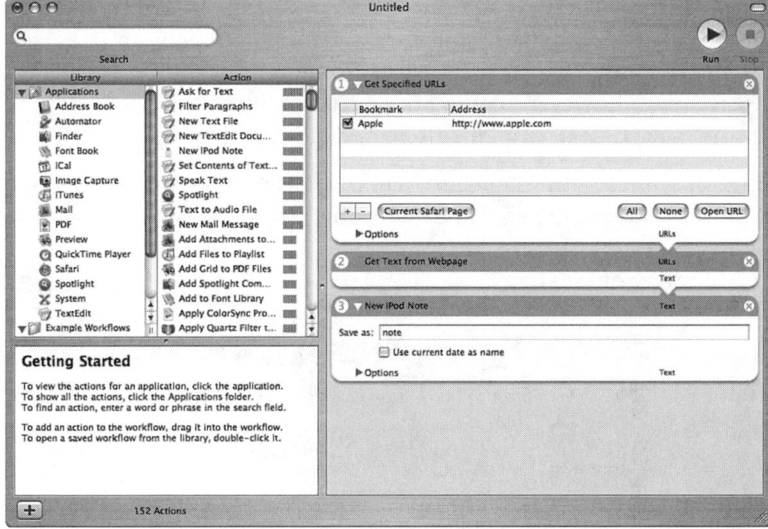

FIGURE 4.3 Create a simple workflow by dragging the actions into the workflow.

After all the actions have been added, you will need to configure a few properties of the actions.

The first action, Get Specified URLs, requires that you provide it with one or more URLs. Use the + and - buttons to add and remove URLs, respectively. The sole purpose is to feed the URLs you specify into the next action: Get Text from Webpage.

Get Text from Webpage performs the heavy lifting of the workflow and requires no additional settings. This action uses the curl library to download all the text from the URLs that are passed into it from the previous action. When it has finished, it passes information into the third and final action: New iPod Note.

The New iPod Note action, the final step in the workflow, creates a new note that can be read using the scroll wheel on your iPod. By default, the new note will be named `note`. To save the note based on the current date, click the Use Current Date as Name check box.

This workflow is now ready to run. If you have an iPod connected to your system, click the Run button and in a few seconds a text version of the URL you specified will be uploaded to your iPod as a note labeled with the current date.

Now wouldn't it be cool if this workflow could be executed everyday automatically? It can. Find out in the "Managing Workflows" section later in this chapter.

TIP

If a completely linear workflow isn't what you need, you'll be interested to know that Automator's internal actions include the ability to execute AppleScripts and shell scripts, and Automator itself is "AppleScriptable."

Enabling User Control During an Action

The most useful options for an action are always displayed directly in the action block of the workflow—such as the Use Current Date as Name option we just looked at. Many Automator actions also, however, have a Show Action When Run check box. When active, this forces the action to display onscreen dialogs and allow user interaction.

To access these additional settings click the Options disclosure arrow at the bottom of the action block (if available); doing so will expand the block as shown in Figure 4.4.

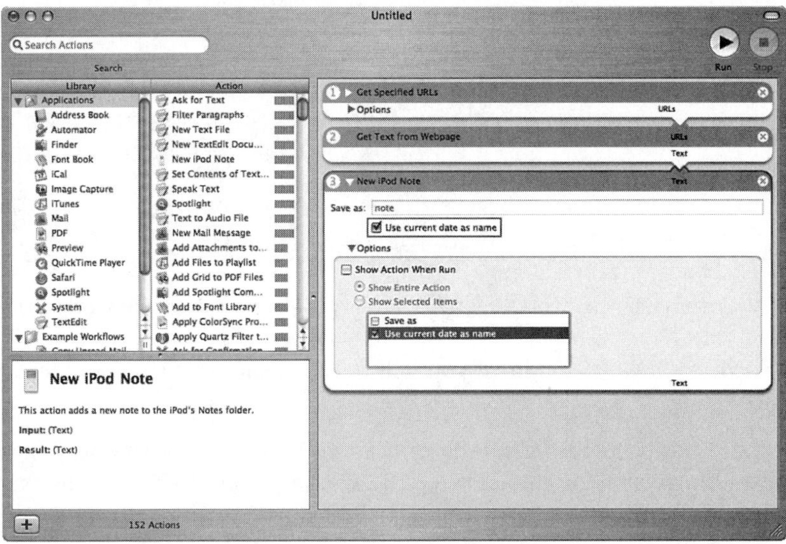

FIGURE 4.4 This is the same New iPod Note action you've seen already, but with additional options displayed.

In this example, you can choose how the iPod note is saved. For example, to show a Save As dialog for the note, you would click the Show Action When Run check box, choose Show Selected Items, and finally click Save As.

NOTE

Strangely, Automator allows you to configure additional options that conflict with the main settings. For example, if you were to use the Use Current Date as Name setting for the New iPod Note action, but also activate Show Action When Run and Save As, you would see a Save as dialog when the workflow is run, but you wouldn't be able to enter any text.

Managing Workflow Actions

After actions have added to a workflow, they can be removed, rearranged, and minimized with only a few clicks. Use these shortcuts to help maintain a clean and manageable workflow:

- Deleting Actions—To delete an action, select it in the list by clicking, then press the Delete key or simply click the X button in the upper-right corner.
- Reordering Actions—To change the order of a group of actions, drag them around within the list. The surrounding actions will automatically renumber as you drag. On some systems, it can be difficult to get an action to properly drop where you want. In such cases, click the action number (or Control-click within the action) and then choose the action you would like it to follow.
- Renaming Actions—By default, actions in the workflow inherit their names from the library. If you would like to rename an action to something specific for your workflow, choose Rename from the pop-up menu displayed by clicking the action's number or Control-clicking within the action body.
- Disabling/Enabling Actions—If you no long want to execute a given step in a workflow, you can disable it rather than delete it. This will keep the action in the flow, but will pass information through it unchanged. Keep in mind that if the action performed a data conversion, the workflow might no longer function. Choose Disable (and Enable) by clicking the action number of control-clicking in the action.
- Collapsing/Expanding Actions—Actions can take up quite a bit of space in the workflow area. After an action has been configured, it can be collapsed, saving a significant amount of screen space. To collapse and expand an action, click the disclosure triangle by the action name.
- Import Actions—If a third party, Apple, or you decide to provide additional actions for an application, you can import them into Automator by Choosing File, Import Actions. See `http://developer.apple.com` for more information on developing Automator actions.

> **TIP**
>
> If you want to have as much space as possible in the workflow, you can choose to have the actions automatically collapse within the Automator application preferences.

Running and Debugging Workflows

As you've discovered already, Workflows can be executed by clicking the Run button in the toolbar or by choosing Run (Command-R) from the Workflow menu. As a workflow executes, a green checkmark appears in the lower-left corner of each successfully completed action. If an action fails, a red X will be displayed instead. Use the Stop button or choose Workflow, Stop (Command-.) to cancel execution in the middle of a workflow.

Workflows don't always work as planned—either because an error occurred somewhere during the execution of an action or there was a logical error during the creation of the flow. As with anything that involves creativity, there is always a need to fix things that didn't quite turn out as you originally envisioned—that is, debug your workflow.

In many cases, errors are caused by either inappropriate or a lack of data being handed off to an action. When this occurs you'll notice that the input and output data types are highlighted in red. You *must* pass compatible data between actions but, at present, Automator doesn't enforce this.

When errors aren't immediately visible in red, there are two ways to track down the problems: through Automator logs and the View Results action.

Viewing Logs

Workflow logs record actions as they are executed, the start and stop time for each, and any error that have been encountered. Since the workflow logs are generated in real-time, you can quickly identify bottlenecks or problems with your workflow. The Workflow log, can be displayed by choosing View, Show Log (Option+Command+L), as seen (with error) in Figure 4.5.

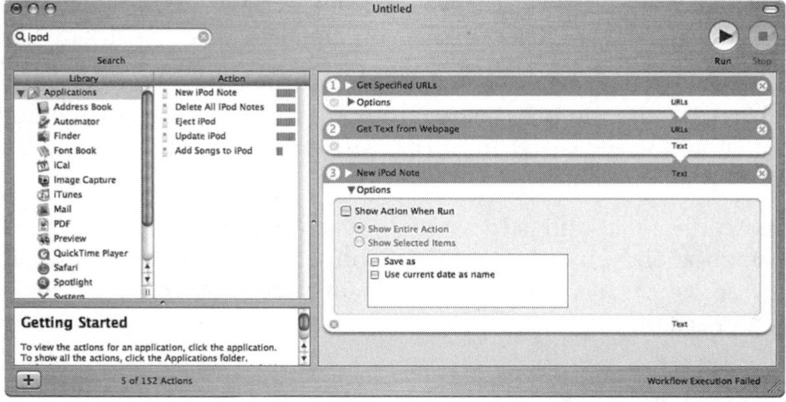

FIGURE 4.5 Use the Automator log to determine where things have gone wrong.

View Results Action

The second error type, a logical workflow error, might not result in an actual visible error, but rather in incorrect information being passed between actions. If you developed a workflow with an action that processes a group of files, but provided it with input of a folder, the action would essentially receive *no* input and probably produce no results. Here, the logical error would be forgetting to insert a Finder Get Folder Contents action before the action expecting the group of files. In these cases, the View Results action can be used as an important debugging tool.

View Results is found in the Automator application's actions and accepts *any* type of Automator input, stops the workflow, and then shows the information that was received from the preceding action. You can use the View Results action to ensure that the data you *think* is entering an action really is. For example, Figure 4.6 shows the results of the View Results action applied to a Finder filter that filters the contents of a folder based on the string `"green"`. Notice that the results are not image files, yet the subsequent action operates on image files—indicating that I've obviously done something wrong with this workflow.

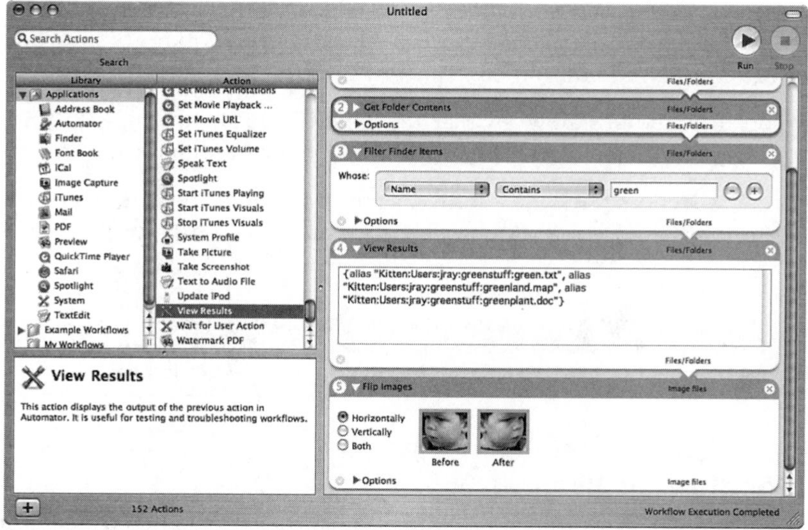

FIGURE 4.6 The View Results action can help debug logical errors in the workflow.

Managing Workflows

After you've developed a workflow, you obviously need to do something with it. Automator gives you quite a bit of flexibility in packaging your final workflows.

Saving Workflows as Documents and Applications

By using File, Save As, workflows can be saved as documents or applications. Double-clicking a document workflow will load it within Automator—just as you'd expect. You can also create double-clickable applications that can be used invoked directly from the Finder by double-clicking or dragging and dropping files onto their icon. Workflows saved as applications cannot be imported into the Automator Library—which you'll learn about directly.

After a workflow has been saved as a document or application, it can be shared with other users who are running Tiger, assuming that they have the appropriate applications and actions installed for the workflow to function.

Adding Workflows to the Automator Library

The Automator Library is seemingly a combination of two rather different functions. I'm sure that Apple is trying to follow the *iApplication* model of collections on the left side of the window, but, in my opinion, this implementation is a bit of a stretch.

First and foremost, the Library provides instant access to the applications that you can automate—you use it to select individual applications to view their actions, or the entire Applications folder to show all actions.

The second role for the Library is to contain collections of workflows. The My Workflows collection contains any workflows placed in the `~/Library/Workflows`. Expand the collection by clicking the disclosure triangle in front of the name. Workflows stored in the collection will be displayed and can be loaded by double-clicking their names.

You can import into My Workflows by placing workflow documents in `~/Library/Workflows`, or by dragging a workflow from the Finder or Automator into the collection.

To create a new collection, click the + button at the bottom of the Automator window. This will create a new empty workflow collection that you can use just like My Workflows.

TIP

Apple provides several sample workflows in the Example Workflows collection.

Saving Workflows as Plug-Ins

Earlier in our discussion of Automator, we mentioned that you could create an Automator action that would repeat on a timed schedule. This is made possible by the ability for workflows to be saved as plug-ins for other applications and tools. Six plug-in options are provided:

- Finder—When saved as a Finder plug-in, an Automator workflow immediately becomes available within an Automator submenu when a contextual menu (Control-click) is invoked in Finder. This enables you create workflows that operate directly on the files selected in the Finder, as shown in Figure 4.7.
- Folder Actions—Folder actions are scripts that are activated based on an action that affects a folder. A workflow could be developed to scale and email all images

dropped into a folder, for example. You'll learn more about configuring folder actions when we talk about AppleScript later in this chapter.

- iCal Alarm—When a workflow is added as an iCal alarm, it can be set as the alarm action for any event. Repeating events can trigger a workflow at any interval you specify. Learn more about setting iCal alarms in Chapter 2, "Useful Tiger Applications and Utilities."
- Image Capture—The Image Capture application has the capability to run a workflow after an image has been imported. This could be used to resize, crop, or otherwise package the images downloaded from your digital devices. Learn more about Image Capture in Chapter 5, "Printer, Fax, and Font Management."
- Print Workflow—A Print Workflow is accessed directly from the PDF menu of the Print dialog box, providing the printing document as the input to the workflow. Learn more about printing settings in Chapter 5.
- Script Menu—The Script Menu is a Menu Extra that can be enabled by the AppleScript utility, discussed later in this chapter. When the Script Menu is active, workflows will appear in this menu and can be accessed from any application at any time.

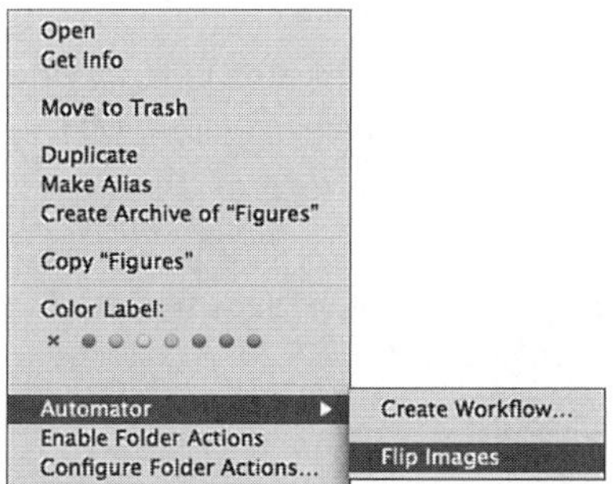

FIGURE 4.7 The Finder plug-in allows you to create your own Finder contextual menus.

The ability to interface and integrate with so many parts of the operating system make Automator an intriguing tool that might very well change how we work with and control our computers.

Creating Advanced Automation with AppleScript

Although Automator is a great tool for stringing together prebuilt actions to create an automated workflow, it is neither the first nor the only means of automating actions on your Macintosh. AppleScript, originally introduced in the early '90s, provides much greater control over your entire system.

AppleScript is intended to provide a means for Macintosh users to develop complex scripts with the ability to evaluate conditions and branch, if needed. The syntax is surprisingly simple and can be understood even if you've never seen a programming language before. For example, consider the following code:

```
tell application "Finder"
    activate
    close window "Applications"
end tell
```

It doesn't look like a programming language, but it is. This small example instructs Tiger to activate the Finder application and then close an open window with the title Applications.

Using a language that can almost be read aloud and understood, normal users can write scripts that combine the capabilities of multiple applications.

Using the Script Editor

The easiest way to get started with AppleScript is with the Script Editor. In addition to being a context-sensitive programming editor, it also acts as a script recorder. A user can open the Script Editor, click Record, and generate an AppleScript by using the editor to monitor his actions while interacting with a recordable application—unfortunately, very few are.

The Script Editor serves as your primary entry and testing point for any AppleScript development, either recorded or entered by hand.

Script Editor Controls

Launch the Script Editor (`/Applications/AppleScript/Script Editor`) to begin scripting. Figure 4.8 shows the initial editor window.

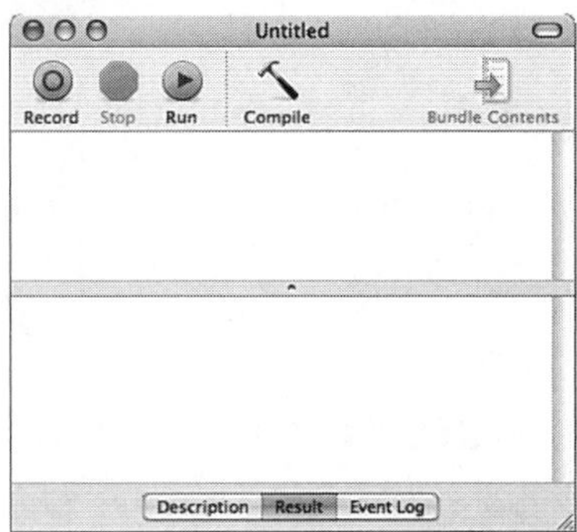

FIGURE 4.8 The Script Editor is used when editing or recording AppleScripts.

The Script Editor recording and editing tools include

- Record/Stop/Run—Similar to a tape deck, these buttons are used to control recording and playback of an AppleScript. Click the Record button (Command-D) to start monitoring your system for Apple events within scriptable applications. These events are then stored in a script. The Stop button (Command-.) is used to stop recording, whereas the Run button (Command-R) executes the actions.
- Compile—Reviews the syntax of the current script for errors and automatically reformats the script if needed.
- Bundle Contents—If the script is saved as an application or script bundle, this button becomes active. A *bundle* is a folder structure that appears as a single file. Clicking Bundle Contents reveals the inner structure of the bundle and allows you to drag in additional script resources, images, and the like so that they can all be distributed as part of your script.
- Content—The content area is used to compose and edit script content. It functions like any text editor, but has the benefit of automatically formatting code when syntax is checked or the script is run.
- Description/Result/Event Log—This area is used to display information from or about the script, depending on the active button at the bottom of the window.

To start using the editor, click the Record button, switch to the Finder, and then open and drag a few windows around. As you work in the Finder, an AppleScript will build in the editor window. Click Stop to finish the code block and prepare it for execution. Figure 4.9 displays a script that has just finished generating.

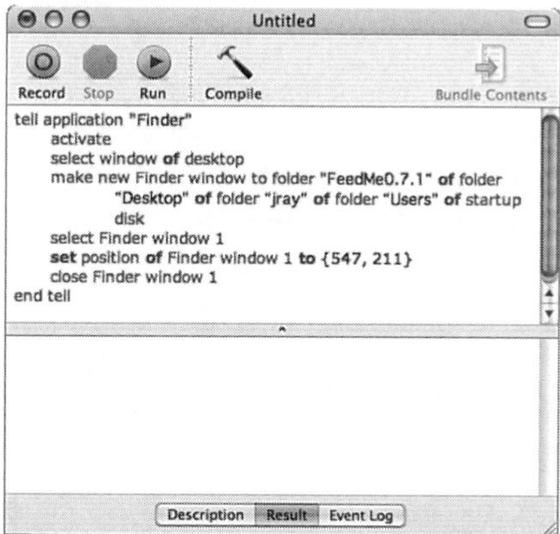

FIGURE 4.9 Click Record to monitor your actions and build an AppleScript; click Stop to finish the script.

You can immediately replay the recorded actions by clicking the Run button.

Exploring the Scripting Dictionary

Obviously, the biggest draw to AppleScript is the capability to create scripts from scratch. Recording is a good way to get a quick start, but it can't be used to generate anything truly useful. The basic AppleScript syntax is covered later in this chapter in the section "Understanding AppleScript Syntax." Even this, however, is useless without knowledge of what commands an application can accept. Thankfully, each scriptable application contains a dictionary that shows the scripting features it supports.

To access a scripting dictionary for any application or scripting addition, choose File, Open Dictionary from the menu. A list of the available scriptable applications is displayed, as demonstrated by Figure 4.10. You can select multiple applications by holding down the Apple key.

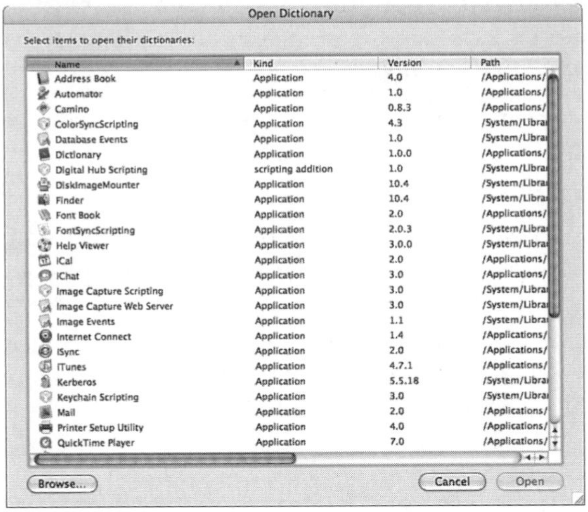

FIGURE 4.10 Choose from the available scriptable applications.

Be aware that some applications might not be shown. The Browse button at the bottom of the window opens a standard File Open dialog for choosing an arbitrary file. After you've picked an application from the default or browse view, a dictionary browser window appears, as shown in Figure 4.11.

The browser toolbar works like many of Apple's other applications: The arrows move back and forth through dictionary entries and the search field provides an instant lookup of any key term you might need.

Below the toolbar are several columns. In the default view mode, the first column allows you to select suites of dictionary entries. A *suite* is simply a categorization for a certain types of AppleScript functionality. The DVD Player, for example, has a DVD Suite that contains all the necessary information for working with DVDs. Some applications might include other suites as well, such as a Standard Suite that provides everything you need to open and close documents, print, and so on. These additional suites are shared throughout the system and enable programmers to use a common syntax when doing everything from creating a new web browser window to creating a new text document.

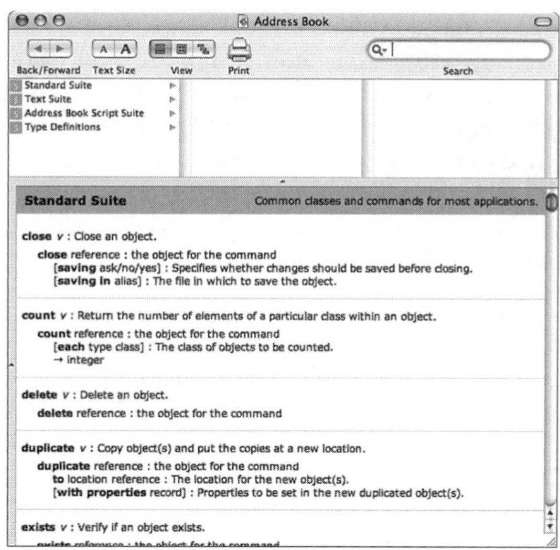

FIGURE 4.11 The dictionary documents the available AppleScript functions.

When a suite is selected, all the available entries within that suite appear to the right and a complete summary of all suite keywords is displayed in the pane below the columns, as shown in Figure 4.12.

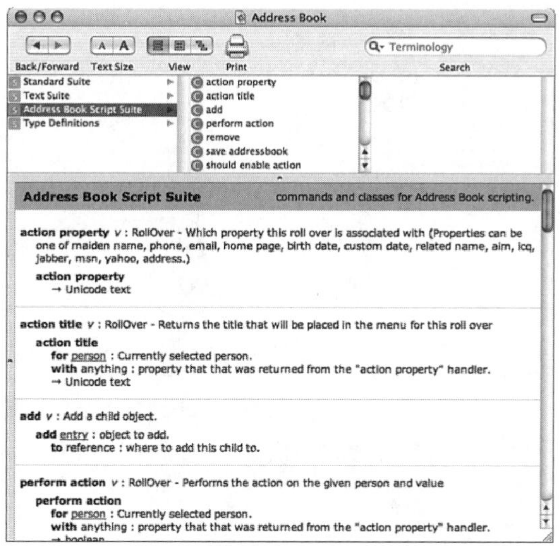

FIGURE 4.12 When a suite is selected, all entries are displayed in the lower pane.

To show a given entry within a suite, select it in the second pane and only its description will appear.

So, what are these entries? What do they represent? Each item within a suite is labeled as either a noun (*n.*) or a verb (*v.*); that is, a command or an event. Nouns are classes that you can either get information about or act on in some way. A *class* is an abstraction of a component of an application you work with, such as a file. When you work with a class, you work with an instance of a class, which is called an *object*. Objects can have properties that can be set or modified to effect changes to the object. In some cases, you might notice additional entries in the far-right column after you've selected an object. These entries are properties of the noun.

Since suites contain classes, commands, and objects contain properties and other objects, and because Apple has decided to refer to commands as *commands, verbs, and events*, and classes as *nouns*...things can get pretty confusing. To help make some sense of it, Apple adds one of five icons to the right of a dictionary entry to help quickly define its role:

Orange "S"—A suite.

Blue "C"—A command (or verb, or event).

Purple "C"—A class.

Purple "P"—An object property.

Orange "E"—An object that is contained in another object.

For example, the Address Book suite contains a Person object. For a given Person, there are many different properties that can be assigned, as can be shown in Figure 4.13, as well as other objects contained within the Person.

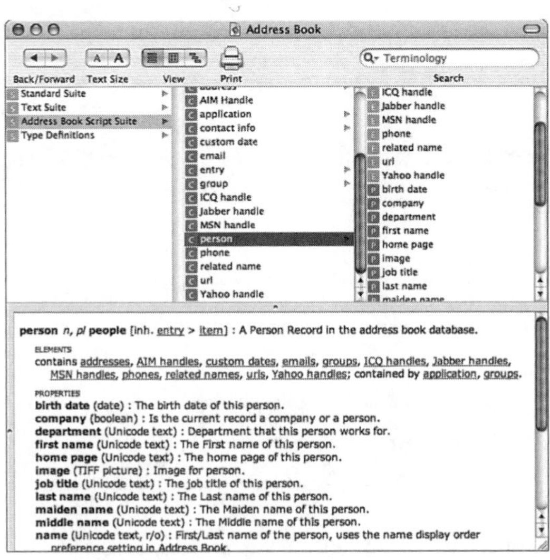

FIGURE 4.13 The Person object contains many attributes that describe a person.

Each property is has a certain data type, such as an integer, image, text string, and so on. In this example, the title attribute of a person is a Unicode text string, whereas the image attribute is a TIFF.

By digging even further through the dictionary, we can find that there is a specific property of the Address Book application called my card, which, in turn, is an instance of the Person class representing the current user, as shown in Figure 4.14.

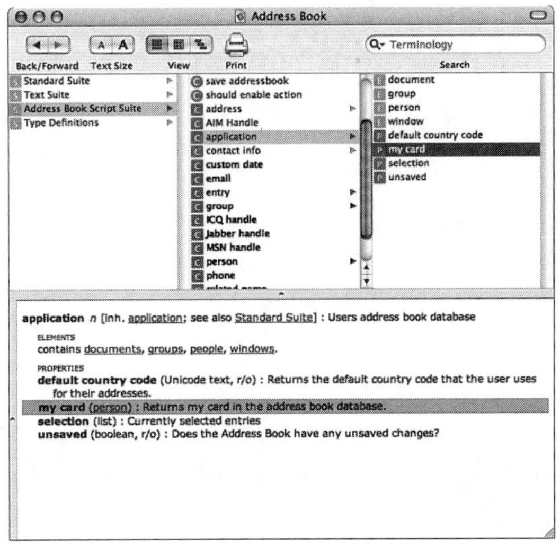

FIGURE 4.14 The my card object represents the currently active user.

The only way to find everything you can do with AppleScript is to dig and experiment. The dictionary browser provides two other browsing modes to help.

Using Alternative Browsing Modes

By default, the dictionary browser shows suites. In some cases, however, you might be more interested in seeing a hierarchical view of what is contained within a given set of objects, or viewing the entire inheritance tree for the application from top to bottom.

What?

The Containment view, the middle button in the view controls of the toolbar, bases its display on how objects are contained within one another. For example, the Address Book application starts with an Application container. Within that container are documents, groups, people, and windows—each of which, in turn, can contain additional elements. Groups, for example, can contain people and more groups. Because groups can contain groups, you could find yourself browsing an infinite loop, as seen in Figure 4.15.

The last viewing mode, Inheritance, uses the object hierarchy of the system to browse a dictionary. AppleScript is an object-oriented environment. This means that the classes you browse can inherit information and features from parent classes and subclasses can, in turn, inherit information from them. Remember earlier we mentioned that the Address

Book application object contains a property called my card that, in turn, is a Person object describing the currently active user. Although this property is specific to the Address Book application, there are other generic properties, such as the application name and version, that are automatically inherited from a parent application object. A view of this inheritance can be seen in Figure 4.16.

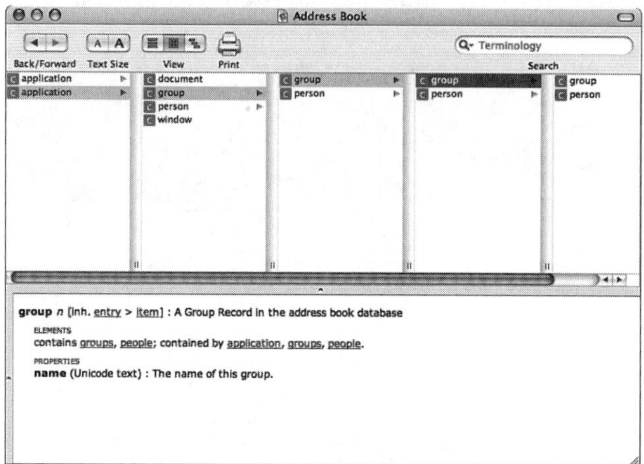

FIGURE 4.15 The Containment view displays elements based on what other elements they contain.

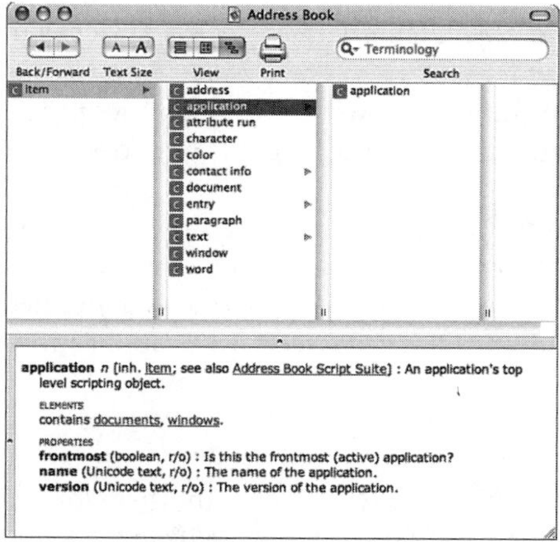

FIGURE 4.16 Objects inherit properties from parent classes.

Unfortunately, object-oriented programming is a bit beyond the scope of this book. If you find these views at all confusing, stick to the Suites view, which provides a much cleaner organization for most users.

Entering a Sample Script

Let's see how the Person class can be used to return an attribute about someone in the Address book. Go back to the main Script Editor window and enter the following code:

```
1: tell application "Address Book"
2:    get the job title of my card
3:    set myTitle to the result
4:    display dialog myTitle
5: end tell
```

When finished, click the Run button and a dialog box will appear with your Address Book title as the contents. Note that if you don't have a Job Title set, you'll need to choose Card, Add Field, Job Title within the Address Book application.

Line 1 indicates that instructions will be sent to the Address Book application. Line 2 `gets` the job title for the Person object contained in the special property "`my card`" (me). Line 3 sets a variable called `myTitle` to the results of the previous `get` command. Line 4 displays a dialog box containing the contents of `myTitle`. Finally, line 5 stops talking to Address Book.

This example introduces the structure you will see in most AppleScript programs. The `tell`, `set`, and `get` statements form the basis of scripts. The objects and the parameters that can be modified, however, must be looked up in the application's dictionary.

TIP

The Script Editor features a Script Assistant that will automatically complete recognized pieces of code as you type. Before you can use the assistant, you must first enable it within the Editing pane of the Script Editor preferences, and then quit and restart the editor.

If the Script Assistant recognizes what you're typing, it places an ellipsis (...) after your cursor. When this is displayed, pressing F5 will show the potential code completions. Use the up and down arrows to choose the one you want, and then press the Return key to insert the code into your script.

Viewing Results

As you saw in the preceding sample script, when an AppleScript function returns a result, it is stored in a special temporary variable called `result`. This variable can be used to access a value without the need for additional variables. For example, lines 3 and 4 of the preceding script could be condensed to

```
display dialog the result
```

To display the contents of the result container within the Script Editor, choose View, Show Result (Command-2) from the menu, or click the Result button at the bottom of the Script Editor window. Tiger displays the current value of `result` below the script.

Tracing Events

To trace the execution of a script as it runs, use the event log. This log keeps track of the events (commands) sent to an application and displays the results that are returned immediately. Click the Event Log button or press Command-3 to show the event log in the lower pane of the Script Editor window. Figure 4.17 shows the event log after replaying a simple script to get the location of a Finder window.

FIGURE 4.17 The event log can be used to monitor script execution.

Saving Scripts

After you've created a script that functions the way you want, you can save it in several different ways. Select File, Save As, and then choose from the following options, depending on what you want to do with the script:

There are five possible file formats for scripts:

- Script—Saves the script as a compiled binary file.
- Application—Saves the script for double-click execution under Tiger.
- Script Bundle—Saves the script in the binary script format but also within a folder bundle, allowing you to add additional resources (other files and so on) within the bundle structure.
- Application Bundle—Saves the script in a double-clickable application format but as a folder bundle, enabling you to add additional files and resources.
- Text—Saves the contents of the script in a plain-text file.

In addition to the file format, you can also choose the line ending format if saving to a text file, and whether the file should be run only (not allow editing), display a startup screen, and stay open (after it has finished executing).

Changing Scripting Preferences

The Script Editor automatically highlights and formats AppleScript as you type. To change the default font styles and formatting, choose Preferences from the application menu.

The five categories of Script Editor preferences are as follows:

- General—The default scripting language to be used. AppleScript is the only language available without installing third-party software.
- Editing—Control line wrap settings, control tab indentation, and enable and disable the Script Assistant.
- Formatting—Choose font size, color, syntax highlighting, and so on.
- History—Enable or disable a running history of AppleScript-generated results and events.
- Plugins—Display any third-party plug-ins that have been installed.

TIP

To use another editor as your AppleScript editor, use the AppleScript Utility (path: `/Applications/AppleScript/AppleScript Utility`) to change the Default Script Editor setting.

Understanding AppleScript Syntax

Describing the AppleScript syntax to a programmer familiar with a traditional language isn't as straightforward as you might think. AppleScript uses an entirely different programming model based on an English-like structure that, after a few minutes of use, leaves the programmer feeling as though he is having a deep, intellectual conversation with his computer.

TIP

Many of the building blocks discussed here can automatically be entered into the Script Editor by Control-Clicking within your script and then choosing from the many prewritten code fragments displayed in the pop-up menu that will appear. You'll still have to fill in the details, but you won't have to remember the exact syntax.

Sending Instructions to an Application: `tell`

The basic building block of an AppleScript is the `tell` statement. `tell` is used to address an object and give it instructions to perform. A `tell` line is written in one of two common forms: a block or a single statement. The block format enables the programmer to send multiple commands to an application without stating its name each time.

Single:

```
tell <object> <object name> to <action>
```

Block:

```
tell <object> <object name>
    <action>
    <action>
    <action>
    ...
end tell
```

For example, the following two statements are identical but are structured using the simple and block forms of `tell`:

```
tell application "Finder" to empty trash
```

and

```
tell application "Finder"
    empty trash
end tell
```

Both of these short scripts cause Finder to empty the trash. Although the second form might seem more verbose, it is likely to be the most commonly encountered form. Most scripts interact with objects to perform complex compound operations rather than simple commands. In addition, the second version of the AppleScript is easier to read and view the functional components. Maintaining readable code is a good idea no matter what programming platform you're using.

TIP

In addition to breaking up code with `tell` blocks, long lines are typically split using a code-continuation character. To break a single long code line across multiple lines, press Option-Return to insert a code-continuation character.

Manipulating Variables: `set/get`

In AppleScript, variables are automatically created when they are `set`. A variable name can be any combination of alphanumerics as long as the first character is a letter. No special prefixes are required to denote a variable within the code.

Although type conversions happen automatically in many cases, a variable type can be explicitly given directly in the `set` statement:

```
set <variable/property> to <value> [as <object type>]
```

For example, both of the following lines set variables (`thevalue` and `thevalue2`) to `5`, but the second line forces the variable to be a string:

```
set thevalue to 5
set thevalue2 to 5 as string
```

In addition to setting variables, the `set` command can act on the properties of an object to effect changes on the system. Earlier you saw how an AppleScript could get the title of the active Person object in Address Book. Similarly, `set` can alter the file type. For example:

```
1: tell application "Address Book"
2:   display dialog "Enter a new job title for yourself:" default answer ""
2:   set myNewTitle to the text returned of the result
3:   set the job title of my card to myNewTitle
4: end tell
```

In line 3 of this code fragment, `set` is used to alter the job title for the active user's card. Previously, we had only read information—now we can change it!

As you've already seen, to retrieve values from variables or properties from objects, you would use the `get` command. `get`, by itself, retrieves the value of an object or variable and stores it in the `result` variable:

```
get the <property/variable> [of <object>]
```

Traditional programmers might feel uncomfortable with retrieving results into a temporary variable (`result`); in that case, they can use an implicit `get` to immediately store the results in another variable or object property:

```
set <variable/property> [of <object>] to the <property/variable> [of <object>]
```

Here the `get` is implied. This form of `get` and `set` is preferred for creating concise and readable code.

Working with Lists

You've seen that variables can take on simple values, such as numbers or strings, but they can also contain more complex values in the form of lists. Lists are equivalent to arrays in more traditional programming languages. A list is represented by a comma-separated group of values, enclosed in curly brackets {}. For example, the following line sets a variable, `thePosition`, to a list containing two values:

```
set thePosition to {50, 75}
```

Lists are often used to set coordinate pairs for manipulating onscreen objects but can contain any object. In fact, lists can even contain lists of lists. For example:

```
set theListOfPositions to {{50, 75}, {65, 45}, {25, 90}}
```

Here, a variable called `theListOfPositions` is set to a list of lists. Item 1 of the list is `{50,75}`, item 2 is `{65,45}`, and so on.

When dealing with list values, you can reference individual items within a list by referring to them as just that: items. For example, assume that you've run the following command:

```
set thePosition to {50, 75}
```

To retrieve the value of the first item in the list, use

```
get item 1 of thePosition
```

When dealing with lists within lists, just embed item statements within one another. Assume, for example, that this list has been entered:

```
set theListOfPositions to {{50, 75}, {65, 45}, {25, 90}}
```

To retrieve the value of the second item of the second list within a list, you could write

```
get item 2 of item 2 of theListOfPositions
```

List Abstraction

In many cases, the names of lists and the elements they contain have been abstracted within the application dictionaries. For example, the Address Book application defines People as the plural form of the Person object. In other words, People is a list of Person elements. Because we know this, we can access any person in the address book by referencing their `item` number in the `people` list.

For example, to reference the name of the first person in the `people` list, I could use:

```
get the name of item 1 of people
```

However, because the system already knows that a Person object is an element of the `people` list, this can also be rewritten as simply:

```
get the name of person 1
```

You can apply this same syntax wherever the dictionary includes an abstraction for a list and its elements.

Again, the power of these commands is based in the dictionaries of AppleScript applications. Exploring the scripting dictionaries is the best way to uncover the capabilities of the AppleScript platform.

Using Flow Control: `If`

A common programming construct is the `If-then-else` statement. This is used to check the value of an item and then react appropriately. The syntax for a basic `If` statement is

```
If <condition> then
    <action>
end if
```

For example, the following code asks the user to input a value, checks to see whether it equals 5, and outputs an appropriate message if it does:

```
1: display dialog "Enter a number:" default answer ""
2: set theValue to (text returned of the result) as integer
3: if theValue = 5 then
4:   display dialog "Five is my magic number."
5: end if
```

Line 1 displays a dialog prompt for a user to enter a value. Line 2 sets a variable `theValue` to the text returned from the dialog and forces it to be evaluated as an integer. Line 3 checks `theValue`; if it is equal to the number 5, line 4 is executed. Line 4 displays an onscreen message, and line 5 ends the `If` statement.

The `If` statement can be expanded to include an `else` clause that is executed if the original condition is not met:

```
1: display dialog "Enter a number:" default answer ""
2: set theValue to (text returned of the result) as integer
3: if theValue = 5 then
4:   display dialog "Five is my magic number."
5: else
6:   display dialog "That is NOT my magic number."
7: end if
```

In this modified version of the code, line 6 contains an alternative message that will be displayed if the condition in line 3 is not met.

Finally, the `else` itself can be expanded to check alternative conditions using `else if`. This enables multiple possibilities to be evaluated within a single statement:

```
1: display dialog "Enter a number:" default answer ""
2: set theValue to (text returned of the result) as integer
3: if theValue = 5 then
4:   display dialog "Five is my magic number."
5: else if theValue = 3 then
6:   display dialog "Three is a decent number too."
7: else
8:   display dialog "I don't like that number."
9: end if
```

The latest version of the code includes an `else if` in line 5. If the initial comparison in line 3 fails, line 5 is evaluated. Finally, if line 5 fails, the `else` in line 8 is executed.

Creating Iteration with repeat

Another common programming construct is the loop. AppleScript uses a single-loop type to handle a variety of looping needs. The repeat statement has several different forms that cover while, until, and other types of traditional loops.

There are six different forms of the repeat statement:

- Repeat indefinitely—Repeat a group of statements indefinitely or until the exit command is called.

```
repeat
  <statements>
end repeat
```

- Repeat #—Using the second loop format, the user can choose the number of times a loop repeats.

```
repeat <integer> times
  <statements>
end repeat
```

- Repeat while—Loop indefinitely while the given condition evaluates to true.

```
repeat while <condition>
  <statements>
end repeat
```

- Repeat until—Loop indefinitely until the given condition evaluates to true. This is the inverse of the repeat while loop.

```
repeat until <condition>
  <statements>
end repeat
```

- Repeat with—Called a *for/next* loop in more traditional languages, this form of the repeat loop counts up or down from a starting number to an ending number. Each iteration updates a variable with the latest loop value.

```
repeat with <variable> from <starting integer> to
<ending integer> [by <increment>]
  <statements>
end repeat
```

- Repeat with list—Like the standard repeat with–style loop, the repeat with list loop runs over a range of values, storing each value in a named variable during the iterations of the loop. The difference is that the value range is specified with a list, rather than an upper and lower integer value. This enables the loop to operate over anything from numbers to strings to lists of lists.

```
repeat with <variable> in <list>
  <statements>
end repeat
```

For example, let's consider a short script that cycles through each of the individuals in your address book and displays the name of each. To do this, we'll need use the second-to-last loop type, and we'll also need to know how many people are in the address book and how to reference each one.

A bit of poking around in the dictionary quickly tells us that we can return the number of elements in any list by using the Standard Suite verb `count` with the syntax `count of <list name>`. We also learned earlier (in the section "List Abstraction") that Address Book abstracts the list of all Person objects as People, and that we can reference an individual element of the `people` list as simply `person <#>` so our script can be written as

```
tell application "Address Book"
    repeat with i from 1 to count of people
         get the name of person i
         display dialog the result
    end repeat
end tell
```

Creating Subroutines

An important building block that you'll need for creating large AppleScripts is the *subroutine*. Subroutines help modularize code by breaking it into smaller, more manageable segments that can return specific results to a controlling piece of code. There are two types of subroutines in AppleScript: those with labeled parameters and those that use positional parameters. A *parameter* is a piece of information passed to a subroutine when it is called.

Positional parameters will be the most familiar to anyone who has used another programming language. This type of subroutine, which is the easiest to define and use, depends on being called with a certain number of parameters in a certain order.

Labeled parameters, on the other hand, rely on a set of named parameters and their values, which can be sent to the subroutine in any order. This can be used to create an English-like syntax but adds a level of complexity when reading the code.

Because positional parameters can be used for almost any type of development and fit in with the structure of other languages discussed in this book, they will be the focus here.

The syntax of a positional parameter subroutine is shown here:

```
on <subroutine name> ([<variable 1>,<variable 2>,<variable n>,...])
  <statements>
  [return <result value>]
end <subroutine name>
```

Each positional parameter-based subroutine requires a name, a list of variables that will be supplied when called, and an optional value that will be returned to the main application. For example, the following `beAnnoying` routine takes a string and a number as parameters, and then displays a dialog box with the message. The display will be repeated until it matches the number given.

```
1: on beAnnoying(theMessage, howAnnoying)
2:   repeat howAnnoying times
3:     display dialog theMessage
4:   end repeat
5: end beAnnoying
```

Line 1 declares the subroutine `beAnnoying` and its two parameters: `theMessage` and `howAnnoying`. Line 2 starts a loop that repeats for the number of times set in the `howAnnoying` variable. Line 3 displays a dialog box with the contents `theMessage`. Line 4 ends the loop, and line 5 ends the subroutine.

As expected, running this piece of code does absolutely nothing. It is a subroutine, and, as such, requires that another piece of code call it. To call this particular routine, you could use a line such as

```
beAnnoying("Am I annoying yet?",3)
```

This causes the subroutine to activate and display the message `Am I annoying yet?` three times.

A more useful subroutine is one that performs a calculation and returns a result. The following example accepts, as input, an integer containing a person's age in years. It returns a result containing the given age in days.

```
on yearsToDays(theYears)
  return theYears * 365
end yearsToDays
```

Because this subroutine returns a value, it can be called from within a set statement to store the result directly into a variable:

```
set dayAge to yearsToDays(90)
```

When working in subroutines, you must explicitly define variables that are used only in the subroutine, as opposed to those that can be accessed from anywhere in the AppleScript application. A variable that is visible to all portions of a script is called a *global variable* and is defined using the `global` declaration. Similarly, the `local` keyword can be used to limit the scope of a variable to only the code contained within a subroutine. For example, try executing the following AppleScript:

```
set theValue to 10
reset()
display dialog theValue
```

```
4:
5: on reset()
6:   local theValue
7:   set theValue to 0
8: end reset
```

In line 1, a variable called `theValue` is set to 10. In line 2, the reset subroutine is called, which appears to set the contents of `theValue` to zero. Yet, when the result is displayed in line 3, the original value remains. The reason for this strange behavior is the inclusion of line 6. Line 6 defines `theValue` as a local variable to the reset subroutine. This means that any changes to that variable will not extend outside the subroutine.

To gain the behavior we expect (the contents of `theValue` are set to zero everywhere), swap the `local` keyword with `global`:

```
1: set theValue to 10
2: reset()
3: display dialog theValue
4:
5: on reset()
6:   global theValue
7:   set theValue to 0
8: end reset
```

This tiny modification tells the reset subroutine that it should use the global representation of the variable `theValue`. When `theValue` is set to zero in line 7, it replaces the initial value set in line 1.

Accessing the Command Line from AppleScript

AppleScript can easily be integrated with shell scripts using the `do shell script` command, which is part of the AppleScript Standard Additions dictionary. This function returns the results of the command in a variable that you can use in your scripts. For example, to return and display the output of the Unix command `date`

```
do shell script "date"
display dialog the result
```

As you work with the command line (see Chapter 9, "Accessing the BSD Subsystem," to get started), you'll learn that sometimes it's useful to execute commands as an administrative user (`root`). There are several additional parameters that you can use with `do shell script` to accomplish this and more. The full syntax follows:

```
do shell script <shell commands>
  [password <admin password> [with administrator privileges]]
```

If the `with administrator privileges` clause is specified, the user is prompted for a password and the script executed with administrative permissions. To eliminate the password prompt, simply use the password keyword followed by your administrator password. For example, to return the contents of `/var/log/secure.log` (which requires administrator access), you could use

```
do shell script "cat /var/log/secure.log" password "mypassword"
  with administrator privileges
```

Combining AppleScript with the power of the command line gives advanced users the ability to control all components of their system.

> **TIP**
>
> Users who just want to activate a shell script can do so by scripting the terminal. This method does not provide a means of returning shell results to the AppleScript.

An example of a Terminal script that uses the `ls` command to display a list of files is shown here:

```
tell application "Terminal"
  do script "ls"
end tell
```

Scripting the Unscriptable

Unfortunately for us, not all applications are directly scriptable. If you attempt to display an application's scripting dictionary and discover that none is available, you'll need to take a slightly different approach to automating its actions—you'll need to use GUI scripting.

First introduced in Panther, GUI scripting allows you to control interface elements directly. You must, in script form, control a virtual user that clicks and types in all the right places. This isn't difficult, but it does require some additional software and the activation of GUI Scripting on your system.

To turn on GUI scripting, open the AppleScript Utility (path: `/Applications/AppleScript/AppleScript Utility`). Click the Enable GUI Scripting checkbox, as shown in Figure 4.18.

After GUI Scripting has been turned on, it's ready to use—but because you must explicitly address each user interface element within an application, you'll need some additional software to identify how these elements are referenced. For example, a GUI script may invoke an action that looks like this:

```
click radio button 3
```

But because the name `radio button 3` is determined by the structure of the application (and not necessarily its visual placement), you can't just guess and expect it to work.

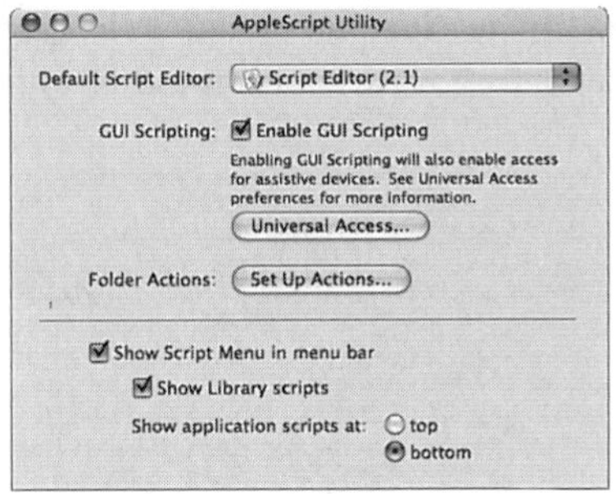

FIGURE 4.18 GUI scripting must be enabled before it can be used.

To correctly identify GUI elements, you can either download Apple's UI Element Inspector from `http://www.apple.com/applescript/uiscripting/02.html`, or use a much (*much*) simpler tool—PreFab Software's PreFab UI Browser found at `http://www.prefab.com/`

Priced at $55, PreFab UI Browser has a 30-day free trial and is much simpler to use than the Apple tool.

As a simple example, let's look at how you might retrieve the version and build number of the Camino browser within a script. This excellent browser (visit `http://camino-browser.org`) isn't yet scriptable, so to retrieve the version, we have to work with directly with GUI scripting and the Camino interface.

First, start Camino and PreFab UI Browser, and choose Camino from the Target pop-up list—this identifies that we will be working with the Camino application. Now, generate your first GUI scripting code by choosing Tell Block Wrapper (Short) from the AppleScript pop-up menu on the right side of the UI browser window. A new window will appear with the GUI scripting code skeleton for Camino, as shown in Figure 4.19.

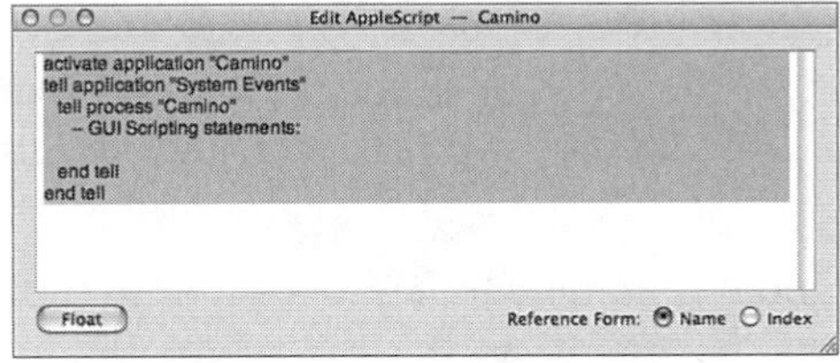

FIGURE 4.19 Start by generating the code block that will work with the application you're trying to script.

Next, determine the path you would normally navigate through to get the information you want. For retrieving the browser version this involves opening the About Camino window and reading the contents of one of the window's text strings.

We start by simulating the mouse click on the About Camino menu item. Using the columns at the top of the PreFab UI Browser, navigate through the selections you would make in the GUI—specifically, `"menu bar 1"`, `"menu bar item," Camino"`, `"menu 1"`, and, finally `"menu item 'About Camino'"`, as demonstrated in Figure 4.20.

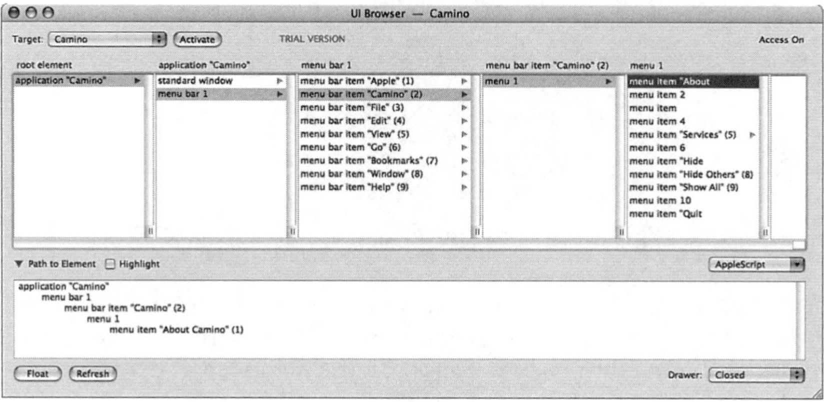

FIGURE 4.20 Navigate to the element you want to operate on.

After you've reached the element that you want to act on, use the AppleScript menu to choose an action. In this case, we want the Click Selected Element action. Choosing this action will generate a line of AppleScript that you can include in the `tell` block that was generated in the first step. The AppleScript should now resemble this:

```
activate application "Camino"
tell application "System Events"
   tell process "Camino"
     -- GUI Scripting statements:
   click menu item "About Camino" of menu 1 of menu bar item "Camino" of menu bar 1
   end tell
end tell
```

Now, if you haven't already, you'll need to either execute this script or manually open the About Camino window because the last step is to identify and retrieve the version string from the window.

After you've opened the About Camino window, click refresh in the UI Browser. You should now see an entry for `"window 1"` in the second column. Now would be a good time to click the Highlight check box in the browser. Doing so will automatically highlight the selected GUI element with a transparent color overlay. After you've turned on this option , click the `"dialog 1"` element and you should see the `"About Camino"` window highlight.

The next step is to identify which of the elements under `"dialog 1"` is the version number. Click through the various text items until the version number highlights, as shown in Figure 4.21. In the current release of Camino, it is `"text 3"`.

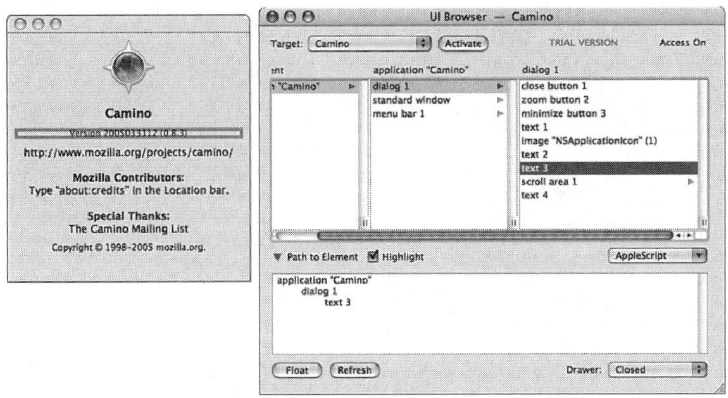

FIGURE 4.21 Identify the text string that contains the version number by selecting each available element then viewing the highlight within the GUI.

Now we've identified the object we're interested in, so choose Reference to Selected Object in the AppleScript menu to generate AppleScript that will identify that object. UI Browser will return `static text "Version 2005033112 (v0.8.3)" of window 1`. Unfortunately, although this is accurate (you *can* reference the object based on its value), it doesn't do us much good if the value changes. Thankfully, we also know that the element can be called `"text 3"` from the UI Browser list of elements. This means our reference can simply become `static text 3 of dialog 1`.

We're not quite done yet, but we're really close. The final step is to retrieve the actual *value* of the element `static text 3 of dialog 1`. This GUI element contains additional attributes such as size, position, and so forth, so we can't simple reference it by its object name. We must identify which of the attributes is the actual text we need. To do this, choose Attributes from the Drawer menu at the bottom of the UI Browser. A list of all the attributes for the selected item is shown, as displayed in Figure 4.22.

Scroll through the attributes until you see the version string. It is stored simply as the `value` attribute of the element. Finally, we can now reference the version string as `the value of static text 3 of dialog 1`!

A complete script that retrieves this value into an AppleScript variable and then displays it is as simple as

```
activate application "Camino"
tell application "System Events"
   tell process "Camino"
     -- GUI Scripting statements:
   click menu item "About Camino" of menu 1 of menu bar item "Camino" of menu bar 1
     set CaminoVersion to the value of static text 3 of dialog 1
   end tell
end tell
display dialog CaminoVersion
```

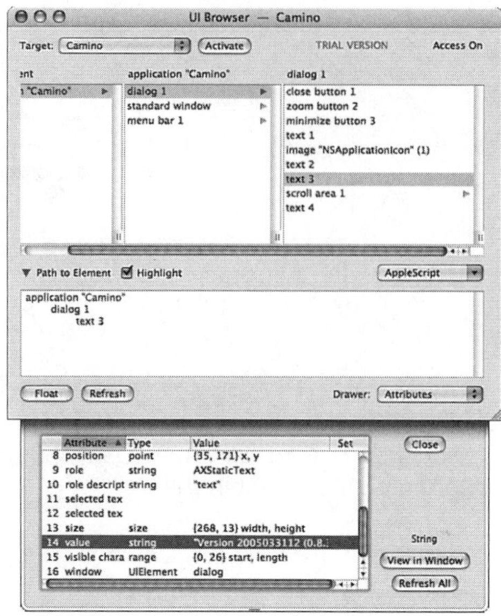

FIGURE 4.22 Identify the attribute of the element that we're really looking for.

Using GUI scripting you can get, set, and use all the other AppleScript features on a normally nonscriptable application. Obviously you will need to spend some time with PreFab's UI Browser to get the job done, but it's better than no scripting at all.

Additional AppleScript Tools and Resources

To finish this chapter, let's look at some additional tools on your system and other resources for AppleScript information. Apple has a strange habit of hiding AppleScript from its users. Although this has improved from Jaguar to Panther and Panther to Tiger, things that you'd expect to be plainly visible are tucked away.

Activating the Script Menu

The Script Menu is a menu extra to your menu bar that can be used to quickly launch AppleScripts from the `/Library/Scripts` folder or `~/Library/Scripts`. Apple has included dozens of scripts you can use with your applications immediately. To turn this feature on, you must run the AppleScript Utility within the AppleScript folder and click the Show Script Menu check box.

Any compiled scripts placed in either of the `Scripts` locations will become accessible from the menu. To create submenus for categorizing scripts, just create multiple folders within the `Scripts` folders. As with everything in Mac OS X, items stored in `/Library/Scripts` are accessible by all users, whereas those in your personal `~/Library/Scripts` folders can be used by only you. If you prefer to see only your own scripts, you can choose to not show library scripts from within the AppleScript Utility.

TIP

The Script Menu can be used to access Perl and shell scripts in addition to AppleScripts. Any script files placed in `Scripts` folders will be added to the list.

To remove the Script Menu, Command-drag it from the menu bar or turn it off within the AppleScript Utility.

Using Folder Actions

Folder Actions are scripts executed when folders are opened, modified, or moved. Actions are configured either via the Script Menu's Folder Actions submenu or by selecting a folder in Finder and invoking the contextual menu (Control-Click).

First, Folder Actions must be enabled. Choose Enable Folder Actions from a folder's contextual menu or the Script Menu.

Next, you can attach a Folder Action to a selected folder using either the Attach Folder Action or Configure Folder Actions option from the same menu.

The Add Folder action prompts you for a Folder Action script to attach to the highlighted folder, whereas Configure Folder Actions opens the Folder Actions Setup application (path: `/Applications/AppleScript/Folder Actions Setup`), shown in Figure 4.23, which provides access to *all* Folder Actions configured for your account.

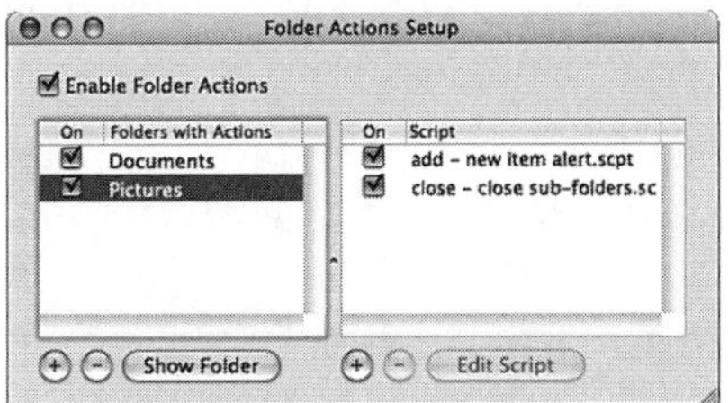

FIGURE 4.23 Configure Folder Actions provides a control center for adding and removing Folder Actions.

Within the Folder Actions Setup window, use the Enable Folder Actions check box to globally enable or disable actions. To add a new action, click the + button below the left column and choose a folder you want to attach an action to. When added to the folder list, highlight it and use the + button in the right column to choose a Folder Action script that you want to attach to the folder. The - button can be used to remove folders and attached scripts, whereas the Open Folder and Edit Script buttons open the highlighted folder and open the selected script in Script Editor, respectively.

To get started with Folder Action scripts, Apple has included three basic scripts in `/Library/Scripts/Folder Action Scripts:`

- `close - close sub-folders.scpt`—Closes any open subfolders when the folder with the attached script is closed.
- `add - new item alert.scpt`—Displays an alert when new items are added to the folder with the attached script.
- `open - show comments in dialog.scpt`—Shows any comments stored when the folder with the attached script is opened.

Also included are several scripts for operating on images, providing simple graphic conversions and alterations just by placing files in a folder.

Properly formed Folder Action scripts should be placed in either `/Library/Scripts/Folder Action Scripts` or `~/Library/Scripts/Folder Action Scripts`. Apple has provided an excellent tutorial on how to set up a Folder Action script at `http://www.apple.com/applescript/folder_actions/`.

Installing Scripting Additions

Enterprising developers who open the power of their software to the AppleScript model constantly expand AppleScript. The most common type of scripting addition is a new application. Applications that you install might or might not be scriptable—be sure to check the documentation or try opening the software's dictionary using the Script Editor.

In addition, some developers might deliver extensions to AppleScript in the form of a scripting extension. These extensions are not applications themselves but libraries of additional functions that can be used in any AppleScript.

Downloaded AppleScript extensions should be stored in `~/Library/ScriptingAdditions` or the system-level directory `/Library/ScriptingAdditions` for access by all users.

Running Command-Line AppleScript Tools

AppleScript compilation and execution has been extended to the BSD shell through the use of the `osacompile` and `osascript` commands.

The `osacompile` utility accepts a text file containing AppleScript as input and outputs a compiled script file using the following syntax:

```
osacompile -o <output file> <script file>
```

Although this is probably the form you'll and use most, several additional command-line options can fine-tune the compile process. Table 4.1 documents several of these options.

TABLE 4.1 Command Documentation Table for `osacompile`

`-l` *<language>*	Override the language for any plain text files. Normally, plain text files are compiled as AppleScript.
`-o` *<name>*	Place the output in the filename. If `-o` is not specified, the resulting script is placed in the file `a.scpt`.
`-t` *<type>*	Set the output file type to type. *type* is a four-character code. If this option is omitted and the output file does not exist, the type is set to `osas`—that is, a compiled script.
`-c` *<creator>*	Set the output file creator to creator. Creator is a four-character code. If this option is omitted and the output file does not exist, the creator is set to `"ToyS"`—that is, Script Editor.
`-x`	Save the resulting script as execute only.
`-s`	Run as a stay-open applet (doesn't exit when finished).
`-u`	Display a startup screen when the script runs.

If no options are specified, `osacompile` produces a classic Mac OS format script file—that is, type `osas` (compiled script), creator `"ToyS"` (Script Editor), with the script data in the `scpt:128` resource and nothing in the data fork. This format is compatible with all Mac OS and Mac OS X systems.

After you've compiled a script, you can run and it from the command line using the `osascript` utility.

`osascript` *<script filename>*

If a filename is not specified on the command line, `osascript` attempts to run AppleScript from standard input. This is a great way to test scripts or run a quick AppleScript command without needing to start the Script Editor. Like the `osacompile` command, `osascript` provides a number of command-line options that advanced users might be interested in. These are displayed in Table 4.2.

TABLE 4.2 Command Documentation Table for `osascript`

`-e` *<command>*	Enter one line of a script. If `-e` is given, `osascript` will not look for a filename in the argument list. Multiple `-e` commands may be given to build up a multiline script. Because most scripts use characters that are special to many shell programs—for example, AppleScript uses single and double quote marks, "(", ")", and "*")—the command has to be correctly quoted and escaped to get it past the shell intact.
`-l` *<language>*	Override the language for any plain text files. Normally, plain text files are compiled as AppleScript.

TABLE 4.2 Continued

`-s <flags>`	Modify the output style. The *`flags`* argument is a string consisting of any of the modifier characters `e`, `h`, `o`, and `s`. Multiple modifiers can be concatenated in the same string, and multiple `-s` options can be specified. The modifiers come in exclusive pairs; if conflicting modifiers are specified, the last one takes precedence. The meanings of the modifier characters are as follows: `h` Print values in human-readable form (default) `s` Print values in recompilable source form `osascript` normally prints its results in human-readable form: Strings do not have quotes around them, characters are not escaped, braces for lists and records are omitted, and so on. This is generally more useful but can introduce ambiguities. For example, the lists `'{"foo", "bar"}'` and `'{{"foo", {"bar"}}}'` would both be displayed as `'foo, bar'`. To see the results in an unambiguous form that could be recompiled into the same value, use the `s` modifier. `e` Print script errors to `stderr` (default). `o` Print script errors to `stdout`.

`osascript` normally prints script errors to `stderr`, so downstream clients see only valid results. When you're running automated tests, however, using the `o` modifier lets you distinguish script errors, which you care about matching, from other diagnostic output, which you don't.

AppleScript Studio

After you've familiarized yourself with basic AppleScript syntax, you might want to consider moving up to the next level of AppleScript development: AppleScript Studio. AppleScript Studio is Apple's integration of the AppleScript programming language with XCode.

Using XCode you can quickly create complete GUI applications powered entirely by AppleScript. Although not appropriate for real-time or graphically intense software, AppleScript Studio can quickly create a GUI around Unix-based commands. In fact, a number of utilities (such as Carbon Copy Cloner, discussed in Chapter 29, "Maintaining a Healthy System") have been written in AppleScript Studio and have received rave reviews.

To get started with AppleScript Studio, install XCode and browse the examples in `/Developer/Examples/AppleScript Studio`. Apple provides a simple tutorial along with PDF reference guides to get you started. Be warned: AppleScript Studio takes advantage of Apple's development tools. These tools, although powerful, have been known to take some time to master.

Other Sources of AppleScript Information

AppleScript is a capable language that offers many advanced features impossible to cover in the amount of space this title allows. What is provided here should be an ample start to creating scripts of your own and editing scripts included with Tiger. If you're interested in more information on advanced AppleScript syntax, I strongly suggest that you check out the following resources:

- *AppleScript Language Guide*— `http://developer.apple.com/documentation/AppleScript/Conceptual/AppleScriptLangGuide/index.html`
- *AppleScript in Mac OS X*—`http://www.apple.com/applescript/macosx/`
- The AppleScript Sourcebook—`http://www.AppleScriptSourcebook.com/`
- *AppleScript in a Nutshell*—Bruce W. Perry, ISBN: 1565928415, O'Reilly

Summary

For a 1.0 release, Automator is an amazing tool. It provides a point-and-click solution for implementing workflow automation between many popular Tiger applications including the iLife suite. Assuming that the technology catches on with developers, we might be on the verge of a completely visual scripting environment in future versions of Mac OS X. In the meantime, what Automator can't do, AppleScript can. For applications that are natively scriptable, you can use their AppleScript dictionaries to explore all the capabilities they offer. For those that don't include scripting features, AppleScript's GUI scripting opens up automation to just about every piece of software on your system.

PART II

Hardware Setup and Configuration

IN THIS PART

CHAPTER 5

Configuring Tiger Hardware Support and Preferences

IN THIS CHAPTER

- Managing Displays: Displays and Display Calibrator Assistant
- Configuring Keyboards and Mice: Keyboard & Mouse
- Tablet Device Input: Ink
- Bluetooth Devices and Services: Bluetooth Preferences and Bluetooth File Exchange
- Disks and Disk Images: Disk Utility
- Scanners, Cameras, and Media Readers: Image Capture
- Audio Input and Output: Sound Preferences and Audio MIDI Setup
- Switching Between Operating Systems: Startup Disk
- Handling Optical Media: CDs and DVDs
- Saving Electricity and the Environment: Energy Saver

Out of the box, Tiger supports hardware such as tablets for handwriting recognition, storage devices, USB sound output devices, even cameras and scanners. Getting these devices working with the operating system, however, can be a bit on the befuddling side because the settings aren't necessarily where you'd expect to find them. This chapter covers the tools available for working with supported devices along with the associated system preference panels that haven't been covered elsewhere.

Managing Displays: Displays and Display Calibrator Assistant

The Displays pane in System Preferences functions in a way that's similar to the Monitors control panel or the Monitors portion of the Monitors & Sound control panel of traditional Mac OS. The options available in the Displays pane vary with the type of display. For example, for a laptop with no other displays attached, expect only the Display and Color sections to be available. For an older iMac, expect to also have a Geometry section. Your system might have options not shown here.

Setting Resolution

In the Display section, shown in Figure 5.1, you can set the resolution, the number of colors displayed, and the refresh rate. There's an option to make the Displays information available in the menu bar and an option to ask the pane to list only modes that the display recommends. You'll probably see some of the options gray out on checking the box.

A slider scale adjuster for brightness might also be available as well as one for contrast. Or your Display section might not have any sliders here. This section might also contain a button to allow you to detect displays. The option to show recent modes might also be available. For some laptops, you also have the option to adjust the brightness as the ambient lighting changes. The Display section in Figure 5.1 is from a laptop and may not reflect what you see in your Displays pane.

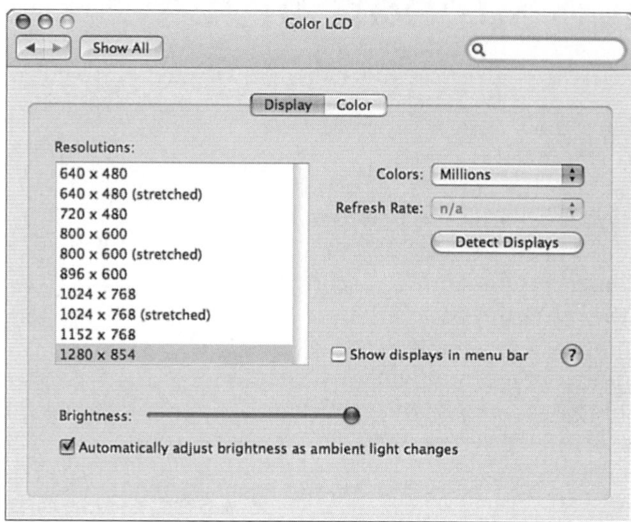

FIGURE 5.1 The Display section of the Displays pane is where you set resolution and color depth.

Fine-tuning Geometry

The Geometry section, shown in Figure 5.2, is where you can set typical monitor geometry settings: position, height/width, pincushion, rotate, keystone, and parallelogram. The buttons surrounding the display depicted in the Geometry tab change with each option. Click on the buttons to make your adjustments. You can also select the factory defaults. Not all monitors have this section. The Geometry example shown in Figure 5.2 comes from an older iMac.

Performing Color Calibration

In the Color section, shown in Figure 5.3, you select a color profile for your monitor. If no ColorSync profile is available for your monitor, you can create a custom profile by clicking the Calibrate option. The Calibrate option starts the Display Calibrator utility, which guides you through the calibration of your monitor. If you have calibrated your monitor, the resulting profile appears as one of your choices here. The exact choices also vary with the display type. Figure 5.3 shows an example of the Color section from a laptop.

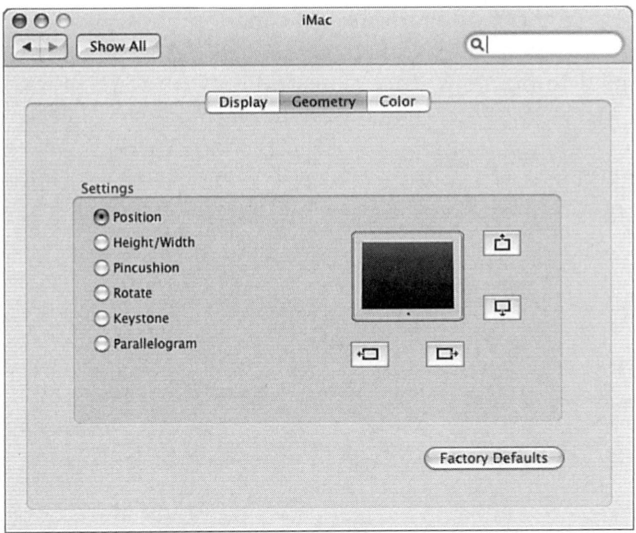

FIGURE 5.2 The Geometry section of the Displays pane is where you set typical monitor geometry settings.

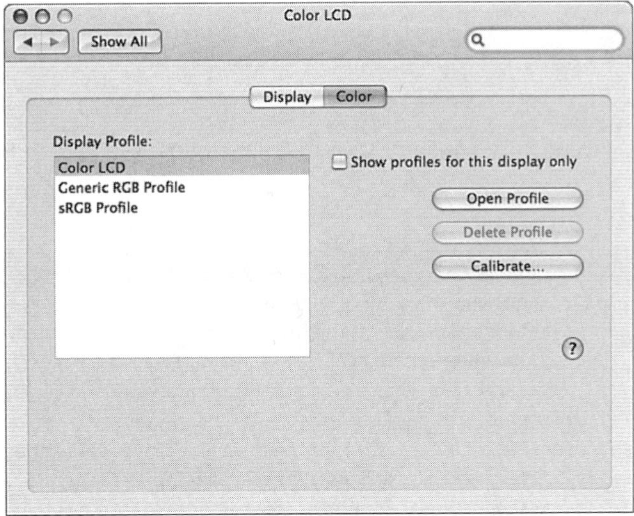

FIGURE 5.3 The Color section of the Displays pane is where you select a color profile for your monitor.

Display Calibrator is the utility that creates a ColorSync profile specific to your monitor. The utility is located in `/System/Library/ColorSync/Calibrators`, but you can also open it from within the Color section of the Displays preferences pane.

Figure 5.4 shows the introductory screen for Display Calibrator. As you can see, the calibrator guides you through adjusting your brightness, contrast, luminance response, gamma, and white point. The calibrator has an expert mode available, which you can select by checking the Expert Mode box. In earlier versions of Mac OS X, expert mode did not necessarily provide more steps, only more options with some of the steps. In more recent versions of Mac OS X, you might expect to perform extra steps in expert mode. Depending on your monitor, you might not have to perform all the steps shown here or you might have additional steps not shown here. To provide some experience with the different modes, we vary the modes shown and try to provide examples of as many of the steps as possible.

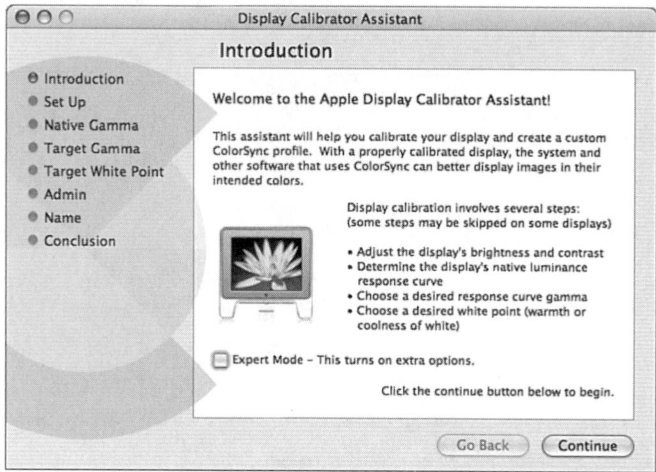

FIGURE 5.4 The introductory screen of Display Calibrator. Here you can choose whether to be in expert mode.

NOTE

Depending on your monitor and the settings you normally worked with, you might be pleasantly surprised, or surprisingly dismayed, at the results of putting together a calibration for your monitor. Calibrating your monitor enables you to see image files and online content as they were intended to be seen, assuming that the person creating the original file had her display calibrated as well. Unfortunately, many users don't have their monitors calibrated, and although the monitors provided by Apple have historically been well behaved with respect to their color response curves, this is by no means a universal constant among all monitor manufacturers. The end result is that if you calibrate your monitor, you see all the errors in everyone else's monitor calibrations in the files they create. Carefully created content looks wonderful, and less carefully created content looks, well...we'll leave that to you to judge.

Overall, we recommend using a carefully and correctly calibrated monitor so that content you create is correct even though much web content created on inexpensive hardware might look better if browsed with an incorrect setting.

The next step might vary. Some monitors might go through the Set Up step, shown in Figure 5.5. In this step, you adjust the display's brightness and contrast. The Display Calibrator assistant instructs you to set your contrast to the highest setting and to adjust your brightness until the oval in the dark square is barely visible. This step is the same in the expert and normal modes. Depending on the capabilities of your monitor, you might or might not have slider controls within Display Calibrator to make these adjustments.

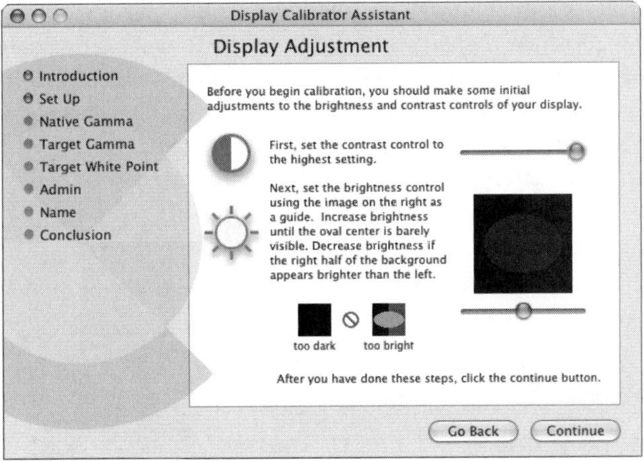

FIGURE 5.5 In the Set Up step, you adjust the contrast and brightness of your display.

The next step for your monitor can be the Native Gamma step in which you determine your display's native luminance response curves. For some displays, the normal mode might not exist, but the expert mode might consist of five separate steps. For other displays, the normal mode might be a one-step version of the expert mode. For both modes, the utility suggests that it might be helpful to squint or stand back from the display to accomplish this task. Figure 5.6 shows the Native Gamma step in expert mode.

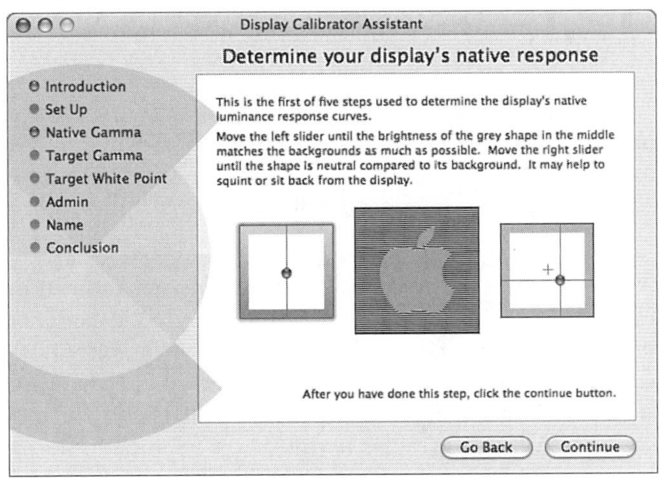

FIGURE 5.6 In the Native Gamma step, shown here in expert mode, you determine the native gamma of your display.

The next step is the Target Gamma step, in which you select a target gamma for your display. Figure 5.7 shows this step in normal mode. In this mode, you select from standard Macintosh gamma, described as Standard Gamma, or standard PC gamma, described as Television Gamma. The target gamma is selected in expert mode on a slider, which has the Macintosh and PC gammas marked as well as an option to use the native gamma. You'll find that your monitor displays a broader and smoother color palette if you choose the Macintosh default gamma of 1.8. If you do a lot of image creation for the World Wide Web, you might find it useful to create two ColorSync profiles: one for a standard Macintosh display and one for a standard PC display. Two such profiles would give you the ability to see approximately how your images appear on each of these common display types.

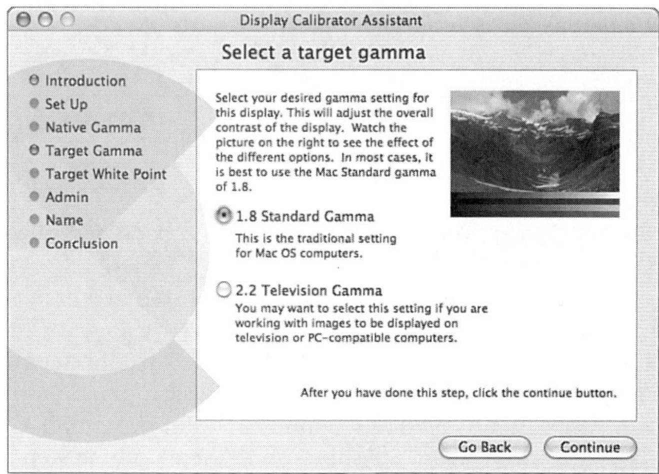

FIGURE 5.7 In the Target Gamma step, shown here in normal mode, you select the target gamma of your display.

In the next step, the Target White Point step, you select a target white point setting for your display. Figure 5.8 shows this step for the normal mode, which provides three basic choices with comments on the choices, as well as a choice for no white point correction. The expert mode provides a slider interface for these choices, but no comments on possibly pertinent choices.

The next step in expert mode is the Administrator Options step, shown in Figure 5.9. You might not experience this step in normal mode. In this step, you can choose to make this color profile available as a possible default for every user on the system. The profile normally becomes available as a possible default for only the user who created it, and is placed in `~/Library/ColorSync/Profiles`. This step, though, puts the profile in `/Library/ColorSync/Profiles/Displays/`. If you set up a profile in normal mode and decide later that you would like to make it available to all users, as an administrative user, copy the profile that was created in your home directory to the systemwide location. If you don't like a profile you created, delete it.

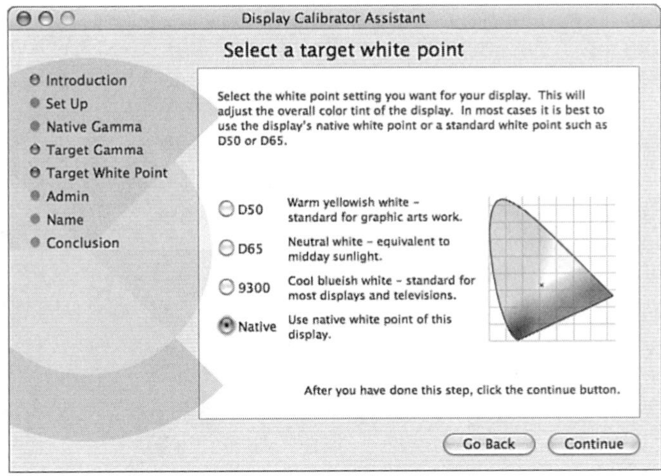

FIGURE 5.8 Select a target white point setting for your display in the Target White Point step, shown here in normal mode.

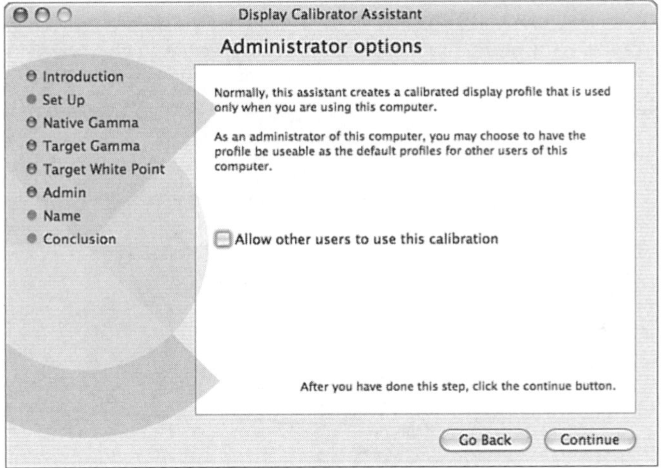

FIGURE 5.9 In expert mode, the Administrator Options step enables you to provide this profile as a possible default to any user on the system.

Figure 5.10 shows the next step, the Name step, which is the same in both expert and normal modes. Here you provide a name for your profile. If you created a profile for a special purpose, such as creating a profile with PC contrast, you might consider including something about the purpose in the name.

The final step, aptly named Conclusion, is shown in expert mode in Figure 5.11. This step is an informational step. In normal mode, the utility indicates that the new profile has been created and set as the default profile, and it provides information about changing your current profile. Changing your current profile can be done in either the Color section of the Displays system preferences pane or in the Devices section of the ColorSync utility. Expert mode provides not only this information, but also a basic summary of the profile you created.

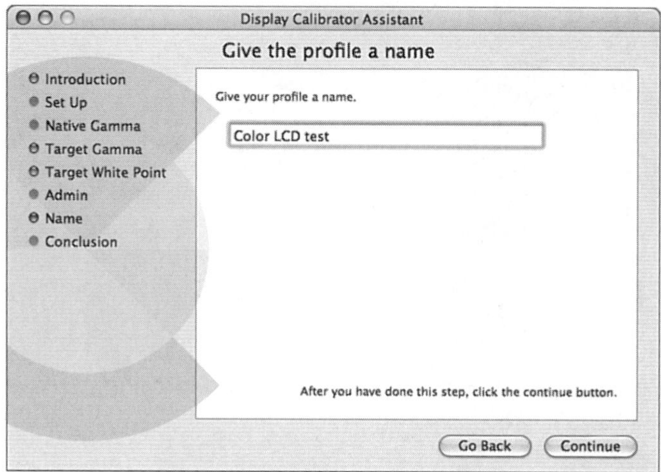

FIGURE 5.10 Provide a name for your new ColorSync profile in the Name step.

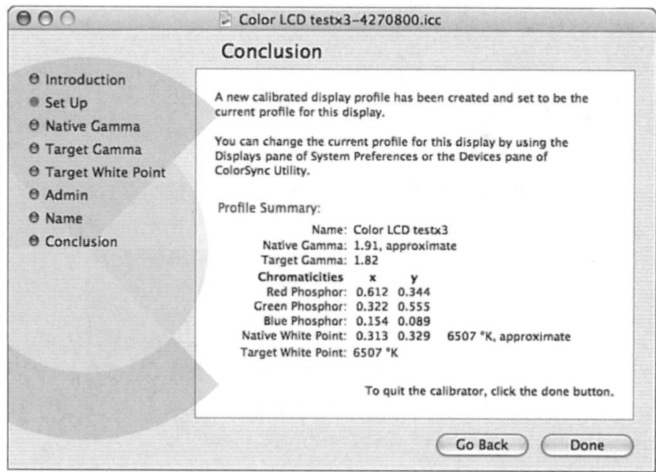

FIGURE 5.11 In the final step, shown here in expert mode, you see comments on the new profile and changing your current profile, as well as a summary of the new profile.

Multiple Monitors

When you open the Displays pane while multiple monitors are attached, the controlling monitor has the extra Arrangement section. At the same time, the other monitors display the normal Displays pane without any additional sections. In this area of the Displays pane, you can select how the monitors are arranged. Drag them around to suit your needs. You can even move them up and down to suit your needs. By default, the main monitor has the menu bar attached to it. To move the menu bar, drag it to the monitor where you would prefer to have it for your needs. You can also choose to mirror the displays.

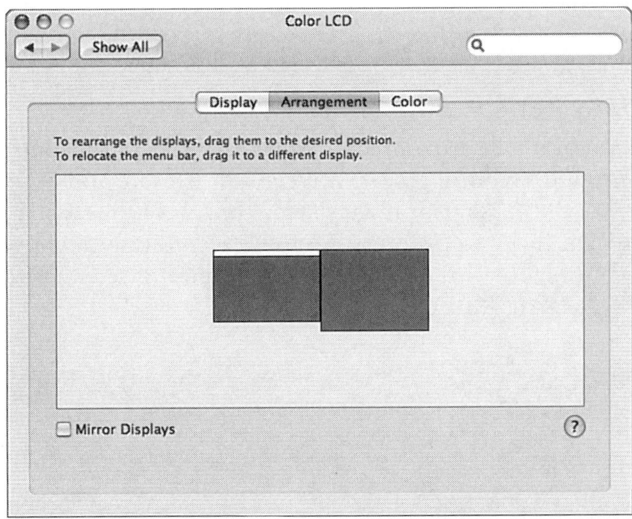

FIGURE 5.12 When you select the Displays pane while multiple monitors are attached, the Displays pane of the main monitor includes an Arrangement section.

Figure 5.13 shows two monitors running something in addition to the Displays pane.

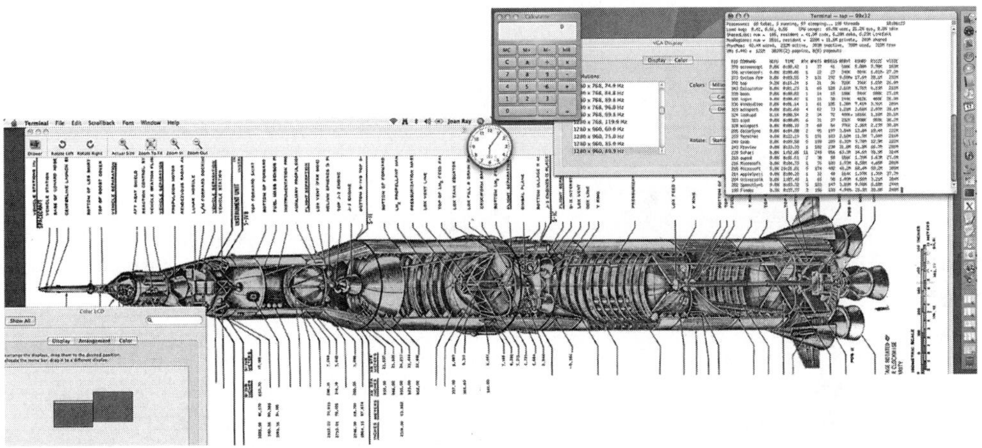

FIGURE 5.13 Here you can see the multiple monitors in active use.

Configuring Keyboards and Mice: Keyboard & Mouse

As with many of the Hardware system preferences, the sections available in the Keyboard & Mouse pane vary with your hardware. Nonetheless, this is the pane in which you specify settings for your keyboard and mouse and/or trackpad, as well as keyboard shortcuts. If you have a Bluetooth keyboard and mouse, the Bluetooth subsection displays the keyboard and mouse names and battery life. Bluetooth devices are covered in more detail in the Bluetooth sections of this chapter.

Setting Keyboard Repeat and Delay

The Keyboard section of the Keyboard pane, shown in Figure 5.14, controls the key repeat rate and the amount of delay until repeat. You can test the rate and delay in a test space within the pane itself. If it takes your fingers some time to release the keys as you're typing, you might want to try some longer settings here. In this day of word processing rather than typing at the typewriter, these controls might not seem important. At the very least, we can reduce Mr. Kitty's typing speed.

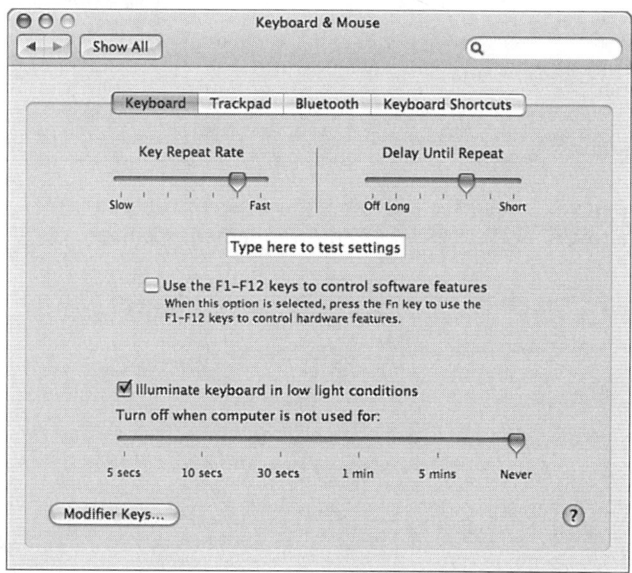

FIGURE 5.14 The key repeat rate and the amount of delay until repeat are set in the Keyboard section of the Keyboard pane.

You can also choose to use the function keys to control software features, and, depending on your hardware, you can choose to illuminate the keyboard under low light conditions. Here there is also an option to turn off the computer after a specified period of time. Finally, in this section you can also customize the actions performed by the Caps Lock, Control, Option, and Command keys.

Setting Trackpad and Mouse Options

If you are using a laptop, you'll have a Trackpad section in the Keyboard & Mouse pane, as shown in Figure 5.15. Here you can control tracking speed and the double-click speed. The pane itself has a space in which you can test the double-click speed.

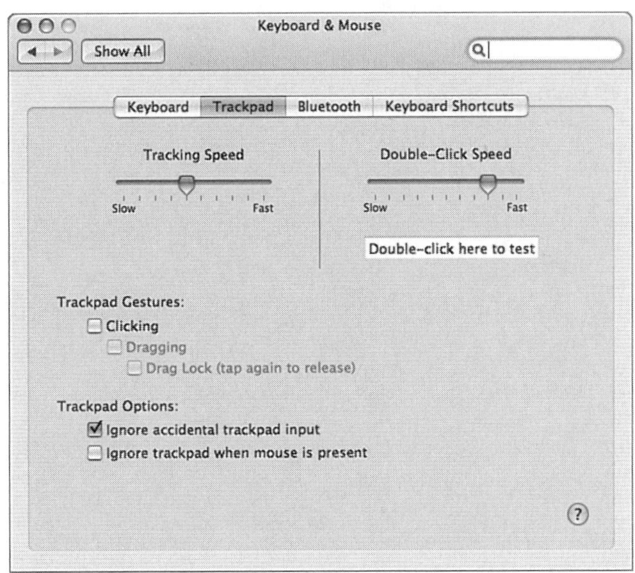

FIGURE 5.15 Trackpad behavior is set in the Trackpad section of the Keyboard & Mouse pane.

The pane also enables you to specify settings involving trackpad use, and we expect that the options available in the section vary with your hardware. You can decide to use the trackpad for clicking and dragging. When you select that option, you replace clicking with tapping. Additionally, you can set the trackpad to ignore accidental trackpad input or to ignore the trackpad completely when a mouse is present. For the newer laptops that offer scrolling by dragging two fingers across the trackpad in the vertical or horizontal direction, we would expect that the ability to further customize that behavior appears here.

If you are dissatisfied with the basic trackpad options, you might consider a third party driver, such as SideTrack, available from `http://www.ragingmenace.com/software/sidetrack/index.html`. It is supported under Tiger and installs as a separate preference pane. It has many powerful features, including the ability to configure vertical or horizontal scrolling on your trackpad as well as the ability to configure left and right clicking on the trackpad. SideTrack's website promises that support for the newer laptops is in progress.

If you are using a mouse on your computer, you'll have a Mouse section in this pane, as shown in Figure 5.16. The tracking, scrolling, and double-click speeds are set here. The pane itself also provides a space in which you can test the double-click speed. If you have a multibutton mouse, set the primary mouse button here.

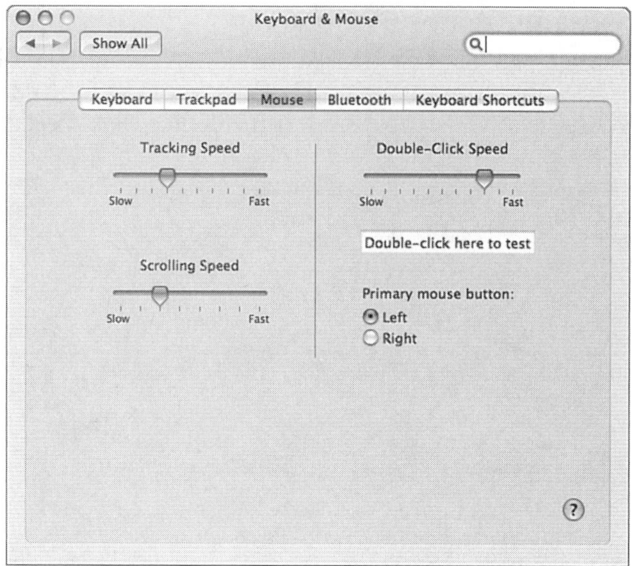

FIGURE 5.16 Mouse behavior is set in the Mouse section of the Keyboard & Mouse pane.

Customizing Keyboard Shortcuts

In the Keyboard Shortcuts section of the Keyboard pane, shown in Figure 5.17, you can choose to use a number of default keyboard shortcuts, or you can change default keyboard shortcuts to shortcuts that you might find more useful. Default keyboard shortcuts are readily available for Screen Shots; Universal Access; Keyboard Navigation; Dock, Expose, and Dashboard; Input Menu; Dictionary and Spotlight.

You can also specify keyboard shortcuts for specific applications. The plus and minus signs enable you to add to and delete items from the list. You can create shortcuts that apply globally to all applications or you can create shortcuts for specific applications. If you don't like what you've done, you can always choose to restore the default settings. Warnings are displayed where there are duplicate shortcuts. In this section, you also control whether in windows and dialogs, the Tab key moves the focus between text boxes and lists only or between all controls instead. Full keyboard access is on all the time by default and can be used for accessing the menu, dock and other screen areas, for highlighting items, and for selecting an action. You can toggle full keyboard access on and off with Ctrl+F1. Check the help system and the Keyboard Navigation section of the shortcuts listing for additional usage tips.

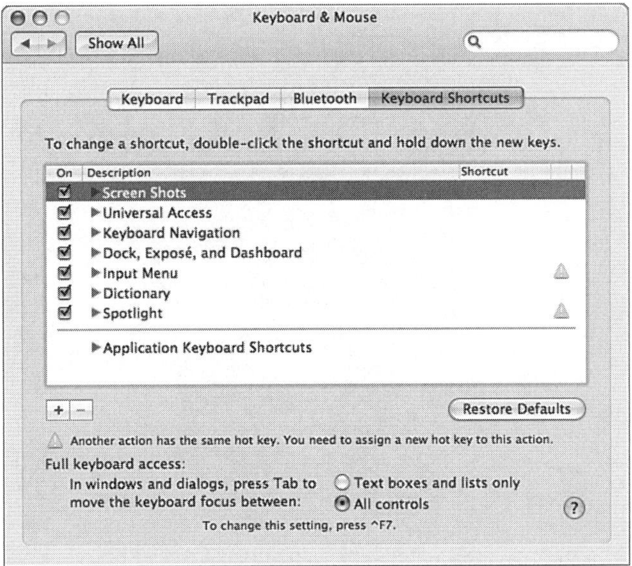

FIGURE 5.17 You can set keyboard shortcuts in the Keyboard Shortcuts section of the Keyboard pane.

Tablet Device Input: Ink

Even though Apple hasn't provided a tablet Mac yet, it has done the preliminary work in creating a handwriting recognition system that you can use with popular graphics tablets: Ink. Built on Apple's Recognition Engine (originally the Newton Recognition Engine), Ink requires no special "graffiti" alphabet—although people with messy handwriting might require practice to understand how Ink interprets characters.

Setting Up Ink

When a recognized graphics tablet is plugged into one of your computer's USB ports, an icon called Ink shows up under the Hardware section of System Preferences. The Ink preferences pane, shown in Figure 5.18, gives you the option to turn on or off handwriting recognition and to change several settings.

The easiest way to access Ink on demand is to add the Ink extra to the menu bar; make sure that handwriting recognition is turned on and that Show Ink in Menu Bar is checked.

Providing Input via Ink

From the Ink menu, you can launch the Ink Window—a toolbar that floats on top of all other application windows. In the Ink Window, use the first button to toggle between full-screen handwriting mode and pointer mode represented by a pen and a cursor, respectively.

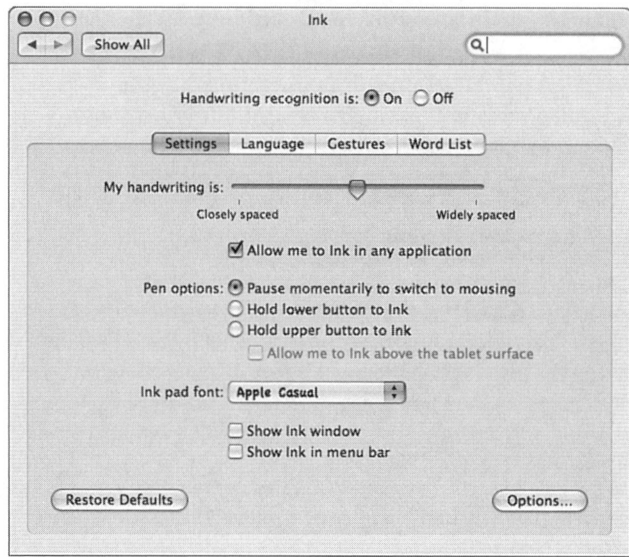

FIGURE 5.18 Ink allows you to set your keyboard and mouse aside.

In handwriting mode, you can write virtually anywhere on the screen. To add text directly to an application, first activate the text area that should receive input. Next, touch the stylus to the tablet to open a writing space with guiding lines and begin writing words. If a writing space doesn't appear, try touching the stylus to the graphics tablet in a different place. Your stylus can also act as a mouse, so some areas of the screen, such as window controls or menus, activate commands instead of opening a writing space. Figure 5.19 demonstrates the handwriting recognition mode of Ink.

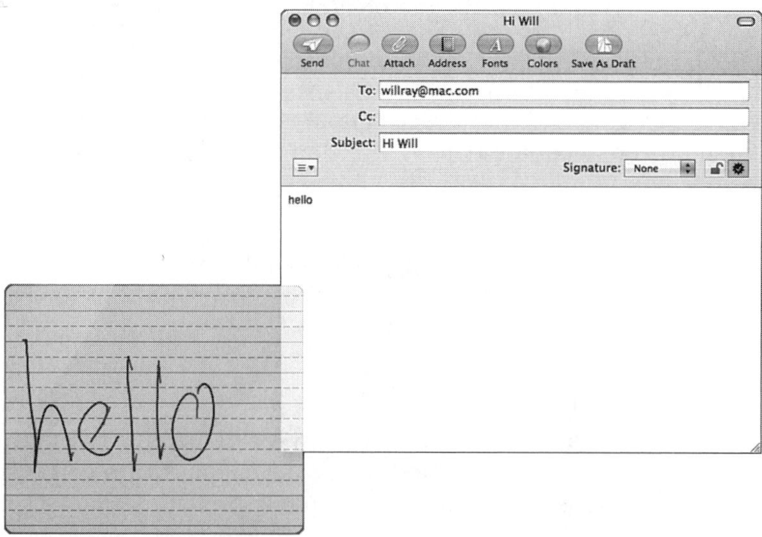

FIGURE 5.19 Handwriting recognition mode provides input across the entire screen.

Using Ink Pad Mode

If you'd prefer to constrain your writing to a smaller area of the screen, you can use Ink Pad mode. To activate Ink Pad mode, toggle handwriting mode off with the first button in the Ink Window, and then open the Ink pad with the notepad icon in the Ink Window. The Ink Window expands to resemble Figure 5.20.

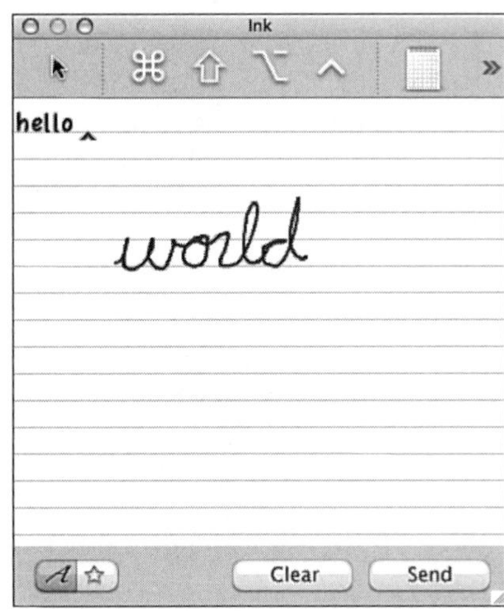

FIGURE 5.20 Use the Ink pad to constrain your writing drawing to a virtual pad of paper.

In Ink pad mode, you can switch between the writing and drawing modes using the A and star buttons at the lower left. All input must be provided within the Ink pad window.

The text or drawings you create in the Ink pad can be inserted into other documents. Simply create the content of your choice in the workspace and click the Send button to add it to the active document at the current insertion point. For example, when you've finished typing a message in Mail, you could sign your name in the drawing view of the Ink pad and insert your signature at the bottom of your message. Obviously, the application must support graphics input to accept graphic images.

Ink doesn't require you to learn special letter forms, but you must write linearly as if you were using paper rather than write overlapping letters as you would on a PDA. When you pause, your markings will be converted to text at the top of the writing space. To correct a mistake, draw a long horizontal line from right to left, and the last character will disappear. If you have larger sections to delete, switch to the pointer mode in the Ink Window, select the part you want to redo, and switch back to writing mode to try again.

TIP

To input special modifier characters, use the Command, Shift, Option, and Control icons in the Ink Window toolbar. Clicking one of these icons turns on that keyboard modifier.

NOTE

Some applications that don't use standard Mac OS X text controls behave unpredictably with Ink's text recognition. If you are using an application in which spaces don't appear between words as needed, try writing your content in the Ink pad and use Send to insert it in the other application.

Configuring Input Options

Ink's input preferences can be changed to suit individual users' writing styles and increase reliability. The following adjustments can be made under the main Settings of the preference pane:

- My Handwriting Is—Move the slider to describe your handwriting as closely spaced, widely spaced, or somewhere in between.
- Pen Options—Choose how Ink will switch between mousing and inking. Note that your tablet might not support all of these features.
- Ink Pad Font—The font to use when providing input via the Ink pad.

Clicking the Options button in the lower right opens a sheet with additional handwriting recognition options, including the amount of delay before writing is converted to type, how much the stylus must move before a stroke is recorded, how long the pen must be held still to act as a mouse, when to recognize handwriting input, whether the pointer should be hidden while writing, and whether Ink should play sounds as you write.

Using Gestures for Common Commands

Ink implements simple handwritten gestures for actions such as Cut, Copy, and Paste. To view, enable, and disable gestures, open the Gestures settings of the Ink preference pane.

Click on an item to see both a demonstration of drawing the shape and a written description of it. Activate or deactivate gesture actions using the check box in front of each item.

NOTE

Apple recommends you provide extra space in front of gesture shapes and exaggerate the ending stroke so that the system does not confuse them with letters.

Providing Input in Other Languages

To change the input language, open the Ink system preference pane and access the Language settings. The Language pop-up menu can be used to choose the input language of choice. Check the Recognize Western European Characters check box if appropriate.

Teaching Uncommon Words to Ink

The Word List settings of the Ink preference pane allows you to add uncommon words that you use frequently. Ink uses a list of common words to help decipher people's input. If you come across a word that Ink doesn't know or has trouble with, click the Add button and type the word in the text box. Use the Edit and Delete buttons to change and remove entries if necessary.

Bluetooth Devices and Services: Bluetooth Preferences and Bluetooth File Exchange

Bluetooth is a popular wireless technology that allows you to form a wireless *PAN—Personal Area Network*. Using this wireless network, you can synchronize PDAs, connect to the Internet through your cell phone, print to printers, use Apple's wireless keyboard and mouse, and so on. Although Bluetooth is an accepted standard, a limited number of devices currently use it, and not all Macintosh systems are Bluetooth enabled. If you're interested in Bluetooth, you can purchase a Bluetooth USB dongle for about $40 that will Bluetooth-enable your Mac.

NOTE

Most third-party USB Bluetooth transceivers work just fine on Tiger. Even Microsoft's Bluetooth adapter is recognized without a hitch.

Getting Ready for Bluetooth

Tiger comes with a suite of Bluetooth tools, including a File Exchange utility, Bluetooth serial utility, and Bluetooth Setup Assistant—all (with the exception of the File Exchange utility) integrated into the Bluetooth System Preference pane. This might seem like a lot of "stuff" just to use a wireless mouse, but it isn't as convoluted as it appears. You should be familiar with three basic terms to use Bluetooth devices:

- *Profiles*—A Bluetooth profile is a categorization of the features that are provided or required by a Bluetooth device—such as a Human Input Device (mouse, keyboard, and so on).
- *Discoverable*—A device is considered discoverable if it can be seen on a Bluetooth network. Nondiscoverable devices are hidden from other Bluetooth devices.
- *Pairing*—To speak to a Bluetooth device, your computer must be paired with it. This prevents any random person from walking into a room with a Bluetooth device and using it to access your computer. Pairing often, but not always, requires a password to be entered on the computer and the device connecting to it.

With that knowledge, and a compatible Bluetooth adapter, you're ready to get started.

Configuring Global Bluetooth Settings

Keyboards, mice, and PDAs are obvious types of Bluetooth devices—but your computer, with a Bluetooth adaptor, is also a Bluetooth device. After plugging a Bluetooth transceiver into your computer, a new Bluetooth System Preferences pane appears, as shown in Figure 5.21. This is the control center for almost everything Bluetooth in Tiger.

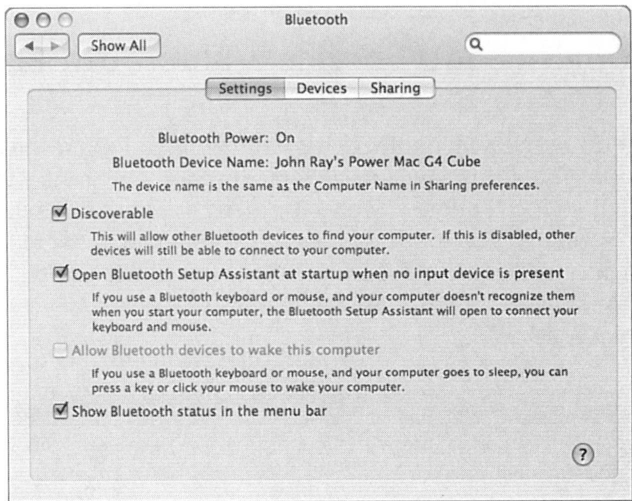

FIGURE 5.21 The Bluetooth System Preferences pane provides control over your wireless devices.

> **WHAT PROFILES DOES TIGER SUPPORT AND PROVIDE?**
>
> On the server side, Tiger supports the Object Push and File Transfer profiles for transferring files and the Serial Port Profile for bidirectional serial communications.
>
> For client devices, Tiger supports the same profiles along with the Dial-up Networking profile for using a phone as a modem, the Human Input Device profile for mice, keyboards, and other input mechanisms, the Headset Profile for audio input and output, and, finally, the Hard Cable Replacement Profile for wireless printing.

Three panes are used to control Bluetooth operation. The first pane, Settings, is shown in Figure 5.21. Here you can see the status of your Bluetooth adapter and make changes to your first Bluetooth device—your Macintosh.

After your Macintosh has an adapter plugged in, it becomes a Bluetooth device on your network. It can speak to other devices, and they, in turn, can speak to it. That being the case, you might want to adjust the discoverability to keep unauthorized users from seeing or pairing with your computer:

- Discoverable—Enables other Bluetooth devices to see your computer on the Bluetooth network. They can, quite literally, browse to your computer. If unchecked, your machine will be invisible to other devices. This does not, however, mean that it cannot be connected, too.

- Open Bluetooth Setup Assistant at Startup When No Input Device Is Present—If Bluetooth is enabled but no input device is paired with your computer, this setting causes the setup assistant to run automatically.
- Allow Bluetooth Devices to Wake This Computer—If enabled and supported by your system, external devices will be able to wake your computer from sleep.
- Show Bluetooth Status in the Menu Bar—Adds a menu extra that can be used to quickly access many of the Tiger Bluetooth settings and functions.

To disable Bluetooth entirely, click the Turn Bluetooth Off button. The adaptor will be disabled until the button is clicked again.

Managing Bluetooth Devices

To manage Bluetooth devices, use the Devices setting pane, shown in Figure 5.22. From here, you can add, delete, disconnect, and otherwise alter the devices that your computer connects to over the Bluetooth network.

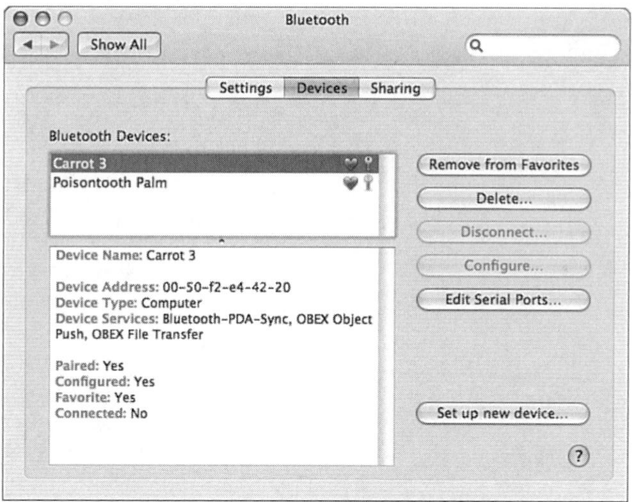

FIGURE 5.22 Use the Devices pane to connect Bluetooth devices to your computer.

In the upper-left corner of the pane is a list of Bluetooth devices paired with your computer. Below the list is a detailed display showing information about the selected device. To the right of the selected device are six buttons used to control the device pairings:

- Add to Favorites/Remove from Favorites—Toggles the device as a favorite. Favorites will automatically be repaired with your computer if they become temporarily unavailable (because of dead batteries and so forth).

- Delete—Removes a device from your list of known Bluetooth devices, effectively causing Tiger to forget about it.
- Disconnect—Disconnects a device but does not delete the pairing. Depending on the device (such as mouse), just using it again causes it to reconnect.
- Configure—Makes configuration changes to the selected paired device.
- Edit Serial Ports—Changes the virtual serial port settings for the selected device. This button is active only if the device pairing requires a serial port.
- Set Up New Device—Creates a new device pairing using the Bluetooth Setup Assistant.

Adding a New Device

To add a new device, click the Set Up New Device button in the Devices settings of the Bluetooth System Preference pane. The Setup Wizard will walk you through the steps of adding a new device. When prompted, as shown in Figure 5.23, choose the type of device you are adding, or, if your device is unlisted, choose Any Device. Click Continue to begin searching for devices.

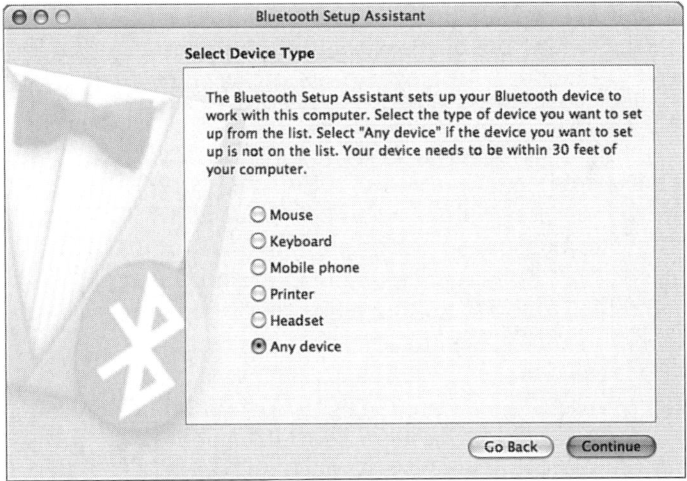

FIGURE 5.23 Set up new Bluetooth connections using the Bluetooth Setup Assistant.

If your Bluetooth devices are set as discoverable and match the chosen type, they will appear in the list at the bottom of the window. If not, the Bluetooth Setup Assistant will display an error message and continue searching.

To finish pairing, you must verify that you have the appropriate permission to create a connection. This is handled by entering a passkey.

Entering a Passkey

Before a pairing is complete, a passkey must typically be provided to verify that a device is authorized to create a connection. If instructions came with your peripheral giving you a specific passkey or telling you to use no passkey at all, click the Passkey Options button below the discovered device listing. Use the options displayed in Figure 5.24 to configure the passkey settings to match those of your device.

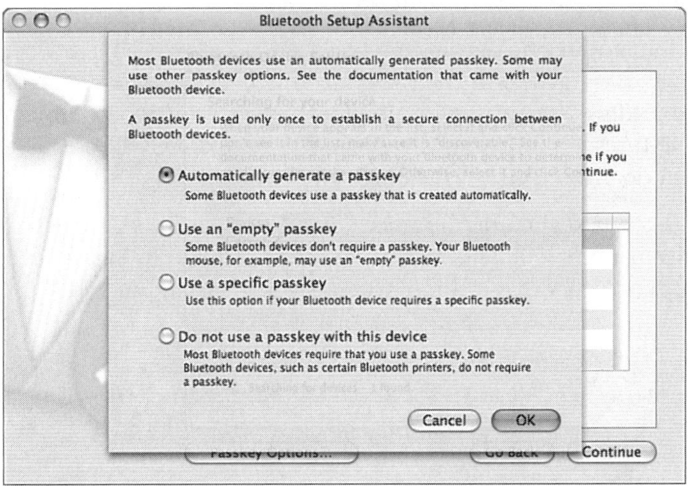

FIGURE 5.24 Configure the type of passkey your device will use.

When ready, click Continue to enter the actual passkey and finish the pairing process, as demonstrated in Figure 5.25.

FIGURE 5.25 Passkeys are used to authoritatively pair two devices.

If the passkey is accepted, the device is considered paired and should be listed in the Devices pane of the Bluetooth System Preferences pane.

Using Paired Devices

So, you've paired a device, now what can you do with it? If you've paired a phone, you can now use Address Book to make and receive phone calls directly from address cards. What the device does is, well, dependant on the device you're using!

When pairing a Bluetooth phone that provides Dial Up Networking, for example, a new modem device will be added to the Networking system preference panel. This device can be configured according to your service provider's specs and used like any other modem to connect to the Internet. Bluetooth headsets will immediately be available as audio input and output devices for use in iChat AV and elsewhere.

Paired Apple Bluetooth keyboards and mice add new settings to the Keyboard & Mouse system preference pane. The Bluetooth setting screen, shown in Figure 5.26, provides status on the battery level of your Apple wireless keyboard and mouse.

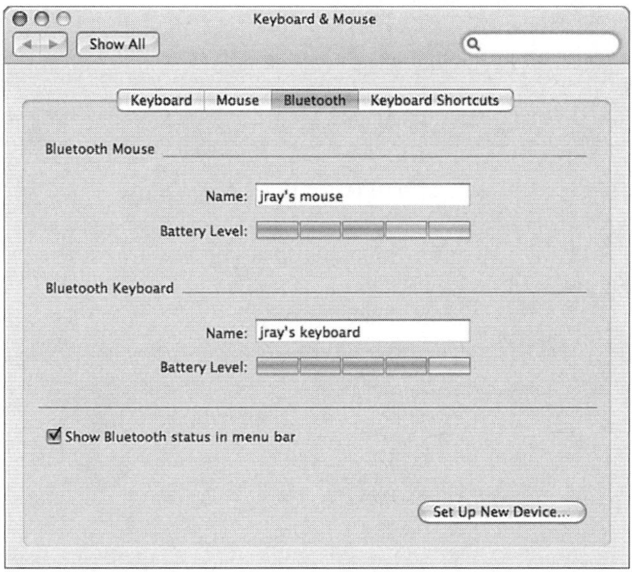

FIGURE 5.26 Use the Bluetooth pane of the Keyboard & Mouse pane to monitor your Apple wireless device battery levels.

Controlling Server-Side Services

As mentioned earlier, installing a Bluetooth adaptor in a computer turns that computer into a Bluetooth device itself. Tiger supports file transfer as well as serial port services—providing a means for external Bluetooth devices to make incoming connections. This is often used for handheld devices to make synch connections back to your computer.

To enable or disable these services, open the Sharing settings of the Bluetooth system preference pane, demonstrated in Figure 5.27.

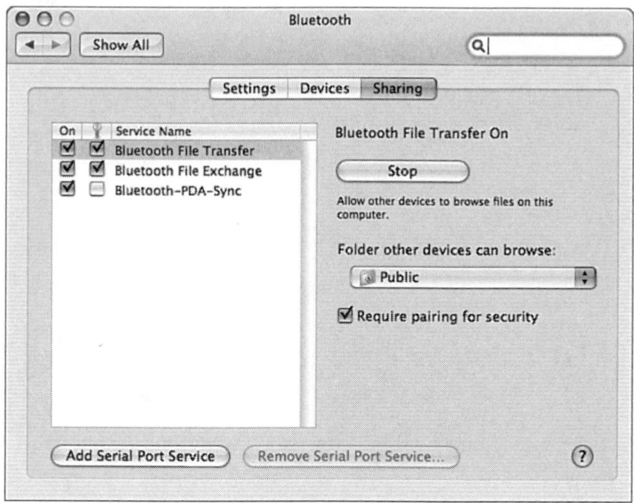

FIGURE 5.27 The Bluetooth Sharing settings work very similarly to the normal Tiger Sharing preferences. Click a service in the list, and then use the Start or Stop buttons or On check box beside its name to enable or disable it.

In addition to starting and stopping a service, you can also force incoming connections to go through the pairing process—that is, the service will be required to generate and validate a passkey. To ensure that only authorized devices connect, click the key check box beside each service name, or highlight the service and then click the Require Pairing for Security check box.

Bluetooth File Transfer

By default, there are two services configured on Tiger. The first, File Transfer, provides basic FTP-like file transfer capabilities between devices. Paired devices can browse the filesystem and put or get files over the Bluetooth connection.

To configure what area of the file system is available to this service, highlight the Bluetooth File Transfer service. The available settings, shown in Figure 5.28, will be displayed.

Use the Folder Other Devices Can Browse pop-up menu to choose an area of the filesystem that is open to other Bluetooth devices. You should, of course, make this a reasonably restricted area of your machine.

Bluetooth File Exchange

The second file service, File Exchange, allows Bluetooth devices to push files to your computer. This is a one-way file transfer that does not provide any filesystem-browsing features. To configure File Exchange, select the File Exchange service. The File Exchange options are displayed as shown in Figure 5.29.

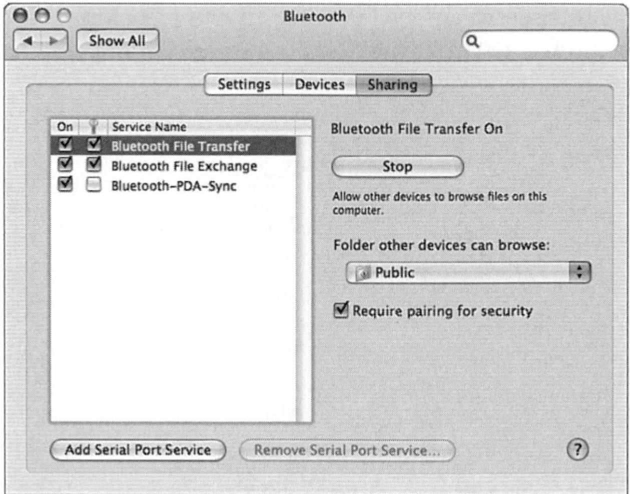

FIGURE 5.28 Control what incoming file transfer connections can see.

FIGURE 5.29 Choose how files sent to your computer should be stored/processed.

The pop-up menus on the right side of the window determine how your computer will react when a file is sent. You can choose to have the system prompt, refuse, or accept all files as well as ask you what to do when it receives certain types of files. You should also set an appropriate folder to which the received items will be saved.

Serial Port Services

In some cases, a device will require a serial port to be configured on your computer to handle incoming connections. By default, no serial port services are configured in Tiger, although the setup assistant might add them as necessary. To manually add a new serial port, click the Add Serial Port Service button at the bottom of the Sharing settings. The serial port configuration will be displayed, as shown in Figure 5.30.

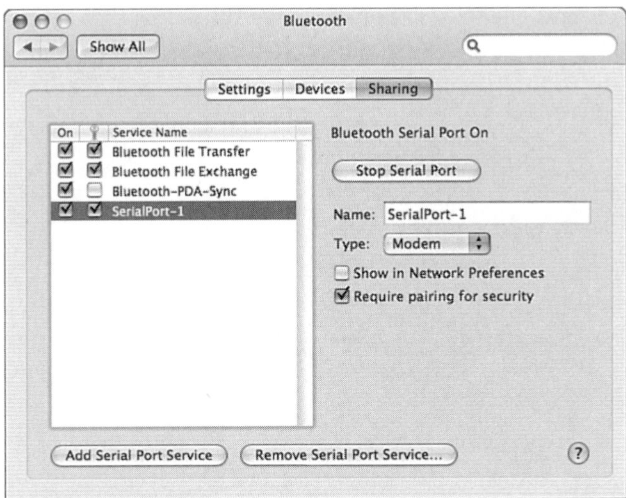

FIGURE 5.30 Configure incoming serial port services.

Provide a name for the serial port. If you are entering this manually, the device connecting to your machine might require a specific name for the port—be sure to check the device documentation.

Next, choose whether the port will act as a modem or a RS-232 industry standard serial port. To include the port in Network preferences, click the Show in Network Preferences check box.

NOTE

Keep in mind that the Sharing settings are for services hosted on your Bluetooth-enabled computer.

To edit serial port settings for a *paired* device, use the Edit Serial Ports button in the Devices settings pane.

Transferring Files over Bluetooth: Bluetooth File Exchange

To transfer files to Bluetooth devices, Tiger natively implements a tool for implementing Object Push and File Exchange profiles. Using the Bluetooth File Exchange application (path: `/Applications/Utilities/Bluetooth File Exchange`), you can browse and transfer files to a Bluetooth device, much like using a simple FTP client.

To use the Bluetooth File Exchange program, first pair with the device you want to transfer files to or from (making sure that it implements either the Object Push or File Exchange profiles); then start the Bluetooth File Exchange application from the Utilities folder, or choose Send File or Browse Device from the Bluetooth menu extra.

Sending Files

By default, Bluetooth File Exchange will prompt you at launch for a file to send (the default action can be disabled from the application preferences). To manually send a file to a device, use File, Send File (Command-O). Tiger displays a dialog box enabling you to choose a file; it then prompts you for the device that the file should be sent to, as shown in Figure 5.31.

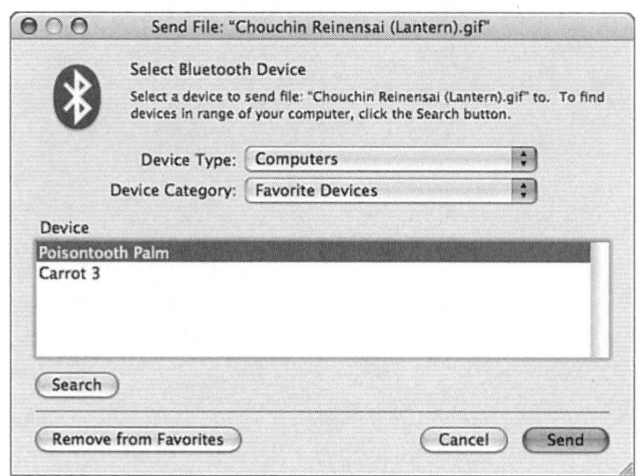

FIGURE 5.31 Choose the device that will receive the file.

Use the Device Type pop-up menu to choose what type of device you're sending to, and then the Device Category to choose among Favorite Devices, Discovered Devices, and recently used devices. When you've identified the Bluetooth device you're looking for, select its name and click Send. If the remote device authorizes the transfer, the file will be sent.

Browsing Files

Browsing is another option for transferring files. To start the file browser, choose File, Browse files within the Bluetooth File Exchange application. You will be prompted for the device you want to connect to (much as in Figure 5.31). After you've selected the device, a file transfer window appears, similar to Figure 5.32.

Navigate through the file listing as you would in the Finder. Using the four buttons in the lower-left corner of the window, you can move to previous folders, jump to the top level (the house icon), create a new folder, or delete the selected item.

To retrieve a file, double-click it in the list, or highlight it and then click the Get button. You can select multiple files with Command or entire folders if you want.

To send a file, click the Send button; then choose the file you want to send.

To log off the device, close the file transfer window.

NOTE

If you commonly find yourself sending or browsing files, you can set Bluetooth File Exchange to default to one of these modes using the application preferences.

FIGURE 5.32 Use the file transfer window to get and send files to or from the remote device.

Disks and Disk Images: Disk Utility

Disk Utility (path: `/Applications/Utilities/Disk Utility`) can be used to prepare disks, create disk images, repair volumes, and more. We'll approach Disk Utility from two sides: the disk imaging aspect and disk repair features.

Launching Disk Utility

Disk Utility combines disk repair with disk formatting and partitioning. As with Mac OS 9, you cannot use either of these functions on your startup partition. If you intend to work with only a secondary disk or partition, launch Disk Utility from the Finder. To use Disk Utility to work on your primary disk, follow these steps:

1. Insert your Mac OS X Install DVD into your computer.
2. Start (or restart) your Macintosh while holding down the C key.
3. Wait for the Installer to boot.
4. Choose Open Disk Utility from the Installer application menu.

After launching Disk Utility, the application opens to display a list of your disk resources in a pane on the left side of the window, as shown in Figure 5.33. To the right of the disk list is the content pane, which displays controls for operating on the selected disk item.

Displaying Disk Information

Disks are listed with each of their partitions displayed under them. Grayed-out partitions are either active system partitions that cannot be verified or repaired or are unmounted partitions.

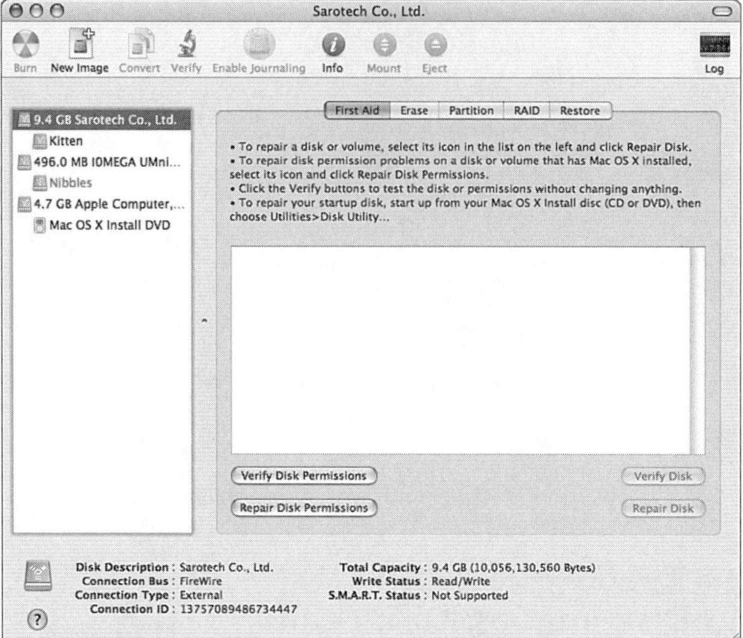

FIGURE 5.33 The left pane contains your disk resources; the right pane displays the operation you are performing on your disk.

TIP

The toolbar contains options for unmounting and mounting volumes. After selecting a disk or partition from the list, you can choose to Mount (Option-Command-M), Unmount (Option-Command-U), or Eject (Command-E) the volume.

At the bottom of the Disk Utility window is a display of the details of the selected disk object. Although most of this information is self-explanatory, of interest is the S.M.A.R.T. (Self-Monitoring Analysis and Reporting Technology) status. A disk that supports S.M.A.R.T. can report potential problems before they occur, warning you of imminent drive failure.

To get more information about a disk or partition, select it in the list and then choose File, Get Info (Command+I) or click the Info icon in the Disk Utility toolbar. All available information about the object is displayed, as demonstrated in Figure 5.34.

When a disk is selected, up to five possible buttons appear above the content area: First Aid, Erase, Partition, RAID, and Restore. Each button opens a pane that performs a different function within the application.

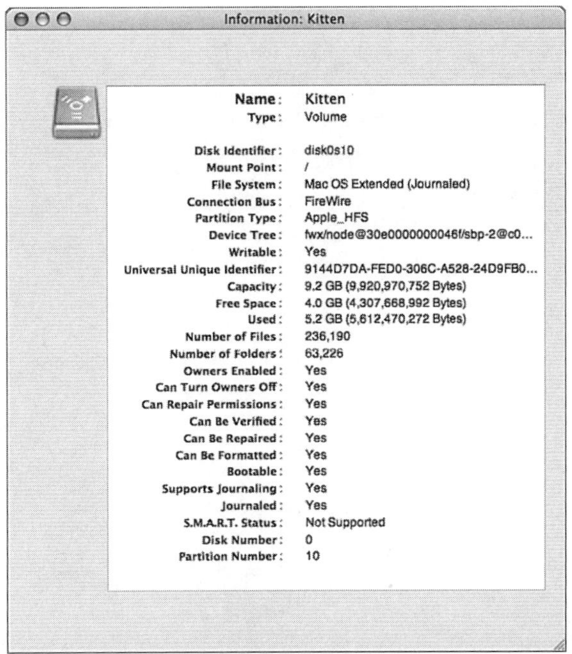

FIGURE 5.34 Get information about a drive or partition.

> **NOTE**
>
> The button bar changes depending on the object you've selected. If you choose a disk, for example, you see *all* the control areas. If you choose a partition, you do *not* see the partition controls because you can't very well partition a partition—nor can you apply RAID settings to a partition and so on.

Verifying and Repairing Disks

To verify the integrity of a volume or attempt to repair it, highlight the disk or partition, and then click the First Aid button. The First Aid pane, shown in Figure 5.35, can perform basic repair operations on a drive. It functions on UFS, HFS+, and HFS volumes—meaning that you can repair both types of Mac OS X partitions and both types of Mac OS 8/9 partitions.

Unfortunately, Disk First Aid is not capable of repairing extensive disk damage, so third-party utilities such as Micromat's Drive 10 and TechTool Pro (`http://www.micromat.com/`) are still important parts of every software library. In addition to basic disk repair, the First Aid tools can also fix any file permissions that might have been accidentally changed while using your computer.

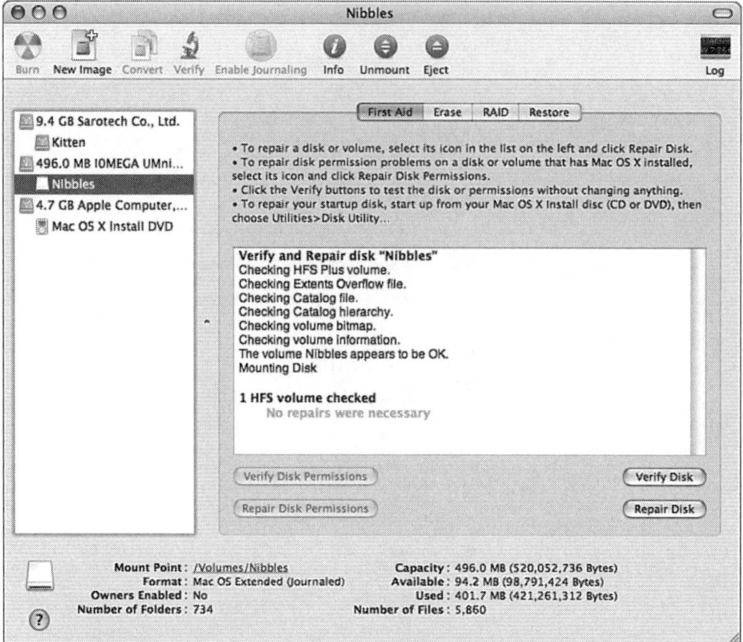

FIGURE 5.35 Use Disk First Aid to repair damaged volumes.

To check or verify a disk, use the four buttons in the lower portion of the pane:

- Verify Disk—Displays any errors found in your disk but does not attempt to repair them.
- Repair Disk—Performs the same tests as Verify but automatically fixes any errors it might find. You can only repair volumes other than your boot disk.
- Verify Disk Permissions—Checks to make sure that your Tiger volume has the proper permissions set. If you're having trouble installing applications or deleting files, you might have a permissions problem.
- Repair Disk Permissions—Repairs any incorrectly assigned permissions. Permissions can be repaired only on your current boot disk.
- Stop—Halts the current action (Verify or Repair).

If errors are found, they will be reported. Several things are checked during this process:

- Extents overflow file—The Extents file keeps track of file information that could not be placed contiguously on a disk. As files become fragmented, the locations of the fragments are stored here.
- Multilinked files—Files incorrectly linked to the same allocation blocks on the disk.

- Catalog—Contains the information that forms the structure (files and folders) of the disk.
- Bitmap—A binary picture of the disk, which records which blocks are allocated to files and which are free space.

If errors cannot be repaired, Disk Utility warns you that it is incapable of fixing your system. If this happens, try rerunning the repair—Disk First Aid often requires two passes to work correctly. If the repair does not work, Apple's suggested course of action is to back up the drive, erase it, and then restore your files. I'd recommend trying another disk repair tool before resorting to such desperate measures.

TIP

You can batch-repair multiple volumes by selecting several disks from the volume list. Just press Command and click the disks/partitions to add to the selection list.

TIP

Use File, Fix OS 9 Permissions to resolve permission problems that might cause OS 9 not to boot or function correctly. This function automatically fixes the permissions where necessary; you do not need to select a volume or partition first.

NOTE

Volumes are repaired from the command line by using the `fsck` tool in single-user mode, as discussed in Chapter 29, "Maintaining a Healthy System."

Apple also offers a command-line utility for mounting, unmounting, ejecting, and renaming disks: `disktool` and a command-line version of Disk Utility: `diskutil`. Learn more about the command line starting in Chapter 9, "Accessing the BSD Subsystem."

Erasing Volumes, Partitions, and Free Space

The Erase pane does exactly what you would think it should: It erases drives and partitions. This is essentially a quick-and-dirty partitioning and initialization tool. If a disk is selected, a single empty partition is created on the selected drive and anything that was previously there is erased. If a partition is chosen, only that partition is erased. You can even use the erase function to securely erase any free space (which might contain previously erased data) on *any* partition, while leaving active data alone.

Figure 5.36 shows the Erase pane.

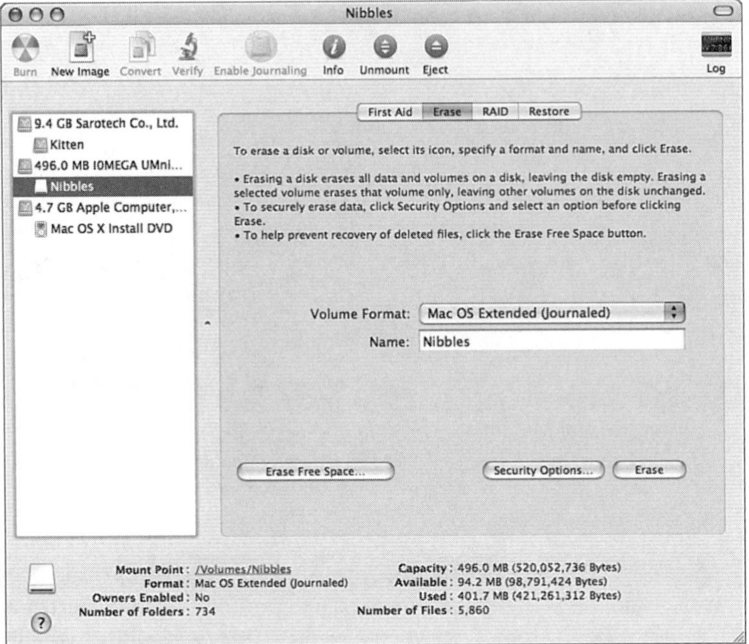

FIGURE 5.36 The Erase pane is used to quickly erase volumes and create a single empty partition.

To erase the selected volume or partition, use the Volume Format pop-up menu to choose between Journaled and non-Journaled Mac OS Extended partitions, Case sensitive and insensitive partitions, MS-DOS, and Unix file systems. Enabling Journaling adds a minor speed hit to the drive, but helps protect your machine from data corruption if the system crashes or is otherwise interrupted.

TIP

You can enable Journaling for a partition at any time by selecting it in the Disk/partition list and clicking the Enable Journaling button in the toolbar, or by using File, Enable Journaling (Command-J).

Journaling can also be *disabled* by choosing File, Disable Journaling (Command-J) or by adding (and using) the Disable Journaling button on the Disk Utility toolbar.

Next, enter a name for the new volume. This will appear as your disk label on the desktop.

If you want to securely erase the volume, click the Options button to force Disk Utility to zero all data on the drive, and write and erase random data 7 times or 35 times across the volume. Refer to Chapter 1, "Managing the Tiger Workspace," for more information about why multiple writes are required for a secure erasure.

Finally, click Erase to remove all existing information from the device and install the selected filesystem.

New to Tiger is the ability to securely erase *just* the free space on any partition without disturbing any active data. To use this feature, select the partition, and then click the button labeled Erase Free Space. You will be prompted with the secure erase options, just as if you were erasing an entire volume. Pick your poison and click the Erase Free Space button, as shown in Figure 5.37.

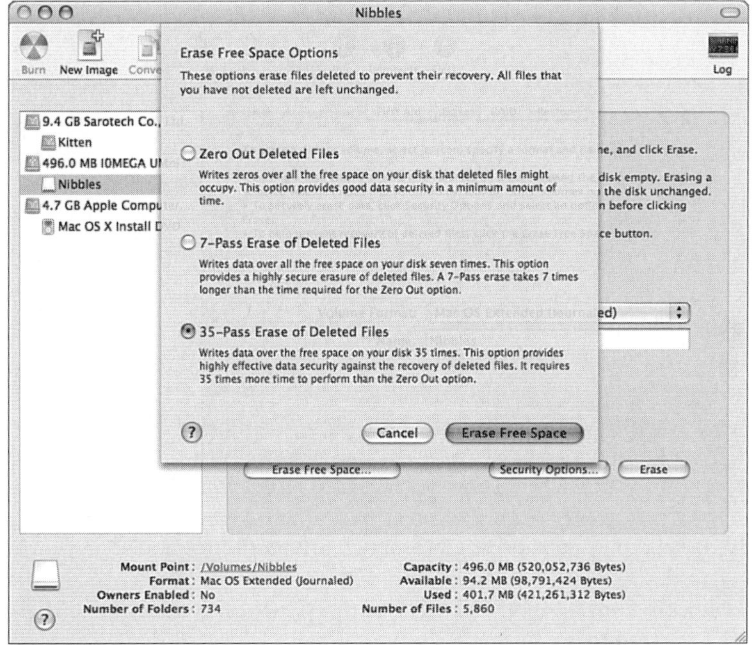

FIGURE 5.37 In Tiger, you can erase only the free space on a volume, securely removing any trace of previously erased files.

Partitioning Volumes

To create a more complex drive layout than what Erase can manage, use the Partition pane shown in Figure 5.38. The Volume Scheme section of the Partition pane contains a visual representation of the partitions on the system. Each box is a partition. The highlighted box is the active partition. Be warned—changes here will make any information on the target drive inaccessible!

TIP

To repartition a volume without destroying the information, you'll need a third-party utility such as iPartition from Coriolis Systems—`http://www.coriolis-systems.com/iPartition.php`.

You can change a partition's size by dragging the dividers between the partitions up and down to shrink or grow the available space. As you drag the bar, the Size field on the right portion of the pane changes to show the current settings.

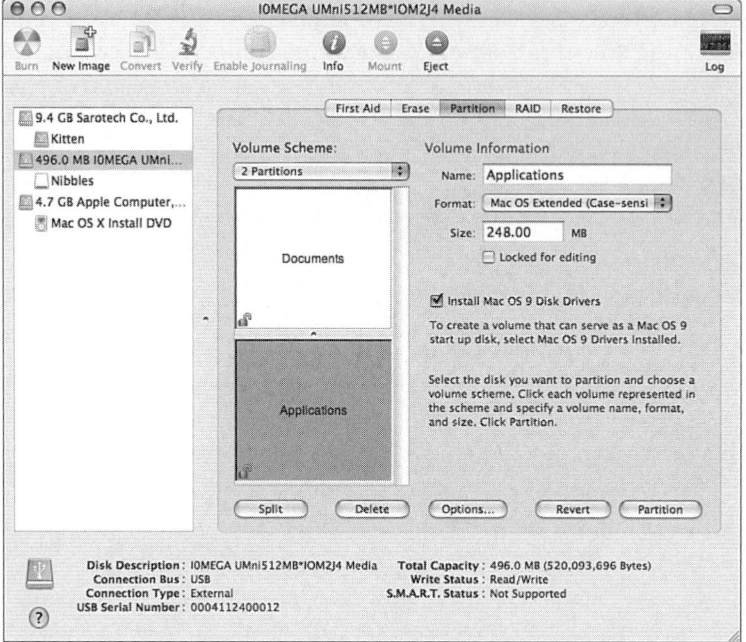

FIGURE 5.38 Partitioning your drive erases any existing information.

In addition to working with the visual view of the partition, you can use the various pop-up menus, fields, and buttons to set other parameters:

- Scheme—Quickly divides your drive into 1–16 equally sized partitions.
- Name—Sets the name of the highlighted partition.
- Format—Sets the highlighted partition to be either HFS, HFS+, HFS+ Journaled, UFS, or free space.
- Size—Manually enter a new size for the selected partition.
- Locked for Editing—When checked, the Locked for Editing setting freezes the current partition's settings. You can continue to work with other partitions but not one that is locked. Clicking the lock icon in the visual view of the partitions also toggles the lock.
- Install Mac OS 9 Disk Drivers—If this option is unchecked, the device is not usable on Mac OS 9.
- Split—Splits the current partition into two equally sized partitions.

- Delete—Removes the active partition.
- Options—Choose between an Apple Partition scheme and a PC Partition scheme. The default, obviously, is Apple. Switching to a PC scheme will create MS-DOS partitions as the default (which is useful when using the Scheme pop-up menu to create multiple partitions).
- Revert—Returns the partition map to its original state.
- Partition—Commits the partition table design to the drive. This destroys all current data on the device.

Clicking the Partition button is the final step to designing your volume's layout. After you've clicked the Partition button, you will be prompted with a final confirmation, and then the changes will be written to the disk.

Using RAID

RAID, or Redundant Array of Independent Disks, is a collection of multiple drives that function together as a single drive. By using drives performing in parallel, the computer can write and read information from the RAID set at a much higher rate than a single drive. Four common types of RAID are available:

- Level 0 – Disk striping—This increases I/O speed by reading and writing to multiple drives simultaneously. It offers no fault tolerance.
- Level 1 – Disk mirroring—Creates a fault-tolerant system by creating an exact mirror of one drive on another drive.
- Level 3 – Disk striping with error correction—This RAID type uses three drives: two operating identically to Level 0, and a third containing error correction information for fault tolerance.
- Level 5 – Striped data and error correction—RAID Level 5 offers the best balance between performance and fault tolerance.

Unfortunately, Tiger supports only Level 0 (striped) and Level 1 (mirrored) in software along with a third, concatenated type that combines the storage space of multiple drives into a single logical partition. This isn't a true RAID volume, but multiple concatenated volumes *can* be used as part of a RAID set. RAID capabilities are easy to configure if you have multiple drives within a machine.

Creating a New RAID Set

To set up a RAID set, you must have at least two matching drives or partitions available. Open the RAID settings pane to begin creating a RAID set definition. Next, enter a RAID Set name, choose a volume format and a RAID type (striped or mirrored). Click the + button to add the configuration to the RAID list, as seen in Figure 5.39.

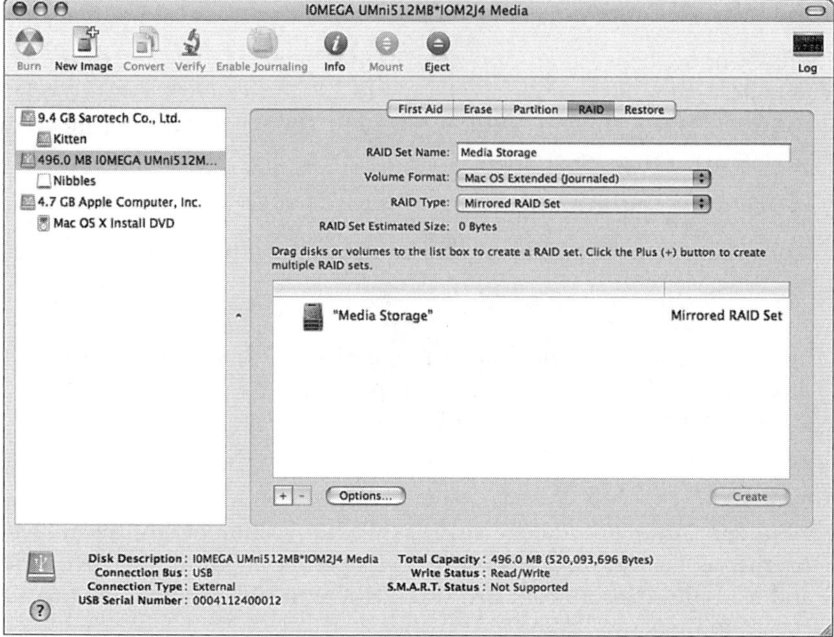

FIGURE 5.39 Define your RAID set using the fields at the top of the window, and then click + to save it.

Now, click the Options button below the RAID definition. From this dialog, shown in Figure 5.40, you can choose to change the default block size of the RAID set and enable autorebuild of a mirrored set if a drive fails.

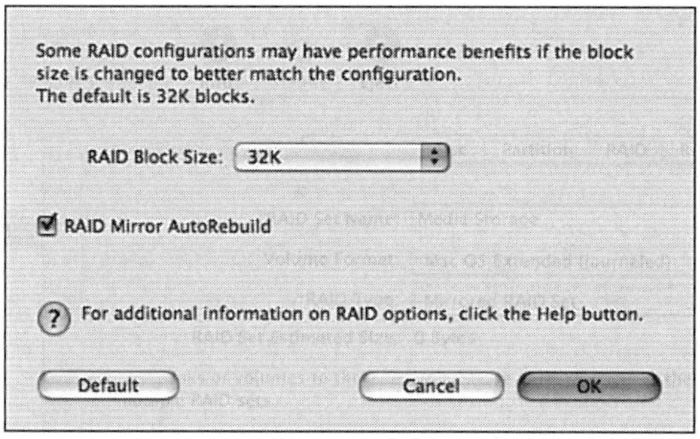

FIGURE 5.40 Choose a block size and autorebuild options.

If you don't know what is being stored on the set, it's best to leave the block size alone. If you know, however, that the drive will be used for small files or large chunks of data (such as video), using a small block size or large block size, respectively, might increase the performance of the set.

The AutoRebuild option is useful only if you are adding at least three volumes to your set. If one of the primary volumes (called a *slice*) in a mirrored set fails, the autorebuild feature will automatically rebuild the set using a spare volume—on the fly. If you have only two drives or are using striping, this option is meaningless. Click OK to save your settings.

TIP

If you do not use the Autorebuild feature, you must launch the Disk Utility manually to rebuild a failed mirror set.

You can continue to add (or remove) RAID set definitions using the + and – buttons at the bottom of the set list. After your sets have been defined, the next step is to add storage.

Adding Drives to a RAID Set

You're now ready to add drives to your set definition. Drag the icons of the drives to add from the volume list on the left to the RAID set definition in the list on the right. If you are adding volumes to a mirrored set, you can select each drive and use the RAID Type pop-up menu (or invoke a contextual menu on that drive) to define whether that drive is a slice or a spare.

You will need two slices for a working RAID configuration. Additional drives can be added as spares and, with the Autorebuild option discussed earlier, will automatically take over in the event of a drive failure.

When you've finished adding volumes, click Create and the new RAID volume will be mounted on the desktop and appear in the volume list on the left.

TIP

Because there is no immediate means of checking the status of a RAID set (other than launching Disk Utility), you can use the command `diskutil checkRAID` to quickly check up on your drives.

Restoring a Volume from a Disk or Disk Image

The Restore pane, shown in Figure 5.41, enables you to completely replace the contents of a disk with the contents of a disk image or another volume. In the case of a disk image, it can even be stored on a web server for retrieving over the network. To use Restore, you must first have either a source drive or disk image. We'll look at creating images later in this section.

Using Restore is simple—either drag the source disk or disk image from the volumes list on the left to the Source field on the right. You can also click the Image button to choose a image file from your filesystem or type in a URL where the image is located.

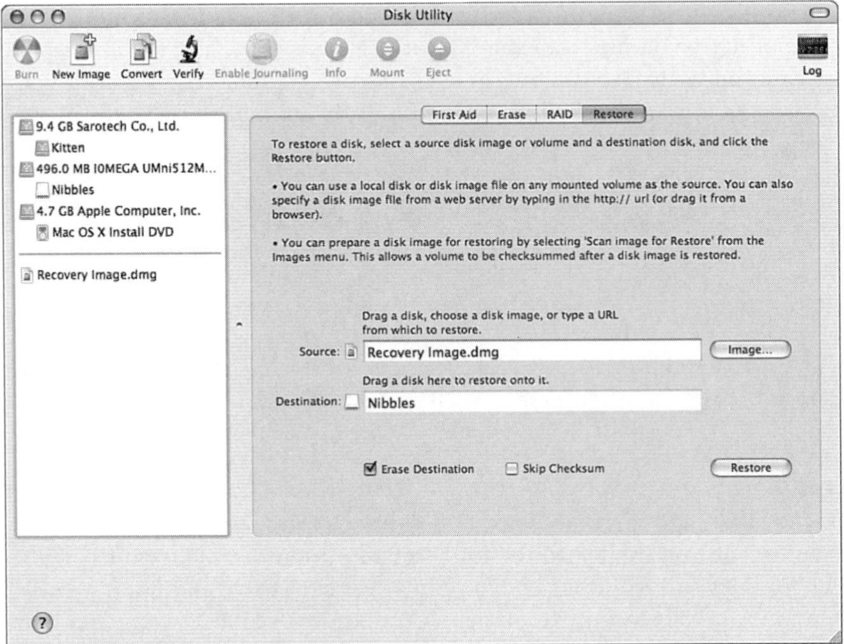

FIGURE 5.41 Restore volumes from disk images.

> **TIP**
>
> In order for a disk image to be used for a restore, it must be specially prepared. Read "Converting and Verifying Disk Images" later in this chapter for more information.

Next, drag a disk or partition to the Destination field. The destination, obviously, must be equal to or greater in size than the source. If you want to erase the destination before copying the image to the drive, click the Erase Destination check box. Finally, click Restore to start the restoration process.

> **TIP**
>
> The Restore feature of Disk Utility uses a command-line tool called `asr`. Apple has provided *excellent* step-by-step instructions for using `asr` and disk images to clone computers for classroom/workplace environments.
>
> Rather than repeat those here, use `man asr` from the command line and read the section entitled "HOW TO USE ASR." Read more about the command line starting in Chapter 9.

Working with Disk Images

Disk images are a common and convenient way to distribute software for Mac OS X. Rather than create an archived folder, developers write their applications to a virtual disk that is loaded into memory when used. This disk appears to the computer as a real disk and can be manipulated like any other disk. For the end user, it is a simple way to work with new applications.

A single disk image file can contain applications, support files, and any other data a program might need—and it never needs to be decompressed. In fact, many applications can actually run directly from disk images, without needing to be copied to your hard drive at all. Disk Utility even has built-in CD burning capabilities to make turning a disk image into a real CD a matter of a few clicks.

Adding Disk Images to the Volume List

To work with an existing disk image, drag the image file into the Disk Utility volume list or use File, Open Disk Image(Option-Command-O). The image is added to an area below your standard hard disks and remains there until you drag it back out (even between executions of Disk Utility).

After the disk image has been added, you can work with it much as you would with any other disk in Disk Utility. You can verify it, repair it, repartition it—even add it to a RAID set.

Creating a Blank Disk Image

Disk Utility can create images as well as mount them. This is useful for creating an exact duplicate of software you don't want to lose, or for making a master image for distributing software over a network with `asr`.

There are three ways to generate an image: copy an existing volume/partition; copy an existing folder; or create an empty image file, mount it, and then copy files to it.

To create an empty image file, choose File, New, Blank Disk Image. Figure 5.42 shows the disk image creation dialog box.

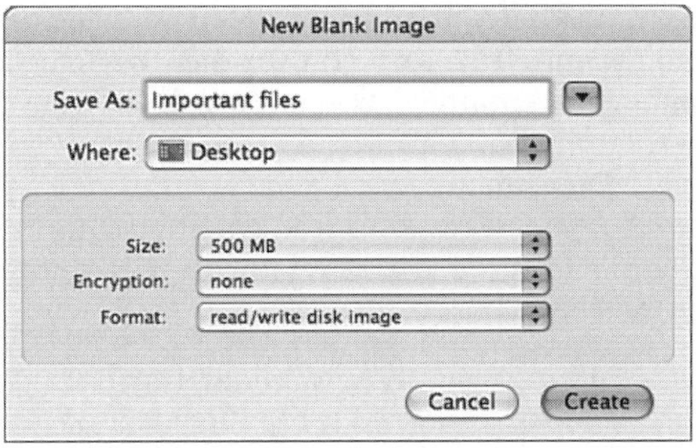

FIGURE 5.42 Generate a new blank image, and then copy files to it.

Fill in the Save As field as you normally would—this is the name of the image file, not the volume that is will be created. Choose a size for the image from the Size pop-up menu. There are a variety of preset sizes for CDs and DVDs, and a Custom setting for arbitrary sizes.

Next, if you want to encrypt the disk image, choose AES-128 from the Encryption pop-up menu.

Finally, choose a volume format with the Format pop-up menu. You can choose between a read/write disk image, which occupies the exact amount of space you've set for the image, or a *sparse* image that grows to accommodate the files you add. Click Create to save the image and add it to the volume list.

Creating a Disk Image from an Existing Partition

Creating an image from an existing drive is even easier. Highlight the partition you want to use; then choose File, New, Image from *Device* where *Device* is the name of your selected partition, or just click the New Image button in the toolbar.

You are prompted for the location to save the image. Using the Image Format pop-up menu, choose the type of image to create: read-only, read-write, compressed, or CD/DVD master. Apply encryption to the image file by choosing AES-128 from the Encryption pop-up menu. Click Save to copy an image of the device onto your hard drive.

TIP

Read-only images are a good way to distribute software because they do not allow any changes to be made to the image. This results in an image that cannot be modified or tainted and can always be assumed to be a working master copy.

Creating a Disk Image from a Folder

The third way to create an image is to copy the *contents* of a folder or volume. This is the easiest means of building a disk image if you already have all the files in a subfolder of your volume, or want to create an image of a mounted network share. It also results in a disk image that is unfragmented because it isn't based on a direct device copy.

Choose File, New, Image from Folder; then use the Mac OS X file browser to pick the folder or volume that you want to use. As with the other two imaging methods, choose the image file and format when prompted, and click Save to create the disk image file.

Converting and Verifying Disk Images

If you have a disk image that you've saved in read/write format, that you'd like to convert to a CDR image, or perhaps encrypt, you can use Images, Convert resave the image in another format or apply AES encryption.

Disk images that will be used for the Apple Software Restore feature are required to be saved as read-only images, and then scanned using the Images, Scan Image for Restore function. This will internally modify the existing image file for use with Restore.

To verify the integrity of an image, use Images, Verify. This will check the image and calculate a CRC for comparison against a known CRC value (such as one published by a site where you downloaded the disk image). If the CRCs match, the image is unchanged from the original. If you are publishing a disk image and want to calculate your own CRC value, you can do this by choosing Images, Checksum, CRC-32 image checksum. The image will be scanned and a CRC value generated.

Burning CDs and DVDs

To burn a CD or DVD from within Disk Utility, you must have your writer connected and powered on. Select the image you want to burn; then choose Images, Burn or click the Burn toolbar icon. If the image is suitable for burning, Disk Utility displays the dialog shown in Figure 5.43.

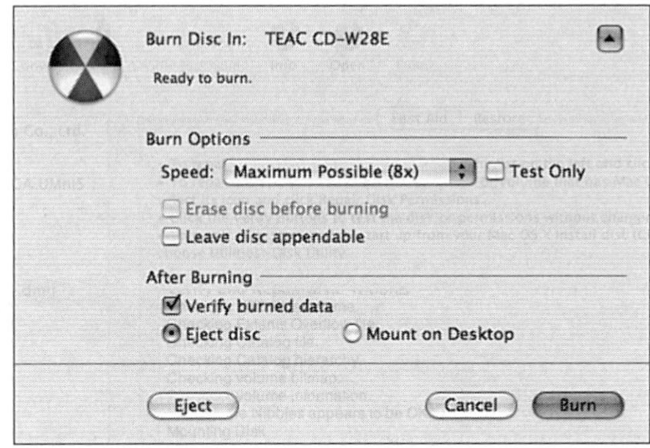

FIGURE 5.43 Insert a CD and click Burn.

Click the disclosure pushbutton to choose the maximum speed you want to use during the burn process, along with whether you want to burn additional copies of the image, verify the burn, and eject or mount the disk after it has finished.

When you're satisfied with your settings, click the Burn button, and Disk Utility begins writing the CD.

Scanners, Cameras, and Media Readers: Image Capture

The Mac OS X Image Capture application (path: `/Applications/Image Capture`) enables you to connect a digital camera, media reader (USB/FireWire), or flatbed scanner to your Mac and import images or even share the device to a remote computer.

NOTE

Surprisingly, Apple provides no free solution for getting video/audio into a computer through FireWire or an audio input source. The new QuickTime Pro for Tiger includes these features at a nominal cost. Refer to Chapter 2, "Useful Tiger Applications and Utilities," for more information about QuickTime.

Although you might opt for the commercial iPhoto solution, Image Capture provides quick-and-dirty import features from the same range of devices as iPhoto. In addition, its capability to control flatbed scanners gives you a single solution for most of your image import needs.

When launched, Image Capture displays a control window for each of the capture devices that you've connected. The digital camera/media reader controls provide the ability to download pictures, whereas the scanner controls allow a user to preview and scan images. Scanner and camera control windows can be seen in Figure 5.44.

FIGURE 5.44 Image Capture displays a window for each connected device.

NOTE

By default, when you use Image Capture, you must launch it manually for digital camera devices (pressing a scanner button will launch the app). Using the Image Capture preferences, however, you can choose to start the application automatically when your camera or media reader is plugged in and activated. You can also choose to display (or not) the scanner window if an appropriate scanner is attached.

Using Cameras and Media Readers

The camera/media reader control window should resemble that of Figure 5.45. The type of camera or media reader and number of images available for download are displayed. Note that the camera icon itself resembles the actual device connected.

FIGURE 5.45 The Image Capture application can be used to download images, audio, and video from cameras and media readers.

To control where images are stored after downloading and what (if any) post processing is performed, use the Download To and Automatic Task pop-up menus.

Selecting a Download Location

The default location for camera downloads is the Pictures, Movies, and Music folders in the current user's home directory (some digital cameras support basic audio and video recording). To change the directory, use the Download To pop-up menu to select Other and then choose the directory to hold the files.

Setting an Automatic Task

After images have been downloaded, Mac OS X can automatically use one of several different AppleScripts or actions to format and arrange your photos. The AppleScripts are located in the `/System/Library/Image Capture/Automatic Tasks` folder and can be modified (or added to). You can learn more about AppleScript in Chapter 4, "Controlling Applications with Automator and AppleScript."

The eleven available default actions are

- Build Slide Show—Displays a slideshow of the downloaded photos after retrieving them from the camera.
- Build Web Page—Builds a complete web page, with thumbnails, for the downloaded images. The web page is stored in a folder named `Index` in the same location as the images used.
- Crop to 3×5—Creates a PNG of the image(s) in your `Pictures` directory where each is cropped to 3×5.
- Crop to 4×6—Creates a PNG of the image(s) in your `Pictures` directory where each is cropped to 4×6.
- Crop to 5×7—Creates a PNG of the image(s) in your `Pictures` directory where each is cropped to 5×7.
- Crop to 8×10—Creates a PNG of the image(s) in your `Pictures` directory where each is cropped to 8×10.
- Fit in 3×5—Creates a PNG of the image(s) in your `Pictures` directory where each is scaled to 3×5.
- Fit in 4×6—Creates a PNG of the image(s) in your `Pictures` directory where each is scaled to 4×6.
- Fit in 5×7—Creates a PNG of the image(s) in your `Pictures` directory where each is scaled to 5×7.
- Fit in 8×10—Creates a PNG of the image(s) in your `Pictures` directory where each is scaled to 8×10.
- Preview—Displays the images in the Preview application.

To choose another script or application, use the Other pop-up menu selection to browse the filesystem and select an alternative.

Downloading the Images

When you're ready to download images, you can choose all the pictures or select from thumbnails of the images stored on the camera. If you choose Download All, Image Capture downloads the files from your camera.

When the download is complete, Image Capture performs your selected automatic task, if any.

To download only certain images from your device, click the Download Some button. After a brief delay, thumbnails appear, as shown in Figure 5.46. Use the Thumbnail Size slider to scale the preview thumbnails within the window. The View buttons can be used to toggle between the thumbnail view and a Finder-like list view with extended image information (size, resolution, and so on).

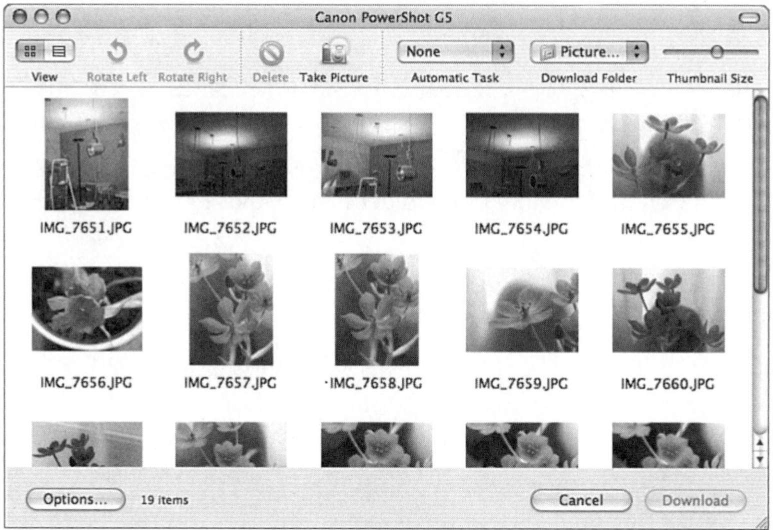

FIGURE 5.46 Choose the images to download.

To perform basic editing, click a thumbnail to select it; then, if necessary, use the Rotate Left/Right and Delete buttons to fix the photo orientation or remove it completely from the device.

Finally, if you didn't get it right on the initial control screen, you can reassign the Download folder and Automatic Tasks using the pop-up menus at the top of the screen.

TIP

If you have a supported camera that allows the computer to trigger a snapshot, you can add a Take Picture toolbar button to the image download window.

Use the Customize Toolbar option under the View menu or Command-Option-Click on the window's toolbar button.

Setting Camera Options

The Image Capture Options button (seen in both the main control window and the Download Some window) configures what happens to images that are downloaded from a camera or media reader and also provides the ability to trigger automatic downloads. These preferences are stored and used each time the device is connected.

There are two panes of settings within the Options dialog: Options and Information. The Options pane, shown in Figure 5.47, customizes the image download process.

Choose from these available settings:

- Delete Items from Camera After Downloading—Removes all image files from the camera or media reader on download.
- Create Custom Icons—Automatically generates custom thumbnail icons for each of the downloaded images.
- Add Item Info to Finder File Comments—Uses the Finder's comment field (accessible from Show Info) to store information (size, name, and so on) about each camera file.
- Embed ColorSync Profile—Adds a ColorSync profile to each image file to ensure consistency across output devices.
- Automatically Download All Items—Automatically starts the download process as soon as a camera or media reader is connected.

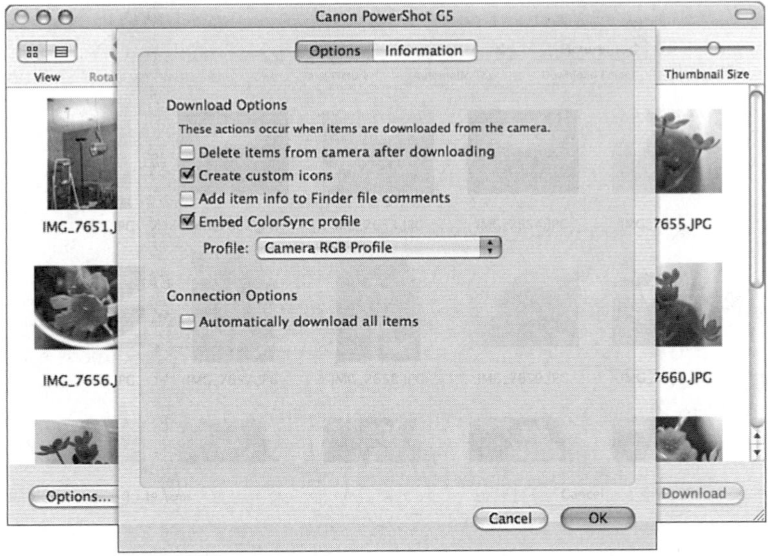

FIGURE 5.47 Download options are used to fine-tune image transfers.

The second pane, Information, lists the connected device and all known information about its capabilities, driver, and manufacturer.

Click OK to save your Device options.

Using Flatbed Scanners

Flatbed scanners work a bit differently from digital cameras. When Image Capture senses that a supported scanner (that is, many Epsons) has been attached and the scanner's Scan button has been pressed, it automatically launches into Scan mode (shown in Figure 5.48) and scans a preview into the Image Capture window.

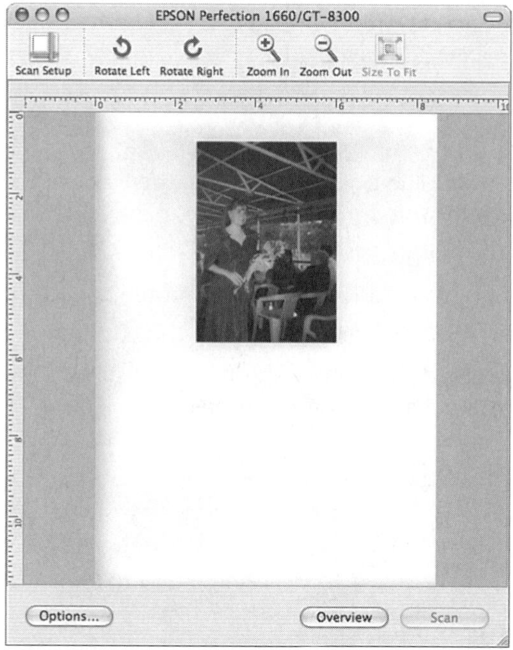

FIGURE 5.48 Image Capture works with some flatbed scanners.

> **TIP**
>
> If your scanner is incompatible with Mac OS X and the manufacturer hasn't made a solution available, your best bet is VueScan (`http://www.hamrick.com/index.html`). VueScan is an excellent flatbed/film scanner that produces amazing results on a wide variety of hardware. The only drawback is the interface, which, although not nearly as elegant as Image Capture, still offers control over the finest details.

The scanner mode of Image Capture is controlled by the toolbar buttons along the top of the window. From left to right, these are

- Scan Setup—Opens a window drawer containing settings for the document type, source, resolution (DPI), source size, percentage scaling, and so on.
- Rotate Left—Rotates the page to the left.
- Rotate Right—Rotates the page to the right.

- Zoom In—Zooms in on Page view in the Image Capture window.
- Zoom Out—Zooms out on Page view in the Image Capture window.
- Size to Fit—Sizes Image Capture's Page view to fit the window.

Scanner and Image Setup

To configure the settings for a scan, click the Scan Setup button in the upper-left corner of the scanner window. Here you can choose the document type, scan resolution, geometry, as well as configure transparency scanning and document feeders (if available). Use the button at the top of the drawer to select the scanner feature to configure. Figure 5.49 displays the Flatbed scanner settings.

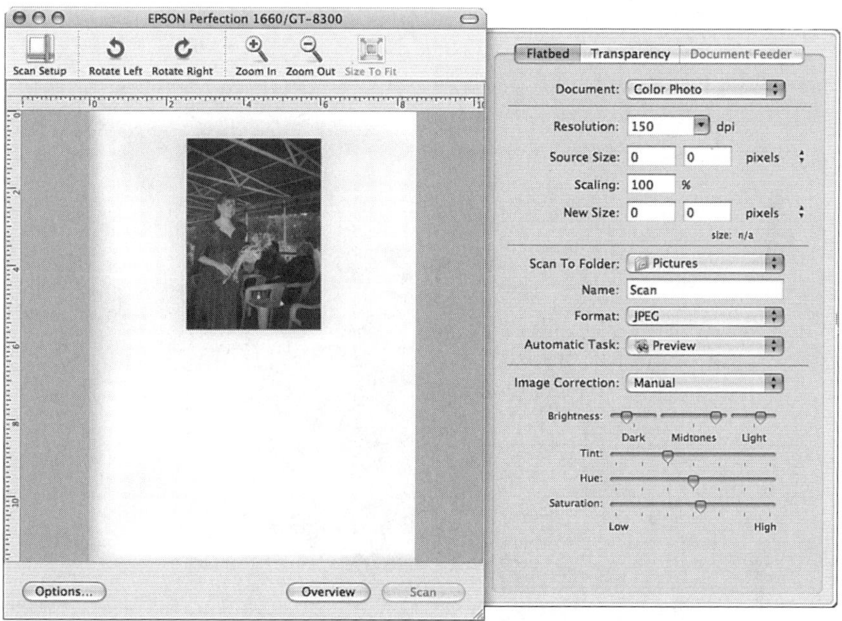

FIGURE 5.49 Use the Flatbed settings to set up the scan type, dimensions, and resolution for a flatbed scanner.

As with images downloaded from a camera, you can choose where scans will be saved and an automatic task to be carried out after a scan is completed. By default, images are opened in Preview after scanning. Image Capture also provides the ability to choose the image file type and a prefix used to label all scans.

New in Tiger is the option to have Image Capture perform basic image correction on your scans. To activate this feature, choose either Automatic or "Manual" from the Image Correction pop-up menu. If set to Automatic, Image Capture will make its best guess for how the images should look. When Image Correction is set to Manual, use the correction sliders (visible in Figure 5.49) to adjust the brightness, hue, tint, and saturation by hand.

Scanning and Previewing

To create a scan, use the two action buttons in the lower-right corner of the scanner control window: Overview and Scan.

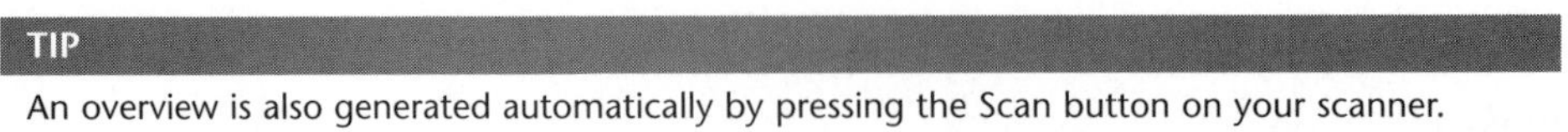

An overview is also generated automatically by pressing the Scan button on your scanner.

An overview is a quick preview scan that is displayed in the scanner window. After an overview has been created, you must draw a scan region around what is important on the page.

Click and drag within the page to create a rectangle that will be the focus of your detailed scan. Areas of the image outside this crop area will not be included in the final image. You can reposition the crop rectangle by clicking and dragging inside it, or resize it using the handles on the rectangle's sides, as shown in Figure 5.50.

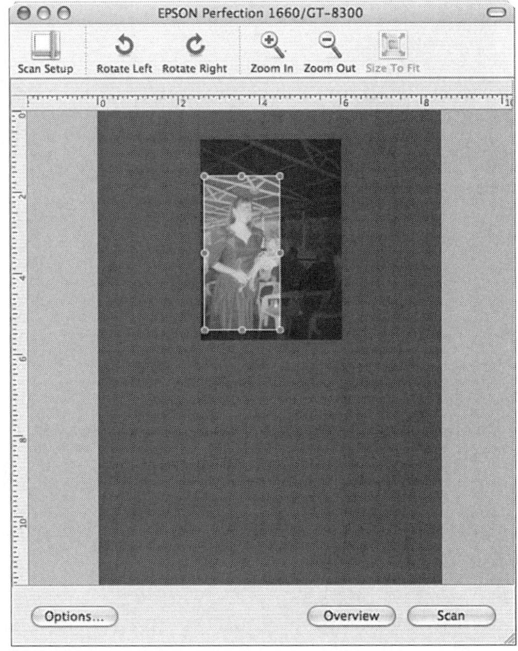

FIGURE 5.50 Choose the region that will be the focus of the scan.

After setting up the scan region, click the Scan button. This creates detailed scan at the resolution specified in the scan setup—saving it to the chosen download folder and processing it with the appropriate automatic task setting.

Setting Scanner Options

As with the digital camera and media reader functions, scanning options are set by clicking the Options button. The main Options pane provides the capability to create custom icons for scanned images as well as store information about the scan in the Finder's comment field and to embed ColorSync profiles in each image. Additionally, the Overview Scan Resolution slider allows you to choose the resolution at which the overview (preview) scan is created.

The second options pane, Buttons (shown in Figure 5.51), allows you to configure what will happen when one of the buttons on the front of your scanner is pushed. Use the pop-up menu to choose an application or script to launch with each button.

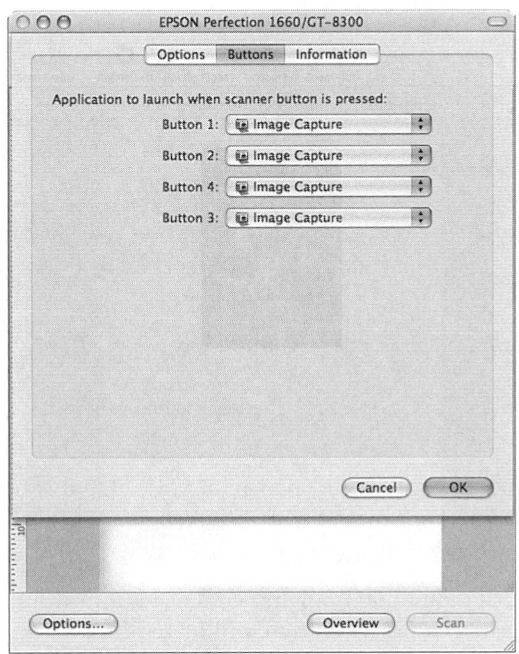

FIGURE 5.51 Choose how Tiger will react to pressing your scanner buttons.

Finally, the Information pane provides information about the connected scanner, its capabilities, and the driver controlling it.

Sharing Image Capture Devices

Tiger can share the devices that Image Capture recognizes. In a bizarre user interface decision, Apple has added these sharing features *not* to the Sharing System Preferences pane but to the Image Capture application preferences.

There are two functions you'll use when sharing devices: sharing and browsing. Sharing allows you to share your scanners and cameras, whereas browsing serves to find and connect shared devices. Sharing is enabled through the Sharing pane of the application preferences. The browsing feature is accessed from the Devices menu.

To set up sharing, open the Image Capture application preferences and switch to the Sharing pane. A screen similar to that shown in Figure 5.52 appears.

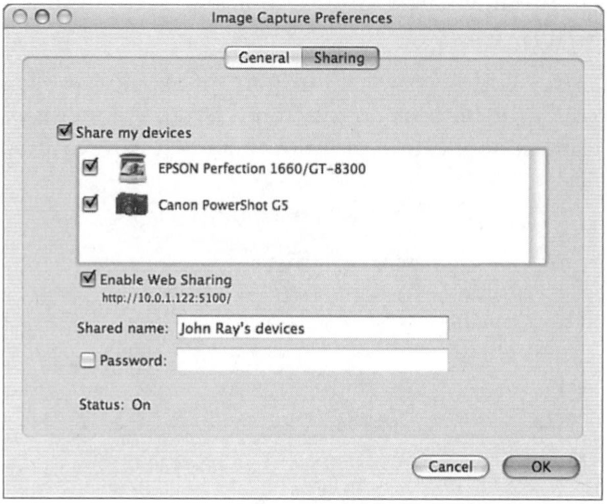

FIGURE 5.52 Configure sharing of image capture devices on Tiger.

Click the Share My Devices check box and the check boxes in front of the devices you want to make available.

Decide whether you want to enable web-sharing of your digital camera (scanners currently aren't supported). If so, click the Enable Web Sharing button—we'll get to exactly what this does shortly.

If you want to change the name that your shared devices appear under, enter a new shared name, and (if desired) a password that will be required to access the resources. The sharing setup is now complete and active.

NOTE

After sharing has been enabled, it is active even after you exit Image Capture.

Browsing and Using Shared Devices

To browse and connect to shared devices (assuming that you've enabled browsing) choose File, Browse from the menu. A window appears, listing each device source, including Remote Image Capture devices and TWAIN devices, as shown in Figure 5.53. To use a remote device, expand the listing by clicking the disclosure arrow in front of Remote Image Capture devices. Choose the device you want from the list that appears, and then click the Connect button.

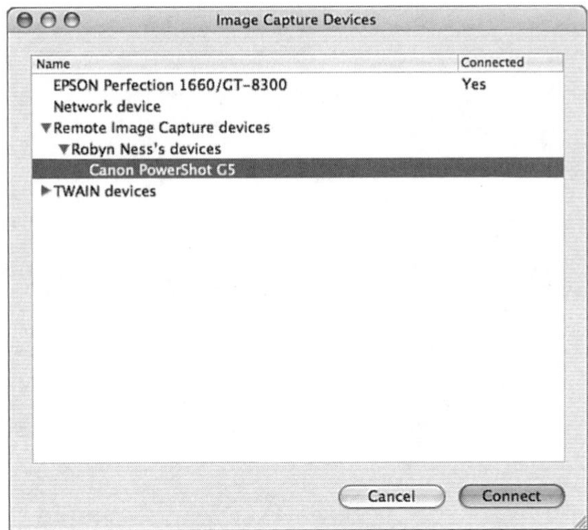

FIGURE 5.53 Find and connect to shared devices.

Within a few seconds, Image Capture displays control windows for each of the devices exactly as if they were directly connected to your computer. Interact with the devices exactly as if they were local. Unfortunately, this might mean having to get up and actually *walk* to swap photos in and out of the office flatbed scanner.

> **TIP**
>
> If you've installed TWAIN drivers for an image capture device, it should appear under the TWAIN Devices category. Choosing the device and connecting will allow Image Capture to use the TWAIN drivers to interact with the device. This can be helpful in overriding the Tiger default drivers for a device.

Web-Sharing of Digital Cameras

Your mind says "what?" and, well, so does mine. If you enable web-sharing, you'll notice that the Sharing setup window (see Figure 5.53) refreshes to display a web-sharing URL. The URL should be the same as your machine hostname/IP and the port 5100—that is, `http://`*`<machine name>`*`:5100`. Visiting the URL from another computer displays a page, shown in Figure 5.54, with controls similar to Image Capture's image download window.

Use your mouse to highlight images just as you would locally (try it—it actually *feels* like an application, not a web page); then click the controls along the top of the window to perform those actions on the selected image.

If your camera supports it, you can use Take Picture to take an instant snapshot. The ability to take a picture remotely is extended even further by the Remote Monitor feature. Access the monitor by clicking the Remote Monitor tab on the web page.

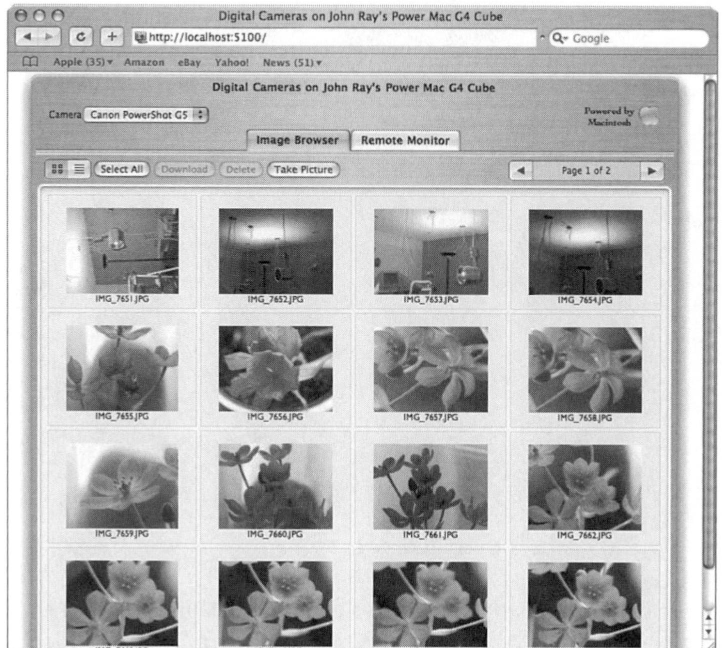

FIGURE 5.54 Control your digital camera over the World Wide Web.

Remote Monitor is a remote image capture function that can be configured to take pictures at a timed interval. Click the icon that resembles a preference panel to change the snapshot frequency. As pictures are taken, thumbnails will automatically begin to appear in the Remote Monitor.

Audio Input and Output: Sound Preferences and Audio MIDI Setup

Tiger sound input and output are controlled primarily through the Sound System Preferences pane. The three subpanes within the Sound preferences are Sound Effects, Input, and Output. These control alert sounds, audio input, and audio output as you would expect. Some addition advanced controls are available through the Audio MIDI tool, also discussed here.

Configuring Sound Effects

The Sound Effects pane provides access to the system alert sounds and other effect sounds that play while you use your computer, as shown in Figure 5.55. Choose the alert sound that you want your computer to play when it needs to get your attention. System sounds are stored in `/System/Library/Sounds`. You can add your own systemwide sounds to the directory `/Library/Sounds`, or personal sounds to `~/Library/Sounds`. These directories probably don't exist on your system, so you might need to create them.

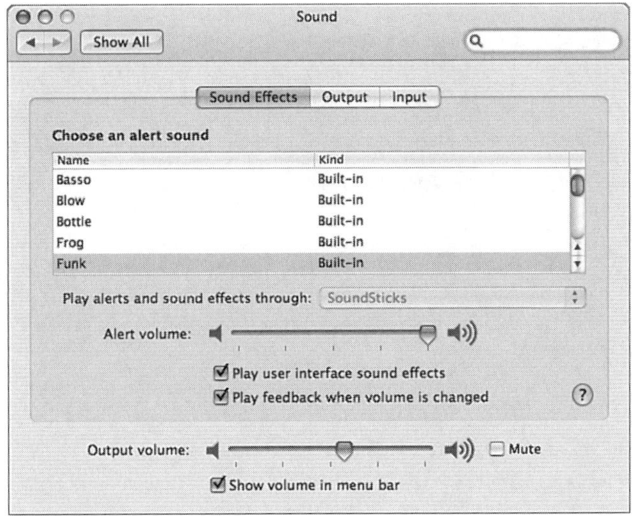

FIGURE 5.55 Choose your system alert sound and output levels.

If there are multiple output devices to your machine, use the Play Through pop-up menu to choose which device alert sounds will play through. Two sliders are provided for controlling output volume. The first controls the output volume of alert sounds, whereas the second determines overall system volume and is available on all the Sound subpanes. Click the Show Volume in Menu Bar check box to add a volume control menu extra to your menu bar. The Mute check box completely disables sound output, if desired.

TIP

Your keyboard also provides volume control and mute capabilities. Use the speaker buttons to raise, lower, or silence your speakers. To play feedback while raising or lowering volume from the keyboard, make sure that the Play feedback check box is selected; otherwise, you might not be able to determine the volume level unless a sound is playing during the adjustment.

A final setting, Play User Interface Sound effects, toggles whether Tiger will make the cute background sounds as you work with the system. When active, you'll hear a few additional noises when you perform actions such as emptying the trash or removing items from the Dock.

Changing Sound Output

The Output subpane is used to choose which output device your computer will use if multiple devices are connected, as well provide balance control over the speaker output. If you have a 5.1 sound output system, you'll have additional controls beyond the standard stereo speakers, shown in Figure 5.56.

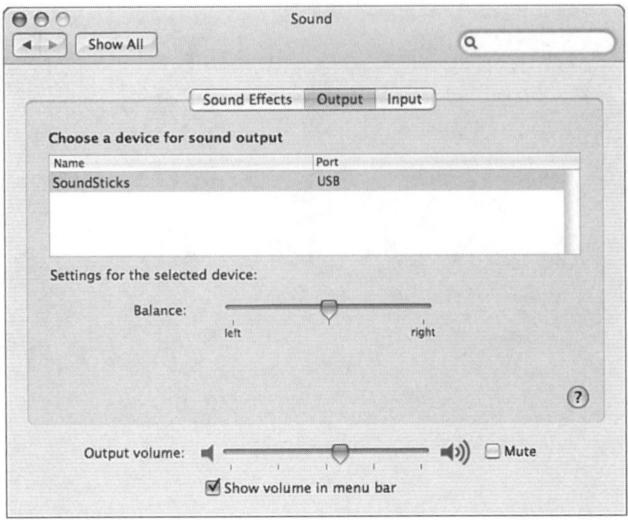

FIGURE 5.56 Choose and configure your output device.

Choosing Audio Inputs

On the third pane, Input, displayed in Figure 5.57, you can pick between the available input devices as well as adjust the gain (input volume) for the chosen source. The Input Level meter is used to help adjust the input volume. This meter displays the current level of sound input. The highest level that has been reached is highlighted within the graph for easy reference.

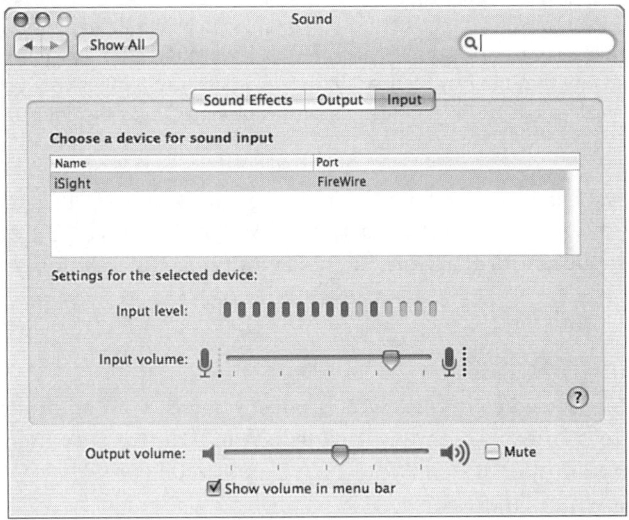

FIGURE 5.57 Choose an input source and adjust the gain.

TIP

Apple doesn't provide a free solution for creating your own sound effects. To get this feature, you'll need to purchase QuickTime Pro; refer to Chapter 2 for more details about QuickTime.

Alternatively, you can download a free program such as Audio In `http://home3.swipnet.se/~w-34826/`. (Click the "Soft" link on the right!)

Advanced Audio and MIDI Settings

The Apple Audio MIDI tool (path: `/Applications/Utilities/Audio MIDI Setup`) is included with Mac OS X but is mainly targeted at individuals using third-party audio hardware with their Macintosh. Shown in Figure 5.58, the Audio Devices pane of the tool allows you to configure your audio input and output settings for a given sound device.

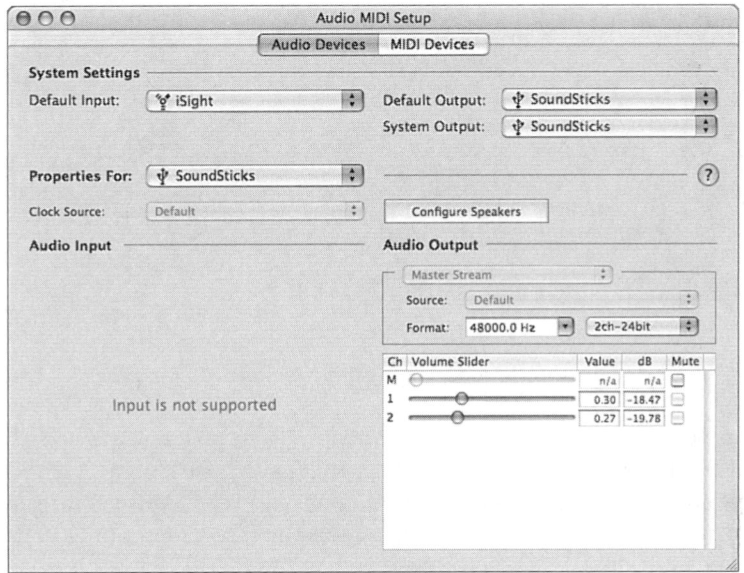

FIGURE 5.58 Use the Audio MIDI tool to configure the audio I/O for third-party sound hardware.

The Audio Devices pane can be considered an expanded version of the Sound System preferences pane that includes the capability to increase input and output volume on a per-channel basis, enables per-channel muting and playthrough, and also offers variety of other pro-audio features. A number of the settings are grayed out on a stock Macintosh because they are not supported by the Apple sound hardware.

The MIDI (Musical Instrument Digital Interface) Devices pane of the Audio MIDI tool is used by musicians to create and map interdevice connections between MIDI devices. Elements such as keyboards and sequencers can be added to the MIDI control view or detected automatically and displayed with a full graphical representation of their physical cabling.

Switching Between Operating Systems: Startup Disk

Tiger makes it simple to choose which operating system you boot into. You can have multiple versions of Mac OS X installed on different drives or partitions and pick and choose between them easily. If you have a G4, you can even boot directly into Mac OS 9.x (Classic).

Choosing Your Boot Device in Tiger

To choose your operating system, open the Startup Disk System Preferences pane, shown in Figure 5.59.

FIGURE 5.59 Boot directly into Mac OS 9.x using the Startup Disk pane.

After searching the available disks and partitions (this can take a while) for viable systems, each of the accessible system folders is listed in the Startup Disk pane. Each icon is labeled with the operating system version and volume name. To select an operating system, click the icon; a status message appears at the bottom of the screen describing your choice.

Quit the System Preferences application when you're finished or click Restart. The next time your computer boots, it boots into the operating system you selected.

TIP

Advanced users might want to use the `bless` command, which chooses what folders can (and should) boot your computer. In short, on a two-partition system, `bless` can be invoked like this to set your Mac's OpenFirmware to boot into Mac OS 9:

```
sudo /usr/sbin/bless/ -folder9 '/Volumes/<path to Mac OS 9 System Folder>'
➥ -setOF
```

Or into Tiger:

```
sudo /usr/sbin/bless/ -folder '/System/Library/CoreServices' -setOF
```

Familiarize yourself with the command line (see Chapter 9) and read the `bless` man page before attempting to use the command.

Sharing Your Drive via FireWire and Target Disk Mode

The Tiger Startup Disk pane provides direct access to Target Disk mode. Target Disk Mode, although not related to choosing your boot operating system, is a unique feature that turns your internal hard drive into the world's most expensive external hard disk.

To clarify, when Target Disk mode is active, your computer acts as an external FireWire drive. You can use a FireWire cable to link it to another computer where it will be recognized and treated as a removable storage device. You can even boot other machines directly from your internal drive.

In addition to the Target Disk Mode button in the Startup Disk pane, you can also enter Target Disk mode by holding down the T key while you turn on your computer. Finally, to exit Target Disk mode, just push your computer's power button.

Choosing Your Boot Device in Mac OS 9.x

To switch back to Tiger after running 9.x, you follow a similar process as switching from Tiger to Mac OS 9. From the Apple menu, choose Control Panels; then select and open the Startup Disk control panel.

Each mounted disk is displayed on a line in the control panel. Disks that include a bootable system folder have a disclosure arrow directly in front of them. Clicking the disclosure arrow displays the operating systems located on that disk, along with each operating system's path and version.

To boot into Tiger, highlight the appropriate system within the list and then click the Restart button in the lower-right corner. If you don't want to restart immediately, close the control panel. The next time the system restarts, it will boot into the selected operating system.

TIP

One alternative means of choosing your startup devices is to hold down the Option key when restarting your computer. The boot manager built into your Macintosh firmware will load, displaying all recognized boot devices.

Handling Optical Media: CDs and DVDs

In the CDs & DVDs pane, shown in Figure 5.60, you choose an insert action for different types of CDs and DVDs. For blank CDs and DVDs, you can set the system to ask you what to do; open the Finder, iTunes, or Disk Utility; open another application; run a script; or simply ignore. By default, a music CD is set to open with iTunes. A picture CD is set to iPhoto by default if iLife is installed; otherwise, it is set to Ignore. A video DVD is set to DVD Player. For these items, you could instead choose another application, run a script or ignore.

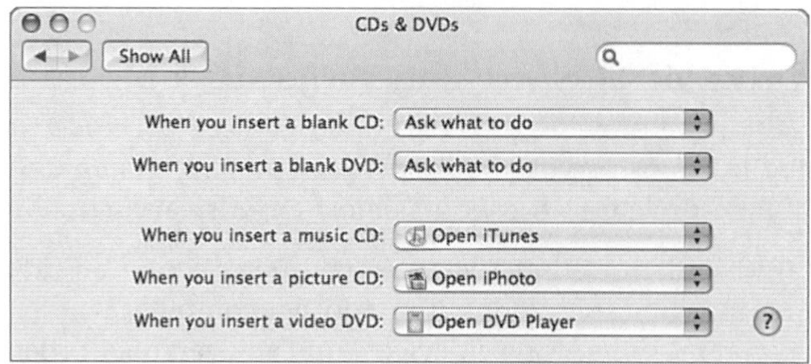

FIGURE 5.60 In the CDs & DVDs pane, you can set what action occurs when you insert a CD or DVD.

Saving Electricity and the Environment: Energy Saver

Like many of the system preferences panes you've seen in this chapter, the contents of the Energy Saver pane varies with the hardware. In short, this is the pane where you can set sleep and wake options as well as set up a startup or sleep schedule. The desktop version of the pane has just the Sleep and Options sections. The laptop version also includes settings for the type of power and optimization settings.

Note that administrative privileges are required to make changes to this pane.

Choosing Preset Energy Settings

For a laptop, you can configure settings for a power adapter or the battery. When set to the power adapter, the preset energy settings are better energy savings, normal, better performance, and custom. When you select among these options, settings change in the Sleep section, shown in Figure 5.61. When set to the battery power, the preset energy times are better battery life, normal, better performance, and custom. Select whichever setting is appropriate for your needs.

When you select a setting, the sleep times listed in the Sleep section for the computer and display change. For a laptop on the power adapter setting, the default computer sleep times range from 10 minutes on the better energy savings setting to Never on the better performance setting. For a laptop on the battery setting, however, the computer sleep times range from 5 minutes on the better battery life setting to 15 minutes on the better performance setting. The default times for putting the display to sleep on the power adapter settings range from 5 to 20 minutes; the battery, 1 to 5 minutes. In the Sleep section, you can also specify that the hard disk be put to sleep when possible.

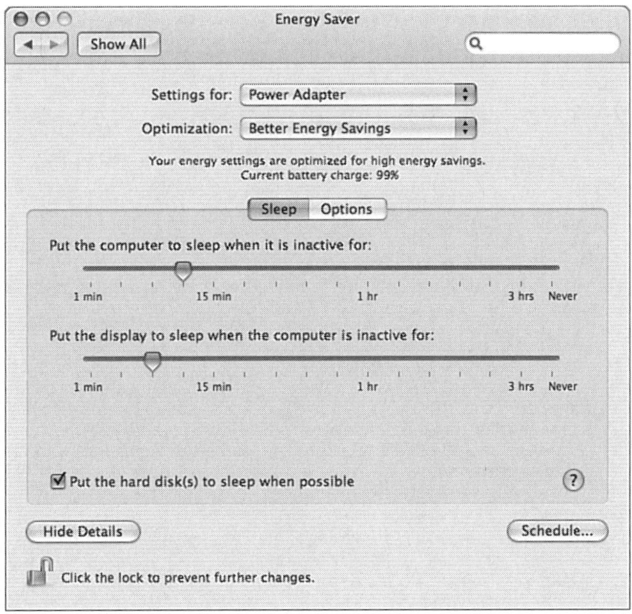

FIGURE 5.61 You can set sleep time for the computer and display in the Sleep section of the Energy Saver pane.

Setting a Startup and Sleep Schedule

Accessible from any section of the Energy Saver pane is the Schedule option. Here you can specify startup, sleep, and shutdown times for the machine. You can set times for weekends, weekdays, every day, or specific days of the week. The options in this section are the same for desktop machines.

Limiting Processor Speed and Other Options

Under the Options section of the Energy Saver pane, shown in Figure 5.62, you can limit your processor speed, if you have hardware for which that can be configured. Choices are Automatic, Highest, or Reduced. The Highest setting allows the computer to work at its highest speed, whereas the Reduced setting causes the computer to work at a lower speed. The Automatic setting allows the computer to switch back and forth between the settings as appropriate for its tasks.

The other options in this section also vary with the hardware. For a laptop set to the power adapter, you can set the computer to wake when the modem rings or to wake for ethernet network administrator access. For the latter option, `ssh` commands are not sufficient. The administrator has to send a wake-on-LAN packet. Apple's online documentation recommends Apple Remote Desktop, Wake550 (`http://www.tc.umn.edu/~olve0003/wake550.html`), or Wakeonlan (`http://gsd.di.uminho.pt/jpo/software/wakeonlan/`) for accomplishing this. Other options you can configure here include automatically reducing the brightness of the display before display sleep, restarting automatically after a power failure, and showing the status of the battery in the menu.

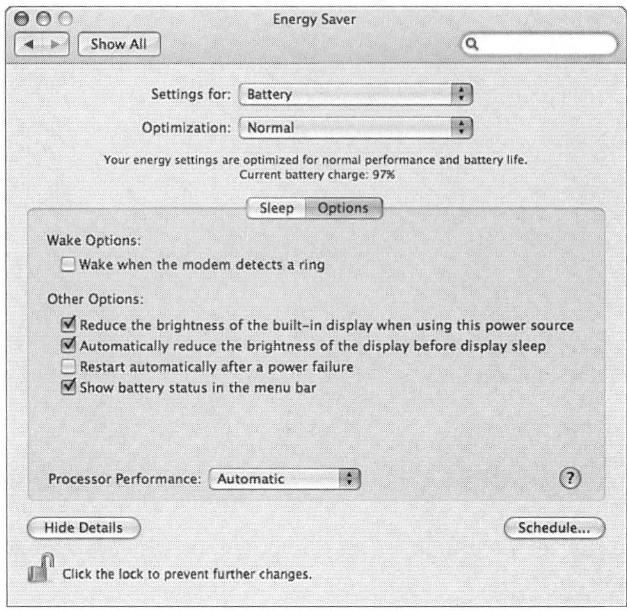

FIGURE 5.62 You can limit processor speed and specify other energy-related options in the Options section.

For a laptop set to the battery, the only wake option is the option to wake when the modem rings. The other options for the battery are the same as those for the power adapter, except that there is also an option to reduce the brightness of the display when using the battery.

For a desktop machine, the Options section might include only the options to use the power button to go to sleep and to restart automatically after a power failure.

Summary

Tiger gives you quite a bit to play with without installing additional third-party software. With each successive release of Tiger, Apple has refined peripheral support and eliminated redundancy throughout the operating system. Although not *everything* might work when you first plug it in, many popular USB, Bluetooth, and storage devices will function without a hitch.

CHAPTER 6

Printer, Fax, and Font Management

IN THIS CHAPTER

- Using Print Center/Printer Setup Utility
- Setting Printing System Preferences
- Using the Tiger Fax Capabilities
- The CUPS System Interface
- Managing Fonts
- Font Websites

In this chapter, we look at printer and font management in Mac OS X. Because printing spans the GUI and underlying command-line functionality, and it's a bit early to be talking about the fine details of the command line, we'll cover the Aqua GUI interface to configuring and using printing resources here, and defer discussion of the command line details until Chapter 13, "Using Common Command-Line Applications and Application Suites."

First, you will see how to add a local or network printer. Then you will learn more about your printer and its queue, as well as settings for your print job and sending it to a printer. After a brief examination of the printer, we look at font management. You'll see how to manage your font collections, add a new font, and manipulate the keyboard inputs available in Mac OS X.

One of the neatest additions Apple put into Mac OS X starting with 10.2 was the CUPS (Common Unix Printing System) printing system. With 10.3, Apple expanded support for more CUPS features, and 10.4 has continued this trend with further consolidation of settings and expansion of printing features. With almost any other printing system you might have encountered, support for a printer depends on whether the printer manufacturer decides to write a driver for your machine. And, with typical printer drivers, whether the output you get from one printer looks similar to that from another depends on how the different manufacturers have implemented their drivers. CUPS is different. CUPS is a system that makes every printer look like a PostScript printer from the application's point of view, completely eliminating all the weirdness that has long been associated with using PostScript or TrueType (scalable) fonts, or natively vector graphics from programs such as Illustrator, on inherently bitmapped printing devices such as ink-jet printers. "Drivers" for CUPS can be written by interested users, manufacturers, or third-party retailers, and are relatively simple modules that plug into the main printing system and instruct it in how to talk to a particular type of printer. Between the various sources of printer descriptions for CUPS, more than 5,000 different models of printers are supported.

NOTE

Complete and complex configurations of CUPS are covered in considerable detail by Michael Sweet in *CUPS: Common Unix Printing System*, ISBN 0-672-32196-3, from Sams Publishing. What we cover here should be sufficient for most users setting up systems with a few printers. CUPS is capable, however, of so much more. If you've a complicated printing setup, want to exert more control over your print jobs than is clear from these details, or need to manage a printing network involving many printers, this book can help.

Apple has neatly wrapped the CUPS system into both its GUI and command-line printing environment. Where Apple's tools stop and CUPS begins is completely hidden to the user and really of no consequence. The integration is sufficiently seamless that unless you really want to dig around in its guts, you'll never have to even know that CUPS exists—printing simply works, and works much better now than ever before.

Using Print Center/Printer Setup Utility

The once-familiar Chooser is not a part of Mac OS X. Instead, the heart of the Mac OS X GUI environment printing system is the Printer Setup Utility, which also appears as the Print Center. The Print Center/Printer Setup Utility is used for adding and deleting printers, setting the default printer, and interacting with the queues. The Print Center combines the printer tasks it once took both the Chooser and a desktop printer icon to accomplish. Desktop printer icons are still available, however, and provide a sort of limited view into the Printer List of the Printer Setup Utility. The rest of the familiar printing activities are available under the File menu of each application. The Print Center/Printer Setup Utility is located in `/Applications/Utilities`.

Note that just adding a printer in the Print Center is sufficient to enable both GUI and command-line printing under modern versions of Mac OS X. Under the original releases, this was not true, and information needed to be added to the NetInfo database as well. Now, almost any configuration you could want can be handled through the Printer Setup Utility or an auxiliary configuration interface accessed via a web page. A small number of Print and Page Setup dialog preferences can also be configured via the Print & Fax control pane.

Adding a Local USB or FireWire Printer

Because all modern Macintosh hardware comes with USB and FireWire ports, a local USB or FireWire printer is easy to add. Talking to printers on either of these local interfaces is conceptually similar, so the same instructions apply to either connection type.

When you open the Printer Setup Utility (sometimes called *Print Center*), a list of already configured printers should appear. If no Printer List window appears, you can select Show Printer List from the View menu to check for, or set up your USB, or FireWire printer. Your printer, if plugged in, turned on, and supported, should appear in the Printer List window automatically. If you don't see your printer listed, or if it is listed as unsupported, check the software CD that came with your printer for Mac OS X drivers. If it does not have any, check the manufacturer's website for the latest drivers and instructions. Mac OS X comes with some third-party USB printer drivers. If the drivers that come with Mac OS X work with your printer, you should be ready to print. If none of these sources have driver modules available, there are still a few other possibilities, but they're a bit more complicated, so we'll cover them later in the section on installing CUPS modules.

After the drivers have been properly installed, your local USB printer should be available for printing. You can either use the automatically discovered and configured printer queue that's created for it by the Printer Setup Utility, or you can add your own queue for the printer and sometimes assert more control over the system.

The advantage of just working with the automatically created printer is that it's essentially already configured and correct, and you don't need to do anything more than turn on the printer and plug it in to have it work. The advantage of creating your own queue is that you can name it something more useful than just the literal name/model of the printer. Additionally, a manually created queue will be available even when the printer is off or unavailable, so you can print to its queue, and save up print jobs destined for it, until it's available again.

If you'd like to manually add a queue for a USB or FireWire printer, click the Add icon in the Printer List, and you will be presented with the top-level interface to the Printer Browser window. By default, this window opens, showing automatically discovered printers—that is, local printers attached directly to your machine via USB and other "wired" solutions, or remote printers that are being auto-discovered via Bonjour (nee Rendezvous) or by CUPS's internal printer sharing/discovery module. If your printer is further away than can be automatically discovered (there's no problem, other than the hike to pick up your printouts, with configuring your system to print via a friend's machine in Bangladesh—CUPS couldn't care less where a configured printer physically lives), you can switch the window to IP Printer mode, where you can configure a specific IP address, and type of remote printing service to which CUPS should direct print requests. If neither option works for getting to your printer, you can also click the More Printers button, which will bring up a printer configuration dialog that's similar to that used in Mac OS X 10.2 and 10.3. In this configuration dialog, you can configure most automatic-discovery printer types, as well as local and remote printer types that can't be discovered automatically. This includes types such as serial-port printing, where data is sent out over a serial interface and one hopes (expects) that there is a printer listening that will do something with it, and print-via-file type printing, where a printer device sits around watching a particular file on disk, and prints any information that shows up in the file.

For most people and most purposes, simply selecting an auto-discovered printer or pointing to a remote IP printer should be all that's necessary. Printers that don't advertise their presence are becoming few and far between. On the other hand, people who might never have thought about, or thought they might need, advanced printing configurations might benefit by considering how some of the new capabilities that Mac OS X and CUPS bring to the printing world fit into their workflow. It would, for example, be a rather easy task to configure a system so that for every document printed, one copy popped out of a locally connected USB printer, and another copy popped out of a central printer in your company's records room, conveniently marked with "file copy." Likewise, a system could be configured to save a local PDF file as a copy of every fax that passes through the printing system. Because CUPS is open and extendable, the possibilities are limited only by your imagination.

Figure 6.1 shows the printer browser with local and shared printers that can be added to the Printer List.

FIGURE 6.1 The printer browser lets you add local and network-visible printers to the list of printers available in the Print dialog.

Mac OS X also allows you to share your locally connected printers to the network. This capability is enabled via selection of the Printer Sharing check box under the Services pane of the System Preferences Sharing pane. If you share your printer, it appears in other local network users' Printer Setup Utility Printer lists automatically.

Browsing or Specifying Network Printers

If you do not have a local USB printer, or if remote (network) printers also are available, you might want to add a network printer to your Printer List. Due to the way CUPS works, you won't need to do anything to add some network printers to your Printer List—nearby "shared" printers, and independently network-aware printers will automatically appear, preconfigured, in your printer list. Similar to the way the Chooser used to discover AppleTalk printers on your network, the CUPS system automatically knows about shared printers available through the CUPS system on other local machines (including non-Apple machines using CUPS, such as Linux boxes). Unlike the Chooser, the CUPS system also knows and shares the configuration information for those printers, so you've no need to select printer models or configure CUPS printers that are automatically discovered; they are simply available as already-configured printer choices whenever they can be found on the local network.

TIP

As a matter of fact, unless you want to do something like specify an automatically discovered printer as the default printing destination or as a desktop printer, you don't really even need to set up printers for any automatically discovered printers. All of them that are visible at any point in time automatically appear under a Shared Printers submenu of every Print dialog, so any that are on/visible are always available when you need to print.

The printers shown in Figure 6.1 as "Shared Printer" items are automatically discovered shared printers, and their configuration will be adopted from whatever machine is sharing them. Automatically discovered shared printers are also automatically available any time you print in an application, under a Shared Printers pop-up submenu in the Printing dialog.

Network-connected printers that are either too remote to be automatically discovered (automatic discovery is generally limited to your local network subnet), or that are less vociferous about their presence, must be specifically identified to your system if you want to use them. To do this, you need to know their network identification, so that you can tell the CUPS system where to find them.

Most—with the exception of Samba/SMB printers shared from Windows machines—can be configured by clicking on the IP Printer icon at the top of the Printer Browser, and switching to manual configuration of network printing. When in IP Printing mode, you are presented with several choices of network connection type, a place to specify the hostname or IP address of the printer, and a place to specify the queue for the printer, in case the printer supports the idea of multiple different print queues with different priorities, or other distinct features.

For this type of connection, you are also required to specify the type of printer so that the CUPS system can send the correct type of data over the network for it, and so that the printing dialog is aware of any special capabilities or limitations of the printer. You can also optionally give the printer a more mnemonic name to appear in your Print dialogs than the default hostname/IP address, and optionally specify a location, in case it's helpful to have a note regarding where to go to find your printout.

Figure 6.2 shows the IP Printer version of the interface, configuring a LPR-based printer at IP address `192.168.1.3`. The printer is an HP LaserJet 4MV, and I want to print to it using its native PostScript support, rather than using Tiger's built-in GIMP-Print capabilities.

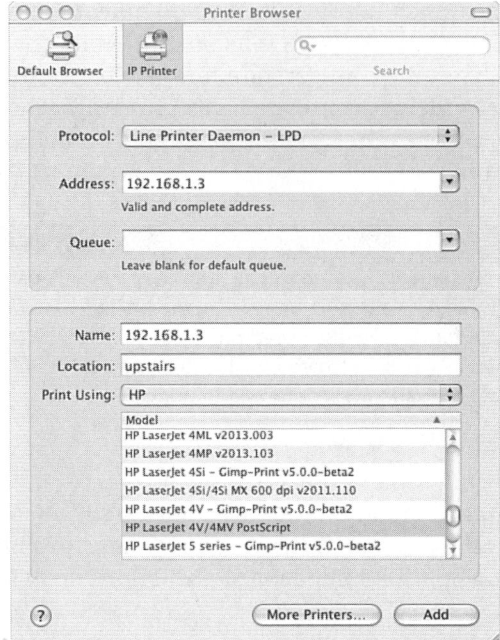

FIGURE 6.2 IP-based printers can't be browsed, so you need to tell the system how to find them.

In this interface, you have the option of choosing between the following three types of network-connected printers:

- LPD (Line Printer Daemon) printers—LPD printing is the long-standing Unix printer sharing mechanism, and is likely to be available at any established Unix facility, and with many Linux installations. LPD provides only the most basic printer-control capabilities, but its near-ubiquitous availability across platforms makes it a popular way to provide printing services in large or widespread, potentially heterogeneous clusters of machines. LPD printers are often PostScript capable, but occasionally are limited to literally line-printer (plain, old, unadorned text) capabilities, so it's important to have at least a general knowledge of the type of printer you're pointing to, when you set up a queue for a LPD printer in Printer Setup Utility.
- IPP (Internet Printing Protocol) printers—IPP printing is fast-replacing LPD printing as the default Unix printing method. IPP is the basic transport system for CUPS, so it will be found anywhere that CUPS printers are installed. IPP provides a far more complete printer-control solution than LPD, and almost any IPP printer can be treated as a generic PostScript printer, if you don't know more specific configuration information.
- HP JetDirect printers—HP created their own proprietary network transport system for their network-capable printers, and this interface can also be configured through the IP Printing interface of Printer Setup Utility. Most JetDirect-enabled printers also

support LPD, or have more friendly queues configured through server computer's printer-sharing preferences, so you'll only rarely need to know about configuring this type of printer interface, and then the appropriate information should be available from the network staff that configured these limitations on the printer.

Configuring Printers Through the Printer Setup Utility More Printers Interface

For some printing setups, neither the automatically discovered nor simple network configuration options are sufficient. For these, additional and advanced printing configurations are available by clicking on the More Printers button in the Printer Browser dialog. Apple's hidden even more, More Printers, in a secret Advanced pop-up item that appears in the menu only if you hold down the Option key while clicking the More Printers button. Because the primary use of going to this interface is to get to the advanced options, you might as well just always hold down Option while clicking that button because there doesn't seem to be any downside to doing it that way.

When Option-clicking the More Printers button, a drop-down sheet appears in the Printer Browser, under which you can select from among a number of different auto-discovered printer types. Most of these are already auto-discovered and presented to you under the Default Browser interface, but these can still be useful if you want to select from among a specific type of auto-discovered printer, and the full display is too cluttered. They also provide a few more selection options, such as the ability to specify the AppleTalk zone in which to search for printers.

Under this interface you also have the option of searching for a few semi-discoverable network printer types that don't show up in the Default browser and that aren't configured by IP address. These include Windows SMB-served printers, and unpaired Bluetooth printers. If you have turned SMB/CIFS on in the Directory Access program in `/Applications/Utilities` (be aware that the Windows Printer selection option appears, whether or not you've turned on SMB/CIFS), you'll be able to browse the local Network Neighborhood and local Windows Workgroups for printing resources. When selecting one, you'll need to know the appropriate user and password authentication information for connecting to that resource—the owner of the printer or administrator of the network should be able to give you this information. If you're trying to connect to a Bluetooth printer that you haven't previously used, you should be able to select among currently visible Bluetooth devices, and set up pairing with new devices that you want to use. Apple's overall interface (and seemingly its interface philosophy) for Bluetooth is in flux, however, so pairings might eventually be constructed elsewhere and only printer selection handled here.

Getting Information on Configured Printers

The Printer Setup Utility's Printer List itself is the place to examine known, configured, available printers. Each entry in the Printer List shows, by default, the printer name and its status. Under the View menu of the Print Center, the Columns submenu allows you to select from other information to display in the list. The available columns are as follows—the Name column is not optional, and you can't turn it off:

- In Menu (previously called *Favorites*)—A column allowing you to enable and disable printer availability in the Print dialog of applications, without removing them from the Printer List. Checked printers are available for printing to in the pop-up printer-selection menu in the Print dialog. Unchecked printers do not show up. Selected printers can be sorted to the top of the list for your convenience. The check box for one will be grayed out because you can't disable the display of your default printer.
- Name—The configured name of the printer. For printers you control, you can edit this value under the Name and Location pane of the Show Info option of the Printers menu.
- Status—The status information the printer reports.
- Jobs—The number of current print jobs waiting on the printer.
- Kind—The printer model as configured.
- Host—The host serving the printer, or local, if the printer is directly connected to your machine.
- Location—The location information reported by either the machine serving the printer or the directory service describing the printer. If the printer is local to your machine (including network printers incorrectly identified as local), you can edit the location information by using Get Info from the Printer List, selecting the Name and Location pane, and changing the location.

Figure 6.3 shows a sample Printer List. In this Printer List, five printers are shown. One (`lp`) is a remote Apple LaserWriter Select 360 that was automatically discovered through the Directory Services (NetInfo) method of specifying network resources. This method is useful if you want to propagate a specific printer configuration to a large group of client machines, and involves setting up a printer description in your NetInfo domain, and then subscribing the clients to the domain so that they all have a copy of the same description. One is an HP Color LaserJet connected via AppleTalk. One (`192.168.1.3`) is an HP LaserJet 4MV connected via direct IP printing (LPR/LPD). In versions 10.3 and 10.4, these have no host information at all, even though all three are network printers: two having a fixed IP and the other having a fixed AppleTalk ID. In 10.2, these show `local` as their host, despite the fact that they're network printers. In earlier versions of Mac OS X, these would identify themselves as being served via NetInfo, AppleTalk, and from a particular IP address, respectively. The fact that this information is not correctly displayed is probably a bug, but it's been around for a while. Based on the ongoing changes to the printing system interface, this area is probably under active development, and you should expect to eventually start seeing more useful information regarding the printers and their current states in this window

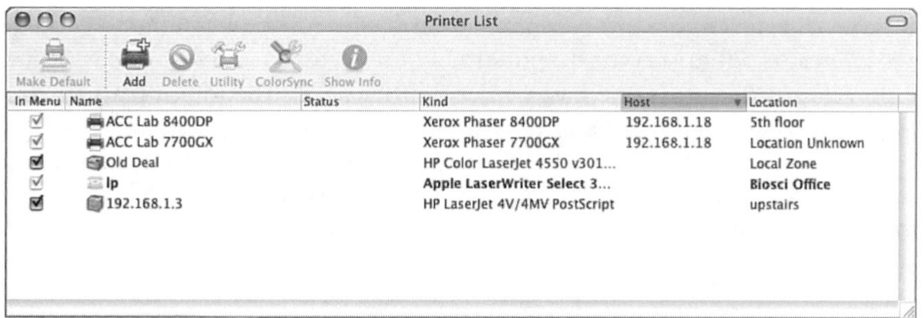

FIGURE 6.3 This Printer List shows five printers, three of which are configured locally (though they're remote printers), and two of which are discovered from other computers on the network.

The other two printers are CUPS printers that are shared from `192.168.1.18`. Under Mac OS X 10.2, these would have displayed shaded entries to indicate that they're automatically discovered remote printers. Under 10.4, only the In Menu check box gets shaded (because you don't have any choice about these—printers that are automatically discovered and configured are always shown in all applications' Printer Setup and Print dialog menus). Also, unfortunately, the printer list doesn't display the queue name for these printers, and it's the queue name that you'll need to know if you want to access them from the command line. Under the print dialog in GUI applications, selecting them by the names shown here is sufficient identification.

The bolded line indicates that printer `lp` is currently my default printer. Each time you add a printer, the newly added one automatically becomes the default. To make a specific printer your default, select the printer in the Printer List and then choose the Make Default icon, or choose Printers, Make Default from the menu. Selecting a printer as a destination in an application's Print dialog also currently changes the default. To delete a printer, select it in the Printer List and click the Delete icon.

Creating Desktop Printers

A desktop printer is nothing more than an icon you can create (essentially an optional button) in the Finder (and it doesn't even have to be in the Desktop folder), that opens up an individual printer's job list/status/control window. To see an individual printer's job list (things printing, or waiting to print in its queue), select the printer in the Printer List, and then select Show Jobs from the Printers menu, or simply double-click on the printer you want to examine in the Printer List. The window that appears functions as a diagnostic indicator for the printer, telling you how it and/or the current job are doing; a job list for the printer, showing what print jobs are pending in the queue; and a control center for the printer allowing the printer to be taken out of service, or individual jobs to be managed. Figure 6.4 shows a sample print queue that has experienced an error and is retrying the send. According to the status entry, it hasn't yet given up. If the job had experienced a serious error, the Stop Job button would have changed to Retry, and there would be a more serious-sounding error report displayed in the window. Some print configurations will never give up, even if they can't contact the printer or remote host at all. Others will error out and give you potentially useful diagnostics in this window. When a job gets stuck, as this one has, you can either delete the job or pause it by selecting the print job and clicking the appropriate button. If something happens and the printer or CUPS system thinks that the job is completely broken, your options change to deleting or retrying the job. If there's a known printer problem that will take some time to fix, you can stop the printer, or put the job on hold, and re-enable the job after the printer's working properly again.

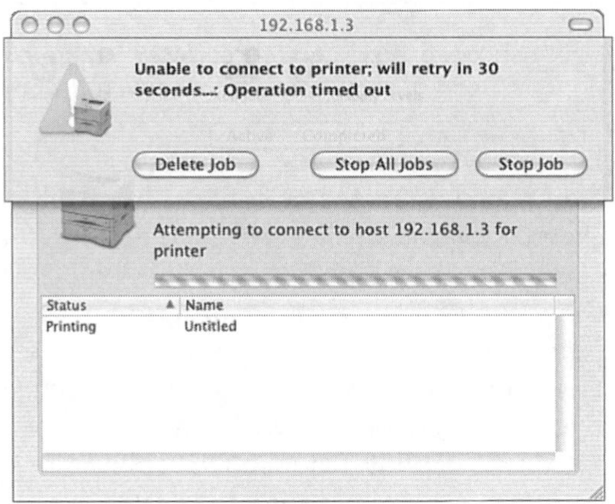

FIGURE 6.4 The print queue for printer `192.168.1.3` shows that the current print job has encountered an error in communications but is still retrying the connection. You could choose to delete the job or put it on hold. If it had fully errored out, you could retry it.

> **TIP**
>
> Alternatively, you can drag print jobs out of a malfunctioning printer's queue, and onto another printer, if you want to redirect stalled output to a functioning machine.

The printing status window for each specific printer shows a number of visual diagnostics regarding the printer's behavior and current and recent activity, as well as controls to pause or stop printing on that printer, and to rearrange or delete individual print jobs. While a successful job is printing, a blue status bar appears, and a status message alternately flashes Processing Job and Preparing Data for the duration of the print time. The Delete, Hold, and Resume buttons are grayed out unless you select a specific print job. Figure 6.5 shows a sample status window for a normal printer with several jobs in its queue.

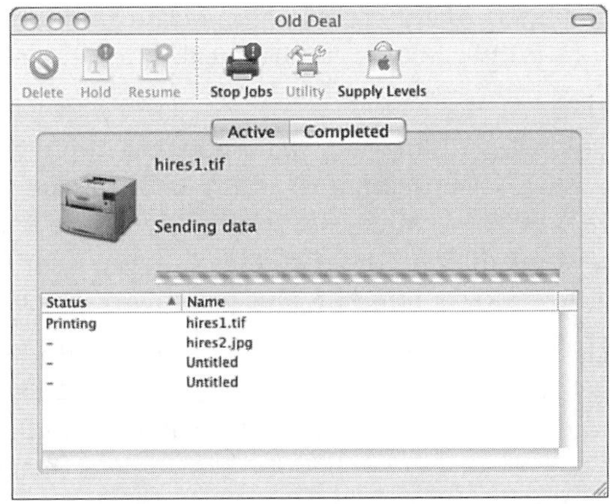

FIGURE 6.5 The print queue for printer `Old Deal` shows that the current print job is proceeding normally.

If you'd like to be able to get to this informational window more quickly, and without needing to navigate the Printer Setup Utility, you can create a Desktop Printer icon that, when clicked, will open directly to this printer job list/control window. To create a desktop printer, simply select the printer for which you want a desktop printer icon from the Printer List of Printer Setup Utility, and then select the Create Desktop Printer from the Printers menu. You will be prompted for a name and location to save the icon. After it has been created, the Desktop Printer icon will appear as an alias. It might look like a simplified picture of your printer or it might look a bit like a generic laser printer or ink jet. Double-clicking this alias icon will launch directly to the job list/status/control window for the associated printer. You can also print certain documents by dragging them directly to the desktop printer, without needing to first open them in an application. When printing this way, you have no control over finer details of the print jobs (such as can be addressed from the Print dialog in most applications), but it is far more convenient than using Preview, for example, for printing quick copies of 50 screen capture images.

At the top of each printer's window, you can choose to stop the jobs for a printer. When you do that, the status entry for the printer in the Printer List reflects that the queue has stopped by listing the status as Stopped. After you have stopped a printer queue, the Stop icon changes and becomes Start Jobs. When a job is printing, Hold and Delete activate, allowing you to place an individual job on hold or delete it entirely. When a job is on Hold, the Resume button activates, allowing you to restart the individual job.

Printer Classes

New in 10.3, Apple added support for CUPS printer classes. Printer classes are user-created groupings of printers that can be treated like a single printer from the perspective of applications that want to print output. Classes appear in the Print dialog's list of printers just like any other individual printer. When selected and a print job sent to a printer class, CUPS delivers the print job to the first available printer in the class.

This capability to group printers might sound unimportant from the perspective of a home user with only a few printers, but it can be a real time- and labor-saver for a business with many shared networked printers.

To place printers in a class, select all of them that you want to put into the class in the Printer Setup Utility and then select Printers, Pool Printers. You are presented with a dialog where you can confirm the printer selections you've made and give the class a name. You can create multiple printer classes and place any printer into any number of classes as well, allowing flexible groupings of your printing resources.

When created, printer classes look to the rest of the system like individual printers, but are handled by CUPS by load-sharing the print jobs across the available printers. In any place that the system expects to see a specific printer name (including command-line commands such as `lpr`—see Chapter 13—that don't document this feature), you can substitute a printer class, and CUPS manages the actual destination in the background.

Setting Printing System Preferences

The printers that are available to the system are one type of printing preference, but there are also printer-specific preferences, and specialty CUPS preferences that can be imposed on printing as well. You are almost certainly already familiar with configuring per-print-job setting regarding things like the number of copies to be printed, or, if you have a printer that can print on both sides of a page, whether to use this feature for a particular print job. Surprisingly, many users don't realize that the settings that they choose for a print job can be configured to be the default settings for all documents printed from an application, or, with some care, for the printer in general. This lack of recognition hasn't been helped by Apple's choice of hiding the ability to save printer preferences under the enigmatic printing dialog pop-up menu labeled Presets. It's even further obscured in Tiger, by a redesign of the Printing dialog itself, so as to eliminate the preference saving option entirely from the Standard dialog, and to make it available only under the Advanced version of the Printing dialog.

Nonetheless, forewarned is forearmed, and once you know how to get to the option to save your print job preferences, creating, and reusing printer settings is a simple task.

Choosing a Default Printer and Page Setup

As mentioned previously, the default system printer can be configured through the Printer Setup Utility, simply by selecting a printer and clicking the Make Default button. Insidiously however, Apple has added a Printing and Fax control-pane option that also influences the apparent default printer. Using it, you can select a particular printer—which has the same effect as selecting that printer and making it the default through the Printer Setup Utility, or you can select the Last Printer Used option, in which case the system tries to determine the last printer used *for each application*, and sets each application to use the printer that was most recently used *in it*. The system default printer, however, does not change, and applications that haven't been used before or that don't obey the last-used option, are still controlled by the system default that was configured in the Printer Setup Utility. Overall, this might be a good way to do things, having an overall default, and the option to override that default (by default) for any application in which you choose to do so, but to have to configure it through two different interfaces, with no mention of the features of the other in either, seems like a recipe for user confusion.

The Page Setup settings remain as an artifact of Apple's ancient printing system design that doggedly persists, version after version, despite being outmoded by newer printing considerations. Page Setup is used to configure information about what printer properties to use for configuring a job (things such as the printable margins), paper size, paper feed orientation, and print scaling. Unfortunately, if you have more than one printer, each of them probably requires different settings, and you can save only one collection of settings as the default. The result is that you will still need to remember to open the Page Setup dialog for every print job, and select the proper printer under Format For, or your margins and other important size-related details will be wrong.

Under the File menu of an application, choose Page Setup to set basic paper dimensions/printer specific dimensioning information. Figure 6.6 shows what Page Setup looks like in Tiger—it keeps losing functions to more appropriate homes, but it still hasn't gone away. Page Setup appears as either a sheet or a window, depending on the application. Sometimes it can be accessed only from the File menu, and in other applications it is available through an icon-bar selection or with Shift-Command-P. The Settings option has been essentially reduced to Save As Default, although application-specific settings still do force themselves into this menu on occasion. The menus and options in the middle of the dialog change, depending on whether there's anything else to choose (such as an application-specific item) under the Settings menu. At the bottom of Page Setup, there is a button for direct access to the Help Center, as well as buttons for Cancel and OK. We will break down our examination of Page Setup according to the Settings choices.

Page Attributes

The Settings option is set to Page Attributes (the only available option) by default. This menu is really a status line telling you what option set is currently being displayed in the Page Setup dialog or pane. The only other option, unless you're running an application such as Microsoft Word, which forces its own configuration settings to appear here as well, is to select Save As Default, which saves the displayed settings as the default selection for future use.

Format For When displaying the Page Attributes section of Page Setup, you can select which printer to format for. The available printer choices are Any Printer and whatever printers are included as part of your Printer List. Page Setup formats for Any Printer by default. When you select a printer in the Format For List, a more specific description appears. Note that in our example, Page Setup describes printer `192.168.1.3` as an HP LaserJet 4V/4MV. Selecting the correct printer here is important because this is the portion of the printing system interface that controls what the system thinks that printer's allowable margins and other properties are. If you have a printer that really can't print within one inch of the page margins, and select a printer here that has quarter-inch margins, you will be able to print and format print jobs as though your printer has quarter-inch margins, but the outside edge will be missing. Likewise, if you have a printer that can handle borderless printing and you have selected a printer that has margins larger than zero, the system, and therefore your applications, won't let you actually print to the edges of the page.

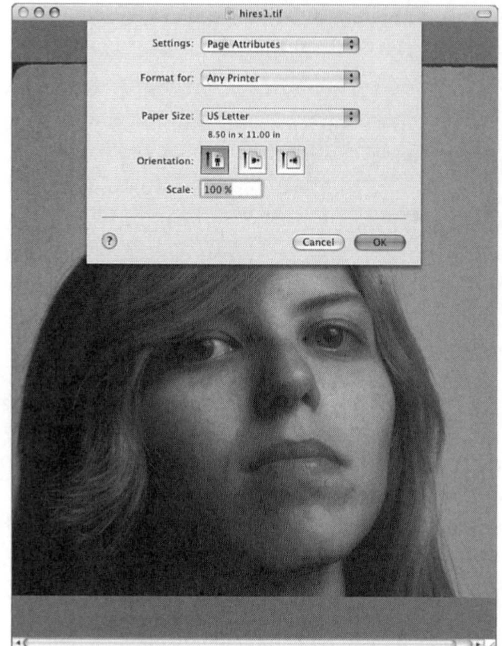

FIGURE 6.6 Page Setup can still be found under the File menu in Mac OS X. There are fewer attributes that can be configured, but their use is identical to previous versions of Mac OS and Mac OS X.

Paper Size

Page size is also specified in Page Setup. The available paper sizes vary with the selected printer. The default page sizes available for Any Printer range from 3×5 to 13×19—obviously not all of which are possible on some printers. So, although Any Printer is fine to use as a general default, don't be surprised if its settings don't literally work for any printer. Whenever you select a paper size, its dimensions appear as an additional description. For Any Printer, US Letter, 8.5"×11", is the default paper size. Keep an eye on the setting that this option comes up with. Some specific printers seem to default to US Letter Small as their default paper size, which can wreak havoc with page layouts that you've constructed for full-size US Letter paper.

The Paper Size menu also has a Manage Custom Sizes option that brings up a dialog allowing you to configure custom paper sizes. This is a surprisingly unnecessary option for most users on a day-to-day basis, but as printers get larger, this option becomes more important. Specifying a custom paper size is also an incredibly useful option to have when you're trying to force particular output to fit on a single page, yet don't want to tweak a bunch of formatting and font-size options until it all fits. It's a kind of hackish trick, but if you're presented with a program like MS Excel that wants to break up your output horizontally onto multiple pages, and you really want all your columns on one page, regardless of how small the font gets, playing with Custom Sizes can be a life saver. Simply set up a page size that's large enough to contain all of your columns at whatever the display characteristics are set to in Excel, and then "Print" it, but instead of printing to paper, print to a PDF. Load the PDF up in Preview, specify your real printer and paper size in Page Setup, and when you go to print the PDF, Preview will ask and then automatically scale everything to fit on the paper.

Orientation

The Orientation setting controls which edge of the paper is "up" with respect to the print. Portrait, the norm for written-text type output, is available as well as two forms of landscape (more commonly used for photographs). For landscape orientation, you can specify whether the top of the printout should be at the right or left side of the paper. Simply select the appropriate icon to suit your needs. Portrait is the default orientation. This option, despite its utility, is becoming less relevant as more applications, such as MS PowerPoint, try to ignore it and try to force page orientation settings internally (often with unexpected and undesirable results).

Scale

Scale is a box where you can input the desired scaling. The default is 100%. Because few applications make it easy to determine at what size they're trying to print a document, it's often difficult to figure out a good scaling setting. The fact that Preview (through which much printing is managed) invisibly munges print scales to fit the size of the available margins doesn't help the situation at all. (Preview will ask, if your print is too large for the current page setup, whether you want to scale it down to fit, but under some circumstances, if the print is smaller than the page setup, it will scale the print up to fit, without asking permission.)

Application Specific

Page setup dialogs might also include application-specific entries in the Settings menu. These can include almost any configuration option and can override the settings in other panes of the Print Setup dialog, if the application-specific and normal options overlap. Microsoft Word, for example, duplicates almost all the regular page setup options in its own application-specific pane. It further allows the page setup options configured there to apply to sections of the document, and to have different page setup options for different sections of a document.

Setting and Storing Print-Job/Document Printing Preferences

Document-specific sorts of print preferences, such as which pages of, and how many copies of the printout are needed, are configured by selecting Print from the File menu, and setting options in a set of Print dialog panes. With Tiger, Apple has created a simplified Print dialog that appears for some applications (such as Preview); it provides a sort of instant preview and access to some commonly used settings, but it removes your access to many important Print dialog options. The complete Print dialog, with all of its familiar and useful options, is still available in these applications by clicking on the Advanced button. Because the options available in the simplified interface are just limited-capability versions of the ones in the Advanced interface (which is the Standard interface in most other applications), we'll show an example of the simplified interface that Apple's working on (see Figure 6.7), but document the options available in the Advanced interface. The simplified interface seems to still be under development, so please remember to look for the Advanced button if you find a printing option that you need, but that doesn't seem to be available in the interface you're looking at.

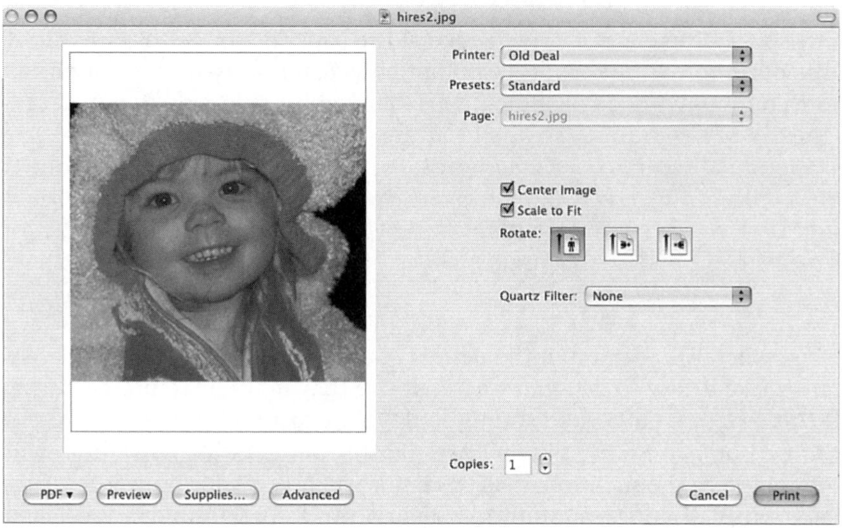

FIGURE 6.7 The simplified Print dialog provides access to a limited range of typically useful options, as well as an instant preview of your output page. The Advanced button takes you to the familiar Advanced Print dialog.

The Print dialog itself is accessed through the File menu, under Print, and is typically also attached to the Command-P keystroke. Select this menu option to print a file. Depending on the application, choosing Print opens either the Simplified/Standard (refer to Figure 6.7), or Advanced (see Figure 6.8) Print dialog box. Also depending on the application, the Print dialog appears either as a sheet or as a separate, movable (dialog style) window.

In the top part of the Print dialog, using the Printer pop-up menu, you can select what printer you want to route the printout to (or edit the Printer List to include it, if it's not available for selection). Using the Presets pop-up, you can select among (or save) collections of Print configuration settings.

The options necessary to configure a number of printing preferences appear in the middle part of the Print dialog box. From a pop-up menu, you can select among the options you want to configure (not all of which will be available for every printer): Copies & Pages, Layout, Output Options, (print) Scheduler, Paper Handling, ColorSync, Cover Page, Error Handling, Paper Feed, Color Options, Finishing, Printer Features, Preview, Application Specific, and Summary can all be configured or viewed here. Settings that you make here can be saved by under the Presets pop-up menu.

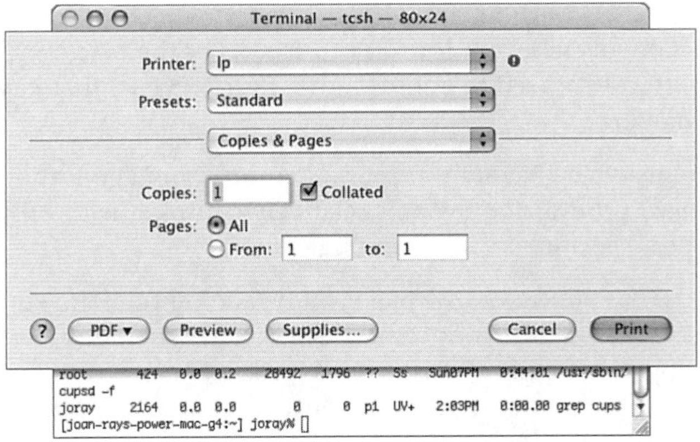

FIGURE 6.8 Choosing File, Print opens the Print dialog box, where you can select a printer and various options for your print job. Note the small stop sign (the tiny octagon with an exclamation point in it) to the right of my chosen printer, indicating that this print queue is currently stopped.

The bottom section of the Print dialog box has buttons for Preview, Supplies, Cancel, and Print, and a button labeled PDF that really isn't a button, but a toggle to pop up a menu of PDF-related functions, such as saving the document as a PDF. A standard ? button linking to the help system also sometimes appears, depending on whether there is enough room for it. If the application you are printing from supports both a Standard and Advanced Print dialog, buttons to switch between these also appear here.

Curiously, the option to send the document as a fax, if your machine is able to send faxes, has migrated from a convenient FAX button to a menu item on a menu that appears if you click the PDF button. Actually other things have strangely migrated under this PDF button as well—some of which have as little to do with PDFs as faxing. Save PDF as PostScript has a bizarre ring to it. Other items in this PDF menu however, make it sound like this could be an insidiously useful little three-letter button—even if Apple has misguidedly started labeling everything the print system touches as PDF.

The Preview button runs processes the print as though it was going to send it to the printer, but instead sends it to Preview as a PDF, allowing you to view a relatively faithful rendition of what should hit paper when you actually do send the print job. Print Preview is sometimes available under the File menu of an application, but it always appears as a button in the Print dialog box.

The Supplies button opens a page in your web browser for ordering new printer supplies. It appears that Apple's attempting to integrate supplies monitoring into the Printer status/job list/control windows, so this is probably supposed to inform you when you're about to run out of ink in your inkjet or toner in your laser printer, and help you go directly to an ordering page. Right now, most of it appears to be experimental and of demo functionality, and none of it works with any of the printers we have, so we don't know how well it will really work. Probably reasonably well, for supplies for current, popular printers, but the real test will be how well they support the oddball white elephants we all still have chugging away in back rooms. On the other hand, there have been other "order more of these" buttons in other parts of the Mac OS X interface (such as the Buy Fonts button that used to appear in the font preview) that have disappeared over time without fanfare.

Note that the contents of the Standard print dialog vary from application to application, but that the Advanced print dialog remains relatively constant, with only the material under the Application-Specific section changing.

The Settable options that appear on the page will be among the following items—although the exact capabilities of your printer will dictate whether some panes appear, and what options appear on each of them. There probably are even a few preferences panes that we've never seen; ones that appear only on printers to which we don't have access for testing.

The Printer Menu

Whichever printer is listed in your Printer List as your default printer appears here initially. You can also select from any of the other printers available in your Printer List, and from any shared printers, or other automatically discovered and configured printers that are currently visible. Or you can choose Add Printer at the bottom of the menu of available printers to add to or modify your Printer List. This option immediately takes you to the Printer Setup Utility, where you can add or delete printers. The selection for Print & Fax Preferences opens the system preferences panel for print and fax items.

The Presets Menu

Presets are collections of Print dialog option settings that you've saved. The default is Standard, which is your plain vanilla one-copy, all pages, no special options setting. You'll probably use this one most of the time. If you find, however, that for a particular printer you like to have a setting, such as the print quality, set to a nondefault value, you can set that option, and then save a preset, which will remember and set that setting whenever you select that preset in the future. After you have saved a customized setting, you can select Standard or any of your customized setting collections by name. The Save, Save As, Rename, and Delete options available under the Presets menu allow you to manage the presets you have constructed. Custom presets that you construct are available from all applications, although application-specific options for seemingly identical preferences might not be transferred between different applications. Less usefully, custom presets that you construct are also available for all printers, whether they apply to that printer or not. Sometimes this is no big deal—if you've set a preset for duplex printing on one printer and accidentally select that preset on another printer that can't do two-sided printing, nothing bad happens. If you have two printers with *very* similar, but not quite identical printer-specific options, a preset configured for one can select unexpected configuration options in the other.

The Unlabeled Menu in the Middle of the Page

In the vertical middle of the Print dialog is a section (bounded by lines above and below) that displays one of a number of possible print configuration pages. The contents of this section are initially the Copies & Pages pane, and the menu that controls the contents is labeled Copies & Pages. The options available in this menu vary depending on the capabilities of the printer that you have, and the application that you're using to print, but most should be among the following items:

- Copies & Pages—This is the first item in a pop-up menu of many items, and is the default pane in the center of the Print dialog. Here you specify the number of copies you want to print, whether the pages should be collated, and a page range. For the page range, you can select either All, to print the entire document, or you can specify an actual range of page numbers. On some applications, a Current option also appears, to select only the currently visible page in the application.
- Layout—Here is where you select layout settings. The first available option is Pages Per Sheet, where you can select 1, 2, 4, 6, 9, or 16 pages per sheet. The next option is Layout Direction. There are four layout direction options: horizontally from left to right, horizontally from right to left, vertically from left to right, and vertically from right to left. The available layout directions are indicated with helpful icons. The final layout option is Border. Available options for Border are None, Single Hairline, Single Thin Line, Double Hairline, and Double Thin Line.

  If you have a printer that can print both sides of the page (called *duplex printing*), you might be able to set that print option in the Layout pane under Two Sided Printing, or you might have a separate configuration pane for duplex printing. The duplex options allow you to select between binding edges for the prints. This controls which way the two-sided prints "flip" so that you can turn the page either at the top or at the side.
- Output Options—The previously available Output options pane has disappeared. The ability to save as PostScript (the only thing this pane previously provided) has moved to the funny PDF button in the main interface.
- Paper Handling—This section allows you to specify whether to print all, just even or odd pages, or to reverse the printing order. This might not seem a particularly useful collection of options, but in fact it's a convenient way to get two-sided printing out of a printer that can only print on one side of the page. Using the options here, you can print first the odd pages, take the stack of paper directly out of your printer's output stack, put it back in the input tray, and then print the even pages onto the other side of the stack.

  A new section of the pane has appeared in Tiger, providing some control over rescaling for final output. With all the options to scale in applications, and additionally scale in Page Setup, this might seem like a bizarre feature to add, but it could prove to be quite useful. It's not at all uncommon to set up a document to print natively to a particular page size (say, perhaps a poster print for a presentation), and then want a scaled-down copy of it for previewing. Changing the paper size in the application can (and will!) completely mess up all of your careful formatting, whereas using this option to rescale to different paper will allow you to leave all of your other print settings alone, and just do an at-print-time rescale onto different paper.

- Scheduler—This divergently named pane (why isn't it Scheduling? Apple's usually much more careful than this) allows you to control when your printout gets printed. It also lets you set a print priority for the printout. These settings interact in such a way as to make the when portion of the setting mostly a suggestion, and the priority portion of the setting a control as to how serious the timing suggestion actually is. The higher the priority you set, the stronger the time portion of the suggestion and the closer to the set time that your printout is likely to appear. The lower the priority, the less important your time suggestion becomes (subject to the fact that it won't ever print *before* you set the time to print), and the more subject to being delayed by other printouts it becomes. You could, for example, set the printout to be printed Now and set the priority to Low, and end up with your printout not appearing for several hours, as other more important print jobs repeatedly bump it out of the way in the queue.
- ColorSync—The ColorSync pane controls options related to Apple's ColorSync color-workflow process, and the contents of the pane are contextually dependent on the capabilities of the application doing the printing. In addition to a number of Quartz filters that can generate subtly different output presentations by filtering the input, this pane might give you some contextually available options that appear only for certain types of prints or for certain printers. For example, with our black-and-white laser printer we can choose between having colors mapped to grays in software or directly in the printer's hardware. It might seem that there's little difference in where one discards the color information to create a grayscale print from a color image, but in fact there are sometimes significant visual consequences—instances where an image would be simply unusable printed one way, and acceptable when printed the other.
- Cover Page—This pane controls options related to printing a cover-page for your print job. Some printers and printer configuration sets won't support this option. Currently there are only the options of setting some banner text regarding the document's confidentiality, of placing the banner page before or after your printout, and of adding some text to the cover page regarding appropriate billing. We expect this page to mature over time, as many print systems allow the cover page to be printed from a separate paper bin (letterhead for example), and other useful manipulations of that type.
- Error Handling—Some printers have more brains than others, allowing them to get quite verbose about problems they've encountered when printing a file. This pane is conditionally available, depending on whether your printer can be configured to do something other than simply "not print right" when it encounters an error. (Many inkjet printers won't provide this dialog.) The Error Handling options that appear for this printer are for PostScript Errors and Tray Switching. The PostScript error choices are to either have No Special Reporting, which is the default, or to Print Detailed Report. The Tray Switching error options are Use Printer's Default, Switch to Another Cassette with the Same Paper Size, or Display Alert. Unfortunately, because the authors have only PostScript printers readily available to test, we can't tell you whether another error handling option might appear in place of the

PostScript Errors option, or whether that option is simply grayed out for non-PostScript printers.

- Paper Feed—This option group is where you set any special paper feed options. You can either choose to specify that all your pages come from a particular paper feed option, or that the first one comes from one location and the remaining pages from a different location. This could be useful, for example, if you have a tray dedicated to letterhead. The actual paper feed choices available for the different categories vary with the printer.

  If you want to print your job on special paper, either the first page or all of it, the manual feed for the first page option can be a useful tool to have in your bag of tricks. More than once, we've sent a print job down to the networked color laser to be printed on a batch of high-quality stock for correspondence, only to find that the 87th revision of a grad student's dissertation has gotten in ahead of ours and eaten up a bunch of our high-quality paper. If your printer supports it, you can use the first-page-manual option to delay your print job until you're actually at the printer and can make sure that it's going through under your control, on your desired paper.

  This works because most printers will pause indefinitely waiting for a piece of paper to be dropped in the manual feed slot. If you select Manual for the first page, the effect is not only that you get to feed it your first page separate from the cassette (allowing you to use letterhead if you choose), but also that the printer waits to grab that page out of the manual feeder before it starts loading pages from the normal tray for the rest of your job. This makes for a nice pause in the process during which you can load whatever special paper you want to use, drop your manual-feed page in the manual feed tray, slap in the cassette of quality paper that you don't want to lose to someone else's printouts of email messages and web funny pages, and be relatively certain that your job is going to proceed immediately and with no break in the middle for someone else to use the paper you've loaded.

- Finishing—This option set appears only for some printers, and seems to be an "end of print job paper handing" pane, allowing you to specify whether you want a job sent to an automated collator and stapler feature (if your printer has one), or to an alternate output tray.

- Image Quality—This optional pane controls printer-specific settings related to how your printout is sent to and rendered at the printer, especially for, but not necessarily limited to, "images" (more things are printed as images than most people realize). Here again you can configure some color correction settings (that interact peculiarly and unpredictably with the ColorSync settings—either leave ColorSync on In Printer and change these, leave these on Automatic and mess with ColorSync, or be prepared for some long nights debugging color output), and other potentially printer-specific image rendition controls. If you have a Print Quality option on this pane, you might be surprised at how bad Standard quality printouts look, compared to Enhanced or High Resolution prints.

- Troubleshooting—This optional pane seems to be intended for links to printer-specific resources that might be useful for solving print problems.
- Application-specific panes—Sometimes an application will have a category for additional special options unique to it. This is always a good place to check if you find that your print results are a bit unexpected. For example, if you print something created in color to a color printer, but it prints in grayscale, you would want to check here for additional options for your particular application because the application itself might have some default control that forces grayscale output, despite the other printing settings.
- Printer Features—Printers with special capabilities might register printer-specific menu items and panes under this pane as well. These can include anything from special handling for different paper stocks, to control of built-in color profiles. Sometimes a printer-specific subpane will contain multiple subpanes of its own, each of which will have assorted options specific to the selected printer. These options can range from relatively useful, such as specifying how you want the in-printer processing to interpret your colors, to relatively useless, such as pop-up menus labeled only with undocumented acronyms and populated only with unlabeled numbers. If you encounter the latter variety, we recommend that you stick with whatever undocumented settings appear by default because some of these are service-type settings that can permanently alter the way that your printer behaves, sometimes in a quite undesirable fashion.
- Print Summary—This pane doesn't contain configurable options, but does give you a convenient summary overview of all the settings you've made on the myriad other panes available for configuration here. This is sometimes a real life-saver because noticing the one out-of-place check box among the gadjillion places to look is often a task accomplished only after a bad printout has already been produced.

The Strange PDF Menu

A surprising amount of functionality hides under the little PDF button at the lower left of the Print dialog. This is where the Save as PDF option has moved, as well as the Save as PostScript option that used to be available from the Output Options pane. Apple seems to have decided that anything touched by the printing system is a PDF, and that therefore all alternative functionality related to doing things that are printing-like can be labeled as PDF related. This is literally sort of true—internally Apple manages just about everything in PDF format, and the printing system seems to process everything through PDF before sending it off to be printed. Still, when you open a JPEG file, being presented with the option to save the PDF as PostScript is not exactly the user-friendly abstraction of function for which Apple is known.

Despite its odd naming, this will turn out to be a quite useful menu. Among its options (which appear to be extendable by the construction of additional printing workflows), are the following items:

- Save as PDF—Exactly what you'd expect for a PDF menu—the option to save the print job as a PDF file, instead of sending it off to a pile of paper.

- Save PDF as PostScript—Ignore the fact that they say PDF as PostScript. Save as PostScript, whether or not you're starting with a PDF. If you have to exchange printable documents portably with a system that isn't quite so cozy PDFs as Mac OS X (primarily with other Unix systems), PostScript is a good option.
- Fax PDF—Again, ignore the PDF part—fax whatever you're trying to print. This allows you to send your print job off to a fax machine and have it printed there. If the receiving machine is actually a Macintosh, it could well be automatically saving an electronic copy of the data when it's received, but there is nothing that forces the transaction to be with another computer.

  You have effectively acquired the ability to treat any fax machine that you can find a phone number for, as a printer for your system. When you click the Fax PDF item, the Print dialog changes to present options required for faxing. Where previously you could select a printer, there is now a To line, where the fax system wants you to enter a phone number. This field is tied directly to the Address Book through the icon/button that looks like a person's head and shoulders. Clicking this button allows you to select from your known contacts, and have that person's fax information automatically inserted. The form additionally allows you to specify a prefix that you need to dial out on the local phone network (many businesses require that you dial 9 before an outgoing number), to select what modem to use for faxing, and to specify text to be included as a cover page. The Fax version of the Print dialog, shown in Figure 6.9, also includes a number of the same configurable central option panes available under the normal Print dialog.

6

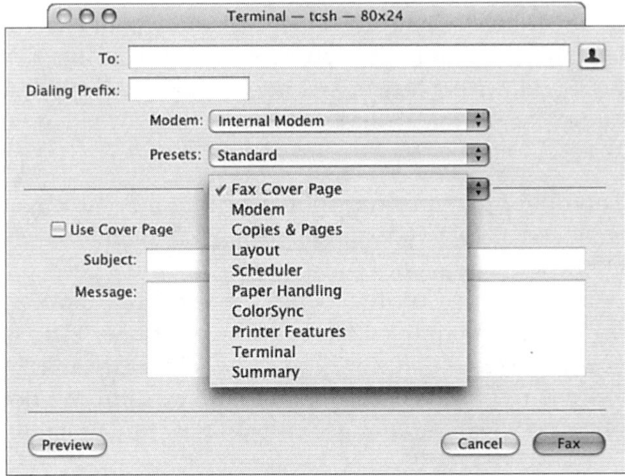

FIGURE 6.9 The Print dialog changes into a Fax dialog if you click the Fax PDF option in the PDF menu.

Below a horizontal divider in the pop-down PDF menu is a set of extendable PDF-based workflows for PDF files. Essentially they convert the current document to a PDF file, and then do something with it. At the bottom of the list, the menu provides the option to edit itself and add/delete PDF workflows. As we write, the following options are available. Some are far more useful than others, but this feature definitely looks like it will bear watching, as Apple (hopefully) documents the workflow creation process in the future.

- Compress PDF—Save a compressed version of the PDF file. Because PDFs are already highly compressed internally, they don't tend to compress well at all, so this is probably not going to be a very useful option, and we can't begin to guess what effect compression might have on cross-platform compatibility.
- Encrypt PDF—Save an encrypted version of the PDF file. This uses internal, rather than external, encryption (the data in the PDF file is encrypted, rather than the PDF file being itself encrypted). Hopefully this means that Apple is using Adobe's internal encryption and password-protection mechanism for the PDF.
- Mail PDF—Send the PDF to someone as an email attachment. This requires that you have Mail configured on your system.
- Save as PDF to iPhoto—Didn't know that iPhoto could catalog PDFs as images, did you? This could be useful! Save the PDF into iPhoto for storage and indexing, and you have a catalog of your printouts that you can return to, and reprint whenever you need a new copy! Of course, you could always do that by saving a PDF and keeping it around in a directory of potentially useful printouts, but this would let you visually index the printouts, and seems like a great idea.
- Save PDF to Web Receipts Folder—I didn't even know I had a Web Receipts folder—well, that's not true—for about six years now I've been saving virtual printouts (PDFs) or screen captures of all my online receipts into a yearly folder for tax purposes—and now Apple's gone and added a feature to do exactly that, directly to the Print dialog. This is going to be even more useful than the Save PDF to iPhoto option! For the record, with a little searching, the `Web Receipts` folder appears to live under your `Documents` folder, and will be auto-created when you first use this Print option.
- Edit Menu—This option provides a cryptic little interface into creating additional workflows that would allow you to automatically do different useful things with PDFs. It's pretty easy to figure out how to get a PDF into a particular application—just click the + button to add an item, and then select the application you want to use to open the PDF. If you find yourself passing print-only PDFs through PhotoShop for a little creative editing, you can easily set up a PDF printing workflow that allows you to print PDFs directly into PhotoShop. We hope Apple provides more information on advanced uses of this workflow functionality soon!

Configuring CUPS Server-Specific Options

There are also a number of printing settings that aren't specifically related to either a printer's setup, or a print-job's settings. Things such as where the printing system should store logging information, and other print-server specific settings are configured in the file `/etc/cups/cupsd.conf`. Most users won't have any reason to touch the settings in this file, but there are a few things that can be configured that are quite useful, especially in a multiprinter, multiuser network environment. Among these are controls such as the maximum number of print jobs allowed per user, who and/or what machines can access the CUPS administrative web interface, and where to store temporary files that are generated by the printing process. There are more than 100 server-specific options in that can be configured in this file, and they range from the entirely practical ability to limit a user to only a half-dozen simultaneous print jobs so that one user can't monopolize a printer all day, to the somewhat whimsical ability to cause every print-out that is handled by the server to have a Classified banner emblazoned across the top and bottom of every page. If you're interested in controlling this type of setting, read through the file—it has good internal comments that explain what parameters control what print behaviors, and how to change them.

Sharing Printers with Other Mac OS X Systems

Apple has not yet implemented particularly sophisticated controls for printer sharing. If you're willing to fiddle with the CUPS server configuration, you can enact some more fine-grained rules as to what machines can see your printers, and what printers are shared, by looking in the #<Location /classes/...> and #<Location /printers/...> areas of the /etc/cups/cupsd.conf configuration file. If you don't feel comfortable editing Apache-style Allow/Deny rules (see Chapter 23, "Creating a Web Server"), the only controls you have are to click the Printer Sharing check box (or click the Start button, which will check the box for you) in the Services pane of the Sharing Control Panel, and to select printers to share from the Print and Fax Control Panel. Checking the Printer Sharing check box in Sharing turns on (by default) printer sharing for all of your configured printers, to all machines on your local network. The printers you share will automatically appear in everyone's Printer List, and be available for them to select when they click Print, under a Shared Printers submenu. You can restrict the printers that everyone sees, by going to the Sharing pane of the Print and Fax control panel, where you can turn off access to specific printers (or turn it back on, if you've turned it off).

Using the Tiger Fax Capabilities

In addition to the ability (if you have a modem) to send anything that you can print as a fax to any fax machine, Mac OS X provides some relatively sophisticated tools for using your computer as a Fax machine. You have built-in capabilities to send, receive, print, reprocess, and reroute faxes.

Sending Faxes by Printing

As covered in the section detailing the Print dialog earlier in this chapter, sending a printout as a fax requires nothing more than issuing the Print command in an application, and when presented with the standard Print dialog, clicking the cryptic PDF button in the lower-left corner of the window. Under the menu that appears, select Fax PDF, and you will be presented with an interface that lets you specify what number to dial, cover-page options, and other details for the fax job. Clicking the Fax button that appears in this interface dials up the indicated fax machine, and sends off your printout to be printed on the remote fax.

Receiving, Emailing, and Printing Faxes

Receiving faxes is no more complicated than sending them. All you need to do for basic functionality is to open the Faxing pane of the Print and Fax control panel and check the Receive faxes on this computer check box. Also available on this page are a number of options to configure basic fax machine parameters, and to control optional things you choose to do with received faxes in addition to receive them. Among the options are the following:

- My Fax Number—The number that the fax software should claim as the originating number on delivered pages.
- Answer After [] Rings—The number of rings that should be allowed before the modem picks up the call. If this is also your voice line, you probably want to leave enough time for a human to pick up the phone, unless you want to subject your callers to shrieking fax noises.
- Save To—A check box enabling a selection menu where you can specify a folder where incoming faxes should be stored. Because there's no way for an incoming fax to identify what user on your system it should belong to, these, by default, go into a communal shared faxes folder located in `/Users/Shared/Faxes`.
- Email To—A check box enabling a text field where you can enter an email address where received faxes should be re-sent as PDFs. Very convenient! Want to be able to receive faxes on the road, and you don't want to have to constantly call someone to have them check the fax machine to see if you've gotten that important document? Just configure this so that your computer will receive the document, and then wrap it up as a PDF and forward it off to your .Mac account, and anywhere you can find network access, you can receive your fax. Whoever sent it will never even know you were out of the office.
- Print on Printer—A check box that enables a selection menu where you can choose a printer for the fax to be printed on. How completely boring—a way to make your computer/fax-modem/printer combination act just like an old-fangled paper-based fax.
- Show Fax Status in the Menu Bar—Selecting this check box will create a little Fax icon in the menu bar, where you can see real-time status information on the fax system (sending, receiving, retrying, and so on).
- Set Up Fax Modem—Clicking this button opens the Fax List, which is similar to the Printer List, but contains available fax modems. Few users will have anything different than Apple's already-available Internal Modem option that comes preconfigured here, but if you have multiple fax modems installed, you can choose among them here.

The CUPS System Interface

Despite its ubiquitous presence, printing, as a process, is not a simple or conveniently packaged application. The interfaces need to be universally available, flexible, and extendable, without that flexibility jeopardizing the software that relies on it. It needs to seamlessly operate over group of devices that range in sophistication from knowing how find a particular point on a sheet of paper and place a black dot, to having complete operating systems and internal programming languages, and it needs to present all of these to the user with a cohesive, consistent interface. This calls for a considerable amount of programming glue, in the form of little programs that live between larger applications, and between parts of the operating system itself, and which handle the job of ironing out printing process details so that everything thinks it's talking to a single, cohesive interface.

Most of the software acting as glue between the Print Center interface, the command line, and GUI applications is based on or related to CUPS. CUPS is a general printing solution that's been being developed on other Unix variants for several years, and now is available on Mac OS X. Because one of the goals of CUPS is to bring AppleTalk-like printing simplicity to Unix, and because the other Unix systems don't have the Print Center built in, CUPS itself has a nice configuration and control system of its own. This system is accessed through a web page interface that you should be able to find via the URL `http://127.0.0.1:631/`. As the Print Center/Printer Setup Utility matures, this interface becomes more and more redundant. It still, however, presents a few capabilities not available through the Print Center. Perhaps more interestingly, it allows GUI-based remote configuration and administration of printers via a web browser, so it's worth being familiar with, even if you don't use it regularly.

As mentioned previously, one really nice feature of CUPS is the availability of an enormous number of printer drivers through a range of sources. Installation and configuration aren't exactly as friendly as Mac users will prefer, but the steps necessary to install an incredible number of printing devices under Mac OS X should be comfortable actions to you by the time you're halfway through this book. Here, we'll show you how to extend the range of your system's printing capabilities by using some of the publicly available tools, and how to configure the CUPS printing system through the web interface. Specifically, we'll carry out some of the one-time setup necessary to use the full power of CUPS. (Apple leaves out a few important bits, apparently assuming that all you're interested in printing with is relatively recent printers.) The following procedure really isn't overly complex even without reading ahead, so if you're mildly adventurous and have a printer that you can't configure through the Print Center and you want to see it printing, have at it.

In the following example, I'll install the components necessary to get a 1984 Apple ImageWriter I dot-matrix, serial-interface printer to function as a USB-connected PostScript printer on a brand-new Mac Mini. Yes, this is a ludicrous printing combination. The printer reaches somewhere around a roaring four pages per hour, and if you can find ribbons for it, they probably cost more than a new "disposable brand" ink-jet at your local Wally World, but it demonstrates just how flexible CUPS really is as a printing environment, and it covers each of the steps necessary to get any other CUPS-supported printer up and running on your system. If you have a different model printer, the only substantial change in the following instructions is to substitute your printer type at the step where you create the PPD file describing the printer to the system. If you just want to use the web interface for controlling your printer setup, you can skip all of this installation business and skip ahead to the section on configuring printers with CUPS. The installation details here are important to you only if you want to use one of the several thousand printer models that are supported only through the efforts of the CUPS user community and the custom/open-source printing solutions that they have created.

Installing CUPS `foomatic` Drivers and Support Software

To install the underlying drivers to tie new (or old) community-supported printer types into the system, download the foomatic-rip filter set from `http://www.linuxprinting.org/foomatic.html`. The current version as we're writing lives at `http://www.linuxprinting.org/download/foomatic/foomatic-filters-3.0.2.tar.gz`. The goal is to get a script that lives in this file (`foomatic-rip`) into the directory `/usr/libexec/cups/filter/`. At this point, the authors haven't made this exactly Mac Standard easy. Hopefully, that'll change eventually, but if it doesn't, you can always follow these instructions:

1. Install Ghostscript. Ghostscript is a software PostScript and PDF interpreter that also contains an amazing number of output drivers for assorted printers. Apple includes many bits of the Ghostscript suite by necessity because the rest of CUPS depends on it, but for reasons we haven't been able to fathom, Apple has so far omitted the critical `gs` command-line driver that almost every other Ghostscript-compatible application expects to be able to use.

   For many printers, Ghostscript can convert directly from PostScript to the printer's natural binary language. For others, it can be used to convert from PostScript into a generic intermediate image format that can be used as input by a printer-specific driver. Ghostscript, compiled with almost every supported printer type enabled, as well as some special printer-driver software is available from the GIMP-Print project at `http://gimp-print.sourceforge.net/MacOSX.php3`. With 10.3, Apple even started providing most of the GIMP-Print software, but even as of this writing, it doesn't provide the crucial Ghostscript module. From the looks of things, Apple is convincing the GIMP-Print folks to mutate their software to work without Ghostscript when run on Mac OS X, rather than the GIMP-Print project convincing Apple to include the industry-wide standard solution, so don't expect this omission to change any time soon.

   Download and install the most recent version of EPS Ghostscript that the GIMP-Print folks have listed—even though they say it isn't necessary for GIMP-Print under Panther or newer versions of Mac OS X, it's still necessary just to have Ghostscript functionality.

2. Open a Terminal window (that's the `Terminal` program in `Applications/Utilities`, if you haven't worked with it before). You're about to use the command line, but you don't need to know what any of this means right now; you'll learn about it all in a few chapters. Type the following command at the prompt that appears, and then press the Return key:

   ```
   curl -O http://www.linuxprinting.org/download/foomatic/
   ➥foomatic-filters-3.0.2.tar.gz
   ```

(All on one line, no returns in it, despite the fact that we can't get Sams to print it properly in the book.)

If this complains that the file's not found, check your typing very carefully. If that's not the problem, point Safari at `http://www.linuxprinting.org/download/foomatic/` and check to see whether the version number has changed. If so, make the appropriate change in the Terminal and try again.

3. In the Terminal window, type **`gunzip foomatic-filters-3.0.2.tar.gz`** and press the Return key (if the version has changed, replace `foomatic-filters-3.0.2.tar.gz` with the name of the `foomatic-filters` file you've downloaded).
4. Type **`tar -xf foomatic-filters-3.0.2.tar`** and press the Return key.
5. In the Terminal window, type **`cd foomatic-filters-3.0.2`** and press the Return key. Now type **`ls`** and press the Return key. You should see a list of files that looks something like this:

```
COPYING          config.cache              foomatic-rip
CVS              config.log                foomatic-rip.1
ChangeLog        config.status             foomatic-rip.1.in
Makefile         configure                 foomatic-rip.in
Makefile.in      configure.in              install-sh
README           filter.conf               makeMan
TODO             foomatic-gswrapper        makeMan.in
USAGE            foomatic-gswrapper.1      make_configure
acinclude.m4     foomatic-gswrapper.1.in
aclocal.m4       foomatic-gswrapper.in
```

In the Terminal window, type **`./configure`** and press the Return key. Next type **`make`** and press Return, and finally type **`sudo make install`** and press the Return key. (You've just built a piece of Unix software from scratch—a subject you'll learn much more about in the chapters to come.)

To finish up, type **`cd /usr/libexec/cups/filter/`** into the terminal and press Return. Then type **`sudo ln -s /usr/local/bin/foomatic-rip ./`** and press Return. You're now finished with the terminal for a while.

The base software necessary to support the community-written and other specialty drivers for CUPS is now installed. Now it's time to install a PPD *(PostScript Printer Description)* to tell CUPS specifically how to speak to your printer. In my case, again, I'm going to find one that will let me treat my ancient tractor-feed dot-matrix Imagewriter as a PostScript printer. Amazingly, enough code can be stuffed into a PPD to allow even this transformation to take place.

1. Point your browser to `http://www.linuxprinting.org/printer_list.cgi`. Select an appropriate PPD file for your printer. This PPD contains not only information on the details of printer capabilities but also the information necessary to have CUPS translate into the language that this printer understands.

For example, `http://www.linuxprinting.org/show_printer.cgi?recnum=Apple-ImageWriter` points to a page with printer definitions to feed into CUPS and the `foomatic-rip` driver to allow you to print PostScript to the ancient but indestructible Apple ImageWriter I dot-matrix printer. If you were installing this, you'd follow the link, for example, to the `iwhi` driver, and select the Download PPD file option from the Recommended driver section of the page.

2. Wherever this file lands on your machine, you need to copy it to `/usr/share/cups/model/<filename>`, where `<filename>` is the PPD file that you downloaded. In my case (for the ImageWriter I), the file is `Apple-ImageWriter-iwhi.ppd`. After you have the PPD file in the `/usr/share/cups/model` directory, you're almost finished with the installation.
3. Some printers require a separate, printer-specific filter installation in addition to the `foomatic-rip` filter and the PPD. The same page that points to the PPD contains instructions on downloading and installing this filter. Follow these if necessary for your printer.
4. If your system does not include back-end files named `serial` and `file` in `/usr/libexec/cups/backend/`, download the `serial` and `file` CUPS drivers from `http://www.macosxunleashed.com/downloads/` and install them in this location. Make sure that the files have execute permission (`chmod 755 /usr/libexec/cups/backend/file; chmod 755 /usr/libexec/cups/backend/serial`, or use the Finder's Get Info permissions dialog). If we've gotten a working `parallel` driver by the time you read this, it will be available from the same location.

   To enable file-type output, you need to edit `/etc/cups/cupsd.conf` and change the line that reads

```
#FileDevice No
```

   so that it reads

```
FileDevice Yes
```

CAUTION

This change could incur some security problems. For example, it potentially allows users to write into any file that the CUPS system can write into. It's the most debuggable of the interfaces, however, and we're going to show you how to write your own basic printer driver, so if you're inclined to hack at your system or want to get a freaky old printer to work, you might need to temporarily enable it. Unfortunately, the pipe-output back-end type, which is almost as nice for debugging, doesn't seem to currently be supported, or as straightforward to hack into working condition.

6. All that now remains to do is restart the cups daemon (`sudo killall -HUP cupsd`, or just restart your machine if that doesn't make sense), and you should be able to add a printer using this new information.

CAUTION

You might find it necessary to restart your machine regardless of whether you're comfortable restarting the daemon. We've experienced some erratic behavior when restarting the CUPS daemon both through the simple `kill` statement and through the `StartupItems` script.

Now you have CUPS installed and printer drivers for a number of printers available as well. If you need additional drivers for other printers, you can continue creating PPDs at `http://www.linuxprinting.org/` and installing them on your system or you can wait until later; you can always add others whenever you need them.

Configuring Printers Through the CUPS Administrative Web Interface

After the `cupsomatic/foomatic-rip` drivers and support software have been installed and a proper driver for your printer is available, setting up the printer requires a number of steps through the CUPS administration web interface, accessed through `http://127.0.0.1:631/`:

1. The first is adding a few identifying bits of information to the system. Figure 6.10 shows the first step reached under the CUPS Add Printer item. This item is linked from a number of places in the CUPS administrative web pages. The easiest to access is under the Do Administration Tasks item from the main `http://127.0.0.1:631/` page. You will need to enter your user name and password to use the administrative settings.

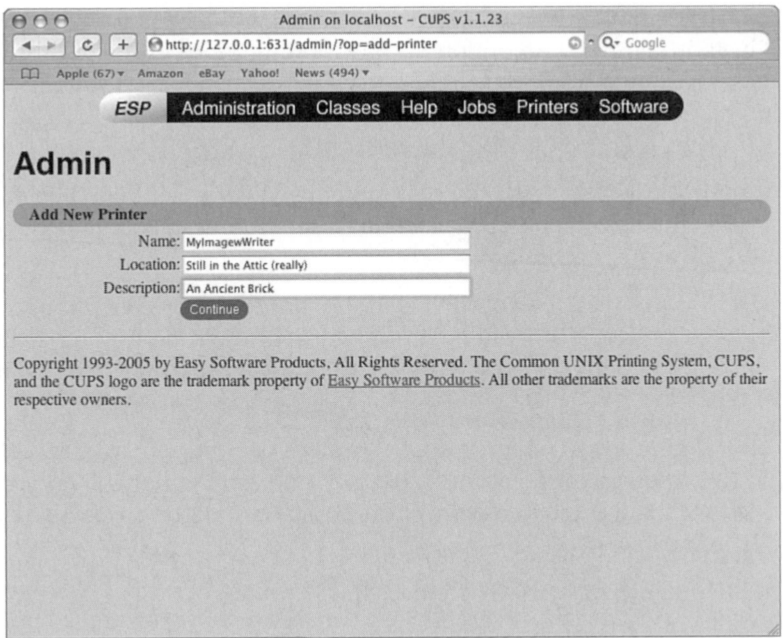

FIGURE 6.10 The first step of setting up a printer under CUPS is defining a name, location, and description.

2. The next step is selecting the type of connection, as shown in Figure 6.11. This is moderately cryptic because several connection types seem to overlap. For my printer, I'm going to use the `file` connection type. On Unix systems, serial devices just look like files that you can write data into. I have a serial device that appears to be working, and the latest CUPS also appears to directly detect `/dev/` directory devices as potential print targets, so I probably don't need to use this less secure way of running the printer. However, by using the file device, I can conveniently point the output at a different file if I choose, and that will let me debug; or, if I'm feeling hackish, add additional processing to the print pipeline without needing to significantly modify the printer. If you really just want to get an older printer working, using either the serial or direct-device drivers would be a smarter long-term choice. The point of making an over 20-year-old printer pretend it's a modern PostScript device, however, is rarely rooted in practicality!

   The following list details the known printer connection types that CUPS can use. Not all of these might be available on your system, and what you can use will depend on a number of configuration choices you make, and optional software that you might have installed.

   - AppleTalk Printer Access Protocol is standard AppleTalk printing, which should also include LaserWriter printers. Most of these can probably also be added through the Print Center.
   - AppSocket/HP JetDirect is an option to talk to HP JetDirect servers. Most of these support AppleTalk or LPR printing, so there's little reason to use this option.
   - Bluetooth Printer is an option for Bluetooth linked printing devices. There is no provision for creating a link in the CUPS web interface, so this will be useful only for already linked printers.
   - Internet Printing Protocol (HTTP) is for IPP printers accessible via HTTP. Currently, CUPS is about the only system you'll see using IPP, and your local CUPS printers will appear in the Print Center. You can configure remote printers here using this option.
   - Internet Printing Protocol (IPP) is for IPP printers accessible through IPP's own protocol. Again, CUPS will be hosting most of these, and you can access them through the Print Center if they're local, or set them up here if you need to provide a remote address.
   - LPD/LPR Host or Printer is for Line Printer Daemon printers accessible via TCP/IP. You can configure these in the Print Center, or, if you're running an Mac OS X Server environment, this information can be pushed over the NetInfo database.
   - USB Printer covers directly connected USB devices.

- FireWire Printer covers directly connected FireWire printing devices.
- Serial is for printers attached to serial ports. You might not have this option unless you've downloaded the serial driver from `http://www.macosxunleashed.com/downloads/` or Apple's started including it in the distribution again. In some versions of Mac OS X, it's there; in some, it's missing. This driver should work with real serial ports and with USB-adapter serial ports, if your USB port reports the existence of a serial port in a syntax that the driver understands.

  The Serial interface option will add itself to the list of connection types, as well as add items for each serial port that it discovers. These will have cryptic names like `USA28X1913P1.1`. Although not documented, it looks like you can either select the serial interface, and then enter a `serial://` device URI for the driver or select the direct `USA28X...` name, and get slightly more automated control and a friendlier interface to the driver.
- Parallel is for printers attached to parallel ports. This is the choice if you have a USB-to-parallel adapter being used to hook up your printer.
- FAX and Modem are a CUPS interface into the Mac OS X print-to-fax system.
- Depending on the version of Mac OS X you're running, you might have an option labeled either Zeroconf or Rendezvous, which configures the system to automatically discover available printers being shared by other Zeroconf-capable systems.
- Windows Printer via Samba is for network printers attached to Microsoft Windows machines and served via the Samba resource sharing protocol.
- Zeroconf Registered Printer is for network-available printers that are being shared out using the Zeroconf protocol. Zeroconf is the technology that Apple adopted and rebranded as Rendezvous in earlier versions of Mac OS X, and that is now apparently being called Bonjour. Printers served from Tiger, and from other flavors of Unix using Zeroconf, should be able to interoperate seamlessly from all platform's points of view.
- File is a catch-all last-ditch option to be used for printing to printers that can be accessed by writing data to a named file (this isn't as weird as it sounds—most peripherals in Unix can be accessed by reading from, or writing to, specific files in the `/dev/` directory. When the operating system recognizes the existence of a peripheral—a printer, for example—a special file is created in `/dev/` that is connected to the printer. Read from the file, and you'll get any status information the printer cares to share. Write to it, and what you put in it gets printed. You won't have the File device unless you install the file driver as shown earlier in this chapter.

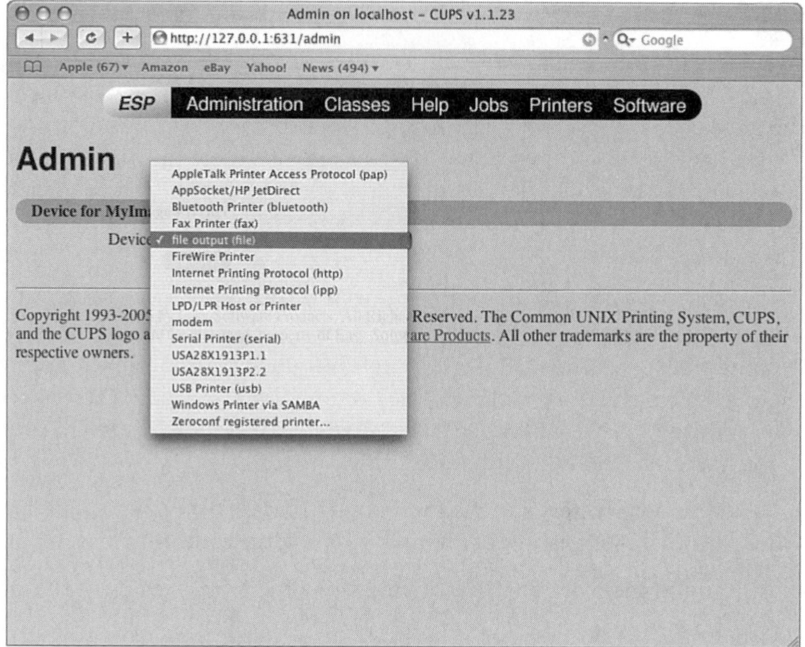

FIGURE 6.11 The second step in configuring the printer is selecting the type of connection being used.

3. Next you need to provide distinct connection information for the printer. In my case, I'm using a USB serial adapter, which appears as `/dev/tty.USA28X1913P1.1` and `/dev/tty.USA28X1913P2.2`. (Try checking your network pane to see what your serial ports are named. If you're trying to install a serial printer, you might need to quit and restart your System Preferences utility to get it to detect the adapter, and the name might be incomplete—missing the information after the second decimal—as shown in the Network Interfaces pane.) These can be selected in the web interface several different ways. I'm using the file interface with the URIs `file:/dev/tty.USA28X1913P1.1` and `file:/dev/tty.USA28X1913P2.2`, but they can also be used directly through the serial interface, and, not surprisingly, through the USB interface.

   Figure 6.12 shows this configuration page, including some syntax examples for printers connected via other methods. I could also select them as serial devices using the serial connection mode, or raw pipe devices. From the end user's perspective, there's little difference between these options, but from someone inclined to poke at the system's guts, the ability to treat the printer either as a file that can be written to, a "pipe" into which data can be pumped, or as a serial communications device, gives great power and flexibility for sophisticated control.

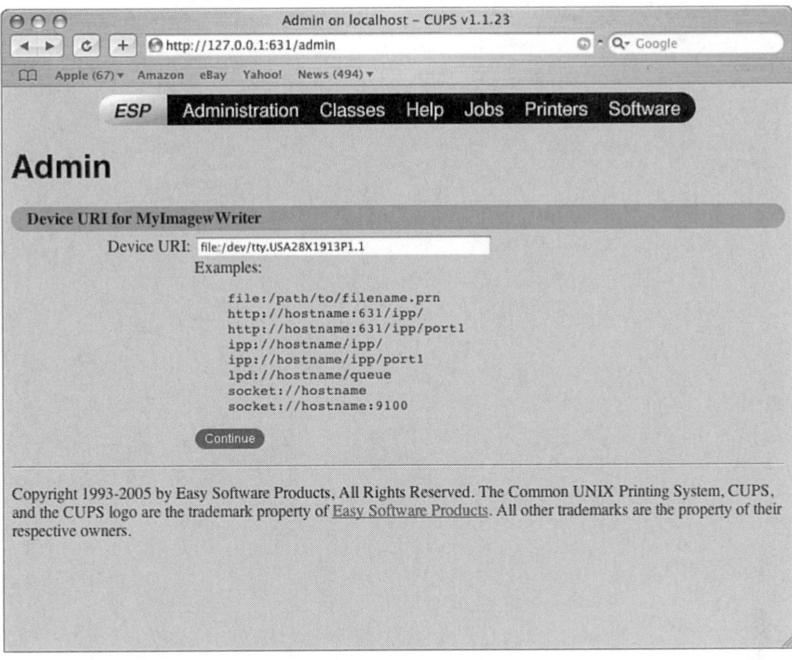

FIGURE 6.12 The third step is providing a rather cryptic definition of how the software can contact and interact with the printer description. In this case, it's an URI for a file, where the Unix side of Mac OS X can write directly to the serial interface.

4. The fourth step is selecting the printer's manufacturer, as shown in Figure 6.13. If the manufacturer of your printer isn't shown, either you haven't downloaded and installed the PPD properly or your PPD doesn't report the correct information to CUPS.

NOTE

Don't expect your list of available manufacturers or printers to look like mine. The PPDs that you configure and install from `linuxprinting.org`, or from GIMP-Print, control the options you see on your system.

5. Given a manufacturer, the interface constructs a list of printers, from which you can choose your specific printer, as shown in Figure 6.14. Hopefully, after you click Continue at this step, you'll get a page saying your printer has been installed and configured properly. At this point, your printer should be available in the Print Center for printing in both GUI and command-line applications.

After you have configured a printer, you can visit its configuration page to make modifications to the printer's connection, location, and description; turn the queue for it on and off; and manage jobs on it. Figure 6.15 shows the web interface to this functionality. The Print Center can make most of these modifications as well, when the printer is visible to it.

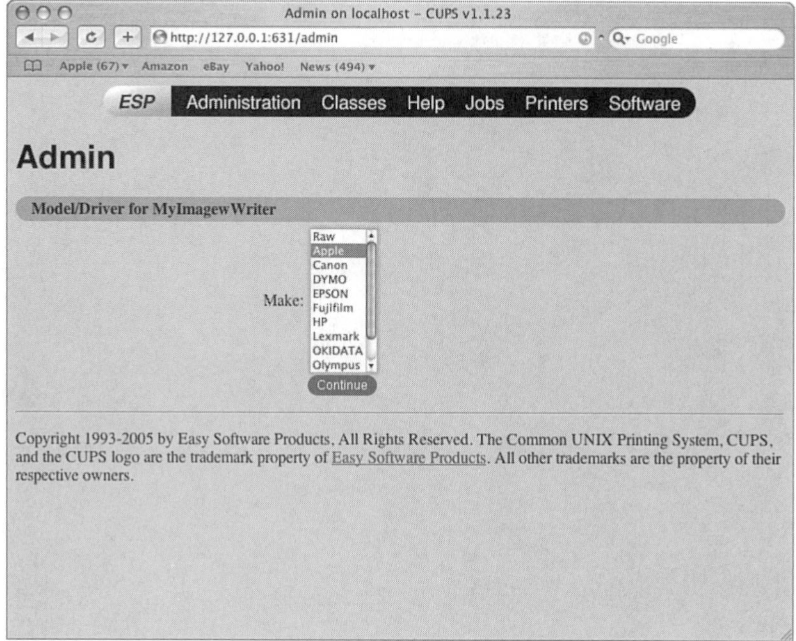

FIGURE 6.13 The fourth step is selecting the printer's manufacturer. This selection modifies the list of printers available on the next page.

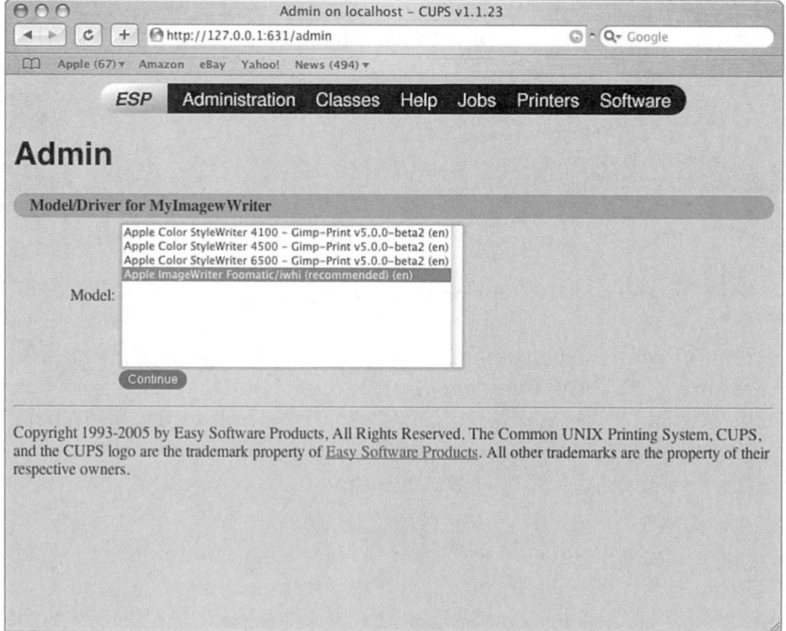

FIGURE 6.14 Finally, you can select the specific printer type you're installing. The Foomatic part of the name is generated by the Foomatic PPD generator.

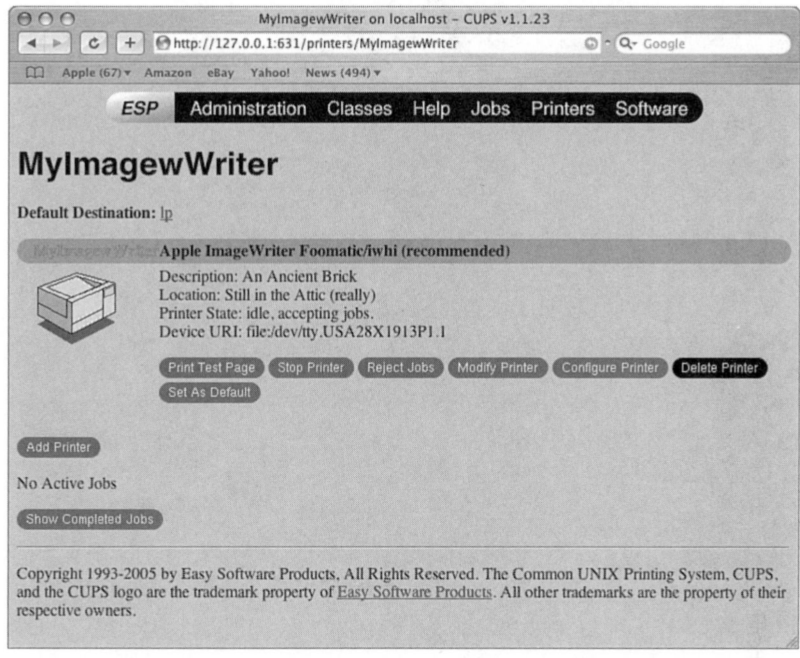

FIGURE 6.15 The printer status page for MyImageWriter, under the CUPS web interface. You can start and stop the printer queue, send test pages, reconfigure the printer's connection, and make some modifications to the printer's behavior from this page.

Under the Configure Printer option shown in the previous Admin page, you have control over a number of simple options regarding the printer. For the ImageWriter, a page like that shown in Figure 6.16 appears, with settings to control the default printing resolution, default page size, and whether to print banners or trailer pages for each job. The banners and footers are contained in PostScript files stored in the directory `/usr/share/cups/banners`.

A printer with 120×144 resolution and dot-gain approaching 100%, is not the most beautiful output device for printing PostScript data. However, it *does work*. Other, more capable printers work better and there is active development in the GIMP-Print community of quite high-quality drivers for a number of high-resolution ink-jet devices. With CUPS, PostScript printing support for the modern photo-quality ink-jet printers is only a few open-source mouse-clicks away.

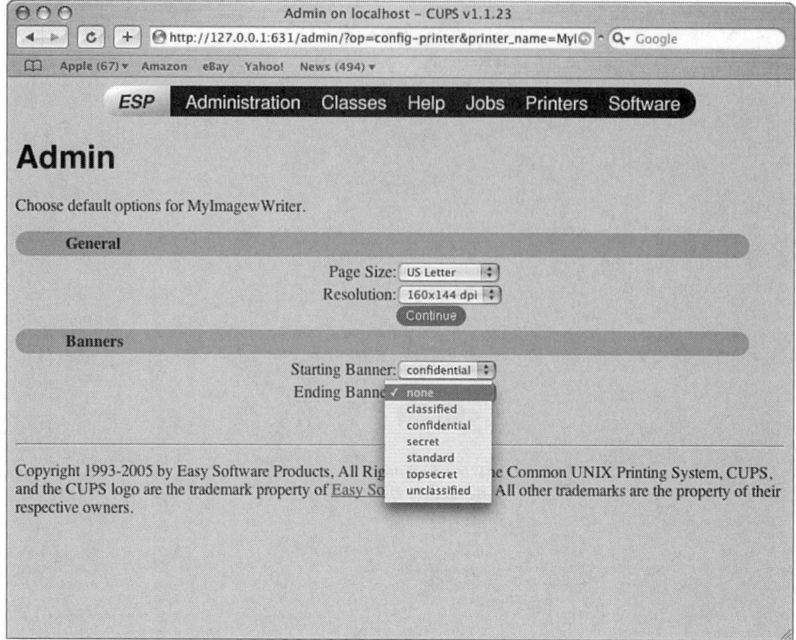

FIGURE 6.16 Some of the printing options that can be configured for an ImageWriter type printer, according to the PPD-O-Matic PPD.

NOTE

Most of the same configuration options for CUPS printers specified by URI connection are also available under a hidden Advanced dialog option in the Print Center. If you hold down the Option key while clicking Add to add a new printer, you have the option of choosing Advanced from the list of printer connection types. The dialog that appears gives you access to the same installation and configuration options as adding a printer through the CUPS administrative interface, although it provides much less hinting as to what valid responses are.

These same options, and a few more, are available via the command-line interface to CUPS administration, which is covered in Chapter 13.

Administering CUPS Printers from Remote Locations

One of the nice things about having a web-based interface to the CUPS printing system is that if you configure the server to allow it, you can check on your printers and perform any administration tasks from any place you can find a web browser (such as a web-enabled cell-phone) just as easily as you can from the console of your machine. All that is required to enable remote administration is to modify the CUPS configuration file that tells it what machines it should allow to connect to the administrative web interface. This file lives in `/etc/cups/` and is named `cupsd.conf`. The syntax is identical to normal

Apache web server configuration syntax, so you'll learn considerably more about things you can do to customize its operation when Apache is covered in Chapter 23. For now, the options you're interested in examining are the `Listen` option (by default set to `127.0.0.1:631`), the `BrowseAllow` option (by default set to `127.0.0.1`), and the `Allow From` option, which is also `127.0.0.1` by default.

If you want to allow another specific machine to connect, you can extend the access to the administrative web interface by adding `<your ip address>:631` as an additional `Listen` option, and adding `BrowseAllow` and `Allow From` lines for the IP address of the specific machine you want to allow to connect. You can set up considerably more sophisticated access restrictions and allowances, such as password-restricted access, and selective access to different parts of the web interface, if you explore the full options available for Apache web server configuration.

CAUTION

Changes to this file can break printing if you move your machine from network to network!

If you enter your machine's real IP as an IP to `Listen` at, and your machine's IP address changes, the `cupsd` server won't be able to bind that network address and it will quit. This will leave your machine without printing services. Usually though, there's little reason to want to enable remote printer administration on a machine that's moved from place to place, so this is likely to be a problem only for the experimenter and not a practical limitation.

Managing Fonts

With the initial releases of Mac OS X, Apple introduced a new type of font suitcase designed to reduce the incompatibilities between the many different font systems available for different computers. With 10.3, Apple continued to upgrade the font system and has added sort-of convenient new font manager: Font Book. In 10.4, Font Book has evolved slightly, but, as a major (missing) feature most users will still notice, lacks any way for you to conveniently print out what would classically be called *type books*, so that you can compare the features of similar fonts.

Outside of that glaring omission, Font Book gives you a simple and intuitive way to preview what fonts you have installed, group your installed fonts into useful collections, and to install new fonts into your system. In addition to using the new font format, Mac OS X supports these Windows font formats: TrueType fonts with extension `.ttf`, TrueType collections with extension `.ttc`, and OpenType fonts with extension `.otf`. Mac OS X also supports PostScript Type 1, legacy bitmap fonts, and Unicode. Unicode is a universal character-encoding standard for multilingual text support across multiple platforms. Supporting Unicode enhances Mac OS X's multilingual support. Mac OS X's multilingual support is most clearly seen in the available keyboards in the International System preferences pane. At this point, though, you might wonder if your old collection of fonts will work in Mac OS X. Fortunately, Mac OS X also supports older font suitcases used in earlier versions of the operating system without any conversion.

Installing a New Font

Installing a new font on your system is not difficult. For example, to install the Pushkin handwriting font from the ParaType free fonts page (`http://www.paratype.com/store/free/`), download the following file to your drive:

```
http://www.fontstock.com/softdl/PushkinTT.zip
```

This is actually a Windows TrueType font, but as we know, Mac OS X conveniently understands these, as well as many traditional Mac OS font types. You can uncompress the Zip file by double-clicking on it, dropping it on StuffIt Expander, or, if you're inclined to manage your system from the command line, you can use the `unzip` command:

```
unzip PushkinTT.zip

Archive:  PushkinTT.zip
  inflating: Pushkin.ttf
```

The first line shown here is the command you type. The next two lines are lines of output that the command produces as it unzips the file. You can then install it from the command line by copying it into the appropriate directory on your system. If you want this font to be available to all users on your machine (our recommended configuration), copy it to the `/Library/Fonts/` directory. If you want the font to be available for your use only, copy it to your `~/Library/Fonts/` directory. Alternatively, you can simply double-click the `Pushkin.ttf` file, and Apple's new Font Book application opens, shows you a sample of the font, and allows you to install it with a simple button click.

If you want to use the command line to copy the file, use the following syntax:

```
ditto Pushkin.ttf /Library/Fonts/
```

> **NOTE**
>
> Unix-heads note: Early in the Tiger announcements (and still appearing in various places in the literature) Apple claimed that Tiger was going have some tweaks to the underlying filesystem access routines that would allow more-typical Unix commands for file management (such as `cp` and `mv`) to be used seamlessly with files that have resource forks. If these tweaks have happened, they aren't working. As of the end of March 2005, `cp` still breaks files with resource forks, and you've got to use `ditto` or `CpMac` to safely handle files that might have resource content.

If you've only ever worked in a graphical user environment and have never used a command line, you might not see much point to being able to do something like install a font from a command line. After all, it's much easier to just double-click the font file, right? Right. Well, usually right, but not always. Consider the situation in which you want to install dozens, or even hundreds of fonts that you've accumulated. Suddenly you're faced with double-clicking a multitude of files, or, if you select them all and open them simultaneously, at least clicking Install in a great number of font-sample windows. As you will learn in the coming chapters, telling the command line to execute the appropriate commands over and over, for each font you're interested in, takes only slightly more effort than telling it to do a single file. For one or two fonts, working through the Finder and Font Book might indeed be faster, but at the command line, there is only a keystroke or two difference between installing 2 fonts and installing 200. For large administrative tasks, the command line quickly takes the lead.

NOTE

You will find some online Mac OS X references that indicate that you can or should install fonts into the `/System/Library/Fonts` folder. These are antiquated instructions generated during the earliest releases of Mac OS X. At the time, Apple's filesystem layout was not well understood, and almost everyone was writing instructions and documentation based on what worked, as determined by experimentation. Now we know that the `/System` folder is intended for Apple's use alone, whereas the `/Library` folder is intended to be an area where you as an administrator can add files that should be available systemwide.

If you installed the font by dragging and dropping in the Finder or by clicking Install in Font Book, that's it—you're finished with the install. You'll need to restart some applications that you want to be able to use the font, but you shouldn't need to restart your machine, or even log out. Unfortunately, as of the current version of 10.4, if you install from the command line, things aren't so nice, and you need to restart the machine before the new fonts will be recognized. Because this is a step backward from the convenience of font installation under prior versions of Mac OS X, it wouldn't be surprising to find this fixed again in some future version. Figure 6.17 shows what the terminal looks like in the Pushkin handwriting font.

CAUTION

Macintosh suitcases and PostScript fonts need to be copied into the `/Library/Fonts/` or `~/Library/Fonts/` directory by using the `ditto` command, by dragging and dropping in the Finder, or by using Font Book to do the install, rather than using the `cp` command, because these fonts can contain resource-fork data, which is not correctly handled by the `cp` command.

Browsing and Managing Fonts with Font Book

Figure 6.18 shows the Font Book application's interface. If you've already used the font selection interface in previous versions of Mac OS X, the Font Book application's interface will be very familiar. Like many Mac OS X information-navigation interfaces, it consists of a set of vertically scrolling panes proceeding from the most general information in the leftmost pane to the most specific in the rightmost. In Font Book's case, the leftmost pane contains a list of font collections, the middle pane lists individual fonts or families that are members of the collection selected in the left pane, and the right pane shows a sample of a particular selected font and the font's associated information. As seen in the figure, any given font can contain a number of font styles (typefaces). The previous functionality of mousing over the listed fonts to see additional information on the font features seems to have disappeared. Likewise, you no longer seem to be able to see the number of fonts and typefaces in a collection by mousing over the listed collections. Hopefully Apple will decide to return these features sometime soon.

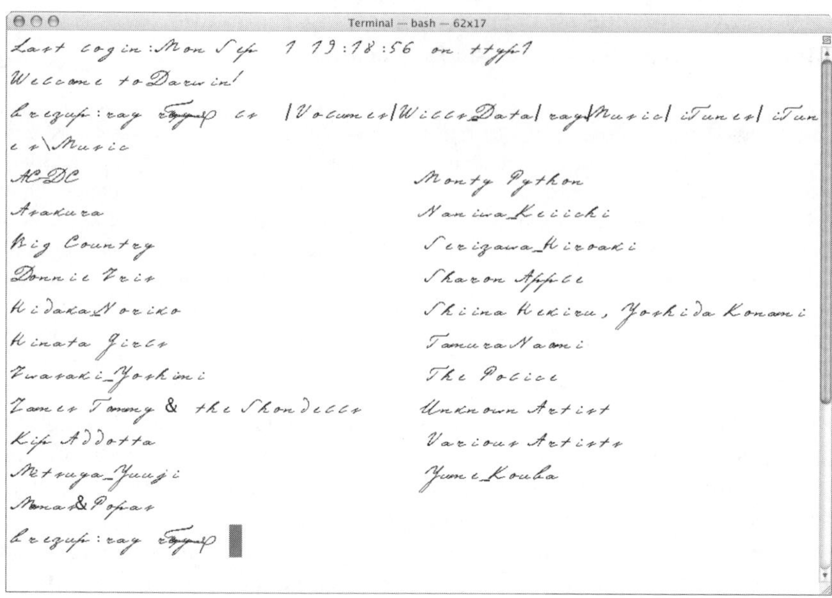

FIGURE 6.17 A terminal window set to use the Pushkin handwriting font. Although this is an amusing change for a terminal, it is perhaps not the best font choice for regular terminal usage.

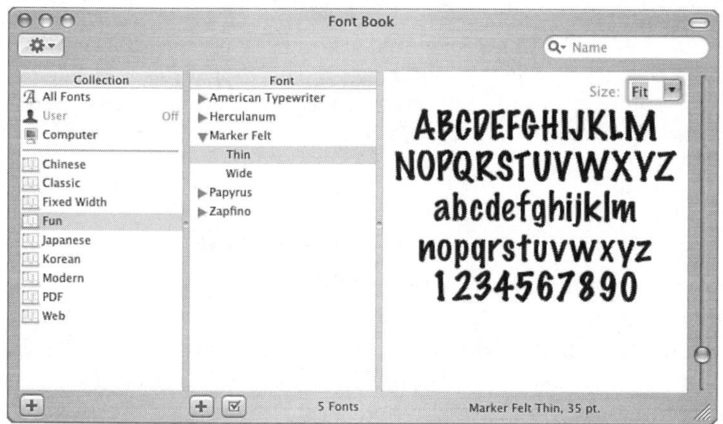

FIGURE 6.18 The Font Book application, browsing fonts.

The + buttons under the column of collections and under the column of fonts allow you to add new collections or fonts, respectively. Fonts can be added to a collection (and can be members of multiple collections) by selecting them and dragging them from the font list into the desired target collection. Collections and fonts can be deleted by selecting them and pressing the Delete key on the keyboard. You can also disable fonts and collections without deleting them. This is useful if you find that some of your fonts are cluttering up your font menus and interfering with work, but you still need them for specific uses and don't want to delete them. Disabling a collection is accomplished by Control-click-and-hold, and then selecting the option to disable the collection from the contextual menu that will appear. Disabling a font is accomplished by selecting the font and clicking the "semi-grayed-out-check box" button (now that's an intuitive interface element!) next to the + button for the fonts column.

Under the Preview menu, you have the option of choosing to preview fonts in a number of ways. The Sample option is essentially the collection of uppercase and lowercase letters and numerals available in the font. The font's Repertoire is the complete collection of characters available in the font. Custom Display allows you to set the text displayed for the preview. Custom defaults to an upper/lower/numerals lists but can be edited by clicking in the font-preview window. There's also a nice info panel available that gives far more information than you probably realized ever got stored about each font. Figure 6.19 shows the info panel for one of my favorites, Adobe Jenson. The information in this panel can be extremely useful if you've stumbled across a font you like, but don't know who made it, where it came from, or where you can get more like it.

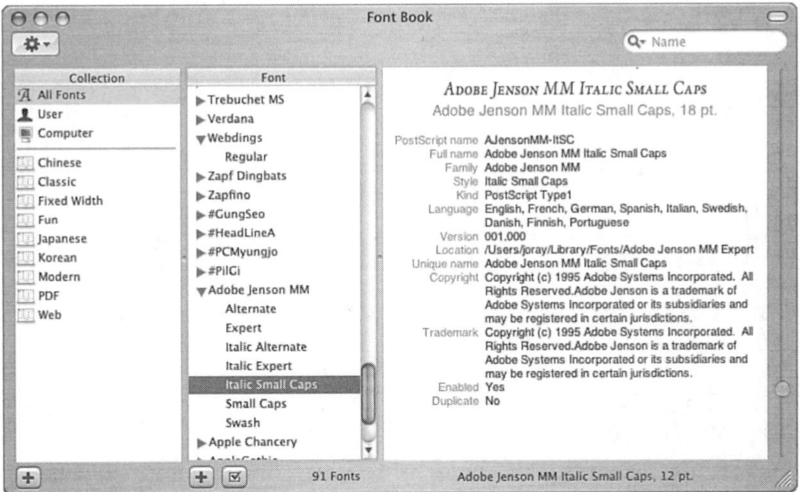

FIGURE 6.19 The font info page (found under the Preview menu) of the Font Book application is a good place to look if you are sleuthing for more information on where to get more fonts like the one at which you're currently looking.

Almost the only thing confusing about the Font Book interface is the slider at the right side of the page, which, if you look, is clearly not a vertical-scroll slider. Yet in practice, many users seem to click on it and drag it up and down expecting the preview display to scroll. In actuality, it's a size slider, controlling the displayed size of the font in the preview. If you adjust it until your font preview doesn't all fit in the window, a vertical (and/or horizontal) scrollbar appears as needed.

Under the Edit menu there is an option to Resolve Duplicates. Under some versions of Font Book, this option becomes enabled only if you have fonts or typefaces selected that contain duplications. The annoying limitation that *you* find the duplicates for *it*, which was present in earlier versions of Font Book, appears to have been corrected in the Tiger version. You can now select your entire collection of fonts, resolve duplicates, and have the whole thing cleaned up in one step. For informational purposes, if you do have duplicates, Font Book places a dot to the right of any font or typeface that appears to contain duplicates. In Figure 6.20, the font Verdana is indicated to contain duplicates, and in it, apparently each of the typefaces has been duplicated.

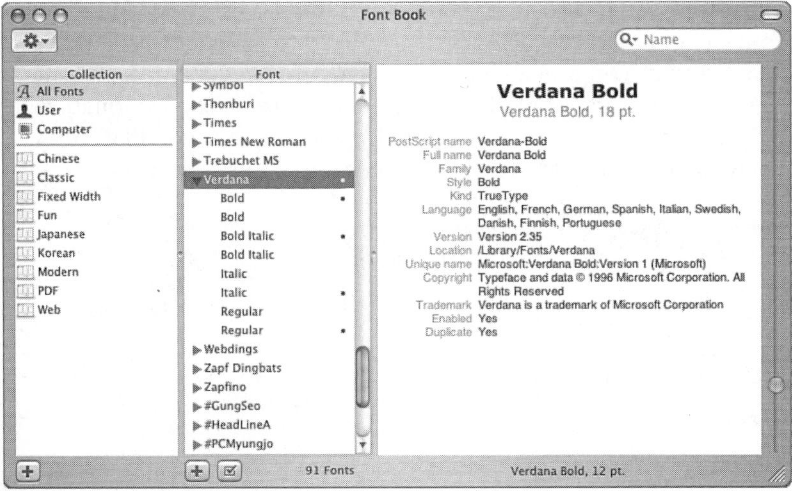

FIGURE 6.20 The Font Book application, browsing the Verdana font, shows that I've apparently duplicated every typeface in this font.

Using Fonts with the Font Pane

You can access your fonts in the Font pane, which is available in many of the typical Mac OS X applications. The location of the Font pane varies with the application. For example, some applications include Font as a menu bar item, and you select Show Fonts under that menu or a hierarchical submenu of it. Other applications include the Font pane as an option, although it might be a nested option under another menu bar category, such as Format. Others attach it to a keystroke or to a button somewhere in the interface. This lack of consistency is annoyingly painful because having convenient, consistent access to fonts should be one of the things that distinguish Mac OS X as a standout operating system.

The Font pane has divisions for Collections, Family, Typeface, and Size. Because the default collection is All Fonts, you can indeed see your entire collection of available fonts with ease. However, the Font pane also displays the collections you've created through Font Book, so you can group your fonts together, as well as use some precreated groupings that Apple provides.

The Font pane also includes a number of font display and rendering options and some styling options such as colors, strikethrough and underline, and character spacing options. Sometimes these options are a little confusing because there can be application-specific additions to this pane, yet the applications don't necessarily obey all the options that are set. For example, the Terminal includes a pane containing character spacing options (to spread the characters apart or condense them closer together) at the bottom of the Font pane. It, however, doesn't obey any of the character rendering options that create drop-shadows or even the font color setting from the Font pane (this might be a bug?). In general, however, in most applications these options control the onscreen selection and rendering of fonts, and are primarily available for the purpose of customizing your display and making information easier (or at least more enjoyable) to read.

Applications that are more typesetting or graphics/layout oriented have their own way of specifying font rendering options. Figure 6.21 shows the Font pane interacting with TextEdit. In this figure, different drop-shadow rendering options have been applied to different portions of the text. We've included snapshots of the drop-shadow rendering controls from the Font pane directly above each quote on which they were used.

To switch between collections, just click the desired collection in the Collections column. Although this sounds obvious, it is not so obvious if you don't see the Collections column. If you shrink the Font pane horizontally too far, the similarity to Finder multi-column view disappears, and the Collections column does too, and you don't get a horizontal scrollbar with which to browse the different levels of the hierarchy.

The little "gear wheel" (Apple calls it an *action button*) icon at the bottom left of the Font pane gets you to a menu with a number of useful settings. Hiding the preview and/or effects (or showing them if they're hidden) has exactly the expected effect: The font sample at the top of the Font pane or the rendering controls are hidden (or shown).

The Add to Favorites option under the pop-up enables you to add fonts directly to a collection of favorite fonts, without having to go through Font Book. Actually, because Favorites doesn't appear as a collection in Font Book, the Add to Favorites option is your only route to adding fonts to this collection. When you select a font from the Favorites collection, the Add to Favorites pop-up menu button becomes Remove from Favorites, allowing editing of your Favorites list.

The Edit Sizes option under the action section of the Font pane allows you to choose whether you want to see font sizes listed as fixed sizes, a size slider, or as both. It also enables you to edit the available sizes. For a fixed view, you can add or delete a specific size from the fixed list. For a sliding scale, you can edit the minimum and maximum font sizes. Figure 6.22 shows the Font – Sizes window that appears for editing sizes.

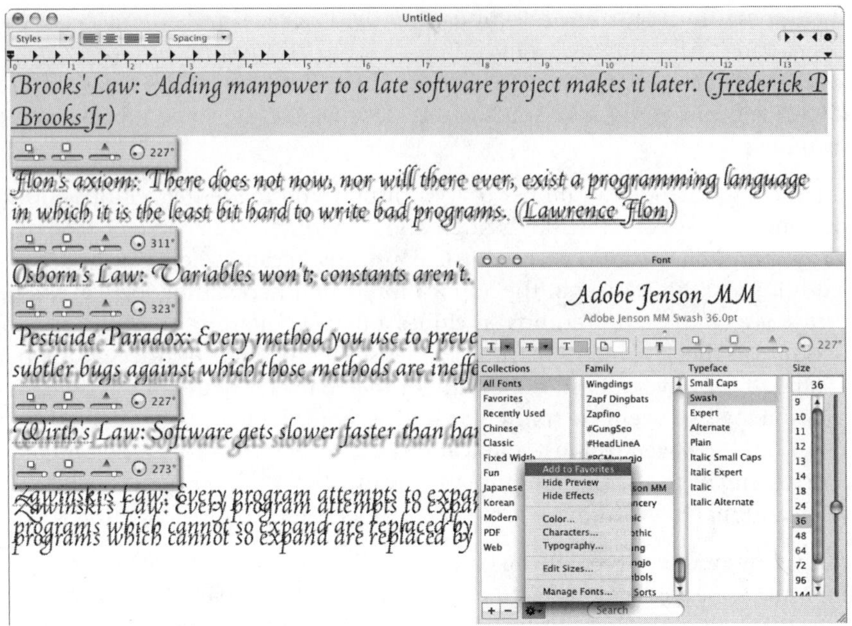

FIGURE 6.21 The Font pane is your interface to selecting fonts and onscreen rendering options.

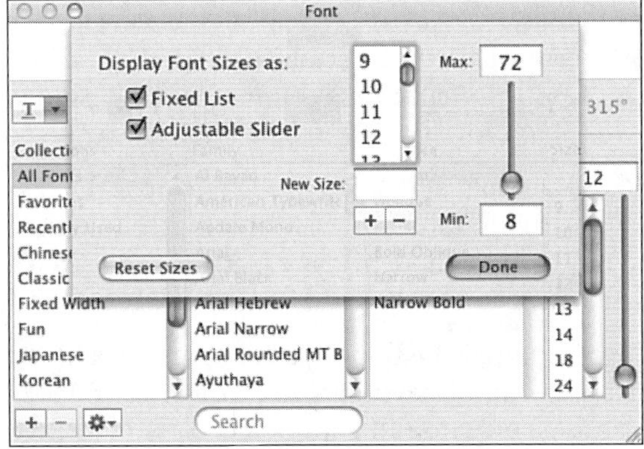

FIGURE 6.22 The Font – Sizes window, which appears when you select Edit Sizes under the Extras section in the Font pane, is where you select how the font size options will be displayed.

The Color option under the action button pop-up, as well as the button in the rendering options with the pea-soup yellow-green box on it, opens a standard color browser where you can specify, by a wheel, spectrum, color scales, and so on, a color for the font you are using. Be aware, when playing with these, that (depending on the application) the settings you create as you fiddle with the colors, are "live" settings—they take effect immediately as you change things. This can make unexpected changes to your document!

Finally, there is a rather cryptic typography option under the action button pop-up. This currently opens what looks intended to be a set of typography-related options, that is populated (at the moment) by only a single item:—ligatures. That item, in turn, is populated only by a check box option for Common Ligatures. Neither of these is documented, but they are interesting. Ligatures are what make the output from MS Word look like, well, the output from MS Word, and make this appearance somehow subtly less satisfying than the appearance of a professionally typeset page, no matter what you do playing with fonts, font sizes, and so on.

The difference, or a large portion of it, is due to the fact that typesetters learned, long ago (before the advent of moveable type) that certain characters "blend" when placed on the page. Recognizing this, they created special character pairs, and in some cases character triples, that are used when certain combinations of characters are used next to each other. Look closely at a real book—this one probably won't do, as I think our publisher prints out of Word—but something from O' Reilly probably will, as will most hard-bound textbooks and quality leisure-reading books. Some major newspapers are still adhering to proper kerning and ligatures as well. Look at character combinations such as "fi"—that is, where there is a "f", followed by an "i", as in "finish." If you look closely at the way these characters were put on paper before we had mechanical devices that allowed us all to be our own print shops (and the way that places that still care about good-looking type produce their output today), you'll see that (in many fonts) the "fi" pair isn't a pair of distinct characters—the cross-bar of the f becomes the serif-top of the i, and the dot of the i merges onto the end of the curved top of the f. The "f" "i" pair, becomes the "fi" ligature. Others ligatures exist as well. They not only change the display of the characters, but they subtly change the intercharacter spacing, and the appearance of lines of printed text. The visible difference is subtle, or even difficult to define, if you don't know exactly what you're looking for, but the effect on reading speed, reading comfort, and comprehension is profound. Repeated studies of reader's ability to read, understand and concentrate on text that follows good typographic conventions, versus text layed out by today's "ignore the context, just slap the next character on the page" printing systems, have led researchers to conclude as much as a 10% improvement in reader comprehension and so forth with proper typography. It looks as if Apple's trying to re-introduce some proper typographic conventions into the Mac OS X text rendering system, such that all applications could take advantage of better quality typographic output. This is quite exciting—currently undocumented, and unspecific in terms of what it's going to do, but exciting nonetheless.

In earlier versions of Mac OS X, there used to be an Extras section to the Font pane, with a Get Fonts option that took you to `http://www.apple.com/fonts/buy/`, which appeared to be a site where Apple was intending to sell additional fonts. This option no longer appears, and the website was offline during the 10.2 release, but it's back again with a "Coming Soon" banner, so perhaps Apple is once again hoping to implement this option.

As you shrink the Font pane by dragging the bottom-right corner inward, it selectively shrinks various elements, hides others, and also changes elements into more compact forms such as pop-up menus instead of scrolling lists. This can be very convenient if you need some settings visible for working in your document but don't want to waste all the screen real-estate that would be lost to the full-sized pane. This can also be really annoying if you can't get to the Action pop-up menu because it has decided to disappear, and the only solution is dragging the window out to a large size to convince the interface that it'll fit again.

The appearance of the Font pane is saved on a per-application basis, so you can have it customized in size to what you need in each application, and when you use it from that application again, it will appear as you last left it. When you quit the application associated with a particular Font pane, that Font pane also closes.

As for actually using a font in your application, select the font you want to use from the Font pane and start typing. If you need to switch the font of a section of text, select the text you want to change, and select the desired font. The font switches to what you want, and you can continue typing. If you want to see the Font pane in action, although the presentation is a little dated, check the QuickTime movie at `http://www.apple.com/macosx/theater/fonts.html`.

Using the Keyboard Menu and Alternative Input Scripts

Apple has, for several generations of Mac OS, made a clever feature available as an optional part of the operating system. This software, WorldScript, and the various language kits it supported, was a way of putting a layer of abstraction between what you type on the keyboard, and what is actually entered into a document that you are working with. The system was modeled on the notion that a computer might have only one physical keyboard, but a knowledge of the language and locale in which the user is working would enable a translation between what keys are physically pressed and contextually correct data output. This functionality is now a default part of Mac OS X and is embodied in a two-part system comprised of key-mapping tables called *keyboards* and locale-sensitive processing software known as *input scripts*.

Keyboard mapping tables are used to map between a particular key that is pressed and an output symbol that is generated. For example, you might have heard of the Dvorak keyboard, a more efficient alternative to the QWERTY keyboard that you are probably already familiar with. A keyboard mapping might be used to remap the keys on your QWERTY keyboard so that they function as though your keyboard were a Dvorak keyboard instead. A keyboard mapping can also be used to do things such as change the currency indicator to the appropriate currency for the locale—British pounds for U.K. English and American dollars for American English, for example.

Input scripts, on the other hand, can perform more sophisticated, context-sensitive alterations of data as it is entered. This modification can be anything from changing the font used to display all or certain characters, to providing phonetic ways of entering symbols not directly available from the keyboard.

These two pieces of functionality, accessed jointly through the Keyboard menu (discussed in the following section) and the International pane of the system controls, give you the ability to enter data in character sets appropriate for other languages, whether they are English-like languages or languages with completely different symbol sets and entry needs.

The use and utility of this are probably not immediately apparent from just a description, but working through the following example should give you an idea of just how powerful the keyboard tables and input scripts can be.

The first place to examine when configuring or customizing your input environment is the International pane. Figure 6.23 shows the Input Menu tab of the International pane. The list of available languages and input scripts might initially look intimidating, but it's mostly informational, and a place for you to turn on selected input types. If you're running a standard U.S. release of Mac OS X, you'll almost undoubtedly have the US (with little United States flag) item selected in the Name column, and it'll indicate that it's using the Roman input script. The US/American (and most related European languages) use the Roman input script because they all have generally similar printed-language characteristics; a similar number of characters, left-to-right printing, uppercase and lowercase characters, a phonetic notion of character alphabetization, and so on.

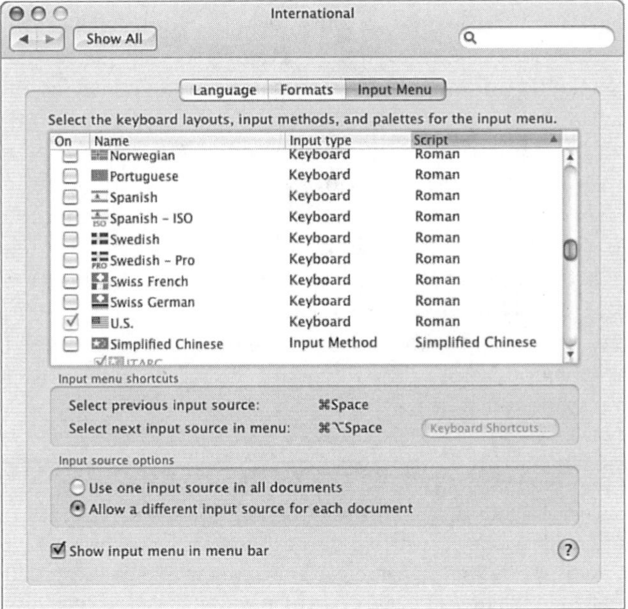

FIGURE 6.23 The Input Menu tab of the International pane is where you select what input types and languages are available on your system.

Other languages might use their own particular input scripts, which can provide language-specific input functionality, or they might use the Unicode input script. Unicode is an internationally standardized way of providing input in a number of symbol sets that cannot be conveniently represented on a standard keyboard. The Unicode input script cannot provide customized input processing in a language-contextual manner but does provide a standardized way to input many characters from a keyboard with only a limited number of keys. To use Unicode, therefore, you need to have a mapping between keyboard sequences and output symbols. As a demonstration of the power available in other input scripts, we'll take a look at the Japanese input script, and how it maps from phonetic keyboard input in Romanji, into natural Japanese Katakana, Hiragana, and Kanji.

If you don't read Japanese, it's the one with characters that look like a chest of drawers, a strange telephone pole with slanty bars, and an indescribable pictogram.

For the examples in the following section, open the Input Menu tab of the International Control Panel and select a few interesting languages that use the Roman script. Also select the Character Palette and Keyboard Viewer. Finally, if you want to follow our example of how an input script can interact with a keyboard layout in a sophisticated manner, select the Japanese layout, which is the one named Kotoeri, and the Japanese Kana Palette. Make sure that the Hiragana and Katakana keyboards are selected for it the Kotoeri input.

With previous versions of the system, when you select more than one keyboard, a little menu consisting of flags signifying your chosen script and keyboard appeared automatically. Now you need to select the Show Input Menu in Menu Bar option in the International pane to get this menu to appear. This little "flag menu," shown in Figure 6.24 is the Input, or Keyboard menu, which shows what keyboard layouts are available and which one is chosen. The Open International option takes you to the Input Menu tab of the International pane. After it has been enabled, the most obvious way to switch between keyboard layouts is to select the one you want from the Input/Keyboard menu itself. However, if you check the Options section of the Input Menu tab of the International pane, you see that you could also use Command-Option-Space to rotate to the next keyboard in the Input menu, and Command-Space should swap keyboards with the previously most recently used keyboard. Unfortunately, these now collide with the default keys to bring up Spotlight, so they'll be disabled, and you'll need open the Keyboard & Mouse Control Panel to the Keyboard Shortcuts pane, and edit the key combinations if you want to use these.

CAUTION

This feature now works subtly differently than it previously did (again). Earlier (better) versions used Command-Option-Space to switch to the next keyboard available *in the currently active script*. In other words, if you were in a keyboard that used the Roman script interface, the key combination rotated to the next Roman keyboard in your menu. You could use Command-Space to rotate to the default keyboard of the *next* script. Now Command-Option-Space rotates to the top keyboard of the top script of your input menu and then rotates sequentially through all the keyboards available in the menu. Command-Space, thankfully, isn't as brain-damaged as it was in 10.3. Now it swaps you literally to the most recently used input method/keyboard. This isn't as useful (in my opinion) as the most recently used input that uses the current script, but it's far better than 10.3's notion of swapping to the most recent input that *doesn't* use the current script!

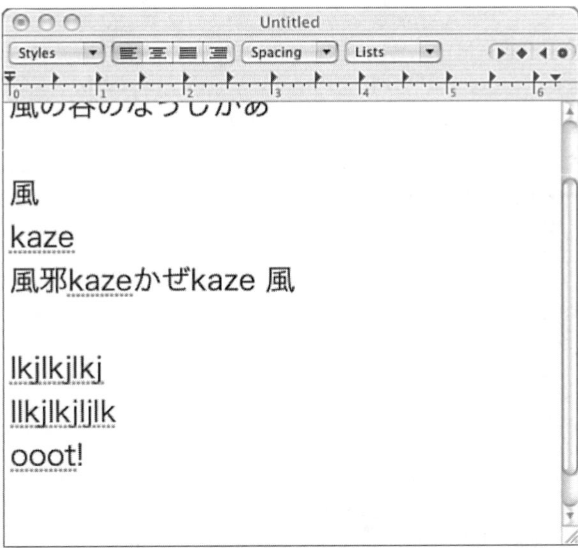

FIGURE 6.24 This is the Input menu/Keyboard menu that appears in the Finder when you have enabled more than one keyboard layout under the Input menu tab of the International pane and made the Input menu visible in the Finder.

Take a few moments to play with the Roman script keyboard layouts in an application such as TextEdit. A simple example to check is the British keyboard. If you switch to it and type **#**, you will discover that you get £, the British pound. Switch to the French keyboard and start pressing the number keys. You get many characters with accents instead. To get a number, hold down the Shift key while pressing a number key.

Hopefully, you have gotten used to the idea of the script interpreting your input as appropriate for the keyboard layout you have selected. Although these modifications of your input might seem relatively simple, this is because you've been working in your already familiar Roman input script.

Now, let's take a look at a more interesting keyboard layout and input script—the one for Japanese. As you go through the example, notice where the input script is interpreting the input that you type, and attempting to produce contextually correct output for you. Apple has historically produced some fantastic software for mapping between QWERTY-type keyboards and nonromance languages. These software packages were once priced far outside the range of students of the languages, and often of many professional users, predominantly because they included enormously expensive fonts as a part of the package. Now, through marketing magic we won't pretend to understand (but that we love—these packages, only a few years ago, would have cost tens of thousands of dollars—now you get them all, built-in, for free!), Apple is providing an ever-expanding collection of these language kits as well as the associated fonts as a standard part of Mac OS X. We'll use Japanese as an example of how these input scripts and keyboards interact, primarily because as authors we understand a bit about how this language works with the system, but please feel free to experiment in whatever language you're comfortable with.

Figure 6.25 shows a Japanese phrase. For those who don't read Japanese, the pronunciation is (as close as we can represent in English) Kazenotaninonaushika, which translates as "Nausicaä of the Valley of the Wind," the title of a popular Japanese children's film.

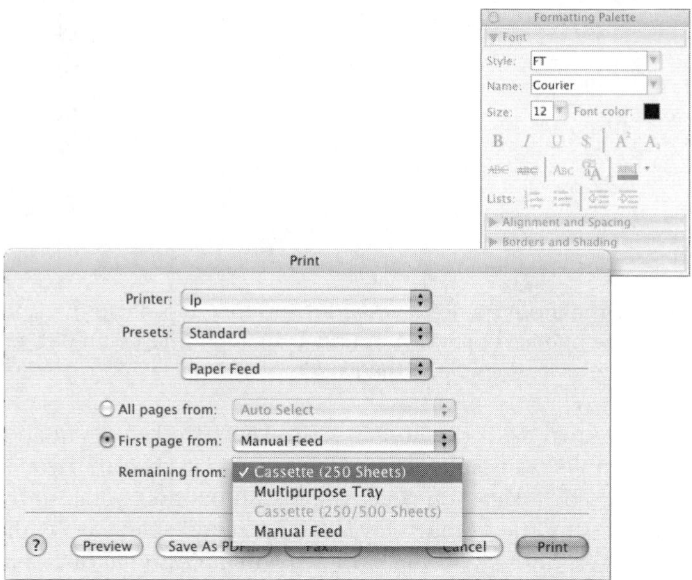

FIGURE 6.25 The Japanese phrase *Kaze no tani no Nausicaä* serves as our example of using the input system.

Without the functionality available in the language kit, typesetting this phrase from the keyboard would be very difficult. It contains characters from three different Japanese alphabets. Not three different fonts, but three completely different alphabets, two of which are phonetic, and one that consists of stylized ideographs and contains thousands of characters. Entering this without a language kit would entail finding the right keys to produce the characters from the two small phonetic alphabets, all the while switching between fonts and picking from a huge list of characters in the thousand-plus character alphabet. With the Japanese kit, typesetting this is only a little more complex than typing the phrase phonetically as it is pronounced in English.

Using TextEdit and the Japanese language kit, we can easily reproduce the text shown in Figure 6.25. Although this example is in Japanese, the same steps can be used for any language you use. From within the application where you want to use an alternative input script, choose the keyboard layout from the Input menu. The input script for that keyboard takes over the input for the application.

CAUTION

This functionality is now even enabled in the Finder and the Terminal. Be careful if you're working in an alternative keyboard and input script, and switch between applications, because the language you're working in can follow you around the system. This can produce unexpected results, especially in applications that have traditionally been ASCII/English-alphabet based, such as the Terminal. You can slightly ameliorate this behavior by making sure that you have the Allow a Different Source for Each Document option selected in the International Control Panel/Input Menu pane, but you'll still need to set the input method you want for each application and/or document before it'll use its own settings, rather than adopting the settings from the most recently used application.

NOTE

Mac OS X 10.3 changed the way that some language kits interoperate with the system in some significant ways. Primarily among these, some input scripts and keyboards carried along with them language-specific interfaces to the system. These could be accessed from a little floating Operations Palette that appeared when in a language that provided them. In 10.3, Apple dropped the Operations Palette, and instead added various language-specific options to the Input menu when in the associated keyboard. 10.4 continues this new style of interface. Because of this, you can expect new Input menu options to appear in the menu itself when working in different languages. The proper use of these is beyond the scope of this book, but hopefully the in-language Help sections that Apple provides for each will be sufficient for users who want to use these features. Given that Apple keeps expanding the capabilities of Mac OS X, we strongly suspect that all the language-specific features such as in-language file management that used to exist under the Operations Palette are still hidden in here somewhere!

To reproduce the Japanese phrase in our example, all we need is to make sure that the appropriate keyboard is selected, and that we know how to say (phonetically) what we want to type. The one you want is the Hiragana keyboard, which puts the input script in a mood to accept phonetic input in an English-like form, and then converts it to "Native" Japanese phonetics if possible, and "Foreign" Japanese phonetics if not. Further, it converts appropriate groupings of native phonetics into pictogram/ideogram characters if there are pictograms with the appropriate composite pronunciation.

For the sample phrase, the characters we are looking for break up partly as words and partly as phonetics (words for the pictogram-based parts of the phrase, and phonetics for the phonetic character parts), as follows

```
kaze no tani no na u shi ka
```

In the Font pane, pick a fairly large size for the font so that you can easily read what you are typing. Then type the letter **k**. So far, nothing unexpected happens. Type the letter **a**.

As soon as you type this, the input script recognizes that you have entered a phoneme and replaces it with the appropriate phonetic character for the selected alphabet. The character for the sound ka has appeared and replaced the k and a characters. Type the letter **z**. Now you have a Hiragana character and the letter z, as shown in Figure 6.26. Now type the letter e. Again, the input script recognizes a phoneme. The character for the ze sound has appeared. Note the characters have an underscore. This means that the input script recognizes that other possible representations in the language could also be appropriate ways of displaying *both* of these phonemes, and is prompting that we might want to change the current representation—in this case, from a phonetic representation to a pictographic representation.

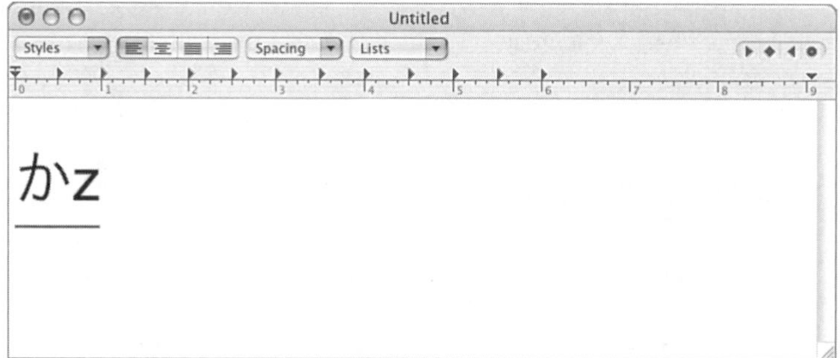

FIGURE 6.26 The Japanese character for *ka* followed by the letter *z* are showing after typing *ka*, and then *z*. The underscore means that we have not picked any final representations yet.

To select from possible representations that fit the current input, press the spacebar. The input system selects a character for you. If the character is not correct, press the spacebar again. This opens a little window, as shown in Figure 6.27, from which you can manually select a character. You can scroll the selection up and down in the list by using the arrow keys on your keyboard, and you can select a character by clicking on it. You can accept the current selected character or characters by pressing the Return key, and select and exit the menu by double-clicking your desired character. When you have the character that you want and are back to the TextEdit window, just start typing from the example again.

If the scrolling list of alternative representations doesn't provide what you're looking for, you can also bring up the Character Palette. This appears in many applications as an option labeled Special Characters that appears under the Edit menu but is also universally available through the Input menu itself, if you have it selected as a Keyboard/Input method via the International pane.

The Character Palette provides access to a large selection of characters in a number of fonts, styles, and groups. If you needed a Kanji numeral, for example, you'd select Japanese from the View pop-up menu, and then select from either categorized input (By Category pane), as shown in Figure 6.28, or if you're a dedicated user of Kanji, by stroke and radical (shapes and styles of the lines that make up the characters) from the By Radical pane.

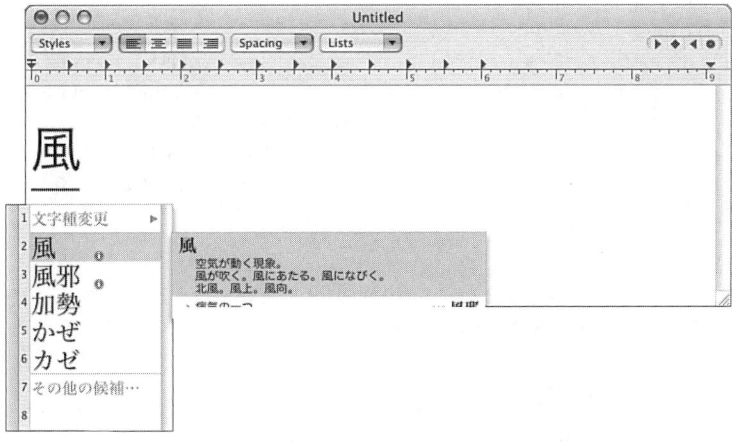

FIGURE 6.27 Press the spacebar twice to get a menu that allows you to choose another character.

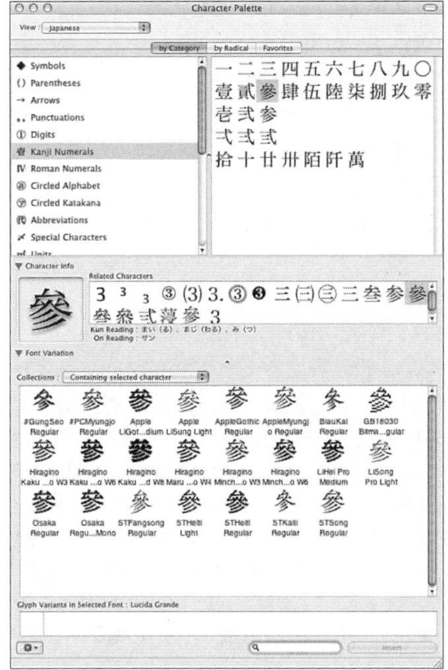

FIGURE 6.28 The Character Palette provides categorized access to a great number of characters in useful groupings.

NOTE

The Kanji items in the By Radical pane of the Character Palette are listed by radical (base character) in increasing stroke order. These characteristics are specific to a traditional method of characterizing and specifying Japanese Kanji characters. If your language kit uses a similar method of characterizing pictogram or other characters, you can expect a similar presentation in the Character Palette. Otherwise, expect the ordering to be as the characters would be traditionally alphabetized in the language.

To select an item from the Character Palette, select the desired character in the grid and drag it into your document, or double-click the character, and it will be inserted automatically.

The Character Palette has more (many more) than just Japanese language items, so you might be interested in playing with it more later. These currently include Cyrillic, Greek, and a number of pictorial symbols such as boxes and lines. The available categories, and even the available panes from which to select categories, vary depending on the language view type you've selected. This palette provides access to an immense number of character types and manipulations. You can access categorized characters in areas as diverse as the symbols used for marking up dental x-rays and charts regarding treatments, to characters for drawing in-text boxes and grids, and from fractions to alphabets or numerals drawn in circles or squares.

A particularly nice feature of the Character Palette is the ability to view what a particular character looks like in all the fonts that have it available. This can be useful for selecting the best font from which to get selected special characters to put into a presentation or chart.

The example we're working on can be successfully completed without the help of the Character Palette, so continue through the rest of the phrase, picking and choosing characters using the spacebar as you go. You should be able to get through the kazenotanino part with just a few keystrokes, a couple spaces, and a couple returns. The final part of the title we're working on, Nausicaä, is written in the other Japanese phonetic alphabet, Katakana. To work in this character system, select the Katakana keyboard type from the Input menu. Now type **na** and press Return. Next, type **u** and press Return. Then type **shi** and press Return. Finally, type **ka** and press Return. Pressing Return after each indicates to the input script that you're finished entering a phonetic equivalent, and that you want to accept the symbol that it has chosen. Now you have finished typing the title. What you have typed should match what is shown in Figure 6.29.

This particular title was a convenient example for you to try because it uses characters from all three Japanese alphabets, giving you the opportunity to see examples of each of the input script methods and the way they interact. Even if you're interested in working in a different language kit, we hope you find this information useful. If you understand the functionality we've presented here, you should be able to find similar functions in the language kit of your choice.

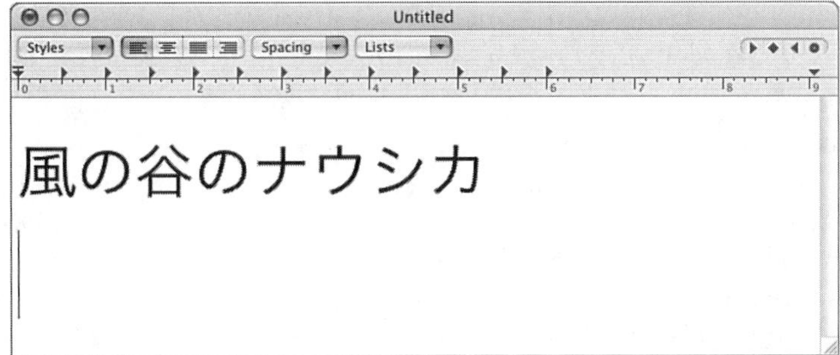

FIGURE 6.29 Now we have successfully converted `kazenotaninonaushika` into correctly written Japanese.

> **NOTE**
>
> After having spent the time to type the Japanese for the Nausicaä title, you might be interested in learning more about the animated film. Check `http://www.nausicaa.net/` to learn more about this and other films by the same studio.

Finally, Figure 6.30 shows just a small sampling of the types of characters available in the Character Palette, with some of these entered into the TextEdit application. This palette provides a significant resource for picking and choosing characters appropriate to different languages, even if you don't know how to pronounce the symbol phonetically.

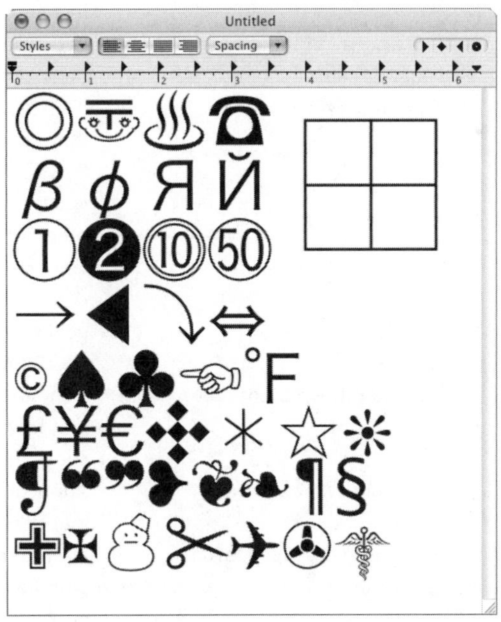

FIGURE 6.30 The Character Palette provides access to many additional characters through a number of categorized lists.

Hopefully, this section has provided a fun way to learn about the way different keyboard inputs can work under Mac OS X. If you want to watch your system type right-to-left instead, enable the Hebrew input method and experiment with it.

When you have multiple enabled keyboards, the Input menu appears in the menu bar. You can easily select a desired keyboard by selecting it from the Input menu. For keyboards that belong to the Roman script input, the changes in the behavior of your keyboard might be subtle. With the Japanese script input keyboard, however, the input method is far more interactive than the Roman script input keyboards. Other input scripts and keyboards are available, and we hope that the techniques you've learned in experimenting with the Japanese system will help you to work in any other input systems that you need.

Font Websites

There are many places that you can download fonts, including free fonts. Just do a search on your favorite web search site, and you should be pleased with the results, perhaps even overwhelmed. Table 6.1 includes a few sites here to get you started. However, for your reference, we include sites other than ones with just downloadable fonts.

TABLE 6.1 Font-Related Websites

Website	URL	Content
iFree Top Font Sites	`http://www.ifree.com.au/top/fonts/index.html`	Lists many links to font sites.
WebFontList	`http://www.webfontlist.com/`	Lists many links to font sites, both free and shareware.
Karen's Koncepts Free Fonts Resources	`http://www.netmegs.com/koncepts/freefont.htm`	Lists many links to sites with fonts, both free and shareware.
MyFonts.com	`http://www.myfonts.com/`	A site where you can buy fonts through participating foundries. Provides some font utilities to help you find the right font. Has links to other font sites and font utility sites.
MyFonts.com: WhatTheFont	`http://www.myfonts.com/WhatTheFont/`	The direct link toMyFonts.com's WhatTheFont utility. This interesting utility can be used to try to identify a font from a scanned image.
Identifont—identify fonts and typefaces	`http://www.identifont.com/identify.html`	A site that helps you identify a font by asking a series of questions about the font.
Apple—Fonts/Tools	`http://fonts.apple.com/`	Apple's technical site on fonts and font development.
TrueType Typography: TTF fonts & technology	`http://www.truetype.demon.co.uk/index.htm`	An informative site onTrueType typography. Includes info about history and specification.

TABLE 6.1 Continued

Website	URL	Content
Adobe Solutions Network: OpenType Specification	`http://partners.adobe.com/asn/tech/type/`	Lists the Adobe type specification, including OpenType.
Free Fonts, TrueType, OpenType, ClearType Microsoft Typography	`http://www.microsoft.com/typography/default.asp`	Microsoft's Typography site. Includes technical information as well as a link to Microsoft's free fonts.
Microsoft Typography Fonts and products	`http://www.microsoft.com/typography/fonts/default.asp`	Provides a listing of what fonts come in what Microsoft products. Does not include images of the fonts.
Unicode Home Page	`http://www.unicode.org/`	Includes information on Unicode and the Unicode standard.

Summary

In this chapter, you learned a variety of basics involving printer and font management. You learned about the Print Center, which enables you to add and delete printers, select a default printer, and work with the print queues. You learned that printing from an application works the same as in traditional Mac OS. Under the File menu, Page Setup enables you to set the attributes for your page or view a summary of the attributes. Also under the File menu, Print enables you to send a job to the printer. You can also specify further options about your printout, including an output option to print to a PDF file. After learning basics about the printer, you learned how to manage fonts. You learned how to install a new font and how to use the Font pane, including using it to manage font collections. Finally, you enhanced your font experience by learning about input methods that use multilingual characters. You experimented with switching between various Roman script inputs as well as the Japanese script input.

PART III

Advanced User and Network Settings

IN THIS PART

CHAPTER 7

Configuring Network Connectivity

IN THIS CHAPTER

- Understanding TCP/IP Basics
- Configuring Network Connections
- Connecting to a VPN
- Sharing a Single Internet Connection with Multiple Computers
- Using the Built-in Tiger Firewall

Unix, as a rule, is happiest when it gets to run as an always-on, always-network-connected operating system. Unix machines tend to run continuously (talking to other machines via the network) for months or years at a time, and the underpinnings of the networking system are designed for this mode of operation. Surprisingly, Apple has managed to pin a reasonable facsimile of the Mac OS as-needed picture of networking at the user level onto the Unix networking framework. You've already learned how to set up basic networking functions during the install process. In later chapters, you'll learn how this was accomplished at the Unix level, and how to perform even more sophisticated network tricks at the command line. In this chapter, we'll cover some of the GUI network controls.

Understanding TCP/IP Basics

TCP/IP, the acronym that has become a de facto name for a network communications protocol, stands for Transmission Control Protocol/Internet Protocol. TCP/IP has become so ubiquitous that many think of it, not just as a communications protocol, but as the *only* network communications protocol. Although not the only protocol out there (AppleTalk, covered later in this chapter, is one of the others), TCP/IP has proven flexible enough to support different types of data with a large range of requirements for delivery, timing, and reliability.

Basically, the TCP/IP protocol can be thought of as specifying the manner in which pieces of data should be transferred between two machines. This protocol includes the notion that the transmission of data can be broken down into a number of separate and abstract layers. Figure 7.1 shows the TCP/IP protocol stack, the conceptual breakdown of the protocol into layers. This is commonly referred to as the *OSI (Open Systems Interconnect)* model of networking. Because the functions of the layers are conceptually separate, the manner in which the function of any layer is accomplished does not matter, as long as it cooperates with the layers above and below it in the manner that each layer expects.

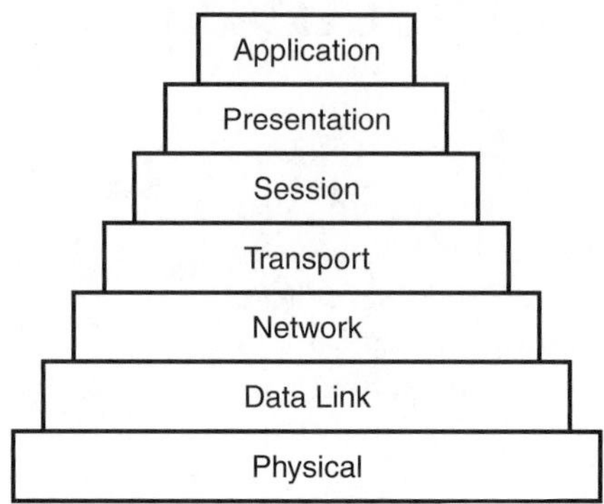

FIGURE 7.1 The OSI network model on which the TCP/IP stack is built.

For example, it doesn't matter whether the physical layer is carried by twisted-pair ethernet cabling, radio waves, or even with data written on slips of paper and handed back-and-forth between people sitting at terminals. As long as the data transmitted by the Physical layer gets retrieved from or inserted into data structures correctly at the Data Link layer, the rest of the TCP/IP stack functions identically.

This separation of functionality into independent and abstract pieces is typical of Unix technologies and allows the TCP/IP protocol to handle the transmission of a wide range of data types. Whether the data is equipment control where real-time transmission is critically important, or financial transactions where security and error-free transmissions are more important than speed, it is likely that the data can be fit into the TCP/IP model.

Going forward in the chapter, there are several TCP/IP-related terms you should be familiar with. These items define your connection to the Internet:

- IP address—The address that uniquely identifies your computer on the Internet. An IP address is typically represented in the form `###.###.###.###`, such as `192.168.0.1`. An IP address is assigned either by your network administrator or automatically via a DHCP *(Dynamic Host Configuration Protocol)* or BOOTP *(Bootstrap Protocol)* server.

  The IP address shown in the preceding paragraph is for the IPv4 protocol (Internet Protocol Version 4). This protocol uses a 32-bit address space and has been around for the last 20 years. As the popularity of the Internet increases, the number of addresses available in the IPv4 address space decreases. To address the impending address shortage, NAT *(Network Address Translation)* is regularly implemented in businesses and at home. This creates a private internal network that uses addresses that the IPv4 protocol has already specified are acceptable to use for this purpose, whereas another machine with NAT software, or a NAT hardware device, has a unique IP that the outside world recognizes and handles the negotiations between the outside world and the private network. The dynamic IP addresses that your ISP serves also assist with coping with the address shortage by providing addresses for machines as they need them, rather than uniquely assigning an IP address for each customer's machine.

To also help fix this address space shortage, the IETF *(Internet Engineering Task Force)* has introduced the next version of the Internet Protocol, IPv6 *(Internet Protocol Version 6)*. IPv6 uses a 128-bit address space, vastly increasing the number of addresses available. Additionally, it provides some improvements in routing and network configuration. It is expected that IPv4 and IPv6 will coexist for many years as the Internet transitions from one protocol to the other.

- Hostname—Typically, a hostname simply refers to the network name of your computer. Some people might use the term *hostname* to refer to the FQDN *(fully qualified domain name)* as well. This is the entire Internet name of your machine as registered with a DNS *(domain name server)*, such as `www.poisontooth.com`. If you have a name registered with a DNS, your machine will use this as the hostname; otherwise, it will use the name configured as your Computer Name (from Sharing Preferences) by default. The default can be overridden by adding a *`HOSTNAME`* entry to `/etc/hostconfig` with whatever name you'd prefer your machine to use. If you have a name registered with a DNS, this name should be used because a number of important networking features will not work properly if this value appears to be misconfigured.
- Subnet mask—Similar in appearance to an IP address, a subnet mask tells your computer which part of the IP address identifies the network it is on and which is the individual computer. Most users will be part of a Class C network with the subnet mask `255.255.255.0`. The last segment of the IP address identifies the computer, whereas the first three segments identify the network.
- Gateway/router address—The gateway address is an IP address of a network device that connects your local network to the rest of the Internet. A gateway handles any necessary translation between different types of networking media.
- DNS—Domain name servers are Internet servers that provide translation between IP addresses and fully qualified domain names. Each request for a machine using its FQDN requires an interaction with a DNS before a connection can take place.
- Network interface—The device that connects your computer to the network. This can be an ethernet port, AirPort card, and so on. Some computers might have

multiple network interfaces. Mac OS X names its interfaces sequentially. The `en0` interface is built-in ethernet, and `en1` is typically AirPort.

In addition to the canonical TCP/IP terms common to all Unix networking configurations, it will be helpful to know a few Apple-specific networking terms for discussion and comparison:

- AppleTalk—AppleTalk is a network protocol with goals similar to those of TCP/IP but designed for less general-use applications, and with features to make it more friendly to nonexpert users. Instead of requiring each computer to have an assigned, distinct identification number, AppleTalk was designed to allow each computer to independently choose its own identification number, and to advertise its identification and services that it provides to the network. With only normal TCP/IP network methods, there is no convenient way for one computer to discover that another provides a service (such as a shared printer). The reason is that, although the service might be provided, there isn't any networkwide broadcast of this information. To use a remote printer in this networking model, you need to know the TCP/IP address of the machine to contact regarding the use of the printer. AppleTalk overcomes this problem by each computer continuously and repeatedly advertising all the services it provided, but this results in continuous traffic on your network. Because of this, it is usually limited to local networks only because you probably don't want to know about all the printers available on Macs all across the country.

- Computer Name—In the AppleTalk world, each computer can claim a name for itself and advertise this on the network. The names do not have to be different. This value is configured through the Sharing control pane or manually through the `/etc/hostconfig` file.

- Bonjour—Bonjour is an Apple product based on the Zeroconf project (`http://www.zeroconf.org`, a project of the Internet Engineering Task Force, `http://www.ietf.org`). Zeroconf is an attempt to provide AppleTalk-like networking simplicity with TCP/IP networking services. Although the ultimate goal of Zeroconf is fully automated network configuration, with Mac OS 10.2, Apple began promoting Bonjour, then Rendezvous (née Zeroconf), as a service-discovery protocol carried over TCP/IP. This provides an open-API method for computers to communicate in a manufacturer-agnostic manner about services that they provide or require. Using Bonjour services is as simple as using the Bonjour Computer Name as a URL in a web browser.

- Bonjour Computer Name—Yet another name for your computer. This parameter, configurable through the Sharing pane, defaults to a value similar (excluding illegal characters) to your Computer Name, with `.local` appended. The Bonjour Computer Name, also called your *local hostname,* is used by your computer when advertising services to the network and when trying to connect to your computer from others that want to use services you provide. The Bonjour Computer Name is also used, possibly incorrectly, in a number of other networking contexts, such as the name that Postfix (see Chapter 26, "Creating a Mail Server") attempts to report for the machine.

Using these pieces of information, you can configure your computer to access the Internet. Although most dial-in accounts automatically set these parameters for you, users connecting directly to a network via ethernet or AirPort need to know the appropriate settings for their network to continue.

If you want more information on the TCP/IP protocol and its use, I recommend *Special Edition Using TCP/IP* (ISBN: 0789718979).

Configuring Network Connections

The Network preferences pane is the GUI brain center of the OS X interface to TCP/IP. This pane, in actuality, just provides a series of hints to the underlying Unix TCP/IP control software, but it does so in a much prettier and often more convenient fashion than twiddling configuration parameters at the command line. The primary control with which you should familiarize yourself is the Configuration menu. In previous versions of Mac OS, various portions of the networking software were configured by separate control panels, and each panel was controlled by its own independent saved configuration setting. Mac OS X has instead placed all network configurations under a single parent control pane, with an umbrella configuration setting that covers TCP/IP, modem control, AppleTalk, and location settings.

The two main options in this pane are the Location and Show options. Location can be set to Automatic, New Location, Edit Locations, and any locations that you've already created. What appears by default under the Show menu varies with your system's hardware. Options include Network Status, Internal Modem (dial-up connection, if you have a modem), IrDA modem (infrared port, if you have this interface), Built-in Ethernet, AirPort (if your machine has an AirPort), and Network Port Configurations. The collection of these that are visible to you may also be modified by enabling and disabling each connection type on a per-location basis.

Available to each subpane are Assist Me and Apply Now options as well as the Help Viewer. The Assist Me option takes you directly to the Network Assistant. Note that this System Preference requires administrative access to change.

Viewing Network Connection Status

To view your network connection status, select Network Status in the Show option of the Network preferences pane. This subpane shows you the status of your network ports. For an active network port, you can see such information as your machine's current IP address. Additionally, you can select a network port here, and configure it or connect using it. Figure 7.2 shows the Network Status subpane for a PowerBook. The appearance of this subpane varies with your hardware and what hardware you have disabled and whether you have any virtual private networks (VPNs) configured.

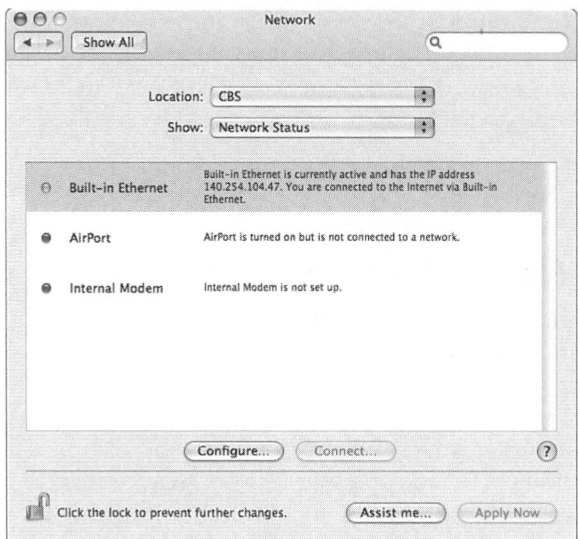

FIGURE 7.2 The Network Status subpane of the Network preferences pane.

Network Port Configurations

Most of the available selections in the Show menu switch between subpane groups specifying configurations for particular network interfaces. The Network Port Configurations subpane doesn't provide network configuration but allows you to enable and disable already existing configurations for the interfaces and create new configuration sets. Figure 7.3 shows the Network Port Configurations subpane of the Network control pane. To make network configuration as easy as possible, Mac OS X attempts to automatically detect and select the correct network configuration for any given situation. This convenience comes at a slight cost in startup time, so unless you actually intend to use all the available configurations, we don't recommend leaving all the configurations enabled as shown in Figure 7.3.

If you've already experimented enough to find the location settings and mastered the ability to switch between them, the capability to save multiple configurations for a single interface assigned to the same "location" might seem redundant. It becomes useful, however, in situations in which you have multiple IP addresses at the same conceptual location on a single network interface. Without requiring you to iterate through different location settings, setting up several different configurations would allow the system to automatically search through each until it found a working set of parameters. This might occur if you have multiple in-building networks with different IP ranges on each, but with each connected to share resources. Another possible use is if you have a number of different dial-up service providers and want your machine to try each until it finds an open one.

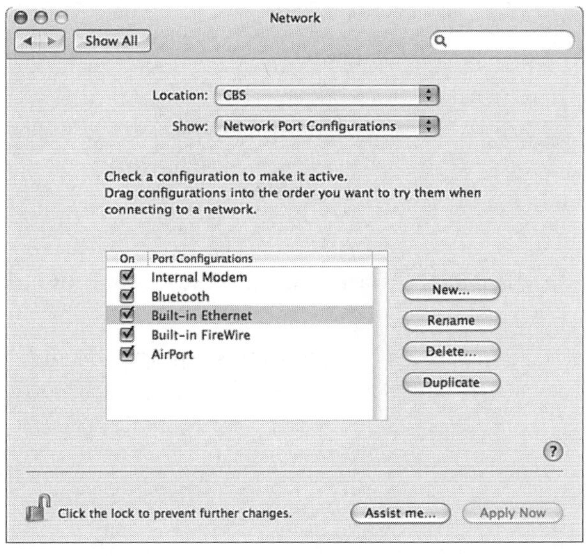

FIGURE 7.3 The Network Port Configurations subpane of the Network preferences pane.

Setting Up Network Interfaces

The available network interfaces you may configure varies with your hardware and whether you have configured any VPNs. We will briefly look at setting up the built-in ethernet, built-in FireWire, internal modem, Bluetooth modem and AirPort interfaces. The available subpanes under each interface vary, but the interfaces tend to use some subset of the same subpanes. Table 7.1 details which subpanes and interfaces go together by sorting on the subpane. Because the table is based on the G4 PowerBook, you might not necessarily see an interface that is on your system listed in the table. The TCP/IP Network subpane is listed twice at the end of Table 7.2 to show that the options are the same for different groups of network interfaces. Table 7.2 details the same information by sorting on the network interface. Table 7.2 reflects the experience you have as you use the Network preferences pane. This section details the information by Network subpane in the expectation that as you are configuring your interfaces, it will be easier to look for each subpane, rather than to look for an interface whose description might contain one or more comments to see another section.

TABLE 7.1 Summary of Network Preferences Subpanes and Network Interfaces

Network Subpane	Network Interface
AirPort	AirPort
AppleTalk	AirPort, Built-in Ethernet
Bluetooth Modem	Bluetooth
Ethernet	Built-in Ethernet
Modem	Internal Modem
PPP	Internal Modem, Bluetooth

TABLE 7.1 Continued

Network Subpane	Network Interface
PPPoE	AirPort, Built-in Ethernet
Proxies	AirPort, Built-in Ethernet, Built-in FireWire, Bluetooth, Internal Modem
TCP/IP	AirPort, Built-in Ethernet, Built-in FireWire
TCP/IP	Bluetooth, Internal Modem

TABLE 7.2 Summary of Network Interfaces and Network Preferences Subpanes

Network Interface	Network Subpanes
AirPort	AirPort, TCP/IP, PPPoE, AppleTalk, Proxies
Bluetooth	PPP, TCP/IP, Proxies, Bluetooth Modem
Built-in Ethernet	TCP/IP, PPPoE, AppleTalk, Proxies, Ethernet
Built-in FireWire	TCP/IP, Proxies
Internal Modem	PPP, TCP/IP, Proxies, Modem

AirPort

The AirPort subpane, available only for the AirPort interface, is shown in Figure 7.4. In this subpane, you can choose your default AirPort network either automatically or by specifying one, and enter your network password if one is required. Note that when there is a preferred list of networks, the subpane says that the AirPort will connect to the first wireless network in the list. This subpane also displays your AirPort ID.

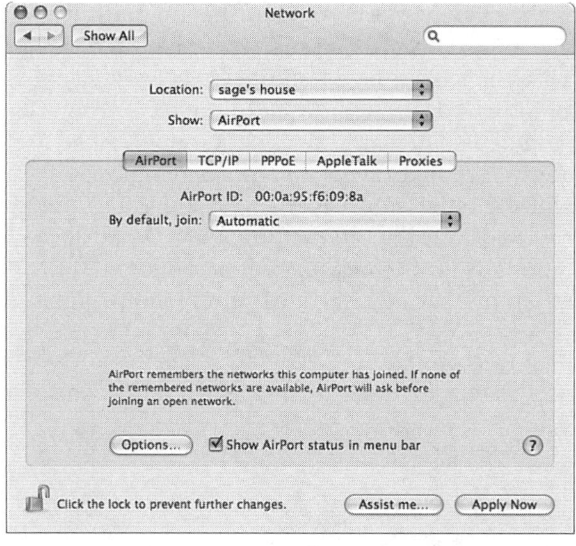

FIGURE 7.4 The AirPort subpane of the AirPort interface in the Network preferences pane.

The Options section contains a variety of options you can configure. If the AirPort finds no preferred network, you can specify whether it should ask before joining an open network, automatically join an open network, or whether it should keep looking for recent networks. Here you can also set whether an administrative password should be required to change wireless networks and to create computer-to-computer networks. Additionally, you can set the AirPort to automatically add new networks to the preferred network list, disconnect from the wireless network when you log out, and enable interference robustness.

You can also choose to show AirPort status in the menu. This is a recommended convenience, particularly because it allows you to see at a glance what your AirPort signal is like and which network you are connected to. From the menu, you can also turn the AirPort on or off, create networks, use interference robustness or open the Internet Connect application.

AppleTalk

AppleTalk is a communications protocol pioneered by Apple in the era of the Macintosh Plus. This protocol was designed for networking small collections of computers on relatively small networks. Because it was designed to facilitate network-building by people with no interest in being network designers or administrators, AppleTalk is a rather chatty and inefficient protocol. Because of its ease of use, it has survived the transition to a mostly ethernet-based world and prospered in environments where its inefficiencies do not impair other network services.

Because of its intimate association with Apple's printing and file-sharing software, AppleTalk is sometimes thought of as actually being disk services and print services. In reality, it's a communications protocol, over which disk, print, and other services can be delivered. Because of this, like TCP/IP, AppleTalk connectivity is configured from the Network control pane, and services that need to use AppleTalk are configured elsewhere. AppleTalk is enabled and configured from the AppleTalk subpanes of the Built-in Ethernet and AirPort configuration sets.

7

TIP

Remember that these subpanes, although they contain identical options, are configurations for two different interfaces. You can configure different parameters for each, to be used with each of the interfaces as appropriate.

Information entered in one interface configuration set does not automatically become the default information for any other interface. Therefore, you might need to enter such things as proxies, for example, in more than one place, depending on how your network is set up.

Figure 7.5 shows the AppleTalk subpane for the Built-in Ethernet configuration (the AirPort version looks identical). The AppleTalk settings configured here are specific for the interface configuration set that you're editing. You can choose to configure AppleTalk automatically or manually. Unless otherwise directed, automatic is probably sufficient.

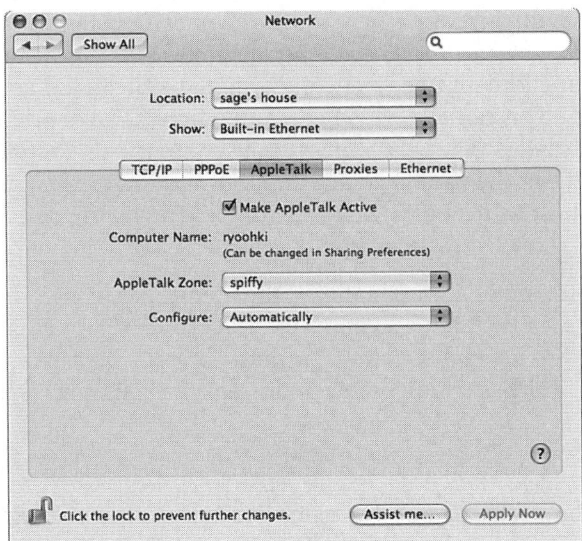

FIGURE 7.5 The AppleTalk subpane of the Network pane.

In the AppleTalk subpane, the following options can be configured:

- Make AppleTalk Active—Activate AppleTalk for this interface. AppleTalk must be activated for an interface if you need to share your files via AppleShare on that interface.
- Computer Name—This is your AppleTalk Computer Name, which is also your Hostname, but is different from your Bonjour Computer Name. This parameter is configured from the Sharing preferences pane.
- AppleTalk Zone—If your AppleTalk network has multiple zones, you can select the zone you want your computer to join from this menu. If you're on a network with multiple zones, your network administrator should be able to tell you what the proper setting is for your computer.
- Configure—Gives you the option of manually configuring your AppleTalk network parameters or automatically determining the information. The AppleTalk Network ID and Node ID are similar to a TCP/IP subnet and IP address. The difference is AppleTalk is designed so that the computers in a network can cooperatively and automatically work out this information for themselves, without needing it to be specified by the users or administrators. There are very few instances in which you should need to set up the system for manual configuration.
- Node ID—If your network administrator tells you that you need to configure your machine for fixed rather than automatically determined AppleTalk network information, the node ID goes here. This option is available only in the manual configuration.
- Network ID—If your network administrator tells you that you need to configure your machine for fixed AppleTalk network information, the Network ID goes here.

If your network administrator gives you the network ID as ###.###, instead of a number between 1 and 65534, multiply the first by 256 and add the second to it. If you are given the number as ##.##.##, multiply the first by 256, the second by 16, and then add the those two results with the third number. This option is only available in the manual configuration.

Bluetooth Modem

The Bluetooth Modem subpane, shown in Figure 7.6, is available only for the Bluetooth network interface. In this subpane, you configure which modem you have. You can also specify whether to enable error correction and compression in the modem and whether to wait for the dial tone before dialing. Finally, you can specify whether to show Bluetooth status in the menu bar and whether to show modem status in the menu bar.

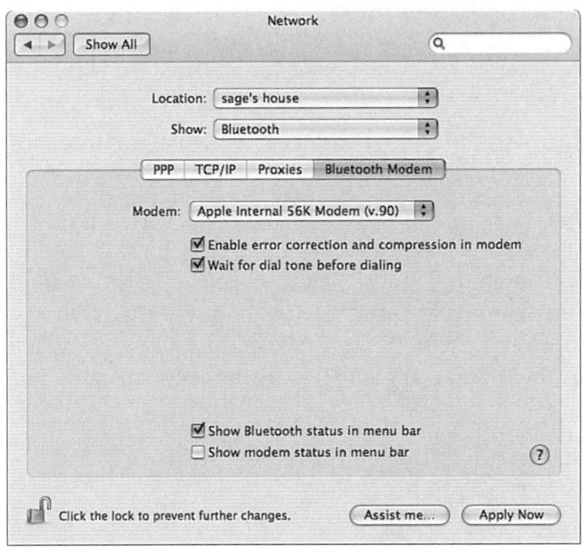

FIGURE 7.6 The Bluetooth Modem subpane of the Bluetooth interface in the Network preferences pane.

Ethernet

Shown in Figure 7.7 is the Ethernet subpane, available only for the Built-in Ethernet interface. It displays your machine's ethernet ID and allows you to configure the hardware either automatically or manually. Unless told otherwise by your network administrator, always choose automatically. Choosing the wrong settings manually can cause a lot of unnecessary headaches for you.

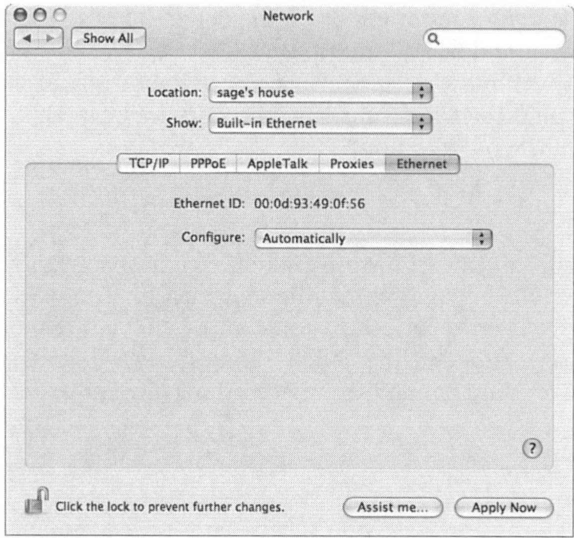

FIGURE 7.7 The Ethernet subpane of the Built-in Ethernet interface in the Network preferences pane.

Modem

The Modem subpane, shown in Figure 7.8, allows you to select your modem, configure the dialing type, determine whether you want to hear your connections as they progress, and indicate whether you want to be notified of incoming calls while you are connected to the Internet. Additionally, here you can choose to display modem status in the menu bar.

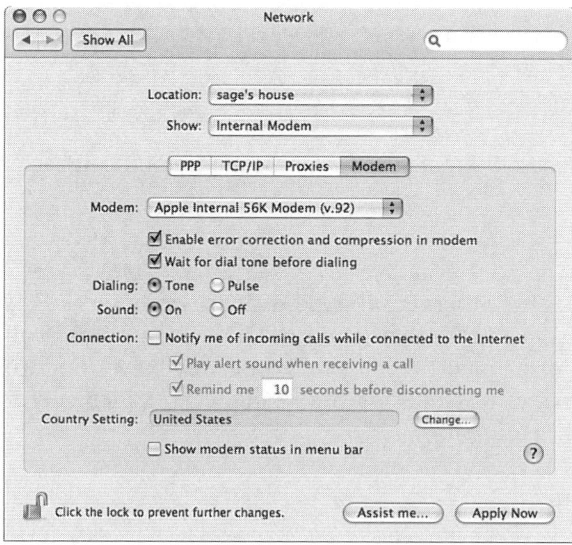

FIGURE 7.8 The Modem subpane of the Internal Modem interface in the Network preferences pane.

PPP

The PPP (*Point-to-Point Protocol,* carried over a dial-up connection) subpane is available for the Bluetooth and Internal Modem interfaces. Figure 7.9 shows the PPP subpane for the Internal Modem interface; however, the Bluetooth interface uses and identical PPP subpane. Under this subpane, you can configure how to connect to your ISP. Almost all ISPs use PPP to provide TCP/IP over dial-up connections. If yours does not, you will need to follow its instructions, which will probably include installation of some custom software.

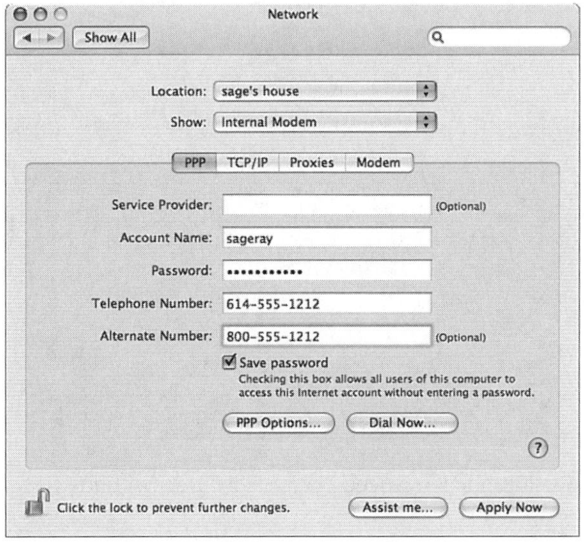

FIGURE 7.9 The PPP subpane of the Internal Modem and Bluetooth configurations allows you to specify your dial-up account information.

The PPP subpane has the following fields:

- Service Provider—An optional field where you can specify a name for the service provider. This option is useful if you have multiple providers that your machine needs to dial, and you need a better way to keep track of them than just by phone number.
- Account Name—The username or account name that you have with this ISP.
- Password—The password for this account and ISP.
- Telephone Number—The telephone number to dial.
- Alternate Number—An alternative number to dial for the same service provider. If your ISP doesn't have alternative dial-in numbers, leave this field blank.
- Save Password—If your machine is going to be used by multiple users and you don't want them to be able to connect to the Internet using your account information and password, don't check this box.

The PPP subpane also has a PPP Options button and corresponding sheet that enables you to configure several other options with respect to the dial-up connection, as shown in Figure 7.10. This figure is shown for the Internal Modem interface, but an identical Options sheet appears for the Bluetooth interface.

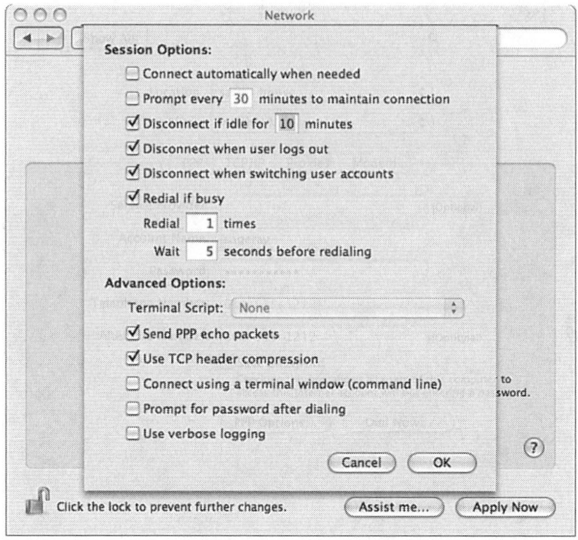

FIGURE 7.10 The Session and Advanced options drop-down pane for dial-up connections.

The sheet enables you to configure the following:

- Whether to automatically dial and make a connection when an application starts that needs TCP/IP services.
- Whether, and how frequently, to prompt you to stay connected if there hasn't been any recent network activity.
- How long to wait before disconnecting when there's no network activity.
- Whether to disconnect when there's no user logged in on the console.
- Whether to disconnect when switching users at the console.
- Whether to, how many times to, and how rapidly to redial the phone if the ISP is busy.
- Whether to send PPP echo packets. Some ISPs periodically send little "are you really there?" messages to connected computers to make sure that everything is working properly—this option controls whether to respond. Unless you have been told by your ISP to do otherwise, leave this option checked.
- Whether to compress TCP header information. TCP/IP information is carried in packets, with a significant amount of meta-information about the contents of the packet. Compressing this information can speed your network connection but

requires processor power. On a fast machine, you'll probably get a network speedup from compressing headers, unless your ISP is using some ancient hardware that takes more time to perform the compression/decompression than the savings in transmission time.

- Whether to use a manual terminal window for connection. If your ISP doesn't use a standard PPP server, you might need to carry on some textual dialog with the server during connection. Selecting this option opens a terminal for you to interact with the host during connection.
- Whether to prompt for a password after dialing.
- The verbose logging option increases the amount of information regarding dial-up connections stored in the system logs.

PPPoE

As mentioned earlier, TCP/IP is just one of a number of communications protocols. It's actually possible to run multiple communications protocols over the same piece of wire at the same time. In a clever use of this capability, it's possible to establish a PPP connection via ethernet wiring rather than a phone line; hence the name *PPP over ethernet* or simply *PPPoE*. If your service provider gives you this option, you can configure it with the subpane shown in Figure 7.11. This subpane is available for the Built-in Ethernet and AirPort interfaces. The options available in this subpane are exactly analogous to the options under the dial-in PPP configuration. Here you can also choose to show the PPPoE status in the menu bar.

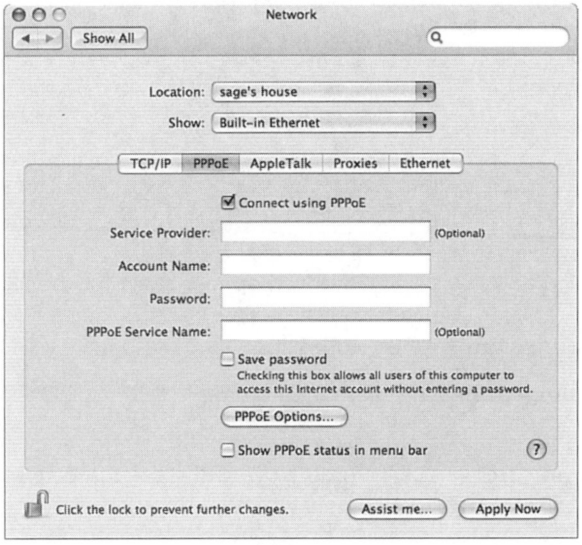

FIGURE 7.11 The PPPoE subpane of the Built-in Ethernet configuration set.

In this subpane, you have the following fields to fill in:

- Service Provider—An informational field similar to the service provider field for a dial-in connection.
- Account Name—The user or account name for your PPPoE ISP.
- Password—The password for your account.
- PPPoE Service Name—Another informational field.
- Save Password—If you want this account to function automatically without requiring you to specify a password at each network connection, select this option.

The PPPoE subpane has a number of advanced options that can be configured from a sheet that appears when the PPPoE Options button is clicked. Shown in Figure 7.12, these options allow you to configure the behavior of your PPPoE connection.

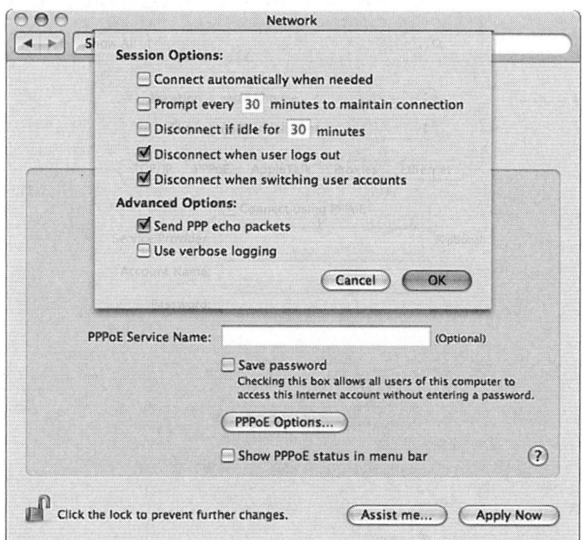

FIGURE 7.12 The PPPoE Session and Advanced options sheet for the PPPoE subpane.

The pane enables you to configure the following:

- Whether to automatically connect when an application starts that needs TCP/IP services.
- Whether, and how frequently, to prompt you to stay connected if there hasn't been any recent network activity.
- How long to wait before disconnecting when there's no network activity.
- Whether to disconnect when there's no user logged in on the console.
- Whether to disconnect when switching users on the console.

- Whether to send PPP echo packets. Some ISPs periodically send little "are you really there?" messages to connected computers to make sure that everything is working properly—this option controls whether to respond. Unless you have been told by your ISP to do otherwise, leave this option checked.
- The verbose logging option increases the amount of information regarding dial-up connections stored in the system logs.

Proxies

If you're on a network segment where you must connect to proxy servers instead of directly to outside services such as FTP and web servers, the Proxies subpane is the place to tell the system about the proxies. Shown in Figure 7.13, the Proxies subpane, available for all the network interfaces, allows you to select what is needed and how to contact the proxy types.

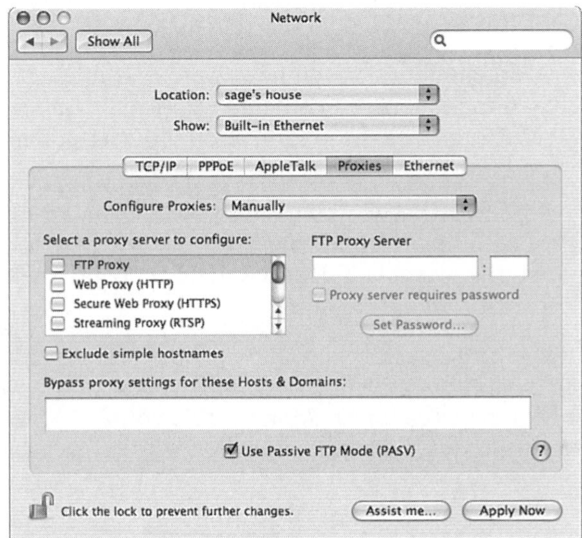

FIGURE 7.13 The Proxies subpane of the Built-in Ethernet configuration option.

Under the Proxies submenu, you can choose to configure your proxies using a PAC *(Proxy Auto Configuration)* file, and point the system to it, or you can configure your proxies manually. The Proxies submenu proxy types are

- FTP Proxy—If you need to contact a proxy to use FTP, enter its IP address and the proxy port here.
- Web Proxy (HTTP)—Configure this if you need to go through a proxy to access the web. There are occasions when you might want to use a web proxy even if you don't have to. For example, if you want to make your server connections anonymous by going through one of the web's anonymous proxy servers.

- Secure Web Proxy (HTTPS)—If you need to go through a secure proxy to access the web, configure this option.
- Streaming Proxy (RTSP *[real time streaming protocol]*)—Most types of proxy setups are designed to prevent a remote host from having any chance of connecting back to your machine. This makes it difficult for streaming services that need to send a lot of data as quickly as possible; hence, a specific proxy type for streaming data. If you're behind a firewall, you probably need to configure this—if your network services allow streaming data through at all.
- SOCKS Proxy—The SOCKS *(SOCKet Secure)* firewall system can be used to proxy for a number of different network services. If your network uses a SOCKS-type firewall, enter its information here.
- Gopher Proxy—Gopher was an early browser based way of serving data around the Internet, and has been all but completely supplanted by Web servers. If you've found one of the world's few remaining Gopher servers and need to access it through a proxy, this is where you tell the system about it.
- Automatic Proxy Configuration—If you have a proxy configuration file with all of your needed proxy information and you didn't notice the option to choose configurations using a PAC file, choose this option and point the system to the file.

Here you can also set whether to exclude simple hostnames. Additionally, you can configure your machine to use PASV (passive) FTP mode for transferring data, an option that will probably be required if you are behind a firewall or on a NAT (network address translation) private local network.

Finally, you can configure hosts and domains in which the proxy settings should be ignored. If you contact servers both inside and outside your local firewall, you might want to provide your local network information for this option. Therefore, your machine doesn't need to contact the proxy and then reconnect inside your local network for interior connections.

TCP/IP

If you are connected to your network via an ethernet connection (a physical chunk of wire, typically twisted pair, which looks like a bulky phone cable), you need to configure your connection under the Ethernet configuration option. Because switching from one physical transport to another requires changing only a little bit in a few protocol layers, it's similar to dial-up configurations you've already seen.

Under the TCP/IP subpane, by default, you have the option to configure IPv4 and/or IPv6. Generally, you have the option of providing manual configuration settings or of getting your configuration parameters from a server. For IPv4, which you will most likely be using, you can configure your Ethernet port manually, using DHCP with a manual address, using DHCP, or using BOOTP, or you can turn it off. For IPv6, you can configure automatically or manually, or you can turn it off.

Under the TCP/IP subpane, shown in Figure 7.14, you can configure how your TCP/IP stack gets its control and configuration information. The manual configuration settings for IPv4, shown in the figure, allow you to configure individual options by hand.

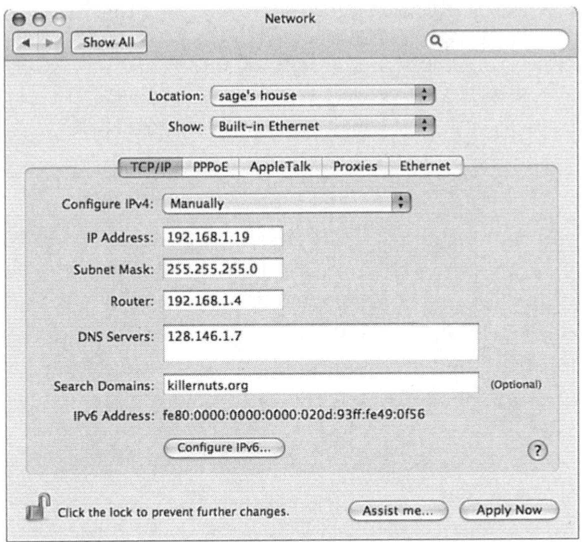

FIGURE 7.14 The TCP/IP subpane, showing available options for the Built-in Ethernet configuration set.

If you need to provide manual configuration information for IPv4, you need to know and fill in the following information—you should be able to get this information from your network administrator:

- IP Address—Your computer's IP address. This should be four sets of digits, separated by periods, such as `192.168.1.19`.
- Subnet Mask—This should be four sets of numbers separated by periods, as well. Most likely it will be `255.255.255.0` or `255.255.0.0`.
- Router—The machine that your machine must contact to reach the outside network world. This will frequently (but not always) be similar to your IP address, but with the final number replaced by a `1`. Your network administrator might also call this machine a *gateway*.
- DNS Servers—The IP addresses of machines that translate between IP addresses and fully qualified domain names (FQDNs), such as `www.apple.com`.
- Search Domains—Partial domain names to append to machine names, if you give less than an FQDN. For example, you might frequently work with machines on the domains `macosxunleashed.com` and `apple.com`. If you want your machine to try to connect to `info.macosxunleashed.com` or `info.apple.com` whenever you ask it to connect to `info`, you can enter the domains here. Your machine will try them both when it discovers that you've asked for a name that does not resolve as an FQDN.

This section automatically displays an IPv6 address for your machine, but you can choose to automatically or manually configure it. If you need to provide manual information for IPv6, you need to be able to manually fill in the IP address, the router, and the prefix. Get this information from your network administrator and write it down carefully.

NOTE

To bind another IP address to your network card, you can just duplicate your interface in the Network Preferences pane and assign another IP address to the duplicate entry. You will see uses for this in Chapters 22 and 23.

For modem TCP/IP configuration, you have essentially the same options available as you do for ethernet. Figure 7.15 shows the options available for TCP/IP setup under a modem connection. Most dial-up Internet service providers use PPP to service connections, so you'll probably be selecting the Using PPP option. Under this pane, you have partial manual configuration of the network parameters, but it would be unusual if an ISP did not provide the information for these settings automatically, by using PPP.

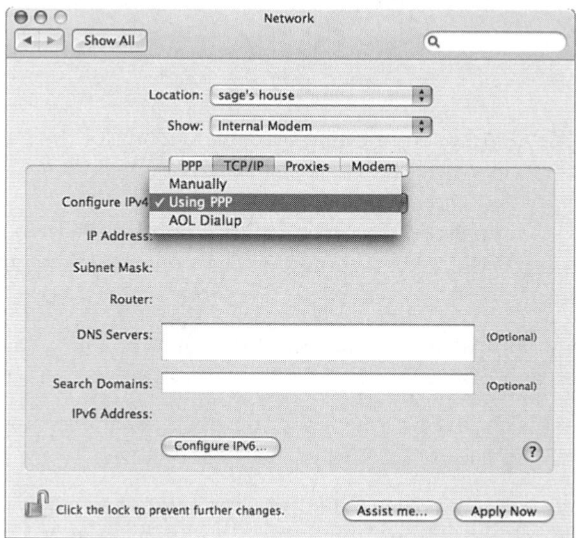

FIGURE 7.15 The TCP/IP options for the modem configuration sets are essentially identical to those for the Built-in Ethernet configuration.

Using the Location Manager

With Mac OS X, Apple has made location management considerably easier than it was with previous versions of the Macintosh operating system (although somewhat less powerful). Instead of managing configurations for each protocol in its own pane and then switching between different collections of the configurations with the Location Manager tool, interface configurations in Mac OS X are accessed directly under the location setting.

Figure 7.16 shows the entirety of the location management interface in Mac OS X. Selecting a location from this menu switches between location-specific settings in the subpanes below it. From this menu, locations can be chosen, duplicated, and edited.

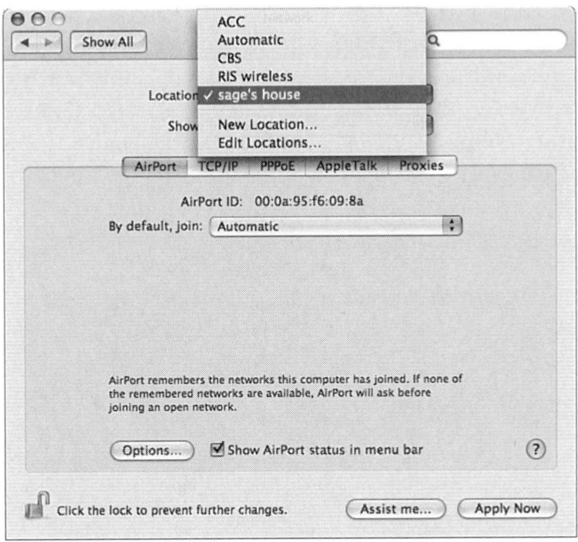

FIGURE 7.16 The location management menu in the Network preferences pane.

Each location in the Locations menu carries with it settings for the Configure menu and the subpanes that it switches through. That is, when you are entering information into the specific interface configuration panes, it is assigned to the currently displayed location. If you switch to a new location, you get new information and configurations in the interface configuration panes.

If you set the location setting to Automatic, the system attempts to guess the correct location information and switches between locations, based on what it can determine regarding its network environment.

TIP

Using the Location submenu from the Apple menu, you can switch between locations that you've configured through the Network preferences pane.

Connecting to a VPN

Your office might tell you it has a virtual private network (VPN) to which you may connect. A VPN is a collection of cooperating software that simulates a situation in which your machine is directly wired into some remote network via an unbroken cable. Additionally, the traffic on this virtual wire is encrypted, protecting it against prying eyes. Only machines that are also members of this virtual (and private) network can talk to the services provided on this network.

To connect to a VPN, use the Internet Connect application. Internet Connect allows you to connect to PPTP (Point-to-Point Tunneling Protocol)–type VPNs, which include VPNs served by Mac OS X Server, Microsoft Windows XP/2000, and to L2TP (Layer 2 Tunneling Protocol) over IPSec (IP Security Protocol), which is supported by Linux, Microsoft operating systems, and hardware VPNs by companies such as Cisco. Setting up your Mac OS X machine as a member of a VPN network is almost anticlimactically simple. Almost all the configuration is handled on the server side, so as a client, you've little to do other than fill in a few pieces of information in a dialog and a VPN connection is installed automatically. You can also set up and save multiple VPN configurations. Figure 7.17 shows the connection dialog for setting up a VPN connection. You can also edit the configuration as needed.

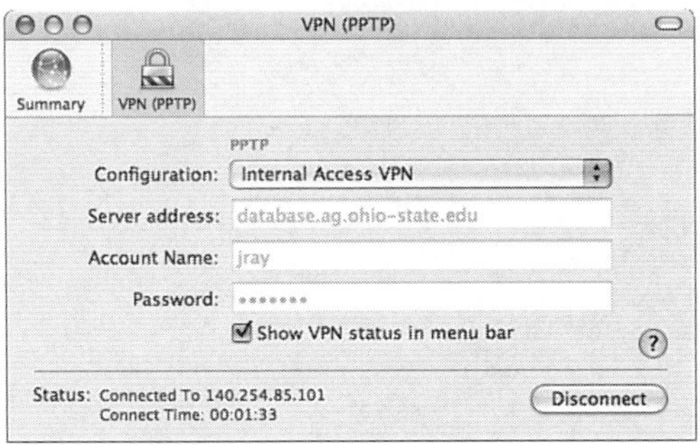

FIGURE 7.17 Setting up a VPN in the Internet Connect application.

Additionally, you can choose to show VPN status in the menu bar. From the menu bar, you can connect or disconnect, choose to show time connected, choose to show status while connected, and open Internet Connect.

After you have configured a VPN, its configuration is added to the Network preferences pane. Figure 7.18 shows the Network Status subpane with a VPN interface included.

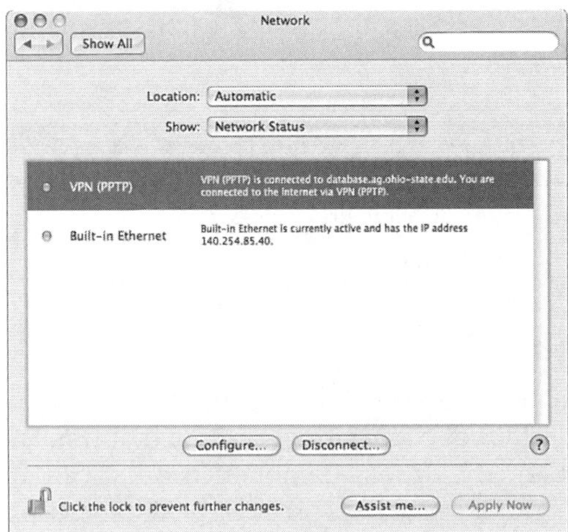

FIGURE 7.18 The VPN interface is now included in the Network preferences pane.

Sharing a Single Internet Connection with Multiple Computers

If you have multiple computers on which you want to be able to access the Internet, and only one convenient connection to the Internet itself, you can now easily configure Mac OS X to share the connection it has to the Internet with other machines connected to it on other interfaces. Yet again, more sophisticated options are available at the command line, but being able to just click a button and turn your machine into an AirPort base station or allow all your local machines to communicate with the Internet through your modem is wonderfully convenient.

Figure 7.19 shows the Internet subpane of the Sharing preferences pane. Clicking the Start button enables a number of things under Mac OS X's hood and makes useful automatic configuration choices based on the rest of your Network preferences. When enabled, Internet connection sharing allows any computers connected to this one to use this machine's primary connection to connect to the Internet. If your primary connection is via AirPort, any machines connected to this one via ethernet can connect to the Internet by using this machine's AirPort connection. If your primary connection is an ethernet connection, your machine becomes an AirPort base station, and shares its connection to others using AirPort, as well as allowing others on the same ethernet network to connect through it. You can configure typical AirPort base station options, such as the name, a password, whether to enable WEP (Wired Equivalent Privacy) encryption, and, if enabled, whether to use 40-bit or 128-bit encryption. If your connection is a modem, your machine becomes an AirPort base station, as well as shares the modem connection through the ethernet.

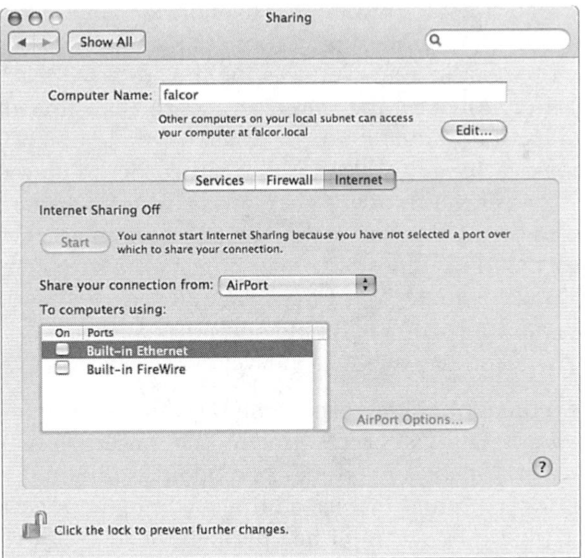

FIGURE 7.19 Sharing your network connection has never been easier.

CAUTION

You have limited configuration options here. You can't enable or disable DHCP services for the shared connection, and you can't configure what interfaces you want to allow sharing on or through. DHCP runs by default when you enable Internet connection sharing, and DHCP IP-address service is provided on any interfaces where your machine hasn't made a DHCP connection itself. This can cause problems if you're using a fixed IP address on a network on which there is also a DHCP server providing addresses for transient clients. Enabling connection sharing when using such a network causes your machine to become a DHCP server to the network, and in doing so, to compete with the legitimate DHCP server. This can cause confusing results and possible network errors.

Using the Built-in Tiger Firewall

A firewall is something interposed between the stuff that's important and the stuff that's dangerous. In a vehicle, this is the bit of the car that separates the passenger compartment from the engine, protecting the riders from dangers that might occur under the hood. In the world of computers, the firewall sits between the outside network and network services on your computer to protect the computer from network-based attacks. Not that long ago, firewalls were seldom seen, annoying things that got in your way, hindered your work, and generally annoyed everyone, including the seemingly dictatorial network administrators who imposed them on their users. Now, everyone wants one.

The most effective firewalls are completely separate devices, physically separating the protected network from the exterior network and its dangers. Much less expensive, and somewhat less effective, is firewall software that lives on the same machine it's protecting. Although a hardware firewall can interrupt network traffic upstream of the protected computer and prevent the traffic from ever reaching the protected machines, a software firewall must transparently intercept traffic as it reaches the machine, determine whether to accept it, and then hand it to the service for which it was destined. This method doesn't prevent the traffic from reaching the machine, but rather tries to prevent the traffic from reaching the services it was headed for. It's not always a successful way of trying to do things, as demonstrated by the fact that there have been a number of commercial software firewalls for a certain other operating system that provide less than complete protection. The firewall software running under Mac OS X's Firewall pane (ipfirewall, sometimes called *ipfw*) is well respected, however. Although not conceptually as secure as a separate firewall device, it's quite powerful and provides a good level of protection.

As with many of the more powerful aspects of the Unix underpinnings of Mac OS X, the GUI interface to the firewall provides access to only the simplest functionality of the software. The ipfw software is capable of considerable sophistication in its control of your network connection, but it requires manual editing of configuration files. More sophisticated configuration than can be accomplished through the GUI is covered in Chapter 28, "Implementing Server and Advanced Network Configuration."

Under the Firewall subpane of the Sharing preferences pane, shown in Figure 7.20, you can enable Mac OS X's built-in firewall software and perform simple configuration and control. You can't actually select the check boxes for services that are enabled/enabled via the Services subpane—they're automatically checked if you enable the service.

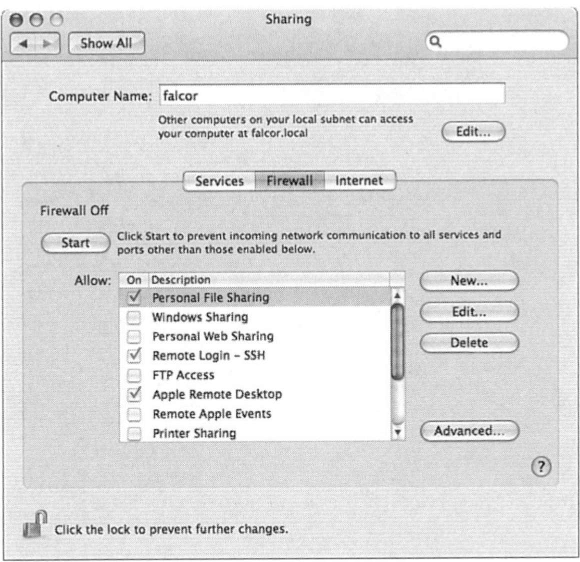

FIGURE 7.20 The Firewall subpane of the Sharing preferences pane.

Click the Start (or Stop) button to enable (or disable) the firewall. If the firewall is disabled, all services on your machine are on their own as far as network security goes, and all ports on your machine can be reached from the network. When enabled, the firewall prevents network clients from accessing any port that it isn't explicitly configured to allow. This can protect your machine against compromise by malicious software that might open a port and allow access without your knowledge (again, much more sophisticated configuration is possible from the command line). The check boxes shown in the scrolling list activate and disable access for certain services or port ranges. Those for known services enabled through the Services subpane, however, are automatically checked when the service is enabled and unchecked when the service is disabled, and cannot be edited through the Firewall subpane. These entries for known services also cannot be edited.

If you click the New button, you are presented with a dialog like that shown in Figure 7.21. This is where you can configure other services that you want the firewall to allow connections to. Select either a known service-type entry from the shown pop-up list, or the Other entry to configure for unknown services. The dialog automatically fills in the port or port range for known services in the list. For the Other entry, you fill in the applicable port(s) and a description of the service, which is the name that will be used when it is added to the list in the subpane.

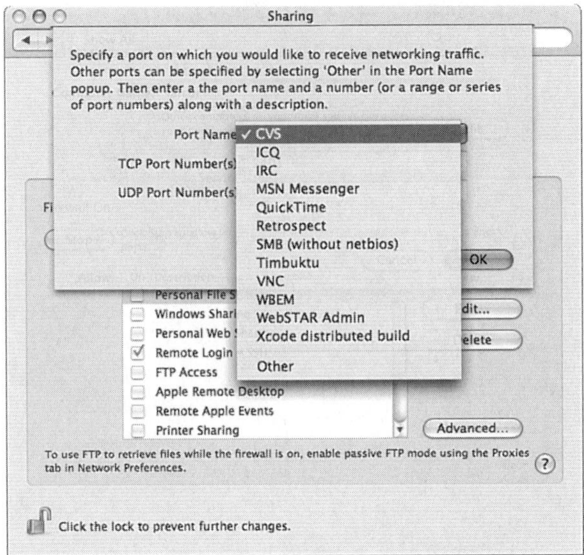

FIGURE 7.21 Adding a new service to those passed by the firewall.

> **NOTE**
>
> Remember, if you've enabled the firewall and haven't added an entry to pass traffic for a network client type, that traffic will be blocked by the firewall and the client might not work. Put another way, if you're trying to use a new network client and it's not working, check whether your firewall is enabled!

The Firewall subpane includes an Advanced options section. In that section, which is shown in Figure 7.22, you can choose to block UDP (User Datagram Protocol) traffic, enable firewall logging, and enable stealth mode, which ensures that traffic to your machine does not even receive notification that your machine exists. You can also open the log, which is located in `/var/log/ipfw.log`, through the Advanced options section. The five-digit number that you will notice with much of the activity is the rule number that the firewall enforced.

The built-in firewall can protect your machine from incoming connections, but if you are also interested in protecting your machine from outgoing connections, you might take a look at a commercial package called Little Snitch, available at `http://www.obdev.at/products/littlesnitch/index.html`. Little Snitch notifies you whenever an application tries to make an outgoing connection. You can then allow or deny the connection, or create a rule for Little Snitch to follow the next time. An application such as this can assist in protecting your machine from downloading harmful software such as trojans and worms.

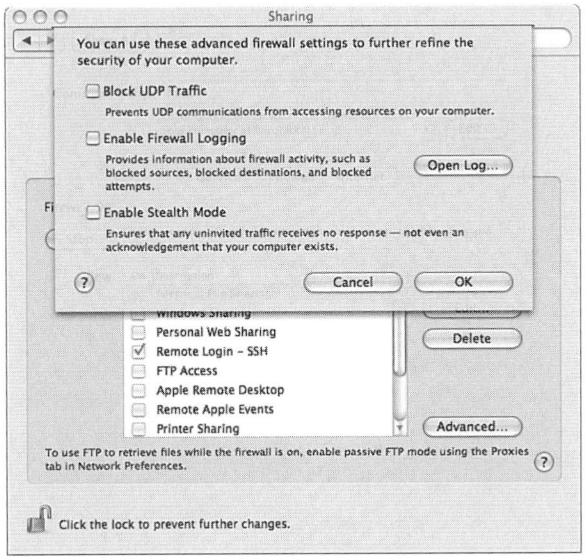

FIGURE 7.22 Advanced options for the firewall.

Summary

Linux and Unix operating systems have a history of being difficult to configure for online use. Users must often understand the complexities of TCP/IP to correctly set up their devices. Mac OS X puts a clean, user-friendly interface on network setup and enables the user to get online without ever seeing a command line.

This chapter covered the Mac OS X network configuration utilities and how they can be used to create a connection through modem, ethernet, and wireless interfaces. Macintosh users are accustomed to quickly and easily finding and connecting to network resources. Although the interface has changed, the process is just as easy as it has always been.

In addition to network setup, we covered enabling sharing your internet connection through the Sharing preferences pane and protecting your information with Apple's firewall. Macintosh networking has never had a more solid and stable base than it does in Mac OS X.

CHAPTER 8

Customizing User and System Settings

IN THIS CHAPTER

- Creating Multiple User Accounts: Accounts
- Applying Account Security: Security
- Setting International Options
- Configuring Voice and Accessibility Options: Speech and Universal Access
- Setting System Time and Date
- Using Spotlight to Search System Preferences

Mac users wouldn't be happy without the ability to customize their systems. Although Mac OS X is a secure multiuser operating system, it gives individuals a great deal of freedom to customize their settings. Even though some restrictions might initially seem odd to users more familiar with a single-user OS, in some ways, Mac OS X users have considerably more freedom than was available in the past. As in versions of the Mac OS before Mac OS X, different desktop backgrounds, screen savers, color profiles, and even speech recognition settings can be customized. However, with Mac OS X, these settings can be customized on a per-user basis so that from any individual's point of view, the machine appears to be configured to exactly his favorite state.

As in previous versions of the Mac OS, a large portion of a user's personalization of his environment is stored in preference files. Under Mac OS X, these files are stored in the user's home directory, which enables each user to personalize his own settings. This also provides a very useful service in allowing those customizations to be shared across multiple machines, although the details of this are a topic for a later chapter. The notion of control panels has given way to the Mac OS X System Preferences panel, but the idea is still very much the same. Using System Preferences, users can choose an individual panel to change a series of related configuration options. Unlike previous versions of Mac OS, however, some user settings and preferences are stored in a network-accessible database. This database (NetInfo) enables certain user settings to be more easily shared among groups of machines.

This chapter covers the available System Preferences panels, as well as an introduction to the NetInfo database. You learn how to interact with the NetInfo database, how System Preferences controls work, and what they change on your system. If you want to fine-tune any areas of the operating system, this is the first place to look.

Creating Multiple User Accounts: Accounts

In this section, we touch on some of the basics involved in user account creation. First we will take a look at the multi-user system nature of Mac OS X, and then we will look at adding a user, setting user limitations, enabling fast user switching, understanding administrative user capabilities, and removing users.

Introduction to Multiuser Systems

Mac OS X is a Unix-based operating system. As such, it's a multiuser operating system; that is, everyone who uses the machine may do so by having an account on the machine. A user can use his account on the machine either at the console or via a network connection—if you choose to enable remote login from the sharing pane of System Preferences, which we discuss in further detail in Chapter 21, "Accessing and Controlling Tiger Remotely."

A particularly nice feature of a multiuser system is that multiple users can use the machine at the same time. While each user is using the system, it seems to each user as if he's the only user on the system.

Each user has a home directory where he stores his files. In Mac OS X, the users' home directories are located in the `/Users` directory. Figure 8.1 shows the `/Users` directory on a sample Mac OS X client.

> **NOTE**
>
> Although the text of this book often shows directories using their full pathname (such as `/Users`), the Mac OS X Finder shows only the name of the directory at the end of the path. In the case of `/Users`, this would simply be Users. The shortening of pathnames isn't critical, but to successfully interact with the system, it's important to understand how the Mac OS X directory structure looks and works.

When a user logs in to the system, the default area where he is logged in is his home directory; hence, the use of the house as an icon in the Finder window. Additionally, you see the same icon in Figure 8.1 among the user directories. Users can still see most areas on the machine, although they might not necessarily be able to see all of another user's files. In a multiuser system, users can set permissions on their files to allow different types of access. Even if other users can see your files, they can't modify them unless you've set permissions to allow them to do so. For example, Figure 8.2 shows how the home directory for user `nermal` looks to another user. A number of folders have a white minus in a red circle on them. Directories so marked aren't viewable by this user. The other files and directories, however, can be viewed by this user.

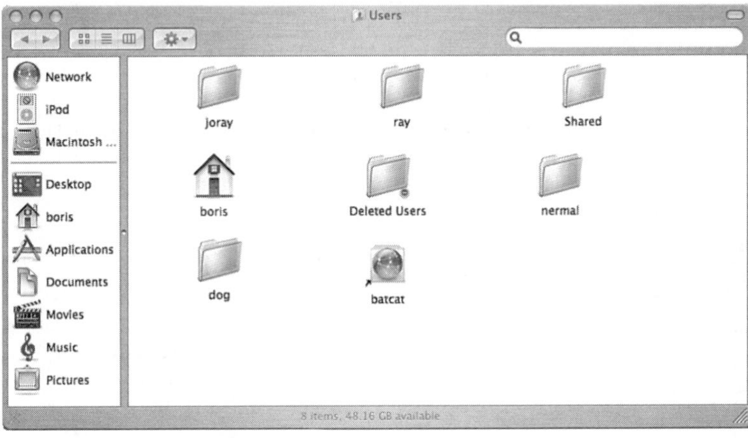

FIGURE 8.1 You can get to the `/Users` directory by clicking on your OS X drive in your finder view and opening the Users folder.

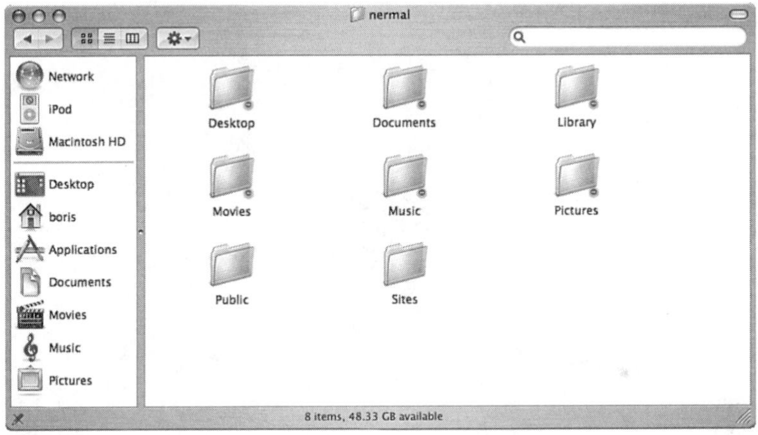

FIGURE 8.2 Depending on how the owner grants permissions on his files and directories, other users might not be able to view them.

Adding a New User

When you install Mac OS X, you're asked to provide your name and a short name that can be used as your login name. During the installation process, you create an account. Specifically, you create an administrator account. Adding another user account is much like creating the original administrator account that you create at installation time.

Because it can be used to modify the machine settings or install software, the administrator account is a rather powerful account. When you add a new user, you have the choice of adding a regular user or adding one with administrator capabilities. Although it's helpful to have more than one user with administrator capabilities, don't give administrator access to every user account that you create. Otherwise, every user on the machine can modify your system.

You create a new user account using the Accounts pane in the System section of System Preferences as follows:

1. Open the Accounts pane in System Preferences.
2. Click the make changes lock icon if it's set not to allow changes, and enter your administrator username and password. Click the plus sign in the lower left. This adds a user in the Other Accounts section along the left whose privileges are automatically listed as Standard. Figure 8.3 shows the Accounts pane as it appears before starting to add a new user.

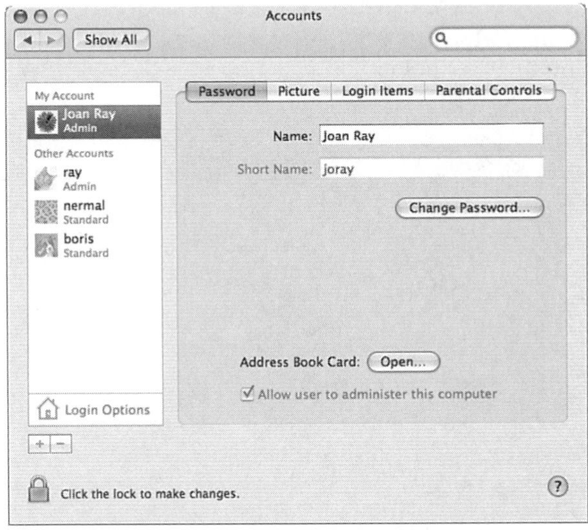

FIGURE 8.3 The Accounts pane, where you can create and delete users, or edit user information.

The first section for adding a new user, the Password section, shown in Figure 8.4, has the following fields:

- Name—This is where you enter your user's name. In Mac OS X, this is a name that the user can use to log in to the machine.
- Short Name—The short name is the username; that is, the name of the account. This is also a name that the user can use to log in to the machine. This name can be up to eight characters in length, must have no spaces, and must be in lowercase letters. This name is used by some of the network services.
- Password—The password should be at least four characters. Many systems recommend at least six characters with a variety of character types included in the password. If you're feeling uninspired on passwords, new with Tiger is the little key

button associated with this field. You can use this to have the system generate a new password for you. Clicking this button brings up the Password Assistant, which allows you to select the type of password, from choices such as Memorable and Random, and you can select a password length on a slider. The assistant generates a selection of passwords for you. Using the Password Assistant can be especially useful if you have to create a lot of user accounts. You could also use the assistant to get feedback on the quality of the password that you are thinking about manually assigning.

- Verify—This is where you re-enter the password for verification purposes.
- Password Hint—This is an optional field. The password hint is displayed if the user enters an incorrect password three times. If you include a hint, make sure that the hint is not so obvious that other users can guess the password.

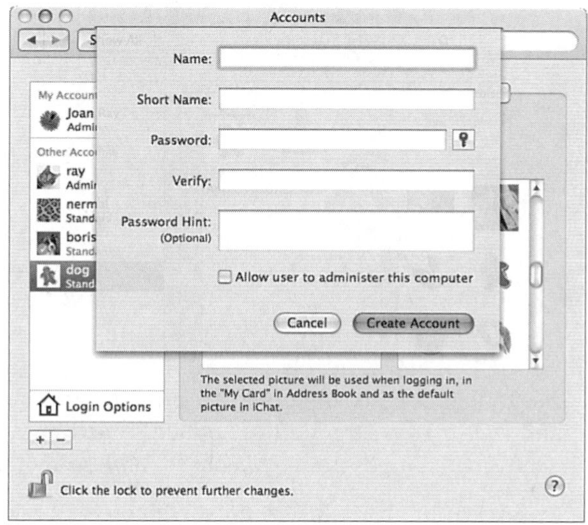

FIGURE 8.4 Complete the fields in this sheet to start to create a new user.

When you have entered the information for the new user, the pane returns to the Password section, where you can now see the name and short name of your new user. Here you can also reset the password and choose to allow this user to administer the computer.

Continue to the next section, Picture. When you complete the Password section and continue to another section, your new user's identification as shown in the left column is updated to include the user's name. In Chapter 20, "Configuring Advanced Multiuser/Multisystem Cooperation Features," you learn how to create a specific user called `software` with a specific user ID and group ID.

The Picture section, shown in Figure 8.5, is where you select a picture for the new user. This picture is used in the login window, in the My Card in the Address Book, and as the default iChat picture. Either select one of the default images, choose a custom picture elsewhere on your machine, or choose to take a video snapshot by selecting Edit.

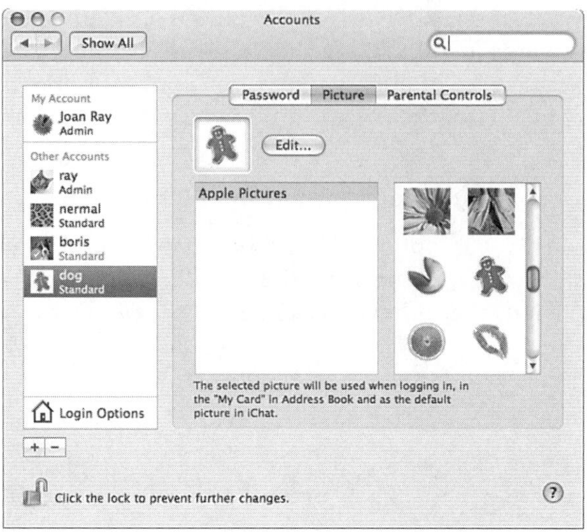

FIGURE 8.5 Select a picture for the new user in the Picture section.

Setting User Limitations

For standard users, there is quite an extensive set of user limitations that you can apply. They are available under the Parental Controls section of the Accounts pane, shown in Figure 8.6. The categories to which you can apply user limitations are Mail, Finder & System, iChat, Safari, and Dictionary. After you've applied some limitations, the description for the user in the left side changes from *Standard* to *Managed*.

Under the Mail category, shown in Figure 8.7, you list which email addresses are acceptable for this user to communicate with, and you have the option of having permission emails emailed to a specified address.

The Finder & System category, shown in Figure 8.8, is similar to the Limitations section of Mac OS X 10.3. In this section you set the user to Some Limits or Simple Finder. Some Limits, shown in Figure 8.8, enables you to specify whether the user can open all of System Preferences, modify the Dock, change his password (this becomes available if you choose to allow the user to open all system preferences), burn CDs and DVDs, administer printers, or allow supporting programs. Additionally, the user can be restricted to use only certain applications. The Simple Finder option restricts the user to a simplified dock and allows him to use only those applications showing in the My Applications folder in the Dock. Figure 8.9 shows a sample desktop for a user who has been restricted to the Simple Finder.

FIGURE 8.6 Set user limitations in the Parental Controls section.

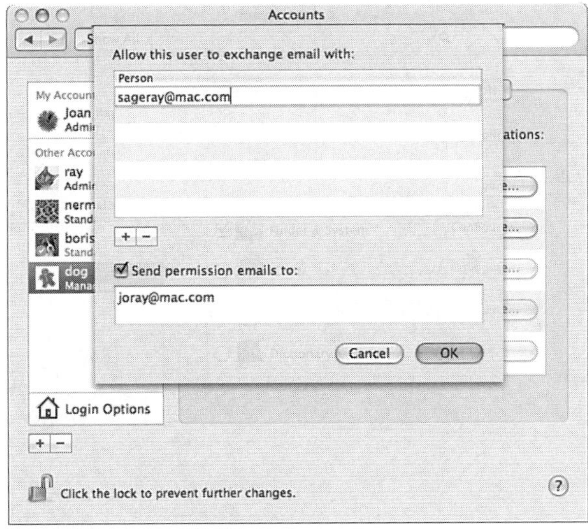

FIGURE 8.7 List acceptable email addresses to which the user can communicate.

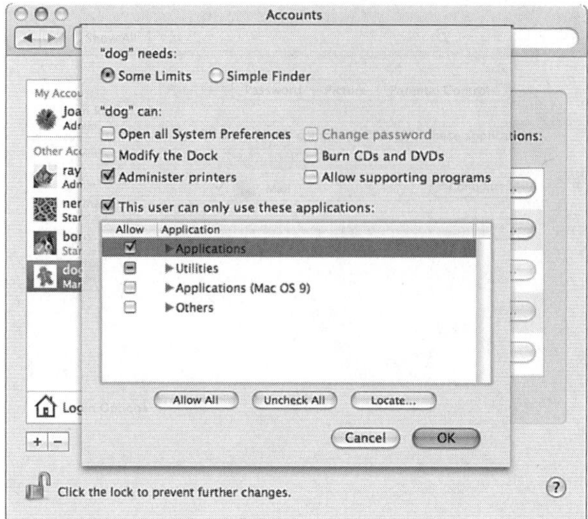

FIGURE 8.8 The Finder & System category of limitations.

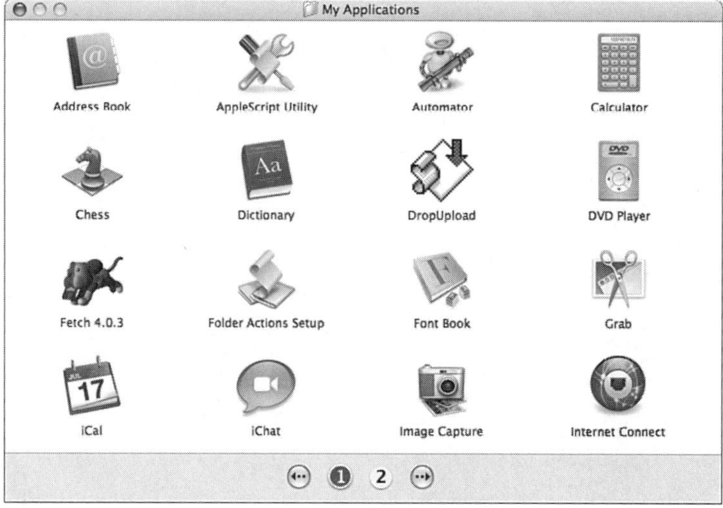

FIGURE 8.9 Desktop of a user restricted to the Simple Finder.

Under the iChat category, you list acceptable names and AIM addresses that the user may communicate with. The interface for this category looks much like that for the Mail category. If you turn on the Safari limitation, the pane tells you to log in as the user to add acceptable Safari sites that the user may visit. Log in as that user and browse the acceptable sites. Safari will ask for your administrator username and password when you visit the sites. By default, though, some sites, such as Apple's, CNN's, and eBay's are considered acceptable. If you select the Dictionary category, the Configure changes to Info, which tells you that the user is prevented from viewing certain words, such as profanity.

Enabling Fast User Switching and Other Login Options

Under the Login Options section of the Accounts pane, shown in Figure 8.10, you can choose to enable fast user switching. Fast user switching allows multiple users to be logged in to the console at the same time. This can be particularly useful in a family environment because it allows everyone to be able to use the computer at the console, even if someone is logged in but not there. When you enable fast user switching, you can choose to have the users for the machine displayed by name, short name, or icon. When fast user switching is enabled, the menu bar includes, in whatever way you specified, a login window menu item. Both in the pull-down menu and the login window of the machine, users who are logged in are shown with a checkmark. Users who are logged in are also shown with a checkmark in the Accounts pane. You cannot make changes for users who are currently logged in at the console.

There are some drawbacks to fast user switching. You might experience some resource conflicts. For example, one user could be using the digital camera, so the other users will not be able to access the digital camera during that time. Additionally, some applications might not let multiple users at the console use them.

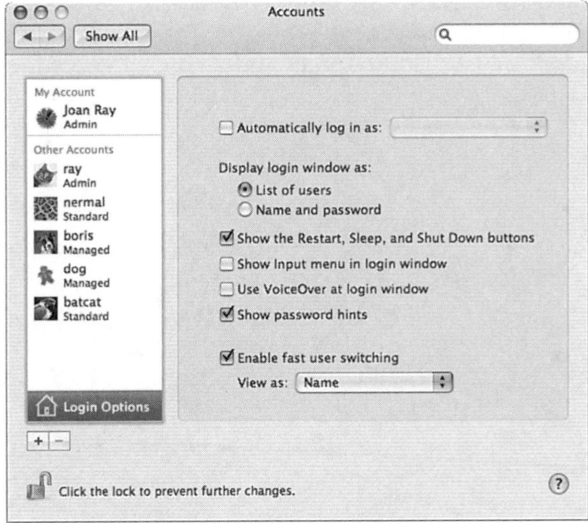

FIGURE 8.10 Fast user switching can be enabled under the Login Options section as well as the behavior of the login window.

In addition to enabling fast user switching, you can specify who to automatically log in as, or you can disable automatic login. This option is not recommended if your machine is truly serving as a multiuser machine because anyone can easily modify the automatically logged-in account without having to know anything about the username or password for the account. You can also select whether the login window displays a list of users or displays just the name and password fields to be filled in by the user when she logs in. In this section, you can choose to hide the Sleep, Restart, and Shut Down buttons. If your machine is serving as a multiuser machine, especially in a public location, this option is recommended. This provides you a little more control over the machine's uptime, but does not prevent anyone from turning the machine off at the power button.

Additionally, you can specify whether to use the Input menu at login, use VoiceOver at login, or to show password hints. The Show Input Menu at Login option shows the keyboard section of the Input menu. The Input menu was covered in Chapter 6, "Printer, Fax, and Font Management." We will cover VoiceOver later in this chapter. If you choose to show password hints, a user who has a password hint will be shown his password hint after three unsuccessful login attempts.

Note that the login window also displays the hostname. You can click on this and rotate though a series of information about the machine that includes hostname, operating system version, operating system build, serial number, and date.

Login Items

Unless a user has been denied access to the Accounts pane in one way or another, that user can access the Password and Login Items sections. When you are creating accounts, there is not a Login Items section for the different users. Each individual user has access to his own Login Items section when he is logged in. For example, the administrator has a Login Items for himself, but he cannot make those adjustments for the user whose account he is creating.

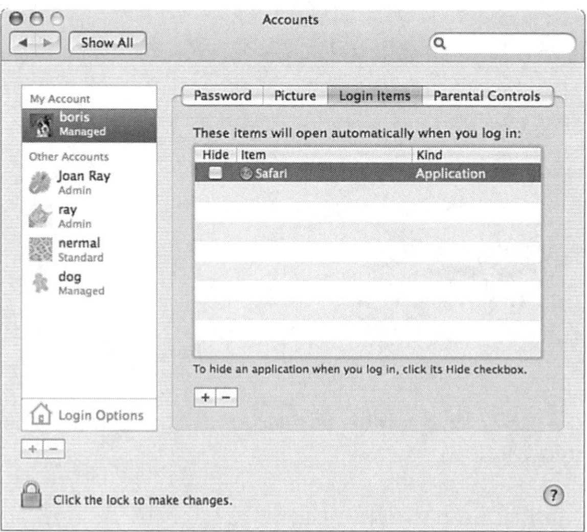

FIGURE 8.11 Under the Login Items section, list any applications that you would like to automatically start when you log in.

Understanding Administrative User Capabilities

The first account that is created on your machine is an administrative account. In the Accounts pane, under the Password section, you can turn any existing user into an administrative user by checking the box to allow the user to administer the computer. It is often useful to have at least one administrative user in addition to the first administrative user, but you do not want to give administrator capabilities to all of your users. Why is this?

An administrative user can do anything on your machine. Only an administrative user can adjust system settings in Security, Energy Saver, Printer & Fax, Network, Sharing, Accounts, Date & Time, Software Update, and Startup Disk. These are just some of the places where an administrator has the authority to make changes.

Administrators also belong to the group called `admin`. Users in this group are also allowed to execute the `sudo` command, which allows them to run commands as `root`, the most powerful user on the system. More information on `sudo` and `root` is included in Chapter 20.

You must trust any user to whom you give administrator access. An administrator can not only adjust your system settings and fix a broken system—an administrator can also accidentally wipe out your system.

Removing User Accounts

To remove a user account, open the Accounts preferences pane, unlock it, select the user whose account should be removed, and click the minus sign that appears beneath the list of users. A dialog then appears, asking how you want to handle deleting the account. You can choose to delete the account immediately, archive the account and delete it, or cancel the action. Click Delete Immediately to delete the account without saving its contents. Click OK to archive the contents of the account before deleting it.

When you choose the option to archive the contents of the account, user information for the account is removed from the system, but the actual contents of the account are saved as a disk image in the `/Users/Deleted Users` directory. If you need to access the files that were in the account, go to that directory and mount the user's disk image. Only administrators have access to the Deleted Users folder.

Applying Account Security: Security

As you might expect, in the Security preferences pane, shown in Figure 8.12, you can configure a number of options regarding system security. You can specify whether a password is required to wake up from sleep or screen saver. If you are running a truly multi-user machine, or if your machine is located in a rather public place, this option is recommended. For all accounts, you can also disable automatic login, require a password to unlock each secure system preference, require that a user be logged out after a specified period of inactivity, or use secure virtual memory. *Secure virtual memory* is a mechanism by which the system encrypts the virtual memory being used by the applications you are running. Finally, you can enable FileVault protection in this pane.

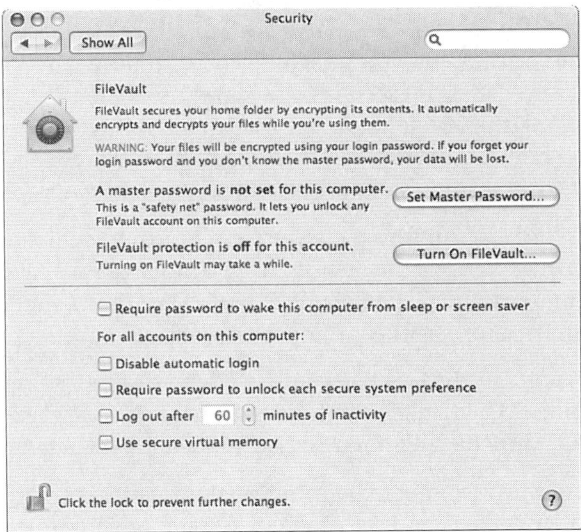

FIGURE 8.12 In the Security pane, you can turn on FileVault protection and set other basic security preferences.

FileVault Protection

FileVault protection is a means by which users can encrypt their home directory data using their login password. Using FileVault protection allows a user to protect her files from anyone on the system, including administrative users. Under the FileVault protection system, a user's home directory is stored as an encrypted disk image. When the user logs in, her home directory is decrypted and mounted in the `/Users` directory. When the user logs out, her home directory is unmounted and again stored as an encrypted disk image. To use FileVault protection, the system must have at least as much free disk space as the size of the user's home directory; otherwise, the conversion cannot take place.

When a FileVault-protected user is logged in, her account looks to other users like an aliased network account, as shown in Figure 8.1. The `batcat` user is a FileVault user who is currently logged in. When you click on that account, the system says that it can't find the source of the alias, even for an administrator. However, via `sudo`, the administrator can see the contents of the directory of a logged-in FileVault user. When the user is not logged in, her home directory looks like a normal folder to other users, and the contents look like an encrypted disk image. There does not appear to be a convenient way for a FileVault user to use her account remotely.

Enabling FileVault Encryption

To enable FileVault encryption, an administrative user has to set the master password for the system. A master password is required so that if a user forgets his password, an administrative user can use the master password to reset that user's password. After the master password has been set, a user will need the administrator to help with the process. When you turn on FileVault, the system asks for an administrator user and password to unlock the Security preferences pane. The user then has to enter his password to start the FileVault encryption, and indicate that he really wants to enable it. While the encryption takes place, the user is logged out. No other users can be logged in at the console at the time. When the user logs back in, his home directory icon is replaced by a FileVault icon.

Disabling FileVault Encryption

The process for disabling FileVault protection is much like the process for enabling it. The user will again need the assistance of an administrator. When the option to Turn Off FileVault is clicked, the system asks for an administrator username and password to unlock the Security preferences pane. The user then enters his own password, and tells the system that he really wants to disable FileVault. The user is logged off while the decryption occurs. No other users can be logged in at the console while this takes place.

Overriding Encryption with the Master Password

For enabling FileVault on a given system, the administrator must provide a master password. This master password can assist with password issues for a FileVault protected account.

If a user forgets his password, the administrator can assist in resetting that user's password by using the master password. The user tries to log in. After three unsuccessful attempts, the login window displays the user's password hint. If the password hint doesn't help, the system requests the master password. If the user does not have a password hint, the system goes continues directly on to the request for the master password. After that has been entered, the login window forces a password change. The user changes his password and finishes the login process.

If a user already knows her password and would like to change it, she can do so in the Password section of the Accounts pane. However, if the user would like to have the administrator reset her password, the administrator cannot do so from within the Accounts pane. The administrator must attempt to log in as the user and then reset the password after the master password has been given.

If you need to delete a FileVault-protected account but archive it, the account is archived with the password of the user account. If the account contains sensitive material that must remain encrypted, make sure that you reset the password for the account via the master password mechanism before you delete and archive the account. If the account does not contain sensitive material, but does contain material that your organization might need, reset the password for the account and then disable FileVault before deleting the account.

If you need to change the master password, you can do so by using the Change option under the FileVault section. The system will ask for the old password, the new password, verification of the new password, and a hint for it.

If the administrator has forgotten the master password, reset it by deleting `/Library/Keychains/FileVaultMaster.keychain` and creating a new master password in the FileVault section. Changing the master password can have repercussions that might cause you to have to reset the passwords of the FileVault-protected accounts, but so far we have not experienced such a situation.

Setting International Options

Settings involving language, date format, keyboard layouts, and so on are set in the International pane. The Input menu was discussed in Chapter 6. In this section we will look at the Language and Formats sections.

Setting User Languages

In the Language section of the International pane, shown in Figure 8.13, you can set your preferred order for languages used in applications menus, dragging, and sorting. Just drag the languages around until you've achieved the desired order. If not all the languages you want to rank are shown, click the Edit List button to edit the language listing. Select the languages of interest and then rank their order.

For example, if you list French as the preferred language, you will see your system menus in French, but your Word application might use English, if you installed the English edition.

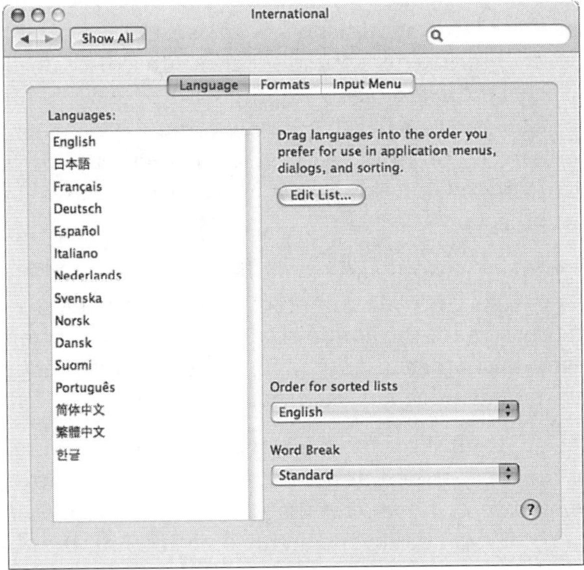

FIGURE 8.13 The preferred language order for application menus and dialogs is set in the Language section of the International pane.

Modifying Date, Time, and Monetary Formats

The Formats section enables you to set preferences involving dates, times, and numbers displays. First select a region. Some regions will display a note that they are available only in Unicode applications. This sets defaults for the Dates, Times, and Numbers categories. The short, medium, long and full date format can be further customized in the Date section under Customize. You can set such items as the date separator, whether to use a leading zero, and the preferred order of month, day, and year. Just drag the elements around, select what you would like for each element, and type separator characters to create whatever you would like to see here. This section also includes a calendar section. The calendar options are Gregorian, Buddhist, Hebrew, Islamic, Islamic Civil, and Japanese. This is a way for you students of Japanese language to learn what the date is in the Japanese calendar. In the Times section, you can customize such items as whether to use a 12-hour or a 24-hour clock, the separator, and whether to use a leading zero for the hour for the short, medium, long, and full formats using the same drag and text entry method as is used for the date. How the numbers appear in the Numbers section is guided by the base region you select. In the Currency section, select something suitable if the default is not what you want. Finally, you can select either English or metric measurement units. Figure 8.14 shows the Formats section set for the defaults for the Austria (German) region. This particular region was accessed by checking the Show All Regions box and selecting the region.

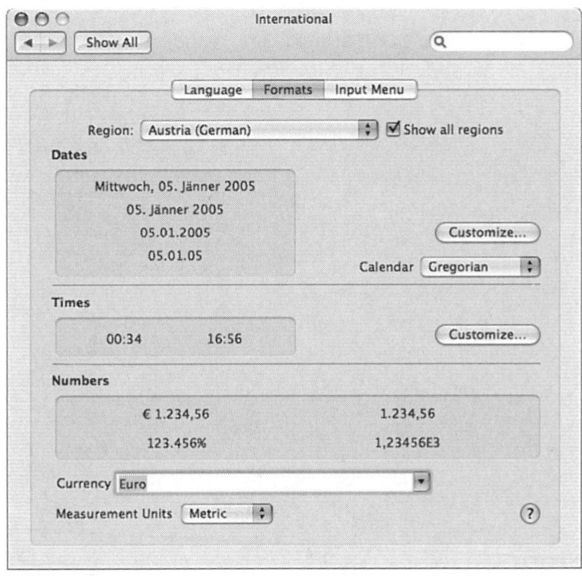

FIGURE 8.14 The Formats section of the International pane is where you set your preferences for dates, times, and numbers displays.

Configuring Voice and Accessibility Options: Speech and Universal Access

By using the Speech and Universal Access panes, you can configure your system to be more accessible to any needs you have. With the Speech pane, you can configure the voice recognition system, which can be used to assist you in controlling your computer by letting you speak commands to it. The Universal Access pane provides access to a variety of ways to configure your machine to be more usefully accessible to you.

Using Voice Recognition

The voice recognition system is controlled by the Speech preferences pane, which itself has a Speech Recognition section and a Text to Speech section. The Speech Recognition section is further divided into the Settings and Commands subsections. Available to both sections is the capability to turn speakable items on or off. This turns the voice recognition system on or off.

In the Settings section, shown in Figure 8.15, you set which microphone the system should use. If the system has trouble recognizing your commands, you might try the Calibrate option. Under this option, you speak a phrase and adjust a slider until the phrase flashes. Repeat this for all the phrases. Additionally, you can set your listening key either to the default key, Escape, or as a key combination out of the set listed in the configuration sheet. You also select your listening method, which can be to listen only when the listening key is pressed or to listen continuously with keyword. You can set the keyword to be optional, a requirement before each command, required 15 seconds after the last command, or required 30 seconds after the last command. Finally, you can select how the system acknowledges your command. It can respond by playing a sound or by speaking a command acknowledgement and playing a sound.

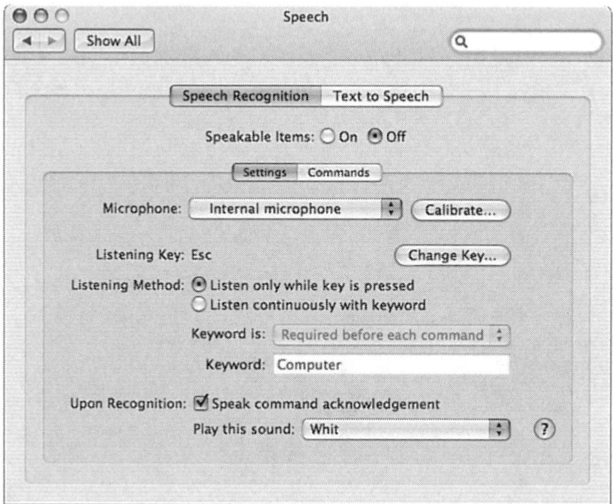

FIGURE 8.15 The Settings subsection of the Speech Recognition section of the Speech pane.

In the Commands section of the Speech Recognition section, shown in Figure 8.16, you can select which commands are available when Speakable Items is by selecting command sets. Available command sets currently are Address Book, Global Speakable Items, Application Specific Items, Application Switching, Front Window, and Menu Bar. Each set may also include a configure option. The Address Book set provides access to names contained in your address book, and the configure option allows you to set which names are speakable. The Global Speakable Items provides access to commands that may be spoken in any application, and the configure option allows you to choose whether exact wording is required for the speakable items. The Application Specific Items set allows you to access commands that may be spoken when an application is in the front, but there is no configure option at this time. The Application Switching set allows you to switch between running applications or to launch a recently run application, and does not have a configure option at this time. The Front Window set allows you to speak front window controls, such as push button names and radio names. This command set does not have a configure option at this time. The Menu Bar set enables you to speak names of any menu or menu item, and also does not have a configure option at this time.

In this section you can also open the Speakable Items folder, and see some tips with the Helpful Tips option. The Helpful Tips option displays the set of tips that is displayed when you first turn on speech recognition.

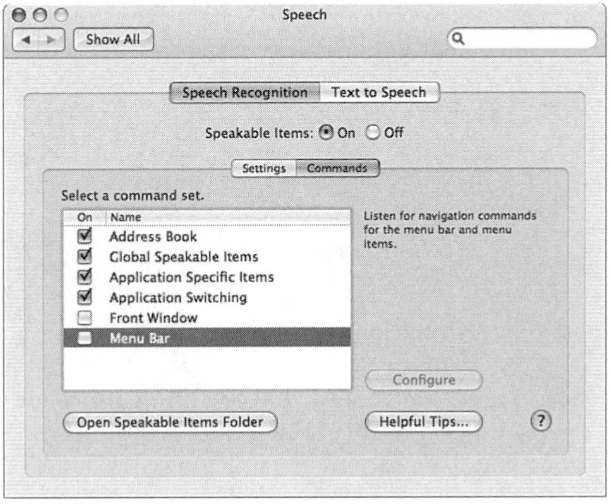

FIGURE 8.16 The Commands subsection of the Speech Recognition section.

The other main section of the Speech pane is the Text to Speech section, shown in Figure 8.17. In this section, you select the voice the speech recognition system should use and set its speaking rate. You can also test voices and rates here. Additionally, you can choose to have announcements made when there are alerts or when an application requires your attention. Under the Alert Options section, you can further customize how you want your announcement. You can choose to have the system speak selected text to you and set a key combination to trigger the action. Finally, you can access the Date & Time pane to have the clock announce the time, and you can access the Universal Access pane to change VoiceOver settings.

When you turn on voice recognition, the Speech Feedback window appears. It is a small round window. While you're speaking, the microphone image changes and the horizontal lines, which start as gray lines, display the microphone level, and the feedback on what key to press or phrase to speak to cause the computer to listen disappears. The bottom line is a blue color. The next two lines are green and the top line is red. The Helpful Hints recommends that you try to speak in the green levels. The arrow at the bottom of the window has links to the Speech Commands window and the Speech Preferences pane.

You can open the Speech Commands window by either saying "Open Speech Commands window" or by clicking on the arrow. The Speech Commands window shows the commands that you may speak to the computer in the bottom portion. This is updated as you change which application you're using.

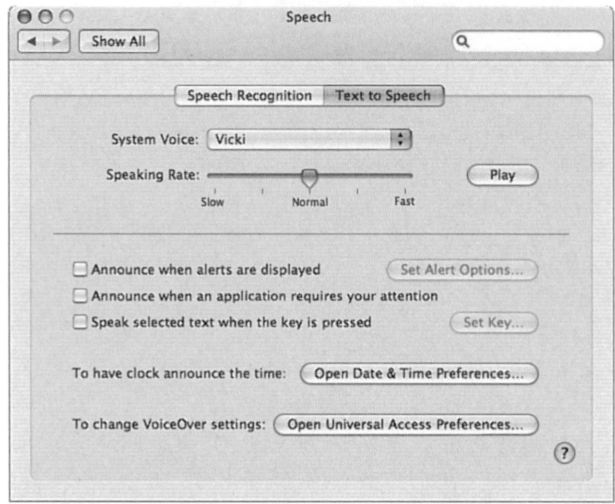

FIGURE 8.17 The Text to Speech section of the Speech pane.

Figure 8.18 shows what to expect when Speech Recognition works for you. The Speech Commands window shows not only which commands you may speak to the computer, but also which commands you have spoken so far. Figure 8.19 shows the Safari windows that were opened using the voice recognition system.

FIGURE 8.18 Speaking to the computer.

FIGURE 8.19 Here voice recognition was used to open and control Safari. Note that the Speech Commands window shows which commands have been spoken so far.

Universal Access

The Universal Access pane is where you can customize the computer to assist you with any difficulties that you have in seeing or hearing the computer, as well as set some keyboard and mouse behaviors to assist with any difficulties you experience with those devices.

All the subdivisions of the Universal Access pane include the ability to enable access for assistive devices for the Universal Access preferences pane.

Using Voiceover Navigation Features

New with Tiger is the VoiceOver system, a screen-reading system. It is especially helpful if you have difficulty reading the screen. Even if you don't have difficulty reading the screen, you might enjoy having the computer read to you. VoiceOver currently works only with English language Apple keyboards. The VoiceOver system is enabled in the Universal Access pane, and from there you can open the VoiceOver utility.

There are quite a few preferences that can be set in the VoiceOver utility. All the sections have access to the Reset option. Under the Verbosity section, you can set how verbose the system ought to be. You can set such options as what it should say when you type, if and when it should speak text under you mouse, announce when the mouse enters a window, or when a modifier key or Caps Lock key is pressed. Under the Navigation section, you can control general features about the VoiceOver cursor and its tracking. Under the Voices section, you set the default voice and its rate, pitch, and volume. You can additionally set voices for content, status, type, attributes, and VoiceOver menu. By default, they are set to the default voice. Under the Display section, you can set the size of the VoiceOver cursor and whether to show it, the degree of magnification of the VoiceOver menu, the size of the caption panel and whether to show it, the number of rows that should be in the caption panel, and captional panel transparency. The final preference section is the Pronunciation section, where you can specify how terms can be pronounced. You can add or remove terms. Fortunately, you can edit the terms that are already there, such as fixing the GIF entry.

Depending on what settings you pick for VoiceOver, when you enable it, you might find that you now have black boxes around things, and that your computer gives you a running monologue of what you're doing. The black box is the VoiceOver cursor. You can navigate around by using Ctrl+Opt and the arrow keys. As you navigate, VoiceOver will describe what you have just navigated to. In scrollable areas, tables, lists, HTML content areas, you can begin the same sort of interactive with Ctrl+Opt+Shift+Down Arrow, and you can end the interactive mode in those areas with Ctrl+Opt+Shift+Up Arrow. Then navigate interactively with Ctrl+Opt and the arrow keys.

To access the VoiceOver menu, shown in Figure 8.20, use Ctrl+Opt+F7. The VoiceOver menu can assist you in figuring out how to use VoiceOver. VoiceOver help, which you can get to using Ctrl+Opt+?, will also be useful. The figure also shows what the caption panel can look like. Figure 8.21 shows using Safari with VoiceOver enabled. The black box is the VoiceOver cursor and the gray section is the caption panel, which is detailing what VoiceOver is saying.

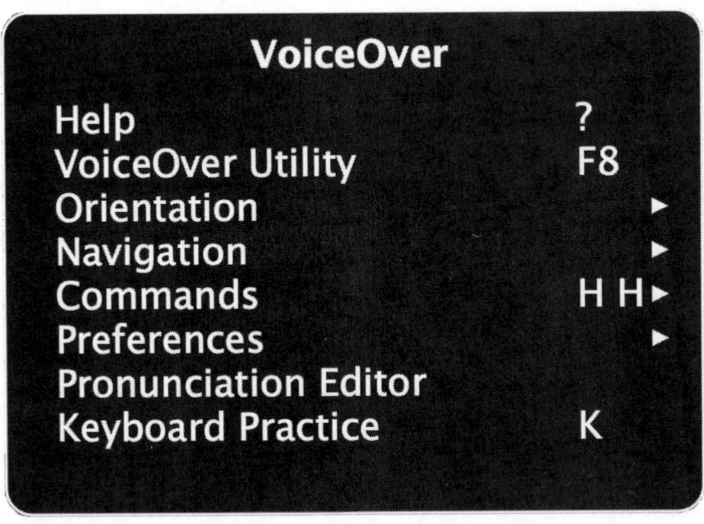

FIGURE 8.20 You can get to the VoiceOver menu with Ctrl+Opt+F7.

FIGURE 8.21 Using Safari with VoiceOver enabled.

Seeing

In the Seeing section of the Universal Access pane, shown in Figure 8.22, you can enable VoiceOver, set options for zooming in and out, or set options for the display. You can set your monitor to display white on black or to display in grayscale. The Option+Command+= combination zooms in, whereas Option+Command+- zooms out. You might find it easier to think of the zoom-in option as Option+Command++, which was the original notation that Apple used for zooming in, but please note that the + in that notation is not literally a +. The combination does not and never did require a shift to literally get the +, but was simply used to depict the key that contains the +, which is a more intuitive symbol for zooming in than the =. After you've zoomed, you can navigate.

Hearing

In the Hearing section, shown in Figure 8.23, you can set the screen to flash whenever a sound occurs. To get an idea of what to expect, you can test the behavior with the Flash Screen button. Finally, you can adjust the volume with the Adjust Sound button, which opens the Input section of the Sound pane for you.

Keyboard

In the Keyboard section, shown in Figure 8.24, you can set the Sticky Keys on or off. If you set the Sticky Keys on, you can also choose to have the machine beep when a modifier key is set and to show pressed keys onscreen. The Sticky Keys option is useful if you have trouble executing multiple key combinations, such as Command+I. The keys are displayed in the same fashion as the keyboard volume controls. Note that you can also set the toggle on and off for the Sticky Keys behavior by pressing the Shift key five times.

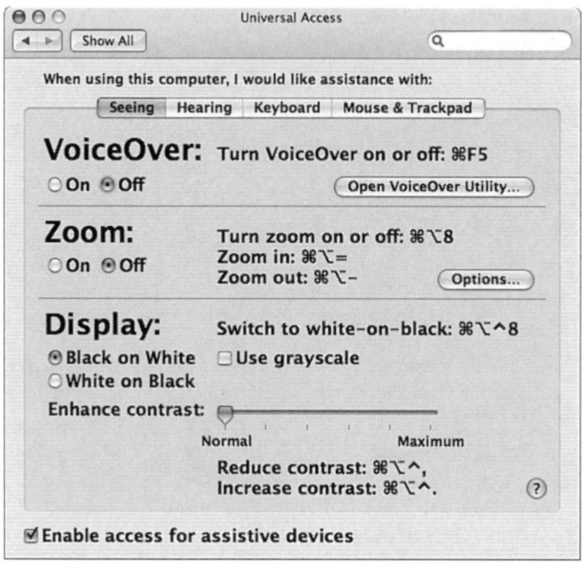

FIGURE 8.22 Select settings to help you see your display better under the Seeing section of the Universal Access pane.

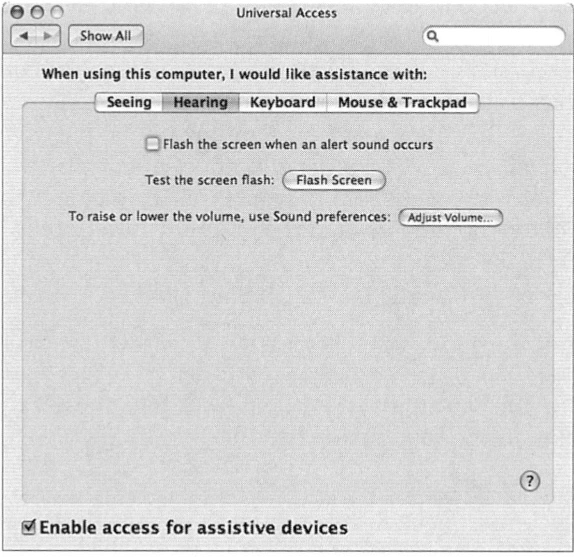

FIGURE 8.23 Set the screen to flash whenever an alert sound occurs in the Hearing section of the Universal Access pane.

From the Keyboard section, you can also adjust settings for difficulties with keystrokes being repeated. You can turn Slow Keys on or off here. If Slow Keys is on, there's a delay between when the key is pressed and when it's accepted. This delay time is set in the

Acceptance Delay slider scale. Additionally, you can choose to enable click key sounds while you're typing or otherwise interacting with the keyboard. It sounds much like you're typing at a typewriter when that option is enabled. Finally, you can adjust repeat timing through the Set Key Repeat button, which brings up the Keyboard section of the Keyboard & Mouse pane.

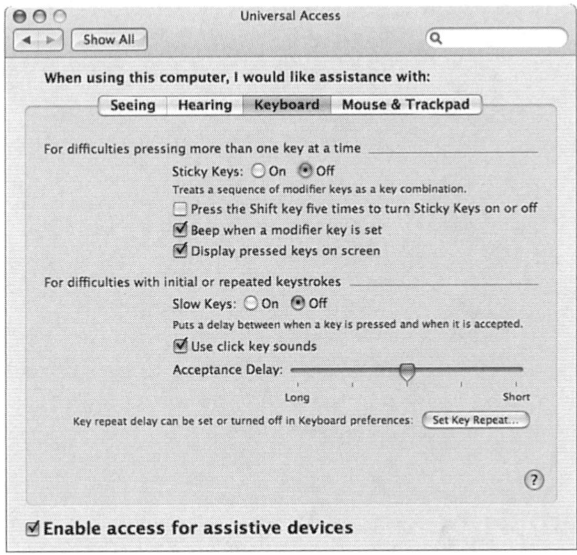

FIGURE 8.24 If you have difficulties pressing more than one key at a time or with keystrokes being repeated, make keyboard adjustments to assist you under the Keyboard section of the Universal Access pane.

Mouse & Trackpad

Depending on what hardware you have, this section might be a Mouse section instead. If you have difficulties using the mouse, you can turn on Mouse Keys in the Mouse section, shown in Figure 8.25. When you turn Mouse Keys on, the numeric keypad is what you use to move the cursor around. The Mouse section also enables you to customize mouse pointer movement by setting a preferred initial delay and maximum speed using slider controls. Note that you can also choose to enable the toggle on and off setting for the Mouse Keys by pressing the Option key five times. If you have a trackpad, you can choose to ignore the trackpad when Mouse Keys is on. If you have difficulty seeing the cursor, you can adjust the cursor size here. In this section, you can also enable full keyboard access by clicking on the Open Keyboard Preferences, which takes you to the Keyboard pane.

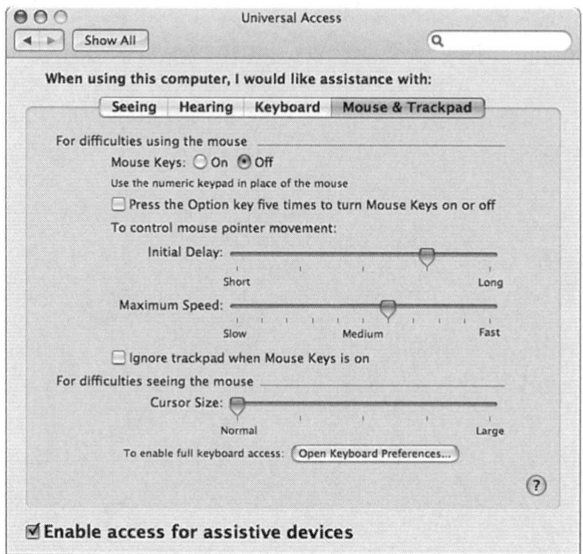

FIGURE 8.25 Set the Mouse Keys on in the Mouse or Mouse & Trackpad section of the Universal Access pane if you have difficulties with the mouse.

Setting System Time and Date

Various aspects of the date and time are specified in the Date & Time pane of System Preferences.

Date & Time

In the Date & Time section of the Date & Time pane, you actually set the date and time. If your computer gets time from a network time server, you don't need to set the time, but you do need to set the server. Select one of Apple's network time servers or provide an address for another one. You can also access the International pane from here to set date and time formats. Figure 8.26 shows the Date & Time section. Note that if you receive your time setting from a network time server, you might have trouble when your machine boots up if it can't find the network time server.

Time Zone

The Time Zone section, shown in Figure 8.27, is where the time zone is set. You just click on your approximate area on the map, and select a nearby city from the pop-up window. If you don't like scrolling through the list of cities, you can also type in nearby cities. If a city is recognized, the time zone information is filled in and the time changes to the time for that city. This method can be useful if you are having trouble determining what the correct time zone is.

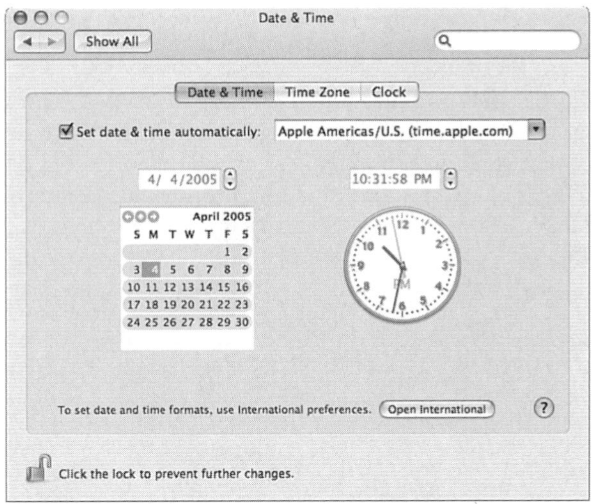

FIGURE 8.26 The current date and time are set in the Date & Time section of the Date & Time pane.

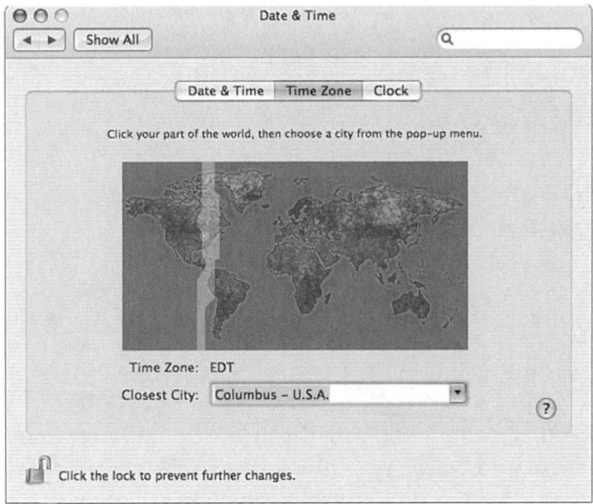

FIGURE 8.27 Select your time zone in the Time Zone section of the Date & Time pane.

Clock

Figure 8.28 shows the Clock section, where you set specifics about displaying and announcing date and time. You can choose to have date and time displayed. If you choose this option, you can select various ways they are displayed. The date and time can be displayed in the menu bar or in a window. If you choose to display date and time in a window, you can set the window's transparency using the Transparency slider. You can also choose whether the display is digital or analog. If you choose a digital display, you can select various options for how it is displayed.

In this section, you can also choose to have the time announced, and you can select an interval of on the hour, half hour, or quarter hour for the announcement, as well as an announcement voice. For the voice, you can select the default voice or various other voices. You can set a custom rate and volume for the voice and play the settings until you find something you like.

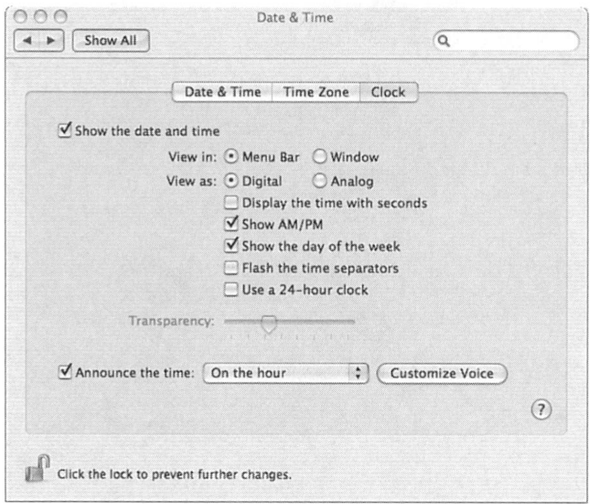

FIGURE 8.28 Preferences involving displaying and announcing date and time are set in the Clock section of the Date & Time pane.

Using Spotlight to Search System Preferences

As you have already seen, the Spotlight search system is new with Mac OS X 10.4. Also new with Tiger is the ability to search the System Preferences directly in the System Preferences. Just type what you are looking for in the Spotlight search box at the top right of the System Preferences and watch the interactivity. With each stroke you type, you can see the matches change. When you've finished, the most likely result has the strongest spotlight, whereas other pertinent results are dimly lit. Figure 8.29 shows a Spotlight search for the term *keyboard*.

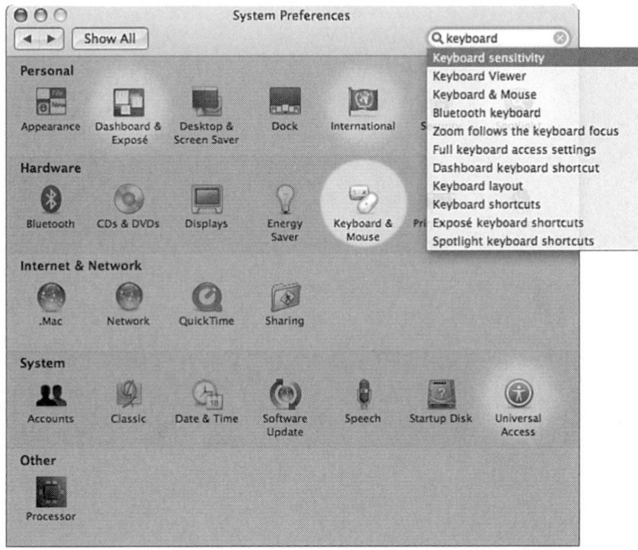

FIGURE 8.28 The results of a search for *keyboard* using Spotlight in the System Preferences.

Summary

In this chapter, we looked at customizing user and system settings. First we took a look at user account creation. Then we looked at account security options available in the Security pane, with concentration on FileVault. We also looked at some more general system settings, including the International and Date & Time panes. In addition to general settings, we looked at some voice and accessibility options that can make your computer easier for you to use. These included the voice recognition system, which is a control system for your computer that allows you to speak to your machine, and the VoiceOver system, which describes what is on your screen for you. Lastly, we saw that we can run Spotlight searches directly in the System Preferences.

PART IV

Introduction to BSD on Tiger

IN THIS PART

CHAPTER 9

Accessing the BSD Subsystem

IN THIS CHAPTER

- Getting Started with the Command Line
- Interacting with Unix: Basic Unix Commands
- Terminal Preferences and Configuration

In this chapter, we reach the topic of the underlying BSD Unix subsystem, something that some Mac enthusiasts eagerly awaited for years, while others dreaded since they heard about the underpinnings of Mac OS X. As OS 9 fades into history, a good number of you have been living happily with BSD for four years now, whether you've known that it's there or not. If you're a little uncomfortable with the idea of conversing directly with the underpinnings of the operating system, this is an important point to remember: It's there if you need it, but Apple's done such a good job of putting an elegant GUI on top of it, that you don't have to know about it if you don't want to. The material in the following chapters is for users who want to know more about how to completely customize their machines, enable features that aren't available through the graphical user interface, or get under the hood and just plain tinker. We've enough experience with helping formerly-GUI-only users learn to use the command line that we're confident that almost anyone can enhance their computing experience by learning a bit about the BSD subsystem and how to work directly with it.

Berkeley Software Distribution (BSD) is one of the two major philosophical variants of Unix. Apple has named its version Darwin, so you'll see this term used frequently to refer to both the open source effort Apple has underway to further develop the base of Mac OS X, and the underlying system as accessed at the command line.

If you're a longtime Unix user, you'll probably find much of the rest of this book familiar, and you should consider it a reference to those places where the Apple implementation differs from what you're already familiar with. If, on the other hand, you're new to Unix, you'll soon have to decide whether you're satisfied with Mac OS X as simply a more stable, more powerful flavor of the Mac OS you've grown to know and love, or whether you want to learn even more. In this chapter, we cover the primary concepts that you need to understand to use the BSD subsystem and introduce some of the most important command-line programs.

Getting Started with the Command Line

If you're not familiar with Unix, you've probably heard and read enough to have developed any number of preconceptions regarding what using it will be like. Almost all of them are probably at least a bit intimidating. You've probably heard that Unix commands are cryptic and that the learning curve is steep. Even worse, it uses a command-line interface—you've actually got to *type* at the thing to tell it what to do, and we all know how archaic that mode of controlling a machine is.

It might be archaic, but that does not mean that there's anything wrong with it or that it's not the best way to accomplish certain tasks. We know—many of you poked fun at that *other* operating system for years because its unfortunate users had to type to make it work. Don't worry; we've laughed, too. You're just going to have to be courageous and admit that you've used the keyboard in the Mac OS Finder to do things such as jump a Finder window to a file with a particular name. The mouse is a wonderful tool for doing things where the brain's visual processing machinery can come into play. The keyboard is also a powerful tool for other types of interaction, and it would be silly to intentionally restrict yourself to only one type of interface when other complementary interfaces are available. In many ways, what Apple has given you is analogous to being provided with a high-end sports car, and a fully equipped machine shop and garage to work on it. If buzzing around in the fancy car is your pleasure, you are free to do so without ever opening the hood. On the other hand, if you feel like working on the engine, all the tools are there to enable you to further customize and enhance your ride to your heart's content.

Regardless of what you've heard, the idea that learning and using Unix will be fun and rewarding is likely to be furthest from your mind. We hope that in this and upcoming chapters, we'll be able to convince you differently. If we can't, don't worry. Nothing about Mac OS X requires you to learn and use anything other than the graphical interface that we've already covered. You can live with your Mac OS X machine, use it for the same type of applications you always have, and love it in all its "nontypishness," without ever having to learn any of this Unix stuff. However, if you want to learn how to make your machine even more powerful, make yourself more productive, and customize everything to an exquisite extent, give this command-line stuff a try.

CAUTION

Having just told you that we think you'll like the Unix side of your machine if you give it a fair chance, and encouraged you to try it out, we'll turn around and caution you about its use. Unix is not for everyone. Although we'd love to see every Macintosh user graduate to the power available in the BSD subsystem, we can't avoid the reality that Unix is more complicated and powerful than some users will ever want to use. Just as some of us are safer not owning super-fast sports cars, some are less a threat to ourselves and others if we don't have a big box of firecrackers, and some would be better off if we couldn't buy donuts by the dozen, Unix is just too much for some people. It might be too much power, or too much flexibility, or too much information to remember, but Unix seems specially designed to create a user who epitomizes the phrase "knows just enough to be dangerous."

Evaluate your needs honestly. We're firmly convinced that everyone can learn Unix, and everyone can use it safely, but the reality is that not everyone will. If you're hesitant about trying out the Unix side of your new operating system because you think it might be too difficult, we suggest that you give it a try because we think we can convince you that it's not as tough as you think. If you're not sure that Unix is a good match for what you do, you might be right: It might be better if you use Mac OS X as the super-stable, more flexible operating system on which to run your GUI-based programs, and leave the BSD subsystem alone.

Understanding the BSD Philosophy

One of the complaints you might have heard from people regarding Apple's new operating system is that it is based on immensely old operating system technology. They're right! The roots of Unix lie almost in the roots of modern computing itself. The thing that they're wrong about is their claim that this is a "Bad Thing." Unix development started more than three decades ago, and the operating system that you can use today is the product of the work and improvements of thousands upon thousands of developers. Along the way, Unix has picked up some powerful design concepts and some wonderful solutions to problems common in the computing world.

Much of the "Unix way" is based on the idea of abstracting interfaces into the simplest possible terms. Initially, this was simply because the operating system was experimental, and the simplest possible interface—one that wouldn't need to be fiddled with later—was the most expedient to construct. Over time, this "do it the easy way" methodology has evolved into a powerful design concept: abstraction. This concept will be mentioned time and again as it makes its appearance in different topics throughout the book.

As an initial explanation, though, an example provides immediate understanding. Among many other concepts, Unix abstracts the notion of things that can be read from, or written to, as files. To Unix, everything from which data can be read is treated as though it were a file, and everything to which data can be written is treated as though it were also a file. Why? Because after you've developed an in-OS methodology to control reading and writing to files, it's a nuisance to have to implement almost identical methodologies for reading and writing to the network, or writing data to printers, or reading data from the keyboard. Instead, it's considerably easier to write an abstraction layer that talks to the particular device and makes it appear to the operating system as just another file. If you make your printer look like a file, printing is simply "writing to a file" for any application. If you make your keyboard input look like it's coming from a file, any application can automagically accept input from either the keyboard or an actual on-disk file, without knowing the difference.

What starts as a time-saving implementation turns into a powerful interface feature, allowing the addition of arbitrary devices, without needing to implement new OS features—just write something that makes the device "look like a file," and suddenly the operating system can use it. This notion of abstraction ends up being powerful for the end user, and similar abstractions are pointed out in the sections to come.

More information on Unix and its role in computing can be found at `http://www.macosxunleashed.com/unixhistory.html`.

Additionally, the Unix design philosophy drives programs that are used in day-to-day interaction with a Unix machine to be small, single-purpose, and non-overlapping in functionality. The presence of a vast array of these single-purpose programs, designed so that they can be combined in near-infinite combinations, allows the user to construct customized solutions for most any problem. The necessity for some programs to provide more complicated functionality, requires them to be less-single purpose, and to allow somewhat more overlap. Finally, just as in other operating systems that you're used to, there are programs that are large, multifunctional, and monolithic. Typically, Unix users think of the small, single-purpose programs as *commands*, and the large, multifunctional programs as *applications*. Although they're all programs, the term *program* itself is frequently reserved for a program that doesn't fit the description of a command or an application. This somewhat muddy semantic distinction between types of programs might seem confusing at first, but as you become more comfortable using Unix, it will make more sense to you. As an example to get you started, you can think of a Unix command as a small program with a single function such as listing files. A Unix application is typically a much larger program, perhaps something like a word processor or a web browser. Moreover, although both are programs, the term *program* itself is infrequently used to describe anything that falls into either of these categories.

Thankfully for the beginning Unix user, making complete sense of the semantic distinctions isn't necessary for anything other than conversing with other Unix users.

Finally, it is important to understand that almost nothing to do with the Unix way of thinking about things, BSD design philosophy, or the command line, has anything to do with Apple's Tiger specifically. The command line sections of this book are not about Tiger's command line, or even Mac OS X's command line particularly. We're using Tiger and other versions of Mac OS X as our primary examples, but the Unix shell is the Unix shell, is the Unix shell. You could apply 99.9% or more, of this information directly to Linux, or Sun's Solaris, or any of a dozen other flavors of Unix, or the information from their related reference materials for working with Tiger. As a matter of fact, you'll find examples here that span from the most recent beta release of Tiger, to output from a version of Unix that Sun Microsystems hasn't produced since 1993. Unless you're incredibly astute, you won't be able to tell the difference (which is entirely in the detail of dates displayed for some files in the output). Apple has applied its own little tweaks and flavor to things, but when looking at these examples, it's important to concentrate on the ideas. The details are window dressing.

Using Terminal to Access the Command-Line Interface

The Terminal program, found in the Utilities subfolder of the Applications folder, is the primary method for communicating with the BSD subsystem of the Mac OS X installation, via the Unix command line. Some tricks and nifty applications are already appearing to insulate you from the need to work with the command line for some applications that are essentially command line based. We cover these as well, but the Terminal itself will probably be your primary mode of interaction.

Simply put, `Terminal.app`, which appears to the Finder as simply Terminal, and being an application bundle, to the command line as a directory named `Terminal.app`, is a virtual terminal by which you can type commands to your machine. It's the software version of what used to be implemented as a dedicated hardware device, one that understood how to display data and put it in specific positions on a screen. A terminal itself isn't particularly interesting but provides the mechanism for communication between you and programs that are more interesting to talk to.

Terminal itself has a number of useful preferences that you can set that modify how several things in this and subsequent chapters work, but before we go into those details, let's see just what Terminal can do for you. The preferences for Terminal, as well as some of the additional functionality available through the menus are covered at the end of this chapter.

Interacting with Unix: Basic Unix Commands

You've already learned how to interact with Unix using Mac OS X's Aqua interface and the GUI tools discussed throughout the earlier chapters of this book. Much of the rest of the book provides the information you need to interact with Unix textually, through the command line. Unix commands, programs, and applications are all run by typing their names at the command line. The remainder of this chapter covers what you need to know to start interacting with the command line and how to get help for what you're trying to do.

Introduction to the Unix Shell

As mentioned previously, a terminal alone isn't sufficient to enable you to interact with your machine. The terminal needs something to talk to, and that thing is usually a program called a *shell*. Unix shells provide text-based interaction between the user and the rest of the operating system. For those who have experience with the DOS environment, you can think of a Unix shell as similar to a very powerful version of `COMMAND.COM`. Please don't let that put you off. `COMMAND.COM` does not approach being a fair comparison for a Unix shell, but both do let you type commands to the computer.

Although it is text-based, you can think of a shell running in a terminal as sharing a few conceptual similarities with a Finder window.

Any running shell can be thought of as "being in a place" in the filesystem, just as a Finder window is open to a certain folder in the system. This place is the *current working directory*.

Each shell can navigate through the filesystem by moving to parent or higher-level directories, or by moving to child or lower-level directories. Again, this is much like the functionality provided in each Finder window, by command-clicking the folder icon to reveal the enclosing folder structure or clicking a folder displayed in the window to navigate to an enclosed folder.

Unlike a Finder window, a shell in a terminal is not restricted to running a command that is present in the same directory that the terminal is "at"—it can run commands located anywhere on the machine.

Also unlike Finder windows, shell commands that you execute in terminal windows (usually) run within the Terminal window, and they (usually) consume the resources of the shell such that the shell becomes "preoccupied" and can't run another command until the current one finishes (although you can always open another Terminal window to launch another shell to work in while other commands complete).

Most flavors of Unix come with a number of different shells from which the user can choose, and the BSD version underlying Mac OS X is no exception. With Mac OS X, you can choose from the following five shells, or possibly more, if Apple or another source makes them available.

- `sh`—The Bourne shell. The Bourne shell is ubiquitously available on Unix, but does not have syntax or features particularly friendly to the user. It is most frequently used for writing shell scripts (programs written to run using the shell language itself, rather than a more traditional programming language; how to write them is covered in Chapter 15, "Shell Configuration and Programming (Shell Scripting)") that are expected to run on any version of Unix. Sometimes it is used for the login shell of particularly important accounts, such as `root`.
- `csh`—The C shell (yes, it's pronounced *seashell*). The `csh` shell is a more user-friendly shell that takes its name from the C programming language. `csh` syntax is similar to the C language, and it provides significant power for both shell programming and for users. `csh` is almost as omnipresent as `sh`, and considerably less annoying to use.
- `tcsh`—Enhanced C shell. Many people considered `csh` to have been a botched implementation in a number of ways and wanted something with similar syntax, but less broken. `tcsh` was born to fix the bugs, and extend the functionality, of `csh` and includes nice features such as automatic command completion and a command history. `tcsh` is appearing as a standard available on more and more distributions, but although it's a frequent favorite for day-to-day use as a login shell, many traditional Unix users are still shy of using it for writing shell scripts that they might want to distribute widely. Early versions of Mac OS X used `tcsh` as the default shell, but with Panther, the default switched to `bash`.
- `bash`—The Bourne again shell (and yes, Unix programmers frequently have a twisted sense of humor). The Bourne again shell is a modern shell that takes the enhancements that make `csh` and `tcsh` more useful for user interaction and implements them in a shell with the `sh` syntax. `bash` is popular among Linux users because it's the default login shell for many Linux distributions. `bash` users and `tcsh` users tend to engage in heated and sometimes hostile debate over their shells of choice; `bash` users tend to think of `tcsh` as an undisciplined and poorly arranged set of hacks that is unsuited for any but the most trivial day-to-day tasks, and `tcsh` users tend to think of `bash` as a product of zealots who are unable to see the utter misanthropy of the interface they've designed.

- zsh—zsh is designed to be an interactive user shell that incorporates powerful programming features. The intent in its creation seems to have been to build an amalgam of the most powerful features of the other shells, and to introduce a number of new features as well. The shell has been described as suffering from "feeping creaturism" (see the Jargon File, sometimes called the "Hacker's Dictionary"—available at http://www.catb.org/jargon/html/F/feeping-creaturism.html, among a plethora of other locations), and of having a few more features than even the author knows about.

Despite the fact that you'll find references and diatribes on the Internet that make the issue seem to take on almost religious significance, shell preference is just that, personal preference. There are well-considered reasons for picking any of them, and a user's personality as well as the type of work that he is doing ultimately dictates the shell environment in which he'll be most effective and happy. Starting with 10.3, Apple chose to make bash the standard shell for Mac OS X. The previous default was tcsh, and the change will aggravate a great many users because many do not like the syntax of sh. Thankfully, if you have a preference for a different shell, changing yours is a simple matter of resetting a terminal preference or a NetInfo setting. On the other hand, being forced to perform day-to-day work in the same shell language that you would need to use if you wanted to distribute your work to users of other systems is a strong plus for bash because its syntax is based on sh.

Examples in this book are shown using the default bash shell in most places, with tcsh samples where the usage diverges significantly. Regardless of what shell you choose, interaction with each is similar. To issue a command to the computer using a shell, you type the name of the command and press the Return key. In general, the command you requested will be executed by the shell and that shell will be occupied until the command is finished. After the command finishes executing, you'll be returned to the shell prompt. If the command requires additional information, it might be required on the command line in the form of flags or arguments, or interactively in the terminal as the program runs. *Flags* are usually individual letters or words preceded by a dash (-) that indicate the turning on or off of an option; *arguments* are words or data provided on the command line for the command to process. Some commands also require that data be provided at internal prompts or data entry areas created by the command when it is run. As mentioned previously, we'll discuss more complex programs and applications in following chapters.

NOTE

When documenting commands throughout the book, we will use the following syntax:

```
commandname <required options> [optional options] <arg1> <arg2>
```

and

```
commandname <required> [optional] <arg1> <arg2> ...
```

These mean that you type *commandname* at the prompt, must choose one or more entries from the *<required parameters>*, and may choose one or more options from the *[optional* *options*]. In the first invocation form, two additional required arguments are expected on the command line; in the second, the command accepts a variable number of arguments. In general, single-letter flags (options or parameters), usually preceded by a `-` (minus) sign, when enclosed in <> brackets are required, and when enclosed in `[]` brackets are optional. The brackets shown in the syntax examples are not actually entered on the command line—they are shown only to distinguish required parameters and optional options. Arguments are required if shown, and an alternative form of the command is displayed with no parameters or arguments if this is also an allowable syntax. Options or parameters separated by a vertical bar, ¦, are exclusive; you must, or may, pick one or the other (depending on whether they're required or optional), but you cannot specify both.

For example, the fictitious command documentation shown in Table 9.1 indicates that a command named `silly` can be invoked as `silly`, `silly -L`, and `silly -P`. Invoked as `silly`, it does the same thing as `silly -L`; that is, it makes a silly laugh. Invoked as `silly -P`, it makes a silly picture. Each form also can be called with an arbitrary number of filenames following the command, in which case `silly` will place its output in the specified files.

TABLE 9.1 Command Documentation Table for the Fictitious `silly` Command

`silly`	Does something silly, optionally into files.
`silly [-L¦P] <filename> <filename2> ...`	
`silly [-L¦P]`	
`-L`	Default: Makes a silly laugh.
`-P`	Makes a silly picture.

Please be aware that the command documentation tables we've provided here are abstracted from the documentation, experimentation on the system, and our experience. Sometimes things don't really work quite like the online manual pages say that they do. Sometimes they include documentation for ridiculous options that you are unlikely to want to know about (for example, the `man` command, discussed later in this chapter, includes a `-d` option that means "Don't actually display the man pages, but do print gobs of debugging information"). We're correcting the documentation where necessary, simplifying it where possible, and leaving out many of the options that you probably don't care about in the tables themselves. If you see options listed in the syntax section, but not described in the rest of the table, these are probably items that seemed unlikely to be useful to most readers. If it seems that the command ought to do something that it can't quite do with the available options, check the built-in man pages, because it's always possible that we omitted exactly the option you're looking for. We'll do our best to keep our online PDF appendix complete with updated man pages that document all command options, even the seemingly useless ones, as well.

Shell Rules and Conventions

In dealing with the shell, it helps to remember a few rules. The first rule you need to know is that things that you type in Unix are case sensitive. This includes commands. Unlike with Mac OS and Windows, you cannot mix case and still have a command function. You must type the name exactly as it is stored on the system. Mac OS X has the option (the default, actually) of using HFS+, which isn't case sensitive, but this creates some odd behavior in its interaction with the BSD subsystem. There are classical Unix commands included in the BSD subsystem that have names that differ only by capitalization and that normally do different things. For example, `Mail` and `mail` are two different traditional Unix programs, and they traditionally have different functionality (both deal with email, but do different things). On Mac OS X installed over an HFS+ filesystem, it is indeterminate which program runs when you type `mail` (or `Mail`) at the command line. Apple has gone a long way to making the capitalization issue transparent to the user, but there are still places where capitalization sensitivity (or lack thereof) comes back to bite people. Because there's no obligation for Mac OS X to be running on HFS+, and it's quite possible that you will be mounting drives from other machines that aren't running Mac OS X at all, you really should treat everything in the BSD subsystem as though it were case sensitive, even if your installation actually isn't. It might seem initially inconvenient to remember the exact capitalization that's been used for various commands (really, they're *almost* all lowercase, so it's not that difficult), but with time it will become second nature to you. Regularly practicing good form with respect to case specificity will almost certainly save you considerable headaches eventually.

Next, when you type at the command line, characters that you type become part of the command. Most alphanumeric characters, as well as underlines and hyphens, are valid parts of commands. Most symbols aren't valid parts of commands, and some have special meanings to the command line. Table 9.2 shows some of the symbols with special meaning to the command line.

TABLE 9.2 Command-Line Symbols

Symbol	Meaning
*	When used as part of a filename, the * character substitutes for zero or more characters in a filename. This is called a *wildcard*. For example, specifying a filename of `*.gif` as an argument to a command-line program tells the shell to search the current directory for all files that have names ending in `.gif` and substitute all these filenames on the command line at this point in the command.
?	A single-character wildcard. Functions like *, except that it substitutes for a single character in filenames, instead of any number of characters. If you need some specific number of wildcarded positions, you can use multiple ? characters, one for each wildcard substitution.
Tab	If you press the Tab key at the command line, the shell attempts to complete the command for you. If the portion of the command or filename that you've typed is unique, the shell fills in the rest of the information for you. For example, if you're in your home directory, and you want to specify the `Documents` directory on the command line, typing `Docu` and then pressing the Tab key will most likely fill out the command line to include the full `Documents` name.
space	Unix interprets a space between words on the command line as a separator between parts of the command. This is not always what you want because Macintosh filenames can have spaces. The Unix command line usually interprets the space in a Mac filename such as `My File` as indicating two different files: one named `My` and one named `File`.
\	The shell escape character. If you need to insert a character into a Unix command or filename that is usually interpreted by the shell (such as a space or * character), you can place the \ character before the character that would usually be interpreted by the shell. This is called *escaping* the special character. You frequently see this on the command line to specify Mac filenames such as `My File`, which in Unix must be specified as `My\ File`.

9

NOTE

Note that you can use the shell escape character \ to allow inclusion of usually special characters into a single command argument, or, alternatively, you can often place the argument in quotes. Therefore, if you wanted to list the directory *`My Big Directory`*, you could either specify it as *`My\ Big\ Directory`*, or as "*`My Big Directory`*" when used in a command. Although the quoted version is a little easier to read, we recommend familiarizing yourself with the escaped version because this is what the shell will use when automatically expanding arguments when you press the Tab key.

Most useful shells provide a history mechanism whereby previous commands can be recalled and reused. Previous commands may be recalled to the command line by use of the up arrow key. If you need the last command you typed, just press the up arrow key, and it will be recalled to the command line. You can rotate through the command history with the up arrow and down arrow keys to pick the command you need.

The command line also provides editing capabilities. You can use the left arrow and right arrow keys to move around in the command line currently displayed, and edit it by typing new characters or deleting existing characters with the Delete key. This also applies to commands that you've recalled via the command history with the arrow keys.

When you type a command, the system searches for a command with that name in the list of directories known as the `PATH`. This is done because a complete search of the entire filesystem could take a long time, and restricting the portions of the filesystem examined to only a small subset speeds up things significantly. Unfortunately, the current directory, where the shell "is," isn't necessarily in the `PATH`. Because of this, you might be in a directory named `/Users/wizbot/spin/`, and there might be a command named `spinnin` in the directory, but typing `spinnin` produces only the error `command not found`. In this case, you can run the command by specifying either the full name of the path to the command (`/Users/wizbot/spin/spinnin`), or by specifying the relative path to the command (`./spinnin`). You can also solve the problem by adding the path to the directory holding `spinnin` to the `PATH` list, or by adding the current directory to the `PATH`. You learn about this and more in Chapter 15. You also learn considerably more about paths in the immediately following sections, covering the filesystem and basic navigation.

CAUTION

Understanding the location of command executables with respect to the current directory is one of the most common problems that new users encounter at the command line. It is quite common to see a user become furious at a shell prompt because it insists on reiterating `command not found` when the user types the name of a command. They'll demonstrate that the command most certainly does exist by listing the contents of the directory, and pointing out that it's right there, plain as day. The fact that the places that the shell itself looks to find commands might not include that directory, seems insidiously hard to remember, and we've seen some users return a half-dozen times to ask the same question of other commands, before they truly understood the necessity of specifying either the full path, or `./`*`<commandname>`* for commands in the current directory.

The difficulty isn't limited to novice users, either. We've seen professional programmers who ought to be able to teach classes on this material, befuddled for days by a slight variant of this error, and even after almost 20 years of working daily with the command line, still experience brief moments of annoyance with this issue ourselves.

Some might wonder, given that we're saying this is a common complaint, why we don't simply recommend adding the current directory to the list of places a shell should look for commands. This is a security-related issue, and while on the surface it sounds like an appealing idea, it's actually a rather dangerous practice. Adding the current directory to the PATH, allows a malicious user to install a trojan horse that has the same name as a real command, that will accidentally be executed instead of what you intended, if you happen to be in the same directory as it is when you attempt to execute the command you wanted. This also has the side effect (which kept our professional programmer mentioned above occupied for a whole weekend) that if you're used to a command running from your current directory, and a command by the same name gets added elsewhere in the system, it might start executing instead when you type its name.

All in all, it's safest to leave the current directory out of your path, and remember to use `./` in front of commands that you want to execute in your current directory.

Occasionally, you might do something that leaves your shell in an apparently unusable state. Frequently, this is because you've started a process that is expecting input from you. If you don't have the appropriate information to give it to keep it happy, you can try several key combinations that might help you regain control of your shell:

- Ctrl-D—This key combination sends an End Of File (EOF) signal to the current process, usually terminating input. If the process is designed to continuously accept data until reaching the EOF, sending it this key combination causes it to stop accepting input and go about whatever it was designed to do next.

CAUTION

Be careful with Ctrl-D. If you're not currently running a process in the shell, you'll send the EOF to the shell itself, which tells it that you're finished sending input (typing commands to it) and it will summarily stop. If you've set your Terminal preferences to close the window when the last process running in it stops, that Terminal window goes away as well.

- Ctrl-Z—This key combination suspends the current foreground process (more on foreground and background processes in Chapter 12. The process won't continue to run; it simply sits there in suspended animation until you either close the shell (perhaps by logging out), thereby killing it, or until you reenable it using one of the techniques discussed in "Process Management."
- Ctrl-C—This key combination is the Unix break character. This usually (you can configure the behavior) kills the current process and returns you to the shell prompt.

Don't be afraid to test the commands shown in this book. The system can do a pretty good job of protecting itself from anything a normal user can type, and we'll be sure to place conspicuous warnings with any commands capable of causing mischief in any case. With a little experimenting, we think you'll find that you can do a surprising number of things with only a few keystrokes.

Issuing Commands

So, now that we've taken all that time to provide background on using the shell, you might think that this is going to be confusing, intimidating, or difficult. It's not. It might seem confusing for a bit, but it's not difficult, and if you don't let it become intimidating, you'll find that you can quickly pick up techniques that make day-to-day use of your machine more convenient and productive. There's absolutely no need for you to learn everything that you can do with the shell all at once. As a matter of fact, there's no need to learn more than a handful of commands and techniques at any one time. We've written this section of the book as though you were going to start it as a shell novice, and graduate after seven chapters as an experienced shell programmer. Next to nobody is going to follow that path. This, however, isn't a bad thing; almost nobody follows anybody else's path with learning to use the command line, except in a very general sense.

You start off doing a few things that are useful to you, and as you become proficient with those, it's natural to start adding new abilities and knowledge to your repertoire. Exactly what you learn when isn't really at all important. We've presented the material in an order that we think makes learning to use most commands and utilities (including ones that we haven't room to cover in this book) straightforward, but don't feel that you need to learn it all before you can start utilizing what you've learned. Unless you really want to, don't even try to learn it all before you become comfortable with the parts that help you right now, with whatever you're regularly doing.

That being said, what exactly does this Terminal and shell thing do? It gives you a place to type things, and a place for the machine to respond. Before we get started on specifics, let's look at the sorts of things you can do in a shell running in Terminal. First, when you start Terminal, it gives you a friendly message and a prompt indicating that it's time for you to type something:

```
Last login: Sat Sep 20 22:50:19 on console
Welcome to Darwin!
/Volumes/Wills_Data/ray
bash-2.05a$
```

That's not too interesting. What's the point of telling me what version of `bash` I'm running. If I cared, I could probably ask it, right? Let's make that prompt into something more useful. How about our machine name, our username, and the directory we're currently in:

```
bash-2.05a$ PS1='\h:\u \W \$ '
brezup:ray ray $
```

Well, that's a little better, at least now I know who and where I am when I look at the terminal. `PS1` is a shell variable that customizes your prompt. `\h` calls out your machine name, `\u` calls out your username, \W (capitalization is important) calls out the name of the current directory, and \$ places the traditional bash $ character at the end of the prompts. If you're following along, believe it or not, you're customizing your shell environment already. It's not quite the same type of tweaks that you can get out of the Appearance control pane, but this is exactly the sort of small utility command that makes your life easier. And you don't need to read all the way up to Chapter 15 where we cover many other variables like PS1 that can be set to make your life easier, for you to start making productive use of what you know now. We use this prompt (and a slight variation on it) throughout the book.

So now you've customized a bit of your environment. What sort of useful things can you do now? How about a calendar?

```
brezup:ray ray $  cal 2005
                               2005

       January               February               March
 S  M Tu  W Th  F  S   S  M Tu  W Th  F  S   S  M Tu  W Th  F  S
                   1         1  2  3  4  5         1  2  3  4  5
 2  3  4  5  6  7  8   6  7  8  9 10 11 12   6  7  8  9 10 11 12
 9 10 11 12 13 14 15  13 14 15 16 17 18 19  13 14 15 16 17 18 19
16 17 18 19 20 21 22  20 21 22 23 24 25 26  20 21 22 23 24 25 26
23 24 25 26 27 28 29  27 28                 27 28 29 30 31
30 31
        April                  May                   June
 S  M Tu  W Th  F  S   S  M Tu  W Th  F  S   S  M Tu  W Th  F  S
                1  2   1  2  3  4  5  6  7            1  2  3  4
 3  4  5  6  7  8  9   8  9 10 11 12 13 14   5  6  7  8  9 10 11
10 11 12 13 14 15 16  15 16 17 18 19 20 21  12 13 14 15 16 17 18
17 18 19 20 21 22 23  22 23 24 25 26 27 28  19 20 21 22 23 24 25
24 25 26 27 28 29 30  29 30 31              26 27 28 29 30

        July                 August               September
 S  M Tu  W Th  F  S   S  M Tu  W Th  F  S   S  M Tu  W Th  F  S
                1  2      1  2  3  4  5  6               1  2  3
 3  4  5  6  7  8  9   7  8  9 10 11 12 13   4  5  6  7  8  9 10
10 11 12 13 14 15 16  14 15 16 17 18 19 20  11 12 13 14 15 16 17
17 18 19 20 21 22 23  21 22 23 24 25 26 27  18 19 20 21 22 23 24
24 25 26 27 28 29 30  28 29 30 31           25 26 27 28 29 30
31
       October               November              December
 S  M Tu  W Th  F  S   S  M Tu  W Th  F  S   S  M Tu  W Th  F  S
                   1         1  2  3  4  5               1  2  3
 2  3  4  5  6  7  8   6  7  8  9 10 11 12   4  5  6  7  8  9 10
 9 10 11 12 13 14 15  13 14 15 16 17 18 19  11 12 13 14 15 16 17
16 17 18 19 20 21 22  20 21 22 23 24 25 26  18 19 20 21 22 23 24
23 24 25 26 27 28 29  27 28 29 30           25 26 27 28 29 30 31
30 31
```

Know another quick way to get a calendar for all of any year with only eight keystrokes?

How about a peek at how long your machine's been running?

```
brezup:ray ray $ uptime
 0:04  up 11 days,  4:56, 8 users, load averages: 0.10 0.03 0.01
```

Not only does it tell me how long it's been booted this time around (only one hour, two minutes right now), but also how many users are using the system, the time, and how hard the processor's working (.16 processes running during the command's averaging period, which is not working too hard at all).

How about what your current IP address is and the state of your network?

```
brezup:sageray Documents $ ifconfig -a
lo0: flags=8049<UP,LOOPBACK,RUNNING,MULTICAST> mtu 16384
        inet6 ::1 prefixlen 128
        inet6 fe80::1 prefixlen 64 scopeid 0x1
        inet 127.0.0.1 netmask 0xff000000
gif0: flags=8010<POINTOPOINT,MULTICAST> mtu 1280
stf0: flags=0<> mtu 1280
en0: flags=8863<UP,BROADCAST,SMART,RUNNING,SIMPLEX,MULTICAST> mtu 1500
        inet6 fe80::230:65ff:feaa:37ae prefixlen 64 scopeid 0x4
        inet 192.168.1.19 netmask 0xffffff00 broadcast 192.168.1.255
        ether 00:30:65:aa:37:ae
        media: autoselect (10baseT/UTP <half-duplex>) status: active
        supported media: none autoselect 10baseT/UTP <half-duplex>
➥10baseT/UTP <full-duplex> 10baseT/UTP <full-duplex,hw-loopback>
➥ 100baseTX <half-duplex> 100baseTX <full-duplex> 100baseTX
➥<full-duplex,hw-loopback>
fw0: flags=8822<BROADCAST,SMART,SIMPLEX,MULTICAST> mtu 2030
        tunnel inet  -->
        lladdr 00:30:65:ff:fe:aa:37:ae
        media: autoselect <full-duplex> status: inactive
        supported media: autoselect <full-duplex>
```

Okay, so there's a bunch of information that you're not interested in there, but buried in the middle is a line that says `inet 192.168.1.19`, which is my current IP address. Actually, a couple of lines look like that, because those are all valid IP addresses by which this machine knows itself (127.0.0.1 exists on every machine, and always points back to itself). There's a 426-kilobyte application that you can find on the net that can retrieve this information and show it to you when you double click it. Is the convenience of double-clicking worth the difference between 11 keystrokes and 426KB? Okay, so maybe the trouble of looking through that output is worth spending some disk space on. What if we add 15 more keystrokes (for a total of 26), and get the output down to only the IP address lines?

```
brezup:sageray Documents $ ifconfig -a ¦ grep "inet "
        inet 127.0.0.1 netmask 0xff000000
        inet 192.168.1.19 netmask 0xffffff00 broadcast 192.168.1.255
        tunnel inet  -->
```

Still worth nearly half a megabyte of disk space? Well, the 426KB application also can monitor your IP address and email you when it changes, but by the time you're finished with Chapter 15, you'll know how to add that capability to what you've seen here, and how to store it as your own little application that you can run with whatever name you care to call it. This'll cost you a one-time payment of another 100 or so keystrokes, depending on the length of your email address. It's rarely the functionality that takes up the room in these sorts of utility applications. Instead it's all the additional trimmings that must be layered around a simple utility to make it into a nice double-clickable GUI-driven application.

Hardly a day goes by when we don't see one or more utilities that someone's published for Mac OS X that aren't amazingly overcomplex and oversize for the capabilities that they bring to the end user. It's truly wonderful that people are willing to write little applications that perform useful actions and post news about them on macnn.com, and we wish their authors only the best. But it would often be of much more use for the author to just show the handful of lines of shell commands necessary to duplicate the effect. You can help change this landscape and further educate yourself at the same time, by learning how to construct simple utilities yourself (which you will be doing before you know it), and by urging utility authors to tell you how they did it, instead of just asking for impenetrable double-clickable applications.

Other command-line commands that you learn about in this and the following chapters are usually similarly designed. They do some small utility task, but they do it flexibly, and with a minimum of muss, fuss, or effort. By the end of Chapter 15 you will learn how to string them together into arbitrarily complex collections of commands that perform custom operations for you, and that can make use of your computer significantly more enjoyable and productive. Remember as you read through these chapters that it's not imperative for you to learn all the commands as you read about them. We've presented the commands in such an order that the topics build on each other, so paying attention to the general concepts helps a lot, but a multitude of commands are available in the shell, and even the most experienced Unix users rarely use more than a few percent on a regular basis.

Getting Help Through Online Manual Pages

The very first command that you should become familiar with is the `man` (manual) command. All good Unix systems provide an online collection of manual pages that detail almost every command available in the system. Mac OS X is no exception. Simply type **`man`** ***`<commandname>`*** at any shell prompt, and if there is a manual page documenting the command, it will be shown to you. For example, to see the man pages for the `date` command (which tells you the date and time), you could type

```
brezup:sage Documents $ man date
DATE(1)                   BSD General Commands Manual                  DATE(1)

NAME
     date -- display or set date and time

SYNOPSIS
     date [-nu] [-r seconds] [+format]
     date [-u] mmddhhmm[[cc]yy]

DESCRIPTION
     date displays the current date and time when invoked without arguments.
     Providing arguments will format the date and time in a user-defined way
     or set the date.  Only the superuser may set the date.

     The options are as follows:

     -n      The utility timed(8) is used to synchronize the clocks on groups
             of machines.  By default, if timed is running, date will set the
             time on all of the machines in the local group.  The -n option
             stops date from setting the time for other than the current
             machine.

     -r      Print out the date and time that is seconds from the Epoch.

     -u      Display or set the date in UTC (universal) time.

     An operand with a leading plus (``+'') sign signals a user-defined format
     string which specifies the format in which to display the date and time.
     The format string may contain any of the conversion specifications
     described in the strftime(3) manual page, as well as any arbitrary text.
:
```

TIP

If your terminal shows you a line that says `more` at the bottom of the window, a pathname and a percentage figure, or simply a `: character`, it means that there is more output to be seen. Press the spacebar and the next page of output scrolls into view. Which of the versions is displayed depends on what pager is being used. The first two are displayed when the pager is `more`, but `:` is displayed when the pager is `less`. If `less` is used as the pager, you will be able to search the man pages. As of Mac OS X 10.3, the functionality of `more` has been wrapped into an enhanced version of less, though both behaviors remain available to the user. The most important operating characteristics of both are discussed in the next chapter.

There's a vast quantity of information available in the `man` pages, books and books worth of it. In 1993, I had a complete printed set of the `man` pages that were shipped with an early version of Sun Microsystems' flavor of Unix. These manuals completely filled a 4-foot by 6-foot bookcase of 8.5×11 three-ring binders, and the quantity of information provided in the man pages has only been expanding. Once upon a time, this quantity of information was actually a significant burden to store on expensive and scarce disk space, and so it was stored in a mildly compressed format that wasn't easily human-readable, and the man page reading software was written to unpack this data and display it as necessary. Processors weren't so fast back then either, so the "unpack and display" step made the process a little slower than most people liked. To accommodate, the system was also designed to allow a duplicate set of man pages, in an unpacked format as well, which could be transparently (and more quickly) pulled up if they were available on the system, and an additional database of keywords and important terms that could be searched to find related man pages.

For reasons seemingly lost in the depths of time, someone also made the decision that the creation of a searchable database for the man pages would be left to the same process as the act of unpacking (known as "formatting") the man pages. The result of this is that now, even as machines have become fast enough that on-the-fly formatting is an imperceptible delay, and the disk space occupied by uncompressed (formatted) copies is insignificant, we're still saddled with a man system where man pages are typically delivered in a file format in which they can't be easily read or searched, and where creating a searchable version usually requires an additional step beyond what comes native on your machine. Thankfully, modern systems such as Tiger can build the keyword database independently of the formatted man pages, so now updating the database is at least a more convenient process.

By default, Mac OS X is delivered without formatted man pages, and without the database of keywords and terms built. Apple's Xcode (Developer Tools) installer now takes the initiative to run the formatting and database-building commands when it finishes the install process, but this doesn't mean that you no longer need to know about the process because other software that you might install on the system probably won't insert its information into the database or run preformatting commands. Because of this you can end up in a situation where some of your man page system is searchable, and some invisible to the search software. You can only remedy this by running the database building commands manually yourself when you install new software that adds pages to the man page system, or by running Apple installers that update the system as part of their installation process.

9

If you needed to build the searchable database for your Apple-supplied man page collection, either because you haven't installed the XCode distribution or because you'd like to update the pages with additional information that has been recently installed, you can do it like this:

```
brezup:ray Documents $ sudo makewhatis -v
Password:
man directory /usr/share/man
  /usr/share/man/man1
        reading /usr/share/man/man1/open.1
        reading /usr/share/man/man1/slp_reg.1
```

```
        ignoring junk description ""
        reading /usr/share/man/man1/slpd.1
        ignoring junk description ""
        reading /usr/share/man/man1/authopen.1
        reading /usr/share/man/man1/hdiutil.1
        reading /usr/share/man/man1/createhomedir.1
... <lots of output deleted>
        reading /usr/share/man/mann/while.ntcl
        reading /usr/share/man/mann/Widget.n
        reading /usr/share/man/mann/winfo.ntcl
        reading /usr/share/man/mann/wm.ntcl
        reading /usr/share/man/mann/yencode.n
        reading /usr/share/man/mann/zero.n
        reading /usr/share/man/mann/zip.n
brezup:ray Documents $
```

That might look like a lot of output, but the only really important thing is that it didn't toss up any serious errors, and that it came back to the command prompt when it finished. Many commands produce a wealth of diagnostic information when they're run, in addition to performing their intended function. Mostly, as with this, unless you're really interested in the intermediate steps and status, you can just ignore it.

Even if Apple's XCode install has already run the `makewhatis` step for you on the man page set Apple provides, you won't hurt anything if you decide you'd like to run it again yourself. You'll eventually want to run `makewhatis` on the `/usr/local/man` directory into which most third-party Unix applications will install their man pages (`sudo makewhatis /usr/local/man`) so that non-Apple man page information is searchable as well. When you run this command, don't worry too much about the warning messages that you see. So long as the warning messages don't suggest that something went terribly wrong everything is working okay.

NOTE

For the inquisitive, the `sudo` command used at the beginning of the examples here is used to cause the command that follows it to run with `root` (administrative) privileges. If you have enabled the `root` account, you could also do this by using the `su` command to switch to a shell running as the `root` user, which is an even more powerful administrative user than the normal Mac OS X Admin user group. We don't recommend that you spend much time in an sued shell because you can do a lot of damage in this mode, but some way to run commands as `root` is required for doing certain sorts of maintenance like this. We cover the advantages and disadvantages of `sudo` and `su`, and the intricacies and requirements for their use, in later chapters.

The `makewhatis` command that follows the `sudo` command is the name of a program that does the actual uncompressing, and indexing of the contents of the compressed man page data files. Using `sudo` before the command allows it to run with the permissions it requires to do the job in directories where your user ID would normally not be allowed to write.

After you have a formatted man page set (the default for Apple's man pages, if you've installed Xcode, but remember you'll need to format your own for other software you install), you can use the -k option to man. (This is equivalent to the apropos command; wherever you see man -k, you can substitute apropos, if that's easier for you to remember. There's also a similar program, whatis, that works just like these, but constrains the results to only whole-word matches of the query.) This option searches the man pages for pages with keywords matching what you've entered. For example, if you want to know which man pages might have information on the subject of time, you could issue a man command like this:

```
brezup:ray Documents $ man -k time
BIO_f_ssl(3o), BIO_set_ssl(3o), BIO_get_ssl(3o), BIO_set_ssl_mode(3o)
...
Benchmark(3)             - benchmark running times of Perl code
CPAN::FirstTime(3), s-1CPAN:s0 - Util for s-1CPAN:s0:Config file Initialization
...
Time::localtime(3)
➥- by-name interface to Perl's built-in localtime() function
Time::tm(3)
➥- internal object used by Time::gmtime and Time::localtime
ac(8)                    - display connect time accounting
adjtime(2)
➥- correct the time to allow synchronization of the system clock
alarm(3)                 - set signal timer alarm
...
sleep(1)                 - suspend execution for an interval of time
...
strftime(3)              - format date and time
time(1)                  - time command execution
time(3)                  - get time of day
time2posix(3), posix2time(3) - convert seconds since the Epoch
times(3)                 - process times
timezone(3)              - return the timezone abbreviation
touch(1)                 - change file access and modification times
tzfile(5)                - time zone information
tzset(3)                 - initialize time conversion information
ualarm(3)                - schedule signal after specified time
uptime(1)                - show how long system has been running
utime(3)                 - set file times
utimes(2)                - set file access and modification times
vtimes(3)                - get information about resource utilization
zdump(8)                 - time zone dumper
zic(8)                   - time zone compiler
...
```

This command lists each of the man pages that the system knows about that match the keyword (in this case, `time`) that you've requested. We've used ellipses in the output shown here to limit the output to only some of the most interesting time-related functions and commands you might want to know about. The listing you'll see when you run the command is (sometimes unfortunately) as comprehensive as your system can find, with respect to the query.

To be able to limit that listing down to just commands, or to just programming-library functions, or any of several other general categories of time-related information, it's important to know that the man page system has several sections into which the content is divided. Because of this, there might be commands that have multiple man pages, each in a different section. The system is divided into sections roughly segregated into the following topics:

- `Man1`—Typical user commands. Documentation of commands that can be executed by the normal user at the command line.
- `Man2`—System calls. Documentation of routines internal to the system that programmers can use in programs.
- `Man3`—User-level library calls. Documentation of C and other library functions for programmers.
- `Man4`—Device drivers, protocols, and network interfaces. Documentation of the internals of hardware support and software APIs for these items.
- `Man5`—File formats. Documentation of file format details for both system control files and certain program data files.
- `Man6`—Games and demos. Documentation for amusement software.
- `Man7`—Miscellaneous. Various tables of useful information, such as ASCII tables.
- `Man8`—Maintenance commands. Documentation for maintenance and system administration commands.
- `Man9`—System kernel developer's commands. Documentation for system kernel developer commands.

CAUTION

The segregation of the man pages into the directories `Man1`–`Man9` is not absolute. Third-party software providers have a bad habit of breaking convention and placing their man pages in inappropriate sections.

There are also a growing number of specialty sections that are devoted to the segregation of particular programming languages, or operating system features, and these have arbitrary names that aren't easily guessed. The only way that you might know, for example, that there is an `ntcl` section into which TCL scripting-language documentation is segregated, is because you notice `(ntcl)` appended to some of the commands that are related to your time query.

If you look at the earlier listing for the `man -k time` command, you will notice that each topic listed includes a number or letter in parentheses after the name of the topic. This is the man page section in which the item occurs. Unfortunately, although you can display man pages from specific sections by specifying the section before the item to read about (for example, `man 1 time`), there isn't a good way to tell `man -k` to search in only a particular section. This often makes the output of `man -k` less than appealing. By the time you learn how to use a few more features of the command line (the `grep` program and pipes, specifically), you'll know how to construct your own filters to select exactly the results you really want.

NOTE

Your system might not (and probably won't!) show exactly these same items. The available man pages depend on whether you've installed the developer toolkit and on any other software installed on the system. If the following examples using manual section 3 do not work for you, read through them now, and try them again after you've installed the developer tools (Chapter 14). We're including them here because we expect that many users will have "installed ahead," or are reading this book while trying to learn on a completely configured machine at work or school. If you're following along in a from-the-ground-up installation, bookmark this section on man pages, and try it out again after finishing the developer tools install.

To look at man pages in specific sections of the manual, specify the numeric or textual identifier for the section between the `man` command and the item you want to look up. For example, the system includes man pages for both the `time` command and the `time()` C library function. `man time` defaults to showing you the man page for the command-line–related item, if one exists, so both `man time` and `man 1 time` show you the man page for the `time` command:

```
brezup:ray Documents $ man time

TIME(1)                    BSD General Commands Manual                    TIME(1)

NAME
     time -- time command execution

SYNOPSIS
     time [-lp] utility

DESCRIPTION
     The time utility executes and times utility.  After the utility finishes,
     time writes the total time elapsed, the time consumed by system overhead,
     and the time used to execute utility to the standard error stream.  Times
     are reported in seconds.

     Available options:
```

```
     -l      The contents of the rusage structure are printed.

     -p      The output is formatted as specified by IEEE Std 1003.2-1992
             (``POSIX.2'').

     The csh(1) has its own and syntactically different builtin version of
     time.  The utility described here is available as /usr/bin/time to csh
:
```

The following man command produces identical results:

```
brezup:ray Documents $ man 1 time
```

If you want to know about the C library function named `time()`, however, you will need to look in the program-functions–related section of the man pages, using `man 3 time` as your command:

```
brezup:ray Documents $ man 3 time

TIME(3)                   BSD Library Functions Manual                 TIME(3)

NAME
     time -- get time of day

LIBRARY
     Standard C Library (libc, -lc)

SYNOPSIS
     #include <time.h>

     time_t
     time(time_t *tloc);

DESCRIPTION
     The time() function returns the value of time in seconds since 0 hours, 0
     minutes, 0 seconds, January 1, 1970, Coordinated Universal Time, without
     including leap seconds.

     A copy of the time value may be saved to the area indicated by the
     pointer tloc.  If tloc is a NULL pointer, no value is stored.

     Upon successful completion, time() returns the value of time.  Otherwise
     a value of ((time_t) -1) is returned and the global variable errno is set
:
```

NOTE

If you add any software to the system, it might place man pages into the system `man` directories (located in `/usr/share/man` on OS X), or into the local `man` directories (located in `/opt/man`, `/usr/local/man`, or both). If you do this, you will need to rebuild the `makewhatis` database before the new manual pages will show up when you use the `man -k` option.

The `man` system is self-documenting, of course, so if you want to read further about the `man` command, simply type **`man man`**.

A command documentation table (our revised and sometimes corrected version of the man pages, with most esoteric or uninteresting options pared out) for `man` is shown in Table 9.3, which lists the syntax and selected options for `man`. The complete documentation table is located in Appendix A.

TABLE 9.3 Syntax and Selected Options for `man`

`man`	Formats and displays online manual pages.
`man [-acdfFhkKtwW] [--path] [-m system] [-p string] [-C config_file] [-M pathlist] [-P pager] [-S section_list] [section] name ...`	
`-a`	Displays all the manual pages for a specified section and name combination. (The default is to display only the first page found.)
`-d`	Displays debugging information, rather than manual pages. Not really useful for the end user, but included here because it's important to understand the range of options that these commands typically provide.
`-f` *<keyword>*	Displays a list of manual pages that contain complete word matches to the *<keyword>*. Same as `whatis`.
`-h`	Displays the help for `man`.
`-k` *<keyword>*	Displays a list of manual pages that contain the *<keyword>*. Same as `apropos`.
`-w`	Lists the pathnames of manual pages that would be displayed for the specified section and name combination. Don't display the pages themselves.
`-S` *<list>*	Searches the specified colon-separated sections in *<list>*. Overrides `MANSECT` environment variable.

The optional *<section>* argument restricts `man`'s results to the specified section. Multiple sections can be listed using the `-S` *<section list>* option, and providing a comma-separated list of sections to search.

As you can see, there are copious additional options that we aren't detailing here. These, again, are likely to be of minimal interest to most readers, and we direct your attention to the built-in versions for those cases where you might find it useful to know about such things as how to specify an alternative configuration file or an alternative location to search for `man` pages.

Terminal Preferences and Configuration

As with most Mac OS X GUI tools, a number of things about Terminal can be customized. Because you're probably familiar with configuring GUI apps by now, we'll just hit the highlights and give you an overview of what is configured where.

In Preferences under Terminal, shown in Figure 9.1, you configure the shell to use for interaction in the terminal. Because the default shell from Apple is in `bash`, it's probably best to keep the default setting, `Execute the default login shell using /usr/bin/login`, rather than specifying another shell, unless you really want something else. If you do decide to specify another shell, you need to set it, close the Terminal Preferences, and open a new terminal window. In the past we've seen this preference take longer than expected to take effect, so you might quit Terminal and re-launch it if you keep landing in the previous shell. Also, here you can set Terminal to open a saved terminal settings file upon launching. You can also configure the type of (hardware) terminal that Terminal claims to be. If you remember, we said that Terminal is a software version of what used to be hardware devices used to talk to machines. There were many different hardware terminal types, and they all spoke their own hardware-specific languages. This setting in the Terminal's preferences enables you to tell Terminal what type of hardware appliance to claim to be, in case the software at the other end of the communications pipe wants to take advantage of special features that a given hardware terminal appliance might have had. We recommend that you leave this with Apple's default setting unless you meet a system that claims to not know how to speak to your Terminal. A setting of VT100 or VT52 is also likely to be widely compatible.

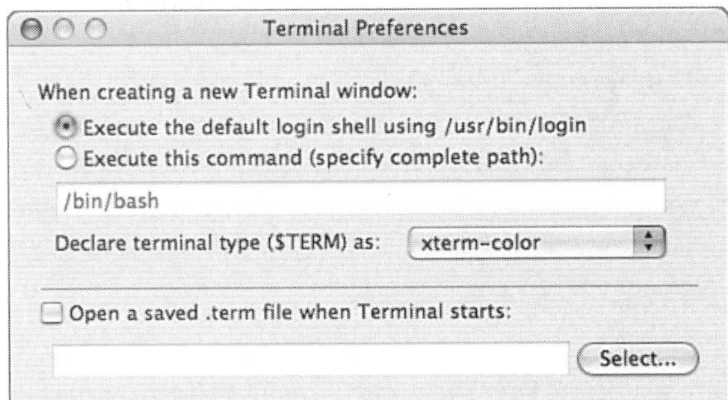

FIGURE 9.1 The shell is configured in the Terminal Preferences, located under Preferences under the Application (Terminal) menu.

Additional preferences can be chosen by selecting Window Settings under the Terminal menu, or by selecting File, Show Info under the File menu. This brings up the Terminal Inspector, where you can set the following settings via a pop-up menu:

- Shell, shown in Figure 9.2, enables you to configure the behavior of the terminal window when the shell or application running in it exits. You can choose to close the window, not close the window, or close the window only if the shell exited cleanly. If you change your shell in Terminal Preferences, you see that shell listed rather than `bash`.

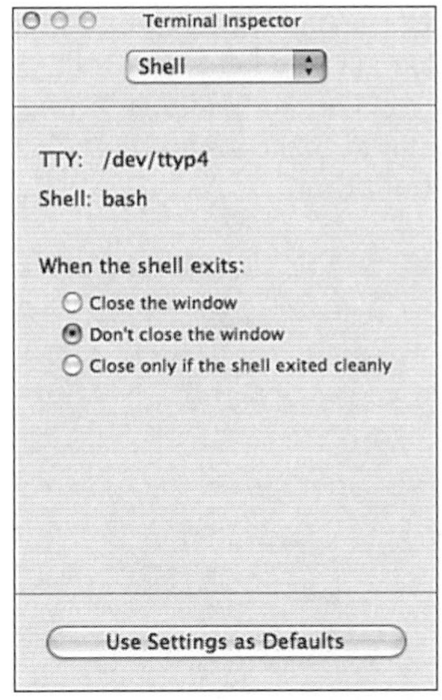

FIGURE 9.2 Under the Shell pop-up of the Terminal Inspector, the terminal's behavior upon exiting is specified.

- Processes, shown in Figure 9.3, shows you any current processes that that terminal is the parent of. As you'll learn later in this chapter, Unix commands run "in" terminals. If you were to run `ls`, which we will also see later in this chapter, `ls` would be added to the current process listing for that terminal window. Here you can also specify the behavior of a terminal window upon closing it. Because Unix commands run "in" terminals, closing a terminal when an application running "in" it is still active can have undesirable results. You can choose to have Terminal prompt you always, never, or only if commands other than the ones listed are running. You can also modify that command list.
- Emulation, shown in Figure 9.4, allows you to configure input and output options. You can configure a number of input options. Here you can translate between Unix newline only and Macintosh carriage return when pasting between Terminal and other applications, as well as configure several other features of the way that the Terminal emulates hardware devices. If your text gets pasted as all one line rather than multiple lines, you probably need to change the newline pasting setting. Another input option is to use Escape Non-ASCII Characters in the stream, which is to say, cause the Terminal to specially mark nonprinting characters. Whether you need to enable or disable this depends on the applications you're trying to run in the Terminal. If weird characters are being displayed instead of formatted text, or your Terminal output is positioned oddly around the screen instead of some characters appearing, try toggling this setting. Reverse Linewrap enables you to travel back up a wrapped line, instead of backspace stopping at the left edge of the window. Strict VT-100 Keypad Behavior emulation configures whether your numeric keypad behaves as defined for the VT-100 terminal, or whether it makes some common, but

9

nonconforming changes in the behavior. Again, the setting you need depends on the software you run. If you get odd behavior from your keypad keys in the software you need, toggle this setting. The Audible Bell setting, as you might expect, causes "bell" events in the terminal to make a sound. The visual bell flashes the terminal when the terminal bell would ring.

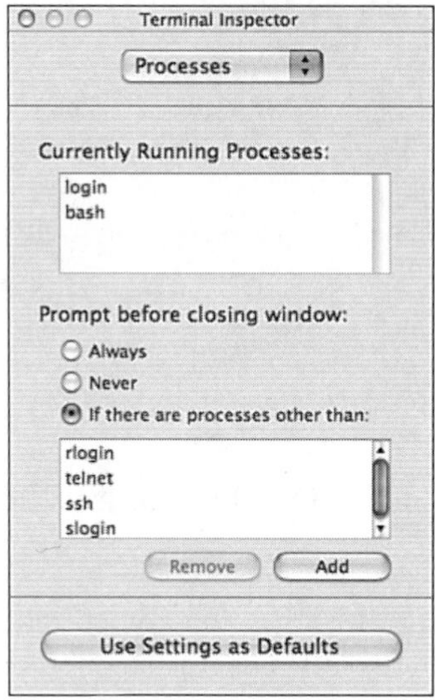

FIGURE 9.3 The Processes section of the Terminal Inspector.

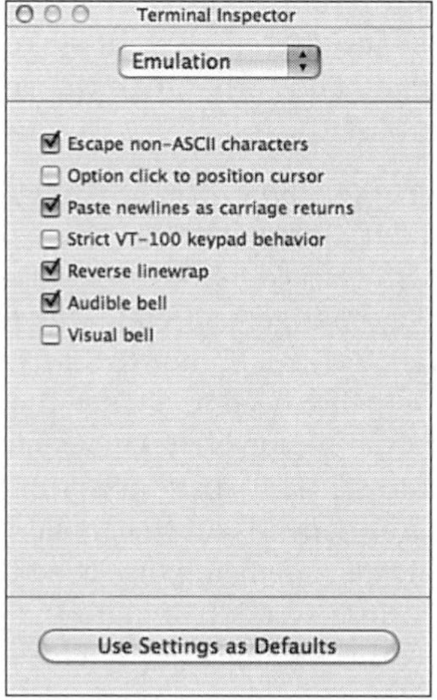

FIGURE 9.4 The Emulation section enables you to configure input and output options.

- The Buffer section of the Terminal Inspector, shown in Figure 9.5, lets you disable the scrollback buffer, or set how many lines to keep in the buffer. We suggest you use many, many lines! We couldn't live with a scrollback buffer of fewer than 3,000 lines. As memory and disk space become cheaper every day, you'll probably find that you want, and can use, even more. Whether to wrap lines is your choice, as is whether you want the terminal to scroll to the bottom when you enter data into it. You can also choose whether to rewrap lines when resizing a window.

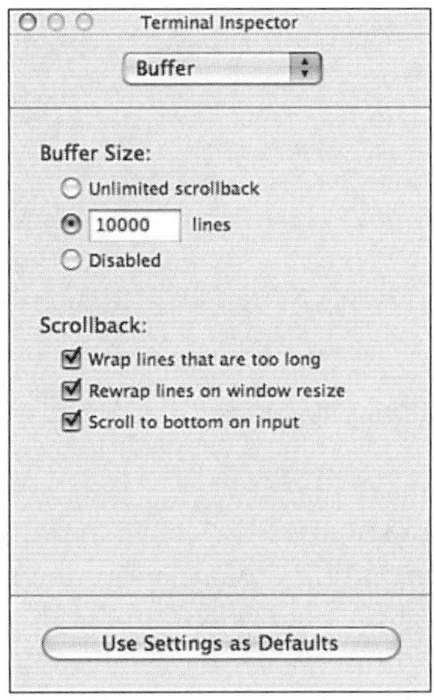

FIGURE 9.5 The Buffer section allows you to configure the scrollback buffer.

- The Display section of the Terminal Inspector, shown in Figure 9.6, lets you specify the type of cursor you want and whether it blinks. Additionally, you can configure the font. Be sure to pick a monospace font, such as Monaco or Courier, because the formatting you see in the terminal is typically based on spaces. Output, documentation, and so on will look better in the terminal. Proportional fonts are better suited for applications such as word processors. Character set encoding is also configured here. We recommend you leave it at `Unicode (UTF-8)` because some applications require it. With the Unicode setting, however, you might see some characters translated as question marks in a diamond. For those applications, you might want to experiment with other character encoding sets. Drag and drop copy/pasting allows the terminal to interact conveniently with more traditional Macintosh programs but causes some interesting effects if you drop in text that you couldn't have typed in the Terminal.

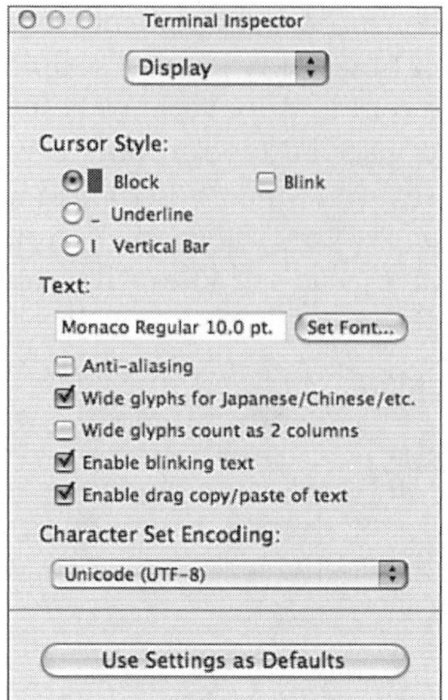

FIGURE 9.6 In the Display section, you can set the cursor style, text, and character set encoding.

- The Color section, shown in Figure 9.7, lets you configure the colors of many features of the terminal, including the background and selection. Additionally, you can set a transparency level for the background and/or an image to use as the terminal background. If you find the colors that some command-line software chooses to use for its text to be annoying or unreadable, you can disable the color and force it all to nice clean black by disabling ANSI color here.

  If you want to quickly change colors in the terminal, in addition to the custom option, preset options are available: black on white, white on black, green on black, black on light yellow, white on blue, or blue on white. One of those preset color selections might bring back fond memories of your Apple IIe, or other computer.

- The Window section, shown in Figure 9.8, lets you configure the window's dimensions by specifying the number of columns and rows displayed. You can also customize what is displayed in the title bar by giving a custom name and checking boxes for what additional data you want to have displayed, such as the shell command name, the window's dimensions, or the current process running in the terminal window. Selecting the current process is particularly useful if you minimize terminals into the dock because this will let you quickly scan through many minimized terminals to find the one you want, instead of needing to open each one to figure out what it's doing.

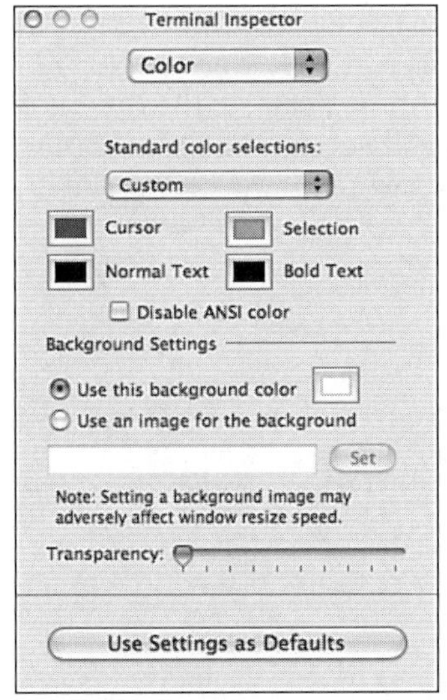

FIGURE 9.7 The Color section of the Terminal Inspector.

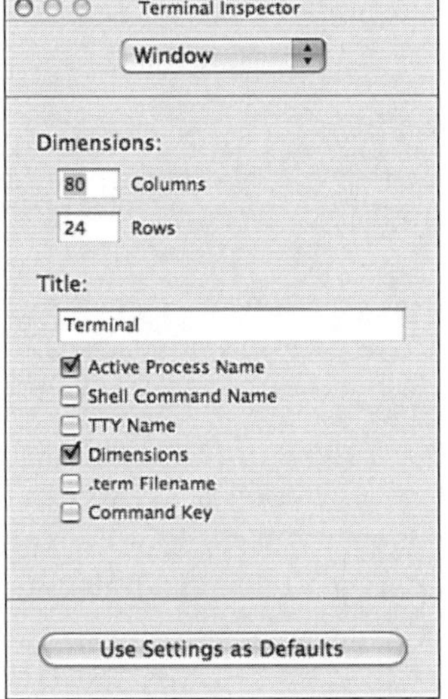

FIGURE 9.8 In the Window section, you can set window dimensions and the title bar display.

- The Keyboard section, shown in Figure 9.9, lets you configure the actual data sent when you press almost any key or key combination on the keyboard. This can be handy both for customizing the keyboard to work with your software, and for finding out just what the keyboard is doing for certain key combinations when you're trying to customize other software to match it. You can also configure whether the Delete key sends backspace (in Unix, backspace typically deletes to the left of the cursor) or delete (which typically deletes to the right of the cursor). If you have software that requires a meta key (a virtually obsolete keyboard key once popular on some terminals), you can set the option to send the meta sequence. Typically this is not needed because almost all software that expected to see meta as a character sent from the keyboard now uses the escape key instead.

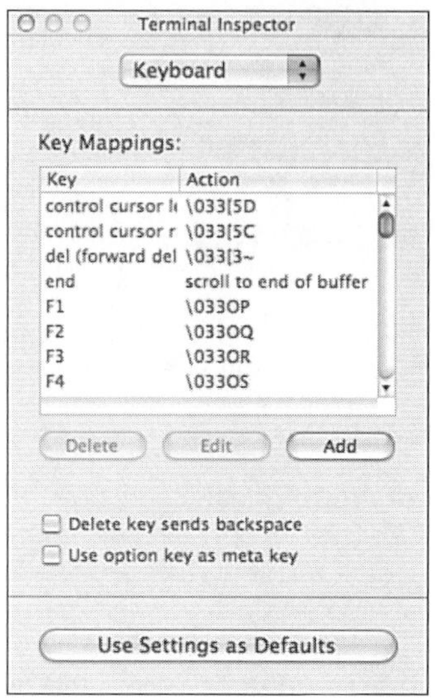

FIGURE 9.9 In the Keyboard section, you can set keyboard mappings and the behavior of Delete and Option keys in the Terminal.

The Use Settings as Default button that appears at the bottom of each item in the Terminal Inspector allows you to save those settings as your default settings, so that whenever you open a terminal, it opens with those saved settings.

The Save and Save As items are accessible from the File menu. These allow you to save the preferences of a Terminal window or window set. This can be useful, for example, for saving different colored terminals that you use for different purposes, or terminals that are preconfigured to open running a particular command.

Open allows you to open a terminal window using settings that you saved to a `.term` file.

Also accessible are the Save Text As and Save Selected Text As items. These allow you to save the complete text buffer of the terminal, or whatever text you have selected in the terminal.

The New Command item of the File menu produces a dialog box in which you can enter a command to run in a new terminal window. If the command doesn't produce an interactive environment, the new window just tells you that the command ran, which isn't very useful. If the command is an interactive one such as `emacs` (`emacs` is a powerful text editor that you'll learn about in Chapter 13, "Using Common Command-Line Applications and Application Suites"), it produces a new window and runs the specified command in that window.

TIP

Although the New Command item might not sound particularly useful at first, it is actually a powerful tool. The point isn't to give you yet another way of running a program in a terminal, but rather to give you a way to *save a preference* for what program is running in a terminal. If you use the New Command to start a program in a terminal, and then Save that terminal from the File menu, you'll get a Terminal document that you can double-click, and have that command executed for you. If you're constantly using a terminal to log in to another system, or to run an editor, and so forth, you can save Terminal documents for each, and just double-click the saved document to launch each application in its own terminal as necessary. This becomes a real time-saver when the commands you run have a large number of command line options, and take a long time to type without errors.

The File menu item Set Title is another way to bring up the Terminal Inspector. Of course, the Terminal Inspector comes up with the pop-up menu set to Window, but you can still navigate through the inspector.

Additionally, the File menu includes the option to send a Break signal to the terminal, which can be invaluable for stopping a program that has gone awry without taking the drastic step of closing the terminal.

Most of the items in the Edit menu are familiar. The Find item, however, leads to an option to bring up the Find panel, from which you can search for data in the Terminal's buffer.

The Font and Windows menus have the properties you already expect.

Each terminal window itself has an option to view it as a split window. Click on the icon (little square with a squiggle in it) at the upper right of the terminal window. You can adjust the vertical height of the resulting split window sections by dragging the bar. The top section stores your buffer, and the lower window generally contains your current activity. The split window may be especially useful for running an editor and using the scrollback buffer for items to copy and paste into the editor. Figure 9.10 shows an example of the split window.

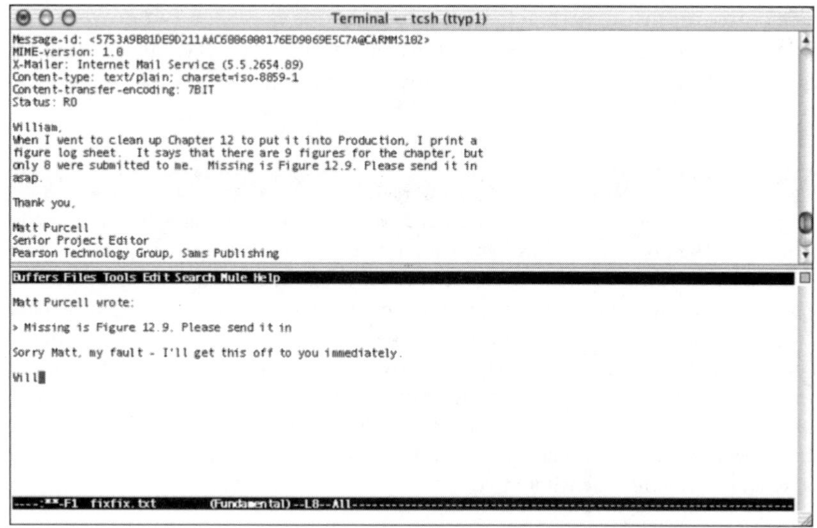

FIGURE 9.10 The Terminal window includes an option to be displayed as a split window.

Summary

In this chapter, we began the introduction to what is, for most practical purposes, a second operating system living under the hood of your Mac OS X computer. The BSD Unix variant underlying the graphical interface to Mac OS X is a fully featured Unix and provides a command-line interface to your operating system.

This chapter covered some of the background information that you need to know for interacting with the command line, and getting help. However, the most important thing to remember from this chapter is not the particular commands or syntax detailed here, but rather the general way that these commands work and feel. You'll get much more exposure to the Unix experience in the coming chapters. The most powerful tool in a Unix user's toolbox is an understanding of "The Unix Way." The best method of learning about Unix is by experience and experimentation. You will soon find that you can use your understanding of the way things work in Unix to rearrange and recombine examples that we've shown to synthesize new solutions.

CHAPTER 10

Common Unix Shell Commands: File, Directory, and Disk Operations

IN THIS CHAPTER

- Understanding Tiger, HFS+, and BSD Command Interaction
- Basic Tiger Filesystem Navigation
- Managing Files and Directories
- Examining File Contents
- Searching for Files, Directories, and More
- File Compression and Archiving
- Getting Disk and Directory Information: `du`, `df`
- Mounting/Unmounting Volumes: `diskutil`

A large fraction of the truly good uses for a command-line application revolve around manipulating files in some fashion. It's immediately obvious that a command-line–based painting program sounds like a rather cumbersome tool (although we will talk about a command-line photo-editing suite in Chapters 13, "Using Common Command-Line Applications and Application Suites," and 14, "Command-Line Software Installation and Troubleshooting"), but a point-and-click based file renaming system, such as is used by the Finder, is a similarly less-than-optimal solution. The command line provides better ways to perform this type of action, so we will begin our in-depth coverage of the command line with the simple file-manipulation commands that are ubiquitously necessary to get almost anything done. You'll almost certainly find that you use the commands from this chapter more frequently than any other, when working at the command line. Augmented with the material from Chapter 15, "Shell Configuration and Programming (Shell Scripting)," you might find that there is little else that you want or need to do at the command line. This could easily be enough to save you hours of mousing or driving a trackpad every day.

Understanding Tiger, HFS+, and BSD Command Interaction

To the novice Unix user—especially one coming from a GUI environment as nice as the Mac's—venturing into the

Unix filesystem will probably feel like a journey back to the Stone Age. Files upon files, nothing to indicate what any of them do, and not a friendly icon in sight. Although the filesystem might initially appear cryptic and primitive, you will find that with experience, it actually affords you considerable sophistication and control. This sophistication comes from the ability to combine the functions of many small programs into larger programs with arbitrarily complex functions.

Before the use of most Unix commands will make sense, you need to understand a few things about the design of the standard Unix filesystem, and the ways that the Mac OS X HFS+ filesystem differs. Apple doesn't strictly adhere to the model that most forms of Unix use, but from the point of view of the BSD subsystem, it functions similarly enough that almost everything works without modification. You'll find a number of differences between the way Unix thinks of files, and what you're probably used to, but after you get used to them, you'll probably find these differences are to your liking.

CAUTION

One important caution and caveat with respect to almost all basic Unix commands we're going to be covering: As you'll soon see, Unix doesn't know a resource fork from a salad fork. Apple's legacy way of storing the information for a particular file in two physically disparate locations on the disk is completely foreign to Unix, and although Apple has performed some clever kluges to allow the Mac OS X to live atop a filesystem that inherently doesn't understand portions of what the operating system is talking about, there are still some rough edges. Apple originally promised most of these would be worked out in Tiger, but as we're writing, it doesn't look like everything's quite as polished as it could be.

What you as the user will notice, as a result of these rough edges, is that it's sometimes a bad idea to use Unix file manipulation commands on files that were created by or that belong to the GUI. For example, some programs still keep their preferences in files with resource forks, and if you try to move or copy what seems to be the preferences file with the Unix command line tools, the resulting file will be damaged. Apple has provided workarounds via some specialty commands that we'll cover in several places as appropriate, but it would be nice if these fixes were melded into the traditional tools so that you didn't need to use different tools to work with different file types—that's definitely not the Unix way. Even in this slightly rough state, the vast majority of things will work exactly as expected, and in four years of using Mac OS X, I've only run into a single instance in which the incompatibilities irreparably damaged a file. You should still be aware that there are some limitations, and that you should probably use the Finder for doing things such as copying, moving, and backing up critical files like applications, preferences, and documents from Cocoa/Carbon applications.

Basic Unix File Principles

Unix filesystems have a single root directory. Unlike Macintosh filesystems with their multiple drive icons on the desktop, and Windows machines with their ABCs, Unix filesystems have only a single top-level designator for the filesystem. This is the root directory named /. Unix considers all its files to belong to a tree-shaped structure, with the root directory at its base and files as the leaves. Directories are the branching points between the branches. Unix trees are upside down with respect to real trees because Unix users speak of the root directory as being at the top of the tree, and other directories and files as being under it. Any directory can contain files and other directories.

NOTE

The term *root* is used for multiple meanings in Unix. The `root` user is the most authoritative user of the system, with essentially absolute control over any process or configuration. The root of the filesystem is the top directory of the filesystem, beneath which all other files and directories occur.

Every file in the Unix filesystem has a unique and unambiguous name that points to it. This complete name is known as the *full path* to the file and can be specified from any directory in the filesystem to indicate any file in the filesystem. The full path to a file always starts with the root directory and ends in the filename, indicating directory names along the way, separated by the separator character `/`. A full path can be thought of as the shortest list of directories that must be traversed from the root to reach the file. A file with the full path `/home/wizbot/spin/spinnin` is named `spinnin` and is located in the directory `spin`, which is located in the directory `wizbot`, which is located in the directory `home`, which is located in the root directory `/`.

Files have both full paths and relative paths. A *relative path* is a path from the current directory, instead of from the root directory. There are two special relative directory names. One of these is `.`, which indicates the current directory; the other is `..`, which indicates the directory that is the parent of this directory. For example, assume that there is a directory named `spun` in the same directory as the directory named `spin` in the earlier path (it would have a full path of `/home/wizbot/spun`). If we are in the directory `spun` and want to specify the relative path to the file `spinnin`, we can do so with the relative path `../spin/spinnin`. Likewise, if we're in the directory `wizbot`, we can use any of `/home/wizbot/spin/spinnin`, `spin/spinnin`, or `./spin/spinnin` to address the file `spinnin`. The importance of being able to specifically address the current directory in a file path specification is probably not immediately obvious. It is related to an occasional necessity to differentiate between items in situations where there are duplicated names, and one item happens to be in the current directory.

TIP

Full (or absolute) paths always start with `/`; relative paths never do.

Not only do you not have multiple drives at the top level of the system (although the Finder makes it look like you do), but you, as the user, don't need to know which drives are where. Additional drives (or, more properly, *partitions*) appear as directories and can be mounted at any point in the filesystem to appear as an extended branch in the system. Sound strange? After a while it won't. In one of the nice feats of Unix abstraction, the system removes from the user's sphere of concern what hardware devices actually exist, and where they are or how they're connected. After you get used to this idea, you'll see that it makes really good sense. So long as you can uniquely identify a file by name in the filesystem, why would you care which spinning chunk of metal it lives on? This system has additional nice features. If you find one day that you've run out of space to put files in some particular location, you can simply add a drive to the system and mount it—that is, make it appear as the directory—where you need space. There's no need to reconfigure things or move files around because the additional space will simply appear as new space in whatever directory you mount it as.

If the importance of that isn't clear, imagine a situation in which you've been downloading a lot of information from the Internet. You've been storing everything in a directory named `Macintosh HD/Web Stuff/Downloads`, and you've just run out of space on Macintosh HD. In other operating systems, including the old familiar pre-OS X Mac OS, even if you had another disk available and ready to add to the system, you would need to rearrange things, perhaps creating `Macintosh HD2/Web Stuff/Downloads` and moving everything from the original directory over to the new one. With Unix-based operating systems, including Mac OS X, this is unnecessary. You would still need to move your files, but you could add the new drive and make it appear (mount it) as the directory `Macintosh HD/Web Stuff/Downloads`. Suddenly, that directory would have plenty of space, and you wouldn't need to rearrange the filesystem, reconfigure your Internet applications to download to a new location, or develop a new set of downloading habits.

As a matter of fact, you don't even need to know what country your files physically reside in. Again, Unix abstraction comes into play, and a remote file server is mounted as a directory under the local filesystem just as additional physical storage is. From your point of view, a remote file server is just another directory; the only difference between accessing files on it and on local storage is the possible network delay associated with transporting the files.

Regardless of whether you know where your files actually are, the shell, as previously mentioned, is always somewhere in the filesystem structure. Just like a Finder window that is showing file icons is open to and currently displaying some particular location on your system, a shell displaying a prompt is in some specific location. Commands that use files reference files from the point of view of being "in" that directory. The `pwd` command causes the shell to tell you what directory it's currently in.

Also as previously mentioned, Unix is a case-sensitive system, and Unix filenames are usually case sensitive from the command line. From Mac OS X, this isn't absolutely the case (depending on which base disk format you chose for your installation), but when you're working from the command line, remember that what you type must have the correct capitalization.

A file has three primary attributes that control who can access the file. These attributes control access at the level of whether the file can be read, written to, and executed. Additionally, these attributes can be specified separately for the user who owns the file, a group of selected users, and everybody on the system. These attributes can be set to any combination of values, although some combinations do not make much sense. For example, you would expect an application to be executable, a configuration file for a program to be readable, and something like your daily schedule to be both readable and writable. Unix, however, will do whatever you tell it to with the file permissions. If you make your daily schedule executable, Unix will do its best to execute it, which most likely will result in an error message and no damage done. If you tell Unix that an application is writable, it will be happy to let you edit it in a word processor, which will probably make the application useless. We cover file permissions in more detail later in the "Introduction to File Permissions" section of Chapter 11, "Using File Permissions and Access Control Lists."

Everything in the filesystem has an owner. Every file and directory in the Unix filesystem has auxiliary information attached to it that specifies the individual user who owns it, and also the group of users that it belongs to (also known as *group ownership* or *group ID*). Depending on the permissions, this user or group of users can access the file. The individual owner of the file can control the group it belongs to, and the access privileges that the group, and all other users on the system, can use in accessing the file.

Each user has a home directory. This is one special directory in the filesystem that is owned by the user and is used to contain configuration files and other content specific to the user. From the point of view of the filesystem, the user's home directory is no different than any other directory, but it is significant in that it is the directory where you start when you open a terminal and shell on the system. To make things simpler for you, Unix doesn't require that you remember the path to your directory; it can always be specified by the special path `~<username>`.

Keep these basic principles in mind when reading about the commands to work within the filesystem. We cover some of them in more detail later in this chapter, but it helps to have a basic understanding of them as we move to the explanations and examples of commands.

NOTE

When discussing your interaction with the shell, we frequently use the word *you* interchangeably with the shell. It's much shorter to write "in the directory where you type the command" than "in the current working directory of the shell that you're interacting with when you type the command."

Basic Tiger Filesystem Navigation

The most basic commands for dealing with the Unix filesystem are those for moving around the filesystem (changing that "somewhere" that the shell always is) and for listing the contents of directories (finding out what's in the same location as the shell or in some other directory). Before you start moving around, however, it's a good idea to be able to find out where you are.

Finding Your Current Location: `pwd`

The `pwd` command (print working directory) prints the full path to the current working directory—the location where you are at the moment in this particular shell.

```
brezup:nermal Documents $ pwd
/Users/nermal/Documents
```

Table 10.1 shows the complete command documentation table for pwd.

TABLE 10.1 The Command Documentation Table for pwd

pwd	Prints current working directory.
pwd [-L¦P]	
-L	Prints the logical path to the current working directory, as defined by the shell in the environment variable PWD.
-P	Prints the physical path to the current working directory, with symbolic links resolved. This is the default under tcsh, but from bash, pwd appears to execute as pwd -L instead.

NOTE

Sometimes pwd doesn't respond with identical information to what you expect. For example, if you cd (change directory—a command covered shortly) to the directory named /var/tmp, and issue the pwd -P command, you get /private/var/tmp as an answer. This is because Apple has put some of the normal Unix directories in weird places and pulled some trickery to get them to appear as though they're where they should be. This is a compromise forced on the system because it must be able to coexist with Mac OS on the same drive. If you want to see pwd return the same information as where you ceded to, use pwd -L.

Listing Files in Various Locations: ls

The ls command lists files in the directory where you currently are. More properly, the ls command lists files anywhere in the filesystem, presuming that you have permissions with which to do so. If you don't specify any other directory for it to list, ls defaults to listing the files in the current working directory.

For example, to list the files in the current working directory, simply type **ls**.

```
brezup:nermal Documents $ cd /
brezup:nermal / $ pwd
/
brezup:nermal / $ ls
AppleShare PDS             Network                    etc
Applications               System                     mach
Applications (Mac OS 9)    System Folder              mach.sym
Cleanup At Startup         TheFindByContentFolder     mach_kernel
Desktop DB                 TheVolumeSettingsFolder    private
Desktop DF                 Trash                      sbin
Desktop Folder             Users                      tmp
Developer                  Volumes                    usr
Documents                  bin                        var
Late Breaking News         cores                      vol.tar
Library                    dev                        ???T+???Blank1
```

This example shows that the directory / contains 33 things. From this listing, you can't tell which of those things are directories and which of those things are files.

There's really no need to issue the pwd command as shown in the preceding example. If you don't know where you are in the filesystem, pwd tells you. If you already know, there's no need to ask the computer to tell you.

NOTE

Many of the command listings shown here are based on a user account we've created for demo purposes, with the username nermal. You're welcome to use your own account instead of nermal for the examples.

If you want to list the files in a directory other than the one that you are currently in, simply specify the path to the directory after the ls command. The path to specify can be either a relative or an absolute path. For example, to list the files in a directory named /Users/nermal/ if you're in the directory /Users/, simply type **ls nermal/**.

```
brezup:nermal / $ cd /Users/
brezup:nermal /Users $ ls
Shared joray  miwa   nermal
brezup:nermal /Users $ ls nermal/
Desktop                    Network Trash Folder      chown-output
Documents                  Pictures                  myfile
Library                    Public                    output-sample6
Movies                     Sites                     su-output
Music                      TheVolumeSettingsFolder   typescripts
```

You could also produce this same output by using the absolute path. Instead of the relative path nermal/ from the current directory /Users/, you could look explicitly in /Users/nermal/:

```
brezup:nermal / $ cd /Users/
brezup:nermal /Users $ ls
Shared joray  miwa   nermal
brezup:nermal /Users $ ls /Users/nermal/
Desktop                    Network Trash Folder      chown-output
Documents                  Pictures                  myfile
Library                    Public                    output-sample6
Movies                     Sites                     su-output
Music                      TheVolumeSettingsFolder   typescripts
```


Or, if you're in the directory /Users/nermal/Documents/ and want to list the files in the directory that is the parent of this directory (/Users/nermal/), you can use the relative path .. (the parent directory) to access it. To do this, use **ls ../**.

```
brezup:nermal nermal $ cd /Users/nermal/Documents
brezup:nermal Documents $ ls ../
```

```
Desktop                  Network Trash Folder      chown-output
...looks the same, still!
```

Likewise, if you want to list the contents of `/Users/nermal/typescripts/`, and you're in `/Users/nermal/Documents/`, you could type

```
brezup:nermal nermal $ cd /Users/nermal/Documents
brezup:nermal Documents $ ls ../typescripts/
typescript           typescript-copy-2   typescript2          typescript5
typescript-copy      typescript-copy-3   typescript4
```

Like most Unix commands, the `ls` command has a plethora of options from which to choose. These options enable you to specify which files you want to list and what information you want to list about them. Table 10.2 shows the syntax for `ls` as well as some common and interesting options.

TABLE 10.2 Syntax and Selected Options for `ls`

`ls`	Lists directory contents.
`ls [-ABCFGHLPRTWZabcdefghiklmnopqrstuwx1] [<file1> <file2> ...]`	
For each operand that names a file of a type other than directory, `ls` displays its name as well as any requested, associated information. If no operands are given, the contents of the current directory are displayed. If more than one operand is given, nondirectory operands are displayed first; directory and nondirectory operands are sorted separately and in lexicographical order.	
`-A`	Lists all entries except for `.` and `..`. Always set for superuser.
`-C`	Forces multicolumn output. This is the default when output is to a terminal.
`-F`	Displays a slash (`/`) immediately after each pathname that is a directory, an asterisk (`*`) after each that is executable, an at sign (`@`) after each symbolic link, an equal sign (`=`) after each socket, a percent sign (`%`) after each whiteout, and a vertical bar (`¦`) after each that is a FIFO.
`-G`	Enables colorized output. Equivalent to defining `CLICOLOR` in the environment.
`-R`	Recursively lists subdirectories encountered.
`-T`	When used with the `-l` option, displays complete time information for the file, including month, day, hour, minute, second, and year.
`-a`	Includes directory entries whose names begin with a dot (`.`).
`-c`	Uses time when file status was last changed for sorting or printing.
`-d`	Lists directories as plain files (not searched recursively).
`-e`	Prints the Access Control List associated with a file, if one exists.
`-h`	When used with the `-l` option, uses unit suffixes—byte, kilobyte, megabyte, gigabyte, terabyte, and petabyte—to reduce the number of digits to three or less using base 2 for sizes.
`-l`	Lists in long format. Long format lists the following: file mode, number of links, owner name, group name, number of bytes in the file, abbreviated month, day-of-month file was last modified, hour file last modified, minute file last modified, and the pathname.
`-r`	Reverses the order of the sort to get reverse lexicographical order or the oldest entries first.
`-t`	Sorts by time modified (most recently modified first) before sorting the operands by lexicographical order.

TABLE 10.2 Continued

`-u`	Uses time of last access, instead of last modification of the file for sorting (`-t`) or printing (`-l`).
`-x`	The same as `-C`, except that the multicolumn output is produced with entries sorted across, rather than down, the columns.

You can use an `ls` command like this to produce a listing that shows the contents of the root directory and indicates the following for each file (or directory): who the owner of the file is, what group the file belongs to, and the size of files.

```
brezup:nermal / $ ls -l
total 13232
-rwxrwxrwx   1 root  wheel   106496 Apr 20 14:59 AppleShare PDS
drwxrwxrwx  25 root  admin      806 Apr 18 11:05 Applications
drwxrwxrwx  18 root  wheel      568 Apr 20 14:54 Applications (Mac OS 9)
drwxrwxrwx   2 root  wheel      264 Apr  6 12:24 Cleanup At Startup
-rwxrwxrwx   1 root  wheel   212992 Apr 20 14:59 Desktop DB
-rwxrwxrwx   1 root  wheel  1432466 Apr 20 14:57 Desktop DF
drwxrwxrwx   6 root  staff      264 Apr  4 11:51 Desktop Folder
drwxrwxr-x  12 root  admin      364 Mar  1 20:29 Developer
drwxrwxrwx   6 ray   staff      264 Apr  4 14:20 Documents
-rwxrwxrwx   1 root  wheel        0 Apr  4 14:11 Late Breaking News
drwxrwxr-x  21 root  admin      670 Apr 18 11:04 Library
drwxr-xr-x   6 root  wheel      264 Apr  4 12:47 Network
drwxr-xr-x   3 root  wheel       58 Apr 12 00:51 System
drwxrwxrwx  40 root  wheel     1316 Apr 20 14:50 System Folder
drwxrwxrwx   2 ray   staff      264 Mar 23 14:59 TheFindByContentFolder
drwxrwxrwx   4 ray   staff      264 Mar 23 14:46 TheVolumeSettingsFolder
drwxrwxrwx   2 ray   staff      264 Apr 20 14:58 Trash
drwxr-xr-x   6 root  wheel      160 Apr 16 12:37 Users
drwxrwxrwt   6 root  wheel      264 Apr 20 15:00 Volumes
drwxr-xr-x  33 root  wheel     1078 Apr 16 09:40 bin
lrwxrwxr-t   1 root  admin       13 Apr 20 15:00 cores -> private/cores
dr-xr-xr-x   2 root  wheel      512 Apr 20 15:00 dev
lrwxrwxr-t   1 root  admin       11 Apr 20 15:00 etc -> private/etc
lrwxrwxr-t   1 root  admin        9 Apr 20 15:00 mach -> /mach.sym
-r--r--r--   1 root  admin   652352 Apr 20 15:00 mach.sym
-rw-r--r--   1 root  wheel  4039744 Mar 30 23:46 mach_kernel
drwxr-xr-x   7 root  wheel      264 Apr 20 15:00 private
drwxr-xr-x  56 root  wheel     1860 Apr 16 09:41 sbin
lrwxrwxr-t   1 root  admin       11 Apr 20 15:00 tmp -> private/tmp
drwxr-xr-x  10 root  wheel      296 Apr 12 14:45 usr
lrwxrwxr-t   1 root  admin       11 Apr 20 15:00 var -> private/var
-rw-r--r--   1 root  admin    10240 Apr 16 09:35 vol.tar
-rwxrwxrwx   1 root  wheel   221696 Apr  4 13:57 ???T+???Blank1
```

The output might look a little confusing at first, but it breaks down into parts that are easy to understand.

The first line contains information telling you the total sum for all the file (not including directories) sizes contained in the directory. The total is in 512-byte blocks—divide by 2 if you prefer your answer in kilobytes.

Next come lines detailing the contents of the directory, one file or directory listed per line.

At the beginning of each line are 10 characters. These indicate the values of 10 flags that belong to the file. The first flag indicates whether the file is a directory, a symbolic link (Unix for *alias*), or just a plain normal file. If the first flag is a `d`, the indicated item is a directory. If it is an `l`, the item is a link. If it is only a `-`, the item is a file. Next is a set of three values, `r`, `w`, and `x`, repeated three times. These three values specify the read flag, the write flag, and the execute flag for each user who owns the file, the group that owns the file, and all other users on the system. If a `-` is shown instead of an `r`, `w`, or `x`, the user, the group, or everybody on the system is not allowed to perform whatever action—read, write, or execute—that the flag is missing for.

Shortly following the 10 flag characters, each line contains an entry indicating the user who owns the file; in this case, `root` owns many of the files shown. The user `ray` owns a few.

Following the information indicating the owner of the file is another entry indicating the group that owns the file. Group ownership of a file is not as stringent as the user ownership of a file. The individual owner of a file is the only user allowed to modify the permissions of a file. So, although a user who belongs to the group that owns the file might be able to write to the file, that user cannot modify the flags indicating what the permissions are for the file.

Next is an entry indicating the size of the file in bytes. Entries for files indicate the full size of the file on disk. Entries for directories indicate another value loosely associated with the number of entries that the directory contains.

Following the size of the file comes an entry indicating the date of the most recent modification of the file. If the file was modified within the last year, the date and time are given; otherwise, the month, day, and year are given.

Finally, each entry lists the filename. Note that the filenames are identical to the name shown by the use of `ls` from our first example, with the exception of `core`, `etc`, `tmp`, `mach`, and `var`. Each of these entries is followed by an odd arrow that points to a path. Note that the file type for these is indicated by `ls` as a symbolic link. Just as a Mac OS alias points to a file or directory in another location, a symbolic link also points to a file or directory in another location. The information shown following the arrow is the path to which each particular entry points.

To prevent clutter, the `ls` command, by default, does not show certain files and directories that are expected to be configuration files or to contain maintenance or control information. Specifically, files or directories whose names begin with a dot (`.`) are not shown. Still, if you want to see them, there is an `ls` option that will allow this. If you want to see absolutely everything in the directory, add the `-a` option to the `ls` command; for example, `ls -la` (or `ls -al`, the order of options doesn't typically matter in most commands).

```
brezup:nermal / $ ls -al
total 13264
drwxrwxr-t  39 root  admin     1282 Apr 20 15:00 .
drwxrwxr-t  39 root  admin     1282 Apr 20 15:00 ..
-rwxrwxrwx   1 root  admin     8208 Apr 18 11:05 .DS_Store
d-wx-wx-wx   2 root  admin      264 Apr  4 12:20 .Trashes
-r--r--r--   1 root  wheel      142 Feb 25 03:05 .hidden
dr--r--r--   2 root  wheel      224 Apr 20 15:00 .vol
-rwxrwxrwx   1 root  wheel   106496 Apr 20 14:59 AppleShare PDS
drwxrwxrwx  25 root  admin      806 Apr 18 11:05 Applications
drwxrwxrwx  18 root  wheel      568 Apr 20 14:54 Applications (Mac OS 9)
drwxrwxrwx   2 root  wheel      264 Apr  6 12:24 Cleanup At Startup
-rwxrwxrwx   1 root  wheel   212992 Apr 20 14:59 Desktop DB
-rwxrwxrwx   1 root  wheel  1432466 Apr 20 14:57 Desktop DF
drwxrwxrwx   6 root  staff      264 Apr  4 11:51 Desktop Folder
drwxrwxr-x  12 root  admin      364 Mar  1 20:29 Developer
drwxrwxrwx   6 ray   staff      264 Apr  4 14:20 Documents
-rwxrwxrwx   1 root  wheel        0 Apr  4 14:11 Late Breaking News
drwxrwxr-x  21 root  admin      670 Apr 18 11:04 Library
drwxr-xr-x   6 root  wheel      264 Apr  4 12:47 Network
drwxr-xr-x   3 root  wheel       58 Apr 12 00:51 System
drwxrwxrwx  40 root  wheel     1316 Apr 20 14:50 System Folder
drwxrwxrwx   2 ray   staff      264 Mar 23 14:59 TheFindByContentFolder
drwxrwxrwx   4 ray   staff      264 Mar 23 14:46 TheVolumeSettingsFolder
drwxrwxrwx   2 ray   staff      264 Apr 20 14:58 Trash
drwxr-xr-x   6 root  wheel      160 Apr 16 12:37 Users
drwxrwxrwt   6 root  wheel      264 Apr 20 15:00 Volumes
drwxr-xr-x  33 root  wheel     1078 Apr 16 09:40 bin
drwxrwxrwt   1 root  admin       68 Jun 28 23:09 cores
dr-xr-xr-x   2 root  wheel      512 Apr 20 15:00 dev
lrwxrwxr-t   1 root  admin       11 Apr 20 15:00 etc -> private/etc
lrwxrwxr-t   1 root  admin        9 Apr 20 15:00 mach -> /mach.sym
-r--r--r--   1 root  admin   652352 Apr 20 15:00 mach.sym
-rw-r--r--   1 root  wheel  4039744 Mar 30 23:46 mach_kernel
drwxr-xr-x   7 root  wheel      264 Apr 20 15:00 private
drwxr-xr-x  56 root  wheel     1860 Apr 16 09:41 sbin
lrwxrwxr-t   1 root  admin       11 Apr 20 15:00 tmp -> private/tmp
drwxr-xr-x  10 root  wheel      296 Apr 12 14:45 usr
lrwxrwxr-t   1 root  admin       11 Apr 20 15:00 var -> private/var
-rw-r--r--   1 root  admin    10240 Apr 16 09:35 vol.tar
-rwxrwxrwx   1 root  wheel   221696 Apr  4 13:57 ???T+???Blank1
```

Notice that several new files have appeared at the top of the listing relative to our previous output. These all start with `.` characters at the beginnings of their filenames. They aren't shown in the normal `-l` listing because files that start with `.` are understood by convention to be configuration files, and other types of content that the average user doesn't want to be troubled with seeing on a day-to-day basis when looking at the directory contents. You can make any file "slightly invisible" at the command line by adding a `.` to the beginning of its name.

Moving Around the Filesystem: `cd`, `pushd`, `popd`

Now that you know how to determine where you are in the filesystem and how to list the files in a particular location, it's time to learn how to change your location. Unix provides two primary mechanisms by which you can do this. The first of these is the `cd` (change directory) command. This command does exactly what you would expect from its name: It changes your location in the filesystem to whatever location you ask it. If you want to change the current working directory from `/var` to `/var/log/`, you can type **`cd /var/log/`**. Because `cd`, like most Unix commands, accepts either relative or absolute paths, you can also make this change by typing **`cd log/`**, as shown here:

```
brezup:nermal var $ cd /var/log/
brezup:nermal log $
```

or:

```
brezup:nermal var $ cd log/
brezup:nermal log $
```

TIP

Remember that you can always use `~` as a quick absolute path to your home directory. You can also use `~` to construct absolute paths to directories or files beneath your home directory. If you want to change into the directory named `fizbin` located in your home directory, you can use the `cd` command `cd ~/fizbin`.

The `cd` command can also be used without an argument, in which case it assumes that you want to go to your home directory, and takes you to that location:

```
brezup:nermal log $ cd
brezup:nermal nermal $
```

Table 10.3 show the command documentation table for `cd`.

TABLE 10.3 The Command Documentation Table for `cd`

`cd`	Changes working directory.
`cd [-L¦-P] [<dir>]`	
`cd`	
`<dir>` is an absolute or relative pathname. The interpretation of the relative pathname depends on the `CDPATH` environment variable.	
`-L`	Forces symbolic links to be followed.
`-P`	Uses physical directory structure instead of following symbolic links.
An argument of `-` is equivalent to `$OLDPWD`, which essentially takes you back to wherever it is that you last came from.	

The `bash` and `tcsh` shells (similar to most others) also support a considerably more powerful way of navigating through the filesystem. This method, accessed through the `pushd` and `popd` commands, uses a computer structure called a *stack*. Using a stack enables you to go to another location and return to wherever you came from, without needing to remember the location and `cd` back.

NOTE

Computer scientists use the term *stack* as a friendly term for a data structure also known as a Last In, First Out (LIFO) structure. A classical LIFO structure has a single place where data can be put into or retrieved from the structure. If you put one piece of data into the structure, and then put in a second, you can't get the first back out again until you remove the second. See? The last thing you put in must be the first thing you take out. It's also called a stack because it works just like a stack of plates at a cafeteria. The last plate put on the stack (the one at the top of the stack) is the one that you take off first.

The `pushd` and `popd` commands work in concert. `pushd` puts the current directory on the stack and takes you to whatever directory you tell it to. `popd` takes you to whatever directory is on top of the stack and removes that directory from the stack.

For example, if you're in `/var/tmp/` and you want to temporarily change to the directory `/etc/httpd/`, you could do so by issuing `cd` commands that you already know about, like so:

```
brezup:nermal tmp $ pwd
/private/var/tmp
brezup:nermal tmp $ cd /etc/httpd
brezup:nermal httpd $ pwd
/private/etc/httpd
...
(do some work here perhaps)
...
brezup:nermal httpd $ cd /var/tmp
brezup:nermal tmp $ pwd
/private/var/tmp
```

10

This works, but has the strong disadvantage that you need to use the wetware in your head to remember where you were and how to get back. It's also tedious if you're doing something that requires you to make this flip back and forth between the directories frequently. It seems like there should be a way to let the computer leave a trail of breadcrumbs for you, marking the waypoints of your travels about the directories as it were, and then to use this information to be able to automatically backtrack whenever needed. There is—the solution is the `pushd` and `popd` commands.

As mentioned previously when discussing `pwd`, the results of looking at where you are might not agree entirely with where you think you've gone. This is the cause of the discrepancy seen between the locations `cd`'ed to, and the results of the `pwd` location checks shown here.

To do the same thing using `pushd` and `popd` is easier:

```
brezup:nermal tmp $ pwd -L
/var/tmp
brezup:nermal tmp $ pushd /etc/httpd
/etc/httpd /var/tmp
brezup:nermal httpd $ pwd -L
/etc/httpd
brezup:nermal httpd $ popd
/var/tmp
brezup:nermal tmp $ pwd -L
/var/tmp
```

Because the stack of directories is arbitrarily deep, you can push multiple items on before you start popping them off. For example:

```
brezup:nermal tmp $ pushd /etc/httpd
/etc/httpd /var/tmp
brezup:nermal httpd $ pwd -L
/etc/httpd
brezup:nermal httpd $ pushd /Users
/Users /etc/httpd /var/tmp
brezup:nermal Users $ pwd -L
/Users
brezup:nermal Users $ popd
/etc/httpd /var/tmp
brezup:nermal httpd $ pwd -L
/etc/httpd
brezup:nermal httpd $ popd
/var/tmp
brezup:nermal tmp $ pwd -L
/var/tmp
```

To be able to switch back and forth between a pair of directories, simply don't give an argument to `pushd`. It will pop the directory on top of the stack, push the current directory on, and switch you to the directory that it popped off. If that's a little confusing, just remember that if you've just come from somewhere using pushd, you can get back again using pushd with no arguments. When you're back, you've again just come from somewhere using pushd, so to get back to where you came from, you just pushd. For example, you might do something like this:

```
brezup:nermal tmp $ pushd /etc/httpd
/etc/httpd /var/tmp
brezup:nermal httpd $ pwd -L
/etc/httpd
brezup:nermal httpd $ pushd
/var/tmp /etc/httpd
brezup:nermal tmp $ pwd -L
/var/tmp
brezup:nermal tmp $ pushd
/etc/httpd /var/tmp
brezup:nermal httpd $ pwd -L
/etc/httpd
( And this can go on forever)
```

Finally, note that the stack used by tcsh isn't technically a classical LIFO structure because it has a side door. You might have noticed that pushd prints out the stack of directories after it's used each time. If you need to switch to a directory that's not at the top, issue pushd +*n*, where *n* is the depth of the directory you want to go to. Doing so shuffles that directory out to the top of the stack, and switches you to it.

Tables 10.4 shows the complete command documentation table for pushd.

TABLE 10.4 The Command Documentation Table for pushd

pushd	Pushes a directory onto the directory stack.
pushd [-**n**] [dir]	
pushd [-**n**] [+n] [-n]	
Adds a directory to the top of the directory stack, or rotates the stack, making the new top of the stack the current working directory. With no arguments, exchanges the top two directories and returns 0, unless the directory stack is empty.	
-**n**	Suppresses the normal change of directory when adding directories to the stack, so that only the stack is manipulated.
+n	Rotates the stack so that the *n*th directory (counting from the left of the list shown by dirs, starting with zero) is at the top.
-n	Rotates the stack so that the *n*th directory (counting from the right of the list shown by dirs, starting with zero) is at the top.
<dir>	Adds *<dir>* to the directory stack at the top, making it the new current working directory.

Table 10.5 shows the complete command documentation table for popd.

TABLE 10.5 The Command Documentation Table for popd

popd	Removes entries from the directory stack.
popd [-**n**] [+n] [-n]	
With no arguments, removes the top directory from the stack, and performs a cd to the new top directory.	
-**n**	Suppresses the normal change of directory when removing directories from the stack so that only the stack is manipulated.
+n	Removes the *n*th entry counting from the left of the list shown by dirs, starting with zero. For example: popd +0 removes the first directory; popd +1, the second.
-n	Removes the *n*th entry counting from the right of the list shown by dirs, starting with zero. For example: popd -0 removes the last directory; popd -1, the next to last.

Managing Files and Directories

Having mastered navigating about the filesystem, it's now time to learn how to interact with some of the files. We'll start with basic file manipulation commands that do things such as rename files and make copies of them, and then cover more complicated things such as finding files, extracting portions of their contents, and archiving them.

As mentioned previously, Unix commands tend to be small, single-function commands that can be combined to form more complex functionality. You see this demonstrated by many commands in this chapter; their functionality might seem oddly limited if you're not used to the Unix command philosophy. By the time you're finished with this chapter, however, you should begin to see how the commands could be fit together, and you should be able to abstract what you learn here to most Unix commands.

Moving and Renaming Files: mv

If you're a longtime Macintosh user, you are probably familiar with the notion of moving files about by way of the Macintosh's drag-and-drop formalism. Unix and its command line might not seem like a particularly appealing way to deal with moving files—having to type the names and paths to directories can't possibly be much fun! There's no denying that there are certain tasks for which the drag-and-drop way works much better than the command line. But, although you might not have thought about it, there are also situations in which drag-and-drop makes your life much more difficult. Interestingly, these are frequently situations in which the command line works particularly well; for example, when a folder contains many files of the same type, and you're interested in using a number of them that are related by name rather than by icon position. In a situation such as this, rearranging things in the Finder, or Shift-clicking your way through the list of files to pick the ones you want, is usually less efficient than choosing them from the command line by using a shell filename wildcard. Similarly, it's frequently faster to type a filename, if you know it, than to scroll around in a Finder window looking for the file. For these reasons, as well as conveniences that really become apparent only from experience rather than explanation, the command line makes for a useful complement to the Finder for certain operations.

Renaming files in Unix is accomplished with the `mv` (move) command. It might seem odd at first that renaming a file is accomplished by moving it, but it makes sense in the Unix philosophy of accomplishing things in simple, abstract ways. Why create two commands that do essentially the same thing, when one command can do both with the same syntax, the same way? To rename a file from one name to another, simply use `mv` *<oldfilename> <newfilename>*. For example, if you're in a directory with a file named `mynewfile`, and you want to rename it as `myoldfile`, you might do something like this:

```
brezup:nermal Documents $ ls
lynx       lynx.cfg   mynewfile  test
brezup:nermal Documents $ mv mynewfile myoldfile
brezup:nermal Documents $ ls
lynx       lynx.cfg   myoldfile  test
```

Remember that most commands can take absolute paths or relative paths to files? Well, being in the same directory and using just the filenames is using the relative paths. On the other hand, you can accomplish the same thing using the absolute paths to the files. Starting from where we left off in the previous example, this might look like the following:

```
brezup:nermal Documents $ pwd
/Users/nermal/Documents
brezup:nermal Documents $ mv /Users/nermal/Documents/myoldfile
➥/Users/nermal/Documents/myevenolderfile
brezup:nermal Documents $ ls
lynx       lynx.cfg   myevenolderfile  test
```

Because you can do that, why should you need to be in the same directory as the files at all? As a matter of fact, because you can specify the full paths to the files, what is to stop you from changing something other than the filename when you use the `mv` command? What if you decide to change one of the directories in the full path while you're at it? For example, let's look at what happens if you move a file from the `Documents` directory at the same time that you change its name:

```
brezup:nermal Documents $ cd ~
brezup:nermal nermal $ ls
Desktop                    Network Trash Folder      chown-output
Documents                  Pictures                  myfile
Library                    Public                    output-sample6
Movies                     Sites                     su-output
Music                      TheVolumeSettingsFolder   typescripts
brezup:nermal nermal $ ls Documents
lynx       lynx.cfg   myevenolderfile  test
brezup:nermal nermal $ mv /Users/nermal/Documents/myevenolderfile
➥/Users/nermal/Public/myolderfile
```

```
brezup:nermal nermal $ ls Documents/
lynx      lynx.cfg test
brezup:nermal nermal $ ls Public/
Drop Box   myolderfile
```

The end result is that Unix's abstraction of file access and naming causes the full path to the file to be, essentially, the full proper name of the file. "Renaming" it using the `mv` command can result in a change to any part of that name, including the parts that indicate the directory in which the file exists. See? Nothing odd about using the same syntax to rename files as used to move them about at all.

NOTE

Moving or renaming directories is exactly the same as moving or renaming files, with the exception of trying to move a directory from physical media that belongs to one disk partition or network device to media belonging to another. If you try to do this, the system warns you that you're trying to move a directory across partition boundaries and disallows the action. There's no simple way around this, so we'll cover a trick that you can use to get around this limitation of the filesystem in the section on `tar` later in the chapter. The obvious, and somewhat brute-force solution, is to do it the way it's always been done on the Mac: Copy the directory to the location on the other drive or partition and then delete the original. But doing so changes the modification times of the files, and you might not want that.

CAUTION

You can't create a directory structure by the action of a move command. If you try to move `/usr/local/wizbot` to `/usr/remote/wizbot`, and the directory `/usr/remote/` does not exist, the `mv` command exits and notifies you of the error.

Table 10.6 lists the syntax and primary options for `mv`.

TABLE 10.6 The Syntax and Primary Options for `mv`

`mv`	Moves files.
`mv [-f¦-i¦-n] [-v] <source> <target>`	
`mv [-f¦-i¦-n] [-v] <source1> <source2> <source3> ... <directory>`	
In the first form, `mv` renames `<source>` to the name provided by `<target>`. If `<source>` is a file, a file is renamed. Likewise, if `<source>` is a directory, a directory is renamed.	
In the second form, `mv` moves the list enumerated by `<source1> <source2> <source3> ...` to the directory named by `<directory>`.	
`-f`	Forces an existing file to be overwritten.
`-i`	Invokes an interactive mode that prompts for a confirmation before overwriting an existing file.

Creating Directories: `mkdir`

The `mkdir` command is used to create directories. The usual syntax is simple, being most commonly used as

```
mkdir <new directory name>
```

This creates a new directory named *<new directory name>* in the current directory. Full and relative paths are allowed to the new directory being specified. If the path to the directory that you are attempting to create does not completely exist, `mkdir` does not (by default) create the entire directory structure. For example, if you want to create `/usr/local/tmp/testing/morefiles/`, and the directory `/usr/local/tmp/testing/` does not exist, you either have to create it before you can create `/usr/local/tmp/testing/morefiles/` or use the `-p` option to `mkdir`. The `-p` option causes `mkdir` to create the entire path (if any of it's missing), as well as the final directory. This can be both a great convenience and a real nuisance. If you're an accurate typist, you don't need to issue multiple `mkdir` commands to create a deep directory hierarchy. On the other hand, because it creates directories that don't exist, a typo in a higher-level directory name just causes the mistyped name to be created, making typing errors annoyingly invisible when they're committed. Users new to Unix might like to add the `-v` flag as well so that `mkdir` reports what it's doing as it goes. Table 10.7 shows the syntax and primary options for `mkdir`.

TABLE 10.7 The Syntax and Primary Options for `mkdir`

`mkdir`	Makes directories.
`mkdir [-pv] [-m <mode>] <dir1> <dir2> ...`	
`mkdir` creates the named directories in the order specified. The permissions on the directories are controlled by the current `umask`.	
The user must have write permission in the parent directory.	
`-p`	Creates all nonexistent parent directories first. If this option is not specified, the full path prefix of each intended target directory must already exist. Intermediate directories are created with permission bits `rwxrwxrwx (0777)` as modified by the current `umask (2)`, plus write and execute permission for the owner.
`-m <mode>`	Sets the permission bits of the created directory to *<mode>*. *<mode>* can be in any formats specified to the `chmod (1)` utility. If a symbolic mode is specified, the operation characters `+` and `-` are interpreted relative to an initial mode of `a=rwx`.
`-v`	Be verbose about what `mkdir` is doing.

Copying Files: `cp`

The `cp` (copy) command functions similarly to the `mv` command, but instead of renaming a file between two locations, the `cp` command creates a duplicate of the file. The syntax is also similar, copying a file from one location to another or copying a number of files into a directory.

If our user `nermal` wants to copy some images to the `/Users/shared` directory so that all users can conveniently find the images without having to remember which user has the images, she can copy them with the `cp` command to the desired location.

Because nermal is new to Unix, she first decides to double-check that the images are located where she thinks they ought to be with the following:

```
brezup:nermal Documents $ ls -l Public/Drop\ Box/shar*tiff
-rw-r--r--  1 nermal  staff  872714 Apr 16 16:17 Public/Drop Box/sharing-1.tiff
-rw-r--r--  1 nermal  staff  873174 Apr 16 16:17 Public/Drop Box/sharing-2.tiff
```

Then she actually copies them and verifies that they copied:

```
brezup:nermal Documents $ cp Public/Drop\ Box/shar*tiff /Users/shared/
brezup:nermal Documents $ ls -l /Users/shared
total 3424
-rw-r--r--  1 nermal  wheel  872714 Apr 23 11:08 sharing-1.tiff
-rw-r--r--  1 nermal  wheel  873174 Apr 23 11:08 sharing-2.tiff
```

She could have copied each file individually, but cp can fortunately take multiple files in its arguments, so she can use shar*tiff to refer to both files. Note that the copies in the /Users/shared directory show the date that they were copied, rather than the original date. If everyone knows that the images from April 16 are the ones they need to use, they might be confused by the April 23 date. nermal could remove this confusion by specifying the -p option, which preserves as much as possible of the original modification time, user information, and so on:

```
brezup:nermal Documents $ cp -p Public/Drop\ Box/shar*tiff /Users/shared/
brezup:nermal Documents $ ls -l /Users/shared
total 3424
-rw-r--r--  1 nermal  staff  872714 Apr 16 16:17 sharing-1.tiff
-rw-r--r--  1 nermal  staff  873174 Apr 16 16:17 sharing-2.tiff
```

Note the use of the \ character to escape the space in the folder named Drop Box so that the shell doesn't interpret Public/Drop as one argument and Box/shar*.tiff as another.

If user joray has promised nermal some test data in a subdirectory named tests-for-nermal in joray's home directory, nermal can recursively copy the test directory to her own home directory as follows:

```
brezup:nermal Documents $ cp -R ~joray/tests-for-nermal ./
```

A check shows that a directory was indeed copied:

```
brezup:nermal Documents $ ls -ld tests-for-nermal
drwxr-xr-x  9 nermal  staff  262 Apr 23 11:29 tests-for-nermal
```

Not only that, but there was a directory under that directory, and cp copied it:

```
brezup:nermal Documents $ ls -l tests-for-nermal
total 48
-rw-r--r--  1 nermal  staff   15 Apr 23 11:29 broken
-rw-r--r--  1 nermal  staff   20 Apr 23 11:29 broken-again
```

```
-rw-r--r--  1 nermal  staff   23 Apr 23 11:29 fix
-rw-r--r--  1 nermal  staff   17 Apr 23 11:29 fix2
-rw-r--r--  1 nermal  staff  848 Apr 23 11:29 test
drwxr-xr-x  4 nermal  staff   92 Apr 23 11:29 test-data
-rw-r--r--  1 nermal  staff  848 Apr 23 11:29 test2
```

You have seen just some of what you can do with `cp`. The complete syntax and options for `cp` are shown in Table 10.8, the command documentation table.

TABLE 10.8 The Command Documentation Table for `cp`

`cp`	Copies files.
`cp [-R [-H ¦ -L ¦ -P]] [-f ¦ -i ¦ -n] [-pv]` *<source> <target>*	
`cp [-R [-H ¦ -L ¦ -P]] [-f ¦ -i ¦ -n] [-pv]` *<source1> <source2>* ... *<directory>*	
In its first form, `cp` copies the contents of *<source>* to *<target>*.	
In its second form, `cp` copies the contents of the list enumerated by *<source1> <source2>* ... to the directory named by *<directory>*. The names of the files themselves are not changed. If `cp` detects an attempt to copy to itself, that attempt fails.	
`-R`	If *<source>* is a directory, `cp` recursively copies the directory. This option also causes symbolic links to be copied as links, rather than indirected through. Created directories have the same mode as the corresponding source directory.
`-H`	If `-R` is specified, symbolic links on the command line are followed, but symbolic links in the tree traversal are not.
`-L`	If `-R` is specified, all symbolic links are followed.
`-P`	If `-R` is specified, no symbolic links are followed.
`-f`	Forces an existing file to be overwritten.
`-i`	Invokes an interactive mode that prompts for a confirmation before overwriting an existing file.
-n	Do not overwrite any existing file.
`-p`	Causes `cp` to retain as much of the modification time, access time, file flags, file mode, user ID, and group ID information as permissions allow.
`-v`	Be verbose about the copy process and the results.

NOTE

Apple has added a bit of Apple flavor to a number of Unix command-line utilities and has created a few of its own that merge the world of Apple's GUI and HFS+ filesystem with traditional Unix command-line functionality. If you've a need to copy files with resource forks (such as Classic Mac OS applications and similar files), see Chapter 29, "Maintaining a Healthy System," for documentation on the `ditto` command. If you've installed the developer tools, and have added the path `/Developer/Tools/` to your path, you also have access to `CpMac` and `MvMac`, which are Mac-resource-fork-aware versions of `cp` and `mv`, as well as a number of other resource-fork-related command-line tools.

Creating Symbolic Links: ln

Sometimes it is useful to link an alternative name with a particular file or directory, or make a file appear to be in two places at once, without actually creating a duplicate of that item. You're already used to this idea from the Finder notion of aliases. At the command line, the same thing can be done with the ln command. It is especially useful for administrative purposes, but even a regular user might need to link a filename or directory name to some other particular name. The best way to do this is to use a symbolic link. The simplest syntax for making a symbolic link is

```
ln -s <source> <target>
```

Because the syntax is similar to the basic cp syntax, you won't have much trouble remembering it.

You might be wondering just what sort of use you might have for symbolic links. An instance in which you might use a symbolic link is for your website. Suppose that you are using a web editing suite that uses home.html for the default name for the main page of your website. Suppose, however, that your web server is set to read only files named index.html as the default page for a directory. If you use home.html, you might have to give out something like http://ryoohki.biosci.ohio-state.edu/~nermal/home.html as your URL. If, on the other hand, your home.html file were really called index.html, you could give out a slightly shorter URL instead: http://ryoohki.biosci.ohio-state.edu/~nermal/.

What could you do to get an index.html file in your directory if your web editing suite won't create one? And how could you keep it conveniently updated to match home.html? Well, as you just saw, you could copy home.html to index.html. But the next time you edited home.html, you would then have to remember to copy home.html to index.html when you were finished. Although you might be good about remembering to do that, you undoubtedly will eventually forget, probably when it matters most. If you simply link index.html to home.html, every time you update home.html, you don't have to remember to do anything else! To create the symbolic link, do the following:

```
brezup:nermal public_html $ ln -s home.html index.html
```

A quick check shows us that index.html is now a link to home.html.

```
brezup:nermal public_html $ ls -l
total 16
-rw-r--r--  1 nermal  staff  52 Apr 23 11:56 home.html
lrwxr-xr-x  1 nermal  staff   9 Apr 23 11:56 index.html -> home.html
```

NOTE

You will need to set your Apache web server followsymlinks option for symbolic links to work properly as shown. See Chapter 23, "Creating a Web Server," for information on how to do this.

A common administrative use for symbolic links is to move a directory from one partition to another, while leaving the path that a user would use to get to the directory the same. This makes the administrator's change transparent to the user for most purposes. An example of this follows. On this machine, obup, the /usr partition was getting full, so the local directory of /usr/local was moved to a partition named /home. After the directory was moved, the /usr/local directory was replaced with a symbolic link that points to /home/local.

```
obup:joray / $ ls -l /usr/local
lrwxrwxrwx   1 root     other     11 Mar 20  1997 /usr/local -> /home/local
```

If a user changes to the /usr/local directory and then checks his location with pwd, he finds the following:

```
obup:joray / $ cd /usr/local
obup:joray local $ pwd
/home/local
```

So, as the user might have grown to expect, he can still cd to /usr/local but without having to know any of the "administrivia" behind its actual location.

Table 10.9 shows the syntax and primary options for ln.

TABLE 10.9 The Syntax and Primary Options for ln

ln	Makes links.
ln [-fhinsv] *<source>* *<target>*	
ln [-fhinsv] *<source1>* *<source2>* *<source3>* ... *<directory>*	
In the first form, ln links *<source>* to *<target>*. If *<target>* is a directory, a link named *<source>* is placed in *<target>*.	
In the second form, ln makes links to the files enumerated by *<source1>* *<source2>* *<source3>* ... in *<directory>*. The links have the same names as the sources in the list.	
There are two types of links: hard links and symbolic links. The default is hard links. A hard link to a file is indistinguishable from the original entry. Hard links may not normally refer to directories and may not span filesystems. Although infrequently necessary, hard link properties make them ideal for creating what are essentially duplicate "real" names for a given file, where the properties of an "alias-like" name are not sufficient. The consequences of this are subtle; for example, with a hard link, you can delete the original file, and it will still exist and take up disk space under its linked name. Because of this, we recommend using soft links unless you're positive that a hard link is necessary for your needs.	
A symbolic link refers by name to the file to which it is linked. Symbolic links may refer to directories and may span filesystems.	
-f	Forces the link to occur by unlinking any already existing links.
-h	If *<target>* or *<directory>* is a symbolic link, it is not followed.
-i	If the target already exists, prompt the user via the error-reporting mechanism (STDERR) regarding the action to take.
-s	Creates a symbolic link—this is most like the idea of aliases, with which you're already familiar.

Changing Modification Times and Creating Empty Files: `touch`

The `touch` command is used to update the last-modified time for a file. This command also has the side effect of creating a new, empty file if the file that you attempt to `touch` does not exist.

Neither of these functionalities probably sounds particularly interesting at the outset, but, in fact, they both have good uses. For example, most archiving and backup software is frequently configured to back up only files that have changed since the last backup. Using `touch` on a file makes it appear to have been changed, which results in it being flagged for backup. Because the `touch` command can be quickly applied from the command line to a large number of files, it enables you to conveniently force some files to be backed up without having to open and resave each in its parent applications.

Creating empty files doesn't have much use at the command line but turns out to be useful when you start writing programs in the shell scripting language (see Chapter 15). In this case, multiple simultaneously running scripts can be made to talk to each other by the creation of empty files known as *flag files*—essentially the electronic equivalent of a script raising a flag to tell another script that something has happened.

To create a new (empty) file with `touch`, or to update the modification date of the file to the current time, the syntax for the `touch` command is simply

```
touch <filename to modify>
```

The `touch` command can actually update files to have any modification time that you want, although the preceding is by far the most common usage. Table 10.10 shows the syntax and options for `touch`.

TABLE 10.10 The Command Documentation Table for `touch`

`touch`	Changes file access and modification times.
`touch [-acfm] [-r <file>] [-t [[CC]YY]MMDDhhmm[.SS]] <file> ...`	
`touch` sets modification and access times of files to the current time of day. If the file does not exist, it is created with default permissions.	
`-a`	Changes the last-access time of the file, rather than the last-modification time.
`-c`	Does not create the file if it does not exist.
`-f`	Attempts to force the update, even if file permissions do not currently permit it.
`-m`	Changes the modification time of the file.
`-r <file>`	Replaces access and modification time with that of `<file>` instead of using the current time.
`-t`	Changes the access and modification time to the specified time.
`CC` is the century (20, for dates in the 2000s), `YY` is the last two digits of the year (2005 can be specified as either 2005 or 05).	
`MM` is the month, `DD` is the day of the month. `hh` is the 24-hour version of the hours, `mm` is minutes, and `SS` is seconds.	
Therefore, to set the date and time of the last change of file `fizbin` to have occurred on March 2nd, 2002, at 13 seconds after 1:10 AM, you could specify your touch command as `touch -t 200203020110.13 fizbin`. Alternatively, `touch -t 0203020110.13 fizbin` would also do.	

Removing Files and Directories: rm, rmdir

Removing files and removing directories with Unix are fairly straightforward tasks, so you need to know only two commands to accomplish them.

Now that you have filled up your directory with many files, it is time to learn how to clean it up a bit. You can remove a file with `rm`. Our user `nermal` has decided that her file called `myfile` is no longer needed. To remove it, she does the following:

```
brezup:nermal Documents $ ls -l myfile
-rw-r--r--  1 nermal  staff  51 Apr 12 15:11 myfile
brezup:nermal Documents $ rm myfile
remove myfile? Y
```

As you notice in this example, `rm` prompts for confirmation before removing the file. Your system might not be configured to make `rm` prompt you for the removal of files. You can cause `rm` to ask for confirmation by aliasing `rm` to `rm -i`. Aliasing is a technique covered in more depth in Chapter 15. For now, you want to add either the first or second lines that follow to the `.bashrc` file or `.cshrc` file in your home directory (the first if you're using `bash`, and the second if you're using `tcsh`). Alternatively, you could add them to `/etc/bashrc` or `/etc/csh.cshrc` to make the change for all users of your system.

For `bash`:

```
alias rm='rm -i'
```

For `tcsh`:

```
alias rm 'rm -i'
```

We highly recommend that you follow these instructions to make your `rm` command interactive at the first possible opportunity. After you're a seasoned Unix user, you're welcome to run with `rm` in noninteractive mode by default; but until you've been sure that you're ready a long, long time, it's probably safest to have it operate interactively by default.

> **CAUTION**
>
> Okay, so perhaps suggesting that you put something like a few years of Unix experience under your belt before using `rm` in the noninteractive mode is a bit facetious and silly. On the other hand, I don't think I know a single longtime Unix user who *hasn't* entered an `rm` command, pressed the Return key, and then felt his stomach bounce off the floor as he realized that the reason the command didn't return immediately was because it was currently deleting his entire filesystem. I've seen this happen to seasoned system administrators, so I really do want to stress that with `rm`, overconfidence can be deadly.

Our user `nermal` has also decided that she is finished with the data that she copied from user `joray`'s directory and that she wants to remove the entire directory. The easiest way to do this is to force rm to recursively remove the directory, using options -r for recursive, and -f to override the interactive mode she has enabled by default, as shown here:

```
brezup:nermal Documents $ ls -ld tests-for-nermal
drwxr-xr-x  9 nermal  staff  262 Apr 23 11:29 tests-for-nermal
brezup:nermal Documents $ rm -rf tests-for-nermal
[localhost:~] nermal% ls -ld tests-for-nermal
ls: tests-for-nermal: No such file or directory
```

Removing a directory and all its contents using the recursive and force options to rm is easy, but it is also silent and very fast. Remember to use those options only when you really mean it. Double-check everything before you run it. As you can see in the example, there is no recourse if you type the wrong thing.

Table 10.11 shows the syntax and primary options for rm.

TABLE 10.11 The Syntax and Primary Options for rm

rm	Removes directory entries.
rm [-dfiPRrvW] *<file1>* *<file2>* ...	
unlink *<file>*	
-f	Forces the removal of files without prompting the user for confirmation. The -f option overrides any previous -i options.
-i	Invokes an interactive mode that prompts for confirmation before removing a file. The -i option overrides any previous -f options.
-d	Attempts to remove directories as well as other types of files.
-R	Attempts to recursively remove files. Implies -d option.
-W	Attempts to undelete files. This option can be used to recover only files covered by whiteouts.

rm removes symbolic links, but not the files referenced by the target of a link.

Attempting to remove the files (directories) . and .. is an error because they are virtual placeholders for the current and parent directories, respectively. You can, however, remove the directory that you're currently in by using other valid names for it. If you do this, you'll find that many shell commands suddenly don't work, and produce only an error such as can't stat .. You can usually rescue the situation by issuing a cd ~/ command.

TIP

unlink is a synonym for rm, but it accepts fewer options. This might seem like a bizarre thing to want, but it actually is sometimes an important feature to not have rm's flag options. For example, if you've managed to create a file with a name that starts with a -, using rm to remove it is all but impossible because rm insists on interpreting the - as a marker indicating the presence of a flag, rather than as part of the name. unlink doesn't suffer from this problem, and can let you delete files that have names that confuse rm.

There is also a command available for removing directories: rmdir. It is useful only for removing empty directories, but this is also a valuable limitation on its capabilities. It lets you `rmdir` rather indiscriminately, and know for certain that it will delete only unoccupied directories, and never any real files. Table 10.12 shows its complete syntax and options.

TABLE 10.12 The Command Documentation Table for `rmdir`

`rmdir`	Removes directories.
`rmdir [-p] <directory1> <directory2> ...`	
`rmdir` removes each *<directory>* argument specified, provided it is empty. Arguments are processed in the order listed on the command line. To remove a parent directory and subdirectories of the parent directory, the subdirectories must be listed first.	
`-p`	Attempts to remove the specified directory and its parent directories, if they are empty.

Examining File Contents

Moving around the filesystem, and moving files around the filesystem, isn't all that interesting if you can't look at what's in the files. Unix provides a number of facilities for examining the contents of files, and frequently these are more convenient to use than their graphical counterparts. BBEdit, for example, is a wonderful text editor, and it's light enough in memory footprint to load quickly. However, if you want to see whether the file you're thinking about deleting is really the file you mean to delete, and the information is readily apparent by looking at the beginning of the text, there are much more efficient ways to examine the contents from the command line than starting up a GUI program just to glance at the file.

Looking at the Contents of Files: `cat`, `more`, `less`

Now that you have learned a little bit about how to list and copy your files, it is time to learn how to examine the contents of your files.

`cat` reads files and displays their contents. In this example, you see that `myfile` is short.

```
brezup:nermal Documents $ cat myfile
Hi.  this is nermal.

I hope you enjoyed myfile.
```

If the file were longer, it would keep scrolling by on the screen either until you pressed Ctrl-C to break the process or the file came to an end.

It might seem odd that anyone would want a program that just dumped all the output to the terminal, with no convenient way to slow it down or page through it. However, this is part of the Unix philosophy. The `cat` command reads files and sends their contents to the terminal. (Actually, `cat` sends their contents to `STDOUT`, a way of connecting commands that you'll learn more about in Chapters 12 and 15. `STDOUT` just happens to be connected to the terminal, unless you tell the command line otherwise.) In the Unix way of doing things, it is the job of some other program to provide a paged display of data.

10

Table 10.13 shows the complete syntax and primary options for cat.

TABLE 10.13 The Syntax and Primary Options for cat

cat	Concatenates and prints files.
cat [-nbsvetu] <*file1*> <*file2*> ...	
cat [-nbsvetu] [-]	
cat reads files in sequential, command-line order and writes them to standard output. A single dash represents reading the standard input, rather than an on-disk file.	
-n	Numbers all output lines, starting with 1.
-b	Numbers all output lines, except blank lines.
-s	Squeezes multiple adjacent empty lines, causing single-spaced output.
-v	Displays nonprinting characters. Control characters print as ^X for Control-X; delete prints as ^?; non-ASCII characters with the high bit set are printed as M- (for meta) followed by the character for the low 7 bits.

You could also use cat to read the contents of longer files. However, the contents of your file scroll quickly. If you hope to read the contents as they appear, it would be better to use more, which also reads and displays files, but it pauses the display after a screenful.

The contents of nermal's short file look the same when viewed with more:

```
brezup:nermal Documents $ more myfile
Hi. this is nermal.

I hope you enjoyed myfile.
```

With a longer file, though, more pauses after a screenful:

```
brezup:nermal Documents $ more /var/log/system.log
Sep 11 16:00:54 localhost syslogd: restart
Sep 11 16:00:54 localhost syslogd: kernel boot file is /mach_kernel
Sep 11 16:00:54 localhost kernel: /IOFireWireSBP2LUN/com_apple_driver_LSI_FW_
➥500/IOSCSIPeripheralDeviceNub/IOSCSIPeripheralDeviceType00/I
OBlockStorageServices/IOBlockStorageDriver/Maxtor
➥1394 storage Media/IOApplePartitionScheme/untitled@3
Sep 11 16:00:54 localhost kernel: BSD root: disk1s3, major 14, minor 9
Sep 11 16:00:54 localhost kernel: HFS: created HFBT on Maxtor 38 GB HD
Sep 11 16:00:56 localhost kernel: Jettisoning kernel linker.
.
.
.
Sep 11 16:01:13 localhost kernel: obtaining ID
Sep 11 16:01:13 localhost kernel: from Registry
Sep 11 16:01:13 localhost kernel: ATIRage128: using AGP
Sep 11 16:01:15 localhost lookupd[136]: lookupd
➥(version 322) starting - Thu Sep 11 16:01:15 2003
```

```
Sep 11 16:01:17 localhost diskarbitrationd[106]:
➥disk1s3  hfs   E14C9FFC-2328-3ACB-98DC-EA27AD8B1880 Maxtor 38 GB HD   /
Sep 11 16:01:17 localhost SystemStarter: Welcome to Macintosh.
Sep 11 16:01:17 localhost kernel: UniNEnet: Ethernet address 00:30:65:aa:37:ae
Sep 11 16:01:17 localhost kernel: IOFireWireIP:
➥FireWire address 00:30:65:ff:fe:aa:37:ae
/var/log/system.log (3%)
```

In this display, we can see at the bottom of the screen that we are looking at a file called `system.log`, and that we have viewed about 3% of the file. After we've finished looking at that screenful, we can press the spacebar and look at the next screenful of text. The most common syntax you will use for `more` is

```
more <filename>
```

Another way of looking at files with a paged view is by using the command `less`. `less` started off live as a more advanced pager that was named as a Unix-style pun on `more`. Now, `more` is actually just an alternative functionality of the `less` executable, and traditional `more` isn't included as an independent application. `more` and `less` have traditionally had several differences in their behaviors, and the new `less` appliction preserves these differences when it's invoked under each name.

For example, `more` traditionally scrolls data off the top of the screen when you press the spacebar to move to the next page, and `less` traditionaly erases the screen and repaints it with the new page of data. This difference might not seem significant at first, but it means that in `more`, you can scroll back to something that's earlier in the file by using Terminal's scrollbar. In `less`, on the other hand, things don't accumulate in the scroll buffer. If your terminal type supports it, `less` erases the screen back to what it was before you ran `less`, when it exits, leaving no mess from the pager in your Terminal window or buffer at all. These modes of operation both have advantages and disadvantages. `more`'s output accumulates as part of a Terminal's history, whereas the output from `less` is displayed only temporarily, and leaves you back at a clean Terminal with all of your previous activity right where it previously was before you ran the command.

Another difference is that `more` traditionally exits after hitting the bottom of the file, whereas `less` traditionally remains in the pager, enabliing you to issue in-pager searches and move throughout the file even after it's hit bottom. Both of these behaviors are annoying, when you're expecting the other!

`less`'s commands are based both on traditional `more` and `vi`, a text editor we introduce in Chapter 13. Although `less` is frequently thought of as a command, it has enough complex functionality for the user who wants it that `less` might be better called an *application*. The fact that it is most frequently used for its command-like capabilities leads to its inclusion here.

The appearance of `less` output is similar to that from `more`:

```
brezup:nermal Documents $ less system.log
Sep 11 16:00:54 localhost syslogd: restart
```

```
Sep 11 16:00:54 localhost syslogd: kernel boot file is /mach_kernel
Sep 11 16:00:54 localhost kernel: /IOFireWireSBP2LUN/com_apple_driver_LSI_FW_
➥500/IOSCSIPeripheralDeviceNub/IOSCSIPeripheralDeviceType00/I
OBlockStorageServices/IOBlockStorageDriver/Maxtor
➥1394 storage Media/IOApplePartitionScheme/untitled@3
Sep 11 16:00:54 localhost kernel: BSD root: disk1s3, major 14, minor 9
Sep 11 16:00:54 localhost kernel: HFS: created HFBT on Maxtor 38 GB HD
Sep 11 16:00:56 localhost kernel: Jettisoning kernel linker.
.
.
.
Sep 11 16:01:13 localhost kernel: obtaining ID
Sep 11 16:01:13 localhost kernel: from Registry
Sep 11 16:01:13 localhost kernel: ATIRage128: using AGP
Sep 11 16:01:15 localhost lookupd[136]: lookupd
➥(version 322) starting - Thu Sep 11 16:01:15 2003
Sep 11 16:01:17 localhost diskarbitrationd[106]:
➥disk1s3    hfs      E14C9FFC-2328-3ACB-98DC-EA27AD8B1880 Maxtor 38 GB HD
/
Sep 11 16:01:17 localhost SystemStarter: Welcome to Macintosh.
Sep 11 16:01:17 localhost kernel: UniNEnet: Ethernet address 00:30:65:aa:37:ae
Sep 11 16:01:17 localhost kernel: IOFireWireIP: ➥FireWire address
00:30:65:ff:fe:aa:37:ae
```

Like `more`, `less` pauses after a screenful. At the bottom, we also see that the file is called `system.log`, but it is not displaying the percentage of the file that we have examined.

The most common syntax you will use for `less` is

`less` *<filename>*

`less` is powerful. The most important thing to remember about `less` is how to invoke help, which can be done by issuing either `less -?` or `less --help`. Depending on how your shell interprets a question mark, you might have to try `-\?` or `"-\?"` for help. The man page is overwhelming, but the `--help` option is easy to read and organized nicely. Some of the highlights from the output of the `--help` option are included in Table 10.14.

Many options are available in `less`, and there is much that you can do after you are in `less`. Table 10.14 shows the syntax for `less`, as well as some basic information on movement and pattern searching in `less`.

TABLE 10.14 The Command Documentation Table for `less`

`less`	Opposite of `more`.
Pages through data or text files.	
`less -?`	
`less --help`	
`less -V`	
`less --version`	

TABLE 10.14 Continued

```
less [-[+]aBcCdeEfFgGiIJmMnNqQRrsSuUVvwX~][-b <space>][-h <lines>][-j <line>] [-k
<keyfile>] [--{oO} <logfile>] [-p <pattern>][-t <tag>] [-T <tagsfile>] [-x <tab,...>]
[-y <lines>] [-[-z] <lines>][-# <shift>][+[+]<cmd>] [--] [<file1>...]
```

Summary of `less` Commands

Commands marked with * may be preceded by a number, *N*.

Notes in parentheses indicate the behavior if *N* is given.

h	H					Display this help.
q	:q	Q	:Q	ZZ		Exit.
MOVING						
e	^E	j	^N	CR	*	Forward one line (or *N* lines).
y	^Y	k	^K	^P	*	Backward one line (or *N* lines).
f	^F	^V	SPACE		*	Forward one window (or *N* lines).
b	^B	ESC-v			*	Backward one window (or *N* lines).
z					*	Forward one window (and set window to *N*).
w					*	Backward one window (and set window to *N*).
ESC-SPACE					*	Forward one window, but don't stop at end-of- file.
d	^D				*	Forward one half-window (and set half-window to *N*).
u	^U				*	Backward one half-window (and set half-window to *N*).
ESC-(		RightArrow			*	Left eight character positions (or *N* positions).
ESC-)		LeftArrow			*	Right eight character positions (or *N* positions).
F						Forward forever; like "`tail -f`".
r	^R	^L				Repaint screen.
R						Repaint screen, discarding buffered input.
Default window is the screen height.						
Default half-window is half of the screen height.						
SEARCHING						
/pattern					*	Search forward for (*N*-th) matching line.
?pattern					*	Search backward for (*N*-th) match- ing line.
n					*	Repeat previous search (for *N*-th occurrence).
N					*	Repeat previous search in reverse direction.

TABLE 10.14 Continued

JUMPING				
g	<	ESC-<	*	Go to first line in file (or line *N*).
G	>	ESC->	*	Go to last line in file (or line *N*).
p	%		*	Go to beginning of file (or *N* percent into file).

NOTE

Those who find the technical underpinnings of the command line to be interesting (c'mon, admit it—the stuff you can do in here is fascinating!), should note that when they run `less` or `more` on recent versions of Mac OS X, they're actually running the exact same program. The command itself looks to see which name was used to invoke it, and assumes the traditional behavior of whichever is appropriate when it runs. This would be kind of like having icons in the Finder for both Mail and Safari, but both of them being aliases for a single application that can act as either a mail reader or a web browser—they do share a lot of functionality, so why not disk space as well?

Looking at Portions of the Contents of Files: `head`, `tail`

Sometimes you need to see only a portion of a file, rather than the entire contents. To see only portions of a file, use either `head` or `tail`. As the names suggest, `head` displays the first few lines of a file, whereas `tail` displays the last few lines of a file.

Let's look at the first few lines of `system.log`:

```
brezup:joray log $ head system.log
Sep 11 16:00:54 localhost syslogd: restart
Sep 11 16:00:54 localhost syslogd: kernel boot file is /mach_kernel
Sep 11 16:00:54 localhost kernel: /IOFireWireSBP2LUN/com_apple_driver_LSI_FW_
➥500/IOSCSIPeripheralDeviceNub/IOSCSIPeripheralDeviceType00/
➥IOBlockStorageServices/IOBlockStorageDriver/Maxtor 1394 storage ➥Media/IOAp-
plePartitionScheme/untitled@3
Sep 11 16:00:54 localhost kernel: BSD root: disk1s3, major 14, minor 9
Sep 11 16:00:54 localhost kernel: HFS: created HFBT on Maxtor 38 GB HD
Sep 11 16:00:56 localhost kernel: Jettisoning kernel linker.
Sep 11 16:01:02 localhost kextd[86]: registering service
➥"com.apple.KernelExtensionServer"
Sep 11 16:01:03 localhost kernel: Resetting IOCatalogue.
Sep 11 16:01:04 localhost kernel: Matching service count = 0
Sep 11 16:01:08 localhost kernel: AppleRS232Serial:
➥0       0 AppleRS232Serial::start - returning false early, Connector or
➥machine incorrect
brezup:joray log $
```

Nothing other than the first few lines of the file is displayed. Because head is not a pager, we do not see the name of the file displayed at the bottom of the screen, and the system prompt returns immediately when head is finished displaying its output. Table 10.15 shows the complete syntax and options for head.

TABLE 10.15 The Syntax and Options for head

head	Displays the first lines of a file.
head [-n *<number>*] *<file1> <file2>* ...	
head [-n *<number>*]	
-*n <number>*	Displays the first *<number>* of lines. If *n* is not specified, the default is 10.
If more than one file is specified, the output for each file is preceded by a short header indicating the file number that is about to be displayed.	

tail behaves in the same way as head, except that only the last few lines of a file are displayed, as you see in this sample. The line Sep 16 23:58:42 localhost xinetd[329]: START: ssh pid=1010 from=192.168.1.4 is the last one in the file:

```
brezup:joray log $ tail system.log
Sep 16 11:31:32 localhost sshd[891]:
➥Accepted password for sageray from 192.168.1.4 port 2260 ssh2
Sep 16 22:58:32 localhost xinetd[329]:
➥service ssh, IPV6_ADDRFORM setsockopt() failed: Protocol not available
➥(errno = 42)
Sep 16 22:58:32 localhost xinetd[329]:
➥START: ssh pid=906 from=192.168.1.4
Sep 16 22:58:52 localhost sshd[906]:
➥Accepted password for sageray from 192.168.1.4 port 2272 ssh2
Sep 16 23:54:18 localhost xinetd[329]:
➥service ssh, IPV6_ADDRFORM setsockopt() failed: Protocol not available
➥(errno = 42)
Sep 16 23:54:18 localhost xinetd[329]:
➥START: ssh pid=1004 from=192.168.1.4
Sep 16 23:54:25 localhost sshd[1004]:
➥Accepted password for sageray from 192.168.1.4 port 2274 ssh2
Sep 16 23:58:42 localhost xinetd[329]:
➥service ssh, IPV6_ADDRFORM setsockopt() failed: Protocol not available
➥(errno = 42)
Sep 16 23:58:42 localhost xinetd[329]:
➥START: ssh pid=1010 from=192.168.1.4
```

Table 10.16 shows the complete syntax and options for tail.

TABLE 10.16 The Syntax and Options for `tail`

`tail`	Displays the last part of a file.
tail [-f ¦ -F ¦ -r] [-b *<number>* ¦ -c *<number>* ¦ -n *<number>*] *<file>* ...	
`-f`	Waits for and displays additional data that *<file>* receives, instead of stopping at the end of the file.
`-F`	Similar to `-f`, except that every five seconds, `tail` checks whether *<file>* has been shortened or moved.
`-r`	Displays the file in reverse order, by line. This option also modifies the `-b`, `-c`, and `-n` options to specify the number of units to be displayed, rather than the number of units to display from the beginning or end of the input.
-b *<number>*	Specifies location in number of 512-byte blocks.
-c *<number>*	Specifies location in number of bytes.
-n *<number>*	Specifies location in number of lines.
If *<number>* begins with +, it refers to the number of units (512-byte blocks, bytes, or lines) from the beginning of the input. If *<number>* begins with - or no explicit sign, it refers to the number of units from the end of the input.	
If more than one file is specified, the output for each file is preceded by a short header indicating the file number that is about to be displayed.	

Searching for Files, Directories, and More

Unix traditionally has provided useful tools for searching for files by name and content, and Apple has expanded on these by making available a command-line interface into the same databases that the Finder uses to locate files. Unix's traditional tools don't work from a database like the Finder's file searching function does, so they run more slowly. On the other hand, they aren't hampered by needing a database to run or by being only as current in their results as the last database update.

Finding Files: `locate`, `find`, `mdfind`

Sometimes you want to find some files, but you are not sure where they are. Three tools are available to search for files: `locate`, `find` and `mdfind`. Despite having the same purpose, these commands all behave a little bit differently. `locate` works from a database of file names that is updated periodically, and is aware of your user permissions and places that you'd typically look for files. It sometimes won't show you files that have been added recently, or that are in odd corners of the system, but it works quickly. `find` actually goes to look at everything on the system when you run it, so it can take a very, very long time to search, but it's always up to date, and always returns information on all files that you can see. `mdfind` uses Tiger's new Spotlight search facility, which also uses a database, but one that's supposed to be updated continuously for every change that is made to any file, and is capable of searching file contents as well as file names - unfortunately (as of April 2005) it's too easy to accidentally break Spotlight's indexing and have files that match, get lost.

Using `locate`

If you know some of the name of a file, you can use the `locate` utility to try to find it.

For example, our user `nermal` looked earlier at a file called `system.log`. Does our machine have other files that have `log` in their name? You bet! The syntax for `locate` is

```
locate <pattern>
```

We encourage you to try the `locate` command for files with `log` in them (`locate log`) to see the output, but it is much too long to include here. `locate` searches a database of pathnames on the machine.

> **NOTE**
>
> If you try `locate log` and produce no output, it's because your machine hasn't generated the database of paths yet. This database starts off empty and is automatically rebuilt once a week. If you're particularly adventurous, you will find what you need to know to build it by hand in the `/etc/weekly` script, but this is a bit more complex than a novice will want to face.

Further information on `locate` is shown in the command documentation table, Table 10.17.

TABLE 10.17 The Command Documentation Table for `locate`

`locate`	Finds files.
`locate <pattern>`	

Searches a database for all pathnames that match *<pattern>*. The database is rebuilt periodically and contains the names of all publicly accessible files.

Shell and wildcard (globbing) characters (`*`, `?`, `\`, `[`, and `]`) may be used in *<pattern>*, although they must be escaped, to prevent the shell from interpreting and expanding them before handing them to the command. Preceding a character by `\` eliminates any special meaning for it. No characters must be explicitly matched, including `/`.

As a special case, if you specify a pattern with no wildcard/globbing characters (such as a search for `foo`), the pattern actually is matched as though it was surrounded by `*` wildcard characters; that is, matched as `*foo*`.

Useful files:

`/var/db/locate.database`	Database
/usr/libexec/locate.updatedb	Script to update database

Using `find`

A more powerful and more ubiquitous tool for finding files is `find`. It is much slower than the `locate` command because it actually searches the filesystem every time it's used instead of consulting a database, but that also means that it doesn't depend on a database for its information and the information is always completely up-to-date.

After running her search for files containing `log` in the name, our sample user `nermal` was overwhelmed by the results. However, she thinks that she might have heard that general system log files might be located in /usr or /var. To check whether what she recalls is correct, she decides to run find:

```
brezup:nermal Documents $ find /var /usr -name \*log\* -print
/usr/bin/grep-changelog
/usr/bin/logger
/usr/bin/login
/usr/bin/logname
/usr/bin/rcs2log
/usr/bin/rlog
/usr/bin/rlogin
/usr/bin/slogin
/usr/bin/xmlcatalog
/usr/include/httpd/http_log.h
/usr/include/libxml2/libxml/catalog.h
/usr/include/php/ext/standard/php_ext_syslog.h
/usr/include/php/main/logos.h
/usr/include/php/main/php_logos.h
/usr/include/php/main/php_syslog.h
... there's a mess o' files in the middle here,
... none of which are system.log, trust us!
/usr/share/vim/vim62/syntax/prolog.vim
/usr/share/vim/vim62/syntax/purifylog.vim
/usr/share/vim/vim62/syntax/rcslog.vim
/usr/share/vim/vim62/syntax/verilog.vim
/usr/share/zsh/4.1.1/functions/_logical_volumes
/usr/share/zsh/4.1.1/functions/_rlogin
/usr/X11R6/bin/xlogo
/usr/X11R6/include/X11/bitmaps/xlogo11
/usr/X11R6/include/X11/bitmaps/xlogo16
/usr/X11R6/include/X11/bitmaps/xlogo32
/usr/X11R6/include/X11/bitmaps/xlogo64
/usr/X11R6/lib/X11/doc/html/xlogo.1.html
/usr/X11R6/lib/X11/xedit/lisp/progmodes/xlog.lsp
/usr/X11R6/man/man1/xlogo.1
brezup:nermal Docuements $
```

In the preceding statement, nermal searches /usr and /var. The results, though, do not include the system.log file that nermal knows user joray was looking at earlier. According to these results, many files in /usr contain log, but nothing in /var. This seems slightly odd—so many files (some of them not even really log files, but just containing *log* in their names) in the filesystem below one directory, but nothing in the other. nermal is sure that /var is the other possibility she has heard for a location for the file, so perhaps there's something about /var that's different, and the reason nothing at all shows up isn't because nothing's there, but rather because it isn't being searched. It turns out that if you look closer:

```
brezup:nermal Documents $ ls -l /var
lrwxrwxr-t  1 root  admin  11 Sep 17 23:47 /var -> private/var
```

/var is actually a symbolic link to another directory. If you read find's man page, you'll discover that in its default behavior, find won't traverse symbolic links. Adding -H, as one of the options for find causes it to return information on the referenced file (target of the link), rather than for the link itself:

```
brezup:nermal Documents $ find -H /var -name \*log\* -print
find: /var/backups: Permission denied
find: /var/cron: Permission denied
find: /var/db/dhcpclient: Permission denied
find: /var/db/netinfo/local.nidb: Permission denied
find: /var/db/openldap/openldap-data: Permission denied
find: /var/db/openldap/openldap-slurp: Permission denied
find: /var/db/shadow: Permission denied
/var/log
/var/log/cups/access_log
/var/log/cups/error_log
/var/log/ftp.log
/var/log/httpd/access_log
/var/log/httpd/error_log
/var/log/install.log
/var/log/ipfw.log
/var/log/lastlog
/var/log/lookupd.log
/var/log/lpr.log
/var/log/mail.log
/var/log/netinfo.log
/var/log/secure.log
/var/log/system.log
/var/log/windowserver.log
find: /var/root: Permission denied
find: /var/run/sudo: Permission denied
/var/run/syslog
/var/run/syslog.pid
find: /var/spool/cups: Permission denied
find: /var/spool/mqueue: Permission denied
find: /var/spool/postfix/active: Permission denied
find: /var/spool/postfix/bounce: Permission denied
find: /var/spool/postfix/corrupt: Permission denied
find: /var/spool/postfix/defer: Permission denied
find: /var/spool/postfix/deferred: Permission denied
find: /var/spool/postfix/flush: Permission denied
find: /var/spool/postfix/hold: Permission denied
find: /var/spool/postfix/incoming: Permission denied
```

```
find: /var/spool/postfix/maildrop: Permission denied
find: /var/spool/postfix/private: Permission denied
find: /var/spool/postfix/public: Permission denied
find: /var/vm/app_profile: Permission denied
```

There, in the middle of that output, is the `system.log` file, as well as some additional files with `system.log` in their name. As we see from the output, `nermal` does not have permission to search everywhere, but `find` responds with information for areas where permissions permit it. `nermal` was lucky that her machine's logs appear to include `log` in the name. That is not the case on all systems.

FOCUSING YOUR RESULTS

If you think seeing all the errors regarding places that `find` isn't allowed to look is a space-consuming waste of time, keep reading. Because the Unix philosophy breaks functionality down into little indivisible actions, filtering the errors out of the output isn't rightly `find`'s job. The next command we discuss in this chapter, plus a little Unix wizardry called a *pipe* (from Chapter 12 and 15), will enable you to construct a version that doesn't report the errors.

Numerous options are available in `find`. In addition to being able to search on a pattern, `find` can also run searches based on ownership, file modification times, file access times, and much more. Table 10.18 shows the complete syntax and some useful options for `find`.

TABLE 10.18 The Syntax and Primary Options for `find`

`find`	Finds files.
`find [-H ¦ -L ¦ -P] [-EXdsx] [-f <file>] <file> .... <expression>`	
`find` recursively descends the directory tree of each file listing, evaluating an `<expression>` composed of *primaries* and *operands*.	
Options	
`-E`	Causes `find` to interpret regular expression patterns specified with `-regex` or `-iregex` as standard modern regular expressions, rather than as basic regular expressions (BREs). See `re_format(7)` manual page for a description of each format.
`-P`	Causes the file information and file type returned for each symbolic link to be those of the link itself. This is the default.
`-d`	Causes a depth-first traversal of the hierarchy. In other words, directory contents are visited before the directory itself. The default is for a directory to be visited before its contents.
`-x`	Excludes `find` from traversing directories that have a device number different from that of the file from which the descent began.
`-f`	Specifies a file hierarchy for `find` to traverse. File hierarchies may also be specified as operands immediately following the options listing.

TABLE 10.18 Continued

Primaries (in Expressions)	
All primaries that can take a numeric argument allow the number to be preceded by +, -, or nothing. *n* takes on the following meanings:	
+*n*	More than *n*
-*n*	Less than *n*
n	Exactly *n*
`-atime` *n*	True if the file was last accessed *n* days ago. Note that `find` itself changes the access time.
`-ctime` *n*	True if the file's status was changed *n* days ago.
`-mtime` *n*	True if the file was last modified *n* days ago.
`-newer` *XY* *<file>*	True if the current file has a more recent last access time (X=a), change time (X=c), or modification time (X=m) than the last access time (Y=a), change time (Y=c), or modification time (Y=m) of file. In addition, if Y=t, then file is instead interpreted as a direct date specification of the form understood by `cvs(1)`.
`-name` *<pattern>*	True if the file or directory name matches *<pattern>*. The pattern may include standard shell globbing wildcards such as `*`, but the shell gets to expand these characters before `find` gets hold of them. This means that if you `find / -name *.log`, the search will actually be for all files beneath the root directory that have the *same name as* files in your *current* directory that end in `.log`. If you want to find all files that end in `.log`, not just ones that also occur in your current directory, you need to escape the wildcard so that it isn't interpreted by the shell, and so that it gets passed on for `find` to work with when it searches. This can be accomplished as shown in the earlier examples by preceding characters that the shell would expand with a \ character (that is, `-name \*.log` would search for all files ending in `.log`). It is also possible in recent versions of the `bash` shell and `find` to use double quotes around a wildcarded string to keep it from expanding in the shell (that is, `-name "*.log"` should be equivalent to `-name \*.log`).
`-iname` *<pattern>*	True if the filename or directory name matches *<pattern>* in a case-insensitive way.
`-exec` *<command>* *[<argument> ...];*	True if *<command>* returns a zero-value exit status. Optional arguments may be passed to *<command>*. The expression must be terminated by a semicolon. If `{}` appear anywhere in the command name or arguments, they are replaced by the current pathname.
`-fstype`	True if the file is contained in a filesystem specified by `-fstype`.

10

Using `mdfind`

The `mdfind` command searches a continuously updated database of "metadata" about files. This metadata database is the same one used by the Spotlight search facility in the Finder, so the type of things that you can search for, and find with it are the same as those that can be found through the GUI. These include both filename searches, file content searches on files of known (and indexable) types, and other associated metadata (data about data) that Apple chooses to index.

The strength of `mdfind` is that the database is connected directly to the file access system at a low level, so as files are created or edited, the appropriate metadata changes are automatically and instantly inserted into the database. There are therefore neither long, and delayed indexing issues such as affect locate, nor long search times as with find. The downside however, is that if the file is *not* indexed for some reason (such as the underlying automated indexing crashing invisibly - a situation that is all too common with the latest developer release we have available, though it may also occur with removable media used on non-Tiger machines), it will *never* be indexed, because the system assumes that all files are indexed at creation. Presuming Apple gets this situation straightened out however, `mdfind` is both faster than `find` and more complete than `locate`.

The syntax for `mdfind` is simply:

```
mdfind <what you want to find>
```

`<what you want to find>` may be a filename, file contents, or more specifically constrained file metadata. If you'd like to constrain the search to only look in a particular directory (which with `find` is important for speed, but with `mdfind` is mostly useful for paring down the returned results), you can add the `-onlyin` *`<directory>`* option. System administrators may find some interesting uses for the `-live` option, that causes `mdfind` to keep running, and display continuously updated results for the search. Keeping track of the number of files matching common metadata features such as images, or `.mov` files that live on your system, can help you monitor and respond to the things your users are doing to your system.

Finding Files with Specific Contents: `grep`

Trying to remember what you've named a file that you need can sometimes be a real chore, especially if you haven't used the file for a long time or its name is similar to many other files on your system. For situations such as these, it is useful to be able to search for files based on patterns contained within the contents of the files themselves, rather than just the filenames. The basic syntax for `grep` is

```
grep <pattern> <files>
```

Here is a sample of using `grep`:

```
brezup:joray Documents $ grep me file*
grep: file1: Permission denied
file2:It's me.  Doing some
file3:Yep, me again..
file4:me again
file5:Another test by me...
```

In the preceding statement, we see that `grep` provides output as permissions permit. We also see that the default output lists only the file, the filename, and the lines containing the searched pattern. A number of options are available in `grep` (enough that entire books have been written on the subject). For example, we could ask grep to list the line numbers on which our pattern, me, appears in the files:

```
brezup:joray Documents $ grep -n me file*
grep: file1: Permission denied
file2:2:It's me.  Doing some
file3:2:Yep, me again..
file4:6:me again
file5:1:Another test by me...
```

Another available option is the recursive option, for descending a directory tree searching all the contents.

The grep command is even more powerful than might be immediately apparent because it is also useful for searching for patterns in the output of other commands. It could, for example, have been used to filter the rather verbose output from the preceding finds to print out only the specific lines containing exact matches to the filename of interest. Although we haven't gotten to the syntax of the more complex matter of chaining Unix commands together to make sophisticated commands, keep grep in mind as a building block, and consider its possible uses when you reach the end of Chapter 15.

Table 10.19 shows the syntax and primary options for grep.

TABLE 10.19 The Syntax and Primary Options for grep

`grep`
`egrep`
`fgrep`
	Prints line matching a pattern.

`grep [options] <pattern> <file1> <file2> ...`	
`grep [options] [-e <pattern> ¦ -f <file>] <file1> <file2> ...`	
grep searches the list of files enumerated by *<file1> <file2>* ..., or standard input if no file is specified or if - is specified. By default, the matching lines are printed.	
Two additional variants of the program are available as egrep (same as grep -E) or fgrep (same as grep -F).	

`-C <num>`
`-<num>`
`--context[=<num>]`
	Prints *<num>* lines of output context. Default is 2.

`--binary-files=<type>`	Assumes that a file is type *<type>* if the first few bytes of a file contain binary data.
Default *<type>* is binary, and grep normally outputs a one-line message indicating the file is binary, or nothing if there is no match. If *<type>* is without-match, it is assumed that a binary file does not match. Equivalent to -I option. If *<type>* is text, it processes the file as though it were a text file. Equivalent to -a option. Warning: Using this option could result in binary garbage being output to a terminal, some of which could be interpreted by the terminal as commands, resulting in unwanted side effects.	
`-c` `count`	Prints a count of matching lines for each file. Combined with -v, counts -- nonmatching lines.

TABLE 10.19 Continued

`-v` `--invert-match`	Inverts matching to select nonmatching lines.hb
`-r` `--recursive`	Recursively reads files under directories. Equivalent to `-d` recurse option.
`-f <file>` `--file=<file>`	Reads a list of patterns from `<file>`, which contains one pattern per line. An empty file has no patterns and matches nothing.
`-e <pattern>` `-regexp=<pattern>`	Uses `<pattern>` as the pattern. Useful for protecting patterns beginning with `-`.
`-G` `--basic-regexp`	Interprets `<pattern>` as a basic regular expression. This is the default behavior.
`-E` `-extended-regexp`	Interprets `<pattern>` as an extended regular expression. Equivalent to `egrep`.
`-F` `--fixed-strings`	Interprets `<pattern>` as a list of fixed strings, separated by newlines, any of which is to be matched. Equivalent to `fgrep`.
`-i` `--ignore-case`	Ignores case in `<pattern>` and input files.
`-n` `--line-number`	Output includes the line number where the match occurs.
`-s` `--no-messages`	Suppresses error messages about nonexistent or unreadable files.
`-w` `--word-regexp`	Selects only lines that have matches that form whole words.
`-x` `--line-regexp`	Selects only those matches that exactly match the whole line.

File Compression and Archiving

As in the Macintosh world, a number of standards have arisen in the Unix world for compressing and archiving files. Unlike the Mac world, however, these programs don't tend to be do-all programs such as StuffIt that can archive, compress, password-protect, and perform a wealth of other useful file archive functions. Following the Unix tradition, software that compresses files mostly just compresses files. Software that collects many files together into a single-file archive mostly just collects many files together into a single-file archive. There are a few exceptions, and some more recent (and some would say misguided) implementations of Unix utilities try to stuff everything but the kitchen sink into their functionality. Primarily though, functions are kept usefully separated into distinct commands and their functionality combined when needed. Even the programs that can do both collection/archiving and compression tend to be used for only one of the functions, with something else appropriate used for the other. For example, the functions of file collection and file compression are used together to collect files into an archive (uncompressed) using one program, and then subsequently something else is used to compress the files into a compressed archive. Likewise, the analogous procedure to "UnStuffIting" a file traditionally requires two steps in Unix because decompression of the archive and unpacking of its contents are two separate steps.

TIP

For those looking for a more seamless solution than the Unix way, take heart. The newer versions of BSD's `tar` program also include compression/decompression facilities. It's not an awfully Unix-like way to do things, but if you insist on the convenience, we won't hold it against you.

NOTE

Every now and then, you'll find a `tar` file that won't `untar` properly, complaining of permission errors writing files or just plain refusing to read properly. This is sometimes caused by incompatibility between some special features available in the GNU (GNU stands for *GNU's Not Unix*, and is the operating moniker for software developed or supported by the Free Software Foundation—the pioneers of the Open Source movement) version of `tar` (now found on Mac OS X 10.3), and the BSD version of `tar` (found on earlier versions of Mac OS X, and many other Unix platforms).

Your best course of action is to complain to the package's authors and get them to `tar` the data up without using either the `BSDtar` or `GNUtar` special options. Alternatively, you could choose to install `BSDtar` on your machine, but if you do, make sure that you install it as `bsdtar`, or some other name that won't conflict with the default system `tar`. Each flavor is unique enough that it will cause problems with software installations if an installer script thinks it's talking to one flavor `tar`, and it's really the other that has assumed the name.

This, by the way, is a perfect example of why it's a bad idea to start adding "special functionality" routines to a program with a simple purpose such as `tar`. The result is files that are no longer universally exchangeable, and software versions that are a nightmare to try to keep in sync.

Common Compression Utilities: `bzip`, `gzip`, `zip`, `compress`

Unix has various tools available for compressing and decompressing files. Compressing files, of course, causes them to take up less space. As drive space becomes cheaper, this is perhaps not as great a concern. However, if you will be transferring files over the network, smaller files transfer faster. In addition, you might find it useful to compress files—especially archives of software packages you have installed—for writing to CD-ROM, where space is limited.

`compress` and `gzip` are the compressing tools available on your system; `uncompress` and `gunzip` are the decompression tools. `compress` and `uncompress` are more widely available by default on systems. The `gzip` tool, however, can compress further than `compress`.

Software packages that you download are frequently distributed as files compressed by compress or gzip. Files that you download ending in .Z are files compressed with compress. Files ending in .gz are compressed with gzip. Decompress files ending in .Z with uncompress; decompress files ending in .gz with gunzip. You also occasionally see files ending in .tgz, which is the result of shoehorning .tar.gz (for tar archive, compressed with gzip) into a three-letter file extension). There's also a zcat utility that performs a function analogous to cat, only it decompresses the files before writing them to standard output (STDOUT). zcat operates on both gzip .gz and compress .Z files.

Here is a sample of compressing a file using gzip:

```
brezup:miwa source $ ls -l sendmail-src.tar
-rw-r--r--   1 miwa  class  4454400 Jul  6  2000 sendmail-src.tar
brezup:miwa source $ gzip -9 sendmail.8.10.2-src.tar
brezup:miwa source $ ls -l sendmail.8.10.2-src.tar*
-rw-r--r--   1 miwa  class  1250050 Jul  6  2000 sendmail-src.tar.gz
```

As we see from the preceding ls listing, the size of the file has been reduced and .gz has been appended to the filename. Table 10.20 shows the syntax and options for compress and uncompress. Table 10.21 shows the syntax and primary options for gzip and gunzip.

TABLE 10.20 The Command Documentation Table for compress and uncompress

compress	Compresses data.
uncompress	Expands data.
compress [-cfv] [-b <*bits*>] <*file1*> <*file2*> ...	
uncompress [-cfv] <*file1*> <*file2*> ...	
compress reduces the size of a file and renames the file by adding the .Z extension. As many of the original file characteristics (modification time, access time, file flags, file mode, user ID, and group ID) are retained as permissions allow. If compression would not reduce a file's size, the file is ignored. uncompress restores a file reduced by compress to its original form and renames the file by removing the .Z extension.	
-c	Writes compressed or uncompressed output to standard output without modifying any files.
-f	Forces compression of a file, even when compression would not reduce its size. Additionally, forces files to be overwritten without prompting for confirmation.
-v	Prints the percentage reduction of each file.
-b <*bits*>	Specifies the upper-bit code limit. Default is 16. Bits must be between 9 and 16. Lowering the limit results in larger, less compressed files.

TABLE 10.21 The Command Documentation Table for gzip, gunzip, and zcat

gzip gunzip zcat	Compresses or expands files.
gzip [-acdfhlLnNrtvV19] [-S <*suffix*>] <*file1*> <*file2*> ... gunzip [-acfhlLnNrtvV] [-S <*suffix*>] <*file1*> <*file2*> ... zcat [-fhLV] <*file1*> <*file2*> ...	
gzip reduces the size of a file and renames the file by adding the .gz extension. It keeps the same ownership modes and access and modification times. If no files are specified, or if the filename is specified, standard input is compressed to standard output. Gzip compresses regular files but ignores symbolic links. Compressed files can be restored to their original form by using gunzip, gzip -d, or zcat. gunzip takes a list of files from the command line, whose names end in .gz, -gz, .z, -z, _z, or .Z and which also begin with the correct magic number, and replaces them with expanded files without the original extension. gunzip also recognizes the extensions .tgz and .taz as short versions of .tar.gz and .tar.Z, respectively. If necessary, gzip uses the .tgz extension to compress a .tar file. zcat is equivalent to gunzip -c. It uncompresses either a list of files on the command line or from standard input and writes uncompressed data to standard output. Zcat uncompresses files that have the right magic number, whether or not they end in .gz. Compression is always formed, even if the compressed file is slightly larger than the original file.	
-d --decompress --uncompress	Decompresses.
-f	Forces compression or decompression, even if the file has multiple links, if the corresponding file already exists, or if the compressed data is read from or written to a terminal. If -f is not used, and gzip is not working in the background, the user is prompted before a file is overwritten.
-h --help	Displays a help screen and quits.
-r --recursive	Traverses the directory structure recursively.
If a filename specified on the command line is a directory, gzip/gunzip descends into the directory and compresses/decompresses the files in that directory.	
-S <*suffix*> --suffix <*suffix*>	Uses <*suffix*> instead of .gz. Any suffix can be used, but we recommend that suffixes other than .z and .gz be avoided to avoid confusion when transferring the file to another system.
A null suffix (-S ") forces gunzip to try decompression on all listed files, regardless of suffix.	
-t --test	Test. Checks the integrity of the compressed file.
-<*n*> --fast --best	Regulates the speed of compression as specified by -<*n*>, where -1 (or --fast) is the fastest compression method (least compression) and -9 (or --best) is the slowest compression method (most compression). Default compression option is -6.

A relatively recent compression utility is the `bzip2` package, developed to provide better compression, data protection, and recovery capabilities, and to eliminate patent and licensing conflicts that have arisen over some aspects of other compression utilities. The `bzip2` package is used much like `gzip` and `gunzip`, compressing with `bzip2`, and decompressing with `bunzip2`, and typically using files suffixed with `.bz2`. There is also a `bzcat` (nope, no 2) utility that is the equivalent of `cat`, only this one uncompresses the file as it is `cat`ted. Because the `bzip2` compression standard compresses data into independent blocks, partial data can be recovered from `bzip2` files that have been corrupted or truncated. The `bzip2recover` program is used to read damaged `.bz2` files and recover what data is still extractable from them. The command documentation table for `bzip2`, `bunzip2`, `bzcat`, and `bzip2recover` is shown in Table 10.22.

TABLE 10.22 The Command Documentation Table for `bzip2` and `bunzip2`

`bzip2`, `bunzip2`
`bzcat`
`bzip2recover` Block-sorting file compressor, v1.0.2
Decompresses files to `stdout`.
Recovers data from damaged `bzip2` files.

`bzip2 [-hcdfkqstvzVL123456789 ] [`*<filename1>* *<filename2>* `... ]`
`bunzip2 [-fkvsVL] [`*<filename1>* *<filename2>* `...]`
`bzcat [-s] [`*<filename1>* *<filename2>* `...]`
`bzip2recover` *<filename>*

`bzip2`, `bunzip2`, and `bzcat` are really the same program. The decision about what actions to take is done on the basis of which name is used.
`bzip2` compresses files using the Burrows-Wheeler block sorting text compression algorithm and Huffman coding.
`bzip2` expects a list of filenames to accompany the command-line flags. Each file is replaced by a compressed version of itself, with the name *<original_name>*`.bz2`. Each compressed file has the same modification date, permissions, and, when possible, ownership as the corresponding original so that these properties can be correctly restored at decompression time.
If no filenames are specified, `bzip2` compresses from standard input to standard output.
`bzip2` reads arguments from the environment variables `BZIP2` and `BZIP`, in that order, and processes them before reading any arguments from the command line. Chapter 15 provides an in-depth discussion of how to set and use environment variables to control your software.
Compression is always performed, even if the compressed file is slightly larger than the original.
`bunzip2` (or `bzip2 -d`) decompresses files. Files not created by `bzip2` are detected and ignored, and a warning is issued. Filenames are restored as follows:

<filename>`.bz2` *<filename>*
<filename>`.bz` *<filename>*
<filename>`.tbz2` *<filename>*`.tar`
<filename>`.tbz` *<filename>*`.tar`
<anyothername> *<anyothername>*`.out`

Supplying no filenames causes decompression from standard input to standard output.
`bzcat` (or `bzip2 -dc`) decompresses all specified files to standard output.

bzip2recover is a simple program whose purpose is to search for blocks in .bz2 files and write each block out into its own .bz2 file. You can then use bzip2 -t to test the integrity of the resulting files and decompress those that are undamaged.

Bzip2recover takes a single argument, the name of the damaged file, and writes a number of files, rec00001file.bz2, rec00002file.bz2, and so on, containing the extracted blocks. The output filenames are designed so that the use of wildcards in subsequent processing—for example, bzip2 -dc rec*file.bz2 > recovered_data—processes the files in the correct order.

Option	Description
-h --help	Displays a help menu.
-d --decompress	Forces bzip2 to decompress, regardless of the invocation name. The bzip family of programs is another collection like the new less, which pretends to be more if invoked under that name. The bzip applications are actually all the same file and all share the same functionality, but determine what they're supposed to do based on the name by which they're invoked. This option enables you to force the nominally compressing invocation bzip2 to decompress instead.
-f --force	Forces overwrite of output files. Normally, bzip2 does not overwrite existing output files. Also forces bzip2 to break hard links to files, which it otherwise doesn't do.

bzip2 normally declines to decompress files that don't have the correct magic header bytes. If forced (-f), however, it passes such files through unmodified. This is how GNU gzip behaves.

Option	Description
-k --keep	Keeps (doesn't delete) input files during compression or decompression.
-t --test	Checks integrity of the specified file(s), but doesn't decompress them.
-z --compress	Forces compression, regardless of the invocation name.
-1 (or --fast) .. -9 (or --best)	Sets block size to 100k .. 900k. The --fast and --best aliases are primarily for GNU gzip compatibility. In particular, --fast doesn't make things significantly faster. --best merely selects the default behavior.

Archiving Files with tar

tar is a useful tool for archiving files. Although originally intended for archiving to tape, tar is commonly used for archiving files or directories of files to a single file. After you have the archive file, it is common to compress it for further storage or distribution.

The most common options that you will probably use with tar are -c for creating a file, -t for getting a listing of the contents, -x for extracting the file, -f for specifying a file to create or act on, and -v for verbose output.

Here is an example of viewing the contents of a `tar` file. It is often useful to look at the contents of a `tar` file before extracting it. Unix commands (if you haven't noticed) tend to be quite literal, so a `tar` file can be an archive of individual files rather than an archive of a directory of files. The consequence is that if you `untar` the contents, they could land, as single files, in whatever your current directory is (or worse, they may have full paths embedded, and write anywhere that you can in the entire filesystem). It is therefore helpful to look at the contents before untarring. That way, you know whether you should create a separate directory for extracting the file so that you have its contents in one place, or whether it will create a directory into which the files will be extracted.

Although not all the output is shown in this example, you can see nonetheless that this archive creates a directory (`sendmail-8.10.2`) into which the files are extracted:

```
brezup:nermal source $ tar -tvf sendmail.8.10.2-src.tar
drwxr-xr-x 103/700       0 2000-06-07 13:01 sendmail-8.10.2/
-rw-r--r-- 103/700     795 1999-09-27 17:39 sendmail-8.10.2/Makefile
-rwxr-xr-x 103/700     327 1999-09-23 17:31 sendmail-8.10.2/Build
-rw-r--r-- 103/700     321 1999-02-06 22:21 sendmail-8.10.2/FAQ
-rw-r--r-- 103/700    1396 1999-04-04 03:01 sendmail-8.10.2/INSTALL
-rw-r--r-- 103/700    8923 1999-11-17 13:56 sendmail-8.10.2/KNOWNBUGS
-rw-r--r-- 103/700    4116 2000-03-03 14:24 sendmail-8.10.2/LICENSE
-rw-r--r-- 103/700   23017 1999-11-23 14:08 sendmail-8.10.2/PGPKEYS
-rw-r--r-- 103/700   13703 2000-03-16 18:46 sendmail-8.10.2/README
-rw-r--r-- 103/700  348392 2000-06-07 03:39 sendmail-8.10.2/RELEASE_NOTES
drwxr-xr-x 103/700       0 2000-06-07 13:00 sendmail-8.10.2/devtools/
...
```

If the archive hadn't been of a directory, it might have looked more like this:

```
brezup:nermal source $ tar -tvf sendmail.8.10.2-messysrc.tar
-rw-r--r-- 103/700     795 1999-09-27 17:39 Makefile
-rwxr-xr-x 103/700     327 1999-09-23 17:31 Build
-rw-r--r-- 103/700     321 1999-02-06 22:21 FAQ
-rw-r--r-- 103/700    1396 1999-04-04 03:01 INSTALL
-rw-r--r-- 103/700    8923 1999-11-17 13:56 KNOWNBUGS
-rw-r--r-- 103/700    4116 2000-03-03 14:24 LICENSE
-rw-r--r-- 103/700   23017 1999-11-23 14:08 PGPKEYS
-rw-r--r-- 103/700   13703 2000-03-16 18:46 README
-rw-r--r-- 103/700  348392 2000-06-07 03:39 RELEASE_NOTES
drwxr-xr-x 103/700       0 2000-06-07 13:00 devtools/
```

This archive would dump files named `Makefile`, `Build`, `FAQ`, (and so on) into whatever directory I uncompressed it in, rather than having the decency to create a subdirectory container for its contents.

Table 10.23 shows the syntax and options for `tar`.

TABLE 10.23 The Command Documentation Table for `tar`

`gnu` `tar`	Tape archiver; manipulates `tar` archive files`tar`

`gnutar [[-]`*`bundled-options Args`*`] [`*`gnu-style-flags`*`] [`*`filenames`*` ¦ -C `*`directory-name`*`] ...`

`tar` is short for *tape archiver*, so named for historical reasons; the `gnutar` program creates, adds files to, or extracts files from an archive file in `gnutar` format, called a *tarfile*. A tarfile is often a magnetic tape but can be a floppy diskette or any regular disk file.

The first argument word of the `gnutar` command line is usually a command word of bundled function and modifier letters, optionally preceded by a dash; it must contain exactly one function letter from the set `A`, `c`, `d`, `r`, `t`, `u`, `x`, for append, create, difference, replace, table of contents, update, and extract, respectively. The command word can also contain other function modifiers, some of which take arguments from the command line in the order they are specified in the command word. Functions and function modifiers can also be specified with the GNU argument convention (preceded by two dashes, one function or modifier per word). Command-line arguments that specify files to add to, extract from, or list from an archive may be given as shell pattern matching strings.

Functions (Exactly one of the following must be specified)

`-A`
`--catenate`
`--concatenate`
	Appends the contents of named file, which must itself be a `gnutar` archive, to the end of the archive (erasing the old end-of-archive block). This has the effect of adding the files contained in the named file to the first archive, rather than adding the second archive as an element of the first.

`-c` `--create`	Creates a new archive (or truncates an old one) and writes the named files to it.

`-d`
`--diff`
`--compare`
	Finds differences between files in the archive and corresponding files in the filesystem.

`-r` `--append`	Appends files to the end of an archive.
`-t` `--list`	Lists the contents of an archive.
`-u` `--update`	Appends the named files if the on-disk version has a modification date more recent than their copy in the archive (if any).

`-x`
`--extract`
`--get`
	Extracts files from an archive. The owner, modification time, and file permissions are restored, if possible.

TABLE 10.23 Continued

Selected Options	
`--overwrite`	Overwrites existing files when extracting.
`-O`	
`--to-stdout`	Extracts files to standard output.
`--owner=<name>`	Forces `<name>` as owner for added files.
`--group=<name>`	Forces `<name>` as group for added files.
`--atime-preserve`	Doesn't change access times on dumped files.
`-m`	Doesn't extract file modified time.
`--modification-time`	
`--same-owner`	Tries extracting files with the same ownership.
`--no-same-owner`	Extracts files as yourself.
`-f [<hostname>:]<file>`	Read or write the specified file (default is `/dev/sa0`). If a hostname
`--file=[<hostname>:]<file>`	is specified, `gnutar` uses `rmt(8)` to read or write the specified file on a remote machine. `-` may be used as a filename for reading or writing to/from `stdin`/`stdout`.
`-[0-7][lmh]`	Specifies drive and density.
`-M`	Creates/lists/extracts multivolume archive.
`--multi-volume`	
`-L <num>`	Changes tape after writing `<num>` x 1024 bytes.
`--tape-length=<num>`	
`-F <file>`	Runs script at end of each tape (implies `-M`).
`--info-script=<file>`	
`--new-volume-script=<file>`	
`-X <file>`	Excludes patterns listed in `<file>`.
`--exclude-from=<file>`	
`-N <date>`	Only stores files newer than `<date>`.
`--newer=<date>`	
`--after-date=<date>`	Only stores files with modification time newer than `<date>`.
`--newer-mtime=<date>`	
`--help`	Prints help information and then exits.

TIP

StuffIt Expander can decompress/unzip/ungzip a file and then `untar` it for you, if you prefer to drag and drop your file archiving tasks. It's not as flexible with respect to what it extracts from an archive, and there are some problems with long, or "weird" filenames, but it's convenient and easy to use. If it doesn't work, don't automatically assume that the archive itself is damaged; give the command-line tools a try.

Getting Disk and Directory Information: du, df

The du and df commands are great examples of where a command-line tool really shines. Finding out how much space your files are using, or how much space is left on your various assorted volumes and drives is not a pleasant process under the Finder. Certainly, the display of drive space on a volume that appears in the bottom of every Finder window is a convenient way to keep track of disk usage, but if you want to find out what drive has the most free space, there isn't a good way to see this information without either clicking through every drive and looking at the window, or running an auxiliary disk-monitoring tool like Disk Utility. At the command line, it's two keystrokes:

```
brezup:~ ray$ df
Filesystem               512-blocks     Used    Avail Capacity  Mounted on
/dev/disk0s3               20447232 16643456  3599304    82%    /
devfs                           186      186        0   100%    /dev
fdesc                             2        2        0   100%    /dev
<volfs>                        1024     1024        0   100%    /.vol
/dev/disk0s5               41418752 28786624 12632128    70%    /Volumes/Software
/dev/disk0s7               54263808 52485896  1777912    97%    /Volumes/Wills_Data
/dev/disk0s9               10223616  8979656  1243960    88%    /Volumes/DVD1
/dev/disk0s11              10223616  6687424  3536192    65%    /Volumes/DVD2
/dev/disk0s13              10223616  8662360  1561256    85%    /Volumes/DVD3
/dev/disk0s15               7665760  1582288  6083472    21%    /Volumes/CD
automount -nsl [299]              0        0        0   100%    /Network
automount -fstab [315]            0        0        0   100%    /automount/Servers
automount -static [315]           0        0        0   100%    /automount/static
```

If you prefer the output in kilobytes, instead of 512-byte blocks (yes, that seems a silly default to us as well), you need to add the -k option.

Likewise, the du command tells you about the disk space being used by various files or directories. If one of your volumes has unexpectedly filled up, and you don't know with what filled it or where the offending files landed, wading through the filesystem with the Finder looking for the large file or files can be tedious. Again, at the command line, getting at the information (sometimes too much of it!) is only a few keystrokes away. The du command will tell you the size of every file on your system with four keystrokes, if you choose:

```
brezup:~ ray$ du /
du: /.Metadata: Permission denied
du: /.Trashes: Permission denied
0       /.vol/234881026
0       /.vol
984     /Applications/Address Book.app/Contents/MacOS
8       /Applications/Address Book.app/Contents/Resources/
➥ABLargeTypeWindow.nib
8       /Applications/Address Book.app/Contents/Resources/
➥da.lproj/ABCarbonLayoutName.nib
```

10

```
8       /Applications/Address Book.app/Contents/Resources/
➥da.lproj/ABConverterProgress.nib
24      /Applications/Address Book.app/Contents/Resources/
➥da.lproj/ABDistribution.nib
16      /Applications/Address Book.app/Contents/Resources/
➥da.lproj/ABDotMacSharingProgress.nib
...
```

This listing goes on and on, and gives the size of every file I currently have permission to read on the entire system.

If I want to limit the output to only a summary for each file or directory, rather than a line of output for every individual item in the hierarchy, I can use the `-s` option, shown here looking only at the files and directories in my home directory:

```
brezup:~ ray$ du -s ~/*
8       ./Adobe SVG 3.0 Installer Log
0       ./Applications
786792  ./Desktop
6078256 ./Documents
896848  ./Library
1236624 ./Mail
0       ./Movies
53632   ./Music
0       ./Network Trash Folder
6269584 ./Pictures
32      ./Public
32      ./Shared
584     ./Sites
0       ./TheFindByContentFolder
16      ./TheVolumeSettingsFolder
32      ./ZaurusBackup
13936   ./joray
0       ./mnt
136     ./output
8       ./tmp
```

If I had issued the command as `du -s ~/`, I would have gotten only a summary response for my home directory as a directory, rather than every file and directory in it. Again, the `-k` option is a good thing to use if you prefer your response in kilobytes, rather than in 512K disk-block units. Table 10.24 shows the syntax and options for `df`, and Table 10.25 shows the syntax and options for `du`.

TABLE 10.24 The Command Documentation Table for `df`

`df`	Displays free disk space.
`df [-ailn] [-b ¦ -h ¦ -H ¦ -k ¦ -m ¦ -P] [-t <type>] [-T type] [<file> ¦ <filesytem> ...]`	
`-a`	Shows information for all filesystems, even if they were mounted with `MNT_IGNORE`, a flag that tells the system to ignore them in normal statistics reporting.
`-i`	Includes statistics on the number of free inodes.
`-l`	Displays statistics only about mounted filesystems with the `MNT_LOCAL` flag set. If a nonlocal filesystem is given as the argument, a warning is issued and no information is displayed.
`-n`	Prints out previously obtained statistics from the filesystem. This option should be used if it is possible that one or more filesystems are in a state such that there is a long delay before they can provide statistics. For example, if you're using `df` as a component of an automated system monitoring your machine, it wouldn't be good for it to hang permanently waiting for data if one of your drives died, or if a volume mounted from a remote server was disconnected. The option allows the `df` to report previously valid statistics, instead of perhaps waiting forever, for a failed resource to report current data.
`-b`	Report the statistics in 512-byte blocks.
`-h`	Reports the statistics in human-readable form, appending appropriate suffixes to the numbers to keep the printed lengths down to convenient sizes; reports the numbers themselves in the base-2 version of kilobyte (1024 bytes), and so on.
`-H`	Reports the statistics in human-readable form, appending appropriate suffixes to the numbers to keep the printed lengths down to convenient sizes; reports the numbers themselves in the base 10 version of kilobytes (1000 bytes), and so on.
`-b`	Reports the statistics in 512-byte blocks.
`-m`	Reports the statistics in megabyte (1048576-byte) blocks.
`-T <type>`	Displays information for filesystems of the specified type. More than one type may be specified in a comma-separated list of the list of filesystem types. Using this option you can limit your responses to only `hfs` for normal Mac filesystems, `nfs` for typical Unix network filesystems, `ufs` for typical Unix local filesystems, `cd9660` for ISO9660 CD ROMs, as well as other filesystem types listed by the `lsvfs` command.
If the environment variable `BLOCKSIZE` is set, and none of the size override options are used, the block counts are displayed according to the environment variable.	

TABLE 10.25 The Command Documentation Table for `du`

`du`	Displays disk usage statistics.
`du [-H ¦ -L ¦ -P] [-I mask] [-a ¦ -s ¦ -d depth] [-c] [-h¦k] [-x] [<file> ...]`	
`du` displays the file system block usage for each file argument and for each directory in the file hierarchy rooted in each directory argument. If no file is specified, the block usage of the hierarchy rooted in the current directory is displayed.	
`-H`	Follows symbolic links on the command line. Symbolic links encountered during tree traversal are not followed.
`-L`	Follows all symbolic links.

TABLE 10.25 Continued

`-P`	Does not follow symbolic links.
`-I <mask>`	Ignores files matching `<mask>`.
`-a`	Displays an entry for each file in the file hierarchy.
`-s`	Displays only the grand total for the specified files.
`-d <depth>`	Prunes the output to only `<depth>` directories deep.
`-c`	Displays the grand total after all the arguments have been processed.
`-h`	Human-readable output as with `df`'s `-h` option.
`-k`	Displays the statistics in 1024-byte blocks. Default is 512-byte blocks.
`-x`	Does not traverse file system mount points.

`du` counts the storage used by symbolic links and not the files they reference unless `-H` or `-L` is specified. If either `-H` or `-L` is specified, the storage used by a symbolic link is not counted and statistics including the target of the link are displayed instead. `-H`, `-L`, and `-P` override each other. The option specified last is the one executed.

Files with multiple hard links are counted and displayed once per `du` execution.

If the environment variable `BLOCKSIZE` is set and the `-k` option is not used, the block counts are displayed according to the environment variable.

Mounting/Unmounting Volumes: `diskutil`

Although the functions of Apple's Disk Utility application aren't a traditional part of the Unix command-line environment—at least not in a single application—Apple has provided an interface to most Disk Utility functions through the `diskutil` program.

`diskutil` lets the user mount and unmount volumes, eject disks, rename volumes, work with RAID sets and do some rudimentary disk repairs. `diskutil` can also be used to good effect in concert with the `hdiutil` command, which we cover in Chapter 29. The syntax and some important options for `diskutil` are shown in Table 10.26.

TABLE 10.26 The Command Documentation Table for `diskutil`

`diskutil`	Modify, verify and repair local disks
`diskutil <verb> [<options>]`	
Renames, ejects, mounts or unmounts disks and volumes.	
Verbs and Their Available Options	
`list [device]`	Lists the disks currently known and available on the system, or on a specific device.
`info [device]`	Get disk information on all, or a specific device.
Managing Disks	
`unmount [force] <device>`	Unmounts a single disk partition (volume) (for example, `diskutil unmount /Volumes/MyDisk` or `diskutil unmount disk2s1`)
`unmountDisk [force] <device>`	Unmounts an entire drive, and all partitions/volumes on it (for example, `diskutil unmountDisk force /dev/disk1`)
`eject <device>`	Ejects a disk

TABLE 10.26 Continued

`mount` *<device>*	Mounts a single volume/partition (for example, `diskutil mount disk2s2`). (Useful when a volume has been unmounted by hand, and you want it back!)
`mountDisk` *<device>*	Mount all volumes on a drive.
Controlling Disk Parameters and State	
`rename` *<device> <newname>*	Renames volume. Renames the volume specified as the first argument. For example, `diskutil rename /dev/disk1s2 Spanky` or `diskutil rename /Volumes/MyDisk /Volumes/YourDisk`.
`reformat` *<device>*	Reformats the *<device>* in the existing format.
`randomDisk [times]` *<device>*	Writes random data to `<device>`, optionally do it [times] times. Useful for wiping sensitive data that you don't want the black-helicopter crowd sniffing from your disk surface.
`secureErase [level]` *<device>*	Erase a disk using even more paranoia than `randomDisk`. Levels 1, 2, and 3 specify one-pass random data, US DoD 7-Pass secure erase mode, and Guttman algorithm 35-pass secure erase mode. Even the black helicopter crowd doesn't know how to get around this one.
`enableJournal` *<device>*	Enable HFS+ journaling on the *<device>*
Checking and Repairing Disks	
`verifyVolume` *<device>*	Verifies the structure of a volume.
`repairVolume` *<device>*	Repairs the structure of a volume.
`repairPermissions` *<device>*	Repairs the permissions of an Mac OS X boot volume. Some people report constant, inexplicable problems with their disk permissions going awry, but we've never seen this happen on our machines.
RAID Tools	
`CreateRAID mirror¦stripe` *<name> <format> <device> <device>* `[`*<device>* `...]`	Creates a RAID set on multiple disks or volumes. Format can be `HFS`, `HFS+`, `JournaledHFS+`, `UFS`, `MS-DOS`. We've seen situations where creating a journaled RAID would not properly install the journal, and creating the RAID in HFS+ then enabling journaling separately was required.
`enableRAID mirror¦concat` *<device>*	Converts a single filesystem or volume into an unpaired mirror RAID set (essentially a degraded mirrored RAID with no existing partner), or the beginning of a concatenated set.
`convertRAID` *<device>*	Converts a RAID converted on Panther or earlier, to Tiger's new 2.x RAID. Personally, we're skeptical that we have the intestinal fortitude to try this with our 2.5 TB XServe RAID!
`repairMirror` *<raidDisk> <newDisk>*	Repairs a failed mirror. *<raidDisk>* is the existing RAID, and *<newDisk>* is the replacement drive/volume to pair into the mirror. *<raidDisk>* and *<newDisk>* need to be a `/dev/` nodes or disk identifiers.

TABLE 10.26 Continued

`<device>` in these commands can be named volumes, such as `/Volume/MyStuff`, device nodes such as `/dev/disk1s3` (disk 1, partiton 3) or `/dev/disk1` (all of disk 1), or just the disk-identifier portion out of the device node name (i.e. `disk1s3` or `disk1`). Some of these don't make sense in certain contexts, such as using the `reformat` verb on a full drive with multiple partitions, or the `mount` verb on a named volume. Apple's documentation doesn't suggest what will happen if you use a peculiar combination, so avoid the ones that don't make sense.

Summary

This chapter introduced the most common Unix command-line file manipulation commands. Commands to copy, move, delete, search, and display files, as well as to archive and compress files were covered. You will most likely type at least one command from this chapter for every other command or application that you invoke from the Unix command line.

These commands also provide a good introduction to the Unix concept of small, single-function commands. What you've learned here about how a task can be accomplished the Unix way should serve you well in determining how to use other Unix commands that we don't have the time to cover in such depth.

CHAPTER 11

Using File Permissions and Access Control Lists

IN THIS CHAPTER

- Introduction to File Permissions
- Applying Advanced Resource Control Using ACLs
- Being Someone Else for a While: `su`, `sudo`

Because Unix is an inherently multiuser environment, it's important for there to be a way to record who owns what, who can look at it, run it, or change it. In Unix, this is accomplished with metadata flags that tell the system what permissions exist for each file. Because the system doesn't actually know a text file from a word processor, these flags are also used to indicate whether the file should be considered executable (and therefore a runnable program or application).

The basic philosophy of the Unix file permission system revolves around the idea of controlling access at three levels: access that's possible for the owner of the file; access that's possible for a group of *owners* (users who aren't the file's individual owner, but who (may) have enhanced privileges with respect to it); and access that's possible for everyone else on the system.

Apple is also working to incorporate Access Control Lists into Mac OS X, but as we are writing this, it's uncertain whether this feature will make it into the release version of Tiger client.

Introduction to File Permissions

This section expands on the topic of file permissions, which were briefly mentioned when we discussed the output from the `ls` command. It's likely that you won't have an immediate use for modifying file permissions, and it's possible that you'll never need to deal with them at all. However, if you want to work with other users on the same system, or decide to start writing your own programs, understanding the permission system will be necessary.

NOTE

A subset of the Unix file permission system can be accessed from the Mac OS X Finder. These are controlled from the Get Info window's Permissions tab.

Read, Write, and Execute

Permissions are specified as a collection of three flags. These flags (also called *bits*) control whether data in the file may be read, written, and executed. Unix takes these flags literally. So, if you have a program and you unset its execute flag, you won't be able to run the program—the system simply won't understand that the program is executable. Likewise, if you set the execute flag for a file containing a word processor document, Unix will assume that the file contents are a program and try its best to run the file. This is unlikely to do anything but produce an error message.

In the case of directories, the same bits apply, but the meanings are slightly different. The read and write bits control whether the contents of the directory may be read, and whether the directory can be written to, respectively. The execute bit, however, controls whether the directory can be `cd`ed to, or otherwise moved into by a shell or program.

The permissions for whether a directory listing can be read or written to are separate from the permission that controls whether you, or programs, can move into it. Also, the permissions for files contained in the directory do not necessarily need to agree with the permissions of the directory. The significance of this might not be immediately apparent, but the meaning is literal. If you have files that have world read permission turned on, you can put them in a directory and set the bits on the directory so that the files in it can be read, but the files can't be listed. Likewise, you can set the permissions so that the directory allows anyone on the system to write files into it, but nobody can read the files or list the contents.

The execute permission for directories interacts with the read and write permission for files in it, in a slightly nonintuitive fashion. Read permission for the directory allows you to read the directory listing but not the files. Read permission for a file in the directory allows you to read the file but not list the directory. However, to be able to read the file, you—or rather the software you're using to read the file—must be able to go into the directory. Because of this, if you turn on read permission for a directory and not execute permission, you can list the directory but not read the files, no matter what the permissions on the files are. Likewise, you (or software under your control) can't write into a directory with only write permission turned on; execute permission must be enabled as well.

If you know that the file `fizbin` exists in the directory `thozbot`, but read permission is turned off for `thozbot` and execute permission is turned on, you can still read `fizbin` (assuming that you have read permission on `fizbin` itself) by using its full or relative path from outside the `thozbot` directory. If you don't know that `fizbin` exists in the directory, there's no way for you to find out because you can't enter the directory or list the contents.

NOTE

Interesting applications for separated directory/file permissions immediately spring to mind. For example, perhaps you want to have a "drop box" directory where people could leave you files, but could not snoop around and see or read what anyone else had written. A directory with permissions set to write and execute only would accomplish this.

Alternatively, a directory set to execute permission only, containing files with read permission enabled, would allow you to distribute files privately from a directory. With this setup, you could use one directory to distribute different files to a number of people privately by giving each person only the filenames of the files he is allowed to read. Nobody can list the contents of the directory, but a person can read files from it, if he knows the correct filenames.

Owner, Group, and World

Adding a layer of complexity to the permission system, the read, write, and execute permissions detailed earlier can be specified separately for three subsets of users. They can be set for each owner of the file, the group owner of the file, and the world.

The owner of a file is, as the name implies, the user who owns the file. Each file on a Unix system has information stored about it that indicates to which user account the file belongs. Files that you create automatically belong to your user ID. Other files on the system belong to other users, or to one of the system accounts that exist to help the operating system keep its processes sorted out and secure.

Files have an additional piece of ownership information: the group ownership of the file. The group ownership specifies, by group name, a collection of users who share the group permissions to the file. This additional information facilitates the sharing of information among more than one user. Interestingly, the group permissions can be *less* than the permissions that are available to everybody, and when they are, the members of that group of users have *restricted* access to the file compared to other users of the machine, rather than enhanced access. Creating groups and controlling their membership are covered in Chapter 20, "Configuring Advanced System Features via NetInfo."

NOTE

Technically, the members of the group don't own the file in the same way that the file's individual owner owns it. Only the individual owner has the ability to change the file's permissions, and can change the group to any group he chooses. For this reason, some documentation (Apple's included) tends to term the group that currently is specified for the file, as the Group ID of the file. This nomenclature is slightly confusing because Group ID is more commonly used for other purposes related to groups, and doesn't apply in quite the same way to files. Regardless, if you see Group Ownership of a file or Group ID of a file, remember that both mean the group of users whose access privileges are affected by the read/write/execute flags for the group to which the file belongs.

Finally, there is a set of permission bits that control the access level enjoyed by the world, or at least all the other users on the system. If you provide any sort of guest access to your machine, it's best to assume that the file's world permissions do in fact apply to just about everyone, independent of location.

TIP

Remember that the permissions allowed each type of user, owner, group, and world do not need to be the same. If you want to allow your friends to look at the data in your daily calendar file and the correlated data in your address/contacts file, you can set permissions on these files so that you (the user) can read and write them, but the group to which your friends belong can only read them. You might even want to let the world read the contents of your schedule, so you could turn on read access for the world for it. However, you probably don't want the world picking through your personal address book, so you could shut off all access from the world by turning off all three flags for the world on that file.

Extended Bits

In addition to the read, write, and execute bits for each file and directory, a few additional bits exist as well. These bits are typically used by system administrators, but they occasionally come in handy for other users.

The complete set of bits, including the extended bits, that control the permissions and properties of a file or directory are called the *mode bits* for the file.

Special Flags

Further extending the classical set of mode bits is a set of special flags. These are definitely not for use by anyone but the administrator, but are mentioned here because one particular bit can sneak up and bite you.

The most important of these for you to watch out for is the immutable flag. This flag is set by Finder's locked status for a file. It's not currently clear why Apple chose this particular flag to map to Finder's locked status, but it causes a few problems on the Unix side. Specifically, if you set a file's immutable flag, it becomes almost impossible to change that file in any way. It can't be modified, it can't be overwritten, it can't be deleted—it becomes, as the name implies, immutable. Although Apple's tech notes indicate that there is a way to override the immutable flag and remove the file, this appears to only work for user-level immutable flags. If the system-level immutable flag (`schg`) becomes set, the only way we've found to remove it is to use ResEdit under Classic.

Checking File Permissions: `ls -l`

Remember that the `ls -l` command shows you the permissions associated with files. To find out the permissions associated with a single file, give it a filename to list:

```
brezup:ray testing $ ls -l /etc/passwd
-rw-r--r--  1 root  wheel  1374 29 Jul 14:15 /etc/passwd
```

Controlling File Permissions: `chmod`

After you are comfortable examining the permissions of files, you'll probably want to be able to change them. This is accomplished with the `chmod` (change mode) command. This command operates in either a "fully specified mode bits" manner, or in a "change this specific mode bit" manner, depending on the arguments you give it on the command line.

The "change this specific mode bit" form is the friendlier of the two, and works by allowing you to specify a bit to change, how to change it, and which type of user to change it for. The complete syntax for this form of the command is

```
chmod <u¦g¦o¦a><+¦-><r¦w¦x> <filename> ...
```

To use it, simply do the following:

1. Choose whether you want to change the permissions for the user (yourself), the group, or the world. If you want to change the user, the first argument is `u`; `g` is for group; and `o` is for other (world).
2. Choose whether you want to add, delete, or absolutely specify a permission. If you want to add a permission, follow your first argument with a `+` sign; if you want to remove a permission, follow it with a `-` sign; otherwise, to set the permissions to an absolute value, use an `=` sign.
3. Indicate the permission or permissions you want to add, delete, or set, using `r` for read, `w` for write, and `x` for execute. Follow these by the names of the files or directories for which you want to change the permissions.

You might also use an `a` to indicate all, in place of the `u`, `g`, or `o` argument, if you want to make the change for the file to all three user types.

For example, consider a file named `fizbin` with the current permission set so that the user has full read, write, and execute permission, and the group and world have no permissions at all.

```
brezup:ray testing $ ls -l
total 0
-rwx------   1 ray  staff  0 Apr 22 23:32 fizbin
```

Perhaps this file is not actually a program, and to prevent yourself from accidentally trying to run it, you want to remove the execute permission from the user.

```
brezup:ray testing $ chmod u-x fizbin
brezup:ray testing $ ls -l
total 0
-rw-------   1 ray  staff  0 Apr 22 23:32 fizbin
```

Now you want to make it readable by both the group and the world.

```
brezup:ray testing $ chmod g+r fizbin
brezup:ray testing $ chmod o+r fizbin
brezup:ray testing $ ls -l
total 0
-rw-r--r--   1 ray  staff  0 Apr 22 23:32 fizbin
```

```
brezup:ray testing $ chmod u+x,g=rx,o=rx fizbin
brezup:ray testing $ ls -l
total 0
-rwxr-xr-x  1 ray  staff  0 Apr 22 23:32 fizbin
```

As you can see, this method of changing file permissions is fairly simple, but it does not lend itself to setting many permissions at once. Although it's possible to say `chmod u=rwx,g=xr,o=xr` *<filename>* to set all the permission bits at once to force the file's mode bits into some particular pattern in a single command, doing so is a bit cumbersome. To solve this, the `chmod` command also includes an "all at once" option, whereby you can specify the full complement of mode bits simultaneously in a more compact form.

This form of the command can appear to be slightly less clear because it requires you to do a little math, but in reality it's no more complicated. In this form, the `chmod` command considers the mode bits for the file to be binary bits. To use the command, you need to specify which bits to set and which to unset.

Unfortunately, you can't do this in a manner as nice as just giving `chmod` a set of nine `rwxrwxrwx` characters or ones and zeros. Instead, you must break up the nine bits of the mode bit set into three sets of three bits (`rwx rwx rwx`), and calculate the decimal equivalent of the bits that you want set.

Put another way, you could think of the elements in `rwx` as specifying where, in a binary string, a `1` occurs. This is done as shown here:

```
100 - read permission.    100 in binary = 4 in decimal.
010 - write permission.   010 in binary = 2 in decimal.
001 - execute permission. 001 in binary = 1 in decimal.
```

To find the decimal value equivalent of a particular combination of `r`, `w`, and `x` bits, you sum the decimal values that correspond to the bit patterns that represent them. So, if you wanted read and execute permission, with no write permission, you would add `4 + 1 = 5`, and for user, group, or world, you would put a `5` in the pattern where needed.

A full example should help to explain this. Let's again consider the `fizbin` file, which, due to the use of `chmod` previously, has mode bits of `rw-r--r--`. That is to say, the user can read and write, and both the group and world can read. If you wanted to change this to mode bits `r-xr-x--x`, the syntax shown for the friendlier mode of `chmod` would require several commands. Instead, you could make this change in a single command by using the "all at once" form. To do so, follow these steps:

1. Split the desired permissions into user, group, and world bits. This results in `r-x` belonging to the user, `r-x` belonging to the group, and `--x` belonging to the world.
2. Calculate the decimal values for each: `r-x` is read permission and execute permission, which is `4+1 = 5`. `r-x` for the group is the same. `--x` for the world is execute permission alone, which is simply `1`.
3. Put these together with the `chmod` command and the filename to change the mode bits for the file. In this case, `chmod 551 fizbin`.

Let's see whether it works:

```
brezup:ray testing $ ls -l
total 0
-rw-r--r--  1 ray  staff  0 Apr 22 23:32 fizbin
brezup:ray testing $ chmod 551 fizbin
brezup:ray testing $ ls -l
total 0
-r-xr-x--x  1 ray  staff  0 Apr 22 23:32 fizbin
```

NOTE

Most people simply get the most useful permission numbers stuck in their heads after a few uses: 7 = read/write/execute, 6 = read/write, 5 = read/execute, 4 = read. 755 is "I get to do everything, everyone else can read and execute it, but not modify it." 700 is "I get to do everything, but nobody else can do anything," and so on. After a while, these numbers become second nature and are much shorter to type than the letter-specified permissions of the first form shown.

Table 11.1 shows the command syntax and the most interesting options for chmod. The complete documentation is available in the online appendix.

TABLE 11.1 The Command Syntax and Most Interesting Options for chmod

chmod	Changes file modes.
	chmod [-R [-H ¦ -L ¦ -P]] [-fv] *<absolute_mode>* *<file1>* *<file2>* ...
	chmod [-R [-H ¦ -L ¦ -P]] [-fv] *<symbolic_mode>* *<file1>* *<file2>* ...
-R	Recursively descends through directory arguments to change file modes.
-H	If -R is specified, symbolic links on the command line are followed. Symbolic links encountered in tree traversal are not followed.
-L	If -R is specified, all symbolic links are followed.
-P	If -R is specified, no symbolic links are followed.

Unless -H or -L is specified, chmod on a symbolic link always succeeds and has no effect. The -H, -L, and -P options are ignored unless -R is specified. Furthermore, -H, -L, and -P override each other. The last option specified determines the action taken.

Some versions of chmod include a -h flag that allows you to change the permissions of a symbolic link, rather than of the target of the link, but the chmod included with Tiger lacks this option.

Permissions are described by three sequences of letters in the order listed here. Each sequence describes the permissions for user, group, and other. If a certain permission has not been granted, a - (dash) appears in its place.

User	Group	Other
rwx	rwx	rwx

The permissions on a file can be viewed using ls -l and changed using chmod.

TABLE 11.1 Continued

Absolute Mode	
Absolute mode is constructed by `OR`ing any of the following modes:	
`4000`	Sets user ID on execution—If this is a program, causes it to run as though the user who owns it is actually running it, regardless of who executes it.
`2000`	Sets group ID on execution—If this is a program, causes it to run with the group ID of the program, regardless of group memberships of the user who executes it.
`1000`	Turns on sticky bit—Has different meanings in different contexts: for directories, protect files from modification by other than owner, even if the user has permissions to write in the directory—overridden by directory ownership.
`0400`	Allows read by owner.
`0200`	Allows write by owner.
`0100`	Allows execute (search in a directory) by owner.
`0600`	Allows read, write by owner.
`0500`	Allows read, execute by owner.
`0300`	Allows write, execute by owner.
`0700`	Allows read, write, execute by owner.
`0040`	Allows read by group.
`0020`	Allows write by group.
`0010`	Allows execute (search in a directory) by group.
`0060`	Allows read, write by group.
`0050`	Allows read, execute by group.
`0030`	Allows write, execute by group.
`0070`	Allows read, write, execute by group.
`0004`	Allows read by other.
`0002`	Allows write by other.
`0001`	Allows execute (search in a directory) by other.
`0006`	Allows read, write by other.
`0005`	Allows read, execute by other.
`0003`	Allows write, execute by other
`0007`	Allows read, write, execute by other.
Symbolic Mode	
Symbolic mode is a comma-separated list, with no intervening white space, of the form:	
`[<who>]<operator>[<permissions>]`	
`<who>` has the following form:	
`< u ¦ g ¦ o ¦ a>`	
`u`	User's permissions.
`g`	Group's permissions.
`o`	Other's permissions.
`a`	All permissions (user, group, other); equivalent to `ugo`.
`<operator>` has the following form:	
`< + ¦ - ¦ = >`	
`+`	Adds `<permissions>`.
If `<permissions>` is not specified, no changes occur.	

TABLE 11.1 Continued

If <*who*> is not specified, <*who*> defaults to a, and <*permissions*> are added as specified, except that `chmod` does not override the file mode creation mask.	
If <*who*> is specified, <*permissions*> are added as specified.	
-	Removes <*permissions*>.
If <*permissions*> is not specified, no changes occur.	
If <*who*> is not specified, <*who*> defaults to a, and <*permissions*> are removed as specified, except that `chmod` does not override the file mode creation mask.	
If <*who*> is specified, <*permissions*> are removed as specified.	
=	Assigns the absolute <*permissions*> specified.
<*permissions*> has the following form:	
`<r ¦ w ¦ x ¦ X ¦ s ¦ t ¦ u ¦ g ¦ o>`	
r	Sets read bits.
w	Sets write bits.
x	Sets execute/search bits.
X	Sets execute/search bits if the file is a directory, or if any execution/search bits are already set in the file before X would act on the file. X is used only with + and is ignored in all other cases.
s	Sets the `set-user-ID-on-execution` and `set-group-ID-on-execution` bits. A process runs as the user or group specified by s.
t	Sets the sticky bit.
u	User permission bits in the mode of the original file.
g	Group permission bits in the mode of the original file.
o	Other permission bits in the mode of the original file.
Operations with <*who*>=o in combination with <*permissions*> s or t are ignored.	

NOTE

`chmod` also controls Tiger's new Access Control Lists *(ACLs)*. ACLs are such an important feature that this functionality is covered separately in a later section of this chapter.

Controlling a File's Permissions Using the Finder

You also have limited access to the permission flags from Finder's Get Info window for a file or directory. Choose the Ownership & Permissions pane of the Get Info window after selecting the file or folder you want to adjust. Your display should look similar to Figure 11.1.

The Finder makes it easy to adjust permissions without getting into nitty-gritty details such as file ownership. By default, the pop-up menu labeled You Can allows you to choose what you want to be able to do with a file. Choose from the following:

- Read & Write—The file or folder can be read, written to, or deleted.
- Read Only—The file or folder can be read but not modified in any way.

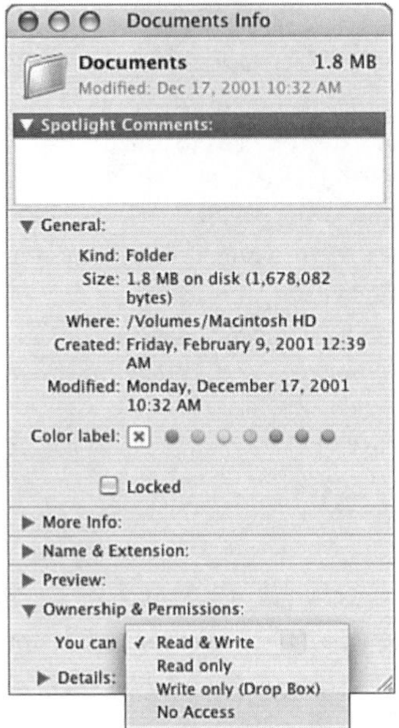

FIGURE 11.1 The Permissions section of the Get Info window allows you to specify what you can do what with a file.

- Write Only (Drop Box)—Available only as an option for folders, write-only access allows users to add files to a folder but not to read what is inside the folder.
- No Access—The file or folder may not be read, written to, deleted, or modified in any way.

If this doesn't suit your fancy, you can gain finer-grained control by expanding the Details section of the Ownership & Permissions pane, as shown in Figure 11.2.

Here, there are three levels of access you can adjust:

- Owner—The person who owns a file. Most files on a default Mac OS X installation are owned by a system user. You own files that you create.
- Group—By default, you are a member of your own group (with the same name as your username). Chapter 20 discusses the creation of additional groups.
- Others—Users who are not the owner and not part of the default group.

For each of these levels of access, there are multiple user rights. Adjusting these rights controls what the owner, group, and everyone else can do to a file or folder. These don't give quite the range of options available through `chmod`, but are good for many common uses. When viewing the file information for a folder, the window also shows an Apply to Enclosed Items button that copies all the access rights on the folder to the files underneath. If a folder has read permission turned off, the files inside the folder may still be accessed or modified unless they too have read permission removed.

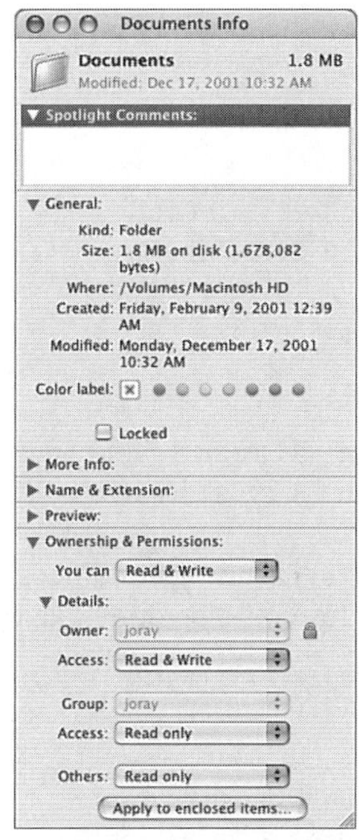

FIGURE 11.2 The Details section of the Get Info window allows you finer-grained control over the permissions.

A final setting exists for nonboot (storage) volumes. If a disk is selected while viewing permission information, an Ignore Ownership on This Volume check box appears. Clicking this box causes the volume to appear as open and unrestricted to the operating system, regardless of what permissions might have previously been applied to a system. Users of your system can modify anything on the drive. Activating this setting is not recommended, but it's sometimes necessary, especially when porting data over from a machine with different users. Keep this in mind when thinking about your files and security—just because you've set your permissions to deny access to other users, are they really secure? Not if potentially nosy users can get their hands on your drive, and attach it to their own system. Your system-level security settings are only as good as your physical security for the device.

Controlling a File's Ownership

Sometimes it's necessary (or useful) to change the users who have control or access to a file. This can be accomplished by changing the file's individual owner or changing the group to which the file belongs. Only `root` can change a file's ownership, but the owner a file can change its group to any valid group in which she is a member.

Controlling a File's Primary Ownership: `chown`

Changing the ownership of a file (possible only for the `root` user) is accomplished using the `chown` command. The usage is `chown <newowner>[:<newgroup>] file`. That is, if `root` wants to change the ownership of a file named `test1` so that it is now owned by `joray`, it might be done like this:

```
brezup:root testing # ls -l
total 0
-rw-r--r--    1 ray  ray  0 Jan  3 20:34 test1
-rw-r--r--    1 ray  ray  0 Jan  3 20:34 test2

brezup:root testing # chown joray test1
brezup:root testing # ls -l
total 0
-rw-r--r--    1 joray  ray  0 Jan  3 20:34 test1
-rw-r--r--    1 ray    ray  0 Jan  3 20:34 test2
```

If `root` would also like to change `test2`, and simultaneously change the group associated with the file to the `staff` group, this could be done like this:

```
brezup:root testing # chown joray:staff test2
brezup:root testing # ls -l
total 0
-rw-r--r--    1 joray  ray    0 Jan  3 20:34 test1
-rw-r--r--    1 joray  staff  0 Jan  3 20:34 test2
```

`chown` also takes several optional command-line flags that control its behavior similarly to the `chmod` flags. That is, optionally causing it to recursively descend directory trees, and controlling its behavior with respect to symbolic links. The command documentation table for `chown` is shown in Table 11.2.

TABLE 11.2 The Command Syntax for `chown`

chmod	Changes file modes.
	chown [-R [-H ¦ -L ¦ -P]] [-fhv] *<owner>*[:*<group>*] *<file1>* ...
	chmod [-R [-H ¦ -L ¦ -P]] [-fhv] :group *<file1>* ...
-R	Recursively descends through directory arguments to change file ownership.
-H	If -R is specified, symbolic links on the command line are followed. Symbolic links encountered in tree traversal are not followed.
-L	If -R is specified, all symbolic links are followed.
-P	If -R is specified, no symbolic links are followed.
-h	If a file is a symbolic link, change the ownership of the link, rather than of the target of the link.

The -H, -L and -P options are ignored unless the -R option is specified.

The *<owner>* and *<group>* parameters can be either names (as in the short name for the user or the group name), or the corresponding numeric IDs. Matches are attempted on name before ID, so if a name is entirely numeric and overlaps an existing numeric ID, the value is interpreted as the name rather than as the ID value.

Controlling a File's Group Ownership: chgrp

As mentioned in Chapter 8, a user may belong to multiple different groups. How these groups are created and managed will be covered in Chapter 20. Each of the groups that are configured on a system, and that a user might belong to, may have different purposes on the system; for example, allowing groups of individual users to collaborate on projects, and allowing some users to belong to multiple different project groups.

By default in Tiger, a new group is created for each individual user, and each normal user belongs only to that group. This is in contrast to more traditional Unix systems where there are "class of user"–type groups, such as Users, Staff, and Guests, and typical users are all members of a common group (in addition to any other groups they may belong to), allowing their permissions to be managed collectively. The "each user gets a group" philosophy seems to have been dragged in by the recent Linux explosion, where this idea was made popular. It is not a favorite of administrators who like to keep their machines organized and manageable, but it does provide significant flexibility if you have users who each want to have an individualized list of buddies with specialized access to their files.

A user who is a member of a group can access files that have that same group as their group owner. Unlike with some real-life groups of people, each user can simultaneously participate in all groups of which they are a member, no matter how many groups that might be. This makes perfect sense for accessing files—you can access a file that belongs to any group of which you are a member at any time.

Creating new files is a little more confusing. A file has only one group ownership, so there has to be some way of determining which of the many groups you belong to the new file gets created as belonging to. In current BSD-derived versions of Unix, this determination is based on the group ownership of the directory you're in. Whatever group owns the directory you're working in, this is the group to which any files you create in the directory will have their group ownership set. This is true regardless of whether you are actually a member of this group.

In addition to being created as belonging to the group owner of the current directory, group ownership of a file can be further controlled by the file's owner. The owner of a file has the ability to change the group ownership of a file to any group to which the owner belongs. Issuing chgrp *<groupname>* *<filename>* switches the group ownership of *<filename>* to *<groupname>*, assuming that you are a member of *<groupname>*. Table 11.3 shows the command syntax and most interesting options for chgrp. The complete documentation is shown in the online Appendix.

TABLE 11.3 The Command Syntax and Most Interesting Options for chgrp

chgrp	Changes group ownership for a file or directory.
chgrp [-R [-H ¦ -L ¦ -P]] [-fhv] *<group>* *<file1>* *<file2>* ...	
-R	Recursively descends through directory arguments to change the group ID.
-H	If -R is specified, symbolic links on the command line are followed. Symbolic links encountered in tree traversal are not followed.
-L	If -R is specified, all symbolic links are followed.
-P	If -R is specified, no symbolic links are followed.

TABLE 11.3 Continued

`-h`	If the `<file>` is a symbolic link, change the group ID of the link instead of the target file.

Unless `-h`, `-H`, or `-L` is specified, `chgrp` on symbolic links exits with no error and has no effect.
The `-H`, `-L`, and `-P` options are ignored unless `-R` is specified. These options also override each other, so the last one specified on the command line determines the action taken by the command.
The group may be either a numeric group ID or a group name. If a group name exists for a group ID, the associated group name is used for the group.
The user invoking `chgrp` must belong to the specified group and be the owner of the file, or be the super user.
Unless invoked by the super user, `chgrp` clears the `set-user-id` and `set-group-id` bits.

Controlling the Special Flags: `chflags`

To modify the special flags, you use the `chflags` command. It's not at all clear what Apple is using the special flags for at the moment, although we do know that the Finder's locked status of a file sets the immutable bit on the Unix side. To make matters even more confusing than the lack of documentation makes things, the behavior in Tiger is (at least with the developer preview) different than the behavior under earlier versions of Mac OS X. In Tiger, it appears that the system-immutable flag (the immutable flag as set by root) is either disabled or broken. In a sense, this is a good thing. Under earlier versions of Mac OS X (and possibly under Tiger as well, if this turns out to be a bug, rather than a feature), the system immutable flag could create a file that was not changeable by anyone, *ever*. For example, using Panther

```
brezup:ray testing 141$ ls -l
total 0
-rw-r--r--   1 ray  staff  -   0 Jun 27 14:22 test
-rw-r--r--   1 ray  staff  -   0 Jun 27 14:22 test2
brezup:ray testing 142$ su
Password:
```

> **NOTE**
>
> Note the use of the `su` command here to switch user IDs to become `root`. By default, the prompt changes to include a trailing `#` rather than the normal `$`, `%`, or `>` character when you're working as `root`. Also notice that the history command number switches from the command number in my history, to the command number for `root`'s command history when I'm working as the `root` user.
>
> Always remember to `exit` from the root subshell when you're finished working as `root`. If you prefer, you could use `sudo` to execute these commands instead of switching user IDs to the `root` user. There are arguments for and against either method, which are discussed in more detail directly following this section.

```
brezup:root testing 21# chflags schg test
brezup:root testing 22# ls -ol
total 0
-rw-r--r--  1 ray  staff  schg 0 Jun 27 14:22 test
-rw-r--r--  1 ray  staff  -    0 Jun 27 14:22 test2
brezup:root testing 23# chflags noschg test
chflags: test: Operation not permitted
brezup:root testing 24# rm test
override rw-r--r--  ray/staff for test? y
rm: test: Operation not permitted
brezup:root testing 25# exit
brezup:ray testing 143$
```

The immutable flag is a relatively recent Unix invention and indicates that the file *cannot* be changed. It's clear from the example that *immutable* really means just that: Even root can't delete the file, and what's more, root can't even remove the system immutable flag after it has been set. If a user sets a user-immutable flag (uchg instead of schg), under previous version of Mac OS X the user can neither unset nor remove the flag, but root can remove the file using rm, whereas in Tiger, both the user and root can (correctly) use chflags nouchg to remove the user immutable flag.

Under Tiger (developer preview), the chflags schg command has no effect, even though it's documented as having one. On one hand, this prevents the file from landing in this limbo state where even root can't touch it again. On the other, it removes the ability to create truly immutable files. We don't know which is the larger problem. Even if Apple has removed the ability to set system-immutable flags for all future version of Mac OS X, the issue is still one that will have to be dealt with in any heterogeneous environment, or on any system where a previous version of Mac OS X has been installed.

When this bit is successfully set using Mac OS X 10.3 or earlier, even booting back into Mac OS 9.2 and trying to unlock the file from a Get Info dialog in Finder turns out to be insufficient. The only successful route that we've found thus far is to remove the locked flag by using the venerable ResEdit program!

We don't really recommend experimenting with the chflags command much because it has the potential to make a real mess of things, and there's no documentation of what Apple is using the rest of the flags for. We've included the syntax and more interesting options in Table 11.4, in case you should run across command examples using this in the future, as adventurous hackers pry the secrets out of Mac OS X.

TABLE 11.4 The Command Syntax and Most Interesting Options for chflags

chflags	Changes file flags.
chflags [-R [-H ¦ -L ¦ -P]] *<flags>* *<file1>* *<file2>* ...	
-R	Recursively descends through directory arguments to change file flags.
-H	If -R is specified, symbolic links on the command line are followed. Symbolic links encountered in tree traversal are not followed.
-L	If -R is specified, all symbolic links are followed.

TABLE 11.4 Continued

`-P`	If `-R` is specified, no symbolic links are followed.
Symbolic links do not have flags. Unless `-H` or `-L` is specified, `chflags` on a symbolic link always succeeds and has no effect. `-H`, `-L`, and `-P` options are ignored unless `-R` is specified. Furthermore, `-H`, `-L`, and `-P` override each other. The last option specified determines the action taken.	
<flags> is a comma-separated list of keywords. Currently available keywords are as follows:	
`arch`	Sets the `archived` flag (super user only).
`opaque`	Sets the `opaque` flag (owner or super user only).
`nodump`	Sets the `nodump` flag, which tells the `dump` archiving system to overlook the file when archiving (owner or super user only).
`sappnd`	Sets the system `append-only` flag, which allows the file to be added to, but not overwritten (super user only).
`schg`	Sets the system `immutable` flag (super user only).
`uappnd`	Sets the user `append-only` flag (owner or super user only).
`uchg`	Sets the user `immutable` flag (owner or super user only).
Prepending the letters `no` to a flag turns off the flag.	

Applying Advanced Resource Control Using ACLs

New with Tiger, Apple has added Access Control Lists *(ACLs)* to the choices a user or administrator has in defining who can do what with a file. ACLs provide significantly more power than traditional Unix permissions. Where a traditional permission set can only detail what's allowable for the owner, the group, or "everyone else" for a particular file, an ACL can be so detailed as to individually define the permissions that are available for each user on the system. The types of permissions that are available are likewise considerably more fine-grained than the read/write/execute permissions controlled by the traditional Unix permissions system.

Understanding ACLs

Despite the considerable additional flexibility that ACLs provide, they are surprisingly simple to manipulate and understand. The primary commands for working with them are the `chmod` command, and the `ls` command with the `-e` flag. The former sets ACL entries, and the `-e` flag to `ls` cause it to list ACL entries for files it shows. The syntax is also simple:

```
chmod <modtype> "<who> <allow¦deny> <what action>" <file or directory>
```

<who> is either a group or user specifier—that is, either a group or username. You can affect the permissions available to all users in the group `staff`, simply by specifying `staff` as the *<who>* parameter. Likewise, you can more specifically target the permission of the user `miwa`, by specifying only `miwa` if you choose.

`<allow¦deny>` simply indicates whether the specified action is permissible or not for the specified user, for that file.

`<what action>` is a permission type that provides fine-grained control over the actions that can be taken with the file or directory. The applicable permissions for files and directories are documented in tables later in this section.

Finally `<modtype>` is a control flag for `chmod` that indicates whether the specified ACL permissions are to be added or deleted from the file's ACL.

Controlling ACLs in Tiger

ACLs provide overrides for the basic permissions supplied by the Unix permissions system. They therefore can be used to allow a select group of users greater access to a file that is relatively restricted by the basic permissions, or to restrict access for specific users on files that are otherwise relatively unrestricted.

The permission types that can be set are as shown in Table 11.5.

TABLE 11.5 The Permissions That Can Be Allowed or Denied via Access Control Lists

These permissions can be set (allowed or denied) for files or directories	
`delete`	Allows (or denies) the named user or members of the named group to delete the file or directory.
`readattr`	Allows (or denies) the named user or members of the named group to read the objects basic attributes.
`writeattr`	Whether the basic attributes may be written.
`readexattr`	Whether the extended attributes may be read.
`writeexattr`	Whether the extended attributes may be written.
`readsecurity`	Whether the security policy (ACL) for the file may be read.
`writesecurity`	Whether the security policy (ACL, ownership, and mode) for the file may be written.
`chown`	Whether the named user or group can change the object's ownership.
These permissions can be set (allowed or denied) only for files	
`read`	Whether the file can be opened for reading.
`write`	Whether the file can be opened for writing.
`append`	Whether the file can be opened for writing, but only to add data, not to allowing overwrites of any existing (previously written) sections.
`execute`	Whether the file can be executed as a script or program.
These permissions can be set (allowed or denied) only for directories	
`list`	Whether listings of the contents are allowed.
`search`	Whether files may be searched for by name in the directory.
`add_file`	Whether new files may be created in the directory.
`add_subdirectory`	Whether new subdirectories may be created in the directory.
`delete_child`	Whether a contained file or directory may be deleted.

ACL `<modtype>`s specify whether the following argument is to be added to or deleted from an existing ACL. The primary `<modtype>`s are `+a` and `-a`, which not surprisingly, add and delete ACL entries. There is also a `+ai` mode to cause inheritance of a property from the ACL of an enclosing directory, and `+a#`, `-a#`, and `=a#` modes to add entries in to specific locations in the list, delete entries from specific locations, or absolutely set specific entries in an ACL, respectively.

To actually use the ACL functionality, simply choose a permission, whether you wants to allow it or deny it to a particular user or group, and the files to which it should be applied. For example, if you have a file (myspecialfile) that you really want to let your friend (and co-user of the system) james edit, but you don't want to make it world-writeable, and you don't want to create a special group containing both you and james, you can use an ACL:

```
chmod +a "james allow write" myspecialfile
ls -le myspecialfile
-rw-r--r--    1 joray  joray      8567 Apr 25 17:27 myspecialfile
owner: joray
1: james allow write
```

Now james has permission to write to your file. Depending on your standard Unix permissions setup, he still might not have permission to read it though! You can fix this by adding another ACL rule, or by chmoding o+r to the file—it all depends on whether you're worried about anyone else seeing the contents.

Perhaps you have a directory of files that you want to share with a bunch of other normal users, but you'd rather not have the admin users snooping around in your files. This, too, can easily be accomplished with ACLs (although if the admin users are stubborn enough, there's hardly anything you can truly prevent them from doing):

```
chmod +a "admin deny list" myhiddendirectory
ls -lde myhiddendirectory/
drwxr-xr-x   2 joray  joray  68 Apr 25 17:40 myhiddendirectory/
owner: joray
1: admin deny list
```

Now anyone in group admin is denied listing permissions for the directory myhiddendirectory. To increase the security, you might want to turn off admin's ability to change the directory security options as well:

```
chmod +a "admin deny writesecurity" myhiddendirectory
chmod +a "admin deny chown" myhiddendirectory
ls -lde myhiddendirectory/
drwxr-xr-x   2 joray  joray  68 Apr 25 17:40 myhiddendirectory/
owner: joray
1: admin deny chown
2: admin deny writesecurity
3: admin deny list
```

If it turns out that james no-longer needs to edit your file, or you no longer want him to have access, the -a mode can be used to remove the permissions you've already created:

```
chmod -a "james allow write" myspecialfile
ls -le myspecialfile
-rw-r--r--    1 joray  joray      8947 Apr 25 18:27 myspecialfile
```

Now you're back to the normal Unix permissions controlling the access to the file.

> **CAUTION**
>
> Unfortunately...
>
> As I write this in early April, ACLs still do not seem to work properly. Worse, despite repeated queries to Apple regarding where the GUI controls for these are located, we've seen no sign of an interface to ACLs in the Finder. In this section, we've documented how they're supposed to work, to the best of our ability, but some aspects of this information might be superceded by new developments as Tiger updates are released.

Being Someone Else for a While: su, sudo

Because Unix is a multiple user operating system, it's sometimes convenient to be able to momentarily switch user IDs so that you can do something as a different user than the one you're currently logged in as. To eliminate the need to log out and log back in under an alternative ID, Unix provides the `su` command (meaning *switch user*), which allows you to briefly act as another user for whom you know the login password. The `su` command is often used to switch to the `root` user ID for the purpose of performing system maintenance, but it can also be used to switch to any other user ID on the system.

The `su` command can be dangerous. When you are running as another user, you have all the permissions that the other user has and all of that user's capabilities. If this is another normal user on the system, you can just as easily damage his files as you can your own. If you've `su`'ed to the `root` user, you can, with a single typo of an `rm` command, delete every file on your drive. Table 11.6 shows the command syntax and options for the `su` command.

> **CAUTION**
>
> This does not mean that you should never use the `su` command. There are operations that you must perform as the `root` user, and you're just as likely to make some terrible mistake and mess up another user's files if you'd logged out and logged in as the other user. Respect the `su` command, be aware of the extra responsibility you have if you're working in someone else's account, realize the danger of careless operation as `root`, and you'll be fine.

TABLE 11.6 The Command Syntax and Most Interesting Options for su

`su`	Substitute user identity.
`su [-flm] [<login>] [-c <shell arguments>]`	
su requests the password for login and switches to that user and group ID after obtaining proper authentication. A shell is then executed, and any additional shell arguments after the login name are passed to the shell.	

TABLE 11.6 Continued

If su is executed with no username as an argument, root is assumed.

If su is executed by root, no password is requested, and a shell with the appropriate user ID is executed.

-c	Invoke the following command in a subshell as the specified user.
-f	If the invoked shell is csh or tcsh, this option prevents it from reading the .cshrc file. This both prevents items in the .cshrc from overriding current environment settings and can be useful if execution of the .cshrc is resource intensive or otherwise would interfere with a proper login.
-l	Simulates a full login. The environment is discarded except for HOME, SHELL, PATH, TERM, and USER. USER is set to the target login. PATH is set to "/bin:/usr/bin". TERM is imported from your current environment. The invoked shell is the target login's, and su changes directory to the target login's home directory. The -l option is synonymous with "-", as in su -.
-m	Leaves the environment unmodified. The invoked shell is your login shell; the current directory is not changed. As a security precaution, if the target user's shell is a nonstandard shell (not listed in /etc/shells), and the caller is not root, su will fail. This option is useful and is the default in many (but apparently not the Mac OS X 10.3) versions of su. Unfortunately, there are some inconsistencies in the way that this currently works. Some of the environment (your prompt, for example) is maintained unchanged without this option and changed with it, whereas other parts are maintained unchanged when -m is set and are overridden without it. Usually, we'd recommend aliasing su to su -m as the best option, but the current behavior is confusing.

The -l and -m options are mutually exclusive; the last one specified overrides any previous ones. Only users in group "wheel" (normally gid 0) or group "admin" (normally gid 20) can su to "root".

By default (unless the prompt is reset by a startup file), the super user prompt will self-modify to end with a # character to remind you of the awesome power of the root shell.

Similar to the su command, the sudo command allows you to execute a single command as another user. Instead of switching user IDs and working as the other user, sudo executes a single command and returns you to working under your own ID. A particularly useful feature of sudo is that it can be configured to allow you to operate as another user without knowing that user's password. Apple has used it this way to allow admin-group users to run commands as root by using their own passwords. To make this happen, sudo's configuration is somewhat complex, requiring a complete specification of what users are allowed to run what commands, under what circumstances, and which user IDs they should appear to run these commands as when they're using them. Table 11.7 shows the command syntax and most interesting options for sudo.

TABLE 11.7 The Command Syntax and Most Interesting Options for sudo

sudo	Execute a command as another user.

sudo -V¦-h¦-l¦-L¦-v¦-k¦-K¦[-H][-P][-S][-b] [-a auth_type] [-c class¦-] [-p *<prompt>*]
[-u *<username>*¦*<#uid>*] *<command>*

sudo -V¦-h¦-l¦-L¦-v¦-k¦-K¦[-H][-P][-S][-b] [-a auth_type] [-c class¦-] [-p *<prompt>*]
[-u *<username>*¦*<#uid>*] -s ¦ -i ¦ -e *<file>* ...

sudo allows a permitted user to execute a *<command>* as root or another user, as specified in /etc/sudoers. The real and effective uid and gid are set to match those of the target user as specified in the passwd file or NetInfo map. By default, sudo requires that users authenticate themselves with a password. (Note: By default this is the user's password, not the root password.) After a user has been authenticated, a time stamp is updated, and the user may then use sudo without a password for a short period of time after the time stamp (five minutes unless overridden in sudoers). The time stamp is updated every time a command is executed through sudo, providing a sliding window during which the user may use commands as the alternative user without re-entering the required password. sudo determines who is an authorized user by consulting the file /etc/sudoers. By giving sudo the -v flag, a user can update the time stamp without running a command.

If a user who is not listed in /etc/sudoers tries to run a command via sudo, mail is sent to the proper authorities, as defined at configure time or /etc/sudoers. Note that the mail will not be sent if an unauthorized user tries to run sudo with the -l or -v flags. This allows users to determine for themselves whether they are allowed to use sudo.

sudo can log attempted sudo sessions as well as errors to syslog(3), a log file, or both. By default, sudo logs via syslog(3).

When used with the -s option instead of a *<command>*, sudo executes the target user's shell in a manner similar to the su command. The change of effective user and execution of the shell are logged, but commands executed while in that shell are not recorded. -i is similar, with the target user's shell executed as a simulated login shell. -e <file> executes a text editor on the named file, rather than running the file as a command.

-l	Lists the allowed (and forbidden) commands for the user on the current host.
-v	Updates the user's time stamp, prompting for the user's password if necessary. This extends the sudo timeout for another five minutes (or whatever the timeout is set to in sudoers).
-k	Invalidates the user's time stamp by setting the time on it to the epoch. The next time sudo is run, a password will be required.

This option does not require a password and was added to allow a user to revoke sudo permissions from a .logout file.

-b	Tells sudo to run the given command in the background. Note that if you use the -b option, you cannot use shell job control to manipulate the process.
-S	Causes sudo to read the password from standard input instead of the terminal device.
-H	Sets the $HOME environment variable to the homedir of the target user (root by default) as specified in /etc/passwd or NetInfo. By default, sudo does not modify $HOME.

TABLE 11.7 Continued

sudo tries to be safe when executing commands. To accomplish this, most shell variables specifying load paths for dynamically loaded libraries, user paths, and similar routes by which commands may be spoofed are ignored when searching for commands and when loading dynamic modules. This will not affect general use of the sudo command, but might result in unexpected behavior in some situations. Carefully read Apple's man page for sudo (which is not quite in sync with the version of the command provided) if you experience difficulty with more sophisticated configurations.

Proper attention to configuration of the `/etc/sudoers` file is outside the scope of this book, but we've tried to cover the basics of the configuration in Chapter 28, where we introduce advanced security concepts. If you need to set up your machine with a sophisticated multiuser configuration that allows for cross-user `sudo`ing, see Chapter 28, and then check out the `sudoers` man page. You also might want to look for *Maximum Mac OS X Security*, also by Will, John, and Joan Ray from Sams Publishing.

Choosing Between `su` and `sudo`: Pick Your Risk

Regarding `sudo`: You'll probably see many references all over the Internet to people doing this, that, or the other thing that requires `root` privileges, using of the `sudo` command instead of `su`ing to `root`. In general, I disagree with this practice on a number of levels. It's okay to do this, if you want, but really, the `sudo` command wasn't intended, and isn't really an ideal solution for what people are using it for.

The `sudo` command is intended to give the `root` user a way to allow nonprivileged users limited access to run very specific commands with `root` permissions. Instead, Apple has used it as a way to allow admin users to run *all* commands as `root`.

Apple's current practice of letting an administrative user use `sudo` to execute *any* command with root privileges is just sort of a kludge that Apple has made available to get around inexperienced users needing to occasionally wear the system-administrator hat. This is okay for users who are only ever going to do one or two things as `root` in their use of the machine, but I don't think that the use of `sudo` inspires the same care as using `su`, where you take a separate action to actually *be* another user.

The real purpose of the `sudo` command is to allow the `root` user to grant the ability to access *specific* `root`-privileged commands to users who don't, and shouldn't, have full `root` access. Typically, this is used to allow, for example, the person who maintains the web server to restart that server, even though restarting the web server requires `root` privileges. The person able to do this wouldn't be given the right to do anything else as `root`, just to restart the web server. The `sudo` command isn't typically used to grant access to all commands as `root`, and for a user used to its traditional usage, this feels sort of sloppy. Feel free to do anything that we write as `su`ing to root, by `sudo`ing every command, if you feel it makes you a safer user.

In a sense, you can't forget to log out of a sued shell if you're using `sudo`. This makes some users, particularly inexperienced users who aren't used to paying attention to security details, into safer administrators of their machines.

In a different sense, you simply can't log out of a sudoed session. For a several-minute period after you use sudo, it'll believe that the person at the keyboard has root permissions, whether it's you sitting there or not. It'll also believe that anything run from any software that you run from the keyboard has identical privileges. A malicious gremlin hidden in an otherwise useful script could lay in wait, watching for this period of relaxed security, and then take advantage of it to do quite unpleasant things to your system.

Actually, there is a way to log out, but nobody ever shows it as part of their examples. Because of this, the normal reader is encouraged, by the uses that you'll see online and in documentation, to use sudo in a very unsafe manner. The style of use that you'll see most often used and recommended for sudo is far less safe for the conscientious user than using su. (Proper use and configuration of the sudo command to limit user access to privileged commands is covered in Chapter 28.)

The major difference for the conscientious user is that you, the conscientious user, know that you absolutely must log out of the sued shell as soon as you've accomplished what you need to do when using su. You can deauthenticate to sudo as well, but sudo deauthenticates itself after a while, and the perception, reinforced by almost all examples you'll see people giving, is that simply using sudo command and allowing it to deauthenticate itself is a safe practice. This is not the case, or at least there is no reason to assume that the lack of exploits that have been reported will continue once Apple's noncanonical use of sudo becomes more widespread.

A secondary but still significant difference is that it's easy to embed a short repetitive pattern into what is often called *muscle memory*. Muscle memory isn't under direct conscious control, and this generates a risk. If you're confronted with commands that require frequent use of sudo, your fingers will eventually learn to type sudo automatically, and you will find that you start using sudo *<command>* any time *<command>* might even possibly need root permission for you to run it. This gets especially risky if *<command>* is something like rm. If you're doing a bunch of drive cleanup and working between different users' directories, you might find that you're sudo rming a great number of files.

If you're doing this, regularly issuing sudo rm *<filename>* commands to accomplish some task, your fingers are going to learn this pattern, whether or not you're consciously aware of it. It's likely that the next time you want to remove a file (even not intending to be root), what will appear at the command line is sudo rm *<filename>*. This can create a disaster.

If your fingers learn to automatically type sudo rm and you make a typo in what you planned to rm the next time around, you can end up doing a large amount of damage to your system. There are good odds that you're going to run it sudoed, whether you intended to or not, and a single-character typo in an rm command, if run as root, can erase every file on your system.

su doesn't cause similar problems (for conscientious users) because it requires considerably more typing than sudo, and because a conscientious user becomes root, does what is necessary, and then gets back out. Even if the commands you're using get embedded in muscle memory, you're just running them as *<command>*, and you won't be running with root permissions if your fingertips happen to type one unrequested.

The sudo command works by initially authenticating that you really are who the shell thinks you are, and then (assuming that sudo believes your account has sufficient privileges), allowing you to run software as the root user. The sudo command then starts a timer, and if you use it again within some short time period of when you ran it last, it simply *assumes* that you still are who it thinks you are, and doesn't ask for your password to authenticate again. This short time period (several minutes by default) during which you can run any command with root privileges, and without entering a validating password, provides the potential for a real security problem. This opens the door for malicious software writers to embed sudoed commands into their applications that can lay in wait for some unsuspecting user to run the software within the timeout window, and then take advantage of the fact that the user has pre-authenticated to run as root.

On the other hand, using su instead of sudo is no panacea either. It's extremely easy to forget to log out of the root shell when you're finished with the parts that necessitate root access. Likewise, it's tempting to just stay in a root shell for tangential operations that don't really require root, if you think you might need the root privileges again soon. Both of these are also dangerous behaviors. The first at least can be somewhat mitigated by configuring your shell to visibly distinguish when you're running as root. The second, however, requires that you consistently place security and safety before convenience at the command line. This is not always easy to do, even for the most conscientious users.

Because of this, although both operating as root with su and operating as root with sudo have risks, the risks are different, and for any given individual, either might be the safer option. sudo's safer for users who can't or won't be bothered by being security conscious, and who would end up opening the door to their machines and then never getting around to closing them if they were using su. sudo is an automatic door closer, and will shut the door for you, but it's slow about it, and it is a short enough command that you'll find your fingers accidentally opening the door even when you didn't intend to. su's safer for users who are security conscious and who close every door they open, every time. If you don't remember to log out from sued shells, and you aren't conscientious enough to never run an unknown/unverified command or program in a sued shell, you'll eventually get bitten either by malicious software, or by a mistake in typing. If you are conscientious, the su command will never be a door for a malicious software writer to attack your machine. On the other hand, if you use the sudo command frequently, and don't use the sudo -k command to deauthenticate after each and every use, your system is vulnerable to opportunistic malicious software that can slip through the (rather large) crack during the period that sudo's holding the door open.

Right now, it probably comes down to personal preference. sudo has been around long enough that if there were any major security concerns with the sudo program itself, someone would have probably found them by now. The potential exploit of malicious scripts taking advantage of the sudo timeout period is not something that we currently see actively affecting users. This lack of activity, however, doesn't imply that the exploit won't be used in the future. I'm extremely sensitive to muscle-memory issues, having had the occasion to train my fingers to type a similar incantation as a prefix to rm to get around the per-file prompting when I was first working with Unix in 1986. This bad habit bit me badly several years later, and since then, I've become very fond of the # prompt for root. I see the # prompt, and I know I had better be darned careful about what I'm doing. I see the $ (or %, or > in other shells) prompt, and I know that I'm generally safe and can't do the system any great harm. It makes me happy and reduces my stress level. If you don't have fingers that type short commands faster than your brain can keep up, and you find worrying about logging out again when you're root more stressful, by all means, use sudo instead of suing to root. The potential problems with being sloppy with su are real, and affect users who aren't paying enough attention every day. No one needs more stress.

Summary

This chapter detailed the permissions systems that interact with other commands and files to control or limit what a user can do with the system. Most users can get by in day-to-day use by just letting the system default permissions stand, and occasionally running Apple's Fix Permissions tweak from Disk Utility when things go unfathomably wrong. If you take the time to learn about the permissions system, however, you can exact much more fine-grained control over who has what type of access to your files and enhance the utility of your system to yourself and for your other users.

CHAPTER 12

Process Management

IN THIS CHAPTER

- Understanding Process Management
- Using Common Process Management Commands
- Communication Between Processes: Redirection, Pipes
- Managing Processes Graphically: Activity Monitor

In this chapter, we will cover the Tiger tools for process management from the command line and the GUI, including how to identify and terminate processes that are causing problems for you.

We'll also cover the notion of input and output redirection. This is the root of much of the real power of the Unix command line. As you read, you should think about how commands that you've already learned might be enhanced by these features; completely independent utilities and applications can often be combined in very unexpected ways.

Understanding Process Management

Tiger is composed of many different cooperating processes. This is not particular to Mac OS X, but is also the norm for Unix. Instead of a monolithic OS and user interface environment, Unix and (even more so) the Mach kernel on which Mac OS X is based both operate as collections of a large number of cooperating programs. These programs create the illusion and functional experience of a seamless interface but provide considerably more flexibility in the user's ability to modify things to suit his particular needs.

For example, with Classic Mac OS, you're used to having a clock in the menu bar, and having the option to turn it on or off and perhaps set the font. This functionality is a built-in part of the operating system and user interface. With Unix, if you want a clock, you run a separate program that displays a clock. Because the clock is a program and not an integral part of the operating system, it can be any program. By selecting different programs, the clock can be made to appear as any type that you choose, anywhere on the screen that you choose.

It might take a while for you to come to appreciate the flexibility that this "everything is a process" idea of building operating systems provides for you. Monolithic operating system and user interface environments have the advantage of being able to guide the user somewhat more strictly. They also are able to "guarantee" some types of responsiveness in ways that can't be done when all the user interface components are controlled by separate programs. Many of the things we will say are advantages of the Unix environment—such as processes that run and provide some sort of functionality with no user interface (background processes), or programs that start at some prespecified time—you might think are not so impressive because they were available in earlier versions of Mac OS. It is true that these advantages have been available. But as much as we love the Mac OS, we have to admit that they have been, at best, hacks; attempts to implement what you now have available to you: the Unix way of managing processes.

Using Common Process Management Commands

There are many mechanisms for working with processes in Tiger. In this section we will cover some of the most useful tools at your disposal. Because process management and input/output control are intimately linked to the shell itself, there are some differences between how you do these things that depend on the shell you've picked. Fortunately, the capabilities of both `csh` and `sh`-type shells are similar with respect to basic process and input/output control, so the differences are mostly cosmetic.

Listing Processes: `ps`

The `ps` command is used for listing the process status report. This is the command-line version of the Process View utility. There are many options to `ps`, but you will probably find issuing `ps` with the `a`, `u`, and `x` options to be most useful (this combination produces one of the more complete and informative, yet relatively concise displays):

```
ps -aux
```

The following provides a sample of what to expect the output to look like:

```
brezup:ray testing $ ps -aux

USER       PID %CPU %MEM    VSZ   RSS  TT STAT STARTED    TIME  COMMAND
williamr   483 11.4  4.2 349852 43580 ?? S    11:40PM 1:21.21 /Volumes/S
williamr   451 10.2  0.5  94172  4892 ?? S    11:29PM 0:03.09 /Applicati
williamr   186  0.1  1.5  66904 15228 ?? Ss   11:26PM 0:23.20 /System/Li
root        82  0.0  0.1  28304  1264 ?? Ss   11:26PM 0:02.10 kextd
root       104  0.0  0.2  29820  1872 ?? Ss   11:26PM 0:01.47 /usr/sbin/
root       105  0.0  0.1  27852   876 ?? Ss   11:26PM 0:00.61 /usr/sbin/
root       107  0.0  0.0  18064   104 ?? Ss   11:26PM 0:00.58 update
.
.
.
williamr   453  0.0  0.1  18648   760 std S   11:29PM 0:00.08 -bash
williamr   480  0.0  0.4  29908  4000 ??  S   11:32PM 0:00.12 /System/Li
```

```
williamr  484  0.0  1.1  92732 11156 ??  S   11:40PM  0:00.62 /Volumes/S
root      488  0.0  0.0  18108   336 std R+  11:44PM  0:00.00 ps -aux
root        1  0.0  0.0  18080   300 ??  Ss  11:25PM  0:00.06 /sbin/init
root        2  0.0  0.0  18616   200 ??  Ss  11:25PM  0:00.11 /sbin/mach
root       76  0.0  0.0  18096   200 ??  Ss  11:26PM  0:00.07 /usr/sbin/
```


If your terminal window is narrower than the complete width of the output, it will be truncated on the right edge of your terminal. This is apparent in the previous output on most lines. If you want to see more of the command, you can add the w flag to ps, to cause it to ignore your terminal width and output 132 columns of information regardless of wrapping:

```
brezup:ray testing $ ps -auxw
USER       PID %CPU %MEM    VSZ   RSS TT STAT STARTED    TIME COMMAND
williamr  483 16.0 4.5  326612 46884 ?? S   11:40PM  1:56.68_
➥ /Volumes/Software/Work_Software/Microsoft Office X/Microsoft W
williamr  451  9.5 0.5  94628  5540 ?? S   11:29PM   0:06.90_
➥ /Applications/Utilities/Terminal.app/Contents/MacOS/Terminal -
root      489  6.0 0.0  18108  336 std R+  11:47PM  0:00.02_
➥ ps -auxw
williamr  186  3.0 1.5  67108 15364 ?? Ss  11:26PM  0:26.99_
➥ /System/Library/Frameworks/ApplicationServices.framework/Frame
root      307  1.1 0.0  18328  268 ?? Ss   11:26PM   0:00.13
➥ ntpd -f /var/run/ntp.drift -p /var/run/ntpd.pid
root      105  0.0 0.1  27852  876 ?? Ss   11:26PM   0:00.61_
➥ /usr/sbin/diskarbitrationd
root      107  0.0 0.0  18064  104 ?? Ss   11:26PM   0:00.66_
➥ update
.
.
.
williamr  480  0.0 0.4  29908  3996 ?? S   11:32PM   0:00.12_
➥ /System/Library/Services/AppleSpell.service/Contents/MacOS/App
williamr  484  0.0 1.1  92732 11220 ?? S   11:40PM   0:00.62_
➥ /Volumes/Software/Work_Software/Microsoft Office X/Office/Micr
root      452  0.0 0.0  27544  508 std Ss  11:29PM  0:00.03_
➥ login -pf williamray
root        1  0.0 0.0  18080  300 ?? Ss   11:25PM   0:00.06_
➥ /sbin/init
root        2  0.0 0.0  18616  200 ?? Ss   11:25PM   0:00.11
➥ /sbin/mach_init
root       76  0.0 0.0  18096  200 ?? Ss   11:26PM   0:00.07_
➥ /usr/sbin/syslogd -s -m 0
root       82  0.0 0.1  28304  1264 ?? Ss  11:26PM  0:02.10_
➥ kextd
root      104  0.0 0.2  29820  1872 ?? Ss  11:26PM  0:01.47_
➥ /usr/sbin/configd
```

If you have more wordy commands in deeper directories that need even more than 132 columns to display, the w flag can be specified twice (as in ps -auxww), causing ps to completely ignore column-width issues.

The output from ps using these flags includes the owner of the process (USER), the process ID (PID), the percentage of the CPU (%CPU) and memory (%MEM) being consumed by the process, the virtual size of the memory space used by the program (VSZ) as well as the amount of that size that's resident in main memory (RSS), the controlling terminal (TT = ?? for no terminal), the run state of the process (STAT = R for running, S for short sleep, others), the time the process started (STARTED), the accumulated CPU time (TIME), and the command that is running (COMMAND). The output is sorted by the percentage of the CPU that's being used for each command. More display options and orderings are available with the ps command, and command options, syntax, and keyword definitions for ps are included in the command documentation table—Table 12.1.

TABLE 12.1 The Command Syntax and Most Interesting Options for ps

ps	Displays process status report.
ps [-aCcefhjlMmrSTuvwx] [-O *<fmt>*] [-o *<fmt>*] [-p *<pid>*] [-t *<tty>*] [-U *<username>*]	
ps [-L]	
-a	Includes information about processes owned by others in addition to yours.
-c	Changes the command column output to contain just the executable name rather than the full command line.
-f	Shows command line and environment information about swapped-out processes. This is honored only if the user's user ID is 0 (root).
-j	Prints information associated with the following keywords: user, pid, ppid, pgid, sess, jobc, state, tt, time, and command.
-l	Displays information associated with the following keywords: uid, pid, ppid, cpu, pri, nice, vsz, rss, wchan, state, tt, time, and command.
-M	Prints the threads corresponding with each task.
-m	Sorts by memory usage, rather than by process ID.
-r	Sorts by current CPU usage, rather than by process ID.
-T	Displays information about processes attached to the device associated with standard output.
-u	Displays information associated with the following keywords: user, pid, %cpu, %mem, vsz, rss, tt, state, start, time, and command. The -u option implies the -r option.
-v	Displays information associated with the following keywords: pid, state, time, sl, re, pagein, vsz, rss, lim, tsiz, %cpu, %mem, and command. The -v option implies the -m option.
-w	Uses 132 columns to display information, instead of the default, which is your window size. If the -w option is specified more than once, ps uses as many columns as necessary, regardless of your window size.
-x	Displays information about processes without controlling terminals.
-p *<pid>*	Displays information associated with the specified process ID *<pid>*.
-t *<tty>*	Displays information about processes attached to the specified terminal device *<tty>*.
-U *<username>*	Displays information about processes belonging to the specified *<username>*.

The following is a list of the definitions of the keywords that some of the options already include. More keywords are available than are defined here.

`%cpu`	Percentage CPU usage (alias `pcpu`).
`%mem`	Percentage memory usage (alias `pmem`).
`command`	Command and arguments.
`cpu`	Short-term CPU usage factor (for scheduling).
`jobc`	Job control count.
`lim`	Memory use limit.
`nice`	Nice value (alias to `ni`).
`pagein`	Pageins (total page faults).
`pgid`	Process group number.
`pid`	Process ID.
`ppid`	Parent process ID.
`pri`	Scheduling priority.
`re`	Core residency time (in seconds; 127 = infinity).
`rss`	Resident set size (real memory).
`rsz`	Resident set size + (text size/text use count) (alias `rs-size`).
`sess`	Session pointer.
`sl`	Sleep time (in seconds; 127 = infinity).
`start`	Time started.
`state`	Symbolic process state (alias `stat`).
`tsiz`	Text size (in kilobytes).
`tt`	Control terminal name (two-letter abbreviation).
`uid`	Effective user ID.
`user`	Username (from `uid`).
`vsz`	Size of process in virtual memory in kilobytes (alias `vsize`).
`wchan`	Wait channel (as a symbolic name).

Listing Shell Child Processes: `jobs`

The term *jobs* and the term *processes* are frequently used interchangeably when discussing programs running on a Unix machine. But there is also a more specific meaning of jobs that has to do with processes that are run within, or by, a shell process.

Unix processes have the notion of parent and child processes. For example, consider `Terminal.app`. If you run a shell in a terminal window (which is what you most frequently will do to get access to a shell), the running process that is that shell will be a child of `Terminal.app`. If you run a process in the shell, such as `ls`, or any other commands we discuss in this book, the process that is that command will be a child of the shell. Likewise, the shell will be the parent of the `ls` command run in it, and `Terminal.app` will be the parent of the shell. `Terminal.app`, in this case, is the child of the Window Server (which controls the Tiger user interface), and the Window Server is the child of `/sbin/launchd`. Every process in this way can trace its execution lineage back to the ancestor of all executing programs, `/sbin/launchd`, which will have process ID 1.

Therefore, a *user's jobs* refers to all processes running on a machine that belong to a particular user. *Shell jobs*, on the other hand, refers to processes that are children of (that is, were run by) a particular running instance of a shell.

The `jobs` command displays current processes that are children of the shell where the command is issued. This might not make much sense just yet because we haven't introduced any way for you to run a command and have it execute to completion before returning to the command prompt, but we will cover this material shortly. The `jobs` command gives you the ability to find out what jobs are present and what state they are in. For example, the shell shown in the following output has three jobs running in the background, and one job that is stopped:

```
brezup:ray testing $ jobs
[1]   Running                 ./aaa.csh &
[2] - Running                 ./bbbb.csh &
[3]   Running                 ./test.csh &
[4] + Stopped                 ./test2.csh
```

`Stopped` (`tcsh` uses the label `Suspended` instead of `Stopped`) jobs are jobs that are not executing for one reason or another. In this case, the suspended job was stopped with the Ctrl+Z shell key sequence (discussed shortly) and is waiting for the user to resume it, send it to the background, or kill it off.

The `+` and `-` characters between the job number and the status indicate the most current job, and the previously most current job, respectively. *Most current* in this case means either the most recent job stopped that had been running in the foreground or the most recent job that was started into the background.

The command documentation for `jobs` in Table 12.2 also includes information on how a job may be referenced, based on the output of `jobs`, for use in other job-control commands.

TABLE 12.2 The Command Syntax and Most Interesting Options for `jobs`

`jobs`
`jobs [-lnprs] [<jobspec>]`
`jobs -x <command> [<args>]`
	Displays the table of current jobs.

`-l`	Lists jobs in long format. This includes the job number and its associated process ID, in case, for example, you want to use various `kill` signals, discussed in the following section, against jobs you have running in the shell.
`-p`	`bash/sh` specific: Lists the process ID of the job's process group leader.
`-n`	`bash/sh` specific: Lists only information for jobs whose status has changed since the last time the user has queried the status.
`-r`	`bash/sh` specific: Lists only running jobs.
`-s`	`bash/sh` specific: Lists only stopped jobs.

After you know what jobs belong to the current shell, there are several ways to construct a proper `<jobspec>` to refer to a job. `%` introduces a job name. Job number `1` is `%1`. An unambiguous string of characters at the beginning of the name can be used to refer to a job; the form is `%<first-few-characters-of-job>`. An unambiguous string of characters in the job name can also be used to refer to a job; for example, the form `%?<text-string>` specifies a job whose name contains `<text-string>`. These `<jobspec>` references can be used with a number of commands that interact with running processes to specify which, out of a collection of running jobs, the command needs to work with.

If `<jobspec>` is supplied, the output is restricted to only that job. For example, assume that you have a stopped `emacs` job. You can match the job using just the first few characters with `%ema`:

```
brezup:ray testing $ jobs %ema
[1]+  Stopped                 emacs
```

Alternatively, you can match based on *any* characters in the job name, such as `%?mac`:

```
brezup:ray testing $ jobs %?mac
[1]+  Stopped                 emacs
```

With the `-x <command>` option, `jobs` functions as a meta-command, and rewrites, and then executes `<command>` such that any `<jobspec>` that appears in `<command>` or `<args>` is first replaced by the appropriate process ID. This gives you an easy way to use commands that want to work on process IDs with shell-job `<jobspec>`s. This usage is particularly useful with commands such as `kill` (discussed later in this chapter), which can be issued as `jobs -x kill <jobspec>` to execute `kill` against a particular job, instead of requiring the job's process ID.

Output pertaining to the current job is marked with `+`; output from a previous job, `-`. `%+`, `%`, and `%%` refer to the current job. `%-` refers to the previous job.

NOTE

In `tcsh`, the `jobs` command provides only the `-l` option. The syntax for job listings and `<jobspec>` references, however, is similar.

Backgrounding Processes: `bg`

The `bg` command backgrounds a suspended job. The process continues, only in the background. The most noticeable effect for the user is the return of the command prompt. Backgrounding processes is particularly useful for commands and programs that do not produce command-line output. Although the user's prompt returns, the process continues. It does not make sense to background something like `ls`, which is trying to show you output to the terminal. On the other hand, backgrounding the process responsible for a long `cp` or `compress` can be very convenient. The usual method for suspending a running process is to press Ctrl+Z, which stops, but does not kill, the process. For example:

```
brezup:ray testing $ jobs
[1] - Running              ./aaa.csh &
[4] + Running              ./test.csh &
brezup:ray testing $ ./test2.csh
^Z
[5] + Stopped              ./test2.csh
brezup:ray testing $ jobs
[1]   Running             ./aaa.csh &
[4] - Running             ./test.csh &
[5] + Stopped             ./test2.csh
brezup:ray testing $ bg
[5]  ./test2.csh &
brezup:ray testing $ jobs
[1] - Running             ./aaa.csh &
[4] + Running             ./test.csh &
[5]   Running             ./test2.csh &
```

When stopped with Ctrl+Z, bash automatically lists the job you've just stopped, whereas tcsh provides the complete current list of jobs.

CAUTION

If you're running multiple jobs in a single terminal, there's only one place (that terminal) for them, and any job-control software you're using, to display output. The result is that all the output from the programs living in the terminal is interleaved into the same display. This can occasionally produce some confusing-looking output. It's not so bad when you have a bunch of programs all babbling at the same time, and you know that it's all gibberish. Sometimes, however, it can be insidiously confusing. For example, output-timing issues sometimes result in the shell displaying its prompt just before another command prints information to the terminal. This causes the information to be printed as though it were a command, sitting after the prompt at the command line.

For example, in the case of the previous bg command, with certain shell configurations, running bg produces not only a line detailing the job that's just been put in the background but also a line telling you what directory you're currently working in. This directory display has an annoying habit of landing at the (empty) command-line prompt when it appears. The result is output that looks like this:

```
localhost ray 188> bg
[5]  ./test2.csh &
localhost ray 189> /Users/ray
```

This looks, on the screen, as though I'd typed /Users/ray at the prompt for command number 189, but in fact that's just output from the bg command, and there is currently nothing on the command line for command number 189. Pressing the Return key if this happens will not harm anything, and you'll just get your prompt back, safe and ready to work again.

If there were multiple suspended jobs, I could pick which one to send to the background by the use of a job specifier *<jobspec>* (as defined in the discussion of the `jobs` command), using the syntax `bg` *<jobspec>*. Table 12.3 shows the `bg` command syntax.

TABLE 12.3 The `bg` Command

`bg`	Backgrounds a job
`bg [`*<jobspec>*` ...]`	
<jobspec> `&`	

`bg`

`bg` backgrounds the jobs specified by the given *<jobspecs>*, or if no argument is given, the current job. *<jobspec>* may be any acceptable form described in `jobs`. A job that is currently a foreground job may be backgrounded simply by referring to it using the % notation—that is, `%1 &` backgrounds job `1`.

Backgrounding Processes with `&`

Processes can also be put in the background by using the `&` symbol at the end of the command line. Simply add this symbol to the end of any command line, and the resulting process will be run in the background automatically.

```
brezup:ray testing 190$ jobs
[1] - Running              ./aaa.csh &
[4] + Running              ./test.csh &
[5]   Running              ./test2.csh &
brezup:ray testing 191$ ./bbbb.csh &
[6] 691
brezup:ray testing 192$ jobs
[1] - Running              ./aaa.csh &
[4]   Running              ./test.csh &
[5]   Running              ./test2.csh &
[6] + Running              ./bbbb.csh &
```

When a job is put into the background using the `&` suffix for a command line, it automatically prints out its job number and process ID.

This syntax is also an abbreviation for the `bg` command as used on stopped jobs.

```
brezup:ray testing 193$ ./ccc.csh
^Z
[7] + Stopped              ./ccc.csh
brezup:ray testing 194$ jobs
[1]   Running              ./aaa.csh &
[4]   Running              ./test.csh &
[5]   Running              ./test2.csh &
[6] - Running              ./bbbb.csh &
[7] + Stopped              ./ccc.csh
brezup:ray testing 195$ %7 &
```

```
[2]+ ./ccc.csh &
brezup:ray testing 196$ jobs
[1]   Running             ./aaa.csh &
[4]   Running             ./test.csh &
[5]   Running             ./test2.csh &
[6] + Running             ./bbbb.csh &
[7] - Running             ./ccc.csh
```

Foregrounding Processes: `fg`

The command `fg` returns a job to the foreground, where it continues to run. The command may be either a background job or a suspended job. If you don't specify a <*jobspec*>, the current job (the one indicated by the + in the jobs listing) is brought to the foreground.

```
brezup:ray testing 207$ jobs
[1] - Running             ./aaa.csh &
[5] + Running             ./test2.csh &
brezup:ray testing 208$ fg %1
./aaa.csh
```

Table 12.4 shows the documentation for `fg`.

TABLE 12.4 The Command Syntax and Most Interesting Options for fg

`fg`	Foregrounds a job.
`fg [<jobspec>...]`	
`<jobspec>`	
`fg`	

Brings the specified jobs (or, if no argument is given, the current job) to the foreground. <*jobspec*> may be any acceptable form as described in `jobs`. Like backgrounding jobs, referring to a backgrounded or stopped job in `%` notation (that is, simply referencing its <*jobspec*>) brings it to the foreground—that is, entering `%1` on the command line foregrounds background job `1`.

Stopping Processes, Sending Signals: `kill`, `killall`

The `kill` command sends a signal to a process or terminates a process. It is most commonly used in conjunction with `ps`, which provides the process ID of the process to which you want to send a signal.

You will probably most often use this command either to terminate a process, or to send a hang up signal (HUP) to force a process to reread its configuration file.

The syntax that you will probably most often use is one of the following forms:

```
kill -9 <pid>
kill -HUP <pid>
```

In the first example, the -9 sends an explicit termination (KILL) signal to the process specified. This is a request that the operating system cause the process to stop, now, no questions asked. Unless the process is in such a state that it cannot be terminated (certain types of operations cannot be interrupted by design), it will cease to execute immediately. Effectively, this is much like pulling the power-plug for the process. In the second example, the -HUP sends a hangup signal to a process. This signal is frequently used by the operating system to indicate to programs that some other piece of software to which they've been speaking, has, so to speak, hung up the phone. Some programs interpret this as a sign that they should tidy up whatever they've been doing and then quit, whereas others have been designed to interpret HUP as an indication that they should reread their configuration files and restart themselves. You will see at least one example of this second behavior later in the book.

Table 12.5 shows the command syntax and options for kill.

TABLE 12.5 The Command Syntax for kill

kill kill [-*<signal>*] %*<job>* ¦ *<pid>* kill -l [exit-status]	Sends a signal to a process or terminates a process.
-l [exit-status]	With no argument, lists the all the signal names; otherwise, lists the signal associated with the status exit-status.
<signal>	Specifies which signal to send to a process. If *<signal>* is not specified, the TERM (terminate) signal is sent. *<signal>* may be a signal number or signal name.
%*<job>*	csh/tcsh specific: Specifies the job that should receive a signal. In bash, use jobs -x kill *<jobspec>* to cause jobs to rewrite the argument to kill from a *<jobspec>* to a *<pid>*.
<pid>	Specifies the process ID that should receive a signal. The process ID can be determined by running ps.

The killall command is similar to the kill command, except that it kills (or sends various signals to) processes by name, instead of by process ID. This can be considerably more convenient if you want to kill the execution of a command you've just run, or if you want to wipe all copies of some server running on your machine simultaneously. However, although it's usually more convenient for you to remember a command name than to look up a process number, killall is less specific than kill, in that it has no way to differentiate between multiple running copies of the same program. Instead, when you killall mail, you kill all running copies of mail owned by your user ID. If you're currently operating as root, you kill all copies of mail that anyone's running on the machine. Table 12.6 shows the command syntax and most interesting options for killall.

TABLE 12.6 The Command Syntax and Most Interesting Options for `killall`

`killall`	Kills processes by name
`killall [-d ¦ -v] [-help] [-l] [-m] [-s] [-u <user>] [-t <tty>] [-c <procname>] [-<SIGNAL>] [<procname> ...]`	
`killall` kills processes selected by name, as opposed to the selection by `pid` as done by `kill`. By default, it sends a `TERM` (software termination) signal to all processes with a real UID identical to the caller of `killall` that match the name *<procname>*. The `TERM` signal gives the target application the capability to close down on its own. The `root` user is allowed to kill any process.	
`-l`	Lists the names of the available signals and exits, like in `kill`.
`-m`	Matches the argument *<procname>* as a (case-insensitive) regular expression against the names of processes found. Caution! This is dangerous; a single dot matches any process running under the real UID of the caller.
`-<SIGNAL>`	Sends the specified *<SIGNAL>* instead of the default `TERM`. The signal may be specified either as a name (with or without a leading SIG), or numerically.
`-u <user>`	Limits potentially matching processes to those belonging to the specified *<user>*.
`-t <tty>`	Limits potentially matching processes to those running on the specified *<tty>*.
`-c <procname>`	When used with the `-u` or `-t` flags, limits potentially matching processes to those matching the specified *<procname>*.

Listing Resource-Consuming Processes: `top`

The `top` command displays system usage statistics, particularly of those processes making the most use of system resources. Processes are displayed at one-second intervals. The `top` command can be useful for diagnosing unusual behavior with a process. It is worthwhile to run `top` from time to time so that you learn what the typical behavior for your system is.

When `top` is displaying processes, it takes over your screen. You can quit the display by pressing the Q key. The following is a sample of what `top` output looks like:

```
Processes: 49 total, 2 running, 47 sleeping.. 112 threads      22:00:10
Load Avg: 1.14, 0.96, 1.07   CPU usage: 74.8% user, 15.5% sys, 9.7% idle
SharedLibs: num = 107, resident = 24.5M code, 2.80M data, 7.56M LinkEdit
MemRegions: num = 3665, resident = 50.9M + 7.60M private, 69.7M shared
PhysMem: 56.3M wired, 70.9M active, 132M inactive, 259M used, 764M free
VM: 2.36G + 72.3M  18452(0) pageins, 0(0) pageouts

 PID COMMAND     %CPU  TIME   #TH #PRTS #MREGS RPRVT RSHRD RSIZE VSIZE
 990 top         3.8% 0:00.61  1  15       24  240K  428K  604K 26.9M
 989 bash        0.0% 0:00.02  1  12       15  172K  880K  780K 18.2M
 988 login       0.0% 0:00.05  1  12       35  140K  420K  508K 26.9M
```

```
963 pickup     0.0% 0:00.03  1  12     19  132K  512K  580K 26.9M
904 bash       0.0% 0:00.09  1  12     16  180K  880K  796K 18.2M
903 login      0.0% 0:00.05  1  12     35  140K  420K  508K 26.9M
878 sleep      0.0% 0:00.01  1  11     15  72K   340K  276K 17.6M
877 tcsh       0.0% 0:00.02  1  12     18  180K  644K  648K 22.1M
864 sleep      0.0% 0:00.00  1  11     15  72K   340K  276K 17.6M
863 tcsh       0.0% 0:00.03  1  12     18  180K  644K  648K 22.1M
848 Terminal  45.0% 0:35.40  4  70    156 1.94M+ 10.1M 7.39M+ 95.3M+
668 lookupd    0.0% 0:01.16  2  33     55  340K  956K 1.11M 28.5M
596 Microsoft  0.7% 0:02.77  1  68     97 1.81M 7.90M 4.41M 90.5M
595 Microsoft 26.9% 24:30.31 4  89    240 25.2M 40.9M 40.5M  146M
396 Finder     0.0% 0:14.44  1  80    133 3.48M 15.2M 12.3M  112M
395 SystemUISe 0.0% 0:05.96  1  192   191 1.57M 8.48M 5.38M 93.3M
```

Table 12.7 shows the command syntax and most interesting options for top.

TABLE 12.7 The Command Syntax and Most Interesting Options for top

top	Displays system usage statistics.
top [-u] [-w] [-k] [-s *<delay>*] [-e ¦ -d ¦ -a] [-l *<samples>*] [*<number>*]	
top	
-u	Sorts by CPU usage and displays usage starting with the highest usage.
-s *<delay>*	Samples processes at the specified *<delay>*. Default is one-second intervals.
-e	Switches to event-counting mode where counts reported are absolute counters. Options -w and -k are ignored.
-d	Switches to an event-counting mode where counts are reported as differences relative to the previous sample.
-a	Switches to an event-counting mode where counts are reported as cumulative counters relative to when top was launched. Options -w and -k are ignored.
-l *<samples>*	Switches from default screen mode to a logging mode suitable for saving the output to a file. If *<samples>* is specified, top samples the number of samples specified before exiting. The default is 1.
<number>	Limits the number of processes displayed to *<number>*.
Pressing the Q key causes top to exit immediately.	
Columns displayed in default data mode:	
PID	Unix process ID.
COMMAND	Unix command name.
%CPU	Percentage of CPU used (kernel and user).
TIME	Absolute CPU consumption (min:secs.hundredths).
#TH	Number of threads.
#PRTS (delta)	Number of MACH ports.
#MERG	Number of memory regions.
VPRVT (-w only)	Private address space currently allocated.
RPRVT (delta)	Resident shared memory (as represented by the resident page count of each shared memory object).
RSHRD (delta)	Total resident memory (real pages that this process currently has associated with it; some may be shared by other processes).

TABLE 12.7 Continued

VSIZE (delta)	Total address space currently allocated (including shared).
Columns displayed in event-counting modes:	
PID	Unix process ID.
COMMAND	Unix command name.
%CPU	Percentage of CPU used (kernel and user).
TIME	Absolute CPU consumption (min:secs.hundredths).
FAULTS	Number of page faults.
PAGEINS	Number of requests for pages from a pager.
COW_FAULTS	Number of faults that caused a page to be copied.
MSGS_SENT	Number of mach messages sent by the process.
MSGS_RCVD	Number of mach messages received by the process.
BSDSYSCALL	Number of BSD system calls made by the process.
MACHSYSCALL	Number of MACH system calls made by the process.
CSWITCH	Number of context switches to this process.

TIP

top, by default, often uses enough CPU time to place itself at the top of the list. A less resource-intensive means of invoking top is `top -ocpu -R -F -s 2 -n30`. You might want to consider aliasing this to something like ttop, with `alias ttop='top -ocpu -R -F -s 2 -n30'`.

Automating Process Execution with cron

Oftentimes it isn't desirable to have to manually start processes in the Finder or at the command line. Automating repetitive tasks, after all, is one of the reasons we have computers in the first place. To this end, the crond service can be set to automatically run applications and scripts by adding entries to either a user or system crontab file. Let's start by looking at the system-level file, /etc/crontab:

The default crontab file looks like this:

```
# /etc/crontab
SHELL=/bin/sh
PATH=/etc:/bin:/sbin:/usr/bin:/usr/sbin
HOME=/var/log
#
#minute hour  mday  month  wday  who   command
#
#*/5   *     *     *     *     root   /usr/libexec/atrun
#
# Run daily/weekly/monthly jobs.
15    3     *     *     *     root   periodic daily
30    4     *     *     6     root   periodic weekly
30    5     1     *     *     root   periodic monthly
```

At the start of the file, a handful of environment variables are set (SHELL, PATH, HOME), which are made available to the commands executing from the file. Additional environment variables can be added using the same syntax: *<variable name>*=*<value>*.

One special crontab variable is the MAILTO variable, which can be set to a user account name. Output from the crontab commands (errors, and so on) is sent via email to that user's account.

The body of the crontab file is laid out in seven columns, separated by spaces or tabs. These seven fields control different aspects of when a command is run:

- Minute—The minutes after an hour that a command should be executed (0–59).
- Hour—The hour a command should run (0–23).
- Day of the month—The day of the month to run the command (0–31).
- Month—The month, specified numerically (1–12), or by name that the command should execute.
- Weekday—The day of the week the command should execute, set numerically (0–7, 0 or 7 specifies Sunday) or by name.
- User—The user ID to use while executing the command.
- Command—The command string to execute. This field can point to a shell script or other file to run a sequence of commands.

Fields that contain an asterisk (*) indicate that the command will run whenever the other columns' values are matched. For example, assume that there is an asterisk in every column (except for the User and Command fields, obviously):

```
* * * * * <my user> <my command>
```

The command will be started every minute, of every hour, of every day, of every day of the week, and so on. In addition, you can set a command to run at multiple different intervals within a time period without having to use additional lines. Just use integers separated by commas to set off multiple times within one of the columns.

For example, to run a command every 10 minutes, you could use

```
0,10,20,30,40,50 * * * * <my user> <my command>
```

Even this, however, can be shortened to be a bit more manageable. Regular intervals can be shortened using the syntax */*<interval length>*. The previous example could be rewritten like this:

```
*/10 * * * * <my user> <my command>
```

Additions made to the /etc/crontab file are read every minute without additional user interaction.

Three jobs are run by default from the Tiger `/etc/crontab` file: periodic daily, periodic weekly, and periodic monthly. As the names suggest, these are run at repeating intervals each day, week, and month, respectively. The periodic program is used to execute periodic `cron` tasks—in this case, daily, weekly, and monthly scripts located in the `/etc/daily`, `/etc/weekly`, and `/etc/monthly` files, respectively. They handle cleaning up temporary system files, log rotation, and other menial maintenance tasks. You can take advantage of these files or add additional script files to perform other common tasks.

CAUTION

It might be tempting to set up scripts that run in tight intervals (for monitoring system activity and so forth). If you set up commands to execute at frequent intervals, make absolutely sure that they can finish executing within that interval. If a command tends to run long, you might find that your system slowly grinds to a halt as more copies are started and system resources are exhausted.

Providing `cron` Services to Normal User Accounts

The systemwide `/etc/crontab` file should be used only for system tasks. Users, however, might want to add their own commands and scripts that are executed within their accounts. To do this, a user can create a `crontab`-style file within his directory. This file should contain all the fields as the previously documented `/etc/crontab` file, with one notable exception: there is no User field. Any commands executed from a personal `crontab` file are executed with the permissions of that user.

For example:

```
*/15 * * * * /Users/jray/myscript.pl
```

Putting this line in a file gives me a personal `crontab` that executes a Perl script in my home directory every 15 minutes.

Unlike the system-level `crontab` file, personal `crontab` files are loaded into a privileged system area rather than run directly from the file you've created. To load a personal `crontab` file into the system, use the `crontab` utility followed by the name of your personal file: `crontab` *`<my crontab file>`*.

Assuming that I've stored my `crontab` entries in `mycrontab`, I can load them into the system with

```
brezup:jray jray $ crontab mycrontab
```

After the file is loaded into the system, you can safely delete the local copy of your `crontab` file—it is no longer needed. A user can display the loaded `crontab` information (and thereby regenerate the original file) by typing **`crontab -l`**:

```
brezup:jray jray $ crontab -l
# DO NOT EDIT THIS FILE - edit the master and reinstall.
# (mycrontab installed on Sun Jul 1 10:01:20 2001)
```

```
# (Cron version -- $FreeBSD: src/usr.sbin/cron/crontab/crontab.c,v 1.12
# 1999/08/28 01:15:52 peter Exp $)
*/15 * * * * /Users/jray/myscript.pl
```

Users can also use the `-e` option to edit the currently stored `crontab` information, or use `-r` to remove it entirely.

> **NOTE**
>
> The root user (or a user executing `sudo`) can work with the contents of any user's personal `crontab` file by adding `-u`*<username>* to the `crontab -l` command-line utility.
>
> The `crontab` information is stored in `/etc/cron/tabs/`*<username>* if you want direct access to the data.

Those wanting to access `cron` services from a GUI interface might want to check out the donation-supported CronniX application, shown in Figure 12.1. CronniX can create and edit `crontab` files for any user from within a point-and-click environment. Download it from `http://h5197.serverkompetenz.net/cronnix/`.

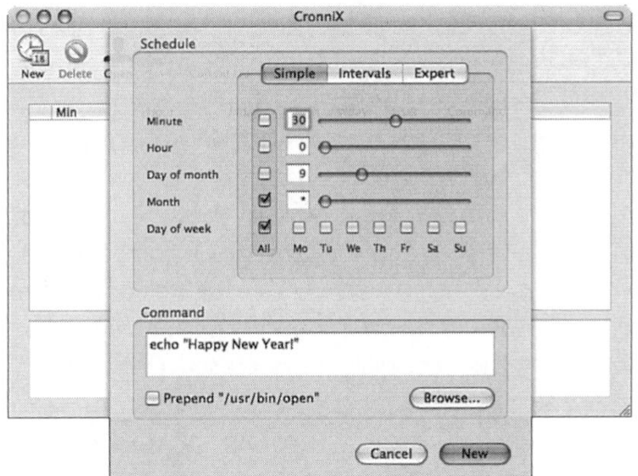

FIGURE 12.1 The CronniX application can graphically edit system and user `crontab` files.

If you are at all hesitant about the format of the `crontab` file or interval scheduling, CronniX is highly recommended. A simple matter of mistyping an `*` where you didn't intend could ultimately result in serious performance issues or other problems on your system.

Limiting Access to `cron` Services

On a system with many users, it isn't necessarily a good idea to give all of them access to `cron` services. You might find that your poor system performance is due to a few hundred copies of `SETI@home` that start automatically every night. To limit access to the `crontab` command for adding personal `crontab` entries, use either `/var/cron/allow` or `/var/cron/deny`.

As you might infer, the `allow` file controls who is allowed to access `crontab`. Adding entries to this file denies access for anyone who isn't listed. Likewise, the `deny` file, if it exists, provides access to `crontab` for anyone who isn't listed.

This isn't intentionally tricky, but it is important to note that the act of creating one of these files implicitly denies or allows access to all the accounts on the system. Obviously, you should not be running a system where both files exist simultaneously because it leads to an ambiguity of what happens to everyone else who isn't listed in one of the files.

Over time, you'll discover that there are small tasks you carry out on a day-to-day basis. Using the power of the `cron` daemon along with shell scripts, Perl, or AppleScript can automate many of these processes.

Communication Between Processes: Redirection, Pipes

Building an operating system out of a multitude of small, cooperating processes would not provide such flexibility and power to the user were it not for a simple method of making all of these processes speak to each other. At the heart of the interprocess communications model of Unix is a simple but amazingly effective abstraction of the idea of input and output.

To paraphrase the model on which Unix bases input and output, you can imagine that Unix thinks of user input to a program as a stream—a stream of information. Output from the program back to the user can be thought of in the same way. A stream of information is simply a collection of information that flows in or out of the program in a serial (ordered) fashion. A user can't send two pieces of information to a program at the same time—two key presses, no matter how closely they occur, are ordered, one first and one second. A cursor moving across a screen provides information serially as to where it is now, and where it was then. Even if two events manage to occur simultaneously, the electronics of the machine can't really deal with simultaneous events, and so they end up being registered as separate events occurring very close in time. Output must be similarly serially ordered. Whether you are drawing data to the screen or sending data over an Internet connection, no two data items leave a program at exactly the same time; therefore, they are also a serial stream of information.

Because both input and output from processes are streams of information, and every function of the system from user programs to reading files to parts of the operating system is a running process, Unix models the implementation of communication between the processes as simply tying the output stream of one process to another's input stream. Tying the standard output stream (named `STDOUT`) from one process to the standard input stream (named `STDIN`) of another is called *creating a pipe* between them. When you understand the view of data moving into or out of a process as being a data stream, it is immediately obvious that there is no need for the system to concern itself over the endpoints of the stream. Data simply moves about the system between programs in streams, as though each program had input and output spigots, and someone had connected garden hoses between them. The input spigots all look the same, and the output spigots all look the same, so the operating system can tie any output into any input, and let the programs worry about whether they know what to do with the data in the stream.

For example, one endpoint of a stream might be connected to the output (STDOUT) of a process that is taking input from a user at a keyboard, and the other endpoint might be connected to the input (STDIN) of a process manipulating that information and writing it into a file. On the other hand, the same information could be placed in a file, and we could replace the user entering information with a process that could read the file and write the same information onto its STDOUT. If we tie the stream created in this fashion into the STDIN of the same manipulation program, there would be absolutely no difference between these two situations from the operating system's point of view.

In short, this abstraction provides that so long as the input coming to a process looks like the input the process expects; it does not matter to the process or the operating system where that input comes from. Likewise, provided that the destination of the output from the process acts as expected, it does not matter where the output is actually going.

Redirection: STDIN, STDOUT, STDERR

Unix makes this input/output model available to the user through a concept known as *redirection*. This is implemented as a requirement that all processes adhere to certain conventions regarding input and output.

At the base is the notion that input and output from programs is generally from, and to, a user typing information at the command line. Even programs that are not intended to be used by a person at a command line are expected to adhere to the model that input comes from a user, and output goes to a user.

This might seem counterintuitive, but further conventions are required that allow this seeming restriction to be less restrictive, while generalizing the input/output model sufficiently that it can be applied to almost any need. Two of these are the idea of input arriving in a program through a virtual interface known as STDIN (standard input), and output leaving the program through a virtual interface known as STDOUT (standard output). It also requires the convention of a third virtual interface by which error messages can be conveyed, which is STDERR (standard error).

Redirection is accomplished by attaching these virtual interfaces to each other in various combinations—essentially redirecting the input or output from a process to a different location than to a user or from a user.

Standard In: STDIN

The virtual input interface to programs is called STDIN, for standard input. A program can expect the incoming data stream from the user (or any other source) to arrive at STDIN.

When you interact with a command-line program, the program is reading the data you are entering from STDIN. If you prefer not to enter the data by hand, you can put it in a file and redirect the contents of the file into the program's STDIN—the program will not know the difference.

A program that you can use for an example is the spell program. Apple hasn't distributed spell with Mac OS X as of this writing, but we've provided instructions on how to install it in Chapter 13, "Using Common Command-Line Applications and Application Suites."

If you're using a system on which it's already been installed, follow along here. Also, the installation's not too difficult if you care to glance ahead and just trust us on the commands you don't recognize yet to perform the install. If not, `spell` still makes a good program for explanation because it has exactly the features we want to exhibit—just read along and imagine that it's really working until you get to Chapter 13.

The `spell` command finds misspellings. Given input from `STDIN`, `spell` parses through it, checks the input against a dictionary, and returns any misspellings it finds. To issue the `spell` command from the command line, you might type something like the following:

```
brezup:ray testing $ spell
Now is the tyem for all good authors to come to thie ayde of some very
good Unix users
Ctrl+D
```

Pressing Ctrl+D finishes the input, sending an end-of-data signal into `STDIN`, effectively telling the program that no further information is to come. The `spell` program goes to work, and returns the following:

```
tyem
thie
ayde
```

Each of the misspelled words (or at least words that aren't in the dictionary) is displayed, exactly as expected.

This might not seem to be a particularly useful program at first glance—how often do you want to type a sentence, just to find out what words are misspelled in it? The key to its usefulness, however, is that the `spell` program does not care whether you typed the input, or whether the input came from a file.

NOTE

Actually, it's more proper to think of `spell` as not caring whether the input comes from a file or from you instead. The `spell` program is designed to work with input coming from a file or a program. It just happens that because of the input/output model abstracting all system input and output as from/to a user-like interface, in operation, `spell` doesn't care whether the input comes from a user or from a file instead. Many programs you'll find available for Unix fall into this category—they are designed to take input or provide output to or from other programs or files rather than from users. The input/output model, however, enables a user to interact with the software anyway. Because of this, you might occasionally find the syntax in which these programs converse to be slightly odd. Just remember, they weren't really designed to talk directly to you.

Now try it with data from a file. Fire up your favorite text editor, and create a file containing the same text you typed to spell previously. Then try `spell` by redirecting this file into its `STDIN` interface. If you named your file `reallydumbfile`, you can run `spell` on it by typing the following:

```
brezup:ray testing $ spell < reallydumbfile
tyme
thie
ayde
```

This looks a little more useful. The < character redirects `STDIN` for the program to its left to come from the file named to its right. Here, it redirects `STDIN` for the `spell` program so that it comes from the file `reallydumbfile` rather than from your keyboard.

Standard Out: `STDOUT`

The virtual output interface that Unix provides to programs is called `STDOUT`, for standard output. Just as you can redirect `STDIN` from a file, if you want to store the output of a command in a file, you can redirect `STDOUT` from the program into the file. The > character directs the `STDOUT` of the program to its left into the file named to its right. For example, if you want to collect the last few lines of `/var/log/system.log` into a file in your home directory, you could type

```
brezup:ray testing $ tail -20 /etc/services > ~/my-output
```

This command directs the shell to create a file named `my-output` in your home directory, and to redirect `STDOUT` from the `tail` command (that is, the data `tail` would print if you just issued the command `tail -20 /etc/services`) into the file. If `my-output` already exists in your home directory, it will be overwritten by the output from `tail`.

If you want to collect and archive the data, by appending it to `my-output` instead of overwriting it, the shell can be directed to append rather than replace the data. In this case, `STDOUT` is redirected with >> rather than the single >. The >> character pair appends the `STDOUT` of the program to the left into the file named on its right.

You can also simultaneously redirect `STDOUT` and `STDIN`, like this:

```
[localhost:~/Documents] nermal% spell < reallydumbfile > reallydumbspelling
[localhost:~/Documents] nermal% ls
get_termcap      lynx.cfg       reallydumbspelling termcap-1.3.tar
lynx         reallydumbfile   termcap-1.3     test
[localhost:~/Documents] nermal% cat reallydumbspelling
tyem
thie
ayde
```

Standard Error: `STDERR`

To make your life easier, Unix actually has two different output interfaces that it defines for programs. The first, `STDOUT`, has just been covered. The second, `STDERR`, is used to allow the program to provide error and diagnostic information to the user. This is done for two reasons. First, it allows error information to be reported in such a way that it does not interfere with data on the `STDOUT` interface. Second, if you are redirecting `STDOUT` from a program to another program or to a file, you would not see error messages if they were carried on STDOUT. By providing a separate error channel, Unix gives the user the choice of how and where error and diagnostic information should be displayed, independent of information that is actually correct output data.

tcsh and bash syntax disagree rather significantly here. In tcsh if you want to redirect STDERR into the same stream as STDOUT, effectively combining these two different pieces of information, you can do so by using the character pair >& to indicate redirection in the command, instead of >. bash allows this syntax for combining the streams (though it prefers the use of &>), but in bash you also have the option of redirecting STDERR independently of STDOUT. To redirect just STDERR, use 2> as the redirection specifier rather than >.

As mentioned earlier, both bash and tcsh are vastly more complex than can be completely covered in a book of this size, and input/output redirection is one of the principal areas of complexity. If you want to perform more complex manipulations of your command's input and output, see your online man pages to learn how the shell of your preference behaves.

Pipes

Finally, there is nothing in the input/output model that restricts redirection to coming from or going into files/users (if everything looks like a user or a file, letting software talk to anything else is just as good). STDIN and STDOUT can just as easily be tied together instead of being tied into files or the command line.

Perhaps more correctly, the operating system never really redirects to or from files. What the operating system is really doing when you redirect into a file is invisibly creating a process that writes into a file, and redirecting your output to the STDIN of the process writing the file. Likewise, when you redirect a file into a program's STDIN, the operating system is invisibly creating a process that opens and reads the file, and is tying the STDOUT from this process into your process's STDIN (and now you see why we said the model was based on input and output being attached to users, rather than to files). For the user's convenience, these common actions are abbreviated into the < and > redirection characters.

Programs, on the other hand, are connected by directly redirecting their STDOUT and STDIN interfaces with a pipe. To create a pipe in Unix, you simply use a ¦ character between the programs on the command line.

Again, an example is more illustrative than a considerable amount of explanation. Consider a situation in which you want to examine the content of a file that is larger than will fit on one screen. You can accomplish this easily by piping the output from the cat command into a pager, such as the more command.

```
brezup:ray testing $ cat /usr/share/file/magic ¦ more
# Magic
# Magic data for file(1) command.
# Machine-generated from src/cmd/file/magdir/*; edit there only!
# Format is described in magic(files), where:
# files is 5 on V7 and BSD, 4 on SV, and ?? in the SVID.
```

```
#------------------------------------------------------------------------------
# Localstuff: file(1) magic for locally observed files
#
# $Id: Localstuff,v 1.1 2003/07/02 18:00:17 eseidel Exp $
# Add any locally observed files here. Remember:
# text if readable, executable if runnable binary, data if unreadable.
#------------------------------------------------------------------------------
# acorn: file(1) magic for files found on Acorn systems
#

# RISC OS Chunk File Format
# From RISC OS Programmer's Reference Manual, Appendix D
# We guess the file type from the type of the first chunk.
0     lelong      0xc3cbc6c5   RISC OS Chunk data
>12   string      OBJ_       \b, AOF object
>12   string      LIB_       \b, ALF library

byte 920
```

Of course, you already know that you could have accomplished this by just using `more /usr/share/file/magic`. The point, though, is that although we told you how to use `more` to read a file before, `more` *actually* wants to take its input from `STDIN` and uses a file specified as an argument only as a last resort.

Knowing this, you now know how to make any other output from any other program viewable with the `more` pager. This enables you to do things such as look at the full contents of your filesystem without needing an immensely large scroll buffer in your terminal:

```
brezup:ray testing $ ls -lRaF / ¦ more

total 8721
drwxrwxr-t 39 root wheel    1326 16 Aug 17:16 ./
drwxrwxr-t 39 root wheel    1326 16 Aug 17:16 ../
-rwxrwxr-x  1 ray  unknown   6148 16 Aug 17:15 .DS_Store*
d-wx-wx-wt  4 ray  admin    136 12 Aug 01:09 .Trashes/
-rw-r--r--  1 ray  admin   39568 11 Aug 22:42 .VolumeIcon.icns
-r--r--r--  1 root wheel    156 29 Jul 14:15 .hidden
dr--r--r--  2 root wheel    256 16 Aug 17:16 .vol/
drwxrwxr-x 28 root admin    952 11 Aug 23:50 Applications/
drwxr-xr-x  2 ray  unknown    68 11 Aug 23:54 Calendars/
drwxr-xr-x  4 ray  unknown   136 11 Aug 23:54 Contacts/
-rw-r--r--  1 root admin    1024 11 Aug 23:50 Desktop DB
-rw-r--r--  1 root admin     2 11 Aug 22:43 Desktop DF
drwxr-xr-x  2 ray  unknown    68 13 Aug 10:58 Desktop Folder/
drwxrwxr-x 13 root wheel    442 2 Jul 17:22 Developer/
```

```
-rw-r--r--  1 ray  admin     0 11 Aug 22:42 Icon
drwxrwxr-x 35 root wheel  1190 13 Aug 20:45 Library/
drwxr-xr-x  1 root wheel   512 16 Aug 23:19 Network/
drwxr-xr-x  5 root wheel   170 2 Jul 17:22 System/
drwxr-xr-x  3 ray  unknown  102 13 Aug 10:58 TheVolumeSettingsFolder/
drwxr-xr-x  2 ray  unknown   68 13 Aug 10:58 Trash/
drwxrwxr-t  9 root admin   306 16 Aug 16:28 Users/
drwxrwxrwt  8 root admin   272 16 Aug 17:16 Volumes/
byte 1356
```

One particularly useful use of such piping of commands together comes when you want to filter the output of a command so that you only see the most interesting parts. For example, if you want to find files in your current directory that were edited in August, you could refer to Chapter 9, "Accessing the BSD Subsystem," and look up how to filter dates in `ls`, or you could use what you probably already remember about `grep`. Adding a pipe from `ls -l` into a `grep` command looking for the string `Aug` is as simple as entering both commands on the command line, separated by a ¦ character.

```
brezup:ray Documents $ ls -l
total 16456
-rw-r--r--   1 ray staff 4925440 Jun 11 00:11 BTS.tar
drwxr-xr-x  17 ray staff     578 Jun 13 08:57 BTS_folder
drwxr-xr-x  28 ray staff     952 Jun 12 11:27 Core
drwxr-xr-x   4 ray staff     136 Mar 9 02:13 DnD_data
drwxr-xr-x  10 ray staff     340 Jul 2 10:43 Mailsmith User Data Backup
drwxr-xr-x  17 ray staff     578 Aug 15 23:58 Microsoft User Data
drwxr-xr-x   7 ray staff     238 Jul 16 2002 Software_Docs
drwxr-xr-x  48 ray staff    1632 Aug 15 00:19 buying_the_farm
drwxrwxrwx  39 ray staff    1326 Apr 24 19:02 dna_demos_2002
drwxr-xr-x   4 ray staff     136 May 29 13:12 games
-rw-r--r--   1 ray staff  610678 Aug 15 02:24 hd_genes_aa.fa
-rw-r--r--   1 ray staff 1645031 Aug 15 02:24 hd_genes_nt.fa
-rw-r--r--   1 ray staff  609071 Jun 9 21:06 lumberjk.mp3
drwxr-xr-x  17 ray staff     578 May 21 16:56 openGL
drwxr-xr-x  36 ray staff    1224 Aug 15 00:19 research
drwxr-xr-x 104 ray staff    3536 Jun 26 10:39 security
drwxr-xr-x   5 ray staff     170 Dec 27 2002 source
-rw-r--r--   1 ray staff  623484 Jan 18 2002 squirrel.mpg
drwxrwxrwx  16 ray staff     544 Sep 16 2002 stylewriter
drwxrwxrwx   7 ray staff     238 Aug 16 15:56 unleashed

brezup:ray Documents $ ls -l ¦ grep "Aug"
drwxr-xr-x  17 ray staff     578 Aug 15 23:58 Microsoft User Data
drwxr-xr-x  48 ray staff    1632 Aug 15 00:19 buying_the_farm
-rw-r--r--   1 ray staff  610678 Aug 15 02:24 hd_genes_aa.fa
-rw-r--r--   1 ray staff 1645031 Aug 15 02:24 hd_genes_nt.fa
```

```
drwxr-xr-x  36 ray staff    1224 Aug 15 00:19 research
drwxrwxrwx  7  ray staff     238 Aug 16 15:56 unleashed
```

Sometimes, you want to filter both `STDOUT` from the command and `STDERR`. `find`, for example, has an annoying tendency to report all manner of errors about directories that you're not allowed to look in. This often clutters up the output such that you can't actually find what it was that you wanted to find. Here, redirecting `STDOUT` using only the ¦ character is insufficient because find helpfully puts the error messages on `STDERR`, where they won't be captured by the ¦ pipe (which only works on `STDIN`).

In `tcsh`, redirecting both `STDIN` and `STDERR` simultaneously is simply a matter of using the `¦&` pipe combination instead of the single ¦ character. In `bash`, it's just slightly more complex. `bash` can't redirect both at once, but it can redirect `STDERR` into `STDOUT`. The syntax for that looks like `2>&1`. After `STDERR` has been redirected into `STDOUT`, the combined stream can then be redirected into `grep` with the ¦ character.

```
brezup:ray testing $ find / -name 702_fall_grades -print
find: cannot read dir /lost+found: Permission denied
find: cannot read dir /usr/lost+found: Permission denied
find: cannot read dir /usr/local/lost+found: Permission denied.
.
.
.
^C
brezup:ray testing $ find / -name grades1 -print 2>&1 ¦ grep "702_fall_grades"
/Users/ray/Biophysics/702_fall_grades
```

These are, of course, simplistic examples of connecting programs, but keep an eye out for how pipes are used throughout the rest of the book. The ability to create small programs with small functions and to tie these together into arbitrarily large programs with arbitrarily complex behaviors is powerful. This is one of the main reasons that having access to the BSD half of your new operating system is so valuable.

Think back to programs such as `grep`, and you can probably begin to see how you could apply this to creating custom solutions to problems that you might have encountered. You should also begin to see why this functionality cannot be conveniently duplicated with a GUI-only interface.

Joints in Pipes: `tee`

On occasion, you might want to redirect `STDOUT` to both a file and another program at the same time. In such a case, you can use the `tee` command. This command accepts data on `STDIN`, writes it to a filename specified on the command line, and continues to send the data, unaltered on `STDOUT`.

Consider an example in which you want to search through your files, looking for files that match a particular name pattern. You want to both browse the found names as they appear, and collect the names into a log file so that you can use the information again later. In this example, we will look in a rather inefficient fashion for files with names that contain java. Because many of them are probably on the system, we want the output piped through a pager (more). We also want to collect the filenames into a file in our home directory named my_output.

```
brezup:ray testing $ find / -name \*java\* -print | tee ~/my_output | more

/Applications/Utilities/Java/Java Web Start.app/Contents/MacOS/javaws.cfg
/Applications/Utilities/Java/Java Web Start.app/Contents/MacOS/javaws.jar
/Applications/Utilities/Java/Java Web Start.app/Contents/MacOS/javaws.policy
.
.
.
```

It might take some time for this to start printing output to the screen because it could take find a while to start finding appropriately named files. If you let this run to completion, you can then look at the file my_output, and it will have all the stuff you just scrolled through with more. If you press Ctrl+C to stop the find and the listing, you'll kill the tee process, and it won't write its output. Because this isn't a valuable listing, you might prefer to kill it off rather than actually wait for this to finish just to see the output, but you wouldn't want to do this if it were important to capture the output.

The tee command is invaluable if you need to split one STDOUT stream to be used by multiple different processes, or if you need to collect logging or partial output from intermediate steps in a large, multiprogram piped command. Table 12.8 shows syntax and options for tee.

TABLE 12.8 The tee Command

tee	A pipe fitting
tee [-ai] *<file>*	
-a	Causes tee to append to *<file>* rather than overwriting it
-i	Causes tee to ignore SIGINT signals (the signals you learned earlier with the kill and killall commands)

The tee command accepts input on STDIN and writes the same output to both STDOUT and to a *<file>*.

Managing Processes Graphically: Activity Monitor

As you know, pressing Option-Command-Escape opens a process list and enables you to force-quit open applications from the Tiger Finder. This is fine for many end-user applications, but doesn't provide the same depth of features that you can get from the command-line process management utilities.

For those seeking more control, Apple's Activity Monitor application (path: /Applications/Utilities/Activity Monitor) provides information on all the system's processes, not just the GUI software that is running; consider it a much-improved graphical version of the `top` command discussed earlier in this chapter.

Figure 12.2 shows the default Activity Monitor display.

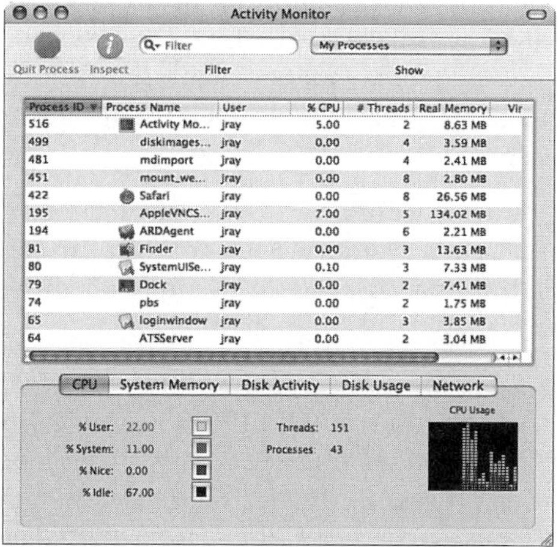

FIGURE 12.2 The Process Listing can show you everything that is running on your computer.

Controlling the Process Listing

Using the controls in the Process Listing screen, you can configure the type of output and amount of the information displayed.

The Filter and Show features help limit the amount of data shown within the process listing. Typing into the Find field filters processes that match the given string. For example, typing **Safari** would limit the displayed processes to those that have the word Safari in their name. The Show pop-up menu filters processes based on the owner. You can change the setting to show the following categories:

- All Processes—All the processes running on the system.
- All Processes Hierarchically—All the processes running on the system, sorted into a parent/child hierarchy.
- My Processes—The processes running under your user account.
- Administrator Processes—The processes running with administrative rights.
- Other User Processes—Processes running from other user accounts (not including root).
- Active Processes—Processes that are currently running and active.
- Inactive Processes—Processes that are running, but sleeping (not consuming CPU time).

- Windowed Processes—Processes running under the Tiger windowing system (your GUI applications).

The process listing is not, as you might first think, a real-time view of the programs running on the system. The process information is always changing. To avoid overwhelming the user with a list that jumps all over the place, the process list is only updated every few seconds. Using the View, Update Frequency menu selection, you can change the rate at which the list is refreshed. The larger the number, the longer you must wait for updates.

Processes are listed based on seven columns: Process ID, Process Name, User, % CPU, # Threads, Real Memory, and Virtual Memory. Each column can be sorted by clicking on the column heading. Click the small triangle in the upper-right corner of the process list to reverse the sorting order.

A unique feature of Tiger's Activity Monitor is the ability to view *process deltas* (changes) rather than just the standard column readings. If, for example, you feel that a process might have a memory leak and you want to see whether the memory consumption is increasing, you can select the process in the list, choose View, Show Deltas for Process. The row will change to show only changes (+ or –) from the values displayed at the time you switched viewing modes.

To export the current process listing to an XML file, choose File, Save.

Killing and Signaling Processes

There are a number of ways that you can interact with processes through Activity Monitor. Using the toolbar icons or the View menu, you can inspect a process in the listing and, of course, quit it.

As you learned earlier, telling the operating system to kill a process is really just a matter of sending a signal, such as `TERM` or `HUP`. To send a specific signal using Activity Monitor, choose View, Send Signal to Process. A dialog will appear listing the available signals to choose and send, as seen in Figure 12.3.

Displaying Process Details

If you want even more information about a process, you can double-click it within the listing or highlight it and click the Inspect (I) icon in the toolbar, or View, Inspect Process (Command-I). A detail window, shown in Figure 12.4, appears.

At the top of the detail window you can view the following information:

- Parent Process ID—The process that started the selected process. For example, if a user starts a program from the command line (the shell), the ID of the shell is listed as the program's parent process ID. Processes started at boot time list the parent process ID of 1 (launchd). Note that the parent process name is a hyperlink—clicking it opens the details window for the parent process.
- Process Group ID—The ID of the group used to start the process.

- %CPU—The amount of CPU time that the process is taking.
- User—The user who owns the process.

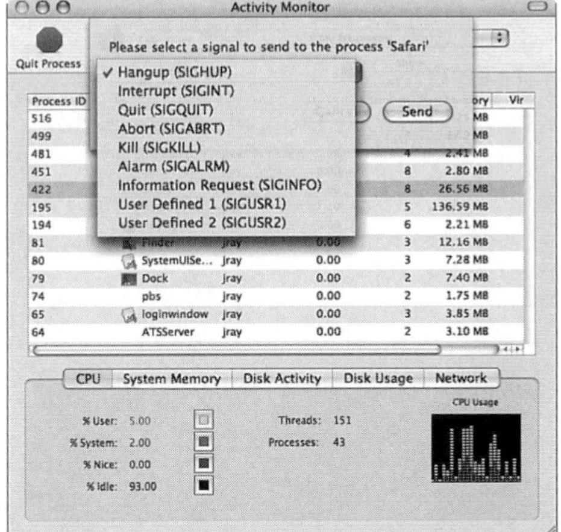

FIGURE 12.3 Tiger's Activity Monitor can send specific signals to processes.

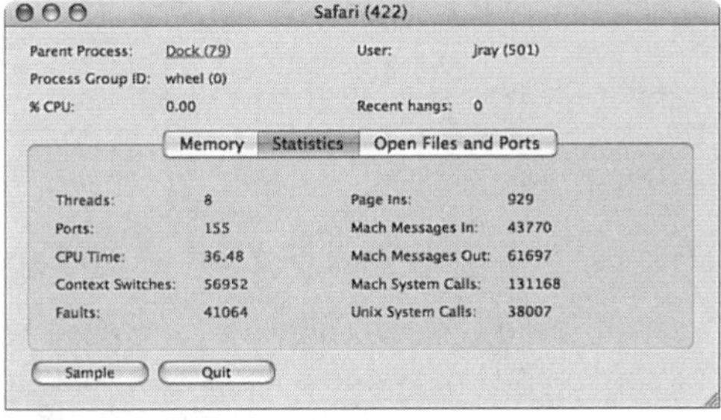

FIGURE 12.4 View details about a selected process.

The middle portion of the process details window displays information about one of up to three categories, depending on which button in the button bar is highlighted: Memory, Statistics, or Open Files and Ports (not visible for all applications):

- Memory—The amount of memory (real and virtual) being used by the process. For information on memory types, visit (`http://developer.apple.com/documentation/Performance/Conceptual/ManagingMemory/index.html`).
- Statistics—Information about how the process is behaving on your system, including threads, CPU time used, and the number of Unix system calls processed.
- Open Files and Ports—A list of resources that are open and in use by the process.

At the bottom of the details window are two buttons: Sample, and Quit. The Sample button takes a sample trace of the process execution over several seconds (this is mostly useful only for developers). The Quit button, as you might expect, offers you the options of quitting (gracefully) or force-quitting the process.

Monitoring System Statistics

At the bottom of the Activity Monitor window are controls for viewing CPU usage, System Memory, Disk Activity, Disk Usage, and Network activity. These provide an overview of *all* activity and usage across the entire system; they are not dependent on the processes selected in the process listing. Let's run through each pane and the information it contains.

CPU Usage

The CPU pane, shown in Figure 12.5, displays the current activity level of the CPU(s) on your system.

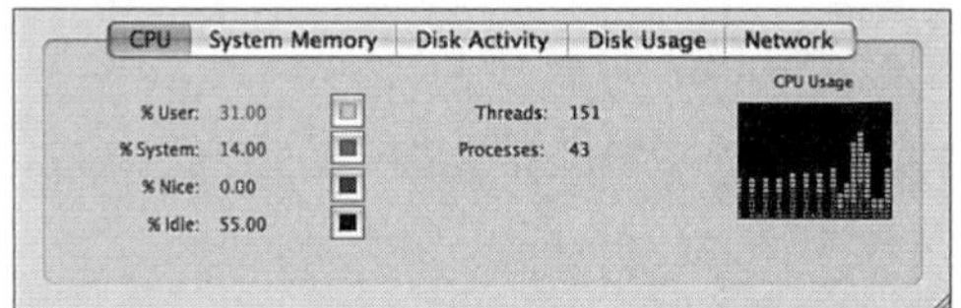

FIGURE 12.5 View your system activity level in the CPU pane.

Three types of activity are monitored:

- User—CPU time that is used by user-started processes and applications.
- System—Processor usage by the system processes, such as the Window Server and other components of the operating system. The system CPU time often correlates directly to the user activity. Dragging objects within an application, for example, places a load on the application and on the Tiger graphics and event-processing subsystem.
- Nice—CPU time used by processes running with an altered scheduling priority. All user processes start with the same priority of execution. This priority can be adjusted with the nice and renice commands to provide them with more or less access to CPU time.

The fourth value (idle) is actually just a lack of activity (100% minus the other three values). The total number of threads and processes is also displayed.

To the right of the readouts is a scrolling graph that displays the three types of CPU activity.

TIP

In the CPU pane and any other pane, you can alter the colors used in the graph by clicking the color wells to the right of each graphed value.

System Memory

The System Memory pane shows the overall memory usage for the system, as displayed in Figure 12.6.

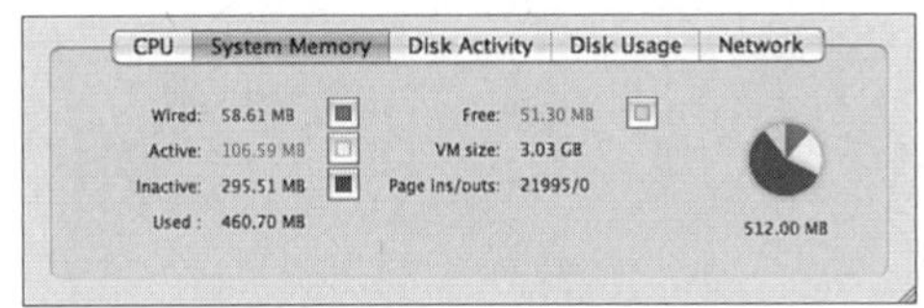

FIGURE 12.6 Monitor your system's memory usage.

Although most of the data labels should be obvious (active memory, inactive memory, total used, and so on), the Wired reading might be confusing if you've never encountered it before. Wired memory cannot be written to virtual memory and *must* remain in real memory by the system. A properly operating idle system should not display an increase in real memory over an extended period of time. If it *does*, a memory leak in a system component (such as a device driver) might be slowly eating away at your resources.

Disk Activity

The third pane, Disk Activity, tracks your disk usage—reads/writes on your drives. This pane is demonstrated in Figure 12.7.

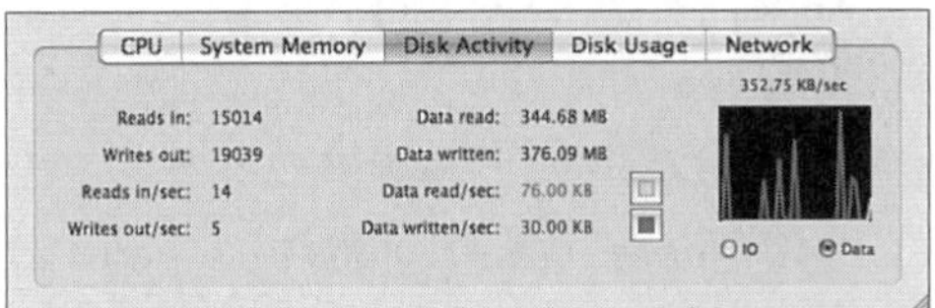

FIGURE 12.7 View the read/write activity on your local drives.

Disk Usage

The Disk Usage pane, shown in Figure 12.8, displays the amount of available free space on any of your currently mounted volumes.

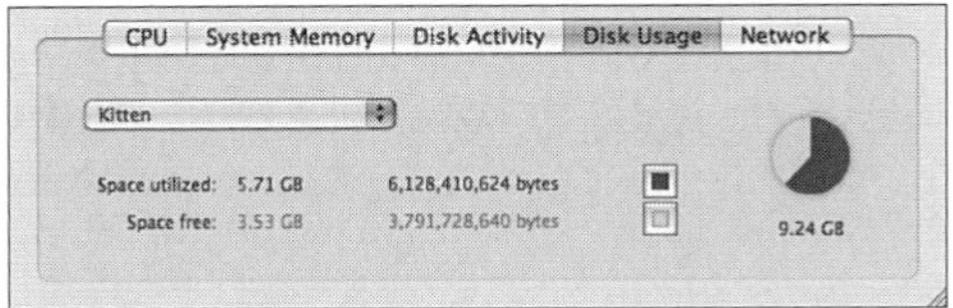

FIGURE 12.8 Monitor how much remaining space is available on your local and network volumes.

Use the pop-up menu in the Disk Usage pane to choose the drive you want to monitor.

Network

The final pane, Network, displays the amount of data and packets going in and out of your active network interfaces. Figure 12.9 shows the Network pane.

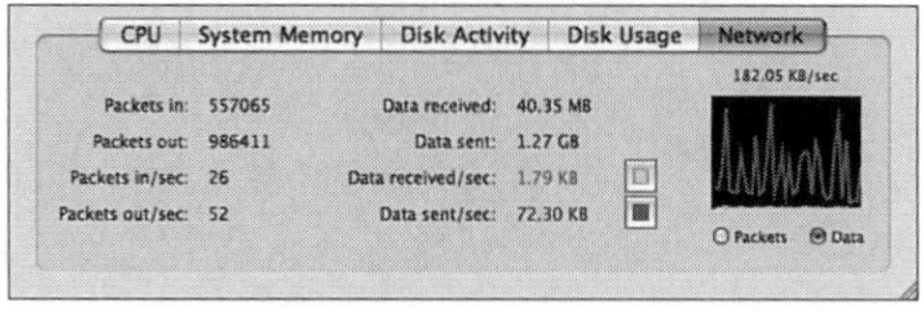

FIGURE 12.9 The Network pane can be used to monitor incoming and outgoing data.

Creating Activity Graphs

You've already seen that the Activity Monitor is capable of producing graphs to display your CPU usage, among other things. However, keeping the Activity Monitor window open to view the graphs isn't realistic if you plan to use your computer for actual work.

Thankfully, Apple provides a number of ways of displaying *some* of the information in floating windows or within the Dock icon. The View, Dock Icon menu provides access to most of these functions:

- Show CPU Usage—Displays an instantaneous view of the CPU usage.
- Show CPU History—Displays a growing graph of CPU usage over time, just like the CPU pane discussed earlier.
- Show Network Usage—Displays incoming and outgoing network traffic.
- Show Disk Activity–Graphs the read/write activity of your system drives.
- Show Memory Usage—Graphs the amount of memory used over time.
- Show Application Icon—Just shows the standard Activity Monitor icon.

If you prefer floating windows rather than a Dock icon, use the CPU Usage and CPU History options under the Window menu. These create small windows with the normal close controls and so forth.

You can also create an even *smaller* floating window that can be positioned on the menu bar or oriented horizontally or vertically by using the Window, Show Floating CPU Window submenu.

Summary

This chapter detailed some of the general concepts and commands that can be used to interact with and control the behavior of processes in Tiger. Process management and output redirection are all fundamental Unix concepts, although ones that many Unix users frequently choose to ignore. We recommend that you familiarize yourself with these ideas and commands—they are fundamental to using Unix effectively, if not to simply using it.

CHAPTER 13

Using Common Command-Line Applications and Application Suites

IN THIS CHAPTER

- Networking Applications
- Browsing the Web: `lynx`
- Mail Clients
- Text Editors
- Printing Tools
- Bridging the GUI to Command Line Gap: Hybrid Software

In the last few chapters, we covered what you need to know to get around in the command-line-based BSD environment. We also introduced you to the use of simple programs. In this chapter, we cover command-line programs with more complex interfaces. If you're from a classic Mac background, the previous chapters' small building block-type programs are probably a slightly foreign concept because most Mac applications have historically been self-contained. The Unix applications introduced in this chapter will be somewhat more familiar because they are more similar to the functionally complete programs you're used to.

Networking Applications

Many of the command-line network applications are simply textual equivalents of graphical network applications with which you're likely to already be familiar. There are command-line applications for browsing the World Wide Web, transferring files over the Internet, reading your email, and most other network functions you're familiar with. Most of these have both advantages and disadvantages with respect to their graphical counterparts.

The mouse has proven to be an efficient tool for tasks involving complex selections, and command-line applications fail in situations that would require fast and furious mousing. On the other hand, if you're using a terminal and at a command-line prompt, it's almost always faster to use a textual tool to do something quick, such as transfer a file via FTP, than it is to start a graphical client. An additional difference is that some command-line applications can function in both an interactive fashion and as a building-block program. This allows many of them to be used in shell scripts or other programs to provide their functionality to a more complex program that needs to use it.

NOTE

URLs are one of the most ubiquitous formalized ways of specifying the place a program should look for a particular network resource. You're almost certainly familiar with URLs in a practical sense—many of them look like this, for example: `http://www.apple.com/`. What you might not be aware of is that this string `http://www.apple.com/` has meaning beyond simply specifying the name of a machine, `www.apple.com`, to which software should connect. The `http://` part of the expression is also used, and specifies the connection protocol, which should be used for accessing this resource. Other connection protocols can be specified by the use of other prefixes before the machine name, such as `ftp://`.Technically, the URL actually has three parts: a protocol specifier (`http`, `ftp`, `gopher`, and so on), followed by a host specification, followed by a path, with the syntax *`<protocol>`*`://`*`<host><absolute path>`*. It is technically an error for the path to be empty, and as an absolute path, it must begin with a `/`. This means that URLs that you occasionally see as `http://www.someplace.com` are actually incorrect, and properly should be specified as `http://www.someplace.com/`. As a matter of fact, when you enter a URL that's missing the trailing `/` character into your web browser, the result is an error from the server—browsers have just been written to disguise this fact from the casual computer user. Instead of returning the top of the website directory, as you might have come to expect when using a URL such as `http://www.someplace.com`, the web server returns an error indicating that your web browser might want to try a syntactically correct URL, and your browser is obliged to try again. This costs extra load on the server, extra data transmitted, and extra time—all of which are annoying to someone at some level.

As we've pointed out previously, Unix is a particular and precise environment. Specifying `www.apple.com` as a URL to a web browser is sloppy and imprecise, and works only in certain cases in which the browser manufacturer has decided to write its software to try to compensate for poor habits on the part of the user.

A considerable amount of Unix software isn't written to support sloppy usage on the part of the user and requires that you enter complete and correct URLs, including the `http://`, or other prefix, part of the URL to function correctly.

Some recent Unix software is starting to go the route of the large browsers and support the sloppy usage without a specified protocol, but much still does not, and we don't believe this is a positive trend. We've made every effort to provide complete and correct URLs in the text here, and we hope that you'll get used to using them properly—it will eventually save you a considerable headache when you meet an application that requires you to be as precise as it is.

Browsing the Web: `lynx`

`lynx` is a command-line web client. Surprising as it might seem, many people prefer browsing the World Wide Web in a text-only application. There are, of course, many pages that simply can't be browsed without a graphics-capable application, but those pages are written by people who aren't concerned with making their information as widely available as possible and don't seem to be of interest to people who prefer to browse in text only.

NOTE

There's a reasonable chance that lynx isn't installed on your system. It's currently not distributed by Apple. It's a favorite, however, among command-line aficionados, so you might find it already installed at work or school. We're going to use it for a few things later in the chapter, so if you don't have it, you'll be installing it in Chapter 14, "Command-Line Software Installation and Troubleshooting." The install we do for lynx will be of the easiest possible command-line install style, so you might even want to flip forward a few pages and do the install now.

The basic syntax of `lynx` is `lynx <URL>`. This gives you a textual representation of the page and a few lines of prompting information as to what you can do from there. For example, looking at `http://www.apple.com/`, `lynx` produces the following output:

```
[ryoohki:~] sage% lynx http://www.apple.com/

#                                                                       Apple

   #home index

   Apple The Apple Store iPod+iTunes .Mac QuickTime Apple Support Mac OS X
   Hot News Switch Hardware Software Made4Mac Education Pro business
   Developer Where to Buy

   Our hearts reach out to those hurt by the Indian Ocean tsunamis.

   Help survivors and their families by making monetary donations to these
   organizations:
     * American Red Cross International Response Fund
     * AmeriCares South Asia Earthquake Relief Fund
     * CARE USA Asia Quake Disaster
     * Direct Relief International International Assistance Fund
     * M?decins Sans Fronti?res International Tsunami Emergency Appeal
     * Oxfam Asian Earthquake & Tsunami Fund
     * Sarvodaya Relief Fund for Tsunami Tragedy
     * Save the Children Asia Earthquake/Tsunami Relief Fund
     * SEVA South Asia Emergency Fund
     * UNICEF South Asia Tsunami Relief Efforts
     * World Food Programme Tsunami Disaster Appeal

   United States Agency for International Development Donate to the
   International Response Fund Support South Asia Tsunami Relief Efforts
   Information resource for the humanitarian relief community
```

```
     * Important Safety Recall -- Rechargeable Battery for 15-inch
       PowerBook G4
     * Expanded iBook Logic Board Repair Extension Program (12/17/2004)

   _________________________ Search
   Site Map ¦ Search Tips

   Visit the Apple Store online or at retail locations.
   1-800-MY-APPLE

   Find Job Opportunities at Apple.
   Visit other Apple sites around the world:
   [Choose...____]

   Contact Us ¦ Terms of Use ¦ Privacy Policy

   Copyright ? 2005 Apple Computer, Inc. All rights reserved.

   Powered by MacOSXServer

(NORMAL LINK)   Use right-arrow or <return> to activate.
  Arrow keys: Up and Down to move.  Right to follow a link; Left to go back.
 H)elp O)ptions P)rint G)o M)ain screen Q)uit /=search [delete]=history list
```

Not bad, it's useable, and it sure loads faster than all those fancy graphics if you've got a slow connection!

If you want to move down the page, you can press the spacebar. Use the up- and down-arrow keys to move from link to link. Use the right-arrow key or press the Return key to select a link. The right-arrow and left-arrow keys take you, somewhat predictably, to the target of the currently selected link or back to the previous page. As you might have noticed, some of the comments we have made here appear at the bottom of the screen output. As you use `lynx`, it provides helpful hints on what you might want to do. These appear near the bottom of the screen and contain helpful information, such as how to enter text in a text entry field or move to the next page by using the spacebar.

TIP

I mentioned that `lynx` provides helpful hints on what to do because a significant amount of human-computer-interface research indicates that, to many people, omnipresent onscreen help is almost invisible. Keep your eye on the onscreen hints—even if it's not the best user interface design, it is there to help, and it's a lot faster than searching the help pages.

Because you don't have a mouse and cursor with which to navigate pages being displayed in `lynx`, a number of keyboard commands are available to perform various actions. Table 13.1 shows common one-key commands within `lynx`.

TABLE 13.1 Common One-Key Commands Within the lynx Interactive Web Browser

Key	Action
+	Move up the page.
-	Move down the page.
b	Move up the page.
<space bar>	Move down the page.
<right arrow>, <return>	Go to selected link.
<left arrow>	Go back.
<up arrow>	Select previous link, downloadable element, or form field.
<down arrow>	Select next link, downloadable element, or form field.
d	Download the target of the currently selected link or downloadable element.
H	Go to the lynx help pages. These pages are implemented as HTML pages, so you can go forward and back in them with the forward and back arrows.
O	Go to the lynx Options page. Here you can set an assortment of internal parameters such as where your lynx bookmarks are stored.
P	Print the current page.
G	Go to a new URL.
M	Go back to the Main page, by which lynx means the page that you first started on.
Q	Quit the program.
/	Search in the page.
<delete>	Show the history for the current browser window.

A veritable plethora of additional one-key options are explained in the lynx help, under the Key-stroke Commands heading.

The lynx browser also sports a wide range of command-line options that enable or modify advanced behaviors. These include items such as sending the data to STDOUT and collecting a list of the URLs contained in the document.

Finally, it should be mentioned that lynx, like much Unix software, works great as a command-line building-block utility. Ever wanted to process the contents of a web page, perhaps to do something such as collect all the links from someone's page of interesting links, without having to dig through the source by hand? Using the -dump option causes lynx to send the target document of the URL to STDOUT, followed by a list of the URLs in the document. For example, if you wanted to collect a list of URLs to the files available on http://www.macosxunleashed.com/ (specifically, the stuff in the downloads subdirectory), you could use lynx like this:

```
[ryoohki:~/downloads] sage% lynx -dump http://www.macosxunleashed.com/downloads/

                                Index of /downloads

     * [1]Parent Directory
```

```
    * [2]26FIG112.gif
    * [3]26FIG133.gif
    * [4]CGvirusscan.tgz
    * [5]Python-2.2.tgz
    * [6]addme.c
    * [7]appendix.pdf
    * [8]arpwatch.tar.Z
    * [9]clref.pdf
    * [10]cupsomatic
    * [11]file
    * [12]gdbm-1.8.0.tar.gz
    * [13]ispell-3.1.20.tar.gz
    * [14]ispell-english.zip
    * [15]jpegsrc.v6b.tar.gz
    * [16]libpng-1.0.10.tar.gz
    * [17]logsentry-1.1.1.tar
    * [18]lynx.1
    * [19]lynx.10_1.gz
    * [20]lynx.cfg
    * [21]lynx.gz
    * [22]majora.tar.gz
    * [23]netpbm-9.12.tgz
    * [24]nmap-2.54BETA25.tar.gz
    * [25]page1440.pdf
    * [26]parallel
    * [27]pine4.43.tar.Z
    * [28]portsentry-1.0.tar.gz
    * [29]portsentry-2.0b1.tar.gz
    * [30]postpipe
    * [31]serial
    * [32]serial-darwin
    * [33]spell-1.0.tar.gz
    * [34]termcap-1.3.tar.gz
    * [35]unleashed.jpg


   Apache/1.3.33 Server at www.macosxunleashed.com Port 80

References

   1. http://www.macosxunleashed.com/
   2. http://www.macosxunleashed.com/downloads/26FIG112.gif
   3. http://www.macosxunleashed.com/downloads/26FIG133.gif
   4. http://www.macosxunleashed.com/downloads/CGvirusscan.tgz
   5. http://www.macosxunleashed.com/downloads/Python-2.2.tgz
```

```
  6. http://www.macosxunleashed.com/downloads/addme.c
  7. http://www.macosxunleashed.com/downloads/appendix.pdf
  8. http://www.macosxunleashed.com/downloads/arpwatch.tar.Z
  9. http://www.macosxunleashed.com/downloads/clref.pdf
 10. http://www.macosxunleashed.com/downloads/cupsomatic
 11. http://www.macosxunleashed.com/downloads/file
 12. http://www.macosxunleashed.com/downloads/gdbm-1.8.0.tar.gz
 13. http://www.macosxunleashed.com/downloads/ispell-3.1.20.tar.gz
 14. http://www.macosxunleashed.com/downloads/ispell-english.zip
 15. http://www.macosxunleashed.com/downloads/jpegsrc.v6b.tar.gz
 16. http://www.macosxunleashed.com/downloads/libpng-1.0.10.tar.gz
 17. http://www.macosxunleashed.com/downloads/logsentry-1.1.1.tar
 18. http://www.macosxunleashed.com/downloads/lynx.1
 19. http://www.macosxunleashed.com/downloads/lynx.10_1.gz
 20. http://www.macosxunleashed.com/downloads/lynx.cfg
 21. http://www.macosxunleashed.com/downloads/lynx.gz
 22. http://www.macosxunleashed.com/downloads/majora.tar.gz
 23. http://www.macosxunleashed.com/downloads/netpbm-9.12.tgz
 24. http://www.macosxunleashed.com/downloads/nmap-2.54BETA25.tar.gz
 25. http://www.macosxunleashed.com/downloads/page1440.pdf
 26. http://www.macosxunleashed.com/downloads/parallel
 27. http://www.macosxunleashed.com/downloads/pine4.43.tar.Z
 28. http://www.macosxunleashed.com/downloads/portsentry-1.0.tar.gz
 29. http://www.macosxunleashed.com/downloads/portsentry-2.0b1.tar.gz
 30. http://www.macosxunleashed.com/downloads/postpipe
 31. http://www.macosxunleashed.com/downloads/serial
 32. http://www.macosxunleashed.com/downloads/serial-darwin
 33. http://www.macosxunleashed.com/downloads/spell-1.0.tar.gz
 34. http://www.macosxunleashed.com/downloads/termcap-1.3.tar.gz
 35. http://www.macosxunleashed.com/downloads/unleashed.jpg
```

If you wanted to parse just the URLs out of this output, you could simply run **lynx** and pipe the output though grep looking for URL patterns. Something like `lynx -dump http://www.macosxunleashed.com/downloads/ | grep "http:"` will produce the following output:

```
[ryoohki:~ downloads] sage% lynx -dump
➥http://www.macosxunleashed.com/downloads/ | grep "http:"
  1. http://www.macosxunleashed.com/
  2. http://www.macosxunleashed.com/downloads/26FIG112.gif
  3. http://www.macosxunleashed.com/downloads/26FIG133.gif
  4. http://www.macosxunleashed.com/downloads/CGvirusscan.tgz
  5. http://www.macosxunleashed.com/downloads/Python-2.2.tgz
  6. http://www.macosxunleashed.com/downloads/addme.c
  7. http://www.macosxunleashed.com/downloads/appendix.pdf
  8. http://www.macosxunleashed.com/downloads/arpwatch.tar.Z
```

```
 9. http://www.macosxunleashed.com/downloads/clref.pdf
10. http://www.macosxunleashed.com/downloads/cupsomatic
11. http://www.macosxunleashed.com/downloads/file
12. http://www.macosxunleashed.com/downloads/gdbm-1.8.0.tar.gz
13. http://www.macosxunleashed.com/downloads/ispell-3.1.20.tar.gz
14. http://www.macosxunleashed.com/downloads/ispell-english.zip
15. http://www.macosxunleashed.com/downloads/jpegsrc.v6b.tar.gz
16. http://www.macosxunleashed.com/downloads/libpng-1.0.10.tar.gz
17. http://www.macosxunleashed.com/downloads/logsentry-1.1.1.tar
18. http://www.macosxunleashed.com/downloads/lynx.1
19. http://www.macosxunleashed.com/downloads/lynx.10_1.gz
20. http://www.macosxunleashed.com/downloads/lynx.cfg
21. http://www.macosxunleashed.com/downloads/lynx.gz
22. http://www.macosxunleashed.com/downloads/majora.tar.gz
23. http://www.macosxunleashed.com/downloads/netpbm-9.12.tgz
24. http://www.macosxunleashed.com/downloads/nmap-2.54BETA25.tar.gz
25. http://www.macosxunleashed.com/downloads/page1440.pdf
26. http://www.macosxunleashed.com/downloads/parallel
27. http://www.macosxunleashed.com/downloads/pine4.43.tar.Z
28. http://www.macosxunleashed.com/downloads/portsentry-1.0.tar.gz
29. http://www.macosxunleashed.com/downloads/portsentry-2.0b1.tar.gz
30. http://www.macosxunleashed.com/downloads/postpipe
31. http://www.macosxunleashed.com/downloads/serial
32. http://www.macosxunleashed.com/downloads/serial-darwin
33. http://www.macosxunleashed.com/downloads/spell-1.0.tar.gz
34. http://www.macosxunleashed.com/downloads/termcap-1.3.tar.gz
35. http://www.macosxunleashed.com/downloads/unleashed.jpg
```

The `-dump` option turns out to be useful for doing things that don't relate to processing the URLs as well, such as downloading files from FTP or HTTPD servers. You see examples of this use of `lynx` during the software installs in Chapter 14. Table 13.2 shows the `lynx` syntax and most interesting options.

TABLE 13.2 The Command Documentation Table for `lynx`

`lynx`	Textual web browser
`lynx [options] [`<*file*>`]`	
You can find out which options are available by running `lynx -help`. Here is the listing of command-line options for the current version of `lynx`:	
`-`	Receive options and arguments from `STDIN`.
`-accept_all_cookies`	Accept cookies without prompting if `Set-Cookie` handling is on (off).
`-auth=`<*id*>`:`<*pw*>	Authentication information for protected documents.
`-base`	Prepend a request URL comment and BASE tag to `text/html` for `-source` dumps.
`-book`	Use the bookmark page as the start file (off).

TABLE 13.2 Continued

-cache=<NUMBER>	<NUMBER> of documents cached in memory.
-cfg=<FILENAME>	Specify a lynx.cfg file other than the default.
-cmd_log=<FILENAME>	Log keystroke commands to the given file.
-cmd_script=<FILENAME>	Read keystroke commands from the given file.
-connect_timeout=<N>	Set the <N>-second connection timeout (18000).
-cookie_file=<FILENAME>	Specify a file to use to read cookies.
-cookie_save_file=<FILENAME>	Specify a file to use to store cookies.
-cookies	Toggle handling of Set-Cookie headers (on).
-core	Toggle forced core dumps on fatal errors (off).
-crawl	With -traversal, output each page to a file. With -dump, format output as with -traversal, but to STDOUT.
-dont_wrap_pre	Inhibit wrapping of text in <pre> when -dumping and -crawling, mark wrapped lines in interactive session (off).
-dump	Dump the first file to STDOUT and exit.
-from	Toggle transmission of From headers (on).
-get_data	User data for get forms, read from STDIN, terminated by '---' on a line.
-help	Print this usage message.
-homepage=<URL>	Set home page separate from start page.
-image_links	Toggles inclusion of links for all images (off).
-index=<URL>	Set the default index file to <URL>.
-localhost	Disable URLs that point to remote hosts (off).
-mime_header	Include MIME headers and force source dump.
-nobold	Disable bold video attribute.
-nobrowse	Disable directory browsing.
-nocolor	Turn off color support.
-nofilereferer	Disable transmission of referer headers for file URLs (on).
-nolist	Disable the link list feature in dumps (off).
-noredir	Don't follow Location: redirection (off).
-noreferer	Disable transmission of referer headers (off).
-noreverse	Disable reverse video attribute.
-nostatus	Disable the miscellaneous information messages (off).
-nounderline	Disable underline video attribute.
-number_fields	Force numbering of links as well as form input fields (off).
-number_links	Force numbering of links (off).
-pauth=<id>:<pw>	Authentication information for protected proxy server.
-popup	Toggle handling of single-choice SELECT options via pop-up windows or as lists of radio buttons (off).
-post_data	User data for post forms, read from STDIN, terminated by '---' on a line.
-pseudo_inlines	Toggle pseudo-ALTs for inlines with no ALT string (on).
-realm	Restrict access to URLs in the starting realm (off).
-reload	Flush the cache on a proxy server (only the first document affected) (off).

13

TABLE 13.2 Continued

`-source`	Dump the source of the first file to `STDOUT` and exit.
`-traversal`	Traverse all HTTP links derived from start file.
`-useragent=<Name>`	Set alternative Lynx User-Agent header.
`-verbose`	Toggle `[LINK]`, `[IMAGE]`, and `[INLINE]` comments with filenames of these images (on).
`-width=<Number>`	Screen width for formatting of dumps (default is 80).
`-with_backspaces`	Omit backspaces in output if `-dumping` or `-crawling` (like `man` does) (off).

Accessing FTP Servers: `ftp`

`ftp` is the command name for the program that implements the FTP protocol (creative, no?). On the Macintosh, the `Anarchie` and `Fetch` programs have historically been the FTP clients of preference, and both of these provide features sadly lacking in the default command-line `ftp` interface. The command-line interface, however, is again a quick and convenient way to get or put a file or three without needing to launch a graphical client. It also tends to be better for diagnosis purposes when an FTP transfer fails or when a file can't be found. All the messages from the server can be seen immediately and are directly in response to the commands you issue, so if something's wrong, it's much clearer at what point it went that way.

To connect to a remote site using `ftp`, simply issue the command as **`ftp <ftp site>`**. Presuming that all goes well, this command connects you to the remote site and requests your user ID and password. If you're trying to connect to a public site, the default guest user ID is `anonymous`. After that, the site asks you for a password, which if you're connecting as an anonymous user, should be given as your email address. Responding properly to both these queries (`anonymous` and your email address or your correct user ID and password) takes you to an internal prompt in the `ftp` program from which you can traverse the site's directories and upload or download files.

Following is a sample of what you might see after connecting to a site that doesn't really want you there. This sort of information is largely hidden in the graphical FTP clients, frequently leaving you clicking Retry indefinitely; in reality, the site is trying to give you some helpful information.

```
[ryoohki:~/downloads] sage% ftp ftp.cis.ohio-state.edu
Connected to www.cis.ohio-state.edu.
220 www.cis.ohio-state.edu FTP server (Version wu-2.6.1(1)
Tue Nov 6 12:29:49 EST 2001) ready.

Name (ftp.cis.ohio-state.edu:sage): anonymous
331 Guest login ok, send your complete e-mail address as password.
Password:
530-Sorry, the limit of 30 users logged in has been exceeded (30).
530-We've had to cut back to avoid swamping our outside link.
```

```
530-
530-Please try again later.
530-
530-To report problems, please contact ftp@cis.ohio-state.edu.
530 Login incorrect.
```

And this is an example of what you might see if you have connected properly:

```
[ryoohki:~ downloads] sage% ftp ftp.cis.ohio-state.edu
Connected to www.cis.ohio-state.edu.
220 www.cse.ohio-state.edu FTP server (Version wu-2.6.1(1)
➥Tue Nov 6 12:29:49 EST 2001) ready.
Name (ftp.cis.ohio-state.edu:sage): anonymous
331 Guest login ok, send your complete e-mail address as password.
Password:
230-Hello [unknown]@ryoohki.biosci.ohio-state.edu.
230-
230-This is the anonymous FTP archive of the Computer and Information
230-Science Department and The Ohio State University.
230-
230-You are user 3 out of 30 users currently allowed in.
230-
230-This FTP server is running on a Sun Enterprise 2, with approximately
230-10GB of disk space.  The directory space was recently reorganized
230-and cleaned.
230-
230-Mirrors of other sites are in /mirror
230-Everything else is in /pub
230-
230-Please report any problems to ftp@cis.ohio-state.edu
230-
230 Guest login ok, access restrictions apply.
Remote system type is UNIX.
Using binary mode to transfer files.
ftp>
```

NOTE

If you attempt to access these servers and get different results, don't be alarmed. These are simply examples of various results that can occur, and your results might be different depending on when you connect, where you're connecting from, and whether the site has changed its configuration since these dialogs were captured.

From this `ftp>` prompt, you can issue commands, such as `help`, `rhelp`, `get`, `put`, `cd`, `ls`, `pwd`, and potentially others, depending on the server configuration. The output from the help command gives you a list of commands available to you in your client (don't worry if this looks like a long list; we cover the good ones in the text that follows), and the output of rhelp tells you about commands on the server:

```
ftp> help
Commands may be abbreviated.  Commands are:

!               features        mls             prompt          site
$               fget            mlsd            proxy           size
account         form            mlst            put             sndbuf
append          ftp             mode            pwd             status
ascii           gate            modtime         quit            struct
bell            get             more            quote           sunique
binary          glob            mput            rate            system
bye             hash            mreget          rcvbuf          tenex
case            help            msend           recv            throttle
cd              idle            newer           reget           trace
cdup            image           nlist           remopts         type
chmod           lcd             nmap            rename          umask
close           less            ntrans          reset           unset
cr              lpage           open            restart         usage
debug           lpwd            page            rhelp           user
delete          ls              passive         rmdir           verbose
dir             macdef          pdir            rstatus         xferbuf
disconnect      mdelete         pls             runique         ?
edit            mdir            pmlsd           send
epsv4           mget            preserve        sendport
exit            mkdir           progress        set

ftp> rhelp
214-The following commands are recognized (* =>'s unimplemented).
   USER    PORT    STOR    MSAM*   RNTO    NLST    MKD     CDUP
   PASS    PASV    APPE    MRSQ*   ABOR    SITE    XMKD    XCUP
   ACCT*   TYPE    MLFL*   MRCP*   DELE    SYST    RMD     STOU
   SMNT*   STRU    MAIL*   ALLO    CWD     STAT    XRMD    SIZE
   REIN*   MODE    MSND*   REST    XCWD    HELP    PWD     MDTM
   QUIT    RETR    MSOM*   RNFR    LIST    NOOP    XPWD
214 Direct comments to ftp@cis.ohio-state.edu.
```

Usually, the commands you'll be most interested in are the ones for moving around the filesystem, and for retrieving and sending files. The commands you're most likely to use frequently are the cd and lcd commands (which are analogous to the command-line cd command for the remote and local directories, respectively) and the get and put commands (which retrieve files from the server and send files to it).

Additionally, you can ask for help on specific commands—one of the more interesting ones to ask about in the listing shown is the site command:

```
ftp> rhelp site
214-The following SITE commands are recognized (* =>'s unimplemented).
   UMASK           GROUP           INDEX           GROUPS
   IDLE            GPASS           EXEC            CHECKMETHOD
   CHMOD           NEWER           ALIAS           CHECKSUM
   HELP            MINFO           CDPATH
214 Direct comments to ftp@cis.ohio-state.edu.
```

The site command implements FTP-site-specific command options. You would need to contact the administrator to find out exactly what the command options are and which ones you are allowed to use.

Files that you get from the FTP server are placed into the same directory from which you issued the ftp command unless you specify otherwise by giving a download path along with the get command at the prompt.

An advantage of the ftp client included with Mac OS X is that you can eliminate some of the uses of cd and ls to navigate to where you want to be in the ftp tree simply by issuing the ftp command with a complete URL. For example, to get the gdb-6.3.tar.gz file at ftp.cis.ohio-state.edu, you could navigate the FTP site to get to the file or you could issue this ftp command:

```
ftp ftp://ftp.cis.ohio-state.edu/pub/gnu/gdb/gdb-6.3.tar.gz
```

Table 13.3 shows the syntax and most interesting options for ftp.

TABLE 13.3 The ftp Command Syntax and Useful Options

ftp	File transfer program.

```
ftp [-46AadefginpRtvV] [-N <netrc>] [-o <outfile>] [-P <port>] [-r <seconds>]
[-T <dir>,<max>[,<inc>][[<user>@]<host> [<port>]]] [<host>:<path>[/]]
[file:///<file>] [ftp://[<user>[:<pass>]@]<host>[:<port>]/<path>[/]]
[http://[<user>[:<pass>]@]<host>[:<port>]/<path>] [...]
ftp -u <url> <file> [...]
```

The remote host with which ftp is to communicate can be specified on the command line. Done this way, ftp immediately tries to establish a connection with the remote host. Otherwise, ftp enters its command interpreter mode, awaits commands from the user, and displays the prompt ftp>.

Option	Description
-A	Forces active mode ftp. By default, ftp tries to use passive mode ftp and falls back to active mode if passive mode is not supported by the server.
-a	Causes ftp to bypass normal login procedure and use an anonymous login instead.
-f	Forces a cache reload for transfers that go through the FTP or HTTP proxies.
-g	Disables filename *globbing* (that is to say, it doesn't allow wildcard filename expansions).
-i	Turns off interactive mode when transferring multiple files.

TABLE 13.3 Continued

`-n`	Does not attempt auto-login on initial connection. If auto-login is not disabled, `ftp` checks for a `.netrc` file in the user's directory for an entry describing an account on the remote machine. If no entry is available, `ftp` prompts for the login name on the remote machine (defaults to the login name on the local machine), and if necessary, prompts for a password.
`-p`	Enables passive mode operation for use behind connection filtering firewalls. This option has been deprecated because `ftp` now tries to use passive mode by default, falling back to active mode if the server does not support passive connections.
`-v`	Enables verbose and progress. Default if output is to a terminal (and for progress, if `ftp` is in the foreground). Shows all responses from the remote server as well as transfer statistics.
`-V`	Disables verbose and progress, overriding the default of enabled when output is to a terminal.
`-o` *<output>*	When auto-fetching files, saves the contents in `output`. If `output` is not `-` or doesn't start with `¦`, only the first file specified is retrieved into `output`; all other files are retrieved into the basename of their remote name.
`-P` *<port>*	Sets the port number to *<port>*.
`-r` *<seconds>*	Retries the connection attempt if it failed, pausing for *<seconds>* seconds. Please be kind to the FTP servers and don't set this to a value smaller than 20 seconds or so—larger would be better.
`-T` *<direction>*,*<maximum>* [,*<increment>*]	Sets the maximum transfer rate for *<direction>* to *<maximum>* bytes/second, and if specified, the *<increment>* to *<increment>* bytes/second.
`-u` *<url>* *<file>*	Uploads files on the command line to *<url>* where *<url>* is one of the `ftp` URL types as supported by auto-fetch (with an optional target filename for one-file uploads), and *<file>* is one or more local files to be uploaded.

When `ftp` is in its command interpreter mode awaiting instructions from the user, there are many commands that the user might issue. Some of them include

`ascii`	Sets the file transfer type to network `ASCII`. Although this is supposed to be the default, it is not uncommon for an FTP server to indicate that `binary` is its default.
`binary`	Sets the file transfer type to support binary image transfer.
`image`	Same as `binary`.
`quit`	Terminates the `ftp` session and exits `ftp`. An end of file also terminates the session and exits.
`cd` *<remote_directory>*	Changes the current working directory on the remote host to *<remote_directory>*.
`cdup`	Changes the current working directory on the remote host to the parent directory (same as `cd ../`)

TABLE 13.3 Continued

lcd <*directory*>	Changes the working directory on the local machine. If no directory is specified, the user's home directory is used.
close	Terminates the ftp session with the remote host and returns to the command interpreter.
dir [<*remote-directory*> [<*local_file*>]]	Prints a listing of the directory on the remote machine. Most Unix systems produce an ls -l output. If <*remote_directory*> is not specified, the current directory is assumed. If <*local_file*> is not specified or is -, the output is sent to the terminal.
open <*hostname*> [<*port*>]	Attempts to establish an ftp connection on <*hostname*> at <*port*>, if <*port*> is specified.
glob	Toggles filename expansion for mdelete, mget, and mput. If globbing is turned off, filename arguments are taken literally and not expanded.
delete <*remote_file*>	Deletes the specified <*remote_file*> on the remote machine.
mdelete <*remote_files*>	Deletes the specified <*remote_files*> on the remote machine.
get <*remote_file*> [<*local-file*>]	Downloads <*remote_file*> from the remote machine to the local machine. If <*local_file*> is not specified, the file is also saved on the local machine with the name <*remote_file*>.
mget <*remote_files*>	Downloads the specified <*remote_files*>.
put <*local_file*> [<*remote_file*>]	Uploads the specified <*local_file*> to the remote host. If <*remote_file*> is not specified, the file is saved on the remote host with the name <*local_file*>.
mput <*local_files*>	Uploads the specified <*local_files*>.
help [<*command*>]	Displays a message describing <*command*>. If <*command*> is not specified, a listing of known commands is displayed.
ls [<*remote_directory*> [<*local_file*>]]	Prints a list of the files in a directory on the remote machine. If <*remote_directory*> is not specified, the current working directory is assumed.If <*local_file*> is not specified or is -, the output is printed to a terminal. Note that if nothing is listed, the directory might have only directories in it. Try ls -l or dir for a complete listing.
mkdir <*directory*>	Makes the specified <*directory*> on the remote machine.
rmdir <*directory*>	Removes the specified <*directory*> from the remote machine.
passive [auto]	Toggles passive mode if no argument is given. If auto is given, acts as if FTPMODE is set to auto. If passive mode is turned on (default), the ftp client sends a PASV command for data connections rather than a PORT command. PASV command requests that the remote server open a port for the data connection and return the address of that port. The remote server listens on that port, and the client then sends data to it. With the PORT command, the client listens on a port and sends that address to the remote host, who connects back to it. Passive mode is useful when FTPing through a firewall. Not all ftp servers are required to support passive mode.

TABLE 13.3 Continued

`progress`	Displays a status bar indicating the progress of each transfer as it occurs. Seeing that something is actually happening can be a real comfort when doing large transfers over slow lines.
`pwd`	Prints the current working directory on the remote host.
`rate <direction> [<maximum> [<increment>]]`	Throttles the maximum transfer rate to *<maximum>* bytes/second. If *<maximum>* is `0`, disables the throttle. Not yet implemented for `ascii` mode. *<direction>* may be any one of these: `get` (incoming transfers), `put` (outgoing transfers), or `all` (both). *<maximum>* can be modified on the fly by *<increment>* bytes (default: `1024`) each time a given signal is received: `SIGUSR1` (increments *<maximum>* by *<increment>* bytes, `SIGUSR2` (decrements *<maximum>* by *<increment>* bytes. The result must be a positive number). If *<maximum>* is not supplied, displays current throttle rates.

Terminals in Terminals: `telnet`, `rlogin`, `ssh`

Because one of the primary methods for interacting with a Unix machine that you're sitting in front of is via a textual terminal, it should come as no surprise that a number of network tools are available to allow you to access remote machines through that same interface. The three primary examples of these are the `telnet`, `rlogin`, and `ssh`/`slogin` (secure shell) clients. Each of these provides a connection to a remote machine that is analogous to the one that `Terminal.app` provides to your local machine—you get access to a command prompt and can run software on the remote machine just like software in `Terminal.app` on the local machine.

The `telnet` Program

`telnet` is a venerable connection program that speaks a language compatible with the over-the-wire communication protocol used by many Internet services. The protocol is a fundamental building block of much of the Internet and has been used to provide everything from web services to file transfer services to terminal services. It is, unfortunately, as trivial as it is ubiquitous and provides almost no built-in security. Because of this, terminal services implemented directly in the protocol are inherently insecure, and the `telnet` client and server fall into this category.

The syntax of the `telnet` command is `telnet` *`<host>`* *`[port number]`*.

If you're communicating with a system that's either not connected to the Internet or run by a particularly non-security-conscious system administrator, you might actually be able to use it as a terminal application. In that case, if you issue the `telnet` command, you might see something like the following:

```
ryoohki:~ sage$ telnet krpan.killernuts.org
Trying 192.168.1.10...
```

```
Connected to krpan.killernuts.org (192.168.1.10).
Escape character is '^]'.

Red Hat Linux release 7.0 (Guinness)
Kernel 2.4.2 on a 2-processor i686
login: adam
Password:
Last login: Thu Apr 19 19:36:23 on vc/1
You have mail.

Terminal: vt100.
Printer set to newsioux

krpan adam %
```


At that point, you're at a shell prompt on the remote machine and can interact with it just as you interact with your local machine via its shell prompt in the terminal.

NOTE

Don't expect to actually be able to `telnet` to `krpan.killernuts.org` to test this. We don't know any system administrators who leave `telnet` available on their machine, and we had to enable it specifically for the example.

If everyone you know is concerned about security and has their `telnet` daemons disabled, there are still a number of interesting uses for the `telnet` client. Because many servers for other Internet applications speak the same protocol, you can use the `telnet` protocol to talk to them as well. It might not seem like a useful idea to be able to talk to a web server with a terminal program that doesn't understand anything about the HTTP language and can't display the data properly, but it turns out to have a number of interesting applications.

For example, your web browser tells you that a server isn't responding—can you tell whether it's the web server software that's not responding or the machine that hosts it that's not responding? `telnet` to the HTTP port (port 80) on the server, and see what the response is. If the web server software and machine are both okay, your session should look something like this:

```
ryoohki:~ sage$ telnet www.biosci.ohio-state.edu 80
Trying 140.254.12.240...
Connected to ryoko.biosci.ohio-state.edu.
Escape character is '^]'.
```

If the machine is okay, but the web server software isn't speaking, the session might instead look more like this:

```
ryoohki:~ sage$ telnet rosalyn.biosci.ohio-state.edu 80
Trying 140.254.12.151...
```

```
telnet: connect to address 140.254.12.151: Connection refused
telnet: Unable to connect to remote host
```

If the machine is completely absent from the network, such as `catbert` in the following example, the response gets only to the `Trying` line and hangs there, well, trying—I pressed Ctrl-C in the example to convince it to give up.

```
ryoohki:~ sage$ telnet catbert.biosci.ohio-state.edu 80
Trying 140.254.12.236...
^C
```

Finally, if there really isn't a machine by that name at all, you'll see

```
ryoohki:~ sage$ telnet dingbat.biosci.ohio-state.edu 80
dingbat.biosci.ohio-state.edu: No address associated with nodename
```

CAUTION

Please don't use the `telnet` program as a terminal program unless you are connecting to a machine that has no connection to the Internet. The program transfers all data in plain text, and anyone with physical access to any of the communication hardware involved in the connection (such as the phone lines, ethernet wiring, or the air [if you're using AirPort]) can read everything you type, including user IDs and passwords out of the data stream. There are better alternatives that we'll cover shortly.

The `rlogin` Program

Whereas the `telnet` communication package was conceived with hardly any concern for security, the `rlogin` communications package was developed under the seemingly quaint notion that certain connections could be trusted, based only on their self-proclaimed credentials. Passing its data using the same unprotected protocol as `telnet`, `rlogin` is supposed to give the administrator some confidence in the identity of a connecting visitor by virtue of the fact that the connection came from a trusted port. Using it is similar to `telnet`, except that it doesn't accept an optional connection port and it automatically fills in your user ID on the remote system based on your local system user ID. The syntax is simply `rlogin <remotehost>`.

NOTE

A long, long time ago, in a decade almost two removed, the Internet and the perceptions regarding users who could connect to it were very different. Along with the lack of `this.dot.that.dot.coms` all over the place and the lack of spam in your email, Unix was an expensive commercial operating system. Machines that ran it were expensive, and the people who ran them, even people on different ends of the earth who had never met each other, thought of each other as fellow members of a professional fraternity. Professional courtesies were extended, and if you were a system administrator, a concern about another's security was the same as a concern about your own security.

Because of this expectation that any person running a Unix machine was another security-conscious professional, early security measures were based on utilizing this trust as a form of security credential. Security-conscious professionals were as worried about allowing security risks on others' machines as incurring security risks on their own. A security-conscious professional would never let a "bad" user use his system. The only people who could connect using the `rlogin` client were users on some Unix machine somewhere. Taken together, any user with valid credentials on a Unix machine, verified by their being allowed to run the `rlogin` program, must, by association, be a trustable user.

Taken in the context of today's rampant attacks against system security, this might sound like a naively bad security method, but until the advent of "personal Unixes" such as Linux, it worked surprisingly well. Given that much of today's data is passed around with equally insecure connections, without even a trust-based attempt to verify the authenticity of the content, we probably shouldn't poke too much fun at the naiveté of the early communication packages.

As you are coming into the world of having your own personal Unix machine connected to the Internet, we encourage you to adopt some of the historic notions regarding administrator responsibility and fraternity, but not their naive notions regarding security.

As with the `telnet` program, if you're connecting to machines that aren't connected to the Internet, the `rlogin` client is just as good as any. If you're connecting to machines that are connected to the Internet, please don't use the `rlogin` program, even if the remote machine makes it available. Doing so only risks your accounts and data on both local and remote machines, and the security of both machines as well.

The Secure Shell Software Suite: `slogin/ssh`, `scp`, `sftp` and Others

The Secure Shell collection of programs provides strongly encrypted communications between your machine and a remote server. The implementation that Apple has chosen to provide is based on the OpenSSH (`http://www.openssh.org/`) distribution of the protocols. The protocol requires both client software, which we cover in this chapter, and server software, which is covered in Chapter 21, "Accessing and Controlling Tiger Remotely." Here, we assume that you already have a server to talk to and detail the use of the client software on the Unix side of your Mac OS X machine to talk to your remote server.

`slogin` The starting point for use of the Secure Shell client is the `slogin` (also available under the name `ssh`) program. This program replaces the functionality of the `telnet` and `rlogin` programs and provides some additional capabilities as well. Unlike `telnet` and `rlogin`, `slogin` passes all information between the machines as encrypted data, using a public-key encryption method.

NOTE

Public-key encryption is a clever method of encrypting data. Basically, in public-key encryption schemes, every person interested in exchanging encrypted information creates two keys. One of the created keys is the person's private key and the other is the person's public key. These keys are mathematically related, but one cannot be derived from the other. The cleverness resides in the mathematical relationship between the keys.

When you encrypt data, you encrypt it using two keys: your private key and the public key of the message's intended recipient. The keys are related in such a fashion that data encrypted with your private key, and another's public key, can be decrypted only with a combination of your public key and the other person's private key. This encryption method is used in both systems such as the PGP (Pretty Good Privacy) email encryption software and in data transmission software such as `ssh`. In email encryption, you use your private key and the email recipient's public key to encrypt mail destined for them, and the recipient uses your public key and their private key to encrypt mail destined for you. In the encryption of data transmission in software such as `ssh`, the system again uses your private and public keys and a pair of private and public keys belonging to the remote system to which you are connecting.

The basic use of `slogin` is much like that for `rlogin`—simply issue the command **`slogin <machinename>`**, where *`<machinename>`* is the name or IP address of the remote machine to which you want to connect. If the remote machine is running a Secure Shell server and it is configured to allow you to connect, the server responds by asking for your password. If you respond correctly, you are left at a shell prompt on the remote machine and can type into it and execute commands, just as though you were in a `Terminal.app` window typing to your local machine.

TIP

The command `ssh` is equivalent to the command `slogin`. We use `slogin` in our examples and discussion here to make it clear where we're talking about `slogin` the program, and use SSH as the acronym for the Secure Shell package, but you can substitute the command `ssh` wherever you see `slogin` used here.

A successful `slogin` attempt might look something like this:

```
brezup:ray testing $ slogin rosalyn.biosci.ohio-state.edu
ray@rosalyn.biosci.ohio-state.edu's password:
Last login: Tue May 13 2003 01:16:06 -0500 from dhcp065-024-074-
You have new mail.

...Remote login...

Rosalyn ray 1 >
```

Again, at this point we're at a shell prompt on the remote machine `rosalyn.biosci.ohio-state.edu`.

If you don't want to log in to the remote machine as the same user ID as you are on the current machine, you can specify a user ID using `-l` *`<username>`* after the hostname. Alternatively, you can use *`<username>@<hostname>`* to specify the user and host. If I wanted to log in to `rosalyn` as user `testing` (regardless of what user I am on my local machine), I could use this syntax:

```
brezup:ray testing $ slogin testing@rosalyn.biosci.ohio-state.edu
testing@rosalyn.biosci.ohio-state.edu's password:
Last login: Tue Jun 24 2003 15:30:04 -0500
You have new mail.

...Remote login...

Rosalyn testing 1 >
```


Some system administrators choose not to allow remote logins through simple password authentication. Passwords are generally too short to be difficult for a computer to guess by simple brute-force methods. Instead, the Secure Shell suite allows the use of arbitrarily long, multiword passphrases. An slogin connection requiring this type of login looks like this:

```
brezup:ray testing $ slogin rosalyn.biosci.ohio-state.edu -l joray
Enter passphrase for key '/Users/ray/.ssh/id_dsa':
Last login: Tue Aug 06 2003 14:39:47 -0500 from cvl232015.columb
You have new mail.

...Remote login...

Rosalyn joray 1 >
```

If the remote machine is running this more restrictive security (and we recommend that you do so if you choose to enable remote connections to your machine when we get to Chapter 26, "Creating a Mail Server"), you will be asked, not for your password, but for your passphrase if you have created one. The connection will be refused if you have not created a passphrase.

Creating a passphrase involves a bit of work on your part. This is because if you really want security, you can't allow the encrypted keys that identify you to be seen on the network. Therefore, after the key has been created, you need to transfer it to the remote machine via some old-fashioned, physical method, such as writing it to a floppy disk and taking that disk directly to the remote machine.

TIP

If you're in charge of setting up both machines, you could leave password access under Secure Shell on long enough for you to copy the keys back and forth on the encrypted channel, and then turn off password access to tighten security.

Creating a passphrase for yourself involves the following: On your Mac OS X machine, generate a key pair by running

```
ssh-keygen -t <type>
```

The -t option specifies the key type to be generated. This can be rsa for RSA or dsa for DSA (isn't case sensitivity fun?) RSA is used in SSH1 servers, whereas either RSA or DSA can be used with SSH2 servers. RSA (which stands for *Rivest-Shamir-Adelman*, its developers) is the most commonly used public key algorithm. DSA, Digital Signature Algorithm, is a signature-only algorithm, based on the Diffie-Hellman discrete logarithm problem.

When you run ssh-keygen, you are asked for a passphrase to protect the private key. It is recommended that the passphrase be at least 11 characters long and include as many character types as possible: uppercase letters, lowercase letters, numbers, and special characters. Spaces may be included as part of the passphrase.

Here is a sample run:

```
brezup:miwa miwa $ ssh-keygen -t dsa
Generating public/private dsa key pair.
Enter file in which to save the key (/Users/miwa/.ssh/id_dsa):
Enter passphrase (empty for no passphrase):
Enter same passphrase again:
Your identification has been saved in /Users/miwa/.ssh/id_dsa.
Your public key has been saved in /Users/miwa/.ssh/id_dsa.pub.
The key fingerprint is:
7d:25:3e:87:3b:25:24:cf:5a:05:0e:1d:19:ad:67:10 miwa@brezup
```

As ssh-keygen tells us, user miwa does indeed have the promised keys, as shown in the following output. The private key was saved as id_dsa, and the public key was saved as id_dsa.pub; both are stored in the directory ~/.ssh/.

```
brezup:miwa miwa $ ls -al ~/.ssh
total 16
drwx------   4 miwa  miwa  136 17 Aug 22:09 .
drwxr-xr-x  12 miwa  miwa  408 17 Aug 22:08 ..
-rw-------   1 miwa  miwa  744 17 Aug 22:09 id_dsa
-rw-r--r--   1 miwa  miwa  601 17 Aug 22:09 id_dsa.pub
```

Next, we need to transfer the file id_dsa.pub to the remote host. Because you might be generating different keys for different hosts, it's most convenient if you rename the file first—this also helps prevent you from overwriting it the next time you create a key or overwriting the key on the remote host when you transfer it. You might also want to consider using the -f option to specify a different filename when you generate your public key. However, we wanted to show you what to expect by default. Because it's your public key, it doesn't matter whether the world can see it—you can copy it to your remote host via FTP, move it there with a floppy, or paste it across a logged-in terminal session.

On the remote host, the public key you just created needs to be added to the file authorized_keys (~/.ssh/authorized_keys) in the .ssh directory in your home directory (~/.ssh/). If the file does not exist, it must be created. If you copied the key over in a file, you can do this by simply using the cat command:

```
cat <mynewkeyfile> >> ~/.ssh/authorized_keys
```

When adding the new key to the file, make sure that the key is added as a single long line of data. If your key arrived in one long line of data in a file, the `cat` command shown will work fine. Otherwise, if you're pasting the key in via the terminal or aren't sure it's in a single long line in the file, it's best to check `~/.ssh/authorized_keys` to make sure that it arrived correctly.

TIP

Many terminals will be friendly and line-wrap the key, if you try to paste it through a logged-in terminal window. If your passphrase refuses to work, make sure that there are no extra blank lines in your `~/.ssh/authorized_keys` file, that the key is on a line by itself (rather than attached to the backside of another key), and that the key hasn't accidentally accumulated any line breaks.

Having done all this, if you now try to `slogin` to the remote host where you just added your key (and assuming that the remote host is running `sshd2`!), you should be greeted with a login process asking for your passphrase rather than your password. Enter the passphrase exactly as you did to create the keys, and you will enjoy a data connection that is almost impossible to decrypt, and an access code (your passphrase) that is much more secure than a simple password.

NOTE

There are a number of variations on the movement of the public key and its installation on the remote host. These revolve around the version of server running on the remote machine. Considerably more detail and examples of these options are given in Chapter 21, where we cover getting these outside machines to talk to your Mac OS X box.

The `slogin` program also provides a neat method for protecting data transmissions other than terminals. This is implemented as an encrypted tunnel between the two machines connected by the `slogin` terminal connection. Essentially, `slogin` can be instructed to watch for connections that come to your local machine, package the data from these connections, encrypt it, ship it off to the other end of the tunnel, and unpackage it again. You then use your `ftp`, or any other network connection program, to connect to your local machine (not the remote machine!), and `slogin` tunnels that connection to the remote machine and makes the connection at the other end. Because your user ID and password for the FTP server are carried over the encrypted tunnel, they're never in clear text on the network, and your login information and any data you transmit are protected.

To demonstrate this, the following `slogin` connection sets up a tunnel from the local machine to a remote machine named waashu, over which `ftp` connections can be carried.

```
brezup:root testing # slogin waashu.biosci.ohio-state.edu
➥-l testing -L21:waashu:21
The authenticity of host 'waashu.biosci.ohio-state.edu
➥(140.254.104.239)' can't be established.
DSA key fingerprint is 3d:1d:6b:78:c9:7e:63:b9:8b:6d:13:5f:e5:3b:f1:20.
```

```
Are you sure you want to continue connecting (yes/no)? yes
Warning: Permanently added 'waashu.biosci.ohio-state.edu,140.254.104.239'
➥(DSA) to the list of known hosts.
testing@waashu.biosci.ohio-state.edu's password:
Last login: Tue Jul 15 2003 15:37:15
You have new mail.

/usr/local/testing

WAASHU testing 1 >
```

In this case, we've never connected waashu before, so slogin asks whether we really believe that we're making a connection to the right host and that it's really giving us valid credentials. This is the one point in all our communications where an imposter in the middle of the communication could easily insert false information and fool us into transmitting our information insecurely. Again, this leaves the terminal connected to the remote machine and sitting at a shell prompt on the remote machine. The -L21:waashu:21 part of the command sets up the tunneling magic. It tells slogin to start listening on port 21 (which is the port that the FTP server would usually listen to), capture anything it sees, package it securely, and transmit it to waashu, where it is to be unpackaged and sent to waashu's port 21 (thereby connecting to waashu's FTP server).

NOTE

Note that only the root user can map to ports numbered lower than 1024. For this reason, the slogin forwarding as shown here isn't quite what you want to do for day-to-day use. It's the easiest for basic illustration, though—a more practical example comes a little later.

When slogin is connected like this, it is connecting port 21—the normal ftp port on our machine (localhost)—to port 21 on the remote host we're logged in to. Open another terminal window. The second terminal window is used to invoke ftp to connect over the tunnel (by connecting to our local machine, usually available as localhost and always available as 127.0.0.1) like so:

```
brezup:miwa miwa $ ftp localhost
Connected to localhost.biosci.ohio-state.edu.
220 waashu.biosci.ohio-state.edu FTP server ready.
Name (localhost:miwa): testing
331 Password required for testing.
Password:
230 User testing logged in.
Remote system type is UNIX.
Using binary mode to transfer files.
ftp> passive
Passive mode on.
ftp> cd osx-misc
```

```
250 CWD command successful.
ftp> binary
200 Type set to I.
ftp> put developer-1.tiff
local: developer-1.tiff remote: developer-1.tiff
227 Entering Passive Mode (140,254,12,239,60,59)
150 Opening BINARY mode data connection for 'developer-1.tiff'.
226 Transfer complete.
1255376 bytes sent in 16.2 seconds (77490 bytes/s)
ftp> quit
221 Goodbye.
```


To check whether it arrived okay, we go to the waashu terminal:

```
WAASHU osx-misc 203 > ls -l dev*tiff
-rw-r--r--    1 testing    user    1255376 Apr 21 20:35 developer-1.tiff
```

Note that when we ftp to localhost, ftp reports that we're connected to localhost, but waashu responds. The tunnel is working as expected.

As noted earlier, use of port 21 is restricted to the root user, but for your first introduction, it made sense to direct the ftp port to the ftp port. There is nothing that limits the forwarding to connecting identically numbered ports, though, and ftp can also connect to ports other than the usual port 21. For use on a day-to-day basis, a normal user can replace the -L21:<*machinename*>:21 section of the command with -L2000:<*machinename*>:21. The ftp command then is extended by adding the port number for the local connection as ftp localhost 2000. This probably sounds more complicated than it really is. It really doesn't look much different than just directing the ftp port to the ftp port. In one window, run this:

```
brezup:miwa Documents $ slogin waashu.biosci.ohio-state.edu
➥-l testing -L2000:waashu:21
```

And in another, run the ftp command as like so:

```
brezup:miwa Documents $ ftp localhost 2000
```

This works identically to having root route the tunnel as shown in the first example.

If your machine doesn't know the target by a short name (such as <waashu>), you need to use an IP address or fully qualified hostname for the -L<*sourceport*>:<*target hostname*>:<*targetport*> part of the command as well as the base slogin itself.

Another option, if all you want to do is forward a port without receiving a shell prompt on the remote host, is using the -N option to slogin. This doesn't cause it to return to the command line but is useful in stored terminal scripts if you're not interested in leaving a prompt open and unused (which is usually a good idea for security purposes).

Table 13.4 shows the syntax and additional options for the operation of slogin.

TABLE 13.4 The Syntax and Some Interesting Options for `ssh` and `slogin`

`ssh`	Secure shell remote login client.
`slogin`	
`ssh [-l` *<login_name>*`]` *<hostname>* `¦` *<user>*`@`*<hostname>* `[`*<command>*`]`	
`ssh [-1246AaCfgkNnqsTtVvXxY] [-b` *<bind_address>*`] [-c` *<cipher_spec>*`] [-e` *<escap_char>*`]`	
`[-F` *<configfile>*`] [-i` *<identity_file>*`] [-L` *<port>*`:`*<host>*`:`*<hostport>*`] [-l` *<login_name>*`]`	
`[-m` *<mac_spec>*`] [-o` *<option>*`] [-p` *<port>*`]:`*<hostport>*`] [-R` *<port>*`:`*<host>*`]`	
`[[`*<user>*`@]`*<hostname>*`] [`*<command>*`]]`	
`-a`	Disables forwarding of the authentication agent connection.
`-A`	Enables forwarding of the authentication agent connection. This can also be specified on a per-host basis in a configuration file.
`-f`	Requests `ssh` to go to background just before command execution. Implies `-n`. The recommended way to start X11 programs at a remote site is `ssh -f` *<host>* `xterm`.
`-v`	Verbose mode. Causes debugging messages to be printed.
`-x`	Disables X11 forwarding.
`-X`	Enables X11 forwarding. This can also be specified on a per-host basis in a configuration file.
`-C`	Requests compression of all data.
`-N`	Does not execute a remote command. Useful for just forwarding ports. SSH2 only.
`-P`	Uses a nonprivileged port for outgoing connections. Useful if your firewall does not permit connections from privileged ports. Turns off `RhostsAuthentication` and `RhostsRSAAuthentication`.
`-1`	Forces SSH1 protocol only.
`-2`	Forces SSH2 protocol only.
`-e ch¦^ch¦none`	Sets escape character for sessions with a `pty` (default: ~). The escape character is recognized only at the beginning of a line. Followed by a `.` closes the connection; followed by `^Z` suspends the connection; followed by itself sends the escape character once. Setting it to `none` disables any escapes and makes the session fully transparent. You might want to set this to something other than the default if you find that you're using `mail` and the ~ command in `mail` keeps being absorbed by the `slogin` client.
`-i` *<identity_file>*	Specifies the file from which the identity (private key) for RSA authentication is read. Default is `$HOME/.ssh/identity`.
`-l` *<login_name>*	Specifies the user to log in as on the remote machine. This may also be specified on a per-host basis in a configuration file.
`-o` *<option>*	Can be used for giving options in the format used in the configuration file. Useful for specifying options that have no separate command-line flag. Option has the same format as a line in the configuration file.
`-p` *<port>*	Specifies the port to connect to on the remote host. This can be specified on a per-host basis in the configuration file.

TABLE 13.4 Continued

-F *<configfile>*	Specifies an alternative per-user configuration file. If a configuration file is given on the command line, the systemwide configuration file (/etc/ssh_config) is ignored. Default per-user configuration file is $HOME/.ssh/config.
-L *<port>*:*<host>*:*<hostport>*	Specifies that the given port on the client (local) host is to be forwarded to the given host and port on the remote side.
-R *<port>*:*<host>*:*<hostport>*	Specifies that the given port on the remote (server) host is to be forwarded to the given host and port on the local side.

scp, sftp, and Others In addition to the slogin program, the Secure Shell suite of programs provides additional data encryption and protection functions to the user. There are components (scp) that function analogously to the cp command that you learned about in Chapter 10, "Common Unix Shell Commands: File, Directory and Disk Operations," and to the ftp command that you learned about earlier in this chapter (sftp).

The scp command can copy a file either from or to a Secure Shell remote host. The syntax, like cp, is scp *<from>* *<to>*. Either *<from>* or *<to>* can be specified as a remote machine and file, in the syntax of [*<username>*@]*<remotemachine>*:*<pathtofile>*. For example, the following command copies ~ray/public_html/my_bookmarks.html from the machine soyokaze (soyokaze is a host alias to soyokaze.biosci.ohio-state.edu on this machine) to a file by the same name in the local folder ~/Documents/:

```
brezup:ray testing $ scp ray@soyokaze:public_html/my_bookmarks.html
➥~/Documents/
ray@soyokaze.biosci.ohio-state.edu's password:
my_bookmarks.html                              100%  271KB  45.4KB/s   00:05
```

Likewise, the following copies the file myfile from the current directory to the directory /tmp on the machine known as soyokaze (again, you will need a long name here if your local machine doesn't know the target machine by a short alias) and names it yourfile on the remote machine soyokaze, again logging in using the user ID ray:

```
brezup:ray testing $ scp ./myfile
➥ray@soyokaze.biosci.ohio-state.edu:/tmp/yourfile
ray@soyokaze.biosci.ohio-state.edu's password:
myfile                                        37%  208KB  20.6KB/s   00:17 ETA
```

Note that scp doesn't make complaints about the host key the second time because it has already accepted and stored it.

Table 13.5 shows the syntax and interesting options for scp.

TABLE 13.5 The Syntax and Interesting Options for scp

scp	Secure remote copy.
scp [-1246BCpqrv] [-c *<cipher>*] [-F *<ssh_config>*] [-i *<identity_file>*] [-l <limit>] [-o *<ssh_option>*] [-P *<port>*] [-S *<program>*] [[*<user>*@]*<host1>*:]*<file1>* [...] [[*<user>*@]*<host2>*:]*<file2>*	
-p	Preserves modification times, access times, and modes from the original file.
-r	Recursively copies entire directories.
-C	Enables compression. Passes the flag to ssh to enable compression.
-F *<ssh_config>*	Specifies an alternative per-user configuration file for ssh. Option is directly passed to ssh.
-P *<port>*	Specifies the port to connect to on the remote host.
-i *<identity_file>*	Specifies the file from which the identity (private key) for RSA authentication is read.
-o *<ssh_option>*	Passes specified options to ssh in the format used in ssh_config.

The sftp command can also be used to securely transfer files. It was not available in the original Mac OS X 10.0 distribution but was included in a later update.

The basic syntax for using sftp is

```
sftp [<username>@]<host>
```

This syntax opens an interactive sftp session, which works much like a typical interactive ftp session, as shown here:

```
brezup:sage Documents $ sftp miwa@rosalyn.biosci.ohio-state.edu
Connecting to rosalyn.biosci.ohio-state.edu...
miwa@rosalyn.biosci.ohio-state.edu's password:
sftp> lcd terminal
sftp> cd terminal-misc
sftp> put term-display-1.tiff
Uploading term-display-1.tiff to
➥/home/miwa/terminal-misc/term-display-1.tiff
sftp> ls
drwxr-xr-x    2 miwa     class          512 Aug  6 20:56 ./
drwxr-xr-x   21 miwa     class         1024 Aug  6 20:53 ../
-rw-r--r--    1 miwa     class       921862 Aug  6 20:57 term-display-1.tiff
sftp> quit
```

In this example, an interactive sftp session was used by user sage to transfer the file term-display-1.tiff to user miwa's terminal-misc directory on the remote host rosalyn.biosci.ohio-state.edu. The lcd command was used to change to sage's terminal directory on the local machine, brezup, and cd was used on the remote host to change to miwa's terminal-misc directory. Of course, the sftp command could have been issued directly in sage's terminal directory. Like an interactive ftp session, the interactive sftp session can take commands such as cd, ls, and put. As is the case with scp, if you have the same username on both machines, it is not necessary to supply a *<username>* because the current username is assumed by default.

Table 13.6 shows the syntax and some of the useful options for `sftp`.

TABLE 13.6 The Syntax and Some Interesting Options for `sftp`

`sftp`	Secure file transfer program.

`sftp [-1Cv] [-b <batchfile>] [-o <ssh_option>] [-s <subsystem> ¦ <sftp_server>] [-B <buffer_size>] [-F <ssh_config>] [-P <sftp_server path>] [-R <num_requests>] [-S <program>] <host>`
`sftp [[<user>@]<host>[:<file1> [<file2>]]]`
`sftp [[<user>@]<host>[:<dir>[/]]]`	

The first usage initiates an interactive session. The second usage retrieves files automatically if a noninteractive authentication is used. Otherwise, it retrieves the specified files after interactive authentication. The third usage causes `sftp` to start in an interactive session in the specified directory.	
`-b <batchfile>`	Batch mode. Reads a series of commands from an input batch file instead of `stdin`. Because it lacks user interaction, it should be used in conjunction with noninteractive authentication. `sftp` aborts if any of the following commands fails: `get`, `put`, `rename`, `ln`, `rm`, `mkdir`, `chdir`, `lchdir`, and `lmkdir`.
`-o <ssh_option>`	Passes options to `ssh` in the format used in the `ssh` configuration file. Useful for specifying options for which there is no separate `sftp` command-line flag. For example, to specify an alternative port use: `sftp -oPort=24`.
`-C`	Enables compression via `ssh`'s `-C` flag.
`-F <ssh_config>`	Specifies an alternative per-user configuration file for `ssh`. Option is passed directly to `ssh`.
`-1`	Specifies the use of protocol version 1.
Interactive Commands	
`cd <path>`	Changes remote directory to *<path>*.
`lcd <path>`	Changes local directory to *<path>*.
`chgrp <grp> <path>`	Changes group of file *<path>* to *<grp>*.
`chmod <mode> <path>`	Changes permissions of file *<path>* to *<mode>*.
`chown <owner> <path>`	Changes owner of file *<path>* to *<owner>*.
`get [<flags>] <remote-path> [<local-path>]`	Retrieves the *<remote-path>* and stores it on the local machine. If the local pathname is not specified, it is given the same name it has on the remote machine. If the `-P` flag is specified, the file's full permission and access time are copied as well.
`help`	Displays help text.
`lls [<ls-options> [<path>]]`	Displays local directory listing of either *<path>* or current directory if *<path>* is not specified.

TABLE 13.6 Continued

`lmkdir <path>`	Creates local directory specified by <*path*>.
`ln <oldpath> <newpath>`	Creates a symbolic link from <*oldpath*> to <*newpath*>.
`lpwd`	Prints local working directory.
`ls [<path>]`	Displays remote directory listing of either <*path*> or current directory if <*path*> is not specified.
`mkdir <path>`	Creates remote directory specified by <*path*>.
`put [<flags>] <local-path> [<remote-path>]`	Uploads <*local-path*> and stores it on the remote machine. If the remote pathname is not specified, it is given the same name it has on the local machine. If the `-P` flag is specified, the file's full permission and access time are copied as well.
`pwd`	Displays remote working directory.
`quit`	Quits `sftp`.
`rename <oldpath> <newpath>`	Renames remote file from <*oldpath*> to <*newpath*>.
`rmdir <path>`	Removes remote directory specified by <*path*>.
`rm <path>`	Deletes remote file specified by <*path*>.
`symlink <oldpath> <newpath>`	Creates a symbolic link from <*oldpath*> to <*newpath*>.
`! <command>`	Executes command in local shell.

The "Busload of Useful Tricks" Network Client: `cURL`

`cURL`, more commonly known simply as `curl`, is a command-line tool for getting or sending data to network services using URL syntax. The name is a bit of a play on words, being pronounced either as one word as in "kurl," or as two words as in "see URL" (implying the unspoken "do URL" to those with a Unix sense of humor). `curl` is based on the `libcurl` library, which has the goal of bringing convenient URL-type data access and transfers to software that needs it.

Philosophically, `curl` is a very Unix-friendly program, providing a very specific function, while trying not to overlap the functionality of other programs. We are including it among these other more application-like programs because `curl` makes an excellent assistant program for almost any software that needs network access. As such, it might not fit our definition of an application or application suite, but it does integrate well as a network-access partner for other applications and application suites.

At its simplest, `curl` syntax is `curl [options]` <*URL*>. The complexity and power come from the range of available options. For example, to retrieve the web page `http://www.biosci.ohio-state.edu/` using `curl`, the syntax is simply

```
curl http://www.biosci.ohio-state.edu/
```

The output of this is identical to using `lynx -dump -source http://www.biosci.ohio-state.edu/`. `curl`, however, can grab the name of the remote file from the remote server and write the data into a file by that name locally without you having to do a redirect as you would with `lynx`. Therefore, you could use

```
curl -O http://www.biosci.ohio-state.edu/index.html
```

instead of

```
lynx -dump -source http://www.biosci.ohio-state.edu/index.html  > index.html
```

`curl` isn't a replacement for `lynx` because it isn't a web browser, but, on the other hand, `curl` is bidirectional and can send data as well as receive it. The `-T` *<file>* option directs that the local file named *<file>* be sent to the remote machine and file or directory name as specified in *<URL>*.

```
brezup:ray Unleashed $ curl -T fig18_.gif
➥ftp://192.168.1.143/incoming/
  % Total    % Received % Xferd  Average Speed          Time             Curr.
                                 Dload  Upload Total    Current  Left    Speed
 52  763k    0      0    52  402k      0  27744  0:00:28  0:00:14  0:00:14 34526
```

This command results in `fig18_.gif` being `ftp`ed from the current directory to the machine located at `192.168.1.143` and placed in the `incoming` subdirectory of the `ftp` directory on that machine. Speed and progress statistics are displayed as the file is transmitted.

These are the variations on `curl` that most people will use, most frequently, but the range of available options is truly diverse. Table 13.7 shows the syntax and some of the more useful options for `curl`, including hints on how to access secure servers, track cookie contents, and other useful trivia.

TABLE 13.7 The Syntax and Some Interesting Options for `curl`

`curl`	A utility for getting a URL with FTP, TELNET, LDAP, GOPHER, DICT, FILE, HTTP or HTTPS syntax.
`curl [`*options*`] [`*<URL>*`...]`	
`-a` `--append`	(FTP) When used in an `ftp` upload, this tells `curl` to append to the target file instead of overwriting it. If the file doesn't exist, it is created.
`-A` *<agent string>* `--user-agent` *<agent string>*	(HTTP) Specifies the User-Agent string to send to the HTTP server. Some badly done CGIs fail if it's not set to "Mozilla/4.0". To encode blanks in the string, surround the string with single quote marks. This can also be set with the `-H`/`--header` flag.
`-b` *<name=data>* `--cookie` *<name=data>*	(HTTP) Passes the data to the HTTP server as a cookie. The data is supposedly the data previously received from the server in a `Set-Cookie:` line. The data should be in the format *NAME1=VALUE1*`;` *NAME2=VALUE2*, but there's nothing to say you can't change it.

TABLE 13.7 Continued

	If no = is used in the line, it is treated as a filename to use to read previously stored cookie lines from, which should be used in this session if they match. Using this method also activates the cookie parser, which makes `curl` record incoming cookies too; that can be handy for using this in combination with the `-L/--location` option. The file format of the file to read cookies from should be plain HTTP headers or the Netscape cookie file format. Note that the file specified with `-b/--cookie` is only used as input. No cookies are stored in the file. To store cookies, save the HTTP headers to a file using `-D/--dump-header`.
`-B` `--use-ascii`	Uses ASCII transfer when getting an FTP file or LDAP info. For FTP, this can also be enforced by using a URL that ends with `;type=A`.
`--connect-timeout` *<seconds>*	Specifies how long to wait for a server before giving up.
`-c` `--cookie-jar` *<file name>*	Specifies a file where `curl` should store any cookies it receives. If you set the *<file name>* to a single `-` (dash), the cookies are written to `STDOUT`.
`-C` *<offset>* `--continue-at` *<offset>*	Continues/resumes a previous file transfer at the given offset. The given offset is the exact number of bytes skipped, counted from the beginning of the source file before it is transferred to the destination. If used with uploads, the `ftp` server command `SIZE` is not used by `curl`. Upload resume is for FTP only. HTTP resume is possible only with HTTP/1.1 or later servers.
`--crlf`	Causes `CR` (carriage return) characters to be converted to `CRLF` (carriage return/line feed) on upload. Specifying `--crlf` twice forces this option off.
`-d` *<data>* `--data` *<data>*	(HTTP) Sends the specified data in a `POST` request to the HTTP server (can be changed to `GET` by the `-G/--get` option), in a way that can emulate as if a user has filled in an HTML form and clicked the Submit button. Note that the data is sent exactly as specified with no extra processing (with all newlines cut off). The data is expected to be `url-encoded`. This causes `curl` to pass the data to the server using the content-type `application/x-www-form-urlencoded`. Compare to `-F`. If more than one `-d/--data` option is used on the same command line, the data pieces specified are merged together with a separating `&`-letter. Thus, using `-d name=daniel -d skill=lousy` generates a `post` chunk that looks like `name=daniel&skill=lousy`. If this option is used several times, the ones following the first append data.
`--data-binary <data>`	(HTTP) Posts data in a manner similar to `--data-ascii`, although when using this option the entire context of the posted data is kept as-is. If you want to post a binary file without the `strip-newlines` feature of the `--data-ascii` option, this is for you.

TABLE 13.7 Continued

-D *<file>* --dump-header *<file>*	(HTTP/FTP) Writes the HTTP headers to this *<file>*. Writes the FTP file info to this *<file>* if -I/--head is used. Handy for storing the cookies that an HTTP site sends to you. The cookies could then be read in a second curl invoke by using the -b/--cookie option.
-e *<URL>* --referer *<URL>*	(HTTP) Sends the referer page information to the HTTP server. This can also be set with the -H/--header flag. When used with -L/--location you can append ;auto to the referer URL to make curl automatically set the previous URL when it follows a Location: header. The ;auto string can be used alone, even if you don't set an initial referer. This option lets you lie to servers about the page that directed you to a particular link, potentially bypassing "deep linking" safeguards.
-F --form *<name=content>*	(HTTP) This lets curl emulate a filled-in form in which a user has clicked the Submit button. This causes curl to POST data using the content-type multipart/form-data according to RFC 1867. This enables uploading of binary files and so on. To force the content part to be a file, prefix the filename with an @ sign. To just get the content part from a file, prefix the filename with the character <. The difference between @ and < is that @ makes a file get attached in the post as a file upload, whereas < makes a text field and just gets the contents for that text field from a file.
-G/--get	Use the HTTP GET protocol rather than the POST protocol for sending data.
-h --help	Displays help.
-H --header *<header>*	(HTTP) Extra header to use when getting a web page. You may specify any number of extra headers. Note that if you should add a custom header that has the same name as one of the internal ones curl would use, your externally set header will be used instead of the internal one. This allows you to make even trickier stuff than curl would normally do. Do not replace internally set headers without knowing perfectly well what you're doing. Replacing an internal header with one without content on the right side of the colon prevents that header from appearing.
-I --include	(HTTP) Includes the HTTP-header in the output. The HTTP-header includes things such as server name, date of the document, HTTP version, and more.
-j --junk-session-cookies	Discard session cookies from any cookie data read from a cookie file. This has the effect of starting a new session. Browsers typically discard session cookies when they quit, but it's useful to keep them around until you want to discard them with curl because it's a single-command, single-connection program.

TABLE 13.7 Continued

`-k` `--insecure`	Allows `curl` to perform insecure connections. If this option is not specified, connections to servers with apparently incorrect security certificates will be barred.
`-K` `--config` *`<config file>`*	Specifies which *`<config file>`* to read `curl` arguments from. The *`<config file>`* is a text file in which command-line arguments can be written that then will be used as if they were written on the actual command line. Options and their parameters must be specified on the same line in the file. If the parameter is to contain whitespace, the parameter must be enclosed within quotes. If the first column of a `config` line is a `#` character, the rest of the line will be treated as a comment. Specify the filename as `-` to make `curl` read the file from `stdin`.
`-l` `--list-only`	(FTP) When listing an FTP directory, this switch forces a name-only view. This is especially useful if you want to machine-parse the contents of an FTP directory because the normal directory view doesn't use a standard look or format.
`--limit-rate` *`<speed>`*	Throttles the data connection to a maximum of *`<speed>`* bytes per second. The transfer speed may also be given in *`<speed>`*`K` to specify kilobytes/second or *`<speed>`*`M` to specify megabytes/second. If you're really optimistic, *`<speed>`*`G` asks for gigabytes/second transfer rates.
`-L` `--location`	(HTTP/HTTPS) If the server reports that the requested page has a different location (indicated with the header line `Location:`), this flag instructs `curl` to reattempt the get on the new location. If used together with `-i` or `-I`, headers from all requested pages are shown. If this flag is used when making an HTTP `POST`, `curl` automatically switches to `GET` after the initial POST is done.
`-m` `--max-time` *`<seconds>`*	Specifies the maximum time in seconds that you allow the whole operation to take. This is useful for preventing your batch jobs from hanging for hours due to slow networks or links going down. See also the `--connect-timeout` option.
`-M` `--manual`	Manual. Displays the `curl` man page.
`-n` `--netrc`	Makes `curl` scan the `.netrc` file in the user's home directory for login name and password. This is typically used for `ftp` on Unix. If used with `http`, `curl` enables user authentication. See `netrc(4)` for details on the file format. `curl` does not complain if that file hasn't the right permissions (it should not be world nor group readable). The environment variable `HOME` is used to find the home directory. The basic `.netrc` file syntax looks like this: `machine` *`<host.domain.com>`* `login` *`<myname>`* `password` *`<mysecret>`*

TABLE 13.7 Continued

-o --output <*file*>	Writes output to <*file*> rather than to stdout. If you are using {} or [] to fetch multiple documents, you can use # followed by a number in the <*file*> specifier. That variable is replaced with the current string for the URL being fetched.
-O --remote-name	Writes output to a local file named like the remote file we get. (Only the file part of the remote file is used; the path is cut off.) You may use this option as many times as you have number of URLs.
-q	If used as the first parameter on the command line, the $HOME/.curlrc file will not be read and used as a config file.
-R --remote-time	Attempts to determine the timestamp on the remote file and use that on the local copy.
-s --silent	Silent mode. Doesn't show progress meter or error messages.
-S --show-error	When used with -s, it makes curl show error messages if it fails.
-T --upload-file <*file*>	Transfers the specified local <*file*> to the remote server at <*URL*>. If there is no file part in the specified URL, curl appends the local filename. Note that you must use a trailing / on the last directory to really prove to curl that you aren't providing a filename, or curl thinks that your last directory name is the remote filename to use. That will most likely cause the upload operation to fail. If this is used on an HTTP(S) server, the PUT command is used.
--trace <*file*>	Outputs a full diagnostic trace of all data exchanged between the local and remote hosts. A single - (dash) as <*file*> sends the output to STDOUT.
--trace-ascii <*file*>	Outputs a diagnostic trace of all information in ASCII format. curl claims this is easier for humans to read.
-u --user <*user:password*>	Specifies user and password to use when fetching. See README.curl for detailed examples of how to use this. If no password is specified, curl asks for it interactively.
-x --proxy <*proxyhost[:port]*>	Uses specified proxy. If the port number is not specified, it is assumed at port 1080.
-y --speed-time <*time*>	If a download is slower than speed-limit bytes per second during a speed-time period, the download will be aborted. If speed-time is used, the default speed-limit will be 1 unless set with -y.
-Y --speed-limit <*speed*>	Applies a lower limit to the download speed. If a download is slower than this given speed, in bytes per second, for speed-time seconds, it will be aborted. speed-time is set with -Y and defaults to 30 if not set.

13

TABLE 13.7 Continued

`-Z` `--max-redirs <num>`	Sets the maximum number of server redirections to follow before giving up.
`-3` `--sslv3`	(HTTPS) Forces `curl` to use SSL version 3 when negotiating with a remote SSL server.
`-2` `--sslv2`	(HTTPS) Forces `curl` to use SSL version 2 when negotiating with a remote SSL server.
`-#` `--progress-bar`	Displays progress information as a progress bar instead of the default statistics.

Mail Clients

Depending on how your machine is configured, you might not have a use for the basic email reading command discussed in this chapter, `mail`. It is detailed here partly for historical completeness, and partly because it is an excellent utility for your use, if you have the opportunity.

The `mail` program is an email reading and sending program that works on email that is actually received and managed by your local machine. If all you've ever used is a POPmail or IMAP client, such as Eudora or Mailsmith, you're probably unfamiliar with the idea of your local machine being its own email server. Unix machines have, since the dawn of email, been part of the backbone by which email makes its way around the Internet. Configured properly, they don't need POPmail servers—they *are* POPmail (and IMAP) servers. Email gets around between them by way of the SMTP (Simple Mail Transfer Protocol) and is delivered (with a few minor exceptions) directly from the sender's machine to the receiver's machine.

What does this mean to you? If your machine is set up to receive and deliver mail itself, mail doesn't arrive at 10-minute intervals (or however frequently you have your POPmail client configured to connect). It arrives as instantaneously as it can make its way across the Internet—usually within a few seconds of being sent. It doesn't require your ISP's mail service to be up and running for you to receive mail because you (for email purposes) are your own ISP. Old-time Unix users are frequently amused by the instant messaging services that seem to be all the rage as the hot new Internet technology. Unfettered by the POPmail and IMAP protocols, plain old email *is* an instant messaging technology.

In this section we will look at `fetchmail`, `mail`, and `pine`.

Retrieving Remote Mail: `fetchmail`

As the name suggests, the `fetchmail` command fetches your mail for you. Specifically, it retrieves your mail from a remote server and sends it to your local mail server, where you can use email reading clients such as `mail` or `pine`.

If you are running your own mail server, `fetchmail` provides an easy way to store all of your mail in one place. Even if you prefer to read mail from your various email accounts using different packages or via webmail interfaces, you might still want to use `fetchmail` to retrieve all of your mail to archive it in one place.

The `fetchmail` utility is controlled by a control file, `~/.fetchmailrc`, and command-line arguments. The command-line arguments override the control file.

Before you have `fetchmail` retrieve all of your mail, you can test whatever settings you are considering with the `-V` flag first. Here is a sample of what you might see during such a trial run:

```
ryoohki:~ joray$ fetchmail -V -v -k -u ray.3 pop.service.ohio-state.edu
This is fetchmail release 6.2.5+SSL+INET6
Fallback MDA: (none)
Darwin ryoohki.biosci.ohio-state.edu 8.0.0b2 Darwin Kernel Version 8.0.0b2:
➥Wed Dec  1 23:33:09 PST 2004; root:xnu/xnu-708.1.obj~1/RELEASE_PPC
➥Power Macintosh powerpc
Taking options from command line
Idfile is /Users/joray/.fetchids
Fetchmail will show progress dots even in logfiles.
Fetchmail will forward misaddressed multidrop messages to joray.
Fetchmail will direct error mail to the sender.
Options for retrieving from ray.3@pop.service.ohio-state.edu:
  Mail will be retrieved via pop.service.ohio-state.edu
  True name of server is pop.service.ohio-state.edu.
  This host will be queried when no host is specified.
  Password will be prompted for.
  Protocol is auto (using default port).
  All available authentication methods will be tried.
  Server nonresponse timeout is 300 seconds (default).
  Default mailbox selected.
  Only new messages will be retrieved (--all off).
  Fetched messages will be kept on the server (--keep on).
  Old messages will not be flushed before message retrieval (--flush off).
  Rewrite of server-local addresses is enabled (--norewrite off).
  Carriage-return stripping is disabled (stripcr off).
  Carriage-return forcing is disabled (forcecr off).
  Interpretation of Content-Transfer-Encoding is enabled (pass8bits off).
  MIME decoding is disabled (mimedecode off).
  Idle after poll is disabled (idle off).
  Nonempty Status lines will be kept (dropstatus off)
  Delivered-To lines will be kept (dropdelivered off)
  No received-message limit (--fetchlimit 0).
  Fetch message size limit is 100 (--fetchsizelimit 100).
  Do binary search of UIDs during 9 out of 10 polls (--fastuidl 10).
  No SMTP message batch limit (--batchlimit 0).
  No forced expunges (--expunge 0).
  Messages will be SMTP-forwarded to: localhost (default)
```

13

```
  Spam-blocking disabled
  No pre-connection command.
  No post-connection command.
  Single-drop mode: 1 local name(s) recognized.
        joray
  No plugin command specified.
  No plugout command specified.
  No poll trace information will be added to the Received header.
.
You have new mail in /var/mail/joray
```

You can have `fetchmail` retrieve all of your mail and keep it on the remote server, or delete messages after it has retrieved them, and much more. Table 13.8 contains select command documentation for `fetchmail`.

Here is some sample output showing what you might expect when `fetchmail` is actually fetching mail. The `-v` flag, the verbose flag, has been turned on. In this example `fetchmail` retrieves mail, but leaves messages on the remote server. If I weren't expecting to erase and install various incarnations of Tiger on this machine, I would have `fetchmail` delete messages after retrieval.

```
ryoohki:~ joray$ fetchmail -v -k -u ray.3 pop.service.ohio-state.edu
Enter password for ray.3@pop.service.ohio-state.edu:
fetchmail: 6.2.5 querying pop.service.ohio-state.edu (protocol auto)
➥at Tue, 04 Jan 2005 09:52:04 -0500 (EST): poll started
fetchmail: 6.2.5 querying pop.service.ohio-state.edu (protocol IMAP)
➥at Tue, 04 Jan 2005 09:52:04 -0500 (EST): poll started
fetchmail: IMAP< * OK IMAP4 Ready mail-proxy3 00020153
fetchmail: IMAP> A0001 CAPABILITY
fetchmail: IMAP< * CAPABILITY IMAP4 IMAP4REV1 STARTTLS LOGINDISABLED
fetchmail: IMAP< A0001 OK CAPABILITY
fetchmail: IMAP> A0002 STARTTLS
fetchmail: IMAP< A0002 OK Begin TLS negotiation now
fetchmail: Issuer Organization: The Ohio State University
fetchmail: Issuer CommonName: mail-proxy1.service.ohio-state.edu
fetchmail: Server CommonName: mail-proxy1.service.ohio-state.edu
fetchmail: Server CommonName mismatch: mail-proxy1.service.ohio-state.edu
➥!= pop.service.ohio-state.edu
fetchmail: pop.service.ohio-state.edu key fingerprint:
➥F9:29:29:82:CC:B9:89:FE:F8:60:D6:F0:3D:6B:D4:DF
fetchmail: Warning: server certificate verification: self signed certificate
.
.
.
fetchmail: IMAP> A0003 CAPABILITY
fetchmail: IMAP< * CAPABILITY IMAP4 IMAP4REV1
```

```
fetchmail: IMAP< A0003 OK CAPABILITY
fetchmail: IMAP> A0004 LOGIN "ray.3" *
fetchmail: IMAP< A0004 OK You are so in
fetchmail: IMAP> A0005 SELECT "INBOX"
.
.
.
fetchmail: IMAP< )
fetchmail: IMAP< A0636 OK Completed
fetchmail: SMTP>. (EOM)
fetchmail: SMTP< 250 Ok: queued as ADB2992864
 not flushed
fetchmail: IMAP> A0637 STORE 633 +FLAGS (\Seen)
fetchmail: IMAP< * 633 FETCH (FLAGS (\Seen))
fetchmail: IMAP< A0637 OK Completed
fetchmail: IMAP> A0638 LOGOUT
fetchmail: IMAP< * BYE LOGOUT received
fetchmail: IMAP< A0638 OK Completed
fetchmail: 6.2.5 querying pop.service.ohio-state.edu (protocol IMAP)
➥at Tue, 04 Jan 2005 10:01:54 -0500 (EST): poll completed
fetchmail: 6.2.5 querying pop.service.ohio-state.edu (protocol auto)
➥at Tue, 04 Jan 2005 10:01:54 -0500 (EST):  poll completed
fetchmail: SMTP> QUIT
fetchmail: SMTP< 221 Bye
fetchmail: normal termination, status 0
You have new mail in /var/mail/joray
```

TABLE 13.8 The `fetchmail` Program Syntax and Useful Options

`fetchmail`	Fetches mail from a POP, IMAP, ETRN, or ODMR-capable server.

`fetchmail [option...] [<mailserver>...]`

`fetchmail` is a mail retrieval and forwarding utility that retrieves mail from remote mail servers and forwards it to the local mail delivery system, allowing a user to read mail using the local mail clients.

`fetchmail` can retrieve mail from servers running the following protocols: POP2, POP3, IMAP2bis, IMAP4, IMAPrev1. It can also use the ESMTP ETRN extension and ODMR.

As each message is retrieved, `fetchmail` normally delivers it on port 25 of the machine where it is running.

`fetchmail` is controlled by command-line options and a run control file, `~/.fetchmailrc`. Command-line options override `~/.fetchmailrc` declarations.

TABLE 13.8 Continued

General Options	
`-V` `--version`	Displays version information for `fetchmail`. Displays all the information that would be computed for each server specified. Useful for verifying that options are set the way you want.
`-c` `--check`	Returns a status code indicating whether there is mail waiting, without actually fetching or deleting mail. It returns a false positive if you leave read but undeleted mail in your server mailbox and your fetch protocol can't tell kept messages from new ones. Does not work with ETRN or ODMR.
Disposal Options	
`-a` `--all`	(Keyword: fetchall) Retrieves both read and unread messages from the server. Default is to retrieve only messages the server has marked as not read.
`-k` `--keep`	(Keyword: keep) Keeps retrieved messages on the remote server. Default is for messages to be deleted after they have been retrieved. Does not work with ETRN or ODMR.
`-K` `--nokeep`	(Keyword: nokeep) Deletes retrieved messages from the remote mail server. Option is forced on with ETRN and ODMR.
`-F` `--flush`	POP3/IMAP only. Deletes previously retrieved messages from the mail server before retrieving new messages.
Protocol and Query Options	
`-p` *<proto>* `--protocol` *<proto>*	(Keyword: proto[col]) Specifies the protocol to use when communicating with the remote mail server. If no protocol is specified, the default is AUTO.
`-U` `--uidl`	(Keyword: uidl) Forces UIDL use (effective only with POP3). Forces client-side tracking
`-t` *<seconds>* `--timeout` *<seconds>*	(Keyword: timeout) Sets a server-nonresponse timeout in seconds.
`-r` *<name>* `--folder` *<name>*	(Keyword: folder[s]) Causes a specified nondefault mail folder on the mail server (or comma-separated list of folders) to be retrieved. Syntax of the folder name is server-dependent. Not available under POP3, ETRN, or ODMR.
`--ssl`	(Keyword: ssl) Causes the connection to the mail server to be encrypted via SSL. Connects to the server using the specified base protocol over a connection secured by SSL. SSL support must be present at the server. If no port is specified, the connection is attempted to the well known port of the SSL version of the base protocol. This is generally a different port than the port used by the base protocol. For IMAP, this is port 143 for the clear protocol and port 993 for the SSL secured protocol.

TABLE 13.8 Continued

Option	Description
Delivery Control Options	
`-S` *<hosts>* `--smtphost` *<hosts>*	(Keyword: smtp[host]) Specifies a hunt list of hosts to forward mail to (one or more hostnames, comma-separated). Hosts are tried in list order; the first one that is up becomes the forwarding target for the current run. Normally, `localhost` is added to the end of the list as an invisible default.
`-D` *<domain>* `--smtpaddress` *<domain>*	(Keyword: smtpaddress) Specifies the domain to be appended to addresses in RCPT TO lines shipped to SMTP. The name of the SMTP server (as specified by `--smtphost` or defaulted to `localhost`) is used when this is not specified.
`--smtpname` *<user@domain>*	(Keyword: smtpname) Specifies the domain and user to be put in RCPT TO lines shipped to SMTP. The default user is the current local user.
`-Z` *<nnn>* `--antispam` *<nnn[, nnn]...>*	(Keyword: antispam) Specifies the list of numeric SMTP errors that are to be interpreted as a spam-block response from the listener. A value of `-1` disables this option. For the command-line option, the list values should be comma-separated.
`-m` *<command>* `--mda` *<command>*	(Keyword: mda) Forces mail to be passed to an MDA directly (rather than forwarded to port 25).
`--lmtp`	(Keyword: lmtp) Causes delivery via LMTP (Local Mail Transfer Protocol). A service port must be explicitly specified (with a slash suffix) on each host in the smtphost hunt list if this option is selected; the default port 25 will not be accepted (in accordance with RFC 2033).
Resource Limit Control Options	
`-l` *<maxbytes>* `--limit` *<maxbytes>*	(Keyword: limit) Takes a maximum octet size argument and causes messages larger than this size to not be fetched, but left on the server (in foreground sessions, the progress messages note that they are oversized).
`-w` *<interval>* `--warnings` *<interval>*	(Keyword: warnings) Takes an interval in seconds. When `fetchmail` is called with a limit option in daemon mode, this controls the interval at which warnings about oversized messages are mailed to the calling user (or the user specified by the `postmaster` option).
`--fetchsizelimit` *<number>*	(Keyword: fetchsizelimit) Limits the number of sizes of messages accepted from a given server in a single transaction. Useful in reducing the delay in downloading the first mail when there are too many mails in the mailbox. By default, the limit is 100. If set to 0, sizes of all messages are downloaded at the start. Does not work with ETRN or ODMR. For POP3, the only valid nonzero value is `1`.

TABLE 13.8 Continued

`-e <count>` `--expunge <count>`	(keyword: expunge) Arrange for deletions to be made final after a given number of messages. Under POP2 or POP3, `fetchmail` cannot make deletions final without sending QUIT and ending the session—with this option on, `fetchmail` breaks a long mail retrieval session into multiple subsessions, sending QUIT after each subsession.
Authentication Options	
`-u <name>` `--username <name>`	(Keyword: user[*name*]) Specifies the user identification to be used when logging in to the mail server. The appropriate user identification is both server and user-dependent. Default is your login name on the client machine that is running `fetchmail`.
`--auth <type>`	(Keyword: auth[enticate]) This option permits you to specify an authentication. The possible values are `any`, `password`, `kerberos_v5`, `Kerberos`, `kerberos_v4`, `gssapi`, `cram-md5`, `otp`, `ntlm`, and `ssh`.
Miscellaneous	
`-d <interval>` `--daemon <interval>`	Runs `fetchmail` in daemon mode. You must specify a numeric argument which is a polling interval in seconds. In daemon mode, `fetchmail` puts itself in background and runs forever, querying each specified host and then sleeping for the given polling interval. Only one daemon process is permitted per user; in daemon mode, `fetchmail` makes a per-user lockfile to guarantee this.

Building Block Simplicity: `mail`

The `mail` program is a simple command-line program for sending and reading email. Invoked with no arguments, its default behavior is to display the list of messages in your system mailbox and provide a prompt from which further interaction can occur. Used in this fashion, `mail` produces output similar to the code following the note.

> **NOTE**
>
> If you're just setting up your system, you're unlikely to have any mail and will probably get only a message that says `No mail for <username>`. If you never set up your machine as its own mail server, you'll have no reason to read your mail this way. You might still want to set up your machine to do its own mail delivery, which allows you to use the `mail` command as a building block application for shell scripts. We'll talk more about this in Chapter 15, "Shell Configuration and Programming (Shell Scripting)."

```
ryoohki:~ joray$ mail
Mail version 8.1 6/6/93.  Type ? for help.
"/var/mail/joray": 209 messages 209 unread
>U  1 shew.1@osu.edu          Tue Jan  4 09:57 146/7905   "CBSSTAFF mailing list"
 U  2 listproc@lists.acs.o  Tue Jan  4 09:57  49/2105   "WHICH"
```

```
 U  3 server@lists.acs.ohi  Tue Jan  4 09:57  85/3441  "CBSSTAFF: Warning dur"
 U  4 listproc@lists.acs.o  Tue Jan  4 09:57  56/2500  "Subscription approval"
 U  5 shew.1@osu.edu        Tue Jan  4 09:57 5675/432904 "RE: windows ssh stu"
 U  6 cert-advisory@cert.o  Tue Jan  4 09:57 181/7710  "New CERT Coordination"
 U  7 cert-advisory@cert.o  Tue Jan  4 09:57 311/12778 "CERT Advisory CA-2003"
 U  8 OSUToday@osu.edu      Tue Jan  4 09:57 187/8865  "Headlines for Wednesd"
 U  9 OSUToday@osu.edu      Tue Jan  4 09:57 185/8613  "Headlines for Thursda"
 U 10 cert-advisory@cert.o  Tue Jan  4 09:57 251/10400 "CERT Advisory CA-2003"
 U 11 OSUToday@osu.edu      Tue Jan  4 09:57 185/9048  "Headlines for Friday,"
 U 12 OSUToday@osu.edu      Tue Jan  4 09:57 193/9549  "Headlines for Monday,"
 U 13 drake.2@osu.edu       Tue Jan  4 09:57 131/4928  "Fwd: Wellness Tip"
 U 14 OSUToday@osu.edu      Tue Jan  4 09:58 170/7975  "Headlines for Tuesday"
 U 15 OSUToday@osu.edu      Tue Jan  4 09:58 176/8488  "Headlines for Wednesd"
 U 16 listproc@lists.acs.o  Tue Jan  4 09:58 149/6610  "Error Condition Re: U"
 U 17 OSUToday@osu.edu      Tue Jan  4 09:58 209/10204 "Headlines for Thursda"
 U 18 OSUToday@osu.edu      Tue Jan  4 09:58 189/9044  "Headlines for Friday,"
 U 19 OSUToday@osu.edu      Tue Jan  4 09:58 186/8988  "Headlines for Monday,"
 U 20 bobd@araminta.uts.oh  Tue Jan  4 09:58 462/18690 "SGI Security Advisory"
&
```

The & on the last line is the internal `mail` prompt from which you can enter commands. At the & prompt, you have a number of options. These include the expected functions of reading, sending, and deleting messages, as well as a few others. Table 13.9 details the syntax and some useful options in the `mail` program. In this example we are looking at the mail that was just retrieved via `fetchmail`. The `mail` utility displays the date as the download date in this summary view. If you actually look at a message, though, you can see the actual message date in the `Date:` line, as shown in the headers for message 8:

```
& 8
Message 8:
From devnull@osu.edu  Tue Jan  4 09:57:55 2005
X-Original-To: joray@localhost
Delivered-To: joray@localhost.biosci.ohio-state.edu
Date: Tue, 04 Nov 2003 22:01:43 -0500 (EST)
Date-warning: Date header was inserted by mail-mta1.service.ohio-state.edu
From: OSUToday <OSUToday@osu.edu>
Subject: Headlines for Wednesday, Nov. 5, 2003
To: ray.3@osu.edu
MIME-version: 1.0
Content-type: TEXT/PLAIN
Content-transfer-encoding: 8BIT
X-BulkMail-Envelope-From: <devnull@osu.edu>
Original-recipient: rfc822;ray.3@osu.edu
X-Status:
X-Keywords:
X-UID: 8
```

13

TABLE 13.9 The `mail` Program Syntax and Useful Options

`mail`	Sends and receives mail.
`mail [-iInv] [-s` *<subject>*`] [-c` *<cc-addr>*`] [-b` *<bcc-addr>*`]` *<to-addr>*`...`	
`mail [-iInNv] -f [`*<name>*`]`	
`mail [-iInNv] [-u` *<user>*`]`	
`mail`	
`-i`	Ignores `tty` interrupt signals. Especially useful for communication on noisy phone lines.
`-n`	Ignores `/etc/mail.rc` on startup.
`-s` *<subject>*	Specifies the subject. Uses only the first argument after the flag. Be sure to use quotes for any subjects with spaces.
`-c` *<cc-addr>*	Sends a carbon copy to the users specified in *<cc-addr>*.
`-b` *<bcc-addr>*	Sends a blind copy to the users specified in *<bcc-addr>*. The list should be a comma-separated list.
`-f [`*<name>*`]`	Reads the contents of your `mbox` or the file specified by *<name>*. When you quit, `mail` writes undeleted messages back to this file.
`-u` *<user>*	Equivalent to `-f /usr/mail/`*<user>*.

Here are some of the useful options available within `mail`:

`-`*<n>*	Displays the previous message, if *<n>* is not specified; otherwise, displays the *<n>*th previous message.
`?`	Displays a brief summary of commands.
`^D`	Sends the composed message.
`!`*<shell_command>*	Executes the shell command that follows.
`<return>`	Goes to the next message in sequence.
n	
`+`	
`R`	Replies to the sender of the message. Does not reply to any other recipients of the message.
`r`	Replies to the sender and all other recipients of the message.
`mail` *<user>*	Sends mail to the *<user>* specified. Takes login names and distribution
`m`	group names as arguments.
`d`	Takes as its argument a list of messages and marks them to be deleted. Messages marked for deletion are not available for most other commands.
`dp`	Deletes the current message and prints the next message.
`u` *<messages>*	Takes a message list as its argument and unmarks the messages for deletion. A *message list* is a series of space-separated message numbers.
`e`	Takes as its argument a list of messages and points a text editor at each one in turn.
`inc`	Checks for any new incoming messages that have arrived since the session began and adds those to the message list.
`s`	Takes as its argument a list of messages and a filename and saves the messages to the filename. Each message is appended to the file. If no message is given, saves the current message.
`w`	Similar to `save`, except saves only the body of messages.
`U`	Takes as its argument a list of messages and marks them as not read.

TABLE 13.9 Continued

a	With no arguments, prints out the list of currently defined aliases. With one argument, prints out the specified alias. With multiple arguments, creates a new alias or edits an old one.
unalias	Takes as its argument a list of names defined by alias commands and discards the remembered groups of users.
x	Exits `mail` without making any changes to the user's `mbox`, system mailbox, or the `-f` file that was being read.
q	Terminates the session, saving all undeleted messages in the user's `mbox`.

CAUTION

Under some versions of Mac OS X, Apple has provided a program named `Mail`, as well as a program named `mail`. (Remember, capitalization makes a difference in the Unix world; these programs have different capitalization and therefore are not the same thing.) This does not seem to be the case with a fresh install of 10.4, but we can't be sure of the results of every possible upgrade path. In most Unixes, there is a difference in functionality between `Mail` and `mail`. Specifically, `mail` is usually a simple application mostly useful for quick shell-scripting applications—it usually produces a dump of all new messages as its default action. `Mail`, on the other hand, usually provides the interface discussed here. Intentionally or unintentionally, Apple's `mail` acts like the traditional `Mail`. As of this writing, the versions of `Mail` that we can find also act like the traditional `Mail`, but that has not always been the case with Mac OS X. Apple's `mail` program is also the one that is documented.

Full-Featured Power: `pine`

`pine` is a command-line-based modern email client. It provides access to system mailboxes as well as remote (or local if you choose) POPmail and IMAP servers. The `pine` email client provides an interface that will be much more familiar to users of applications such as Eudora. Although text-based, it provides a menu-driven interface with multiple mailboxes, sophisticated filtering, and other friendly conveniences. As of this writing, Apple doesn't distribute `pine` as a default application with Mac OS X, but it's a popular enough mail client that many sites will have it installed. If you're playing system administrator for your own machine, the installation of `pine` is covered in Chapter 14.

`pine`, being a menu-driven, windowed system, doesn't lend itself to command documentation tables, so we give you some output captures. The first output capture shows the first `pine` screen you'll see when you start it up. Unless you have `postfix` working properly, *don't* press the Return key to send the requested statistic information!

```
PINE 4.61   GREETING TEXT                                   No Messages

                    <<<This message will appear only once>>>

          Welcome to Pine ... a Program for Internet News and Email

We hope you will explore Pine's many capabilities. From the Main Menu,
```

```
select Setup/Config to see many of the options available to you. Also
note that all screens have context-sensitive help text available.

SPECIAL REQUEST: This software is made available world-wide as a public
service of the University of Washington in Seattle. In order to justify
continuing development, it is helpful to have an idea of how many people
are using Pine. Are you willing to be counted as a Pine user? Pressing
Return will send an anonymous (meaning, your real email address will not
be revealed) message to the Pine development team at the University of
Washington for purposes of tallying.

             Pine is a trademark of the University of Washington.


                                [ALL of greeting text]
? Help      E Exit this greeting              - PrevPage % Print
          Ret [Be Counted!]                 Spc NextPage
```

As you can see, you can choose from any keys at the bottom to start using the program.

The following is the more typical `pine` top-level screen from which you'll work. You can choose items from the textual menu shown on the screen, and also choose commands from those shown at the bottom of the screen. One thing that you should be aware of is that `pine` usually expects you to "go back" to get out of any particular situation or location you've gotten to in the program. It's sort of like wandering around on the World Wide Web—there isn't necessarily a link back to the first page from any subpages several layers down in the system. Look for options that take you to the previous screen and so on to assist in navigating the system.

```
PINE 4.61   MAIN MENU                         Folder: INBOX  209 Messages


          ?     HELP               -  Get help using Pine

          C     COMPOSE MESSAGE    -  Compose and send a message

          I     MESSAGE INDEX      -  View messages in current folder

          L     FOLDER LIST        -  Select a folder to view

          A     ADDRESS BOOK       -  Update address book

          S     SETUP              -  Configure Pine Options

          Q     QUIT               -  Leave the Pine program


    Copyright 1989-2004.  PINE is a trademark of the University of Washington.
```

```
                    [Folder "INBOX" opened with 209 messages]
? Help                     P PrevCmd                   R RelNotes
O OTHER CMDS > [ListFldrs] N NextCmd                   K KBLock
```

Here is what the mail we downloaded with `fetchmail` looks like as viewed in the `pine` email reader. Note that `pine` displays the actual message date rather than the download date. Again, at the bottom, is a menu that guides you through using the program.

```
PINE 4.61   MESSAGE INDEX               Folder: INBOX  Message 1 of 209 NEW

  N   1 Oct 10 Sandy Shew           (7907) CBSSTAFF mailing list (and list of add
  N   2 Oct 13 OSU ListProcessor    (2022) WHICH
  N   3 Oct 13 server@lists.acs.o   (3396) CBSSTAFF: Warning during message deliv
  N   4 Oct 13 OSU ListProcessor    (2424) Subscription approval request
  N   5 Oct 14 Sandy Shew           (438K) RE: windows ssh stuff
  N   6 Oct 15 CERT Advisory        (7764) New CERT Coordination Center (CERT/CC)
  N   7 Oct 16 CERT Advisory         (13K) CERT Advisory CA-2003-27 Multiple Vuln
  N   8 Nov  4 OSUToday             (8938) Headlines for Wednesday, Nov. 5, 2003
  N   9 Nov  5 OSUToday             (8684) Headlines for Thursday, Nov. 6, 2003
  N  10 Nov 11 CERT Advisory         (11K) CERT Advisory CA-2003-28 Buffer Overfl
  N  11 Nov 13 OSUToday             (9118) Headlines for Friday, Nov. 14, 2003
  N  12 Nov 16 OSUToday             (9627) Headlines for Monday, Nov. 17, 2003
  N  13 Nov 17 Cathy Drake          (4944) Fwd: Wellness Tip
  N  14 Nov 17 OSUToday             (8030) Headlines for Tuesday, Nov. 18, 2003
  N  15 Nov 18 OSUToday             (8549) Headlines for Wednesday, Nov. 19, 2003
  N  16 Nov 19 listproc@lists.acs   (6620) Error Condition Re: Undelivered Mail R
  N  17 Nov 20 OSUToday              (10K) Headlines for Thursday, Nov. 20, 2003
  N  18 Nov 20 OSUToday             (9118) Headlines for Friday, Nov. 21, 2003
  N  19 Nov 23 OSUToday             (9059) Headlines for Monday, Nov. 24, 2003

? Help       < FldrList   P PrevMsg       - PrevPage D Delete      R Reply
O OTHER CMDS > [ViewMsg]  N NextMsg     Spc NextPage U Undelete    F Forward
```

Text Editors

Even though you might think that you'll never have a reason to use anything other than a GUI text editor such as `Alpha` or `BBEdit`, there are a few arguments to be made for text-only mode editing in a terminal. Among them are that the text-only editors can be used even when the system can't display a GUI interface, and that an editor in a terminal can start much faster than most GUI editors. There's also the advantage that if you have occasion to work on Unix machines other than Mac OS X boxes, the command-line editors are what you will have available.

Finally, at this point, the GUI clients available currently seem to have a bit of a problem figuring out whether they should convert a file that they load into Mac-style text (for newlines) or Unix-style text. The Unix command-line editors are a bit more predictable in preferring Unix-format text. Because of this, if you're working with files in the traditional-Unix side of the system, you're probably safer sticking to the command-line editors.

When it comes to editing text on the Unix side, you'll find that many Unix programs use text files as input, create text files as output, or are configured using commands and variables set up in text files. To change the contents of these files, you'll need to use a text editor.

As a matter of fact, most Unix software doesn't know the difference between a text file and any other file. Unlike in Mac OS, from the point of view of Mac OS X's underlying Unix system, files are files are files. If the user chooses to view some of them as containing text and some as containing programs, that's the user's business. An interesting consequence of this lack of concern about a file's contents is that the operating system is just as happy to allow you to use a text editor to edit the contents of your spreadsheet program itself as it is to enable you to attempt to run your email mailbox. Of course, if you actually have execute permission turned on for your email and try to run it, it's almost certainly going to result in nothing more interesting than a bus error and an immediate exit of the command—but the operating system will try to do as you command.

TIP

If you are a programmer, you might find this lack of distinction (yet another example of Unix abstraction at work) to be useful. On occasion, you might find a program that needs a minor change, such as the correction of a misspelling or a change of wording. In these instances, it is sometimes more convenient to simply load the executable file into a text editor and make the correction directly into the binary. This isn't a trick for the faint of heart, but sometimes it's the quick fix you need, and occasionally it's the only fix available for software for which you don't have access to the source.

If you spend much time discussing Unix editors with longtime Unix users, you'll find that there is a disagreement of warlike proportions between the users of the two most common editors: `vi` and `emacs`. Although these editors are actually rather complementary in their functions and are both useful tools to have in your toolbox, chances are that you will run into many users who insist that one or the other editor is completely useless. If you listen to them, instead of keeping both tools handy, you'll be depriving yourself of the better solution to at least some tasks.

Many Unix editors have immense power. `emacs`, for example, not only contains its own built-in programming language but can also function as a complete windowing system, a compiler/debugger interface, a news reader, and many other things. Even with a book of this size, however, there isn't space to do more than address the basics of using these editors. After you've mastered the basics, if you're interested in learning more, we encourage you to stop by your local bookstore or library and choose from among the several books available on each of the major Unix editors.

Quick, Dirty, and Omnipresent: `vi`

The `vi` editor is Unix's most universal editor. Some users pronounce it *vee-eye*, and some pronounce it *vye*, and a growing contingent claim it's pronounced *six*, when used on Mac OS X. There seems to be no concrete consensus which pronunciation is correct (but the people who say *vye* are still wrong). `vi` isn't an easy editor and it isn't friendly. It is, however, a quick-starting editor with a small memory footprint, which you will find on every Unix machine you encounter, regardless of flavor. `vi`, although annoying to learn, is frequently the most convenient editor to use for doing things such as making single-line changes to configuration files.

NOTE

Apple now provides `vim` (`vi` *IMproved*) as a `vi`-replacement. `vim` provides some useful enhancements that are well beyond the design intent of `vi`. `vi` has historically eschewed fancy features such as syntax highlighting and multilevel undo, in favor of speed of use and ubiquity. Although it does have a sophisticated search-and-replace facility, some of `vi`'s strongest points are that it's small, fast, and available everywhere. These features have made `vi` a favorite of system administrators the world over because they know, with almost certainty, that even if all they have to work with on a machine is a paper-terminal (a thing that's much like a printer with a keyboard—no screen, just input on one line, output on the next, repeat...), `vi` will be there and work just like it does everywhere else. `vim` doesn't share these characteristics. It's reasonably fast on today's gigahertz processors, but it's about 20 times the size of `vi` in terms of disk and memory footprint, and it's by no means universally installed on all Unix systems. The improved features available in `vim` allow it to compete with some of the more complex `emacs` features, so you might find that it suits your needs as your day-to-day "power" editor, but we also recommend learning to operate comfortably within the `vi` subset of commands, just in case you ever need to work with the real thing.

When trying to use `vi` (or `vim`), there are a number of things you need to know to make it useful.

`vi` operates in one of two modes: command mode or insert mode. In command mode, you have control over things such as cursor position, deleting characters, and saving files. In command mode, every keyboard character you type will be interpreted as part of a command of some sort. In insert mode, every keyboard key you type is inserted into the file you are editing. This distinction is bound to be confusing at first, but if you use `vi`, you'll find that its speed makes it a preferred editor for quick changes to files. You will find the Return key included in the explanations here because some commands take effect immediately, and some require you to press Return after you enter them.

Table 13.10 shows some of the most used keys and tasks. If you're just coming to `vi` for the first time, *don't look too long at this table yet*; it will just look confusing! Flip past it to the short example of how to use `vi` and then turn back here and see whether, following the table, you understand what each key press did and why.

NOTE

Despite what anyone tells you, `vi`'s not difficult to use; it just looks that way. It looks that way because any way of presenting the separate command and editing interface in a discussion, or at least any way we've ever seen or come up with, looks confusing. Try it. It's not difficult; it *will* make sense.

TABLE 13.10 Common Key Presses and the Resultant Actions in `vi`

Mode	Key(s)/Key Combination(s)	Action
Command	l	Moves right
	h	Moves left
	j	Moves to next line
	k	Moves to previous line
	Put cursor on character and press x key	Deletes character under cursor
	Press d key twice	Deletes an entire line, including an empty line
	A	Enters insert mode at end of current line
	i	Enters insert mode before the character under the cursor
	a	Enters insert mode after the character under the cursor
	:w Return	Saves the file
	:w <*filename*> Return	Saves the file to <*filename*>
	:q Return	Quits
	:q! Return	Quits without saving
	:wq!	Saves file and exit
Insert Mode	Esc key	Switches to command mode
	Backspace or Delete key	Backspaces or deletes, but only for data entered in current insert mode session on the current line
	Any printable keyboard	Inserts the character at the cursor character

Instead of trying to walk through a screenshot-by-screenshot example of using `vi`, try typing the following example. Remember to compare what you're typing to the commands in Table 15.9, and watch what happens. Although the finer details are not revealed by this example, you will pick up enough to get you started doing useful work, and to get out of any sticky situations you might find yourself in while editing a file.

Try typing the following exactly as it appears here, and observe what happens. Where a new line appears in the text, press Return. Remember that `<esc>` is the Escape key.

```
brezup:ray testing $ vi mynewfile
iThis is my new file
This is line one of my new file
This is a test
This is line four of my new file<esc>kddkA
This is line three of my new file<esc>khhhhhhhhhhhhhhhhhxxxitwo<esc>:wq!
```

Your machine should respond

```
"mynewfile" [New file] 4 lines, 119 characters
```

although you might not be able to see that because the line flashes off the screen pretty quickly. Now look at what you have:

```
% cat mynewfile
This is my new file
This is line two of my new file
This is line three of my new file
This is line four of my new file
```


Table 13.11 shows the syntax and common options for the vi (vim) command.

TABLE 13.11 The Syntax and Common Useful Options for vi (vim)

vi	Screen-oriented text editor
ex	Line-oriented screen editor
view	Read-only version of vi

vi [-eFlRrSv] [-c *<cmd>*] [-t *<tag>*] [-w *<size>*] [*<file1>* *<file2>* ...]

ex [-eFlRrSsv] [-c *<cmd>*] [-t *<tag>*] [-w *<size>*] [*<file1>* *<file2>* ...]

view [-eFlRrSv] [-c *<cmd>*] [-t *<tag>*] [-w *<size>*] [*<file1>* *<file2>* ...]

vi/vim is a screen-oriented text editor; ex is a line-oriented editor. vi and ex are different interfaces to the same program. view is equivalent to vi -R, the read-only option to vi.

vim has many more options than vi, but the following are the common ones you'll probably be most interested in:

-e	Starts to edit in ex mode—that is, act like the line-mode ex editor. Few people like it when they land in ex; entering q at the prompt gets you out.
-R	Starts editing in read-only mode.
-r *<recoveryfile>*	Recovers the specified *<recoveryfile>*. If no file is specified, it lists the files that could be recovered. If no recoverable files with the specified name exist, vi starts editing as if the option has not been issued.
-c *<cmd>*	Executes *<cmd>* immediately after starting the edit session. It is especially useful for initial positioning in the file but is not limited to positioning commands.
-t *<tag>*	Starts editing at the specified *<tag>*.
-	Specifies that STDIN should be used as the source of the data to edit. Commands come from STDERR.

vi has two modes: command mode and input mode. Command mode is the initial and normal mode. Exiting from input mode (by pressing the Esc key) returns the user to command mode. Pressing the Esc key while in command mode aborts a partial command.

Some commands for moving around in a file:

h	Moves the cursor one character to the left.

TABLE 13.11 Continued

`l`	Moves the cursor one character to the right.
`j`	Moves the cursor one line down.
`k`	Moves the cursor one line up.
`<arrow keys>`	The arrow keys often also function properly for moving around in a file. Most seasoned uses find the `h/l/j/k` commands faster for navigation.
`<`*`num`*`>G`	Moves the cursor to the line number specified by <*num*>. If <*num*> is not specified, the cursor moves to the last line of the file.
`<`*`num`*`><`*`key1`*`>[<`*`key2`*`>...]`	If <*key1*> is a single-key command, acts as though the user had pressed the <*key1*> <*num*> times. If pressing <*key1*> would switch from command to editing mode, collects <*key2*>...<*keyN*> until the user presses `<esc>`; then acts as though the user had typed these keys <*num*> times in editing mode.
Some commands for inputting text (input mode):	
`i`	Inserts text before the cursor.
`a`	Appends new text after the cursor.
`A`	Appends new text at the end of the line where the cursor is.
`o`	Opens a new line below the line where the cursor is and allows the user to start entering text on the new line.
`O`	Opens a new line above the line where the cursor is, and allows the user to start entering text on that new line.
Some commands for copying text:	
`yy`	Copies the line the cursor is on.
`p`	Appends the copied line after the line the cursor is on.
Some commands for deleting text:	
`dd`	Deletes the line the cursor is on.
`<`*`num`*`>dd`	Deletes <*num*> lines, starting with the line the cursor is on.
`dw`	Deletes the word the cursor is on.
`x`	Deletes the character the cursor is on.
Some other useful text manipulation:	
`r<`*`x`*`>`	Replaces the character the cursor is on with <*x*>.
`J`	Joins the line the cursor is on with the line below.
Some commands for pattern searching:	
`/<`*`pattern`*`>`	Searches forward in the file for <*pattern*>, starting with the location of the cursor.
`?<`*`pattern`*`>`	Searches backward in the file for <*pattern*>, starting with the location of the cursor.
`n`	Repeats the last `/` or `?` pattern search.
`N`	Repeats the last `/` or `?` pattern search in reverse.
Some commands to write the file:	
`:w<return>`	Writes the file back to the filename originally specified when `vi` was started.
`:w <`*`filename`*`><return>`	Writes the file to the filename specified by <*filename*>.

TABLE 13.11 Continued

Some commands to quit editing and exit `vi`:	
`:q<return>`	Exits vi. Refuses to quit if there are any unsaved modifications, or if the file is read-only.
`:q!`	Exits `vi`, even if there are any unsaved modifications.
`ZZ`	Exits `vi`, saving changes.
Miscellaneous functionality:	
`:next`	Switch editing to the next file specified on the command line.

Everything and the Kitchen Sink: `emacs`

On the other end of the spectrum from `vi`'s odd syntax and tiny footprint is `emacs`. In certain circles, it is thought that `emacs` is an acronym for **E**macs **M**akes a **C**omputer **S**low because `emacs` epitomizes the notion of an "everything" package and has the memory footprint to prove it. Including a windowing system, an email-reading client, a news-reading client, a programming language, and an online help database, to name only a few of its features, `emacs` can almost certainly do anything you want a plain text editor to do.

NOTE

Don't believe me? `emacs` also includes an implementation of the aged Eliza psychoanalyst and a *Zippy the Pinhead* quote generator. Do you really think there's anything that's *not* in there? If you're creative, you can convince Zippy to have a conversation with Eliza inside `emacs`. Alternatively, you can play the pong video game, convert text to Morse code, manage your PIM schedule, or automatically insert keywords into your email to cause it to be flagged by the FBI's Carnivore mail-scanner as a possible terrorist threat. Browsing the categorized packages listing by entering `Esc-x help<CR> p` in a fresh `emacs` window should get you started on finding a wealth of interesting features you might never have imagined possible in a text editor.

With today's fast machines and nearly unlimited memory, the major complaints against `emacs` (it's a gargantuan application with a legendary hunger for computer resources—hey it's not all bad—people write haiku about it too!) aren't a significant impediment to its use.

From the point of view of the average user, `emacs` has a much more intuitive interface than `vi`. You're always in insert mode, just as you're used to in GUI-based word processors. Commands are handled by the use of `Control+`*`<key>`* combinations, instead of the use of a separate mode.

To use `emacs`, there are some basics that you need to know—you can get more information from the online tutorial mentioned at the end of this section. In the following list, whenever you see `Ctrl+` preceding a character, it means that you need to hold down the Control key and type that character. Whenever you see `Esc-` preceding a character, it means to press the `Esc` key and then the character.

- The `emacs` editor doesn't have a separate mode for entering commands. You are always either typing a command or typing text—no switching between modes for them. This is just like most word processors that you are probably familiar with. To enter text, just type what you want to appear. To enter a command (usually `Ctrl+`*<key>* or `Esc-x` *<somecommand>*), just type the command as shown.

- You can position the cursor keys in `emacs` by using the arrow keys. If you're working across a network connection, the arrow keys might not work, but you can also position the cursor with `Ctrl+`*<key>* combinations. `Ctrl+f` moves the cursor forward. `Ctrl+b` moves it back. `Ctrl+n` moves to the next line. `Ctrl+p` moves up one line.
- You can delete everything from the cursor to the end of the line with `Ctrl+k`. A second `Ctrl+k` deletes the now blank line.
- `Ctrl+g` is the `emacs` "quit what you're doing" command. If you've started typing a command and change your mind, press `Ctrl+g` to abort.
- If you use `Ctrl+k` to delete a line or lines, you can use `Ctrl+y` to yank it (them) back. You don't have to yank them to the same location from which you deleted them.
- To save the file you're working on, press `Ctrl+x Ctrl+s`.
- To save the file to a new name, press `Ctrl+x Ctrl+w` *<filename>* Return.
- To exit `emacs`, press `Ctrl+x Ctrl+c`. If `emacs` proceeds to ask you about unsaved buffers, it's because you have unsaved work. You can either answer no and save your work, or answer yes to the "quit anyway?" questions and exit without saving.

Beyond the `Ctrl+` commands available in `emacs`, an amazingly extensible set of commands also comes into play if you use the Escape (`Esc`) key. These commands are usually known as `emacs` *meta* commands, even though the machines with the meta key from which the commands draw their name have long since faded into history. These commands, even though they're initiated by pressing the Escape key, are usually abbreviated in the documentation with a leading `M` for `meta`. The complete set of these commands is the subject of more than one book, and we recommend that you investigate your library or bookstore options if you really want to understand the inner workings. If you're a puzzle solver, some of the interesting items are documented in Table 15.10. A good place to start on meta commands will be with testing out the `emacs` online help system. Start `emacs` by simply typing **`emacs`** at the prompt. After it has started, press `Esc-x` and then type **`help-`** and press the spacebar. You will be presented with a list of `emacs` commands starting with `help-`, including useful things such as `help-for-help`—a good place to start.

Instead of a quick example like the one we used for `vi`, we suggest you take the `emacs` tutorial. To enter the `emacs` tutorial, all you need to do is start `emacs` and press `Ctrl+h t` (hold the `Ctrl` key, press the `h` key, release them both, and press the `t` key). If you type a **?** after the `Ctrl+h` instead of the `t`, you'll see that there is actually a whole world of alternatives to the `t` (`Ctrl+h i` is another good place to look). These alternatives give you access to a range of different types of helpful information. For now, take the tutorial. If you're curious, you can probably spend almost eternity exploring the rest of the options available.

Table 13.12 shows a portion of the command documentation table for `emacs` as well as a listing of some of the help topics detailing a number of the available meta commands. The synopses of the help topic areas should give you an idea of some of the things that you can do, and some of the information that you can look for in the online documentation. A vastly more detailed list of capabilities can be accessed in `emacs` itself by typing **`M-x info`** and selecting the `emacs` documentation line. It should be clear even from this highly abridged listing that the complete documentation for `emacs` is voluminous.

TABLE 13.12 The Syntax and Some Useful Options for `emacs`

`emacs`	Editor
`emacs [`*<command-line switches>*`] [`*<file1> <file2>*`...]`	
`emacs` is a powerful editor that can actually do more than edit files. It has an extensive information system, which can be accessed in `emacs` with the key sequence `<Ctrl+h i>` (holding down the Control key and h and then i). The information system can be navigated using the arrow keys to move around and pressing the Return key to make a selection.	
`emacs` has an interactive help facility, `<Ctrl+h>`. The interactive Info information facility, which is a hierarchically organized, (usually) searchable collection of informative topic-related documents, is one type of help available. A help tutorial is available with `<Ctrl+h t>`. Help Apropos `<Ctrl+h a>` helps the user find a command given its functionality. Help Character `<Ctrl+h c>` describes a given character's effect.	
The following are `emacs` options of general interest:	
<file>	Edits the specified *<file>*.
+*<number>*	Moves the cursor to the line number specified by *<number>*. (Do not include a space between + and *<number>*.)
`-q`	Does not load an init file.
`-u` *<user>*	Loads the init file of the specified *<user>*.
`-t` *<file>*	Uses the specified *<file>* as the terminal instead of using `stdin/stdout`. This must be the first argument specified in the command line.
`-nw`	Tells `emacs` not to use its special X interface. When running under X11, some versions of `emacs` default to building an interface with a menu, which interacts (some say poorly) with the X11 cursor, allowing it to act a bit more like the traditional point-and-click editors with which you're familiar. This is sometimes convenient, but also can be incredibly annoying at times. If the `-nw` option is given when invoking `emacs` in an `xterm(1)` window, the `emacs` display is done in that window and `emacs` won't build its special interface. This must be the first option specified in the command line. This is useful if you're running an X server but want `emacs` to display in a terminal rather than the X Windows `xterm` or just plain don't want the special X11 interface.
The following are basic `emacs` key sequences. Remember that two keys pressed simultaneously have a plus sign between them, and a space indicates pressing them sequentially. Most Unix documentation, including the online man pages and info pages, will document `Esc-x` as `M-x` for the Meta key:	
Up Arrow	Move cursor up one line.
Left Arrow	Move cursor to the left one character; to end of previous line if at left side of current line.

TABLE 13.12 Continued

Right Arrow	Move cursor to the right one character; move to the beginning of the next line if at the right side of the current line.
Down Arrow	Move cursor down one line. Adds a new line to the file if currently on the last line of the file.
`Ctrl+p`	Move cursor up one line.
`Ctrl+b`	Move cursor to the left one character; to end of previous line if at left side of current line.
`Ctrl+f`	Move cursor to the right one character, move to the beginning of the next line if at the right side of the current line.
`Ctrl+n`	Move cursor down one line. Adds a new line to the file if currently on the last line of the file.
`Ctrl+v`	Move down one page in file.
`Esc-v`	Move up one page in file.
`Ctrl+l`	Move current line to the center of the page.
`Ctrl+a`	Move cursor to the beginning of the current line.
`Ctrl+e`	Move cursor to the end of the current line.
`Esc-a`	Move cursor to the beginning of the current sentence.
`Esc-e`	Move cursor to the end of the current sentence.
`Ctrl+x Ctrl+h`	Bring up list of `Ctrl+x` prefixed commands. (If you do this, you will see that this table is a *very* abbreviated list!)
`Ctrl+x Ctrl+s`	Save the file.
`Ctrl+x Ctrl+w`	Prompt for new name to save file.
`Ctrl+x Ctrl+c`	Exit `emacs`.
`Ctrl+x Ctrl+f`	Prompt to open file.
`Ctrl+x Ctrl+b`	List current file buffers.
`Ctrl+x b`	Prompt to switch to another buffer.
`Esc-x`	Prompt to open file in literal `find-file-literally` mode—no Mac/Unix linefeed interpretation and so on. This is an important option for Mac users wanting to use `emacs` to convert Mac files to the Unix line-ending style.
`Ctrl+x Ctrl+d`	List directory in `emacs` buffer (allows opening files by browsing directory rather than by typing name).
`Ctrl+x Ctrl+o`	Delete blank lines in file.
`Ctrl+x Ctrl+t`	Transpose lines.
`Ctrl+spacebar`	Set mark at the current cursor position.
`Ctrl+x Ctrl+l`	Downcase region. The region is the area between the cursor, and where the current mark is set.
`Ctrl+x Ctrl+u`	Upcase region. The region is the area between the cursor, and where the current mark is set.
`Ctrl+w`	Delete from mark to cursor. Deleted text goes to kill-ring buffer.
`Ctrl+s`	Enter incremental search mode. Any characters typed after `Ctrl+s` are searched for. Pressing `Ctrl+s` again searches for the next instance of the current search term. Use `Ctrl+g`, a navigation key such as the forward/backward arrows, or `Ctrl+f`/`Ctrl+b` to get out of this mode.

TABLE 13.12 Continued

Ctrl+r	Enter incremental search mode, searching backward in the file.
Esc-w	Copy from mark to cursor into kill-ring buffer.
Ctrl+k	Delete from cursor to end of line. Place deleted text in kill-ring buffer.
Ctrl+y	Yank top data from kill-ring buffer into the text at the current cursor position.
Ctrl+x 2	Split current window vertically into two editing windows (two full-width windows, half the previous height).
Ctrl+x 3	Split current window horizontally into two editing windows (two full-height windows, half the previous width).
Ctrl+x o	Switch to next editing window in split-window mode.
Ctrl+x 1	Switch to single-window mode, keeping the current window open.
Ctrl+x 0	Remove current editing window, keeping others.
Ctrl+x (	Start recording keyboard macro.
Ctrl+x)	Stop recording keyboard macro.
Ctrl+x e	Execute recorded keyboard macro.
Ctrl+u <####>	Create a numeric argument for the next command.
Ctrl+u <####> *<keyseq>*	Execute *<keyseq>* #### times.
Ctrl+x f	Set fill column for word wrap. Requires a numeric argument set with Ctrl+u <####>.
Esc-x fill-region	Word wrap region between cursor and mark.
Ctrl+h Ctrl+h	Bring up menu of help subjects.
Ctrl+h t	Bring up emacs tutorial.
Ctrl+h i	Bring up emacs info-mode manual browser. Browsing through the emacs info through this interface is recommended.
Esc-x info	Bring up emacs info-mode manual browser.
Esc-x apropos	Prompt for command or key sequence to document.
Ctrl+h h	Bring up list of ways to say hello in 34 different languages—we told you emacs had *everything* in it!

The following is a listing of some of the interesting parts of the information system's main menu for emacs. You're supposed to be able to find these and search the subtopics in them by using Esc-x Index-info and entering a search, but there's currently no index distributed for you to search in. Because of this, if you want more information on these topics (there are actually many more than listed here), you'll need to bring up the Info system with Ctrl+h i, navigate (using the down-arrow) to the Emacs section, and then browse the topics included there. We wish we had the space to discuss and document even a fraction of the power that emacs provides, but lacking space, a back-of-the-dustjacket listing of the features we think are most interesting will have to suffice. Think of this listing as a jumping-off place for finding your way to emacs information and a whirlwind tour of some of the options you might never have known were available in a text editor:

Basic Interest

Distrib	How to get the latest emacs distribution.
Copying	The GNU General Public License gives you permission to redistribute GNU emacs on certain terms; it also explains that there is no warranty.

TABLE 13.12 Continued

Intro	An introduction to `emacs` concepts.
Glossary	The glossary.
Mac OS	Using `emacs` in the Mac.
Manifesto	What's GNU? Gnu's Not Unix!
Indexes (Nodes Containing Large Menus)	
Key Index	An item for each standard `emacs` key sequence.
Command Index	An item for each command name.
Variable Index	An item for each documented variable.
Concept Index	An item for each concept.
Option Index	An item for every command-line option.
Important General Concepts	
Screen	How to interpret what you see on the screen.
User Input	Kinds of input events (characters, buttons, function keys).
Keys	Key sequences: what you type to request one editing action.
Commands	Named functions run by key sequences to do editing.
Entering Emacs	Starting `emacs` from the shell.
Exiting	Stopping or killing `emacs`.
Command Arguments	Hairy startup options.
Fundamental Editing Commands and Concepts	
Basic	The most basic editing commands.
Minibuffer	Entering arguments that are prompted for.
M-x	Invoking commands by their names.
Help	Commands for asking `emacs` about its commands.
Important Text-Changing Commands and Concepts	
Mark	The mark: how to delimit a region of text.
Killing	Killing text.
Yanking	Recovering killed text. Moving text.
Accumulating Text	Other ways of copying text.
Rectangles	Operating on the text inside a rectangle on the screen.
Search	Finding or replacing occurrences of a string.
Fixit	Commands especially useful for fixing typos.
Major Structures of `emacs`	
Files	All about handling files.
Buffers	Multiple buffers; editing several files at once.
Windows	Viewing two pieces of text at once.
Advanced Features	
Major Modes	Text mode versus Lisp mode versus C mode.
Indentation	Editing the whitespace at the beginnings of lines.
Text	Commands and modes for editing English.
Programs	Commands and modes for editing programs.
Building	Compiling, running, and debugging programs.
Maintaining	Features for maintaining large programs.
Abbrevs	How to define text abbreviations to reduce the number of characters you must type.

TABLE 13.12 Continued

Picture	Editing pictures made up of characters using the quarter-plane screen model.
Dired	You can "edit" a directory to manage files in it.
Calendar/Diary	The calendar and diary facilities.
Shell	Executing shell commands from `emacs`.
Hardcopy	Printing buffers or regions.
PostScript	Printing buffers or regions as PostScript.
Sorting	Sorting lines, paragraphs, or pages within `emacs`.
Two-Column	Splitting apart columns to edit them in side-by-side windows.
Editing Binary Files	Using Hexl mode to edit binary files.
Saving Emacs	Saving `emacs` state from one
Sessions	session to the next.
Emulation	Emulating some other editors with `emacs`.
Hyperlinking	Following links in buffers.
Dissociated Press	Dissociating text for fun.
Amusements	Various games and hacks.
Customization	Modifying the behavior of `emacs`.
The deeper levels of the documentation include topics covering the following (and many more) useful areas:	
The Organization of the Screen	
Point	The place in the text where editing commands operate.
Echo Area	Short messages appear at the bottom of the screen.
Mode Line	Interpreting the mode line.
Menu Bar	How to use the menu bar.
Basic Editing Commands	
Inserting Text	Inserting text by simply typing it.
Moving Point	How to move the cursor to the place where you want to change something.
Erasing	Deleting and killing text.
Undo	Undoing recent changes in the text.
Files: Basic Files	Visiting, creating, and saving files.
Continuation Lines	Lines too wide for the screen.
Position Info	What page, line, row, or column is point on?
Arguments	Numeric arguments for repeating a command.
The Minibuffer	
Minibuffer File	Entering filenames with the minibuffer.
Minibuffer Edit	How to edit in the minibuffer.
Completion	An abbreviation facility for minibuffer input.
Minibuffer History	Reusing recent minibuffer arguments.
Repetition	Re-executing commands that used the minibuffer.
Help	
Help Summary	Brief list of all Help commands.
Key Help	Asking what a key does in Emacs.
Name Help	Asking about a command, variable, or function name.
Apropos	Asking what pertains to a given topic.

TABLE 13.12 Continued

The Mark and the Region	
Setting Mark	Commands to set the mark.
Transient Mark	How to make emacs highlight the region—when there is one.
Using Region	Summary of ways to operate on contents of the region.
Mark Ring	Previous mark positions saved so you can go back there.
Global Mark Ring	Previous mark positions in various buffers.
Deletion and Killing	
Deletion	Commands for deleting small amounts of text and blank areas.
Killing by Lines	How to kill entire lines of text at one time.
Other Kill Commands	Commands to kill large regions of text and syntactic units such as words and sentences.
Yanking (That Is, *Pasting*, for Mac Folks)	
Kill Ring	Where killed text is stored. Basic yanking.
Appending Kills	Several kills in a row all yanked together.
Earlier Kills	Yanking something killed some time ago.
Controlling the Display	
Scrolling	Moving text up and down in a window.
Horizontal Scrolling	Moving text left and right in a window.
Follow Mode	Lets two windows scroll as one.
Selective Display	Hiding lines with a lot of indentation.
Searching and Replacement	
Incremental Search	Search happens as you type the string.
Nonincremental Search	Specify entire string and then search.
Word Search	Search for sequence of words.
Regexp Search	Search for match for a regular expression.
Regexps	Syntax of regular expressions.
Replace	Search and replace some or all matches.
Replacement Commands	
Unconditional Replace	Replacing all matches for a string.
Regexp Replace	Replacing all matches for a regular expression.
Replacement and Case	How replacements preserve case of letters.
Query Replace	How to use querying.
Commands for Fixing Typos	
Kill Errors	Commands to kill a batch of recently entered text.
Transpose	Exchanging two characters, words, lines, lists.
Fixing Case	Correcting case of last word entered.
Spelling	Apply spelling checker to a word or a whole buffer.
Using Multiple Buffers	
Select Buffer	Creating a new buffer or reselecting an old one.
List Buffers	Getting a list of buffers that exist.
Kill Buffer	Killing buffers you no longer need.
Several Buffers	How to go through the list of all buffers and operate variously on several of them.

TABLE 13.12 Continued

Multiple Windows	
Basic Window	Introduction to `emacs` windows.
Split Window	New windows are made by splitting existing windows.
Other Window	Moving to another window or doing something to it.
Pop Up Window	Finding a file or buffer in another window.
Force Same Window	Forcing certain buffers to appear in the selected window rather than in another window.
Change Window	Deleting windows and changing their sizes.
Major Modes	
Choosing Modes	How major modes are specified or chosen.
Commands for Human Languages	
Words	Moving over and killing words.
Sentences	Moving over and killing sentences.
Paragraphs	Moving over paragraphs.
Pages	Moving over pages.
Filling	Filling or justifying text.
Case	Changing the case of text.
Text Mode	The major modes for editing text files.
Outline Mode	Editing outlines.
TeX Mode	Editing input to the formatter TeX.
Nroff Mode	Editing input to the formatter nroff.
Formatted Text	Editing formatted text directly in WYSIWYG fashion.
Filling (That Is, Automatically Rewrapping) Text	
Auto Fill	Auto Fill mode breaks long lines automatically.
Fill Commands	Commands to refill paragraphs and center lines.
Editing Programs	
Program Modes	Major modes for editing programs.
Defuns	Commands to operate on major top-level parts of a program.
Program Indent	Adjusting indentation to show the nesting.
Comments	Inserting, killing, and aligning comments.
Parentheses	Commands that operate on parentheses.
Documentation	Getting documentation of functions you plan to call.
Hideshow	Displaying blocks selectively.
Symbol Completion	Completion on symbol names of your program or language.
Misc for Programs	Other `emacs` features useful for editing programs.
C Modes	Special commands of C, C++, Objective-C, Java, and Pike modes.
Fortran	Fortran mode and its special features.
Indentation for Programs	
Basic Indent	Indenting a single line.
Multi-line Indent	Commands to reindent many lines at once.
Lisp Indent	Specifying how each Lisp function should be indented.
C Indent	Extra features for indenting C and related modes.
Custom C Indent	Controlling indentation style for C and related modes.

TABLE 13.12 Continued

Documentation Lookup	
Info Lookup	Looking up library functions and commands in Info files.
Man Page	Looking up man pages of library functions and commands.
Lisp Doc	Looking up `emacs` Lisp functions, and so on.
C and Related Modes	
Motion in C	Commands to move by C statements, and so on.
Electric C	Colon and other chars can automatically reindent.
Hungry Delete	A more powerful DEL command.
Other C Commands	Filling comments, viewing expansion of macros, and other neat features.
Comments in C	Options for customizing comment style.
Fortran Mode	
Motion: Fortran Motion.	Moving point by statements or subprograms.
Indent: Fortran Indent.	Indentation commands for Fortran.
Comments: Fortran Comments.	Inserting and aligning comments.
Autofill: Fortran Autofill	Auto fill minor mode for Fortran.
Columns: Fortran Columns.	Measuring columns for valid Fortran.
Abbrev: Fortran Abbrev.	Built-in abbreviations for Fortran keywords.
Compiling and Testing Programs	
Compilation	Compiling programs in languages other than Lisp (C, Pascal, and so on).
Compilation Mode	The mode for visiting compiler errors.
Compilation Shell	Customizing your shell properly for use in the compilation buffer.
Debuggers	Running symbolic debuggers for non-Lisp programs.
Executing Lisp	Various modes for editing Lisp programs, with different facilities for running
Lisp Eval	Executing a single Lisp expression in `emacs`.
Running Debuggers Under `emacs`	
Starting GUD	How to start a debugger subprocess.
Debugger Operation	Connection between the debugger and source buffers.
Commands of GUD	Key bindings for common commands.
GUD Customization	Defining your own commands for GUD.
Dired, the Directory Editor	
Dired Enter	How to invoke Dired.
Dired Navigation	How to move in the Dired buffer.
Dired Deletion	Deleting files with Dired.
Flagging Many Files	Flagging files based on their names.
Marks vs Flags	Flagging for deletion versus marking.
Operating on Files	How to copy, rename, print, compress, and so on. either one file or several files.
Shell Commands in Dired	Running a shell command on the marked files.

TABLE 13.12 Continued

Transforming File Names	Using patterns to rename multiple files.
Comparison in Dired	Running `diff` by way of Dired.
Subdirectories in Dired	Adding subdirectories to the Dired buffer.
Subdirectory Motion	Moving across subdirectories, and up and down.
Dired and Find	Using `find` to choose the files for Dired.
Customization	
Minor Modes	Each minor mode is one feature you can turn on independently of any others.
Variables	Many `emacs` commands examine `emacs` variables to decide what to do; by setting variables, you can control their functioning.
Keyboard Macros	A keyboard macro records a sequence of keystrokes to be replayed with a single command.
Key Bindings	The keymaps say what command each key runs. By changing them, you can redefine keys.
Keyboard Translations	If your keyboard passes an undesired code for a key, you can tell `emacs` to substitute another code.
Syntax	The syntax table controls how words and expressions are parsed.
Init File	How to write common customizations in the `.emacs` file.
Variables	
Examining	Examining or setting one variable's value.
Easy Customization	Convenient and easy customization of variables.
Hooks	Let you specify programs for parts of `emacs` to run on particular occasions.
Locals	Per-buffer values of variables.
File Variables	How files can specify variable values.
Keyboard Macros	
Basic Kbd Macro	Defining and running keyboard macros.
Save Kbd Macro	Giving keyboard macros names; saving them in files.
Kbd Macro Query	Making keyboard macros do different things each time.
Customizing Key Bindings	
Keymaps	Generalities. The global keymap.
Prefix Keymaps	Keymaps for prefix keys.
Local Keymaps	Major and minor modes have their own keymaps.
Minibuffer Maps	The minibuffer uses its own local keymaps.
Rebinding	How to redefine one key's meaning conveniently.
Init Rebinding	Rebinding keys with your init file, `.emacs`.
Function Keys	Rebinding terminal function keys.
Named ASCII Chars	Distinguishing <TAB> from Ctrl+i, and so on.
Mouse Buttons	Rebinding mouse buttons in `emacs`.
Disabling	Disabling a command means confirmation is required before it can be executed. This is done to protect beginners from surprises.
The Init File, `~/.emacs`	
Init Syntax	Syntax of constants in `emacs` Lisp.
Init Examples	How to do some things with an init file.

13

TABLE 13.12 Continued

Terminal Init	Each terminal type can have an init file.
Find Init	How emacs finds the init file.
Dealing with emacs Trouble	
DEL Does Not Delete	What to do if <DEL> doesn't delete.
Stuck Recursive	[...] in mode line around the parentheses.
Screen Garbled	Garbage on the screen.
Text Garbled	Garbage in the text.
Unasked-for Search	Spontaneous entry to incremental search.
Memory Full	How to cope when you run out of memory.
Emergency Escape	Emergency escape—what to do if emacs stops responding.
Total Frustration	When you are at your wit's end.
Command-Line Options and Arguments	
Action Arguments	Arguments to visit files, load libraries, and call functions.
Initial Options	Arguments that take effect while starting emacs.
Command Example	Examples of using command-line arguments.
Environment	Environment variables that emacs uses.
Environment Variables	
General Variables	Environment variables that all versions of emacs use.
Misc Variables	Certain system-specific variables.

Simple and Quick: nano

If you find vi to be unfriendly and emacs to be overwhelming, you might find nano more suitable. The nano editor (the name is derived from *Nano's ANOther* editor, according to the man page) is a small, menu-driven windowed editing system. It is a pico clone that is distributed under the GNU license. The pico editor was developed as the editor for the pine email package. Starting with Mac OS X 10.4, nano, rather than pico, is included, and pico is just a link to nano. This change is most likely a license issue.

Being a menu-driven system, nano does not lend itself to documentation tables, so instead we will show you some output samples. It is worthwhile, though, to take a look at the man page. nano can be run with some options that you might find useful. For example, the -B flag causes nano to write a backup of your file whose name ends in ~. You can also set nano settings in a ~/.nanorc control file, which is documented in the nanorc man page.

When you run nano, you will get output that looks like this:

```
GNU nano 1.2.4                  New Buffer
```

```
                                  [ New File ]
^G Get Help   ^O WriteOut   ^R Read File ^Y Prev Page ^K Cut Text  ^C Cur Pos
^X Exit       ^J Justify    ^W Where Is  ^V Next Page ^U UnCut Txt ^T To Spell
```

As with the pine email reader, there is a menu at the bottom to help you with using the program. After you've started typing something, the [New File] designation in the status line goes away.

When you decide to save your file, press Ctrl+O to save the file. The status line asks for the filename and the menu changes to include options pertinent to saving a file. Here is a sample of the changes you see in the nano interface:

```
GNU nano 1.2.4                New Buffer                            Modified

Hi there.

This is my nano test file.







File Name to Write: nano-test
^G Get Help         M-D DOS Format      M-A Append          M-B Backup File
^T To Files         M-O Mac Format      M-P Prepend         ^C Cancel
```

As you work with nano, you will probably find its help system to be useful. Here is the top-level help system page, which is useful for understanding other nano help pages:

```
GNU nano 1.2.4                New Buffer

 nano help text


 The nano editor is designed to emulate the functionality and ease-of-use
 of the UW Pico text editor.  There are four main sections of the editor:
 The top line shows the program version, the current filename being edited,
 and whether or not the file has been modified.  Next is the main editor
 window showing the file being edited.  The status line is the third line
 from the bottom and shows important messages. The bottom two lines show
 the most commonly used shortcuts in the editor.

 The notation for shortcuts is as follows: Control-key sequences are
 notated with a caret (^) symbol and are entered with the Control (Ctrl)
 key.  Escape-key sequences are notated with the Meta (M) symbol and can be
 entered using either the Esc, Alt or Meta key depending on your keyboard
```

```
 setup.  The following keystrokes are available in the main editor window.
 Alternative keys are shown in parentheses:

^G      (F1)            Invoke the help menu
^X      (F2)            Close currently loaded file/Exit from nano

^Y Prev Page                      ^X Exit
^V Next Page
```

Printing Tools

You already have some printing capability from the Terminal application's printing menu options and built in to the rest of your Mac OS X system. The command line, however, has its own printing facility, allowing you to direct the output of commands to a printer without having to select that output in the terminal and use the menu options to print. These command-line tools are actually fairly sophisticated, although they provide only a minimalist interface to the printing architecture. Print queuing, job-status notification, and print-job logging are all part of the standard Unix `lpr` printing system.

Since Mac OS X 10.2, Mac OS X has included Common Unix Printing System (CUPS) software. This package includes versions of print commands traditionally found on BSD systems as well as versions of print commands traditionally found on System V machines. Mac OS X 10.1 and earlier include only versions of BSD print commands. If you are running Mac OS X 10.1 or earlier, you do not have all the commands listed in this section. The first command listed in each subsection is the BSD-compatible command, and the one that you can find in Mac OS X 10.2 as well as earlier versions. The second command listed in each subsection is the System V–compatible command and is found only in the 10.2 and more recent distributions of Mac OS X.

Sending Jobs to the Printer: `lpr`

The command to send a job to the printer is `lpr`. Although there are a number of options to `lpr`, the most common forms that you will probably use are

```
lpr <filename>

lpr -P<printer> <filename>
```

The first example sends `<filename>` to the system's default printer. The second example sends `<filename>` to an alternative printer named `<printer>`. If your system has more than one printer available to it at the command line, the second form might be of use. Note that there is no space between the `-P` and `<printer>`. This is an example of traditional `lpr` syntax, which we are mentioning in case you encounter it on another system. The `lpr` that ships with Mac OS X 10.2 documents a space between the `-P` and `<printer>`, but the traditional syntax also works. If you are using Mac OS X 10.0 or 10.1, the `lpr` that ships with it documents only the traditional syntax; however, the nontraditional syntax also works. You can send multiple jobs to the printer at once, and they will be queued and printed in sequence.

The command provides no feedback other than a return to your prompt:

```
brezup:ray testing $ lpr my-test
brezup:ray testing $
```

Despite this, it's sent the file my-test off to be printed on my default printer. If I want to send the file to a printer other than my default printer, the -P <*printername*> option allows me to specify any printer configured on my system by name. Table 13.13 shows the syntax and important options for lpr.

TABLE 13.13 The Syntax and Important Options for lpr

lpr	Sends a job to the printer.
lpr [-E] [-P <*printer*>] [-# <*num-copies*> [-l] [-o <*option*>] [-p] [-r] [-C/J/T <*title*>] [<*file1*> <*file2*> ...]	
lpr submits files for printing. Files named on the command line are sent to the specified printer (or the default system printer if none is specified). If no files are listed on the command line, lpr reads the print file from the standard input.	
-P <*printer*>	Specifies <*printer*> as the printer. Otherwise, the site's default printer is used.
-# <*num-copies*>	Sets the number of copies to print from 1 to 100.
-r	Removes the named print files after printing them.
-T <*title*>	Sets the job name.

The other command that you can use to send a job to the printer is lp. The syntax that you will most commonly use is similar to that of lpr, but supports a number of additional options:

```
lp <filename>
lp -d <printer> <filename>
```

Here is a sample of the command in use:

```
brezup:ray testing $ lp term-window-1.tiff
request id is HP_Color_LaserJet_4550-4 (1 file(s))
```

Notice that the command responds by providing the job number, HP_Color_LaserJet_4550-4, in this case. The job number consists of the printer name and a number.

Table 13.14 shows the syntax and important options for lp.

TABLE 13.14 The Syntax and Important Options for lp

lp	Sends a job to the printer.
lp [-E] [-c] [-d *<printer>*] [-h *<hostname>*] [-m] [-n *<num-copies>*] [-o *<option>*] [-q *<priority>*] [-s] [-w] [-t *<title>*] [-H *<handling>*] [-P *<page-list>*] [*<file1>* *<file2>* ...]	
lp [-E] [-c] [-h *<server>*] [-i *<job-id>*] [-n *<num-copies>*] [-o *<option>*] [-q *<priority>*] [-t *<title>*] [-H *<handling>*] [-P *<page-list>*]	
-d *<printer>*	Prints to the specified *<printer>*.
-h *<server>*	Specifies the print server hostname. The default is localhost or the value of the CUPS_SERVER environment variable.
-i *<job-id>*	Specifies an existing job to modify.
-m	Sends email when the job is completed.
-n *<num-copies>*	Sets the number of copies to print from 1 to 100.
-t *<title>*	Sets the job name.
-H *<handling>*	Specifies when the job should be printed. A value of immediate prints the file immediately, a value of hold holds the job indefinitely, and a time value (HH:MM) holds the job until the specified time. Use a value of resume with the -i option to resume a held job.
-P *<page-list>*	Specifies which pages to print in the document. The list can contain a list of numbers and ranges (#-#) separated by commas (for example, 1,3-5,16).

Checking the Print Queue: lpq

Because lpr provides no feedback other than a return to your prompt, you might sometimes find it useful to check the print queue to check on the status of your print job. The lpq command displays the print queue:

```
brezup:ray testing $ lpq
HP_Color_LaserJet_4550 is ready and printing
Rank     Owner   Job     File(s)                         Total Size
active   ray     4       term-window-1.tiff              921600 bytes
```

This actually provides quite a bit of information. From the HP_Color_LaserJet_4550 line you get the printer's name. You might see anything here, depending on how the printer has been named. For example, you might even see location and printer model number.

The output displays each print job on one line. In this example, there is only one print job. The line describing the print job includes a print job number and the filename, size, and owner. If multiple jobs were queued on the printer, however, each would be listed here, along with the job owner, making it convenient to track down who's hogging all the printer time!

Table 13.15 is the command documentation table for lpq.

TABLE 13.15 The Command Documentation Table for `lpq`

`lpq`	Displays the queue of print jobs.
`lpq [ -E ] [ -P <printer> ] [ -a ] [ -l ] [ +<interval> ]`	
`-E`	Forces encryption when connecting to the server.
`-P <printer>`	Specifies `<printer>` as the printer. Otherwise, the site's default printer is used.
`-a`	Displays the queues for all printers.
`-l`	Displays the queue information in long format. Includes the name of the host from which the job originated.
`+<interval>`	Displays a continuous report of the jobs in the queue once every `<interval>` seconds until the queue is empty.

The other command that you can use to check the print queue is `lpstat`:

```
brezup:ray testing $ lpstat
HP_Color_LaserJet_4550-4          ray          1080320   Wed Jan  5 22:36:32 2005
```

The output of `lpstat` is similar to that of `lpq`. It includes the job number, owner, file size, and date.

Table 13.16 shows the syntax and important options for `lpstat`.

TABLE 13.16 Command Documentation Table for `lpstat`

`lpstat`	Prints CUPS status information.
`lpstat [ -E ] [ -h <server> ] [ -l ] [-W <which-jobs>] [-a [<printer(s)>]] [-c [<class(es)>]] [ -d ] [-o [<printer(s)>]] [ -p [<printer(s)>]] [ -r ] [ -R ] [ -s ] [ -t ] [ -u [<user(s)>]] [ -v [<printer(s)>]]`	
`-a [<printer(s)>]`	Shows the accepting state of printer queues. If no printers are specified, all printers are listed.
`-d`	Shows the current default destination.
`-h <server>`	Specifies the CUPS server to communicate with.
`-l`	Shows a long listing of printers, classes, or jobs.
`-o [<printer(s)>]`	Shows the jobs queue on the specified destinations. If no destinations are specified, all jobs are shown.
`-p [<printer(s)>]`	Shows the printers and whether they are enabled for printing. If no printers are specified, all printers are listed.
`-r`	Shows whether the CUPS server is running.
`-R`	Shows the ranking of print jobs.
`-s`	Shows a status summary, including the default destination, a list of classes and their member printers, and a list of printers and their associated `-d`, `-c`, and `-p` options.
`-t`	Shows all status information. This is equivalent to using the `-r`, `-d`, `-c`, `-d`, `-v`, `-a`, `-p`, and `-o` options.
`-u [<user(s)>]`	Shows a list of print jobs queued by the specified users. If no users are specified, lists the jobs queued by the current user.

TABLE 13.16 Continued

-v [<*printer(s)*>]	Shows the printers and what device they are attached to. If no printers are specified, all printers are listed.
-W [<*which-jobs*>]	Shows the current status of jobs that are waiting or being processed, or the completion status of jobs that have finished. <*which jobs*> may be completed or not-completed. This option must appear before -o for it to take effect.

Removing Printer Jobs: lprm

If you decide that you want like to remove a print job from the queue, use the lprm command. You might find it useful to use in conjunction with lpq.

Here is an example of using lprm:

```
brezup:sage Documents $ lpq
_192_168_1_3 is ready and printing
Rank    Owner   Job     File(s)                         Total Size
active  sage    27      view8.tiff                      472064 bytes
1st     sage    28      view9.tiff                      422912 bytes
2nd     sage    29      view7.tiff                      424960 bytes

brezup:sage Documents $ lprm 28
brezup:sage Documents $ lpq
_192_168_1_3 is ready and printing
Rank    Owner   Job     File(s)                         Total Size
active  sage    27      view8.tiff                      472064 bytes
1st     sage    29      view7.tiff                      424960 bytes
```

In this example, we used lpq to get a print job number and then used lprm to cancel a specific job number. Because this version of lprm does not provide feedback on the job cancellation, we again used lpq to verify the job's cancellation.

Table 13.17 is the command documentation table for lprm.

TABLE 13.17 The Command Documentation Table for lprm

lprm	Removes print jobs from the queue.
lprm [-E] [-] [-P <*printer*>] [<*job#1*> <*job#2*> ...]	
-E	Forces encryption when connecting to the server.
-	Removes all print jobs in the queue.
-P <*printer*>	Specifies <*printer*> as the printer. Otherwise, the site's default is used.
<*job#*>	Removes from the queue the print job specified by <*job#*>. The <*job#*> can be determined by using lpq(1).

The other command that you can use to remove a print job from the queue is cancel.

Because the `lp` command provides the print job name when you issue the command, you might not necessarily need to check the queue. However, the `cancel` command does not provide output, so you might want to use `cancel` in conjunction with `lpstat` to verify the job cancellation, as shown in the following example:

```
brezup:sage Documents $ lpstat
_192_168_1_3-31         sage            424960   Wed Jan  5 22:38:54 2005
_192_168_1_3-32         sage            472064   Wed Jan  5 22:39:04 2005
_192_168_1_3-33         sage            422912   Wed Jan  5 22:39:11 2005
brezup:sage Documents $ cancel _192_168_1_3-32
brezup:sage Documents $ lpstat
_192_168_1_3-31         sage            424960   Wed Jan  5 22:38:54 2005
_192_168_1_3-33         sage            422912   Wed Jan  5 22:39:11 2005
```


Table 13.18 is the command documentation table for `cancel`.

TABLE 13.18 The Command Documentation Table for `cancel`

`cancel`	Removes print jobs from the queue.
`cancel [ -a ] [ -h <server> ] [-u <username>] [ <id> ] [ <destination> ] [ <destination-id> ]`	
`-a`	Removes all jobs from the specified destination.
`-h <server>`	Specifies the print server hostname. The default is `localhost` or the value of the `CUPS_SERVER` environment variable.
`-u <username>`	Cancels jobs owned by `<username>`.

Controlling CUPS from the Command Line: `lpoptions`, `lpadmin`, `lpinfo`

Although not strictly part of the command-line suite of printing tools, the CUPS system includes command-line management software that provides administration and control capabilities far beyond what is currently available from either Apple's Print Center or the CUPS web interface. The most important of these, `lpadmin`, `lpoptions`, and `lpinfo`, allow you to create, configure, examine, and delete printers that can be accessed through the standard command-line printing interface (`lpr`) and through GUI applications via the Print dialog.

Configuring a CUPS Printer from the Command Line

Here we will duplicate our example of adding a serial-port-based Apple ImageWriter printer that we used in Chapter 6, "Printer, Fax, and Font Management." It's assumed that the correct PPD file has been downloaded and placed in `/usr/share/cups/model/`, and that the `foomatic-rip` filter is installed in `/usr/libexec/cups/filter/`. The `file` type dummy back end shouldn't be needed, but it shouldn't hurt anything by being present either. (It's necessary for the GUI interface because it generates the list of valid device URIs from the output from the collection of `backend` scripts. If there isn't a `file` script, the GUI doesn't know that it can do `file` printing. But the CUPS printing system knows about file output innately, so the command-line tools simply believe whatever you tell them and don't look in the backend directory to determine what's available.)

> **TIP**
>
> To better understand some of the command-line options, look back to Chapter 6 for more in-depth explanations of the concepts.

In Chapter 6, we specified the printer as printer name test; gave it a location and description; picked a connection type for it; specified the device URI; and finally selected a PPD. These are exactly the same steps we'll take here, only we aren't going to take them on five separate web pages or via dialog box entries. Instead, all this goes onto a single command line.

> **NOTE**
>
> If you didn't do it in Chapter 5, and Apple hasn't started distributing everything necessary to use CUPS and the complete suite of Gimp-Print Ghostscript drivers, you'll need to install the ESP Ghostscript version available from http://gimp-print.sourceforge.net/MacOSX.php3.

Using the -p option to specify a printer that doesn't already exist causes lpadmin to create it. Using the -D option allows the provision of a description. The -L option allows the provision of a location. The -v specification of a device URI provides both the connection type and the specific connection location information. The -m option allows you to pick a PPD from the model directory, and, finally, the -E option enables the printer for access. The command needs to be run as root.

```
lpadmin -p test_again -D "My ImageWriter Again" -L "Still in the Attic"
➥-v file:/dev/tty.USA28X21P1.1 -m Imagewriter.ppd -E
```

It might look a bit long, but it's really no more than a compound of what we did via the GUI into a single command. After executing this command, you could check your Print Center application, and you would see that a new printer had been added and activated. It will appear in the Print Center as My ImageWriter Again and be available from the command line as printer test_again.

Writing Your Own Simple Printer Driver for CUPS

As a matter of fact, from the command line, we've got considerably more power available in configuring the printer. From the Apple Print Center interface and from the CUPS administration web pages, we have only basic options available as to how to get data to the printer. I actually had to cheat a tiny bit in constructing the Chapter 6 demonstration for how to use the Print Center and CUPS interface with my ImageWriter. My serial interface currently refuses to accept any sort of flow control, and it's much faster than my poor old ImageWriter. Because of this, on large pages and images, the end of the page gets garbled because the printer can't keep up with the data stream.

I cheated by making a small modification to the `foomatic-rip` Perl script to throttle the speed down to something my printer can handle. Still, this is inelegant because I might have several printers that use the `foomatic-rip` filter, and I won't necessarily want to throttle them all down to ImageWriter speeds. The `lpadmin` command-line tool, however, gives me the option of saying "chuck all that automagic stuff; I'll run my printer myself, thank you very much," and allows me to specify a driver of my own creation. This comes at the cost of me having to write code to pass my data through Ghostscript (`gs`) for PostScript processing, if I want that functionality, and having to handle spooling the data to the printer myself.

This isn't a particularly appealing portion of the operating system to be messing around with, but it's not that difficult either. And it means that if you have any command-line software that can be made to speak to your printer, you can use it as glue between your printer and the CUPS system. For example, although only a basic vestige of a print spooler, the following code works nicely for passing PostScript code through Ghostscript (a PostScript interpreter) to format it for my ImageWriter, and for spooling the data to the serial port slowly enough that it doesn't overrun the printer's buffer.

```
#!/usr/local/bin/perl
use Time::HiRes qw ( time alarm sleep );
$thispid = $$;
open devfile, (">"."/dev/tty.USA28X1913P1.1");

while(<>)
{
  $infile .= $_;
}

$tmppsname = "/tmp/tempps".$thispid.".ps";
$tmpprnname = "/tmp/tempprint".$thispid.".prn";
open temppsfile, (">".$tmppsname);
print temppsfile $infile;
close temppsfile;

system "/usr/local/bin/gs -q -dNOPAUSE -dBATCH -sDEVICE=iwhi
➥-sOutputFile=$tmpprnname $tmppsname";

open tempprnfile, ("<",$tmpprnname);
while(read(tempprnfile,$line,128))
{
  print devfile $line;
  $line = '';
  sleep(.4);
}

close tmpprnfile;
```

13

```
close devfile;
system "rm -f $tmppsname";
system "rm -f $tmpprnname";
exit;
```

If I've named it `/usr/local/bin/myspooler.pl`, I can load it up as the driver for a CUPS printer named `testsomemore` by using the command line:

```
lpadmin -p testsomemore -D "Ye Olde Printer" -L "Cobweb City"
➥-i /usr/local/bin/myspooler.pl -E
```

The script isn't smart enough to handle data types other than PostScript, and some data streams have sections that still overrun the buffer even with a 0.4 second sleep embedded between every 128 characters (for example, the printer can't feed 128 blank lines in 0.4 seconds), but it's a solid beginning on which you could build a driver for any printer that you know how to access through the command line. If your serial interface (or other printing interface to which your printer is connected) handles flow control, you can safely do away with the makeshift `sleep` command and let the printer worry about pausing the interface when it needs time to catch up.

Don't struggle too hard trying to understand what that code does right now. You'll learn everything you need to know to modify it for your purposes in Chapter 18, "Using Scripting Languages," in the section on Perl programming. For now, simply understand that it does the following:

1. Captures data that software hands to it through CUPS.
2. Writes that to a temporary file with what should be a unique name.
3. Uses Ghostscript (`gs` at the command line) to process the first temporary file into the language supported by my ImageWriter.
4. Writes the result of this processing into a second temporary file with a unique name.
5. Reads that file in, 128 bytes at a time.
6. Sends each 128-byte chunk to the `/dev/` device associated with my serial port.
7. Cleans up after itself by closing connections to the open files and deleting the temporary files it has used.

This method (using `-i` scripts to process data) is unfortunately not entirely satisfactory for all users at this time because it appears that GUI printing does not always interact cleanly with printers specified in this fashion. The `testsomemore` printer created in the previous example is completely functional at the command line. Under some versions of Mac OS X, it's an apparent black hole for data printed by GUI applications. Under version 10.3 and later, it appears to work, but on versions on which it's a problem, GUI applications think that they're printing, but the printer spool never sees the data. I suspect that this is a symptom of some portion of the CUPS system being misconfigured on older versions of

Mac OS X, and it deciding that the target printer does not know how to handle the data type output by the application (as in, CUPS doesn't understand that the printer can handle PostScript, and so trashes the printing job rather than passing it on to the printing script). Lack of documentation prevents a complete diagnosis and correction for 10.2 versions, but Apple seems to have corrected the problem in 10.3 and 10.4.

If you wanted to extend a script like this to handle non-PostScript data, a possible solution would be to hack on a PPD like the `Imagewriter.ppd` file and on the `foomatic-rip.pl` script. Duplicating the `foomatic-rip.pl` script and adding the spooling functionality from this script should be fairly simple. Because `foomatic-rip.pl` already understands how to properly convert each input data format into PostScript for output, this is an easier solution than trying to write your own processing filters around the minimal spooler we've constructed here. A more complex printing script might not be so easy to integrate. We leave the investigation of both of these solutions to the creativity of the reader, should anyone other than myself be interested in whether a 1984 ImageWriter works with a 2005 Mac Mini while using a buggy serial driver that doesn't understand flow control.

Although `lpadmin` is useful for creating and managing printers at the command line, `lpoptions` is useful for examining and setting print configurations. For example, `lpoptions -d testsomemore` sets the default printer for command line `lp` and `lpr` printing requests to the `testsomemore` printer configured in the previous example. This command does *not* affect the default printer for GUI printing.

Finally, `lpinfo` is useful for querying the CUPS system about currently installed printing devices and drivers. `lpinfo -m` is particularly useful for determining the correct model information to hand to the `-m` option of the `lpadmin` command.

The syntax and important options for `lpadmin`, `lpoptions`, and `lpinfo` are shown in Tables 13.19, 13.20, and 13.21, respectively.

TABLE 13.19 The Syntax and Important Options for `lpadmin`

lpadmin	Configures CUPS printers and classes.
lpadmin [-E] [-h *<server>*] -d *<destination>*	
lpadmin [-E] [-h *<server>*] -p *<printer>* *<option(s)>*	
lpadmin [-E] [-h *<server>*] -x *<destination>*	
lpadmin configures printer and class queues provided by CUPS. It can also be used to set the system default printer or class.	
When specified before the -d, -p, or -x options, the -E option forces encryption when connecting to the server.	
The first form of the command sets the default printer or class to *<destination>*. Subsequent print jobs submitted via the lp(1) or lpr(1) commands use this destination unless the user specifies otherwise.	
The second form of the command configures the named *<printer>*.	
The third form of the command deletes the printer or class *<destination>*. Any jobs that are pending for the *<destination>* are removed, and any job that is currently printing is aborted.	

TABLE 13.19 Continued

Printer Queue Configuration Options	
`-c <class>`	Adds the named printer to `<class>`. If `<class>` doesn't exist, it is created automatically.
`-i <interface>`	Sets a System V–style interface script for the printer. This option cannot be specified with the `-P` option (PPD file) and is intended for providing support for legacy printer drivers.
`-o <name>=<value>`	Sets a PPD or server option for the printer. PPD options can be listed using the `-l` option with the `lpoptions` command.
`-o job-k-limit=<value>`	Sets the kilobyte limit for per-user quotas. The `<value>` is an integer number of kilobytes; one kilobyte is 1024 bytes.
`-o job-page-limit=<value>`	Sets the page limit for per-user quotas. The `<value>` is the integer number of pages that can be printed; double-sided pages are counted as two pages.
`-o job-quota-period=<value>`	Sets the accounting period for per-user quotas. The `<value>` is an integer number of seconds; 86,400 seconds are in one day.
`-r <class>`	Removes the named printer from `<class>`. If `<class>` becomes empty as a result, it is deleted.

`-u allow:<user>,<user>`
`-u deny:<user>,<user>`
`-u allow:all`
`-u deny:none`
	Sets user-level access control on a printer. The latter two forms turn user-level access control off.

`-v <device-uri>`	Sets the `device-uri` attribute of the printer queue. If `<device-uri>` is a filename, it is automatically converted to the form `file:/file/name`.
`-D <info>`	Provides a textual description of the printer.
`-E`	Enables the printer and accepts jobs; this is the same as running the `accept` and `enable` programs on the printer.
`-L <location>`	Provides a textual location of the printer.
`-P <ppd-file>`	Specifies a PostScript Printer Description file to use with the printer. If specified, this option overrides the `-i` option (interface script).

TABLE 13.20 The Syntax and Important Options for `lpoptions`

`lpoptions`	Displays or sets printer options and defaults.
`lpoptions [-h <server>] -d <destination>[/<instance>] [-o <option>=<value> -o <option>=<value>...`	
`lpoptions [-h <server>] [-E] [-p <destination >[/<instance>]] -l`	
`lpoptions [-h <server>] [-E] [-p <destination >[/<instance>]] -o <option>[=<value>] ... -r <option>`	
`lpoptions [-h <server>] [-E] -x <destination >[/<instance>]`	
`-d <destination>[/<instance>]`	Sets the default printer to `< destination >`. If `<instance>` is provided, that particular instance is used. Overrides the system default printer for the current user.
`-E`	Enables encryption when communicating with the CUPS server.
`-h <server>`	Specifies the CUPS server to talk to.

TABLE 13.20 Continued

`-l`	Lists the printer specific options and their current settings.
`-o` *<option>=<value>*	Specifies a new option for the named destination (available options can be seen with `-l`).
`-p` *<destination >*`[/`*<instance>*`]`	Sets the < *destination* > and *<instance>* for any options that follow.
`-r <option>`	Removes the specified option for the named destination.
`-x` *<destination>*`/`*<instance>*	Removes the options for the named destination and instance. This option is useful for a CUPS feature that Apple has apparently not-yet implemented: management of multiple queues with different defaults on the same printer.
	If no options are specified using the `-o` option, the current options for the named printer are reported on the standard output.
	Options set with the `lpoptions` command are used by the `lp` and `lpr` commands when submitting jobs.

TABLE 13.21 The Syntax and Important Options for `lpinfo`

`lpinfo`	Shows available printing devices and drivers.
`lpinfo [ -E ] [ -l ] [ -m ] [ -v ]`	
`-E`	Forces encryption when connecting to the server.
`-l`	Shows a long listing of devices or drivers.
`-m`	Shows the available printer drivers on the system. This option is useful for discovering what `-m` models are available for use with the `lpadmin` command.
`-v`	Shows the available printer devices on the system.

Bridging the GUI to Command Line Gap: Hybrid Software

One final class of software we'll touch on in this chapter is a diverse group of commands, programs, and applications that we've taken to calling *hybrid software*. These programs bridge the gulf between the GUI and command line, bringing GUI interfaces to command-line tools or command-line access to traditionally GUI features. Hybrid software is one of the most interesting and potentially enabling aspects of Mac OS X, and currently seems to be one of the most overlooked as well. We hope we've convinced you by now that command-line software can be incredibly powerful, even if you might still have reservations regarding how user friendly it might be. Many hybrid applications bring the user-friendly graphical mode of interaction you're accustomed to under classic Mac OS, and under Mac OS X Aqua to command-line power and flexibility. Others bring Mac OS accessibility to the command line.

The range of applications possible is limited only by the combinations of command-line software that might be composed, which as you will continue to find throughout this book, is nearly endless. Because we can't hope to document everything available, we'll introduce you to the general concepts by covering the simple tools Apple has made available, an interesting application that lets you put a GUI interface on any command-line tool, and a large suite of tools that blend an old-favorite Mac OS text editor with a traditional Unix text-processing and publication system. The general concepts used in these pieces of software, such as the simple extension of functionality by adding additional command-line parameters to configuration files, should be of general use when you find software of this nature.

The Command Line and the Pasteboard (Clipboard): `pbcopy`, `pbpaste`

Of the tools that Apple has provided, `pbcopy` and `pbpaste` are two that are both subtle and interesting. These command-line tools interact with the same clipboard (or *pasteboard*, as it is being called under Mac OS X) that the GUI Copy/Paste menu actions and keyboard equivalents do. This allows you to move data back and forth between GUI tools and command-line applications with ease. The data is currently limited to textual data types (including formatted text), and EPS, which restricts the utility somewhat, but these commands still play an important role that cannot be accomplished by the traditional Copy and Paste menu actions. Specifically, these commands accept input on the command line's Standard Input, or write their output to the command line's Standard out, allowing them to be used in the construction of small automated programs (you'll learn more about scripting the shell in Chapter 15). The command documentation tables for `pbcopy` and `pbpaste` are shown in Tables 13.22 and 13.23, respectively.

TABLE 13.22 The Command Documentation Table for `pbcopy`

`pbcopy`	Copies data from `STDIN` into the clipboard/pasteboard.
`pbcopy [-help] [-pboard <general¦ruler¦find¦font>]`	
`pbcopy` places data from its standard input (`STDIN`) into the Mac OS X clipboard/pasteboard. Data is placed in the pasteboard as ASCII unless it starts with EPS or RTF headers, in which case it is placed as those datatypes.	
Mac OS X supports multiple pasteboards (clipboards) for different data types. For more information on the different data types, see `http://developer.apple.com/documentation/Cocoa/Conceptual/CopyandPaste/Concepts/DataTypes.html`.	
`-help`	Displays its only option, `-help`.
`-pboard` *<board>*	Specify the pasteboard to use. Options for *<board>* are `general`, `ruler`, `find`, and `font`.

TABLE 13.23 The Command Documentation Table for `pbpaste`

`pbpaste`	Writes textual data from the Mac OS X clipboard/pasteboard to `STDOUT`.
`pbpaste -help`	
`pbpaste [-pboard <general¦ruler¦find¦font>] [-Prefer ascii¦rtf¦ps]`	
`pbpaste` pasts textual data from the clipboard/pasteboard to the command line via `STDOUT`. The `-P` option allows you to suggest a preferred output format but is not necessarily obeyed.	
`-Prefer rtf`	Prefer output in rich text format if available.
`-Prefer ps`	Prefer output in encapsulated PostScript format if available.
`-Prefer ascii`	Prefer American Standard Code for Information Interchange (yes, that's what ASCII stands for) plain text format.
`-pboard` *<board>*	Specify the pasteboard to use. Options for *<board>* are `general`, `ruler`, `find`, and `font`.

Integrating GUI Tools and Command-Line Programs: TurboTool, ScriptGUI, `gnuplot`

There is a set of applications that is best described as integrating GUI tools and command-line programs. In some instances, you use a GUI to perform actions that you could perform at the command line. In other instances, you interact with a command-line tool and GUI tools. In this category, we will look at TurboTool, ScriptGUI, and `gnuplot`. You can use TurboTool for automation, ScriptGUI for running scripts in the Finder, and `gnuplot` for graphing.

Automation with TurboTool

Until you're comfortable with the material in Chapter 15 and have started to write your own shell scripts that can make good use of these, you might find the shareware package TurboTool from `http://www.filewell.com/TurboTool/index.html` to be more immediately gratifying (although it'll be more powerful, too, after you've mastered adding your own shell script functionality to it). This tool allows you to wrap GUI and drag-and-drop interfaces around a number of built-in functions, and even more powerfully, around command-line commands and scripts. Figures 13.1, 13.2, 13.3, and 13.4 show the four components of a TurboTool action that takes a screenshot of a window that you pick, extracts image data from the clipboard, resizes it 75%, and then writes it to disk as a JPEG file. You perform the action in the TurboTool interface, shown in Figure 13.5.

The first component, shown in Figure 13.1, uses `screencapture` to capture the window that you click on when you perform the action. The second component, shown in Figure 13.2, uses a built-in TurboTool action (TurboTool calls them *atomics*) to read image data from the clipboard, using Mac OS's built-in clipboard-conversion capability to extract a TIFF if possible. The third component, shown in Figure 13.3, pulls up a file-request type dialog in which you can enter a filename for the image and sets an internal TurboTool variable to the result so that the next step has a filename to save to. The final component, shown in Figure 13.4, is perhaps the most interesting. It executes a small shell script to perform the functionality of converting the data from the TIFF read from the clipboard into a JPEG and resizing it 75%.

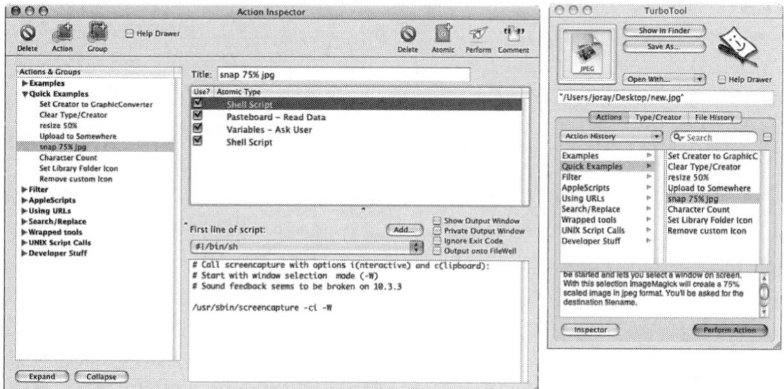

FIGURE 13.1 The TurboTool Action Inspector allows you to examine or build small functional components into complex actions. Here `screencapture` is used to capture a window.

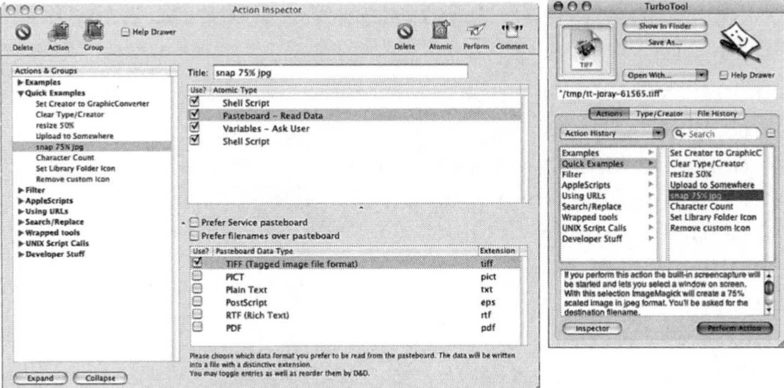

FIGURE 13.2 The second component of the resize to 75% and save as JPEG action is the acquisition of a TIFF format file from data in the clipboard.

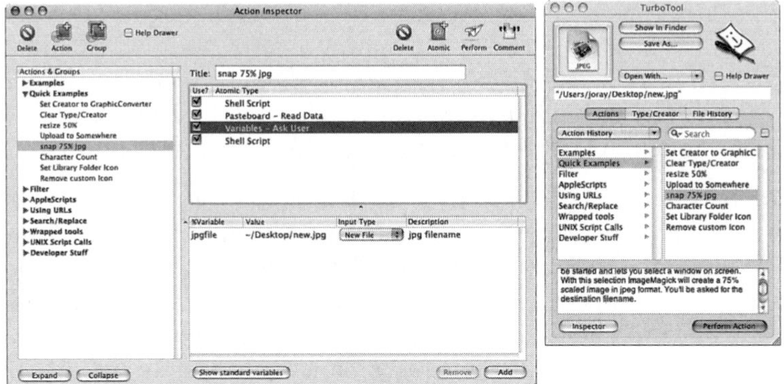

FIGURE 13.3 The third component is to query the user for a filename with which to save the final image.

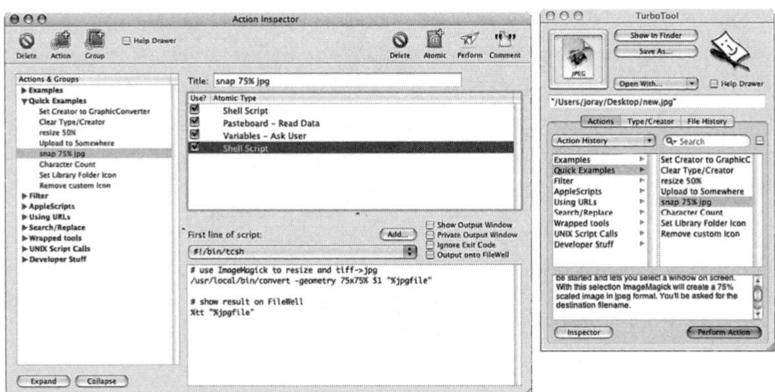

FIGURE 13.4 The fourth component uses a command-line tool to execute the requested resize and save actions.

You can perform any of these actions in the TurboTool interface. Select an action, click Perform Action, and then do anything the action requires of you. In this example, the snap 75% jpg action has an informational section noting that you need to install ImageMagick to perform the action, but it also provides a URL to ImageMagick. When you perform that action, you select what window you want to capture, and provide a name to save the file. Figure 13.5 shows the TurboTool interface after the snap 75% jpg action has been performed. The name of the file that was saved is shown toward the top.

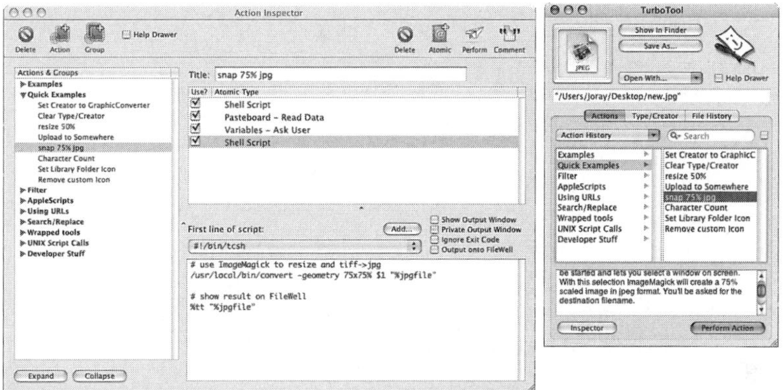

FIGURE 13.5 You can perform actions in the TurboTool window.

Running Scripts in the Finder with ScriptGUI

ScriptGUI, available from `http://www.scriptgui.com/`, lets you run scripts in the Finder. You can use it on existing scripts or you can use its editor to create scripts.

We'll show a simple demonstration of using ScriptGUI to start that Java-based program Haploview, available from `http://www.broad.mit.edu/mpg/haploview/index.php`, which can be used for haplotype analysis.

Figure 13.6 shows the creation of our script, `haploview`, in ScriptGUI. You can click Run to run the script, or you can save it and then click Run. When you save your script, you can choose ScriptGUI Native, Plain Text, or Scriptlet, which saves the script as an application with an .app extension. No matter which format we choose, whenever we click on this script in the Finder, Haploview starts.

In this particular example, we could have named our script `haploview.command`, which would have allowed it to be able to start from the Finder. Clicking on `haploview.command` would start Terminal and run the script in it, which then starts Haploview.

Graphing with `gnuplot`

If you have ever been disappointed in the graphs that you have generated in Excel, you might want to consider `gnuplot` as an alternative. `gnuplot` is a free package available from `http://sourceforge.net/projects/gnuplot`. It is available for many platforms, including Unix and Windows, and for Mac OS X, you can download it as a .dmg file. `gnuplot` supports many output devices, including X11, AquaTerm, printers, epslatex, gif, pdf, png, and jpeg. You can find a wealth of documentation on gnuplot at http://gnuplot.sourceforge.net/. The .dmg file also includes documentation. It might take some time to learn the package, but you will be pleased with its results.

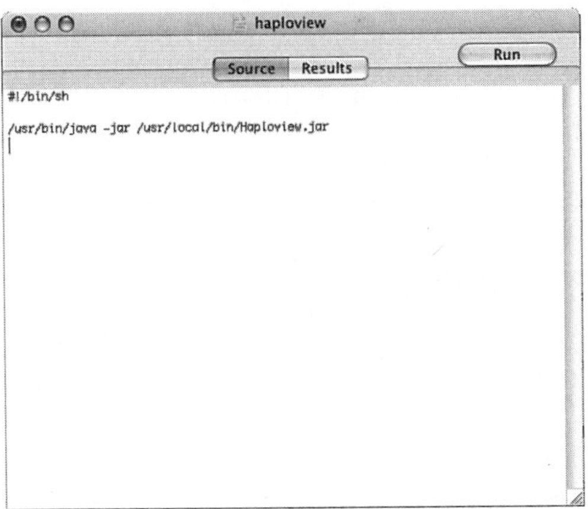

FIGURE 13.6 ScriptGUI can be used to run scripts in the Finder.

The version of gnuplot available for Mac OS X comes already capable of using X11 or AquaTerm as output devices. You can install gnuplot without either, but you will probably want to conveniently display the graphs you are generating, and having at least one of those interfaces available will be a must. Apple's X11 is sufficient for the X11 option. For more information on the X Window system, see Chapter 17, "Using X Window System Applications." If you would like to be able to display to an Aqua application, download AquaTerm, a graphics terminal for Mac OS X, from http://aquaterm.sourceforge.net/.

gnuplot installs in /usr/local/bin. You interact with gnuplot at the command line, but you can display output to either X11 or AquaTerm, among various other devices. In our simple example, we will plot sin(x). To see the result in the X11 interface, start the X11 application. At the command line, type **gnuplot**. Then at the gnuplot> prompt, type **plot sin(x)**. Here is sample output from the terminal:

```
[creampuf:~] joray% gnuplot

        G N U P L O T
        Version 4.0 patchlevel 0
        last modified Thu Apr 15 14:44:22 CEST 2004
        System: Darwin 7.5.0

        Copyright (C) 1986 - 1993, 1998, 2004
        Thomas Williams, Colin Kelley and many others
```

```
        This is gnuplot version 4.0.  Please refer to the documentation
        for command syntax changes.  The old syntax will be accepted
        throughout the 4.0 series, but all save files use the new syntax.

        Type `help` to access the on-line reference manual.
        The gnuplot FAQ is available from
                http://www.gnuplot.info/faq/

        Send comments and requests for help to
                <gnuplot-info@lists.sourceforge.net>
        Send bugs, suggestions and mods to
                <gnuplot-bugs@lists.sourceforge.net>


Terminal type set to 'x11'
gnuplot> plot sin(x)
```


To view results in AquaTerm instead, you can run gnuplot in either the Terminal or X11 applications. Before you run gnuplot, set the GNUTERM environment variable to aqua. For more information on environment variables, see Chapter 15.

If you are running bash, set the environment variable like this:

```
creampuf:~ joray$ GNUTERM=aqua
creampuf:~ joray$ export GNUTERM
```

If you are running tcsh, set the environment variable like this:

```
[creampuf:~] joray% setenv GNUTERM aqua
```

After the environment variable has been set, start gnuplot and then run plot sin(x). When you start gnuplot, you will see a note that the terminal type is aqua.

As you might expect, you can also load files and display them using gnuplot. A site with some interesting gnuplot images is located at http://ayapin.film.s.dendai.ac.jp/~matuda/Gnuplot/pm3d.html. This site demonstrates the use of the palette-mapped 3D terminal, pm3d, which is now included as part of the gnuplot software. Not only does this site include some interesting images, but it also includes the files that were used to generate the images. Information on the pm3d software can be found on Dr. Petr Mikulik's site at http://www.sci.muni.cz/~mikulik/gnuplot.html.

Because we thought you might find an image from this site more interesting to view than sin(x), we slightly modified the file that was used for the turritella image at the bottom right of the first page at this site to display in X11 and AquaTerm. Figure 13.7 shows how the turritella looks in X11, and Figure 13.8 shows how it looks in AquaTerm.

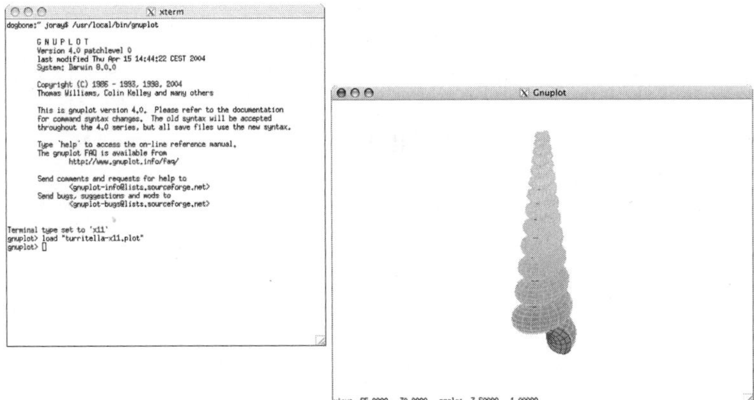

FIGURE 13.7 Here we have slightly modified the turritella `gnuplot` file to display in Apple's X11 application.

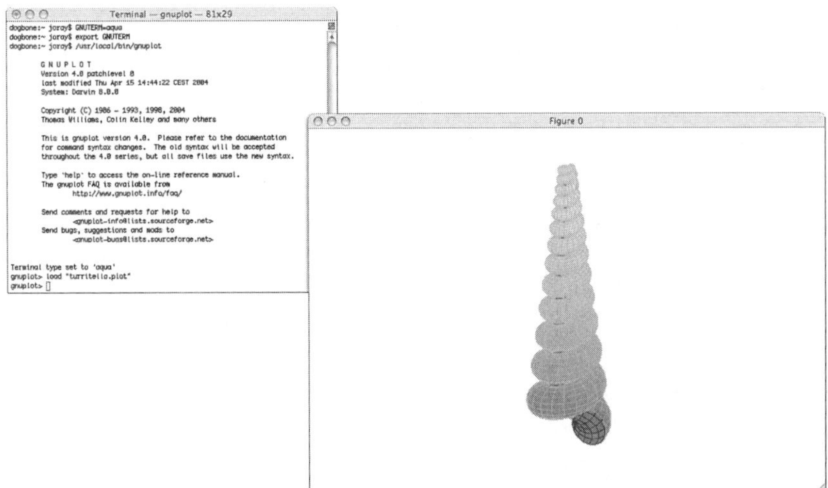

FIGURE 13.8 Here we have slightly modified the turritella `gnuplot` file to display in AquaTerm.

Mixing and Matching to Text-Processing Perfection: AlphaX, OzTeX, and TeX

We've repeatedly written that one of the most significant benefits of the traditional Unix mindset and way of doing things is that it allows you to mix and match the components you need to suit the job you're doing, and your own personal way of working. As a final demonstration of how this benefit carries over to GUI applications in hybrid application suites, we want to mention the combination of AlphaX, OzTeX, and TeX, which together comprise what could be called a word processor.

Reading as far as you have in this book, you might find the notion of a word processor to be somewhat contrary to the "small programs, with specific functions" philosophy that we've been repeating with respect to Unix. In fact, this combination of software works unlike any other word processing application you're likely to be familiar with and fits the Unix philosophy quite well. In fact, it fits it so well that if you decide to try out this system, we almost guarantee that you'll experience some initial discomfort in trying to learn the new patterns of thinking required.

Perhaps the largest single item of culture shock that you'll find is that there is no WYSIWYG (What You See Is What You Get) interface to the formatting of your text. That's right—the wonderfully convenient and powerful paradigm for content editing that Apple brought to light in 1984 with MacWrite, that what you see on the screen as you're editing, is what appears on the page when you print, is conspicuously absent from this system. And this is a *GOOD* thing! WYSIWYG editors revolutionized desktop document creation and turned an entire generation on to writing their own documents, creating their own content, and formatting it how they chose. It was a brilliant decision on Apple's part to foster this as the paradigm for the coming age of personal computing, and a wonderful enabling technology for those who want to create documents rich with personal style. Unfortunately, we aren't all born to be brilliant document formatters, and personal expressions of style aren't always the best way to clearly convey information. Worse, it seems rare that those who have important information and content to convey are also blessed with the necessary stylistic insights to convey that information clearly.

Working in the academic environments that we do, it's common for us to see people using traditional Macintosh or Windows word processors to write letters, papers, or books, who are expending as much effort on trying to format their document professionally as they are on writing the content of the document itself. This creates enormous inefficiency in the dissemination of knowledge. These people are students and faculty and are working hard to clearly and concisely capture their knowledge in written form, and are simultaneously being required by the WYSIWYG word processors to suddenly become professional typesetters if they want to have professional-looking output. This is an unreasonable burden, and one that I believe we, as computer users, willingly assume only because we've become accustomed to the apparent freedom that WYSIWYG editors appear to give by allowing us to endlessly tweak the visual presentation until it is "just so."

As you might imagine, the traditional Unix way of approaching the problem is rather different. Instead of requiring the author to become an expert typesetter, "word processing" in the TeX sense is based on the use of a typesetting program. In this system, the typesetting program itself is the expert typesetter, and the author is free to concentrate on the content. Of course, TeX is also sensitive to the notion that users do desire and deserve significant control over the formatting of their documents. To facilitate this, the author can provide local and global suggestions regarding the formatting to the typesetting program. This system actually provides considerably more control over the final formatting than WYSIWYG word processors do because the typesetter is in fact an interpreter for a programming language designed around the idea of formatting text, and the author has the option of exerting as much or as little control over the system's automated choices as she wants.

Without a doubt, this method of work requires a significant rearrangement of the way one approaches writing problems, and the sense that you're not in control can be irrationally disturbing, especially for someone long-accustomed to the WYSIWYG way. Your humble author came to TeX after having worked in the Unix world for several years, and I still found the transition to be difficult. I spent a long time resisting everyone's suggestions to stop fighting with the system, concentrate on my writing, and "let go" so that the system could do what it was designed to do. It took probably a year of working in TeX on a daily basis before I discovered that I was no longer fighting for control.

Having cleared that mental hurdle, however, I can safely say that I have no desire to ever return to WYSIWYG word processors for any serious writing. If clearly conveying information is the paramount concern for a document, I find it tremendously liberating to not have to worry about formatting, and to be able to concentrate on what I am writing rather than how it appears onscreen. The TeX system's expert typesetting rules almost always make good formatting choices, and I can override them in those specific instances where I am displeased with the final appearance of the result. Only if a document's physical layout is of similar importance to the content (such as with advertising, flyers, leaflets, and similar material), will I resort to a WYSIWYG editor (and even these documents could be accomplished with the TeX typesetting system if the investment in time to write the layout rules for an advertising flyer could be justified by its repeated use).

This having been explained, a short description is in order regarding how AlphaX, OzTeX, and TeX are interrelated in this Unix-style word processing suite.

- AlphaX, available from `http://www.maths.mq.edu.au/~steffen/Alpha/AlphaX/`, is a text editor. That is, it edits text. Not styled text, not text in different fonts, not text in different colors or sizes, just "plain old text" text. It's a Mac OS X incarnation of the venerable Alpha editor from the days of Mac OS. One of the neatest things about Alpha is that in spirit, it should have been a Unix application all along. Alpha, available in a number of variations on a number of platforms, is a text editor built out of a graphics-enabled scripting language. When you run Alpha, what you run is essentially a collection of scripts that cooperatively create a text-editing interface. If you're so inclined, you can edit and add to the scripts, changing the functionality of the editor to suit your particular needs.

  As a text editor, Alpha is oriented toward the editing of various types of programming languages, including the TeX and LaTeX typesetting languages. Conveniently, it provides a multitude of options for syntax highlighting in different languages and automatic insertion of assorted syntactic constructs. This allows you to, in HTML language mode, do things such as select `HTML Menu->Lists->Unordered List`, and have Alpha automatically insert a syntactically correct `<UL>` item as a neat little form into which you can fill elements to create the unordered list you need. In TeX mode, it lets you do things such as select `TeX Menu->"Document->Insert Document ->Letter"`, and it inserts all the necessary control code to define a business letter, into which you only need to fill your specific content.

- OzTeX is an implementation of the TeX typesetting system as a GUI application, but more importantly, it's a viewer for the results of TeX typesetting and a front-end application that integrates a number of different tools that must be run to handle all aspects of typesetting a document using the TeX system. OzTeX currently contains an internal implementation of the TeX system because of its heritage as a Mac OS application, and additionally can use command-line TeX tools. It is expected to eventually transition to a more Unix-like application, when it will make full use of the command-line TeX tools and be relieved of the burden of the internal implementation. OzTeX is available from `http://www.trevorrow.com/oztex/`. Because all of TeX is community supported, many useful little packages are contributed by different authors, and it sometimes takes a while to accumulate all the useful bits that you might want for a project. On the OzTeX CD, Andrew Trevorrow distributes many useful TeX-related tools and auxiliary packages, so if you find TeX and LaTeX to be useful to your work, but find that you'd like more third-party utilities than you really want to install, Andrew's OzTeX CD is a great convenience.

- TeX, as has been previously explained, is an expert typesetting system embodied in a suite of several traditionally command-line applications. The input that you provide to TeX is a plain text document containing the content you want to typeset and, optionally, small fragments of code in the typesetting language that TeX speaks, to describe to the system any nondefault formatting that you want to apply. You mark up your content in plain text using a simple syntax to indicate the content's structure. TeX reads your marked-up text, applies either its default rules for formatting the structures you've marked up or any variant formatting you've requested, and writes out a formatted version of the document in a `.dvi` (device independent) file. This file can then be read by DVI viewers (such as OzTeX) to show you what the formatted output will look like, or converted into any number of printer-driver languages (such as PostScript) for delivery to a hard copy output device.

  LaTeX is a macro package that lives on top of TeX and provides a number of advanced document formatting features to the author. All major TeX implementations include the LaTeX macro package as a standard component.

  Gerben Wierda's TeX implementation is a blend of a number of TeX distribution lineages packaged as a convenient Mac OS X `.dmg` installer, or as a network-aware installation program that downloads and installs needed components when run. It is available from `http://www.rna.nl/tex.html` (and also on Andrew's OzTeX CD). The i-Installer version of the installation program is recommended.

Taken together, these packages allow the following chain of events to occur relatively seamlessly: You author TeX and LaTeX documents in AlphaX. When you're satisfied with the content (not the appearance—the content—what you have to say) you've created and want to see how it will look printed, you trigger AlphaX to hand off these documents to OzTeX by use of a menu selection, or a key press combination. OzTeX determines the document type and invokes TeX or the LaTeX macro package, as appropriate. TeX formats the document and writes a `.dvi` file. OzTeX recognizes the creation of the `.dvi` file and opens a viewer showing you exactly what your document will look like when printed.

This might sound like a long and cumbersome sequence of events, but by now, it should seem like a perfectly logical Unix way of proceeding. Also by now, you should be getting the idea that Unix allows the programmer to hide many of these interactions from the user, if the user wants to ignore them. From the user's perspective, it turns out that this interaction is not particularly cumbersome at all. Instead, in practice, the process looks like you type some content into an AlphaX window and press Command-T. A second or two later (faster if you have a machine with more horsepower than my G4 PowerBook), a preview of your document, exactly as it will print, appears in a window. Note that this is actually much more WYSIWYG than what you get from a normal WYSIWYG word processor. With this system, what you see is directly rendered from the code that will be used to drive your printer. If you've ever fought with the weird "What You See Is (Kind of Like, But Not Quite) What You Get" problems some word processors seem to always have with font widths not being quite right and character alignments being ever so slightly off between the display and the printout, you'll find this display to be refreshingly accurate. Being derived from the code that drives the printer, it contains all the same positioning and formatting as what will print. Your display might not have the resolution of your printer, and so might not be able to display characters exactly identically, but they should be pixel-perfect in their formatting and alignment.

Figure 13.9 shows the code of a simple LaTeX document to construct a business letter, as shown by AlphaX. If this book were in color, you'd see the syntax coloring indicating that the editor knows which parts of the document are LaTeX commands, which are comments, and which are my actual content. The entire structure of this document was set up for me by AlphaX; all I've done is filled in my textual content where I needed it and a bit of code to pull in my digital signature file. It may be of interest to note that lines starting with `%` symbols are comments in TeX/LaTeX. Being a programming language, I can comment out parts of the document to keep them from displaying or printing, while still keeping them unaltered in the text document itself. This can be useful when working on multiple versions of the same document or when making sweeping changes to a document where large sections need to be deleted or rearranged, but you don't want to lose track of important points made in the original.

Also remember, this is a plain text document. I can edit it at the command line with `vi` or `emacs`. I can typeset it at the command line using the command-line TeX tools. If I'm away from home and I need to edit it and print a copy for my secretary, my PCS-modem phone and my PDA are all I need to connect to my desktop machine, fire up a text editor, make the edits, typeset, and print a new copy. Editing the document is location and software independent, and because TeX runs on almost every hardware platform conceivable, if I want to take it with me, typesetting it is location and hardware independent as well.

Figure 13.10 shows OzTeX's view of the output from Figure 13.9's LaTeX code. If you have particularly good eyes, you'll notice that the text formatting displays the characteristics of text layout done by a typesetting professional. Character pairs such as *fi* show proper ligatures, and line lengths are massaged, by minute variation of intercharacter and interword spacing, to avoid widow words at the end of paragraphs. Considerably more is going on behind the scenes that isn't apparent from this partial-page display, such as paragraph balancing to avoid widow lines at the top of pages, proper formatting of oblique as well as italic typefaces, and too many more careful optimizations of the layout to name.

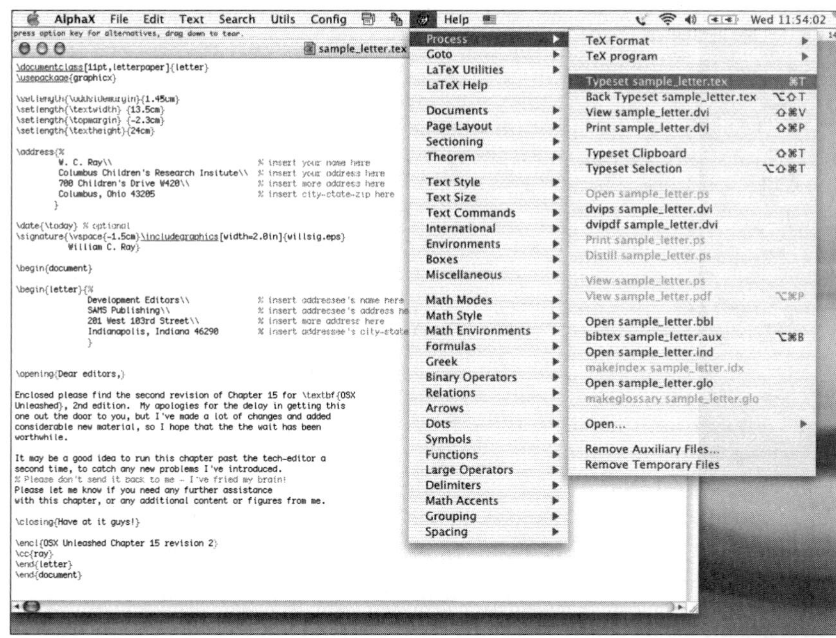

FIGURE 13.9 Editing a LaTeX document in AlphaX.

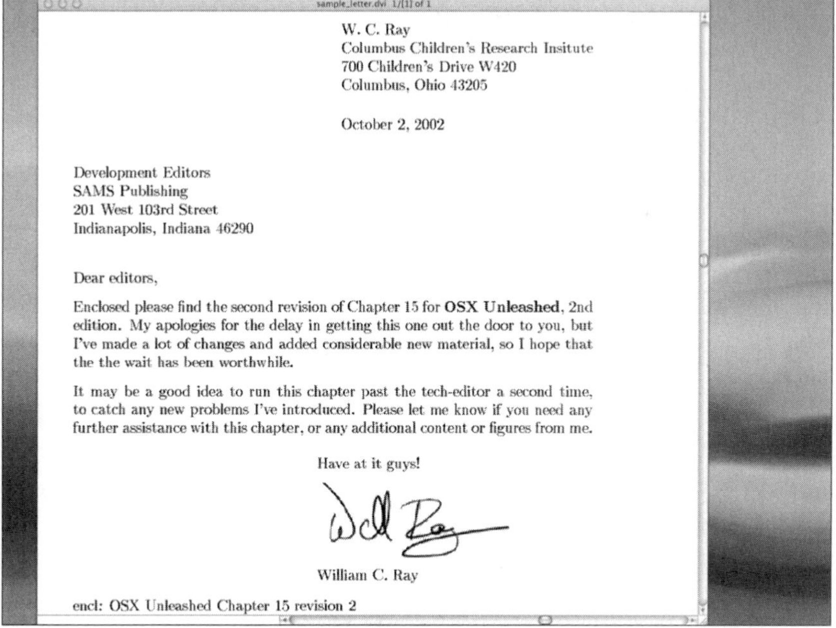

sample_letter.dvi 1/[1] of 1

W. C. Ray
Columbus Children's Research Insitute
700 Children's Drive W420
Columbus, Ohio 43205

October 2, 2002

Development Editors
SAMS Publishing
201 West 103rd Street
Indianapolis, Indiana 46290

Dear editors,

Enclosed please find the second revision of Chapter 15 for **OSX Unleashed**, 2nd edition. My apologies for the delay in getting this one out the door to you, but I've made a lot of changes and added considerable new material, so I hope that the the wait has been worthwhile.

It may be a good idea to run this chapter past the tech-editor a second time, to catch any new problems I've introduced. Please let me know if you need any further assistance with this chapter, or any additional content or figures from me.

Have at it guys!

William C. Ray

encl: OSX Unleashed Chapter 15 revision 2

FIGURE 13.10 The result of LaTeX formatting the code shown in Figure 13.9.

NOTE

If you've found this notion of a plain-text, programmatic typesetting language to be of interest, we encourage you to check out Donald Knuth's definitive work on TeX *The TeXbook* and Leslie Lamport's definitive work on LaTeX, *LaTeX: A Document Preparation System.* Helmut Kopka's *A Guide to LATEX: Document Preparation for Beginners and Advanced Users* is also a good book that actually covers a fair bit of what you need to know about both LaTeX and the underlying TeX system. If you're tempted by the idea, think back to this system after you've read through Chapter 15 on shell scripting, and Chapter 18's section on Perl programming. The ability to automate changes to documents and build formatted text structures with software can be useful. The plain text nature of TeX's input lends itself nicely to such manipulation.

We don't expect the majority of our readers to decide to become TeX hackers based on this short introduction, but even if it doesn't sound interesting enough to install the software to try it out, we hope you come away from this discussion with an idea of what is possible if the power of the GUI and the command line are taken together. Even if TeX just isn't your thing, understand that what this specific-programs-for-specific-functions system allows is complete customization of a word processor environment.

Due to the newness of Mac OS X, you're currently rather limited in your choices for filling out this suite, but imagine if all word processing applications were handled in a similar fashion, instead of as monolithic applications like MS Word. If you didn't like a component, you could easily switch it out and use a different one that provided better functionality for your use in its place. In this instance, you can switch out AlphaX for BBedit or any other command-line editor. It makes no difference to the system, choose whichever one you like. If you don't like OzTeX, there are a half dozen other TeX front ends (see Weirda's list at `http://www.rna.nl/tex.html` for details) that can sit between your editor of choice and the TeX command-line software. If you don't like LaTeX/TeX as a typesetter, you could use PDFTeX (typesets LaTeX directly to PDF files), or one of the *roff family of text formatters (an unpleasant group of text formatters primarily used for formatting Unix man pages these days; see the man page for `groff` if you want the gory details), or `txt2pdf` (`http://www.sanface.com/txt2pdf.html`). If the major software vendors get on board with this way of doing things, you'll suddenly be able to pick the best components from each to meet your own personal working style and the requirements of the work you need to do.

Summary

In this chapter, you were introduced to command-line tools for accessing network resources of a number of types. The chapter also covered the two premier Unix text editors, the Unix printing environment that functions as a small suite of cooperating commands, and a sampling of tools that interoperate between the command line and other parts of Mac OS X.

As of now, you have been introduced to a range of command-line programs representative of the types of interactions you will experience with almost any Unix software at the command line. Many of these commands and applications probably still seem cumbersome, and you will probably need to refer to the book frequently to remember an option. Don't be discouraged by this. There is probably not a single person alive who actually remembers all the possible commands in the `emacs` environment. Use the commands when the opportunity occurs, and reference the book or the man pages to help recall what you've forgotten. Even the best Unix users refer to the man pages or a book with considerably more frequency than Mac OS users look at their user manuals. Eventually the parts of the programs that you use with regularity will sink in to muscle memory, and you'll be able to whiz around the command line doing what you do on an everyday basis without needing to consult your references at all.

CHAPTER 14

Command-Line Software Installation and Troubleshooting

IN THIS CHAPTER

- Installing Xcode, Apple's Developer Tools
- Installing Software at the Command Line
- Installing Some Additional Interesting Software
- Troubleshooting Software Installs, and Compiling and Debugging Manually
- Using Common Sense and Configuration Options
- Fiddling with File Locations and Fighting with Installers
- Tracing Software Problems to the Source: Using the `gdb` Debugger

This chapter introduces software installation at the command line. You're almost undoubtedly familiar with installing software in the graphical user interface: double-click the installer, answer a few questions, and away it goes. You might be surprised to find that installing at the command line isn't much more difficult: type a few relatively standard command-line incantations and away it goes. We'll focus specifically on command-line installs for command-line software because that is the variety that will be the least familiar. You should be aware, however, that some GUI software might require you to install it by using a command-line program such as `tar`. And, peculiarly, some command-line software is only distributed for Mac OS X as a packaged GUI installer.

Although it might sound like an entirely foreign concept because of the long-standing position of Unix at the forefront of the Open Source software movement, the majority of traditional Unix programs are distributed as source code rather than as executable applications. That is, when you download the installer for a Unix application, you get a recipe, not a finished cooked product. You (and the automated systems on your machine) are expected to cook (compile) it yourself to turn it from the recipe (source) into the product (application). If you're like most classic Macintosh users, you've probably never even looked at the code it takes to create a program, let alone tried to convince a machine to turn it into a fully functional application. As Mac OS X becomes more popular and more prevalent in the market, we're seeing much more software distributed in precompiled form to satisfy those who really don't want to know this stuff. There are, however, still many useful applications that haven't been built into nice, neat, clickable Mac OS X installers (actually, there are many, many more that haven't been built than have), and until they are, building your own really isn't that difficult.

The components needed to compile and install many pieces of Unix software right out of the box (or more accurately, right out of the `ftp` directory) are already located on your system. You need some support files that tell software how to interact with the hardware, the source for whatever application you want to build, and a compiler to build it with. In the good tradition of Unixes everywhere, Apple has provided the first and last of these for you; all that remains is for you to pick the software you want and issue a few fairly standard commands.

NOTE

Just so that you don't take this the wrong way—not all Unix software compiles as easily as what we demonstrate here. Apple has arranged some things in a sufficiently nonstandard fashion that some software seemed almost impossible to compile in Mac OS X version 10.0.4. Although things definitely got better in 10.2, and 10.3 and 10.4 have further improved, it's still not as easy as using a Unix that's been around for 15 years. We expect that things will continue to improve over time and that more software will compile cleanly. For the adventurous, the second half of this chapter details some of the steps that can be taken if the standard procedures at the beginning of this chapter don't work properly for the software you want. Even if you're comfortable rolling up your sleeves and jumping into the code, we can't guarantee that everything you try can be compiled.

Installing Xcode, Apple's Developer Tools

This install is necessary. You will need it to follow most of the rest of this book, and it will allow you to make use of a far wider world of Mac OS X/Unix software than will be available to you if you don't install Xcode. The Mac OS X Xcode developer tools include compilers, libraries, and assorted programs. You might be tempted to skip this install, thinking that if you aren't a developer, the benefits won't be worth the disk space. Install Xcode anyway, even if you're not planning on doing any development. Because of the previously mentioned "delivered as a recipe" nature of most Unix software, your system will need parts of the Xcode installation whether or not you plan to use it. The parts that we'll cover in this chapter are the compilation and debugging tools. If you're interested in details regarding the libraries and so forth, remember those man commands, and spend some time digging around in the system man pages to learn what other neat things exist after the installation.

Installation of Xcode is much like installing other software from the GUI. Insert the CD and click the installer package. Be aware that the developer tools can be installed only on your startup volume, and that the installer, like the installer for the operating system itself, has a rather poor notion of the amount of time the install will take.

Installing Software at the Command Line

The majority of the Unix software you'll find that hasn't been specifically made for Mac OS X is created by other users just like you. Some of them are professional programmers, but the vast majority of them are simply hobbyists who've put together an application because they wanted a program that did something, and they've made it available for you to install out of the sense of team spirit that pervades the Unix and open source communities. Because of the wide range of individuals involved, the possibilities for how the software might be delivered and what you will need to do to install it are truly limitless. We'll do our best to give an overview of the techniques used, but pay attention to the author's instructions to see whether or where they differ from our suggestions. Also, don't be afraid to use your own common sense if you find something that doesn't have instructions and our samples don't appear to apply.

Regardless of the actual steps involved in the installation, there are some things to keep in mind if you want to keep your system in some semblance of order.

- You'll usually have as much flexibility, and often even more flexibility, about where you install software in Unix as you do in Mac OS. Unfortunately, although the Mac OS Finder invisibly and automatically updates the database of software that's installed for you, Unix doesn't. If you install command-line software in random places throughout the system, you will need to continuously update your `PATH` variable to reflect the changes. For this reason, despite having the option to install just about anywhere, you'll probably be happiest if you confine your installs to a few common and highly recommended locations. Specifically, those locations are the `/usr/local/` and `/opt/` directory trees. The popular DarwinPorts installer uses `/opt/local/`, and the equally popular Fink distribution installer adds `/sw/`. These are the most common and best places to install software if you want convenience in your system.

- If you have multiple users on the system, even if you update your own `PATH`, other users' paths won't be updated, and, consequently, they might not be able to run the software. This can be an advantage or a disadvantage, depending on whether you want to hide the software from others or make it publicly available. If you want the software to be available to your user only, extend your `PATH` variable in your own `.login` / `.cshrc` or `.profile` / `.bashrc` files. If you want to make the software available to everyone on the system, extend the systemwide `/etc/csh.login` / `/etc/csh.cshrc` or `/etc/profile` / `/etc/bashrc` files.

- If you decide to reconfigure your system or reinstall something, it will be much easier if you keep a complete copy of the distribution and any special options you picked to make it work. Use the `tar` command and `compress` or `gzip` commands (explained in Chapter 10, "Common Unix Shell Commands: File, Directory and Disk Operations," after you've successfully managed to install it. You'll probably want to `make clean` the distribution first, if possible—that incantation will be explained shortly.

- If you want to maintain your sanity, it will help if you always download software packages into the same location, and do all your configuration and software building in subdirectories of the same directory.
- Avoid compiling or installing software as the `root` user. We know, you're going to ignore that suggestion, and compile, install, and run random bits of software you've downloaded as `root`. Everybody ignores it—on occasion we do to. It'll come back and bite you on the butt. Trust us, we've been there. One day you'll run a poorly written (or maliciously written) install script, and it'll go off and damage your system. You'll think, "Why, oh, why did I just run that command as `root`? Nothing about it required `root` privileges. If only I'd been a bit more careful." We won't tell you "we told you so," but we will tell you that a lot of the pain is avoidable if you're willing to have some discipline about how you run your system.

  Some software might insist that you install it as `root` (Fink does, for example), but the `root` user is the single user with the capacity to destroy your system with a single command (although Apple's done a fair bit of work towards making any group-Admin user have the same capability). It might be preachy to suggest that you're probably better off without most software that requires you to be `root` to install it, but until you *know* when it's safe to ignore this suggestion, you'll be much safer following it.

INSTALLING SOFTWARE AS `root` IS A BAD IDEA!

Some readers with Unix experience, and particularly those experienced in the Linux flavor, might find this caution peculiar in that a considerable amount of third-party software ends up installed in privileged system directories these days. These users are accustomed to needing to be `root` to do simple installs. Fortunately, this is the wrong way to do things, and it's a rare Unix application that forces you to do things in a poorly thought-out fashion. Almost all non-OS-vendor (in this case non-Apple) software should be installed and owned by non-`root` users. Even vendor-supplied copies of third-party applications (such as the Apache web server or the Perl programming language) are best owned and installed by non-`root` users.

This model makes life a bit more difficult than just having `root` own everything (and so the vendors of Unix-come-lately versions seem to be leaning toward making everything owned by `root`), but the benefits of behaving in a responsible and secure fashion far outweigh the minor inconvenience. If you conscientiously make sure that everything that isn't distinctly part of the operating system is owned by a nonprivileged user, you can allow nonprivileged users to modify and maintain those parts of the system with no fear that they are going to damage the OS itself. Even if you, as the person at the keyboard, aren't personally different in any way when you're operating as `root`, you're inherently putting your machine in more danger than when you're operating as a nonprivileged user. If non-OS-vendor software is installed and owned by a non-`root` user, any time spent working with and installing that software, and any unfortunate things that happen as a result of code that it runs, are done by a nonprivileged user. The machine is more secure and the danger of a malicious script or an errant keystroke causing damage to the system is significantly reduced. If you have a true multiperson, multiuser system, the workload of managing software can be safely distributed, and users who need to be able to modify configurations (such as changing the web server settings), can do so without having to annoy `root` or having to develop the meticulous operating habits that someone running as `root` must conscientiously maintain.

Implementing this model on your system takes a little additional effort on your part. You won't be able to follow people's simple-minded instructions to `sudo make install` bits of software. But your machine will be better managed, more secure, and you'll be helping to keep mushy-headed thinking from taking hold of the Mac OS X platform if you just take the time to follow these suggestions and set up a nonprivileged software account to own and install the majority of your third-party software.

- Another useful trick for keeping your system in order is to create a special user ID that is used solely for software installations and management. The ownership of the `/usr/local` and `/opt` directories, as well as the ownership of wherever you download software and where you store it, can be set to this user ID. This user ID does not need to have (and definitely *should not* have) administrator privileges on the system. This minimizes the risk of simply doing something wrong or accidentally damaging the running system. It also minimizes the impact that a malicious user, distributing damaging scripts in the guise of useful software, can do to your system.

Downloading

You'll find Unix software being distributed in Usenet newsgroups, on web pages, FTP servers, through email, and other mechanisms. No matter how it's distributed, you are going to need to transfer a copy of the software, from wherever it is stored, to your local machine.

You've got all the tools necessary to accomplish any of these in the command-line programs discussed here and in the previous chapter, as well as in the GUI clients covered earlier.

While acquiring software, keep in mind that things will go smoothest if

- The software is downloaded by the user who will be responsible for the installation.
- The software is downloaded into a directory where it can be unpackaged and compiled, if necessary. This includes the requirement for sufficient disk space, as well as the appropriate permissions for the user ID that will be doing the installation. If you have a tendency to download software as your primary logged-in user ID and then try to manage it as a special, limited software-install user, the software user probably won't be able to read or modify your downloaded copies, and you'll just get annoyed with the requirements to move everything around in circles so that both you and the software-install user can access the files. Learn to use `curl` or `lynx` for downloading your software so that you can paste links from a web browser that you are running to a terminal where you're logged in as the software user for downloads. Alternatively, make the directory where you download the software group-writeable and put yourself and the software-install user in the same group.
- If you're using `ftp`, remember to use binary mode.
- Put StuffIt Expander in your Dock, so that you can drag and drop onto it conveniently. You'll normally want to use the command-line utilities `gunzip` and `tar`, but

sometimes StuffIt Expander is just the ticket for getting a packaged-up software distribution out of an archived newsgroup posting that you've found via Google.

- Sometimes StuffIt Expander eats `.tar.gz` (or other Unix-compressed) files or at least it regurgitates useless bits after trying to process the file. If you try to build a Unix application from an archive that you've uncompressed through StuffIt Expander, and it complains of things like missing files, remember to try the command-line tools before giving up. StuffIt Expander has problems with some filenames and it's not always forthcoming about the fact that it changed something.

Unarchiving

Some software comes as source code (the language that compilers read) that explains to the compiler how to create a finished program. Some comes as final executable programs. Either way, most software comes as a tarfile compressed with either the compress program (usually denoted by a `.Z` file suffix) or the `gzip` program (usually denoted by a `.gz` suffix).

The first thing you'll need to do after downloading, therefore, is usually to `uncompress` or `gunzip` the tarfile.

Next you'll usually need to untar the tarfile (with `tar -xvf` *<tarfile>*). Before you do that, however, it's usually a good idea to make sure what's in the tarfile. You're interested in the contents as well as where the tarfile wants to put the stuff that's in it. The second item is of particular importance—some software authors have the sloppy habit of letting their tarfiles place files in the current directory rather than a subdirectory. Additionally, some packages are distributed as tarfiles that are designed to untar "in place" in the system. That is, they place files directly into their final locations (such as `/usr/local/bin`) rather than into a temporary subdirectory for subsequent installation.

TIP

Some web browsers insist on uncompressing and untarring files for you without asking. This leaves a directory with the contents sitting on your desktop, or elsewhere, where you've specified that downloads should go. This functionality is okay, as far as it goes, but it's not uncommon for file permissions and other important information to get lost or broken when the web browser does this. If everything works properly in the directory as unarchived by the web browser, you're home free; but if it doesn't, don't panic: Delete the directory that the web browser created, redo the `uncompress`/`untar` by hand, and try again.

TIP

Also keep in mind that if you download with a web browser, it isn't unusual for the browser to remove the file suffix without actually doing anything to the file. This results in downloaded `gzip` files that are missing their `.gz` suffix and so on. This confuses some utilities designed to work with these files. If you have downloaded a piece of software with a web browser that arrives as a `.tar` file but `tar` refuses to unpack it, try adding a `.Z` or `.gz` suffix and see whether `uncompress` or `gunzip` will process the renamed file.

If you've downloaded a precompiled application that needs you only to unpack it in place or put it in a final location after unpacking the distribution, you're all set. If you've downloaded a package that is distributed as source code, skip to the next section on compiling software.

Installing a Precompiled Binary by Unarchiving and Putting It Where It Belongs: `lynx`

The `lynx` command-line web browser is such a useful tool that we'll do a download and unarchive install right now. A precompiled version of `lynx` is available from `http://www.macosxunleashed.com/downloads/`.

Before you install `lynx`, we recommend that you make a change in your system's configuration that helps keep your system safe from malicious software and accidents during software installs. Use the Accounts control pane discussed in Chapter 8, "Customizing User and System Settings," to create a new user to own all your software. There we showed how to create the unprivileged `software` user with the custom group `tire`. This is the user who will own and install our programs for us. Because `software` is not an administrative user and has privileges only in her home directory and in `/usr/local/`, `software` can't damage anything outside those locations. At worst, a malicious script or accident at the keyboard will just screw up what `software`'s already installed, leaving the rest of the machine safe.

Next, su to the `root` user. Finally, change the ownership of the directory `/usr/local/` on your machine to belong to the `software` user and group. If you're using unprivileged user `software` with group `tire`, ifrom the command line, the process looks like the following:

```
brezup:ray testing $ su
Password:
brezup:root testing # cd /usr
brezup:root usr # chown software.tire /usr/local
brezup:root usr # ls -ld local
drwxr-xr-x  4 software  tire  92 Apr 21 22:00 local
```

1. Now, log out and log back in as the unprivileged `software` user that you created. If you prefer, you can start multiple terminals, or use Apple's User Switching technology to flip between sessions logged in as yourself and the unprivileged `software` user.

2. Start a terminal and create the directories `/usr/local/lib`, `/usr/local/man`, `/usr/local/man/man1`, and `/usr/local/bin` (`mkdir /usr/local/lib`; `mkdir /usr/local/man`; `mkdir /usr/local/man/man1`; `mkdir /usr/local/bin`).

3. Next, point your browser at `http://www.macosxunleashed.com/downloads/` and download the files `lynx.gz`, `lynx.1`, and `lynx.cfg`.

   Chances are, if you're using Safari or Internet Explorer, it's going to insist on decompressing `lynx.gz` automatically. If not, you will need to find the file (double-click `lynx.gz` in the download manager and click Reveal in Finder) and then drag it to your `software` user's `Documents` folder.

4. In the terminal, `cd ~/Documents`. Uncompress the `lynx.gz` archive with the command `gunzip lynx.gz`. If your browser already did this for you, a file named `lynx` might be in your `Desktop` folder.

5. Wherever the file `lynx` ends up, copy it to `/usr/local/bin/`. Use `cp <path to lynx> /usr/local/bin/`. `<path to lynx>` might just be `lynx` or it might be `~/Desktop/lynx`.

   In the same directory, you should find ithe `lynx.1` file that you downloaded—this is the man page for `lynx` and belongs in `/usr/local/man/man1`; copy it there with `cp lynx.1 /usr/local/man/man1/`. If you want to be able to find it with the `whatis` or `man -k` commands, you can `makewhatis /usr/local/man` now as well.

6. Read the beginning of `lynx.cfg`. You can do this with `less lynx.cfg`. You can set a lot of configuration defaults in this file, but for now, leave the defaults as they are and copy the file to its intended destination. It should tell you that it belongs in `/usr/local/lib/lynx.cfg`, so `cp <path to lynx.cfg> /usr/local/lib/lynx.cfg`.

7. Just to make sure that the `lynx` file is executable, `chmod 755 /usr/local/bin/lynx`.

8. Log out and back in as your normal user. You might need to set your path to include `/usr/local/bin`, if it doesn't already. The easiest way to do this, as explained in Chapter 10 and detailed in 15, is to extend your path with `PATH="$PATH:/usr/local/bin/"` in your `.bashrc` file or `set path=($path /usr/local/bin)` placed in your `.cshrc` file, depending on which shell you're using. If you want this path to be available to everyone, all the time, you could put those statements in the systemwide `/etc/` versions of the files: `/etc/bashrc` and `/etc/csh.cshrc`.

The `lynx` application should now be executable and behave just as detailed in Chapter 13, "Using Common Command-Line Applications and Application Suites," although there is a bit of weirdness with the man page that we're going to have to fix in the next few pages.

Before you go on, stop and think fori a moment about what you've just done. If the terminal is still a strange place to you, you might be feeling as if you've just uttered some magic incantations and not be too sure you could do this again without the explicit instructions. Most things you come across will have instructions that are relatively explicit, but that's not the point. All that you've done is this: You've downloaded the software—you're used to doing that for other software installs in your web browser, FTP client, or the like—you've done nothing different here. Then you unpackaged it—nothing new there either—you've used StuffIt Expander before, right? Finally, you made a few new directories and copied the software where you wanted it to go. None of this was difficult for you and it won't be difficult for you in the future either. Don't let the fact that you're using unfamiliar tools now get in the way of the fact that you know what to do every step of the way. Soon you'll find this way of working to be just as second nature to you as double-clicking an "install" icon.

Building Software from Source Code: Compiling

Compiling source code is still complicated enough—and there are plenty of places it can go wrong—that most users will at least initially find it less than fun. It'll be the last *scary* topic we introduce in this book, though—everything after this is an application of what you've learned in the last few chapters and this one and the introduction of new programs for you to use. Actually, this stuff isn't that scary either. If you make it through this chapter and we haven't scared you away from the BSD subsystem, you're home free—we promise!

NOTE

Compilation is the process that a program-language compiler uses to take a source code "recipe" and convert it into an actual executable application. It is also used to describe the act of running the compiler to perform the compilation. To those coming from a Macintosh or Windows background, the idea of having to cook your own software from the raw ingredients probably evokes images of impossibly cryptic commands and more headaches than you would ever want to deal with. Thankfully, compiling prepackaged source code isn't quite cooking from the raw ingredients—it's usually more like warming up a TV dinner.

If you're interested in learning to cook software from scratch, we recommend Kernigan and Ritchie's excellent *The C Programming Language* and Donald Knuth's *The Art of Computer Programming* books on software architecture. There are far simpler books on programming, but nothing beats these seminal and indispensable references on the practice and principles of software design and engineering.

NOTE

In addition to installing software using GUI installers and compiling your own at the command line, there's a third major way of installing software under Mac OS X. This method, using a software package management system, is explained later in this chapter, when we will use the Fink ports package management system to install some X11 software for the X Window System and the DarwinPorts system to install a spell checker.

Much of what you can install at the command line in this chapter can be more easily installed using the Fink package manager or DarwinPorts. So, if you find this chapter's manipulations to be more than you're willing to deal with, don't worry; there are easier ways to install most of this and other software. The downsides of using the ports systems are that the software in them is rarely as up-to-date as what you can download directly from the authors and you're stuck with whatever compilation options and settings the port maintainers chose for their compilation. Still, despite these limitations, software installed from the Fink or DarwinPorts system is more than adequate for most uses, and the convenience of just typing **`fink install`** ***<package>*** usually outweighs the flexibility you get from installing manually.

Think of the manual installation examples here mostly as a practice and learning experience. There is more software that's not in either major port system than there is in both put together, so the techniques you'll learn are indispensable, even if these particular applications can be acquired somewhat more easily. We've selected some software that demonstrates many of the characteristics you'll find common among most manual software installs. If you think of building your system this way as an exciting challenge, you'll be able to go well beyond what's available from GUI or package-manager installations. If you look at playing with the guts of the system as an unpleasant exercise best avoided, you probably won't mind trading a bit of a wait for someone else to do the dirty work of fitting new software into Fink or DarwinPorts.

Basic Steps: `configure`, `make`

Let's start with an example of a simple software install that requires compilation—things can get more complicated than this, but for many applications written by conscientious programmers, these steps will suffice. Installs shown here are also done assuming that you're logged in as your `software` user and that you've downloaded software into the `Documents` directory.

Almost universally, the first command you'll issue to compile software is either `./configure` (if it's present) or `make` (if `./configure` is not present). For `pine`, the only things you have to type are

```
make
build osx
cp bin/pine /usr/local/bin/
mkdir /usr/local/man/
mkdir /usr/local/man1/
cp docs/pine.1 /usr/local/man/man1/
```

That doesn't look too hard, does it? The basic operations are simply `make`, `build`, and copying some files into standard locations in the file system.

If you want to follow along with this example, the `pine` package shown here can be downloaded from `ftp://ftp.cac.washington.edu/pine/pine.tar.gz`. The simplest way to do this is with `curl`:

```
cd ~/Documents
curl -O ftp://ftp.cac.washington.edu/pine/pine.tar.gz
gunzip pine.tar.gz
tar -xf pine.tar
```

NOTE

If you prefer to use the command-line Internet client `lynx`, you could issue the same download request by using the following command in place of the curl command:

```
lynx -dump ftp://ftp.cac.washington.edu/pine/pine.tar.gz > pine.tar.gz
```

The developers of `lynx` are changing and rearranging the way that some of the download functions work in the program. If your version of `lynx` produces files that can't be `gunzipped` as shown in the examples, you've been unlucky and gotten one of the versions that automatically uncompresses and `gunzips` files on download, even when storing them to disk. In this case, remove the `gunzip` step from the process and start off with the file as a `.tar` file instead.

`ftp://ftp.cac.washington.edu/pine/pine.tar.gz` is always a link to the most recent version, so `pine` might have advanced beyond 4.61 by the time you're reading this. We know `pine4.61` compiles okay, so if you download a more recent version and have problems, you should be able to get 4.61 from its `old` directory—most likely at the URL `ftp://ftp.cac.washington.edu/pine/old/pine4.61.tar.gz`.

After you've downloaded and unpacked your distribution, it's time to dig in and build some software.

```
brezup:software source $ cd pine4.61/
brezup:software pine4.61 $ ls -l
total 136
-rw-r--r--     1 software  tire   2866 May  7  2004 CPYRIGHT
-rw-r--r--     1 software  tire  12229 May  7  2004 README
-rwxr-xr-x     1 software  tire  18070 May 17  2004 build
-rwxr-xr-x     1 software  tire   6039 Mar 15  1996 build.cmd
-rwxr-xr-x     1 software  tire  17118 May  7  2004 buildcyg
drwxr-xr-x    10 software  tire    340 Apr 27  2004 contrib
drwxr-xr-x    13 software  tire    442 Jul 15 13:38 doc
drwxr-xr-x    16 software  tire    544 Jul 15 14:29 imap
-rw-r--r--     1 software  tire   1574 Oct  3  2003 makefile
drwxr-xr-x     5 software  tire    170 Jul 14 15:28 packages
drwxr-xr-x    86 software  tire   2924 Jul 14 15:37 pico
drwxr-xr-x   101 software  tire   3434 Jul 15 13:37 pine
```


There's no file named `configure`, so try `make`:

```
brezup:software pine4.61 $ make
Use the "build" command (shell script) to make Pine.
You can say "build help" for details on how it works.
```

So, this software install isn't quite standard—it doesn't use `make`, other than to tell us that it doesn't use `make`. If you read the `README` and look at the output of `build help`, which points you to `docs/pine-ports`, you'll observe that an `osx` option already is available, so give that a try:

```
brezup:software pine4.61 $ ./build osx
make args are CC=cc  osx

<much output deleted>

Building c-client for osx...
echo `cat SPECIALS`  > c-client/SPECIALS
cd c-client;make osx EXTRACFLAGS='\
 EXTRALDFLAGS='\
 EXTRADRIVERS='mbox'\
.
.
.
Building OS-dependent module
If you get No such file error messages for files x509.h, ssl.h,
pem.h, buffer.h, bio.h, and crypto.h, that means that OpenSSL
is not installed on your system. Either install OpenSSL first
```

```
or build with command: make osx SSLTYPE=none
`cat CCTYPE` -c `cat CFLAGS` `cat OSCFLAGS` -c osdep.c
`cat CCTYPE` -c `cat CFLAGS` mail.c
.
.
.
Building bundled tools...
cd mtest;make
cc -I../c-client `cat ../c-client/CFLAGS`   -c -o mtest.o mtest.c
.
.
.
Making Pico and Pilot
make CC=cc -f makefile.osx
rm -f os.h
ln -s osdep/os-osx.h os.h
cc   -g -DDEBUG  -Dbsd -DJOB_CONTROL   -c -o main.o main.c
cc   -g -DDEBUG  -Dbsd -DJOB_CONTROL   -c -o attach.o attach.c
.
.
.
Making Pine and rpload/rpdump.
make CC=cc LDAPLIBS=-lldap LDAPCFLAGS=-DENABLE_LDAP -f makefile.osx
rm -f os.h
ln -s osdep/os-osx.h os.h
./cmplhlp2.sh  < pine.hlp > helptext.h
cc   -g -DDEBUG -DDEBUGJOURNAL  -DENABLE_LDAP -Dconst=
➥ -DSYSTYPE=\"OSX\"   -c -o addrbook.o addrbook.c
.
.
.
Links to executables are in bin directory:
__TEXT  __DATA  __OBJC  others  dec     hex
4272128 319488  0       3248128 7839744 77a000  bin/pine
684032  12288   0       684032  1380352 151000  bin/mtest
724992  77824   0       720896  1523712 174000  bin/imapd
278528  12288   0       286720  577536  8d000   bin/pico
274432  12288   0       282624  569344  8b000   bin/pilot
946176  20480   0       946176  1912832 1d3000  bin/rpdump
950272  20480   0       950272  1921024 1d5000  bin/rpload
684032  12288   0       679936  1376256 150000  bin/mailutil
684032  12288   0       679936  1376256 150000  bin/ipop2d
688128  12288   0       679936  1380352 151000  bin/ipop3d
Done
```

Wow, that's a lot of output! If you were watching closely, you'll have seen some warnings fly by in there. But as long as it didn't explicitly say "Error" and, at the end, it tells you that there are executables in the bin directory, you're in good shape. Let's look in the bin directory and see what you've got.

```
brezup:software pine4.61 # ls -l bin
total 36848
total 38456

-rwxr-xr-x   2 software  tire  1453756 Jan  5 12:25 imapd
-rwxr-xr-x   2 software  tire  1368304 Jan  5 12:25 ipop2d
-rwxr-xr-x   2 software  tire  1375420 Jan  5 12:25 ipop3d
-rwxr-xr-x   2 software  tire  1371568 Jan  5 12:25 mailutil
-rwxr-xr-x   2 software  tire  1372536 Jan  5 12:25 mtest
-rwxr-xr-x   2 software  tire   566500 Jan  5 12:26 pico
-rwxr-xr-x   2 software  tire   559768 Jan  5 12:26 pilot
-rwxr-xr-x   2 software  tire  7787980 Jan  5 12:28 pine
-rwxr-xr-x   2 software  tire  1902860 Jan  5 12:28 rpdump
-rwxr-xr-x   2 software  tire  1910980 Jan  5 12:28 rpload
```

14

We were building pine, and in fact there is an executable pine in the bin directory, as well as a number of other applications. Installing pine now is simply copying it to /usr/local/bin with cp bin/pine /usr/local/bin. After that, pine should function as shown earlier.

```
brezup:software pine4.61 $ cp bin/pine /usr/local/bin/
```

A number of other executable applications are in that bin directory, too. You might want to spend the time to find out whether they do anything that you'd find useful—for example, along with pine, you've just built pico, which is a popular text editor that's been gaining on emacs and vi for quite a while. If you check the version of pico, a fairly popular and friendly terminal-based text editor included with Mac OS X 10.2 and 10.3, you'll find that it's version 2.5, and you've just built pico version 4.6—possibly a worthwhile upgrade. We'll leave the exercise of reading about the rest of the utilities you've just built up to you.

To make this a little easier, you might have noticed at the first listing of the directory, there is a doc directory. Things such as man pages are probably found there, so let's take a look:

```
brezup:software pine4.61 $ ls doc
brochure.txt    pico.1          pine.1          tech-notes
mailcap.unx     pilot.1         rpdump.1        tech-notes.txt
mime.types      pine-ports      rpload.1
```

Great! Things that end in .<#> are usually man pages that belong in the man# section of the manual. Let's put the pine.1 page for pine into the appropriate man1 directory in

/usr/local/man. If you didn't already create the /usr/local/man/man1 directory when you installed lynx earlier, you'll get a response something like this:

```
brezup:software pine4.61 $ cp doc/pine.1 /usr/local/man/man1/
cp: /usr/local/man/man1: No such file or directory
```

In such a case, you simply need to make the directory:

```
brezup:software pine4.61 $ mkdir /usr/local/man/man1
mkdir: /usr/local/man/man1: No such file or directory
```

Of course, if you didn't create these directories already, there's probably no /usr/local/man directory either. Thankfully, you only have to do this kind of directory creation steps once—most other command-line software will want the same directory structure, and this will be the only time you have to create these directories.

```
brezup:software pine4.61 $ mkdir /usr/local/man
brezup:software pine4.61 $ mkdir /usr/local/man/man1
```

Alternatively, you could make both directories with the same command, by using the -p "make intermediate directories" (that is make the entire path) option of mkdir:

```
brezup:software pine4.61 $ mkdir -p /usr/local/man/man1
```

If another application needs another directory, of course you'll need to create it, but you've got almost everything standard covered by now.

```
brezup:software pine4.61 $ cp doc/pine.1 /usr/local/man/man1
```

And now we can try looking at the man page. If you're using a version of Mac OS X that doesn't include the manpath command (versions more recent than 10.2.5 appear to include it) or you don't have /usr/local/bin added to your executable search path, you'll see something like the following; otherwise, you should see the man page for pine appear, just like any other man page on your system:

```
brezup:software pine4.61 $ man pine
man: no entry for pine in the manual.
```

CAUTION

Depending on your system configuration, system versions more recent than 10.4 might produce this error as well, but for a different reason: Apple has changed a previously working configuration from something that makes sense in the wide world of standard installations to something that might make sense if the rest of the world didn't exist, but breaks things because it the world won't go away. If you see this on 10.4, run the manpath command at the command line. Chances are you'll see /usr/local/share/man in the list instead of /usr/local/man. You have a choice of adjusting the configuration that causes this mis-choice of paths, putting your man pages where Apple has decided that everyone should have been putting them all along, or faking the system into thinking that they're in /usr/local/share/man despite their real, traditional location. The vast majority of the software you install will put its man files in /usr/local/man, so it makes more sense to either change the configuration or add a link from /usr/local/share/man back to /usr/local/man, rather than trying to adjust every installation to meet Apple's new silliness. You can make this adjustment in /usr/share/misc/man.conf (or /etc/manpath.config, depending on the version).Edit the lines that say MANPATH_MAP /usr/local/bin /usr/local/share/man so that they point to /usr/local/man instead, or just comment them out altogether. Alternatively, mkdir /usr/local/share; ln -s /usr/local/man /usr/local/share/man should work.

If you already have both directories, and files living in each, you can copy the contents of one into the other before repairing the configuration, or linking the directories.

This error indicates that the man command doesn't know where to find the man page for pine—specifically, that it hasn't been informed of the /usr/local/man/man1 directory that you just put it in. On recent versions of Mac OS X, all you need to do to make that directory visible to man is to include the /usr/local/bin directory in your executable search path (and perhaps fix the configuration as mentioned in the preceding caution), and the manpath command will automatically provide man with likely sounding directory names that are near the executable directories.

14

NOTE

Be aware that the automatic manpath finding algorithm can be a little dense. It will look for man directories that parallel any directories in your path that end in <*somepath*>/bin—note that there's no trailing forward slash, despite the fact that it's a directory. If you add /fizbin/wozbot/bin to your PATH environment variable, manpath will correctly identify /fizbin/wozbot/man as a possible location to search for man pages. If you specify /fizbin/wozbot/bin/ in your PATH, manpath will ignore its existence.

If for some reason you really want to stuff man pages off in weird corners where the manpath command can't find them automatically, you can always set the MANPATH environment variable as a way of explicitly telling man where to look.

NOTE

With bash, the shell is supposed to automatically discover new programs that have been added to directories in your PATH and let you immediately run them by name. This doesn't always work, and the only cure we're aware of is to quit the shell and start another one. With tcsh, you can tell the shell that it's time to refresh its list of available commands by running the rehash command.

In this case, I've deliberately forgotten to set the executable search path to include /usr/local/bin, so the manpath command doesn't know about /usr/local/man as a place to find man pages. Again, fixing these things is best done in your .bashrc or .cshrc file or the system equivalents. Setting it by hand now can be accomplished as follows:

```
brezup:software pine4.61 $ echo $PATH
/bin:/sbin:/usr/bin:/usr/sbin
brezup:software pine4.61 $ PATH=$PATH:/usr/local/bin
```

```
brezup:software pine4.61 $ echo $PATH
/bin:/sbin:/usr/bin:/usr/sbin:/usr/local/bin
brezup:software pine4.61 $ man pine
pine(1)                                                          pine(1)

NAME
       pine - a Program for Internet News and Email

SYNTAX
       pine [ options ] [ address , address ]
       pinef [ options ] [ address , address ]

DESCRIPTION
       Pine  is  a screen-oriented message-handling tool.  In its default con-
       figuration, Pine offers  an  intentionally  limited  set  of  functions
       geared  toward  the  novice  user,  but  it  also has a growing list of
       optional "power-user" and personal-preference  features.   pinef  is  a
       variant  of  Pine  that uses function keys rather than mnemonic single-
       letter commands.  Pine's basic feature set includes:
.
.
.
```

If you install other programs from the `bin` directory, you'll want to copy their man pages as well. Finally, clean up after yourself, and put the `pine` stuff into your `installed` software directory in case you need it again:

```
brezup:software pine4.61 $ make clean
./build clean
make args are CC=cc  clean
Cleaning c-client and imapd
Removing old processed sources and binaries...
<deletia>
Cleaning Pine
rm -f *.o os.h os.c helptext.c helptext.h pine pine.exe
➥ rpdump rpdump.exe rpload rpload.exe
<more deletia>
Cleaning pico
rm -f *.a *.o *~ pico_os.c os.h pico pico.exe pilot pilot.exe
<and more deletia>
Done
brezup:software pine4.61 $ cd ../
brezup:software source $ tar -cf installed_pine4.61.tar pine4.61/
brezup:software source $ gzip installed_pine4.61.tar
brezup:software source $ mkdir installed
brezup:software source $ mv installed_pine4.61.tar.gz installed/
```

```
brezup:software source $ \rm -rf pine4.61
brezup:software source $ \rm -rf pine.tar
```

That's it! If you've been following along, you've just compiled and installed a piece of software. Is your heart racing or are your palms sweaty? Do you feel like a different person? No? Didn't think so. Most software installations, by and large, are exactly this anticlimactic.

TIP

Curious about the `\` before the `rm` in the last command of that example? Remember when we suggested aliasing `rm` to `rm -i` to help avoid deleting things unintentionally? Remember also that the `\` character escapes things in the shell? If you precede an `alias`ed command with an `\` escape character, the effect is that the command, as the command line sees it, isn't exactly the same as the command that you set up the `alias` for. Effectively, for the execution of this command, the `alias` does not exist. In this case, it allows us to recursively delete the entire `pine4.61` directory and all its contents without needing to repeatedly answer `Y` to delete each file.

TIP

Why did I throw away the tarfile that I downloaded and create another one of the directory I was just working in for archiving in my `installed` directory? Because I have a terrible time remembering what installation options I might have used, files that I might have edited, and tweaks that I might have had to make to configure and install the software the way that I want it. By archiving a copy of the install directory in exactly the condition it is in when I run my final successful `make` (or in this case, `build`), I don't need to remember these things; they're preserved right there for me in the `tar` file.

Next, let's do a couple of quick installs that use a more standard installation protocol. They're a collection of steps to get you set up for a considerably more difficult install we'll do in the troubleshooting section of this chapter. The first of these is `libjpeg` and the second is `libpng`. These are library packages that will be needed later to support the `netpbm` package—an amazingly powerful command-line graphics processing program. The complete standard invocation for configuration and compiling is usually the following:

```
configure
make
make test
make install
```

If you read the `README` file for this software, you'll see it gets an additional `make install-lib` step—always read the `README` and `INSTALL` files if they are present!

1. Download both `libjpeg` and `libpng` with `curl`:

   ```
   cd ~/Documents/
   curl -O ftp://ftp.uu.net/graphics/jpeg/jpegsrc.v6b.tar.gz
   curl -O ftp://swrinde.nde.swri.edu/pub/png/src/libpng-1.2.8-config.tar.gz
   ```

2. Uncompress and unarchive the `libjpeg` archive:

```
brezup:software source $ gunzip jpegsrc.v6b.tar.gz
brezup:software source $ tar -xf jpegsrc.v6b.tar
```

TIP

If you prefer to uncompress and untar the file in one step, you can use `tar -xvzf jpegsrc.v6b.tar.gz` instead. I habitually do this process as two separate steps because I work between a number of Unix-based platforms, and not all of them have `tar`s that include the uncompress option. Rather than be somewhere in the middle of typing `make` when I notice that the `tar` command returned an error, it's easier for me to simply always use two steps.

3. `cd` into the directory, check to see whether there's a `configure` file or only a makefile, and either `./configure` or `make`, as appropriate:

```
brezup:software source $ cd jpeg-6b/
brezup:software jpeg-6b $ ls

README          jcmarker.c     jdhuff.h      jpegint.h      maktjpeg.st
ansi2knr.1      jcmaster.c     jdinput.c     jpeglib.h      makvms.opt
ansi2knr.c      jcomapi.c      jdmainct.c    jpegtran.1     rdbmp.c
cderror.h       jconfig.bcc    jdmarker.c    jpegtran.c     rdcolmap.c
cdjpeg.c        jconfig.cfg    jdmaster.c    jquant1.c      rdgif.c
cdjpeg.h        jconfig.dj     jdmerge.c     jquant2.c      rdjpgcom.1
change.log      jconfig.doc    jdphuff.c     jutils.c       rdjpgcom.c
cjpeg.1         jconfig.mac    jdpostct.c    jversion.h     rdppm.c
cjpeg.c         jconfig.manx   jdsample.c    libjpeg.doc    rdrle.c
ckconfig.c      jconfig.mc6    jdtrans.c     ltconfig       rdswitch.c
coderules.doc   jconfig.sas    jerror.c      ltmain.sh      rdtarga.c
config.guess    jconfig.st     jerror.h      makcjpeg.st    structure.doc
config.sub      jconfig.vc     jfdctflt.c    makdjpeg.st    testimg.bmp
configure       jconfig.vms    jfdctfst.c    makeapps.ds    testimg.jpg
djpeg.1         jconfig.wat    jfdctint.c    makefile.ansi  testimg.ppm
djpeg.c         jcparam.c      jidctflt.c    makefile.bcc   testimgp.jpg
example.c       jcphuff.c      jidctfst.c    makefile.cfg   testorig.jpg
filelist.doc    jcprepct.c     jidctint.c    makefile.dj    testprog.jpg
install-sh      jcsample.c     jidctred.c    makefile.manx  transupp.c
install.doc     jctrans.c      jinclude.h    makefile.mc6   transupp.h
jcapimin.c      jdapimin.c     jmemansi.c    makefile.mms   usage.doc
jcapistd.c      jdapistd.c     jmemdos.c     makefile.sas   wizard.doc
jccoefct.c      jdatadst.c     jmemdosa.asm  makefile.unix  wrbmp.c
jccolor.c       jdatasrc.c     jmemmac.c     makefile.vc    wrgif.c
jcdctmgr.c      jdcoefct.c     jmemmgr.c     makefile.vms   wrjpgcom.1
jchuff.c        jdcolor.c      jmemname.c    makefile.wat   wrjpgcom.c
jchuff.h        jdct.h         jmemnobs.c    makelib.ds     wrppm.c
```

```
jcinit.c        jddctmgr.c      jmemsys.h       makeproj.mac    wrrle.c
jcmainct.c      jdhuff.c        jmorecfg.h      makljpeg.st     wrtarga.c
```

Yes, that's a bunch of files—it's nothing to worry about, though. The configuration and build scripts put together by the author will take care of the details; all you need to do is remember the general steps for building and respond as requested if there's something the software or READMEs ask you to do. There's a configure file, so call `./configure`:

```
brezup:software jpeg-6b $ ./configure
checking for gcc... gcc
checking whether the C compiler (gcc  ) works... yes
checking whether the C compiler (gcc  ) is a cross-compiler... no
checking whether we are using GNU C... yes
checking how to run the C preprocessor... gcc -E
checking for function prototypes... yes
checking for stddef.h... yes
checking for stdlib.h... yes
checking for string.h... yes
checking for size_t... yes
checking for type unsigned char... yes
checking for type unsigned short... yes
checking for type void... yes
checking for working const... yes
checking for inline... __inline__
checking for broken incomplete types... ok
checking for short external names... ok
checking to see if char is signed... yes
checking to see if right shift is signed... yes
checking to see if fopen accepts b spec... yes
checking for a BSD compatible install... /usr/bin/install -c
checking for ranlib... ranlib
checking libjpeg version number... 62
creating ./config.status
creating Makefile
creating jconfig.h
```


NOTE

Why `./configure` instead of just `configure`? Because there might be many different executables named `configure` on your machine and you want to be sure to run only this one in this directory. As a matter of fact, on most competent Unix installations, typing **`configure`** (or any program name) at the command line will most frequently *not* run a version of that command that's in the current directory. Mac OS X seems currently to be reasonably well configured with respect to default paths, so if you want the command line to search the current directory for executables, you'll have to add it to your path.

configure runs and drops you back to the command line with no complaints, so now it's time to run make:

```
brezup:software jpeg-6b $ make
gcc -02  -I.   -c -o jcapimin.o jcapimin.c
gcc -02  -I.   -c -o jcapistd.o jcapistd.c
gcc -02  -I.   -c -o jctrans.o jctrans.c
gcc -02  -I.   -c -o jcparam.o jcparam.c
gcc -02  -I.   -c -o jdatadst.o jdatadst.c
.
.
.
rm -f libjpeg.a
ar rc libjpeg.a  jcapimin.o jcapistd.o jctrans.o jcparam.o jdatadst.o \
jcinit.o jcmaster.o jcmarker.o jcmainct.o
➥jcprepct.o jccoefct.ojccolor.o \
jcsample.o jchuff.o jcphuff.o jcdctmgr.o
➥jfdctfst.o jfdctflt.o jfdctint.o \
jdapimin.o jdapistd.o jdtrans.o jdatasrc.o
➥jdmaster.o jdinput.o jdmarker.o \
jdhuff.o jdphuff.o jdmainct.o jdcoefct.o
➥jdpostct.o jddctmgr.o jidctfst.o \
jidctflt.o jidctint.o jidctred.o jdsample.o
➥jdcolor.o jquant1.o jquant2.o \
jdmerge.o jcomapi.o jutils.o jerror.o jmemmgr.o jmemnobs.o
ranlib libjpeg.a
gcc -02  -I.   -c -o cjpeg.o cjpeg.c
gcc -02  -I.   -c -o rdppm.o rdppm.c
.
.
.
gcc -02  -I.   -c -o wrjpgcom.o wrjpgcom.c
gcc  -o wrjpgcom wrjpgcom.o
```

Again, you arrive back at the command line, so it's time to try make test:

```
brezup:software jpeg-6b $ make test
rm -f testout*
./djpeg -dct int -ppm -outfile testout.ppm  ./testorig.jpg
./djpeg -dct int -bmp -colors 256 -outfile testout.bmp  ./testorig.jpg
./cjpeg -dct int -outfile testout.jpg  ./testimg.ppm
./djpeg -dct int -ppm -outfile testoutp.ppm ./testprog.jpg
./cjpeg -dct int -progressive -opt -outfile testoutp.jpg ./testimg.ppm
./jpegtran -outfile testoutt.jpg ./testprog.jpg
cmp ./testimg.ppm testout.ppm
cmp ./testimg.bmp testout.bmp
```

```
cmp ./testimg.jpg testout.jpg
cmp ./testimg.ppm testoutp.ppm
cmp ./testimgp.jpg testoutp.jpg
cmp ./testorig.jpg testoutt.jpg
```

If there was a problem, `make test` would have spit out some error diagnostics and told you that it had encountered trouble. Because it didn't, you're ready to move on to `make install`:

```
brezup:software jpeg-6b $ make install
/usr/bin/install -c cjpeg /usr/local/bin/cjpeg
/usr/bin/install -c djpeg /usr/local/bin/djpeg
/usr/bin/install -c jpegtran /usr/local/bin/jpegtran
/usr/bin/install -c rdjpgcom /usr/local/bin/rdjpgcom
/usr/bin/install -c wrjpgcom /usr/local/bin/wrjpgcom
/usr/bin/install -c -m 644 ./cjpeg.1 /usr/local/man/man1/cjpeg.1
/usr/bin/install -c -m 644 ./djpeg.1 /usr/local/man/man1/djpeg.1
/usr/bin/install -c -m 644 ./jpegtran.1 /usr/local/man/man1/jpegtran.1
/usr/bin/install -c -m 644 ./rdjpgcom.1 /usr/local/man/man1/rdjpgcom.1
/usr/bin/install -c -m 644 ./wrjpgcom.1 /usr/local/man/man1/wrjpgcom.1
```

Notice that it's using the `/usr/local/man/man1` directory that you created earlier. If you hadn't done so, it would be complaining here.

14

NOTE

Sometimes `make install` rules automatically create directories needed for installation, but this particular install doesn't do this. Many authors assume that any sane version of Unix would already have directories such as `/usr/local/bin` and `/usr/local/man` and that creating them should never be necessary. Within a few installations, you'll have created all the directories that are customarily present, and then things should take care of themselves because authors tend to be more careful to explicitly create directories that aren't in the "normally present" tree.

Finally, if you read the README, you'd see that we need a `make install-lib` step here, too:

```
brezup:software jpeg-6b $ make install-lib
/usr/bin/install -c -m 644 jconfig.h /usr/local/include/jconfig.h
/usr/bin/install: /usr/local/include/jconfig.h: No such file or directory
make: *** [install-headers] Error 1
```

What did I say about that installer not creating directories? Now it needs a `/usr/local/include` directory as well:

```
brezup:software jpeg-6b $ mkdir /usr/local/include
brezup:software jpeg-6b $ make install-lib
/usr/bin/install -c -m 644 jconfig.h /usr/local/include/jconfig.h
/usr/bin/install -c -m 644 ./jpeglib.h /usr/local/include/jpeglib.h
```

```
/usr/bin/install -c -m 644 ./jmorecfg.h /usr/local/include/jmorecfg.h
/usr/bin/install -c -m 644 ./jerror.h /usr/local/include/jerror.h
/usr/bin/install -c -m 644 libjpeg.a /usr/local/lib/libjpeg.a
```

Then you're finished. To tidy things up, `make clean`, delete the original `tar` file, `tar` and then delete the directory you've been working in, `gzip` the new `tar` file, and store it in your `installed` directory.

Now let's take a look at what you just did. Other than creating a directory to fix the not-quite-functional installer, the entire process was: `./configure`, which guessed a few settings about your machine, and then a series of `make`, `make test`, `make install`, and `make install-lib`. Other than the `./configure`, the actual program called in each case was `make`, and it was directed to make different things with each call. The identities of these things are defined by the software author in a control file called a *makefile* and named, unsurprisingly, either `Makefile` or `makefile`. With any well-written software package, the makefile will direct `make` (called with no arguments) to compile the software with default settings. Frequently, but not always, a test suite is provided that can be invoked with `make test`.

Finally, an installer routine is invoked, by convention, with `make install`. In the case of `libjpeg`, the package provides both a few small executables and some library functions for other software, should you want them. The basic `make install` process puts the small executables in `/usr/local/bin` but doesn't install the libraries because not everyone wants them. Therefore, there's an optional `make install-lib` step to install the libraries and support files. If you've followed along this far, your `/usr/local` structure should be fairly mature and most software won't need you to create any more directories for it.

NOTE

Some software that you try to install will want you to use the `bsdmake` version of the `make` program instead of just `make` (which in Apple's case is currently `GNUmake`). Apple has also provided a separate `gnumake` executable should you find software that wants GNUmake to be named `gnumake` or `gmake`. If you find a request for `bsdmake` in a `README` file (or software that complains about syntax errors in the makefile), try substituting `bsdmake` or `gnumake` for `make` at the command line. If you find a program that outputs what seems to be incomprehensible gibberish when you type `make`, give the other versions a try and see whether they do any better.

The `configure` step is typical as well, although the mechanics vary depending on the application you're compiling. Most of the time, `configure` can examine your system and either determine or make an educated guess about configuration options. Occasionally, it requires you to provide it with some information, but in most cases it's all right to accept the default answers suggested by `configure` if you don't have a better answer or don't know the answer.

Finally, let's run through the install of `libpng` because without it, the broken `netpbm` we're going to fix in the next section is truly hopeless:

```
brezup:software source $ gunzip libpng-1.2.8-config.tar.gz
brezup:software source $ tar -xf libpng-1.2.8-config.tar
brezup:software source $ cd libpng-1.2.8-config
brezup:software libpng-1.2.8 $ ls
ANNOUNCE         config.sub       png.c            pngrutil.c
CHANGES          configure        png.h            pngset.c
INSTALL          configure.ac     pngbar.jpg       pngtest.c
KNOWNBUG         contrib          pngbar.png       pngtest.png
LICENSE          depcomp          pngconf.h        pngtrans.c
Makefile.am      example.c        pngerror.c       pngvcrd.c
Makefile.in      install-sh       pnggccrd.c       pngwio.c
README           libpng.3         pngget.c         pngwrite.c
TODO             libpng.txt       pngmem.c         pngwtran.c
Y2KINFO          libpngpf.3       pngnow.png       pngwutil.c
aclocal.m4       ltmain.sh        pngpread.c       projects
autogen.sh       missing          pngread.c        scripts
config.guess     mkinstalldirs    pngrio.c         test-pngtest.sh
config.h.in      png.5            pngrtran.c
```

It has a `configure`, so use it:

```
brezup:software libpng-1.2.8 $ ./configure
checking for a BSD-compatible install... /usr/bin/install -c
checking whether build environment is sane... yes
checking for gawk... no
checking for mawk... no
...
config.status: creating Makefile
config.status: creating config.h
config.status: executing depfiles commands
brezup:software libpng-1.2.8 $
```

Well, that's pleasant. It seems to have configured itself. Now it's time to try `make`:

```
brezup:software libpng-1.2.5 $ make
make  all-am
if /bin/sh ./libtool --mode=compile gcc -DHAVE_CONFIG_H -I. -I. -I.
➥      -g -O2 -MT png.lo -MD -MP -MF ".deps/png.Tpo" \
  -c -o png.lo `test -f 'png.c' || echo './'`png.c; \
then mv ".deps/png.Tpo" ".deps/png.Plo"; \
else rm -f ".deps/png.Tpo"; exit 1; \.
...
echo R_opts=\"-Wl,-rpath,/usr/local/lib\"; \
echo libs=\"-lpng12 -lz -lm\"; \
cat ./scripts/libpng-config-body.in ) > libpng-config
cp libpng-config libpng12-config
brezup:software libpng-1.2.8 $
```

If I had been working with an earlier version of `libpng`, that command would have stopped with an error, and I would have had to search around the documentation and FTP site to discover that there was an updated, custom `makefile` available for Mac OS X. Now, due to the magic of open source development, someone's fixed the bug for me and it all appears to have worked neatly.

Because there were no errors, and the installer doesn't appear to have a `make test` step, we're on to `make install`:

```
brezup:software libpng-1.2.8 $ make install
/bin/sh ./mkinstalldirs /usr/local/bin
 /usr/bin/install -c libpng-config /usr/local/bin/libpng-config
 /usr/bin/install -c libpng12-config /usr/local/bin/libpng12-config
/bin/sh ./mkinstalldirs /usr/local/lib
...
----------------------------------------------------------------------
Libraries have been installed in:
   /usr/local/lib

If you ever happen to want to link against installed libraries
in a given directory, LIBDIR, you must either use libtool, and
specify the full pathname of the library, or use the `-LLIBDIR'
flag during linking and do at least one of the following:
   - add LIBDIR to the `DYLD_LIBRARY_PATH' environment variable
     during execution

See any operating system documentation about shared libraries for
more information, such as the ld(1) and ld.so(8) manual pages.
----------------------------------------------------------------------
...
mkdir -p -- /usr/local/man/man5
 /usr/bin/install -c -m 644 ./png.5 /usr/local/man/man5/png.5
/bin/sh ./mkinstalldirs /usr/local/include/libpng
mkdir -p -- /usr/local/include/libpng
 /usr/bin/install -c -m 644 png.h /usr/local/include/libpng/png.h
 /usr/bin/install -c -m 644 pngconf.h /usr/local/include/libpng/pngconf.h
brezup:software libpng-1.2.8 $
```

All done. You've survived yet another software install. By now, this should be starting to look a bit more tedious than double-clicking an installer but no more threatening. Unfortunately, Mac OS X isn't as well supported in the `configure` scripts as some major Unix flavors just yet, so there are still a few rough spots like the makefile you would have needed to discover with the earlier versions. It's catching on quickly though, so soon, expect that 90% of all software will install with `./configure`, `make`, `make test`, and `make install`, and no further interaction from you.

> **NOTE**
>
> How can you enhance your chance of compilation success? You can make more installs work using the `configure` command by copying some files that Apple has provided into the software directory where you will be running `configure`. None of the installs shown here benefit from this, but copying `/usr/share/automake-1.6/config.guess` and `/usr/share/automake-1.6/config.sub` to the directory where you run `configure` might help with some compilations.

Installing the `fink` Ports and Packages Manager

Fink is a porting project, and `fink` is the software package manager it has produced for Mac OS X. It's an open source community project intended to bring the wide wild world of Unix applications to Mac OS X at a level of difficulty that the average Macintosh user won't find frustrating or, hopefully, even annoying. Because this book is being written on the bleeding edge of the release of Mac OS X 10.4, `fink` itself hasn't yet been updated to work with Tiger. Overall this isn't a large problem; `fink` will work in Tiger much like it works in earlier versions of the Mac OS, it simply might have some different defaults and might require a few months after the release to come up to full speed with respect to supporting applications. Hopefully, by the time you're reading this, everything will be working exactly as shown. If not, check the `fink` home page periodically (`http://fink.sourceforge.net/`), because being able to use a package manager to facilitate large, multipackage software installs really is a huge convenience. There's even a GUI front end (available from `http://finkcommander.sourceforge.net/`) that makes the installation of hundreds of useful applications that were historically installed from the command line into a point-and-click experience.

> **NOTE**
>
> DarwinPorts, which we cover in the next section, is another, complementary ports management system for Mac OS X. At one point DarwinPorts was supposed to be incorporated directly into the operating system, but we've seen neither hide nor hair of this plan since Steve Jobs announced it at one of the MacWorld Expos. Still, installing it yourself isn't difficult and it's an incredibly useful tool to have for software installation.

When using `fink`, you have the choice of installing precompiled binary applications out of Fink's library or using `fink` as an automated system to work out and apply compilation details, building the software on your own system. Because the binary application library always lags a few versions behind what's available through the source distribution, and sometimes doesn't even provide versions of some software, we'll cover how to use the source distribution in this chapter. Using the source distribution is relatively easy—easier than any of the command-line software installations you've seen. Using the binary distribution is even easier, if you've a reason to prefer to work with it (for example, it doesn't require that you have the developer tools installed).

Because we seem to constantly be revising this book on the cusp of major operating system changes, we've gotten used to the fact that the corresponding Fink version is rarely finished when we're writing. As a result, you get to have the most grueling introduction possible to using `fink`—pretty much building everything from scratch, straight from the command line. Don't let this bother you. The Fink system is a study in automation—the "most grueling introduction possible" requires you to type about a half-dozen commands, press the Return key to accept a few default prompts, and go have dinner. After you've done this, you can build entire applications with the simple command `fink install` *<packagename>*. The maintainers of Fink application porting projects do all the hard work of figuring out the quirks of making software work with Mac OS X and then package it so that all the interdependencies are known and codified. When a package is made available, all you need to do is ask `fink` to install it, and, along with any other required software, it'll be automatically downloaded, configured, and installed.

CAUTION

As the Tiger release approaches, we're becoming certain that these instructions won't exactly match what you'll see when you try to use the Fink system. Fink hasn't been updated to use the most recent Xcode (gcc) compilers, so portions of this will almost definitely not work on April 29th. Hopefully, Fink will catch up with Apple's changes again quickly!

NOTE

Fink (`http://fink.sourceforge.net/`) and DarwinPorts (`http://darwinports.opendarwin.org/`) aren't the only package systems being promoted for Mac OS X, but they're among the best supported and the most honest. The `gnu-darwin` group (`http://www.gnu-darwin.org/`) is also doing very nice work. There's also a collaboration going on between a number of the porting projects, with news and links maintained at `http://www.metapkg.org/`. There are, however, other groups out there operating less from a desire to help further open source computing and Mac OS X than to line their own pockets by preying on the fact that many traditional Macintosh users find the command line intimidating.

If you're really willing to pay $30 to avoid having to type one single line at the command prompt, these people provide the service you're looking for. If you're not too intimidated by the command line, however, be mildly suspicious of people who want to sell you ported Unix software. Some of them are doing a fine job of providing ported software and additional value-added features or documentation that make their commercial distribution of free software well worth the money. However, the migration of Mac users to a Unix-based operating system has brought a whole crowd of vultures out of the woods hoping to make a quick buck. If it's a Unix application, there's a good chance you can find it for free from Fink, DarwinPorts, `gnu-darwin`, or another porting group on the Net. This isn't to say that `gnu-darwin`'s ports CD is not a great deal at $30—that's only five cents per megabyte that you don't have to download and install. But when someone tries to charge you $30 for 5MB, or is downloading and selling web access to packages compiled and provided for free by Fink, DarwinPorts, and `gnu-darwin`, it should raise some eyebrows.

The first step in using `fink` to install software is to install `fink` itself. You need to do this only once, and despite the large volume of interaction we show here, it's really a simple process.

```
brezup:ray Software $ mkdir finkcvs
brezup:ray Software $ cd finkcvs
```

```
brezup:ray finkcvs $ cvs -d:pserver:anonymous@
➥cvs.fink.sourceforge.net:/cvsroot/fink login


(Logging in to anonymous@cvs.fink.sourceforge.net)
CVS password:
```

The CVS password for anonymous, download-only access is empty, so just press the Return key at the password prompt.

```
brezup:ray finkcvs $ cvs -d:pserver:anonymous@
➥cvs.fink.sourceforge.net:/cvsroot/fink checkout fink
cvs server: Updating fink
U fink/.cvsignore
U fink/AUTHORS
U fink/COPYING
U fink/ChangeLog
U fink/INSTALL
U fink/INSTALL.html
.
.
.
cvs server: Updating fink/update
U fink/update/ChangeLog
U fink/update/Makefile.in.in
U fink/update/config.guess
U fink/update/config.sub
U fink/update/ltconfig
U fink/update/ltmain.sh
```


Alternatively, you might be able to avoid the CVS checkout step and download a tarfile of the base `fink` installer source from Fink's downloads page as well (`http://fink.sourceforge.net/download/srcdist.php`). This has the advantage of getting you the base system in a lump, but it will be several revisions behind the most recent, and you'll have to remove and install new versions to update, rather than simply being able to ask the CVS version to update and rebuild itself. Regardless of how you obtain the base distribution, your next step is to `cd` in to the directory (which might be named different things, depending on how you acquired it) and run the `bootstrap.sh` script to get everything configured.

```
brezup:ray finkcvs $ cd fink
brezup:ray fink $ ./bootstrap.sh
Welcome to Fink.

This script will install Fink into a directory of your choice,
setup a configuration file and conduct a bootstrap of the installation.
```

```
Found perl version 5.008004.
Checking package... looks good.
Checking system... powerpc-apple-darwin8.0.0b2
This system was not released at the time this Fink release was made.
Prerelease versions of Mac OS X might work with Fink, but there are no
guarantees.
Distribution 10.3

Fink must be installed and run with superuser (root) privileges. Fink can
automatically try to become root when it's run from a user account. Avaliable
methods:

(1)  Use sudo
(2)  Use su
(3)  None, fink must be run as root
Choose a method: [1] 3
ERROR: Can't continue as non-root.
brezup:ray fink $
```

`fink` must have some way to run by the `root` user so that it can modify various things in semiprivileged directories. This is a poor design, but it's because Apple put things that shouldn't be `root`-owned, in places that only `root` can write. The `bootstrap.sh` script halted here because I don't like giving software the option of "becoming root itself," and I forgot to `su` or `sudo` at the start of the `bootstrap.sh` process. `fink` is capable of updating many Apple-supplied packages to more current versions, and the maintainers seem committed to keeping their software as Apple-friendly as possible. They appear to be making a conscientious effort to keep their installers from conflicting with Apple installations while providing updated versions of Apple-supplied software. I'm not a big fan of running installations as `root`, but given the level of attention that the `fink` project maintainers are paying to the quality of their code, I feel better about giving this software the go-ahead.

```
brezup:ray fink $ sudo ./bootstrap.sh
Password:
Welcome to Fink.

...

Fink must be installed and run with superuser (root) privileges. Fink can
automatically try to become root when it's run from a user account. Avaliable
methods:

(1)  Use sudo
(2)  Use su
(3)  None, fink must be run as root
```

```
Choose a method: [3] 3
Checking cc... looks good.
Checking make... looks good.
Checking head... looks good.
Please choose the path where Fink should be installed. [/sw] /sw
OK, installing into '/sw'.

Creating directories...
mkdir -p /sw
mkdir /sw/etc
mkdir /sw/etc/alternatives
.
.
.
mkdir /sw/fink/10.2/local/main/finkinfo
mkdir /sw/fink/10.2/local/main/binary-darwin-powerpc
Copying package descriptions...
.
.
.
USAGE.html ChangeLog VERSION fink.in fink.8.in install.sh setup.sh
postinstall.pl.in perlmod update mirror
Creating initial configuration...

OK, I'll ask you some questions and update the configuration file in
'/sw/etc/fink.conf'.
```


A considerable number of configuration choices follow, enabling you to suggest preferred locations of where you want to download various software bits as the system needs them. If you change your mind later, you can modify these choices with the command `fink configure`. Make choices that are appropriate for your system—I've mostly just chosen the default values here.

```
In what additional directory should Fink look for downloaded tarballs? []
(1)  Quiet (don't show download stats)
(2)  Low (don't show tarballs being expanded)
(3)  Medium (shows almost everything)
(4)  High (shows everything)
How verbose should Fink be? [4] 4
Proxy/Firewall settings
Enter the URL of the HTTP proxy to use, or 'none' for no proxy. The URL should
 start with http:// and may contain username, password or
➥port specifications. [none] none
Enter the URL of the proxy to use for FTP, or 'none' for no proxy. The URL
should start with http:// and may contain username, password
or port specifications. [none] none
```

```
Use passive mode FTP transfers (to get through a firewall)? [Y/n] Y
Mirror selection
Choose a continent:

(1)  Africa
(2)  Asia
(3)  Australia
(4)  Europe
(5)  North America
(6)  South America, Middle America and Caribbean
Your continent? [1] 5
Choose a country:

(1)  No selection - display all mirrors on the continent
(2)  Canada
(3)  Mexico
(4)  United States
Your country? [1] 4
```

A dozen or so configuration options sets go by, but despite the volume of options, accepting the defaults appears to work just fine. Next the program starts downloading and building the bits and pieces that it needs to construct itself. Self-collecting and building software—neat, huh?

```
BOOTSTRAP PHASE ONE: download tarballs.

pkg gettext  version ###
pkg gettext  version 0.10.40-3
pkg tar  version ###
...
gcc -DHAVE_CONFIG_H -I. -I. -I.. -I../intl  -I/sw/bootstrap/include \
-g -02 -c `test -f hash.c ¦¦ echo './'`hash.c
source='human.c' object='human.o' libtool=no \
depfile='.deps/human.Po' tmpdepfile='.deps/human.TPo' \
depmode=gcc /bin/sh ../depcomp \
gcc -DHAVE_CONFIG_H -I. -I. -I.. -I../intl  -I/sw/bootstrap/include \
-g -02 -c `test -f human.c ¦¦ echo './'`human.c
source='modechange.c' object='modechange.o' libtool=no \
depfile='.deps/modechange.Po' tmpdepfile='.deps/modechange.TPo' \
depmode=gcc /bin/sh ../depcomp \
...
```

(A very long time passes—go have dinner!)

```
...
BOOTSTRAP DONE. Cleaning up.
```

```
rm -rf /sw/bootstrap
dpkg-scanpackages dists/local/main/binary-darwin-powerpc override ¦
gzip >dists/local/main/binary-darwin-powerpc/Packages.gz
...
dpkg-scanpackages dists/local/bootstrap/binary-darwin-powerpc override ¦
gzip >dists/local/bootstrap/binary-darwin-powerpc/Packages.gz
 Wrote 14 entries to output Packages file.

You should now have a working Fink installation in '/sw'. You still need
package descriptions if you want to compile packages yourself. You can get
them from CVS or by installing the packages.tar.gz tarball.

Run 'source /sw/bin/init.csh ; rehash' to set up this Terminal's environment
to use Fink. To make the software installed by Fink available in all of your
shells, add 'source /sw/bin/init.csh' to the init script '.cshrc' in your
home directory. Enjoy.
```


NOTE

If you're running `tcsh`, the `rehash` command is necessary. If you're running `bash`, it's not.

Now you almost have a working copy of the `fink` software installation system. The first thing to do when the prompt returns is to edit the file `/sw/etc/fink.conf` and change the line that reads

```
Trees: local/main stable/main stable/crypto local/bootstrap
```

to

```
Trees: local/main stable/main stable/crypto local/bootstrap unstable/main
➥ unstable/crypto
```

NOTE

The exact list of trees that you'll want to configure is somewhat variable and depends on the state of the `fink` ports for both your current operating system and your version of the developer tools. This list shown is representative of a Mac OS X 10.2 installation using `gcc` 3.1, and allows `fink` to make available a number of applications that haven't been thoroughly tested but that largely work well nonetheless.

If you're interested in only stable release software (by stable, `fink` means "well tested"; much of the unstable software is considerably more stable than many commercial packages you probably use every day, but it hasn't been examined and tested to verify that it qualifies as stable by the rules of the project maintainers), you don't need to add the `unstable/*` entries. There's a fair quantity of interesting software that lives in the unstable branches, though, so it's probably worth leaving in there. You aren't obliged to install any of the software in those branches, but having the entry in the `.conf` file enables you to see the software in them from the installation interface, and you can make an informed choice.

The next thing to do is make that recommended change to your `.bashrc` or `.cshrc` file (add `. /sw/bin/init.sh` or `source /sw/bin/init.csh` to the bottom of the appropriate shell startup file —or watch to see what `fink` recommends as it finishes its run— this syntax changes occasionally), and at the command line execute the file to load its configuration into your running shell (`. /sw/bin/init.sh` or `source /sw/bin/init.csh ; rehash`, as appropriate).

NOTE

This is important! `fink` installs software in a number of noncanonical places and a number of places that won't be in your path as provided by Apple or your previous modifications of your `.bashrc`/`.cshrc` file. `/sw/bin/init.csh` and `/sw/bin/init.sh` set up a number of directory paths that `fink` uses, and if you don't add lines that run these files in your shell startup file, you won't be able to run any of the software the next time you log in.

Now you need to tell `fink` to update portions of itself using the software it just constructed in the bootstrap phase. (Again, `tcsh` syntax is used here because we can't stand `bash` as a user shell. If you're running `bash`, use `. /sw/bin/init.sh`, and ignore the `rehash` command.)

```
brezup:ray fink $ source /sw/bin/init.csh ; rehash
brezup:ray fink $ sudo fink selfupdate-cvs
The selfupdate function can track point releases or it can set up your Fink
installation to update package descriptions from CVS. Updating from CVS has
the advantage that it is more up to date than the last point release. On the
other hand, the point release may be more mature or have less bugs.
Nevertheless, CVS is recommended. Do you want to set up direct CVS updating?
[Y/n] Y
Fink has the capability to run the CVS commands as a normal user. That has
some advantages - it uses that user's CVS settings files and allows the
package descriptions to be edited and updated without becoming root
Please specify the user login name that should be used: [root] root
For Fink developers only: Enter your SourceForge login name to set up full CVS
access. Other users, just press return to set up anonymous read-only
access. [anonymous] anonymous
mkdir -p /sw/fink.tmp
Checking to see if we can use hard links to merge the existing tree. Please
ignore errors on the next few lines.
touch /sw/fink/README; ln /sw/fink/README /sw/fink.tmp/README
Now logging into the CVS server. When CVS asks you for a password, just press
return (i.e. the password is empty).
cvs -d:pserver:anonymous@cvs.sourceforge.net:/cvsroot/fink login
(Logging in to anonymous@cvs.sourceforge.net)
CVS password:
Now downloading package descriptions...
cvs -z3 -d:pserver:anonymous@cvs.sourceforge.net:/cvsroot/fink
➥checkout -d fink dists
cvs server: Updating fink
```

```
U fink/.cvsignore
U fink/ChangeLog
...
pkg apt-shlibs  version ###
pkg apt-shlibs  version 0.5.4-5
pkg storable-pm  version ###
pkg storable-pm  version 1.0.14-1
No packages to install.

The core packages have been updated. You should now update the other packages
using commands like 'fink update-all'.
brezup:ray fink $
```


When this step finishes, you're ready to start using `fink` to install software. `fink` is also done with the `finkcvs` directory (it's the source and build directory for the `fink` command and related software, not for the software `fink` installs), so you can delete it now as well. All other installing, configuring, and updating is carried out in the `/sw` directory (or another location that you specified instead).

You have a choice of using `fink` to carry out software installations directly from the command line or from a menu-driven interface to the `fink` system. These options differ in a fundamental way: The command-line version uses the `fink` system to download and compile source directly on your computer, whereas the menu-driven system downloads precompiled binaries and installs them. There are advantages and disadvantages to each approach. A precompiled binary is usually quicker to download and install, but it might be out of phase with the software on your system, and you could be stuck waiting for someone else to submit a compiled version before you can download something that works on your system.

Using `fink` to compile, on the other hand, is generally slower, and you run a different but similarly annoying risk of the compilation parameters supplied by `fink` not being in sync with the compilers and libraries available on your machine. The maintainers of `fink` packages do a wonderful job of making installation via compilation simple and painless, but regardless of how carefully they try, there are always going to be machines configured by users who "think just a little more differently" than the `fink` maintainers anticipated in their installer scripts.

NOTE

When we were writing for release 10.2 of Mac OS X, (September 17, 2002), the argument for the command-line compilation option won: The binaries available through `fink` hadn't been updated to be 10.2 compatible yet, but the source distribution had been updated to compile on 10.2. As of Sept 14, 2003, the binaries were winning for 10.3, as most of the binaries that worked on 10.2 also worked on 10.3, whereas the source distribution wasn't quite working yet. By the middle of 2004, the source distribution was back in the lead, and now that we're on the cusp of a Tiger release, it looks like binaries will have an advantage again for a short while. By the time you're reading this, though, the binary distribution will probably be behind again (being largely stuck in an earlier version of the compiler `gcc`), and the source distribution will be updated to work with your new operating system and corresponding new developer tools.

Installing Some Additional Interesting Software

After getting you all excited about how easily the `fink` system installs software, you didn't think we were going to just leave you hanging without showing you around a bit more of the system, did you? Just for kicks, let's use the `fink` system to see what's available (remember, `fink` is always adding new packages) in the way of games. To do this, we use the `fink list` command. `fink list` takes a single argument: a pattern to match in the package name. Here we'll look for some additional software to play with under X11, the alternate (traditional Unix) windowing system that Apple's incorporated seamlessly with Aqua.

> **FINK ISN'T JUST FOR X11**
>
> The `fink` system isn't just for installing X11 software. That's what we're primarily using it for in our examples, but `fink` can install programming languages, networking software, utilities, spreadsheets, you name it. If there's a Unix application that can be ported to Mac OS X, the `fink` project will try to wrap it into its package management system.

To start, let's try looking for packages with game in the name:

```
brezup:root Documents # fink list game

Information about 1449 packages read in 1 seconds.

     gnome-games        1.4.0.4-2     GNOME games collection.
     gnome-games-dev    1.4.0.4-2     GNOME games collection.
     gnome-games-shl    1.4.0.4-2     GNOME games collection.
     kdegames3          3.0.7-2       KDE - games
     kdegames3-commo    3.0.7-2       KDE - shared libraries used by KDE games
     kdegames3-dev      3.0.7-2       development headers and libraries for KDE...
```

That's not particularly impressive for a port system boasting more than 1,400 packages, is it? Well, let's see what one of them is before we dig further:

```
brezup:root Documents # fink describe gnome-games

Information about 1449 packages read in 1 seconds.

pkg gnome-games  version ###
pkg gnome-games  version 1.4.0.4-2

gnome-games-1.4.0.4-2: GNOME games collection.
 The gnome-games package contains a collection of simple games for your
 amusement.
 .
 Web site: http://www.gnome.org/
 .
 Maintainer: Masanori Sekino <msek@users.sourceforge.net>
```

Okay, that could be interesting, let's give it a whirl:

```
brezup:root Documents # fink install gnome-games

Information about 1449 packages read in 1 seconds.

pkg gnome-games  version ###
pkg gnome-games  version 1.4.0.4-2

fink needs help picking an alternative to satisfy a virtual dependency. The
candidates:

(1)  giflib: GIF image format handling library, LZW-enabled version
(2)  libungif: GIF image format handling library, LZW-free version

Pick one: [1]
```


`fink` needs help? It's just asking you to make a choice, and it's already suggesting a default, so press the Return key and let it go:

```
fink needs help picking an alternative to satisfy a virtual dependency. The
candidates:

(1)  giflib-bin: GIF image format handling library, LZW-enabled version
(2)  libungif-bin: GIF image format handling library, LZW-free version

Pick one: [1]
```

Repeat as necessary!

```
fink needs help picking an alternative to satisfy a virtual dependency. The
candidates:

(1)  giflib-shlibs: GIF image format handling library, LZW-enabled version
(2)  libungif-shlibs: GIF image format handling library, LZW-free version

Pick one: [1]

The following package will be installed or updated:
 gnome-games
The following 53 additional packages will be installed:
 audiofile audiofile-bin audiofile-shlibs db3 db3-shlibs docbook-dsssl-nwalsh
 docbook-dtd esound esound-bin esound-common esound-shlibs gdk-pixbuf
 gdk-pixbuf-shlibs giflib giflib-bin giflib-shlibs glib glib-shlibs
 gnome-games-shlibs gnome-libs gnome-libs-dev gnome-libs-shlibs gtk+
 gtk+-data gtk+-shlibs gtk-doc guile guile-dev guile-shlibs imlib
 imlib-shlibs libjpeg libjpeg-bin libjpeg-shlibs libpng libpng-shlibs libtiff
```

```
 libtiff-bin libtiff-shlibs libxml libxml-shlibs netpbm netpbm-bin
 netpbm-shlibs openjade orbit orbit-bin orbit-shlibs passwd readline
 readline-shlibs scrollkeeper sgml-entities-iso8879

Do you want to continue? [Y/n] Y
```

Do you want it to install 53 packages for you automatically? Perhaps a better question is, "Do you want to install 53 packages manually, the way that you did in earlier chapters?" Press Y and let it roll!

Much time now passes...

```
The following group entries will be added to your NetInfo database:
news:*:250:
mysql:*:251:
pgsql:*:252:
games:*:253:
canna:*:254:
postfix:*:255:
maildrop:*:256:
tomcat:*:257:
jabber:*:258:

Existing entries with these names or numbers will be overwritten or
otherwise affected by this. On the other hand, some Fink packages will
not work unless these entries are in the NetInfo database. You can make
adjustments to the files /sw/etc/passwd-fink and
/sw/etc/group-fink now (from another window), then say yes here. Or
you can say no here and add the users and groups manually (e.g. on your
central NetInfo server). If you don't know what all of this is about,
just say yes.

Do you want to continue? [Y/n] Y
```

Again, accept the default. After this step, and more time, you come back to your command prompt with not much information regarding exactly what software has been installed. Remember that `fink` likes to store its executables in `/sw/bin`. Libraries go in `/sw/lib`. Looking in those directories, you'll find many files. If you look at the names of the programs and libraries, some of them might strike you as familiar. Look back at the list of packages `fink` told you it was going to install—do you recognize `libjpeg`? `libtiff`? How about `netpbm`? All to install a few sample games (`gnometris` is one of them—a simple Tetris-like puzzle-piece game), `fink` has installed some 400 programs and associated libraries, include files, man pages, and so on. The rest of this software is available for you to use as well, so it might be worth a bit of your time to look at some of what's been installed and check out the man pages—there's far more interesting stuff in there than could be documented here, even if we devoted the entire book to it! All of this, and you only had to answer a few questions and wait a while.

If you want to try out the software that `fink` installed, start X11 (in case what you choose is an X Window application) and run some of it. Try out some of the games; `gnometris`, `mahjongg`, `iagno`, `gnibbles`, and `gnobots2` are a few of them. Try out some of the `netpbm` applications—see whether they produce the same output as the ones you built by hand. Figure 14.1 shows a number of the `gnome-game` samples running alongside Aqua windows.

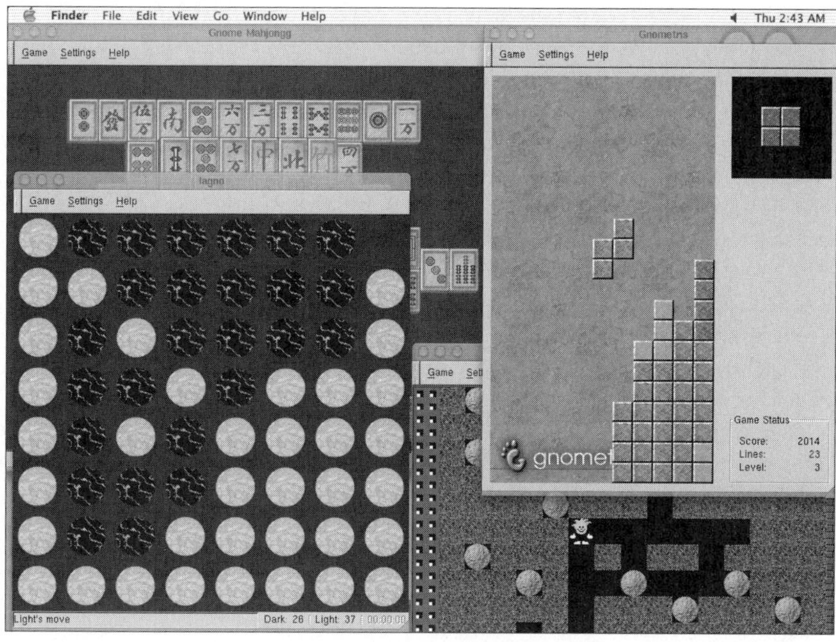

FIGURE 14.1 X11 games running beside Aqua applications.

Let's return to `fink` and see whether there are more games. If you've peeked ahead to see what X11 is all about, you already know from looking at the screenshots that there's an X11 version of the arcade game Galaga, so let's see whether it's in `fink`:

```
brezup:root Documents # fink list galaga
Information about 1449 packages read in 2 seconds.

     xgalaga            2.0.34-1     Clone of the classic game of galaga
```

Nifty! Now you know how to install `xgalaga` if you want it. More importantly, you should observe that although it's a game, `xgalaga` doesn't have the word `game` in its name, only in the comment. This and the `grep` command should get you started on finding much more software that you might want:

```
brezup:root Documents # fink list | grep "game"
        amaze   0.0-2   3D maze game in curses.
        atlantik        3.0.7-2 KDE - monopoly-like game
        cgoban  1.9.12-1        X11 frontend for the game of Go
```

```
     connect4         1.1-2   Text-based Connect Four game.
     crafty-tb-four  18-1     Four piece endgame tablebases for crafty
     crafty-tb-three 18-1     Three piece endgame tablebases for crafty
     crossfire        1.3.0-1 Graphical role-playing adventure game for X11.
     dama    0.5.4-1 Turkish draughts board game. (checkers-like)
     danican 0.5.2-1 International draughts board game. (checkers-like)
     dopewars         1.5.4-1 Drug dealing game set in New York
i    gnome-games      1.4.0.4-2       GNOME games collection.
     gnome-games-dev 1.4.0.4-2       GNOME games collection.
i    gnome-games-shlibs      1.4.0.4-2       GNOME games collection.
     gnuboy  1.0.3-2 Opensource gameboy emulator
     gnugo   3.2-12  Plays the game of Go
     grhino  0.6.0-1 Strong othello game for GNOME.
     gtkmonop         0.3.0-5 Client for something resembling the well known
                      ➥board game
     katomic 3.0.7-2 KDE - sokoban-like game
     kbackgammon      3.0.7-2 KDE - backgammon board game
     kde-panel-fifteen        3.0.7-2 KDE - moving squares panel game
     kdegames3        3.0.7-2 KDE - games
     kdegames3-common         3.0.7-2 KDE - shared libraries used by KDE games
     kdegames3-dev    3.0.7-2 development headers and libraries for KDE games
     kenolaba         3.0.7-2 KDE - strategy board game
     khangman         3.0.7-2 KDE - hangman word game
     kjumpingcube     3.0.7-2 KDE - tactical game
     klickety         3.0.7-2 KDE - tetris-like game
     klines  3.0.7-2 KDE - Color Lines-like logic game
     kmahjongg        3.0.7-2 KDE - pick-up game based on the ancient
                              ➥mandarin Mah Jong
     kmessedwords     3.0.7-2 KDE - mind-training word game
     kmines  3.0.7-2 KDE - minesweeper-like game
     kolf    3.0.7-2 KDE - mini-golf game
     konquest         3.0.7-2 KDE - multi-player strategic war game
     kpat    3.0.7-2 KDE - collection of solitaire-like card games
     kpoker  3.0.7-2 KDE - poker card game
     ksame   3.0.7-2 KDE - simple game inspired by SameGame
     kshisen 3.0.7-2 KDE - Shisen-So - a Mah Jong-like game
     ksokoban         3.0.7-2 KDE - sokoban-like game
     kspaceduel       3.0.7-2 KDE - 2-player space arcade game
     ktuberling       3.0.7-2 KDE - Mr. Potato Head-like game
     lskat   3.0.7-2 KDE - 2-player card game like Offiziersskat
     megami  3.0.7-2 KDE - blackjack card game
     monopd  0.5.0-3 Monopoly-like game server
     nethack 3.4.0-1 Console/X11 based graphical adventure game
     nibbles 1.1-2   Text-based color snake game.
     robotournament  01.20.02-1      Robot board game inspired by RoboRally
     teg     0.10.1-12       Strategy game similar to Risk
```

```
        xdigger 1.0.10-1        Boulderdash like game for X Windows
        xfrisk  1.2-2   Computer version of the Risk boardgame
        xgalaga 2.0.34-1        Clone of the classic game of galaga
        xlightoff       1.1-1   Light switching game for X11.
        xpilot  4.5.4-1 Multi-player 2D space game.
        xscorch 0.1.15-2        Scorched Earth - "the mother of all games"
        xscrabble       0901-1  Scrabble game for X
```

That's more like it. (Although I'll give you a hint: That isn't all the games either. Some of them, such as `kbattleship`, don't have `game` in either the name or the description.) Something to note in the listing is that the lines for both `gnome-games` and `gnome-games-shlibs` now have the letter `i` before them. This indicates that they're already installed. If there were newer versions available that you might want to install, these would be shown as `(i)` instead of just `i`.

Should you ever need to update your installed `fink` software to newer versions, you can use `fink update-all`, which automatically downloads everything necessary to update any installed `fink` packages on your system.

Before we leave our quick tour of `fink`, let's look at just a few other types of applications.

Spreadsheets?

```
brezup:root Documents # fink list ¦ grep "pread"
        abs     0.908-1 Opensource spreadsheet
        gnumeric        1.0.9-1 Spreadsheet program for gnome, reads many formats
        kspread 1.2.0-2 KDE - spreadsheet
```

Graphics?

```
brezup:root Documents # fink list ¦ grep "raphics"
        autotrace       0.30-4  Converts bitmap to vector graphics
        gd      1.8.4-11        Graphics generation library
        gd-bin  1.8.4-11        Graphics generation library
        gd-pm   1.33-3  Perl interface to the GD graphics library
        gd-shlibs       1.8.4-11        Graphics generation library
        gd2     2.0.1-4 Graphics generation library
        gd2-bin 2.0.1-4 Graphics generation library
        gd2-shlibs      2.0.1-4 Graphics generation library
        gif2png 2.4.6-1 GIF to PNG graphics file conversion
        gqview  1.0.2-1 Graphics file browser utility
        gri     2.10.1-2        Language for scientific graphics programming.
        kde-kfile-image-plugins 3.0.7-2 KDE - graphics
        kdegraphics3    3.0.7-2 KDE - graphics
        libart2 2.3.9-1 Library for high-performance 2D graphics
        libart2-shlibs  2.3.9-1 Library for high-performance 2D graphics
 i      netpbm  9.25-1  Graphics manipulation programs and libraries
 i      netpbm-bin      9.25-1  Graphics manipulation programs and libraries
```

```
 i      netpbm-shlibs   9.25-1  Graphics manipulation programs and libraries
        pgplot  5.2-3   Fortran- or C-callable scientific graphics package.
        pgplot-perl     2.18-2  Perl interfaces for the PGPLOT graphics library
        pymol   0.82-2  Molecular graphics system
        r-base  1.5.1-2 Environment for statistical computing and graphics
        rasmol  2.7.1.1-3       Molecular graphics visualisation tool
        sketch  0.6.13-3        Vector graphics editor
        sodipodi        0.24.1-2        Gnome vector graphics application
        transfig        3.2.3d-7        Converts xfig objects to various
                                ➥graphics formats.
```

Text?

```
brezup:root Documents # fink list ¦ grep "text"
        autogen 5.4.2-1 Tool for automated text generation from templates
        bluefish        0.7-1   Web-oriented text editor
        context 2001.11.13-2    Full-featured macro package written in TeX
        dosunix 1.0.13-1        Converts DOS text files to unix text format
        ee      1.4.2-3 Easy to use text editor.
        emacs-w3        4.0.47-2        Emacs text-based web browser
        emacs21 21.2-9  Flexible real-time text editor, v21.2 with X11 support
        emacs21-nox     21.2-9  Flexible real-time text editor, v21.2 for
                       ➥terminal only
        enscript        1.6.1-1 Converts text files to PostScript
        figlet  22-3    Makes large letters out of ordinary text
        gd-textutil-pm  0.82-1  Perl package for text utilities of GD
 i      gettext 0.10.40-3       Message localization support
        gnotepad+       1.3.3-1 Simple and feature-rich HTML/text editor
        grep    2.4.2-3 Search text files for patterns
        gtranslator     0.43-1  Gettext po file editor for the GNOME
                        ➥desktop environment
        html-fromtext-pm        1.005-2 Text2html function marks up
                        ➥plain text as HTML
        hyperref        6.72-2  Hypertext marks (clickable links) in LaTeX
        ircii   20020912-1      Popular text based irc client
        jless   358-iso254-1    Featureful text pager with ISO 2022 code extension.
        kbabel  3.0.7-2 KDE - edit and manage gettext PO files
        kedit   3.0.7-2 KDE - simple text editor
        kinput2 3.0-3   Input server for easy input of Japanese text
        kterm   6.2.0-2 X11terminal emulator that can handle multi-lingual text.
        less    376-1   Featureful text pager
        links   0.96-2  Lynx-like text WWW browser with tables
        links-ssl       0.98-1  Lynx-like text WWW browser with tables
        locale-maketext-pm      1.03-1  Perl framework for localization
        mutt-ssl        1.4i-11 Sophisticated text-based mail user agent
        nano    1.0.9-11        Improved clone of the Pico text editor.
```

```
        nedit   5.3-5   Multi-purpose text editor X Windows.
        pango1  1.0.3-2 System for Layout and rendering of internationalized text
        pango1-dev      1.0.3-2 System for Layout and rendering of
                        ➥internationalized text
        pango1-shlibs   1.0.3-2 System for Layout and rendering of
                        ➥internationalized text
        text-delimmatch-pm      1.03-1  Perl extension to find regexp
                                ➥delimited strings
        textutils       2.0-4   Text file processing utilities
        vile    9.3-2   Enhanced vi-like text editor.
        w3m-ssl 0.3-13  Pager/text-based WWW browser, with SSL support
        wrap    1-3     Fast text wrapping
        xemacs  21.5.4-3        Highly customizable text editor.
```


Viewers?

```
brezup:root Documents # fink list ¦ grep -i "view"
        aview   1.3.0rc1-4      Ascii art image viewer
        eog     0.6-4   Image viewing and cataloging program
        epstool 2.1-1   Utility to manipulate preview images in EPS files.
        geomview        1.8.1-5 Interactive 3D viewing program
        gkrellkam       0.3.4-1 Gkrellm plugin - Webcam viewer.
        gqview  1.0.2-1 Graphics file browser utility
        kdvi    3.0.7-2 KDE - DVI print file previewer
        kfax    3.0.7-2 KDE - fax file viewer
        kghostview      3.0.7-2 KDE - postscript viewer
        kugar   1.2.0-2 KDE - business report viewer and creator
        kview   3.0.7-2 KDE - image viewer
        lv      4.49.4-2        Powerful Multilingual File Viewer
        mgv     3.1.5-3 Motif PostScript viewer loosely based on Ghostview 1.5.
        mlview  0.0.1.11-1      Simple XML editor for gnome
        orrery  0.9.2-3 Digital model of the solar system, a geomview module
        xmakemol        5.05-2  View atomic and molecular systems
        xmltv   0.5.0-1 Set of utilities to manage your TV viewing
        xpdf    1.01-2  Viewer for Portable Document Format (PDF) files.
        xv      3.10a-2 Image viewer
```

Finally, because this one would be difficult to guess what to search for unless you knew what you were looking for, I want to point out the GIMP (GNU Image Manipulation Program):

```
brezup:root Documents # fink describe  gimp
Information about 1449 packages read in 1 seconds.

pkg gimp  version ###
pkg gimp  version 1.2.3-10
```

```
gimp-1.2.3-10: The GNU Image Manipulation Program
 .
 Web site: http://www.gimp.org/
 .
 Maintainer: Alexander Strange <astrange@ithinksw.com>
```

The GNU Image Manipulation Program is such a diminutive understatement for a program that many fancy to be an open source Photoshop killer. The GIMP is an ongoing project aimed at developing a free-software product to compete with Adobe's Photoshop application. It's definitely not Photoshop CS, but it's an amazingly powerful and configurable application. One of the neatest features is that it's not a closed proprietary application. That means the source is available, the interface to create plug-ins and so on is well documented, and many sample files are floating around the Net containing code that can be used to make custom filters that do exactly what *you* want them to do. You can buy a copy of the GIMP for your Mac if you want to or you can type **`fink install gimp`** at the command line. Pretty easy, huh?

Installing the DarwinPorts Ports and Packages Manager

DarwinPorts is another large, well-supported (by the open-source community) port and package manager for Mac OS X. It is in many ways complementary to Fink, and there are a significant number of programs that are distinct to each. If you can't find it in Fink, check DarwinPorts, and conversely, if you can't find it in DarwinPorts, check Fink.

Again, because everyone's working with developer prerelease versions of Tiger as we write, many software packages are in a state of flux and are being rebuilt to accomodate Tiger. DarwinPorts is no exception. What you see here, therefore, should be representative of how DarwinPorts works when you're trying it out on your system, but don't be surprised when there are minor differences.

Like Fink, DarwinPorts installs the base system using CVS:

```
cvs -d :pserver:anonymous@anoncvs.opendarwin.org:/Volumes/src/cvs/od login
(Logging in to anonymous@anoncvs.opendarwin.org)
CVS password:

cvs -d :pserver:anonymous@anoncvs.opendarwin.org:/Volumes/src/cvs/od
➥co -P darwinports
```

When asked for your CVS password, just press the Return key. After you've run the second `cvs` command, a long list of files will be downloaded. When your command prompt returns, you need to execute a fairly standard installation:

```
cd darwinports/base
./configure
make
sudo make install
```

Finally, add /opt/local/bin to your path, preferably by editing the appropriate private or system-global shell startup script. You should now have a working DarwinPorts installation, and can start using it to browse and install software. Let's see how it does at installing the spell-checker we used to demonstrate pipes:

```
port search 'spell'
aspell          textproc/aspell 0.50.3
                           ➥Spell checker with better logic than ispell
aspell-dict-de  textproc/aspell-dict-de 0.50     German dictionary for aspell
aspell-dict-dk  textproc/aspell-dict-dk 0.50     Danish dictionary for aspell
aspell-dict-en  textproc/aspell-dict-en 0.50     English dictionary for aspell
aspell-dict-es  textproc/aspell-dict-es 0.50     Spanish dictionary for aspell
aspell-dict-fr  textproc/aspell-dict-fr 0.50     French dictionary for aspell
aspell-dict-it  textproc/aspell-dict-it 0.50     Italian dictionary for aspell
aspell-dict-nl  textproc/aspell-dict-nl 0.50     Dutch dictionary for aspell
aspell-dict-ru  textproc/aspell-dict-ru 0.50     Russian dictionary for aspell
aspell-dict-sv  textproc/aspell-dict-sv 0.50     Swedish dictionary for aspell
ispell          textproc/ispell 3.2.06
                ➥An interactive spelling checker for multiple languages
```

Well, that's pretty neat—the last time I tried to install aspell manually, it had me beat, I've been using ispell instead for a while. Now aspell is a simple DarwinPorts install:

```
sudo port install aspell
Password:
--->  Fetching aspell
--->  Attempting to fetch aspell-0.50.3.tar.gz from ftp://ftp.gnu.org/gnu/aspell
--->  Attempting to fetch aspell-0.50.3.tar.gz from
      ➥ ftp://gatekeeper.dec.com/pub/GNU/aspell
--->  Verifying checksum(s) for aspell
--->  Extracting aspell
--->  Configuring aspell
--->  Building aspell with target all
--->  Staging aspell into destroot

You must install one of the language dictionaries after installing
this port in order for it to work.

--->  Packaging tgz archive for aspell 0.50.3_1
--->  Installing aspell 0.50.3_1
--->  Activating aspell 0.50.3_1
--->  Cleaning aspell
```

Nifty! It compiled, installed, and cleaned up after itself, all in one neat command, and I *know* that wasn't a trivial install from the command line. One thing to note: It wants me to install a dictionary, so I'll also instruct the port command to pull down the English version for me:

```
port install aspell-dict-en
```

And, theoretically, I'm done. Let's see what I've actually installed in /opt/local/bin:

```
ls /opt/local/bin/
aspell          port        portindex       run-with-aspell
aspell-import   portall     pspell-config   word-list-compress
```

Not much in there so far, but there's the aspell program, and if I run it, it prints out a humongous list of options. To get it to behave neatly as spell (the canonical Unix name for this command), as shown in Chapter 12, "Process Management," we can use an alias (more on aliases in Chapter 15, "Shell Configuration and Programming (Shell Scripting)"). In tcsh this is simply alias spell aspell -l. In bash it's alias spell='aspell -l':

```
brezup:ray testing $ aspell -l
Now is the tyem for all good authors to come to thie
ayde of some very good Unix users
Ctrl-D
tyem
thie
ayde
brezup:ray testing $
brezup:ray testing $ alias spell 'aspell -l'
brezup:ray testing $ spell
Now is the tyem for all good authors to come to thie
ayde of some very good Unix users
Ctrl-D
tyem
thie
ayde
brezup:ray testing $
```

What other useful software might DarwinPorts have hiding in its more than 2,000-port-long list of Unix applications for Mac OS X? How about security applications:

```
port list | grep "security"
cryptlib          devel/cryptlib      cryptlib is a powerful security toolkit
flawfinder        devel/flawfinder    Examines C/C++ source code for sec. flaws
fuzz              devel/fuzz          software security checking tool
libnasl           net/libnasl         Nessus security scanner
nessus-core       net/nessus-core     Nessus security scanner
nessus-libraries          net/nessus-libraries      Nessus security scanner
nessus-plugins    net/nessus-plugins                Nessus security scanner
aescrypt          security/aescrypt      A program for encryption/decryption.
```

```
aesutil          security/aesutil      command line program to encrypt and
                                       ➥decrypt data via AES
authforce        security/authforce    A HTTP authentication brute forcer.
checkpassword-pam        security/checkpassword-pam  implementation of
                         ➥checkpassword-compatible auth program
cracklib         security/cracklib     A ProActive Password Sanity Library
ctool            security/ctool     ctool is a checksumming application
gpg-agent        security/gpg-agent GPG key agent
hydra            security/hydra     parallized login hacker utility
ike-scan         security/ike-scan  ike-scan can discover and identify
                                    ➥IPsec VPN systems running IKE.
jailkit          security/jailkit   utilities to create limited user
                                    ➥accounts in a chroot jail
libident         security/libident  Ident protocol library
libprelude       security/libprelude Prelude Network Intrusion Detection
                                    ➥System librairies
logsentry        security/logsentry logfile auditing tool
md5deep          security/md5deep   Recursively compute digests on
                                    ➥files/directories
murk             security/murk      rsync friendly encryption tool
otr              security/otr       Off-the-Record Messaging Library
outguess         security/outguess  steganographic tool
pgpdump          security/pgpdump   PGP packet visualizer
pinentry         security/pinentry  Passphrase entry dialog utilizing the
                                    ➥Assuan protocol
portsentry       security/portsentry port scan detection and active defense
prelude-lml      security/prelude-lml     Prelude Network Intrusion Detection
                                          ➥System Log Monitoring Lackey
prelude-manager security/prelude-manager Prelude Network Intrusion Detection
                                          ➥System central logging point
prelude-nids     security/prelude-nids    Prelude Network Intrusion Detection
                                          ➥System sensor
prelude-piwi     security/prelude-piwi    Prelude Network Intrusion Detection
                                          ➥System PIWI
putty            security/putty     ssh tools pscp, psftp and plink from the
                                    ➥Putty project
racoon           security/racoon    an IKE (IPSec) daemon
scponly          security/scponly   Limited shell which wraps scp/sftp
sign             security/sign      sign is a file signing and signature
                                    ➥verification utility
stegdetect       security/stegdetect tool for detecting steganographic
                                    ➥content in jpeg images.
stunnel          security/stunnel   SSL tunneling program
tor              security/tor       anonymizing overlay network for TCP
tor-devel        security/tor-devel anonymizing overlay network for TCP
```

14

```
tripwire        security/tripwire   integrity assurance and intrusion
                                    ➥detection tool
mod_security    www/mod_security    intrusion detection and prevention
                                    ➥engine for web applications
```

Wow. That's a lot of stuff. Notably, it contains (today) 41 security-related packages to Fink's 4. Especially interesting are the `tripwire` and `portsentry` items because you'll have the opportunity to learn more about using them in Chapter 28, "Implementing Server Security and Advanced Network Configuration."

> **TIP**
>
> DarwinPort's `port` command `search` functionality is somewhat lacking. Just as `fink` doesn't look in descriptions when you use a keyword for `list`, the `port` command doesn't look in the categories field or the descriptions field when you `search`. Instead, use the `list` command, and `grep` for the category you're interested in.

How about multimedia applications?

```
port list | grep "multimedia"
acme            gnome/acme      Tool to make multimedia keys work on laptops
avidemux        multimedia/avidemux     Avidemux is an avi and mpeg editing pgm
emotion         multimedia/emotion      A Evas smart-object library for video
ffmpeg          multimedia/ffmpeg       Digital VCR and streaming server
libmatroska     multimedia/libmatroska  Matroska is an extensible open
                                        ➥standard audio/video container format.
libmpeg2        multimedia/libmpeg2     A free library for decoding mpeg-2
                                        ➥and mpeg-1 video streams.
libtheora       multimedia/libtheora    Video codec based on libogg / libvorbis
mkvtoolnix      multimedia/mkvtoolnix   Matroska media files manipulation
mpeg2vidcodec   multimedia/mpeg2vidcodec  MPEG-2 Video Encoder / Decoder
mpgtx           multimedia/mpgtx        MPEG audio/video/system file toolbox
MPlayer         multimedia/MPlayer      The Unix movie player
ogmtools        multimedia/ogmtools     OGG media streams manipulation tools.
smpeg           multimedia/smpeg        a general purpose MPEG A/V player/lib
vcdimager       multimedia/vcdimager    Free software (Super) video CD
                                        ➥authoring solution
xine-lib        multimedia/xine-lib     xine-lib is a free multimedia engine
XviD            multimedia/XviD         High performance and high quality
                                        ➥MPEG-4 video library
py-ogg          python/py-ogg           Python module for the ogg multimedia
                                        ➥interface
```

Only 17, but `MPlayer` is something you're going to be interested in—it plays (just about) anything you can throw at it. Obscure Windows media files that you can't open with Quicktime got you down? `MPlayer` plays them with ease. Can't keep up with the annoying "codec of the week club" that the DiVX/XViD/3ViX crowd change faster than underpants? `MPlayer` has just about all of them built-in, so you don't have to worry about finding the right one, or about what'll break if you install it. `ffmpeg` is pretty neat too—it'll let you read video files that Quicktime either can't or won't touch (such as MPEG-2), and re-encode them into formats that you can then import into iMovie/Final Cut, embed in web pages, or otherwise edit more conveniently—and it's fast.

There are many, many more categories and applications available through DarwinPorts. You can most easily browse by checking the port listing on the DarwinPorts web page (`http://darwinports.opendarwin.org/ports/`).

Troubleshooting Software Installs, and Compiling and Debugging Manually

Sometimes when you try to compile and install a program, it won't work as easily as the examples at the beginning of this chapter. Sometimes it's a matter of the program not being tweaked to run properly on Mac OS X. Sometimes the program is just poorly written. Most often, however, it's because the vast majority of software written for Unix is in a constant state of revision, and minor bugs are introduced, squashed, and often re-created again in some other subroutine, on a regular basis. If you're in no hurry to use the software, don't worry that it doesn't compile. As long as you've obeyed the mantra *Never compile or install software as a user with a privileged account*, the attempt to compile and run it has done nothing more than occupy some disk space and cause a little frustration. Write to the program's author, let him or her know that something's not right, and it will probably be fixed in a reasonable amount of time.

If you're in a hurry, or are either inquisitive or stubborn, there are some things that you can try to get the software working. A few of these involve updating certain parameters in your environment, and one involves rolling up your sleeves and digging around in the program's guts. If the latter is something you've never imagined doing, don't worry—it's your choice! Just remember that as long as you're working in a nonprivileged account, you can't really do much damage—the software is already broken; you can't hurt the system. The worst that will happen is you don't improve anything.

This section outlines a few common things to check when an install doesn't seem to work and takes you through an example of what is necessary to fix one particularly troublesome install. Because every problem install is different, we can't give you an exhaustive list of things to look for. Instead, we hope the tour of a problematic install and the example of using the GNU debugger gives you an idea of what to look for and how to solve the problem.

If you find this material too complicated, don't let it bother you. This chapter provides an example of the routes of attack that you can take if you choose to pursue the issue. If you aren't inclined to fight with a recalcitrant install, feel free to skip the rest of this chapter. Nothing in the remainder of the book requires that you be comfortable with the troubleshooting material.

At the end of the chapter, we've provided a short section outlining a number of useful applications that you might like to install at the command line. When possible, we've included copies of the source and compiled binaries of all that we can (copyright restrictions prevent us from distributing some packages because the authors prefer you to download the source from their sites only) at `http://www.macosxunleashed.com/downloads/`. In general, the precompiled software will work for you, but if you want the most current and complete version of a piece of software, it's always best to go to the source and build it yourself.

Using Common Sense and Configuration Options

A reasonable number of problems can be solved by a suitable application of common sense. The biggest problem with this is that users appear to have a difficult time figuring out what sense is common, and what is not. I repeatedly have seen users who were convinced their problems were the fault of a program or machine, and were hopping mad at the system for treating them poorly. Most frequently, however, it turns out that they've mistyped some command or entered an incorrect parameter and fixing this also fixes the problem. Conversely, I've seen users who have spent hours fighting with a problem, firmly convinced that they were making some trivial error and were simply incapable of seeing it. Almost to the user, these cases turn out to be actual machine or software errors rather than user errors. If you're new to the Unix environment, watch for this tendency—if you think something is the system's fault, stop to consider whether you really have done everything properly. If you think you're doing something wrong but can't figure out what it is after suitable inspection, don't forget that the people who wrote the software are users too and could have made an error.

That being said, we'll provide a general list of things that might help you figure out what's going wrong with a piece of compiled software. There is no such thing as a complete list, but these are relatively good places to start.

- The absolute first thing to try, if software doesn't install, is reading the instructions. I know, you've already read the instructions. Read them again.

> **TIP**
>
> Try taking out a marker and highlighting the specific places where it says "type this" and "enter that." I've been coding on Unix machines for, good grief, I think it's 20 years now, and I still religiously highlight all relevant sections of installation and configuration instructions. Get into the habit—it's good for you.

- Make sure while reading the instructions that you've read any sections dealing specifically with Mac OS X. If there's nothing that deals specifically with Mac OS X or Darwin, the instructions for BSD, NextStep, or OpenStep installation might be of interest.
- Examine the evidence of a problem. Error messages are generally trying to tell you something beyond the simple fact that there was an error. They sometimes do an

abysmally bad job of it, but the average error message contains at least some clue as to what the error is and how to fix it.

- If the error involves something going wrong well after the compile—for example, when the program is running—check whether the program outputs log files. Many programs write progress reports and debugging information into log files. The location of these files is frequently defined in the program's configuration options, but programs can also log via the SYSLOG facility and write log information into files in the `/var/log/` directory.

TIP

I can't stress strongly enough how important or useful log entries can be. I know, in the throes of fighting with an error it's difficult to remember to look at the logs, but at least 50% of the time I'm having a problem, if I remember to look, the logs have an answer for me.

- If the program doesn't have a log file, check to see whether it has a Debug or Verbose mode (usually invoked with `-d` or `-debug` and `-v` or `-verbose`, respectively). Adding these to the program's invocation either enables log output to a file or causes the program to produce useful output to the terminal.

- If the problem is that at the compilation step, the program makes a complaint that it can't find a library (typically a file ending in `.o`, `.so`, or `.dylib`), it might be because the compiler doesn't know where to find it, not because it doesn't exist. If you can find the file it's complaining about, you can attempt to fix the problem in one of two ways. The first approach involves editing the makefile. If you can find where the library is used in the makefile (look for the `<filename>.o` string in the makefile), you can try adding `-L<pathtodirectory>` to the makefile. `<pathtodirectory>` should be the full path to the directory that the library was found in. The second approach is to copy the library file to the directory where the compilation is going wrong (be careful—sometimes the compiler wanders down into subdirectories of the directory where you actually typed **`make`**, and it's the subdirectory where it's working that you'll need to put the library). This is a clunky attempt, and prone to failure if the library was a shared (`.so` or `.dylib`) library, but sometimes, in a fix, it's easier than trying to do it right—especially if you're not sure that the compile is even possible, and all the work of fixing a possibly quite cryptic makefile could be in vain for other reasons.

- Similarly, at runtime, you might occasionally find programs that refuse to execute with errors that indicate an inability to find a dynamically loaded library (typically `<filename><revision>.dyld` or `<filename><revision>.so`). If you encounter this, you need to search your system (use `find` from the root directory) for a version of the missing library (anything with the same major version should work fine—dynamic and shared libraries have a number of revision levels, typically indicated by a triple of dot-separated numbers appended to the filename `<major>.<minor>.<bugfix>`). Add the path to directory containing the library to your DYLD_LIBRARY_PATH and/or LD_LIBRARY_PATH. The DYLD_LIBRARY_PATH setting should typically be sufficient (set this to a colon-separated list of paths to the directories where you've found the missing files), but some software might require the LD_LIBRARY_PATH instead. At the command line, enter DYLD_LIBRARY_PATH=<*paths_to_libraries*>, or (setenv DYLD_LIBRARY_PATH <*paths_to_libraries*> if you're using tcsh) to make the setting.

- The configure script frequently pulls some options and makes some decisions based on the contents of two files in the current directory where it's run. Because not everyone has updated their scripts to correctly handle Darwin-based systems, sometimes it helps to copy the versions that Apple provides in cp /usr/share/automake-1.6/config.* into the current directory before running configure.

- A syntax error from the compiler that indicates a line number is a warning from the compiler that invalid code has been found in the file. This is an indication that there's something wrong with the program, or perhaps that you've downloaded it incorrectly, or that it has become corrupted on your local machine. Sometimes these are fixable without too much trouble—for example, something you can easily repair in the syntax is the damage that's done when a Mac-OS-side editor has saved a file with Macintosh end-of-line characters rather than Unix end-of-line characters (or has accumulated an assortment of each through the use of different editors).

- "Downloaded incorrectly" problems can frequently be traced to the fact that Unix and Macintosh applications use two different symbols to indicate the end of a line of text. Apple is trying to rewrite many command-line utilities so that they're platform agnostic with respect to the carriage-return versus linefeed issue, but Apple can't do it for every application that you might compile. If you use Macintosh applications such as text editors or web browsers to download or modify code or configuration files, expect to see the occasional compilation or execution error as a result of having the line endings changed (it happens to all of us, more frequently than we like to admit).

  Similar problems pop up from time to time when you've used a text editor that saves state information along with the data. If you find yourself in a situation in which a compiler or program complains that the syntax of a file is incorrect, or the software just plain dies while reading files, check your line endings, and then check to see whether your editor has saved metadata regarding the file in its first few bytes. Pure plain text editors such as BBedit and Alpha both include the option to save files with Unix line endings in their Save As dialogs. Both also include the option to discard state information. The command-line emacs editor tells you whether your file has Macintosh line endings in its status line. If you use the emacs M-x find-file-literally option to load a file, it loads with the Mac's control-M line endings as control-M, and you can use M-x replace-string to switch them to Unix line endings (control-J).

- Apple has supplied make as a version of GNUmake. Some software makefiles are designed for the BSD version of make instead and break when GNU's make is used. If you get weird errors during compilations that seem to indicate a syntax error with the makefile itself, try using `bsdmake` rather than `make`.

- A number of the `configure` scripts and makefiles out there assume that if they're using GNU's `make`, it'll be named `gmake`, or `gnumake`, and that if `make` is named just plain `make`, it's a BSD-derived version. Calling GNUmake `make` on Mac OS X can cause problems with makefiles that are (poorly) designed to detect which `make` system they're running under, and that try to automatically use the correct syntax for the version of `make` that's in use. Sometimes it helps to put a `gmake` link in `/usr/local/bin` and point it to `/usr/bin/make` or to invoke your compilations explicitly with `gmake`.

- Yet another inconsistency results in the occasional inability for `make` to proceed properly through the entire hierarchy of directories where it needs to be run. One of the first things to try, if you're seeing messages from `make` that say `entering directory` *`<dirname>`* followed shortly by a compilation error, is to manually `cd` to that directory and run `make` in it by hand. You might need to do this several times, with directories at each level in the hierarchy. If `make` turns out to work properly when manually run in the subdirectory where it was previously breaking, repeat this step as necessary throughout the directory structure of the program, return to the top-level directory for the compile, and then run `make` there again. This should use all the subparts you've hand-assembled and correctly finish the process. Occasionally, it'll find yet something else wrong in a subdirectory due to some cross-dependency with another subdirectory. If that's the case, try stepping through the process again and see whether the final `make` at the top level gets further the next time. If it does, you're making progress. If it doesn't, it's time to look elsewhere for the source of the trouble.

- Due to differences between compiler and linker versions, and the fact that any given compilation process could have been designed for something other than what you've got on your system, it's sometimes necessary to add certain flags to compile and link steps. These are usually defined in the makefile as `CFLAGS` and `LDFLAGS` variables. The most common flags of interest are `-flat_namespace`, `-undefined suppress`, `-no-cpp-precomp`, and `-fno-common`. The exact combination of flags that you need to either add or remove from the `CFLAGS` and `LDFLAGS` definitions varies from package to package. In general, if you get complaints regarding undefined symbols, try adding `-undefined suppress` and, potentially, `-flat_namespace`. `-fno_common` makes the compiler more strict about certain things but also makes it behave more like the default behavior on some other systems, which allows certain "smart" makefiles to recognize what's going on and adjust properly, where they'd fail under more lenient settings. Unless the software was designed for Darwin, `-no-cpp-precomp` is usually safe to add and is a good try if you're seeing complaints about syntax.

14

CARGO-CULT COMPILING

Many of the recommendations we've made in this section amount to what a programmer would consider to be *cargo-cult compilation* (the uneducated application of various "magic" incantations to a problem, with no real understanding of what any of them do, in the hopes that one or more might solve the problem). The term comes from the story of primitive island cultures that supposedly picked up the habit of building mock airstrips, radio shacks, and barracks in an attempt to induce planes and ships to land there, having once seen planes and ships land near similar structures during wartime occupations.

In the world of real programmers, cargo-cult programming is generally looked down on. Programming is a precise art, and those who denigrate that art by cutting and pasting bits of code that they don't understand, but that they believe has some functionality, aren't real programmers regardless of what they've put on their resume.

You, however, aren't expected to be a real programmer. It's great if you are, but if you're not and you're not trying to be, using cargo-cult techniques to try to solve a compilation error is a valid approach to the problem. We've given you some of the best general-purpose incantations we know. If you're not trying to be a real programmer, and you have software that won't compile, try out some of them. The worst that can happen is that the compile still doesn't work. And never let a real programmer knock the result if you get something working. If he'd done his job, you wouldn't have had to fix it!

Fiddling with File Locations and Fighting with Installers

For this example, you need the `netpbm` package, available from `http://www.macosxunleashed.com/downloads/netpbm-9.12.tgz` or from its original home at `http://download.sourceforge.net/netpbm/netpbm-9.12.tgz`. A more recent version of `netpbm` is available, and it's the one you'll actually want to install and use eventually, but this older version makes for a nice tour through the underbelly of a software install. The easy download solution is

```
curl -O http://download.sourceforge.net/netpbm/netpbm-9.12.tgz
```

The file should be 2057293 bytes in length. Uncompress it, untar it, and check whether it wants `configure` or `make`:

```
brezup:software source $ gunzip netpbm-9.12.tgz
brezup:software source $ tar -xf netpbm-9.12.tar
brezup:software source $ cd netpbm-9.12
brezup:software netpbm-9.12 $ ls

COPYRIGHT.PATENT          README.VMS         pbmplus.h
GNUmakefile               amiga              pgm
GPL_LICENSE.txt           compile.h          pnm
HISTORY                   configure          ppm
Makefile                  empty_depend       scoptions
Makefile.common           installosf         shhopt
Makefile.config.djgpp     libopt.c           stamp-date
```

```
Makefile.config.in       libtiff              stamp-date.amiga
Makefile.depend          magic                testgrid.pbm
Netpbm.programming       make_merge.sh        testimg.ppm
README                   mantocat             urt
README.CONFOCAL          mkinstalldirs        version.h
README.DJGPP             netpbm.lsm           vms
README.JPEG              pbm                  zgv_bigmaxval.patch
```

There's a `configure` file, so run it. This one is going to make some guesses and ask you some questions. Pick the options shown in the following example because they're necessary to get the rest of the example to work:

```
brezup:software netpbm-9.12 $ ./configure
su: ./configure: /bin/perl: bad interpreter: No such file or directory
```

14

Hold on; problem number one—that wasn't the expected behavior. The file `configure` is right here in the directory with you; what's with this "no such file" business? Actually, it's complaining about something else, not the `configure` script itself. (If you are running `tcsh`, you get an even less useful error—simply `tcsh: ./configure: Command not found`).

```
brezup:software netpbm-9.12 $ head ./configure
#!/bin/perl -w

use strict;

# This program generates Makefile.config, which is included by all of the
# Netpbm makefiles.  You run this program as the first step in building
# Netpbm.  (The second step is 'make').

# This program is only a convenience.  It is supported to create
# Makefile.config any way you want.  In fact, an easy way is to copy
...
```

The problem is that Mac OS X doesn't have Perl as `/bin/perl`; it's `/usr/bin/perl`. Fire up `vi` (or your favorite text editor) and change that first line to `#!/usr/bin/perl -w`. A more permanent solution to the fact that different systems have Perl in `/bin/`, `/usr/bin/`, or `/usr/local/bin/` is to make a link back to `/usr/bin/perl` in each of these places where it isn't, so that software written on other systems can run without modification. If you want, the following should fix Perl for most scripts:

```
brezup:root netpbm-9.12 # ln -s /usr/bin/perl /bin/perl
brezup:root netpbm-9.12 # ln -s /usr/bin/perl /usr/local/bin/perl
```

NOTE

Of course, you do need to be `root`, or `sudo` your way to the first of those commands, should you choose to make these links.

Because Perl is only the most common thing you'll find that might be affected by this type of configuration problem, and you're unlikely to want to use the link solution for all of them, we'll take the route of fixing the `configure` script instead.

```
brezup:software netpbm-9.12 $ head ./configure
#!/usr/bin/perl -w

use strict;
...
```

Now try again:

```
brezup:software netpbm-9.12 $ ./configure
Which of the following best describes your platform?
1) GNU/Linux
2) Solaris or SunOS
3) AIX
4) Tru64
5) Irix
6) Windows (Cygwin or DJGPP)
7) BeOS
8) NetBSD
9) none of these are even close

Your choice ==> 1

Enter the installation directory (the prefix on all installation
paths for 'make install'). This is not built into any programs;
It is used only by 'make install'.

install prefix (/usr/local/netpbm)=>

Do you want static-linked Netpbm libraries or shared?

static or shared (shared)=> static

Can't exec ""ginstall"": No such file or directory at ./configure line 195.

We have created the file 'Makefile.config'. You can now
proceed to enter the 'make' command.

Note, however, that we have only made a rough guess at your
configuration, and you may want to look at Makefile.config and
edit it to your requirements and taste before doing the make.
```

NOTE

By the way, we picked GNU/Linux—even though Mac OS X is a BSD flavor—because many of the tools are GNU tools. Still, this will cause problems later because Linux typically has things in nonstandard places with respect to BSD, and Apple has maintained a lot of the typical BSD filesystem structure.

The results of the `configure` script are better, but there's an ominous complaint in there about `can't exec ginstall`. To get things working will take editing that `Makefile.config` and making a few changes—mostly to patch things back to standard locations from where Linux tends to store them. Start `vi` and look through `Makefile.config` for lines that look similar to the following; then change them until they're exactly as shown in the following listings:

- It seems to have ignored the `static` option given to `configure`, so set it here, too.

  ```
  # STATICLIB = N
  STATICLIB = Y
  ```

- `ginstall` is GNU's installation program. Apple probably uses it, but has probably named it `install` instead, so comment out the `ginstall` line and uncomment the `install` line.

  ```
  #INSTALL = ginstall
  #Solaris:
  #INSTALL = /usr/ucb/install
  #Tru64:
  #INSTALL = installbsd
  #OSF1:
  #INSTALL = installosf
  #Red Hat Linux :
  INSTALL = install
  ```

This version of the software and the current version of the C compiler don't quite get along. Adding `-no-cpp-precomp` and `-fno-common` to the arguments that are handed to the C compiler—usually via a `CFLAGS` variable—helps in many cases. The flag `-flat_namespace` helps with some things as well, and the flag `-undefined suppress`, which used to help make the linker happy for this software under 10.1, now seems to cause problems (although it's necessary for some other compiles). Add the `-no-cpp-precomp` and `-fno-common` for a first try. Add the `-flat_namespace` and the `-undefined_suppress` options if it still bombs.

```
CFLAGS = -pedantic -no-cpp-precomp -fno-common -O3 -Wall
➥-Wno-uninitialized $(CDEBUG)
```

Linux installations tend to have taken a wrong turn in filesystem design, and include the binaries, libraries, and headers for optional packages in the `/usr/bin/`, `/usr/lib/`, and

/usr/include directories. This makes system maintenance a real problem because your unprivileged software management user would need root privileges to work in those directories. Fix the defaults so that the jpeglib stuff comes from /usr/local, where we put it not too long ago:

```
#JPEGLIB_DIR = /usr/lib/jpeg
#JPEGHDR_DIR = /usr/include/jpeg
# Netbsd:
#JPEGLIB_DIR = ${LOCALBASE}/lib
#JPEGHDR_DIR = ${LOCALBASE}/include
# OSF, Tru64:
#JPEGLIB_DIR = /usr/local1/DEC/lib
#JPEGHDR_DIR = /usr/local1/DEC/include
# Typical:
JPEGLIB_DIR = /usr/local/lib
JPEGHDR_DIR = /usr/local/include
# Don't build JPEG stuff:
#JPEGLIB_DIR = NONE
#JPEGHDR_DIR = NONE
```

Do the same for the libpng stuff:

```
#PNGLIB_DIR = /lib
#PNGHDR_DIR = /usr/include/png
# NetBSD:
#PNGLIB_DIR = $(LOCALBASE)/lib
#PNGHDR_DIR = $(LOCALBASE)/include
# OSF/Tru64:
#PNGLIB_DIR = /usr/local1/DEC/lib
#PNGHDR_DIR = /usr/local1/DEC/include
# Typical:
PNGLIB_DIR = /usr/local/lib
PNGHDR_DIR = /usr/local/include
# No PNG:
#PNGLIB_DIR = NONE
#PNGHDR_DIR = NONE
```

Now you're ready to try the make. If you're running an older version of Mac OS X, and someone hasn't fixed this peculiar problem already, you'll run into a problem with the compiler. If you're running 10.2 or later, you can skip ahead a couple paragraphs to where it says to "try the make again":

```
[Racer-X:~/Documents/source/netpbm-9.12] software% make

make -C pbm -f /Users/software/Documents/source/netpbm-9.12/pbm/Makefile all
ln -s ../pbmplus.h pbmplus.h
ln -s ../version.h version.h
```

```
../stamp-date
gcc -c -I../shhopt -pedantic -O3 -Wall -Wno-uninitialized
➥-o atktopbm.o ../pbm/atktopbm.c
make[1]: gcc: Command not found
make[1]: *** [atktopbm.o] Error 127
make: *** [pbm] Error 2
```

This is not the output we wanted! If the results of your make are more voluminous, skip ahead to where we run make again; otherwise, you need to deal with this complaint that it can't find the compiler. cc is the standard name for a C compiler, but gcc is the GNU C Compiler, and many software packages are written to take advantage of special features that the GNU compiler provides. Apple has been nice enough to provide the GNU compiler with the development tools, but on some versions of Mac OS X, Apple has named it cc instead of gcc. This causes programs that try to accommodate the compiler to break because they don't realize that they're working with gcc, and make the wrong assumptions about what the compiler wants. It also causes problems with software that simply assumes that everyone out there has gcc installed. The error for this program could be fixed by modifying the Makefile.config file again to call cc instead of gcc, but a similar problem will frequently crop up with installations wondering where gcc is, and many installers won't know that they can use the special gcc features unless the compiler is called gcc. If your system is missing a properly named gcc, a better fix is to create an alias (symbolic link) named gcc instead and point it at the cc compiler:

14

```
[Racer-X:~/Documents/source/netpbm-9.12] software% pushd /usr/local/bin
/usr/local/bin ~/Documents/source/netpbm-9.12
[Racer-X:/usr/local/bin] software% which cc
/usr/bin/cc
[Racer-X:/usr/local/bin] software% ln -s /usr/bin/cc ./gcc
[Racer-X:/usr/local/bin] software% popd
~/Documents/source/netpbm-9.12
```

Try the make again:

```
brezup:software netpbm-9.12 $ make
make -C pbm -f /Users/software/Documents/source/netpbm-9.12/pbm/Makefile all
ln -s ../pbmplus.h pbmplus.h
ln -s ../version.h version.h
../stamp-date
gcc -c -I../shhopt -pedantic -no-cpp-precomp -fno-common -O3 -Wall
➥-Wno-uninitialized  -o atktopbm.o ../pbm/atktopbm.c
../pbm/atktopbm.c: In function `ReadATKRaster':
../pbm/atktopbm.c:307: warning: unsigned int format, int arg (arg 3)
../pbm/atktopbm.c:314: warning: implicit declaration of function `strcmp'
gcc -c -I../shhopt -pedantic -no-cpp-precomp -fno-common -O3 -Wall
➥-Wno-uninitialized   -o libpbm1.o ../pbm/libpbm1.c
gcc -c -I../shhopt -pedantic -no-cpp-precomp -fno-common -O3 -Wall
➥-Wno-uninitialized   -o libpbm2.o ../pbm/libpbm2.c
```

```
gcc -c -I../shhopt -pedantic -no-cpp-precomp -fno-common -O3 -Wall
➥-Wno-uninitialized   -o libpbm3.o ../pbm/libpbm3.c
gcc -c -I../shhopt -pedantic -no-cpp-precomp -fno-common -O3 -Wall
➥-Wno-uninitialized   -o libpbm4.o ../pbm/libpbm4.c
gcc -c -I../shhopt -pedantic -no-cpp-precomp -fno-common -O3 -Wall
➥-Wno-uninitialized   -o libpbm5.o ../pbm/libpbm5.c
cd ../shhopt; make shhopt.o
gcc  -o shhopt.o -c -pedantic -no-cpp-precomp -fno-common -O3 -Wall
➥-Wno-uninitialized   -I. shhopt.c
rm -f libpbm.a
ar rc libpbm.a libpbm1.o libpbm2.o libpbm3.o libpbm4.o libpbm5.o
➥../shhopt/shhopt.o
ranlib libpbm.a
make -C .. libopt
...
ln -s ../../pbmplus.h pbmplus.h
ln -s ../../pbm/pbm.h pbm.h
gcc -pedantic -no-cpp-precomp -fno-common -O3 -Wall -Wno-uninitialized
➥-I../../shhopt -c pbmtoppa.c -o pbmtoppa.o
gcc -pedantic -no-cpp-precomp -fno-common -O3 -Wall -Wno-uninitialized
➥-I../../shhopt -c ppa.c -o ppa.o
gcc -pedantic -no-cpp-precomp -fno-common -O3 -Wall -Wno-uninitialized
➥-I../../shhopt -c pbm.c -o pbm.o
gcc -pedantic -no-cpp-precomp -fno-common -O3 -Wall -Wno-uninitialized
➥-I../../shhopt -c cutswath.c -o cutswath.o
cd ../../pbm ; make libpbm.a
make[3]: `libpbm.a' is up to date.
gcc  -o pbmtoppa pbmtoppa.o ppa.o pbm.o cutswath.o \
  `../../libopt ../../pbm/libpbm.a`
make -C pgm -f /Users/software/Documents/source/netpbm-9.12/pgm/Makefile all
ln -s ../pbmplus.h pbmplus.h
ln -s ../pbm/pbm.h pbm.h
ln -s ../pbm/libpbm.h libpbm.h
gcc -c -I../shhopt -pedantic -no-cpp-precomp -fno-common -O3 -Wall
➥-Wno-uninitialized  -o asciitopgm.o
➥/Users/software/Documents/source/netpbm-9.12/pgm/asciitopgm.c
gcc -c -I../shhopt -pedantic -no-cpp-precomp -fno-common -O3 -Wall
➥-Wno-uninitialized   -o libpgm1.o
➥/Users/software/Documents/source/netpbm-9.12/pgm/libpgm1.c
gcc -c -I../shhopt -pedantic -no-cpp-precomp -fno-common -O3 -Wall
➥-Wno-uninitialized   -o libpgm2.o
➥/Users/software/Documents/source/netpbm-9.12/pgm/libpgm2.c
rm -f libpgm.a
ar rc libpgm.a libpgm1.o libpgm2.o
ranlib libpgm.a
```

```
...
gcc -o pgmtexture pgmtexture.o -lm `../libopt libpgm.a ../pbm/libpbm.a`
gcc -c -I../shhopt -pedantic -no-cpp-precomp -fno-common -O3 -Wall
➥-Wno-uninitialized  -o rawtopgm.o
➥/Users/software/Documents/source/netpbm-9.12/pgm/rawtopgm.c
gcc -o rawtopgm rawtopgm.o -lm `../libopt libpgm.a ../pbm/libpbm.a`
gcc -c -I../shhopt -pedantic -no-cpp-precomp -fno-common -O3 -Wall
➥-Wno-uninitialized  -o pgmkernel.o
➥/Users/software/Documents/source/netpbm-9.12/pgm/pgmkernel.c
gcc -o pgmkernel pgmkernel.o -lm `../libopt libpgm.a ../pbm/libpbm.a`
make -C ppm -f /Users/software/Documents/source/netpbm-9.12/ppm/Makefile all
ln -s ../pbmplus.h pbmplus.h
ln -s ../pbm/pbm.h pbm.h
ln -s ../pbm/libpbm.h libpbm.h
ln -s ../pbm/pbmfont.h pbmfont.h
ln -s ../pgm/pgm.h pgm.h
ln -s ../pgm/libpgm.h libpgm.h
gcc -c -I../shhopt -I/usr/local/include -pedantic -no-cpp-precomp
➥-fno-common -O3 -Wall -Wno-uninitialized  -o 411toppm.o
➥/Users/software/Documents/source/netpbm-9.12/ppm/411toppm.c
cc1: warning: changing search order for system directory "/usr/local/include"
cc1: warning:   as it has already been specified as a non-system directory
/Users/software/Documents/source/netpbm-9.12/ppm/411toppm.c:60:20: malloc.h:
➥No such file or directory
make[1]: *** [411toppm.o] Error 1
make: *** [ppm] Error 2
```

Did I mention that I chose this install because it wasn't easy? Those error messages are just `gcc` being pedantic about the code. The C programming language has gone through a few revisions, and some programs still don't adhere to the most recent standards. The warnings won't hurt anything, but the error at the bottom of the output will. A few lines above the error is the complaint `header file malloc.h not found`. This is the actual source of the error. If you were a programmer, you'd be expected to clean up all those warnings as well, but for your purposes, just fixing the error is enough. If you were to read the code looking for occurrences of `malloc.h` (`grep` might help with this), you'd find there are comments detailing the ambiguities of different Unix flavors and their oddball `malloc.h` implementations. In Apple's case, it's that `malloc.h` isn't where the source expects it to be. You've got a choice of fixing all the code to point to `/usr/include/sys/malloc.h` instead of `/usr/include/malloc.h`, or cheating a little and making it available somewhere that the makefile already has the compiler looking. We're going to take the cheating route and make a link to `/usr/include/sys/malloc.h` in `/usr/local/include/malloc.h`, where the compiler should be able to find it. There's actually another option, adding a path to the places that the compiler will search for header files, but it turns out that fix will break something else later on, so stick with our cheat:

```
brezup:software netpbm-9.12 $ pushd /usr/include
/usr/include ~/Documents/source/netpbm-9.12
brezup:software include $ find ./ -name malloc.h -print
.//malloc/malloc.h
.//objc/malloc.h
.//sys/malloc.h
brezup:software include $ popd
~/Documents/source/netpbm-9.12
brezup:software netpbm-9.12 $ pushd /usr/local/include
/usr/local/include ~/Documents/source/netpbm-9.12
brezup:software include $ ln -s /usr/include/sys/malloc.h ./
brezup:software include $ popd
~/Documents/source/netpbm-9.12
```

CAUTION

Note that you might want to remove that link to `malloc.h` after you're finished with the compile. You can always put it back later if you need it, but there are many pieces of software out there that try to figure out what system they're being built on by checking where various files appear to be located. This one doesn't know about Apple's locations, and other bits of the install will break if you make the build find `malloc.h` where Apple has it stored. Others will misidentify your system if they see a copy in `/usr/local/include`. Apparently, you simply can't win them all—at least not all simultaneously. Because such files only need to be in place while an application's being built, you can put any file anywhere to satisfy the `make` process and then remove it later, so at least you can win them one at a time.

Back to `make` again:

```
brezup:software netpbm-9.12 $ make
make -C pbm -f /Users/software/Documents/source/netpbm-9.12/pbm/Makefile all
make -C pbmtoppa all
cd ../../pbm ; make libpbm.a
make[3]: `libpbm.a' is up to date.
make -C pgm -f /Users/software/Documents/source/netpbm-9.12/pgm/Makefile all
cd ../pbm ; make libpbm.a
make[2]: `libpbm.a' is up to date.
make -C ppm -f /Users/software/Documents/source/netpbm-9.12/ppm/Makefile all
gcc -c -I../shhopt -I/usr/local/include -pedantic -no-cpp-precomp
➥-fno-common -O3 -Wall -Wno-
...
gcc  -o ppmtojpeg ppmtojpeg.o `../libopt libppm.a ../pbm/libpbm.a
➥../pgm/libpgm.a` \
  -L/usr/local/lib -ljpeg
/usr/bin/ld: table of contents for archive: /usr/local/lib/libjpeg.a
➥ is out of date; rerun ranlib(1) (can't load from it)
make[1]: *** [ppmtojpeg] Error 1
make: *** [ppm] Error 2
```

Well, at least this time it not only tells us what the error is but also how to fix it.

```
brezup:software netpbm-9.12 $ ranlib /usr/local/lib/libjpeg.a
```

NOTE

Your system might or might not encounter the error with `libjpeg.a` and the other subsequent `ranlib`-related problems. It depends on the order in which you've done a number of things on your system. If you do encounter complaints about library tables of contents being out of date, just follow the instruction given and `ranlib` it.

You also might or might not encounter this next error in `parallel.c`. This depends more on which compiler your system is currently set to use, and which set of `include` and library files it's using. Because Mac OS X ships with a number of `gcc` versions, and cross-compilation setups for previous versions of the operating system, it's possible to get the system into a situation in which it actually won't experience this error.


```
brezup:software netpbm-9.12 $ make
 .
 .
 .
gcc -c parallel.c -o parallel.o -pedantic -no-cpp-precomp -fno-common -O3
➥-Wall -Wno-uninitialized  -I. -Iheaders
➥-I../../shhopt -I/usr/local/include
cc1: warning: changing search order for system directory "/usr/local/include"
cc1: warning:   as it has already been specified as a non-system directory
In file included from parallel.c:89:
/usr/include/sys/socket.h:77: parse error before "sa_family_t"
/usr/include/sys/socket.h:77: ISO C forbids data definition with no type
➥or storage class
/usr/include/sys/socket.h:212: parse error before "u_char"
/usr/include/sys/socket.h:213: ISO C forbids data definition with no type
➥or storage class
/usr/include/sys/socket.h:215: parse error before '}' token
/usr/include/sys/socket.h:223: parse error before "u_short"
...
parallel.c:1764: storage size of `nameEntry' isn't known
parallel.c:1790: sizeof applied to an incomplete type
parallel.c:1764: warning: unused variable `nameEntry'
make[2]: *** [parallel.o] Error 1
make[1]: *** [all] Error 2
make: *** [ppm] Error 2
```

If you see this one, it's a tough problem—tough enough that this would be where most people would throw up their hands and decide they don't need the software that badly. It hasn't complained that there's a file missing, but it's making some noise about parse errors and undefined types. It's bad to have parse errors and undefined things in programs, and there doesn't seem to be anything missing to have caused things to be undefined. Still, it's not as if doing some poking around is going to do anything worse than waste a bit of time, and you never know when you might get lucky, so let's press ahead. First, find the file it's complaining about:

```
brezup:software netpbm-9.12 $ find ./ -name parallel.c -print
.//ppm/ppmtompeg/parallel.c
```

Looking at this file, we see

```
#include <sys/types.h>
#include <sys/socket.h>
#include <sys/times.h>
#include <time.h>
#include <netinet/in.h>
#include <unistd.h>
#include <netdb.h>
```

The `make` process complained that there were undefined things in `socket.h`, and the only thing included before `socket.h` that could have defined them is `types.h`. `types.h` almost certainly lives in `/usr/include/sys`, based on the angle brackets surrounding the `include` filename in `parallel.c`. Searching in `/usr/include/sys/types.h` for the undefined `u_char` type, we find

```
#ifndef _POSIX_SOURCE
typedef unsigned char   u_char;
typedef unsigned short  u_short;
typedef unsigned int    u_int;
typedef unsigned long   u_long;
typedef unsigned short  ushort;         /* Sys V compatibility */
typedef unsigned int    uint;           /* Sys V compatibility */
#endif
```

Interestingly, the type is defined, but there's a cryptic `#ifndef POSIX_SOURCE ... #endif` surrounding the definition. If you were a programmer, the problem would be almost immediately obvious at this point. Because you're probably not a programmer, the most information you can get is that if something named `POSIX_SOURCE` is *not* defined, the needed `u_char` type *is* defined. Presumably, if `POSIX_SOURCE` is defined, `u_char` doesn't get defined here. Armed with this knowledge, if you search in `parallel.c` again, you'll find the following lines:

```
#define _POSIX_SOURCE
#define _POSIX_C_SOURCE 2
```

What do you know! Right there in `parallel.c`, it's shooting itself in the foot. Let's see what happens if we just comment that out and have at it again. It already doesn't work, so the most that can go wrong is that it still won't work, right? Fire up your editor again, and change those lines so that they look like this:

```
/* #define _POSIX_SOURCE */
/* #define _POSIX_C_SOURCE 2 */
```

NOTE

No, I'm not sure what the `#define _POSIX_C_SOURCE 2` line is doing—I'm playing nonprogramming user here. If I were playing programmer, I'd spend the time to figure out what it's doing, and whether there's anything I can do to correct the particular condition we're seeing. You might not want to be a programmer, so let's play around and see what a nonprogrammer can accomplish. I commented the `POSIX_SOURCE` lines out on a nonprogrammer-like hunch, and things seem to have worked. There are undoubtedly numerous other possible solutions. You're welcome to try other solutions without commenting out the line and see what happens. I can't guarantee that the rest of the install will follow the course shown if you do, but it's just as possible that it will work better.

14

And `make` again:

```
brezup:software netpbm-9.12 $ make
.
.
.
/usr/include/ppc/ansi.h:94: warning: ISO C89 does not support `long long'
In file included from
        ➥/Users/software/Documents/source/netpbm-9.12/pnm/pbmplus.h:115,
                 from /Users/software/Documents/source/netpbm-9.12/pnm/pbm.h:7,
                 from /Users/software/Documents/source/netpbm-9.12/pnm/pgm.h:7,
                 from /Users/software/Documents/source/netpbm-9.12/pnm/ppm.h:7,
                 from /Users/software/Documents/source/netpbm-9.12/pnm/pnm.h:7,
                 from
        ➥/Users/software/Documents/source/netpbm-9.12/pnm/pnmtopng.c:58:
/usr/include/stdlib.h:206: warning: ISO C89 does not support `long long'
/usr/include/stdlib.h:208: warning: ISO C89 does not support `long long'
/usr/include/stdlib.h:210: warning: ISO C89 does not support `long long'
/usr/include/stdlib.h:212: warning: ISO C89 does not support `long long'
gcc  -o pnmtopng pnmtopng.o `../libopt libpnm.a ../ppm/libppm.a
➥../pgm/libpgm.a ../pbm/libpbm.a ` \
  -L/lib, -lz -L/usr/local/lib -lpng -lm
ld: warning -L: directory name (/lib,) does not exist
ld: table of contents for archive: /usr/local/lib/libpng.a is out of date;
➥rerun ranlib(1) (can't load from it)
make[1]: *** [pnmtopng] Error 1
make: *** [pnm] Error 2
```

You've already seen that one before:

```
brezup:software netpbm-9.12 $ ranlib /usr/local/lib/libpng.a
brezup:software netpbm-9.12 $ make
.
.
.
ar -rc libfiasco_lib.a arith.o bit-io.o dither.o error.o image.o list.o
➥misc.o rpf.o
make -C ../../pnm libpnm.a
make[3]: `libpnm.a' is up to date.
make -C ../../ppm libppm.a
make[3]: `libppm.a' is up to date.
make -C ../../pgm libpgm.a
make[3]: `libpgm.a' is up to date.
make -C ../../pbm libpbm.a
make[3]: `libpbm.a' is up to date.
gcc  -o pnmtofiasco binerror.o cwfa.o getopt.o getopt1.o params.o \
`../../libopt codec/libfiasco_codec.a input/libfiasco_input.a
➥output/libfiasco_output.a lib/libfiasco_lib.a ` \
 `../../libopt ../../pnm/libpnm.a ../../ppm/libppm.a ../../pgm/libpgm.a
➥../../pbm/libpbm.a ` -lm
ld: archive: codec/libfiasco_codec.a has no table of contents, add one with
➥ranlib(1) (can't load from it)
ld: archive: input/libfiasco_input.a has no table of contents, add one with
➥ranlib(1) (can't load from it)
ld: archive: output/libfiasco_output.a has no table of contents, add one with
➥ranlib(1) (can't load from it)
ld: archive: lib/libfiasco_lib.a has no table of contents, add one with
➥ranlib(1) (can't load from it)
make[2]: *** [pnmtofiasco] Error 1
make[1]: *** [all] Error 2
make: *** [pnm] Error 2
```

That's getting a little boring! Don't you wish it would just run `ranlib` for you, instead of telling you it needs to be run? Actually, the installers are supposed to take care of that stuff for you. Like one of the earlier installs not creating the needed directories, this one also seems to have trouble running `ranlib`, so for some things you have to do it by hand:

```
brezup:software netpbm-9.12 $ ranlib codec/libfiasco_codec.a
ranlib: can't open file: codec/libfiasco_codec.a (No such file or directory)
```

Oops! That wasn't expected. Something else you don't (usually) need to worry about is that `make` might be recursively making things in subdirectories. The path shown in an error might not be the relative path from your location, but rather the relative path from wherever `make` is currently operating. In this case, we can just find the directories by name and `ranlib` them that way:

```
brezup:software netpbm-9.12 $ find ./ -name libfiasco_codec.a -print
.//pnm/fiasco/codec/libfiasco_codec.a
brezup:software netpbm-9.12 $ find ./ -name libfiasco_input.a -print
.//pnm/fiasco/input/libfiasco_input.a
brezup:software netpbm-9.12 $ find ./ -name libfiasco_output.a -print
.//pnm/fiasco/output/libfiasco_output.a
brezup:software netpbm-9.12 $ find ./ -name libfiasco_lib.a -print
.//pnm/fiasco/lib/libfiasco_lib.a
brezup:software netpbm-9.12 $ ranlib .//pnm/fiasco/codec/libfiasco_codec.a
brezup:software netpbm-9.12 $ ranlib .//pnm/fiasco/input/libfiasco_input.a
brezup:software netpbm-9.12 $ ranlib .//pnm/fiasco/output/libfiasco_output.a
brezup:software netpbm-9.12 $ ranlib .//pnm/fiasco/lib/libfiasco_lib.a
```

And make again:

```
brezup:software netpbm-9.12 $ make

gcc  -o pnmtofiasco binerror.o cwfa.o getopt.o getopt1.o params.o \
`../../libopt codec/libfiasco_codec.a input/libfiasco_input.a
➥output/libfiasco_output.a lib/libfiasco_lib.a ` \
 `../../libopt ../../pnm/libpnm.a ../../ppm/libppm.a ../../pgm/libpgm.a
➥../../pbm/libpbm.a ` -lm
ld: multiple definitions of symbol _mv_code_table
codec/libfiasco_codec.a(mwfa.o) definition of _mv_code_table in section
➥ (__DATA,__data)
output/libfiasco_output.a(mc.o) definition of _mv_code_table in section
➥ (__DATA,__common)
make[2]: *** [pnmtofiasco] Error 1
make[1]: *** [all] Error 2
make: *** [pnm] Error 2
```

And we encounter another new problem. Here, it complains that a variable, `mv_code_table`, has been defined in multiple places. Programs can't get built very cleanly when that happens because a specific memory location is used for each thing defined, and the system has no way of knowing which location is intended if a variable name is defined in multiple places. Again, this is a place where many would stop, but we intrepid few will forge ahead. Always remember—it's already broken, what more harm can you do? Note that the system's been nice enough to tell you the `.c` files where the multiple definitions occur: `mwfa.c` and `mc.c`. Apparently, there's a definition of `mv_code_table` in both. The codec (that stands for enCOder/DECoder) is probably the more important one to keep the value defined in, so let's dig around in the definition in the output module.

```
brezup:software netpbm-9.12 $ find ./ -name mc.c -print
.//pnm/fiasco/input/mc.c
.//pnm/fiasco/output/mc.c
```

If you look in the input/mc.c file, you'll see that mv_code_table is defined as a static int and has a bunch of data included in it. If you look in the codec/mwfa.c file, you'll see something similar (with a note that this variable is supposed to be local). The version in the output directory, however, just defines the variable and stores no data in it. One of these things is not like the other—one of these things just doesn't belong. The one that's different looks like fair game to me. Change the line for mv_code_table in mc.c of the output directory so that it reads:

```
extern int mv_code_table [33][2];      /* VLC table for coordinates, mwfa.c */
```

This tells the compiler "go look somewhere else for this data." It's already defined somewhere else; the compiler told you so. Somewhere else must be a good place to look, right? And try the make, yet again.

```
brezup:software netpbm-9.12 $ make
.
.
.
make -C output libfiasco_output.a
gcc -c -I.. -I../lib -I../codec -pedantic -no-cpp-precomp -fno-common -O3
➥-Wall -Wno-uninitialized  -o mc.o
➥/Users/software/Documents/source/netpbm-9.12/pnm/fiasco/output/mc.c
ar -rc libfiasco_output.a matrices.o mc.o nd.o tree.o weights.o write.o
make -C lib libfiasco_lib.a
make[3]: `libfiasco_lib.a' is up to date.
make -C ../../pnm libpnm.a
make[3]: `libpnm.a' is up to date.
make -C ../../ppm libppm.a
make[3]: `libppm.a' is up to date.
make -C ../../pgm libpgm.a
make[3]: `libpgm.a' is up to date.
make -C ../../pbm libpbm.a
make[3]: `libpbm.a' is up to date.
gcc  -o pnmtofiasco binerror.o cwfa.o getopt.o getopt1.o params.o \
`../../libopt codec/libfiasco_codec.a input/libfiasco_input.a
➥output/libfiasco_output.a lib/libfiasco_lib.a ` \
 `../../libopt ../../pnm/libpnm.a ../../ppm/libppm.a ../../pgm/libpgm.a
➥../../pbm/libpbm.a ` -lm
ld: table of contents for archive: output/libfiasco_output.a is out of date;
➥rerun ranlib(1) (can't load from it)
make[2]: *** [pnmtofiasco] Error 1
make[1]: *** [all] Error 2
make: *** [pnm] Error 2
```

You know what to do:

```
brezup:software netpbm-9.12 $ ranlib ./pnm/fiasco/output/libfiasco_output.a
```

and make again.

```
[Racer-X:~/Documents/source/netpbm-9.12] software% make

.
.
.
gcc  -o palmtopnm palmtopnm.o palmcolormap.o `../../libopt ../../pnm/libpnm.a
➥../../ppm/libppm.a ../../pgm/libpgm.a ../../pbm/libpbm.a ` \
gcc -c -I../../shhopt -pedantic -no-cpp-precomp -fno-common -O3 -Wall
➥-Wno-uninitialized  -o pnmtopalm.o ../../pnm/pnmtopalm/pnmtopalm.c
../../pnm/pnmtopalm/pnmtopalm.c: In function `main':
../../pnm/pnmtopalm/pnmtopalm.c:42: warning: implicit declaration of
➥function `strcmp'
../../pnm/pnmtopalm/pnmtopalm.c:220: warning: implicit declaration of
➥function `memset'
../../pnm/pnmtopalm/pnmtopalm.c:290: warning: implicit declaration of
➥function `memcpy'
gcc  -o pnmtopalm pnmtopalm.o palmcolormap.o `../../libopt ../../pnm/libpnm.a
➥../../ppm/libppm.a ../../pgm/libpgm.a ../../pbm/libpbm.a ` \

[Racer-X:~/Documents/source/netpbm-9.12] software%
```

Hard to believe, but it just finished the compile. Now if you do a make install, you'll be all set. netpbm installs its applications into /usr/local/netpbm/bin/; its man pages and so on go into directories in /usr/local/netpbm. Because of this, you'll again need to extend your path: PATH=$PATH:/usr/local/netpbm/bin or set path=($path /usr/local/netpbm/bin/), depending on whether you're using bash or tcsh, respectively.

Finally, if you want to see whether it works, find something like a JPEG file, and try out the following:

```
pnm/jpegtopnm < ~/Pictures/<oldfile>.jpg | pnm/pnminvert |
➥ppm/ppmtojpeg > ~/Pictures/<newfile>.jpg
```

If you've installed it, that'd be just

```
jpegtopnm < ~/Pictures/<oldfile>.jpg | pnminvert |
➥ppmtojpeg > ~/Pictures/<newfile>.jpg
```

Now take a look at the new file in your Pictures directory. The netpbm package is a large collection of programs that perform specific graphics manipulations. They can be chained together in arbitrary combinations to create arbitrarily complex graphics manipulations. We'll cover a few of the things it can do in Chapter 15. The number of uses is almost unlimited, so you really should read through the man pages for more ideas.

Now that you've gone through all of that, remember that this is an older version of netpbm. Installing the most recent version is much easier, but rather than have you go through the compile, you can even more easily install it with fink.

Tracing Software Problems to the Source: Using the gdb Debugger

If thinking about the problem, trying to do things as correctly as possible, and examining all the debugging information yields only an application that doesn't run correctly, you still have the option of digging around in the code. Thankfully, Apple has provided the GNU debugger, `gdb`, as part of the development tools. The GNU debugger is to the Unix debugging world what the GNU compiler is to the Unix programming world—a flexible, community-supported, de facto standard for programmer productivity.

The easiest way to explain how to use `gdb` is to demonstrate its use. The program has copious online help, as well as man pages and an INFO section available through the `emacs M-x info` command. Before the demonstration, however, Table 14.1 contains a summary of command-line options and common internal commands.

> **NOTE**
>
> When following this debugging example, an almost overwhelmingly large number of details appear in the output. These all have important meanings to someone studying the inner workings of the program, but for the purpose of just trying to see what might be wrong, and whether you understand enough to fix it, you really only need to follow along with the details discussed in the example.
>
> *Don't* let the other details intimidate you and convince you to ignore the possibilities the debugger presents. Even accomplished programmers sometimes let the apparent complexity of debugging output sidetrack them into using less effective tools and wasting time. You can learn an incredible amount and get good at cleaning up little software errors by starting from these humble beginnings. All it takes is a willingness to experiment and pay attention to deeper details each time you learn something new.
>
> In light of this, don't consider or expect this example to be a comprehensive discussion of how you use `gdb` to debug software. It's designed to show you what real errors look like and to demonstrate that if you pay attention, it really is within the grasp of ordinary, everyday users to hunt for, and potentially to fix, software errors.

TABLE 14.1 The Command Documentation Table for the gdb Debugger

`gdb`	GNU debugger
`gdb [-help] [-nx] [-q] [-batch] [-cd=`*<dir>*`] [-f] [-b `*<bps>*`] [-tty=`*<dev>*`] [-s `*<symfile>*`] [-e `*<prog>*`] [-se `*<prog>*`] [-c `*<core>*`] [-x `*<cmds>*`] [-d `*<dir>*`] [`*<prog>*` [`*<core>*` ¦ *<procID>*`]]`	
`gdb` can be used to debug programs written in C, C++, and Modula-2.	
Arguments other than options specify an executable file and a core file or process ID. The first argument encountered with no associated option flag is equivalent to the `-se` option; the second, if any, is equivalent to the `-c` option, if it is a file. Options and command-line arguments are processed in sequential order. The order makes a difference when the `-x` option is specified.	
`-help` `-h`	Lists all options with brief explanations.
`-symbols=`*<file>* `-s `*<file>*	Reads symbol table from file *<file>*.

TABLE 14.1 Continued

`-write`	Enables writing into executable and core files.
`-exec=`*<file>* `-e` *<file>*	Uses *<file>* as the executable file to execute when appropriate, and for examining pure data in conjunction with a core dump.
`-se=`*<file>*	Reads symbol table from *<file>* and uses it as the executable file.
`-core=`*<file>* `-c` *<file>*	Uses *<file>* as a core dump to examine.
`-command=`*<file>* `-x` *<file>*	Executes `gdb` commands from *<file>*.
`-directory=`*<directory>*	Adds *<directory>* to the path to search for source files.
`-d` *<directory>*`-nx` `-n`	Does not execute commands from any `.gdbinit` files. Commands in these files are normally executed after all the command options and arguments have been processed.
`-quiet` `-q`	Quiet mode. Does not print the introductory and copyright messages. Also suppresses them in batch mode.
`-batch`	Batch mode. Exits with status `0` after processing all the command files associated with the `-x` option (and `.gdbinit`, if not inhibited). Exits with nonzero status if an error occurs while executing the `gdb` commands in the command files.
`-cd=`*<directory>*	Runs `gdb` using *<directory>* as the working directory rather than using the current directory as the working directory.
`-fullname` `-f`	Outputs information used by `emacs-gdb` interface.
`-b` *<bps>*	Sets the line speed (baud rate or bits per second) of any serial interface used by `gdb` for remote debugging.
`-tty=`*<device>*	Runs using *<device>* for your program's standard input and output.

These are some of the more frequently needed `gdb` commands:

`break [`*<file>*`]`*<function>*	Sets a breakpoint at *<function>* (in *<file>*).
`run [`*<arglist>*`]`	Starts your program (with *<arglist>*, if specified).
`bt`	Backtrace. Displays the program stack.
`print` *<expr>*	Displays the value of an expression.
`c`	Continues running your program (after stopping, such as at a breakpoint).
`next`	Executes the next program line (after stopping); steps over any function calls in the line.
`step`	Executes the next program line (after stopping); steps into any function calls in the line.
`help [`*<name>*`]`	Shows information about `gdb` command *<name>*, or general information about using `gdb`.
`quit`	Exits `gdb`.

To use gdb, you first need something on which to use it. Type in the little program shown in Listing 14.1, just as it appears here. Alternatively, you can download it from macosxunleashed.com's downloads directory:

```
curl -O http://www.macosxunleashed.com/downloads/addme.c
```

Name the file addme.c.

LISTING 14.1 The Source for the addme.c Demo C Program

```
/* addme.c   A really silly C demo program */
/* 990325 WCR                              */
/* Usage is <progname> <filename>          */

#include <stdio.h>

int addem(a,b)
int a, b;
{
  return a+b;
}

void main(argc,argv)
int argc;
char *argv[];
{
  int i;
  char infilename[8];
  int j;
  FILE *infile;
  char number[100];
  char *infilename2=infilename;
  strcpy(infilename2,argv[1]);
  i=0; j=0;
  infile = fopen(infilename2,"r");

  if(infile==NULL)
  {
     printf("couldn't open file %s please try again\n",infilename2);
     exit(1);
  }

  i=0;
  while (fgets(number,90,infile) != '\0')
  {
     sscanf(number,"%d",&j);
     i=addem(i,j);
```

LISTING 14.1 Continued

```
  }
  printf("Your total is %d\n",i);
  exit(0);
}
```

This simple little C program takes a list of integers from a file, one per line, and adds them together. So that you'll have a file to work from, create a file named `numbers` with the following contents:

```
1
2
13
15
```


Make sure that there are no blank lines above or below the data.

Also create a file with a very long name, such as `supercalifragilisticzowie`, and put the same data in it.

Note there's a bit of trickery involved in the way this code is written that's specifically there to generate an error. Even though there are a few errors in this code, some systems are sloppy enough with memory management that the program might run intermittently. Also, if you rearrange the definition of the variables `i` and `j`, you decrease the likelihood of a crash. Weird, huh?

So, let's see what we have. Time to compile the program. We don't have a makefile, so we'll have to do it by hand. Issue the command

```
cc -g -o addemup addme.c
```

After a few seconds, your machine should return you to a command line. The compiler should respond with a warning similar to the following:

```
addme.c: In function `main':
addme.c:16: warning: return type of `main' is not `int'
addme.c:40: warning: incompatible implicit declaration of built-in function 'exit'
```

It should return you to the command line. If it does anything else, for instance, outputs

```
addme.c: In function `main':
addme.c:15: parse error before `char'
addme.c:23: subscripted value is neither array nor pointer
```

that means you've typed the program in incorrectly, or have otherwise messed up your downloaded version. Specifically, if you got this error, in all likelihood you forgot the semicolon after the line that says `int argc;`.

The warning that's returned when it's correct is just that: a warning, not an error. The most recent revision of the C programming language has a preference for a particular return type for the main program, and the compiler is just being pedantic and reminding me that having a void return value is archaic.

After you get the program to compile cleanly with no errors, you're ready for the next step—trying it out. Issue the command ./addemup and see what happens. Note that the command is addemup, not something related to addme. I could actually have named it anything I wanted, simply by changing the -o addemup part of the cc command. If you don't specify any output filename, cc names the output file a.out by default. Also, just so that you know, the -g flag tells the compiler to turn on the debugging output. This slows the program but gives the debugger important information.

```
./addemup
Bus Error
```

Well, that doesn't sound good. What could be wrong? You can probably figure it out just by looking at the code at this point, but on a more complicated program, that would be impossible. Instead, let's start the gdb debugger and take a look.

```
brezup:software source $ gdb ./addemup
GNU gdb 5.3-20030128 (Apple version gdb-365) (Sun Oct 24 12:57:07 GMT 2004)
Copyright 2004 Free Software Foundation, Inc.
GDB is free software, covered by the GNU General Public License, and you are
welcome to change it and/or distribute copies of it under certain conditions.
Type "show copying" to see the conditions.
There is absolutely no warranty for GDB.  Type "show warranty" for details.
This GDB was configured as "powerpc-apple-darwin"...
Reading symbols for shared libraries
 .. done
(gdb)
```

Okay, we're at a prompt. What do we do? The gdb debugger actually has a complete selection of online help available. To access the help system, simply enter the command help.

```
(gdb) help
List of classes of commands:

aliases -- Aliases of other commands
breakpoints -- Making program stop at certain points
data -- Examining data
files -- Specifying and examining files
internals -- Maintenance commands
obscure -- Obscure features
running -- Running the program
stack -- Examining the stack
status -- Status inquiries
support -- Support facilities
tracepoints -- Tracing of program execution without stopping the program
user-defined -- User-defined commands
```

```
Type "help" followed by a class name for a list of commands in that class.
Type "help" followed by command name for full documentation.
Command name abbreviations are allowed if unambiguous.
(gdb)
```

I'll leave some of the interesting items here for you to explore, rather than walk you through them. Right now, let's get back to debugging our program. To start the program, simply issue the command `r`.

```
(gdb) r
Starting program: /Users/software/Documents/source/addemup
Reading symbols for shared libraries . done

Program received signal EXC_BAD_ACCESS, Could not access memory.
Reason: KERN_PROTECTION_FAILURE at address: 0x00000000
0x978c6168 in strcpy ()
(gdb)
```


So, gdb knows something. Not a very intelligible something at this point, but something none the less. That address `0x00000000` is most disturbing (above and beyond the errors). It's almost impossibly unlikely that a program would actually have data at location zero. If it had any other value, I might suspect a logic error, but an address of zero ***for anything*** suggests that something somewhere isn't being assigned to what it should be. Let's see whether gdb can be a bit more informative.

```
(gdb) where
#0  0x978c6168 in strcpy ()
#1  0x00002bb0 in main (argc=1, argv=0xbffffcb6) at addme.c:23
(gdb)
```

gdb says the program broke in a procedure named `strcpy`, which was called from a procedure named `main`, in line 23 of our file `addme.c`. Depending on the compiler version and gdb version, you might also see a line or two for `start()`, which is Mac OS X and gdb initializing and starting the program. Let's take a look at the region of the code in your file (line 23) that gdb indicates was the last place that things were working.

```
(gdb) l 23
18        char infilename[8];
19        int j;
20        FILE *infile;
21        char number[100];
22        char *infilename2=&infilename;
23        strcpy(infilename2,argv[1]);
24        i=0; j=0;
25        infile = fopen(infilename2,""r"");
26
27        if(infile==NULL)
(gdb)
```

Line 23 has a function `strcpy` on it (this C function copies the contents of one character array [string] variable to another). The debugger seems to be on to something here. Let's set a *breakpoint* (a place we want the program to stop running and wait for us) at line 23 and see what happens.

> **TIP**
>
> C functions have man page entries too. You can get documentation on most anything you see as a function in a C program like this. If you're not a programmer, the meat of the documentation might not be much use to you, but for something like `strcpy`, knowing that the function is supposed to copy the contents of one argument into another can be useful when looking at debugging output.

```
(gdb) b 23
Breakpoint 1 at 0x2b9c: file addme.c, line 23.
(gdb)
```

So far, so good. Now let's run the program again and see where this takes us.

```
(gdb) r
The program being debugged has been started already.
Start it from the beginning? (y or n) y
Starting program: /Users/software/Documents/source/addemup numbers

Breakpoint 1, main (argc=1, argv=0xbffffcb6) at addme.c:23
23          strcpy(infilename2,argv[1]);
(gdb)
```

Note that `gdb` asked me whether I wanted to restart from the beginning, and I told it to go ahead. Now it has run up to our breakpoint and is waiting for me to do something. Even if I don't know what `strcpy` does, there's still something obviously wrong with this line. I know I've got a variable named `infilename2` and a funny variable named `argv[1]`. Let's see what `gdb` has to say about them.

```
(gdb) p infilename2
$1 = 0xbffffb58 "????"
(gdb)
```

The `$1` indicates that it's telling us about the first variable we asked about. The `0xbfff99c` is the memory location where it's stored. Don't be surprised if yours is different, or your version of `gdb` doesn't show the location without tweaking some customization settings—the default behavior depends on a number of factors outside the scope of this discussion. If you use `gdb` much, you'll pick up how to set your configuration to display the data you like in the format you want. The built-in help system is, well, helpful here. The `????` is the current content of this variable, which, other than not being anything you might expect, might appear to be meaningless. Depending on your `gdb` settings, you might see other gibberish instead, which will probably look something like `L\000\000@`. Other than the fact that there's nothing interpretable at that memory location, this might not seem to be too informative yet. It will make more sense shortly. (Don't be surprised if yours has something else in whatever memory location shows up on your machine.)

Moving on, what can we tell about this `argv[1]` variable?

```
(gdb) p argv[1]
$2 = 0x0
(gdb)
```

Hmmm... `0x0` is a hexadecimal 0, or `NULL` in the C world. Examining the code again certainly suggests that something useful should be happening here. It looks as if `infilename2` gets used to open a file in just a few lines, and neither `L\000\000@` nor `NULL` looks promising as a filename. Nulls are used in C, but frequently they're signs of a problem, so let's think about this.

The program is trying to do something with a variable named `argv[1]`. The only other place this variable (`argv`) appears is in the `main` statement—the statement that starts the actual program execution. It certainly looks as if there should be something other than a `NULL` here. Wait a minute, what did it say in the comments at the top? It said I need to give it a filename at the command line when I run it! I didn't give it a filename, and it's trying to copy something that doesn't exist to get one. Aren't programmers supposed to check for that?

Let's see whether I'm right. I'll rerun the program with a filename this time.

```
(gdb) r numbers
The program being debugged has been started already.
Start it from the beginning? (y or n) y
Starting program: /Users/software/Documents/source/addemup numbers

Breakpoint 1, main (argc=2, argv=0xbffffca2) at addme.c:23
23          strcpy(infilename2,argv[1]);
(gdb)
```

I started it over, but I forgot to turn off my breakpoint. Still, this is a good opportunity for me to check whether I was right.

```
(gdb) p infilename2
$3 = 0xbffffb38 "???\236"
(gdb)
```

That's different, but just as useless as before.

```
(gdb) p argv[1]
$4 = 0xbffffd3a "numbers"
(gdb)
```

Now we're getting somewhere! If we remember to give it a filename, it actually gets one! To continue past the breakpoint, I can enter c.

```
(gdb) c
Continuing.
Your total is 31

Program exited normally.
(gdb)
```

The program now does exactly what it should. If I want to test it again without stopping at the breakpoint, I can delete the breakpoint and run it again.

```
(gdb) d 1
(gdb) r
Starting program: /Users/software/Documents/source/addemup numbers
Your total is 31

Program exited normally.
(gdb)
```

The command d 1 deletes breakpoint 1 (you can have multiple breakpoints if you need them). Note that I didn't have to give it the command-line argument numbers this time when I entered **r** because gdb conveniently remembers command-line arguments between runs. As you can see, it runs properly to completion.

Quitting gdb with the quit command and trying it on the command line produces the same results.

```
brezup:software source $ ./addemup numbers
Your total is 31
brezup:software source $
```

Now let's see whether we can demonstrate another type of error. Do you still remember what your very long filename is? Try using that filename instead of numbers and see what happens.

```
brezup:software source $ ./addemup supercalifragilisticzowie
couldn't open file supercal please try again
brezup:software source $
```

Huh? I didn't call it supercal. Something happened to my filename. Time to break out gdb again and have another look.

```
brezup:software source $ gdb ./addemup
GNU gdb 5.3-20030128 (Apple version gdb-365) (Sun Oct 24 12:57:07 GMT 2004)
Copyright 2004 Free Software Foundation, Inc.
GDB is free software, covered by the GNU General Public License, and you are
welcome to change it and/or distribute copies of it under certain conditions.
```

```
Type "show copying" to see the conditions.
There is absolutely no warranty for GDB.  Type "show warranty" for details.
This GDB was configured as "powerpc-apple-darwin"...
Reading symbols for shared libraries
 .. done
(gdb) r supercalifragilisticzowie
Starting program: addemup supercalifragilisticzowie
Reading symbols for shared libraries .. done
couldn't open file supercal please try again

Program exited with code 01.
(gdb)
```


Basically, it says the same thing. There must be something more we can find out, though. Let's look at the code and see whether we can figure out where that weird truncation came from.

```
(gdb) l
13      void main(argc,argv)
14      int argc;
15      char *argv[];
16      {
17        int i;
18        char infilename[8];
19        int j;
20        FILE *infile;
21        char number[100];
22        char *infilename2=infilename;
(gdb)
23        strcpy(infilename2,argv[1]);
24        i=0; j=0;
25        infile = fopen(infilename2,"r");
26
27        if(infile==NULL)
28        {
29           printf("couldn't open file %s please try again\n",infilename2);
30           exit(1);
31        }
32
(gdb)
```

Line 29 seems to be where the error message is coming from. Let's set a breakpoint there and see what happens.

```
(gdb) b 29
Breakpoint 1 at 0x2be4: file addme.c, line 29.
```

```
(gdb) r
Starting program: addemup supercalifragilisticzowie

Breakpoint 1, main (argc=2, argv=0xbffffc80) at addme.c:29
29          printf("couldn't open file %s please try again\n",infilename2);
(gdb)
```

We're at our breakpoint. `infilename2` is supposed to be `supercalifragilisticzowie`, and it is...

```
(gdb) p infilename2
$1 = 0xbffffb18 "supercal"
(gdb)
```

...not!. Something's wrong here! Time to back up to our trusty breakpoint at line 23 and watch what happens from the top down.

```
(gdb) b 23
Breakpoint 2 at 0x2b9c: file addme.c, line 23.
(gdb) r
The program being debugged has been started already.
Start it from the beginning? (y or n) y
Starting program: addemup supercalifragilisticzowie

Breakpoint 2, main (argc=2, argv=0xbffffd2c) at addme.c:23
23        strcpy(infilename2,argv[1]);
(gdb) p argv[1]
$2 = 0xbffffd18 "supercalifragilisticzowie"
(gdb) p infilename
$3 = "???¦\000\000\000\f"
```

So, the previous culprit isn't a problem here.

```
(gdb) p infilename2
$4 = 0xbffffb18 "???¦"
(gdb)
```

There's nothing interesting there. Let's see what happens on the next line—use the `gdb` command `n` to step to the next line. Before you step to the next line, the line you are currently on executes, so you should expect to see the results of that `strcpy` on line 23 after stepping forward to line 24.

```
(gdb) n
24        i=0; j=0;
(gdb) p infilename2
$6 = 0xbffffb18 "supercalifragilisticzowie"
(gdb)
```

As expected, `infilename2` contains our atrociously long filename. Nothing wrong here now, but when we ran all the way through, by the time execution hit line 29, it was broken. Let's step forward again and see what happens.

```
(gdb) n
25          infile = fopen(infilename2,""r"");
(gdb) p infilename2
$8 = 0xbffffb18 "supercal"
(gdb)
```

Wait a minute! Now it's wrong! What happened? All that the program did between those two lines was to assign both the variables `i` and `j` to be zero, and somehow it affected `infilename2`. You wouldn't think this could happen, variables just changing their values willy-nilly.

In fact, if the program were written properly, this wouldn't happen. As a nonprogrammer, this is where you usually give up. That isn't to say that the exercise has been useless. With this information, you can more easily explain to the author or online support community what problems you've observed so that they can fix it more easily and quickly. Program authors hate it when they get bug reports that say, "it didn't work." This doesn't mean anything to them because if they could duplicate the problem on their end, they'd probably have found and fixed it already. Instead, you say, "it doesn't work because for some reason, between line 23 and line 25, the `infilename2` variable contents get tromped on," and help the author find the bug by localizing it to a very small portion of the code.

By taking these extra steps, the information you can provide about the program's problems can mean the difference between a fix that takes a few minutes to appear and a fix that never appears.

NOTE

If you're curious, and you keep a C handbook around, fixing this particular error isn't that difficult. The error here is that the variable `infilename` has been defined to hold only eight characters. `infilename2` is essentially an alias to `infilename1` and is needed to fool the debugger into not telling you about the problem immediately. The assignment of the very long filename to `infilename2` actually works most of the time, despite the fact that there theoretically isn't enough room to hold it. It works because there's enough slop in the assignment of memory space that it's unlikely that it will write over anything important, although the `supercalifragilisticzowie` value hangs out the end of it and into unknown memory space, and as long as it doesn't write over anything important, the operating system doesn't really care what a program does in its own memory space.

The thing that actually makes the error show up almost all the time is the placement of the definitions of `i` and `j` around the definition of `infilename`. Most compilers will arrange variables in memory in the same order they were defined in the program. Because the compiler doesn't know you're going to stuff a huge string into `infilename`, it chooses memory close to `infilename` for the storage of `i` and `j`. With optimization turned off, most compilers will place `i` and `j` flanking `infilename` in memory, and a sufficiently long value in `infilename` will overlap the memory used by `i` and `j`. By assigning both `i` and `j` to 0 after assigning `infilename`, it's almost guaranteed that part of `infilename` will be damaged and that the program will fail. To fix the program so that this can't occur with any reasonable filename, simply change the definition of `infilename` to something like `char infilename[256];` instead of `char infilename[8];`.

DEBUGGING IN GORY DETAIL

Although details of kernel process tracing are a subject for a book on advanced system programming, experienced programmers reading here might be interested in knowing that Mac OS X ships with kernel tracing enabled. The `ktrace` command writes kernel trace logs for processes and the `kdump` command reads `ktrace` logs and formats them into human-readable output. For the nonprogrammer interested in seeing just what the operating system is doing when a program is running (as opposed to the program-centric view shown by `gdb`), run `ktrace` on a command such as `ls` (`ktrace ls; kdump ¦ less`). Working through the meaning of each call used in a program such as `ls`, by using the man pages to look up functions, is an excellent excercise if you're interested in really understanding how the system works.

This command can also be a real lifesaver when you have a program that fails with some cryptic "can't open file" error message, but doesn't inform you as to what file it was trying to open. Digging through the `ktrace` output can sometimes give you enough clues to determine, for example, that the program was trying to read a configuration file that has gone missing or write a log file into a directory that doesn't exist. That information is sometimes enough to let you find or reconstruct the data that the program needs to get up and running again.

Summary

In this chapter, you did something the vast majority of Macintosh users have never done: compile and install your own software. We hope that you found this experience completely anticlimactic. Mac OS X is still rough enough around the edges that if you try to install every program out there, you will run across some that raise your blood pressure. But on Unix flavors that have existed for a longer time, almost every piece of source can be compiled with the same standard installation procedure: `./configure`, `make`, `make test`, and `make install`. We expect that Mac OS X will mature rapidly to the point that all installs are as simple as the straightforward installations that we've gone through here.

For those installs that aren't so simple, you've had a tour of several installation, compilation, troubleshooting, and debugging issues. We have found that a large percentage of Unix users, after they have developed the necessary mindset regarding software installation, can productively fight through troublesome installs such as these by successively attacking small parts of the problem as shown here. The keys to remember are that the messages and errors reported by the compilers and debuggers *do have meaning*, and that the worst that can happen by attempting to logically determine the cause of an error is that it doesn't get any better. Surprisingly often, a problem in a programming language can be fixed by working with error messages and making logical guesses, even if you don't know the language in the slightest.

Always remember: It all looks more difficult than it really is, and if it's already broken, you can't make it work any worse.

PART V

Advanced BSD Concepts

IN THIS PART

CHAPTER **15**

Shell Configuration and Programming (Shell Scripting)

IN THIS CHAPTER

- Customizing Your Shell Environment and Storing Data
- Automating Tasks with Shell Scripts
- Setting Up Automatic Script Execution

In the preceding several chapters, we have introduced you to the wide range of possibilities inherent in being able to access the Unix subsystem at the command line. Although we've said that being able to type to the command line can give you the power to do things that you've never been able to do before, we've also repeatedly hinted that there were ways that you could automate much of the typing and build your own mini-programs. In this chapter, we'll cover the final things you need to know to make this a reality.

With Mac OS X 10.3, Apple changed the default user shell from `tcsh` to `bash`. 10.4 maintains this default. Because of this, not all of you will be using the same shell. Unfortunately, the mechanical details of these shells are different enough that they can't both be easily covered in a single discussion without becoming confusing. The concept of shell scripting itself, and of automating your command-line tools, is universal, however, and does not depend on what shell you're using to work in. Therefore, this chapter is divided into sections that discuss scripting as a concept—and in which we'll use one shell or the other, whichever is most illustrative of the scripting point at hand, to generate our primary examples—and subsections that discuss the mechanistic and syntactic details of the `bash` and `tcsh` shells themselves, as well as how these relate to the general scripting concepts. When you come to one of these shell-specific sections, concentrate on the version that deals with your shell.

We wish we could put enough pages in this book to provide identical coverage of both. Unfortunately, if our popular reviews are correct, we'd need to put wheels and a tow-handle on the book if we did. To cut down on the bulk and weight a little bit, we'll confine most extended discussions, examples, and listings to one, or the other shell sections (the `bash` section, whenever it's possible to make the point clearly in `bash`). Because of this, regardless of which shell you're using, you'll want to skim the other section after reading the specifics of yours to catch any places where the other goes into greater detail. You'll be able to generate the analogous examples for each by following along with what is done in the other shell and applying the details regarding differences that we've provided in the section specific to your shell.

If you're interested in using a different shell, you'll find that the concepts and capabilities we cover here are almost universal, though the syntax and advanced features of these and other shells will differ somewhat. Some shells, such as `zsh`, have so many additional features beyond what we can cover there that a complete description of their use is sufficient to fill a book or two of their own.

Don't let the idea of multiple differing shell syntaxes sound intimidating to you. Even if you don't realize it yet, for whatever shell you're working in, you already know shell syntax. It's what you've been using for the last six chapters. To make the best use of the command-line environment, you'll also need to know about shell variables, conditional statements, and looping structures. At this point in your command-line experience, these will not be difficult details to master.

Customizing Your Shell Environment and Storing Data

Variables are a way of addressing bits of the computer memory so that we can store random pieces of information in it. It would be difficult to do much productive work with a computer if all we could store in any location was one particular, predetermined piece of information. Variables give us the ability to name a region `X`, store whatever value we want in `X`, and change the value whenever we want. Variables in the shell are used both to hold data to be used in commands and programs written in the shell and to control the behavior of certain aspects of the shell. You've already been introduced peripherally to this second use by way of the `PATH` variable, which affects where the shell looks to find executable programs. We'll go into somewhat more detail on this use in the next section and cover the former later in this chapter.

Setting Environment and Shell Variables

Many shells make a distinction between environment variables and shell variables in one way or another. Both are variables that you can set and use in a shell. The difference is that environment variables are inherited by any programs (such as subshells) that are children of (Unixism for "run by") that shell, whereas shell variables are not inherited. This might not seem a useful distinction, but there are significant uses for each type. Noninherited shell variables don't cost memory and startup time for subshells, and can be expected to be empty in any shell until they are used to store something. Inherited environment variables, on the other hand, must be copied into the memory space of child programs, taking room and time, and they can be used to pass information between a parent shell and programs that it executes.

NOTE

It is traditional to use uppercase variable names for environment variables and lowercase variable names for shell variables, although there is no requirement that this tradition must be followed in your own scripts.

Setting Variables in bash

In bash, all variables start out as shell variables, and then are upgraded to environment variable status using the export command. To set a shell variable, the syntax is as follows:

```
<shellvariablename>=<value>
```

TIP

There are no spaces between the *<shellvariablename>*, the = character, or the *<value>*. Spaces that creep unannounced and unwanted into statements that you're typing will be one of the most common problems you encounter when working in bash.

To set a shell variable named x to contain the value 7, the bash shell expression is simply

```
x=7
```

To make a shell variable into an environmental variable, the syntax is

```
export <shellvariablename>
```

To make the shell variable x (that we previously set to contain the value 7) into an environment variable, the shell expression is

```
export x
```

This makes the variable x available to other programs we start from within this shell.

Setting Variables in tcsh

In tcsh one uses an explicit command to tell the shell to put a value into a variable, instead of just an = sign. Setting shell variables uses a different command than setting an environment variable: Shell variables use the command set, and environment variables use the command setenv. To set a shell variable, the syntax is as follows:

```
set <shellvariablename> = <value>
```

To set a shell variable named x to contain the value 7, the shell expression is simply

```
set x=7
```

TIP

tcsh is not as particular as bash about spaces, but it does require that the spaces be balanced. That is, you can use either x=7 or x = 7, but not x= 7 or x =7. The error that tcsh reports if you use either of these latter two constructs is a seemingly irrelevant complaint about a variable name needing to start with a letter.

To set an environment variable to a particular value, the syntax is

```
setenv <environmentvariablename> <value>
```

To set an environment variable named Y to contain the value 8, the shell expression is

```
setenv Y 8
```

Note that with setenv, no = sign is used.

CAUTION

In tcsh it's quite possible for you to create a shell variable and an environment variable with the same name, each containing a distinct value. In this case, most shell commands will see the variable as having the value of the shell variable rather than the value of the environment variable.

Using Shell and Environment Variables

Both shell and environment variables are addressed for use by the prepending of a $ sign before the variable names. A simple demonstration can be accomplished with the echo command, which prints to the STDOUT of the shell, the value of the expression following it.

NOTE

Observe the shell prompt in the command-line examples in this chapter. It's probably not what you're used to seeing as a shell prompt. The shell prompt can be customized to a significant extent. See Table 15.2 (bash) or Table 15.4 (tcsh) in this chapter, and the man pages for bash and tcsh for information on how you can customize your prompt to include the information you find most useful. For many of the examples in this chapter, I'm using a shell prompt that includes a sequentially increasing number. This number is useful not only for demonstrations such as are being done in this chapter, but also for access to the command history list, discussed later in this chapter.

Using Variables in bash

The shell use of variables is simultaneously both rather simple and often annoying in its requirement for attention to detail. Variables are case sensitive, and the spacing between variables and operators such as the = sign in assignment statements is critical to the correct functioning of the statement. The habits necessary to work with shell variables however aren't hard to develop, and it's easy enough to experiment and try again if something doesn't work:

```
brezup:ray Documents 351 $ echo "Hi There"
Hi There
brezup:ray Documents 352 $ echo x
x
brezup:ray Documents 353 $ echo $x

brezup:ray Documents 354 $ x=7
brezup:ray Documents 355 $ echo x
x
brezup:ray Documents 356 $ echo $x
7
brezup:ray Documents 357 $ Y=8
brezup:ray Documents 358 $ export Y
brezup:ray Documents 359 $ echo $y

brezup:ray Documents 360 $ echo $Y
8
brezup:ray Documents 361 $ z=$x+$Y
7+8
brezup:ray Documents 362 $ let z=$x+$Y
brezup:ray Documents 363 $ echo $z
15
```


Here, a shell variable `x` and an environment variable `Y` have been set to values `7` and `8`, respectively, and their values have been printed to the terminal. There are a few lines of "mistakes" interspersed to demonstrate the behavior of the shell if you don't get your variable names quite right when you're trying to use them. It's important to note that `bash` doesn't provide error diagnostics for a simple misuse such as asking for the value of a variable that's never been set. This can make finding errors in scripts more challenging.

Notice the result of the command numbered 361? `bash` automatically expands variables to their values (that is, replaces them in the expression with whatever value they contain), but it doesn't automatically evaluate arithmetic expressions. Because of this, the assignment done in command 361, `z=$x+$Y`, is treated as a string assignment: `$x` and `$Y` are replaced by their values to the left and right of the `+` sign, and the resulting string is stored in `z`. To tell `bash` to treat the expression as an arithmetic expression instead, the `let` command is used. This signals `bash` that the following arguments should be expanded, and then evaluated arithmetically, rather than as a string.

`bash` also supports the notion of array variables. An array can be created simply by assigning values to subscripted variables:

```
brezup:ray Documents 364 $ z[3]=12
brezup:ray Documents 365 $ z[$x]=14
```

```
brezup:ray Documents 366 $ echo $z[3]
15[3]
```

NOTE

Remember, the value of $x and $z have been set earlier.

Unfortunately, the syntax for retrieving the values isn't quite what you'd probably like it to be. Command number 366 reports `15[3]` in the preceding example because `$z` has previously been set to the value `15`, and `bash` (annoyingly) expands that value, instead of noticing that the `[3]` calls up an array subscript of `z`.

```
brezup:ray Documents 367 $ echo ${z[3]}
12
brezup:ray Documents 368 $ echo $z
15
brezup:ray Documents 369 $ z[$x+Y]=2
brezup:ray Documents 370 $ echo ${z[15]}
2
```

When setting an array value, the variable may be specified as `<varname>[<subscript>]`, but when using it, curly braces must be placed around the `<varname>[<subscript>]` portion to prevent the shell from interpreting it as `$<varname>` followed by the string `[<subscript>]`. Inside the square braces specifying the subscript, expressions are treated as arithmetic and evaluated to determine the final subscript value.

TIP

Peculiarly, the arithmetic expansion inside `[]` means that you don't need to use a $ in front of a variable name, when you want to use that variable's value inside the `[]` braces. This allows the expression `z[$x+Y]=2` to be written as `z[x+Y]=2` and `z[$x+$Y]=2` as well. Leaving out the $ is a good way to make what you write visually confusing, so we recommend against this, even though it's valid syntax.

Accessing the zeroth value of an array variable is the same as accessing the variable without an array subscript:

```
brezup:ray Documents 371 $ echo ${z[0]}
15
brezup:ray Documents 372 $ z[0]=32
brezup:ray Documents 373 $ echo $z
32
```

Finally, you can force the shell to recognize a portion of a command line as some variable and a portion as some other information by insulating the variable name with curly braces. For example, if you have a variable named `zz` and a variable named `zzygy`, you'd have trouble printing the value of `$zz`, followed by the characters `ygy` without this facility:

```
brezup:ray Pictures 453 $ zz="howdy neighbor"
brezup:ray Pictures 454 $ zzygy="plonk"
brezup:ray Pictures 455 $ echo $zz
howdy neighbor
brezup:ray Pictures 456 $ echo $zzygy
plonk
brezup:ray Pictures 457 $ echo ${zz}ygy
howdy neighborygy
```

The most common ways of using shell and environment variables in bash command lines are shown in Table 15.1.

TABLE 15.1 Useful bash Syntax Options for Setting and Accessing Shell and Environment Variables

Expression syntax	Effect
<word>	Used as a part of a command-line expression, *<word>* is a string of nonwhitespace characters or a quoted string that possibly contains spaces.
<variable>	The name of a variable. Variable names are composed of alphanumeric and underscore characters and begin with an alphabetic character or underscore.
$*<variable>*	Expands to the contents of *<variable>*. This will typically be a *<word>* or *<wordlist>*. A *<wordlist>* is a series of words separated (in the default case) by spaces.
${<variable>[n]}	Expands the *n*th value of the array-variable named *<variable>*. The curly braces are required.
<variable>=*<word>*	Sets the value of *<variable>* to *<word>*.
<variable>[*n*]=*<word>*	Treats *<variable>* as an array of words, and sets the *n*th value to *<word>*. This has the effect of setting the *n*th word of a wordlist to *<word>*.
<variable>[*<expression>*]=*<word>*	Treats *<variable>* as an array of words and *<expression>* as an arithmetic expression. Evaluates *<expression>* and sets the *<expression>*th value of *<variable>* to *<word>*.
export *<variable>*	Makes *<variable>* available to other processes as an environment variable.
let *<variable>*=*<expression>*	Treats *<expression>* as a mathematical expression, attempts to evaluate it, and assigns the result to *<variable>*.
let *<variable>*=(*<expression>*)	Same as the previous item. Parentheses can be used to order the execution of parts of the expression, and it's frequently helpful to use them around any expression on general principles.
let *<variable>[n]*=*<expression>*	Treats *<variable>* as an array and sets the *n*th value of it to the value of *<expression>*.

CAUTION

The spacing between the parts of a command, like the `let z=$x+$Y` command in the example, is one of the largest sources of difficulty to the beginning shell programmer. Making matters worse, the spacing that's required is different between shells, and what's required in one, breaks others. In `bash`, the lack of spaces between "words" that are being operated on—for example the `z`, the `=`, `$x`, `$y`, and the `+` symbol—are critical to the command being understood properly. The only place where there's much leniency is between the `let` and the arithmetic expression part of the command. Inserting spaces in other places will cause the arithmetic expression to be evaluated differently than you intend or cause the entire command to fail.

To demonstrate the difference between shell and environment variables, you can create a subshell and test the variables you used in the previous example in it:

```
brezup:ray Documents 373 $ bash
brezup:ray Documents 151 $ echo $x

brezup:ray Documents 152 $ echo $Y
8
```

As you can see, after the subshell is started (notice that the command number in the prompt drops to 151—the size of the retained history prior to the parent shell), the environment variable `Y` maintains its value and the shell value `x` goes back to being undefined.

Using Variables in `tcsh`

`tcsh` syntax for everything but the most basic variable operations is similar to `bash` syntax, but not quite identical.

```
brezup Documents 200> echo "Hi There"
Hi there
brezup Documents 201> echo $x
tcsh x: Undefined variable.
brezup Documents 202> set x=7
brezup Documents 203> echo $x
7
brezup Documents 204> setenv Y 8
brezup Documents 205> echo $y
tcsh y: Undefined variable.
brezup Documents 206> echo $Y
8
brezup Documents 207> @ z = ( $x + $Y )
brezup Documents 208> echo $z
15
```

Here, a shell variable x and an environment variable Y have been set to values 7 and 8, respectively, and their values have been printed to the terminal. tcsh is more strict about variable name use than bash, and complains when you try to access the value of a variable that hasn't previously been set. The @ command is a tcsh shell built-in command, similar to the set command. However, the set command treats all its arguments as strings, whereas the @ command treats them as numbers, allowing math operations such as +, -, /, and *. The @ command, like the set command, sets a shell variable (or creates it if it does not exist). The set and @ commands can also be used as [set or @] *<variablename>*[*n*] = *<expression>*. In this form, the command attempts to treat the variable *<variablename>* as an array and set item *n* (the *n*th word, if echoed) to the value of *<expression>*. Table 15.2 lists the most frequently used methods for setting variable values.

TABLE 15.2 tcsh Syntax Options for Setting Shell and Environment Variables

Expression syntax	Effect
<word>	Used as a part of a command-line expression, *<word>* is a string of nonwhitespace characters, or a quoted string that possibly contains spaces.
$*<variable>*	Expands to the contents of *<variable>*. This will typically be a *<word>* or *<wordlist>*. $*<variablename>* preferentially expands to the value of the shell variable by the name *<variablename>* if both shell and environment variables with this name exist.
set *<variable>* = *<word>*	Sets the value of *<variable>* to *<word>*.
set *<variable>*[*n*] = *<word>*	Treats *<variable>* as an array of words, and sets the *n*th value to *<word>*. This has the effect of setting the *n*th word of a wordlist to *<word>*.
setenv *<variable>* *<word>*	Sets the environment variable *<variable>* to contain the value *<word>*. Most variable manipulations must be done in shell variables, and the values transferred into environment variables if needed.
@ *<variable>* = *<expression>*	Treats *<expression>* as a mathematical expression, attempts to evaluate it, and assigns the result to *<variable>*. Most forms of errors in attempts at this result in the response @: *Expression Syntax*.
@ *<variable>* = (*<expression>*)	Same as the previous item. Parentheses can be used to order the execution of parts of the expression, and it's frequently helpful to use them around any expression on general principles.
@ *<variable>[n]* = *<expression>*	Treats *<variable>* as an array, and sets the *n*th value of it to the value of *<expression>*.

CAUTION

The spacing between the parts of a command, like the `@ z = ( $x + $Y )` command on line 207 of the preceding example, is one of the largest sources of difficulty to the beginning shell programmer. The spaces between "words" that are being operated on—here the `$x`, the `$y`, and the `+` symbol—are critical to the command being understood properly. You can have more spaces, but if you remove a space, the words become indistinct, and the shell becomes confused. For example, if you remove the space between the `$x` and the `+` sign, `tcsh` will no longer see a variable named `$x`, a `+` sign, and a variable named `$y`. Instead, it will see a variable named `$x+` and a variable named `$y`, with no mathematic operation between them. This turns out to be two errors because the `+` symbol isn't a valid part of a variable name, and some math operation is required in the expression.

Peculiarly, while `tcsh` requires balanced spaces around the `=` character in `set` and `setenv` statements, it does not require balanced spaces around the `=` in `@` statements. There must be a space between the `@` and the variable into which the value is being placed, but you can write `@ z=3`, `@ z = 3`, `@ z= 3`, and `@ z =3` to the same effect.

To demonstrate the difference between shell and environment variables, you can create a subshell and test the variables you used in the previous example in it:

```
localhost ray 210> tcsh
/Users/ray
localhost ray 151> echo $x
x: Undefined variable.
localhost ray 152> echo $Y
8
```

As you can see, after the subshell has been started (notice that the command number in the prompt drops to `151`—the size of my retained command history list), the environment variable `Y` maintains its value and the shell value `x` becomes undefined.

Reserved Variables in the Shell

As mentioned earlier, certain shell and environment variables are reserved by the shell and used to either report various values to the user or to control the behavior of some parts of the shell or of programs that run as children of the shell. Tables 15.3 and 15.4 list the `bash` and `tcsh` shell variables that affect the behavior of `bash`, `tcsh`, and a few intimately related programs. Remember that any program you run in a shell may be additionally affected by environment variables. For example, the `man` command determines where to look for man pages by examining the `MANPATH` environment variable. This variable isn't set or controlled by either `bash` or `tcsh`, but if you set this environment variable to some path in your shell, the `man` command will inherit it and search in that path for man pages. Because every program may independently choose to examine any environment variables it chooses, it's best to look at the man pages for any programs to determine whether there are environment variables with which you can affect the program's behavior.

TABLE 15.3 The bash Reserved Shell Variables

Shell Variable	Effects
BASH	Expands to the full filename used to invoke this instance of bash.
BASH_VERSINFO	A read-only array variable whose members hold version information for this instance of bash. The values assigned to the array members are as follows: BASH_VERSINFO[0] The major version number (the release) BASH_VERSINFO[1] The minor version number (the version) BASH_VERSINFO[2] The patch level BASH_VERSINFO[3] The build version BASH_VERSINFO[4] The release status (for example, beta1) BASH_VERSINFO[5] The value of MACHTYPE
BASH_VERSION	Expands to a string describing the version of this instance of bash.
COMP_CWORD	An index into ${COMP_WORDS} of the word containing the current cursor position. This variable is available only in shell functions invoked by the programmable completion facilities.
COMP_LINE	The current command line. This variable is available only in shell functions and external commands invoked by the programmable completion facilities.
COMP_POINT	The index of the current cursor position relative to the beginning of the current command. If the current cursor position is at the end of the current command, the value of this variable is equal to ${#COMP_LINE}. This variable is available only in shell functions and external commands invoked by the programmable completion facilities.
COMP_WORDS	An array variable consisting of the individual words in the current command line. This variable is available only in shell functions invoked by the programmable completion facilities.
DIRSTACK	An array variable containing the current contents of the directory stack. Directories appear in the stack in the order they are displayed by the dirs builtin. Assigning to members of this array variable may be used to modify directories already in the stack, but the pushd and popd builtins must be used to add and remove directories. Assignment to this variable will not change the current directory. If DIRSTACK is unset, it loses its special properties, even if it is subsequently reset.
EUID	Expands to the effective user ID of the current user, initialized at shell startup. This variable is read-only.
FUNCNAME	The name of any currently executing shell function. This variable exists only when a shell function is executing. Assignments to FUNCNAME have no effect and return an error status. If FUNCNAME is unset, it loses its special properties, even if it is subsequently reset.
GROUPS	An array variable containing the list of groups of which the current user is a member. Assignments to GROUPS have no effect and return an error status. If GROUPS is unset, it loses its special properties, even if it is subsequently reset.
HISTCMD	The history number, or index in the history list, of the current command. If HISTCMD is unset, it loses its special properties, even if it is subsequently reset.

TABLE 15.3 Continued

Shell Variable	Effects
HOSTNAME	Automatically set to the name of the current host.
HOSTTYPE	Automatically set to a string that uniquely describes the type of machine on which bash is executing.
LINENO	Each time this parameter is referenced, the shell substitutes a decimal number representing the current sequential line number (starting with 1) within a script or function. When not in a script or function, the value substituted is not guaranteed to be meaningful. If LINENO is unset, it loses its special properties, even if it is subsequently reset.
MACHTYPE	Automatically set to a string that fully describes the system type on which bash is executing, in the standard GNU cpu-company-system format.
OLDPWD	The previous working directory as set by the cd command.
OPTARG	The value of the last option argument processed by the getopts builtin command.
OPTIND	The index of the next argument to be processed by the getopts builtin command.
OSTYPE	Automatically set to a string that describes the operating system on which bash is executing.
PIPESTATUS	An array variable containing a list of exit status values from the processes in the most recently executed foreground pipeline (which may contain only a single command).
PPID	The process ID of the shell's parent. This variable is read-only.
PWD	The current working directory as set by the cd command.
RANDOM	Each time this parameter is referenced, a random integer between 0 and 32767 is generated. The sequence of random numbers may be initialized by assigning a value to RANDOM. If RANDOM is unset, it loses its special properties, even if it is subsequently reset.
REPLY	Set to the line of input read by the read builtin command when no arguments are supplied.
SECONDS	Each time this parameter is referenced, the number of seconds since shell invocation is returned. If a value is assigned to SECONDS, the value returned upon subsequent references is the number of seconds since the assignment plus the value assigned. If SECONDS is unset, it loses its special properties, even if it is subsequently reset.
SHELLOPTS	A colon-separated list of enabled shell options. Each word in the list is a valid argument for the -o option to the set builtin command. The options contained in/displayed by SHELLOPTS are those reported as being on by the command set -o. If this variable is in the environment when bash starts up, each shell option in the list will be enabled before reading any startup files. This variable is read-only.
SHLVL	Incremented by one each time an instance of bash is started.
UID	Expands to the user ID of the current user, initialized at shell startup. This variable is read-only.

TABLE 15.3 Continued

Shell Variable	Effects
BASH_ENV	If this parameter is set when bash is executing a shell script, its value is interpreted as a filename containing commands to initialize the shell, as in ~/.bashrc. The value of BASH_ENV is subjected to parameter expansion, command substitution, and arithmetic expansion before being interpreted as a filename. PATH is not used to search for the resultant filename.
CDPATH	The search path for the cd command. This is a colon-separated list of directories in which the shell looks for destination directories specified by the cd command. A sample value is ".:~:/usr".
COLUMNS	Used by the select builtin command to determine the terminal width when printing selection lists. Automatically set upon receipt of a SIGWINCH.
COMPREPLY	An array variable from which bash reads the possible completions generated by a shell function invoked by the programmable completion facility.
FCEDIT	The default editor for the fc builtin command.
FIGNORE	A colon-separated list of suffixes to ignore when performing filename completion. A filename whose suffix matches one of the entries in FIGNORE is excluded from the list of matched filenames. A sample value is ".o:~".
GLOBIGNORE	A colon-separated list of patterns defining the set of filenames to be ignored by pathname expansion. If a filename matched by a pathname expansion pattern also matches one of the patterns in GLOBIGNORE, it is removed from the list of matches.
HISTCONTROL	If set to a value of ignorespace, lines which begin with a space character are not entered on the history list. If set to a value of ignoredups, lines matching the last history line are not entered. A value of ignoreboth combines the two options. If unset, or if set to any other value than those documented here, all lines read by the parser are saved on the history list, subject to the value of HISTIGNORE. This variable's function is superseded by HISTIGNORE. The second and subsequent lines of a multi-line compound command are not tested and are added to the history regardless of the value of HISTCONTROL.
HISTFILE	The name of the file in which command history is saved (see HISTORY variable). The default value is ~/.bash_history. If unset, the command history is not saved when an interactive shell exits.
HISTFILESIZE	The maximum number of lines contained in the history file. When this variable is assigned a value, the history file is truncated, if necessary, to contain no more than that number of lines. The default value is 500. The history file is also truncated to this size after writing it when an interactive shell exits.
HISTIGNORE	A colon-separated list of patterns used to decide which command lines should be saved on the history list. Each pattern is anchored at the beginning of the line and must match the complete line. (No implicit * is appended.) Each pattern is tested against the line after the checks specified by HISTCONTROL are applied. In addition to the normal shell pattern matching characters, & matches the previous history line. & may be escaped using a backslash (\); the backslash is removed before attempting a match. The

15

TABLE 15.3 Continued

Shell Variable	Effects
	second and subsequent lines of a multiline compound command are not tested, and are added to the history regardless of the value of HISTIGNORE.
HISTSIZE	The number of commands to remember in the command history (see HISTORY variable). The default value is 500.
HOME	The home directory of the current user; the default argument for the cd builtin command. The value of this variable is also used when performing tilde expansion.
HOSTFILE	Contains the name of a file in the same format as /etc/hosts that should be read when the shell needs to complete a hostname. The list of possible hostname completions may be changed while the shell is running; the next time hostname completion is attempted after the value is changed, bash adds the contents of the new file to the existing list. If HOSTFILE is set, but has no value, bash attempts to read /etc/hosts to obtain the list of possible hostname completions. When HOSTFILE is unset, the hostname list is cleared.
IFS	The internal field separator that is used for word splitting after expansion and to split lines into words with the read builtin command. The default value is "<space><tab><newline>".
IGNOREEOF	Controls the action of an interactive shell on receipt of an EOF character as the sole input. If set, the value is the number of consecutive EOF characters that must be typed as the first characters on an input line before bash exits. If the variable exists but does not have a numeric value, or has no value, the default value is 10. If it does not exist, EOF signifies the end of input to the shell.
INPUTRC	The filename for the readline startup file, overriding the default of ~/.inputrc.
LANG	Used to determine the locale category for any category not specifically selected with a variable starting with LC_.
LC_ALL	This variable overrides the value of LANG and any other LC_ variable specifying a locale category.
LC_COLLATE	This variable determines the collation order used when sorting the results of pathname expansion and the behavior of range expressions, equivalence classes, and collating sequences within pathname expansion and pattern matching.
LC_CTYPE	This variable determines the interpretation of characters and the behavior of character classes within pathname expansion and pattern matching.
LC_MESSAGES	This variable determines the locale used to translate doublequoted strings preceded by a $.
LC_NUMERIC	This variable determines the locale category used for number formatting.
LINES	Used by the select built-in command to determine the column length for printing selection lists. Automatically set upon receipt of a SIGWINCH.
MAIL	If this parameter is set to a filename and the MAILPATH variable is not set, bash informs the user of the arrival of mail in the specified file.

TABLE 15.3 Continued

Shell Variable	Effects
`MAILCHECK`	Specifies how often (in seconds) `bash` checks for mail. The default is `60` seconds. When it is time to check for mail, the shell does so before displaying the primary prompt. If this variable is unset or set to something other than a positive integer, the shell disables mail checking.
`MAILPATH`	A colon-separated list of filenames to be checked for mail. The message to be printed when mail arrives in a particular file may be specified by separating the filename from the message with a `?`. When used in the text of the message, `$_` expands to the name of the current mailfile (for example: `MAILPATH='/var/mail/bfox?"You have mail":~/shell-mail?"$_ has mail!"'`.) `bash` supplies a default value for this variable.
`OPTERR`	If set to the value `1`, `bash` displays error messages generated by the `getopts` built-in command. `OPTERR` is initialized to `1` each time the shell is invoked or a shell script is executed.
`PATH`	The search path for commands. It is a colon-separated list of directories in which the shell looks for commands.
`POSIXLY_CORRECT`	If this variable is in the environment when `bash` starts, the shell enters posix mode before reading the startup files, as if the `--posix` invocation option had been supplied. If it is set while the shell is running, `bash` enables posix mode, as if the command `set -o posix` had been executed.
`PROMPT_COMMAND`	If set, the value is executed as a command prior to issuing each primary prompt.
`PS1`	The value of this parameter is expanded and used as the primary prompt string. The default value is `"\s-\v\$ "`. We like to use `"\h:\u \W \! \$ "` or `"\h:\u \W \$ "`.
`PS2`	The value of this parameter is expanded as with `PS1` and used as the secondary prompt string. The default is `"> "`.
`PS3`	The value of this parameter is used as the prompt for the `select` command.
`PS4`	The value of this parameter is expanded as with `PS1`, and the value is printed before each command `bash` displays during an execution trace. The first character of `PS4` is replicated multiple times, as necessary, to indicate multiple levels of indirection. The default is `"+ "`.

`TIMEFORMAT`	The value of this parameter is used as a format string specifying how the timing information for pipelines prefixed with the `time` reserved word should be displayed. The `%` character introduces an escape sequence that is expanded to a time value or other information. The escape sequences and their meanings are as follows; the braces denote optional portions.
	`%%` A literal `%`
	`%[p][l]R` The elapsed time in seconds
	`%[p][l]U` The number of CPU seconds spent in user mode
	`%[p][l]S` The number of CPU seconds spent in system mode
	`%P` The CPU percentage, computed as `(%U + %S) / %R`
	The optional `p` is a digit specifying the precision, the number of digits after a decimal point. A value of `0` forces no decimal point or fraction to be output.

15

TABLE 15.3 Continued

Shell Variable	Effects
	At most, three places after the decimal point may be specified; values of `p` greater than `3` are changed to `3`. If `p` is not specified, the value `3` is used. The optional `l` specifies a longer format, including minutes, of the form `MMmSS.FFs`. The value of `p` determines whether the fraction is included. If this variable is not set, `bash` acts as if it had the value `$'\nreal\t%3lR\nuser\t%3lU\nsys%3lS'`. If the value is `null`, no timing information is displayed. A trailing newline is added when the format string is displayed.
`TMOUT`	If set to a value greater than zero, `TMOUT` is treated as the default timeout for the read built-in. The select command terminates if input does not arrive after `TMOUT` seconds when input is coming from a terminal. In an interactive shell, the value is interpreted as the number of seconds to wait for input after issuing the primary prompt. `bash` terminates after waiting for that number of seconds if input does not arrive.
`auto_resume`	This variable controls how the shell interacts with the user and job control. If this variable is set, single word simple commands without redirections are treated as candidates for resumption of an existing stopped job. No ambiguity is allowed; if more than one job begins with the string typed, the job most recently accessed is selected. The name of a stopped job, in this context, is the command line used to start it. If set to the value `exact`, the string supplied must match the name of a stopped job exactly; if set to `substring`, the string supplied needs to match a substring of the name of a stopped job. The `substring` value provides functionality analogous to the `%?` job identifier. If set to any other value, the supplied string must be a prefix of a stopped job's name; this provides functionality analogous to the `%` job identifier.
`histchars`	Two or three characters that control history expansion and tokenization. The first character is the history expansion character, the character that signals the start of a history expansion; normally this is the character `!`. The second character is the quick substitution character, which is used as shorthand for rerunning the previous command entered, substituting one string for another in the command. The default is `^`. The optional third character is the character that indicates that the remainder of the line is a comment when found as the first character of a word, normally `#`. The history comment character disables history substitution for the remaining words on the line. It does not necessarily cause the shell parser to treat the rest of the line as a comment.

TABLE 15.4 The tcsh Reserved Shell Variables

Shell Variable	Effects
addsuffix	Controls addition of / to the end of directory paths and spaces after normal filenames when expanded by shell filename autocompletion.
afsuser	If set, this is the username to autologout under Kerberos authentication.
ampm	If set, shows time in 12-hour AM/PM format.
argv	The list of arguments passed to the shell on startup.
autocorrect	If set, attempts to fix command misspellings.
autoexpand	If set, passes command completion attempts through the expand-history processor. (See the tcsh man page for more details.)
autolist	If set, lists possible expansions for autocompletion if the expansion is ambiguous. If the value is set to ambiguous, lists possibilities only when an autocompletion attempt does not add any new characters.
autologout	The number of minutes of inactivity before autologout. Optionally, the number of minutes before automatic locking of the terminal.
backslash_quote	If set, backslashes (\ characters) are automatically inserted before any backslash or quote character in a command completion.
cdpath	A list of directories in which cd should look for subdirectories if they aren't in the current working directory.
color	If set, enables color display for the ls command and shell built-in command ls-F.
command	If set, contains the command that was passed to the shell with a -c flag.
complete	If set to enhance, completion ignores filename case and considers periods, hyphens, and underscores to be word separators, and hyphens and underscores to be equivalent.
correct	If set to cmd, attempts automatic spelling correction for commands. If set to complete, commands are automatically completed. If set to all, the entire command line is corrected.
cwd	The full path of the current working directory.
dextract	If set, pushd +*n* extracts the *n*th subdirectory from the stack, rather than rotating it to the top.
dirsfile	The default location in which dirs -S and dirs -L look for their history.
dirstack	An array of all directories in the directory stack.
dspmbyte	If set to euc, enables display and editing of EUC-Kanji (Japanese) code. If set to sjis, enables display and editing of Shift-JIS (Japanese) code. Other options are available—see the tcsh man page for more details.
dunique	If set, pushd removes any instances of the pushed directory from the stack, before pushing it onto the top of the stack.
echo	If set, each command and its arguments are echoed to the terminal before being executed.
echo_style	The style of the echo built-in. May be set to bsd, sysv, both, or none to control the behavior of the echo command. See the tcsh man page for more details on behavior affected.
edit	If set, allows command-line editing.
ellipsis	If set, use an ellipsis to represent portions of the path that won't fit in the prompt.

15

TABLE 15.4 Continued

Shell Variable	Effects
`fignore`	List of filename suffixes to be ignored in completion attempts.
`filec`	An unused `tcsh` shell variable, included to maintain backward compatibility with `csh`, which used this variable to control whether completion should be used.
`gid`	The user owning the shell's real group ID.
`group`	The user owning the shell's group name.
`histchars`	A string determining the characters used in history substitution. The first character replaces the default `!` character, and the second replaces the default `^` character.
`histdup`	Controls handling of duplicate entries in the history list. If set to `all`, only unique history events are entered into the history. If set to `prev`, a run of identical commands is reduced to a single entry in the history list. If set to `erase`, a repeat of a command already in the history list removes the previous occurrence from the history.
`histfile`	The default location in which `history -S` and `history -L` look for a history file. If unset, `~/.history` is used.
`histlit`	If set, the shell built-in, editor commands, and history-saving mechanism use the literal (unexpanded) form of lines in the history list.
`history`	The first word indicates the number of history events to save. The optional second word indicates a format for printing the history. See the `tcsh` man page for more details on format control strings.
`home`	Initialized to the home directory of the user. Command-line expansion of `~` refers to this variable for its action.
`ignoreeof`	If set to the empty string or `0` and the input is a terminal, an end-of-file command sent to the terminal causes the shell to print an error rather than exit.
`implicitcd`	If set, the shell treats a directory name entered on the command line as though it were entered as the argument of a `cd` command.
`inputmode`	Can be set to insert or overwrite to control the behavior of command-line editing.
`listflags`	Contains command-line flags to include with any used when issuing the `ls-F` shell built-in.
`listjobs`	If set, all current jobs are listed when a running job is suspended.
`listlinks`	If set, the `ls-F` shell built-in command shows the time of file to which symbolic links point.
`listmax`	The maximum number of items that the list-choices command-line editor and autocompletion will list without prompting.
`loginsh`	Set by the shell if it is a login shell.
`logout`	Set by the shell to `normal` before a normal logout, `automatic` before an automatic logout, and `hangup` if the shell was killed by a hangup signal (typically generated by `kill -HUP`, or by a terminal connection being interrupted rather than cleanly exited).

TABLE 15.4 Continued

Shell Variable	Effects
mail	The name of the files or directories to check for incoming mail. See both the tcsh and mail man pages for more information on the behaviors controlled by this variable.
matchbeep	Controls whether and when command-line completion rings the bell. Setting it to never prevents all beeps. nomatch beeps when there is no current match. ambiguous beeps when there are multiple matches. notunique beeps when there is an exact match, as well as other longer matches. If unset, the behavior is the same as ambiguous.
nobeep	If set, beeping is completely disabled.
noclobber	If set, the shell attempts to prevent output redirection from overwriting existing files. See the tcsh man page for more details.
noglob	If set, filename substitution and directory substitution are inhibited. Normally used only as a performance enhancement for shell scripts where filenames are already known.
nokanji	If set, disables kanji support so that the meta key is used.
nonomatch	If set, a filename or directory substitution that doesn't match any files does not cause an error.
nostat	A list of directories, or patterns that match directories, that should not be examined for matches during completion attempts.
notify	If set, announces job completions immediately rather than waiting until just before the next command prompt appears.
owd	The previous working directory.
path	A list of directories in which to look for executable commands. The path shell variable is set at startup from the PATH environment variable.
printexitvalue	If set and a program exits with a nonzero status, prints the status.
prompt	The string that is printed as the prompt for command-line input. This can contain both literal strings for display as well as a number of special patterns indicating the substitution of everything from the current directory to the username. See the tcsh man page for the (rather extensive) list of options available.
prompt2	The string to use for the inner prompt in while and foreach loops. The same format sequences as used in the prompt variable may be used in prompt2.
prompt3	The string to use for prompting regarding automatic spelling corrections. The same format sequences as used in the prompt variable may be used in prompt2.
promptchars	If set, specifies a pair of characters to substitute between for a shell prompt when a normal user and when su-ed to the super user.
pushdtohome	If set, pushd without any arguments is equivalent to pushd ~.
pushdsilent	If set, pushd and popd don't print the directory stack.
recexact	If set, completion is finished with an exact match even if a longer one is available.

TABLE 15.4 Continued

Shell Variable	Effects
`recognize_only_executables`	If set, command listings display only executable files in the path.
`rmstar`	If set, the user is prompted before `rm *` is allowed to execute.
`rprompt`	The string to print on the right side of the screen when the prompt is displayed on the left. This prompt accepts the same formatting controls as the prompt variable. In your author's opinion, this is a bizarre shell capability.
`savedires`	If set, the shell does a `dirs -S` before exiting.
`savehist`	If set, the shell does a `history -S` before exiting.
`sched`	The format in which the `sched` built-in prints scheduled events. The string format is the same as that for `prompt`.
`shell`	The file in which the executable shell resides.
`shlvl`	The nested depth of the current shell beneath the login shell for this session.
`status`	The status returned by the last command to exit.
`symlinks`	Can be set to several different values to control the resolution of symbolic links. See the `tcsh` man page for more details.
`tcsh`	The version number of the `tcsh` shell.
`term`	The terminal type currently being used to work in the shell.
`time`	If set to a number, executes the `time` built-in after any command that takes longer than that number of seconds. Can also control the format of the output of the time commands so executed. See the `tcsh` man page for further information.
`tperiod`	The period, in minutes, between executions of the `tcsh` special alias, `periodic`.
`tty`	The name of the `tty` for the current terminal, or `empty` if the current shell is not attached to a terminal.
`uid`	The user's real numeric user ID.
`user`	The user's login name.
`verbose`	If set, causes the words of each command to be printed after any history substitution. Can be set on startup by executing the shell with the `-v` command.
`version`	The shell's version ID stamp, as well as a considerable amount of information regarding compile-time options that were specified when the shell was compiled. See the `tcsh` man page for more information on interpreting the output.
`visiblebell`	If set, flashes the screen instead of using an audible terminal bell.
`watch`	A list of user/terminal pairs to watch for logins and logouts.
`who`	The format string for `watch` messages. See the `tcsh` man page for specific format information.
`wordchars`	A list of nonalphanumeric characters to be considered part of a word by the command-line editor.

The use of bash and tcsh reserved environment variables is similar in each shell: Values that the shells set may be read and used in commands, and the values that the user can specify may be set to control certain aspects of the operation of the shell. For example, in tcsh, we like to customize our command-line prompt using the prompt variable:

```
# pwd
/Users/ray/Documents
# set prompt="$HOST $cwd:t \! >"
brezup Documents 151 >
```

In bash, we use the PS1 variable:

```
bash-2.05b$ pwd
/Users/ray/Pictures
bash-2.05b$ PS1='\h:\u \W \! \$ '
brezup:ray Pictures 440 $
```

Some of the options that are controllable in the shells are incredibly specific and provide considerable power only to a subset of users who need their unique functionality. Others, such as the tcsh's visiblebell setting or bash's MAILCHECK variable, allow every user to exert a considerable amount of control and apply significant customizations to their commandline environments.

On the other hand, reserved variables that are automatically set by the shell provide values for you to feed into custom tools and commands that you construct at the command line. The availability of variables such as tcsh's $cwd and bash's $PWD are instrumental in automating repetitive tasks in your environment.

NOTE

The VISUAL and EDITOR environment variables don't specifically affect the shell, but are customarily used to affect the operation of many command-line programs. These are used to suggest appropriate editors to use when some command-line program needs you to edit something, and wants to open an editor in which you can work. The VISUAL variable typically specifies an editor to use when you have screen-formatting capability, and the EDITOR variable is used to specify an editor to use when you are working in a shell that has no formatting capability (think of the difficulty with working in an editor like emacs in the days of paper terminals). Thankfully, this is an almost unheard of situation today, and the VISUAL editor should almost always be available and functional, if you have it set. If you don't have VISUAL or EDITOR set, each application will default to its own preferred editor, which can be confusing.

Alternative Variable Addressing Methods

Both bash and tcsh shell and environment variables can also be addressed in a number of ways other than with the simple $<*variablename*> method used to return the contents of the variable. These alternative addressing methods can provide a range of information about the variable, allowing you to access everything from its contents to a count of the number of characters that it contains. Table 15.5 provides bash alternatives for accessing other information in the shell or other information regarding the variable, such as the number of words in the variable or whether the variable actually has a value. Table 15.6 provides the analogous information for tcsh.

TABLE 15.5 Alternative Variable Addressing Methods for bash

Addressing a Variable As	Returns
$*name* ${*name*} ,	The value of the variable. If the variable contains multiple words, each is separated by a blank. The braces insulate name from characters following it, causing ${zz}ygy to be distinct from $zzygy.
${*name*[*selector*]}	Treats *name* as an array of words and returns only the selected element from the list of words.
$0	Substitutes the name of the shell or of the file from which command input is being read (used in shell scripts).
$*number* ${*number*}	Expands to the *number*th argument on the commandline when the shell was invoked.
$*	Expands to the complete list of arguments passed to the shell/shell script, starting with argument 1. If IFS is set, and the expansion occurs within double quotes (that is, "$*"), the arguments are separated by the first character of the value of the IFS variable.
$@	Expands to the complete list of arguments passed to the shell/shell script, starting with argument 1. If the expansion occurs within double quotes, each command-line argument is output as a separate word, separated by spaces.
$#	Expands to the number of parameters supplied on the command line.
$?	Expands to the status of the most recent foreground command/pipeline.
$~	Expands to the current option flags, including both those set at shell invocation and those set by the set built-in command.
$$	Expands to the process ID of the running shell. In a subshell executed as part of a command by use of parenthesis on the command line, it expands to the process ID of the parent shell, not the subshell.
$!	Expands to the process ID of the most recently executed background job started by this shell.
${#*name*}	Expands to the length, in characters of the value of *name*.
${#@} ${#*}	Expands to the number of command-line parameters passed to the shell.

TABLE 15.5 Continued

Addressing a Variable As	Returns
`${#name[*]}` `${#name[@]}`	Expands to the number of elements in the array *name*. Note that this is not necessarily equal to the maximum array subscript, but instead counts only populated array positions.
`${name:-word}`	Expands to the value of *name* if *name* is set; otherwise expands to *word*.
`${name:-$name2}`	Expands to the value of *name* if *name* is set; otherwise expands to the value of *name2*.
`${name:=word}`	Expands to the value of *name* if *name* is set; otherwise sets *name=word* and expands to *word*.
`${name:?word}`	Expands to the value of *name* if *name* is set; otherwise writes *word* to STDERR. Causes noninteractive shells to exit if an error is generated.
`${name:+word}`	Expands to the value of *word* if *name* is set; otherwise expands to nothing.
`${name:offset:len}`	Expands to a substring of the value of *name*, starting from position *offset* and extending for *len* characters. If name is @, expands to *len* values from the command line parameters, starting with the *offset*th parameter.
`${name:offset}`	Expands to a substring of the value of *name*, starting from position *offset* and extending to the end of the value.

TABLE 15.6 Alternative Variable Addressing Methods for `tcsh`

Addressing a Variable As	Returns
`$name` `${name}`	The value of the variable. If the variable contains multiple words, each is separated by a blank. The braces insulate name from characters following it, causing `${zz}ygy` to be distinct from `$zzygy`.
`$name[selector]` `${name[selector]}`	Treats name as an array of words and returns only the selected element from the list of words.
`$0`	Substitutes the name of the file from which command input is being read (used in shell scripts).
`$number` `${number}`	Equivalent to `$argv[number]`. Remember that `argv` is a variable containing an array of command-line arguments passed to the shell.
`$*`	Equivalent to the `$argv` array.
`$?name` `${?name}`	Substitutes `1` if variable *name* is set; `0` if it is not (that is, true or false, depending on whether the variable exists).
`$?0`	Substitutes `1` if the name of the program running the shell is known. This is specifically applicable to shell scripts and is always `0` for interactive shells.

15

TABLE 15.6 Continued

Addressing a Variable As	Returns
`$#name`	Substitutes the number of words in *name*.
`${#name}`	
`$#`	Equivalent to `$#argv`.
`$%name`	Substitutes the number of characters in *name*.
`${%name}`	
`$?`	Expands to the status of the most recent foreground command/pipeline. Equivalent to the `$status` variable.
`$$`	Substitutes the process number of the parent shell.
`$!`	Substitutes the process number of the most recent background process started by the shell.
`$<`	Substitutes a line from `STDIN`. This can be used to read input from the keyboard into a shell script.

Variable Substitution Modifiers

Along with the capability to set variables to specific values and to manipulate variable values by the use of external programs, the shell also contains some capability to modify variables internally as well. This capability is mainly targeted to modification of command, filename, and path-like contents in variables. For example, this allows you to parse the extension part of a filename off a file with a name such as `myfile.jpg`—keeping either the extension, `jpg`, or the main name, `myfile`.

In `tcsh` these manipulations are an independent mechanism layered on top of the assorted variable addressing methods and effected by appending to the variable one or more sets of a colon followed by a modifier string.

In `bash` these manipulations are handled by a set of substitution methods that are part of the variable addressing and expansion syntax. The `tcsh` way of doing it is much less powerful than the `bash` way, but it's also far more readable and easier to remember for the sorts of manipulations that you'd do at the command line or in simple shell scripts. This is one of the areas of difference in which `tcsh` fans typically feel that `bash` is a highly unfriendly user environment.

Because the `tcsh` syntax is easier to follow, we'll cover it first this time around. Table 15.7 shows the `tcsh` variable substitution modifiers and their effects. Table 15.8 shows `bash` equivalents where available and some of the syntax of `bash`'s more general substitution methods.

TIP

If the contents of these tables look intimidating, read ahead to the examples, and then come back here to see more specifically what was done. These are really quite powerful capabilities of the shell, and ones that you won't want to be without. They're also not nearly as confusing to use, as they are to explain!

TABLE 15.7 Shell and Environment Variable Substitution :<*modifier*> Options

Modifier String	Effect
h	Removes a trailing pathname component, leaving the head.
t	Removes all leading path components, leaving only the trailing file component.
r	Removes a filename extension .xxx, leaving the head portion of the filename before this.
e	Removes everything from a filename except for the extension.
u	Changes the case of the first lowercase letter to uppercase.
l	Changes the case of the first uppercase letter to lowercase.
s/l/r/	Substitutes l for r. l can be any simple string, as can r.
g	Applies the next modifier to each word, rather than just to the first occurrence.
a	Applies the next modifier as many times as possible to a single word. Beware of creating modification loops with this option.

TABLE 15.8 bash Shell and Environment Variable Substitution :<*modifier*> Options

Modifier String	Effect
${*name*%/*}	Removes a trailing pathname component from *name*, leaving the head. This is equivalent to tcsh's <*variable*>:h.
${*name*##*/}	Removes all leading path components from *name*, leaving only the trailing file component. This is equivalent to tcsh's <*variable*>:t.
${*name*%.+([!/])}	Removes a filename extension such as .xxx from name, leaving the head portion of the filename that occurs before this. This is equivalent to tcsh's <*variable*>:r.
${*name*##*.}	Removes everything from filename *name* except for the extension. This works unless the filename has no extension, but was specified in a path format in which one or more directories have extensions (periods in their names). In that case, it will return the portion of the path after the rightmost period in the full pathname. This is almost equivalent (with the exception of where it doesn't work) to tcsh's <*variable*>:e.
${*name*%*pattern*}	Expands to the value of *name*, with the shortest match to *pattern* removed from the right-hand side. This substituion is how the head-of-a-path operator at the beginning of this table is constructed.
${*name*[@]%*pattern*}	Expands to a list of all values of the array *name*, with the shortest match to *pattern* removed from the right hand side of each.
${*name*%%*pattern*}	Expands to the value of *name*, with the longest match to *pattern* removed from the right-hand side.
${*name*[@]%%*pattern*}	Expands to a list of all values of the array *name*, with the longest match to *pattern* removed from the right-hand side of each.
${*name*#*pattern*}	Expands to the value of *name*, with the shortest match to *pattern* removed from the left-hand side.
${*name*[@]#paittern}	Expands to a list of all values of the array *name*, with the shortest match to *pattern* removed from the left-hand side of each.
${*name*##*pattern*}	Expands to the value of *name*, with the longest match to *pattern* removed from the left-hand side.

TABLE 15.8 Continued

Modifier String	Effect
`${name[@]##pattern}`	Expands to a list of all values of the array *name*, with the longest match to `pattern` removed from the left-hand side of each.
`${name/pat/repl}`	Expands to the value of *name*, with the first occurrence of `pat` replaced by `repl`. If `repl` is ommitted, `pat` is replaced by nothingness, deleting the first occurrence of it from the value.
`${name[@]/pat/repl}`	Expands to a list of all values of the array *name*, with the first occurrence of `pat` replaced by `repl` in each.
`${name//pat/repl}`	Expands to the value of *name*, with all occurrences of `pat` replaced by `repl`.
`${name[@]//pat/repl}`	Expands to a list of all values of the array *name*, with all occurrences of `pat` replaced by `repl` in each.

NOTE

Some `bash` pattern matching expressions are disabled by default. For example the "remove a trailing file extension" syntax shown in Table 15.8 won't work in `bash`'s default configuration because it uses a repeated character class pattern option. (A complete treatment of regular expressions is beyond the scope of this book—the `bash` man page provides some information, but a much better reference is *Mastering Regular Expressions* from O'Reilly Publishing.) To enable extended pattern options, you need to tell `bash` to turn on the `extglob` shell flag-variable by using the command `shopt -s extglob`.

There are a number of additional behaviors that can be configured in `bash` using the `shopt` command, but these move into the realm of being so `bash`-specific that they're best left for a book specifically on `bash`. `bash` users might wonder why these aren't controlled by variables in the shell, as are many other shell behaviors and capabilities. Your authors wonder this too.

As a simple example in `tcsh`, if the variable x contains `/home/ray/testfile.jpg`, we can extract and act upon several different parts of this variable by using the modifiers shown in Table 15.7.

```
brezup Documents ray 152> set x=/home/ray/testfile.jpg
brezup Documents ray 153> echo $x
/home/ray/testfile.jpg
brezup Documents ray 154> echo $x:h
/home/ray
brezup Documents ray 155> echo $x:t
testfile.jpg
brezup Documents ray 156> echo $x:r
/home/ray/testfile
brezup Documents ray 157> echo $x:e
jpg
brezup Documents ray 158> echo $x:u
/Home/ray/testfile.jpg
brezup Documents ray 159> echo $x:s/test/special/
```

```
/home/ray/specialfile.jpg
brezup Documents ray 171> set y=( /home/ray/testfile.jpg /home/ray/filetest.jpg )
brezup Documents ray 172> echo $y
/home/ray/testfile.jpg /home/ray/filetest.jpg
brezup Documents ray 173> echo $y:u
/Home/ray/testfile.jpg /home/ray/filetest.jpg
brezup Documents ray 174> echo $y:gu
/Home/ray/testfile.jpg /Home/ray/filetest.jpg
brezup Documents ray 175> echo $y:au
/HOME/RAY/TESTFILE.JPG /home/ray/filetest.jpg
```

In bash, the analogous commands look like this:

```
brezup:ray ray 499 $ x=/home/ray/testfile.jpg
brezup:ray ray 500 $ echo $x
/home/ray/testfile.jpg
brezup:ray ray 501 $ echo ${x%/*}
/home/ray
brezup:ray ray 502 $ echo ${x##*/}
testfile.jpg
brezup:ray ray 503 $ echo ${x%.+([!/])}
/home/ray/testfile.jpg
brezup:ray ray 504 $ shopt -s extglob
brezup:ray ray 505 $ echo ${x%.+([!/])}
/home/ray/testfile
brezup:ray ray 506 $ echo ${x##*.}
jpg
brezup:ray ray 507 $ echo ${x/test/special}
/home/ray/specialfile.jpg
brezup:ray ray 508 $ y=([0]="/home/ray/testfile.jpg"
➥[1]="/home/ray/filetest.jpg")
brezup:ray ray 509 $ echo ${y/test/special}
/home/ray/specialfile.jpg
brezup:ray ray 510 $ echo ${y[0]/test/special}
/home/ray/specialfile.jpg
brezup:ray ray 511 $ echo ${y[@]/test/special}
/home/ray/specialfile.jpg /home/ray/filespecial.jpg
```

bash doesn't include options analogous to tcsh's capitalization controls as built-in functions. To perform a maniupulation such as changing the case of a value in bash, you would pass the value to an external program such as sed or awk and retrieve the processed value back into a shell variable.

15

NOTE

The four most important things to remember for working with variables in the shell are how to put values into variables, how to make the variables accessible to other shells and programs, the special treatment necessary to use a variable expression as an arithmetic expression, and how to get values back out of the variables you've set.

In `bash`, putting values in just uses the = sign, making them available to other programs uses the `export` command, treating them as math requires the `let` command, and getting values back out uses `$`, with a number of optional extra syntax bits on the expression.

In `tcsh`, these are matched by the `set` command, the `setenv` command, the `@` expression prefix, and the `$` prefix for accessing variables.

Nearly everything you want to do with variables will involve permutations of these.

Command History Substitution

As briefly mentioned earlier, good user shells maintain a history of commands that you have executed at the command line. Although we've only mentioned selecting previous commands out of the history by use of the arrow keys up to this point, both `bash` and `tcsh` actually provide a number of options for the use of previous commands from the history in more sophisticated ways. Primary among these is the ability to select among the previous commands and substitute new information for previous information in the commands.

In `tcsh`, the modification strings for variables detailed earlier can be applied to commands in the history, and some additional history-specific modifiers can be used as well.

In `bash`, the modification expressions for variables don't work on commands in the history, but instead, a set of history-modification commands almost identical to the `tcsh` universal (variable and history) modification set is available for use on the command history.

The basic form of history substitution in both shells is simply the exclamation point, which indicates that a history substitution is to take place at that point in the command line. The characters following the exclamation point specify which item from the history is to be used and, optionally, what modifications need to be made to it. Table 15.9 lists the history item specifiers that can follow the exclamation point history substitution indicator.

TABLE 15.9 History Substitution Options for Both `bash` and `tcsh`

Item Following `!` Character	Meaning to the History Mechanism
n (*n* is a number)	Executes the item with that number out of the history list.
`-`*n* (*n* is a number preceded by a minus sign)	Executes the command *n* items before the current one.

TABLE 15.9 Continued

Item Following ! Character	Meaning to the History Mechanism
# (the pound sign)	The current command. This allows recursion, so be careful! To indicate a modification of the current event, the # sign indicating the current command can be omitted if a substitution modifier is used also.
!	The previous command (equivalent to -1).
s (*s* is a character)	Executes the most recent command whose first word begins with *s*.
?s? (*s* is a string)	The most recent event that contains the string *s*.
Quick substitution (Do Not Prepend the ! Character)	
*^pattern^replacement^*	Reissues the most recent command, replacing the first occurrence of pattern in the command with replacement.

For example, a user's command history (which can be listed by use of the history command) is shown in part here:

```
brezup:ray Documents 543 $ history | tail -5
  539  ls -l
  540  cp file1.ps file1.ps.bak
  541  cp /usr/test/storage/file1.ps ./
  542  lpr file1.ps
  543  history | tail -5
```

We could execute another lpr file1.ps simply by typing **!l** on a command line. Alternatively, !?ora? would execute the copy from /usr/test/storage by matching the string ora from storage. !! would re-execute the most recent command, which is history at command number 544, but will be whatever I issue as command 544 when I'm at the 545 prompt. !-4 would execute the command 4 prior to the current command, which is currently the copy to file1.ps.bak, but this also changes as more commands are issued. !540 reissues the cp to file1.ps.bak, but this resolution doesn't change over time, and !540 will always produce that result in this instance of the shell. These are shown here:

```
brezup:ray Documents 544 $ !l
lpr file1.ps
brezup:ray Documents 545 $ !?ora?
cp /usr/test/storage/file1.ps ./
brezup:ray Documents 546 $ !!
cp /usr/test/storage/file1.ps ./
brezup:ray Documents 547 $ !-4
history | tail -5
  543  history | tail -5
  544  lpr file1.ps
```

```
  545  cp /usr/test/storage/file1.ps ./
  546  cp /usr/test/storage/file1.ps ./
  547  history | tail -5
brezup:ray Documents 548 $ !540
cp file1.ps file1.ps.bak
```

These commands can be combined with substitution modifiers as detailed earlier to further reduce the amount of typing effort needed. In the history, `bash` doesn't use its variable substitution syntax, and instead uses the same `:`*<modifier>* syntax that `tcsh` does. See the `tcsh` variable substitution modifiers in Table 15.7 for history substitution modifiers that work in `bash`:

```
brezup:ray Documents 549 $ !?ora?:s/1/2/
cp /usr/test/storage/file2.ps ./
brezup:ray Documents 550 $ !540:gs/1/2
cp file2.ps file2.ps.bak
brezup:ray Documents 551 $ !540:r.newbak
cp file1.ps file1.ps.newbak
```

Table 15.10 shows some `history`-specific `:`*<modifier>* strings that can be applied to history substitutions.

TABLE 15.10 History-Specific `:<modifier>` Options Available in both `bash` and `tcsh`

Modifier String	Action
`&`	Repeat the previous substitution in this position.
`p`	Print out a history substitution with expanded substitutions, rather than execute the command.
`q`	Quote the value after this modification, preventing further modifications.
`0`	The leftmost argument of the command (typically, the command itself).
n	The *n*th argument of the command.
`^`	The first argument, equivalent to `1`. The colon can be omitted from before this modifier.
`$`	The last argument. The colon can be omitted from before this modifier.
`%`	The word matched by an `?s?` search. The colon can be omitted from before this modifier.
x-*y*	A range of arguments from the *x*th to the *y*th.
-*y*	Equivalent to `0`-*y*. In `tcsh` the colon can be omitted from before this modifier.
`*`	Equivalent to `^-$`, but returns nothing if the command is the only argument. The colon can be omitted from before this modifier.
`x*`	Equivalent to `x-$`.
`x-`	Equivalent to `x*`, but omits the last word `$`.

NOTE

These tables and examples cover only the most commonly used history and variable modification options. The bash and tcsh man pages alone would occupy more than 200 pages of this book, and they are tersely written, to say the least. Entire books have been written on effectively using shells, and if you're interested in making the absolute best use of a shell, we recommend that you pick up one book, or even a handful.

Don't let the volume of options available overwhelm you, though. Most people who use Unix don't make use of even 10% of the options shown in the abbreviated discussion here, and are perfectly happy with their productivity at that level. Be aware that these options exist; they can make your life much easier if you find that you need them, but don't feel obliged to try to actually learn them until you do find a need.

Aliases and Shell Functions

The alias command is a simple tool that can help you customize your environment. At its simplest, it is the textual equivalent of the graphical Mac OS icon aliases (or Windows shortcuts) that you're probably already familiar with. alias makes it possible for you specify a new name by which you can refer to an existing command. If you don't like typing history to list your command history, you can use the alias command to make typing h equivalent to typing history.

We could have introduced this command much earlier in the discussion, but the information you have just learned about history and variable substitution makes the alias command much more powerful than just creating alternate names for commands—alias can create alternative names, with alternative options for commands, and simultaneously make preprogrammed modifications to the command and its arguments before invoking the target command itself

At its simplest, the alias command has an almost trivial syntax: In bash it's alias *<newname>=<definition>*, and in tcsh it's alias *<newname> <definition>*. It accepts no command-line options and has no arguments or flags to control it. To alias h so that it calls history as described earlier, simply use alias h='history' (or in tcsh, alias h 'history').

TIP

Single quotes aren't absolutely necessary here, but they are generally used around the thing to which you want to make an alias to prevent variable and history expansion in the alias. You generally want an alias to use variables as they'd expand at the current command-line prompt—that is, when you issue the aliased command, rather than have those variables and substitutions occur when you type the alias command itself.

The real power of being able to compress a collection of typing down into a single manageable command, however, is in what you can do to customize and automate your shell by making use of variable substitutions in those commands. In tcsh this ability is built into the alias command itself, whereas bash makes it available through a separate ability to define functions that behave like (very powerful, but strangely limited in their ability to deal with the command history) `tcsh` aliases. `bash` functions are defined much like aliases, but have the syntax `<funcname>() { <commands>; }` instead of the simpler `alias` syntax.

For example, there are a number of machines in another domain that I access on a regular basis. It's inconvenient to type `slogin oak.cis.ohio-state.edu`, `slogin shoe.cis.ohio-state.edu`, and so on whenever I need to access one of these machines. Using the trivial application of `alias`, I could change `slogin` so that I could type something shorter, such as `scis` instead of `slogin`. That's a minor improvement, but really not all that much help. This would still leave me typing `scis oak.cis.ohio-state.edu`, and so on. Using the power of substitution, however, this can be made much more useful.

In `bash` I can use the shell's capability to parse out command-line parameters into variables named `$<num>` to get at values that I put on the command line after calling a function:

```
brezup:ray ray 506 $ scis() { slogin $1.cis.ohio-state.edu; }
brezup:ray ray 507 $ scis oak
ray@oak.cis.ohio-state.edu's password:
brezup:ray ray 507 $ scis pear
ray@pear.cis.ohio-state.edu's password:
```

The first line of this example defines a function that causes `bash` to execute a little program for me whenever I type `scis`. The program's extremely short, and consists of only the following: parsing off the first argument after the `scis` command; building a new expression that consists of `slogin`, followed by the value of the first argument, with `.cis.ohio-state.edu` appended to the end; and finally executing the command it has built. The result is that when I type `scis <machinename>`, the actual command that the shell executes, after going through all the substitutions, is `slogin <machinename>.cis.ohio-state.edu`.

In `tcsh` I can use similar facilities to get to command-line arguments, or I can alternatively access the command history. This can get a bit more convoluted visually (in terms of how I construct the command), but allows you more flexibility in generating useful aliases on the fly as you're working in the shell. `bash`'s function paradigm is quite a bit more powerful, but requires significantly more forethought to use. For example, in `tcsh`, I can use the `*` modifier to the history (which returns all the arguments from the specified command in the history), executed against the current command in the history (`#`). Using these, I can pass the arguments given to my alias to another command of my choice. Specifically, I could use an alias such as `alias scis 'slogin \!#:*.cis.ohio-state.edu'`. That might look a little ugly the first time you see something like it, but it all breaks down into understandable parts with just a little thought.

`tcsh` supports using the command-line parameters as `bash` does, but this example should give you an idea of how the command history might be used in constructing useful aliases. In this case, it's using the `!#` history expansion, which expands to the entire current command line as typed so far, and the `:*` modifier that pares off the command-word portion and returns the rest of the arguments. The backslash before the history expansion prevents it from being expanded immediately at the prompt when I entered the `alias` command. Now, all I have to do is type `scis oak`, and the `alias` command expands the command to `slogin !#:*.cis.ohio-state.edu`. The history substitution then replaces the `!#:*` with the argument given to the command, which in this case is `oak`. The final command executed is `slogin oak.cis.ohio-state.edu`.

NOTE

Several comments in the tables on history substitution and modifiers relate to the `!#:*` expression suggested here, and can make this less ugly looking. Most notably, if a modifier is acting on the current history event, the # can be omitted, and the : can be omitted before *. This history substitution specifier therefore abbreviates to `!*`, and the alias could therefore be written `alias scis 'slogin \!*.cis.ohio-state.edu'`.

Also, the `!*` substitution specifier substitutes the entire remainder of the command line from the current command. This is fine as long as I type `scis oak`, but if I type `scis oak apple pear`, the expansion is probably not going to be what I want. I could limit it to the first argument to the command with the ^ modifier, or the last argument with the $ modifier, instead of the * all-arguments modifier I have used. It's a little bit sloppy, but I normally find it sufficient to just use the all modifier and to remember to issue commands within the restrictions that doing so imposes. For me, this is easier than remembering to use the proper modifier when I need it, but you're welcome to use whatever you find easiest.

15

NOTE

Nothing in the `bash` documentation suggests that history substitution isn't possible inside functions, but there doesn't seem to be a way to make it work. If you try to build a history-substituting function in `bash`, you'll find that it either substitutes the history at the moment of the function creation rather than at the point when you invoke it, or that it escapes the special characters that should cause history substitution and just prints them out instead of expanding them to the proper substitution. Maybe it's a bug, or maybe we just can't figure out the proper syntax.

Because `bash` undergoes frequent revisions, it's not unusual for portions of the behavior to change between releases. By the time you're reading this, `bash` might support history substitution inside functions as well.

To remove an alias, simply use the `unalias` command on the *<newname>* that you've created for your command. `bash` doesn't seem to have the facility to undefine functions that you've created.

Automating Tasks with Shell Scripts

With as many times as we've mentioned how powerful shell scripting can be and how much time and effort it can save you, you might be expecting that writing shell scripts is going to require dealing with some additional level of complexity on top of what you've already learned. Shell scripts are simple programs that you write in the language of the shell, and if you've made it this far in the book, you've been learning and working in the language of the shell for a few chapters now. If you consider this fact, and the notion that Unix, by design, attempts to abstract the notion of input and output so that everything looks the same to the operating system, you might have a good guess at what we'll say next: That's right—you *already know* how to write shell scripts. There are a few more shell techniques that you can learn to enhance your ability to program the shell, but Unix itself doesn't care whether it's you typing at a command prompt or commands being read out of a file on disk. Everything you've typed so far in working with the shell could have been put in a file, and the computer could have typed it to itself—voilá, a shell script.

At its most trivial, a shell script can be exactly what you type at a prompt to accomplish some set of tasks. If you find that you have a need to repeatedly execute the same commands, you can type them once into a file, make that file executable, and forever after execute them all just by typing the name of the file.

It really is as simple as it sounds, but just in case it's not quite clear yet, an example should help. Consider the following situation: Let's say that every day when you log in to your computer, you like to check the time (with `date`), check to see who's online (using the `who` command), check to see how much space is left on the drive with your home directory (with `df`), and finally check who's most recently sent you mail (with `from` - this command might not work for you on a default install, because it relies on my particular mail setup).

You could type each of these things to a command prompt when you log in to your machine, or you could put them in a file, make it executable, and let the file "type" them for you.

```
brezup:ray Documents 165 $ date
Mon Jun 18 23:35:55 EDT 2003
brezup:ray Documents 166 $ who
joray    ttyp0   Jun 14 18:22   (140.254.12.151)
ray      ttyp1   Jun 18 21:49   (24.95.74.211)
ray      ttyp2   Jun 15 10:00   (rodan.chi.ohio-s)
radman   ttyp3   Jun 18 23:33   (ac9d3e22.ipt.aol)
brezup:ray Documents 167 $ df .
Filesystem    512-blocks     Used    Avail Capacity  Mounted on
/dev/disk0s11   12581856 12224784   357072    97%    /Volumes/Wills_Data
brezup:ray Documents 168 $ from ¦ tail -10
From vanbrink@home.ffni.com  Mon Jun 18 16:20:23 2003
From billp@abraxis.com  Mon Jun 18 17:28:33 2003
From douglas_mille70@hotmail.com  Mon Jun 18 18:34:28 2003
From owner-c-r-ffl@serge.shelfspace.com  Mon Jun 18 19:23:42 2003
From owner-c-r-ffl@serge.shelfspace.com  Mon Jun 18 20:42:53 2003
From owner-c-r-ffl@serge.shelfspace.com  Mon Jun 18 21:24:00 2003
From buckshot@wcoil.com  Mon Jun 18 22:02:15 2003
From jray@poisontooth.com  Mon Jun 18 22:28:56 2003
From jray@poisontooth.com  Mon Jun 18 23:15:28 2003
From owner-c-r-ffl@serge.shelfspace.com  Mon Jun 18 23:34:43 2003
```

```
brezup:ray Documents 169 $ cat > imhere
#!/bin/bash
date
who
df .
from | tail -10
^D

brezup:ray Documents 170 $ chmod 755 imhere
brezup:ray Documents 171 $ ./imhere
Mon Jun 18 23:36:51 EDT 2003
joray     ttyp0    Jun 14 18:22    (140.254.12.151)
ray       ttyp1    Jun 18 21:49    (24.95.74.211)
ray       ttyp2    Jun 15 10:00    (rodan.chi.ohio-s)
Filesystem     512-blocks      Used     Avail Capacity  Mounted on
/dev/disk0s11    12581856 12224784    357072     97%    /Volumes/Wills_Data
From billp@abraxis.com  Mon Jun 18 17:28:33 2003
From douglas_mille70@hotmail.com  Mon Jun 18 18:34:28 2003
From owner-c-r-ffl@serge.shelfspace.com  Mon Jun 18 19:23:42 2003
From owner-c-r-ffl@serge.shelfspace.com  Mon Jun 18 20:42:53 2003
From owner-c-r-ffl@serge.shelfspace.com  Mon Jun 18 21:24:00 2003
From buckshot@wcoil.com  Mon Jun 18 22:02:15 2003
From jray@poisontooth.com  Mon Jun 18 22:28:56 2003
From jray@poisontooth.com  Mon Jun 18 23:15:28 2003
From owner-c-r-ffl@serge.shelfspace.com  Mon Jun 18 23:34:43 2003
From owner-c-r-ffl@serge.shelfspace.com  Mon Jun 18 23:36:48 2003
```

15

As you can see, executing the file `imhere`, containing my commands, produces essentially the same output with much less typing. (The output has a few changes because one user has left the system, and new mail has arrived between the by-hand runs and the execution of the shell script.)

The only part of the `imhere` script that might be confusing is the first line: `#!/bin/bash`. The shell interprets the first line of a shell script in a special manner. If a pattern such as `#!`*`<path to an executable file>`* is found, the executable file named in that line is used as the shell for executing the contents of the script.

NOTE

The C shell, `csh`, and the Bourne shell, `sh`, are probably the best shells for you to write shell scripts in if you think you might be trying to use those scripts on other machines (especially if they might have different versions of Unix), or giving them to other people. Some shells offer somewhat more power in their scripting capability, but `csh` and `sh` are the only shells that can be considered ubiquitous. This might not be a concern if you never intend your scripts to run anywhere but on your own personal machine or on other identically configured Mac OS X boxes. But if you think you might ever use another machine, or are interested in distributing your scripts to other people, you can't rely on any specialty shells being available.

In the world of real programmers and writers of fancy shell scripts, we'd be considered heretical for including `csh` (or `tcsh`) as a potential shell you might want to script in. The Bourne shell is the shell of choice for tasks that truly must be able to be run anywhere, but it's not a particularly friendly shell language to live in for day-to-day shell use. Some might say it's downright horrific. Because Apple has changed the default user shell to `bash`, many users will want to use it for scripting anyway. If you have the patience to use its complicated variable substitution syntax and function definitions for your work, you'll definitely have quite powerful scripting capabilities at your disposal. If on the other hand you prefer `tcsh`'s less powerful, but considerably more user-friendly style, you're not alone. Despite its Bourne-shell heredity, many long-time Unix users are now calling `bash` the "least-standard" shell because of the sometimes dramatic changes in behavior that occur between versions.

In the end, it all boils down to user preference—don't let anyone tell you that you shouldn't use `bash` because it's too complicated or that you shouldn't use `tcsh` because it isn't complicated enough. If it works for you, and you're comfortable with it, use it.

TIP

In many scripting languages—`tcsh`/`csh`/`bash` shell scripting being no exception—anywhere a `#` appears indicates that the rest of the line is a comment. A `#!` on the first line of a file being executed by the shell is a special comment to the system, indicating which program is the intended interpreter for the script contained in the file.

Single-Line Automation: Combining Commands on the Command Line

Before we go too far with the notion of storing collections of commands in files, however, let's look at what can be done at just the command-line level. You already know about using pipes and variables. These concepts can be combined to produce very powerful expressions directly at the command line, without any need to store the collection of commands in a file.

Consider for a moment the `netpbm` collection of graphics manipulation programs that was installed in Chapter 14, "Command-Line Software Installation and Troubleshooting." Included in the capabilities of the suite are a number of conversions among various file formats, as well as a range of manipulations of the image content itself. With Mac OS, if you want to convert a GIF file into a PICT file, and convert it to four-color grayscale along the way, you have a number of options. You could fire up PhotoShop or GraphicConverter, perform the changes there, and save the file. Alternatively, you could program a conversion filter in DeBabelizer to perform this manipulation for you. With `netpbm`, you can perform the manipulation from the command line as shown in the code following the note.

NOTE

In the following examples, we're using `tcsh` syntax in the running text because it's much easier to read, and considerably easier to translate from `tcsh` into the `bash` version than it is to go the other direction. `bash` equivalents of the code will be called out only in notes.

```
brezup Documents 277> ppmtogif < sage.ppm > sage.gif
ppmtogif: computing colormap...
ppmtogif: 192 colors found
brezup Documents 278> giftopnm  < sage.gif > sage.pnm
brezup Documents 279> ppmtopgm  < sage.pnm > sage.pgm
brezup Documents 280> ppmquant 4 < sage.pgm > sage.pgm2
ppmquant: making histogram...
ppmquant: 120 colors found
ppmquant: choosing 4 colors...
ppmquant: mapping image to new colors...
brezup Documents 281> ppmtopict < sage.pgm2 > sage.pict
ppmtopict: computing colormap...
ppmtopict: 4 colors found
```

Figure 15.1 shows a comparison of the original image `sage.gif`, and the four-color grayscale image, `sage.pict`.

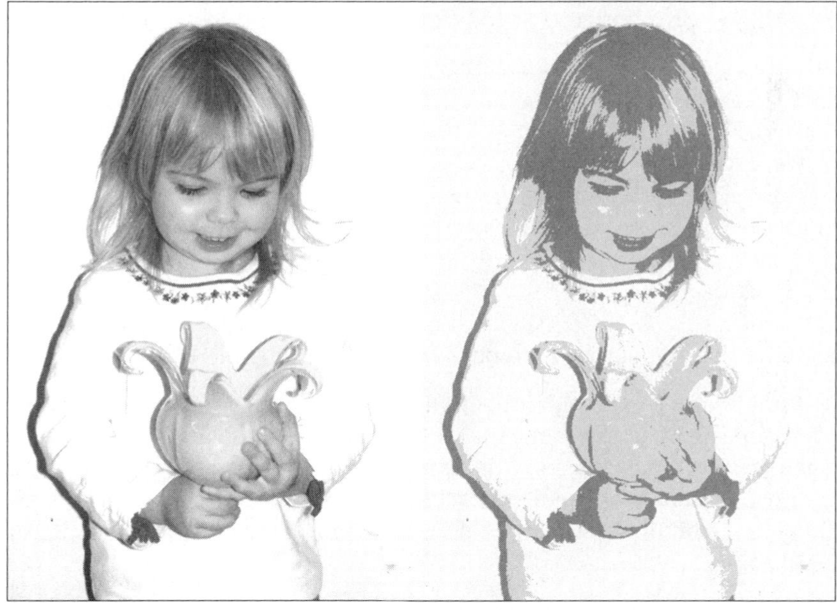

FIGURE 15.1 A comparison of an original file and the result of processing it through one of a number of different `netpbm` filters.

NOTE

The `netpbm` suite provides most of its manipulation facilities on an internal format, variably named `.ppm`, `.pgm`, or `.pnm`. It provides a number of filters that can read data into this format, a number of filters that can act upon and modify the contents of files in this format, and a number of filters that can output into other file formats. Together, these facilities enable a wide range of image formats to be read, manipulated, and written. Additionally, the file format is well documented and simple for a programmer to write code to parse. This makes it easy for a programmer to write her own filters to perform any manipulations that the provided software cannot. If you've installed this suite, refer to the netpbm man pages for considerably more information on the use of netpbm.

From the brief discussion at the beginning of this section, you should already have an idea of how you could combine all that into a single file, if for some reason you wanted to perform that conversion to the sage.gif file over and over and over.

This does not seem to be a very useful thing to automate, and takes quite a bit of typing to boot (although, frankly, not nearly as much work as starting up Photoshop to do something this simple). Let's see what we can do with pipes and shell variables though to cut down on the amount of typing.

First, observe that all the programs are taking the input files on STDIN and are producing output on STDOUT. Unix command-line programs are frequently like this, and it's a very good thing. Using the power of pipes to connect one program's STDOUT to another program's STDIN, we can shorten that collection of commands to a single command line:

```
brezup Documents 287> giftopnm < sage.gif | ppmtopgm | ppmquant 4 |
➥ ppmtopict > sage.pict
ppmquant: making histogram...
ppmquant: 120 colors found
ppmquant: choosing 4 colors...
ppmquant: mapping image to new colors...
ppmtopict: computing colormap...
ppmtopict: 4 colors found
```

I'll let you verify that the output is graphically identical on a file of your own.

You might think that it's probably not very likely that you'll want to perform this single manipulation repeatedly to the same image. However, there are many times when you'd like to be able to perform a collection of manipulations like that on a number of different images. With what you know about shell variables, you can come up with several ways to abstract that command line so that it could be reused for any GIF file. You might try something like this:

```
brezup Documents 288> set infile=sage.gif
brezup Documents 289> giftopnm < $infile | ppmtopgm | ppmquant 4 |
➥ ppmtopict > $infile:r.pict
ppmquant: making histogram...
ppmquant: 120 colors found
ppmquant: choosing 4 colors...
ppmquant: mapping image to new colors...
ppmtopict: computing colormap...
ppmtopict: 4 colors found
```

NOTE

Note how I used the `:r` modifier to the shell variable `$infile` to remove the `.gif` suffix and added text after it to replace it with my new `.pict` suffix.

NOTE

In `bash`, this looks like

```
shopt -s extglob
infile=sage.gif
giftopnm < $infile ¦ ppmtopgm ¦ ppmquant 4 ¦
➥ ppmtopict > ${infile%.+([!/])}.pict
```

Disgusting syntax, yes?

You could simply use new values for `$infile`, and you'd have a reusable command that could perform the same manipulation on any GIF image. It's still too much work though, right? Well, remember aliases? We can further automate things by using an `alias` command to compact that large command-line expression into something more manageable.


```
brezup Documents 290> alias greyconvert 'set infile=\!#:* ; giftopnm < $infile ¦
➥ppmtopgm ¦ ppmquant 4 ¦ ppmtopict > $infile:r.pict '
brezup Documents 291> greyconvert sage.gif

ppmquant: making histogram...
ppmquant: 120 colors found
ppmquant: choosing 4 colors...
ppmquant: mapping image to new colors...
ppmtopict: computing colormap...
ppmtopict: 4 colors found
```

NOTE

Notice how I've used the history substitution `\!#:*` to get the arguments passed into the alias, and then put those arguments (although I only expect one, a filename) into `$infile`?

NOTE

In `bash` we can't do variable expansion in aliases. We also can't do history substitution in functions. To accomplish the `tcsh` equivalent, we have to define a function for `greyconvert` and use the command-line parameters to capture the file to be converted:

```
shopt -s extglob
greyconvert() { infile=$1; giftopnm < $infile ¦ ppmtopgm ¦ ppmquant 4 ¦
➥ ppmtopict > ${infile%.+([!/])}.pict; }
greyconvert sage.gif
```

That command is getting pretty long, isn't it? The good news is that for almost any task in Unix, you can figure out how to build up to an expression like this, just as shown here. Start by figuring out how to do it one step at a time on the command line, and work your way up to an elegant solution that solves the problem for you with as little repetitive work as necessary.

After you've invented useful aliases or functions such as this one for yourself, remember to store them in your `.cshrc`, `.tcshrc`, or `.bashrc` file in your home directory so that you can use them again whenever you log in to your computer.

Multiline Automation: Looping at the Prompt

Creating customized commands that perform special functions such as the `greyconvert` command built in the previous sections is useful, but it still doesn't address the need to automate tasks. For that, we need some sort of looping command, and `bash` and `tcsh` both offer two basic types of loops: the `for` loop and the `while` loop. Both commands repeat a block of shell commands. The first executes it "for each" of its arguments, and the second executes it "while" some condition is true.

Looping in `tcsh`

The `foreach` and `while` shell commands are unlike other shell commands in that they require additional information beyond the first command line. For example, the syntax of the `foreach` command in `tcsh` is

```
foreach <variablename> ( <item list> )
  <first command to execute>
  <second command to execute>
  .
  .
  .
  <nth command to execute>
end
```

The `tcsh` `while` command, on the other hand, has the syntax

```
while ( <comparison> )
  <first command to execute>
  <second command to execute>
  .
  .
  .
  <nth command to execute>
end
```

In the `foreach` command, the *`<item list>`* can be a space-separated list of items, a command that produces a space-separated (or return-separated) list of items, or a command-line wildcard that matches a list of files. As a demonstration, consider a situation in which we want to execute our previous `greyconvert` command on every GIF file in a directory containing many files. This can be accomplished in several ways by the use of the `foreach` command.

Looping in `bash`

The syntax for the `for` command in `bash` is

```
for <variablename> in <words> ; do
  <first command to execute> ;
  <second command to execute> ;
  .
  .
  .
  <nth command to execute> ;
done
```

The `bash` `while` command, on the other hand, has the syntax

```
while <commands> ; do
  <first conditional command to execute> ;
  <second conditional command to execute> ;
  .
  .
  .
  <nth conditional command to execute> ;
done
```

In the `for` command, bash steps throught the list of *<words>* and sets the value of *<variablename>* sequentially to each. After *<variablename>* has been set to any given value from *<words>*, the list of commands is executed. When the final value has been extracted from *<words>* and the commands have been run the final time, the `for` loop terminates.

In the `while` command, `bash` executes *<commands>* (which can be a single word command, or a parenthesized, colon-separated list of commands). If the final command in *<commands>* returns a `true` (`1`) value, the `while` loop executes the conditional commands in the loop. This repeats until the final command in *<commands>* evaluates to `false` (`0`).

Using Looping Constructs at the Command Line

Using looping constructs at the command line is relatively powerful and allows you to execute a collection of commands many times, for many files (again, `tcsh` examples are somewhat clearer to read). The following example uses a wildcard to match all the files of interest in the current directory, and then runs our `greyconvert` alias on each of them:

```
brezup amg 246> ls
AMG_cal-cover.gif          AhMyGoddess-v05.gif        AhMyGoddess-v10-f1.gif
AhMyGoddess-v01-f1.gif     AhMyGoddess-v06-f1.gif     AhMyGoddess-v10-i1.gif
AhMyGoddess-v01.gif        AhMyGoddess-v06.gif        AhMyGoddess-v10-i2.gif
AhMyGoddess-v02-f1.gif     AhMyGoddess-v07-f1.gif     AhMyGoddess-v10-i3.gif
AhMyGoddess-v02.gif        AhMyGoddess-v07.gif        AhMyGoddess-v10.gif
```

15

```
AhMyGoddess-v03-f1.gif     AhMyGoddess-v08-f1.gif     amg-nt0694_cover.gif
AhMyGoddess-v03.gif        AhMyGoddess-v08.gif        amg-nt0694_i1.gif
AhMyGoddess-v04-f1.gif     AhMyGoddess-v09-f1.gif     amg-nt0694_i2.gif
AhMyGoddess-v04.gif        AhMyGoddess-v09.gif
AhMyGoddess-v05-f1.gif     AhMyGoddess-v10-b.gif
brezup amg 247> foreach testfile ( *.gif )
foreach -> greyconvert $testfile
foreach -> end
ppmquant: making histogram...
ppmquant: 165 colors found
ppmquant: choosing 4 colors...
ppmquant: mapping image to new colors...
ppmtopict: computing colormap...
ppmtopict: 4 colors found
ppmquant: making histogram...
ppmquant: 159 colors found
.
.
.
ppmquant: making histogram...
ppmquant: 163 colors found
ppmquant: choosing 4 colors...
ppmquant: mapping image to new colors...
ppmtopict: computing colormap...
ppmtopict: 4 colors found
brezup amg 248> ls
AMG_cal-cover.gif          AhMyGoddess-v05-f1.pict    AhMyGoddess-v10-b.gif
AMG_cal-cover.pict         AhMyGoddess-v05.gif        AhMyGoddess-v10-b.pict
AhMyGoddess-v01-f1.gif     AhMyGoddess-v05.pict       AhMyGoddess-v10-f1.gif
AhMyGoddess-v01-f1.pict    AhMyGoddess-v06-f1.gif     AhMyGoddess-v10-f1.pict
AhMyGoddess-v01.gif        AhMyGoddess-v06-f1.pict    AhMyGoddess-v10-i1.gif
.
.
.
AhMyGoddess-v04-f1.gif     AhMyGoddess-v08.pict       amg-nt0694_i1.gif
AhMyGoddess-v04-f1.pict    AhMyGoddess-v09-f1.gif     amg-nt0694_i1.pict
AhMyGoddess-v04.gif        AhMyGoddess-v09-f1.pict    amg-nt0694_i2.gif
AhMyGoddess-v04.pict       AhMyGoddess-v09.gif        amg-nt0694_i2.pict
AhMyGoddess-v05-f1.gif     AhMyGoddess-v09.pict
```

In this example, the `foreach testfile ( *.gif )` line could have been replaced with the following variants to achieve identical results:

```
foreach testfile ( `ls *.gif` )
```

```
foreach testfile ( AMG_cal-cover.gif AhMyGoddess-v01-f1.gif ...
➥ amg-nt0694_i2.gif )
```

NOTE

The second variant should be understood to contain a list of *all* GIF files in the directory, not just the three shown. The presence and direction of the single back quotes in the first line are also critical. Single back quotes around a command on the command line cause that command to be executed and its results to be *substituted into the current command line in the place of* the quoted command.

NOTE

In bash, the for command looks much the same:

```
for testfile in *.gif ; do
greyconvert $testfile
done
```

In bash, other equivalent expressions are

```
for testfile in `ls *.gif` ; do greyconvert $testfile; done

for testfile in AMG_cal-cover.gif AhMyGoddess-v01-f1.gif ...
➥ amg-nt0694_i2.gif ; do greyconvert $testfile ; done
```

The `while` command works similarly, executing its code block while some <*condition*> holds:

```
brezup Documents 249> set x = 10
brezup Documents 250> while ( $x > 0 )
while -> echo $x
while -> @ x = ( $x - 1 )
while -> end
10
9
8
7
6
5
4
3
2
1
brezup Documents 251> echo $x
0
```

15

NOTE

In bash, this would be written as follows:

```
x=10
while (( $x > 0 )) ; do
echo $x ;
let x=$x-1 ;
done
```

The double parentheses are required around the comparison portion of the while statement to cause $x > 0 to be evaluated arithmetically and a true or false value to be returned. One or more commands could also be embedded in the while condition as well—for example, the following while command produces identical results to the preceding code:

```
x=10;
while ( echo $x ; (( $x > 0 )) ) ; do let x=$x-1; done
```

This example obviously doesn't have much day-to-day applicability. Most while expressions that are actually useful do things like watch for particular events to occur, such as the existence of temporary files or disk space usage of more or less than some value. None of these is particularly easy to demonstrate in a text-only format such as a book, but we expect that you'll get the idea fairly quickly. Table 15.11 shows the conditional operators that can be used to construct the *<condition>* part of while loops and if conditional statements.

TABLE 15.11 Logical, Arithmetical, and Comparison Operators

<table>
<tr><th>Operator or Symbol</th><th>Function</th></tr>
<tr><td>||</td><td>Boolean OR arguments.</td></tr>
<tr><td>&&</td><td>Boolean AND arguments.</td></tr>
<tr><td>|</td><td>Bitwise Boolean OR.</td></tr>
<tr><td>^</td><td>Bitwise Exclusive OR.</td></tr>
<tr><td>&</td><td>Bitwise Boolean AND.</td></tr>
<tr><td>==</td><td>Equality comparison of arguments ($x == $y is true if the value in $x equals the value in $y).
Compares arguments as strings.</td></tr>
<tr><td>!=</td><td>Negated equality comparison of arguments ($x != $y is true if the value in $x is not equal to the value in $y).
Compares arguments as strings.</td></tr>
<tr><td>=~</td><td>tcsh-only: pattern-matching equality comparison (matches shell wildcards).
Compares arguments as strings.</td></tr>
<tr><td>!~</td><td>tcsh-only: pattern-matching negated equality comparison.
Compares arguments as strings.</td></tr>
<tr><td><=</td><td>Less than or equal to.</td></tr>
<tr><td>>=</td><td>Greater than or equal to.</td></tr>
<tr><td><</td><td>Less than.</td></tr>
</table>

TABLE 15.11 Continued

Operator or Symbol	Function
>	Greater than.

<<	Bitwise shift left. To avoid the shell interpreting this as redirection, it must be in a parenthesized subexpression.
	For example,
	`set y = 32;`
	`@ x = ( $y << 2 )`

>>	Bitwise shift right. See preceding comment.
+	Adds arguments.
-	Subtracts arguments.
*	Multiplies arguments.
/	Divides arguments.
%	Modulus operator (divides and reports remainder).
!	Negates argument.
~	Ones complement (bitwise negation) of argument.
(	Opens parenthesized subexpression for higher-order evaluation.
)	Closes parenthesized subexpression for higher-order evaluation.

Another common use for the `while` command is to create infinite loops in the shell. This is a way to do things such as cause a shell command to execute over and over, potentially creating something like a "drop directory" that automatically processes files that are copied to it. For example, if we want to create a directory into which we could copy GIF files, and any file copied into it would have the `greyconvert` process run on it automatically, and then the GIF files would be deleted, we might try something like the following:

```
brezup Documents 252> while (1)
while -> foreach testfile (*.gif)
while -> greyconvert $testfile
while -> rm $testfile
while -> end
while -> sleep 60
while -> end
```

NOTE

The first four lines, with the `while->` prompt, are actually part of the `foreach` command, but it doesn't display its prompt while the `while->` prompt is active.

This `while` command attempts to loop perpetually (the value of `1` is `true` for the purposes of a comparison expression) and to internally execute our previous `foreach` loop to convert any files that match the `*.gif` pattern in the current directory. An `rm` command has been added to the `foreach` loop to remove the GIF file after it has been converted. The `sleep 60` command after the `foreach` command's `end` causes the `while` loop to pause for `60` seconds before going on to its `end` statement and relooping to the top of the `while`.

Unfortunately, from the command line, this does not quite work properly in all cases; when there are no files that match `*.gif`, the `foreach` line fails without creating its loop, and the `end` on line 4 is mistaken as intended to `end` the `while` loop.

NOTE

In `bash`, the equivalent `while` loop looks like this:

```
while (( 1 )) ; do
> for testfile in `ls *.gif` ; do
> greyconvert $testfile ;
> rm $testfile ;
> done
> sleep 60 ;
> done
```

`bash` doesn't suffer from the same problem creating the inner `for` loop that `tcsh` has with the `foreach`, so this actually turns into a useful piece of command-line code.

Thankfully, even in `tcsh` you can work around this problem by applying the final topic in our discussion of shell scripts.

Storing Your Automation in Files: Proper Scripts

With all the power available to you directly at the command line, the move to putting shell scripts in files should seem almost anticlimactic in its lack of complexity. As mentioned at the beginning of this chapter, anything that you can type on the command line, you can put in a file, and the system will quite happily execute it for you if you make the file executable. It really is that simple. There is really little more to say, except that putting your script in a file allows you to conveniently separate parts of the execution into separate shells, preventing conflicts such as those just demonstrated earlier with the `while` and `foreach` loops.

Any script that is put in a file and directly executed (rather than `source`d in your current shell) creates its own shell in which to execute. To use this to make the previous example function properly, we can put the `foreach` section of the command into its own file:

```
brezup Documents 253> cat > greyconv.csh
#!/bin/csh
foreach testfile (*.gif)
greyconvert $testfile
rm $testfile
end
brezup Documents 254> chmod 755 greyconv.csh
brezup Documents 255> ls -l greyconv.csh
-rwxr-xr-x  1 ray  staff  75 Jun 23 01:58 greyconv.csh
brezup Documents 256> cat greyconv.csh
#!/bin/csh
```

```
foreach testfile (*.gif)
greyconvert $testfile
rm $testfile
end
```

Then our perpetual `while` command can be run as

```
brezup Documents 257> while (1)
while -> ./greyconv.csh
while -> sleep 60
while -> end
```

NOTE

Of course, these examples as written require the previous definition of the `greyconvert` alias, or function. If you're using `bash`, you'll additionally need to `export greyconvert` for the function to be visible in the subshell created when you run the script.

There's nothing to prevent you from embedding the `alias` in a `tcsh` version of this script, or the function in the `bash` version if you don't feel like having it defined in your command-line environment. If you go with the idea of embedding the definition, you can make the script truly portable so that it can be given to other users and executed in other environments.

As a matter of fact, there's no reason to leave the `while` at the command line either—it might as well be embedded in the script too. In `bash`, this might look something like this:

```
#!/bin/bash

greyconvert() {
infile=$1;
giftopnm < $infile ¦ ppmtopgm ¦ ppmquant 4 ¦
➥ ppmtopict > ${infile%.+([!/])}.pict; }

while (( 1 )) ; do
for testfile in `ls *.gif` ; do
greyconvert $testfile ;
rm $testfile ;
done
sleep 60 ;
done
```

It's important to note that the `$1` used inside the `greyconvert` function defined in this script refers to the first argument passed to the `greyconvert` function, not to the first argument passed to the script.

TIP

Remember to chmod the script file so that it's executable. The shell won't let you run the script if it's not set to be executable.

This command will loop perpetually in the current directory, executing the greyconv.csh shell script every 60 seconds. Any file with a .gif extension that is placed in the directory will be discovered and passed through the greyconvert alias that we created earlier, and then the original file will be deleted. This will run perpetually in the directory, enabling any file dropped in to be converted (within 60 seconds) automatically. Because the end of the foreach is in a completely separate shell, it can't accidentally end the while, and everything will work as expected. Of course, if there were a reason to do this on a regular basis, you could put that while loop into its own shell script file. It could be stored and executed as a single command from the command line just like any other command.

NOTE

Particularly astute readers will observe that the script does not attempt to make sure that the entire GIF file actually exists in the directory before the script executes upon it. You might also expect that the behavior of the script could be rather unpredictable if the greyconv.csh script takes longer than a minute to execute. Shell scripts are generally an exercise in successive refinement to eliminate potential problems such as these, and these examples should be considered nothing more than the first step to a final application. You can get quite a bit of functionality out of simple scripts such as this. But if you're inclined to tackle the more complicated "correct" solutions, **we can't recommend strongly enough that you read the man pages and check out some books specifically on shell scripting**.

Using Shell Parameters and Conditional Execution in the Shell

Two final things to note now that we've introduced independent shells invoked as the result of placing scripts in files: the `$argv[1]...$argv[n]` list and the corresponding `$1...$n` command-line argument variables. (Refer to the table of shell variables and the table of alternative variable addressing methods for a refresher on these.) These parameters that can be passed into a shell script by placing values on the command line after the script name. They also provide a good mechanism for us to introduce the if shell command, allowing conditional execution of code blocks.

If we'd like to make the greyconv.csh script somewhat more general, we can make use of the ability to pass arguments into the script. For example, it would be nice to be able to use greyconv.csh on the GIF files in a directory without actually having to be in the directory when we run the while loop. Simultaneously, we might like to have the ability to convert all the files in the current directory without needing to specify a directory name. There is no need to write two different scripts to do this. One script can perform both actions by using conditional statements and checking to see whether a parameter has been passed on the command line. If there is a shell parameter, it can be taken as the directory name in which to work; if there is no shell parameter, the script can operate in the current working directory. The modified version of greyconv.csh is as follows:

```
#!/bin/csh

if ( $?1 == 1 ) then
cd $1
endif

foreach testfile (*.gif)
greyconvert $testfile
rm $testfile
end
```

This version of `greyconv.csh` demonstrates both an `if` conditional expression and the use of a command-line argument. The `if` statement checks whether the variable `$1` is set (using the `$?<variablename>` alternative variable addressing to check for existence). If it is set, the script assumes that the value in `$1` is the name of a directory, and it `cd`s into that directory before executing the `foreach` loop to convert and delete the GIF files. `greyconv.csh` can now be called with a directory, to operate in that directory, or without a directory specified, to operate in the current directory.

> **NOTE**
>
> In `bash`, we would write a `greyconv.sh` script instead. It might look something like this:
>
> ```
> #!/bin/bash
>
> greyconvert() {
> infile=$1;
> giftopnm < $infile | ppmtopgm | ppmquant 4 |
> ➥ ppmtopict > ${infile%.+([!/])}.pict; }
>
> if (( $# == 1 )) ; then
> cd $1
> fi
>
> while (( 1 )) ; do
> for testfile in `ls *.gif` ; do
> greyconvert $testfile ;
> rm $testfile ;
> done
> sleep 60 ;
> done
> ```
>
> Here, it's even more important to keep the use of `$1` straight in your head because it's used twice with two different meanings. The `$1` that means the first command-line argument passed to the command is used inside the `if` conditional to `cd` into the directory named in `$1` if it's provided. The `$1` that means the first argument passed to the `greyconvert` function is used inside the `greyconvert` function to assign the value of `infile`. The portions of the script in

which each definition apply are called the *scope* of that definition. Functions get their own definition scope and redefine the positional parameter variables `$1..$n` as the values of their arguments *only for the commands contained in the function itself.*

We hope that gives you a few ideas for how powerful shell scripts can be, and how you can use them to make your use of Mac OS X much more productive. We've only just scratched the surface in this chapter, and have trivialized some explanations to their simplest case to avoid a chapter that takes half the book. What's here can get you quite a way into shell scripting, and many Unix users with years of experience don't use more than a fraction of what we've covered. Still, if you're looking for more power and more capabilities, don't hesitate to go to the man pages and shell programming–specific reference books.

Setting Up Automatic Script Execution

After you've mastered the skill of building useful automated process into scripts, you'll start wanting to set things up so that they run themselves automatically as well, instead of requiring you to start them manually. Not surprisingly, the Unix side of Mac OS X provides several flexible ways for you to set up the automation you need.

Making Shell Scripts Start at Login or at System Startup

Now that you know how to write shell scripts and run them as commands, making them start when you log in to your account, or making them start when the system starts, is straightforward.

You're already familiar with the login preferences settings and your ability to customize what programs start when you log in from it. An executable shell script is just another program as far as Unix is concerned, so you can configure scripts to start on login from there. If you're going to be working from the command line with any frequency, you might want to consider adding a single shell script to your login preferences and using that script to execute other scripts as necessary.

To add a shell script as an item that starts at system startup is also quite simple. Create a subdirectory for the script you want to run in the `/Library/StartupItems/` folder and place the script or a link to the script in the directory, giving it the same name as the directory. When the system starts, the script will execute. Remember that it's not going to have a terminal attached, so if it does things such as `echo` data, the data will have nowhere to appear. In the next chapter, we'll cover the contents of the `plist` (properties list) file that you can add to the directory with your script to customize some of its behavior.

Executing Scripts at Timed Intervals: `cron` and `at`

In addition to the ability to construct convenient little (or arbitrarily large) programs of your own for the command line, Unix also provides a simple and powerful method for automatically running them at specific times when you want them to run. This method is embodied in the cron facility, which gives every user on the system a way to individually configure timing for executing arbitrary commands. The timing can be expressed in terms of minutes, hours, day of the week, day of the month, and month of the year. These parameters can be mixed and matched, allowing considerable flexibility in the specification of command timing.

For example, if you knew that your boss always wandered through the office looking over people's shoulders to see whether they're being productive on Monday mornings and Friday afternoons, you could configure a shell script to clean all the suspicious files off your desktop (swap in a clean ~/Desktop/ folder, and hide the other one), launch Word and Excel with some important-looking files, and hide iTunes, iChat, and your current favorite video game. So that you don't forget to run it, you could configure cron to automatically execute it at 9:00 a.m. on Mondays, and 1:00 p.m. on Fridays. If you're bad at remembering to copy important files from your desktop to your laptop before leaving work, you could use cron to schedule a snapshot of your desktop Documents folder and copy it to your laptop every workday afternoon at 4:30 p.m.. Although it might be more useful to schedule a reminder in iCal, you could even remind yourself to file your tax return by configuring cron to automatically launch Safari, pointed at the TurboTax website, on April 14th every year. Apple extensions to the standard Unix cron facility allow you to selectively prevent scheduled commands from running when a laptop is operating on battery power, and to schedule a command execution to occur after reboots, regardless of time, day, or date.

In addition to scheduling regularly occurring events, the cron facility can be used to schedule events that need to occur at a single specific time. To do this, the list of events and times are stored in a file, and a special cron job periodically checks the file to see when and if anything needs to be run in the near future. Finally, the same facility can be used to check the system load, instead of the time, and to hold execution of particular jobs until the system load is low and more CPU can be devoted to the task.

To access the time/day/date scheduling facility, you use the crontab command. The crontab command edits files (unsurprisingly called *crontabs*), that contain per-user scheduling information, and the always-running cron system reads these file and acts on them accordingly. The crontabs live in /var/cron/tabs/ in files named after each user, and are in a human-readable standardized format used by all Unix versions of cron (although they should not be edited by hand). Invoking the crontab command opens the file belonging to your user, in the command-line editor of your choice (or at least the one specified by your VISUAL or EDITOR environment variable). When the file is open, you can edit its content just as you normally would with that editor. When you quit out of the editor, your crontab file is saved, and the cron system is informed of the changes so that it can begin working with them.

All this probably sounds far more complicated than it is in reality. Sophisticated crontab schedules are built up in little uncomplicated bits, just like complicated Unix shell commands. For example, if you have a program named backup that you would like to run at 4:45 every afternoon, you'd run the crontab command, and edit the (possibly empty) crontab it presents you with to contain a line like this:

```
45  16  *  *  *  backup
```

Positionally, this specifies the time you at which you want to fire the rule in the following form:

```
minute  hour  day-of-month  month  day-of-week  <command>
```

Run the backup command on the 45th minute of the 16th hour of the day (counting from midnight as zero). The * characters indicate that these are "don't care" values, so the rule will fire on any day of the month, any month of the year, and any day of the week.

Perhaps this is a work machine and you'd only want it to run (and expend drive space making backups) on work days. You could limit it to only running Monday through Friday like this:

```
45  16  *  *  1,2,3,4,5  backup
```

Sunday is the zeroth day (or the seventh day, either are acceptable syntax), so this runs your backup command at the 45th minute of the 16th hour of the first (Monday), second, third, fourth, and fifth days of the week.

Perhaps you're a school teacher and it makes sense to run this only while school is in session from September to June:

```
45  16  *  9-12,1-6  1,2,3,4,5  backup
```

Now it runs on the 45th minute of the 16th hour of weekdays, in months that are in the range September to December or January to June.

Finally, Apple has extended the crontab syntax to allow you to prevent a rule from firing if the computer is currently running on battery power (as a laptop might). If you need this additional flexibility, you simply prepend @AppleNotOnBattery to the command section and separate it from the command by a space:

```
45  16  *  9-12,1-6  1,2,3,4,5  @AppleNotOnBattery backup
```

There are additional, still more sophisticated ways to specify scheduling options available, and they are mentioned in the command documentation table for crontab (see Table 15.12). Most of these, such as the ability to specify a counting base for ranges (for example, do *<command>* on any minutes in the range 10-45, counting by 7s) are rather esoteric in purpose, and won't see extensive use at the hands of most users.

TABLE 15.12 The Command Documentation for the crontab Command, and the Basic Format of a crontab File

crontab	Maintains crontab files for individual users.
crontab [-u *<user>*] *<file>*	
crontab [-u *<user>*] [-l ¦ -r ¦ -e]	

crontab is the program that installs, removes, and lists the tables the cron facility executes for users. Each user can have his own crontab, which is stored in /var/cron/tabs/ by username. These files are not to be edited directly.

If /var/cron/allow exists, the *<user>* trying to use cron, or that was specified to run the command in

TABLE 15.12 Continued

the `crontab`, must be listed in `/var/cron/allow` to be able to use `cron`. If `/var/cron/allow` does not exist, but `/var/cron/deny` exists, *<user>*s listed in `/var/cron/allow` cannot use the `cron` facility. If neither file exists (depending on site-dependent configuration), either only the super user may use this command or all users may be able to use this command.

The first form of the command installs a `crontab` from *<file>* or standard input if `-` is given instead of *<file>*. The second form of the command displays, removes, or edits the installed `crontab`.

`-u` *<user>*	Specifies the name of the user. If not specified, the user issuing the command is assumed. If `crontab` is being used inside an `su` or `sudo` command, `-u` should be specified to reduce confusion regarding whose `crontab` to edit.
`-l`	Lists the current `crontab` on standard output.
`-r`	Removes the current `crontab`.
`-e`	Edits the current `crontab` using the editor specified by the environment variables `VISUAL` and `EDITOR`. On exiting the editor, the modified `crontab` is automatically installed.

The basic format of an in-`crontab` scheduling statement looks like this:

`minute hour day-of-month month day-of-week [<user>] <command>`

The valid ranges for the time specifiers are as follows (Sunday may be 0 or 7):

`0-59 0-23 1-31 1-12 0-7`

Fields may be separated by spaces or tabs. `*` may be used as the value of a field to mean all possible values for that field. A field value may be further specified by providing a single value, a comma-separated list of values, a range of values, or a comma-separated list of single values or ranges of values.

Step values may be specified by use of *<range>*`/`*<number>*. For example, `0-23/2` would specify every other hour. `0-23/2` is equivalent to the value list `0, 2, 4, 6, 8, 10, 12, 14, 16, 18, 20, 22`. Step values may also be specified by `*/`*<number>*. For example, every other hour could also be specified by `*/2` in that field.

Names may also be used for the `month` and `day-of-week` fields. Names are the first three characters of the actual name. Case does not matter. Lists or ranges of names, however, may not be used.

The *<user>* field is specified only in a system (root user) `crontab`.

Although `crontab` files allow the scheduling of repeating events, they're not well suited for scheduling something that you want to happen once. For this situation, there is that `at` command. The `at` command schedules something to happen *at* some particular time.

CAUTION

Use of the `at` command, or the related `batch` command, requires that that `root` have a specific command (the `atrun` command) configured in `root's crontab`. Without this command, `at` will schedule events, but they will never actually fire. To configure `atrun` for root, insert a line into `root's crontab` that contains the following:

```
*/10 * * * * root /usr/libexec/atrun
```

`sudo crontab -u root -e` should get you editing the right `crontab` file.

This is *not* configured by default because including it will force your system to access the `at` files once every 10 minutes, and prevent things such as drive sleep from functioning properly. You can change the /10 stepping to something finer, or less-fine grained, if you like. With /10, at's precision is to the nearest following 10-minute mark—a job scheduled for 4:45 will fire at 4:50. One scheduled at 2:29 will fire at 2:30, and so on.

Also be aware that although root is always able to run at jobs, the privileges for normal users are controlled by a pair of allow/deny files for the system and might not have permission to schedule at jobs, depending on the system configuration. The default on Mac OS X is to allow all users access.

The syntax for using at commands is simple: at <time> <command>. For example, if you really need to send a friend a copy of a file you've been working on before going home for the day, but you're worried that you'll forget to do it, you can write a short shell script that can do the mailing (mailfred), and then set up an at command like this, to fire it off in the afternoon at 4:45:

```
at 04:45pm mailfred
```

So long as you've configured root's crontab with atrun, that should fire off your mailfred script at about 4:45 p.m.. If you'd like to run it on a particular date, instead of simply the next 4:45 p.m. that comes around, you can use month, day, and, optionally, year specifiers as well. January 14th at 4:45 p.m. would look like this:

```
at 04:45pm jan 14 mailfred
```

If you're really thinking ahead, you can make it run January of 2008, if you like:

```
at 04:45pm jan 14 2008 mailfred
```

There are additional less-used options for specifying the at time, such as the ability to put the trigger into various queues that control the priority level of the job when it runs, and that let you specify times in silly increments, such as running at "teatime" (which means 4:00 p.m.), as well as different formats in which the time and date can be specified. These are discussed in the command documentation table for at (see Table 15.13).

TABLE 15.13 The Command Documentation Table for at, atq, atrm, and batch

at	Executes commands at a specified time.
atq	Lists the user's pending jobs, unless the user is super user. If the user is super user, lists all users' jobs.
atrm	Deletes jobs.
batch	Executes commands as soon as system load levels permit. This is either when the average load drops to below 1.5 or the value specified at the invocation of atrun.

Using any of these commands requires the configuration of the atrun command in root's crontab.

at [-q *<queue>*] [-f *<file>*] [-m] *<time>*

atq [-q *<queue>*] [-v]

atrm [-q *<queue>*] *<job>* [*<job2>*...]

TABLE 15.13 Continued

batch [-f *<file>*] [-m]	
Both at and batch take input from either standard input or the file specified by -f option. The working directory, environment (except for the variables TERM, TERMCAP, DISPLAY, and _) and umask are retained from the time of invocation. Any at or batch command invoked from an su shell retains the current user ID.	
Permission to use these commands depends on the files /var/at/at.allow and /var/at/at.deny. The super user may use these commands. If /var/at/at.allow exits, only the users (one per line) listed in the file may use these commands. If /var/at/at.allow does not exist, /var/at/at.deny is checked. Users listed in /var/at/at.deny may not use these commands. If an empty /var/at/at.deny exists, all users may use these commands. If neither file exists, only the super user may use these commands.	
-q *<queue>*	Uses the specified queue. A queue consists of a single letter. Valid queue ranges are a to l. The a queue is the default, and b is the batch queue. Queues with higher letters run with increased niceness. If atq is given a specific queue, it shows only the pending jobs in the specified queue.
-f *<file>*	Executes commands in the specified *<file>* rather than from standard input.
-m	Sends mail to the user when the job is complete, whether or not there was any output.
-v	For atq, shows completed, but not yet deleted, jobs in the queue. Otherwise, shows the time the job will be executed.
<time>	*<time>* may be given in a variety of formats. Times may be of the form *<HHMM>* or *<HH:MM>* for a specific time of day. If the time has already passed, the next day is assumed. You may also specify midnight, noon, or teatime (teatime for 4:00 p.m.). You may also append AM, am, PM, or pm to a specific time. A time may also include a date in any of the following forms: *<month-name>* *<day>* [*<year>*], MMDDYY, MM/DD/YY, or DD.MM.YY. The date must follow the time specification. Time may also be given in increments, such as *<now>* + *<count><time_units>*, where *<time_units>* can be minutes, hours, days, or weeks. Terms today and tomorrow may also be used.

Summary

This chapter rounded out the remainder of the general topics you need to know to productively use the Unix command-line shell. We described environment variables and shell variables—both those that affect the behavior of the shell directly and those that can be used in scripts. The chapter also expanded on the use of STDIN and STDOUT, as well as pipes on the command line. The use of loops, conditional expressions, and the storage of your command-line expressions in executable files rounds out your ability to create powerful and completely customized solutions to problems that you encounter. Finally, the job scheduling cron facility was outlined, giving you the ability to run your scripts automatically when, and how you want. With these tools, there is little that you won't be able to do in the world of Unix.

CHAPTER 16

Managing System Services and Configuration

IN THIS CHAPTER

- Locating the Mac OS X Configuration Files
- Managing User Preferences
- Managing System Services
- Strong-Arming the System—Brute Force Behavior Modification

You've already been introduced to configuring and controlling the system through GUI utilities such as the control panes. When using older versions of Mac OS, the only access you have to the configuration for the system is through the GUI interface. Now, you have the option of using a GUI or modifying things through the command line. Although you might wonder whether you'd ever want to use the command line for configuration when Apple has provided such nice GUI tools for configuration, we think there are a few arguments to be made for the command line.

- Generally, we agree that Apple's GUI tools are nice. Still, they're GUI tools, and that means you need access to the GUI to use them. If you're trying to manage your machine from a remote location (more on this in Chapter 21, "Accessing and Controlling Tiger Remotely"), access to the GUI might not be possible.
- Even if you're at the console, it generally takes more time for GUI tools to load and display their interface than it takes to tweak configuration files. Sometimes this doesn't make any difference, but sometimes it's simply annoying to wait for a GUI interface to load when only a few keystrokes are necessary to make the same change.
- Configuration files don't need you to change them. A piece of software can make changes to configurations for you. More interestingly, software can change your configurations on a schedule or based on changes that it detects in the operation of the system. This

can let you automate things such as location or network settings, as well as a range of other possibilities.

- Finally, just to be pedantic, we'll point out that the GUI interface is software running on top of a non-GUI interface. It's possible for the software that creates the GUI interface to be damaged, and for the rest of the system still to be intact enough to run. If you're limited to knowledge of the GUI tools only, you're limited in your ability to fix the situation. Generally, when dealing with Unix-based things, it's safest to have a handle on the command-line configuration and administration tools. For a pure Unix book, we'd say that it is imperative that you avoid the GUI tools and learn to do everything with the command line. For this book, we'll say that it's a good idea to know the command-line tools—Apple has done a *very* good job.

This chapter introduces you to the tools that you need to modify your machine's configuration from the command line and gives you a few examples of things that you can do. You learn further specifics about the use of these tools in chapters such as Chapter 20, "Configuring Advanced Multiuser/Multisystem Cooperation Features," where we detail specific system configuration topics. Specifically, this chapter addresses where to find configuration files, interacting with the `defaults` database to customize some user preferences, how to manage system services, and how to brute-force your system into doing what you want.

Locating the Mac OS X Configuration Files

Locating Mac OS X configuration files and figuring out what can be put in them can sometimes be a bit of an adventure. It's difficult to determine the correct information to provide for some items in this chapter. Many configuration options and files that exist in Mac OS X are not actually intended for you to use in the Mac OS X client version. These parts of the configuration system are actually managed by tools provided only (for the moment, at least) by Mac OS X Server. It's possible to diddle around with them, and to do some interesting things, but Mac OS X doesn't provide the tools or the information to do a complete job of documentation or configuration. We'll do our best to provide you with up-to-the-minute information on what's been discovered to be tweakable in the system as of when this book hits the shelves. Do check online information sources such as `http://www.macosxunleashed.com/` and `http://www.macosxhints.com/`, and understand that it seems clear that Apple doesn't intend for the user to ever understand or modify some of these things.

Preference Locations

Unlike previous versions of Mac OS, which kept almost all its preferences in the Preferences folder of the System folder, Mac OS X keeps its preferences in several different locations. Primarily these are the `/etc/` folder, the NetInfo database, the `/System/Library/LaunchDaemons/` folder and the `~/Library/Preferences/` folders. Many preferences that affect the running of the system, such as what network services are started, the machine name, and global information that does not change from login to login, are kept in the `/etc/` folder or its subfolders or in `/System/Library/LaunchDaemons/`. Other preferences of this nature are kept in the NetInfo database. Preferences that affect individual user configuration are primarily kept in files stored in `~/Library/Preferences/`.

Preference Format

Preferences stored in files in the `/etc/` directory generally follow long-standing Unix tradition and are formatted according to their own individual file formats. The `/etc/inetd.conf` and `/etc/xinetd.d` files are discussed in depth later in the chapter.

Other `/etc/` directory preference and configuration files that you should be familiar with are

- `/etc/services`—Configures the service name to port number mapping required for `inetd` and some other network-based services.
- `/etc/hosts`—Configures the set of other machines that this machine knows about, without having to go to the DNS server to get a hostname or IP address.
- `/etc/passwd`—Configures user IDs and associated home directories, passwords, and shells.
- `/etc/group`—Configures groups and group memberships.

16

All these files use specific configuration formats rooted in Unix tradition and documented in the man pages. In Mac OS X, these files are directly used only in single-user mode because Apple has replaced their use with databases from NetInfo. Learning about them isn't completely irrelevant, though. It's often much easier to load the NetInfo database from these files with well-defined formats than it is to enter the data directly into NetInfo. In Chapter 20, we show how to use the traditional `/etc/` configuration file formats to load data into NetInfo.

You might also want to be familiar with the formats for `/etc/fstab` and `/etc/exports`. These files traditionally control the mounting of disks and the serving of disks, respectively. Apple, however, doesn't seem to use them even in single-user mode. But the NetInfo server can load data from these file formats, so it might be useful to learn them if you will be interacting with other types of Unix machines.

One of the more significant `/etc/` preferences files in Mac SO X, however, is not a common file in the Unix world. This file, `/etc/hostconfig`, contains a number of variable assignments that provide information to assorted programs that run on your behalf. We will also take an in-depth look at this file later in the chapter.

Files contained in `/System/Library/LaunchDaemons` and in `~/Library/Preferences` are mostly stored in XML (Extensible Markup Language), an emerging data storage standard. Readers familiar with HTML (Hypertext Markup Language) will find many similarities in the structure of the HTML document and of documents written in XML. The primary differences are that HTML is intended to be (but has wandered away from being) a structurally tagged language in a specified tag set, whereas XML is a language in which structural tagging can be arbitrarily defined. Specifically, these preferences are stored as `plist` files, which are XML files with unstructured data about a file or application.

For those unfamiliar with either language, both are essentially languages in which the content of a document is indicated by surrounding content items with tags. The beginning tag is usually of the form `<TAGNAME>`, where the < and > are required parts of the tag. The ending tag is of the form `</TAGNAME>` where the `TAGNAME` part of the begin/end pair must match. Tags in both languages can be nested, but neither supports tag pairs that overlap. (That is, `<TAG1> some data <TAG2> more data</TAG1> and more data</TAG2>` is not acceptable.) HTML has a defined set of tags that are part of the language, but XML is actually a language in which arbitrary tags can be defined. HTML tags also imply to a browser that the data enclosed by the tags has certain intended display characteristics. XML tags, however, imply only document structure and require an additional style definition to provide display properties. Finally, through design and through degeneration by lack of standards, HTML has come to include a number of tags with purposes and syntaxes outside the logic described earlier. For example, HTML allows "half tags" for certain types of tags because it uses some tags exclusively for display control, rather than for structural tagging. HTML's `<P>` (paragraph) tag, for instance, can be used alone with no closing `</P>` tag because it specifies only that the browser should move down and start a new line with the next text. It does not delimit the boundaries of a paragraph.

Where HTML allows implicitly closed tags for items such as `<P>` (paragraph), XML requires explicitly closed tags. For completely nonenclosing tags, such as HTML's `<HR>` tag (horizontal line), XML substitutes a tag type that is understood to open and close itself in the statement. The XML equivalent would look like `<HR/>`, which is read by the parser as `<HR></HR>`. Apple uses this type of tagging frequently in its XML preferences files.

The `plist` files can contain portions that aren't human readable or easily guessable as to how they relate to preference settings. The `plist` files are more readable using the Property List Editor that is included in the Developer Tools. If you would like to learn more about property lists, check `http://developer.apple.com/documentation/CoreFoundation/Conceptual/CFPropertyLists/index.html`.

Managing User Preferences

Your preferences, located in `~/Library/Preferences` are `plist` files, a form of XML file. In this section we will take a look at some sample `plist` files and learn ways to manage them. Listing 16.1 shows the `Terminal.app` preference file (located in `~/Library/Preferences/com.apple.Terminal.plist`) from an installed, but little-used user account.

LISTING 16.1 An Almost Bare Preference File for `Terminal.app`

```
<?xml version="1.0" encoding="UTF-8"?>
<!DOCTYPE plist PUBLIC "-//Apple Computer//DTD PLIST 1.0//EN"
➥"http://www.apple.com/DTDs/PropertyList-1.0.dtd">
<plist version="1.0">
```

LISTING 16.1 Continued

```
<dict>
        <key>StartupFile</key>
        <string></string>
</dict>
</plist>
```

The terminal preferences currently contain little of interest other than a reference to a startup file.

> **NOTE**
>
> With Mac OS X 10.4, many of the `plist` files have been encoded into binary. To read any of these `plist` files, make a copy of the `plist` file that you are about to convert, and then run this command:
>
> ```
> plutil -convert xml1 <file-to-be-converted>
> ```
>
> If you want to convert the file back to binary, replace `xml1` with `binary1`.

Listing 16.2 shows the `Terminal.app` preferences from a considerably more used account. As you can see, the `plist` files are not required to contain all the preferences for an application and can grow as the user specifies more preferences that aren't just the defaults. One annoyance that this causes is that sometimes hidden preferences aren't accessible through any of the application's Preferences panes. These preferences can find their way into the XML `plist` files only if somebody discovers their existence and adds the preference line to the `plist` file manually.

16

LISTING 16.2 A Preferences File for `Terminal.app` That Has Accumulated Some Settings over Time

```
<?xml version="1.0" encoding="UTF-8"?>
<!DOCTYPE plist PUBLIC "-//Apple Computer//DTD PLIST 1.0//EN" "http://www.apple.
➥com/DTDs/PropertyList-1.0.dtd">
<plist version="1.0">
<dict>
        <key>AutoFocus</key>
        <string>YES</string>
        <key>Autowrap</key>
        <string>YES</string>
        <key>BackgroundImagePath</key>
        <string></string>
        <key>Backwrap</key>
        <string>YES</string>
        <key>Bell</key>
        <string>YES</string>
```

LISTING 16.2 Continued

```
        <key>BlinkCursor</key>
        <string>YES</string>
        <key>BlinkText</key>
        <string>YES</string>
        <key>CleanCommands</key>
        <string>rlogin;telnet;ssh;slogin</string>
        <key>Columns</key>
        <string>118</string>
        <key>CursorShape</key>
        <string>0</string>
        <key>CustomTitle</key>
        <string>Terminal</string>
        <key>DeleteKeySendsBackspace</key>
        <string>NO</string>
        <key>DisableAnsiColors</key>
        <string>NO</string>
        <key>DoubleBold</key>
        <string>YES</string>
        <key>DoubleColumnsForDoubleWide</key>
        <string>NO</string>
        <key>DoubleWideChars</key>
        <string>YES</string>
        <key>EnableDragCopy</key>
        <string>YES</string>
        <key>ExecutionString</key>
        <string></string>
        <key>FontAntialiasing</key>
        <string>NO</string>
        <key>FontHeightSpacing</key>
        <string>1</string>
        <key>FontWidthSpacing</key>
        <string>1</string>
        <key>IsMiniaturized</key>
        <string>NO</string>
        <key>KeyBindings</key>
        <dict>
                <key>$F708</key>
                <string>ESC[25~</string>
                <key>$F709</key>
...
                <key>~F712</key>
                <string>ESC[34~</string>
        </dict>
        <key>Meta</key>
```

LISTING 16.2 Continued

```
        <string>-1</string>
        <key>NSColorPanelMode</key>
        <string>6</string>
        <key>NSColorPanelVisibleSwatchRows</key>
        <integer>1</integer>
        <key>NSFixedPitchFont</key>
        <string>Monaco</string>
        <key>NSFixedPitchFontSize</key>
        <real>10</real>
        <key>NSFontPanelPreviewHeight</key>
        <real>0.0</real>
        <key>NSWindow Frame Inspector</key>
        <string>102 311 268 435 0 0 1024 746 </string>
        <key>NSWindow Frame NSColorPanel</key>
        <string>325 263 201 309 0 0 1024 746 </string>
        <key>OptionClickToMoveCursor</key>
        <string>NO</string>
...
        <key>TermCapString</key>
        <string>xterm-color</string>
        <key>TerminalOpaqueness</key>
        <real>1</real>
        <key>TextColors</key>
        <string>1.000 1.000 1.000 0.000 0.000 0.000 1.000 1.000 1.000 1.000 1.00
➥0 1.000 0.000 0.000 0.000 1.000 1.000 1.000 0.667 0.667 0.667 1.000 1.000 1.000C
</string>
        <key>TitleBits</key>
        <string>78</string>
        <key>Translate</key>
        <string>YES</string>
        <key>UseCtrlVEscapes</key>
        <string>YES</string>
        <key>VisualBell</key>
        <string>NO</string>
        <key>WinLocULY</key>
        <string>471</string>
        <key>WinLocX</key>
        <string>67</string>
        <key>WinLocY</key>
        <string>0</string>
        <key>WindowCloseAction</key>
        <string>1</string>
</dict>
</plist>
```

Listing 16.3 shows a preferences file for a shareware product called GraphicConverter. As you can see in Listings 16.2 and 16.3, the items stored in the `~/Library/Preferences/` files are many and varied. You also can see that some preferences are not intuitively parseable.

NOTE

The truly observant might notice that the big block of characters in the middle of Listing 16.3 displays a vague pattern. In fact, it's an icon, encoded and stored in text form. This might give you an idea or two about how you could customize program icons automatically from a script.

LISTING 16.3 The `plist` File for GraphicConverter

```
<?xml version="1.0" encoding="UTF-8"?>
<!DOCTYPE plist PUBLIC "-//Apple Computer//DTD PLIST 1.0//EN"
➥"http://www.apple.com/DTDs/PropertyList-1.0.dtd">
<plist version="1.0">
<dict>
<key>AppleNavServices:ChooseFolder:0:HomeDirectoryPath</key>
        <string>file://~/Documents/</string>
        <key>AppleNavServices:ChooseFolder:0:Path</key>
        <string>file://localhost/MacHD/Users/joray/Documents/</string>
        <key>AppleNavServices:ChooseFolder:0:Position</key>
        <data>
        ATkBaA==
        </data>
        <key>AppleNavServices:ChooseFolder:0:Size</key>
        <data>
        AAAAAAFvAjA=
        </data>
        <key>AppleRecentFolders</key>
        <array>
                <string>file://localhost/MacHD/Users/joray/Documents/</string>
        </array>
...
        <key>custom color table</key>
        <data>
        //////////////8zM/////5mZ/////2Zm/////zMz/////wAA//MzP/////MzMzM///M
        zJmZ///MzGZm///MzDMz///MzAAA//+Zmf////+ZmczM//+ZmZmZ//+ZmWZm//+ZmTMz
        //+ZmQAA//9mZv////9mZszM//9mZpmZ//9mZmZm//9mZjMz//9mZgAA//8zM/////8z
        M8zM//8zM5mZ//8zM2Zm//8zMzMz//8zMwAA//8AAP////8AAMzM//8AAJmZ//8AAGZm
        //8AADMz//8AAAAAzMz/////zMz//8zMzMz//5mZzMz//2ZmzMz//zMzzMz//wAAzMzM
        zP//zMzMzMzMzMzMzJmZzMzMzGZmzMzMzDMzzMzMzAAAzMyZmf//zMyZmczMzMyZmZmZ
        zMyZmWZmzMyZmTMzzMyZmQAAzMxmZv//zMxmZszMzMxmZpmZzMxmZmZmzMxmZjMzzMxm
        ZgAAzMwzM///zMwzM8zMzMwzM5mZzMwzM2ZmzMwzMzMzzMwzMwAAzMwAAP//zMwAAMzM
        zMwAAJmZzMwAAGZmzMwAADMzzMwAAAAAmZn/////mZn//8zMmZn//5mZmZn//2ZmmZn/
```

LISTING 16.3 Continued


```
        /zMzmZn//wAAmZnMzP//mZnMzMzMmZnMzJmZmZnMzGZmmZnMzDMzmZnMzAAAmZmZmf//
        mZmZmczMmZmZmZmZmZmZmWZmmZmZmTMzmZmZmQAAmZlmZv//mZlmZszMmZlmZpmZmZlm
        ZmZmmZlmZjMzmZlmZgAAmZkzM///mZkzM8zMmZkzM5mZmZkzM2ZmmZkzMzMzmZkzMwAA
        mZkAAP//mZkAAMzMmZkAAJmZmZkAAGZmmZkAADMzmZkAAAAAZmb/////Zmb//8zMZmb/
        /5mZZmb//2ZmZmb//zMzZmb//wAAZmbMzP//ZmbMzMzMZmbMzJmZZmbMzGZmZmbMzDMz
        ZmbMzAAAZmaZmf//ZmaZmczMZmaZmZmZZmaZmWZmZmaZmTMzZmaZmQAAZmZmZv//ZmZm
        ZszMZmZmZpmZZmZmZmZmZmZmZjMzZmZmZgAAZmYzM///ZmYzM8zMZmYzM5mZZmYzM2Zm
        ZmYzMzMzZmYzMwAAZmYAAP//ZmYAAMzMZmYAAJmZZmYAAGZmZmYAADMzZmYAAAAAMzP/
        ////MzP//8zMMzP//5mZMzP//2ZmMzP//zMzMzP//wAAMzPMzP//MzPMzMzMMzPMzJmZ
        MzPMzGZmMzPMzDMzMzPMzAAAMzOZmf//MzOZmczMMzOZmZmZMzOZmWZmMzOZmTMzMzOZ
        mQAAMzNmZv//MzNmZszMMzNmZpmZMzNmZmZmMzNmZjMzMzNmZgAAMzMzM///MzMzM8zM
        MzMzM5mZMzMzM2ZmMzMzMzMzMzMzMwAAMzMAAP//MzMAAMzMMzMAAJmZMzMAAGZmMzMA
        ADMzMzMAAAAAAAD/////AAD//8zMAAD//5mZAAD//2ZmAAD//zMzAAD//wAAAADMzP//
        AADMzMzMAADMzJmZAADMzGZmAADMzDMzAADMzAAAAACZmf//AACZmczMAACZmZmZAACZ
        mWZmAACZmTMzAACZmQAAAABmZv//AABmZszMAABmZpmZAABmZmZmAABmZjMzAABmZgAA
        AAAzM///AAAzM8zMAAAzM5mZAAAzM2ZmAAAzMzMzAAAzMwAAAAAAAP//AAAAAMzMAAAA
        AJmZAAAAAGZmAAAAADMz7u4AAAAA3d0AAAAAu7sAAAAAqqoAAAAAiIgAAAAAd3cAAAAA
        VVUAAAAAREQAAAAAIiIAAAAAEREAAAAAAADu7gAAAADd3QAAAAC7uwAAAACqqgAAAACI
        iAAAAAB3dwAAAABVVQAAAABERAAAAAAiIgAAAAAREQAAAAAAAO7uAAAAAN3dAAAAALu7
        AAAAAKqqAAAAAIiIAAAAAHd3AAAAAFVVAAAAAERERAAAAACIiAAAAABER7u7u7u7u3d3d
        3d3du7u7u7u7qqqqqqqqiIiIiIiId3d3d3d3VVVVVVVVREREREREIiIiIiIiERERERER
        AAAAAAAA
        </data>
...
        <key>general</key>
        <data>
        AAADcAAVABIBAAAAAAAAAAAADAAkAAAAAAAAAAAADAAkAAAAAAAAAAAD/pmZmZmZmaP+mZ
        mZmZmZo/6ZmZmZmZmj/pmZmZmZmaAQAAAAAMAAAAAAAAAAAAABAAAAAQEBAAEBAQAAAQBk
        AAEAAgACAAEAAQABAAEBAQEAAQAAAAABAAAFAAAAA7UAAAAAAAEAAAABUlNFRAEAAAAA
        MgABAAAAAAAABAAEBAAEAAAAAAAAAAAAAAAAAAAAAAAAAAAAABAAAAAoAAAAHgAAAABAAA
        AAgAAABIAAAAAQAABAAAAAAAAAAAEAAAABAAAAAAKAAAAB4AAAAAAAAAAAAAAAAAAAAAAAAA
        AAAAAAAAAAAAAAAAAAAAAAAAAAAAAAAAAAAAAAAAAAAAAAAAAAAAAAAAAAAAAAAA
        AAAAAAAAAAAAAAAAAAAAAAAAAAAAAAAAAAAAAAAAAAAAAAAAAAAAAAAAAAAAAAAA
        AAAAAAAAAAAAAAAAAAAAAAAAAAAAAAAAAAAAAAAAAAAAAAAAAAAAAAAAAAAAAAAA
        AAAAAAAAAAAAAAAAAAAAAAAAAAAAAAAAAAAAAAAAAAAAAAAAAAAAAAAAAAAAAAAA
        AAAAAAAAAAAAAAAAAAAAAAAAAAAAAAAAAAAAAAAAAAAAAAAAAAAAAAAAAAAAAAAA
        AAAAAAAAAAAAAAAAAAAAAAAAAAAAAAAAAAAAAAAAAAAAAAAAAAAAAAAAAAAAAAAA
        AAAAAAAAAAAAAAAAAAAAAAAAAAAAAAAAAAAAAAAAAAAAAAAAAAAAAAAAAAAAAAAA
        AAAAAAAAAAAAAAAAAAAAAAAAAAAAAAAAAAAAAAAAAAAAAAAAAAAAAAAAAAAAAAAA
        AAAAAAAAAAAAAAAAAAAAAAAAAAAAAAAAAAAAAAAAAAAAAAAAAAAAAAAAAAAAAAAA
        AAAAAAAAAAAAAAAAAAAAAAAAAAAAAAAAAAAAAAAAAAAAAAAAAABQAFABGAF8AQEA
        AAABAQAAAQAOAQEAAAABAAAAAAAAAAAAADwEBAAAAAAAAAAAAAAAAAAAAAAAAQAA
        AAAAAAAAAAAAAAAAAABAAABAQAAAAEAAAA/8AAAAAAAAAAAAP+zMzMzMzM0/6ZmZmZmZ
        mj/pmZmZmZmaP+mZmZmZmZoBLAAAAIAAAwADAABqcGVnAAAAAAAAAAAADAHJwemEAAAAA
```

LISTING 16.3 Continued


```
AAAAAAMAAAADAAAMAAAAAAAAYAAfQAAAAAAAAAAMAAAADAAAAAAAABAAAAP9AAAAAAAAAA
AAAAAAA/1mZmZmZmZgAAAAAAAD/gAAAAAAAAAAAAAAAAP+ZmZmZmZmYAAAAAAAA/8AAA
AAAAAAAAAAAAAD/zMzMzMzMzAAAAAAAAP/MzMzMzMzMAAAAAAAA/8zMzMzMzMwAAAAAA
AD/QAAAAAAAAAQFmAAAAAAAAAAAz/wAAAAAAAAAAAAAAAAAAAAAAAAAJagAABvQAQEAAAAA
AAAAAAAAAAAAAAAAAAAAAAAAAAAAAAAAAAAAAAAAAAAAAAAACAAAAyAAAAAAAAAAABAAEA
AAADAAAAAAABkAAAAAQAAAAEAAAAAAAAAAAAAAAAAAAAABAAAAAQAAAAAAAAAABAAAAAAAA
AUAAAADwAAAABQAAAAAAAAAAA////////AAAACQAAAAAAAAAAAAAAAAAAAAEAAAABAAAA
AQAAAAAAAAAAAAAAAAAAAAAAAAAAAAAAAAA//8AAP//AAAAAP///////wAAAAD//wAA
//9ERAAAAAD///////93d3d3d3d3d3d3//93d///d3d3d/////////3d3d3f//3d3////
////AAD////////8AAAABAAAAAQAAAAAAAAAAAAAAAQAAAAQAAAAAAAAAAAQAAAAAAAAAAB
AAAAAAAAAAwAAAAAAAAAAAAAAAAAAAAAAAAAAAAAAAAAAAAAAAAAAAAAWgAAAAAAAAAACAAAA
AAAAAAAAAAKAAAAB4AAAAAUAAAABAAAAQAAAADQAAAADAAAACQAAAAAAAP///////wAA
AAAAAAAAAAAAAAAAUAAAADIAAAAAQAAAAAAAAAAAAAAAAAAQAAAAEAAAABAAAAAAAAAAAUA
AAAAAAAAAAAAAAAAAAAAAAAAAAAAAAAAAAAAAAAAAAAAAAAQAAAABAAAAAAAAAAAAAAAAA
AAAAAAAAAAAAAAAAAAAAAAAAAAAAAAAAAAAAAAAAAAAAAAAAAAAAAAAAAAAAAAAAAAAAAAAA
AwAAAAEAAAAAAAAAAAAAAAAwAAAAIAAAAAAAAAAAAAEAAAAAAAAAAAAQAAAAEAAAAAAAAAAAAAAA
AAEAAAAAAAAAAAAQAAAAAAAAAAAAAAAAAQAAAAAAAAAAAAAAAAAAAAAIAAAABAAAAAAAAAAAAAA
AAAAAAAAAAAAAAAAAAAAAAAAAAAAAAIAAAAAAAAAAAAAAAAAAAAAAAAAAAAAAAAAAAAAAAAB
AAAAAAAAAAcAAAABAAAAlgAAACAAAAAAAAAAAAAAAAAoAAAAAAAAAAAAAAAAAAEAAAAAAAAAAA
AQAAAAEBcgAAAAAAAAAFnAAAAAAAAAAAWIAAAAAAAAAADcGFsAAAAAAAAAAAAAAAAAAAAAAAAAD
AAAAAAAAAAMAAAAMAAAACQAAAAAAAAAABAAAAAAAAAAAAAAAAAAAAAAAAAAAAAAAAAAQAAAAAA
AAAAAAAAAAAAAAAAAAAAAAAAAAAAAAAAAAAAAAAAAAAAAAAAAAAAAAAAAAAAAAAAAAEAAAAA
AAAAgAAAAAAAAAAAAAAAAAAAAAAEAAAAAAAAAAAAQAAAAEAAAABAAAAAAAAAAAAAAAAAAABAAAA
AQAAAAAAAAAAAABAAAAAAAAAAAAAAAAABAAAAAQAAAAoAAAAKAAAAAAAAAAAAAoAAAAFAAAAAQAA
AAAAAAAAAAAAAAQAAAAAAAAAAAAAAAAAAAAAAAAAAAAAAAAAAAAAAAAAAAAAAAAAAAAAAAAAAAAAA
AAABAAAABQAFAAAAAQAAAAAAAAAAAAAAAAZAAAAGQAAAABAAAAAwAAAAEAAAAAAAAAAAAAAAQAA
AAAAAAABAAAABQAAAAMAAAAAAAAAAAAAAAAzM0AAAABAAAAAQAAAAAAAAAAAAAAAAAAAEdLT04A
AAAAAAAAAAAAAAAAAAABAAAAAAAAAAAAAAAAAABAAAAAAAAAAAAAEAAAABAAAAAQAAAAEAAAAA
AAAAAAAAAAAAAAAAAAAAAAAAAAAAAAAAAAAAAAAAAAAAAAAAAAAAAAAAAEqKioqKioqKgAAAAAA
AAAAAAAAAAAAABAAAAAAFAAAABQAAAAAAAAAAAAAAAAABLAAAAMgAAAAAAAAAACCAAAAZQAAAAAA
AAAAAAAAAAAAAAAAAAAAAAAAAAAAEAAAAAAAAAAAAFIqY2gAAAADAAACAAAAAgAAAAAAAAAAAA
AAAAAAMAAAABAAAAAAAAAAAAAAAAAAAAAAAAAAAAAAAAEAAAABAAAAAQAAAAEAAAABAAAAAQAA
AAEAAAABAAAAAQAAAAAAAAAAAABAAAAAQAAAAEAAAABAAAAAQAAAAEAAAAAAAAAAAAAQAAAAEA
AAAAAAAAAAAAAAAAAAAAACAAAAAwAAAAAAAAAAAAAAAAAAAAAAAAEAAAABAAAAAAAAAAAAAAAAAAB
AAAAAQAAAAEAAAABAAAAAAAAAAAAAAAAAAAAAAAAAAQAAAAIAAAAAAAAAAAAAAAAAAAEAAAAAAAAA
AAAAAAAAAAAAAAAAAAAAAAAAAEAAAAAAAAAABAAAAAEAAAAyAAAAMgAAAAAAAAAAAAAAAEAAAAA
AAAAAQAAAAEAAAAAAAAAAAFAAAAAAAAAAAABAAAAAAAAAAAAEAAAABAAAAAQAAAABNT1NTAAAA
AQAAAB4AAAABAAAAAQAAAAAAAAAAAAAQYAAQAAABQAAAAUAAAAAAAAAAAAAAAAAAAAABAAAAAAAA
AAQAAAADAAAAAAAAAAAAAEAAAABAAAAAAAAAAAAAEAAAAAAAAAAAAAAAAAAAAAAAAAAAAAAQAAAyAA
AAMgAAAAAAAAAAAAoAAAAAAAAAAAAAAAAAAAAAAAAAAAAAAAAAGQAAAAAAAAAAAAAAAAAEAAAAA
AAAAAAAAAAAAAAAAAAAAAAAAAAAAAAAAAAAAAAAAAAAAAAAAAAAAAAAAAAAAAAAAAAAAAAAA
AAAAAAAAAAAAAAAAAAAAAAAAAAAAAAAAAAAAAAAAAAAAAAAAAAAAAAAAAAAAAAAAAAAAAAAA
AAAAAAAAAAAAAAAAAAAAAAAAAAAAAAAAAAAAAAAAAAAAAAAAAAAAAAAAAAAAAAAAAAAAAAAA
AAAAAAAAAAAAAAAAAAAAAAAAAAAAAAAAAAAAAAAAAAAAAAAAAAAAAAAAAAAAAAAAAAAAAAAA
```

LISTING 16.3 Continued


```
AAAAAAAAAAAAAAAAAAAAAAAAAAAAAAAAAAAAAAAAAAAAAAAAAAAAAAAAAAAAAAAAAAAA
AAAAAAAAAAAAAAAAAAAAAAAAAAAAAAAAAAAAAAAAAAAAAAAAAAAAAAAAAAAAAAAAAAAA
AAAAAAAAAAAAAAAAAAAAAAAAAAAAAAAAAAAAAAAAAAAAAAAAAAAAAAAAAAAAAAAAAAAA
AAAAAAAAAAAAAAAAAAAAAAAAAAAAAAAAAAAAAAAAAAAAAAAAAAAAAAAAAAAAAAAAAAAA
AAAAAAAAAAAAAAAAAAAAAAAAAAAAAAAAAAAAAAAAAAAAAAAAAAAAAAAAAAAAAAAAAAAA
AAAAAAAAAAAAAAAAAAAAAAAAAAAAAAAAAAAAAAAAAAAAAAAAAAAAAAAAAAAAAAAAAAAA
AAEAAAABAAAAAAAAAAAAAD6AAAAAAAAAAAAAAAAAAAAAAAABACwAAwHqBAYAAAC0AAAA
AAAAAAAAAAAyAAAAAUAEAAAAAAAAQAAAAAAAAAAAAAAABAAAAAAAAAAAAAAAAAAAAbgAA
AG4AAAABAAAAAwAAAAQAAAAAAAAAAAAAAAAAAAAAAAAABQAAAAEAAAAAAAAAAQAAAAAA
AAAAAAAAAAAAAAH///////8AAAAAAAAAAAAAAAgAAAABAAAAAgAAAAEAAAABAAAAMv//
/////wAAAAEAAAAAAAAAAQAAAAEAAAABAAAAAQAAAAEAAAABAAAAAQAAAAEAAAABAAAA
AQAAAAEAAAABAAAAAQAAAAEAAAABAAAAAQAAAAEAAAABAAAAAQAAAAEAAAABAAAAAQAA
AAEAAAADAAAAAAAAAAAAAAAAAAAAAAAAAAAAAAAAAAAAAAAAAAAAAAAAAAAAlgAAAAEA
AAABAAAAAwAAAAAAAAAAAAAAAAAAAAAAAAAAAAAAAAAAAAAAAAAAAAAAAAAAAAAAAAAA
AAAAAAAAAAEAAAAAAAAAAAAAAAAAAAAAAAACWAAAADIAAAAAAAAAAAAAAAEAAAe9AAAA
AAAAAAAAAAAAAAAAAAAAAAAAAAAAAAAAAgAAAAEAAAABAAAAAAAAAAAAAAAAAAAAAAAA
AAEAAAAeAAAAAQAAAAAAAAAAAAAAAAAAAAAAIAAAAAAAAAAMAAAAAQAAABQAAAAUAAAA
AAAAAAAAAAAAAAAAAAAAAAAAAAAAAAAAAAAAAAAAAAAAAAAAAAAAAMgAAAAAAAAAAAAA
AAAAAAAAAAAAAAAAAAAAAAAAAAAAAAAAAAAAAAAAAAAAAAAAAAAAAAAAAAAAAAAAAAAA
AAAAAAAAAAAAAAAAAAAAAAAAAAAAA+gAAAAAAAAACwAAAFAAAAAAAAAAAAAAAAAAAAAB
AAAAAQAAAAAAAAAAAAAAAAAAAAEAAAAAAAAAAAAAAAEAAAAAAAAAAAAAAADw8PDw8PAP
Dw8PDw8AAACWAAAAAQAAAAEAAAABAAAAAQAAAAEAAAABAAAAAAAAAAAAAAABAAAAAQAA
AAEAAAAAAAAAAAAAAAAAAAABAAAAAAAAAAAAAAAeAAAAAQAAAAAAAAAABAAAAAAAAAAAA
AAAAAAAAAAAAAAAAAAABAAAAAQAAAAAAAAAAAAAAAAAAAAAAAAAAAAAAAAgAAAAAAAAAB
AAAAAQAAAAAAAAABAAAAAQAAAAAAAAAAAAAAAQAAAAEAAAABAAAAAT/wAAAAAAAAAAAA
AAAAAAAAAAABAAAAAAADDUAAAAARAAAAAAAAAAAAAAAAAAAAAAAAAAAAAAABAAAAAQAA
mZoAAQAAAAEAAAABAAAAAAAKAAAAAAAAAAMAAAABAAAAAQAAAAQAAAAAAAAAAAAAAAAA
AAAAAAAAAQAAAAAAAAAAAAAAAAAAAAAAAAAAAAAAAAAAAAAAAAAAAAAAAAAAAAAAAAAA
AAAAAAAAAAAAAAAAAAAAAAAAAAAAAAAAAAAAAAAAAAAAAAAAAAAAAAAAAAAAAAAAAAAA
AAAAAAAAAAAAAAAAAAAAAAAAAAAAAAAAAAAAAAAAAAAAAAAAAAAAAAAAAAAAAAAAAAAA
AAAAAAAAAAAAAAAAAAAAAAAAAAAAAAAAAAAAAAAAAAAAAAAAAAAAAAAAAAAAAAAAAAAA
AAAAAAAAAAAAAAAAAAAAAAAAAAAAAAAAAAAAAAAAAAAAAAAAAAAAAAAAAAAAAAAAAAAA
AAAAAAAAAAAAAAAAAAAAAQAAABkAAAABAAAAAAAAAEAAAAAAAAAAAQAAAAEAAAABAAAA
AAAAAAEAAAABQCgAAAAAAAAAAAABAAAAAAAAAAAAAAABAAAAAQAAAAAAAAAAEAAAAAAAA
ABQAAAABAAABQAAAAPAAAABIAAAAAQAAAAAAAAAAAAAAAAAAAAAAAAAAAAAAAAAAAAAA
AAAAAAAAAAAAAAAAAAAAAAAAAAAAAAAAAAAAAAAAAAAAAAAAAAAAAAQAAAAGAAAAXwAA
AAAAAAAAAAAAUAAAAAAAAAAAAAAAAAAAAAAAAAAJAAAAAAAAAAAAAAAAAAAAAAAAAAEA
AAABAAAAAQAAAAAAAAAAAAAAAAAAAAAAAAABAAAAAAAAAAAAAAABAAAAAAAAAAAAAAAA
AAEAAAAAAAAAAAAAAAAAAAABAAAAAQAAAAEAAAABAAAAAQAAAAAAAAAAAAAAAAAAAAEA
AAAAAAAAAQAAAAEAAAABAAAAAAAAAAAAAAAAAAAAAAAAAAEAAAAAR0tPTgAAAAEAAAAB
AAAAAQAAAAFqampqamoAAAAAAAAAAAAAAAEAAAAAAAAAAAAAAAAAAAAAAAAAAQAAAAEA
AAAAAAAAAAAAAAAAAAAAAAEgAAAAAAAAAAAAAAAABLAAAAAAAAABAAAAAAAAAAAAAAAB
AAAABAAAAAAAAAABAAAAAQAAAAEAAAAAAAAAAAAAAAAAAAAeAAAAAAAAB9QAAAACAAAA
GAAAAAwAAAAAAAAAAAAAAAAEAAAABAAAAAQAAAAAAAAAAAAAAAAAAAMAAAAAAAAAAQAA
```

LISTING 16.3 Continued

```
        AAEAAAAAAAAAAAAAAAEAAIAAAAAAAQAAAAAAAABAAAAAAAAAAAAAAAAA//8AAAAAAAAA
        AQAAAAEAAACFAAAAAQAAAAAAAAAAAAAAAAAAAQAAAAFAUgAAAAAAAAAEBSAAAAAAAAA
        AAAAAQAAAAEAAAAAAAAAAAHd3d3dwAAAAAAAAAAAAAAAAAgAAAAIAAAAAAAAAAAAAA
        AAAAAAAAAQAAAAAAAAAAAAAAAAQAAAAEAAAABAAAAAQAAAAAAAAAAAAAAAAAAAAAAAAB
        AAAAAQAAAAAAAAAAAAAAAAAADwAAAACAAAAAAAAAAAAAAMgAAACWAAAAAAEAAAAAAAAAA
        AAAAAAEAAAAAAAAAAAAAAAAAAAAAAAAAAAAAAAAAAAAAAAAAAAAAAAAAAAAAAAAAAAAA
        AAAAAAAAAAAAAAAAAAAAAAAAAAAAAAAAAAAAAAAAAAAAAAAAAAAAAAAAAAAAAAAAAAAA
        AAAAAAAAAAAAAAAAAAAAAAAAAAAAAAAAAAAAAAAAAAAAAAAAAAAAAAAAAAAAAAAAAAAA
        AAAAAAAAAAAAAAAAAAAAAAAAAAAAAAAAAAAAAAAAAAAAAAAAAAAAAAAAAAAAAAAAAAAA
        AAAAAAAAAAAAAAAAAAAAAAAAAAAAAAAAAAAAAAAAAAAAAAAAAAAAAAAAAAAAAAAAAAAA
        AAAAAAAAAAAAAAAAAAAAAAAAAAAAAAAAAAAAAAABAAAAAAAAAAAAAAAFAAAAAb4oQgwA
        AAAAAAAAAQAAAAAAAAAAAEAAAAAwAAAAEAAAACAAAAAwAAAAQAAAACAAAAAQAAAAAAAAAAAA
        AAAAAAAAAAAAAAAAAAAAAAAAAAAAAAAAAAAAAAAAAAAAAAAAAAAAZAAAAAIAAAAyAAAA
        AQAAAAEAAAAAAAAAAAQAAAAIAAAADAAAABAAAAAUAAAAGAAAABwAAAAAAAAAAAAAAAAAA
        AAAAAAAAAAAAAAAAAAAAAAAAAAAAAAAAAAAAAAAAAAAAAAAAAAgAAAABAAAAAAAAAAAA
        AAAAAAAAAAAAAAAAAABkAAAACQAAAAH///////8AAAABAAAAAQAAAAQ/Pz8/AAAAAAAA
        AAAAAAAAAAAAAAAAAAEAAAABAAAAAQAAAAMAAAAOAAAAAAAAAAAAAAAAASlBFRz8/Pz8A
        AAADAAAAAA==
        </data>
...
        <key>serial 2</key>
        <string></string>
        <key>string 0</key>
        <string></string>
        <key>string 1</key>
...
        <key>string 23</key>
        <string></string>
        <key>string 24</key>
        <string>Movie</string>
        <key>string 25</key>
        <string>YYYY-MM-DD HH.NN.SS</string>
        <key>string 26</key>
        <string>THM TXT HTM HTML EXE DLL P C PAS CC ASM COM SYS LST DOC XLS PST
OST INI PPT INF SIT ZIP TAR MIM GZIP ARJ</string>
        <key>string 27</key>
        <string>THM TXT HTM HTML EXE DLL P C PAS CC ASM COM SYS LST DOC XLS PST
OST INI PPT INF SIT ZIP TAR MIM GZIP ARJ</string>
        <key>string 28</key>
        <string></string>
        <key>string 29</key>
        <string>n-cc-rr.x</string>
        <key>string 3</key>
        <string>en</string>
```

LISTING 16.3 Continued

```
        <key>string 30</key>
        <string>target="_blank"</string>
        <key>string 31</key>
        <string>ftp://</string>
        <key>string 32</key>
        <string></string>
        <key>string 33</key>
        <string></string>
        <key>string 34</key>
        <string>/</string>
        <key>string 35</key>
        <string>grab</string>
...
</dict>
</plist>
```

As we mentioned, some application preferences are hidden. However, if you are interested, you can spend some time discovering possible preferences. Using the `strings` command can assist in discovering hidden preferences. You see a list of all textual strings in the program. It's reasonable to expect that for the program to read strings out of a `.plist` file, it must contain the string, so the strings found in the program make for potentially interesting things to try as preferences. For example, to try to discover some of the available hidden preferences in the Dock, you might run

```
strings /System/Library/CoreServices/Dock.app/Contents/MacOS/Dock | more
```

Some of the output you get includes the following excerpts:

```
__dyld_mod_term_funcs
__dyld_make_delayed_module_initializer_calls
__dyld_image_count
__dyld_get_image_name
__dyld_get_image_header
__dyld_NSLookupSymbolInImage
__dyld_NSAddressOfSymbol
libobjc
__objcInit
The kernel support for the dynamic linker is not present to run this program.
showhidden
showshadow
DoesPointToFocusCursorUpdate
ClientMayIgnoreEvents
com.apple.finder
DockProxyPSNLoHack
en_US
```

16

```
Info.plist
trashlabel
owensdock
dock
.dock
AppleShowAllExtensions
AppleShowAllFiles
notfound
trashfull
trashempty
finder
openfolder
wvousfloat
wvousfloatselected
wvouscornertl
wvouscornertr
wvouscornerbl
wvouscornerbr
shadow
/System/Library/CoreServices/Finder.app
SetsCursorInBackground
.app
autohide
magnification
/System/Library/PreferencePanes/Dock.prefPane
poof.png
...
TrashName
TrashRemoveFromDock
Trash
Remove From Dock
default.plist
com.apple.dock
version
persistent-apps
...
orientation
bottom
left
right
pinning
middle
start
mineffect
genie
```

```
scale
suck
...
size-immutable
magnify-immutable
autohide-immutable
position-immutable
mineffect-immutable
contents-immutable
...
```

As you can see, the resulting output contains a variety of items, from comments to filenames to possible preference names and possible preference values. From the output, we might guess that `orientation` is a preference and that possible values are `bottom`, `left`, or `right`. We might also guess that `mineffect` is another preference with possible values of `genie`, `scale`, or `suck`. From the Dock control pane, however, we have only the choices of `genie` or `scale`, so we've probably already discovered a sort of hidden preference. In that same section of output is `pinning`, which looks as if it might have possible values of `middle` or `start`. In the final section of the shown output, a number of entries that end in `immutable`, making it seem as if there might be a way to set some preferences so that they don't change. Without experimenting, though, we can't be sure what behavior, if any, to expect. In the middle, there's an entry for `poof.png`, which is an image file—wonder if that's the Dock "poof" for when you remove things from it by dragging, and whether we could customize that little animation by finding and editing this graphics file?

16

Instead of requiring you to edit XML files directly, Apple has provided a convenient command-line program for editing the preferences stored in these files. The `defaults` command allows you to specify a preference to be modified and a value with which to modify it. If the application whose preferences you are trying to modify is currently running, restart the application. As an example of the `defaults` command in use, the following command pins the Dock at the beginning side of the Dock, as shown in Figure 16.1:

```
defaults write com.apple.dock pinning start
```

Specifically, this command modifies the preference `pinning` in the file `~/Library/Preferences/com.apple.dock.plist` and sets the value to `start`. Logging out and logging back in is one way to cause changes to the Dock to take effect. More easily, you can run `killall Dock`. Now this file contains these lines:

```
<key>pinning</key>
<string>start</string>
```

FIGURE 16.1 Here is an example of the Dock with the pinning preference set to start.

If you decide you don't like the pinning that you've just enable, you can always remove it. To remove the change run:

```
defaults delete com.apple.dock pinning
killall Dock
```

Suppose that you don't want to have available the option to hide the Dock. You might try enabling the `autohide-immutable` item we saw earlier in the output by using the following command:

```
defaults write com.apple.dock autohide-immutable -bool true
```

The command modifies the preference `autohide-immutable` to have the Boolean value `true` by adding these lines to the file:

```
<key>autohide-immutable</key>
<true/>
```

In the Dock control pane, the option to hide the Dock is no longer available, and the option no longer appears under the Apple menu. Figure 16.2 shows the modified Dock control pane.

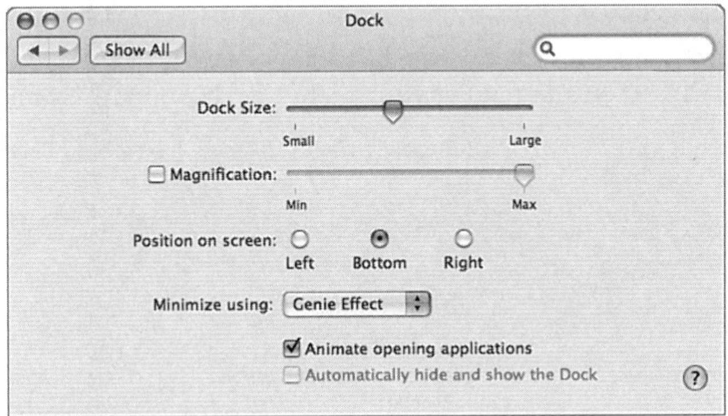

FIGURE 16.2 After setting the `autohide-immutable` preference to `true`, the option to hide the Dock is no longer available.

As you have seen, preferences files can vary in their complexity. You might sometimes find it easier to edit the actual `plist` file or use the graphical `/Developer/Applications/Utilities/Property List Editor.app`. For example, from the earlier `strings` output on the Dock preferences, we notice the `persistent-apps` string. This suggests that there might be a way to remove icons that permanently appear in the Dock. However, just from the `persistent-apps` string, it is difficult to guess what you might have to do to remove one of those icons. Because that section in the `~/Library/Preferences/com.apple.dock.plist` file also looks complicated, it might be difficult to guess what the appropriate `defaults` command may be. However, in your favorite text editor, or in the Property List Editor, you can easily locate the section for the application you no longer want to have in your Dock and simply delete it. Figure 16.3 shows removing the `AddressBook` section of the `persistent-apps` section of the file using the Property List Editor. You can tell that item 4 of the `persistent-apps` section, the item to be removed, is the Address Book based on the file-label value.

Unfortunately, Apple hasn't provided a definitive list of preferences options for each application. Even a listing of the options that each file contains would not be complete because some applications accept preferences that are not yet stored in the XML files. There are preferences options that some programs take as defaults but that can be overridden by the insertion of specific preferences into the XML files. Because no current preference is stored, we can only make intelligent guesses as to what preference names and values might be accepted. As a matter of fact, making intelligent guesses is exactly what the online community is doing regarding these preferences. With this brief look at discovering and manipulating some preferences in the Dock, you can also start to make some intelligent guesses regarding preferences.

Table 16.1 lists a number of preferences options that have been reported to be interesting, when configured using the `defaults` command. Not all these have known or well-documented functions. We have primarily tested those for the Finder and the Dock. In our testing of the `NSUserKeyEquivalents` preference, we had success in building key equivalents with the `Command` and/or `Shift` characters. However, we list all the reported information on `<keystring>` values, in case it should indeed prove useful. Figure 16.5

shows `Terminal.app`'s Terminal menu modified so that About Terminal, which normally does not have a keyboard equivalent, now has a keyboard equivalency of Shift-Command-b. You can set this particular equivalency by running this `defaults` command:

```
defaults write com.apple.Terminal NSUserKeyEquivalents '{"About Terminal"="$@b";}'
```

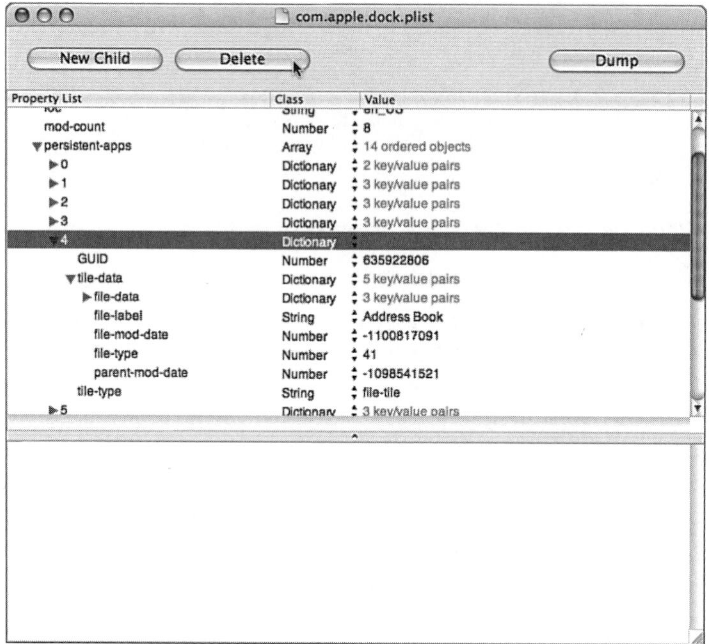

FIGURE 16.3 Using the Property List Editor to remove the Address Book icon from the Dock.

TABLE 16.1 A Number of the Interesting `defaults` Preferences Options That Have Been Reported as Having Interesting Effects on the Interface

Issue command as

`defaults write` *`<domain> <key> <value>`*

<domain>	*<key>*	*<value>*	**Effect**
`com.apple.finder`	`Finder.HasDarkBackground`	`-bool true` `-bool false`	Some text appears as white with a black outline or as solid black.
	`ShowHardDrivesOnDesktop`	`-bool true` `-bool false`	Does or does not show hard drives on the desktop.
	`ShowRemovableMediaOnDesktop`	`-bool true` `-bool false`	Does or does not show removable media on the desktop.

TABLE 16.1 Continued

<domain>	*<key>*	*<value>*	**Effect**
	`ProhibitEmptyTrash`	`-bool true` `-bool false`	Does or does not remove the option to empty the trash.
	`ProhibitFinderPreferences`	`-bool true` `-bool false`	Does or does not remove the Finder preferences option.
	`ProhibitEject`	`-bool true` `-bool false`	Does or does not remove the option to eject removable media.
	`ProhibitBurn`	`-bool true` `-bool false`	Does or does not remove the option to burn recordable media.
	`ProhibitGoToiDisk`	`-bool true` `-bool false`	Does or does not remove the option to go to the iDisk.
	`ProhibitGoToFolder`	`-bool true` `-bool false`	Does or does not remove the option to go to a folder.
	`ProhibitConnectTo`	`-bool true` `-bool false`	Does or does not remove the option to connect to a server.
	`AppleShowAllFiles`	`-bool true` `-bool false`	Does or does not show all files. Normally false, which hides some files.
	`AnimateWindowZoom`	`-bool true` `-bool false`	"Zoom" windows open from their icon locations, or make them simply appear in place.
`com.apple.loginwindow`	`Finder`	*<path>*	Launches the application specified by *<path>* at login instead of the Finder.
`com.apple.dock`	`showhidden`	`-bool true` `-bool false`	Does or does not dim Dock icons for hidden applications.
	`showshadow`	`-bool true` `-bool false`	Does or does not display a slight drop shadow along the edge of the Dock.

16

TABLE 16.1 Continued

<domain>	*<key>*	*<value>*	**Effect**

	`mineffect`	`genie`
		`suck`
		`scale`
			Known values for different Dock minimization effects.

	`orientation`	`left`
		`bottom`
		`right`
			Known values for Dock position.

	`pinning`	`start`
		`middle`
		`end`
			Known values for anchoring the Dock in its position.

	`autohide-immutable`	`-bool true` `-bool false`	Does or does not make available the option to automatically hide and show the Dock.

`NSGlobalDomain`	`NSInterfaceStyle`	`nextstepdefaults`
		`macintoshdefaults`
		`windowdefaults`
			Turns off antialiasing below *<size>*—can be set higher than the prefs menu allows (16 is sufficient for finder menus).

	`NSFixedPitchFontSize`	*<fontsize>*	
	`NSFontSize`	*<fontsize>*	
	`NSSystemFontSize`	*<fontsize>*	
	`AppleAntiAliasingThreshold`	*<size>*	
<any application domain>	`NSUserKeyEquivalents`	`'{"`*<menuitem>*`"=` `"`*<keystring>*`";}'`	*<menuitem>* is any named menu item in a Cocoa application.

<keystring> is built from:
@ = Command
$ = Shift
~ = Option
^ = Control
and any other character.
Modifies the key equivalent for a menu item.

NOTE

This table includes information from our own investigation as well as excerpts from information collected on the Internet from a variety of places, including

`http://www.macosxhints.com/search.php?query=defaults+write&mode=search&datestart=0&dateend=0&topic=0&type=stories&autho=0`

`http://www.macnn.com/`

`http://www.pixits.com/defaults.htm`

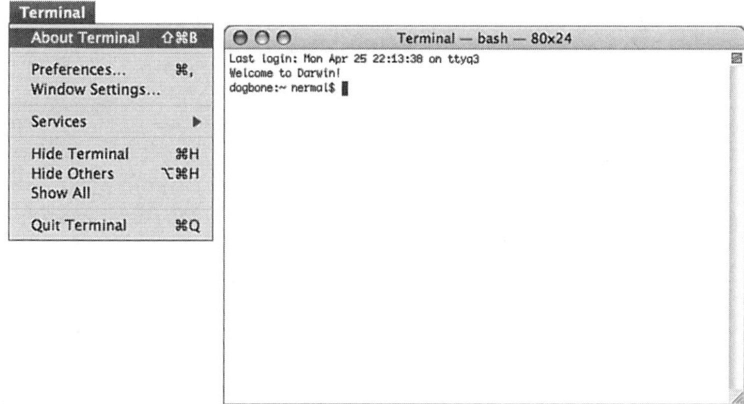

FIGURE 16.4 About Terminal under the Terminal menu of `Terminal.app` now has a keyboard equivalency of Shift-Command-b after issuing the appropriate `defaults` command.

Table 16.2 shows select documentation for the `defaults` command. Note that not only can you use the `defaults` command to write preferences, but you can also use it to read, delete, and search preferences.

TABLE 16.2 Select Documentation Table for the `defaults` Command

defaults	Accesses the Mac OS X user defaults system.
`defaults [currentHost ¦ -host` *<hostname>*`] read [`*<domain>* `[`*<key>*`]]`	
`defaults [currentHost ¦ -host` *<hostname>*`] read-type` *<domain>* *<key>*	
`defaults [currentHost ¦ -host` *<hostname>*`] write` *<domain>* `{'`*<plist>*`' ¦` *<domain>* *<key>* `[']`*<value>*`[']}`	
`default [currentHost ¦ -host` *<hostname>*`] rename` *<domain>* *<old-key>* *<new_key>*	
`defaults [currentHost ¦ -host` *<hostname>*`] delete [`*<domain>* `[`*<key>*`]]`	
`defaults [currentHost ¦ -host` *<hostname>*`] { domains ¦ find` *<word>* `¦ help }`	
`defaults` allows users to read, write, and delete Mac OS X user defaults from the command line.	
Applications use the `defaults` system to record user preferences and other information that must be maintained when applications aren't running, such as the default font for new documents. Because applications do access the `defaults` system while they are running, you should not modify the defaults of a running application.	
User defaults belong to domains, which typically correspond to individual applications. Each domain has a dictionary of keys and values to represent its defaults. Keys are always strings, but values can be complex data structures made up of arrays, dictionaries, strings, and binary data. These data structures are stored as XML property lists.	
Although all applications, system services, and other programs have their own domains, they also share a domain called `NSGlobalDomain`. If a default is not specified in the application's domain, it uses the default listed in the `NSGlobalDomain` instead.	
<domain> is specified as follows:	
<domain_name> `¦ -app` *<application_name>* `¦ -globalDomain`	
Subcommands	
`read`	Prints all the user's defaults for every domain to standard output.

TABLE 16.2 Continued

read *<domain>*	Prints all the user's defaults for the specified *<domain>* to standard output.
read *<domain>* *<key>*	Prints the value for the default of the *<domain>* identified by *<key>*.
write *<domain >* *<key>* '*<value>*'	Writes *<value>* as the value for *<key>* in *<domain>*. *<value>* must be a property list, and must be enclosed in single quotes. For example: `defaults write com.companyname.appname "Default Color" '(255, 0, 0)'` sets the default color in com.companyname.appname to the array containing 255, 0, 0 (red, green, blue components). Note that the key is in quotes because of the space in its name.
write *<domain>*	Overwrites the defaults information in '*<plist>*' *<domain>* with that specified in *<plist>*. *<domain>* must be a property list representation of a dictionary, and must be enclosed in single quotes. For example, `defaults write com.companyname.appname '{ "Default Color" = (255, 0, 0); "Default Font" = Helvetica; }'` Overwrites any previous defaults for com.companyname.appname and replaces them with the ones specified.
delete *<domain>*	Deletes all default information for *<domain>*.
delete *<domain>* *<key>*	Deletes the default named *<key>* in *<domain name>*.
domains	Prints the names of all domains in the user's defaults system.
find *<word>*	Searches for *<word>* in the domain names, keys, and values of the user's defaults, and prints out a list of matches.
help	Prints a list of possible command formats.
Options:	
-g	When specifying a domain, -g can be used as a synonym for NSGlobalDomain.
Specifying *<value>* for Preference Keys	
<value>	Specifies *<value>* as a string value to use.
'*<value>*'	Specifies *<value>* as a string value to use.
-string *<string_value>*	Specifies *<string_value>* as the string to use.
-data *<hex_digits>*	Specifies *<hex_digits>* as the data to use.
-int[eger] *<integer_value>*	Specifies *<integer_value>* as the integer value to use.
-bool[ean] true ¦ false ¦ yes ¦ no	Specifies the Boolean value to use.

Managing System Services

Many programs run on your system to provide an assortment of services to you as a local user and to remote users contacting your system. These services range from obvious things (such as terminal services that allow you to connect to your machine from remote locations and file-sharing services) to less obvious but still useful services (such as the ones that provide wall-clock time information and remote machine status information).

Programs that provide service for all users on a machine are generally started by one of two different mechanisms. Either they are started at machine startup, by a series of shell scripts that execute programs during boot, or they are executed by a daemon that waits for requests for service and starts the appropriate program to handle the request.

Traditional Unixes manage most system services through `inetd` and/or `xinetd`. Early releases of Mac OS X used `inetd` and `SystemStarter` as the primary mechanisms for managing system services. Starting with Mac OS X 10.3, `xinetd` and `SystemStarter` were the primary mechanisms. Starting with Mac OS X 10.4, `launchd` has become the primary mechanism for managing system services. However, vestiges of `xinetd` and `SystemStarter` remain in Tiger. In this section, we will take a look at the basic files involved in stopping and starting services, the services used to stop and start services, and commands used to stop and reboot the machine itself.

Starting and Stopping Services: `launchd`

New with Tiger is the `launchd` service. This is Apple's own home-grown service-control daemon, and `xinetd`, discussed in a later section, is becoming a legacy-support option. For new services support, and for older services that have been tested with the new launch configuration, Apple is gravitating toward the use of `launchd`.

16

Understanding Files in `/System/Library/LaunchDaemons`

The system stores the information that `launchd` needs for determining what services to start in `/System/Library/LaunchDaemons`. This directory now contains files for a number of services that were previously controlled either by `SystemStarter` or `xinetd`. The following is a listing of the `/System/Library/LaunchDaemons` directory:

```
dogbone:/System/Library/LaunchDaemons joray$ ls
bootps.plist                            finger.plist
com.apple.KernelEventAgent.plist        ftp.plist
com.apple.atrun.plist                   login.plist
com.apple.mDNSResponder.plist           nmbd.plist
com.apple.nibindd.plist                 ntalk.plist
com.apple.periodic-daily.plist          org.isc.named.plist
com.apple.periodic-monthly.plist        org.postfix.master.plist
com.apple.periodic-weekly.plist         org.xinetd.xinetd.plist
com.apple.portmap.plist                 printer.plist
com.apple.syslogd.plist                 shell.plist
com.apple.xgridagentd.plist             smbd.plist
com.apple.xgridcontrollerd.plist        ssh.plist
com.vix.cron.plist                      swat.plist
eppc.plist                              telnet.plist
exec.plist                              tftp.plist
```

These services are described in Table 16.3.

TABLE 16.3 Typical Items in the `/System/Library/LaunchDaemons` Directory

File	Description
`bootps.plist`	`bootp` is a way of transmitting network configuration information to clients. Chances are you'll use DHCP for this, if you have the need to do so, although it's possible that Mac OS X server could use `bootp` for `netboot` clients. Formerly started out of `xinetd`.
`com.apple.KernelEventAgent.plist`	Starts the kernel event agent. This is an undocumented service. Perhaps it involves communication between parts of the kernel. Formerly started out of `SystemStarter`.
`com.apple.atrun.plist`	Starts `atrun`, which runs jobs queued for later execution by `at`, which is usually invoked by `cron`.
`com.apple.mDNSResponder.plist`	Starts the multicast DNS Responder, the part of the Bonjour system that listens for and responds to DNS-format query packets. Formerly started out of `SystemStarter`.
`com.apple.nibindd.plist`	Starts the NetInfo binder, which is responsible for finding, creating and destroying NetInfo servers.
`com.apple.periodic-daily.plist`	Runs periodic system functions daily. These actions usually occur daily at 3:15 a.m.. It is intended to be called by `cron`.
`com.apple.periodic-monthly.plist`	Runs periodic system functions monthly. These actions occur on the first day of the month at 5:30AM. It is intended to be called by `cron`.
`com.apple.periodic-weekly.plist`	Runs periodic system functions weekly. These actions occur on Saturdays at 3:15 a.m It is intended to be called by `cron`.
`com.apple.portmap.plist`	Provides connectivity between remote machines and services on your machine that don't have defined TCP/IP ports that they run on. Formerly started out of `SystemStarter`.
`com.apple.syslogd.plist`	Starts the system logging daemon. Formerly started out of `SystemStarter`.
`com.apple.xgridagentd.plist`	Starts `xgridagentd`, the service then connects to an `xgrid` controller. `xgrid` is the Apple product that sets up a cluster of machines for distributed computing. The product is similar to the Sun Grid Engine.
`com.apple.xgridcontollerd.plist`	Starts the `xgrid` controller service, which controls how `xgrid` jobs are handled.
`com.vix.cron.plist`	A service that starts various programs at specified times or specified intervals. Formerly started out of `SystemStarter`.

TABLE 16.3 Continued

`eppc.plist`	Starts the Apple Event Server, which handles incoming AppleEvents. AppleEvents are communications between applications and the system. Originally started out of `SystemStarter` and then out of `xinetd` in 10.3.
`exec.plist`	Starts `rexecd`, a service that allows for the remote execution of parts of programs. Apple claims that it isn't known to be useful, but a programmer can make good use of this service to perform distributed processing tasks by sending parts of the programs to many different machines. Of course, it is a security risk. Originally run out of `inetd` and then `xinetd`.
`finger.plist`	The `fingerd` daemon allows external users to finger a user ID and find out whether the ID exists; if it does, how recently, and on what terminals the ID has been logged in. Originally started out of `inetd` and then `xinetd`.
`ftp.plist`	The `ftpd` daemon provides an FTP *(File Transfer Protocol)* server. Originally started out of `inetd`, and then `xinetd`. You can find more information on `ftpd` in Chapter 22.
`login.plist`	Provides service for the `rlogin` remote login terminal program. Don't turn this on. Originally started out of `inetd` and then `xinetd`.
`nmbd.plist`	The NetBIOS name server provides NetBIOS over IP naming services to clients. It is a part of the samba suite. Formerly started out of `xinetd`. You can find more information on providing Windows services in Chapter 27.
`ntalk.plist`	The `ntalk` (new protocol talk) daemon provides for real-time chat services. If you're familiar with ICQ, iChat or IRC, this service is somewhat similar. Originally started out of `inetd` and then `xinetd`.
`org.isc.named.plist`	Starts the name server. Previously started out of `SystemStarter`.
`org.postfix.master.plist`	Starts the postfix mail server. Previously started out of `SystemStarter`.
`org.xinetd.xinetd.plist`	A service that starts and controls other services. It is a more secure replacement for the traditional `inetd`, and it first entered the Mac OS X distribution with 10.2. Commonly used on many Unix platforms, but is being phased out of Mac OS X. Previously started out of `SystemStarter`.

TABLE 16.3 Continued

`printer.plist`	Starts the CUPS *(Common Unix Printing Service)* line printer daemon printing service that provides some legacy printing support. For more information on printing, see Chapter 6.
`shell.plist`	Starts `rshd`, a service that provides remote shell access. This service is required to use certain remote services, such as remote tape archive storage. Because Apple hasn't provided all the software necessary to make full use of these services, we suggest that this be left off as well; it's almost as large a security risk as `rlogin` and `telnet`. Originally started out of `inetd` and then `xinetd`.
`smbd.plist`	Provides printing and file share services to Windows clients. Originally started out of `SystemStarter` and then `xinetd`. You can find more information on providing Windows services in Chapter 27.
`ssh.plist`	Starts SSH, the secure shell service. This service provides remote terminal access over an encrypted channel. Originally started out of `SystemStarter` and then `xinetd`. For more information on SSH, see chapter 21.
`swat.plist`	Starts `swat`, the Samba Web Administration Tool. Previously started out of `xinetd`. You can find more information on providing Windows services in Chapter 27.
`telnet.plist`	Provides the `telnet` daemon to allow remote `telnet` terminal access. Don't turn this on.
`tftp.plist`	`tftp` is trivial file transfer protocol and is one of the methods of providing file service to completely disk-less network clients. You won't need to enable this service unless you're providing network boot services for diskless Unix clients.

Because the FTP server is one that you might consider replacing, we will look at the default `ftp.plist`. Listing 16.1 shows a sample `plist` file from this directory.

NOTE

The numbers shown in Listing 16.4 are shown here to make the description of the file easier to follow. The line numbers are not and should not be in the actual file. This is also the case for all the listings in this chapter with line numbers.

LISTING 16.4 The Default `/System/Library/LaunchDaemons/ftp.plist` File

```
 1 <?xml version="1.0" encoding="UTF-8"?>
 2 <!DOCTYPE plist PUBLIC "-//Apple Computer//DTD PLIST 1.0//EN"
   ➥"http://www.apple.com/DTDs/PropertyList-1.0.dtd">
 3 <plist version="1.0">
 4 <dict>
 5         <key>Disabled</key>
 6         <true/>
 7         <key>Label</key>
 8         <string>com.apple.ftpd</string>
 9         <key>Program</key>
10         <string>/usr/libexec/ftpd</string>
11         <key>ProgramArguments</key>
12         <array>
13                 <string>ftpd</string>
14                 <string>-l</string>
15         </array>
16         <key>inetdCompatibility</key>
17         <dict>
18                 <key>Wait</key>
19                 <false/>
20         </dict>
21         <key>Sockets</key>
22         <dict>
23                 <key>Listeners</key>
24                 <dict>
25                         <key>SockServiceName</key>
26                         <string>ftp</string>
27                         <key>Bonjour</key>
28                         <true/>
29                 </dict>
30         </dict>
31 </dict>
32 </plist>
```

From this file we learn the following:

- Lines 5–6 show that the `Disabled` key is true. Because the default for the `Disabled` key is `false`, when a service has been enabled, the `Disabled` key is removed.
- Lines 7–8 show how the program will be listed when you list all the jobs loaded into `launchd`. This one will be listed as `com.apple.ftpd`.
- Lines 9–10 list where the service is located. In this case, the default `ftpd` is in `/usr/local/libexec/ftpd`. This is the equivalent of the sixth column of an `/etc/inetd.conf` file's `ftp` line.

- Lines 11–15 list how the program will be run, including any runtime options. This is equivalent to the final column in an /etc/inetd.conf file.
- In lines 16–20, the inetdCompatibility key indicates to launchd that the service expects to be run as though it were launched from inetd. The Wait flag for that key is set to false, which is the equivalent of the nowait entry in /etc/inetd.conf.
- Lines 21–28 are the Sockets section, which specifies launch on demand sockets that can be used to let launchd know when to run the job. The ftp entry tells launchd to connect to the ftp service. The Bonjour key enables the FTP server to be found via Bonjour.

Understanding launchd

There are various ways to start services that run via launchd. First try /sbin/service. For example, to replace the default ftpd with a new one, stop the FTP server using /sbin/service, if it was already running. Keep a copy of your original ftp.plist, and then edit the file with appropriate changes for the new FTP server. Start the ftp service with /sbin/service. As long as you keep the ftp.plist name for your new FTP server, you can also start and stop the FTP server via launchd by using the Sharing preferences pane.

If /sbin/service does not work for you, you can try to unload the old ftp job, if it was already loaded, and then load your new ftp job. Note that you must be root or use sudo to do this.

```
localhost:/System/Library/LaunchDaemons root# launchctl list
com.apple.KernelEventAgent
com.apple.launchd_helperd
com.apple.mDNSResponder
com.apple.nibindd
com.apple.portmap
com.apple.syslogd
com.openssh.sshd
com.apple.ftpd
localhost:/System/Library/LaunchDaemons root# launchctl unload /System/Library/
                                             ➥LaunchDaemons/ftp.plist
localhost:/System/Library/LaunchDaemons root# launchctl list
com.apple.KernelEventAgent
com.apple.launchd_helperd
com.apple.mDNSResponder
com.apple.nibindd
com.apple.portmap
com.apple.syslogd
com.openssh.sshd
localhost:/System/Library/LaunchDaemons root# launchctl load /System/Library/
                                             ➥LaunchDaemons/ftp.plist
localhost:/System/Library/LaunchDaemons root# launchctl list
```

```
com.apple.KernelEventAgent
com.apple.launchd_helperd
com.apple.mDNSResponder
com.apple.nibindd
com.apple.portmap
com.apple.syslogd
com.openssh.sshd
com.apple.proftpd
```

What we have done here is, as `root`, we have looked at what jobs are loaded into `launchd` already with `launchctl list`. In this case, the default FTP server was running. With the `launchctl unload` command, we removed the current FTP server job and then we verified with `launchctl list` that the job was indeed removed. Next we edited the `ftp.plist` file (not shown). Included in our edits was a change in the job name, so that we could tell at a glance which FTP server is running. With `launchtl load`, we loaded our new `ftp.plist`, and then verified that the new job was loaded with `launchctl list`. Listing 16.5 shows an example of a modified `ftp.plist` that enables `proftpd` as the default FTP server. In this example, the `Disabled` key could have been omitted.

Please note that you should probably more properly store your modified `ftp.plist` in `/Library/StartupItems/`, to ensure that system updates do not overwrite your modified file, but you might not be able to start and stop the FTP server from the Sharing preferences pane.

16

LISTING 16.5 A Modified `/System/Library/LaunchDaemons/ftp.plist`

```
<?xml version="1.0" encoding="UTF-8"?>
<!DOCTYPE plist PUBLIC "-//Apple Computer//DTD PLIST 1.0//EN"
➥"http://www.apple.com/DTDs/PropertyList-1.0.dtd">
<plist version="1.0">
<dict>
        <key>Disabled</key>
        <false/>
        <key>Label</key>
        <string>com.apple.proftpd</string>
        <key>Program</key>
        <string>/usr/local/sbin/proftpd</string>
        <key>inetdCompatibility</key>
        <dict>
                <key>Wait</key>
                <false/>
        </dict>
        <key>Sockets</key>
        <dict>
                <key>Listeners</key>
                <dict>
```

LISTING 16.5 Continued

```
                    <key>SockServiceName</key>
                    <string>ftp</string>
                    <key>Bonjour</key>
                    <true/>
               </dict>
          </dict>
</dict>
</plist>
```

If you decide to run a new FTP server via `xinetd` rather than `launchd`, stop the current FTP server, if you have it running. Then move the default `ftp.plist` file elsewhere, such as `/System/Library/LaunchDaemons-disabled/`. We find that moving `ftp.plist` completely out of its default location makes everything work together better. Create your `/etc/xinetd.d/ftp` control file, and then start the FTP server with `/sbin/service`. Please note that if you decide to run the replacement FTP server via `xinetd`, the Sharing preferences pane FTP control can no longer be used. If you do decide to replace your FTP server, we recommend running it out of `xinetd` rather than `launchd`. At this time, you have a lot more control over the FTP server through `xinetd`.

Command documentation for `launchd` is included in Table 16.4, and select command documentation is included for `launchctl` in Table 16.5. Be sure to take a look at the `launchctl` documentation table. It suggests a couple ways that you could probably start and stop jobs via `launchctl`.

TABLE 16.4 Command Documentation for `launchd`

`launchd`	Systemwide and per-user daemon/agent manager.
`launchd [-vsx]`	
`launchd` manages daemons, both for the system as a whole and for individual users. Ideal daemons can launch on demand based on criteria specified in their respective XML property lists specified in the Files section. During boot, `launchd` is invoked by the kernel to run as the first process on the system and to further bootstrap the rest of the system.	
Extra Options When Run as PID 1	
`-s`	Single-user mode. Instructs `launchd` to give a shell prompt before booting the system.
`-v`	Verbose mode.
`-x`	Safe mode. Instructs the system to boot conservatively.
Files	
`~/Library/LaunchAgents`	Per-user agents provided by the user.
`/Library/LaunchAgents`	Per-user agents provided by the administrator.
`/Library/LaunchDaemons`	Systemwide daemons provided by the administrator.
`/System/Library/LaunchAgents`	Mac OS X per-user agents.
`/System/Library/LaunchDaemons`	Mac OS X systemwide daemons.

TABLE 16.5 Select Command Documentation for `launchctl`

`launchctl`	Interfaces with `launchd`.
`launchctl` interfaces with `launchd` to load, unload daemons/agents and generally control `launchd`. `launchctl` supports taking subcommands on the command line, interactively, or even redirected from standard input. These commands can be stored in `$HOME/.launchd.conf` or `/etc/launchd.conf` to be read at the time `launchd` starts.	
`load [-w]` *<paths>*	Loads the specified configuration files or directories of configuration files. The optional `-w` removes the disabled key and write the configuration files back out to disk.
`unload [-w]` *<paths>*	Unloads the specified configuration files or directories of configuration files. The optional `-w` add the disabled key and write the configuration files back out to disk.
`start` *<joblabels>*	Starts the specified jobs by label.
`stop` *<joblabels>*	Stops the specified jobs by label. Jobs may restart automatically if demand driven.
`list`	Lists all the jobs loaded into `launchd`.
`limit [cpu ¦ filesize ¦ data ¦ stack ¦ core ¦ rss ¦ memlock ¦ maxproc ¦ maxfiles] [both [soft ¦ hard]]`	With no arguments, this command prints all the resource limits of launchd as found via `getrlimit`. When a given resource is specified, it prints the limits for that resource. With a third argument, it sets both the hard and soft limits to that value. With four arguments, the third and forth argument represent the soft and hard limits respectively. See `setrlimit`.
`shutdown`	Tells `launchd` to prepare for shutdown by removing all jobs.
help	Prints out a quick usage statement.

Starting and Stopping Services: `SystemStarter`

The only mechanism for starting and stopping services that has been included with Mac OS X since its inception is `SystemStarter`. This mechanism is being phased out, but is still persists in the Tiger release. In this section, we will look at some of the important files associated with `SystemStarter` and how to use it.

Understanding `/etc/hostconfig`

As mentioned earlier, `/etc/hostconfig` is an important configuration file for a Mac OS X machine. It configures variables that are primarily used by services that start via `SystemStarter`. The values in the `/etc/hostconfig` come partly from settings in the System Preferences panes and partly from manual modification (even though the file says that it should be touched only by the controls). The `/etc/hostconfig` on your machine should look similar to Listing 16.6.

LISTING 16.6 A Typical `/etc/hostconfig` File

```
 1 AFPSERVER=-NO-
 2 AUTHSERVER=-NO-
 3 AUTOMOUNT=-NO-
 4 CUPS=-AUTOMATIC-
 5 NFSLOCKS=-YES-
 6 NISDOMAIN=-NO-
 7 TIMESYNC=-YES-
 8 QTSSERVER=-NO-
 9 WEBSERVER=-NO-
10 SMBSERVER=-NO-
11 SNMPSERVER=-NO-
12 SPOTLIGHT=-YES-
13 ARDAGENT=-YES-
14 CRASHREPORTER=-YES-
```

Briefly, the lines in this listing specify the following information:

- Line 1 indicates that the machine isn't providing AppleShare Filing Protocol services, which are necessary for serving files via AppleShare.
- Line 2 specifies that the machine isn't providing authentication services.
- Line 3 controls whether the NFS Automounter will run. If you're not using NFS, it seems to make no difference. We aren't fans of NFS automounting for normal Unix installations and aren't sure what to think of it on Mac OS X. You learn more about NFS in Chapter 20.
- Line 4 controls whether the machine has printing services running.
- Line 5 controls whether or not NFS locking support is available for the machine, but when it functions as an NFS client and as an NFS server.
- Line 6 specifies which, if any, NIS domain the machine belongs to. NIS is the traditional Unix way of distributing user ID and password information to multiple machines in a cluster. If you have an existing Unix installation, you can subscribe your Mac OS X machine to the Unix machine's account information.
- Line 7 determines whether the machine should use a remote time server to synchronize its clock.
- Line 8 specifies whether the machine functions as a QuickTime streaming server. This technology is detailed in Chapter 25, "Darwin Streaming Server and QuickTime Broadcaster."
- Line 9 controls whether the machine functions as a web (HTTPD) server. How to enable and configure your machine as a high-powered web server is covered in Chapter 23, "Creating a Web Server."

- Line 10 configures whether the machine can serve files to Windows machines. How to enable and configure your machine to serve a Windows network is covered in Chapter 27, "Working with Windows-Based Systems."
- Line 11 configures whether the machine runs SNMP *(Simple Network Management Protocol)*. This protocol is used to manage network devices, such as routers.
- Line 12 sets whether the machine has Spotlight, the new searching technology, running. Details on Spotlight can be found in Chapter 1, "Managing the Tiger Workspace."
- Line 13 configures whether the machine functions as an Apple Remote Desktop client. Chapter 21, "Accessing and Controlling Tiger Remotely," has more details on Apple Remote Desktop.
- Line 14 determines whether the machine reports crashes.

NOTE

We've abbreviated the language in the preceding list a bit. The first few entries are worded correctly—the file literally sets the values of variables, and these variables are used elsewhere to configure the properties of the system described. Later items that state that the line *controls* something should be read to mean that it sets a variable that is used by a program elsewhere to control the item.

16

Understanding Files in `/System/Library/StartupItems`

Many of the variables configured in `/etc/`hostconfig are used by files in `/System/Library/StartupItems`. Services that need to be continuously present, such as the software that configures and maintains network connections, are started from startup scripts. These startup scripts are kept in subdirectories of the `/System/Library/StartupItems` directory and are simply shell scripts (such as you learned about in Chapter 15, "Shell Configuration and Programming (Shell Scripting)") that perform simple logic to make sure that everything is right with the system and start the appropriate software.

NOTE

Remember that, in Unix, if you can type it at the command line, you can write it into a shell script. Anything you find that you want to run whenever the system is running can simply be placed in a shell script and that script executed at system startup.

As shipped, your Mac OS X machine should have a complement of items in the `StartupItems` folder similar to that shown in Table 16.6. Don't worry if your `/System/Library/StartupItems/` doesn't contain exactly these items. Depending on what installation options you've chosen, and whether any additional software has been installed by the time you're reading this, your system might display some differences.

TABLE 16.6 Typical Items in the `/System/Library/StartupItems/` Directory

Apache	The web server.
`AppServices`	Assorted support services for the overall GUI interface.
`AppleShare`	AppleShare file sharing.
`AuthServer`	User authentication services.
`CrashReporter`	Reports system crashes to Apple, if desired.
`Disks`	Controls disk operations.
`FibreChannel`	Updates system settings for fibre channel controllers and targets.
`IFCStart`	Controls `ifcstart`, the daemon responsible for rebuilding file caches used by international components of the operating system.
`IPServices`	Controls some services related to TCP/IP networking.
Metadata	Starts the Spotlight service.
`NFS`	Controls use of and access to the NFS (Network File System) Unix file sharing protocol.
`NIS`	Starts NIS *(Network Information Service).*
`NetworkTime`	Interacts with the network time server.
`PrintingServices`	Starts the CUPS *(Common Unix Printing System)* printing service.
`RemoteDesktopAgent`	Starts the Apple Remote Desktop Client.
`SNMP`	Starts the SNMP (Simple Network Management Protocol) service. This protocol is used to manage network devices, such as routers.

Each of these directories contains a number of items—typically a file named after the name of the directory, a directory named `Resources`, and a file named `StartupParameters.plist` (which, oddly, isn't an XML file—it uses the old NeXT-style `plist` format). The file named after the directory (and service) is the actual shell script that is run at system boot time. The `Resources` directory typically contains directories of "resource-like" information, such as files that contain language-replacement strings for language localization. The `StartupParameters.plist` contains a collection of variables and associated values that affect the operation of the service started. To add your own startup script, you need only the startup script itself and a `StartupParameters.plist` file.

Listing 16.7 shows a simple `StartupItems` shell script—this one starts the Apache web server.

LISTING 16.7 The Apache `StartupItems` Shell Script

```
#!/bin/sh

##
# Apache HTTP Server
##

. /etc/rc.common

StartService ()
{
```

LISTING 16.7 Continued

```
    if [ "${WEBSERVER:=-NO-}" = "-YES-" ]; then
        echo "Starting Apache web server"
        if [ ! -e /etc/httpd/httpd.conf ] ; then
                cp -p /etc/httpd/httpd.conf.default /etc/httpd/httpd.conf
        fi
        apachectl start
        if [ "${WEBPERFCACHESERVER:=-NO-}" = "-YES-" ]; then
            if [ -x /usr/sbin/webperfcachectl ]; then
                echo "Starting web performance cache server"
                /usr/sbin/webperfcachectl start
            fi
        fi
    fi
}

StopService ()
{
    if [ -x /usr/sbin/webperfcachectl ]; then
        echo "Stopping web performance cache server"
        /usr/sbin/webperfcachectl stop
    fi
    echo "Stopping Apache web server"
    apachectl stop
}

RestartService ()
{
    if [ "${WEBSERVER:=-NO-}" = "-YES-" ]; then
        echo "Restarting Apache web server"
        apachectl restart
        if [ "${WEBPERFCACHESERVER:=-NO-}" = "-YES-" ]; then
            if [ -x /usr/sbin/webperfcachectl ]; then
                echo "Restarting web performance cache server"
                /usr/sbin/webperfcachectl restart
            fi
        fi
    else
        StopService
    fi
}

RunService "$1"
```

In this listing, items starting with the # sign are comments. The meaning of the lines in the script can be summarized in a simple manner:

- Line 7 sources the script `/etc/rc.common`, where many systemwide definitions are made.
- Line 9 starts the section for the `StartService` case.
- Line 11 checks for the value of the variable `WEBSERVER`, and determines whether the value is `YES` or `NO`. This value is actually extracted from the `/etc/hostconfig` file shown in Listing 16.3.
- If Line 11 finds a yes, line 12 sends a message to the console that says `Starting Apache web server`.
- Furthermore, line 13 checks for the nonexistence of `/etc/httpd/httpd.conf`. If it does not exist the default `/etc/httpd/httpd.conf.default` is copied to `/etc/httpd/httpd.conf`.
- Line 15: `fi` is *if* backwards, and it terminates the conditional expression started by the `if` on line 13.
- Line 16 executes the program `apachectl` with the argument `start`. `apachectl` is actually another shell script, specific to the Apache installation, which handles all the real work of starting the service.
- Line 17 checks for the value of the variable `WEBPERFCACHESERVER`, and determines whether the value is `YES` or `NO`. This value is actually extracted from the `/etc/hostconfig` file shown in Listing 16.3. Mac OS X server includes this variable in `/etc/hostconfig`.
- If Line 17 finds a yes, line 18 starts the process of looking for whether an executable called `/usr/sbin/webperfcachectl` exists.
- If Line 18 finds that the file exists, line 19 sends a message to the console that says `Starting web performance cache server`.
- Line 20 executes the program `/usr/sbin/webperfcachectl` with the argument start. `webperfcachectl` is included in Mac OS X Server.
- Line 21 terminates the conditional expression started by the `if` on line 19.
- Line 22 terminates the conditional expression started by the `if` on line 17.
- Line 23 terminates the conditional expression started by the `if` on line 11.
- Line 26 starts the section for the `StopService` case.
- Line 28 checks for the existence of an executable file called `/usr/sbin/webperfcachectl`.

- If line 28 finds a yes, then line 29 sends a message to the console that says `Stopping the web performance cache server.`
- Line 30 actually executes `webperfcachectl stop` to stop the web performance cache server.
- Line 31 terminates the conditional expression started by the `if` on line 28.
- Line 32 displays a message that says `Stopping Apache web server.`
- Line 33 actually executes `apachectl` stop to stop the Apache web server.
- Line 36 starts the section for the `RestartService` case.
- Line 38 checks for the value of the variable `WEBSERVER`, and determines whether the value is `YES` or `NO`.
- If Line 38 finds a yes, line 39 sends a message to the console that says `Restarting Apache web server.`
- Line 40 actually executes `apachectl restart` to restart the Apache web server.
- Line 41 checks for the value of the variable `WEBPERFCACHESERVER`, and determines whether the value is `YES` or `NO`.
- If line 41 finds a `YES`, line 42 starts the process of looking for whether an executable called `/usr/sbin/webperfcachectl` exists.
- If line 42 finds that the file exists, line 43 sends a message to the console that says `Restarting web performance cache server.`
- Line 44 executes `/usr/sbin/webperfcachectl` restart to restart the web performance cache server.
- Line 45 terminates the conditional expression started by the `if` on line 42.
- Line 46 terminates the conditional expression started by the `if` on line 41.
- If line 38 finds a `NO`, line 47 starts the `else` section for what to do instead.
- Line 48 goes to the `StopService` case.
- Line 49 terminates the conditional expression started by the `if` on line 38.
- Line 52 specifies that `RunService` execute the first command-line argument it receives. For this line to make more sense, it is helpful to look at the `RunService` section of `/etc/rc.common`, where you can see that the expected options are `start`, which executes `StartService`; `stop`, which executes `StopService`; and `restart`, which executes `RestartService`. If none of the expected arguments is given, it returns a response that the argument is an unknown argument. Listing 16.8 shows the `RunService` section of `/etc/rc.common`.

16

LISTING 16.8 The `RunService` section of `/etc/rc.common`

```
RunService ()
{
    case $1 in
      start  ) StartService   ;;
      stop   ) StopService    ;;
      restart) RestartService ;;
      *      ) echo "$0: unknown argument: $1";;
    esac
}
```

The `StartupParameters.plist` file for Apache is shown in Listing 16.9. The `StartupParameters.plist` file for Apache makes use of three of the types of available key types: Description, Provides and Uses. As you might guess, the Description is a brief description of the service. The Provides key lists what kind of service the service provides, and the Uses key lists any other services that this service may use. The services that it uses should start before it does, but they are not necessarily required for this service to start. For more information on the `StartupParameters.plist` file, see `http://developer.apple.com/documentation/MacOSX/Conceptual/BPSystemStartup/Tasks/CreatingStartupItems.html`.

LISTING 16.9 The `StartupParameters.plist` File for Apache

```
{
  Description       = "Apache web server";
  Provides          = ("Web Server");
  Uses              = ("Disks", "NFS");
}
```

In Chapter 22, "Creating an FTP Server," it is mentioned that you could choose to run the new FTP server as a standalone FTP server by adding a startup script to your system. You will need to create a directory to store your startup script. We recommend something like `/Library/StartupItems/ProFTPD/`. As we have seen in this section, the startup script would have to be called `ProFTPD` for this example. Include a line in the script that starts the new FTP server. Also required is a `StartupParameters.plist` file. Recommended ownership for items in `/Library/StartupItems/` is to have the items owned by `root`, in group `admin`. The startup script, `ProFTPD`, should be executable. Reboot the machine to test that the new FTP server does indeed start at startup.

Here is a listing of our files:

```
localhost:/Library/StartupItems joray$ ls -l
total 16
-rwxr-xr-x   1 root  admin  115 Feb  7 11:25 ProFTPD
-rw-r--r--   1 root  admin  216 Feb  7 11:29 StartupParameters.plist
```

Listing 16.10 shows our sample startup script, and Listing 16.11 shows our sample `StartupParameters.plist` for the replacement FTP server.

LISTING 16.10 Sample `/Library/StartupItems/ProFTPD/ProFTPD`

```
#!/bin/sh

. /etc/rc.common

##
# Start up ProFTPD
##

ConsoleMessage "Starting ProFTPD"

/usr/local/sbin/proftpd
```

LISTING 16.11 Sample `/Library/StartupItems/ProFTPD/StartupParameters.plist`

```
{
  Description     = "ProFTPD";
  Provides        = ("proftpd");
  Requires        = ("Resolver");
  OrderPreference = "None";
  Messages =
  {
    start = "Starting ProFTPD";
    stop  = "Stopping ProFTPD";
  };
}
```

Unfortunately, the Apache web server, like many of the services in `/System/Library/StartupItems`, does not have a Resources directory. The English language locale configuration for the `CrashReporter` `StartupItems` (`CrashReporter/Resources/English.lproj/Localizable.strings`) is shown in Listing 16.12.

LISTING 16.12 The English Language Locale Configuration for the `CrashReporter` `StartupItems`

```
<?xml version="1.0" encoding="UTF-8"?>
<!DOCTYPE plist SYSTEM "file://localhost/System/Library/DTDs/PropertyList.dtd">
<plist version="0.9">
<dict>
        <key>Starting crash reporter</key>
        <string>Starting crash reporter</string>
</dict>
</plist>
```

16

This XML file specifies a key, the expression `Starting crash reporter`, and a local (English) replacement string for that expression `Starting crash reporter`. If everything works as intended, whenever the program attempts to print the key value, the system instead outputs the replacement string value. Because this isn't quite obvious from the English example, Listing 16.13 shows the `Italian.lproj` version of the `Localizable.strings` file.

LISTING 16.13 `Italian.lproj` Version of the `Localizable.strings` File for the `CrashReporter` Service

```
<?xml version="1.0" encoding="UTF-8"?>
<!DOCTYPE plist PUBLIC "-//Apple Computer//DTD PLIST 1.0//EN"
➥"http://www.apple.com/DTDs/PropertyList-1.0.dtd">
<plist version="1.0">
<dict>
        <key>Starting crash reporter</key>
        <string>Avvio resoconto blocco sistema</string>
</dict>
</plist>
```

Here, it is more obvious that the localization file is requesting a search to find `Starting crash reporter` and replacing it with the Italian equivalent.

Understanding `SystemStarter`

`SystemStarter` is used for starting and stopping services whose controls are located in `/System/Library/StartupItems` or `/Library/StartupItems`. If you need to manually start, stop, or restart one of these services, the `SystemStarter` utility may be used. Basic syntax is

```
SystemStarter <action> <service>
```

The action can be `start`, `stop` or `restart`, and the service is whatever is listed as the `Provides` variable in the `StartupParameters.plist` file. For example,

```
dogbone:~ joray$ sudo SystemStarter restart "Web Server"
Password:
Restarting Apache web server
/usr/sbin/apachectl restart: httpd restarted
```

restarts the Apache web service.

If you have any trouble with `SystemStarter`, try sending the action you want to occur directly to the startup script with this basic syntax:

```
<startup-script> <action>
```

For example, you can restart the Apache web service by running:

```
dogbone:~ joray$ sudo /System/Library/StartupItems/Apache/Apache  restart
Password:
```

```
Restarting Apache web server
/usr/sbin/apachectl restart: httpd restarted
```

This latter syntax is common in certain flavors of Unix and can therefore be useful to you outside Mac OS X. Depending on the startup script, even the latter syntax might not work properly. In that case, try manually executing the appropriate command from the section of the appropriate portion of the script. For something that requires detailed configuration, you might have to properly configure the service before you get the desired results. Table 16.7 includes command documentation for `SystemStarter`.

TABLE 16.7 Syntax and Selected Options for `SystemStarter`

`SystemStarter`	Starts, stops and restarts system services.
`SystemStarter [-gvxdDqn] [<action> [<service>]]`	
The `SystemStarter` utility can be used to start, stop, and restart system services, which are described in `/Library/StartupItems/` and `/System/Library/StartupItems/` paths.	
The optional `<action>` argument specifies which action `SystemStarter` performs on the startup items.	
The optional `<service>` argument specifies which startup items to perform the action on. If no service is specified, all startup items are acted on; otherwise, only the item providing the service, any items it requires, or any items that depend on it will be acted on.	
Actions	
`start`	Starts all items, or starts the item that provides the specified `<service>` and all items providing services it requires.
`stop`	Stops all items, or stops the item that provides the specified `<service>` and all items that depend on it.
`restart`	Restarts all items, or restarts the item providing the specified `<service>`.
Options	
`-g`	Graphical startup.
`-x`	Safe mode startup (runs only Apple-provided items).
`-n`	Doesn't actually perform action on items (no-run mode).

Starting and Stopping Services: `inetd` and `xinetd`

In traditional Unixes, `inetd` is the service that starts other services. The `inetd` service is typically available on any Unix system. Mac OS X 10.0 and 10.1 included `inetd`. However, some administrators choose to install `xinetd`, the extended Internet services daemon, as a replacement for `inetd`. Mac OS X 10.2 included both `inetd` and `xinetd` as equivalent peers. Starting with Mac OS X 10.3, `inetd` was not included, but `xinetd` ran in `inetd`-compatibility mode. In Mac OS X 10.4, `xinetd` is included, and can run in `inetd`-compatibility mode.

Although the current release of Mac OS X does not use `xinetd` much, we still feel that a discussion of both types of configuration files is important. Understanding the basic format of those files will mostly be helpful in dealing with third-party applications that might prefer to run out of `xinetd`. The `launchd` documentation also includes some dire warnings regarding certain actions that services could take, which would break the `launchd` system, so `xinetd` might remain the only option for some network services.

If you are thinking about replacing a default service that can be run out of `xinetd` rather than `launchd`, pick `xinetd` as the startup mechanism. If the service will have so much traffic that you feel it should be a constantly running service, run it out of `/System/Library/StartupItems`.

In this section we will take a look the basic configuration files used for `inetd` and `xinetd` and how to start services through `xinetd`.

Controlling `inetd/xinetd` Managed Processes

As mentioned earlier, the `inetd` service, configured by the `/etc/inetd.conf` file, actually is a service that starts and controls other services. It's not practical to start an unlimited number of some types of network services and leave them running, right from startup. Depending on the use of your machine, some services might be needed in great numbers; for example, the `ftpd` FTP server processes, if you serve particularly interesting data and have many people connecting simultaneously. Others might be used hardly at all, such as the `sprayd` network diagnostic daemon. Or, on your system, the use pattern might be the opposite—but regardless of the use, patterns are likely to vary over time. For many of these types of services, the system relieves you of the task of trying to provide the right number of these servers in some manual configuration process, by using the `inetd` daemon to configure and run them on an as-needed basis.

> **NOTE**
>
> If you want to learn much more about network services in general, you're invited to check out Que Publishing's *Special Edition Using TCP/IP* (ISBN 0-7897-1897-9), another book by John Ray.

The `inetd.conf` file is the file that tells `inetd` which services it should start and how. Starting with Mac OS X 10.3, however, Apple no longer provides an `inetd` service, but the provided `xinetd` runs in `inetd` compatibility mode. The `/etc/inetd.conf` file can still be used, but instead it can configure `xinetd`.

The default `inetd.conf` file as it comes from Apple is shown in Listing 16.14. The # symbol in front of each item indicates that the line is commented out and will not be run. Many of the services that run out of `inetd/xinetd` are security holes.

LISTING 16.14 A Typical `/etc/inetd.conf` File

```
# WARNING
#
# Mac OS 10.2 and forward uses xinetd instead of the traditional inetd.
# See xinetd.conf(5) if you need to add a service to run out of xinetd.
# Please use /sbin/service to interface over editing the shipped files
# in /etc/xinetd.d directly. For example:
# /sbin/service telnet start
# /sbin/service telnet stop
# /sbin/service --list
#
```

LISTING 16.14 Continued

```
# Internet server configuration database
#
#       @(#)inetd.conf  5.4 (Berkeley) 6/30/90
#
# Items with double hashes in front (##) are not yet implemented in the OS.
#
#finger stream  tcp  nowait  nobody  /usr/libexec/tcpd  fingerd -s
#ftp    stream  tcp  nowait  root    /usr/libexec/tcpd  ftpd -l
#login  stream  tcp  nowait  root    /usr/libexec/tcpd  rlogind
#nntp   stream  tcp  nowait  usenet  /usr/libexec/tcpd  nntpd
#ntalk  dgram   udp  wait    root    /usr/libexec/tcpd  ntalkd
#shell  stream  tcp  nowait  root    /usr/libexec/tcpd  rshd
#telnet stream  tcp  nowait  root    /usr/libexec/tcpd  telnetd
#uucpd  stream  tcp  nowait  root    /usr/libexec/tcpd  uucpd
#comsat dgram   udp  wait    root    /usr/libexec/tcpd  comsat
#tftp   dgram   udp  wait    nobody  /usr/libexec/tcpd  tftpd /private/tftpboot
#bootps dgram   udp  wait    root    /usr/libexec/tcpd  bootpd
##pop3  stream  tcp  nowait  root  /usr/libexec/tcpd  /usr/local/libexec/popper
##imap4 stream  tcp  nowait  root  /usr/libexec/tcpd  /usr/local/libexec/imapd
#
# "Small servers" -- used to be standard on, but we're more conservative
# about things due to Internet security concerns.  Only turn on what you
# need.
#
#chargen stream tcp     nowait  root    internal
#chargen dgram  udp     wait    root    internal
#daytime stream tcp     nowait  root    internal
#daytime dgram  udp     wait    root    internal
#discard stream tcp     nowait  root    internal
#discard dgram  udp     wait    root    internal
#echo    stream tcp     nowait  root    internal
#echo    dgram  udp     wait    root    internal
#time    stream tcp     nowait  root    internal
#time    dgram  udp     wait    root    internal
#
# Kerberos (version 5) authenticated services
#
##eklogin   stream tcp   nowait root     /usr/libexec/tcpd    klogind -k -c -e
##klogin    stream tcp   nowait root     /usr/libexec/tcpd    klogind -k -c
##kshd      stream tcp   nowait root     /usr/libexec/tcpd    kshd -k -c -A
#krb5_prop stream tcp   nowait root     /usr/libexec/tcpd    kpropd
#
# RPC based services (you MUST have portmapper running to use these)
#
```

LISTING 16.14 Continued

```
55 ##rstatd/1-3    dgram rpc/udp wait root /usr/libexec/tcpd        rpc.rstatd
56 ##rusersd/1-2   dgram rpc/udp wait root /usr/libexec/tcpd        rpc.rusersd
57 ##walld/1       dgram rpc/udp wait root /usr/libexec/tcpd        rpc.rwalld
58 ##pcnfsd/1-2    dgram rpc/udp wait root /usr/libexec/tcpd        rpc.pcnfsd
59 ##rquotad/1     dgram rpc/udp wait root /usr/libexec/tcpd        rpc.rquotad
60 ##sprayd/1      dgram rpc/udp wait root /usr/libexec/tcpd        rpc.sprayd
61 #
62 # The following are not known to be useful, and should not be enabled unless
63 # you have a specific need for it and are aware of the possible implications.
64 #
65 #exec    stream  tcp     nowait  root    /usr/libexec/tcpd        rexecd
66 #auth    stream  tcp     wait    root    /usr/libexec/identd      identd -w -t120
```

Briefly, the intent of the services on each line is as follows:

- Lines 1–9—This section provides a comment that Mac OS X now uses `xinetd` by default and lists the syntax for using `/sbin/service` to enable and disable services through `xinetd`.
- Line 17—The `fingerd` daemon allows external users to finger a user ID and find out whether the ID exists; if it does, how recently, and on what terminals the ID has been logged in.
- Line 18—The `ftpd` daemon provides an FTP *(file transfer protocol)* server.
- Line 19—The `login` service provides service for the `rlogin` remote login terminal program. Don't turn this on.
- Line 20—The `nntp` service is a Usenet newsgroups server. If your machine is configured to receive news from other servers, you can point your newsreader to your local machine to read news.
- Line 21—The `ntalk` *(new protocol talk)* daemon provides for real-time chat services. If you're familiar with ICQ, iChat, or IRC, this service is somewhat similar.
- Line 22—Provides remote shell service—another way to remotely access machines. This service is required to use certain remote services, such as remote tape archive storage. Because Apple hasn't provided all the software necessary to make full use of these services, we suggest that this be left off as well; it's almost as large a security risk as `rlogin` and `telnet`.
- Line 23—Provides the `telnet` daemon to allow remote `telnet` terminal connections. Don't turn this on.
- Line 24—The `uucpd` service implements the Unix-to-Unix Copy Protocol. This is an antiquated method for networking Unix machines that can't always be connected to the network. Essentially, it allows network traffic between two sites to be queued until both sites are available on the network and then exchanges the data. This

service is of limited utility today and presents a significant security risk because it hasn't really been maintained since the days of 1200-baud modems.

- Line 25—The `comsat` daemon provides notification of incoming mail to mail-reader clients.
- Line 26—`tftp` is trivial file transfer protocol and is one of the methods of providing file service to completely diskless network clients. You won't need to enable this service unless you're providing network boot services for diskless Unix clients.
- Line 27—`bootp` is a way of transmitting network configuration information to clients. Chances are you'll use DHCP for this, if you have a need to do so, although it's possible that Mac OS X Server could use `bootp` for netboot clients.
- Line 28—`pop3` is a POPmail (Post Office Protocol Mail) server. In the file, Apple indicates that this service is not yet available.
- Line 29—`imap4` is an IMAP mail server. Again, this service is not available as of the 10.4 release.
- Lines 35–42—Provide a number of network and network-software diagnostic servers. Unless you are performing network diagnosis and specifically need these, leave them off. They do not cause any known security problems, but if you're not using them, they occupy resources needlessly.
- Lines 43 and 44—Provide the time service (some servers require both stream and datagram connectivity, and these must be defined on separate lines). If you want your machine to be a time server, these can be turned on.
- Lines 48–51—Start a number of Kerberos (security authentication) related servers, but most are unavailable from Apple as of the 10.4 release. The `krb5_prop` service (starting `krpropd`) is the server that propagates a master Kerberos server's database to slave servers.
- Line 55—The `rstatd` daemon allows systems to connect through the network and get machine status information.
- Line 56—The `rusersd` daemon allows systems to connect through the network and to find information about this system's users. This is generally considered to be a bad idea.
- Line 57—The `walld` daemon allows users to write to the screens of all users on the system. This facility is nice if you're root and need to tell your users that the machine is going to go down for maintenance. It's annoying if one of your users starts using it to incessantly ask anyone connected to the machine for help with trivial Unix problems.
- Line 58—The `pcnfsd` daemon provides service for a PC network filesystem product named `pcnfs`. Almost everybody uses `samba` instead nowadays.
- Line 59—The `rquotad` daemon provides disk quota information to remote machines so that they can enforce quotas that your machine specifies on disks that it is serving to them.

- Line 60—sprayd is another network diagnostic server. Simply put, it responds as rapidly as it can to packets placed on the network by some other machine's spray process, which places packets on the network as fast as it can. This one would be nice if Apple provided it in a later release because it can be useful for finding problem hardware in your network.
- Line 65—The rexecd daemon allows for the remote execution of parts of programs. Apple claims that it isn't known to be useful, but a programmer can make good use of this service to perform distributed processing tasks by sending parts of programs to many different machines. Of course, it is also a security risk.
- Line 66—Another service that Apple considers to be of no practical use. The identd daemon provides a method for a remote machine to verify the identity of a user causing a connection, inasmuch as any identity can be verified over the network. The service was created because it is easy for a user accessing, for example, a remote FTP site, to pretend to be a different user on your system and potentially cause trouble for the person he is pretending to be.

The service specification lines consist of a set of fields separated by tabs or spaces. The fields that must occur on each line are shown in the following list, with a brief description of the data that belongs in them.

- Service name (used to look up service port in NetInfo services map)
- Socket type (stream, dgram, raw, rdm, or seqpacket)
- Protocol (tcp or udp, rpc/tcp, or rpc/udp)
- Wait/nowait (for dgrams only—all others get nowait; should the socket wait for additional connections)
- User (user to run the service as)
- Server program (actual path to binary on disk)
- Server program arguments (how the command line would look, if typed, including server name)

Listing 16.15 shows an inetd.conf file from a running machine, with a few useful network services enabled.

LISTING 16.15 An inetd.conf File from a Running Machine, with a Few Useful Network Services Enabled

```
#
# Internet server configuration database
#
#    @(#)inetd.conf    5.4 (Berkeley) 6/30/90
#
# Items with double hashes in front (##) are not yet implemented in the OS.
```

LISTING 16.15 Continued

```
#
#finger  stream   tcp   nowait    nobody  /usr/libexec/tcpd          fingerd -s
ftp      stream   tcp   nowait    root    /usr/libexec/tcpd          ftpd -l
#login   stream   tcp   nowait    root    /usr/libexec/tcpd          rlogind
#nntp    stream   tcp   nowait    usenet  /usr/libexec/tcpd          nntpd
ntalk    dgram    udp   wait      root    /usr/libexec/tcpd          ntalkd
#shell   stream   tcp   nowait    root    /usr/libexec/tcpd          rshd
#telnet  stream   tcp   nowait    root    /usr/libexec/tcpd          telnetd
#uucpd   stream   tcp   nowait    root    /usr/libexec/tcpd          uucpd
comsat   dgram    udp   wait      root    /usr/libexec/tcpd          comsat
#tftp    dgram    udp   wait      nobody  /usr/libexec/tcpd
   ➥      tftpd /private/tftpboot
#bootp   dgram    udp   wait      root    /usr/libexec/tcpd          bootpd
##pop3   stream   tcp   nowait    root    /usr/libexec/tcpd
   ➥      /usr/local/libexec/popper
##imap4  stream   tcp   nowait    root    /usr/libexec/tcpd
   ➥      /usr/local/libexec/imapd
```

Because this machine doesn't provide many network services to the outside world, the majority of the services are turned off. Only the `ftpd` (ftp server), `ntalkd` (talk daemon, provides chatlike services), and `comsat` (provides new mail notification service) are turned on. To turn on additional services, simply uncomment (remove the # sign) the line and restart `xinetd`:

16

```
kill -HUP <xinetd_pid>
killall -HUP xinetd
```

We strongly recommend that you leave your `telnet` daemon and `rlogin` daemon disabled because these are both significant security risks. You're already familiar with the `ssh` (Secure Shell) programs for connecting to remote machines. Chapter 21, "Accessing and Controlling Tiger Remotely," covers configuring the `sshd` daemon on your own machine, and this service provides a secure replacement for the functionality of the `telnet` and `shell` daemons. For any services that currently start via `launchd`, see the section on `launchd` for some additional advice on starting `xinetd` if it is not already running.

Notice that according to the file format definition given earlier, the program started by many of the lines is exactly the same: `/usr/libexec/tcpd`. This is part of a security mechanism, whereby `xinetd` doesn't start the actual service, but instead starts yet another service, which starts the desired final service. The intermediate service, the program `/usr/libexec/tcpd`, is the TCP Wrappers program. This program can be configured to intercept requests for network services and allow them to continue only if the request comes from an authorized remote host. TCP Wrappers lives as an intermediate service between the `xinetd` service and the end services that it delivers because the `xinetd`-to-end-service method of providing network services was well established before the magnitude of potential Internet security problems was discovered. It turned out to be easier to sneak a wrapper around the end service, and not worry about modifying the model or about having to add security-conscious code to each and every possible service. Chapter 28, "Implementing Server Security and Advanced Network Configuration," covers how to configure TCP Wrappers to increase your system security.

Table 16.8 shows select runtime options available for xinetd. In Mac OS X, it runs by default with the -inetd_compat and -pidfile options: xinetd -inetd_compat -pidfile /var/run/xinetd.pid. The -inetd_compat option is an especially interesting option. With this option enabled, xinetd can also read the /etc/inetd.conf file. It processes /etc/xinetd.conf first and then /etc/inetd.conf. For users who prefer the /etc/inetd.conf file, this is a way to use a familiar file without any extra work.

TABLE 16.8 Select Runtime Options for xinetd

Option	Description
-d	Enables debug mode.
-syslog *<syslog_facility>*	Enables syslog logging of xinetd-produced messages using the specified syslog facility. The following syslog facilities can be used: daemon, auth, user, local[0-7]. Ineffective in debug mode.
-filelog *<log_file>*	Specifies where to log xinetd-produced messages. Ineffective in debug mode.
-f *<config_file>*	Specifies which file to use as the config file. Default is /etc/xinetd.conf.
-pidfile *<pid_file>*	Writes the process ID to the file specified. Ineffective in debug mode.
-stayalive	Tells xinetd to stay running even if no services are specified.
-inetd_compat	Causes xinetd to read /etc/inetd.conf in addition to the standard xinetd config files. /etc/inetd.conf is read after the standard xinetd config files.

The default /etc/xinetd.conf file that comes with Mac OS X 10.4 is shown again in Listing 16.16.

LISTING 16.16 The default /etc/xinetd.conf File

```
# man xinetd.conf for more information

defaults
{
          instances             = 60
          log_type              = SYSLOG daemon
          log_on_success        = HOST PID
          log_on_failure        = HOST
          cps                   = 25 30
}

includedir /etc/xinetd.d
```

The /etc/xinetd.conf file looks different from the /etc/inetd.conf file. This file has two major sections: a defaults section and a services section. The defaults section has controls that are basic defaults for the services. Each service has further controls and can also override or augment controls listed in the defaults section. Briefly, the intent of the lines of this file is as follows:

- Line 3 labels the defaults section of the file.
- Line 4 starts the configuration for the defaults section of the file.
- Line 5 sets the first defaults attribute, instances, which specifies the limit of servers for a given service, to 60.
- Line 6 sets the log_type attribute to the SYSLOG facility at the daemon level.
- Line 7 sets the log_on_success attribute to HOST, which logs the remote host's IP address, and PID, the process ID of the server.
- Line 8 sets the log_on_failure attribute to HOST, which logs the remote host's IP address.
- Line 9 sets the cps attribute, the one that limits the connections per second, to 25 connections per second. When this limit is reached, the service disables itself for the number of seconds specified in the second argument, 30 seconds in this case.
- Line 10 ends the defaults configuration section.
- Line 12 starts the services section by using the includedir directive to specify that every file in the /etc/xinetd.d directory, excluding files containing . or ~, is parsed as an xinetd configuration file. The files are parsed in alphabetical order according to the C locale.

16

Already you can tell that xinetd has more functionality than the traditional inetd. For instance, inetd cannot limit the number of connections per second. The items listed in this default /etc/xinetd.conf file are not the only ones that can be listed in this section, nor are the default values necessarily the only possible values. Table 16.9 shows a listing of select attributes for xinetd. Notice that xinetd can be set to restrict access based on hosts and even time, redirect services, and display banners.

TABLE 16.9 Select Attributes for xinetd

Attribute	Description
id	Used to uniquely identify a service. Useful for services that can use different protocols and need to be described with different entries in the configuration file. Default service ID is the same as the service name.
type	Any combination of the following can be used: RPC: Specifies service as an RPC service. INTERNAL: Specifies service as provided by xinetd. TCPMUX/TCPMUXPLUS: Specifies a service that is started according to the RFC 1078 protocol on the TCPMUX well-known port.

TABLE 16.9 Continued

	UNLISTED: Specifies that the service is not listed in a standard system file, such as /etc/services or /etc/rpc.
flags	Any combination of the following can be used: INTERCEPT: Intercepts packets or accepted connections to verify that they are coming from acceptable locations. Internal or multithreaded services cannot be intercepted. NORETRY: Avoids retry attempts in case of fork failure. IDONLY: Accepts connections only when the remote end identifies the remote user. Applies only to connection-based services. NAMEINARGS: Causes the first argument to server_args to be the name of the server. Useful for using TCP Wrappers. NODELAY: For a TCP service, sets the TCP_NODELAY flag on the socket. Has no effect on other types of services. DISABLE: Specifies that this service is to be disabled. Overrides the enabled directive in defaults. KEEPALIVE: For a TCP service, sets the SO_KEEPALIVE flag on the socket. Has no effect on other types of services. NOLIBWRAP: Disables internal calling of the tcpwrap library to determine access to the service. SENSOR: Replaces the service with a sensor that detects accesses to the specified port. Does not detect stealth scans. Should be used only on services you know you don't need. Whenever a connection is made to the service's port, adds the IP address to a global no_access list until the deny_time setting expires. IPv4: Sets the service to an IPv4 service. IPv6: Sets the service to an IPv6 service. REUSE: The REUSE flag is deprecated. All services now implicitly use the REUSE flag.
disable	Has a value of yes or no. Overrides the enabled directive in defaults.
socket_type	Has a value of stream, dgram, raw, or seqpacket.
protocol	Specifies the protocol used by the service. Protocol must exist in /etc/protocols. If it is not defined, the default protocol for the service is used.
wait	Specifies whether the service is single-threaded or multithreaded. If yes, it is single-threaded; xinetd starts the service and stops handling requests for the service until the server dies. If no, it is multithreaded; xinetd keeps handling new service requests.
user	Specifies the UID for the server process. Username must exist in /etc/passwd.
group	Specifies the GID for the server process. Group must exist in /etc/group. If a group is not specified, the group of the user is used.
instances	Determines the number of simultaneous instances of the server. Default is unlimited. The value can be an integer or UNLIMITED.
nice	Specifies server priority.

TABLE 16.9 Continued

server	Specifies the program to execute for this service.
server_args	Specifies arguments to be passed to the server. Server name should not be included, unless the NAMEINARGS flag has been specified.
only_from	Specifies to which remote hosts the service is available.
no_access	Specifies the remote hosts to which this service is not available.
access_times	Specifies time intervals when the service is available. An interval has the form: hour:min-hour:min. Hours can range from 0–23; minutes can range from 0–59.
log_on_success	Specifies what information is logged when the server is started and exits. Any combination of the following can be specified: PID: Logs the server process ID. HOST: Logs the remote host's address. USERID: Logs remote user ID using RFC 1413 identification protocol. Available for multithreaded stream services only. EXIT: Logs the fact that the server exited along with the exit status or termination signal. DURATION: Logs the duration of the server session. TRAFFIC: Logs the total bytes in and out for a redirected service.
log_on_failure	Specifies what is logged when a server cannot start, either from lack of resources or access configuration. Any combination of the following can be specified: HOST: Logs the remote host's address USERID: Logs remote user ID using RFC 1413 identification protocol. Available for multithreaded stream services only. RECORD: Logs as much information about the remote host as possible. ATTEMPT: Logs the fact that a failed attempt was made. Implied by use of any of the other options.
env	Value of this attribute is a list of strings of the form *<name>*=*<value>*. These strings are added to the server's environment, giving it xinetd's environment as well as the environment specified by the env attribute.
passenv	Value of this attribute is a list of environment variables from xinetd's environment to be passed to the server. An empty list implies passing no variables to the server except those explicitly defined by the env attribute.
port	Specifies the service port. If this attribute is listed for a service in /etc/services, it must be the same as the port number listed in that file.
redirect	Allows a TCP service to be redirected to another host. Useful for when your internal machines are not visible to the outside world. Syntax is redirect = *<IP address or host name> <port>* The server attribute is not required when this attribute is specified. If the server attribute is specified, this attribute takes priority.
bind	Allows a service to be bound to a specific interface on the machine.
interface	Synonym for bind.

LISTING 16.9 Continued

`banner`	Name of the file to be displayed to the remote host when a connection to that service is made. The banner is displayed regardless of access control.
`banner_success`	Name of the file to be displayed to the remote host when a connection to that service is granted. Banner is displayed as soon as access to the service is granted.
`banner_fail`	Name of the file to be displayed to the remote host when a connection to a service is denied. Banner is printed immediately on denial of access.
`per_source`	Specifies the maximum number of connections permitted per server per source IP address. May be an integer or `UNLIMITED`.
`cps`	Limits the rate of incoming connections.
`groups`	Takes either `yes` or `no`. If `yes`, the server is executed with access to the groups to which the server's effective UID has access. If `no`, server runs with no supplementary groups. Must be set to `yes` for many BSD-flavored Unixes.
`enabled`	Takes a list of service names to enable. Note that the service disable attribute and `DISABLE` flag can prevent a service from being enabled despite its being listed in this attribute.
`include`	Takes a filename in the form of `include /etc/xinetd/service`. File is then parsed as a new configuration file. May not be specified from within a service declaration.
`includedir`	Takes a directory name in the form of `includedir /etc/xinetd.d`. Every file in the directory, excluding files containing `.` or ending with `~`, is parsed as an `xinetd.conf` file.
`rlimit_cpu`	Sets the maximum number of CPU seconds that the service may use. May either be a positive integer or `UNLIMITED`.
`deny_time`	Sets the time span when access to all services to an IP address are denied to someone who sets off the `SENSOR`. Must be used in conjunction with the `SENSOR` flag. Options are `FOREVER`: IP address is not purged until `xinetd` is restarted. `NEVER`: Just logs the offending IP address. *<number>*: A numerical value of time in minutes. A typical time would be 60 minutes, to stop most DoS attacks while allowing IP addresses coming from a pool to be recycled for legitimate purposes.

Mac OS X no longer has any default configuration files in `/etc/xinetd.d`.

Traditionally, services that require two lines in `/etc/inetd.conf`, such as `time`, require two files in `/etc/xinetd.d`. Now that Apple has gone to using `launchd` as a replacement for `inetd/xinetd`, we do not see this phenomenon.

In Chapter 22, we mention that one of the options you can use to replace the default FTP server is to have the new one start via the `xinetd` service. Mac OS X no longer comes with a default `/etc/xinetd.d/ftp` file, but we have included a basic one that you could use, shown in Listing 16.17.

LISTING 16.17 A Sample `/etc/xinetd.d/ftp`

```
 1 service ftp
 2 {
 3         disable = no
 4         socket_type     = stream
 5         wait            = no
 6         user            = root
 7         server          = /usr/local/sbin/proftpd
 8         groups          = yes
 9         flags           = REUSE
10 }
```

Let's take a brief look at this sample `/etc/xinetd.d/ftp` file:

- The third line sets the first attribute, `disable`, to `no`. This enables the FTP service. In the `/etc/inetd.conf` file, this is equivalent to uncommenting the `ftp` line.
- The fourth line sets the `socket_type` attribute to `stream`. This was the second item in the `ftp` line of `/etc/inetd.conf`.
- The fifth line sets the `wait` attribute to `no`. This was the third item in the `ftp` line of `/etc/inetd.conf`.
- The sixth line sets the `user` attribute to `root`. This was the fourth item in the `ftp` line of `/etc/inetd.conf`.
- The seventh line sets the `server` attribute to `/usr/local/sbin/proftpd`. This was the fifth item in the `ftp` line of `/etc/inetd.conf`.
- In the default `/etc/inetd.conf` file, the default `ftpd` starts with the `-l` argument. If we wanted to include an argument for the replacement FTP server, we would use the `server_args` attribute, set to whatever arguments we wanted. For the default `ftpd`, we would assign `-l` to the attribute.
- The eighth line sets the `groups` attribute to `yes`. This is required for BSD-flavored Unixes. Because this attribute is required for all your `xinetd` services, you could also move it to the `defaults` section of `/etc/xinetd.conf` and then remove it from the individual service files.
- Finally, the ninth line sets the `flags` attribute to `REUSE`, which according to the man page is actually deprecated because all services use this flag.

Perhaps one of the most notable differences between the default `/etc/inetd.conf` file and this `/etc/xinetd.d/ftp` file is that the server is set to `/usr/libexec/tcpd` in the `inetd.conf` file, but in the `ftp` file, it is set to the new FTP server's binary,

/usr/local/sbin/proftpd. Because inetd is not as configurable, it is important to use TCP Wrappers. However, you can configure host access information directly in xinetd without having to use TCP Wrappers. We recommend that you use that built-in capability.

If you want to enable any of the default services controlled by xinetd or enable a service that you are adding, using only the xinetd configuration files, run /sbin/service <service> start. To start any service that otherwise runs out of launchd using xinetd instead, see some additional details in the launchd section before running the command.

If you prefer a more manual method, change the disable entry to no and restart xinetd by sending it a HUP signal using either of the following methods:

```
kill -HUP <xinetd_pid>
killall -HUP xinetd
```

If you are running a service using /etc/inetd.conf rather than /etc/xinetd.d/, start xinetd, after looking at comments in the launchd section. The /sbin/service command already takes care of this for services running out of xinetd.

If you want to change any of the configuration files in /etc/xinetd.d/, simply restart xinetd to have the changes take effect.

Restarting and Shutting Down: shutdown, reboot, halt

After you have played quite a bit with starting and stopping services, you can sometimes have your machine so confused about your services that it is necessary to reboot. To do so from the command line, you can use the shutdown command. It is a convenient command to use to shut down the machine or to reboot, especially when users are on the system. The shutdown command notifies users that the system is about to go down and gives them the opportunity to save what they are doing. Additionally, it does not allow logins five minutes before shutdown, or immediately, if the impending shutdown is in less than five minutes. The two most common uses of shutdown are

```
shutdown -r <time>
shutdown -h <time>
```

The -r option reboots the machine, and -h option halts the machine. The specified *<time>* can be now or in minutes or a specific date. Table 16.10 shows the command documentation for shutdown.

TABLE 16.10 Command Documentation for shutdown

shutdown	Closes down the system at a given time.
shutdown [-] [-h¦-r¦-k] [-o [-n]] *<time>* [*<warning_message>*]	
shutdown provides an automatic way for the superuser to nicely notify users of an impending shutdown.	
-h	Halts the system at the specified *<time>*.
-r	Reboots the system at the specified *<time>*.

TABLE 16.10 Continued

`-k`	Kicks everybody off. The `-k` option does not actually halt the system, but does leave the system multiuser with logins disabled for all users except the superuser.
`-o`	If one of the `-h`, `-p`, or `-r` is specified, `shutdown` executes `halt` or `reboot` instead of sending signal to `init`.
`-n`	Prevents normal `sync` before stopping.
`<time>`	The time when the system is to be brought down. `<time>` can be the word `now` for immediate shutdown, or a future time in one of two formats: *<+number>* or *<yymmddhhmm>*, where the year, month, and day may be defaulted to the current system values. The first form brings the system down in *<number>* minutes and the second at the absolute time specified.
`<warning_message>`	Any other arguments comprise the warning message that is broadcast to users currently logged on the system.
`-`	Reads the warning message from standard input.

In addition to `shutdown`, `halt` and `reboot` can also be used to halt or reboot the system, as appropriate. The `shutdown` command is more polite for the users and is therefore the recommended command to use. However, if you do end up using `halt` or `reboot`, they are traditionally invoked in combination with `sync`, as follows:

```
sync;sync;sync;reboot
sync;sync;sync;halt
```

The `sync` command forces the completion of disk writes. `halt`, `reboot`, and `shutdown` also do this before closing down the machine. However, the wisdom of defying tradition is left to you. Table 16.11 shows command documentation for `halt` and `reboot`.

TABLE 16.11 Command Documentation for `halt` and `reboot`

`halt`	Stops the system.
`reboot`	Restarts the system.
`halt [-lnq]`	
`reboot [-lnq]`	
The `halt` and `reboot` utilities flush the system cache to disk, send all running processes a `SIGTERM` and subsequently a `SIGKILL` and, respectively, halts or restarts the system. The action is logged, including adding a shutdown record into the login accounting file.	
`-l`	Does not log the `halt` or `reboot` to the system log. Intended for applications, such as `shutdown`, that call `reboot` or `halt` and log this themselves.
`-n`	Does not flush the file system cache. This option probably should not be used.
`-q`	Quickly and ungracefully halts/restarts the system, and only flushes the file system cache. This option probably should not be used.
Normally, `shutdown` is used when the system needs to be halted or restarted to warn users of their impending doom and to cleanly terminate specific programs.	

Strong-Arming the System—Brute Force Behavior Modification

Sometimes, there just isn't a configuration option available to let you make something work the way you want it to. The GUI tools don't have a button for you to click, the configuration files for the software don't list an option for you, and the `Defaults` database contains no useful parameters. If you're willing to apply what you've learned so far in this book, there still might be ways for you to make your system do what you want. The key is remembering that underneath it all, Mac OS X is running Unix, and the Unix user experience is fundamentally the product of many programs running simultaneously, each providing specific functionality. If you can localize the behavior you want to modify to a single program, you can approach reaching your configuration goal as an exercise in replacing that program's functionality with something that does what you want, instead of what the current version does.

The Sneaky Way—Inserting Imposters

Depending on exactly what you're trying to change, there are two primary ways to go about this. The less obnoxious way is to interpose some software of your own devising between what the system is trying to do and what it's actually doing. Because most everything is a small, special-purpose program, you can often insert an imposter program that looks and talks to the system like the program it thinks it's calling. The imposter can then call the actual program (or not, if you don't need to) with any modifications to inputs that you want, unrestricted by what the system allows you to conveniently configure.

Let's take the Command-Shift-3/Command-Shift-4 screen capture facility that's built into the operating system as an example. Pressing Command-Shift-3 takes a screenshot of what currently appears on the screen. Command-Shift-4 lets you select a region of the screen or a particular window to save an image of instead. Both of these functions unfortunately save their output as Portable Network Graphics PNG files, or Adobe Portable Document Format `.pdf` files. Darned inconvenient, right? If you want to use images captured this way in some truly portable fashion, for example to build a web page, you have to use Preview to export them as some more universally supported image-file format, such as GIF or JPEG, or find some other way to post-process the `.png` or `.pdf` files. Wouldn't it be more convenient if the system just saved the screenshots in TIFF format, as it did in Mac OS X 10.1 and earlier?

If you really want that functionality, you're willing to strong-arm the system into giving it to you even though it doesn't appear to be an option, and you accept the consequences of the changes you'll be making, there is a way to accomplish your goal. The solution requires replacing bits of the software underlying the user interface with things that do what you want, instead of what Apple made them do. The consequence is that your system will no longer be quite as Apple delivered it, and there's no telling what an Apple software update will do when it encounters these modified files.

CAUTION

We can't in good conscience suggest that you make this particular modification or other modifications of this style. We've seen Apple's update installers balk at far less important things, and we wouldn't want to encourage anyone to make a modification that might leave their system in a state that could require a complete reinstallation. Still, we think it's a good example of what can be done with the system if you can keep track of changes you might have to back out to run an update, or if you're willing to live on the wild side and make your system your own. There are many things that we think are pretty cool, that we would be pretty irresponsible if we actually suggested....

The key to solving the problem is to recognize that when you press Command-Shift-3 or Command-Shift-4, the GUI invokes a command-line application, `/usr/sbin/screencapture`. The easiest way to find this out is by running `top` at the command line and watching the process listing while taking a few screenshots. Armed with this tidbit of information, you should already begin to see the possibilities. At the command line, `screencapture` indicates that its options are as shown in Table 16.12. In Mac OS X versions prior to 10.4, none of these options gave any hope that you could control the file type. The `-t <format>` option appeared in early developer releases of Tiger, but Apple so far (as of March, 2005) admits no knowledge of how a user would control the settings for this parameter. No matter: If you have administrative access to your machine, there's hardly anything that you *can't* do with it if you put your mind to it.

TABLE 16.12 Command Documentation for `screencapture`

`screencapture`	Takes pictures of the current state of the screen.
`screencapture [-[i¦m]wsWCx] [-t <format>] <file>`	
`screencapture [-[i¦m]cwsWx] [-t <format>]`	
`screencapture` takes pictures of the current state of the screen or screens present on the machine, or of windows or selectable regions of the screen. `screencapture` saves its output in `.pdf` format, or places it on the clipboard.	
`screencapture` lists a `[cursor]` parameter as following the `<file>` parameter when displaying its options, but this parameter is undocumented, and an examination of the `screencapture` executable does not reveal any obvious candidates for parameter values. `screencapture` also accepts an undocumented `-f` option, which is apparently a placeholder option that can be used in `<file>` mode.	
`-i`	Captures the screen interactively, by selection or window. Pressing the spacebar toggles between Region selection (crosshair cursor) Window selection (camera cursor) Pressing `<control>` causes the screenshot to go to the clipboard. Pressing `<esc>` cancels the capture.
`-c`	Places the screen capture on the clipboard, instead of into a file.
`-m`	Captures only the main monitor. Undefined if `-i` is present.
`-w`	Allows only window selection mode.
`-s`	Allows only mouse selection mode.
`-t<format>`	Captures in `<format>` format; viable options appear to be `png`, `pdf`, `pct`, `tif`
`-C`	Captures the cursor in the saved picture.
`-W`	Starts interaction in window selection mode.
`-x`	Does not play sounds.

The fact that the screen image is captured by a command-line application should immediately bring to mind a possible way that a solution might be approached. You can write small command-line programs, right? You learned how to do this in Chapter 15, when you learned about shell scripts. A shell script looks for all the world just like any other program, but you can fill it with the automated execution of any command-line commands that you want.

So, what would happen when you press Command-Shift-3, if you were to find the `screencapture` program as delivered by Apple, rename it so that the system couldn't find it, and then replace it with a shell script of your own devising? Presuming that you write a syntactically correct shell script, no more and no less than exactly what you put in your shell script. Let's see what happens: You'll find the `screencapture` program in `/usr/sbin/`. As `root`, move it to `/usr/sbin/screencapture-o`.

```
brezup:ray ray $ su
Password:
brezup:root ray # cd /usr/sbin
brezup:root sbin # mv screencapture screencapture-o
```

Now replace it with a small shell script so that you can see what's being passed to the `screencapture` program when Command-Shift-3 and Command-Shift-4 are pressed.

```
brezup:root sbin # cat > screencapture
#!/bin/csh

echo "option 0 $0" > /tmp/screencapopts
echo "option 1 $1" >> /tmp/screencapopts
echo "option 2 $2" >> /tmp/screencapopts
echo "option 3 $3" >> /tmp/screencapopts
```

Press Control-d to end the `cat` session; then make the new `screencapture` script executable.

```
brezup:root sbin # chmod 755 screencapture
```

Press Command-Shift-3 and see what happens—depending on whether you're Tiger, or a previous version of Mac OS X, you'll see two slightly different behaviors:

On Tiger:

```
<Command-Shift-3>
brezup:root sbin # cat /tmp/screencapopts
option 0 /usr/sbin/screencapture
option 1 -f
option 2 -tpng
option 3 /Volumes/Wills_Data/ray/Desktop/Picture 1.pdf
```

Previous versions:

```
<Command-Shift-3>
brezup:root sbin # cat /tmp/screencapopts
option 0 /usr/sbin/screencapture
option 1 -f
option 2 /Volumes/Wills_Data/ray/Desktop/Picture 1.pdf
option 3
```

NOTE

Note that the Tiger version passes an argument that specifies an image file type. Users of earlier versions of Mac OS X don't have it so lucky. For them, `screencapture` writes only a single type, PDF, and they've got to work around this. Still, even with Tiger, despite the option apparently existing for setting a different file type, there is, as yet, no way for the user to control this directly. Bending the system to our will still requires some hackish programming.

Also check Command-Shift-4 and both variants with Control held down as well (the Control variants are supposed to place the capture on the clipboard):

```
<Command-Shift-4>
brezup:root sbin # cat /tmp/screencapopts
option 0 /usr/sbin/screencapture
option 1 -i
option 2 -tpng
option 3 /Volumes/Wills_Data/ray/Desktop/Picture 2.pdf

<Command-Control-Shift-3>
brezup:root sbin # cat /tmp/screencapopts
option 0 /usr/sbin/screencapture
option 1 -c
option 2 -tpng
option 3

<Command-Control-Shift-4>
brezup:root sbin # cat /tmp/screencapopts
option 0 /usr/sbin/screencapture
option 1 -ic
option 2 -tpng
option 3
```

(Panther, and earlier-version users will see similar output, lacking the `-tpng` parameter.)

From these, it's clear that the options are always passed as the first parameter to the command (which is apparently what that do-nothing `-f` option is for—filling space as parameter 1 when no real parameter is required), and the filename, if there is one, is always parameter 3 on Tiger, and parameter 2 in earlier versions. This is lucky for us. We don't need to do any fancy option parsing. So long as we can figure out how to either pass the parameters we want, instead of the hard-coded PNG format, or to convert the output of Apple's `screencapture` (now `screencapture-o`) into a friendlier file format, we can just pass options and parameters straight from our script to it, and all should be well.

If we are working with Tiger, our immediate task is now simple: how to change the `-tpng` parameter to something we prefer. This requires nothing more than rewriting our new `screencapture` script so that it calls Apple's `screencapture` (now `screencapture-o`), and passes a `-t<format>` option with our preferred format instead of `-tpng`. To summarize, the following things must be done to make a completely functional shell script wrapper for `screencapture-o`, which will force the output into whatever file format we prefer:

- Our wrapper needs to be named `screencapture` and be found by the system when we press the Command-Shift-3/4 key combinations.
- It is going to call the original `screencapture` program, now known as `screencapture-o`, to do the actual work of capturing the screen images.
- It must accept and store the options and parameters that the system thinks it's handing to the (original) `screencapture` program, so that it can in turn pass these options and parameters on to `screencapture-o` itself.

A script, stored in `/usr/sbin/screencapture`, such as this would do the trick:

```
#!/bin/csh

set options="$1";
set type="-ttif";
set filename="$3";

/usr/sbin/screencapture-o $options $type "$filename";

exit
```

The only problem with this, is that parameter 3, the filename, is being passed in by some external process, and it's still being sent in the form of `Picture #.png`, rather than `Picture #.<ourformat>`, as we'd prefer. There are a number of ways to work around this problem. Because we're already overwriting the type information, the method that comes to mind first might be to also overwrite the supplied filename with one of our own choosing. Using what you know about shell scripting and rewriting file suffixes, you might construct a script such as this:

```
#!/bin/csh

set options="$1";
set type="tif";
set typeoption = "-t$type";
set filebase="$3:r";
```

```
set filename="$filebase.$type";

/usr/sbin/screencapture-o $options $typeoption "$filename";

exit
```

This comes *so close* to working perfectly that it hurts. Unfortunately, whatever is passing in the filename is also what's controlling the `<#>` part of the `Picture <#>.<format>` name. It knows about only `png` (or in earlier Mac OS Xs, `pdf`) file extensions, so it picks the number for the file based on the already existing `Picture <#>.png` files on your Desktop, regardless of what `<format>` you've told `screencapture` to write.

All is not lost, however. There are few things a computer can do to keep a determined user from realizing his perfect configuration. If the computer won't create nice incremental numbers for us, we can always come up with ways to make our own incrementing filenames. Substituting the date for the `<#>` portion seems like a quick and dirty way of doing things—how many times are you going to capture multiple pictures in the same second? Possibly even better, this would make all your screencapture filenames completely unique, so you'd no longer need to rename them from `Picture #` to something useful when you moved them off your desktop.

```
#!/bin/csh

set options="$1";
set toldtype="$2";

if ( $%3 > 0 ) then
 set type="tif";
 set typeoption = "-t$type";
 set toldfile = "$3"
 set datestr=`date "+%y%m%d-%H:%M:%S"`
 set wrkdir  = "$toldfile:h"
 set outfile="$wrkdir/Picture $datestr.type"

 \rm -f "$toldfile"
 /usr/sbin/screencapture-o $options $typeoption "$outfile"
 exit
endif

/usr/sbin/screencapture-o $options $toldtype
exit
```

This might be beginning to look a little bit complex, and it contains a couple things that we haven't discussed in the text, but it's actually pretty easy to understand when broken down into parts.

16

To most quickly begin to understand what the script does, take the case where the `if` statement fails—that is, when the third option, `$3`, contains no text (there is no filename). In this case, execution falls through to the `endif` statement, and the only thing executed is `/usr/sbin/screencapture -o $options $typeoption`. It's as if this script weren't even there, which is exactly what we want to happen. If there is no filename, it's because the user held down the Control key, and wants the data to go to the clipboard, so we don't want to fiddle with the call in any way (if you look back at the things we caught in our `screencapopts` experiments earlier, however, you'll see that Apple sets a file type even when sending the data to the clipboard, so this might be a parameter that could be usefully modified in some situations as well).

If there is a filename in `$3`, we need to process it as follows:

1. First it is stored in the shell variable `$toldfile`.
2. A formatted date is acquired into the shell variable `$datestr`. This date string is necessary because the portion of the `screencapture` process that prevents filename collisions is not part of `screencapture` but instead is part of the GUI server. We'll use this to create a unique filename for the final `.tif` image. (We're trying to create `.tif` files, but the system passes `.png` names, so it'll happily keep passing `Picture 1.png` forever because our `.tif` names will never conflict with it.) The date format specified is `YYMMDD-HH:MM:SS`. You can change this to something more to your liking at your leisure.
3. We get the working directory for saving the file by parsing the path off the `$toldfile` specified by the system.
4. We build a final name for our TIFF file from these components.
5. We remove the file pointed at by `$toldfile` because the system creates it before starting `screencapture` in an attempt to make it show up on the user's desktop more quickly. Unfortunately, we're not going to be using that file, we're building a TIFF file. I suppose that we could `touch` our own `$outfile` here to simulate the same behavior.
6. We run `screencapture-o`, with the options passed to our script, and dump its output in the temporary file we've created.

It's a little difficult to demonstrate in the static text of a printed book, but when installed, this works exactly as described. Using the Command-Shift-3/4 key combinations in the system now results in a file with a name such as `Picture 050309-03/00/58.tif` appearing on the desktop in the Finder.

NOTE

The observant reader who pays attention to man pages will note that the date format we specified and what ends up in the filename as shown by the Finder are not identical. We asked for colons separating hour, minute, and second, and instead the Finder is showing / characters. If you look at the filename at the command line, it is as expected, and contains colons. This is probably a symptom of Apple's attempt to graft the larger Macintosh set of acceptable filename characters onto the Unix filesystem. Those truly bothered by the discrepancy can play with the date format string and pick something they like better than this.

If you're working in Panther or some other earlier version of Mac OS X, you don't have the option of directly controlling the file type that Apple's `screencapture` writes. Instead, you would need to find a way to convert the fixed format output from Apple's `screencapture` into whatever format you preferred. Because Tiger gives you the ability to control the format, that isn't necessary here, but the general technique is applicable to any other situation where you're hoping to more completely control the system's operation. If you find yourself in this situation, it's easy to extend the script to do internal processing on the file. Simply have `screencapture` write it to a temporary filename, process that file to your heart's content, and then write it to the final filename you're hoping to use. In the case of converting the old-style `.pdf` files from `screencapture` into TIFFs, this can easily be accomplished by using the Ghostscript application that was installed for supporting additional printing features. When we previously visited this software in Chapter 5, "Configuring Tiger Hardware Support and Preferences," we were interested only in using it to convert between different printer-language formats, for driving oddball, unsupported printers. In fact, it's good for converting between all manner of image file formats (examine the output of `gs -h` for a listing of supported output formats), and lends itself nicely to grabbing the output from `screencapture` and making it into whatever you prefer.

I'm partial to storing my images as TIFFs, so I'm going to use the `tiff24nc` output format, which is uncompressed 24-bit TIFF. Fiddling around at the command line, I find that the syntax shown in the following line, converts a `.pdf` file into a TIFF format file for me.

```
/usr/local/bin/gs -q -dBATCH -dNOPAUSE -sDEVICE=tiff24nc
➥-sOutputFile=<tiffile> <pdffile>
```

For example,

```
brezup:root Desktop # /usr/local/bin/gs -q -dBATCH -dNOPAUSE -sDEVICE=tiff24nc
➥-sOutputFile="Picture 1.tif" "Picture 1.pdf"
```

creates the file `Picture 1.tif` in my current directory, and it is a properly formatted TIFF file (there's a reason I've used `.tif` instead of `.tiff`, which will be explained shortly).

NOTE

Of course, you aren't restricted to using TIFF files. If you prefer some other format of output on your end, simply replace the appropriate bits of the filenames, and select the Ghostscript device you require to suit your purposes.

```
brezup:root Desktop # file Picture\ 1.tif
Picture 1.tif: TIFF image data, big-endian
```

Even with a screencapture that insists on writing PDFs (and doesn't accept a -t parameter as option 2), the TIFF file final format version of our little hack can be accomplished with a relatively simple script, like this:

```
#!/bin/csh

set options="$1";

if ( $%2 > 0 ) then
 set pdffile = "$2"
 set datestr=`date "+%y%m%d-%H:%M:%S"`
 set wrkdir  = "$pdffile:h"
 set tmpfile="$wrkdir/.Picture $datestr.tmp"
 set tiffile="$wrkdir/Picture $datestr.tif"

 \rm -f "$pdffile"
 /usr/sbin/screencapture-o $options "$tmpfile"
 gs -q -dBATCH -dNOPAUSE -sDEVICE=tiff24nc -sOutputFile="$tiffile" "$tmpfile"
 \rm -f "$tmpfile"
 exit
endif

/usr/sbin/screencapture-o $options
exit
```

Note that there's very little change from the version that uses screencapture's new -t option. This version needs only to save the output from screencapture into a temporary file (named much like the final file, only with a . preceding the name, to prevent it from appearing in the Finder), and to pass that temporary file through Ghostscript (gs) as a filter, to convert it into the TIFF file output I want. If I wanted to string together a bunch of netpbm filters to tweak the image further, send it to Mail to have it automatically emailed somewhere, or dump it to the printer so that Command-Shift-3 saved, and simultaneously printed a copy, all of this can be easily added to the script after it has the capture saved to disk.

The Brutal Way—Organ Transplants

Sometimes, inserting imposters isn't a clean solution. Other times, it just can't give you all the functionality you really want. In the screencapture example given previously, the most annoying issue remaining is that the filename is a bit clunky. Apple's default "Picture #" names are elegant, if somewhat less than informative. There's no easy way to get that functionality out of a screencapture script, though, because it's actually some part of the GUI that's working out what the next available filename is, and it's doing it based on a .png (or .pdf) suffix. We could work out some csh syntax to list all .tif files and find the highest numbered instance, but that would be some ugly csh code, and Apple's already done the work, it's just not *quite* accessible to us. Fixing Apple's software so that it does what we want would be more elegant, but how can we do this without Apple's source code?

CAUTION

This is one of those places where the product carton should say "Kids, don't try this at home—all stunts performed by professional stunt actors." If you try this, or other tweaks of this nature, and you make a mistake, there's a reasonable chance you'll leave your machine unable to boot into anything but single-user mode (see Chapter 29, "Maintaining a Healthy System," for more information about what to do if that happens). You can really, really make a mess of things if you try these techniques and you make a mistake. You also can make some useful customizations if you get it right, but *always* make backups, and never say we didn't warn you!

Remember back in the early chapters covering Unix when we said that Unix doesn't really know or care what's in a file; that if you tried to execute a datafile, Unix would let you; and that likewise you could read applications like they were giant text files with text editors? Well, `emacs` is your application-modifying friend.

If you dig around the `/System/Library/CoreServices/` directory, you'll eventually find that `SystemUIServer` is the part of the system that's calling `screencapture` when you press the Command-Shift-3/4 key combinations. I found it by using `grep` from `/System/Library/CoreServices/`, as in `grep screencapture /System/Library/CoreServices/*/*/*/* 2>&1 | grep "matches"`.

TIP

I've piped `grep` back into `grep` (with `STDERR` wrapped into `STDOUT`), so that I don't see all the complaints from the first `grep` about directories.

If you run `strings` on the file that matches, the following interesting tidbits show up:

```
brezup:root sbin # strings -3
➥ /System/Library/CoreServices/SystemUIServer.app/Contents/MacOS/SystemUIServer
.
.
.
screen capture threw exception while handling hot key
-fC
-cC
-ic
dvderror
Screen grabs are unavailable during DVD playback.
dvderrormessage
Please quit DVD Player first.
grabicon.icns
OSXDisableScreenGrab
location
```

```
Picture
png
screen capture: Unable to get directory (Desktop) to write files to.
%@ %@
%@ %@(%@)
%@%@.%@
ScreenCapture.m
.
.
.
```

The particularly interesting bits are the `Picture` and `png` lines. There are a few other bits that look suspiciously like Apple's planning on making this an option that you can configure, but right now this appears to be bits of the `SystemUIServer` that specify chunks of the filename we're trying to control. If this is how `SystemUIServer` finds and picks names for `screencapture`, why not just change the contents of `SystemUIServer` itself?

If you're sure that you want to try this, make a backup copy of `/System/Library/CoreServices/SystemUIServer.app/Contents/MacOS/SystemUIServer`; then fire up `emacs` on the file (not the backup) and search for and change the bit of the file containing `png` so that it contains `tif` instead. I used Control-s to incrementally search for `png`, and found only a single instance of it in the file. I then carefully replaced just the letters `png` with `tif`, and saved the file. If you're following along, reboot your machine, and if you can still log on, things are going well.

CAUTION

If you don't know how to make these edits, don't even try until you're more comfortable with your `emacs` skills. One wrong keystroke and it's good-bye to your interface.

CAUTION

Never change the size of a string when you're editing it this way. There's a good chance that the program knows exactly where in itself the various bits of information such as the string specifying the format of the `screencapture` filename are stored. If you changed the `png` to `tiff`, everything after that string would be off by one position from where the program expects it, and there's no telling exactly what the effect might be. You can bet, however, that it won't be good.

Presuming that you've successfully made the modification, what you've just done is modify a part of the GUI server so that it no longer passes `Picture #.png` to `screencapture`. Instead, it passes `Picture #.tif`. Because the UI handles the collision detection and incrementing the internal number properly, we no longer need to deal with that in our `screencapture` script. As a matter of fact, presuming we're not trying to convert into a file format that `screencapture` can't write itself, we don't need our `screencapture` imposter script at all—the system should now pick an appropriate filename, and send along the `tif` file type for the original `screencapture` just as though Apple built it to do that from the start.

Even if we're trying to do something more complicated and still require the `screencapture` imposter, it can be a significantly less complicated script. The `SystemUIServer` code will be handling collision detection and creating a good filename for us, so that's no longer necessary. All we require now is the code to do whatever additional modifications we desire on the file, and to put it in its final resting place. And, as before, it does in fact work as you might hope—TIFF files, or files of whichever type you've specified in your modifications to `SystemUIServer`, with convenient "Picture #" names appear on the desktop in response to Command-Shift-3/4.

These examples could, of course, be made much more sophisticated if you were inclined to experiment with the shell scripts. Want Command-Shift-3 to both make a screen capture and print a copy of the file? Easy! Just send the file that `screencapture -o` writes off to `lpr` in your script. Need all of your `screencaptures` to be reduced to grayscale? Pipe them through some `netpbm` tools before writing them. The possibilities are just about limitless.

CAUTION

Although the benefits available through these sorts of tweaks have been explained, we'll still close with a repeat of our previous warning. There's no telling what an Apple update will do if it sees a modified `screencapture`, or even worse, a modified `SystemUIServer`. It is a good idea to keep a list of modifications that you make to Apple software, and move original copies back in before trying to update your system.

Actually, if you've become a sophisticated enough script writer and Unix user to make these sorts of modifications, you should also have become a wise enough Unix user to be maintaining an automated script that lets you back out all your changes to Apple system files with a single command before you execute any system update scripts.

Summary

This chapter provided an overview of the preferences and configuration controls available from and through the command line. Because so much of the system is currently undocumented by Apple, we can't guess whether these items will remain in these places or continue to contain the same options. However, we have a pretty good guess that the general form and style of how the configuration is controlled will remain the same. With the tools provided here, you should be able to cope with any changes that might come your way.

CHAPTER 17

Using X Window System Applications

IN THIS CHAPTER

- Introduction to the X Window System
- Installing the X Window System
- Using X

In this chapter, we introduce the X Window System, Unix's favored graphical user interface *(GUI)*. If we haven't convinced you that this Unix stuff is too confusing (and we hope we haven't!), you shouldn't be bothered by the fact that the X Window System is rather different from both the Mac OS GUI and the Mac OS X Aqua GUI, and that frequently it exists best as a completely separate graphical interface.

NOTE

We have a few too many Xs to go around. The X Window System, though, has had its X for two decades longer than Mac OS X, so we have to get used to the nomenclature. The X Window System is usually referred to as X#, where # is the major revision number. Alternatively, you might see X#R*n*, where # is the major revision, and *n* is the minor revision. As of this writing, X11R6 is the current version, but it is generally referred to as *X11*, or more simply, just *X*. X for the X Window System is pronounced as the letter X, not the number 10, as Mac OS X is supposed to be said.

Both a bit of a boon and a bane to the new Mac OS X user, the X Window System will be an important, if somewhat confusing, feature of Mac OS X for some time to come. As the de facto standard for Unix GUI applications, you'll find that a considerable amount of software has been written to use the X Window System. Much of this software will probably be slow in being ported to the Aqua GUI interface, and some might not be ported at all. Because of this, if you want to make the most use of the available Unix software, it's necessary for you to install the software to enable you to use the X Window System and get to know a little about the way that the interface works.

In earlier versions of Mac OS X, if you wanted to use X11, you needed to invest a bit of effort in installing it, or purchase a commercial product that installed it and integrated it with Aqua. With Mac OS X 10.3, Apple has started providing its own version of X11. Actually, it's a modified version of an open source X11 product. As an actively developed open source application, Apple's X11 version can be installed as a custom installation option, and either it or some other version of X11 for Mac OS X, is necessary to use applications written for X11. The new Apple installer, potentially combined using Fink or DarwinPorts to install applications, makes installation and use of X11 software a completely painless experience.

This chapter provides a basic introduction to X11, an explanation of how the X Window System interacts with the Mac OS X Aqua interface, and a brief discussion of some interesting X applications.

Introduction to the X Window System

In many ways, it's easier to explain how the X Window System is different from the interface that you're accustomed to than it is to explain how it's similar. Whether you're from a Mac or a PC background, you're certainly used to a graphical user interface, and both the X Window System and the interface to which you're accustomed display windows with program content and information in them. But beyond this, the X Window System is fundamentally a different interface than the GUI present on either of the popular desktop operating systems.

At the most obvious level, the X Window System is not a built-in part of the operating system. Whereas the Mac OS and Windows graphical user interfaces are intimately tied to the underlying operating system, the X Window System is a completely separate system with no real attachment to the operating system underneath it. This separation makes for inefficiencies in the way the window system interacts with the operating system and is the cause of certain performance issues that are of some annoyance. As you'll see, however, this separation between display and operating system also provides a level of flexibility that cannot be readily accomplished with integrated systems.

Also different is the fact that the X Window System functions as a client/server system. Unlike operating systems with integrated GUI functionality, programs that use the X Window System interface functionality don't actually display GUI elements. Instead they contact a completely separate program, the X server, and request that the server perform whatever display functions they require. This might seem like a bizarre and inefficient way of handling GUI element display, but it leads to the abstraction that's another major difference and one of the sources of the extreme flexibility of the system.

The client/server model utilized for X Window System communication is a network-capable system. Messages requesting display functionality can be passed from client to server over a network connection. In fact, even connections from a client application running on the same machine as the display server are processed as though the client were speaking to the server over the network. A benefit of this model that isn't immediately obvious is that to a user sitting in front of a machine running the X Window System, it's completely transparent whether the programs being displayed on the machine are actually running on that machine or on some other machine. Other than possible delays due to delays in the network, the X Window System server responds identically to programs running on other machines as it does to programs running on its own.

Still not sure what this means to you? It means that you can display programs running on any machine anywhere (well, any machine running a Unix-like operating system) on any other machine running an X Window System server. Applications running on remote systems aren't trapped in their own view of another system's desktop, but instead are full peers on the desktop right beside applications running on the same machine as the X server. This intermingling of clients displayed from local and remote hosts also isn't limited to just one remote host at a time; instead, any X11 program from any remote host can be displayed and interacted with simultaneously with all the other client programs being displayed by the server. This doesn't require some high-priced and proprietary commercial application or an experimental program and protocol; it uses well-established and open source software that has been under development by the online community for decades.

An additional difference between personal computer windowing systems and the X Window System is that the interface's look and feel are controlled by yet another separate program, rather than by the X Window System server or the operating system itself. In the X Window System model, the X server is responsible for handling client display requests for displaying windows. Unless a client specifically draws things such as title bars for itself, X doesn't give them to it. The convention with the X Window System is that a separate program is run to create title bars and to manage user interactions such as moving windows around, iconizing and minimizing windows, and providing an application dock or other similar functionality.

The X11 software based on the XFree86 that Apple currently provides contains both a completely separate interface to the X11/Unix side of Mac OS X and also a mode to commingle applications running X11 with Mac OS X–native Aqua interface applications. This mixed mode will be the most comfortable for many Mac users because it provides almost seamless integration of X11 clients into the Aqua interface. It does, however, mildly break the normal X11 paradigm because the window management is handled by Aqua and isn't as accessible to the X11 software as a normal X11 window manager would be. Still, for many uses, the convenience of having your X11 windows available in your normal Aqua interface is probably well worth the small loss of control that comes with tying X11 to Aqua.

Client/Server System

As mentioned briefly earlier, the heart of the X Window System is a server that provides display functionality to client applications. In a slight twist on the terminology that you're used to, the X Window System server is the application that runs on your local machine and physically draws data to your screen, and clients are the programs that run anywhere, including on remote machines. When you consider the functionality, this makes sense because a server provides a service: displaying data locally to you. Clients request the service, which is the display of data regardless of where the clients are. Figure 17.1 shows a typical X11 session with several programs displaying themselves on the X server. Among them are a number of `xterms`—applications similar to Terminal in functionality—as well as a text editor, an application dock, a game, and a mail application. The icons that appear as small computer terminals in the upper left are iconized applications; where the Mac OS uses windowshade title bars or minimizes things into the dock, the X Window System collapses applications into representative icons.

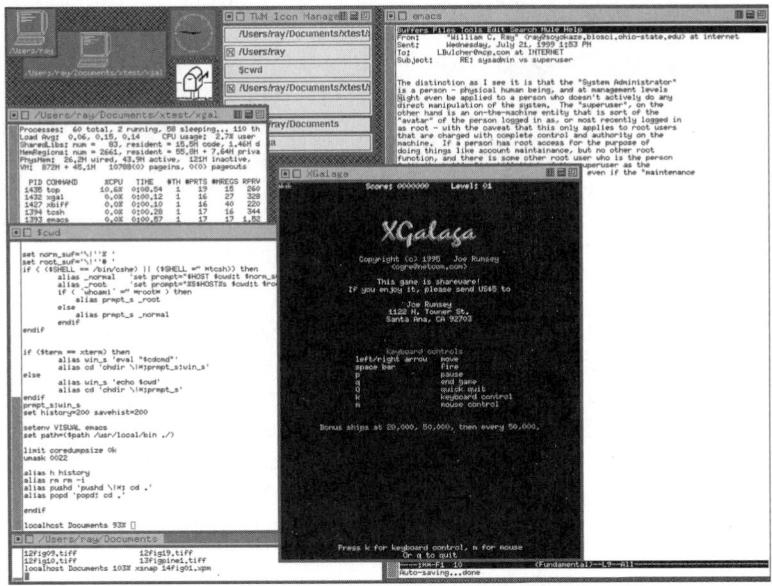

FIGURE 17.1 A typical X11 session with several programs running. The X Window System on a 1024×768 screen is a bit cramped but still usable.

Remote Application Display

Conveniently, this client/server model, like much of the software designed for Unix, is extremely abstract. Just as the input/output model abstracts the notion of where data comes from and goes to (to the point that it doesn't matter whether the data source is a program, user, or file), the X Window System client/server model doesn't care how the client and server are connected. This allows clients to connect to the server from any location and enables you to run software on remote machines and interact with its interface on your local machine.

In Figure 17.2, you again see the X Window System running on a machine. Other than the difference in a few running applications, there's little to distinguish it from Figure 17.1, which is exactly the point. In this screenshot, the web browser, two of the Terminal windows (find the ones with host `soyokaze` in the command prompt), and the game are actually running on a machine on the other side of the city from the actual screen.

Because the X11 client software creating these applications doesn't care what X11 server it's talking to, and the X11 server on my machine doesn't care whether the clients talking to it are running on the same machine, these applications function exactly as if they were running on my local machine instead of across the city. It wouldn't matter—outside possible slowdowns associated with network delays—whether the applications were running across the city or across the planet.

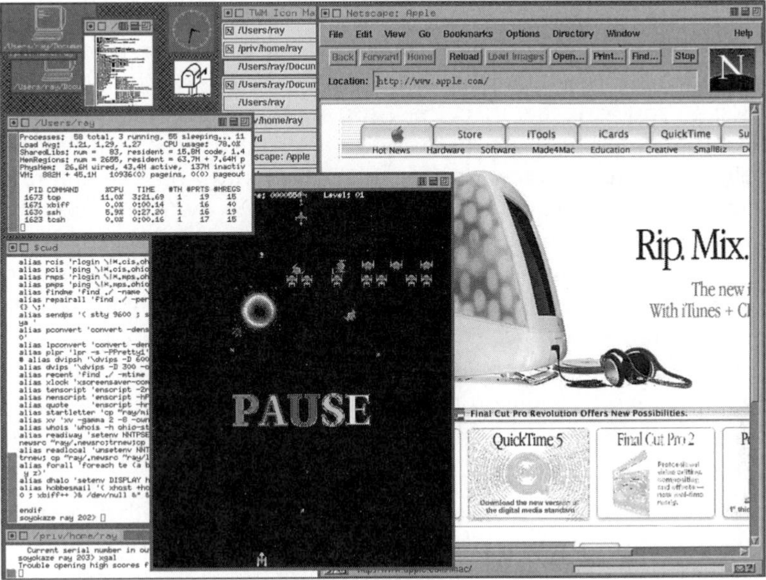

FIGURE 17.2 Another typical X11 session with several programs running. In this image, several of the windows actually belong to applications running on a remote machine.

The impact of this might not be obvious to you yet, but consider that with this capability, the following become possible:

- Have a document at home that you were supposed to edit and email to someone, but you forgot? Just connect to your home machine and fire up your editor with it displayed back to your local machine. Edit your document and send it on its way, all from your home machine, with the software displayed to wherever you are working. No need to transfer files, to create multiple confusing versions, or to work outside your favorite applications.
- Need to change something in a file and you don't have the software on the machine you're sitting at? No problem. Just connect over the network to a machine that has the software and use the software on it. No need to mount remote disks to run the application on your local machine. With X11 you get the ability to display the software's interface wherever you're sitting and run the software on the machine where it's stored.

- Stuck behind a firewall and can't get to eBay to submit a last-minute bid? Don't tell your boss about this, but using what you know about tunneling connections with `slogin` and a web browser running on your home machine, you've got a recipe to browse from home, no matter where you're currently sitting.

Rooted Versus Nonrooted Displays

A quirk forced on the X Window System by attempts to get it to coexist with GUIs such as Aqua is the idea of rooted versus nonrooted displays. The X Window System has existed for years under the same impression that Mac OS has—that it's "the" windowing system running on any particular machine. As such, it includes the idea of a root window, much like the Mac OS desktop. The root window is assumed to be a full-screen window that exists behind all other windows in the system, and into which certain restricted types of information can be placed. To make the X Window System coexist with another windowing system that also wants to have a single whole-screen background window, only a few possible compromises can be made. To coexist, one of the systems has to give up its assumption of supremacy; one or the other could run entirely inside a window in the one that reigns supreme; or both could operate as usual, but display only one at a time, with the user toggling between them. If you've used `Timbuktu` or `VNC` before, you've used a system in which one display runs entirely inside a window on the other. There have been X11 implementations for Mac OS that have provided this option for X as well.

Displaying an entire windowing system rooted inside a window in another windowing system is a less than ideal solution. Outside the problem of not really integrating the functionality, and leaving the user with a poor workflow between applications in each of the environments, handling things such as mouse events destined for windows that are in the in-window system (as opposed to the window containing the system) is difficult.

Toggling back and forth between the systems has some advantages and some disadvantages. The confusion about the proper target for user events is eliminated, and each system can make full use of the hardware as it was intended to, but integration between the systems is even more difficult. The Apple/XFree86 X11 implementation provides one X Window System mode in which X11 exists as an entirely separate windowing system into which you can toggle. Figure 17.1 shows an X Window System session, and Figure 17.3 shows an Aqua session. These two are actually running on the same machine at the same time. The X Window System environment can be toggled to by clicking the X icon in the Aqua dock, and the Aqua environment can be toggled to by pressing Command-Option-A. Even when one of the environments isn't displayed, the applications in it keep on running. Although it's not convenient to interoperate between applications in one environment and applications running in the other, it's not a bad way to work, especially if you're mostly using Unix-side applications and not Aqua-native applications.

The other available mode is a surprisingly successful implementation of nonrooted, or rootless, X11 environments. To produce such an environment, the X Window System model must be gutted of its notion of having a root window, and it isn't entirely clear how doing so might affect all possible X11 applications. However, it's clear that it works surprisingly well for at least most applications at this point. In addition, Apple's provided a way to wrap the X Window System applications with an Aqua interface manager, rather than a native X11 interface manager. Figure 17.4 shows an Aqua session with X11 applications running side by side with native Aqua applications. In fact, the web browser in Figure 17.2 is running on a remote machine and is displaying happily integrated with Aqua applications on the local machine.

FIGURE 17.3 This Aqua session is running concurrently with the X11 session shown in Figure 17.1. The window containing what looks like an X11 session is the Preview application showing the screenshot for Figure 17.2.

> **NOTE**
>
> It's not entirely clear what's been done with the root window in the rootless modes or what the implications of the choice are for all X Window System applications. (For example, what happens to applications that display things in the root window?) The root window is an integral part of the X Window System philosophy, and it's a testimonial to both the creativity of the programmers and the power of Unix-like abstraction models that X11 still seems to work so well without it. There's a good chance that they've done something like implemented an X Window System server so that it displays the root window "somewhere else." *Somewhere else* is probably something like into an invisible and unused buffer in memory, and the programmers have fooled the applications into thinking that they're working in a normal X11 environment. We know it's geeky, but we think that the ability to do things like that with Unix applications is pretty cool.

FIGURE 17.4 X11 and Aqua applications can now coexist in the Aqua GUI, all managed by the Aqua user environment.

Installing the X Window System

Now that you have been exposed to a little bit of the X Window system, you might be wondering where to get it and how to install it. There are a few versions of X11 available for Mac OS X. The one that will probably be suitable for most uses is Apple's X11. You can install it from your operating system CD, or you can download it from Apple at `http://www.apple.com/macosx/features/x11/`. Apple's X11 is based on XFree86. If you want the latest X11, XFree86 source is available from `http://www.xfree86.org/`. If you're looking for something in between, you might be interested in the Fink port, available at `http://fink.sourceforge.net/` or the DarwinPorts version, available at `http://darwinports.opendarwin.org/`. If you discover that you need a full-featured X11, compiling from source or getting an Xfree86 port will be most suitable to your needs.

Using X

Whether you've installed X11 from Fink or `xfree86.org` or DarwinPorts, or are using Apple's version, starting it is simply a matter of running the `startx` command from the shell or clicking the appropriate icon for the application. When started from the X11 application, you get preference choices between rooted or rootless display and a few other useful features. If you choose to run your X11 server in rooted mode (completely separate from Aqua windowing system), you can switch between the X11 desktop and your normal Aqua environment by pressing Command-Option-A.

CAUTION

If it appears that you can't type into any of the windows (you move your cursor over the window and the in-window text cursor highlights, but nothing you type appears), congratulations! You've found a Mac OS X bug. Some versions of the Mac OS X kernel have a bug in which it randomly unloads a table that contains a list of which keys exist on the keyboard. X11 needs this table to map what you type into data to be provided to a program. If you experience this bug, our recommendation is to kill X11, sleep the machine, wake it up, and start X11 again. Apparently, the keymap table is reinjected into the kernel on wake up, and starting X11 immediately afterward seems to be the only consistent fix.

The look and feel of the X Window System are mostly the responsibility of the particular window manager you've chosen to run. (You learn more about window managers in the immediately following section.) But in the general operation of the environment, you'll find that there are a number of constants to the way the X Window System works, regardless of what the interface looks like. Some of these are familiar to anyone who has previously used a computer with a mouse. A few, however, are likely to be new even to users who've been happily using a mouse since the earliest days of the Mac. The significant things to remember are described in the next section.

Exploring Common X11 Interface Features

The X Window System is designed for a three-button mouse. Most X software uses the left button for pointing, clicking, and selection. X uses the center button for general functions such as moving or resizing windows, and the right button for application-specific functions such as opening in-application pop-up windows. Of course, any application is capable of modifying these uses, so examination of a program's documentation is always in order.

X also uses its three-button mouse for selection, copying, and pasting in a way that won't be familiar, but that you'll probably come to appreciate quickly. Unlike Mac and Windows, there's no separate command to perform copy functions. Instead, X functions as though whatever has been most recently selected has been placed on the clipboard and can be pasted. The left mouse button allows click-and-drag type selection and picking the start of a selection region. The right mouse button functions like Shift-clicking on the Mac; that is, it extends the selection. And clicking the center mouse button pastes whatever is selected—or has been most recently selected—into whichever window the cursor is in when clicked. This different paradigm for selection, copying, and pasting turns out to be a wonderfully efficient way of enabling you to work with text with the mouse because it requires no coordinated use of a second hand.

The normal Mac mouse, of course, has no middle or right mouse buttons by default. XFree86 deals with this by enabling you to use keyboard modifiers to emulate the middle and right mouse buttons. To enable this mode, add the argument `-fakebuttons` to the `startx` invocation or select it in the X11 application's preferences. This allows clicking while holding down the Command key to emulate the middle mouse button, and the Option key to emulate the right mouse button. So, that benefit of not needing the second hand goes away again, at least for the time being on the Mac. It might be time to put away that cool pro mouse and buy one with multiple buttons or petition Apple to get with the X program!

OF MICE AND BUTTONS

With a single-button mouse, `-fakebuttons` lets you Command-click to send X11 a middle-mouse-button event, and Option-click to send a right-mouse-button event. With a two-button mouse, the right button sends the X11 right-mouse-button event, and you still need the Command-click to send the middle-mouse-button event. Many scroll-wheel mice send a middle-mouse-button event if you push down on (rather than roll) the scroll wheel.

CLICK EARLY, CLICK OFTEN!

X11 likes to make use of the mouse. Under most window managers, there are control and configuration menus that you can access when left-, middle-, and right-clicking on various screen features. Some applications have special menus that appear for certain types of mouse-clicks as well. The menus and options available are context sensitive and change depending on what interface element you're clicking on, and what mouse button (and possibly keyboard key) you're pressing. Application windows, title bars, and the screen background itself all have (or can have, depending on the configuration) their own contextual behaviors for each type of click and keyboard keys in combination with each click. For example Control-clicking in an `xterm` (X11 terminal program) gives you a number of different menus, with options ranging from resetting the font size for that terminal, to turning its scrollbars on and off.

X has the concept of focused input. On Macintosh and Windows platforms, if you type on the keyboard, you generally expect the typing to appear in whatever window or dialog box is in front. On Mac and Windows, the window in front is the active window. In X, the window manager has the option of directing your input where it chooses. The location into which your input is directed is called the input focus. Most window managers can be configured to focus input on the frontmost window, focus input on a selected window (which, on X, doesn't have to be the front window), or focus input on whichever window the cursor is over. These are usually called, respectively, Focus to Front, Click to Focus, and Focus Follows Cursor modes. The last of these, although most unlike the interface you are probably familiar with, is usually considered to be the most powerful.

With the window manager configured in Focus Follows Cursor mode, you can direct typing into a mostly hidden window (for example, to start a noninteractive program) simply by moving the cursor over any visible part of the mostly hidden window and typing. There's no need to waste time bringing a rear window to the front, typing the command, and then shuffling the window back underneath the window that you really wanted to be working in. Figures 17.5 though 17.7 show several examples of working in the different X11 focus modes. Pay careful attention to where the cursor appears (the cursor is an I-beam style text cursor in each), and which window is active. (The active window usually has a solid-block insertion-point cursor, and inactive ones have hollow block insertion-point cursors.) Configuration methods for the different window managers vary, so we cover the options for several in the next section.

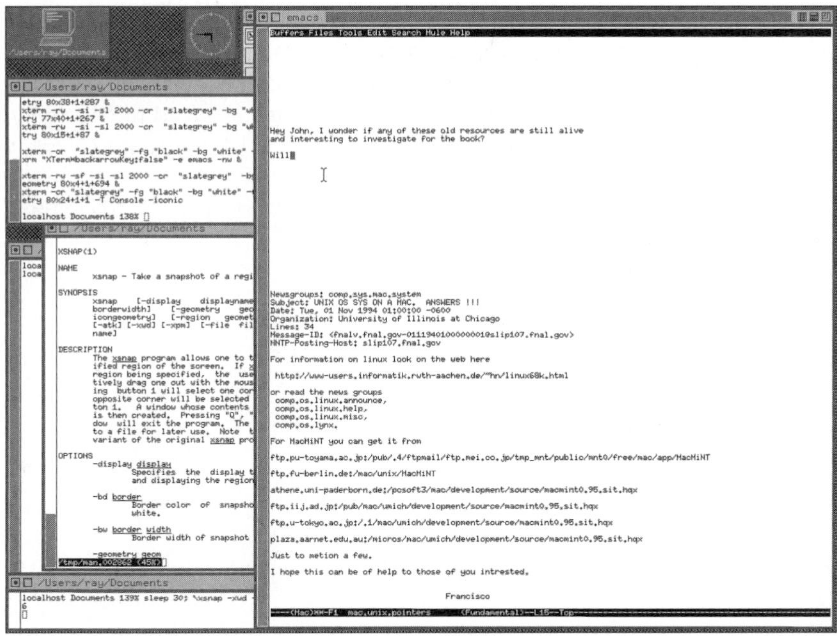

FIGURE 17.5 Focus Follows Cursor mode, with work being done in the frontmost window—this looks like the type of interaction with which you're probably familiar. Note that both the mouse pointer (the I-beam text cursor) and the text insertion point (the dark filled rectangle in the emacs window) are inside the same window.

TIP

If you're typing and you notice that what you're typing isn't appearing where you think it's supposed to, chances are that you've got your input focused in some other window. Make sure that your cursor is where it belongs or, if your system is configured to Click to Focus mode, make sure that you've clicked where you intend to type. It's easy to get confused when moving between platforms using different input focus methods.

In the X Window System, the window manager or any other program can attach arbitrary commands to arbitrary user actions. For example, a program can attach the action of displaying a menu when a user right-clicks on the title bar. The window manager could pop up a variety of menus when the user left-, right-, or center-clicks in the empty background (root window or desktop) of the windowing system. Or it could happen when the user Shift-left-clicks, Shift-right-clicks, or Shift-center-clicks—the possibilities are endless. One popular terminal program, `xterm`, pops up its configuration menus when the user holds down the Control key and left-, right-, or center-clicks in the window.

Some window managers attach a standard menu with common commands such as Close and Resize to icons in each window's title bar. Others attach these functions to pop-up menus in the title bar. You'll find variations in program behavior even among different installations of X11 on the same version of Unix because local configuration options can exert a significant influence over the interface. Don't be too surprised if your installation of X11 doesn't look or behave quite like what is shown here. With the short generation times for open source software, there's plenty of time for the software to be updated a dozen times between me typing this and you reading it. Also, don't be afraid to read the documentation and the FAQs to find out how things work today, regardless of when *today* happens to be.

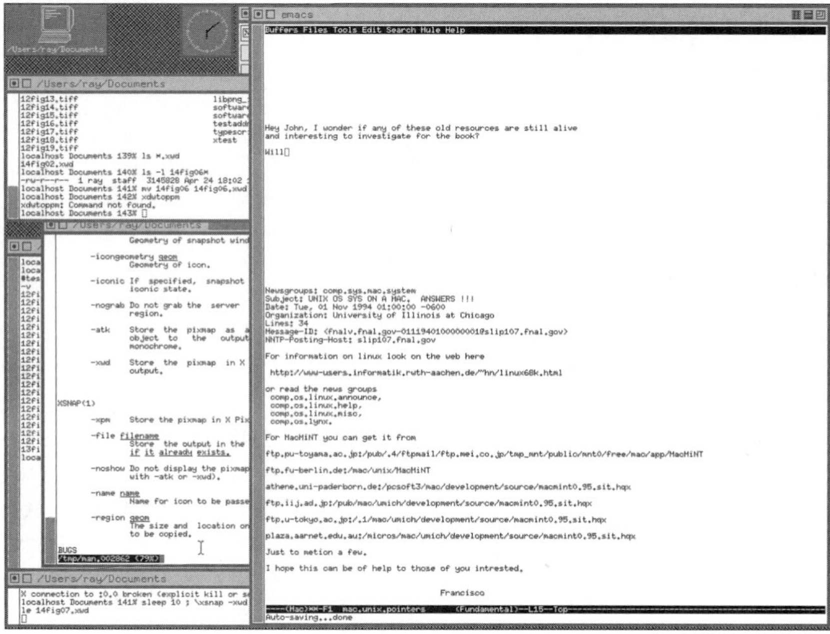

FIGURE 17.6 Focus Follows Cursor mode with work being done in a window that is behind the front window. Notice that the in-window cursor of the `emacs` window (frontmost) has gone hollow to indicate that it's no longer active. The dark active cursor has followed the mouse pointer to indicate that a different window is active. The window border also changes colors, but that probably doesn't show up well in a black-and-white printed image.

Most window managers can iconize windows. Because the actual display of a client's windows isn't handled by the client, but by the server at the request of the client, the X server and window manager are free to make some useful contributions to the user experience. One of these contributions is that when a client requests a window with particular characteristics, the server isn't obliged to represent the window that way to the user. The server is obliged only to treat it as though it had those characteristics. This enables the server, for example, to scale the window arbitrarily or to shrink it down and display it as an icon.

You're familiar with the concept of files and folders being represented with icons. X11 doesn't know a thing about files or folders. It knows about drawing pictures on the screen (there are file browser applications for X11, much like the Mac OS X Finder, and we talk about them later in this chapter), and it knows that you don't always want all those pictures fighting for display space. So, X11 includes the notion that a window can be turned into an icon displayed in the root window if you don't care to have it taking up space. This is sort of like Mac OS X's capability to minimize a running application into the Dock, but you aren't limited to placing things in one location on the screen. (In fact, the window manager Apple provides with its version of X11 uses the Dock for storing the icons that should be on the root window when in rootless mode, and can't minimize at all in root mode.) Likewise, some applications can be dynamically resized to provide different functionality than you are familiar with from Mac OS. The `xterm` terminal window, for example, with most window managers interacts dynamically with the size of the font it's using. Increase the size of the font, and the window increases to show the same data. You can also decrease the font size to a single point—in which case, the terminal shrinks to icon size while remaining a usable terminal and continuing to display output.

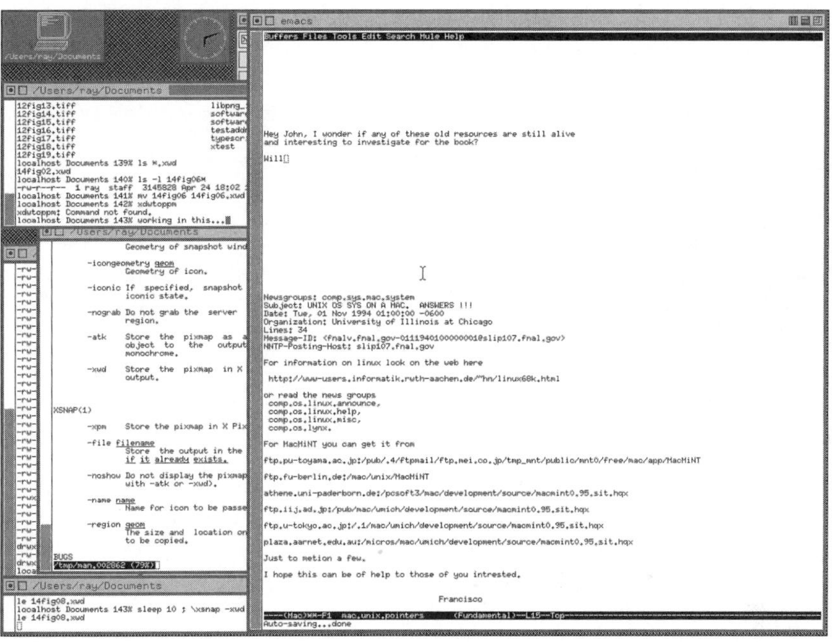

FIGURE 17.7 Click to Focus mode with a window selected other than the one that the cursor is in—this doesn't have to be the front window. Notice that the mouse pointer and active text cursor aren't in the same window. After input has been focused into a window in this mode, it doesn't leave until the mouse is clicked elsewhere.

Configuring the X Window System

Most configuration of the X Window System is handled by a server resource database. When a client makes a request of the server, the server checks the server resource database to determine user preferences for that client. The server resource database is loaded on a per-user basis via the command `xrdb`, which must be executed automatically after starting X11. `xrdb` loads configuration information from a dotfile, usually named `.X11defaults`. `.X11defaults` usually contains lines similar to the following:

```
1    xbiff*onceOnly:                on
2    xbiff*wm_option.autoRaise:     off
3    xbiff*mailBox                  /usr/spool/mail/mymail
```

If you were to include these lines in your `.X11defaults` file, you'd be telling your X server that if `xbiff` (an X11 program that notifies you when you have new mail) starts, it must set certain options.

Line 1 sets an `xbiff`-specific option regarding how frequently to ring the alarm to tell you that you have mail. Here, it's set to ring a single time when mail arrives. Other options are available to set how many times the alarm should ring and at what intervals, if you prefer something other than a single ring.

Line 2 sets an option that belongs to the window manager and tells it how you want `xbiff` treated. Specifically, this tells the window manager not to bring `xbiff` to the front if it's behind other windows when it needs to notify you. Remember, X11 provides the display, and a separate window manager provides such things as window controls.

Line 3 tells `xbiff` where to find the mailbox that it's supposed to look at.

Because each client supports different options and allows the window manager different levels of control, you must consult each client's documentation to learn what you can configure and what you need to do to configure it. As an idea of what you can do, and perhaps as a sample you might like to play with, Listing 17.1 includes a commented listing of my `.X11defaults` file.

LISTING 17.1 A Typical `.X11defaults` File

```
!  ~/.X11defaults
!   This file is used by xrdb to initialize the server resource
!   database, which is used by clients when they start up.
!
! Default defaults
!
*Font:          *-courier-medium-r-*-*-*-120-*-*-*-*-*-*
*MenuFont:      *-courier-medium-r-*-*-*-140-*-*-*-*-*-*
*BoldFont:      *-courier-bold-r-*-*-*-120-*-*-*-*-*-*
!
! GNU Emacs
!
emacs*BorderWidth:      1
! emacs*Font:           9x15
!
! Clock
!
xclock*borderWidth:             0
xclock*wm_option.title:         off
xclock*wm_option.gadgets:       off
```

LISTING 17.1 Continued

```
xclock*wm_option.borderContext: off
xclock*wm_option.autoRaise:     off
!
! Load meter
!
xload*font:                  *-courier-medium-r-*-*-*-100-*-*-*-*-*-*
xload*wm_option.title:          off
xload*wm_option.gadgets:        off
xload*wm_option.borderContext:  off
xload*wm_option.autoRaise:      off
!
! Mail notifier
!
xbiff*wm_option.title:          off
xbiff*wm_option.gadgets:        off
xbiff*wm_option.borderContext:  off
xbiff*wm_option.autoRaise:      off
xbiff*wm_option.volume:         20
!
! Terminal Emulator
!
!XTerm*Font:            9x15
XTerm*c132:             true
XTerm*curses:           true
XTerm*jumpScroll:       true
XTerm*SaveLines:        2048
XTerm*scrollBar:        true
XTerm*scrollInput:      true
XTerm*scrollKey:        true
!
XTerm*fontMenu.Label:                VT Fonts
XTerm*fontMenu*fontdefault*Label:    Default
XTerm*fontMenu*font1*Label:          Tiny
XTerm*VT100*font1:                   nil2
XTerm*fontMenu*font2*Label:          10 Point
XTerm*VT100*font2:          -*-lucidatypewriter-medium-r-*-*-*-080-*-*-*-*-*-*
XTerm*fontMenu*font3*Label:          14 Point
XTerm*VT100*font3:          -*-lucidatypewriter-medium-r-*-*-*-140-*-*-*-*-*-*
XTerm*fontMenu*font4*Label:          18 Point
XTerm*VT100*font4:          -*-lucidatypewriter-medium-r-*-*-*-180-*-*-*-*-*-*
XTerm*fontMenu*font5*Label:          24 Point
XTerm*VT100*font5:                   12x24
XTerm*fontMenu*fontescape*Label:     Escape Sequence
XTerm*fontMenu*fontsel*Label:        Selection
```

17

LISTING 17.1 Continued

```
XTerm*VT100.Translations:       #override \n\
    <Key>L1:    set-vt-font(1) set-scrollbar(off) \n\
    <Key>L2:    set-vt-font set-scrollbar(on) \n\
    <Key>R4:    string("0x1b") string("[211z") \n\
    <Key>R5:    string("0x1b") string("[212z") \n\
    <Key>R6:    string("0x1b") string("[213z") \n\
    <Key>R7:    string("0x1b") string("[214z") \n\
    <Key>R9:    string("0x1b") string("[216z") \n\
    <Key>R11:   string("0x1b") string("[218z") \n\
    <Key>R13:   string("0x1b") string("[220z") \n\
    <Key>R15:   string("0x1b") string("[222z")
!
! Netscape
!
netscape*defaultHeight:     850
netscape*anchorColor:       maroon
netscape*visitedAnchorColor:    blue3
!
! screensaver config
!
xscreensaver*programs: \
    xfishtank -c black -r .1 -f 20 -b 20 \n \
    /usr/local/X11R5/bin/flame -root \n \
    /usr/local/X11R5/bin/maze -root
xscreensaver*colorPrograms:
xscreensaver*monoPrograms:
```

In addition to the server resources database, clients frequently have command-line options that can control the client's interaction with X11. For example:

```
brezup:ray test $ xterm -fg "black" -bg "white" -fn 6x10 -geometry 85x30+525+1
```

This starts an `xterm` terminal session with the following configuration: black as the foreground color, white as the background color (black text on a white window), and a 6×10 point font. It sets the geometry information so that the window is 85 characters wide, 30 characters high, and is placed 525 pixels from the left edge of the screen and 1 pixel down from the top.

Again, different programs have different options available, and your location documentation is your best source for up-to-date information on your exact configuration.

Finally, the applications that start when you start X11 (or most standardized installations of X11, including the default XFree86 installation) are configured by the execution of a file named `.xinitrc` in your home directory. This is a shell script file containing a collection of commands that you want executed when X11 starts. Therefore, you can put in it lines that start xterm terminals, clocks, editors, and any other X11-based applications that you want to start in your environment. The lines are exactly the commands you'd type at the command line to start these applications, so the earlier comments about the wide variability of the configuration options apply here as well.

NOTE

Under Apple's version of X11, if you don't start a window manager yourself in your own .xinitrc file, an Aqua-like window manager is used, giving your X11 applications standard Mac OS X window appearances and controls.

Listing 17.2 shows the contents of my .xinitrc file, which produces the X11 environment shown previously in Figure 17.1.

LISTING 17.2 A Typical .xinitrc File

```
#!/bin/sh

xrdb -load $HOME/.X11defaults
xset m 2 5 s off
xset fp+ /usr/X11R6/lib/X11/fonts

# xmodmap -e 'keysym BackSpace = Delete'
echo  "XTerm*ttyModes:erase ^H" ¦ xrdb -merge

/usr/X11R6/bin/twm &

/usr/X11R6/bin/xclock -bg "slategrey" -fg "lightgrey"  -analog
➥-geometry 60x60+220+1 -padding 4 &

xterm -rw  -si -sl 2000 -cr  "slategrey" -bg "white" -fg "black"
➥-fn 6x10 -geometry 80x38+1+287 &
xterm -rw  -si -sl 2000 -cr  "slategrey" -bg "white" -fg "black"
➥-fn 6x10 -geometry 77x40+1+267 &
xterm -rw  -si -sl 2000 -cr  "slategrey" -bg "white" -fg "black"
➥-fn 6x10 -geometry 80x15+1+87 &

xterm -cr  "slategrey" -fg "black" -bg "white" -fn 6x10 -geometry 82x73+507+1
➥-xrm "XTerm*backarrowKey:false" -e emacs -nw &

xterm -rw -sf -si -sl 2000 -cr  "slategrey"  -bg "white" -fg "black"
➥-fn 6x10 -geometry 80x4+1+694 &
xterm -cr "slategrey" -fg "black" -bg "white" -fn 6x10 -title "CONSOLE"
➥-C -geometry 80x24+1+1 -T Console -iconic
```

17

Window Manager and Application-Specific Configurations

Finally, window managers and applications have their own configuration files that control display options and, possibly, other parameters regarding the user experience. Where and how these are set depends on the window manager and/or application that you are running. Some can be controlled through the server resource database. Others are set in individual control files specific to the window manager or configured through a control pane-like interface. Yet other options are available through combination mouse-button and keyboard actions. (For example, Control-left-, Control-middle-, and Control-right-clicking provides access to a multitude of options for the `twm` window manager and for `xterm` terminals.)

Using Window Managers: `twm`, `mwm`, `quartz-wm`

After you've started the X Window System environment, you're presented with a single `xterm` window in the upper-left side of your screen, managed with an Aqua-like window manager. This is the current default for a user who has no `.xinitrc` file to control what applications to start and where to put them, and no `.twmrc` file to control what the applications look and feel like. Remember that the X Window System provides only interface, component, and display functionality; additional programs are required to provide a useful user interface. In Figure 17.1, you are actually looking at the result of 10 programs running simultaneously (not counting the X Window System server and associated programs necessary for it to function) just to create the interface. Six display windows, one provides an application dock, one is a clock, one is an editor, and finally, the window manager, `twm`, provides the title bars and border controls associated with the windows. Startup of the programs occurs in `.xinitrc`, and the configuration of their appearance is controlled by `twm`.

`twm`

One of the most common window managers is `twm` (*tabbed window manager* or *Tim's window manager*, depending on who you ask). Shown managing the display in Figure 17.1, `twm` provides very basic window management functions and is the default window manager used by XFree86. Even though it's one of the less fancy window managers, `twm` is convenient and allows an extreme amount of user customization of the environment. If you choose to do so, you can create your own standard buttons that appear in your `twm` title bars and cause them to execute arbitrary commands. You can also build your own pop-up menus, automatically execute commands when the cursor enters windows, customize window manager colors and actions by application name and type, and a host of other customizations. Listing 17.3 is a portion of my `.twmrc` file, which gives you an idea of the range of configuration options. The listing is only a portion of my `.twmrc` file because the entire file contains 284 individual configuration parameters. I'm particular about how my interface functions, and `twm` gives me the flexibility to configure every last one of the 284 tweaks it takes to get it how I like it.

LISTING 17.3 A Representative Sample of a .twmrc Configuration File for the twm X Window System Window Manager

```
Color
{
    BorderColor "maroon4"

    BorderTileForeground "bisque4"
    BorderTileBackground "darkorchid4"

    TitleForeground "darkslategray"
    TitleBackground "bisque3"

    DefaultBackground "bisque"
    DefaultForeground "slategrey"

    MenuForeground "slategrey"
    MenuBackground "moccasin"

    MenuTitleForeground "slategrey"
    MenuTitleBackground "bisque3"
    MenuShadowColor "bisque4"
    IconForeground "lightgrey"
    IconBackground "slategray"
    IconBorderColor "darkslategray"
    IconManagerForeground "darkslategrey"
    IconManagerBackground "bisque"
    IconManagerHighlight  "maroon4"
}

BorderWidth     4
FramePadding    2
TitleFont      "8x13"
MenuFont       "8x13"
IconFont       "6x10"
ResizeFont     "fixed"
NoTitleFocus

IconManagerGeometry   "=200x10+290+1"

ShowIconManager

IconManagerFont               "variable"
IconManagerDontShow
{
    "xclock"
```

LISTING 17.3 Continued

```
    "xbiff"
    "perfmeter"
}

ForceIcons
Icons
{
    "xterm"    "terminal"
}

NoTitle
{
  "TWM"
  "xload"
  "xclock"
  "xckmail"
  "xbiff"
  "xeyes"
  "oclock"
}

NoHighlight
{
  "xclock"
  "dclock"
  "xload"
  "xbiff"
}

AutoRaise
{
  "nothing"
}

DefaultFunction f.menu "default-menu"
#WindowFunction f.function "blob"

#Button = KEYS : CONTEXT : FUNCTION
#----------------------------------
Button1 =       : root   : f.menu "button1"
Button2 =       : root   : f.menu "button2"
Button3 =       : root   : f.menu "button3"

Button1 =       : title  : f.function "blob"
```

LISTING 17.3 Continued

```
Button2 =       : title  : f.lower

Button1 =       : frame  : f.raiselower
Button2 =       : frame  : f.move
Button3 =       : frame  : f.lower

Button1 =       : icon   : f.function "blob"
Button2 =       : icon   : f.iconify
Button3 =       : icon   : f.menu "default-menu"
Button1 = m     : icon   : f.iconify
Button2 = m     : icon   : f.iconify
Button3 = m     : icon   : f.iconify
Button3 = c     : root   : f.function "beep-beep"

Function "beep-beep"
{
    f.beep
    f.beep
    f.beep
    f.beep
    f.beep
}

menu "button1"
{
"Window Ops"        f.title
"(De)Iconify"       f.iconify
"Move"              f.move
"Resize"            f.resize
"Lower"             f.lower
"Raise"             f.raise
"Redraw Window"     f.winrefresh
"Focus Input"       f.focus
"Unfocus Input"     f.unfocus
"Window Info"       f.identify
}

menu "button2"
{
"Window Mgr"        f.title
"Circle Up"         f.circleup
"Circle Down"       f.circledown
 "Refresh All"       f.refresh
"Source .twmrc"     f.twmrc
```

LISTING 17.3 Continued

```
"Beep"              f.beep
"Show Icon Mgr"     f.showiconmgr
"Hide Icon Mgr"     f.hideiconmgr
"Feel"              f.menu "Feel"
}

menu "button3"
{
"Clients"              f.title
"Xterm"                ! "xterm &"
"Emacs"                ! "emacs -i &"
"Lock Screen"          ! "xnlock &"
"Xman"                 ! "xman &"
"X Text Exitor"        ! "xedit &"
"Calculator"           ! "xcalc &"
}

menu "default-menu"
{
"Default Menu"         f.title
"Refresh"              f.refresh
"Refresh Window"       f.winrefresh
"twm Version"          f.version
"Focus on Root"        f.unfocus
"Source .twmrc"        f.twmrc
"Cut File"             f.cutfile
"Move Window"          f.move
"ForceMove Window"     f.forcemove
"Resize Window"        f.resize
"Raise Window"         f.raise
"Lower Window"         f.lower
"Focus on Window"      f.focus
"Raise-n-Focus"        f.function "raise-n-focus"
"Zoom Window"          f.zoom
"FullZoom Window"      f.fullzoom
"Kill twm"             f.quit
"Destroy Window"       f.destroy
}

RightTitleButton "down" = f.zoom
RightTitleButton "right" = f.horizoom
LeftTitleButton "icon" = f.destroy
```

mwm

The Motif window manager (mwm) is a popular window manager that evolved from a commercial product, and it's also a popular window manager for others to attempt to emulate. It provides a somewhat different user experience than twm. The difference is partly because twm automatically attaches things such as resize corners to all windows, and partly because of the pretty 3D look it gives to the controls. Figure 17.8 shows mwm managing the same collection of windows managed by twm in Figure 17.1.

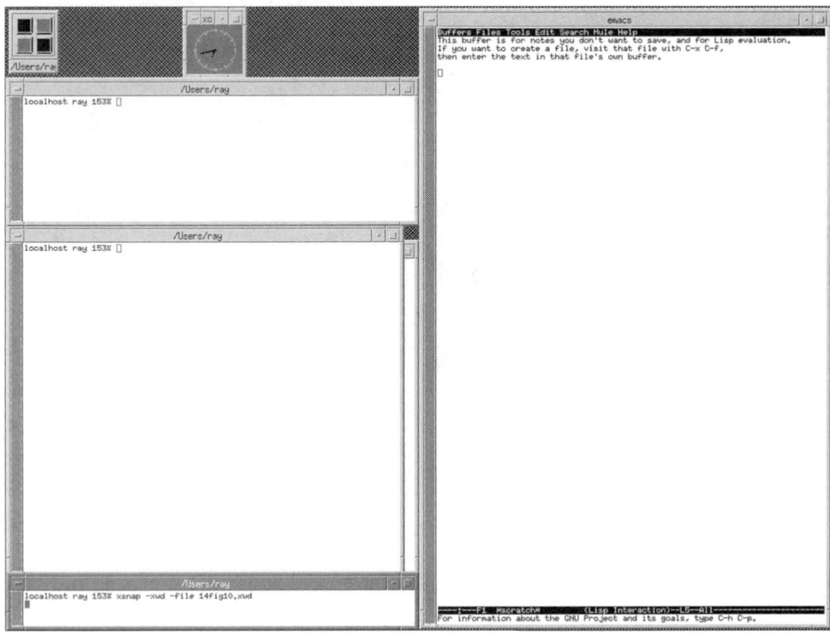

FIGURE 17.8 The mwm window manager, managing the same collection of windows shown in Figure 17.1.

quartz-wm

quartz-wm makes X11 applications look like native Mac OS X applications. Shown managing some of the windows in Figure 17.9, quartz-wm is an Aqua window manager for X11 applications running in either rooted or rootless mode. It makes X11 applications feel almost exactly like normal Aqua applications and generally makes the whole Aqua versus X11 distinction into a nonissue for the Mac-familiar user.

NOTE

quartz-wm is automatically started by Apple's X11 version if you don't start another window manager of your own in your .xinitrc file. If you care to use a different window manager, however, quartz-wm still has one useful feature. If it is started with the option --only-proxy specified, it relinquishes window management to another window manager but provides an integration layer to assist with mapping copy and paste actions between X11 and native Aqua windows. This feature is tremendously useful if you work back and forth between Aqua and X11 windows frequently because X11's native cut-and-paste mechanism is not directly compatible with the normal Macintosh methods.

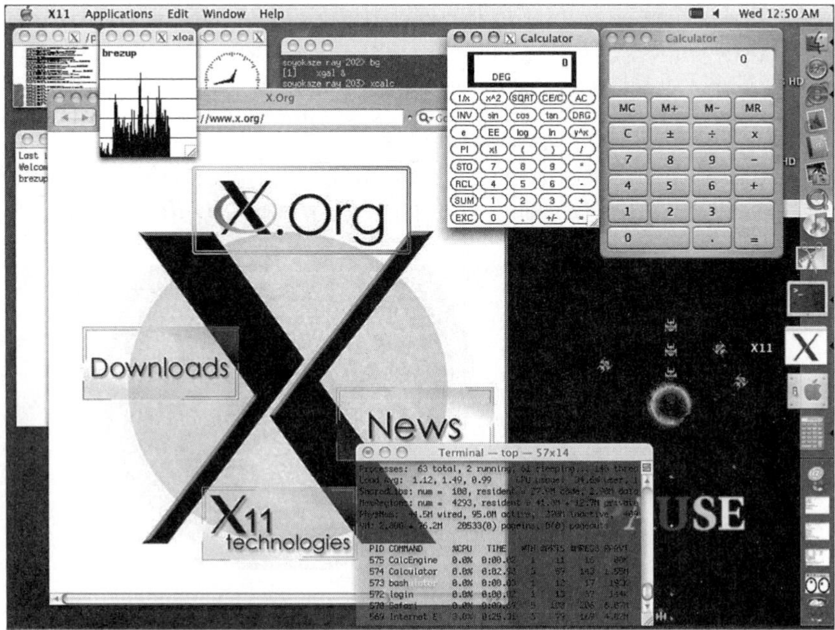

FIGURE 17.9 `quartz-wm` managing some windows. Can you tell which windows are X11 and which are Aqua? What about the minimized applications in the Dock? Visually, and very nearly in any respect, the only clue you get is the odd window names.

Other Window Managers

New window managers and ports of earlier variants are appearing for Mac OS X at a nice pace. Several nice flavors are already available, and more will probably appear by the time this book is published, so here's a quick list of some of the interesting ones to watch for:

- `tvtwm`—An extension of `twm` that enables you to create an arbitrarily large number of virtual windows and switch between them conveniently.
- `fvwm`—A "3D-ish" version of `twm` with even more flexible configuration options.
- `enlightenment`—A heavyweight (some would say bloated) window manager that belongs to the GNOME desktop environment. GNOME and `enlightenment` are popular on the Linux platform because of the user-friendly environment created under X11. Running `enlightenment` with X11 in rootless mode is interesting. `enlightenment` is another window manager that allows you to have multiple virtual screens that you can toggle among. In `enlightenment`'s case, when you run your cursor off the edge of the screen, the screen slides sideways, and you slide over to a new virtual monitor. When run rootless with Aqua, the Aqua applications of course don't slide, so if you keep one virtual monitor empty of X11 applications, the effect is of being able to slide all the X11 applications off the side of your screen to expose just the Aqua versions, whenever you want. `enlightenment`/GNOME tries to pack every bell and whistle available into an interface that makes Aqua look drab.

- KDE—Another heavyweight window manager and desktop environment. KDE is lighter on the fancy polished graphics than GNOME and `enlightenment`, but it provides powerful interface programming capabilities. Many find its look and feel to be more functional than the `enlightenment`/GNOME combination.
- Window Maker—Another heavyweight window manager, Window Maker is designed to give special support for the GNUstep applications and attempts to provide the elegant look and feel of the OpenStep environment.

When running the X Window System, keep in mind that the window controls, such as title bars and scrollbars, are provided by a separate window manager application. The point of repeating this again is that it's possible for the window manager to exit, leaving you with a collection of unmanaged windows. This is a slightly disconcerting state in which to find the X Window System because the window manager also controls the input focus. Figure 17.10 shows an X Window System session that has lost its window manager.

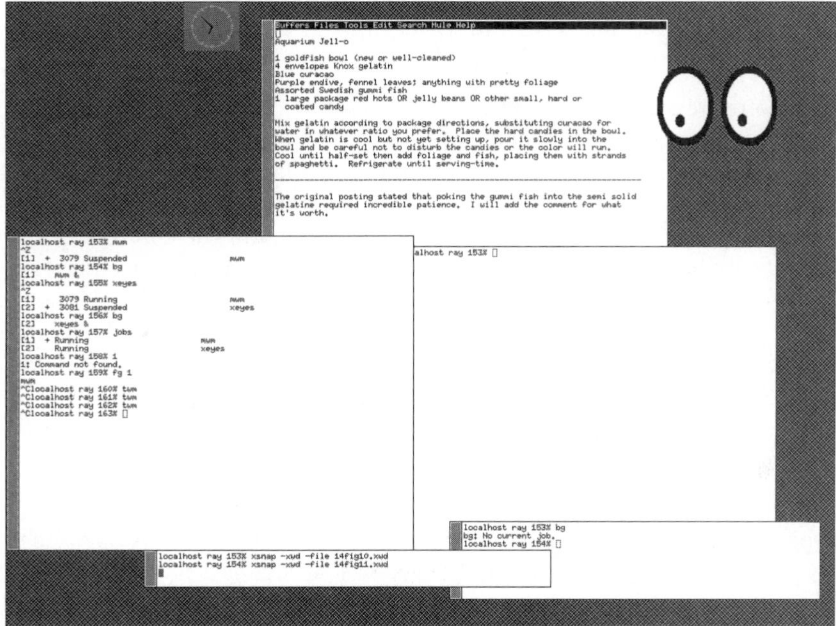

FIGURE 17.10 An X Window System session that has lost its window manager.

NOTE

If your window manager dies while your input is focused somewhere other than a terminal window, you might not be able to refocus. Therefore, you might not be able to type into a window (meaning that you can't type something like `twm` at a prompt, and so you can't restart your window manager). In this case, all is not necessarily lost because the mouse cursor selection and paste method usually still works, even without a window manager. If you can find the letters `t`, `w`, and `m` anywhere on your screen, you can select and paste them at a command prompt, and then select and paste a return/newline, which usually rescues things.

This is a problem with no elegant solution, but if you desperately need to save something you've been working on, it's nice to know there's a fix, even if it's a nuisance. Thankfully, window managers don't frequently die of their own accord. Usually, it takes a user clicking on something like `kill twm` in the menu—in which case, you'll probably be more annoyed at yourself than at having to copy and paste a couple of letters to fix things.

Some Additional Interesting X11 Software

It might not be immediately obvious why you'd want to install an auxiliary windowing system on Mac OS X, when you already have the nice Aqua GUI to work in. If you don't intend to take advantage of the Unix software heritage that's available to you, or to write software that's also compatible with Linux and other Unix variants, there's little reason at all. Remember that the X Window System has been ubiquitous in the Unix world for a long, long time. Because of this, and because it's relatively easy to write software for the X Window System, even things that might not seem like they need GUIs have been written to take advantage of X11.

The range of software available to the X Windows system is amazing—imagine if all the Mac software going back to 1984 could still be run on the Macintosh, only with a far more active user community, all cranking out their own favorite little applications, and all making the software available for download. The result is applications that span from the most obtuse scientific analyses, to hundreds of variants on the common mail-reader, and from office-application suites that rival Microsoft Office, to video games. There isn't room in this book, or a dozen more its size, to cover the whole body of X11 software out there, so we'll simply briefly mention a few applications that you might be interested in, and suggest that you keep an eye on Fink and DarwinPorts for the most easily installable stuff. There is a vast array of X11-capable software out there that's not in either of these sources however, so do keep in mind that much of what you meet on web pages, Usenet newsgroups, or FTP sites can probably be compiled and run on Mac OS X.

Because X11 has been around so long, and because it's a relatively simple GUI to write for, the sophistication of the interfaces that people have created for it vary widely. For example, video games range from simple 2D vector graphics games to fully 3D first-person shooters. An interesting phenomenon to note, however, is that because much X Window System software has been developed using something approximating the open source model, many of the interfaces have been through both testing and troubleshooting to a high degree. This results in interfaces that are sometimes surprisingly effective in their intended role, despite their simplicity.

Unfortunately, this very ease of development and the community effort it inspires sometimes works against intuition. If a given application doesn't do exactly what someone wants, it has often been just as easy to create a new one, tailored to that individual's needs, as it has been to move development of the existing application in the desired direction. Because of this, the user community for a given application is often a small, tightly knit group of individuals who have tuned their application to work exactly how they think it should, and finding the version from the group whose thoughts agree with yours on the matter, is sometimes a bit of work. So, when you're looking at an X11 newsreader and it seems completely counterintuitive, remember that you're probably looking at an application written by people who think your ideas about news-reading-convenience are just as alien, and there is almost certainly something out there that does the same thing, but in a fashion you would find more familiar. It's usually worth your time to go looking for it, rather than to try to "think right" to use software that was written by people from Mars.

Two X11 applications you might be particularly interested in are the GIMP and OpenOffice.org packages. These are both high-productivity packages that many users will find invaluable in doing real work.

GIMP (the Gnu Image Manipulation Program) is a complete photo/image-editing program with layer support, a sophisticated plug-in architecture, and the capability to read, write, and edit most image formats known to man. If you need Adobe Photoshop capabilities, but can't afford software with an Adobe Photoshop price tag, GIMP might be just exactly what you need. If you're interested in photo editing and/or image creation for website design, GIMP is almost definitely something that should be on your list. It's widely used in the Linux community for making website buttons and banners, so there are a great many automated special effect filters available that make three-state (up/clicking/down) buttons, and fancy text effects that are commonly used in website design. Figures 17.11 and 17.12 are GIMP images showing the interface, and some of the text and button effects that can be easily generated using the built-in filters. Because the filter architecture is open and easily extended using only the tools that already come with Mac OS X, you can add your own effects, and you can find many others that interested individuals have written and made available online. GIMP can be installed using either Fink or DarwinPorts, and far more information can be found at `http://www.gimp.org/`. When using GIMP, keep in mind that the primary designers all have three-button mice, and have therefore stuck many functions you probably expect to find in top-of-the-window menus into pop-up menus accessed through the middle and right mouse buttons.

OpenOffice.org (yes, its product is named after its website) is an open source project that was originally a product of StarDivision, distributed as StarOffice. StarDivision was acquired by Sun Microsystems, which continued development and distribution of StarOffice, and eventually released the development effort into an open source project from which it continues to produce both the StarOffice suite and the freely available OpenOffice.org suite. The OpenOffice.org suite and StarOffice are almost identical, with the exception of some third-party components (for which Sun pays license fees for their use in the StarOffice version), a few Sun-proprietary components, and the fact that as a commercial product, StarOffice comes with support. Mac OS X ports of OpenOffice.org are available at `http://porting.openoffice.org/mac/ooo-osx_downloads.html`. One is an X11 implementation and the other is a Carbon and Java implementation. Figure 17.13 shows a snapshot of the OpenOffice.org suite in action. The suite includes a fully functional word processor with Microsoft Word compatibility, a spreadsheet program, a presentation program, and considerable additional office-productivity functionality.

FIGURE 17.11 GIMP.

FIGURE 17.12 GIMP.

Two X11 applications at the opposite end of the spectrum are CannonSmash and xtank. CannonSmash is available through DarwinPorts (or, if you're inclined to build by hand, from the primary source `http://cannonsmash.sourceforge.net/`). xtank is available, precompiled for Mac OS X, from `http://www.macosxunleashed.com/downloads/` (or, via CVS, from `http://alioth.debian.org/forum/forum.php?forum_id=290`).

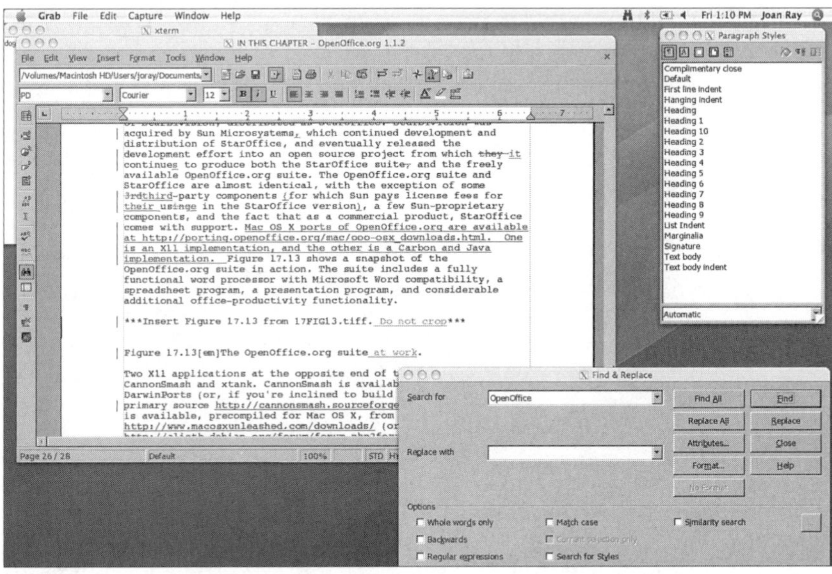

FIGURE 17.13 The OpenOffice.org suite at work.

CannonSmash is a 3D, head-to-head, networkable ping-pong (table tennis) simulator. It's surprisingly addictive, and makes an interesting demonstration of the breadth of development that occurs in the Open Source community. Using OpenGL under X11, CannonSmash is as cross-platform as imaginable, requiring only a competent X11 implementation, and competent OpenGL libraries. This means that you can pop off a quick game or three over a coffee break, playing against a friend who's located half the globe away, running completely a completely different operating system on completely different hardware. Figure 17.14 shows a screenshot out of the CannonSmash training section where you are introduced to the controls and gameplay mechanics.

xtank is a 2D overhead view tank-combat strategy game. Before Half-Life, before Quake, before Marathon, and before DOOM, we had xtank, and it was good. It still is. Lacking, at the time, all the fancy 3D, texture-mapped gee-gaws that are such a large part of today's games, xtank had to find appeal in playability, with which it is amazingly well endowed. In terms of gameplay, xtank is reminiscent of a cross between Space Dungeon and a one-vehicle-per-player version of Total Annihilation. You design and outfit your tank as you see fit (including, if you choose, authoring your own tank designs and weapons-systems code), and then compete in a multiplayer fracas at games that range from outright king-of-the-hill combat to Ultimate Frisbee. The game teaches some interesting things about game design. For example, because it was originally written to run on hardware that couldn't compete with one of today's cell phones in terms of processor power, the game eschews all but the sparest graphics necessary to represent the play. This has surprisingly little effect on its playability. Likewise, the limited map size has interesting implications because it forces players to concentrate on strategy in a close-quarters environment that essentially denies the possibility of camping and other tactics that are playable, but that degrade most players' enjoyment of today's massive combat games. Figure 17.15 shows a screenshot of an xtank game, wherein my oversized, overly slow dreadnought-style tank is being besieged by five faster, lighter, and more maneuverable assault tanks. Now I've waited and absorbed their light gun attacks long enough for all four of my heavy mortars to reload, and they are about to pay the price for buzzing like flies around the guy with the big guns.

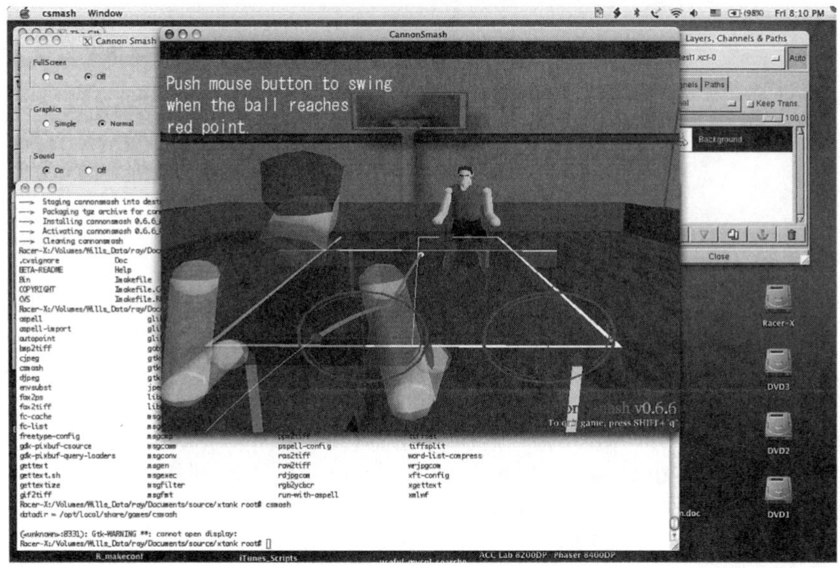

FIGURE 17.14 The training section for CannonSmash, an X11 ping-pong game.

Configuring the Tiger X Window Application

In addition to the general comments we have made about configuring the X Window System, there are a few other points we would like to mention about configuring Apple's X11.

First, as we briefly mentioned earlier, you can choose between a rooted or rootless mode. In the Preferences section of the X11 menu is a subsection called *Output*. Here is where you indicate whether you are interested in a root or rootless display mode. By default, the application is set to a rootless display (like the way the rest of the Mac OS X interface works), but if you would like a rooted display, click the Full Screen Mode box. Recall that if you choose to run your X11 server in rooted mode, you can switch between the X11 desktop and your normal Aqua environment by pressing Command-Option-A. There is also a Colors option in this section as well as an option to use system alert sounds.

Under the Input section, you can choose to emulate a three-button mouse, use the system keyboard, or enable keyboard shortcuts in X11. The section notes that if you select the system keyboard, you can change your X11 keymap settings via the Input menu.

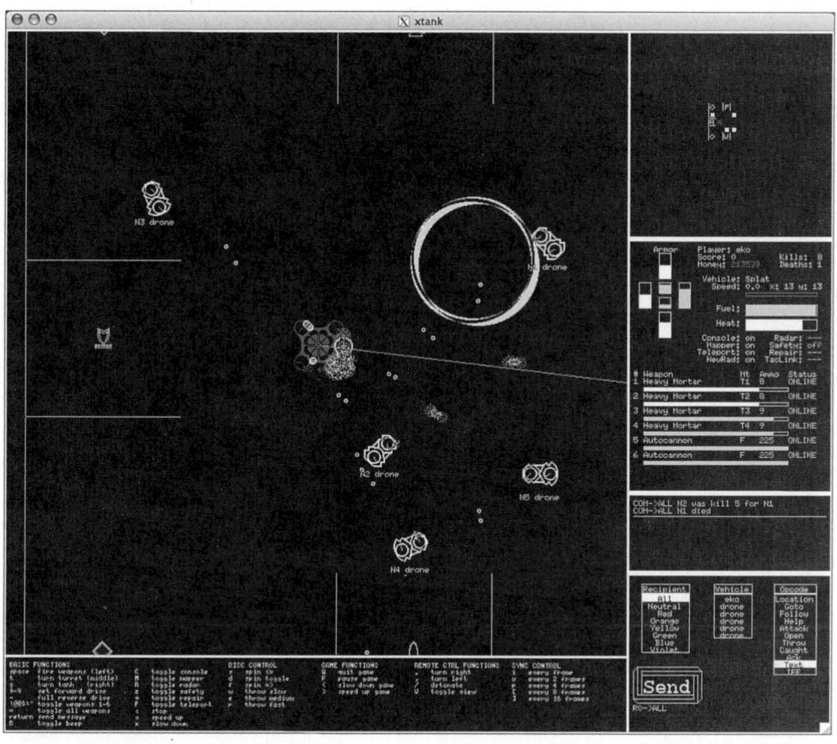

FIGURE 17.15 Five fast, light tanks approach the large tank in this screenshot of xtank, an X11 tank game.

Apple's X11 application provides the ability to create application shortcuts to the more popular applications you use. By default, the menu contains shortcuts for an `xterm` (as Terminal) as well as `xman` and `xlogo`. Under the Customize option, though, you can not only remove a default item, but you can also assign a keyboard shortcut to a default item. Additionally, you can add any other items to that listing that you want and supply keyboard shortcuts for them. This works for applications that do not require any special setup.

Finally, you will experience problems trying to use any X application that also uses the `^h` character combination, such as `emacs`. This is because Apple has mapped `^h`, rather than the customary `^?`, to delete. To correct for this, issue the following command:

```
stty erase ^\?
```

Summary

With the installation of the X Window System on your machine, a whole world of graphical Unix applications has been opened up to you. No matter which X11 server you install, the availability of software that compiles and runs under X11 will only continue to increase. For a taste of the range of X11 applications available, peruse the archives of X.org, located at `http://www.x.org/`.

CHAPTER 18

Using the Perl and Python Scripting Languages

IN THIS CHAPTER

- Perl
- Python

Open source scripting languages open up programming to a wide range of users—from diehard developers to graphic artists. Everyone wants the ability to tell your computer what to do and have it respond appropriately—without having to learn complex development environments or wait for hours while your code compiles. Scripting languages provide instant gratification programming and can be used to create simple data processing applications to complex client/server systems. In Chapter 4, "Managing and Configuring Hardware and Devices," you learned about AppleScript, which has the capability to interact with native Tiger applications. This chapter looks at two popular open source scripting languages that come with your operating system: Perl and Python. Scripts developed in these languages can be used on almost any platform, including Windows.

Perl

Perl, *Practical Extraction and Reporting Language,* is a mouthful to say, but shouldn't be judged by its somewhat bland name. Originally designed to make working with text data simple, Perl has been expanded by developers to handle tasks such as image manipulation and client/server activities. Because of its ease of use and capability to work with ambiguous user input, Perl is a popular web development language.

For example, assume that you want to extract a phone number from an input string. A user might enter 555-5654,

5552231, 421-5552313, and so on. It is up to the application to find the area code, local exchange, and identifier numbers. In Perl, doing so is simple:

```
#!/usr/bin/perl
print "Please enter a phone number:";
$phone=<STDIN>;
$phone=~s/[^\d]//g;
$phone=~s/^1//;
if (length($phone)==7) {
  $phone=~/(\d{3,3})(\d{4,4})/;
  $area="???"; $prefix=$1; $number=$2;
} elsif (length($phone)==10) {
  $phone=~/(\d{3,3})(\d{3,3})(\d{4,4})/;
  $area=$1; $prefix=$2; $number=$3;
} else { print "Invalid number!"; exit; }
print "($area) $prefix-$number\n";
```

This program accepts a phone number as input, strips any unusual characters from it, removes a leading 1, if included, and then formats the result in an attractive manner. Applying this capability to mine data from user input to web development creates opportunities for programmers to write extremely user-friendly software.

Perl programs are similar to shell scripts in that they are interpreted by an additional piece of software. Each script starts with a line that includes the path to the Perl interpreter. In Mac OS X, this is typically `#!/usr/bin/perl`. On entering a script, it must be made executable by typing **`chmod +x`** ***`<script name>`***. Finally, it can be run by entering its complete path at the command line or by typing **`./`*****`<script name>`*** from the same directory as the script. Alternatively, you can invoke a script by passing it as an argument to Perl—that is, **`perl`** ***`<script name>`***. For more information on this process, refer to Chapter 15, "Shell Configuration and Programming (Shell Scripting)."

Although this chapter provides enough information to write a program like the one shown here, it is not a complete reference to Perl. Perl is an object-oriented language with thousands of functions. *Sams Teach Yourself Perl in 21 Days* is an excellent read and a great way to beef up on the topic.

TIP

In addition to this introduction, Chapter 19, "Serving and Connecting to Databases," covers Perl's capability to interact with database systems such as MySQL, and Chapter 24, "Developing Web Applications," discusses using Perl as a web development language.

Variables and Data Types

Perl has a number of different variable types, but the most common are shown in Table 18.1. Perl variable names are composed of alphanumeric characters and are case sensitive, unlike much of Mac OS X. This means that a variable named `$mymacosx` is entirely different from `$myMacOSX`. Unlike some languages, such as C, Perl performs automatic type conversion when possible. A programmer can use a variable as a number in one statement and a string in the next.

TABLE 18.1 Common Perl Variable Types

Type	Description
`$variable`	A simple variable that can hold anything is prefixed with a `$`. You can use these variables as strings or numbers. These are the most common variables.
`FILEHANDLE`	Filehandles hold a reference to a file that you are writing or reading. Typically, these are expressed in uppercase and do not have the `$` prefix.
`@array`	The `@` references an array of variables. The array does not need to be predimensioned and can grow to whatever size memory allows. You reference individual elements of an array as `$array[0]`, `$array[1]`, `$array[2]`, and so on. The array as a whole is referenced as `@array`.
`%array`	This is another type of an array—an associative array. Associative arrays are another of Perl's power features. Rather than using numbers to reference the values stored in this array, you use any string you want. For example, if you have 3 apples, 2 oranges, and 17 grapefruit, you could store these values in the associative array as `$array{apple}=3`, `$array{orange}=2`, `$array{grapefruit}=17`. The only difference between the use of a normal array and an associate array (besides the method of referencing a value) is the type of brackets used. Associative arrays use curly brackets `{}` to access individual elements, whereas standard arrays use square brackets `[]`.

Input/Output Functions

Because Perl is so useful for manipulating data, one of the first things you'll want to do is get data into a script. There are a number of ways to do this, including reading from a file or the Terminal window. To Perl, however, command-line input and file input are much the same thing. To use either, you must read from an input stream.

18

Input Streams

To input data into a variable from a file, use `$variable=<FILEHANDLE>`. This inputs data up to a newline character into the named variable. To read from the command line, the filehandle is replaced with a special handle that points to the standard input stream: `<STDIN>`.

When data is read from an input stream, it contains the end-of-line character (newline) as part of the data. This is usually an unwanted piece of information that can be stripped off using the `chomp` command. Failure to use `chomp` often results in debugging headaches as you attempt to figure out why your string comparison routines are failing. For example, the following reads a line from standard (command line) input and removes the trailing newline character:

```
$myname=<STDIN>;
chomp($myname);
```

To read data in from an actual stored file, it must first be opened with open *<FILEHANDLE>*, "*<filename>*". For example, the following reads the first line of a file named MacOSX.txt:

```
open FILEHANDLE, "MacOSX.txt";
$line1=<FILENAME>;
close FILEHANDLE;
```

When you've finished reading a file, use close followed by the filehandle to be closed.

Outputting Data

Outputting data is the job of the print command. print can display text strings or the contents of variables. In addition, you can embed special characters in a print statement that are otherwise unprintable. For example:

```
print "I love Mac OS X!\n---------------\n";
```

In this sample line, the \n is a newline character—this moves the cursor down a line so that subsequent output occurs on a new line, rather than the same line as the current print statement. Table 18.2 contains other common special characters.

TABLE 18.2 Common Special Characters

Escape Sequence	Description
\n	Newline, the Unix equivalent of Return/Enter
\r	A standard return character
\t	Tab
\"	Double quotes
\\	The \ character

Many characters (such as ") have a special meaning in Perl; if you want to refer to them literally, you must prefix them with \—this is called *escaping* the character. In most cases, nonalphanumeric characters should be escaped just to be on the safe side.

File Output To output data to a file rather than standard output, you must first open a file to receive the information. This is nearly identical to the open operation used to read data, except for one difference. When writing to a file, you must prefix the name of the file with one of two different character strings:

- >—Output to a file, overwriting the contents
- >>—Append to an existing file; creates a new file if one does not exist

With a file open, the print command is again used for output. This time, however, it includes the filehandle of the output file. For example, this code saves "Mac OS X" to a file named MyOS.txt:

```
open MYFILE, "> MyOS.txt";
print MYFILE "Mac OS X\n";
close MYFILE;
```

Again, the `close` command is used to close the file when all output has completed.

External Results (``)

One of the more novel (and powerful) ways to get information into Perl is through an external program. For example, to quickly and easily grab a listing of running processes, you could use the output of the Unix `ps axg` command:

```
$processlist=`ps axg`;
```

Backtick (``) characters should be placed around the command of the output you want to capture. Perl pauses and waits for the external command to finish executing before it continues processing.

This is both a dangerous and powerful tool. You can easily read an entire file into a variable by using the `cat` command with backticks. Unfortunately, if the external program fails to execute correctly, the Perl script might hang indefinitely.

Expressions

Although Perl variables can hold numbers or strings, you still need to perform the appropriate type of comparison based on the values being compared. For example, numbers can be compared for equality using ==, but strings must be compared with `eq`. If you attempt to use == to compare two strings, the expression will evaluate to true because the numeric value of both strings is zero, regardless of the text they contain. Table 18.3 displays common Perl expressions.

TABLE 18.3 Use the Appropriate Comparison Operators for the Type of Data Being Compared

Expression Syntax	Description
`$var1==$var2`	Compares two numbers for equality.
`$var1!=$var2`	Compares two numbers for inequality.
`$var1><$var2`	Checks `$var1` to see whether it is less than `$var2`.
`$var1>$var2`	Tests `$var1` to see whether it is a larger number than `$var2`.
`$var1>=$var2`	Tests `$var1` to see whether it is greater than or equal to `$var2`.
`$var1<=$var2`	Compares `$var1` to see whether it is less than or equal to `$var2`.
`$var1 eq $var2`	Checks two strings for equality.
`$var1 ne $var2`	Checks two strings for inequality.
`$var1 lt $var2`	Checks whether the string in `$var1` is less than (by ASCII value) `$var2`.
`$var1 gt $var2`	Tests the string in `$var1` to see whether it is greater than `$var2`.
`()`	Parentheses can be used to group the elements of an expression together to force an evaluation order or provide clarity to the code.

TABLE 18.3 Continued

Expression Syntax	Description
`&&/and`	Connects two expressions so that both must evaluate to true for the complete expression to be true.
`||/or`	Connects two expressions so that if either evaluates to true, the entire expression evaluates to true.
`!`	Negates an expression. If the expression previously evaluated to true, you can place an `!` in front of the expression to force it to evaluate false or vice versa.

Regular Expressions

Regular expressions *(regex)* are a bit more interesting than the expressions in the preceding section. Like one of the previous expressions, a regex evaluates to a true or false state. In addition, they are used to locate and extract data from strings.

For example, assume that the variable `$mycomputer` contains the information `My computer is a Mac.`

To create a regular expression that would test the string for the presence of the word `mac`, you could write

```
$mycomputer=~/mac/i
```

Although this line might look like an assignment statement, it is in fact looking inside the variable `$mycomputer` for the pattern `mac`. The pattern that a regular expression matches is delimited by the `/` characters (unless changed by the programmer). The `i` after the expression tells Perl that it should perform a case-insensitive search, allowing it to match strings such as `MAC` and `mAC`.

To understand the power of regular expressions, you must first understand the pattern-matching language that comprises them.

Patterns

Regular expressions are made up of groups of pattern-matching symbols. These special characters symbolically represent the contents of a string and can be used to build complex pattern-matching rules with relative ease. Table 18.4 contains the most common components of regular expressions and their purpose.

TABLE 18.4 Use These Pattern-Matching Components to Build a Regular Expression

Pattern	Purpose
`$`	Matches the end of a string
`^`	Matches the beginning of a string
`.`	Matches any character in the string
`[]`	Matches any of the characters within the square brackets
`\s`	Matches any type of whitespace (space, tab, and so on)
`\n`	Matches the newline character

TABLE 18.4 Continued

Pattern	Purpose
`\t`	Matches the tab character
`\w`	Matches a word character
`\d`	Matches a digit

The bracket characters enable you to clearly define the characters that you want to match if a predefined sequence doesn't already exist. For example, if you want to match only the uppercase letters A through Z and the numbers 1, 2, and 3, you could write

```
[A-Z123]
```

As shown in this example, you can represent a contiguous sequence of letters or numbers as a range by specifying the start and end characters of the range, separated by a `-`.

Pattern Repetition

With the capability to write patterns, you can match arbitrary strings within a character sequence. What's missing is the capability to match strings of varying lengths. These repetition characters modify the pattern they follow and enable it to be matched once, twice, or as many times as you want:

- `*`—Match any number (including zero) copies of a character
- `+`—Match at least one copy of a character
- **`{x,y}`**—Match at least `x` characters and as many as `y`

When a repetition sequence is followed by a `?`, the pattern will match as few characters as possible to be considered true. For example, the following expression matches between 5 and 10 occurrences of the numbers 1, 2, or 3:

```
$testnumbers=~/[1-3]{5,10}/;
```

The capability to match an arbitrary number of characters enables programmers to deal with information they might not be expecting.

Extracting Information from a Regular Expression

Although it's useful to be able to find strings that contain a certain pattern, it's even better if the matching data can be extracted and used. To extract pieces of information from a match, you can enclose the pattern within parentheses `()`. To see this in action, let's go back to the original telephone number program that introduced Perl in this chapter. One of the regular expressions extracted the parts of a 10-digit phone number from a string of 10 digits:

```
$phone=~/(\d{3,3})(\d{3,3})(\d{4,4})/;
```

There are three parts to the regular expression, each enclosed within parentheses. The first two parts (`\d{3,3}`) capture strings of three consecutive digits, and the third part (`\d{4,4}`) captures the remaining four.

For each set of parentheses used in a pattern, a $# variable is created that corresponds to the order in which the parentheses are found. Because the area code is the first set of parentheses in the example, it is `$1`, the local prefix is `$2`, and the final four digits are held in `$3`.

Search and Replace

Because you can easily find a pattern in a string, wouldn't it be nice if you could replace it with something else? Perl enables you to do just that by writing your regular expression line a little bit differently:

```
$a=~s/<search pattern>/<replace pattern>/
```

This simple change (adding the `s` [substitute] flag and a second pattern) enables you to modify data in a variable so that it is exactly what you're expecting—removing extraneous data. For example, matching a phone number in the variable `$phone` and then changing it to a standard format can be accomplished in a single step:

```
$phone=~s/(\d{3,3})(\d{3,3})(\d{4,4})/($1) $2-$3/;
```

A new string in the format `(xxx) xxx-xxxx` replaces the phone number found in the original string. This enables a programmer to modify data on the fly, transforming user input into a more usable form.

Regular expressions are not easy for many people to learn, and a single misplaced character can trip you up. Don't feel bad if you're confused at first; just keep at it. An understanding of regular expressions is important in many languages. And if regular expressions are properly used, they can be a powerful development tool.

Implementing Flow Control

Flow control statements give Perl the capability to alter its execution and adapt to different conditions on the fly. Perl uses standard C-like syntax for its looping and conditional constructs. If you've used C or Java before, these statements should look familiar.

`if-then-else`

Perl's `if-then-else` logic is simple to understand. If a condition is met, a block of code is executed. If the condition is not met, a different piece of programming is run. The syntax for this type of conditional statement is

```
if <expression> {
    <statements...>
} else {
    <statements...>
}
```

For example, to test whether the variable `$mycomputer` contains the string `"Mac OS X"` and print `Good Choice!` if it does, you could write the following:

```
if ($mycomputer=~/mac os x/i) {
    print "Good Choice!\n";
} else {
    print "Buy a Mac!\n";
}
```

The curly brackets `{}` are used to set off code blocks within Perl. The brackets denote the portion of code that a conditional, looping, or subroutine construct applies to.

unless-then-else

The `unless` statement is syntactically identical to the `if-then` statement, except that it operates on the inverse of the expression (and uses the word `unless` rather than `if`). To change the previous example so that it uses `unless`, write

```
unless ($mycomputer=~/mac os x/i) {
    print "Buy a Mac!\n";
} else {
    print "Good Choice!\n";
}
```

The `unless` condition is rarely used in Perl applications and is provided mainly as a way to write code in a more readable manner.

while

The `while` loop enables you to execute while a condition remains true. At the start of each loop, an expression is evaluated; if it returns true, the loop executes. If the loop does not return true, it exits. The syntax for a Perl `while` loop is

```
while <expression> {
    <statements>
}
```

For example, to monitor a process listing every 30 seconds to see whether the application Terminal is running, the following code fragment could be employed:

```
$processlist=`ps axg`;
while (!($processlist=~/terminal/i)) {
    print "Terminal has not been detected.\n";
    sleep 30;
    $processlist=`ps ax`;
}
print "The Terminal process is running.\n";
```

Here the output of the `ps axg` command is stored in `$processlist`. This is then searched using a regular expression in the `while` loop. If the pattern `terminal` is located, the loop exits, and the message `The Terminal process is running.` is displayed. If not, the script sleeps for 30 seconds and then tries again.

for-next

The `for-next` loop is the most fundamental of all looping constructs. This loop iterates through a series of values until a condition (usually a numeric limit) is met. The syntax for a `for-next` loop is

```
for (<initialization>;<execution condition>;<increment>) {
    <code block>
}
```

The *initialization* sets up the loop and initializes the counter variable to its default state. The *execution condition* is checked with each iteration of the loop; if the condition evaluates to false, the loop ends. Finally, the *increment* is a piece of code that defines an operation performed on the counter variable each time the loop is run. For example, the following loop counts from 0 to 9:

```
for ($count=0;$count<10;$count++) {
    print "Count = $count";
}
```

The counter, `$count`, is set to 0 when the loop starts. With each repetition, it is incremented by 1 (`$count++`). The loop exits when the counter reaches 10 (`$count<10`).

Creating Subroutines

Subroutines help modularize code by dividing it into smaller functional units. Rather than creating a gigantic block of Perl that does everything under the sun, you can create subroutines that are easier to read and debug.

A subroutine is started with the `sub` keyword and the name the subroutine should be called. The body of the subroutine is enclosed in curly brackets `{}`. For example, here is a simple subroutine that prints `Mac OS X Tiger`:

```
sub printos {
    print "Mac OS X Tiger\n";
}
```

You can include subroutines anywhere in your source code and call them at any time by prefixing their name with `&` (`&printos`). Subroutines can also be set up to receive values from the main program and return results. For example, this routine accepts two strings and concatenates them together:

```
sub concatenatestring {
    my ($x,$y)=@_;
    return ("$x$y");
}
```

To retrieve the concatenation of the strings "Mac" and "OS X", the subroutine would be addressed as

```
$result=&concatenatestring("Mac","OS X");
```

Data is received by the subroutine through the use of the special variable @_. The two values it contains are then stored in local variables (denoted by the my keyword) named $x and $y. Finally, the return statement returns a concatenated version of the two strings.

Expanding Perl Functionality with CPAN Modules

Perl can be extended to offer additional functionality ranging from Internet access to graphics generation. Just about anything you could ever want to do can be done using Perl—you just need the right module. The best place to find the right Perl module is CPAN—the Comprehensive Perl Archive Network. CPAN contains an ever-increasing list of Perl modules with their descriptions and documentation. To browse CPAN, point your web browser to http://www.cpan.org.

There are two ways to install modules located in the CPAN archive. The first is using a built-in Perl module that directly interacts with CPAN from your desktop computer. The second is the traditional method of downloading, unarchiving, and installing—just as with any other software. Perl modules are a bit easier to install than most software because the installed code ends up in the Perl directory instead of needing to be placed in a variety of directories across the entire system hierarchy.

Two Perl modules (DBI::DBD and DBD::mysql) will be used in Chapter 19 to demonstrate Perl/database integration. Conveniently, this corresponds to the two available installation methods. Let's take a look at both methods now and then put them to practice in Chapter 19. Note: These examples are meant to document the process of installing *any* module. If you try to follow these instructions without MySQL installed, you *will* see errors.

CPAN Installation

Using the interactive method of installing Perl modules is as simple as **install *<module name>***. To start the interactive module installation shell, type **sudo cpan** at a command line. The CPAN installer shell starts:

```
cpan shell -- CPAN exploration and modules installation (v1.70)
''
cpan>
```


> **NOTE**
>
> The first time you start the CPAN shell, it prompts you for manual configuration (for network access and so on). To quickly configure the system, reply with *no,* and the shell will automatically configure itself.

NOTE

sudo is used to start the CPAN shell because Perl modules must be installed in privileged directories. If you attempt to use the command without running it as root, it will work through most of the installation and then fail during the final step.

At the cpan> prompt, type **install *<modulename>*** to begin the installation process. For example, to add the DBI::DBD module:

```
cpan> install DBI::DBD

Issuing "/usr/bin/ftp -n"
Local directory now /private/var/root/.cpan/sources/modules
GOT /var/root/.cpan/sources/modules/03modlist.data.gz
...
CPAN: MD5 security checks disabled because MD5 not installed.
 Please consider installing the MD5 module.
...
Installing /usr/bin/dbiproxy
Installing /usr/bin/dbish
Writing /Library/Perl/darwin/auto/DBI/.packlist
Appending installation info to /System/Library/Perl/darwin/perllocal.pod
 /usr/bin/make install -- OK
```

Depending on your Perl installation and version, you might notice a number of messages pertaining to different Perl modules during the installation. Each time the CPAN shell is used, it checks for new versions of itself. If a new version is found, it provides instructions on how to install the update (install Bundle::CPAN). Don't concern yourself too much about these messages unless the installation fails.

TIP

Many Perl modules ask some basic questions during the install process. Even the highly automated CPAN shell installation method pauses to collect information it needs—so pay attention to your screen during installation.

After CPAN has completed the installation process, the module is ready to use—there's no need to reboot. The next time you invoke Perl, the module will be available.

For more control within the CPAN shell, you can use these additional commands:

- **get** ***<module name>***—Download the named module
- **make** ***<module name>***—Download and compile the module, but do not install
- **test** ***<module name>***—Download, compile, and run the named module's tests
- **install** ***<module name>***—Download, compile, test, and install the module

Modules that have been downloaded are stored in the .cpan directory within your home directory. Keep track of the size of this directory because it will continue to grow as long as you install new modules.

Archive-Based Installation

The second form of module installation is archive-based. This is almost identical to installing other types of software, so there shouldn't be many surprises here.

First, download the package to install from CPAN; in this example, I'm using a package called DBD-mysql, which you'll use in Chapter 19 to access the MySQL database system:

```
% curl -O ftp://ftp.cpan.org/pub/CPAN/modules/
     by-module/DBD/DBD-mysql-2.0901.tar.gz
```

Next, unarchive the module:

```
% tar zxf DBD-mysql-2.0901.tar.gz
```

Enter the distribution directory and enter this command: **perl Makefile.PL**. This automatically configures the package and generates a makefile that you can use to compile and install the module:

```
% perl Makefile.PL
This is an experimental version of DBD::mysql. For production
environments you should prefer the Msql-Mysql-modules.

I will use the following settings for compiling and testing:

 testpassword (default   ) =
 testhost    (default   ) =
 testuser    (default   ) =
 nocatchstderr (default    ) = 0
 libs      (mysql_config) = -L/usr/local/lib/mysql -lmysqlclient -lz -lm
 testdb     (default   ) = test
 cflags     (Users choice) = -I'/usr/local/mysql/include'

To change these settings, see 'perl Makefile.PL --help' and
'perldoc INSTALL'.

Using DBI 1.18 installed in /Library/Perl/darwin/auto/DBI
Writing Makefile for DBD::mysql
```

NOTE

Some modules might require additional configuration. Be sure to check any README or INSTALL files that come with your CPAN modules.

18

Now, the installation becomes identical to any other software. The same make commands apply. The best step to take next is to type **make** to compile and then type **make test** to test the compiled software:

```
% make
cc -c -I/Library/Perl/darwin/auto/DBI -I'/usr/local/mysql/include'
     -g -pipe -pipe -fno-common -DHAS_TELLDIR_PROTOTYPE
     -fno-strict-aliasing -O3   -DVERSION=\"2.0901\" -DXS_VERSION=
    \"2.0901\" -I/System/Library/Perl/darwin/CORE dbdimp.c
...

% make test
t/00base...........ok
t/10dsnlist.........ok
t/20createdrop......ok
t/30insertfetch.....ok
t/40bindparam.......ok
t/40blobs...........ok
t/40listfields......ok
t/40nulls...........ok
t/40numrows.........ok
t/50chopblanks......ok
t/50commit..........ok, 14/30 skipped: No transactions
t/60leaks...........skipped test on this platform
t/ak-dbd............ok
t/akmisc............ok
t/dbdadmin..........ok
t/insertid..........ok
t/mysql2............ok
t/mysql.............ok
All tests successful, 1 test and 14 subtests skipped.
Files=18, Tests=758, 25 wallclock secs ( 3.59 cusr + 0.35 csys = 3.94 CPU)
```

Finally, type **sudo make install** to install the Perl module:

```
% sudo make install
Skipping /Library/Perl/darwin/auto/DBD/mysql/mysql.bs (unchanged)
Installing /Library/Perl/darwin/auto/DBD/mysql/mysql.bundle
Files found in blib/arch: installing files in blib/lib into
     ¬architecture dependent tree
...
Installing /usr/share/man/man3/Bundle::DBD::mysql.3
Installing /usr/share/man/man3/DBD::mysql.3
Installing /usr/share/man/man3/DBD::mysql::INSTALL.3
Installing /usr/share/man/man3/Mysql.3
Writing /Library/Perl/darwin/auto/DBD/mysql/.packlist
Appending installation info to /System/Library/Perl/darwin/perllocal.pod
```

The module has been installed and is ready to use. Chapter 19 demonstrates how to use these Perl modules to communicate with a MySQL database.

Accessing Perl Documentation

Retrieving help information on a Perl function or module is as simple as using the `perldoc` command. `perldoc` searches the installed Perl documentation and displays extensive help information on functions, modules, and generalized topics.

There are three common forms for using `perldoc`. The first, `perldoc -f` *<function name>*, returns formatted information about a given built-in Perl function, such as `open`:

```
% perldoc -f open
open FILEHANDLE,EXPR
       open FILEHANDLE,MODE,EXPR
       open FILEHANDLE,MODE,EXPR,LIST
       open FILEHANDLE,MODE,REFERENCE
       open FILEHANDLE
               Opens the file whose filename is given by EXPR, and associates
               it with FILEHANDLE.

               (The following is a comprehensive reference to open(): for a
               gentler introduction you may consider perlopentut.)

               If FILEHANDLE is an undefined scalar variable (or array or hash
               element) the variable is assigned a reference to a new anony-
               mous filehandle, otherwise if FILEHANDLE is an expression, its
               value is used as the name of the real filehandle wanted.  (This
               is considered a symbolic reference, so "use strict 'refs'"
               should not be in effect.)
...
```

Next, `perldoc -q` *<faq topic>* retrieves information from the Perl FAQ. For example, to retrieve information about regular expressions:

```
% perldoc -q expressions
Found in /System/Library/Perl/pods/perlfaq6.pod
    How can I hope to use regular expressions without creating
    illegible and unmaintainable code?

    Three techniques can make regular expressions maintainable
    and understandable.

        Comments Outside the Regex
          Describe what you're doing and how you're
          doing it, using normal Perl comments.
```

Finally, use `perldoc` *`<module name>`* to retrieve information about an installed Perl module:

```
% perldoc Shell
Shell(3)    User Contributed Perl Documentation    Shell(3)

NAME
    Shell - run shell commands transparently within perl

SYNOPSIS
    See below.
...
```

Table 18.5 provides many of the flags for the `perldoc` command.

TABLE 18.5 Command Documentation Table for `perldoc`

`-h`	Prints out a brief help message.
`-v`	Describes search for the item in detail.
`-l`	Displays the filename of the module found.
`-f`	The `-f` option followed by the name of a Perl built-in function extracts the documentation of this function from the `perlfunc` man page.
`-q`	The `-q` option takes a regular expression as an argument. It searches the question headings in `perlfaq[1-9]` and prints the entries matching the regular expression.
`-X`	The `-X` option looks for an entry whose basename matches the name given on the command line in the file `$Config{archlib}/pod.idx`. The `pod.idx` file should contain fully qualified filenames, one per line.
`-U`	Because `perldoc` does not run properly when tainted and is known to have security issues, it will not normally execute as the superuser. If you use the `-U` flag, Perl will execute as the superuser, but only after setting the effective and real IDs to `nobody`'s or `nouser`'s account, or `-2` (if unavailable). If `perldoc` cannot relinquish its privileges, it will not run.
`<PageName¦ ModuleName¦ProgramName>`	The item you want to look up. Nested modules (such as `File::Basename`) are specified either as `File::Basename` or `File/Basename`. You may also give a descriptive name of a page, such as `perlfunc`. You may also give a partial or wrong-case name, such as `basename` for `File::Basename`, but this will result in a slower search. If there is more than one page with the same partial name, you will only get the first one.

Perl's built-in documentation is an excellent comprehensive reference that provides both usage information as well as complete code examples.

Perl Editors and IDEs

Although writing Perl in emacs or vi is completely acceptable, it is not necessarily a Mac-like experience. A few commercial and shareware editors that support syntax highlighting and direct Perl execution can make life easier for the serious Perl developer.

- Affrus—Affrus, shown in Figure 18.1, is a complete Perl IDE for Mac OS X. Written from the ground up for Mac OS X, Affrus offers a debugger, dedicated code editor, command-line interface, Dock integration, and more. Affrus is the best tool for Perl-specific developers. `http://www.latenightsw.com/affrus/`
- BBEdit—The everything-and-the-kitchen-sink editor. Great all-around text editor for HTML, Perl, PHP, and more. `http://www.barebones.com/products/bbedit/`
- TextMate—TextMate, like BBEdit, is a general text editor, but provides a number of advanced features such as project management, macros, triggers, and an innovative "folding" feature that collapses code that doesn't necessary need to be visible. `http://macromates.com/`
- AlphaX—Supporting around 50 languages, AlphaX is a serious editor for developers. AlphaX integrates with the command line for accessing tools such as `diff`, `cvs`, `gcc`, and more. `http://www.maths.mq.edu.au/~steffen/Alpha/AlphaX/`

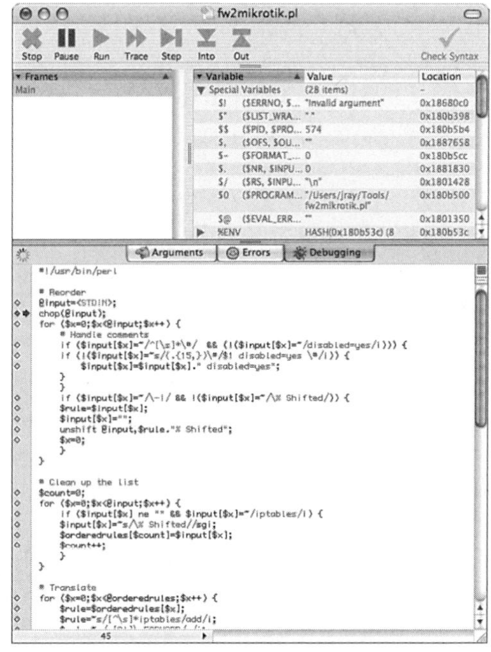

FIGURE 18.1 Affrus provides a complete development solution for Perl programmers.

Additional Perl Information

The information in this chapter should be enough to get you started authoring and editing Perl scripts. In Chapter 19, you'll learn how to extend Perl to control another free software package: MySQL. In Chapter 24, you'll see how Perl can be used to author online applications.

As with many topics in this book, space just isn't available for a completely comprehensive text. If you like what you see, you can learn more about Perl through these resources:

- The Perl Homepage—`http://www.perl.org/`—All that is Perl. This page can provide you with links to the latest and most useful Perl information online.
- CPAN—`http://www.cpan.org/`—The Comprehensive Perl Archive Network contains information on all the available Perl modules (extensions). Later in this chapter, you'll learn how to add modules to your Tiger Perl distribution.
- *Programming Perl*—O'Reilly Publishing, Larry Wall, ISBN: 0596000278. Written by the developer of Perl, you can't get much closer to the source than this.
- *Sams Teach Yourself Perl in 21 Days*—Laura Lemay, ISBN: 0672313057. An excellent step-by-step guide to learning Perl and putting it to use on your system.

Python

Python, like Perl, is an interpreted scripting language included with the system. To quote the Python.org website, Python is defined as

> python, (Gr. Myth. An enormous serpent that lurked in the cave of Mount Parnassus and was slain by Apollo) 1. any of a genus of large, non-poisonous snakes of Asia, Africa and Australia that suffocate their prey to death. 2. popularly, any large snake that crushes its prey. 3. totally awesome, bitchin' language that will someday crush the $'s out of certain *other* so-called VHLL's ;-)

Python was built from scratch to be object-oriented and easy to write and read. Although it has the same features as other popular languages, its syntax is cleaner than most—almost to the point of being scary. As such, it can take a little while for a long-time C or Perl developer to shake the uncontrollable feeling that somehow what they're writing in Python is wrong.

Languages such as Perl—and even AppleScript—have code structure based on explicitly starting and stopping code blocks with braces `{}`, `tell application/end tell`, and so on. In Python, the notion of a code block is still present, but rather than being explicitly stated with a keyword or symbol, it is *implied* by indentation.

Consider the following Perl code that prints the numbers between 1 and 10, and displays a special message when printing the number seven. The code is not indented because doing so is not required in Perl, and it is entirely at the whim of the developer to determine what proper indentation should be.

```
#!/usr/bin/perl

for ($count=1;$count<11;$count++) {
print "The current value is $count\n";
if ($count==7) {
print "I love the number 7!\n";
}
}
print "This program is finished."
```

Rewritten in Python, this simple loop becomes

```
for count in range(1,10):
  print "The current value is",count
  if count == 7:
    print "I love the number seven!"
print "This program is finished"
```

Although there are minor differences in the looping and conditional syntax, the obvious difference is in the actual appearance of the code. We could have formatted the Perl code nicely to be indented and pretty to look at. Python, on the other hand, *requires* the given formatting. The indentation determines which lines of the program belong to a given code block. If lines are at the same level of indentation, they are part of the same block.

Your initial reaction might be to question why you would want to force yourself to write pretty code. The answer should be obvious to anyone who has ever tried to debug layers and layers of loops, conditionals, and so on, all embedded within one another without proper indentation.

Perhaps you've written a program but missed a closing brace somewhere? In Python, doing so is virtually impossible. You must program so that the visual representation of the program mirrors the intended execution. Python programs tend to be shorter, easier to read, and much easier to debug than languages that follow more traditional structures.

18

To create an executable Python script, you should include the Python interpreter in the first line (that is, `#!/usr/bin/python`) and make sure that the script has execute permissions by using `chmod +x` *`<script name>`*.

> **NOTE**
>
> Python lines do not end in a semicolon like Perl, C, PHP, and so on. You can, however, use a semicolon in Python to include more than a single line of code on a single line in the program file, such as `print "Hello"; print "Goodbye"`.

Variables and Data Types

Python's basic variable types are similar to Perl's, and, like Perl, they are case sensitive and do not require a type definition before their use. Unlike Perl, Python variables gain their meaning based on how they are used. A variable is considered numeric, for example, if you store a number in it, and is considered a string if it contains a string. These are the data types we'll be looking at in this introduction:

- String—A variable that contains a text/numeric or mixed value. The line `myString="Macintosh G5"` is an example of a string assignment in Python. The + symbol is the concatenation operator in Python.
- Numeric—An assignment such as `processorG=5` creates a numeric variable with an integer value. By default, Python assumes that an operation performed on integers returns an integer, so you must explicitly use floating-point numbers where appropriate to avoid rounding errors. Python considers any value a floating-point number if it includes decimal places. For example, the assignment `myVal=5/2` normally results in `2`, whereas `myVal=5/2.0` results in `2.5`.
- Lists—A list is the Python equivalent of an array. A list is created by an assignment such as `myList=['This","is","a","test."]`. Individual elements are referenced by indexing into the list starting with 0. For example, `myList[1]` refers to the element `"is"` in the previously defined list. Unlike most array implementations, lists can be modified using insertion and deletion operators, which we'll discuss shortly. Python also supports an immutable list type called a *tuple*. Tuples are assigned just like a list, but use parentheses `()` rather than brackets.
- Dictionaries—A Python dictionary is the equivalent of a Perl associative array. For example, `myDictionary={'Monday': "bad", 'Friday': "good"}`. Here, the strings (keys) `"Monday"` and `"Friday"` are associated with the values `"bad"` and `"good"`, respectively. You can refer to the elements of a dictionary by its keys. The element `myDictionary["Friday"]` returns `"good"`.
- Files—Like a Perl filehandle, a Python file variable provides a reference to an active file for reading or writing. The statement `$myFile=open("file.txt","r")` opens the file `file.txt` for reading and allows file functions to be carried out through the variable `$myFile`.

Python is an *object-oriented* language, and, as such, accessing and manipulating data works a bit differently than in a traditional language. Object-oriented languages apply methods to objects instead of sending data to functions. For example, in Perl I might want to send a string to the `uc()` function to convert it to uppercase:

```
$a="hello";
print uc($a);
```

In Python, however, each of the basic data types is an object, and each has certain methods that that object can perform. String objects, for example, have an `upper()` method that converts them to uppercase. One invokes an object's method by using the syntax *`<object>.<method>`*. For example:

```
a="hello"
print a.upper()
```

The difference becomes apparent when stringing together multiple methods or functions. To convert to uppercase and then back to lowercase in Perl, you'd embed a function call inside another function call:

```
$a="hello'
print lc(uc($a));
```

In Python, it is simply

```
a="hello"
print a.upper().lower()
```

The a.upper() method returns another string object, which also has the lower() method and can subsequently be applied. Object-oriented programming has far more nuances than what we can show here. The ultimate goal of object-oriented programming is to create reusable objects that operate independently of the code that ties them together and that abstracts function from implementation.

Our goal is to give you enough information and incentive to get started using Python right away. If you like what you see, we hope that you will pursue learning the language further.

Input/Output Functions

While you take a few minutes to digest the object-oriented nature of Python, let's take a look at how you can get data into (and out of) Python. I've read dozens of language tutorials that spend far too much time discussing language intricacies rather than introducing basic I/O functions. Personally, I find that a language becomes useful as soon as you learn the basics for moving data in and out of a program.

Reading User Input

Basic user input is carried out through the raw_input(<*prompt string*>) function for strings, or input(<*prompt string*>) for integer and floating-point values. For example:

```
myName=raw_input('What is your name? ')
myAge=input('What is your age? ')
print "Hello",myName+", you are",myAge*365,"days old."
```

This code fragment inputs a name and an age, and then outputs a hello message along with the simple calculation of the person's age in days.

Although the raw_input function always returns a string, you can also use it with numeric values by coercing them to the proper type using the int() and float() functions. The second line of this sample, could be written

```
myAge=float(raw_input('What is your age? '))
```

NOTE

This example uses the `float` function wrapped around `raw_input` instead of using an object method. Certain functions (such as type coercion functions) are global and are not considered an object method. These functions are used just as in Perl.

Because `float()` and `int()` can be used to coerce strings to numbers, it stands to reason that numbers can be coerced to strings. This is performed by simply placing the numeric value within backticks (``). For example, to input `myAge` as a string, you could use the following:

```
myAge=`input('What is your age? ')`
```

Reading from Files

Another common form of input is a text file. To open a file for reading, use the syntax `<filehandle>=open(<filename>,<file mode>)`. In the case of reading, the file mode is simply the string `"r"`. After a file has been opened, you can use the object methods `readline()` and `readlines()` to return a single line of input or a list containing all the lines of input from the file, respectively. After file operations have been completed, the file should be closed with the object method `close()`.

For example:

```
myFile=open('MySpecialFile.txt','r')
firstLine=myFile.readline()
otherLines=myFile.readlines()
myFile.close()
```

This example opens the file `MySpecialFile.txt` for reading and creates the `myFile` object that can be used to refer to the file. The `firstLine` variable is used to store the first line of data from the file (retrieved via `readline()`), whereas `otherLines` contains a list (think "array") of the remaining lines in the file.

Creating Output

If you've been following along, you probably already know how to output to standard out in Python. The `print` statement is used to display information for the user. Unlike Perl's `print`, Python employs a "smart" `print` function that attempts to format output for you as cleanly as possible. For example, in Perl, you could write

```
print "Hello, my name is ",$myName," and I am a Mac user.\n";
```

This would print a hello message with the user's name (spaces before and after) and end the message with a newline (`\n`). In Python, the equivalent statement is

```
print "Hello, my name is",myName,"and I am a Mac user."
```

Spaces are automatically inserted between strings in the print statement, and a newline is generated automatically at the end. If you want to suppress either of the spaces, you can replace the , with +—the Python concatenation character. To suppress the newline, add a lone comma (,) to the end of the line.

NOTE

You can use the same escaped characters such as \n, \r, \t, and so on that you use in Perl to refer to newlines, returns, and tabs—among others.

File Output

Outputting data to a file requires, once again, the file-opening function <*filehandle*>=open (<*filename*>,<*file* mode>), this time used with a file mode of w for writing (and replacing any existing contents) or a for appending to a new or existing file.

The two object methods used to write information to a file are write(<*string*>) and writelines(<*list*>). The former writes a single string to the file, whereas the latter writes all the strings contained in the named list.

```
myFile=open('MySpecialFile.txt','w')
myFile.write("Hello World\n")
myFile.close()
```

This creates or replaces the file MySpecialFile.txt and writes the contents Hello World on a line in the file. Note that the write method includes a newline at the end. Unlike the print function, write requires you to explicitly format the outgoing data.

External Results

One nice feature of Perl is the ease with which you can execute external programs and incorporate their results in your script. You can do the same with Python using the commands.getoutput(<*command to execute*>) method. Before using it, however, you must import the necessary code—simply import commands. For example:


```
import commands
myProcesses=commands.getoutput("ps ax")
```

The resulting process list (generated by ps ax) is stored as a single string within the myProcesses variable.

Expressions

Comparing values in Python is similar but not identical to Perl. Table 18.6 displays common Python expressions.

TABLE 18.6 Common Python Expressions

Expression Syntax	Description
`var1==var2, var1 is var2`	Compares two values for equality.
`var1!=var2, var1 is not var2`	Compares two values for inequality.
`var1><$var2`	Checks `$var1` to see whether it is less than `$var2`.
`$var1>var2`	Tests `var1` to see whether it is a larger number than *var2*, or, when used with strings, whether `var1` is before (based on ASCII value) *var2*.
`var1>=var2`	Tests *var1* to see whether it is greater than or equal to *var2*.
`var1<=var2`	Compares *var1* to see whether it is less than or equal to *var2*.
`()`	Parentheses can be used to group the elements of an expression together to force an evaluation order or provide clarity to the code.
`&,and`	Used to connect two expressions so that both must evaluate to true for the complete expression to be true.
`¦,or`	Used to connect two expressions so that if either evaluates to true, the entire expression evaluates to true.
`not`	Used to logically negate an expression. If the expression previously evaluated to true, you can place a `not` in front of the expression to force it to evaluate false or vice versa.

Slicing

A unique feature of Python is the capability to "slice" lists for the purpose of retrieving specific information, or inserting/deleting data. For example, assume that you have the following assignment:

```
myList=['one','two','three','four','five']
```

You already know that `myList[0]` returns the first element of the list (that is, `one`). It is possible, however, to index into the list using a pair of values, such as `myList[0:2]`. In this case, the first *two* elements of the list (`['one','two']`) are returned. When using this format to dissect a portion of a list, the two numbers specified represent the first element to return and an element to serve as a boundary; the boundary element is *not* returned as part of the results, but the list element preceding it *is*.

As a shortcut for the start and boundary values in a slice, you can leave the first or last number of a slice empty. In the case of an empty initial value, 0 (the first element) is assumed. If the boundary value is left blank, the end of the list (including the final element) is assumed.

For example:

`myList[1:3]` returns `['two','three']`.

`myList[:2]` returns `['one','two']`.

`myList[2:]` returns `['three','four','five']`.

`myList[:]` returns `['one','two','three','four','five']`.

In addition to retrieving information, slicing can be used to delete and insert data in lists.

For example, given the previous list, we could change and insert into the second and third elements (['two','three']) new values (['two','two and a half','three','three and a half']) like this:

```
myList[1:3]=['two','two and a half','three','three and a half']
```

The contents of myList are now

```
['one', 'two', 'two and a half', 'three', 'three and a half', 'four', 'five']
```

Similarly, you can delete elements from the middle of a list by assigning a slice to an empty list. For example, to delete the third, fourth, and fifth elements of the list, use

```
myList[2:5]=[]
```

Common Functions and Object Methods

Being able to store and output information is useful, but the ability to manipulate it makes a computer a truly valuable tool. As you've read about Python data types and I/O, you've already seen a few methods used to for manipulating data, such as readlines and writelines for reading and writing to text files. Table 18.7 contains several more methods and functions, the data types they apply to, and what action they perform.

TABLE 18.7 Common Python Object Methods

Method/Function	Data Type	Description
abs(<#>)	Number	Returns the absolute value of the given number. Example: myABSVal=abs(-35)
hex(<#>)	Number	Returns a string with the hex equivalent of the given number. Example: myHexVal=hex(10)
round(<#>,<*precision*>)	Number	Rounds a given number to the specified number of digits (precision) after the decimal place. Example: MyRoundVal=round(10.05,1). Always returns a floating-point number.
append(<*element*>)	List	Appends an element to the end of a list. Example: myList.append('six')
remove(<*element*>)	List	Removes an element from a list by its value. Example: myList.remove('six')
sort()	List	Sorts a list into alphabetical order. Example: myList.sort()

TABLE 18.7 Continued

Method/Function	Data Type	Description
`pop([`*`index`*`])`	List	Removes and returns the last element in a list. If an index value is provided, it determines the number of elements returned and removed. Example: `myList.pop()`
`count(`*`<element>`*`)`	List	Returns a count of the number of occurrences of a value within a list. Example: `myG5Count=myList.count('G5')`
`reverse()`	List	Reverses the ordering of a list. Example: `myList.reverse()`
`max(`*`<list>`*`)`	List	Returns the list element with the highest value. Example: `myMaxValue=max(myList)`
`min(`*`<list>`*`)`	List	Returns the list element with the lowest value. Example: `myMinValue=min(myList)`
`capitalize()`	String	Capitalizes the first letter in a string and lowercases the rest. Example: `myString.capitalize()`
`find(`*`<search string>`*	String	Searches for a given search string and return the index *`[,<start position>`* value (position) where it starts. Returns `-1` if no match is *`[,<end position>]]`*`)` found. If a start and end are given, the search takes place only between these index positions. Example: `mySearchPos="Find the hidden word.".find('hidden')`
`isalnum()`	String	Returns true if a string is alphanumeric. Example: `myAlphaNumeric.isalnum()`
`isalpha()`	String	Returns true if a string is entirely alphabetic. Example: `myAlpha.isalpha()`
`isdigit()`	String	Returns true if a string is entirely numeric. Example: `myDigit.isdigit()`
`isupper()`	String	Returns true if all characters in a string are uppercase. Example: `myUpper.isupper()`
`islower()`	String	Returns true if all characters in a string are lowercase. Example: `myLower.islower()`

TABLE 18.7 Continued

Method/Function	Data Type	Description
join(<*list*>)	String	Converts the named list to a single string using the object string as the delimiter. Example: myJoinedString=",".join(myList)
upper()	String	Converts a string to uppercase. Example: myString.upper()
lower()	String	Converts a string to lowercase. Example: myString.lower()
rstrip()	String	Removes trailing whitespace from a string. Example: myString.rstrip()
lstrip()	String	Removes leading whitespace from a string. Example: myString.lstrip()
split(<*delimiter*>)	String	Returns a list of strings formed by splitting the object string on the given delimiter. Example: myDateElements="2003-08-25".split('-')
open(<*filename*>, <*file mode*>)	File	Returns a file handle after opening the given filename. The file mode can be r, w, or a for read, write, and append, respectively. Example: myFile=open('filename.txt','r')
close()	File	Closes the file. Example: myFile.close()
readline([bytes])	File	Reads and returns a string containing a line of input from a file. If the optional byte parameter is specified, input is limited to that number of characters. Example: myInputLine=myFile.readline()
readlines([bytes])	File	Reads and returns a list of input lines from a file. If the optional byte parameter is specified, input is limited to that number of characters. Example: myInputLines=myFile.readlines()
write(<*string*>)	File	Writes the contents of the string to a file. Example: myFile.write('Hello\n')
writelines(<*list*>)	File	Writes the contents of the list to a file. Example: myFile.writelines(myList)
range(<*start*>,<*end*>)	List	Returns a list of values between the start and end values. Example: numberList=range(1,10)

Implementing Flow Control

Python's flow control is similar to other languages, with just a few syntactical differences. The biggest change from languages such as C, Perl, JavaScript, and so on is, once again, the use of indentation to denote code blocks. We'll use the same examples as in the preceding Perl introduction so that you can compare and contrast the source.

`if-then-else`

If a condition is met, a block of code is executed. If not, a different piece of programming is run. The syntax for this type of conditional statement is

```
if <expression>:
    <statements...>
else:
    <statements...>
```

For example, to test whether the variable `myComputer` is set to the string `"Mac OS X"` and print `Good Choice!` if it is, you could write

```
if myComputer is "Mac OS X":
    print "Good Choice!"
else:
    print "Buy a Mac!"
```

`while`

The `while` loop enables you to execute while a condition remains true. At the start of each loop, an expression is evaluated; if it returns true, the loop executes. If not, it exits. The syntax for a Perl while loop is

```
while <expression>:
    <statements>
}
```

For example, to monitor a process listing every 30 seconds to see whether the application Terminal is running, the following code fragment could be employed:

```
import commands
myProcesses=commands.getoutput("ps axg")
while myProcesses.find('Terminal') is -1:
    print "Terminal has not been detected."
    commands.getoutput("sleep 30")
    myProcesses=commands.getoutput("ps ax")
print "The Terminal process is running."
```

The output of the `ps axg` command is stored in `myProcesses`. This is then searched using `find` in the `while` loop. If the pattern `Terminal` is located, the loop exits, and the message `The Terminal process is running.` is displayed. If not, the script sleeps for 30 seconds and then tries again.

`for-next`

The Python `for-next` loop is slightly different from other implementations. Rather than loop through a series of numbers, it loops through the elements in a list. Frequently, these are numbers, but any list values will work. The `range` function is commonly used to provide a list of numbers. Using `range(0,11)`, for example, generates the list `[0, 1, 2, 3, 4, 5, 6, 7, 8, 9, 10]`.

The syntax for a `for-next` loop is

```
for <variable> in <list>:
    <code block>
```

For example, the following loop counts from 0 to 9:

```
for count in range(0,10):
    print "Count =",count
```

Creating Functions

Functions (Python's version of subroutines) help modularize code by dividing it into smaller functional units. A Python function is started with the `def` keyword and the name the function should be called followed by a list of parameters it should receive within parentheses. The body of the function is an indented code block. For example, here is a simple function that prints `Mac OS X`:

```
def printos():
    print "Mac OS X"
```

You can include a function anywhere in your source code and call it at any time by its defined name—in this case, `printos()`.

Functions can also be set up to receive values from the main program and return results. This example accepts two strings and concatenates them together:

```
def concatenatestring(x,y):
    return x+y
```

To retrieve the concatenation of the strings `"Mac"` and `"OS X"`, the subroutine would be addressed as

```
myResult=concatenatestring("Mac","OS X")
```

The incoming parameters (`"Mac"` and `"OS X"`) are stored in the variables `x` and `y` and then returned in concatenated form (courtesy of the `return` keyword and the concatenation operator `+`).

Accessing Python Documentation

A great deal of documentation is provided with your Tiger Python distribution and is accessible through the pydoc utility. pydoc has a number of modes of operation, as shown in Table 18.8.

TABLE 18.8 Syntax for Using the pydoc Utility

Option	Description
-k *<keyword>*	Search the Python documentation for modules/classes that match a given keyword.
<name> ...	When used with just a single string argument, pydoc will lookup any documentation for classes, modules, functions, keywords, and so forth that match the value. If the value provided is keyword, modules, or topics, pydoc will list all items that fall within those categories.
-p <port number>	Using pydoc in this manner will start a web server that can be accessed at the given port number to display documentation graphically.
-g	Uses a graphical interface to search documentation and also invokes the web server (much like -p). This function doesn't currently work correctly with Tiger.
-w *<name>* ...	Writes one or more HTML files containing the documentation of the named module.

For example, assume that you want to write a simple web server using Python (this is actually very easy!), you might want to search for HTTP within the Python modules by using the -k option:

```
$ pydoc -k HTTP
BaseHTTPServer - HTTP server base class.
CGIHTTPServer - CGI-savvy HTTP Server.
SimpleHTTPServer - Simple HTTP Server.
httplib - HTTP/1.1 client library
test.test_httplib
```

pydoc returns a several results that match the HTTP keyword. To view the full documentation for a module, simply use pydoc *<name>*:

```
$ pydoc SimpleHTTPServer

Help on module SimpleHTTPServer:

NAME
    SimpleHTTPServer - Simple HTTP Server.

FILE
    /System/Library/Frameworks/Python.framework/Versions/2.3/lib/
    python2.3/SimpleHTTPServer.py
```

```
DESCRIPTION
    This module builds on BaseHTTPServer by implementing the standard GET
    and HEAD requests in a fairly straightforward manner.

CLASSES
    BaseHTTPServer.BaseHTTPRequestHandler(SocketServer.StreamRequestHandler)
        SimpleHTTPRequestHandler
class SimpleHTTPRequestHandler(BaseHTTPServer.BaseHTTPRequestHandler)
      |  Simple HTTP request handler with GET and HEAD commands.
      |
      |  This serves files from the current directory and any of its
      |  subdirectories.  It assumes that all files are plain text files
      |  unless they have the extension ".html" in which case it assumes
      |  they are HTML files.
      |
      |  The GET and HEAD requests are identical except that the HEAD
      |  request omits the actual contents of the file.
      |
      |  Method resolution order:
      |      SimpleHTTPRequestHandler
      |      BaseHTTPServer.BaseHTTPRequestHandler
      |      SocketServer.StreamRequestHandler
      |      SocketServer.BaseRequestHandler
...
```

A more user-friendly approach to browsing the Python documentation is to start the documentation server by using `pydoc -p` *<port number>*. You should use a number greater than 1024 to avoid trampling any system services. For example, to start a server on port 9000:

```
$ pydoc -p 9000
pydoc server ready at http://localhost:9000/
```

18

After the server is started, simply point your web browser at the URL provided (`http://localhost:`*<port number>*) and you can click through all the available Python documentation within a graphical web interface, as shown in Figure 18.2.

Python Distributions

A source of confusion when learning Python on Mac OS X is the presence of a number of competing Python distributions and technologies. There is, of course, the primary Python distribution from Python.org, but a number of other Pythons are available that are either included on your system or can be installed.

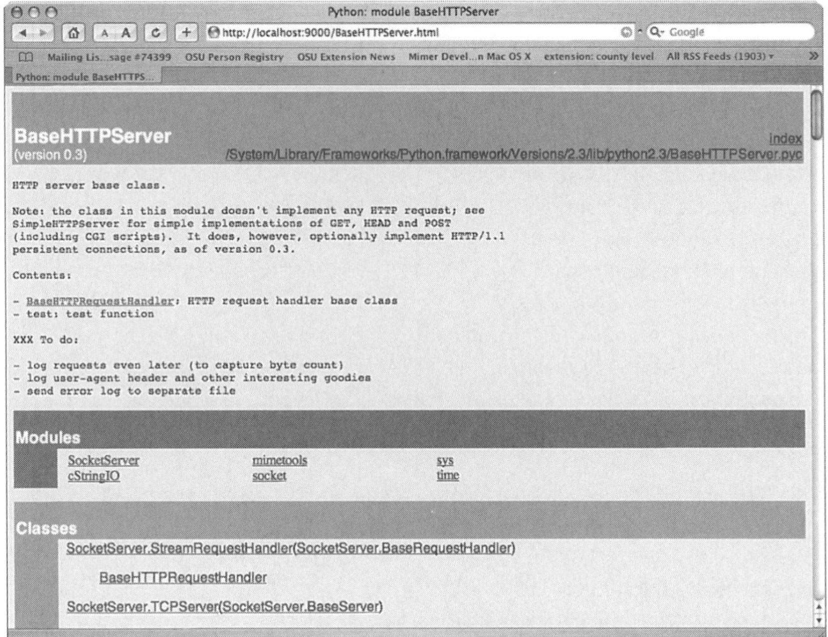

FIGURE 18.2 Use `pydoc -p <port>` to start a personal Python documentation server.

MacPython

The MacPython project works to bring native Mac OS X technologies to Python—such as QuickTime, OpenGL, and so forth and even includes its own IDE and Package Manager for easily adding new features. Unfortunately, Apple chose not to include everything necessary to make MacPython fully useful, but an add-on fix package is available at `http://homepages.cwi.nl/~jack/macpython/download.html` to install the missing components.

MacPython is where you want to be if you are interested in building Tiger-specific applications written in Python. The drawback is that you limit yourself to the Mac OS X platform.

wxPython

Also included in Tiger is the wxPython GUI toolkit (`http://wxpython.org/`). wxPython provides a cross-platform GUI construction set that can be used to build applications across many platforms—Linux, Windows, and so on. The wxWidgets library that the project is built on uses native Cocoa controls and widgets, so applications look native, but can be deployed on other platforms (assuming they've installed wxPython).

tkinter

Apple apparently *really* likes to cover its bases because Tiger provides developer access to tkinter as well. tkinter is the most commonly used toolkit for building GUIs on top of

Python scripts. Like wxPython, tkinter provides a cross-platform means of adding a native GUI onto a Python script. Whereas wxPython provides a more modern GUI toolkit, tkinter's use is widespread and more likely to be available on your deployment platforms.

Jython

Jython is a Java implementation of Python. Scripting languages are wonderful, but they don't package well for execution on other platforms. Providing a script to a user is much different from providing a double-clickable application.

For example, if you want to add GUI support to Python, you can use the proprietary MacPython Cocoa bindings or a third-party windowing/GUI toolkit that would need to be installed (if available) on each client computer. Jython eliminates the problem by providing a full implementation of Python within Java. Although there are a few minor incompatibilities, most Python code runs without any changes in Jython. Additionally, Jython provides easy access to Swing within Python, making it possible to author cross-platform GUI applications with ease.

Completed Jython applications can be compiled into `.jar` files for easy deployment on any Java-compatible system. For a free downloadable Jython installer, visit `http://www.jython.org/`.

Python Editors and IDEs

As with Perl, generic text editors such as AlphaX, BBEdit, and TextMate work well for Python. If, however, you're looking for a full Python development environment, a few solutions are available:

- Wing IDE—Currently the best solution for Mac OS X, the Wing IDE, shown in Figure 18.3, provides a full IDE for Python, but requires and operates within Apple's X11 implementation. If this doesn't deter you, it's well worth the $179 price for large scale development efforts. (`http://wingware.com/doc/howtos/osx`)
- PyOXIDE—Early in development, PyOXIDE is an open source Cocoa-based Python IDE with a number of professional features and a promising future. (`http://projects.gandreas.com/pyoxide/download.php`)
- PythonIDE—Provided as part of the MacPython project, the PythonIDE is a complete development environment. This actually comes with Tiger, but doesn't include all the necessary packages to make it run. You can download an add-on package from `http://homepages.cwi.nl/~jack/macpython/download.html` to fix the broken installation.

Additional Python Information

Like the introduction to Perl, please realize that this should serve as only a basic primer to the Python language. The language is capable of far more than could be reasonably covered in a few introductory pages.

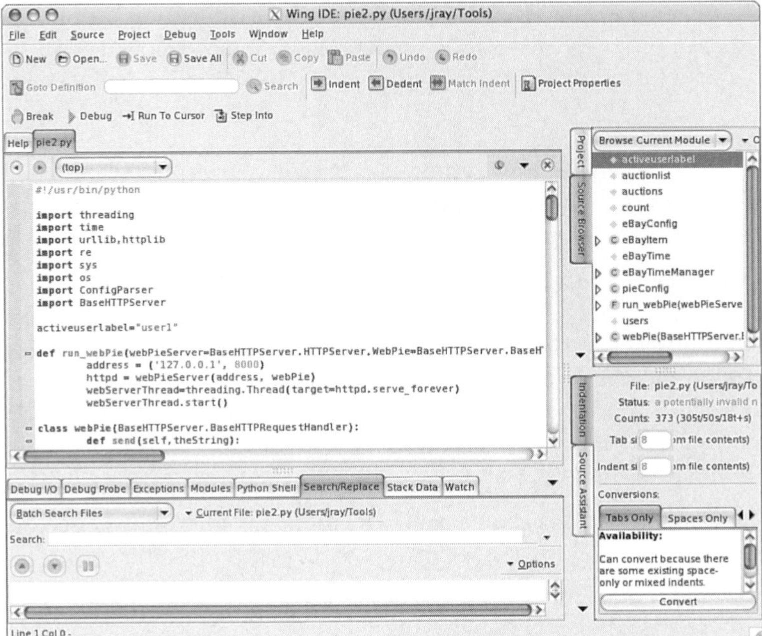

FIGURE 18.3 The Wing IDE runs under X11 and provides a complete Python development environment.

Thankfully, Python information is in abundance both in printed and electronic formats. If you don't mind reading through web pages (or printing off a few PDFs), you can find everything from beginner tutorials to complete references available online. Those looking for published products are also in luck; Python books are in ready supply. The following is a list of resources you might want to look into to learn more about the language and its capabilities:

- `http://www.python.org`—The home of Python and a great source of Python documentation links and tutorials. This is the starting place for both beginners and experienced developers.

- Instant Hacking: Learn How to Program with Python (`http://www.hetland.org/python/instant-hacking.php`)—An excellent tutorial for getting up and running quickly with Python.

- *How to Think Like a Computer Scientist: Learning with Python* (`http://www.ibiblio.org/obp/thinkCSpy/`)—An open source book that teaches the philosophy of programming through Python.

- *Practical Python*, by Magnus Lie Hetland, ISBN: 1590590066—An excellent book by the author of the *Instant Hacking* tutorial. *Practical Python* is easy to read, understand, and apply.

Summary

Python and Perl take over where shell scripting leaves off. These languages are great for writing or controlling command-line processes and provide excellent cross-platform capabilities. With the inclusion of these languages in Mac OS X, potential scripting developers can gain a much wider audience for their software.

Mac OS X has become a wonderful platform for scripting languages, and although only two open source languages are covered here, enterprising users may want to investigate the powers of Ruby (also included on your system), or install Apple's Aqua Tcl/tk, Expect, or any other of the dozens of scripting languages available today.

PART VI

Server and Network Administration

IN THIS PART

CHAPTER 19

Serving and Connecting to Databases

IN THIS CHAPTER

- Installing and Configuring MySQL
- Creating and Working with a MySQL Database
- Accessing Database Information Using Perl
- Accessing Database Information Using ODBC

Thanks to open source projects, Tiger users can enjoy first-class database packages such as MySQL that, only a few years ago we would have never dreamed of running on the Mac OS. Instead of forking over several hundred (or thousand) dollars for a commercial database system, you can take 20 minutes to download and install MySQL and then have a full-featured database at your fingertips.

This chapter covers MySQL, Perl, and iODBC, and discusses how they can be combined to create a powerful database development environment. Without spending a dime, you can host databases capable of handling hundreds of queries a second.

Installing and Configuring MySQL

The MySQL database system is a free implementation of a database system based on Structured Query Language (SQL). MySQL has been successfully deployed for a number of high-end applications on websites such as NASA, Yahoo!, and Slashdot. In addition to the database package itself, MySQL has JDBC and ODBC drivers available, making it accessible from any platform supporting these standards, including Microsoft Windows.

> **NOTE**
>
> The letters SQL are pronounced "S-Q-L," not "sequel," which is typically associated with Microsoft's SQL Server. MySQL, as documented on `http://www.mysql.com`, is pronounced "My S-Q-L."

Downloading the MySQL Distribution

Following the growing trend of providing Macintosh binaries for popular Unix/Linux packages, MySQL has added the Macintosh platform to its officially supported binary distributions. To install MySQL, all you need to do is download the latest binary distribution from `http://www.mysql.com` website and run the installer.

The MySQL software is updated on an ongoing basis, so if you want, you can download the latest source release and compile/install it on your own. We highly recommend, however, that you stick with the official packaged release.

The MySQL disk image can be downloaded from `http://dev.mysql.com/downloads/`.

> **NOTE**
>
> Three binary distributions of MySQL are available: Standard, Max, and Debug. The Standard distribution should be fine for most users. Developers might want to use the Max distribution because it includes some advanced features that will eventually be incorporated into the Standard distribution. The Debug distribution includes debug code and should not be used in a production environment.

Mount the distribution disk image (double-click, or use `hdiutil attach` *<image name>*, enter the resulting MySQL directory, and use either the `installer` command-line utility or GUI installer to set up the software. There are two packages you will need to install: the main MySQL package and a StartupItem that will launch the server at boot.

MySQL is installed in a version-tagged directory within `/usr/local`, such as `/usr/local/mysql-standard-4.1.7-apple-darwin7.5.0-powerpc`. This directory, in turn, is symlinked to `/usr/local/mysql`, so it's best to use the link for referencing commands from scripts and so on.

> **TIP**
>
> If you'd like to compile MySQL from scratch and install it in the same directory structure as the binary distribution, configure it with
>
> ```
> ./configure --prefix=/usr/local/mysql --localstatedir=/usr/local/mysql/data
> --sbindir=/usr/local/mysql/bin
> ```

> **NOTE**
>
> The installer automatically sets the appropriate directory permissions and runs the command `/usr/local/mysql/bin/mysql_install_db`, which sets up the default MySQL databases.
>
> If you've compiled the software by hand, you *must* first use `chown -R mysql /usr/local/mysql/data` to set the data directory ownership. Then run `mysql_install_db` to manually install the initial databases.

Starting the MySQL Daemon

Your MySQL server can be started by changing to the `/usr/local/mysql` directory and then executing the command `./bin/safe_mysqld` as root. Note: You *must* execute `safe_mysqld` from one level above the `/usr/local/mysql/bin` directory, or the daemon will fail to start.

```
brezup:jray jray $ cd /usr/local/mysql ; sudo ./bin/safe_mysqld &
Starting mysqld daemon with databases from /usr/local/mysql/data
```

Alternatively, if you installed the StartupItem, you can simply type:

```
sudo /Library/StartupItems/MySQLCOM/MySQLCOM start
```

You should reset the root MySQL password immediately after the server is started. Use the command

```
/usr/local/mysql/bin/mysqladmin -u root password '<my new password>'
```

For example, to set my password to `john` (an extremely poor password, by the way), I'd use

```
brezup:jray jray $ /usr/local/mysql/bin/mysqladmin -u root password 'john'
```

NOTE

When creating the new root password, be aware that this password has no effect on the actual Tiger root account. For more information on MySQL user management, visit `http://dev.mysql.com/doc/mysql/en/User_Account_Management.html`. I recommend getting a firm grip on MySQL's permissions system before deploying MySQL on a public server.

TIP

The MySQL binaries are installed in `/usr/local/mysql/bin`, which is not part of the default user path. To alter the system to include the directory in your path, see Chapter 15, "Shell Configuration and Programming (Shell Scripting)." This eliminates the need to type the full pathname each time you need to access a MySQL utility. Alternatively, you might want to create a symbolic link from the binaries in `/usr/local/mysql/bin` to `/usr/local/bin`.

Creating and Working with a MySQL Database

The key to using MySQL is an understanding of the SQL syntax itself. If you've used Oracle or another SQL-based system, you'll be right at home interacting with MySQL. For beginners, this introduction should be enough to get started, but we recommend a more complete text such as *MySQL, 2nd Edition* (ISBN: 0-7357-1212-3).

To start MySQL, invoke the client (`mysql`) using `mysql -u<username> -p<password>`. To start, only the root account is available. If you didn't set the password for root, no password is required.

TIP

The MySQL tools (including the client you're using now) can be used to access MySQL servers across a network using the `-h <hostname/ip>` switch. You could, for example, connect to a server named `my.serverwithmysql.com` running MySQL with the username `kitten` and password `fuzzy4` using `mysql -ukitten -pfuzzy4 -hmy.serverwithmysql.com`.

Creating and Deleting Databases

The first step when working with MySQL is to create the database itself. If you've worked with FileMaker Pro or AppleWorks, this is a very different concept. In MySQL, a database is a container that holds a collection of tables. These tables, in turn, hold actual information. The FileMaker database model has a single table in a single database. To create relationships between different collections of data requires multiple databases. In MySQL, a single database can contain multiple tables each with unique data.

To create a database, make sure that you've started MySQL and are at a command prompt:

```
brezup:jray jray $ /usr/local/mysql/bin/mysql -uroot -pjohn
Welcome to the MySQL monitor.  Commands end with ; or \g.
Your MySQL connection id is 1 to server version: 4.1.7-standard

Type 'help;' or '\h' for help. Type '\c' to clear the buffer.

mysql>
```

Next, use `create database <database name>` to set up an empty database. Finally, type `use <database name>` to start working with the new database.

NOTE

The MySQL client requires that all commands end with a semicolon (;). Input can span multiple lines, as long as a semicolon appears at the end.

For example, let's start with an employee database:

```
mysql> create database employee;
Query OK, 1 row affected (0.07 sec)

mysql> use employee;
Database changed
mysql>
```

If you want to delete the database that you've defined, you can use the `drop` command, which works just like the `create` command:

```
drop database <database name>
```

CAUTION

A MySQL database can contain multiple tables, each with its own data. Deleting a database removes all information that has been stored in any of the tables.

Creating Tables

After a database has been created, you need to set up the internal tables that actually hold the data you want to store.

When making a table, use another `create` command to tell the system what type of data you want to store.

```
create table <tablename> (<columns...>)
```

For example, let's create some tables for our employee database:

```
create table tblemployee (
  employeeID int not null,
  firstname  varchar(50),
  lastname  varchar(50),
  titleID   int,
  salary   float,
  primary key (employeeID)
);

create table tbljobclassification (
  titleID   int not null,
  title    text,
  minsalary  float,
  maxsalary  float,
  primary key (titleID)
);
```

The first table, `tblemployee`, holds information about each person in the database, such as his name and salary. The second table, `tbljobclassification`, contains job classification data—a general position description, and the minimum and maximum salary ranges for that position.

TIP

The MySQL commands `show databases`, `show tables`, and `describe` *<table name>* can be used to display the available MySQL database, show the tables within the current database, and provide a detailed description of a named table.

Fields are defined within a table creation statement by using the syntax `<fieldname>` `<datatype>` `<options>`. Two common options are employed to force certain conditions on a table field:

- `not null`—Forces the field to contain a value. If a user attempts to insert data into the database and a not null field is left blank, an error occurs.
- `auto_increment`—When used with an integer field, the value for the field will be determined automatically by MySQL and be incremented with each subsequent record.

The final line of a table creation command should define a primary key (or keys) for the table: `primary key (<fieldname 1,fieldname 2,...>)`. Defining keys is a necessary part of creating a normalized database structure. For more information on normalization, see `http://www.devshed.com/c/a/MySQL/An-Introduction-to-Database-Normalization`. We highly recommend reading through this tutorial, at the very least, before designing large-scale database models.

To remove a table that has been defined, type **`drop table <table name>`**.

MySQL Data Types

When defining a database table, numerous data types are used to build the collection of information that can be stored. Table 19.1 contains a description of the common available data types. This is a summarized version of the documentation supplied at `http://dev.mysql.com/`.

TABLE 19.1 Database Tables Are Built with MySQL Data Types

Data Type	Description
TINYINT [UNSIGNED]	A very small integer. The signed range is –128 to 127. The unsigned range is 0 to 255.
SMALLINT [UNSIGNED]	A small integer. The signed range is –32768 to 32767. The unsigned range is 0 to 65535.
MEDIUMINT [UNSIGNED]	A medium-size integer. The signed range is –8388608 to 8388607. The unsigned range is 0 to 16777215.
INT [UNSIGNED]	A normal-size integer. The signed range is –2147483648 to 2147483647. The unsigned range is 0 to 4294967295.
INTEGER [UNSIGNED]	The same as INT.
BIGINT [UNSIGNED]	A large integer. The signed range is –9223372036854775808 to 9223372036854775807. The unsigned range is 0 to 18446744073709551615.
FLOAT	A small (single precision) floating-point number. Cannot be unsigned. Allowable values are –3.402823466E+38 to –1.175494351E–38, 0 and 1.175494351E–38 to 3.402823466E+38.

TABLE 19.1 Continued

Data Type	Description
DOUBLE	A normal-size (double-precision) floating-point number. Cannot be unsigned. Allowable values are –1.7976931348623157E+308 to –2.2250738585072014E–308, 0 and 2.2250738585072014E–308 to 1.7976931348623157E+308.
DECIMAL	An unpacked floating-point number. Cannot be unsigned. Behaves like a CHAR column: unpacked means that the number is stored as a string, using one character for each digit of the value.
DATETIME	A date and time combination. The supported range is 1000-01-01 00:00:00 to 9999-12-31 23:59:59. MySQL displays DATETIME values in YYYY-MM-DD HH:MM:SS format but enables you to assign values to DATETIME columns using either strings or numbers.
TIMESTAMP	A timestamp. The range is 1970-01-01 00:00:00 to some time in the year 2037.
YEAR	A year in two- or four-digit format (the default is four-digit). The allowable values are 1901 to 2155, and 0000 in the four-digit format and 1970–2069 if you use the two-digit format (70–69).
CHAR(<*M*>) [BINARY]	A fixed-length string that is always right-padded with spaces to the specified length when stored. The range of M is 1 to 255 characters. Trailing spaces are removed when the value is retrieved. CHAR values are sorted and compared in case-insensitive fashion according to the default character set unless the BINARY keyword is given.
VARCHAR(<*M*>) [BINARY]	A variable-length string. Note: Trailing spaces are removed when the value is stored. The range of M is 1 to 255 characters. VARCHAR values are sorted and compared in case-insensitive fashion unless the BINARY keyword is given.
TINYBLOB / TINYTEXT	A BLOB or TEXT column with a maximum length of 255 (2^8–1) characters.
BLOB / TEXT	A column with a maximum length of 65535 (2^16–1) characters.
MEDIUMBLOB / MEDIUMTEXT	A BLOB or TEXT column with a maximum length of 16777215 (2^24–1) characters.
LONGBLOB / LONGTEXT	A BLOB or TEXT column with a maximum length of 4294967295 (2^32–1) characters.

Inserting Records into a Table

There are two ways to insert data into a table; both use the `insert` command with this structure:

```
insert into <table name> [(<field1,field2,...>)]
     values (<'value1','value2',...>)
```

The difference between the methods comes from the optional field listing. If you want to insert into only a few fields of a table, and want to manually specify the order, you would include the field names, as in this example using the `tblemployee` table created earlier:

```
insert into tblemployee (lastname,firstname,employeeID)
    values ('Ray','John','1');
```

In this example, only the `lastname`, `firstname`, and `employeeID` fields are given in the record, and they don't occur in the same order in which they were defined in the original table.

The second way you can use insert is to provide all the field values at once, in the table definition order. This method doesn't require the field names to be listed:

```
insert into tblemployee values ('1','John','Ray','1','35000.00');
```

It is important to note that you must obey the not null clause for a table definition at all times. In these examples, we had to include a value for the `employeeID` field; otherwise, the insert would have caused an error message to be generated.

To demonstrate the rest of the MySQL syntax, you'll need some data to work with. Go ahead and insert some information into the tables:

```
insert into tbljobclassification values ('1','Programmer/Analyst','20000','80000');
insert into tbljobclassification values ('2','Web Developer','20000','50000');
insert into tbljobclassification values ('3','CEO/President','40000','5000000000');
insert into tblemployee values ('1','John','Ray','1','25300.65');
insert into tblemployee values ('2','Will','Ray','1','32100.25');
insert into tblemployee values ('3','Joan','Ray','1','55300.75');
insert into tblemployee values ('4','Robyn','Ness','2','35000.20');
insert into tblemployee values ('5','Anne','Groves','2','35000.65');
insert into tblemployee values ('6','Julie','Vujevich','2','30300.01');
insert into tblemployee values ('7','Jack','Derifaj','1','12000.00');
insert into tblemployee values ('8','Russ','Schelby','1','24372.12');
insert into tblemployee values ('9','Bill','Gates','3','50000.01');
insert into tblemployee values ('10','Steve','Jobs','3','380000000.00');
```

These statements add three different job classifications (Programmer/Analyst, Web Developer, and CEO/President) to the system, as well as 10 employees who fall under these classifications.

After your database has been populated, you can update or delete individual records using the commands update, delete, and replace into.

> **TIP**
>
> MySQL data can be backed up quickly using mysqldump -a -A -u<*username*> -p <*password*> > <*backup filename*>. The resulting file contains all the database, table, and record creation statements.
>
> You can reload an empty MySQL database with this data using the mysql client and mysql -u<*username*> -p<*password*> < <*backup filename*>.

Modifying Records in a Table

Obviously, data in a database must be able to change; otherwise, it would be useful for only a short period of time or for limited applications. There are three types of modification that can be made: updating data already in a table, deleting a record outright, or completely replacing a record with new data.

Updating Existing Records

To change existing data, use the update command:

```
update <table name> SET <field name 1>=<expression 1>,
    <field name 2>=<expression 2>,<field name n>=<expression n>
    [WHERE <search expression>]
```

To use update, you must supply a table name as well as the names of the fields that need to be updated and the new values that they should take on. This leaves one important part of the equation missing: the search expression. If you don't tell update which fields to modify, it modifies all the tables. For example, issuing the command

```
update tblemployee set salary='3000';
```

modifies every listed employee so that the salary field contains '3000'. If this is the desired action, great! If not, you're likely to be smacking your forehead when you discover what you've done.

To be a bit more selective about the update, you must define the WHERE search expression. This selects only the records that you want to update. For example, assume that we want to set the salary for employeeID 1 to equal 30000.99. The update statement would look like this:

```
update tblemployee set salary='30000.99' where employeeID='1';
```

This update statement searches the table for a field where employeeID is equal to 1 and then updates the value in that record's salary field.

In addition to =, there are a number of common ways to select a record based on comparing a field to a value; that is, you can select records by creating an expression that evaluates to true or false. Table 19.2 shows some of the most common expression operators and syntax.

TABLE 19.2 Some Common Expression Operators and Syntax

Expression Syntax	Description
`<fieldname> = <value>`	Selects records based on a direct comparison to a value.
`<fieldname> > <value>`	Selects records where the value of a field is greater than a given value.
`<fieldname> < <value>`	Selects records where the value of a field is less than a given value.
`<fieldname> >= <value>`	Selects records where the value of a field is greater than or equal to a given value.
`<fieldname> <= <value>`	Selects records where the value of a field is less than or equal to a given value.
`<fieldname> LIKE <value>`	Selects records based on a simple SQL pattern-matching scheme. The character % matches any number of characters, whereas _ matches a single character.

These basic expressions can be combined to form more complex searches:

`NOT <expression>`—Evaluates to true if the expression evaluates to false.

`<expression> OR <expression>`—Evaluates to true if either of the expressions is true.

`<expression> AND <expression>`—Evaluates to true if both of the expressions are true.

`(<expression>)`—Use parentheses to combine expressions to force an order of evaluation.

Check the MySQL documentation for further information on available mathematical expressions, string comparisons, and other operators that can be used in expression syntax.

Deleting Records from a Table

To delete data from a MySQL system, you use a command similar to `update` but without supplying new field values:

```
delete from <table name> [WHERE <search expression>]
```

As with the `update` command, you can leave out the `WHERE` portion of the statement entirely. Unfortunately, the result would be the elimination of all data from the named table. Again, if this is your intention, by all means use it! For example, to delete employees who make more than $50,000 from the database, you would enter

```
delete from tblemployee where salary>'50000';
```

Replacing Existing Records

There is one final way to conveniently replace existing records with new data. Using the `INSERT` command to try to save a record more than once when one already exists will result in an error. This happens because only one record with a given primary key can exist at a time. For example, assuming that we've filled the database with the following employee record:

```
insert into tblemployee values ('1','John','Ray','1','25300.65');
```

attempting to insert another record using the same employee ID (1) causes an error:

```
mysql> insert into tblemployee values ('1','Maddy','Green','1','41000.00');
ERROR 1062: Duplicate entry '1' for key 1
```

To circumvent this, you could update the existing record; or delete the record and then rerun the insert; or use the replace into command.

replace replaces an existing record with new data or, if no record exists, simply inserts a record. Think of replace as a more powerful version of the basic insert command. It can be used to add new records to a table or replace existing records with new data. The syntax is identical to insert. For example, let's retry the insert into the tblemployee table—this time using replace:

```
mysql> replace into tblemployee values ('1','Maddy','Green','1','41000.00');
Query OK, 2 rows affected (0.00 sec)
```

Success!

CAUTION

replace is a useful command unique to the MySQL instruction set. Although convenient, it is best to stick to the basic insert statement for most database operations to avoid inadvertently deleting data.

Querying a Database

After you've added data to the tables in a database, you would obviously want to display it. Querying a MySQL database is performed with the select statement. The power of relational databases comes from the capability to relate data in one table to that of another, and select can do just that:

```
select <field name1>,<field name2>,.. from <table name 1>,<table name 2>,..
    [where <search expression>] [ORDER BY <expression> ASC¦DESC]
```

If this isn't confusing for you, fantastic. If you're like the rest of us, however, some explanation is necessary.

The simplest query that select can perform is to pull all the data out of a single table (select * from <*table name*>). For example:

```
mysql> select * from tbljobclassification;
+---------+-------------------+----------+----------+
| titleID | title             | minsalary | maxsalary |
+---------+-------------------+----------+----------+
|    1    | Programmer/Analyst |  20000   |  80000   |
|    2    | Web Developer     |  20000   |  50000   |
|    3    | CEO/President     |  40000   |  5e+09   |
+---------+-------------------+----------+----------+
3 rows in set (0.00 sec)
```

Changing Result Order

To sort the information based on one of the fields, use `order by` with an expression (often one or more comma-separated field names), and `asc` for ascending order or `desc` for descending order:

```
mysql> select * from tbljobclassification order by maxsalary desc;
+---------+-------------------+----------+----------+
| titleID | title             | minsalary | maxsalary |
+---------+-------------------+----------+----------+
|    3    | CEO/President     |  40000   |  5e+09   |
|    1    | Programmer/Analyst |  20000   |  80000   |
|    2    | Web Developer     |  20000   |  50000   |
+---------+-------------------+----------+----------+
```

In this example, the `tbljobclassification` table is displayed, and the records are sorted by the maximum salary in descending order (most to least). Obviously, this is great for getting data out of a single table and manipulating its order, but it still doesn't draw on the relational power of MySQL.

Joining Multiple Tables

To fully exploit MySQL's capabilities, relationships must be created and used. A relationship links two or more tables based on a common attribute. For example, the `tblemployee` and `tbljobclassification` tables share a `titleID` field. Each employee record has a `titleID` field that can be used to relate to the `tbljobclassification` table. The process of relating tables together is called a *join*.

To see a join in action, let's take a look at how you would display a list of each employee's name, along with his or her job title. The `select` statement looks like this:

```
select firstname,lastname,title from tblemployee,tbljobclassification
    WHERE tblemployee.titleID=tbljobclassification.titleID;
```

Translating this query into English is simple: Select the `firstname`, `lastname`, and `title` fields (`select firstname,lastname,title`) from the `tblemployee` and `tbljobclassification` database tables (`from tblemployee,tbljobclassification`). Relate the two tables by matching the `titleID` field in `tblemployee` to the `titleID` field in `tbljobclassification` (`WHERE tblemployee.titleID=tbljobclassification.titleID`).

The result is a neat display of the employees and their corresponding job titles:

```
mysql> select firstname,lastname,title from tblemployee,tbljobclassification
    WHERE tblemployee.titleID=tbljobclassification.titleID;
+-----------+----------+------------------+
| firstname | lastname | title            |
+-----------+----------+------------------+
| Maddy     | Green    | Programmer/Analyst |
| Will      | Ray      | Programmer/Analyst |
| Joan      | Ray      | Programmer/Analyst |
| Jack      | Derifaj  | Programmer/Analyst |
| Russ      | Schelby  | Programmer/Analyst |
| Robyn     | Ness     | Web Developer    |
| Anne      | Groves   | Web Developer    |
| Julie     | Vujevich | Web Developer    |
| Bill      | Gates    | CEO/President    |
| Steve     | Jobs     | CEO/President    |
+-----------+----------+------------------+
10 rows in set (0.03 sec)
```

TIP

In this example, the two `titleID` fields are referenced by an extended version of their name—*<table name>.<field name>*.

By using this syntax, you remove ambiguity in the SQL statements that would result from multiple tables containing the same names. You can use this when referring to any field, and even use it to refer to a database, table, and fieldname: *<database name>.<table name>.<field name>*. In large database projects, with dozens of tables, it helps document the relationships that are being used and is suggested as the standard query format.

A `select` statement can be combined with the `WHERE` search expressions that you've already seen in this chapter. For example, the last query can be modified to show only the employees who earn more than $50,000:

```
select firstname,lastname,title,salary from tblemployee,tbljobclassification
    WHERE tblemployee.titleID=tbljobclassification.titleID
    AND tblemployee.salary>'50000';
```

For example:

```
mysql> select firstname,lastname,title,salary from
    tblemployee,tbljobclassification WHERE
    tblemployee.titleID=tbljobclassification.titleID
    AND tblemployee.salary>'50000';
```

```
+-----------+----------+-------------------+---------+
| firstname | lastname | title             | salary  |
+-----------+----------+-------------------+---------+
| Joan      | Ray      | Programmer/Analyst | 55300.8 |
| Bill      | Gates    | CEO/President     |  50000  |
| Steve     | Jobs     | CEO/President     | 3.8e+08 |
+-----------+----------+-------------------+---------+
3 rows in set (0.00 sec)
```

Of course, expressions can be combined with other expressions to create truly complex queries.

Performing Calculations Within Results

Using built-in MySQL functions, you can create virtual fields that contain data calculated as the query is performed. The syntax for an inline calculation is

```
<expression> as '<variable name>'
```

For example, the expression required to calculate the percentage of the maximum salary that each person makes could be represented by

```
tblemployee.salary/tbljobclassification.maxsalary*100 as 'percent'
```

Adding this code into a query of all the employee names and salaries results in

```
mysql> select firstname,lastname,salary,tblemployee.
    salary/tbljobclassification.maxsalary*100 as 'percent'
    from tblemployee,tbljobclassification where
    tblemployee.titleID=tbljobclassification.titleID;
+-----------+----------+---------+-----------------+
| firstname | lastname | salary  | percent         |
+-----------+----------+---------+-----------------+
| Maddy     | Green    |  41000  |        51.25    |
| Will      | Ray      | 32100.2 |   40.1253125    |
| Joan      | Ray      | 55300.8 |   69.1259375    |
| Jack      | Derifaj  |  12000  |         15      |
| Russ      | Schelby  | 24372.1 | 30.465148925781 |
| Robyn     | Ness     | 35000.2 |  70.0003984375  |
| Anne      | Groves   | 35000.6 |  70.001296875   |
| Julie     | Vujevich |  30300  |  60.60001953125 |
| Bill      | Gates    |  50000  | 0.001000000234375 |
| Steve     | Jobs     | 3.8e+08 |        7.6      |
+-----------+----------+---------+-----------------+
10 rows in set (0.01 sec)
```

Suddenly, the database has provided information that didn't even exist previously! Using these methods, you can use the MySQL database engine to perform much of the mathematical work of database applications, leaving the logic to other programming languages.

NOTE

Just because a database system can be used for calculations doesn't mean that it should be. Database systems are optimized for I/O, not necessarily for numerics. This is, of course, highly dependent on your project and implementation details.

Using Summarization and Grouping Features

Summarizing data is another useful part of any query. Using the summarization functions, you can easily find totals for numeric columns, or count the number of records of a particular type. Here are a few summarization functions that can be used in a query:

- `max()`—The maximum of a given field. Used to match the highest value. For example, if you use `max` on the salary field of the employee table, it should return the highest salary in the group.
- `min()`—The minimum of a given field. Performs the exact opposite of the `max` function.
- `sum()`—The sum of the values in a given field. For example, you could use `sum` to find the total amount paid in salaries.
- `count()`—Provides a count of the number of occurrences of a given field.

For example, you could find the minimum salary of all the employees by typing

```
mysql> select min(salary) from tblemployee;
+-------------+
| min(salary) |
+-------------+
|    12000    |
+-------------+
1 row in set (0.01 sec)
```

Or a count of the occurrences of the `titleID` field:

```
mysql> select count(titleID) from tblemployee;
+----------------+
| count(titleID) |
+----------------+
|       10       |
+----------------+
1 row in set (0.00 sec)
```

This second example obviously isn't very useful—all it did was return the number of times the `titleID` field was used—that is, 10 times, once in each record. Displaying the count of each of the types of `titleIDs` would make more sense. This can be accomplished with one last construct—the `group by` clause.

group by organizes the data based on a field name and then makes it available to the summarization function. For example, the previous query could be modified like this:

```
select titleID,count(titleID) from tblemployee group by (titleID);
```

Instead of simply counting the field occurrences and reporting a result, the query groups the records by the titleID field and then counts the occurrences within each group. The output looks like this:

```
mysql> select titleID,count(titleID) from tblemployee group by (titleID);
+---------+---------------+
| titleID | count(titleID) |
+---------+---------------+
|    1    |       5        |
|    2    |       3        |
|    3    |       2        |
+---------+---------------+
3 rows in set (0.00 sec)
```

As with all queries, this could be turned into a join to provide information from more than one table. To show the actual job titles rather than just ID numbers, you could modify the query like this:

```
mysql> select title,count(tblemployee.titleID) from
    tblemployee,tbljobclassification where
    tblemployee.titleID=tbljobclassification.titleID
    group by (tblemployee.titleID);

+-------------------+--------------------------+
| title             | count(tblemployee.titleID) |
+-------------------+--------------------------+
| Programmer/Analyst |            5             |
| Web Developer     |            3             |
| CEO/President     |            2             |
+-------------------+--------------------------+
```

This output should be a bit more presentable. Note that in the modified query, the extended name (table name and field name) was used to refer to the titleID field. Failure to do this would result in an ambiguity error.

TIP

We highly recommend looking through the official MySQL documentation to get an idea of the full capabilities of the product. This chapter should not be seen as a complete reference to the capabilities of this wonderful application.

Alternative Database Servers

Besides MySQL, Tiger boasts several industrial-strength commercial SQL database solutions. If you're interested in pointing and clicking, take a look at these products:

- FrontBase—A Mac OS X–native SQL database system that features a fully graphical administration and RealBASIC integration. `http://www.frontbase.com/`.
- OpenBase—Another commercial SQL system for Mac OS X. OpenBase features GUI tools for designing database schema, as well as application development using either RealBASIC or RADStudio. `http://www.openbase.com`.
- FileMaker Pro—Apple's "own" database package, FileMaker Pro is available for Mac OS X, Windows, and handheld devices. FileMaker Pro is useful for creating desktop database applications and is available in a Server version for developing web-based applications. `http://www.filemaker.com/`.
- 4D—A high-end database development tool for creating desktop and web applications. 4D provides a far richer development environment than FileMaker Pro but, as a result, has a much higher learning curve. Available on both Windows and Macintosh platforms, 4D is an excellent choice for creating complex data-driven desktop applications. `http://www.4d.com/`.
- PostgreSQL—The PostgreSQL platform is a powerful alternative to MySQL that supports many features that are not yet available in MySQL. PostgreSQL is available from `http://www.postgresql.org/`.
- SQLite—SQLite is an embeddable SQL database engine. It does not require a server, supports a large subset of SQL (including views and subselects!), writes to a flat file on your system, and is very fast for common operations; `http://www.sqlite.org/`.

Accessing MySQL Through a GUI

If you find yourself managing MySQL databases frequently, you might find that the command-line client is a less-than-appealing solution for controlling your database server. GUI clients can provide simpler access to the data and easy editing of MySQL user permissions and database schema.

Two of the best clients for working with MySQL are the native Cocoa application CocoaMySQL and the PHP-based phpMyAdmin. We will take a short look at how you can install and configure these applications to start working with your MySQL server immediately.

CocoaMySQL

CocoaMySQL is a fast and easy way to work with databases directly from a native Tiger GUI. You can download the application for free from `http://cocoamysql.sourceforge.net`.

When starting CocoaMySQL, it will prompt you for connection information for your database server, as seen in Figure 19.1. Enter the hostname (or `localhost`/`127.0.0.1` for the local machine) and the username and password you created when installing the MySQL Server. If you didn't change anything, the default username is `root` with no password.

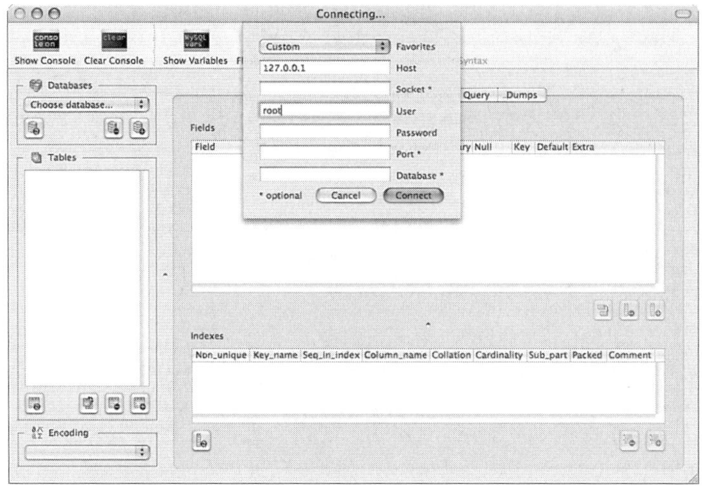

FIGURE 19.1 Enter the information needed to connect to your MySQL server.

You can save the information you've entered by choosing Save To Favorites from the Favorites pop-up menu. Click Connect to connect to the MySQL Server.

The CocoaMySQL interface is divided into three primary components: databases, tables, and information, as shown in Figure 19.2.

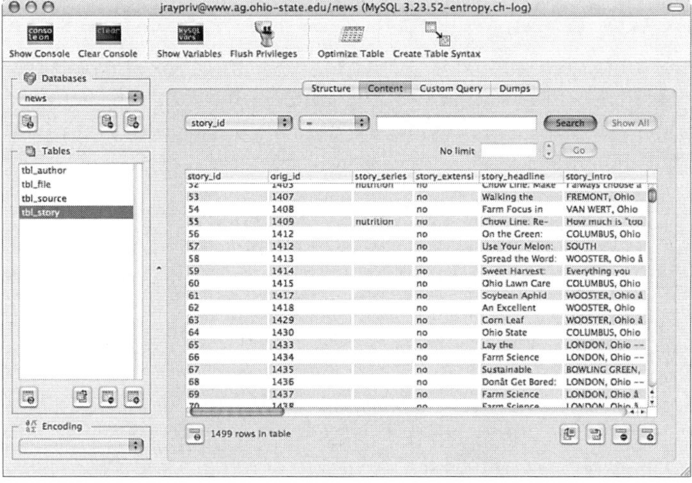

FIGURE 19.2 The CocoaMySQL Windows provides quick access to all the data stored in MySQL.

Use the pop-up menu in the Databases area to select a database to work with. The Tables list will refresh to display all the tables in the chosen database. Selecting a table will display information about the choice in the main viewing area to the right. The Structure, Content, and Custom Query buttons can be used to edit and display the field definitions for the table, the data stored in the table, and create custom SQL queries, respectively.

The buttons below each of the areas can be used to refresh the display, duplicate the selected resources, and delete (drop) or add a new database, table, or record.

Most anything you would commonly need to do from the MySQL command line can be managed within CocoaMySQL. If you find that you would like additional control, however, (such as editing user accounts), a better solution might be phpMyAdmin.

phpMyAdmin

The phpMyAdmin application works through your web browser to provide access to just about every feature MySQL has to offer. To use phpMyAdmin, you must have access to a PHP server or have enabled PHP on your Tiger computer. The instructions to do this are located in Chapter 23, "Creating a Web Server."

Start by downloading the latest phpMyAdmin distribution from `http://www.phpmyadmin.net/home_page/`. Unarchive the distribution in your PHP-enabled server, or the `~/Sites` folder if you've enabled PHP on your desktop. To keep things simple, you may want to rename the distribution folder or create an Apache alias to the distribution folder; the default installation folder includes a version number and patch-level string.

```
[www:~/public_html] jray% mv phpMyAdmin-2.6.0-pl3 phpMyAdmin
```

Next, you'll need to set up a user account in MySQL that can read the MySQL user table—this will enable phpMyAdmin's ability to authenticate users against known MySQL users. To do this, invoke the `mysql` client with the username and password you used to set it up, and then enter the following command. You should replace *<a new password>* with a password of your choice.

```
GRANT USAGE ON mysql.* TO 'pma'@'localhost' IDENTIFIED BY '<a new password>';
GRANT SELECT (
    Host, User, Select_priv, Insert_priv, Update_priv, Delete_priv,
    Create_priv, Drop_priv, Reload_priv, Shutdown_priv, Process_priv,
    File_priv, Grant_priv, References_priv, Index_priv, Alter_priv,
    Show_db_priv, Super_priv, Create_tmp_table_priv, Lock_tables_priv,
    Execute_priv, Repl_slave_priv, Repl_client_priv
    ) ON mysql.user TO 'pma'@'localhost';
GRANT SELECT ON mysql.db TO 'pma'@'localhost';
GRANT SELECT ON mysql.host TO 'pma'@'localhost';
GRANT SELECT (Host, Db, User, Table_name, Table_priv, Column_priv)
    ON mysql.tables_priv TO 'pma'@'localhost';
```

This creates a new MySQL user, `pma`, with the password you've chosen. Finally, you'll need to edit the phpMyAdmin file `config.inc.php` to make a few configuration changes.

Search for the following lines:

```
$cfg['Servers'][$i]['host']          = 'localhost';
// MySQL hostname or IP address
$cfg['Servers'][$i]['port']          = '';
// MySQL port - leave blank for default port
$cfg['Servers'][$i]['socket']        = '';
// Path to the socket - leave blank for default socket
$cfg['Servers'][$i]['connect_type']  = 'tcp';
// How to connect to MySQL server ('tcp' or 'socket')
$cfg['Servers'][$i]['extension']     = 'mysql';
// The php MySQL extension to use ('mysql' or 'mysqli')
$cfg['Servers'][$i]['compress']      = FALSE;
// Use compressed protocol for the MySQL connection
// (requires PHP >= 4.3.0)
$cfg['Servers'][$i]['controluser']   = 'pma';
// MySQL control user settings
// (this user must have read-only
$cfg['Servers'][$i]['controlpass']   = '<pma password>';
// access to the "mysql/user"
// and "mysql/db" tables).
// The controluser is also
// used for all relational
// features (pmadb)
$cfg['Servers'][$i]['auth_type']     = 'http';
// Authentication method (config, http or cookie based)?
```

Edit the lines to reflect the host you are connecting to, the username and password you just set up in MySQL (`pma` and whatever you chose), and finally, set `$cfg['Servers'][$i]['auth_type']` to `http`.

Your phpMyAdmin installation should now be ready to go. Point your web browser at the `phpMyAdmin` directory on your web server, such as `http://127.0.0.1/~jray/phpMyAdmin/` for the installation in my local `Sites` directory. You will be prompted for a username and password—supply the account and password you used when you set up MySQL. If you didn't configure a username and password, the default is `root` with an empty password.

The default phpMyAdmin page, shown in Figure 19.3, provides access to serverwide configuration, including a privileges section for managing user accounts. You can reach this screen at any time by clicking the Home icon.

For most database-specific operations, the phpMyAdmin interface is divided into three primary areas, as shown in Figure 19.4.

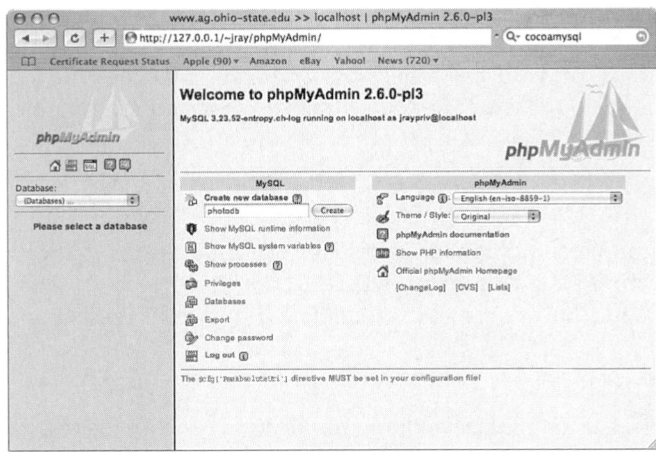

FIGURE 19.3 The phpMyAdmin Home page provides serverwide configuration options.

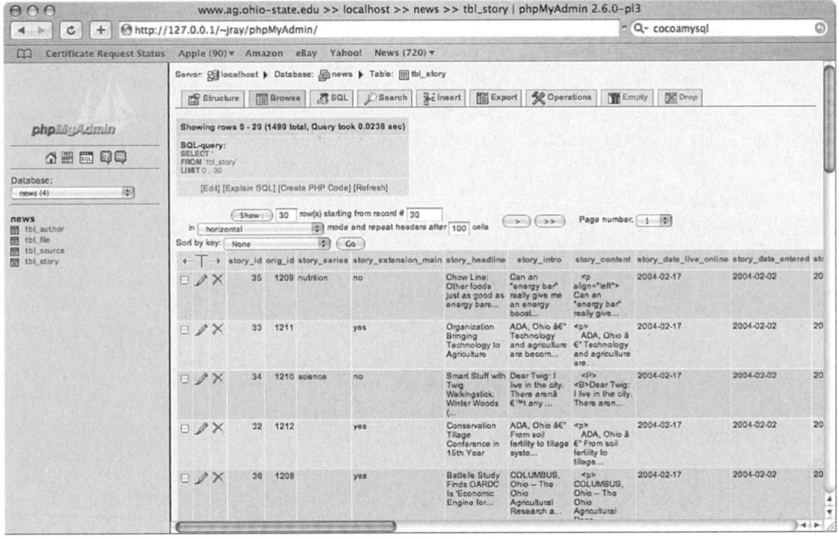

FIGURE 19.4 The phpMyAdmin interface is divided into sections for databases, tables, and overall Information.

Choosing a database in the Databases area will refresh the browser to display the tables within that database. Choosing a table will, in turn, refresh to display information about the database on the right side of the screen. Use the tabs across the top of the information area to browse and edit the table contents, search the data, insert records, and more. A complete guide to using phpMyAdmin can be displayed by pointing your browser at the `Documentation` directory within the phpMyAdmin distribution.

Accessing Database Information Using Perl

So, you've got MySQL on your machine. Now what can you do with it? Obviously, you can use one of the previously mentioned utilities to view and manipulate data, but that isn't nearly as useful as being able to apply programmatic logic to the data. Not surprisingly, Perl can be upgraded using DBI (Database Independent Interface) and DBD (Database Driver) modules to access dozens of database systems, including MySQL.

Perl and MySQL can be combined to create database applications that can be used for anything from storing your personal movie collection to enterprisewide solutions. This portion of the chapter introduces you to the MySQL and Perl connection.

Installing `DBI::DBD`

As you learned in Chapter 18, "Developing Applications and Widgets Using Scripting Languages," installing a Perl module using CPAN requires nothing more than typing **`install`** ***`<module name>`***. To start the interactive module installation shell, type **`sudo perl -MCPAN -e shell`** at a command line.

> **NOTE**
>
> Perl is likely to complain about the version of the CPAN modules you have installed. Although it isn't necessary to upgrade, it won't hurt, and future module installations will be smoother. To upgrade to the latest CPAN modules, type **`install Bundle::CPAN`** at the cpan> prompt.

```
cpan shell -- CPAN exploration and modules installation (v1.7601)
ReadLine support enabled

cpan>''
```

At the cpan> prompt, type **`install DBI::DBD`** to begin the installation process:

```
cpan> install DBI::DBD

Local directory now /Users/jray/.cpan/sources/authors/id/T/TI/TIMB
...
DBI-1.37
DBI-1.37/DBI.xs
DBI-1.37/t
DBI-1.37/t/80proxy.t
DBI-1.37/t/30subclass.t
DBI-1.37/t/70shell.t
DBI-1.37/t/60preparse.t
DBI-1.37/t/20meta.t
DBI-1.37/t/40profile.t
...
Installing /usr/share/man/man3/DBI::Shell.3
```

```
Installing /usr/share/man/man3/DBI::W32ODBC.3
Installing /usr/share/man/man3/Win32::DBIODBC.3
Installing /usr/bin/dbiproxy
Installing /usr/bin/dbish
Writing /Library/Perl/darwin/auto/DBI/.packlist
Appending installation info to /System/Library/Perl/darwin/perllocal.pod
 /usr/bin/make install -- OK
```

Depending on your Perl installation and version, you might notice several additional messages during the installation. Don't concern yourself too much about these messages unless the installation fails. In the event of a failure, be absolutely sure that you have the latest version of the developer tools installed.

TIP

Many Perl modules ask some basic questions during the install process. Even the highly automated CPAN shell installation method pauses to collect information it needs—so pay attention to your screen during an install.

That's it. The `DBD::DBI` module, which provides the basis for database access from within Perl, is now installed.

Installing `DBD::mysql`

To complete the integration of Perl with MySQL, we need the `DBD::mysql` module. Again, using the CPAN shell, this requires no more effort on our part than `install DBD::mysql`.

Again, invoke CPAN with **`sudo perl -MCPAN -e shell`**:

```
cpan shell -- CPAN exploration and modules installation (v1.7601)
ReadLine support enabled
''
cpan>
```

At the cpan> prompt, type **`install DBD::mysql`** to begin the installation process:

```
cpan> install DBD::mysql
GOT /Users/jray/.cpan/sources/authors/id/J/JW/JWIED/DBD-mysql-2.1027.tar.gz
DBD-mysql-2.1027
DBD-mysql-2.1027/t
DBD-mysql-2.1027/t/mysql2.t
DBD-mysql-2.1027/t/akmisc.t
DBD-mysql-2.1027/t/60leaks.t
DBD-mysql-2.1027/t/10dsnlist.t
DBD-mysql-2.1027/t/ak-dbd.t
DBD-mysql-2.1027/t/50chopblanks.t
...
```

```
Installing /usr/share/man/man3/DBD::mysql::INSTALL.3
Installing /usr/share/man/man3/Mysql.3
Writing /Library/Perl/darwin/auto/DBD/mysql/.packlist
Appending installation info to /System/Library/Perl/darwin/perllocal.pod
 /usr/bin/make install -- OK
```

> **NOTE**
>
> If you've already set a root password for MySQL, the install will fail when it attempts to connect to `mysql` as a test. The easiest way around this is to simply force the install by using the command `force install DBD::mysql` within the CPAN shell.

`DBD::mysql` is installed and ready to use. Remember, to view documentation for any of the installed modules, type **`perldoc`** ***<module name>***.

Using Perl with MySQL (`DBD::mysql`)

The `DBD::mysql` module uses an object-oriented model to carry out database translations. Because object-oriented programming is a bit beyond the scope of this book, we'll take a look at two examples: adding information to a database and displaying information contained in a table. You should be able to modify these examples for your own applications, or, if you need more functionality, I recommend adding a Perl book to your library.

Displaying the Results of a Query

The easiest way to retrieve information from a MySQL database is to compose a query and retrieve the results, one record at a time. To be able to do this, you must connect to the database, issue the query, determine the number of results, and loop through a display of each one. Listing 19.1 shows the surprisingly short code necessary to do just that.

LISTING 19.1 Display the Result of a MySQL Query

```
#!/usr/bin/perl

use DBI;

$user="";
$pass="";
$database="employee";
$dsn="DBI:mysql:database=$database;host=localhost";
$sql="select firstname,lastname,title from
      tblemployee,tbljobclassification where tblemployee.titleID=
      tbljobclassification.titleID";

$dbh=DBI->connect($dsn,$user,$pass);
$sth=$dbh->prepare($sql);
$sth->execute;
```

```
14:
15: $numrows=$sth->rows;
16: $numfields=$sth->{'NUM_OF_FIELDS'};
17: $nameref=$sth->{'NAME'};
18:
19: for ($x=0;$x<$numrows;$x++) {
20:   $valueref = $sth->fetchrow_arrayref;
21:   print "--------------------------\n";
22:   for ($i=0;$i<$numfields;$i++) {
23:     print "$$nameref[$i] = $$valueref[$i]\n";
24:   }
25: }
```

The following list describes how the Perl code interacts with the MySQL database through the DBI module:

- Line 3—Use the DBI module. This must be included in any Perl application that accesses MySQL.
- Lines 5–9—Set up the username, password, database name, and SQL that will be used to access the database. The `$dsn` variable contains a string that will be used to set up the connection to MySQL. The format of this string cannot change, although the database and hostname can.
- Line 11—Connect to the database using the previously defined connection string and username and password. The variable `$dbh` is a handle that references the database connection.
- Line 12—Prepare the SQL for execution.
- Line 13—Execute the SQL statement and return a reference to the results in the variable `$sth`.
- Line 15—Store the number of returned rows in the `$numrows`.
- Line 16—Store the number of fields (columns) in the result within `$numfields`.
- Line 17—Store a reference to an array containing the field names in the variable `$nameref`.
- Lines 19–25—Loop through each of the rows in the result.
- Line 20—Fetch a row of the result and return the field values in an array referenced by `$valueref`.
- Line 21—Print a divider between each output record.
- Lines 22–24—Loop based on the number of fields in the result. Display each field name followed by the value stored in that field.

Executing the code (assuming that the employee database from earlier in the chapter is in place) produces output like this:

```
% ./display.pl
----------------------------
firstname = Maddy
lastname = Green
title = Programmer/Analyst
----------------------------
firstname = Will
lastname = Ray
title = Programmer/Analyst
----------------------------
firstname = Joan
lastname = Ray
title = Programmer/Analyst
----------------------------
firstname = Jack
lastname = Derifaj
title = Programmer/Analyst
----------------------------
...and so on...
```

Obviously, the syntax of this code is a bit different from the Perl that you've seen so far, but it should be easy enough to understand that you can modify the code to fit your application.

Storing Data

You probably noticed that the code for displaying the results of a query was very modular. In fact, you can use the same code to insert a record into the database. Listing 19.2 demonstrates the code needed to store data in the `tblemployee` table.

LISTING 19.2 Display the Result of a MySQL Query

```
#!/usr/bin/perl

use DBI;

$user="";
$pass="";
$database="employee";
$id="11"; $firstname="Troy"; $lastname="Burkholder";
$titleID="2"; $salary="45000";
$dsn="DBI:mysql:database=$database;host=localhost";
$sql="insert into tblemployee values ('$id','$firstname','$lastname',
                                        '$titleID','$salary')";

```

```
13: $dbh=DBI->connect($dsn,$user,$pass);
14: $sth=$dbh->prepare($sql);
15: $sth->execute;
```

The only difference between this code and the previous script is the definition of the values for an `insert` (lines 8 and 9) and the definition of the `insert` statement itself (line 11). The SQL statement can be whatever arbitrary SQL code you want. If the statement returns results, they can be read and displayed with the techniques in the previous code.

Accessing Database Information Using ODBC

While Perl's DBI/DBD data abstraction can be used in many cross-platform database scripting solutions, it isn't available outside of Perl. A more universal approach to database abstraction is ODBC (Open Database Connectivity). Starting in Mac OS X 10.2, our favorite platform once again has ODBC support built into the operating system by way of the open source iODBC (Independent Open Database Connectivity) software. Before you get excited (or start scratching your head wondering what this is), let's answer a few of the obvious questions.

First, what is ODBC? ODBC is a programming API that allows developers to interact with many different types of databases without having to create custom code for each system. Each database is made accessible by downloading and installing a driver, which plugs into an ODBC manager and hides the details of the server from the programmer and user. There are numerous alternatives to ODBC—such as JDBC (Java), Apple's own Enterprise Objects Framework, and Perl's DBI module, which you just read about. So, with all these different APIs, each doing something similar, why do we need ODBC? ODBC is (one of) Microsoft's standards for database connectivity. It is widely used on the Windows platform and is an accepted developer standard. Is it better than the other options? Nope—but that hasn't stopped other software supported by a monopolistic company from becoming the standard. The Tiger-included iODBC software is a free implementation of the ODBC standard (`http://www.iodbc.org`).

What can we do with Tiger's ODBC support? To be honest, at the time of this writing, the answer is "not much"—unless you're a programmer. Keep in mind that ODBC is a developer standard for interacting with databases. If developers haven't created applications that use ODBC, users can't do very much with it. ODBC is typically used by software on the Windows platform to allow users to insert live database data into documents. Unfortunately, the support isn't even remotely as pervasive in Tiger. Although this is slowly improving in end-user applications such as FileMaker and Microsoft Office, it isn't nearly as widespread as we might like.

To start using the ODBC productively, you must first install a driver for the database server you want to access. This driver will handle the protocols necessary to talk to the database and subsequently allow iODBC and applications that use it to interact with the server. You'll usually install a driver in one of two ways: either using a point-and-click installer or by compiling your own.

Installing a Prepackaged Driver: MyODBC

If you're lucky, the ODBC driver you need to use will have a GUI installer and a user-friendly configuration tool. Thankfully, this is the case with MyODBC, the official ODBC driver for the MySQL database. To download MyODBC, visit `http://dev.mysql.com/downloads/connector/odbc/`.

To install a packaged driver, double-click the installation package. You will be led through the install process just as with any other Mac application, as demonstrated in Figure 19.5. When the installation finishes, the installed driver might present a GUI for configuring an initial connection to a particular database. If you aren't ready to set the connection up yet, quit out of the setup. We'll look more at this step in later in the "Defining a Data Source Name" section later in this chapter.

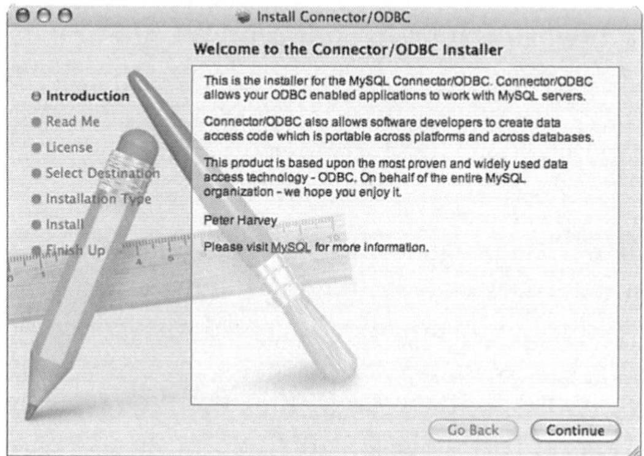

FIGURE 19.5 Some drivers come in prepackaged installers.

> **NOTE**
>
> A good source for database drivers is OpenLink (`http://www.openlinksw.com`). You can download an OpenLink driver packaged to work with Apple's ODBC Administrator from: `http://oplweb.openlinksw.com/product/webmatrixst.asp`. Unfortunately, these drivers cost money. For desktop applications, the price tag is reasonable, but costs go up significantly if you're deploying on a web server. Thirty-day trials are available for free.

To verify that the driver has installed correctly, open the ODBC Administrator utility and click to the Drivers button. Your display should resemble Figure 19.6. We will discuss more about the operation of ODBC Administrator later in this chapter.

Not all driver packages will install the same way, but the end result should be the same: a new driver entry in ODBC Administrator. If you don't see this entry, consult the driver documentation.

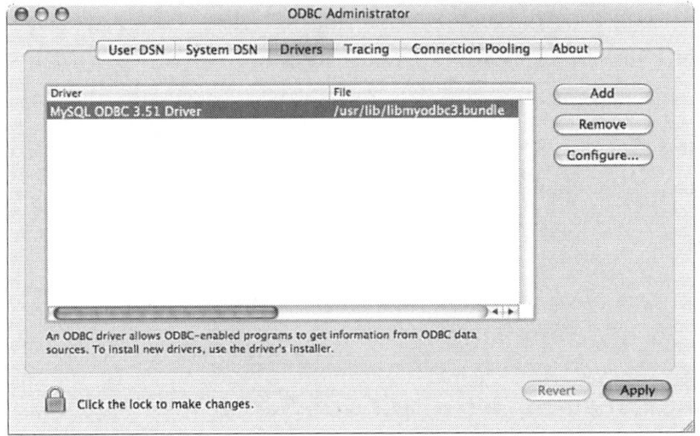

FIGURE 19.6 Use the Drivers pane within the ODBC Administrator to verify that the driver installed correctly.

NOTE

Some ODBC driver installations include their own iODBC manager and support libraries. There is quite a bit of discontinuity at present in the iODBC implementation and developer support for what Apple has included. If you should install a driver only to find that it has installed *another* ODBC Manager tool, you should probably use that tool for configuration.

Building iODBC Drivers from Scratch

Very few packaged drivers are available for Tiger, and many that are available cost money. For those who have to squeeze every penny out of their IT budgets, there are free solutions that can be built without spending a dime.

Most drivers require you to manually compile them, and, before you can do that, you'll need to fix your iODBC installation. Apple, although including iODBC in the system, neglected to include the header files required to compile iODBC-compatible drivers. So, our first step is to retrieve and install the iODBC header files. The good news is that you'll have to do this only once.

First, download the iODBC Manager source code from `http://www.iodbc.org` and unarchive it.

Next, `cd` into the source distribution and run `./configure` to set up the software. We're not going to compile it, but running `configure` is necessary to create one of the header files:

```
brezup:jray libiodbc-3.52.1 $ ./configure
checking for a BSD-compatible install.. /usr/bin/install -c
checking whether build environment is sane.. yes
checking for gawk.. no
checking for mawk.. no
checking for nawk.. no
checking for awk.. awk
...
```

19

Finally, we need to create a directory for the header files (/usr/local/include/iodbc) and copy the contents of the source distribution's include folder to that location. To do this, issue these commands from inside the iODBC source distribution directory:

```
brezup:jray libiodbc-3.52.1 $ sudo mkdir /usr/local/include/iodbc
brezup:jray libiodbc-3.52.1 $ cd include
brezup:jray include $ sudo cp *.h /usr/local/include/iodbc
```

Now you're ready to compile iODBC drivers. Just make sure that the iODBC headers are in the include path during compilation.

Compiling an iODBC Driver for Microsoft SQL Server

A MySQL driver is great for connecting to MySQL, but much of the corporate world relies on Microsoft SQL Server as the database server of choice. As you might guess, there is no Microsoft-supplied ODBC driver for connecting to its products. Thankfully, an open source project named FreeTDS (Tabular Data Stream) provides this functionality remarkably easily on Tiger.

To build a Microsoft SQL Server–compatible driver, you must first download the latest release from http://www.freetds.org/, which offers both nightly snapshots and stable builds. Currently, only the 0.64 nightly snapshots will build cleanly, so download the nightly snapshot.

After unarchiving the source distribution, cd into the directory and use ./configure to prepare the software for compilation:

```
brezup:jray freetds-current $ ./configure
./configure
checking for a BSD-compatible install... /usr/bin/install -c
checking whether build environment is sane... yes
checking for gawk... no
checking for mawk... no
checking for nawk... no
checking for awk... awk
...
```

Next, compile using make, and then install with sudo make install:

```
brezup:jray freetds-current $ make
Making all in include
make  all-am
echo '#define FREETDS_SYSCONFDIR "/usr/local/etc"' >freetds_sysconfdir.h
Making all in src
Making all in replacements
if /bin/sh ../../libtool --mode=compile gcc -DHAVE_CONFIG_H -I. -I.
-I../../include -I../../include  -D_FREETDS_LIBRARY_SOURCE -DIODBC -D_REENTRANT
➥-D_THREAD_SAFE -DDEBUG=1 -Wall -Wstrict-prototypes -Wmissing-prototypes
➥-Wno-long-long  -g -O2 -MT iconv.lo -MD -MP -MF ".deps/iconv.Tpo" \
```

```
...
brezup:jray freetds-current $ sudo make install
Making install in include
make[2]: Nothing to be done for `install-exec-am'.
/bin/sh ../mkinstalldirs /usr/local/include
 /usr/bin/install -c -m 644 bkpublic.h /usr/local/include/bkpublic.h
 /usr/bin/install -c -m 644 cspublic.h /usr/local/include/cspublic.h
...
```

Once finished, your FreeTDS ODBC driver is located at `/usr/local/lib/libtdsodbc.so`. This new driver must be configured in ODBC Administrator before it can be used. Let's find out how that happens now.

Managing Drivers and Data Sources: ODBC Administrator

The command-line interface to iODBC is not user friendly. With the benefits of ODBC support coming to GUI applications, it's unreasonable to think that end users will be opening a command prompt to install and manage database connections. Apple has provided a simple GUI ODBC manager (path: `/Applications/Utilities/ODBC Administrator`) that enables mere mortals to create and edit connections.

ODBC Administrator works (and looks) like Microsoft's ODBC Data Sources control panel, so if you've used ODBC on Windows, you might experience deja vu. If not, a few terms will be helpful to understand going forward:

- ODBC driver—A driver file that abstracts a database behind the ODBC manager. You've just read about how to compile MySQL and Microsoft SQL drivers.
- DSN—A *Data Source Name*. For each drive you install, you can create multiple data source names that connect to different databases/database servers. The DSN is a simple word (such as `mydatabase`) that identifies a database connection and can contain all the information needed to connect and access a given database.
- User DSN—A DSN accessible only by the user who created it.
- System DSN—A DSN accessible by any user on the Tiger system.
- User driver—An ODBC driver accessible only by the user who installed it.
- System driver—An ODBC driver accessible by any user on the Tiger system.

Manually Adding a Driver to ODBC Administrator

There are two ways to add drivers to the ODBC Administrator: either through the GUI, or by editing the appropriate configuration file. Because both methods are simple, let's quickly review each.

The iODBC configuration files consist of `/Library/ODBC/odbcinst.ini`, which contains the installed system drivers, and `/Library/ODBC/odbc.ini`, containing the installed system data source names. The user-level versions of these files are stored in

`~/Library/ODBC/odbcinst.ini` and `~/Library/ODBC/odbc.ini`, respectively. Keep in mind the using the system-level `/Library/ODBC` files results in a systemwide configuration whereas the user level files are accessible to your account only.

> **NOTE**
>
> If you've never used the ODBC Administrator before or have never installed a packaged driver, you will probably need to create the `/Library/ODBC` directory and `odbcinst.ini` files by hand.

To add an ODBC driver to the system, edit the file `/Library/ODBC/odbcinst.ini` and add the lines that follow this pattern:

```
[ODBC Drivers]
<Driver Name> = Installed

[<Driver Name>]
Driver = <path to driver file>
```

The first section `[ODBC Drivers]` is simply a list of each driver installed on the system. The driver name is arbitrary but should describe what is installed.

For each driver listed under `[ODBC Drivers]`, there should be a corresponding section named identically to the driver name, that contains a `Driver =` line set to the location of the installed driver file. There could be additional options that can be set here (see the individual driver instructions for details), but for most cases, this is sufficient.

For example, to add the FreeTDS driver, use:

```
[ODBC Drivers]
FreeTDS = Installed

[FreeTDS]
Driver = /usr/local/lib/libtdsodbc.so
```

An `odbcinst.ini` file that includes both the FreeTDS driver and the MyODBC driver would look like this:

```
[ODBC Drivers]
MySQL ODBC 3.51 Driver = Installed
FreeTDS = Installed

[MySQL ODBC 3.51 Driver]
Driver = /usr/lib/libmyodbc3.bundle
Setup  = /usr/lib/libmyodbc3S.bundle

[FreeTDS]
Driver = /usr/local/lib/libtdsodbc.so
```

After editing the file, start ODBC Administrator and click the Drivers button. You should see the drivers listed, as shown in Figure 19.7.

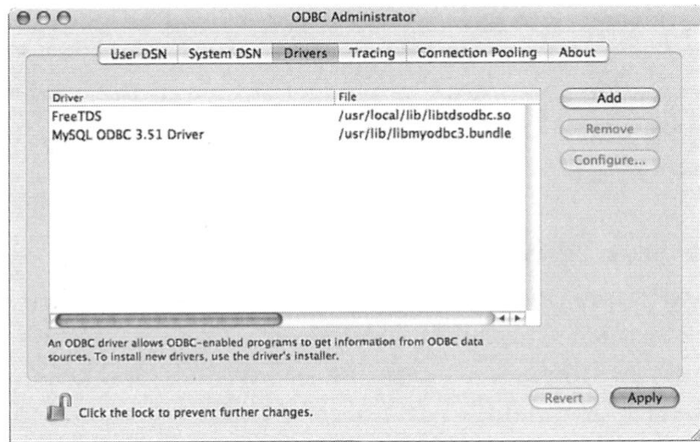

FIGURE 19.7 The Drivers button lists the installed drivers.

If you prefer a more graphical approach to adding the driver, you can avoid editing files altogether by using the Drivers button and the Add button to configure a driver within the Administrator.

First, click Add to display a dialog box where you can specify a description of the driver, the location of the ODBC driver file, and a setup file if one is provided with the driver—such as with MyODBC. The setup file is a GUI wizard that is run to help set up connections to specific databases.

Next, choose whether it will be available as a User or System driver.

Finally, use the Add and Remove buttons within the sheet enable driver-specific variables to be set. Figure 19.8 shows a properly filled-out Add window for adding the FreeTDS driver to ODBC Administrator.

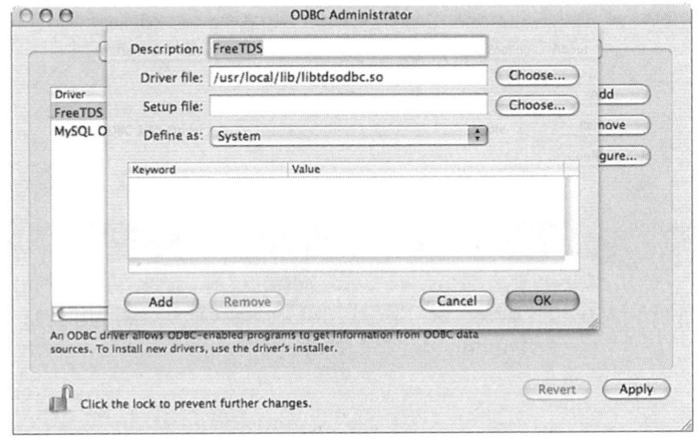

FIGURE 19.8 Use the Add button to add driver files within the ODBC Administrator GUI.

NOTE

System drivers cannot be added unless you first authenticate by clicking the lock icon at the bottom of the ODBC Administrator window.

After a driver has been added, you can change its configuration at any time by highlighting the name in the list and clicking the Configure button. Drivers can be removed altogether by clicking Remove.

Defining a Data Source Name

Regardless of whether you're using an ODBC driver that installed itself via a GUI interface or a driver that you've added manually to an `odbcinst.ini` file, there's still one more step before you can actively *use* the driver—defining a data source name. User data source names and system data source names function identically—it's just a matter of what users have access to them. System DSNs can be accessed by anyone on the machine, whereas user DSNs are limited to the account that installed them.

To define a DSN, click the appropriate DSN button at the top of the ODBC Administrator window. For test purposes, use the User DSN button. Next, click the Add button. You will be presented with a list of the drivers available on your system, as demonstrated in Figure 19.9.

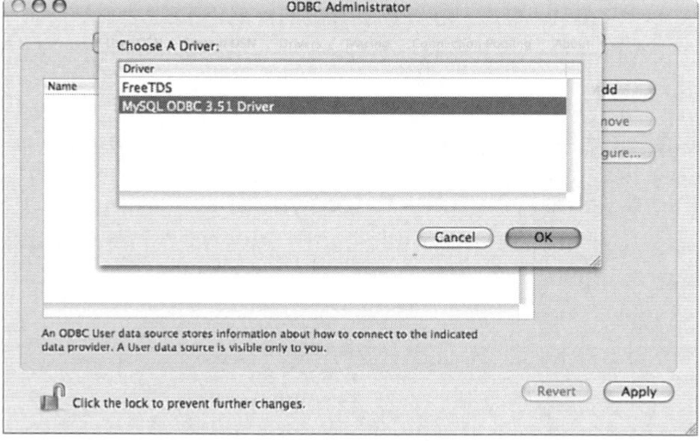

FIGURE 19.9 Choose the ODBC driver you want to use to make a connection.

NOTE

As with adding the ODBC drivers themselves, you cannot add a system DSN unless you first authenticate by clicking the lock icon at the bottom of the ODBC Administrator window.

After you've chosen the driver, one of two things happens. If your driver includes an automated setup tool, such as the MyODBC drivers, you are taken to a GUI setup wizard; otherwise, you are presented with a generic setup screen.

Check with your driver installation instructions to properly complete the setup. In the case of the MyODBC drivers, use the Login tab to configure your connection, as shown in Figure 19.10.

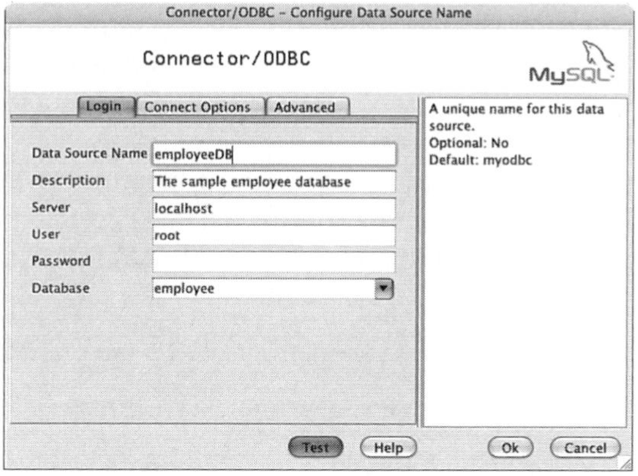

FIGURE 19.10 The MyODBC data source setup is handled through a GUI.

Choose a DSN, such as `employeeDB` for the database we created in this chapter. The hostname should be set to the computer running the database server or `localhost` if it is on the same computer as the ODBC driver. Provide a username and password by which to connect to the database server, and choose the database (such as `employee`) itself. This is all highly dependent on who packaged the driver, so what works with one ODBC driver might not work with another.

Unlike MyODBC, the FreeTDS drivers do not include a setup utility, so they must be configured manually. Drivers such as this show a generic setup screen, similar to that in Figure 19.11.

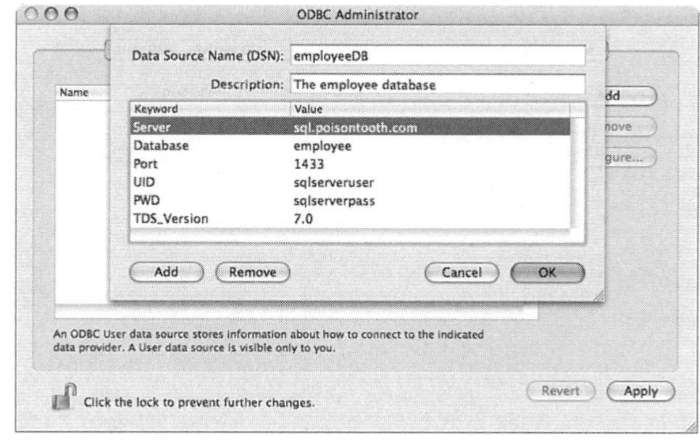

FIGURE 19.11 Drivers without GUI setup wizards must be configured by hand.

Use the DSN field to provide a DSN—`employeeDB`, for our example database. In the Description field, provide a brief description of what the DSN will do. Next, use the Add and Remove buttons to add and remove keywords and values that will be used to define the connection (we'll review these next). Click OK to save the DSN definition.

After a DSN has been added (regardless of the means), it can be reconfigured by clicking the Configure button, or removed entirely by clicking the Remove button.

MyODBC DSN Configuration

Each ODBC driver can (and does) implement different keywords for configuration. You should always check the driver documentation for the settings it supports. Even though MyODBC has a convenient setup utility, it also is easy to configure manually using these keywords:

- `DATABASE`—The name of the database on the MySQL server.
- `SERVER`—The name or IP address of the MySQL server.
- `PORT`—The port that the MySQL server is running on. Always 3306 unless the MySQL Server defaults have been modified.
- `USER`—A MySQL username to connect with.
- `PASSWORD`—The password to use.

NOTE

As noted earlier, actual DSN setup information is stored in the files `/Library/ODBC/odbc.ini` and `~/Library/ODBC/odbc.ini` for system and user DSNs, respectively. You might find that it is often easier to add these definitions by hand rather than use the ODBC Administrator. For example, the MyODBC `employeeDB` DSN is defined in my user DSN `odbc.ini` file as follows:

```
[ODBC Data Sources]
employeeDB = MySQL ODBC 3.51 Driver

[employeeDB]
Driver = /usr/lib/libmyodbc3.bundle
Description = The sample employee database
DATABASE  = employee
SERVER    = localhost
USER      = root
PASSWORD  = mypass
PORT      = 3306
```

This is similar to the `odbcinst.ini` file we saw earlier. The `odbc.ini` file simply lists the DSNs and the drivers they use, and then provides a section for each DSN with the necessary keyword/value pairs to connect to the database server.

FreeTDS DSN Configuration

The settings for FreeTDS are similar, but not identical to MyODBC. Use the following keywords and the appropriate values to define a Microsoft SQL Server connection:

- `Server`—The name or IP address of Microsoft SQL Server.
- `Database`—The name of the default database to use.
- `Port`—The port that Microsoft SQL Server is running on. Always 1433 unless the MS SQL Server defaults have been modified.
- `UID`—The Microsoft SQL Server username to connect with.
- `PWD`—The Microsoft SQL Server password to use.
- `TDS_Version`—Version of the TDS protocol to use. Should always be set to `7.0` for connections to modern Microsoft SQL Server servers.

Testing and Querying the DSN

To test and query a configured DSN, you can either use an ODBC-enabled application or the command-line `iodbctest` utility. To use `iodbctest` to connect to a user DSN, simply invoke it at a command prompt:

```
brezup:jray jray $ iodbctest
iODBC Demonstration program
This program shows an interactive SQL processor
Driver Manager: 03.51.0001.0908

Enter ODBC connect string (? shows list):
Press ? to display a list of the defined DSNs:
Enter ODBC connect string (? shows list): ?
DSN              | Description
-----------------------------------------------------------
employeeDB       | MyODBC

Enter ODBC connect string (? shows list):
```

Finally, type **DSN=<*DSN*>** to connect to a listed DSN:

```
Enter ODBC connect string (? shows list): DSN=employeeDB
Driver: 03.51.0001.0908

SQL>
```

TIP

You can override settings in your DSN definition by supplying them in the ODBC connect string. For example, if you wanted to connect to the `employeeDB` DSN with an alternative username and password, you might use
`DSN=employeeDB;USER=mynewusername;PASSWORD=mynewpassword`.

If the driver has been configured successfully, you'll arrive at an `SQL>` prompt where you can issue SQL commands to the database server. This works just like the `mysql` client application we used earlier:

```
SQL> select * from tblemployee;

employeeID¦firstname¦lastname¦titleID¦salary
----------+---------+--------+-------+---------
1         ¦John     ¦Ray       ¦1      ¦25300.7
2         ¦Will     ¦Ray       ¦1      ¦32100.2
3         ¦Joan     ¦Ray       ¦1      ¦55300.8
4         ¦Robyn    ¦Ness      ¦2      ¦35000.2
5         ¦Anne     ¦Groves    ¦2      ¦35000.6
6         ¦Julie    ¦Vujevich  ¦2      ¦30300
7         ¦Jack     ¦Derifaj   ¦1      ¦12000
8         ¦Russ     ¦Schelby   ¦1      ¦24372.1
9         ¦Bill     ¦Gates     ¦3      ¦50000
10        ¦Steve    ¦Jobs      ¦3      ¦3.8e+08

 result set 1 returned 10 rows.
```

After verifying that the connection works and value results are returned, exit `odbctest` by typing **`exit`**:

```
SQL> exit

Have a nice day.
```

You now have a completely functional ODBC driver and DSN defined. Any software compatible with iODBC should recognize and work with the DSN.

SO NOW WHAT?

You might be asking yourself, "So now what?" The answer, unfortunately, is wait. ODBC-compatible Mac applications will eventually appear. Until then, you'll have to be satisfied with Unix-level utilities.

Perl, for example, provides a DBD ODBC module, `DBD::ODBC`, that can interact with any database using the same syntax discussed earlier with `DBD::mysql`. This is slower than using a native DBD module (it adds an extra layer of work because the DBI module must talk to the DBD driver, which in turn communicates with iODBC and the ODBC driver). However, it is useful for connecting to databases that don't have a native DBD driver.

Advanced ODBC Administrator Settings

Two additional buttons in ODBC Administrator can be used to debug or fine-tune your database connections. The first button, Tracing, is shown in Figure 19.12.

If you are having problems connecting to your database server, you can enable tracing and choose a log file to hold the trace information. The trace file contains all information sent between the driver and the database server, enabling you to pinpoint where the failure is occurring.

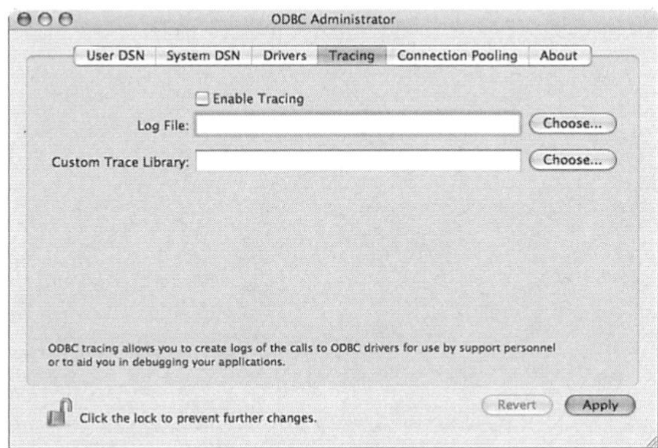

FIGURE 19.12 Enable tracing to debug connection problems.

> **CAUTION**
>
> Trace log files can grow large very quickly and can also slow down the connection to your database server. Enable tracing only when needed.

The second button, Connection Pooling, makes it possible for you to enable pooling for individual drivers. If a driver is pooled, it attempts to reuse open connections instead of relocating connection resources each time they are requested.

To enable pooling, authenticate with ODBC Administrator and then enter a timeout value in the Pool Timeout field. This is the length of time that a pooled connection exists before it is released.

Summary

This chapter introduced MySQL and ODBC for database development and connection management. MySQL provides a powerful database system that can be used to develop commercial solutions for a fraction of the price. Easily integrated with Perl, MySQL can be used for everything from web development to your own custom database applications.

ODBC support is included in Tiger in the form of iODBC and ODBC Administrator. The iODBC software, coupled with Apple's ODBC Administrator, makes it easy to connect to and manage ODBC data sources. Unfortunately, there is still very little end-user software that uses ODBC on the Mac platform. Presumably, the integration of this feature with the Mac OS X will lead to enhanced database functionality in the not-so-distant future.

CHAPTER 20

Configuring Advanced Multiuser/Multisystem Cooperation Features

IN THIS CHAPTER

- Using NetInfo Manager
- Managing Users Through NetInfo
- Command-Line NetInfo Administration Tools
- Using and Sharing Disk Resources with NFS

In this chapter, we will look at configuring advanced multiuser/multisystem cooperation features. We will first explore the NetInfo database, where Mac OS X stores much of this information, using the graphical interface available with the NetInfo Manager application. Next we will look at managing users through the NetInfo database using the NetInfo Manager. Then we will look at one way to manage users via the command-line NetInfo utilities. Finally, we will look at using and sharing disk resources with NFS. This too will involve interacting with the NetInfo database.

Using NetInfo Manager

The Accounts pane is intended to be a simple interface to the user accounts of the system and doesn't provide access to more complex aspects of users' accounts nor to more sophisticated configuration options. For this, you need to use NetInfo Manager. The principles behind the use of NetInfo Manager are very Unix-like, but the NetInfo database itself is unfamiliar to most traditional Unix users. NetInfo is a vestige of Mac OS X's NeXTStep heritage that has been integrated into the more traditional Unix underpinnings of Mac OS X because it's a considerably more powerful information sharing system than its traditional Unix counterparts. The NetInfo database is a hierarchical database that stores information on your machine's configuration and resources.

The NetInfo hierarchy is composed of directories. Each directory has properties. Each property has a name and value. The main directory on a given machine is the root directory, represented by `/`. Each machine has a local database with information about the machine's local resources.

The NetInfo hierarchy can extend beyond your local machine. As you might have guessed, your machine can be part of a NetInfo network. A NetInfo network is a hierarchical collection of domains, where each domain has a corresponding NetInfo database. A NetInfo network could have an unlimited number of domains, but up to three domains is most common. Your machine has its own local domain, but it could belong to a domain comprised of it and other machines. That domain could describe resources available to your local cluster of machines; it could also belong to another domain that might include information on yet another level of resources available, and so on.

Your machine could be part of a larger NetInfo network. However, because NetInfo isn't a widespread network type, it's more likely your machine is using its NetInfo database either as a standalone machine or, possibly, as part of a Unix *cluster* (a cooperating group of machines).

This chapter examines the NetInfo database using the graphical interface, NetInfo Manager, as well as a few command-line tools. You'll learn how to work with the NetInfo database by customizing several aspects of your system, modifying a local user, and adding arbitrary data structures into the NetInfo database.

Using NetInfo Manager to Examine the NetInfo Database

NetInfo Manager (path: `/Applications/Utilities/NetInfo Manager`) is the graphical interface to the NetInfo database. Using NetInfo Manager to examine some of the contents of your NetInfo database is the easiest way to see the hierarchical arrangement of the database.

When you first start NetInfo Manager, it should open to the local domain `/`. If it doesn't, open the NetInfo database on your machine by choosing Open under the Domain menu and selecting the domain `/`. This opens a window from which you can select a domain. If your machine is using the default configuration, the `/` domain is your only choice, as shown in Figure 20.1.

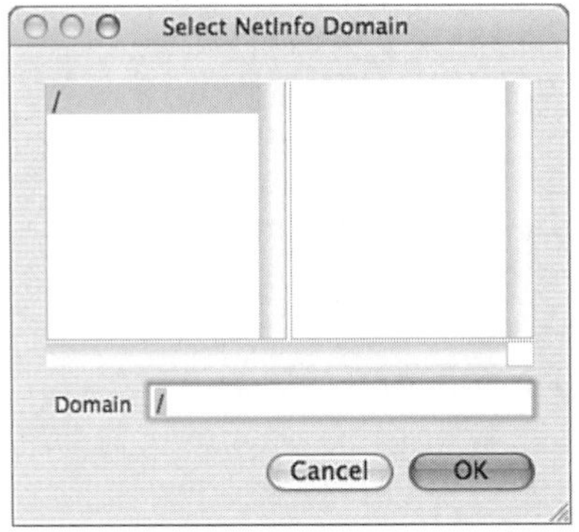

FIGURE 20.1 Opening your machine's NetInfo database from the top level.

Your machine's local NetInfo database also has the name, or tag, `local`. When you looked at the Domain menu, you might have noticed the option to Open by Tag. If you try to Open by Tag rather than Open, the dialog box shown in Figure 20.2 asks for the hostname or IP address and the NetInfo database tag. Possible entries you can use for your own host include its IP address, or `127.0.0.1`, or localhost. For the tag, enter `local`.

FIGURE 20.2 Opening your machine's NetInfo database by tag.

NOTE

If you are trying to serve a NetInfo domain to other machines in addition to your local domain, the NetInfo server should start automatically using the automatic configuration. If it does not, you can override this by changing `NETINFOSERVER=-AUTOMATIC-` to `NETINFOSERVER=-YES-` in `/etc/hostconfig`.

No matter which way you choose to open your NetInfo database, after you have it open, the result is the same except that how the name of the local database is displayed might vary. Figure 20.3 shows what you get if you choose to open your NetInfo database using Open and selecting the default domain. Here the name is displayed as `local@localhost - /`. In our case, the Open by Tag window displays the database as `local@127.0.0.1`.

As you can see in Figure 20.3, the hierarchical nature of the NetInfo database is immediately apparent. You see a directory browser in the top portion of a split view and a properties table in the bottom portion. In the leftmost column, it's in the top level, `/`. In the second column is a list of directories. If you scroll through the list, you'll see some of the types of information that the NetInfo database stores. In the bottom portion are the properties for a given directory. Figure 20.3 shows the properties for the `/` directory. We see that our machine is the master of its local database and that we could add a list of trusted networks.

Let's examine the NetInfo database using NetInfo Manager. If we click the `aliases` directory in the second column, more data appears in the third column. In the properties table, we see the property values for the `aliases` directory. It has only a property called `name` with a value of `aliases`. Yes, the `name` property is indeed the name of the directory. The third column displays the actual contents of the `aliases` directory. The hierarchical information appears directly above the directory browser.

Figure 20.4 shows where we are at this point. Note that above the second column, the one that shows the contents of `/`, is a `/`, and that above the third column, which shows the contents of `aliases`, is `aliases`.

FIGURE 20.3 The top level of your NetInfo database as seen in NetInfo Manager.

FIGURE 20.4 The third column shows the contents of the `aliases` directory. The bottom properties table shows any properties associated with the `aliases` directory.

If we click the postmaster directory in the third column, we see that we have reached the end of the hierarchy. What was the third column is now the second column. The third column has no data. The labels above the directory browser also show in addition to labeling the contents of a column. The bottom split view shows the properties of the `postmaster` directory. In addition to the `name` property, we see that the `postmaster` directory also has a `members` property with a value of `root`. What we learn from Figure 20.5 is that `postmaster` is aliased to `root`. The portion of the NetInfo database that we just looked at is what, in Unix machines, is usually stored in the file `/etc/aliases` or `/etc/mail/aliases`, depending on the system.

FIGURE 20.5 The bottom properties table shows the contents of the postmaster directory. The lack of data in the third column shows that we've reached the end of the hierarchy.

Let's look at something else in the NetInfo database. If we click groups in the left column, we see the same behavior we saw with the `aliases` directory. It has only a `name` property. Similar to the `aliases` directory, it has additional directories under it, as displayed in the third column. The third column has enough directories to have to scroll through the listing. If you scroll to the sshd group and click it, you'll see what's shown in Figure 20.6.

In Figure 20.6, we see that the `/groups/sshd` directory of the NetInfo database contains a `name` property with the value `sshd`, a `passwd` property with the value `*`, and a `gid` property with the value `75`. As you might have guessed, this is NetInfo's way of displaying information that would normally be stored in a file, `/etc/group`, on a typical Unix machine. Unlike the typical `/etc/group` file, though, the NetInfo database currently also includes entries for `generateduid` and `smb_sid`. For a group, the `generateduid` might involve the group's password. For typical Mac OS X users, the `generateduid` is associated with the storage of the user's password. The `smb_sid` entry involves Samba.

FIGURE 20.6 The contents of the `/groups/sshd` directory of the NetInfo database.

As you've have seen in your brief tour of the NetInfo database, the hierarchical nature of the database indeed becomes apparent when viewed in the NetInfo Manager.

Creating a Backup of the Local NetInfo Database

Because the NetInfo database is so important to maintaining the machine's internal world view, it's important for you to make backups of it periodically—especially if you're going to be doing experiments that you might not be able to back out of neatly. Without a properly functioning NetInfo system, Mac OS X is rendered almost inoperable. In Mac OS X 10.2 and earlier, NetInfo Manager provided a graphical way to make a backup of the database. However, starting with Mac OS X 10.3, NetInfo Manager no longer has this feature.

In the command line, you could use `cp` or `tar` to create your backup. The NetInfo database is in the directory `/var/db/netinfo/local.nidb`. When backing up the NetInfo database from the command line, Apple recommends making the backup in single-user mode.

Because the NetInfo database is stored as a collection of data files in a directory, you can make a backup of the NetInfo database either by copying the directory, or by `tar`ring the directory. Apple seems to prefer the recursive copy of the directory, but I find `tar`ring it into a single file to be more useful.

```
brezup:root ray # cd /var/db/netinfo/
brezup:root netinfo # cp -R local.nidb  local.nidb-backup
```

or

```
brezup:root netinfo # tar -cf local.nidb-backup.tar local.nidb
```

No matter which method you use to make your backup, remember to double-check `/var/db/netinfo` to verify that your backups agree with your actual NetInfo database:

```
brezup:root netinfo # ls -l local.nidb-backup
total 200
-rw-r--r--   1 root  wheel     4 Mar  7 09:30 Clean
-rw-r--r--   1 root  wheel     4 Mar  7 09:30 Config
-rw-------   1 root  wheel  5120 Mar  7 09:30 Store.1024
-rw-------   1 root  wheel  4224 Mar  7 09:30 Store.1056
-rw-------   1 root  wheel  1088 Mar  7 09:30 Store.1088
-rw-r--r--   1 root  wheel  4352 Mar  7 09:30 Store.128
-rw-r--r--   1 root  wheel  2880 Mar  7 09:30 Store.160
-rw-------   1 root  wheel   576 Mar  7 09:30 Store.192
-rw-------   1 root  wheel  2240 Mar  7 09:30 Store.224
-rw-------   1 root  wheel  1536 Mar  7 09:30 Store.256
-rw-------   1 root  wheel  6336 Mar  7 09:30 Store.288
-rw-------   1 root  wheel  4160 Mar  7 09:30 Store.320
-rw-------   1 root  wheel  2112 Mar  7 09:30 Store.352
-rw-r--r--   1 root  wheel  8832 Mar  7 09:30 Store.384
-rw-r--r--   1 root  wheel   832 Mar  7 09:30 Store.416
-rw-------   1 root  wheel   672 Mar  7 09:30 Store.672
-rw-------   1 root  wheel  1408 Mar  7 09:30 Store.704
-rw-r--r--   1 root  wheel  1056 Mar  7 09:30 Store.96


brezup:root netinfo # ls -l local.nidb-backup.tar
-rw-r--r--   1 root  wheel  71680 Mar  7 09:33 local.nidb-backup.tar
```

Versions of the NetInfo Manager utility that provide a graphical interface for creating backups created the same types of backups as can be created with `cp -R`. The default name under which the database was stored by the backup was `local.nibak`.

The NetInfo Manager Interface

Now that you've had a chance to explore NetInfo Manager, let's take a brief look at the NetInfo Manager interface itself. NetInfo Manager and the NetInfo database can seem so overwhelming at first that now is a good time to take a step back and look at the interface itself.

As you've seen throughout this chapter, many options are available under the menu items of NetInfo Manager. Because there are so many options, it can be easy to overlook the buttons that are included in the upper left of the NetInfo Manager window.

The buttons provide some useful shortcuts for some actions. Here are descriptions for the buttons, from left to right:

- **Create New Directory**, the button with a folder and a plus sign, is used to add a new subdirectory to the NetInfo database.
- **Duplicate Selected Directory**, the button with two folders, causes the selected folder to be duplicated. You might find this button particularly useful as you create more groups and some types of users.
- **Delete Selected Directory**, the button showing a circle with a slash in the middle, deletes the selected directory when clicked.
- **Open Parent Domain**, the button with an earth and an up arrow, causes NetInfo to move to the parent domain of the current domain. If your machine isn't part of a complicated network, you might not find much use for this button. For the typical user whose machine is only a part of its own local NetInfo domain, this button is grayed out.
- **Show Find Dialog**, represented by button containing a magnifying glass, is used to open the Find dialog box. You might find this button useful for searching the NetInfo database. Figure 20.7 shows the results of using Find on `software` in our NetInfo database.

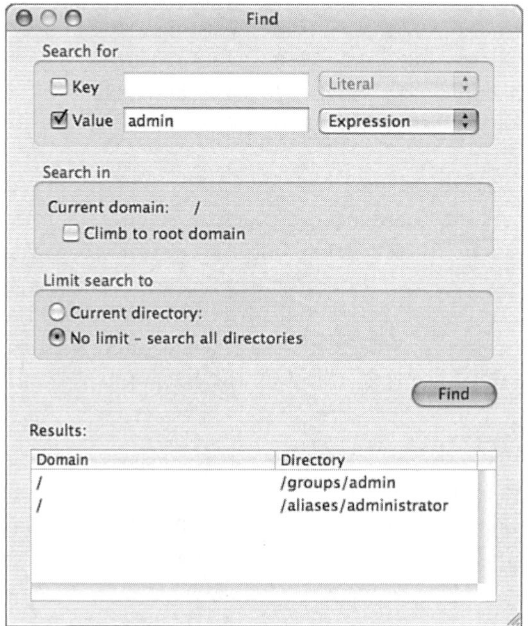

FIGURE 20.7 The Find button can be used to search the NetInfo database.

In addition to the buttons is the folder at the right that we mentioned earlier. The folder was originally used to indicate your present location in the NetInfo database. However, starting with the Mac OS X 10.2 release, that information is displayed above the directory browser in the upper splitview. The folder can be used to drag and drop directories for copying or moving them. The upper split view is where you navigate through the NetInfo database. The lower split view is where you view the contents of a specific directory in the NetInfo database.

Finally, you can control some aspects of the NetInfo Manager through its preferences. You can confirm modifications always or never. The default is always. Additionally, you can select what domain should be opened at startup. Choices are Local, None, or some other specific domain. The default is the local domain. Finally, within the browser itself, you can choose to display directory ID numbers or to display directories with no subdirectories as leaves. When you choose to display the directory ID numbers, you can see some of the same output you see when you run command-line tools. With the other option, you can more easily tell at a glance when a hierarchy ends.

Managing Users Through NetInfo

Although you can create and customize users using the Accounts System Preferences pane, there are some aspects about a user account that can only be customized directly in the NetInfo database, such as the group to which a user belongs.

Understanding Sane User Account Management

It can be very useful to add groups to your system for any logically collected groups of users on your system. The Unix privilege system underlying Mac OS X contains a mechanism to allow groups of users to mutually share access to files within their group, while protecting those files from other users on the same system.

To enable this capability, you must create groups for those users to belong to and you must add their usernames to the `users` value list of the group. A single user can be a member of an arbitrary number of groups and can assign files that he owns to be visible to any one of (or none of) the groups to which he belongs. To make use of this capability, the user must use the command-line group ownership tools discussed in Chapter 15, "Shell Configuration and Programming (Shell Scripting)."

Starting with the release of 10.3, Apple has chosen to follow an administrative philosophy that believes that it's easiest to create a new group for each and every user that's created, and to assign each user to belong, by default, to his own group. This has the advantage that it's easy to assign a small group of users to belong to the same group as some user `jim`, by simply assigning them to the group `jim`. In other words, it makes management of groups that relate to individuals relatively easy—]all of `jim`'s friends belong to group `jim`, and he can easily allow them privileged access to some of his files (although the administrator still must do the work of adding users to group `jim`— there's no current way for `jim` to do this himself).

Unfortunately, this administrative philosophy works well for managing a bunch of individuals, but it doesn't work well for managing things such as project groups or users that are otherwise logically grouped on the system into large "classes" of some sort. For this sort of system use, it's more convenient to have all users that belong to some project, or that have some grouped privilege class, to have the same default group. If an individual wants to have a group-of-friends-type group, `root` can always create an individual group for them as well as the general-class groups. Because `root` has to manually add "`jims` friends" to group `jim` in the new-group-for-each-user design, it's not really any more inconvenient to create additional per-user groups for those individuals who might want to have them when using the general-class group paradigm.

If you decide to dispose of Apple's new-group-for-each-user paradigm for management of your system, you'll want to create at least one general-user group in NetInfo, typically called `users`, into which you can assign users who don't logically seem like `staff` users. Apple's Accounts pane now creates users as members of their own individual groups, and you're welcome to leave them with these default groups, but we'll also show you how you can automate the creation of users and take control of the group assignment process later in the chapter.

On the other systems we run, we have a logical distinction between `staff` users and normal users, so we find it convenient to mirror this with our Mac OS X installations by creating a group to assign new, nonstaff users to. On our Mac OS X machines, we created this as `GID 99`, with group name `users`. We assume this value as a default in various other locations in this book.

NOTE

In more than a few years of managing clusters of Unix machines with aggregate hundreds of users, I don't think I've come across more than a handful of situations where using Apple's current new-group-per-user paradigm would have been helpful in managing users and groups. I've come across many more instances where using the old-style paradigm of assigning all nonadministrative users to the same `users` group, and then creating new specific groups as needed, was a better solution. If you're going to be housing only a small number of users on your system, Apple's method is probably fine, but if you'll have many users, I expect that you'd find limiting things to a smaller number of user groups to be beneficial.

Using the NetInfo Database to Customize a User

Now you've had the opportunity to examine the NetInfo database, back it up, and use several tools to modify it. In the previous section, you saw that changes could be made in the NetInfo database and a small sampling of how these changes interact with and provide information to other tools. We make use of that idea in this section, in which you learn how to customize a user account. We use the Accounts control panel to create a user, but we customize our user by editing information in the NetInfo database.

In our example, we create a user who we want to use as our general software user. This is a specialized user whose account we want to use when compiling software for the system, but we do not want this user to be one of the administrators for the machine. We want our user to belong to a group called `tire` with group ID `100`. We'd also like to have a specific user ID, `502`, for our user, whose account we intend to call `software`. To create this user, do the following:

1. Open the Accounts System Preferences pane. Click the lock icon if it's set not to allow changes. Add a new user with a short name of `software`. Our `software` user's name is `skuld`. Choose whatever password you prefer. Don't give your software user admin privileges.

2. Open NetInfo Manager and select the local domain if it's not already selected. Click the lock to make changes and enter the administrator username and password.

3. Click the `groups` directory and scroll through the list. Because `tire` is not a default group that comes with the system, you should not see a group called `tire`. Therefore, you must make a new group. Click any group to see what values are typically included in a group. Figure 20.8 shows the types of properties that belong to a group.

FIGURE 20.8 Typical properties for a group.

4. Click `groups`. From the Directory menu, select New Subdirectory. A new directory called `new_directory` appears. Edit the `name` property to have the value `tire`. Under the Directory menu, select either New Property or Insert Property to add other property and value pairs as follows:

Property	Value
`name`	`tire`
`passwd`	`*`
`gid`	`100`
`users`	`software`

The `*` in the password field means that a group password is not being assigned. So far, we have only one user in our group: the user named `software`. As the term *group* implies, we can have more than one user in a group. If you wanted to add more than one user to the group, select the `users` property and under the Directory menu, select New Value or Insert Value. Edit the new entry to include the additional user.

5. Select Save Changes from the Domain menu. A question to Confirm Modification appears. Click Update this copy. Now `new_directory` has become `tire`, as shown in Figure 20.9.

FIGURE 20.9 We now have a new group called `tire` with GID 100. At this time, only one user, `software`, belongs to the group.

6. Click `users` and then click `software`. Now the default information about user `software` appears in the bottom window. If this is one of your first users, UID 502 might already be the user ID; otherwise, you can change software's UID shortly. A group ID that is the same as the UID is probably what was made. If you look at the values section for `software`, you can see that the Accounts pane added quite a bit of information about `software` to the NetInfo database.

If software were not one of the first users on my system, I would already have a user with UID 502. Because of this, I would have to either change the UID of my original user or delete the user. If the original user were not an important user, such as a user created to run demonstration commands, rather than a real user who is using the machine, I would just delete the user. If I wanted to keep my user, I could change the UID of the original user to one that wasn't already taken, and then change the UID of software to 502.

NOTE

If I decided to rearrange UIDs instead of simply deleting the user, I would also have to change the ownership of all the files that belonged to my previous user to belong to their new UID. File ownerships are stored based on numeric UID. Changing a user to a previously used UID gives that user access to and ownership of any files that still belong to that numeric UID.

For your purposes, the user ID for software might not be important. Because we want to share some of our resources with another machine that also has a user called software and whose UID is 502, it's important for us to make software's UID 502 for compatibility purposes. In both cases, we want the user software to belong to group tire. Change the GID to 100. Change the UID as appropriate for your situation. Select Save Changes from the Domain menu and click Update this copy in the Confirm Modification box. Figure 20.10 shows the updated information for our user software.

FIGURE 20.10 Now our user software has UID 502 and GID 100. We can see from this information that user software has been assigned a password, a home directory in /Users/software, and a default shell of /bin/bash.

20

7. Click the lock to save your changes and end your ability to make further changes.
8. Open a Terminal window, go to software's home directory, and look at the directory's contents. Take note that the directory was created by the Users pane with the default values. The update to the information in the NetInfo database, however, was not entirely reflected in the system. So, you must manually implement those changes. First, here's the default information for the software user that was created on our system:

```
brezup:sage software $ ls -al
total 8
drwxr-xr-x   11 software  software  374 Mar  7 10:54 .
drwxrwxr-t    6 root      admin     204 Mar  7 11:04 ..
-rw-r--r--    1 software  software    3 Mar  7 10:54 .CFUserTextEncoding
drwx------    3 software  software  102 Mar  7 10:54 Desktop
drwx------    3 software  software  102 Mar  7 10:54 Documents
drwx------   17 software  software  578 Mar  7 10:54 Library
drwx------    3 software  software  102 Mar  7 10:54 Movies
drwx------    3 software  software  102 Mar  7 10:54 Music
drwx------    3 software  software  102 Mar  7 10:54 Pictures
drwxr-xr-x    4 software  software  136 Mar  7 10:54 Public
drwxr-xr-x    5 software  software  170 Mar  7 10:54 Sites
```

In our example, software's original UID was 502, which is still software's UID. Depending on what changes you had to make in the NetInfo database to get the desired UID, you would probably see the original UID number that belonged to software here rather than the username. If you didn't change your software user's UID, you should see software in that column, as shown here. The default GID that the Accounts pane used for creating software was GID 502, the same number as the UID, and has the same group name, software, as well. So, the information that we see for software's home directory is the information that was originally assigned to software. We have to update the information to software's directory to reflect the new information.

As root, or using sudo, in the /Users directory, change the ownership of software's directory to the software user in group tire:

```
brezup:sage Users $ sudo chown -R software:tire  software
Password:
```

Check the results:

```
brezup:sage Users $ ls -ld software
drwxr-xr-x   11 software  tire  374 Mar  7 10:54 software
brezup:sage Users $ ls -l software
total 0
drwx------    3 software  tire  102 Mar  7 10:54 Desktop
drwx------    3 software  tire  102 Mar  7 10:54 Documents
```

```
drwx------   17 software  tire  578 Mar  7 10:54 Library
drwx------    3 software  tire  102 Mar  7 10:54 Movies
drwx------    3 software  tire  102 Mar  7 10:54 Music
drwx------    3 software  tire  102 Mar  7 10:54 Pictures
drwxr-xr-x    4 software  tire  136 Mar  7 10:54 Public
drwxr-xr-x    5 software  tire  170 Mar  7 10:54 Sites
```

If you changed the UID of a user who was originally assigned UID 502, look at that user's home directory and make the appropriate ownership changes.

Enabling the root Account

As mentioned earlier, the administrator account is a powerful account. But the most powerful account on a Unix machine is the account called root. People also refer to root as the super user, but the account name itself is root. On most Unix systems, the first available account is the root account. In Mac OS X, however, the root account is disabled by default as a security precaution.

At some time, however, you might find it necessary to enable the root account. The root account can modify system settings, modify files it does not own, modify files that can't be written to by default, modify a user's password, install software, become another user without having to know the password of that account, and so on. In other words, root can do anything anywhere, making the power of root immense. Because root has so much power, the only users who can become root are users with administrative privileges. Because a user with administrative privileges can become the root user, you should assign these capabilities to only completely trusted individuals.

If you choose to enable the root account, remember to use it with caution. Although the root account might provide some extra utility, you could accidentally wipe out your system if you don't pay careful attention to what you type. In addition, the root password you choose should be difficult to guess. Finally, become the root user for only as long as necessary to complete the task at hand.

With the presence of an administrative user, it might be a long time, if ever, before you discover a need to enable the root user. You can take many approaches for dealing with the root user—from ways to use root without enabling the root account to actually enabling the root account.

Let's take a look at four different ways to gain root access to your system. Although you can choose whichever method you like, it's useful to understand that even though some of these methods appear to work magic, they all accomplish very much the same thing.

The root user is disabled because it does not have a valid password set. Because there are a number of ways to set a password, there are also several ways to enable root, including one method (the first method we'll look at) that was designed specifically for assigning the root account password and *only* the root password. In addition, you'll see how the sudo command can provide root-level access even when the root password is disabled. We recommend that users access the root account only when absolutely necessary.

Using the NetInfo Manager Utility

The NetInfo Manager Utility provides a graphical method for enabling the root user.

1. Start the NetInfo Manager utility and click the lock to make changes.
2. For Mac OS X 10.2 and later, select Enable Root User from the Security menu. For Mac OS 10.1 and 10.0, select Security from the Domain menu. Then choose Enable Root User from the submenu. Unless you've previously set a `root` password, a message appears with a NetInfo error indicating that the password is blank. Click OK.
3. Enter the `root` password you want to use and then click Set. Remember that the `root` password should not be easily guessable.
4. Enter the password again for verification and then click Verify.
5. Click the lock button again to prevent any further changes. Then close NetInfo Manager.

Figure 20.11 shows an example of what an enabled `root` account looks like in NetInfo Manager. Note that the password field no longer has a single `*` in it; instead it has a string of `*`s.

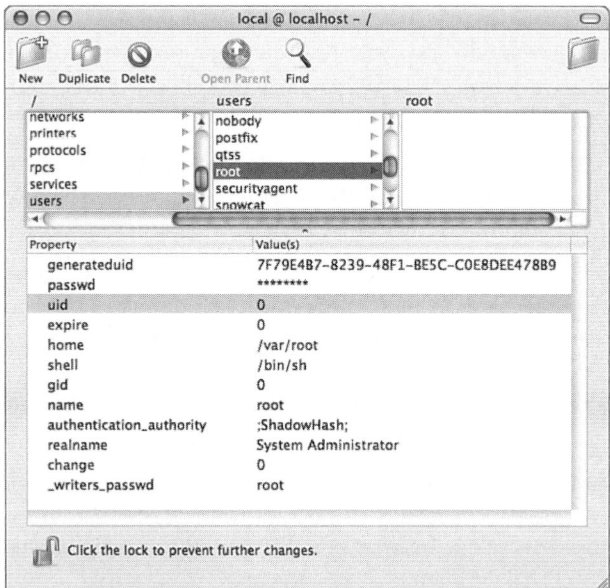

FIGURE 20.11 The `root` account has been enabled on this machine. Note the * that was in the password field has been replaced with several *s.

Using the Mac OS X Installation CD

Because the Mac OS X installation CD comes with an option to reset a user's password, you could use the installation CD itself to enable the `root` user.

To enable the root account using the Mac OS X installation CD, do the following:

1. Insert the Mac OS X CD.
2. With the CD in the CD-ROM drive, reboot the machine. Hold the C key while the machine reboots.
3. Wait for the Installer to appear and then select the Reset Password option under the Installer menu.
4. Select the Mac OS X disk that contains the root account you want to enable. If a spinning CD icon appears after you've chosen the Reset Password option, don't wait for the spinning to end to select your Mac OS X disk.

   The System Administrator (root) user appears as the default user in a pop-up menu that lists all the users.
5. Enter a new password and then reenter the password for verification. Click Save.

   Click OK when the Password Saved box appears.
6. Quit the Password Reset application, quit the Installer, and click Restart.

Using sudo to Enable the root Account

Recall that the sudo command is used to execute a command that root might execute. One way to enable the root account is to use sudo to execute passwd, which is a command used to change passwords.

Here's an example:

```
brezup:sage sage $ sudo passwd root
Password:
Changing password for root.
New password:
Retype new password:
brezup:sage sage $
```

The password that you initially enter is your password. Then you supply a password for root and reenter it for verification. If you mistype the password, you're prompted again, as shown in this example:

```
brezup:sage sage $ sudo passwd root
Password:
Changing password for root.
New password:
Retype new password:
Mismatch; try again, EOF to quit.
New password:
Retype new password:
brezup:sage sage $
```

Command-Line NetInfo Administration Tools

Not only does the NetInfo database have a graphical interface through the NetInfo manager, but there are also command-line tools for interacting with NetInfo. In this section, we will take a practical look at some of the tools by demonstrating the concept of using skeleton accounts to manage user accounts. Then we will take a brief look at other NetInfo command-line tools that you might find useful.

Creating Skeleton User Accounts

If you're going to have any significant number of users on your machine (or machines), you'll soon find that being able to provide a more customized environment than what comes out of the system Accounts control pane by default is a benefit.

Apple has provided a convenient method for you to perform some customization of accounts as created by the Accounts control pane. This is the inclusion of a `User Template` directory, from which the accounts made by the pane are created by duplication. The family of `User Template` directories, individualized by locale, are kept in `/System/Library/User Template`. This system works for simple configuration settings that you might like to configure for each newly created user, but it has some limitations if you want to work with more complex setups. The largest logical limitation is that if you're trying to set up complicated startup scripts and sophisticated environment settings, using a real user account as your default template is nice because you can log in for testing and tweaking. The largest practical limitation is that Apple has put the default templates in the `/System/` hierarchy, where they're Apple-sacrosanct, and system updates are likely to tromp on any customizations that you might make.

The easiest way to solve all the problems at once is to create a skeleton user account as a real user account, and to keep it up-to-date with any environmental customizations that you want to provide for new users when you create accounts. If you create the skeleton user as simply another user account, you can log in to it and then conveniently tweak its settings. Using this method, you can create as many skeleton accounts as you need for different collections of settings.

Even if you prefer to use the Accounts System Preferences pane, the creation of skeleton users as real users on the system can be useful. You can configure skeleton users who you can actually log in as and test their settings, and then populate the `/System/Library/User Template` directories (if you don't mind incurring the wrath of the Apple installers), as required for customizing the configuration of users under the Users pane in System Preferences. Alternatively, you can create the accounts with Apple's default templates and then overwrite the actual user directories with data from your skeleton account.

As covered in Chapter 9, "Accessing the BSD Subsystem," every user's shell environment is configured by the `.profile` and `.bashrc` files (if the user is using `bash`), or `.login` and `.cshrc` (if the user's using `tcsh` or `csh`) shell scripts in the user's home directory. You might also want to provide a more customized starter web page or assorted bits of default data or files in the user's home directory. If you're managing student or employee accounts, you might have basic application preferences that you want to come preconfigured. Consider the wealth of personal customizations that you put into your own account. There are certainly many that other users aren't going to be interested in, but there are also undoubtedly many that would be useful starting places for other users on your system. There is also a lot of work involved in putting these preferences together, so despite the extra work involved in making well-customized user templates, you could be saving many hours of work for your users if you can leverage the work you've already put into the system. If you have many users, this can be a real productivity enhancer and time saver.

After you've configured an account in the fashion you want your new users to have, the hard part is done. It would be nice to have a way to use this account directly from the Users pane as the seed for new accounts as they are created, but, unfortunately, we aren't so lucky yet. Instead, you have two options for how to use the starter account information. First, you can create a new user through the Accounts pane. After the account has been created, you can replace the user's home directory (that the Accounts pane created) with a copy of the skeleton account home directory.

Your other option is to ignore the Accounts pane and create a new user by duplicating an existing user node from the NetInfo hierarchy, making a copy of the skeleton account home directory for the new user's home directory, and then editing the copy of the NetInfo entry for the new user to reflect the correct information for that user.

The first option is probably easier for novice users, but the second has the benefit of being able to be done from the command line with `nidump` and `niload`, and therefore, of being automatable. Table 20.1 contains command documentation for `nidump`. Table 20.2 contains command documentation for `niload`.

For the rest of the discussion, it is assumed that you've created a skeleton account in which you have made any customizations that you want to install for all new users. The account `UID` is assumed to be `5002`, with a home directory of `/Users/skel` and a `GID` of `101`. It is also assumed that you've added the group `users` to your NetInfo `groups` directory, with a `GID` of `101` (we've previously used `99` for this group, but Apple's put a system group on that ID with 10.3), and that you want to use this `GID` for normal, nonprivileged users. If you prefer to use Apple's scheme of having every user in a different, unique group, this method is adaptable to that as well.

To implement the first method of providing local customization for a new user, follow these steps:

1. Create the new user with the Accounts pane. Make any necessary changes to the user's configuration, such as the default `GID`, using NetInfo Manager as shown in earlier chapters.

2. Become `root` (`su`, provide password).

3. Change directories to the skeleton user's directory (`cd ~skel`).

4. Tar the contents of the current directory, using the option to place the output on `STDOUT` (`tar -cf - .`) and then pipe the output of `tar` into a subshell. In the

subshell, cd to the new user's directory, and untar from STDIN (| (cd ~*<newuser-name>* ; tar -xf -)).

> **NOTE**
>
> If you've created preferences in the skeleton user's account that rely on resource forks, you'll want to use the ditto command instead of tar or read ahead to the note regarding hfstar.

5. Change directories to one level above the new user's directory (cd ~*<newusername>* ; cd ../).
6. Change the ownership of everything in the new user's directory to belong to the new user and, potentially, to the user's default group if it's not the same as the skel account default group (chown -R *<newusername>*:*<newusergroup>* *<newuserdirectoryname>*). We'll cover the complete documentation for chown at the end of this chapter.

For example, if you've just created a new user named jim, assigned to the group users with the Accounts pane/NetInfo Manager, and want to put the skel account configuration into jim's home directory, you would enter the following:

```
su (provide password)
cd ~skel
tar -cf - . | ( cd ~jim ; tar -xf - )
cd ~jim
cd ../
chown -R jim:users jim
```

If you'd rather create new users from the command line, either because you can't access the physical console conveniently or because you want to use what you know about shell scripting to automate the process, you can use the second method suggested earlier. You might find this method more convenient for creating users in a NetInfo domain other than localhost/local. The Accounts pane in the nonserver version of Mac OS X seems incapable of creating users in other NetInfo domains, and this makes using it for managing cluster users difficult.

> **CAUTION**
>
> This process creates a new user by manipulating the NetInfo database directly, so the cautions to back up your database frequently are important to remember here.

To implement the second method, follow these steps:

1. Become root (su, give password).
2. Change directories to the directory in which you want to place the new user's home directory (cd /Users, for example).

3. Make a directory with the short name of the user you're about to create (mkdir *<newusername>* to create a directory for a new user named *<newusername>*).

4. Change directories to the home directory of the skel account (cd ~skel).

5. Tar the contents of the current directory and use the option to place the output on STDOUT (tar -cf - .).

6. Pipe the output of the tar command into a subshell. In the subshell, cd to the new user's directory, and untar from STDIN (¦ (cd *<pathtonewuserdirectory>* ; tar -xf -). Note that you can't use ~*<newusername>* because *<newusername>* doesn't actually exist on the system yet.

7. Dump your skel account (UID 5002 here, remember) NetInfo entry, or some other user's entry, into a file that you can edit (nidump -r /name=users/uid=5002 -t localhost/local > ~/*<sometempfile>*). As an alternative to the uid search, you could specify the skel account with /name=users/name=skel.

8. Edit ~/*<sometempfile>*, changing the entries so that they are appropriate for the new user you want to create. You'll want to change at least _writers_passwd, _writers_tim_password, uid, _writers_hint, _writers_picture, gid, realname, name, passwd, and home. It's probably easiest to leave passwd blank for now.

NOTE

If you want to use the "unique group for every user" management paradigm that Apple has moved to (which frankly we think is a management nightmare), you'll want to change GID here as well.

9. Use niutil to create a new directory for the uid that you've picked for the new user (niutil -p -create -t localhost/local /name=users/uid=*<newuserUID>*; give the root password when asked). Table 20.3 shows the command syntax and some of the most useful options for niutil.

10. Use niload to load the data you modified in ~/*<sometempfile>* back into the NetInfo database (cat ~/*<sometempfile>* ¦ niload -p -r /name=users/uid=*<newuserUID>* -t localhost/local).

11. Set the password for the new user (passwd *<newusername>*;). Provide a beginning password—another BSD utility documented at the end of this chapter.

12. Change back to the directory above the new user's home directory (cd ~*<newusername>*; cd ../).

13. Change the ownership of the new user's directory to the new user's *<username>* and *<defaultgroup>* (chown -R *<username>*:*<usergroup>* *<newuserdirectory>*).

That might look like a lot of typing, but that's what shell scripts are for. If you have two users to create, that's a lot of typing. If you have 200 users, it's much less to type the script once and run it 200 times than to create each manually with the Accounts preferences pane and NetInfo Manager.

If you've made a mistake somewhere along the way, just restore your NetInfo database from the backup that you made before you started this. You also might need to find the `nibindd` process, and send it a `HUP` signal (`\ps -auxww ¦ grep "nibindd"; kill -HUP` *`<whatever PID belongs to nibindd>`*, or, `killall -HUP nibindd`, if you prefer to do things the easy way).

RESOURCE FORKS GET LOST IN THE TAR!

The version of `tar` distributed by Apple doesn't understand file resource forks, and some software vendors haven't caught on to the idea of using `plists` properly yet. The unfortunate consequence is that if you've built a highly customized skeleton user (or are trying to use this as an example to move a real user account), and some of the user's preferences are stored in the resource fork of the preference files, `tar` is going to make a mess of things when you use it to duplicate the user's directory to the new location.

To overcome this problem, you currently have two options:

- metaobject has developed `hfstar`, a GNUtar derivative that supports HFS+, allowing it to properly handle resource forks, type and creator codes, and so on. Because Apple is now distributing GNUtar instead of BSDtar, it's probably safe to do a straight-up replacement of Apple's `tar` with `hfstar` if you want (BSDtar and GNUtar have sufficient differences that outright replacement was not previously a good option).Instead of replacement, it would be better to keep both `hfstar` and Apple's `tar` around, just in case there turn out to be unexpected differences. Because metaobject has managed to get resource forks working with GNUtar, I'm hopeful that Apple will follow suit with an updated version of `tar`, obviating the need for replacement. metaobject's `hfstar` can be downloaded from `http://www.metaobject.com/Products.html`.
- Use Apple's already supplied `ditto` command. `ditto` doesn't provide nearly the power of `tar`, but it'll do for copying user directories. More information on `ditto` is provided in Chapter 29, "Maintaining a Healthy System."

To produce results similar to those from the earlier method, the following example creates a new user with the username of `james`, `UID 600`, `GID 70` (the web group `www`), with home directory `/Users/james`. This again assumes the `skel` account with `UID 5002` and characteristics as described earlier.

```
su (provide the password)
cd /Users
mkdir james
cd ~skel
tar -cf - . ¦ ( cd /Users/james ; tar -xf - )
nidump -r /name=users/uid=5002 -t localhost/local > ~/skeltemp
vi ~/skeltemp
```

and change the contents from this:

```
{
  "hint" = ( "" );
  "sharedDir" = ( "Public" );
```

```
  "_writers_passwd" = ( "skel" );
  "authentication_authority" = ( ";ShadowHash;" );
  "name" = ( "skel" );
  "home" = ( "/Users/skel" );
  "passwd" = ( "********" );
  "_writers_hint" = ( "skel" );
  "_writers_picture" = ( "skel" );
  "_shadow_passwd" = ( "" );
  "realname" = ( "Skeleton User" );
  "uid" = ( "5002" );
  "shell" = ( "/bin/bash" );
  "generateduid" = ( "66EA85A3-E1A9-11D7-9893-0030654C2E9C" );
  "gid" = ( "101" );
  "_writers_tim_password" = ( "skel" );
  "picture" = ( "/Library/User Pictures/Animals/Jaguar.tif" );
  "_writers_realname" = ( "skel" );
}
```

to this:

```
{
  "authentication_authority" = ( ";basic;" );
  "picture" = ( "/Library/User Pictures/Nature/Zen.tif" );
  "_shadow_passwd" = ( "" );
  "hint" = ( "boggle" );
  "uid" = ( "600" );
  "_writers_passwd" = ( "james" );
  "realname" = ( "Sweet Baby James" );
  "_writers_hint" = ( "james" );
  "gid" = ( "70" );
  "shell" = ( "/bin/bash" );
  "name" = ( "james" );
  "_writers_tim_password" = ( "james" );
  "passwd" = ( "" );
  "_writers_picture" = ( "james" ) ;
  "home" = ( "/Users/james" );
  "sharedDir" = ( "Public" );
}
```

Then run these commands:

```
niutil -p -create -t localhost/local /name=users/uid=600
(give the root password when asked)
cat ~/skeltemp ¦ niload -p -r /name=users/uid=600 -t localhost/local
(give the root password when asked)
passwd james (fill in a good starting value)
```

20

```
cd ~james
cd ../
chown -R james:www james (GID 70 is group www on this machine)
```

NOTE

Depending on whether your NetInfo daemon is feeling well, you might have to HUP the nibindd process to get it to recognize that you've made the change. Remember that you can always restore your NetInfo database backup to get out of a mess, if you've created one.

TIP

If you need to delete a user account from the command line, you can destroy the NetInfo information for the user by using the command niutil -p -destroy -t localhost/local /name=users/uid=<*userUIDtobedeleted*>. Then \rm -rf the user's home directory to delete it and all its contents from the system.

Just to make sure that your user has been created as you think it should have been, you can use niutil to list the /users NetInfo directory. (Don't be surprised if your listing doesn't look quite like this—this is simply the list of users configured on my machine, so your users are likely to be different.)

```
brezup:root Users # niutil -list -t localhost/local /users
11        nobody
12        root
13        daemon
14        unknown
15        lp
16        postfix
17        www
18        eppc
19        mysql
20        sshd
21        qtss
22        cyrusimap
23        mailman
24        appserver
25        clamav
26        amavisd
27        jabber
28        xgridcontroller
29        xgridagent
30        appowner
31        windowserver
32        tokend
33        securityagent
```

```
92        ray
94        software
97        skel
99        james
101       testme
```

As shown, `james` does now exist in the NetInfo `/users` directory, although this listing shows only the NetInfo node numbers, rather than the users and property values. To see whether `james` has the properties intended, you can use `niutil` to read the info from the node named `james`:

```
brezup:root Users # niutil -read -t localhost/local /users/james
hint: boggle
sharedDir: Public
_writers_passwd: james
authentication_authority: ;ShadowHash;
name: james
home: /Users/james
passwd: ********
_writers_hint: james
_writers_picture: james
_shadow_passwd:
realname: Sweet Baby James
uid: 600
shell: /bin/bash
gid: 70
_writers_tim_password: james
picture: /Library/User Pictures/Animals/Jaguar.tif
_writers_realname: james
```

James can now log in and functions just like a user that you created through the Accounts pane.

NOTE

Frankly, we can't figure out what some values in the output from the `nidump` of the user information are for, or whether they affect the system by being present, absent, or changed. Some of these, such as the `generateduid`, seem likely to change as Apple matures the password authentication system. This value, for example, is an artifact of the way that Apple's chosen to overcome a security vulnerability in earlier implementations of the NetInfo database. It doesn't seem to actually be used for anything (or, rather, it seem to be a unique hash value generated to match between the user's information in NetInfo and an encrypted password stored in a file; it seems, however, to be automatically generated and replaced as needed), and nothing seems to break if we remove it. Unfortunately, the root cause is that Apple's new user password storage system makes a portion of the user authentication information local to each machine, instead of allowing it all to be cleanly served from a remote server. This probably means that Apple will supercede this method, and that the requirement for this value will be changed when Apple implements some secure yet networkable scheme in the future.

TABLE 20.1 The `nidump` Utility Can Export NetInfo Data to Plain Text Formats

`nidump`	Extracts text or flat-file format data from NetInfo.
`nidump [-t] { -r` *<directory>* ¦ *<format>* `}` *<domain>*	
`nidump` reads the specified NetInfo domain and dumps a portion of its contents to standard output. When a flat-file administration format is specified, `nidump` provides output in the syntax of the corresponding flat file. Allowed values for *<format>* are `aliases`, `bootparams`, `bootptab`, `exports`, `fstab`, `group`, `hosts`, `networks`, `passwd`, `printcap`, `protocols`, `rpc`, and `services`.	
If `-r` is used, the first argument is interpreted as a NetInfo directory path, and its contents are dumped in a generic NetInfo format.	
`-t`	Interprets the domain as a tagged name.
`-r`	Dumps the specified directory in raw format. Directories are delimited in curly brackets. Properties within a directory are listed in the form `property = value;`. Parentheses introduce a comma-separated list of items. The special property name `CHILDREN` is used to hold a directory's children, if any. Spacing and line breaks are significant only within double quotes, which can be used to protect any names with meta characters.

TABLE 20.2 The Command Documentation Table for `niload`

`niload`	`niload` populates NetInfo directories with multiple properties at once.
`niload [-v] [-d] [-m] [-p] [-t] {-r` *<directory>* ¦ *<format>*`}` *<domain>*	
`niload` loads information from standard output into the specified NetInfo *<domain>*. If *<format>* is specified, the input is interpreted according to the flat-file format *<format>*. Acceptable values for *<format>* are `aliases`, `bootparams`, `bootptab`, `exports`, `fstab`, `group`, `hosts`, `networks`, `passwd`, `printcap`, `protocols`, `rpc`, and `services`.	
If `-r` *<directory>* is specified instead of a flat-file format, the input is interpreted as raw NetInfo data, as generated by `nidump -r`, and is loaded into *<directory>*.	
`niload` overwrites entries in the existing directory with those contained in the input. Entries that are in the directory, but not in the input, are not deleted unless `-d` is specified. `niload` must be run as the `superuser` on the master NetInfo server for *<domain>* unless `-p` is specified.	
`-v`	Verbose mode. Prints + for each entry loaded, and - for each entry deleted (flat-file formats only).
`-d`	Deletes entries that already exist in the directory, but that aren't duplicated in the input.
`-p`	Prompts for the `root` password of the given domain so that the command can be run from locations other than the master.
`-m`	Merge into an existing NetInfo structure instead of overwriting in the case of collisions.
`-u` *<user>*	Authenticates as *<user>*. Implies `-p`.
`-P` *<password>*	Provides *<password>* on the command line. Overrides `-p`.
`-t`	Interprets the domain as a tagged domain. For example, `trotter/network` refers to the domain `network` on the machine `trotter`. Machine name can be specified as an actual name or an IP address.

TABLE 20.2 Continued

`-r`	Loads entries in raw format, as generated by `nidump -r`. The first argument should be the path of a NetInfo directory into which the information is loaded. The specified directory may be renamed as a result of contents of the input, particularly if the input includes a top-level `name` property. If the specified directory does not exist, it is created.
<domain>	NetInfo *<domain>* that is receiving input. If `.` is the value for *<domain>*, it is referring to the local NetInfo database.

TABLE 20.3 The Syntax and Popular Options for `niutil`

`niutil`	The NetInfo Utility `niutil` is used to edit the NetInfo database.
`niutil -create [`*opts*`]` *<domain> <path>*	
`niutil -destroy [`*opts*`]` *<domain> <path>*	
`niutil -createprop [`*opts*`]` *<domain> <path> <key>* `[`*<val>*`...]`	
`niutil -appendprop [`*opts*`]` *<domain> <path> <key> <val>*`...`	
`niutil -mergeprop [`*opts*`]` *<domain> <path> <key> <val>*`...`	
`niutil -insertval [`*opts*`]` *<domain> <path> <key> <val> <index>*	
`niutil -destroyprop [`*opts*`]` *<domain> <path> <key>*	
`niutil -destroyval [`*opts*`]` *<domain> <path> <key> <val>*	
`niutil -renameprop [`*opts*`]` *<domain> <path> <oldkey> <newkey>*	
`niutil -read [`*opts*`]` *<domain> <path>*	
`niutil -list [`*opts*`]` *<domain> <path>*	
`niutil -readprop` *<domain> <path> <key>*	
`niutil -readval <domain> <path> <key> <index>`	
`niutil -rparent [`*opts*`]` *<domain>*	
`niutil -resync [`*opts*`]` *<domain>*	
`niutil -statistics [`*opts*`]` *<domain>*	
`niutil -domainname [opts]` *<domain>*	
`niutil` performs arbitrary reads and writes on the specified NetInfo *<domain>*. To perform writes, `niutil` must be run as `root` on the NetInfo master for the database, unless `-p`, `-P`, or `-u` is specified. The directory specified by *<path>* is separated by `/` characters. A numeric ID may be used for a path in place of a string. Property names may be given in a path with an `=`. The default property name is `name`. The following examples refer to a user with user ID 3:	
`/name=users/uid=3`	
`/users/uid=3`	
`-t` *<host>*`/`*<tag>*	Interprets the domain as a tagged domain. For example, `parrish/network` is the domain tagged network on machine `parrish`.
`-p`	Prompts for the `root` password or the password of *<user>* if combined with `-u`.
`-u` *<user>*	Authenticates as *<user>*. Implies `-p`.
Operations	
`-create` *<domain> <path>*	Creates a new directory with the specified path.
`-destroy` *<domain> <path>*	Destroys the directory with the specified path.

TABLE 20.3 Continued

`-createprop` *<domain>* *<path>* *<key>* [*<val>*...]	Creates a new property in the directory *<path>*. *<key>* is the name of the property. Zero or more property values *<key>* [*<val>*...] may be specified. The property is created empty if no *<val>*s are provided. If the named property already exists, it is overwritten.
`-appendprop` *<domain>* *<path>* *<key>* *<val>*...	Appends new values to an existing property in directory *<path>*. *<key>* is the name of the property. Zero or more property values *<key>* *<val>*... may be specified. If the named property does not exist, it is created.
`-insertval` *<domain>* *<path>* *<key>* *<val>* *<index>*	Inserts a new value into an existing property in the directory *<path>* at position *<index>*. *<key>* is the name of the *<key>* *<val>* property. If the named property does not exist, it is created.
`-destroyprop` *<domain>* *<path>* *<key>*	Destroys the property with name *<key>* in the specified *<path>*.
`-destroyval` *<domain>* *<path>* *<key>* *<val>*	Destroys the specified value in the property named *<key>* in the specified *<path>*.
`-read` *<domain>* *<path>*	Reads the properties associated with the directory *<path>* in the specified *<domain>*.
`-list` *<domain>* *<path>*	Lists the directories in the specified *<domain>* and *<path>*. Directory IDs are listed along with directory names.
`-readprop` *<domain>* *<path><path>* *<key>*	Reads the value of the property named *<key>* in the directory of the specified *<domain>*.
`-readval` *<domain>* *<path>* *<key>* *<index>*	Reads the value at the given *<index>* of the named *<key>* property in the specified directory.
`-rparent` *<domain>*	Prints the current NetInfo parent of a server. The server should be explicitly given using the `-t` *<host>*/*<tag>* option.
`-statistics` *<domain>*	Prints server statistics on the specified *<domain>*.
`-domainname` *<domain>*	Prints the domain name of the given domain.

Additional Interesting NetInfo Command-Line Utilities

In the previous section, we showed you the NetInfo utilities we find to be the most useful. In this section we will look at `nifind`, `nigrep`, and `nireport`. Another utility that you might find useful, but we will not document, is `nicl`. It is another general NetInfo utility that you can use to perform activities similar to what we did in the previous section. Its most interesting feature is that it has an interactive mode for communicating with the NetInfo database.

The `nifind` utility, documented in Table 20.4, can be used to find a directory ID in the NetInfo database. For example, to see what the directory ID of the software user is, we could run

```
brezup:ray ray $ nifind -a /users/software
/users/software found in ., id = 94
```

This was information that we were also able to find by having `niutil` list the entire `/users` directory, but if you need the directory number for something, `nifind` is a convenient way to get it. You can also have `nifind` print the contents of the directory that it finds with the `-p` option, much like having `niutil` read a specific directory.

TABLE 20.4 The Command Documentation Table for `nifind`

`nifind`	Finds a directory in the NetInfo hierarchy.
`nifind [ -anvp ] [ -t <timeout> ] <directory> [ <domain> ]`	
`nifind` searches for the named directory in the NetInfo hierarchy. It starts at the local domain and climbs up through the hierarchy until it reaches the root domain. Any occurrences of directory are reported by directory ID number. If the optional *<domain>* argument is given, `nifind` stops climbing at that point in the hierarchy. The *<domain>* argument must be specified by an absolute or relative domain name.	
`-a`	Searches for *<directory>* in the entire NetInfo hierarchy.
`-n`	Exempts local directories from the search.
`-p`	Prints directory contents.
`-t <timeout>`	Specifies an integer value to use as the connection timeout.
`-v`	Produces verbose output.

You can search for patterns in the NetInfo database by using `nigrep`, documented in Table 20.5. To find out which users have the pattern `ja`, you could run:

```
brezup:ray ray $ nigrep ja . /users
27 /users/jabber:  name jabber
27 /users/jabber:  _writers_passwd jabber
99 /users/james:  _writers_passwd james
99 /users/james:  name james
99 /users/james:  home /Users/james
99 /users/james:  _writers_hint james
99 /users/james:  _writers_picture james
99 /users/james:  _writers_tim_password james
99 /users/james:  _writers_realname james
```

TABLE 20.5 The Command Documentation Table for `nigrep`

`nigrep`	Searches for a regular expression in the NetInfo hierarchy.
`nigrep <expression> [ -t ] <domain> [ <directory> ... ]`	
`nigrep` searches through the specified *<domain>* argument for a regular expression. It searches the domain's directory hierarchy depth-first starting from the root directory. It can also start from each directory specified on the command line.	
On output, `nigrep` prints the directory ID number of the directory that contains the regular expression, and the property key and values where it was found. A line is printed for each property that contains the regular expression.	
`-t`	Specifies the *<domain>* as a network address or a hostname and a tag.

Perhaps the most interesting of the utilities in this section is `nireport`, whose documentation is in Table 20.6. This utility can be used to provide much nicer views of the data contained in the NetInfo database.

Where you might use `niutil` to list the `/users` directory and then use it again to read properties in certain subdirectories, you could just use `nireport` to generate a table listing of all the properties you are interested in seeing from the subdirectories in `/users`. To quickly see the `uid` and `gid` for users, you could run:

```
brezup:ray ray $ nireport . /users name uid gid
nobody  -2      -2
root    0       0
daemon  1       1
unknown 99      99
lp      26      26
postfix 27      27
www     70      70
eppc    71      71
mysql   74      74
sshd    75      75
qtss    76      76
cyrusimap       77      6
mailman 78      78
appserver       79      79
clamav  82      82
amavisd 83      83
jabber  84      84
xgridcontroller 85      85
xgridagent      86      86
appowner        87      87
windowserver    88      88
tokend  91      91
securityagent   92      92
ray     501     501
software        502     100
skel    5002    101
james   600     70
testme  601     70
```

TABLE 20.6 The Command Documentation Table for `nireport`

`nireport`	Prints tables from the NetInfo hierarchy.
`nireport [ -t ] <domain> <directory> [ <property> ...]`	
`nireport` prints a table of values of properties in all subdirectories of the directory given on the command line. Multiple values of a property are printed in a comma-separated list.	
`-t`	Specifies *`<domain>`* as a network address or hostname and tag.

Using and Sharing Disk Resources with NFS

In this section, we demonstrate ways that your Mac OS X machine can share resources with other Unix machines using NFS, the Network File System. We demonstrate two ways to set up your Mac OS X machine as an NFS client and one way to use it as an NFS server.

A Common Way to Set Up the Tiger NFS Client

In this section, we demonstrate a common method for setting up an NFS client on a Mac OS X machine. We show you this method because you will regularly see references to this type of code, for this and other NetInfo-related activities, on the Internet. Sometimes this type of method is the only method you can choose, so you need to be familiar with it. Sometimes, though, an alternative method might work better. For your Mac OS X machine to be a client machine, there has to be another Unix machine that is an NFS server. In other words, there has to be a Unix machine (Mac OS X or another flavor of Unix) on your network that is willing to export one of its filesystems to your Mac OS X machine. So, you cannot just set up your machine as a client and assume that everything will work fine. Discuss your interest in being able to use your Mac OS X machine to access a filesystem on another Unix machine with that machine's system administrator. There is a security risk involved, particularly for the other machine, when it shares its resources with your machine. Therefore, in that machine's interest, the system administrator might not be willing to export its filesystems to your machine.

There might be some additional details to work out with your NFS server system administrator that we will not discuss in depth here, assuming that he feels you will responsibly control your machine and your use of the NFS server's resources. To avoid confusion on the remote host machine, it would be a good idea for users who are accessing the other machine's filesystem from your machine to have the same user and group IDs that they might already have on the remote host machine. Depending on how the remote host is set up, this might be no problem at all or a considerable annoyance. For example, if the remote host does not have user IDs in the same range as the users on your machine, the unusual user IDs might not be a problem. However, if users on your machine have user IDs in the same range as users on the remote host, files you create on the remote host with your user ID will be viewed by the remote host as being owned by the user native to that system—that is, by whatever user lives on that system and has the same user ID.

At any rate, if the system administrator of the remote machine agrees to export to your machine whichever filesystem you are interested in using, be aware that you still might have to work out some additional details with the system administrator. NFS gives both the client and server considerably more control over exactly how resources are shared (down to details such as how long to wait for a disk to become available again, if the network goes away) than a "point and mount" protocol such as AppleTalk/AppleShare. As your understanding of how to update the NetInfo database continues to improve in this chapter, any changes the system administrator of the remote host might request for your Mac OS X machine should not be difficult to make.

With that said, let's continue to the details of setting up an NFS client on your Mac OS X machine. To be an NFS client, your machine must be running the right services. If you did not turn off any of the major default services, you do not need to worry about this. If you turned off NFS in the /System/Library/StartupItems/ directory, you have to turn it back on to be able to run your NFS client.

NOTE

You're not supposed to need to change these settings, but if your experience is like ours, the AUTOMATIC setting for NFSLOCKS specified in /etc/hostconfig won't actually work automatically for you. To get things working, we needed to edit /etc/hostconfig and set both of this to YES.

It would also be a good idea to read the man pages for mount, mount_nfs, and fstab. The information that you will be adding to the NetInfo database is information regarding where your machine should mount a particular filesystem that resides on a remote host. When you are finished updating the NetInfo database, the remote host's filesystem appears to be local to your own machine.

We include the syntax and primary options for the mount and mount_nfs commands in tables at the end of this section. A complete discussion of how to fully use all the power of NFS is the entire subject of more than one book.

CAUTION

You might need to disable the automounter to get your machine to properly mount NFS directories. This is accomplished by changing the setting in /etc/hostconfig to NO. This change was not necessary under 10.1.x versions of Mac OS X and, based on some information on the Internet, is not the case for all users of 10.2 and 10.3. However, we have seen several machines where the behavior of NFS is pathologically wrong when the automounter is enabled. The symptoms of the problem are

- The directory to which you attempt to mount the remote filesystem is deleted and replaced by a symbolic link to a directory in the /automount/ directory.
- The directory in the /automount/ cannot be entered, lsed, or otherwise read, but mount claims that the remote directory is mounted.
- The remote directory cannot be unmounted without rebooting the machine; you might also find that any attempt to read the supposedly mounted directory (even just trying to get its name to autoexpand at the command line using <TAB>) causes your shell to hang indefinitely.

If you experience these problems and still want to use NFS, disable the automounter by changing its YES entry to NO in /etc/hostconfig, and reboot your machine. With automount off, NFS should work in much more the fashion that the documentation suggests.

AUTOMOUNTER ANTIFANS

We aren't big fans of the automounter (/usr/sbin/automount). Even when it's working, it seems like the wrong thing to do. The automounter is supposed to be this magical (or at least poorly documented) utility that remembers filesystems that have been previously mounted and remounts them automatically whenever they're needed. The problem with this idea, other than the fact that in our cumulative 40-odd years of using Unix we've never seen a nontrivial system using `automount` where `automount` actually worked the way anyone wanted it to, is that `automount` removes control from the machine's administrator. You want to mount a directory of data under `/usr/local/data/`? The automounter, in all its wisdom, will insist on mounting it under `/automounter/` and making a symbolic link to its mount point. Have software that won't work through a symbolic link? Tough. What's worse, on some systems, after it's seen a filesystem once, the automounter will keep mounting (or trying to mount) that filesystem forever, even after you've removed the control definition and tried to make it stop. With the exquisite level to which we're used to being able to configure and control our hardware, this behavior is simply unacceptable for a Unix machine.

No, we aren't fans of the automounter at all, and we generally have it turned off on our systems just as a matter of principle. We won't tell you that you have to turn it off, and for lack of documentation, we aren't even sure what unusual twists Apple might have woven into its version. To make NFS work at all on the machines we tested 10.2 with, the automounter had to be turned off. We haven't had much trouble with 10.3, but it's been enough of a problem that we just don't trust it, so our examples are going to be based on the assumption that it's turned off. Some people make `automount` work on their machines and are happy with how it works, so you very well might be able to make these examples work or manage a setup in your own preferred configuration without shutting off `automount`. If you can, wonderful—perhaps `automount` just hates us old curmudgeons.

To add a filesystem from a remote host to your Mac OS X machine, do the following:

1. Back up your NetInfo database.
2. Plan where you want your Mac OS X machine to mount the remote host's filesystem. Unlike what you might be familiar with on AppleShare volumes, which mount as "drives" on the desktop, NFS filesystems can be grafted into your directory tree anywhere. Essentially, the directory structure rooted at the directory or file system that is exported can be made to appear exactly as it does on the remote host, as though it were any subdirectory of your choosing on your system.

   The purpose of the remote filesystem might guide you in deciding where to mount it on your machine. For example, it is common, when a filesystem with a users' home directories are involved, that a machine mounting such a filesystem frequently does so in a directory hierarchy of `/net/<remote_host>/home`. If the remote filesystem is simply a filesystem used for storage, any way you want to mount it is probably suitable. Temporary mounts that you don't expect to reuse later are frequently done as subdirectories of `/mnt/`. Of course, you can change the name of the mount point and remount the filesystem later if you find that you do not like what you picked. Extra thought up front is particularly important, though, when the remote filesystem is used for users' home directories because more people than just yourself will need to know about and understand any changes that you make later on down the road.

   In our example, we are going to mount a filesystem used for storage. On our machine, we want it to be mounted in a directory called `/morespace/mother` (`mother` is the name of the host that will serve the filesystem). We're creating the mount point in a subdirectory of the `root` directory, rather than directly in the `root` directory, because we might eventually want to add other storage filesystems from other remote hosts, and we want to be able to keep them straight. Another consideration would be a hierarchy similar to typical user hierarchies, such as `/net/<remote_host>/morespace`. If it's the only filesystem of its type that'll be mounted, there's no real need to have the mount point clearly include the host of origin.

After you have decided what to call the mount point, make it—mount points are simply directories. They don't even have to be empty if you want the directory to contain one set of files when you have the remote system mounted and another when it's not. (A particularly nifty option available in the Mac OS X NFS client, `union` filesystems, allows you to see the files in both the local and remote directories simultaneously. See the `mount_nfs` docs for more information.)

```
brezup:root ray # cd /
brezup:root / # mkdir morespace
brezup:root / # mkdir morespace/mother
brezup:root / # ls morespace/mother
brezup:root / #
```

3. Using your favorite text editor, create a file with the contents of the following form:

```
{
"opts" = ( "w" );
"dir" = ( "/<mountpoint>/" );
"name" = ( "<remote_host>:<remote_filesystem>");
"vfstype" = ( "nfs" );
}
```

Save it with Unix line endings rather than Mac line endings. Check again, to make sure that you really did.

Although many options are available for mounting, the one you will probably find most important initially is the read/write option—after you've got that working, tweaking the nearly endless variety of options to customize the connection can be done at your leisure. On most systems, that option is `rw`. In Mac OS X, that option is `w`, although using the traditional `rw` also appears to work.

Here is a copy of the file we used:

```
{
"opts" = ( "w" );
"dir" = ( "/morespace/mother" );
"name" = ( "192.168.1.4:/innerspace");
"vfstype" = ( "nfs" );
}
```

`/morespace/mother` is where I want the remote filesystem to appear, `192.168.1.4` is the machine (also known as `mother`) serving it to me, and on `mother`, the directory that I'll be mounting is named /innerspace. I've named this file mount-test.txt, and it's in my current directory.

4. Run niutil to create a new directory in the mounts directory of the NetInfo database:

```
brezup:root / # niutil -create . /mounts/new1
```

The new1 directory name is not important; it's going to be overwritten by information we're going to load into the database.

5. Run niload to load the file into the NetInfo database:

```
brezup:root / # niload -r /mounts/new1 . < mount-test.txt
```

Notice that because you're providing a name and value in the data you're loading, the niload command renames the new1 subdirectory you just created. If you type as well as we do, you might have to run that statement a few times before it works. You might get messages indicating that there is an error at some line number in your input file. Just look at your file carefully and fix whatever needs to be fixed (especially, watch for things such as having saved the file with Mac line endings rather than Unix line endings).

6. Look at the updates in the mounts section of the NetInfo database either using the command line or the NetInfo Manager. If you are using the command line, you might find it easier to see the values by directory number rather than directory name.

Here are the command-line results in our example as seen using niutil:

```
brezup:root / # niutil -list . /mounts
82       192.168.1.4:/innerspace
brezup:root / # niutil -read . 82
opts: w
dir: /morespace/mother
name: 192.168.1.4:/innerspace
vfstype: nfs
```

7. After you have verified that the updates to your NetInfo database are correct, tell your machine to mount the filesystem, and take a look at what's happened:

```
brezup:root / # ls /morespace/mother/
brezup:root / #
brezup:root / # mount -t nfs -a
brezup:root / # ls /morespace/mother/
apache_1.3.26                    tcpwrappers
apache_1.3.26-src.tar            wu-ftpd-2.6.1-linux-anon
danspage                         wu-ftpd-2.6.1-linux-anon.tar.gz
fcsafiles                        wu-ftpd-2.6.1-linux-both
ftpaccess-mother-anon            wu-ftpd-2.6.1-linux-both.tar.gz
.
```

20

```
.
.
```

Suddenly, there's data in /morespace/mother/. However, it's not actually in /morespace/mother/; it's actually on the remote machine 192.168.1.4. This machine is only on the other side of the room, but there's no reason it couldn't be on the other side of the country.

At this point, you're supposed to be able to reboot your machine, and it should automatically mount that filesystem back up, without you needing to use the mount command. If your automounter is turned on, it'll definitely try (and it'll probably delete your /morespace/mother/ mount point for you while it tries). With automounter turned off, it doesn't appear that Apple takes the customary action of having a mount -t nfs -a command in its startup scripts, so you might need to add your own custom startup script to run mount for you.

When you get this working at startup, or if automount is working for you, it might seem as if it takes your machine a little longer to reboot. This is to be expected.

TIP

If you later notice that it's suddenly taking a lot longer to start up, it might be because the NFS server that you've been mounting is not available. Depending on the options you configure, this can cause your machine to hang indefinitely. Such indefinite hangs aren't inevitable, however; check the man pages for the details regarding retries and under what conditions clients should allow a mount to fail.

In addition to using mount to mount filesystems, you can run mount to see what is mounted where:

```
brezup:root / # mount
/dev/disk1s3 on / (local, journaled)
devfs on /dev (local)
fdesc on /dev (union)
<volfs> on /.vol
/dev/disk0s9 on /Volumes/Racer-9 (local)
/dev/disk0s10 on /Volumes/Racer-X (local)
/dev/disk0s11 on /Volumes/Wills_Data (local)
/dev/disk0s12 on /Volumes/Software (local)
/dev/disk0s13 on /Volumes/Temp (local)
192.168.1.4:/innerspace on /morespace/mother
```

The df command also tells you a bit about your mounts:

```
brezup:root / # df
Filesystem              512-blocks     Used   Avail Capacity  Mounted on
/dev/disk1s3              9715208  9093872  524184    95%    /
```

```
devfs                      196      196       0   100%    /dev
fdesc                        2        2       0   100%    /dev
<volfs>                   1024     1024       0   100%    /.vol
/dev/disk0s9           1258104   994768  263336    79%    /Volumes/Racer-9
/dev/disk0s10         10484800  9073632 1411168    87%    /Volumes/Racer-X
/dev/disk0s11         12581856 12147328  434528    97%    /Volumes/Wills_Data
/dev/disk0s12         10484800  8255520 2229280    79%    /Volumes/Software
/dev/disk0s13          4255160  3333520  921640    78%    /Volumes/Temp
192.168.1.4:/innerspace 799494   677500   80716    89%    /morespace/mother
```

Before we go on, let's look a little more closely at the directory that's coming from the `mother` server. Some of the things that you see with `ls` might be slightly unexpected:

```
brezup:root / # ls -l /morespace/mother/
total 150318
drwxr-xr-x  9 ray       ray          1024 27 Jun  2002 apache_1.3.26
-rw-r--r--  1 ray       ray       9728000 20 Jun  2002 apache_1.3.26-src.tar
drwxr-xr-x  7 software  wheel        1024 26 Jul  1999 danspage
drwxr-xr-x  2 ray       wheel        1024 23 Feb  2000 fcsafiles
-rw-r--r--  1 root      wheel        1918  4 Dec  2001 ftpaccess-mother-anon
-rw-r--r--  1 root      wheel        2046  4 Dec  2001 ftpaccess-mother-w2ftp
drwxr-xr-x  2 ray       ray          1024 23 Aug  2002 ispell
-rw-r--r--  1 ray       ray      14239859 28 Apr  2002 j2re-1_3_1_01-linux-i386-rpm
-rw-r--r--  1 root      wheel    14363657  8 Aug  2001 jre-1.3.1_01.i386.rpm
-rw-r--r--  1 18940     101      29388800 15 Nov  2002
➥krb5-1.2.7-i686-pc-linux-gnu.tar
-rw-r--r--  1 18940     101           303 15 Nov  2002
➥krb5-1.2.7-i686-pc-linux-gnu.tar.gz.asc
.
.
.
drwxr-xr-x  8 ray       10           1024  4 Dec  2001 wu-ftpd-2.6.2-linux-anon
-rw-r--r--  1 root      wheel      956301  4 Dec  2001
➥wu-ftpd-2.6.2-linux-anon.tar.gz
drwxr-xr-x  8 ray       10           1024  4 Dec  2001
➥wu-ftpd-2.6.2-linux-w2ftp
-rw-r--r--  1 root      wheel      956309  4 Dec  2001
➥wu-ftpd-2.6.2-linux-w2ftp.tar.gz
-rw-r--r--  1 600       software   351958  4 Dec  2001 wu-ftpd-2.6.2-src.tar.gz
```

20

Notice how some of the files don't have proper owners and/or groups, and instead show only numeric `UID` and `GID` entries. This is because I don't have the `user` and `groups` list synchronized between these machines. `mother`'s a Linux box that sits in the kitchen and runs my home network, so I have a few users on it that match, but I do most of my work on my Mac OS X laptop. Because of this, I've configured `mother` so that the main user IDs and groups that I use on both machines match, but a number of users on each machine are unique to that system. The `UID/GID` matching for mounted directories is done based on the numeric value of the `UID` and `GID`, so the shared users appear to own their own files, but the nonshared users and groups coming from `mother` have no analogous users on my Mac OS X laptop, so they only show up as numbers. As a matter of fact, from NFS's point of view, there's really no guarantee that `mother` doesn't think that the numeric `UID` that my laptop knows as `ray` is really named `fred`. And from my laptop's point of view, it really doesn't care what `mother` thinks the usernames are; it's just showing names based on what its NetInfo users list says goes with the numeric `UID`s and `GID`s that `mother`'s reporting for the files.

In addition to listing and looking at statistics about the remote filesystem, you can of course now access the remote filesystem as if it were local to your machine.

As mentioned earlier, you might have to work out some details with the system administrator of the remote machine. One of the details you might have to work out is making sure that there is a directory on that filesystem that you are allowed to write to. In our example, there is a public directory on the remote filesystem that we are allowed to use. The `mount` options can be configured to allow all users writing access, only some users, only some users to only some directories, and an assortment of other useful combinations.

An Easier Way to Set Up an NFS Client in Mac OS X

As you might recall from the section on adding a printer through the command line, the `niload` command can recognize some regular Unix flat-file formats. The format we saw earlier, `printcap`, is one of them. It turns out that the file that controls mount points, `fstab`, is another of those formats.

We recommend that, where possible, you use `niload` in combination with formats it might already recognize rather than have it load in raw NetInfo format. Because the Unix flat-file formats are easier to type, you will make fewer typing errors. In addition, if you take the time to familiarize yourself with the regular Unix flat files, you will be even better prepared to understand information that relates to other Unix platforms. Even though the traditional formats are options for your system, most of the rest of the Unix-using world is comfortable with them and will give advice and suggestions using these formats. When you've loaded data from a file in a traditional control format into NetInfo, always take the time to check the information that's landed in the NetInfo database, not only to confirm that everything was done properly, but also to learn the native Mac OS X formats.

In this section, we show you an easier way to enter the mounts information into the NetInfo database than the one we used for `/morespace/mother/`. Although this is easier, be aware that you still have to coordinate with the system administrator of the remote host.

To set up an NFS client on a Mac OS X machine, you can also do the following:

1. Back up the NetInfo database.
2. Create the local mount point for the remote filesystem.

3. Create a one-line file containing the mount information. The one-line file has these fields, which can be separated by spaces or tabs:

Field	Value
1	Remote filesystem to be mounted, including the machine it's being mounted from. The syntax is as shown earlier: `<machine>:<directory to mount>`.
2	Local mount point.
3	Filesystem type (for NFS, it's `nfs`).
4	`mount` options.
5	Interval between dumps.
6	Order in which `fsck` is run at boot time.

Fields `5` and `6` are traditional parts of the format but do not apply to remote filesystems. Those values can either be absent or can be `0`.

Here is the `fstab` used in this examples—note that we can use `rosalyn` as the server name here instead of a fully qualified domain name (complete hostname) because this machine is in the same domain as `rosalyn`, and we have configured this domain as a local search domain via the Network control pane. You might need to use either a FQDN or an IP address for the server, depending on your configuration:

```
rosalyn:/space /extraspace  nfs rw 0 0
```

4. Run `niload` to load the `fstab` format file into the NetInfo database. In our example, we used `fstab-test` as the `fstab` formatted file:

```
brezup:root / # niload fstab . < fstab-test
```

Verify that the data was loaded properly into the NetInfo database using either the command line or the NetInfo Manager.

5. Mount the filesystem with `mount -t nfs -a`, and check your results as previously demonstrated.

Run the same sorts of command-line tools you ran in the previous section, such as `mount` and `ls`. If your automounter is working for you, you might also want to check the list of volumes on your Mac OS X desktop, and/or the `/Computer/Network/Servers` path in the Finder, because you will hopefully find a pleasant surprise there, too. Behavior here seems inconsistent, and what mount points will be seen as remote servers and what won't are still a bit of a mystery to us.

> **NOTE**
>
> Any changes you make to the NFS mounts by tweaking the NetInfo database and manually running `mount` are available immediately via the command line. If you want to make the NFS mounts available via the Finder immediately as well, you might have to reboot after making your changes to the mounts in the NetInfo database. There's undoubtedly a process or two that could be restarted to cause the Finder to recognize the existence of the new network disk resources, but we haven't made this work reliably yet. Restarting is slow, but bulletproof.

Table 20.7 shows the syntax and most useful options for `mount`, and Table 20.8 covers `mount_nfs`, the underlying command that `mount` calls. Table 20.9 covers `umount`.

TABLE 20.7 The `mount` Command Syntax and Important Options

`mount`	Mounts filesystems.
`mount`	
`mount [-adfruvw] [-t ufs ¦ lfs ¦ `*<external_type>*`]`	
`mount [-dfruvw] `*<special>*` ¦ `*<node>*	
`mount [-dfruvw] [-o `*<options>*`] [-t ufs ¦ lfs ¦ `*<external_type>*`] `*<special>*` ¦ `*<node>*	
`mount` invokes a filesystem-specific program to prepare and graft the *<special>* device or remote node (`rhost:path`) on the file system tree at the point *<node>*. If neither *<special>* nor *<node>* is specified, the appropriate information is taken from the `fstab` file.	
The system maintains a list of currently mounted filesystems. If no arguments are given to `mount`, this list is displayed.	
`-a`	All the filesystems described in your NetInfo `mounts` directory or `fstab` control file are mounted. Exceptions are those marked as `noauto` or are excluded by the `-t` flag.
`-r`	Mounts the filesystem read-only (even `root` may not write to it). The same as the `rdonly` subargument to the `-o` option.
`-u`	Indicates that the status of an already mounted filesystem should be changed. Any of the options available in `-o` may be changed. The filesystem may be changed from read-only to read-write or vice versa. An attempt to change from read-write to read-only fails if any files on the filesystem are currently open for writing unless `-f` is also specified.
`-v`	Enables verbose mode.
`-w`	Sets the filesystem object to read-write.
`-t ufs ¦ lfs ¦`*<external_type>*	Specifies a filesystem type. Default is type `ufs`. The option can also be used to indicate that the actions should be performed only on the specified filesystem type. More than one type may be specified in a comma-separated list. The prefix `no` added to the type list may be used to specify that the actions should not take place on a given type. For example, `mount -a -t nonfs,mfs` indicates that all filesystems should be mounted except those of type NFS and MFS. `mount` attempts to execute a program called `mount_XXX` where `XXX` is the specified typename.

TABLE 20.7 Continued

`-o`	Specifies certain options. The options are specified in a comma-separated list.
The following options are available for the `-o` option:	
`noauto`	Skips this filesystem when `mount` is run with the `-a` flag.
`nodev`	Does not interpret character or block special devices on the filesystem. The option is useful for a server that has filesystems containing special devices for architectures other than its own.
`noexec`	Does not allow the execution of any binaries on the mounted filesystem. This option is useful for a server containing binaries for an architecture other than its own.
`nosuid`	Does not allow `set-user-identifier` or `set-group-identifier` bits to take effect.
`rdonly`	Same as `-r`. Mounts the filesystem read-only. Even `root` may not write to it.
`union`	Causes the namespace (that is, the files that appear there) at the `mount` point to appear as the union of the mounted filesystem `root` and the existing directory. Lookups are done on the mounted filesystem first. If operations fail due to a nonexistent file, the underlying filesystem is accessed instead. All new files and directories are created in the mounted filesystem.
Any additional options specific to a given filesystem type may be passed as a comma-separated list. The options are distinguished by a leading `-`. Options that take a value have the syntax `-`*<option>*`=`*<value>*.	

TABLE 20.8 The `mount_nfs` Syntax and Important Options

`mount_nfs`	Mounts NFS filesystems.
`mount_nfs [-23KPTUbcdilqs] [-D `*<deadthresh>*`] [-I `*<readdirsize>*`] [-L `*<leaseterm>*`] [-R `*<retrycnt>*`] [-a `*<maxreadahead>*`] [-g `*<maxgroups>*`] [-m `*<realm>*`] [-o `*<options>*`] [-r `*<readsize>*`] [-t `*<timeout>*`] [-w `*<writesize>*`] [-x `*<retrans>*`] `*<rhost>*`:`*<path>* *<node>*	
`-T`	Uses TCP transport instead of UDP. This is recommended for servers not on the same LAN cable as the client. This is not supported by most non-BSD servers.
`-U`	Forces the `mount` protocol to use UDP transport, even for TCP NFS mounts. Necessary for some old BSD servers.
`-b`	Backgrounds the `mount`. If a `mount` fails, forks a child process that keeps trying the `mount` in the background. This option is useful for a filesystem not critical to multiuser operation.
`-c`	Does not perform a `connect` for UDP mounts. This must be used for servers that do not reply to requests from the standard NFS port number 2049. It might also be required for servers with more than one IP address if replies come from an address other than the one specified in the `mount` request.

TABLE 20.8 Continued

`-d`	Turns off the dynamic retransmit timeout estimator. This might be useful for UDP mounts that exhibit high retry rates; it is possible for the dynamically estimated timeout to be too short.
`-i`	Makes the `mount` interruptible. The filesystem calls that are delayed due to an unresponsive server fail with `EINTR` when a termination signal is posted for the process.
`-s`	Soft `mount`. Filesystem calls `fail` after *<retrycnt>* round-trip timeout intervals.
`-R` *<retrycnt>*	Sets the retry count for doing the mount to *<retrycnt>*.
`-a` *<maxreadahead>*	Sets the read-ahead count to *<maxreadahead>*. This value may be in the 0–4 range, and determines how many blocks are read ahead when a large file is being read sequentially. A value larger than `1` is suggested for `mount`s with a large bandwidth * delay product.
`-o` *<options>*	Options are specified as a comma-separated list of options. See `mount` for a listing of the available options.
`-r` *<readsize>*	Sets the `read` data size to *<readsize>*. It should normally be a power of 2 >= 1024. This should be used for UDP mounts when the fragments dropped due to timeout value are getting large while actively using a `mount` point. Use `netstat -s` to get the fragments dropped due to timeout value. See the `-w` option.
`-t` *<timeout>*	Sets the initial retransmit timeout to *<timeout>*. Might be useful for fine-tuning UDP mounts over networks with high packet loss rates or an overloaded server. Try increasing the interval if `nfsstat` shows high retransmit rates while the filesystem is active, or try reducing the value if there is a low retransmit rate but long response delay observed. Normally the `-d` option is also used when using this option to fine-tune the timeout interval.
`-w` *<writesize>*	Sets the write data size to *<writesize>*. See comments regarding the `-r` option, but using the fragments dropped due to timeout value on the server rather than the client. The `-r` and `-w` options should be used only as a last resort to improve performance when mounting servers that do not support TCP `mount`s.
`-x` *<retrans>*	Sets the retransmit timeout count for soft `mount`s to *<retrans>*.

TABLE 20.9 The Syntax and Primary Options for `umount`

`umount`	Unmounts filesystems.
`umount [-fv]` *<special>* ¦ *<node>*	
`umount -a ¦ -A [-fv] [-h` *<host>*`] [-t` *<type>*`]`	
`-f`	Forcibly unmounts the filesystem. Active special devices continue to work, but all other files return errors if further accesses are attempted. The root filesystem cannot be forcibly unmounted.
`-v`	Enables verbose mode.
`-a`	All the filesystems described in `fstab` are unmounted.

TABLE 20.9 Continued

`-A`	All the currently mounted filesystems except the root are unmounted.
`-h` *<host>*	Unmounts only filesystems mounted from the specified *<host>*. This option implies the `-A` option and, unless otherwise specified with the `-t` option, will only unmount NFS filesystems.
`-t` *<type>*_	Is used to indicate that actions should be taken only on filesystems of the specified *<type>*. More than one type may be specified in a comma-separated list. The list of filesystem types can be prefixed with `no` to specify the filesystem types for which action should not be taken. For example, the `umount` command `umount -a -t nfs,mfs` unmounts all filesystems of the type NFS and MFS.

Serving NFS on Tiger

As the prices of IDE storage continue to drop, the absolute necessity to share disk space is disappearing. Still, it's often convenient if you can share your files and disk space to other machines you use, so that work you do on one is available on all. If you are interested in serving one of your filesystems to another Mac OS X machine, AppleShare might be good enough for some purposes, but NFS works for serving data to any Unix machine. Because we find NFS to be both more powerful and more complicated to get right, and AppleShare to be almost completely automated by the single check box in the Sharing system pane, we'll detail exporting your filesystems as NFS resources. However, if you are interested in powerfully exporting via AppleShare, you might take a look at SharePoints, available at `http://www.hornware.com/sharepoints/`.

Just as setting up your machine to be an NFS client requires coordination with the system administrator of the remote Unix machine, so does serving a filesystem to a remote Unix machine. Remember, this reduces security on both systems, especially yours. Do not consider doing this unless you can trust the remote host.

Depending on the system setups, coordination between user IDs might be necessary, especially if you want to make the drive available to users other than yourself. The other system administrator should be able to guide you through any additional details that might need to be coordinated.

The other Unix system administrator will set up the remote host to be able to mount your filesystem. You will have to set up your machine to export a filesystem to a remote host. At this time, you should read the `exports` man page.

If you plan to create your exports through the command line, you might want to take this opportunity to look at the `nidump` command as well. As the name suggests, `nidump` dumps information from the NetInfo database to standard output. It can dump information to a flat file in a number of traditional Unix configuration file formats. It can also dump information in a format that can be read back into and understood by the NetInfo database. This format is both more general and less conveniently human-readable than the typical Unix flat configuration-file format. Because it's a generalized format that works for any NetInfo data, it can be used to import data for directory structures that don't have an analogous Unix flat-file format. To learn more about this format, you might find running `nidump` on one of the NetInfo directories that you know something about to be a useful way of seeing the syntax used to create a new directory and directories under it.

Here is what the `nidump` output from the `mount` examples in the previous section looks like:

```
[localhost:~] software% nidump -r /mounts .

{
  "name" = ( "mounts" );
  CHILDREN = (
    {
      "vfstype" = ( "nfs" );
      "passno" = ( "0" );
      "dir" = ( "/extraspace" );
      "dump_freq" = ( "0" );
      "name" = ( "rosalyn:/space" );
      "opts" = ( "w" );
    },
    {
      "opts" = ( "w" );
      "dir" = ( "/morespace/mother" );
      "name" = ( "1921.68.1.4:/innerspace" );
      "vfstype" = ( "nfs" );
    }
  )
}
```

Not only does `nidump` provide an example of the syntax used to create a directory and subdirectories, but, as we saw with skeleton user accounts section, the output from a `nidump` command can also provide the basis for a file that you could edit for setting up your exports. This would already provide much of the complicated part of the syntax and enable you to just edit values suitable for exports instead.

To set up your Mac OS X machine to export a filesystem to a remote Unix host, do the following:

1. Back up the NetInfo database.
2. If you plan to export a filesystem that currently contains a space in the name, change its name to something that does not have a space. Mac OS and Mac OS X deal with spaces okay, but they confuse many more traditional Unix systems. If you're only going to be working among Mac OS X systems, spaces might be all right, but you'll probably find that they will eventually be trouble. The same goes for most characters outside basic alphanumerics.
3. Enter `exports` information into the NetInfo database. Unfortunately, despite what the man page says, the `niload` command currently does not understand the typical

exports format. So, in this case, you cannot make an exports format file and load that into NetInfo. You must either make a file that follows the same kind of format you saw in the first mount example (the format with braces, parentheses, and quotes), or you must enter the information into the NetInfo database using the NetInfo Manager.

Because I am so poor at balancing all the appropriate characters, parentheses, and quotes needed to make one of the raw NetInfo files, I prefer to do this through the NetInfo Manager. Our instructions are specifically for the NetInfo Manager. However, you should choose whichever method you are most comfortable with.

Open the NetInfo Manager, and select the `local` domain. Click in the lock to make changes, and enter the administrator username and password. With the root (/) directory selected, select Directory, New Subdirectory from the menu. Change the name of `new_directory` to `exports`, and save the change.

4. Click the `exports` directory. Select Directory, New Subdirectory from the menu. Give this subdirectory the name of the filesystem you want to export. Save it. Now select the new directory and add a `clients` property whose value is a list of clients that the filesystem should be exported to—use `insert value` with the `clients` property selected to add multiple client values. Add an `opts` property with any options you want to specify, based on the `exports` man page—`ro` is common if you want the filesystem to be read-only to remote clients that mount it, whereas `rw` allows read-write access. `alldirs` allows clients to mount arbitrary subdirectories from the filesystem instead of the whole filesystem.

   Figure 20.12 shows the settings that we used for exporting our filesystem. Note that you should not use the `maproot` mapping option we used, *`maproot=root`*, unless you can trust the remote system and administrator as highly as you trust your own.

5. Save your changes to the `exports` directory and then restart the NetInfo servers for your local domain. Click the lock to prevent further changes.

6. Reboot the machine and then test the results. Alternatively, you can (as `root`) run `SystemStarter start NFS` (or, if you've already got NFS exports and are just making changes, `SystemStarter restart NFS`).

   A quick test that you can do on your Mac OS X machine is to run `mount`:

```
brezup:ray ray $ mount
/dev/disk1s3 on / (local, journaled)
devfs on /dev (local)
fdesc on /dev (union)
<volfs> on /.vol
/dev/disk0s9 on /Volumes/Racer-9 (local)
/dev/disk0s10 on /Volumes/Racer-X (local)
/dev/disk0s11 on /Volumes/Wills_Data (local)
/dev/disk0s12 on /Volumes/Software (local)
/dev/disk0s13 on /Volumes/Temp (NFS exported, local)
rosalyn:/space on /extraspace
192.168.1.4:/innerspace on /morespace/mother
```

FIGURE 20.12 Here are the settings we used for exporting our `/Volumes/huge` filesystem.

Note that the Mac OS X machine indicates that `/Volumes/huge` is being served as an NFS export as well as mounted locally.

Another quick test that you can run shows what clients your volume is exported to:

```
brezup:ray ray $ showmount -e
Exports list on localhost:
/Volumes/huge                       192.168.1.13
```

Now you need to add your machine to the remote machine's mount list. If the remote machine is a Mac OS X machine, this is just like adding the `morespace` or `extraspace` mount points we used in earlier examples. If the remote machine is a Linux box or another form of Unix box, the administrator needs to add an `fstab` line similar to what we used to load the `extraspace` mount into our NetInfo database. Here, we're mounting `brezup`'s `/Volumes/Temp` on `rosalyn`, a Sun Solaris machine at the mount point `/net/brezup/huge`. After the mount point has been defined, run `mount -t nfs -a` on the remote machine.

Test that the remote host agrees with the Mac OS X machine:

```
Rosalyn joray 87 > ls /net/brezup/huge
AppleShare PDS          TheFindByContentFolder   osx-misc.tar
Desktop DB              TheVolumeSettingsFolder  test
Desktop DF              Trash                    â¢T+â¢It's HUUUGE
Desktop Folder          lpd-spool-working.tar
```

If we check the filesystem locally, we find the same `ls` listing:

```
brezup:ray ray $ ls /Volumes/huge
AppleShare PDS              TheFindByContentFolder     osx-misc.tar
Desktop DB                  TheVolumeSettingsFolder    test
Desktop DF                  Trash                      ???T+???It's HUUUGE
Desktop Folder              lpd-spool-working.tar
```

NOTE

Notice the file with the weird characters in the name in each listing. They appear to be different because the character sets used by the two machines aren't quite the same, and neither one can display that name properly—it has Macintosh special characters in it.

When you are satisfied that the export is working properly, remember that your machine is now serving data to another machine. Consequently, it might seem as if it takes a little longer for it to shut down at shutdown or reboot time. Do not panic. This is expected. If you plan for your exported filesystem to be of regular use, try to keep the number of reboots to a minimum. After your machine has started serving data to another machine, it is not just your machine or a machine for your local users—it is a machine that users on a remote host could come to rely on.

Table 20.10 shows the syntax and primary configuration options of `exports` entries.

TABLE 20.10 The Syntax and Primary Configuration Options for `exports` Settings

`exports`	Defines remote mount points for NFS requests.
The `exports` file specifies remote mount points for NFS mount protocol per the NFS server specification.	
In a `mount` entry, the first field specifies the directory path within a server filesystem that clients can mount. There are two forms of this specification. The first form is to list all `mount` points as absolute directory paths separated by whitespace. The second form is to specify the pathname of the root of the filesystem followed by the `-alldirs` flag. This form allows hosts to mount at any point within the filesystem, including regular files if the `-r` option is used in `mountd`. The pathnames should not have any symbolic links, or `.` or `..` components.	
The second component of a line specifies how the filesystem is to be exported to the host set. The options specify whether the filesystem is exported read-only or read-write and how the client UID is mapped to user credentials on the server.	
The third component of a line specifies the client host set. The set may be specified in three ways. The first is to list the hostnames separated by whitespace. Standard Internet dot addresses may be used instead. The second way is to specify a netgroup, as defined in `netgroup`. The third way is to specify an Internet subnetwork using a network and network mask.	
Export options are as follows:	
`-maproot=user`	Credential of the specified user is used for remote access by `root`. The credential includes all groups to which the user is a member on the local machine. The user may be specified by name or number.

TABLE 20.10 Continued

`-mapall=user`	
`-r`	Synonym for `-maproot` for backward compatibility with older export file formats.
When neither `-maproot` nor `-mapall` is specified, remote accesses by `root` result in a credential of `-2:-2`. All other users are mapped to their remote credential. If a `-maproot` option is given, remote access by `root` is mapped according to the specified value instead of `-2:-2`. If `-mapall` is given, the credentials of all users, including `root`, are mapped as specified.	
`-ro`	Specifies that the filesystem should be exported read-only.

If the basic ways available to you in Mac OS X for sharing resources seem a bit overwhelming, you might be interested in a shareware product called NFS Manager, available at `http://www.bresink.de/osx/`. It provides GUI interface controls for both NFS `mounts` and `exports`. Figure 20.13 shows a sample of the interface. At the time of this writing, some portions of it seem to rely on the automounter running, so if you've shut off yours, you might be able to use NFS Manager to create configurations, but you'll need to `mount` them manually at the command line. On the other hand, some people are happy with it running hand-in-hand with the automounter, so this could be a good option for you as well. It's also handy for the exploratory purpose of fiddling with settings and then examining the NetInfo database to see exactly what it's done to configure a mount point or export.

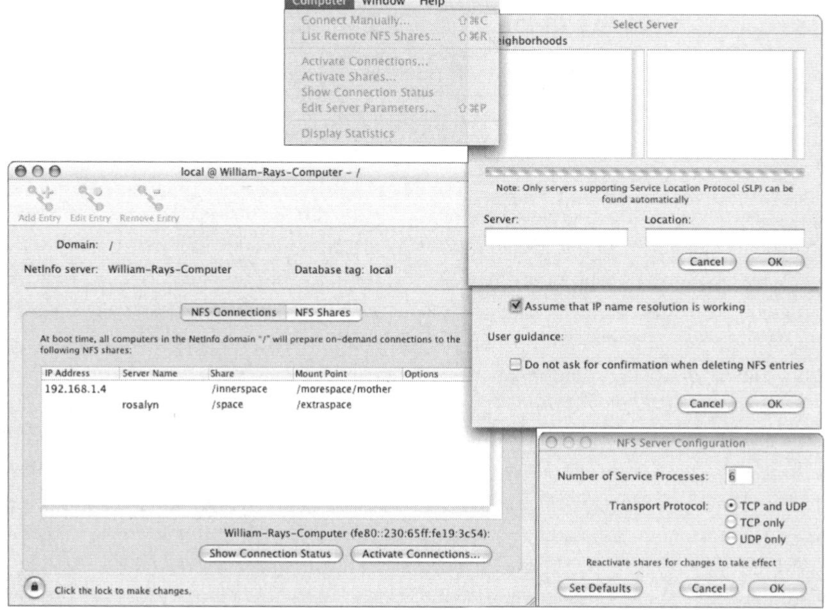

FIGURE 20.13 Here is a sample of what the interface for the shareware product NFS Manager looks like. It can manage both `mount` and `exports` configuration.

Summary

In this chapter we looked at using NetInfo Manager to manage the NetInfo database. We customized users by editing the NetInfo database, and explored the idea of using a skeleton user account to add users via NetInfo command line utilities. We also saw that the NetInfo database also stores information on sharing NFS resources. We learned how to set up our Tiger machine to either subscribe to an NFS resource and/or to serve a resource via NFS.

CHAPTER 21

Accessing and Controlling Tiger Remotely

IN THIS CHAPTER

- Remote Access and Security-Minded Thinking
- Running Shells and Commands Remotely Using SSH
- Accessing Mac OS X Remotely Using Apple Remote Desktop

Apple advertises that with Mac OS X, you now have the power of Unix. With the power of Unix also come some unfamiliar security issues. Many Unix machines run various types of services, such as Telnet, that increase your machine's vulnerability to attacks from crackers. In general, crackers are interested in either wiping your machine or installing a packet sniffer that saves passwords transmitted on your network for future devious uses. To keep your machine most secure, you should not hook it up to the Internet. That solution is rather impractical in an age in which Internet communication is one of the many reasons why people buy computers. Therefore, it becomes your responsibility to pay attention to security issues, if not for yourself, for the other machines on your network.

Fortunately, Apple realizes that Macintosh users are not used to worrying about security issues. In fact, Macintosh users have always had the luxury of knowing that their Macintosh is practically impenetrable. So, unlike some Unix operating systems, Mac OS X ships with all the services turned off. You have to decide, as you start using your machine more, which services, if any, you should try to turn on. Remember that the more services you turn on, the more vulnerable your machine becomes.

In this section, we will look at the Secure Shell suite and Apple Remote Desktop as ways to access and control your machine remotely.

Remote Access and Security-Minded Thinking

Although Chapter 28, "Implementing Server Security and Advanced Network Configuration," goes into security details in considerably more depth, it's a good idea to start thinking about security issues now. In this chapter, you're going to configure your machine so that you can connect to it from other machines. If you can connect to it, so can anyone else, and it's time to start thinking about security. Here are some common sense guidelines that you can use when thinking about your machine's security:

- Regularly apply updates to the operating system. It is common for the Unix vendors to fix security problems and make the fixes available as downloadable updates, usually called *patches*.
- Do not turn on any unnecessary services. If you don't know what the service is, you probably don't need it.
- Do not turn on the `telnet` service. `telnet` transmits passwords in clear text. That is exactly what some of the crackers are looking for.
- Restrict as many of the TCP-based services as possible with `xinetd`'s access attributes or with TCP Wrappers.
- Use secure shell *(SSH)* for remote logins to your machine.

It is the last item, secure shell, that we will discuss in depth in this chapter. You were first introduced to the secure shell software via `slogin`, in Chapter 13, "Using Common Command-Line Applications and Application Suites." In that chapter, you learned how to use `slogin` on your Mac OS X box to connect to outside machines as well as how to use `scp` and `sftp`. In this chapter, we will look at secure shell basic and advanced use and available clients.

Running Shells and Commands Remotely Using SSH

With the Secure Shell suite of utilities you can access your machine remotely via a shell or, if you need to transfer files, via its `scp` and `sftp` features.

What Is Secure Shell?

SSH, also known as *secure shell*, is a protocol for secure remote login, file transfer, and tunneling. It can be used as a secure replacement for the more familiar `telnet` and `rlogin` protocols without any noticeable difference to the user. For file transfers, SSH can be used as a secure replacement for `rcp` and `ftp`. Finally, SSH can be used to tunnel traffic over an encrypted channel. In other words, SSH can be used to transport otherwise insecure traffic more securely. For example, it can be used to encrypt the username and password data transmitted by `ftp`.

SSH is a more secure protocol than the traditional protocols because it encrypts traffic. The other protocols transmit data in clear text, which can then be captured by packet sniffers.

There are two versions of the SSH protocol: SSH1 and SSH2. As you might have guessed, SSH1 is the original version and SSH2 is a later development. The SSH2 protocol is the version currently being developed, although fixes are occasionally released for SSH1 because it is still in use.

The SSH protocol was first developed by Tatu Ylonen in 1995. In that same year he also founded SSH Communications Security and currently serves as its president and CEO. SSH Communications Security offers commercial and free versions of its SSH server and client products. The company originally sold products through another company called Data Fellows, which is now F-Secure. F-Secure has marketing rights for SSH and also sells SSH servers and clients. Both companies work on further developing SSH2.

There is also an SSH open source project called OpenSSH. This is the SSH distribution that Apple includes with Mac OS X. It is also based on Tatu Ylonen's early SSH code. OpenSSH provides support for both SSH1 and SSH2 protocols. There is little noticeable difference in using the SSH servers from one of the companies and from the OpenSSH package.

Because the OpenSSH package is included with Mac OS X, it is the package on which we will concentrate our discussion. Mac OS X 10.4 includes OpenSSH 3.8.1p1.

Activating the SSH Server

If you are just interested in connecting from your Mac OS X machine to another machine running an SSH server, you do not need to activate the SSH server on your machine. However, if you want to be able to access your Macintosh from a remote location, consider turning on the SSH server. To activate the SSH server, check the Remote Login box in the Services section of the Sharing pane.

Behind the scenes, this removes the disabled lines from `/System/Library/LaunchDaemons/ssh.plist` and loads the `ssh` service in `launchd`. The server listed in `ssh.plist` is a script called `/usr/libexec/sshd-keygen-wrapper`, which ultimately runs `/usr/sbin/sshd`. The file also shows that `sshd` is started in `inetd` compatibility mode. Whenever someone connects to the machine via SSH, an SSH server for that session is started. When the user logs out, the session is terminated. In early releases of Mac OS X, an SSH server ran all the time and started `sshd` processes for each login. With Mac OS X 10.3, Apple started running `sshd` out of `xinetd`.

Working with SSH Utilities

The SSH suite provides utilities for making terminal connections, transferring files, tunneling connections and public key authentication. In this section, we will take a look at each of the different types of SSH utilities. Table 21.1 includes a listing of the primary utilities available in OpenSSH.

TABLE 21.1 Primary Utilities in OpenSSH

Utility	Description
`sshd`	SSH server.
`ssh`	SSH client.
`sftp`	An interactive secure file transfer program.

TABLE 21.1 Continued

Utility	Description
`scp`	A copy program for copying files between hosts.
`sftp-server`	SFTP server subsystem started automatically by `sshd`.
`ssh-keygen`	A utility that generates keys for public key authentication.
`ssh-agent`	Authentication agent that manages keys for public key authentication users so that they don't have to enter a passphrase when logging in to another machine. It starts at the beginning of an X11 session or `login` session, and windows and programs start as its children.
`ssh-add`	Utility that adds keys to the `ssh-agent`.

Making Terminal Connections with `ssh/slogin`

SSH provides for secure encrypted traffic transmission across a network. Most SSH software, including that provided by Apple, includes both the encrypted transmission facility and rudimentary tools for making use of that functionality. These tools include the ability to use the encryption to provide secure terminal services and file transfer support. Other functionality can be added as needed by the user, by using just the secure transport portion of the software to encrypt the traffic between otherwise insecure external software packages.

A common use for the SSH package is for making remote terminal connections. Although you can set a number of options to `ssh` in a user configuration file, you will probably find yourself using `ssh` with command-line options initially. This is actually the easiest way to start using `ssh`. After you have been using `ssh` with command-line options for a while, you will get a feel for what options, if any, you may want to specify in either `~/.ssh/config` or `/etc/ssh_config`.

To use the `ssh` client, you can either run `ssh` or `slogin`. If you are used to using `rlogin` on a system, `slogin` will be the natural choice for you. Otherwise, you probably won't have any preferences.

The most commonly used syntax for `ssh` is

```
ssh <username>@<remote_host>
ssh -l <username> <remote_host>
```

To quickly test that `sshd` works on your machine, it is easiest to log in to your own machine, as shown here:

```
creampuf:~ nermal$ slogin 192.168.1.200
The authenticity of host '192.168.1.200 (192.168.1.200)' can't be established.
RSA key fingerprint is f4:2f:a4:46:16:0c:d1:de:f2:88:d6:83:b1:26:b0:52.
Are you sure you want to continue connecting (yes/no)? yes
Warning: Permanently added '192.168.1.200' (RSA) to the list of known hosts.
Password:
Welcome to Darwin!
creampuf:~ nermal$
```

Note that the first time you try an ssh action to a remote host, you are told that the remote machine's identity can't be verified, and you are asked whether it should be trusted.

After you have verified that your SSH server is running, you should be able to connect to your Mac OS X machine from another machine by using an SSH client.

Chapter 13 shows the command documentation for ssh and slogin in Table 13.4.

Transferring Files with scp, sftp

The SSH suite includes the scp (secure copy) and sftp (secure FTP) utilities for securely transferring files.

The basic syntax for scp is

```
scp <from> <to>
```

The *<from>* or *<to>* can be specified as a remote host and file, expanding the basic syntax to

```
scp [[<username>@]<remote_host>:]<pathtofile>
➥[[<username>@]<remote_host>:]<pathtofile>
```

The *<remote_host>* can be a name or IP address. Here is sample output from copying a file on the remote host, ~sage/terminal/term-display-1.tiff, to the current directory on the local machine:

```
creampuf:~ nermal$ scp sage@192.168.1.17:terminal/term-display-1.tiff ./
sage@192.168.1.17's password:
term-display-1.tiff   100% |*********************************|   900 KB    00:01
```

While the transfer occurs, the percentage and amount transferred increase over time. You cannot use scp to copy files from your Mac OS X machine unless you have activated the SSH server.

Chapter 13 shows the command documentation for scp in Table 13.5.

The sftp command can also be used to securely transfer files. Its basic syntax, shown following, initiates an interactive session that works much like regular ftp:

```
sftp [<username>@]<remote_host>
```

Here is sample output from an interactive sftp session:

```
creampuf:~ nermal$ sftp sage@192.168.1.17
Connecting to 192.168.1.17...
sage@192.168.1.17's password:
sftp> get terminal/term-display-2.tiff
Fetching /Users/sage/terminal/term-display-2.tiff to term-display-2.tiff
sftp> quit
```

In this example, sftp is used to transfer a file on the remote host, ~sage/terminal/term-display-2.tiff, to the current directory on the local machine. As with scp, you cannot use sftp to transfer files from your Mac OS X machine unless you have activated the SSH server.

Chapter 13 shows the command documentation for sftp in Table 13.6. Only SSH2 servers include sftp.

Securing Insecure Protocols by Tunneling Connections: Command Line

As you may recall from Chapter 13, Secure Shell can be used to set up an encrypted tunnel between two machines to transfer data. Services that you might be most interested in tunneling include FTP, POP, IMAP, and X11. Note that X11 forwarding is off by default in the /etc/sshd_config file.

When tunneling a connection, you can optionally choose to restrict access to a particular service by restricting it to accept connections only from the server machine. Depending on the service, this can be done as an entry to the appropriate /etc/xinetd.d/ file or as an entry in the /etc/hosts.allow file for the server machine, 127.0.0.1. This type of setup increases the security of your machine.

To set up the tunnel, use an SSH client, such as ssh or slogin.

At the command line on a machine running an OpenSSH version of SSH, such as another Mac OS X machine, you could run the following to set up a tunnel without having a Terminal connection:

```
creampuf:~ nermal$ slogin 192.168.1.17  -l sageray -N -L 2121:192.168.1.17:21
sageray@192.168.1.17's password:
```

In the preceding statement, a tunnel is set up between the local machine and the remote host 192.168.1.17 for user sage. The remote host can be specified as a hostname or an IP address. The tunnel is created between the local host at port 2121 and the remote host at port 21. The -N option allows us to set up a tunnel without initiating a Terminal session. Please note that only root can forward ports under 1024. So, if you wanted to use a port number under 1024 on the local machine, you would have to have root privileges.

After the port forwarding is set up in the SSH client, use the regular client for the service, providing it with the appropriate local port to use and localhost or 127.0.0.1 as the host.

An FTP session over this encrypted channel would look like this:

```
creampuf:~ nermal$ ftp localhost 2121
Connected to localhost.
220 falcor.local FTP server (lukemftpd 1.1) ready.
Name (localhost:nermal): sageray
331 Password required for sageray.
Password:
```

```
230-
    Welcome to Darwin!
230 User sage logged in.
Remote system type is UNIX.
Using binary mode to transfer files.
ftp> cd printing
250 CWD command successful.
ftp> epsv4 off
EPSV/EPRT on IPv4 off.
ftp> binary
200 Type set to I.
ftp> get 13FIG07.tiff
local: 13FIG07.tiff remote: 13FIG07.tiff
227 Entering Passive Mode (192,168,1,17,194,93)
150 Opening BINARY mode data connection for '13FIG07.tiff' (1736394 bytes).
100% |*************************************|  1695 KB  670.55 KB/s    00:02
226 Transfer complete.
1736394 bytes received in 00:02 (669.91 KB/s)
ftp> quit
221-
    Data traffic for this session was 3472788 bytes in 2 files.
    Total traffic for this session was 3501993 bytes in 7 transfers.
221 Thank you for using the FTP service on falcor.local.
```

Although tunneling FTP is pertinent to some of you, tunneling SMTP and a protocol such as POP may be more useful. To tunnel SMTP and POP connections over SSH, use a command such as this one:

```
creampuf:~ nermal$ slogin rosalyn.biosci.ohio-state.edu -l ralph
➥-N -L 2110:rosalyn.biosci.ohio-state.edu:110
➥-N -L 2125:rosalyn.biosci.ohio-state.edu:25
ralph@rosalyn.biosci.ohio-state.edu's password:
```

For the sample statement, in the POP mail client, the POP server is `127.0.0.1`, and its port is 2110. For some POP mail clients, this is entered as `127.0.0.1:2110`. The SMTP server is `127.0.0.1`, and its port is 2125. Again, for some POP mail clients, this is entered as `127.0.0.1:2125`. The 110 and 25 in the preceding statements are the ports where `popper` and `smtp` are listening on the remote host. Those are the standard ports for those services. The administrator of the remote host can tell you which ports the remote host is using. The 2110 and 2125 are port numbers we picked over 1024 so that `root` privileges would not be required for the tunnel. If you are using a POP mail client that does not allow you to specify an alternate port, you may have to use 110 and 25. Figure 21.1 shows the incoming mailbox of a POP account checked using our tunnel and Mail.

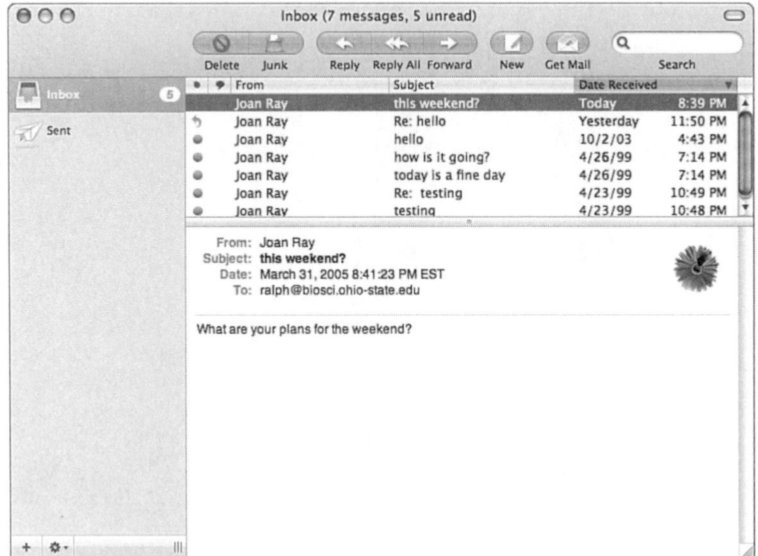

FIGURE 21.1 The incoming mailbox of a POP account checked via SSH tunnels and Mail.

In short, the basic procedure to follow for tunneling a given protocol is as follows:

1. Optionally restrict access by setting up the server to accept connections only from the server machine. Depending on your circumstances, you may have to have this restriction anyway.
2. Set up an `ssh` client with port and server information.
3. Set up the client for the service being tunneled with the local port number to use and `localhost` or `127.0.0.1` as the host.
4. Use the client for the tunneled service as you ordinarily would.

A notable exception to this basic procedure is the procedure for tunneling X11 connections. The SSH server on the remote machine whose display you want to have displayed to your local machine should have X11 forwarding enabled. From your local machine, simply connect with the `ssh` or `slogin` command with the `-X` option, which tunnels an X11 connection. Because SSH takes care of handling everything else to make it work, you don't have to worry about details such as setting the `DISPLAY` environment variable. Figure 21.2 shows remotely running X11 applications being displayed to a Mac OS X machine via SSH tunneling.

Securing Insecure Protocols by Tunneling Connections: Fugu

Although a number of graphical SSH clients are available for Mac OS X, so far only a few include tunneling capability. Fugu, available from `http://rsug.itd.umich.edu/software/fugu/`, and SSH Tunnel Manager, available from `http://projects.tynsoe.org/en/stm/`, are two such clients.

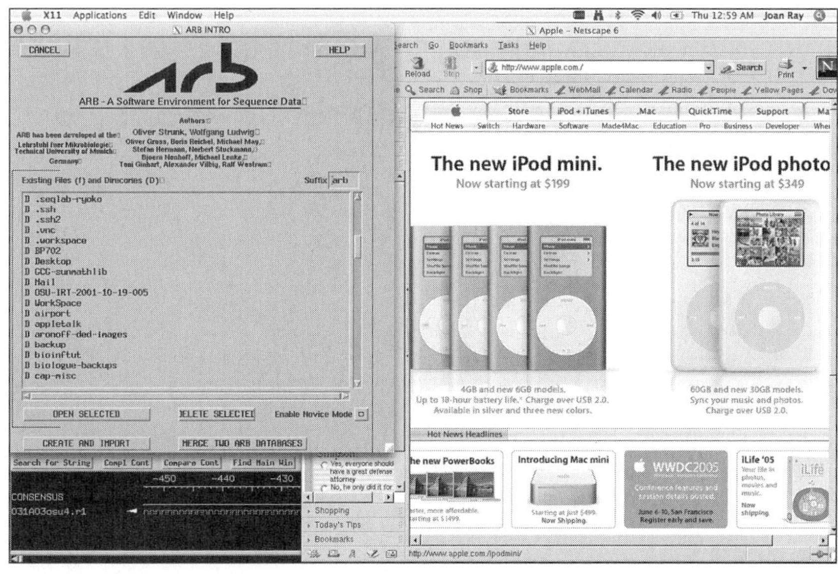

FIGURE 21.2 X11 applications tunneled over SSH.

To tunnel a connection in Fugu, supply the following information: remote host, remote port, local port, tunnel host, username, and port. If you take another look at the example used in the in the previous section for tunneling an FTP connection, `slogin 192.168.1.17 -l sageray -N -L 2121:192.168.1.17:21`, the values to use in Fugu would be

Create a Tunnel to: `192.168.1.17`

Service or Port: `21`

Local Port: `2121`

Tunnel Host: `192.168.1.17`

Username: `sageray`

Port: (Can be left blank if the remote host's SSH server is running on the standard SSH port, 22.)

If you are connecting for the first time, Fugu notes that it can verify the authenticity of the host and asks if you want to continue the connection. After you have established the tunnel, Fugu displays information about the tunnel connection. Once you've established an SSH tunnel, either via the command line or via a graphical SSH client, you can then start the application that needs to use the tunnel, as we saw earlier with Mail. Figure 21.3 setting up the tunnel in Fugu. The ability to use an FTP tunnel in a graphical application is especially useful in web editing suites that include built-in FTP clients. As web editing suites start to support SFTP, the need to use an FTP tunnel may decline.

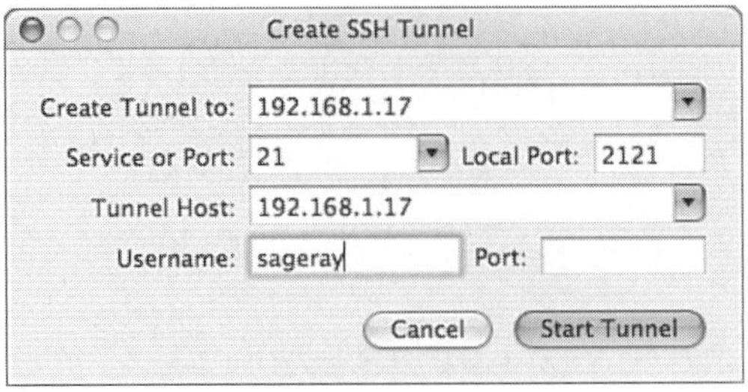

FIGURE 21.3 Setting up a tunnel in Fugu.

Using Public Key Authentication

In addition to the standard method of user authentication—a username and password—SSH provides another method: public key authentication. With the traditional authentication method, the remote host stores a username and password pair for a user. With public key authentication, the user creates a key-pair on a given host. The key-pair consists of a private key and a public key protected with a passphrase. Then the user transfers the public key to the remote host to which she wants to connect. So, the remote host stores a set of public keys for machines on which you have generated a key-pair and transferred a copy of your public key. Furthermore, you protect your keys with a passphrase, rather than a password.

Why might you want to use public key authentication? Passwords do not provide much randomness, even if a user tries to create a password that they think can't be easily guessed. With today's technology, a machine can guess the password space in a matter of months. Passphrases, on the other hand, provide more randomness and are more difficult to guess.

The procedure for enabling public key authentication is similar for both SSH1 and SSH2. Table 21.2 provides select documentation on `ssh-keygen`, the utility that generates key-pairs. To enable public key authentication, do the following:

1. Generate a key-pair on the host from which you want to access another host. (We will call the host from which you want to connect the local host, and the host to which you want to connect the remote host.) Use a good passphrase to protect your key. It is recommended that a good passphrase be 10–30 characters long and not simple sentences or otherwise easily guessable. Include a mix of uppercase, lowercase, numeric, and nonalphanumeric characters.

2. Transfer the public key of the key-pair generated on the local host to the remote host. The public key is public, so you can use any method necessary to transfer it to the remote host. Depending on the SSH servers involved, you might have to convert your key to a different format first.

3. Add the public key you just transferred to the file on the remote host that stores public keys. Depending on the version of SSH that the remote host is running, this could entail actually adding the key to a file, or just adding a reference to the key in the appropriate file.

4. Test logging in to the remote host. You should now be prompted for the passphrase that you used to generate your key-pair because the private key of the local host is paired with its public key that was transferred to the remote host.

TABLE 21.2 Select Documentation for `ssh-keygen`

`ssh-keygen`	Tool for authentication key generation, management and conversion.
`ssh-keygen [-q] [-b` *<bits>*`] -t` *<type>* `[-N` *<new_passphrase>*`] [-C` *<comment>*`] [-f` *<output_keyfile>*`]`	
`ssh-keygen -p [-P` *<old_passphrase>*`] [-N` *<new_passphrase>*`] [-f` *<keyfile>*`]`	
`ssh-keygen -i [-f` *<input_keyfile>*`]`	
`ssh-keygen -e [-f` *<input_keyfile>*`]`	
`ssh-keygen -y [-f` *<input_keyfile>*`]`	
`ssh-keygen -c [-P` *<passphrase>*`] [-C` *<comment>*`] [-f` *<keyfile>*`]`	
`ssh-keygen -l [-f` *<input_keyfile>*`]`	
`ssh-keygen -B [-f` *<input_keyfile>*`]`	
`ssh-keygen` generates, manages, and converts authentication keys for `ssh`. `ssh-keygen` can create RSA keys for use by 1, and RSA or DSA keys for use by SSH2. The type of key to be generated is specified with the `-t` option.	
Normally each user who wants to use SSH with RSA or DSA authentication runs this once to create the authentication key in `$HOME/.ssh/identity`, `$HOME/.ssh/id_dsa`, or `$HOME/.ssh/id_rsa`. Additionally, the system administrator may use this to generate host keys.	
`-b` *<bits>*	Specifies the number of bits in the key to create. Minimum is 512 bits. Generally 1024 bits is considered sufficient, and key sizes above that no longer improve security but make things slower. Default is 1024 bits.
`-e`	Reads a private or public OpenSSH key file and prints the key in a SECSH Public Key File Format to `stdout`. This option allows exporting keys for use by several commercial SSH implementations.
`-f` *<filename>*	Specifies the filename of the key file.
`-i`	Reads an unencrypted private (or public) key file in SSH2-compatible format and prints an OpenSSH-compatible private (or public) key to `stdout`. `ssh-keygen` also reads the SECSH Public Key File Format. This option allows importing keys from several commercial SSH implementations.
`-p`	Requests the changing of the passphrase of a private key file instead of creating a new private key.
`-t` *<type>*	Specifies the type of the key to create. The possible values are `rsa1` for protocol version 1 and `rsa` or `dsa` for protocol version 2.
`-C` *<comment>*	Provides the new comment.
`-N` *<new_passphrase>*	Provides the new passphrase, *<new_passphrase>*.
`-P` *<passphrase>*	Provides the (old) passphrase, *<passphrase>*.

Not only are there differences in public key authentication between SSH1 and SSH2, but there are differences between SSH packages as well. The keys for SSH1 and SSH2 generated by OpenSSH differ from the ones made by SSH Communications Security's SSH servers, the other ones you are most likely to encounter. Be sure to thoroughly read the `ssh-keygen`, `ssh`, and `sshd` man pages for the SSH servers you have to connect to because the information you need to know for connecting via public key authentication will most likely be spread among those man pages. The keys look a bit different for the different protocols and can look quite different between the SSH packages. Fortunately, OpenSSH's `ssh-keygen` can import and export keys.

If you are not sure which type of SSH server a given machine is running, you can always ask its system administrator. If the system administrator is not available, you can also test this by looking at the response you get from telnetting to the machine's port 22, using the command `telnet <host> 22`. Here is a response from an OpenSSH machine:

```
dogbone:~ joray$ telnet localhost 22
Trying ::1...
Connected to localhost.
Escape character is '^]'.
SSH-1.99-OpenSSH_3.8.1p1
^]
telnet> quit
Connection closed.
```

Here is a sample response from an SSH Communications SSH server:

```
dogbone:~ joray$ telnet mother 22
Trying mother...
Connected to mother.
Escape character is '^]'.
SSH-1.99-3.1.0 SSH Secure Shell (non-commercial)
^]
telnet> quit
Connection closed.
```

To give you an idea of how the various public keys look, some sample public keys are shown following. Default file locations were accepted when creating the keys. This first key is a sample SSH2 public key generated in OpenSSH with the DSA algorithm option (`ssh-keygen -t dsa`), stored as `~/.ssh/id_dsa.pub`:

```
ssh-dss AAAAB3NzaC1kc3MAAACBALzT9RbceziStHPmMiHmg78hXUgcMP14sJZ/7MH/p2NX
/fB0cmbULPNgEN8jrs8w9N73J7yUFHSPR/LVfBj+UwkIzwjyXUW/z/VmCs25IDF/UBn1OQK5
PCi16rF0F+Cx0hMN4R3AaFAetXBdLqoom5x4Yo9gdspPqhhB44QnT43JAAAAFQDWTkKDJ2m4
SApHZ/qRnRpMN5whTQAAAIAVADOsHpnUdUOFKjIgxZ0Hwh7IaMQ2ofGt/6PmbmNG/8zXRdxm
u/JrBzieWHq6sSRSkWDSDIjuEuTkZyJ4wx3KsLmhIrtlBw3NCcsJT2GfGQ9gEBm8fkUpeQyK
AQcirbx4Hw93iMFC3g9A8cwqmA4DalKSX3un7cweNU32Irhq+gAAAIAz+lDSjqjFzuTV4vJ/
P83nH2uwb62/iCSIB9cL32hrOm234imaAceu8pN9qqEAPr9AilCWa+lqGvgcdyDK0vZTvKQn
k6KOU3TJfDyMR7i/gzW4P4TA/== miwa@brezup
```

This is a sample SSH2 public key generated in OpenSSH with the RSA algorithm option (`ssh-keygen -t rsa`), stored as `~/.ssh/id_rsa.pub`:

```
ssh-rsa AAAAB3NzaC1yc2EAAAABIwAAAIEAnMV/YAmJdEoRFC3Fa91YVloqivKeAwD62bd4
+zSsd1lMr6JV4oE9EIfVPM3BL98UgmDzfhlh5b2PAP1YFwalXNksPeCQ0TNoBYIO1qloPwGr
00l4sllJDCgMGKphT3saumDCVryGof4g9tm3itMri/c8sA04MqOb0NS2tfBCQRc= miwa@br
ezup
```


This is a sample SSH1 public key generated in OpenSSH with the RSA algorithm, the only choice for SSH1 (`ssh-keygen -t rsa1`), stored as `~/.ssh/identity.pub`:


```
1024 35 1557212985106595841799445393895896855201842965316926480116187178
479312752731786936426534362289883814829220699448695793008292191355256581
252483513540009913562286856320477786490006280726660808370019692878286941
832867913488270433630039854375920434585040342671329990216320744276783576
66438835891174723508102956387 miwa@brezup
```


This key is a sample SSH2 public key generated in SSH Communications Security's SSH server with the DSA algorithm (`ssh-keygen2 -t dsa`), stored in `~/.ssh2/id_dsa_1024_a.pub`:


```
---- BEGIN SSH2 PUBLIC KEY ----
Subject: miwa
Comment: "1024-bit dsa, miwa@Rosalyn, Thu May 16 2002 23:33:30 -0500"
AAAAB3NzaC1kc3MAAACBAIxEJgV24AtDzKyFzMAD5agu/YHOZnhUma12zVX31Ov5Xj9hU/
0VB/FdxtctLKbUMRra5b9azzHFsdJl/f1VqoQ8feEfFZ/4nTcSVbL5f5KydmSe0Mmyq4vq
IqSC4jyDjIHMUcDfj2Z/kRhF9o6VxCdCUd5OvkpZmEfWqLNR9oPlAAAAFQD02rAsEPS2uU
VTAa/pHqKhcrC6mwAAAIB3UDIDjP9TOJNaap34/9o0qW1o7agFMXcJftlUgZEtUfc5v/jX
MplQiL77CggJU+rdv9WQbyefaFjWLQAibV5M71kt2mdkYVtuQzbmBTDW9v8YP1/QMnnjOK
v8xRmrsplC/lv9/rmzS0gI1Hfbbuq60zW/ULdg6c61y7HyZ/Qf5AAAAIArWb/PIWRhMxLR
aY9VZvFZOYjOxcIR66aoybkneODPaAwZsW5yq1q2XEpxxza4q2yTyZ7drTYLCUBbXwG4Cu
RVv3CMTiXQ47AXlKYPECVT0I4bTZyY60GuLI4TUsyHLk5HFF0Ctt/6OB8WEHOn6LGDNNoN
DF4M7MlGbyOVNZnGCw==
---- END SSH2 PUBLIC KEY ----
```


This is a sample SSH2 public key generated in SSH Communications Security's SSH server with the RSA algorithm (`ssh-keygen2 -t rsa`), stored in `~/.ssh2/id_rsa_1024_a.pub`:


```
---- BEGIN SSH2 PUBLIC KEY ----
Subject: miwa
Comment: "1024-bit rsa, miwa@Rosalyn, Sun Sep 08 2002 23:00:14 -0500"
AAAAB3NzaC1yc2EAAAADAQABAAAAgQDenNONzW2v+TB/ZeRHZvKRWJk24Lk7LsA4+uWsYL
5L+bNoPYV0oKD3UMYddEacM47gcSd2e1E511Wlx/+X0MjrvPqEIlqw9owkjwOukm38iISz
qypT4uvawOW9GcKE7c5KH8BD9tfhvCkwZE+oAsJk3jfTBRSdOdxhvhF87RgbcQ==
---- END SSH2 PUBLIC KEY ----
```


This is a sample SSH1 public key generated in SSH Communications Security's SSH server with the RSA algorithm (`ssh-keygen1`), stored in `~/.ssh/identity.pub`:


```
1024 35 150523262886747450533481402006467053649597280355648477085483985
71208317676866466089983419198328656197603216662844372018680273646986695
```

```
561784637378345179225111133633075841684444147236898954804613540972039551
463098346053631424932409374094154707744074894214676103365093267251691315
51506171491685369057102508431 63 miwa@Rosalyn
```

After you have transferred your public key to the remote host, you have to let the remote host know that you want to allow public key authentication from your local host. How this is done depends on the SSH server. For OpenSSH, authorized public keys for SSH1 and SSH2 keys are stored in `~/.ssh/authorized_keys`. Each line of a basic `authorized_keys` file contains a public key. Blank lines and lines starting with # are ignored. However, limitations can be further placed on an authorized public key using options listed in Table 21.3. A sample `~/.ssh/authorized_keys` file follows:

```
1024 35 155721298510659584179944539389589685520184296531692648011618717847931275273178693642653436228988381482922069944869579300829219135525658125248351354000991356228685632047778649000628072666080837001969287828694183286791348827043363003985437592043458504034267132999021632074427678357666438835891174723508102956387 miwa@brezup

ssh-dss AAAAB3NzaC1kc3MAAACBALPMiCqdPDGxcyB1IwPrPXk3oEqvpxR62EsspxGKGGbO
M6mf60i1hwTvjZzDhUSR7ViGeCopKtjJIqn2ljgeLbhFsQUX2UyJ6A1cFVuef0x6GVAsybqb
tJc8JBh41U+iSXJKppEY5BI+REMydpBXJf2qT/8yZeq3NPjiOiMb6TyjAAAAFQDYvvV4WQK1
Zu23q/7iLKg5j/zi5wAAAIBR7vgrQpjKW2cprIUJsnenTm4hnBrEO7NMUomjgezrY23iZdIS
QlU1ESMgx9W9nnZstd2vjeqHDSmmcD2p/aGqhl3N1WlYk8zgFYYJilPwRxVm77Np/vXz/MQp
ygJE7ToXGvfHqVmdBpUyakyfx6DveWhFPis1Ab8N1RCPWm6PMwAAAIAytHjAAMYscqX2tl4i
cw3oOku3HIvoHBCx9D6Q9LjCqt7DqqgMN2e5vuvNz0hzqBaBDJsjNA/A4bI88ZrgLhfJM/Nh
s2xkcb7AYeHEtuGKVbsbB0EjsECtLRHydfmk3wDQjUVT92HsodFvsIl4Je7seWUuiAEe0V1x
fF7XrXuwNQ== miwa@hobbes
```

For an SSH1 server by SSH Communications Security, the authorized public keys are also stored in `~/.ssh/authorized_keys`. An SSH2 server by SSH Communications Security, however, stores references to files that contain authorized public keys in `~/.ssh2/authorization`. Here is a sample `~/.ssh2/authorization` file:

```
Key hobbes.pub
Key ryoohki.pub
```

As an example, suppose that you want to allow public key authentication from a machine running an SSH Communications Security SSH2 server. First, generate a key-pair on the remote SSH2 machine using `ssh-keygen2`. Then transfer the public key of the key-pair to your Mac OS X machine by whatever method you choose.

In this case, because you want to allow public key authentication from a machine running a non-OpenSSH SSH server, you have to convert the public key file that was transferred to something compatible with your OpenSSH server. The `ssh-keygen` utility can convert between SSH formats. Run a command of the following form:

```
ssh-keygen -i -f <transferred_public_key> > <converted_transferred_public_key>
```

The preceding statement imports the transferred public key file and directs the converted output to a file specified by *<converted_transferred_public_key>*. We recommend including the name of the remote host in your filename to make things easier for you. OpenSSH's `ssh-keygen` can also export its keys to the IETF SECSH format.

Then add that file to the `~/.ssh/authorized_keys` file, the file that contains your public keys from machines authorized to connect via public key authentication. This can be done in whatever way you feel most comfortable. Issuing the following statement does this quite neatly:

```
cat <converted_transferred_public_key> >> .ssh/authorized_keys
```

Now that the public key from the non-OpenSSH machine has been transferred and converted to a format used by OpenSSH, you can log in to your Mac OS X machine from the remote host via pubic key authentication.

Logging in to a machine running a non-OpenSSH SSH server from your Mac OS X machine is similar. First generate the key-pair on your Mac OS X machine using `ssh-keygen`. Then convert the public key file to the IETF SECSH format by running a command of the form:

```
ssh-keygen -e -f <public_key> > <converted_public_key>
```

Transfer the converted public key file to the remote host by whatever method you choose. Then add a reference to the `~/.ssh2/authorization` file of the form:

```
Key <public_key_filename>
```

Now that the public key generated on your Mac OS X machine has been transferred to the remote host running a non-OpenSSH SSH server, and a reference to it has been added to the `~/.ssh2/authorization` file, you are logged in to the remote host via public key authentication.

The details provided here address logging in via public key authentication between the major different SSH servers using the SSH2 protocol. Because the SSH1 protocol is not under active development, we are not discussing the details involved there. However, if you need to connect to an SSH1 server via public key authentication, it is easier than what needs to be done for the SSH2 protocol. You do not have to convert the key formats. On the non-OpenSSH machine, the file that contains the public keys is `~/.ssh/authorized_keys`, and you add public keys themselves to the file rather than references to the public key files.

If you don't like the command line, you might try Gideon Softworks' `SSH Helper`, available at `http://www.gideonsoftworks.com/sshhelper.html`. It is a freely available package.

TABLE 21.3 Options for `~/.ssh/authorized_keys`

Option	Function
`From="`*`pattern-list`*`"`	Specifies that in addition to RSA authentication, the canonical name of the remote host must be present in the comma-separated list of patterns. `*` and `?` serve as wildcards. The list may also contain patterns negated by prefixing them with !. If the canonical hostname matches a negated pattern, the key is not accepted.
`Command="`*`command`*`"`	Specifies that the command is executed whenever this key is used for authentication. The command supplied by the user (if any) is ignored. The command is run on a `pty` if the client requests a `pty`; otherwise, it is run without a `tty`. If an 8-bit clean channel is required, one must not request a `pty` or should specify `no-pty`. A quote may be included in the command by quoting it with a backslash. This option might be useful to restrict certain RSA keys to perform just a specific operation. An example might be a key that permits remote backups but nothing else. Note that the client may specify TCP/IP and/or X11 forwarding unless they are explicitly prohibited. Note that this option applies to shell, command, or subsystem execution.
`environment="`*`NAME=value`*`"`	Specifies that the string is to be added to the environment when logging in using this key. Environment variables set this way override other default environment values. Multiple options of this type are permitted. This option is automatically disabled if `UseLogin` is enabled.
`no-port-forwarding`	Forbids TCP/IP forwarding when this key is used for authentication. Any port forward requests by the client will return an error. This might be used, for example, in connection with the `command` option.
`no-X11-forwarding`	Forbids X11 forwarding when this key is used for authentication. Any X11 forward requests by the client will return an error.
`no-agent-forwarding`	Forbids authentication agent forwarding when this key is used for authentication.
`no-pty`	Prevents `tty` allocation (a request to allocate a `pty` will fail).
`permitopen="`*`host:port`*`"`	Limits local `ssh -L` port forwarding such that it may connect to only the specified host and port. IPv6 addresses can be specified with an alternative syntax: `host/port`. Multiple permit open options may be applied separated by commas. No pattern matching is performed on the specified hostnames; they must be literal domains or addresses.

Managing Your Keys with `ssh-agent`

The SSH suite of applications is wonderful for protecting your communications, but while entering a passphrase instead of a password for logins through `ssh` is only a minor inconvenience, repeating it over and over to copy files using `scp` can be a real annoyance. Thankfully, the designers thought of this and have created an auxiliary application that allows you to authenticate yourself once to it. It can then use the stored private keys and the passphrases associated with your SSH identities (SSH keypairs generated by ssh-keygen and authorized on another host), to authenticate to remote hosts for you automatically. Essentially, this software acts as your agent and responds for you whenever a remote host asks for your passphrase. This eliminates any need for you to respond to passphrase queries from remote hosts for which the agent knows a proper response, and can drastically decrease the effort involved in using the SSH applications.

If you're dealing with SSH on a daily basis, using ssh-agent is almost certainly the way you'll want to use the SSH software, as it will make your life much easier. The process for using the agent is simple as well, and can be summarized as follows:

1. Start the ssh-agent.
2. Set up your environment so that SSH applications can find the agent.
3. Add identities to the agent.
4. Use SSH applications (slogin, scp, and so forth), and never get asked for your passphrase.

However, although the difference in practice is significant, the difference in print is subtle. Previously in this chapter you've learned how to perform all the steps necessary to work through SSH, but for the sake of clarity with respect to what ssh-agent can actually do for you, we'll recap from the position of a user who's never used SSH to authenticate to remote hosts. In the examples that follow, we've left the prompt intact so that you can tell which machine and directory we're working in. The input/output fragments that follow were collected as a single stream of actions by our test user miwa, and we've split them up to intersperse some comments on what he's doing. If you follow along, by the end of this section you'll have set up a user with two independent SSH identities that can be used to authenticate against both ssh.com and openssh.org type sshd servers.

1. Let's see what files miwa has in his ~/.ssh directory.

```
brezup:miwa miwa $ ls -l .ssh
ls: .ssh: No such file or directory
```

2. We're starting with a clean slate—we've deleted miwa's ~/.ssh directory so that it's as if he's never used the SSH software before.

```
brezup:miwa miwa $ ssh-keygen -t rsa -b 1024
Generating public/private rsa key pair.
Enter file in which to save the key (/Users/miwa/.ssh/id_rsa):
Created directory '/Users/miwa/.ssh'.
Enter passphrase (empty for no passphrase):
Enter same passphrase again:
Your identification has been saved in /Users/miwa/.ssh/id_rsa.
Your public key has been saved in /Users/miwa/.ssh/id_rsa.pub.
The key fingerprint is:
b3:c9:1f:91:25:ea:31:4d:28:b0:78:34:8a:16:f1:9e miwa@brezup
```

3. To use SSH applications, miwa needs keys. Create his default key as an RSA key of 1024 bits. We enter a passphrase for miwa, but it's not echoed to the screen.

```
brezup:miwa miwa $ ls -l .ssh
total 16
-rw-------  1 miwa  miwa  951  2 Oct 18:50 id_rsa
-rw-r--r--  1 miwa  miwa  221  2 Oct 18:50 id_rsa.pub
```

4. And in his ~/.ssh directory, there are now two files, containing the private and public keypair for his default identity.

```
brezup:miwa miwa $ slogin ryoko.biosci.ohio-state.edu
The authenticity of host 'ryoko.biosci.ohio-state.edu
➥(140.254.104.240)' can't be established.
DSA key fingerprint is 17:07:3d:f6:44:55:7d:8a:a2:00:89:b7:76:43:ad:f4.
Are you sure you want to continue connecting (yes/no)? yes
Warning: Permanently added 'ryoko.biosci.ohio-state.edu,
➥140.254.104.240' (DSA) to the list of known hosts.
 miwa@ryoko.biosci.ohio-state.edu's password:
Last login: Mon Feb 17 2003 19:15:54 -0500 from cvl232015.columb
You have new mail.
ryoko miwa 1 > ls -l .ssh2
.ssh2: No such file or directory
ryoko miwa 2 >mkdir .ssh2
ryoko miwa 3 >exit
Connection to ryoko.biosci.ohio-state.edu closed.
```

5. miwa logs in to ryoko.biosci.ohio-state.edu using his password for the system. ryoko is a Sun Enterprise Server running ssh.com's version of the SSH software. It doesn't keep its key files in the same place as does our Macintosh's openssh.org version. miwa creates the required ~/.ssh2 directory in his home directory on ryoko and then logs off the machine. For the best security, we recommend disabling passworded logins from the network entirely, and only accepting passphrases, but this requires physical access to both machines for at least a little while, or some other way of transferring a public key without being able to log in to the remote machine via the network.

```
brezup:miwa miwa $ cd .ssh
brezup:miwa .ssh $ ls -l
total 24
-rw-------  1 miwa  miwa  951  2 Oct 18:50 id_rsa
-rw-r--r--  1 miwa  miwa  221  2 Oct 18:50 id_rsa.pub
-rw-r--r--  1 miwa  miwa  633  2 Oct 18:56 known_hosts
brezup:miwa .ssh $ ssh-keygen -e -f id_rsa
---- BEGIN SSH2 PUBLIC KEY ----
Comment: "1024-bit RSA, converted from OpenSSH by miwa@brezup"
AAAAB3NzaC1yc2EAAAABIwAAAIEAv09dKFr46dK+U43m8h9hV0JtooRdyf8hbPJcf1y+kX
```

```
cpcOpHWz7NBqGI3FsZZUrJDrgP3Q/1VHa8SiDsCkYFuG55HobfNfrsGVvW7LqHn9ApzYhi
fPUGpLSQnML4/qzTLNn2JmUiEvlcdYrnZoi+b23Om4mLu1zez7nT91EGTnk=
---- END SSH2 PUBLIC KEY ----
```

6. miwa needs to get the public key for the identity he wants to use on ryoko, into a form that ryoko's sshd can understand. Pleasantly, ssh-keygen can not only generate keys, it can also translate them into the standard format that ssh.com's server version wants. A known_hosts file has appeared in miwa's .ssh directory along with his id_rsa identity files. In this file is recorded the public host-key for ryoko.

```
brezup:miwa .ssh $ ssh-keygen -e -f id_rsa > home_rsa.ietf
brezup:miwa .ssh $ ls -l
total 32
-rw-r--r--  1 miwa  miwa  328  2 Oct 19:05 home_rsa.ietf
-rw-------  1 miwa  miwa  951  2 Oct 18:50 id_rsa
-rw-r--r--  1 miwa  miwa  221  2 Oct 18:50 id_rsa.pub
-rw-r--r--  1 miwa  miwa  633  2 Oct 18:56 known_hosts
```

7. Using ssh-keygen, miwa writes out an IETF formatted version of the public key for his id.rsa key, and puts it in his .ssh directory. Because the SSH implementation on Mac OS X won't use this key for anything, he could actually store it just about anywhere, but this seems like as good and safe a place as any.

```
brezup:miwa .ssh $ scp ./home_rsa.ietf
➥miwa@ryoko.biosci.ohio-state.edu:.ssh2/home_rsa.ietf
miwa@ryoko.biosci.ohio-state.edu's password:
scp: warning: Executing scp1 compatibility.
home_rsa.ietf        100% |****************************|   347      00:00
```

8. miwa copies the key to ryoko using scp. Because it's a public key, it wouldn't be a problem even if he had to copy it over a protocol where data is visible. If passworded logins are blocked, this key transfer needs to be done in some other fashion, such as transporting it on removable media.

```
brezup:miwa .ssh $ slogin ryoko.biosci.ohio-state.edu
miwa@ryoko.biosci.ohio-state.edu's password:
Last login: Thu Oct 02 2003 17:56:28 -0500 from dhcp065-024-074-
You have new mail.
ryoko miwa 1 >ls -l .ssh2
total 2
-rw-r--r--   1 miwa     class        328 Oct  2 19:07 home_rsa.ietf
ryoko miwa 2 >cd .ssh2
ryoko .ssh2 3 >cat >> authorization
Key home_rsa.ietf
^D
```

9. An authorization file must be created on ryoko, listing the key miwa just transferred as valid for logins. miwa just cats the line in append mode onto his authorization file. The file doesn't exist, so it'll get created, but if it did exist, this key line would simply be added as new data at the end of the file. The cat command is terminated with a Control-D on a line by itself.

```
ryoko .ssh2 4 >ls -l
total 4
-rw-r--r--    1 miwa     class          18 Oct  2 19:10 authorization
-rw-r--r--    1 miwa     class         328 Oct  2 19:07 home_rsa.ietf
ryoko .ssh2 5 >chmod 600 authorization home_rsa.ietf
ryoko .ssh2 6 >ls -l
total 4
-rw-------    1 miwa     class          18 Oct  2 19:10 authorization
-rw-------    1 miwa     class         328 Oct  2 19:07 home_rsa.ietf
ryoko .ssh2 7 >cat authorization
Key home_rsa.ietf
ryoko .ssh2 8 >exit
Connection to ryoko.biosci.ohio-state.edu closed.
```

10. The authorization file now exists, and contains the data expected. Even through it's a public key and theoretically can't be usefully abused, miwa chmods both files in his .ssh2 directory so that only he can read them, just to be sure.

```
brezup:miwa .ssh $ slogin ryoko.biosci.ohio-state.edu
Enter passphrase for key '/Users/miwa/.ssh/id_rsa':
Last login: Thu Oct 02 2003 18:08:34 -0500 from dhcp065-024-074-
You have new mail.
ryoko miwa 1 >exit
Connection to ryoko.biosci.ohio-state.edu closed.
```

11. Back on brezup, miwa can now slogin to ryoko, and be asked for a passphrase instead of for his considerably weaker password.

```
brezup:miwa .ssh $ ssh-keygen -t rsa -b 1024
Generating public/private rsa key pair.
Enter file in which to save the key (/Users/miwa/.ssh/id_rsa):
➥/Users/miwa/.ssh/internal_rsa
Enter passphrase (empty for no passphrase):
Enter same passphrase again:
Your identification has been saved in /Users/miwa/.ssh/internal_rsa.
Your public key has been saved in /Users/miwa/.ssh/internal_rsa.pub.
The key fingerprint is:
d4:b9:f7:7a:1f:49:96:b4:9d:ac:1a:3a:5d:0a:57:3b miwa@brezup
```

12. For some reason, miwa wants another, separate identity for use on his internal (private) network. Perhaps it's because he's going to allow (against our good advice)

other users to log in to his account and use it for connecting to other machines on the internal network. By using a separate identity, and only giving out the passphrase to his internal identity, he can mitigate the danger in this scheme and protect his external identity. Here, miwa's chosen to create it into the nondefault file internal_rsa, again as a 1024-bit RSA key.

```
brezup:miwa .ssh $ ls -l
total 48
-rw-r--r--   1 miwa   miwa   328   2 Oct 19:05 home_rsa.ietf
-rw-------   1 miwa   miwa   951   2 Oct 18:50 id_rsa
-rw-r--r--   1 miwa   miwa   221   2 Oct 18:50 id_rsa.pub
-rw-------   1 miwa   miwa   951   2 Oct 19:27 internal_rsa
-rw-r--r--   1 miwa   miwa   221   2 Oct 19:27 internal_rsa.pub
-rw-r--r--   1 miwa   miwa   633   2 Oct 18:56 known_hosts
```

13. Now there are files in ~miwa/.ssh/ for both his default id_rsa identity and his internal_rsa identity. miwa needs to transfer the public key from in the internal_rsa keypair to any of our private, internal-network hosts he wants to be able to access via passphrase. In this case, 192.168.1.200, otherwise known as creampuf, will be used as an example.

```
brezup:miwa .ssh $ slogin 192.168.1.200
The authenticity of host '192.168.1.200 (192.168.1.200)'
➥can't be established.
RSA key fingerprint is f3:62:16:8e:25:7f:75:ab:4c:cd:99:5d:39:bc:3c:b7.
Are you sure you want to continue connecting (yes/no)? yes
Warning: Permanently added '192.168.1.200' (RSA) to the list of known hosts.
miwa@192.168.1.200's password:
Welcome to Darwin!
[creampuf:~] miwa% ls -l .ssh
ls: .ssh: No such file or directory
[creampuf:~] miwa% mkdir .ssh
[creampuf:~] miwa% touch .ssh/authorized_keys
[creampuf:~] miwa% chmod 600 .ssh/authorized_keys
[creampuf:~] miwa% exit
Connection to 192.168.1.200 closed.
```

14. Again, miwa hasn't logged in to this host before, so creating the directory to contain SSH keys is necessary. This time it's a Mac OS X machine, so it uses the openssh.org way of specifying authorized remote users, that being a single authorized_keys file of (concatenated) authorized keys. miwa creates the file, and sets its permissions to owner-read/write only.

```
brezup:miwa .ssh $ ls -l
total 48
-rw-r--r--   1 miwa   miwa   328   2 Oct 19:05 home_rsa.ietf
-rw-------   1 miwa   miwa   951   2 Oct 18:50 id_rsa
```

```
-rw-r--r--  1 miwa  miwa  221  2 Oct 18:50 id_rsa.pub
-rw-------  1 miwa  miwa  951  2 Oct 19:27 internal_rsa
-rw-r--r--  1 miwa  miwa  221  2 Oct 19:27 internal_rsa.pub
-rw-r--r--  1 miwa  miwa  856  2 Oct 19:31 known_hosts
```

15. Back on brezup, the `known_hosts` file has grown, as it's accumulated the host key from `192.168.1.200` now as well.

```
brezup:miwa .ssh $ scp internal_rsa.pub
➥ miwa@192.168.1.200:.ssh/miwa_brezup_rsa.pub
miwa@192.168.1.200's password:
internal_rsa.pub     100% |****************************|    240       00:00
brezup:miwa .ssh $ slogin 192.168.1.200
miwa@192.168.1.200's password:
Welcome to Darwin!
[creampuf:~] miwa% cd .ssh
[creampuf:~/.ssh] miwa% ls -l
total 8
-rw-------  1 miwa  staff    0 Oct  2 19:33 authorized_keys
-rw-r--r--  1 miwa  staff  221 Oct  2 19:51 miwa_brezup_rsa.pub
[creampuf:~/.ssh] miwa% cat miwa_brezup_rsa.pub >> authorized_keys
[creampuf:~/.ssh] miwa% cat authorized_keys
ssh-rsa AAAAB3NzaC1yc2EAAAABIwAAAIEAzc9VaVwZEG8lWJ5SO/t1LfCpZK7dHGbz
uTnLXdN2sTLd09Ei0567vLHSxRmDddGej79ShvqKh+4EXXZsCjwvuIyJsQvW61FC/IQJ
HkCJjCxxmrEaxphPEG5Iu5M2k5JsshmoLL89aKYWYadv1vsBLZ5PxgDTtGE2h+pd8PBa
q/0= miwa@brezup
[creampuf:~/.ssh] miwa% chmod 600 miwa_brezup_rsa.pub
[creampuf:~/.ssh] miwa% exit
Connection to 192.168.1.200 closed.
```

16. `miwa` transfers his public key from his `internal_rsa` key-pair to `192.168.1.200`, and saves it as `miwa_sage_rsa.pub` in his `.ssh` directory on `192.168.1.200`. It's good to come up with a standardized naming scheme for keys that gives you some idea of what user the key was for, and what host it will allow them access from. In this case, because `miwa` might be allowing other users to log in to his account, he might eventually have many other users public keys stored in his `authorized_keys` files in his various accounts around our internal network. Keeping a copy of each of them named in terms of who it allows access, and from which machine, gives him the ability to sort through his `authorized_keys` file and delete entries if it becomes necessary to limit access in the future.

    After he's transferred his `internal_rsa` public key to `creampuf`, he logs in to `creampuf` (again using his password) and cats the key (in append mode) onto the end of his `~/.ssh/authorized_keys` file. He also `chmod`s it to owner read/write only, again, just to be safe.

```
brezup:miwa .ssh $ cd ~
brezup:miwa miwa $ slogin 192.168.1.200
```

```
miwa@192.168.1.200's password:
^C
```


17. Back on brezup, miwa tests his setup and lands at a password prompt. That wasn't the expected behavior. Everything was copied over properly, so maybe it's something about slogin that miwa doesn't yet understand—maybe it's not smart enough to pick the correct identity credentials from the ones he's created, and it's trying to authenticate to the internal server with his default ID? Reading the man page, he discovers that you can specify an ID explicitly, and he tries that option.

```
brezup:miwa miwa $ slogin 192.168.1.200 -i internal_rsa
Warning: Identity file internal_rsa does not exist.
miwa@192.168.1.200's password:
^C
```

Again, not the desired response, but this time it's a complaint that the identity doesn't exist. Perhaps slogin's not smart enough to look in the default location for anything other than the default identity as well?

```
brezup:miwa miwa $ slogin 192.168.1.200 -i .ssh/internal_rsa
miwa@192.168.1.200's password:
Welcome to Darwin!
[creampuf:~] miwa% tail -3 /var/log/system.log
Oct  2 21:40:08 creampuf xinetd[283]: START: ssh pid=558 from=192.168.1.119.
Oct  2 21:40:08 creampuf sshd[618]: Authentication refused: bad ownership
➥or modes for directory /Users/miwa
Oct  2 21:40:08 creampuf sshd[618]: Accepted password for miwa from
➥192.168.1.119 port 49656 ssh2
```

Although it doesn't show up in print, there was actually a fairly long pause after miwa issued this slogin command, before it brought up the password prompt. Clearly it knows about the ID, as it didn't complain about the specification this time, so maybe something's wrong with the server on the remote host. A quick look at the diagnostics from sshd in system.log reveals the problem. There's something about the permissions of miwa's home directory that sshd doesn't like, and it's therefore refusing to allow passphrased access.

```
[creampuf:~] miwa% ls -ld /Users/miwa/
drwxrwxr-x  29 miwa  staff  986 Oct  2 19:33 /Users/miwa/
```

The problem is that miwa has been being sloppy with security, and has left his home directory with write access for the staff group. This would enable a malicious user who is a member of group staff to potentially edit or overwrite files in miwa's directory. Because this could allow that user to modify miwa's ~/.ssh/authorized_keys file without permission, sshd recognizes this as a security hole and disables use of that file for authorization.

```
[creampuf:~] miwa% chmod 755 .
[creampuf:~] miwa% ls -ld /Users/miwa/
drwxr-xr-x  29 miwa  staff  986 Oct  2 19:33 /Users/miwa/

[creampuf:~] miwa% exit
Connection to 192.168.1.200 closed.
```

18. miwa changes the permissions on his home directory to disallow write access for anyone except himself, and logs out to try again.

```
brezup:miwa miwa $ slogin 192.168.1.200 -i .ssh/internal_rsa
Enter passphrase for key '.ssh/internal_rsa':
Welcome to Darwin!
```

19. Success! miwa can now login to either ryoko.biosci.ohio-state.edu, or to 192.168.1.200, and each uses an independent ID with independent passphrases. This brings us to the conclusion of the recap, and to where miwa uses ssh-agent to make his life easier, by removing the need for him to constantly type passphrases to use SSH tools.

```
brezup:miwa miwa $ ssh-agent
SSH_AUTH_SOCK=/tmp/ssh-kyJ6HQ6T/agent.6989; export SSH_AUTH_SOCK;
SSH_AGENT_PID=6990; export SSH_AGENT_PID;
echo Agent pid 6990;
```

20. When run, ssh-agent prints out some information regarding how it can be contacted, and forks itself into the background. At that point, it's your agent, ready and willing to answer passphrase requests for you, but it doesn't yet have copies of any of your credentials, and none of the software that needs access to your credentials knows how to find it. The information that it prints out (by default) is commands in the syntax of your shell that will set up a shell so that SSH tools run in that shell can find the agent.

    In tcsh, the preceding output would be

```
setenv SSH_AUTH_SOCK /tmp/ssh-kyJ6HQ6T/agent.6989;
setenv SSH_AGENT_PID6990;
echo Agent pid 6990;
```

    To use the information, simply copy the lines that ssh-agent prints and execute them as commands at the command-line prompt.

```
brezup:miwa miwa $ SSH_AUTH_SOCK=/tmp/ssh-kyJ6HQ6T/agent.6989;
➥export SSH_AUTH_SOCK;
brezup:miwa miwa $ SSH_AGENT_PID=6990; export SSH_AGENT_PID;
```

TIP

Instead of copying and pasting the default `ssh-agent` output, you could just execute `ssh-agent` at the command line as `` `ssh-agent` `` to have that output executed for you.

21. `miwa` runs the two commands to set the environment variables, and ignores the `echo`. The output of `ssh-agent` is designed so that you can wrap it into a script that calls it, and executes its suggested shell commands automatically. The `echo` is only there so that you get diagnostic output to your terminal if you use it in this fashion.

    Next, `miwa` must supply the credentials that he wants the agent to provide in response to queries from SSH programs. This is accomplished with the `ssh-add` command.

```
brezup:miwa miwa $ ssh-add
Enter passphrase for /Users/miwa/.ssh/id_rsa:
Identity added: /Users/miwa/.ssh/id_rsa (/Users/miwa/.ssh/id_rsa)
brezup:miwa miwa $ ssh-add .ssh/internal_rsa
Enter passphrase for .ssh/internal_rsa:
Identity added: .ssh/internal_rsa (.ssh/internal_rsa)
```

22. `miwa` uses `ssh-add` to add his default identity, and then to add his `internal_rsa` identity. Both identities require that he supply the passphrase, just as if he were logging into the remote systems that accept these identities by using `slogin`.

```
brezup:miwa miwa $ ssh-add -L
ssh-rsa AAAAB3NzaC1yc2EAAAABIwAAAIEAv09dKFr46dK+U43m8h9hV0JtooRdyf8
hbPJcf1y+kXcpcOpHWz7NBqGI3FsZZUrJDrgP3Q/1VHa8SiDsCkYFuG55HobfNfrsGV
vW7LqHn9ApzYhifPUGpLSQnML4/qzTLNn2JmUiEvlcdYrnZoi+b23Om4mLu1zez7nT9
1EGTnk= /Users/miwa/.ssh/id_rsa
ssh-rsa AAAAB3NzaC1yc2EAAAABIwAAAIEAzc9VaVwZEG8lWJ5SO/t1LfCpZK7dHGb
z uTnLXdN2sTLd09EiO567vLHSxRmDddGej79ShvqKh+4EXXZsCjwvuIyJsQvW61FC/
IQJ HkCJjCxxmrEaxphPEG5Iu5M2k5JsshmoLL89aKYWYadv1vsBLZ5PxgDTtGE2h+p
d8PBaq/0= .ssh/internal_rsa
```

23. Just for good measure, `miwa` checks the credentials that `ssh-agent` is holding for him, and then goes on to test whether `slogin` now works without requiring him to supply his passphrase:

```
brezup:miwa miwa $ slogin ryoko.biosci.ohio-state.edu
Last login: Thu Oct 02 2003 18:24:46 -0500 from dhcp065-024-074-
You have new mail.
ryoko miwa 1 >exit
Connection to ryoko.biosci.ohio-state.edu closed.
brezup:miwa miwa $ slogin 192.168.1.200
Welcome to Darwin!
[creampuf:~] miwa% exit
Connection to 192.168.1.200 closed.
```

The end demonstration is almost anticlimactic, but it's what miwa doesn't do here that's significant. It looks like there's no authentication— as though ryoko and creampuf simply allowed him to slogin in without bothering to check his credentials. *This isn't the case.* His ID was validated, but it was ssh-agent acting as his assistant that answered the query, and responded with the appropriate credentials. ssh-agent will continue to do so for any SSH commands that are run in this terminal, or for any other terminal that has had the environment variables set so that SSH commands run in it, can find the ssh-agent to talk to it.

Table 21.4 provides documentation for ssh-agent. Table 21.5 provides documentation for ssh-add.

CAUTION

It should be noted that using ssh-agent in this fashion is, as they say, putting all of your eggs in one basket. If a malicious user could find a way to co-opt the use of your ssh-agent, it would allow him to spoof connections as you, and your ssh-agent would happily provide your credentials to verify their false claim. Properly configured file permissions for keys in your .ssh directory will go a long way towards minimizing this problem. However, if a cracker has actually managed to break in to your account, he can access your key files with your permissions, and a running ssh-agent that you've started will have no way to tell you apart. Should this happen, using ssh-agent does materially weaken your security.

If you only use SSH in a mode where the remote systems require you to enter your passphrase directly out of your brain, a cracker who has broken one of your accounts is no closer to cracking your others. If you use ssh-agent to hold all of your credentials, and the cracker happens along while you've a running copy of ssh-agent that's serving credentials for you, the cracker will have full access to your accounts on machines for which ssh-agent holds credentials.

TABLE 21.4 Documentation for ssh-agent

ssh-agent	Authentication agent.
ssh-agent [-a <*bind_address*>] [-c ¦ -s] [-t <*life*>] [-d] [<*command*> [<*args*> ...]]	
ssh-agent [-c ¦ -s] -k	
ssh-agent is a program to hold private keys used for public key authentication (RSA, DSA). ssh-agent is started in the beginning of an X-session or a login session, and all other windows or programs are started as clients to the ssh-agent program. Through use of environment variables the agent can be located and automatically used for authentication when logging in to other machines using ssh.	
-a <*bind_address*>	Binds the agent to the unix-domain socket <*bind_address*>. The default is /tmp/ssh-XXXXXXXX/agent.<*ppid*>.
-c	Generates C-shell commands on stdout. This is the default if SHELL looks like it's a csh style of shell.
-s	Generates Bourne shell commands on stdout. This is the default if SHELL does not look like it's a csh style of shell.
-k	Kills the current agent (given by the SSH_AGENT_PID environment variable).
-d	Debug mode. When this option is specified ssh-agent does not fork.

TABLE 21.5 Documentation for ssh-add

ssh-add	Adds RSA or DSA identities to the authentication agent.
ssh-add [-lLdDxXc] [-t *<life>*] [*<file>* ...]	
ssh-add adds RSA or DSA identities to the authentication agent, ssh-agent(1). When run without arguments, it adds the files $HOME/.ssh/id_rsa, $HOME/.ssh/id_dsa and $HOME/.ssh/identity. Alternative file names can be given on the command line. If any file requires a passphrase, ssh-add asks for the passphrase from the user. The passphrase is read from the user's tty. ssh-add retries the last passphrase if multiple identity files are given. The authentication agent must be running and must be an ancestor of the current process for ssh-add to work.	
-l	Lists fingerprints of all identities currently represented by the agent.
-L	Lists public key parameters of all identities currently represented by the agent.
-d	Deletes the identity from the agent.
-D	Deletes all identities from the agent.
-x	Locks the agent with a password.
-X	Unlocks the agent.
-c	Indicates that added identities should be subject to confirmation before being used for authentication.
-t <life>	Sets a maximum lifetime when adding identities to an agent. The lifetime may be specified in seconds or in a time format specified in sshd.

A Better-Looking, More Helpful Butler: SSH Agent (the GUI Version)

If you're comfortable with the risks that using `ssh-agent` brings, there's a quite useful GUI tool that you might want to consider using. It, the Mac OS X Keychain, and some `Terminal.app` features all working together can make for wonderfully convenient secure remote connections. Xander Schrijen is actively developing a quite useful front end to the `ssh-agent` command-line utility, and endowing it with some nice auxiliary functions. `SSH Agent` acts sort of like a meta-agent for `ssh-agent`. It provides a GUI front end for the features of `ssh-agent`, and further can be configured to use your login credentials to store your passphrases in the Mac OS X Keychain, thereby allowing for `ssh-agent` functionality without you needing to do anything but successfully log in. To try out `SSH Agent`, download it from `http://www.phil.uu.nl/~xges/ssh/` and follow the Quick-Start installation instructions. SSH Agent does take up room on your Dock. If you would prefer to have your agent run in the background, you might be more interested in SSHKeychain, available from `http://www.sshkeychain.org/`. It functions in the background, but is still available as a menu item. Both of these are simply interfaces to the `ssh-agent` command-line application, which is preinstalled and can be configured and used entirely without the GUI. Perform the following steps:

1. Download the software from `http://www.phil.uu.nl/~xges/ssh/`.
2. Mount the disk image and copy the `SSH Agent` application to some convenient place on your drive. If you'd like it to be available to all of your users, putting it in `/Applications/` would be appropriate. Eject the disk image when you're done.

3. Run the `SSH Agent` application and open the Preferences panel.
4. In the Startup tab, shown in Figure 21.4, check the Make Agent Global setting.

FIGURE 21.4 Setting the SSH Agent application to serve credentials globally.

5. In the Environment tab, use the Add Variable button to add a variable named `CVS_RSH`, and set its value to `ssh` (see Figure 21.5).

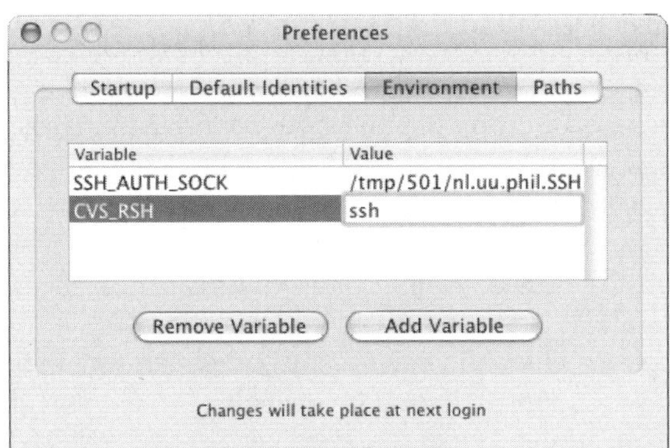

FIGURE 21.5 Setting environment variables through SSH Agent.

6. Log out, log back in, and restart SSH Agent.
7. Open the Preferences panel again, and go to the Default Identities pane.

Initially, it will appear as shown in Figure 21.6. Click on the Add Identity button and the dialog shown in Figure 21.7 will appear. The IDs shown in this dialog should be familiar from our recap of miwa's SSH key generation earlier in this section. Select the private key from the keypair for any identity you want to use by default. In this example, we're adding both IDs that miwa created earlier.

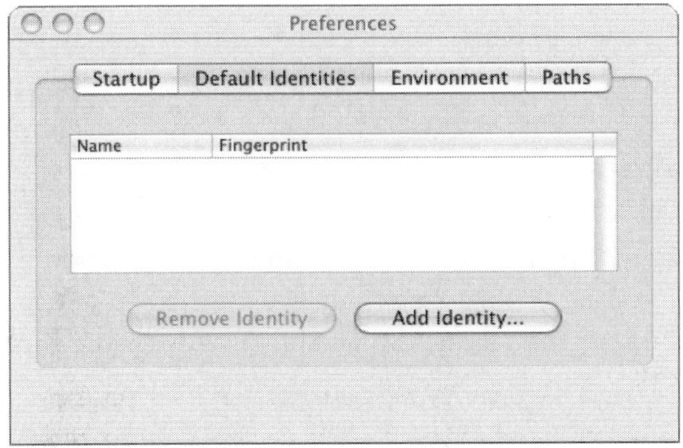

FIGURE 21.6 Like ssh-agent, out of the box, SSH Agent knows no identities.

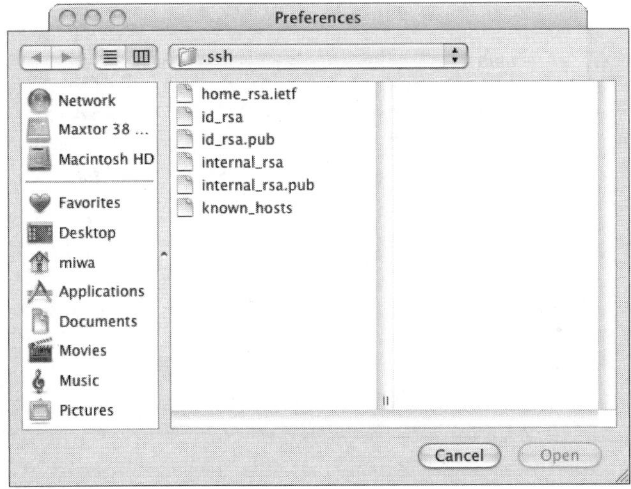

FIGURE 21.7 Clicking the Add Identity button allows you to select among any SSH identities that you've previously created. There's also a New Identity function under the File menu where you can create key pairs in SSH Agent from the beginning. Here, you need to select the private keys of each key-pair you want to use.

After you've selected the identities to add, the IDs will appear in the Default Identities tab, as shown in Figure 21.8.

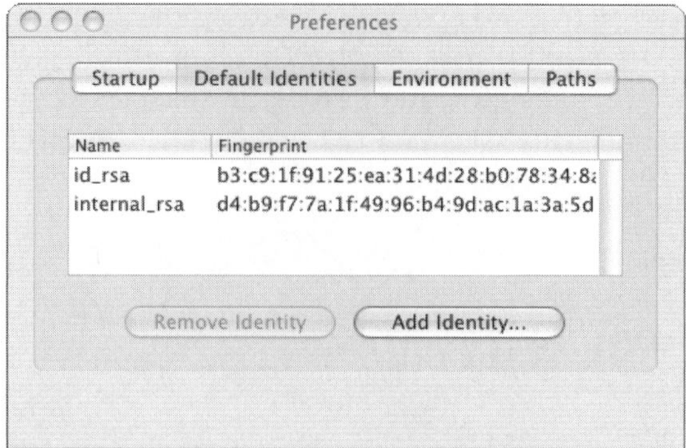

FIGURE 21.8 The Default Identities pane after adding some IDs.

Go back to the Startup pane and select Add Default Identities as shown in Figure 21.9, and then quit SSH Agent again.

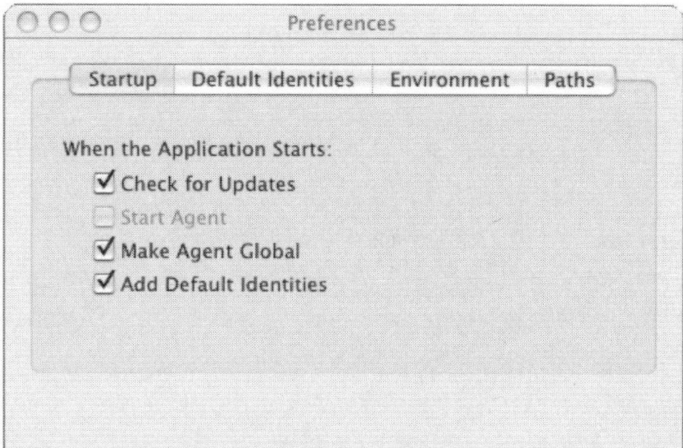

FIGURE 21.9 Setting the final preference that you need to configure before you can start making use of SSH Agent.

When you start SSH Agent again, you'll see a dialog as shown in Figure 21.10, where SSH Agent is asking you for the passphrase for an ID. Pay attention to the path shown for the identity, as SSH Agent will ask you for the passphrase for each identity you've configured it to load by default. Figure 21.11 shows what SSH Agent looks like after you've successfully supplied the requested passphrases.

Now, if you start a terminal you can use the credentials held by SSH Agent, and you don't even need to execute the `setenv` commands like you needed to for the command-line `ssh-agent` (see Figure 21.12).

If you'd like to avoid even the work of having to enter the passphrases once at the startup of SSH Agent, you can select the Add to Keychain option shown in Figure 21.10, and the passphrases you enter for your identities will be saved in your Keychain. If you do this, your default identities will be loaded automatically when you start SSH Agent, and you won't need to enter the passphrases for them again.

FIGURE 21.10 SSH Agent prompts for the passphrases for each identity you've asked it to hold for you.

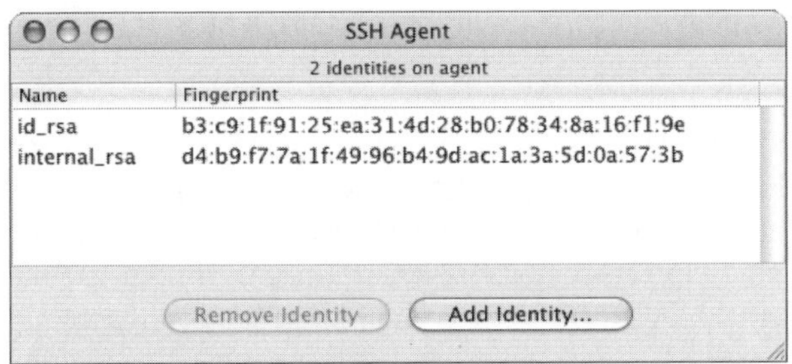

FIGURE 21.11 After you've supplied the requested passphrases, SSH Agent shows the loaded identities. From this window (which you can bring up from the Agent menu if the window is closed), you can also load additional nondefault identities selectively and as needed.

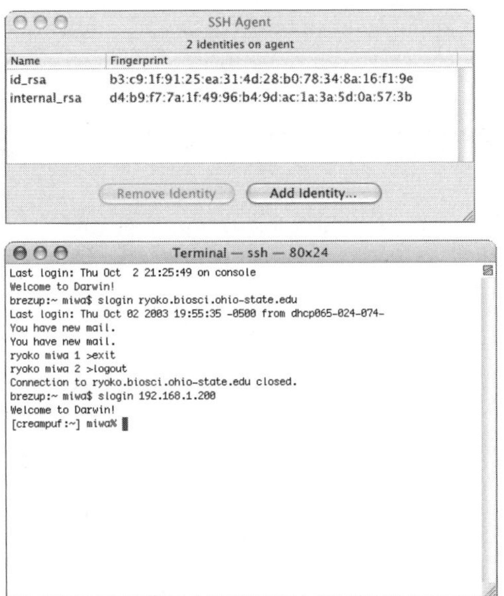

FIGURE 21.12 Now SSH Agent can provide you with the conveniences of `ssh-agent`, without you needing to set environment variables. This is nice, but the good part is still to come.

Combining this capability with some of the capabilities of `Terminal.app` is where the big payoff in ease-of-use comes in. `Terminal.app` has an infrequently-used function under the `File` menu listed as New Command. This function gives you the ability to execute a command and open a Terminal window containing the executing results of that command. Figure 21.13 shows it being used to set up a `slogin` session to `192.168.1.200`.

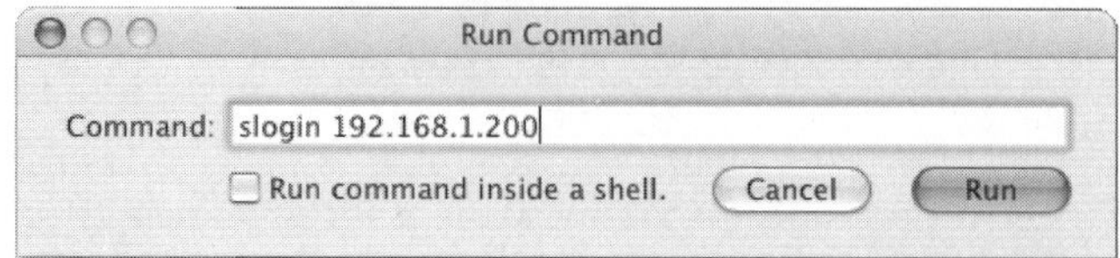

FIGURE 21.13 Setting up a Terminal session to run a command. Usually, you would just run the command in a Terminal session yourself, but this use is special.

Not surprisingly, the result of running the command in a shell, is a connection to `creampuf` (`192.168.1.200`). The neat thing is that we can now use another little-used feature of `Terminal.app` to save this terminal. Select the `Save As` item under `Terminal.app`'s File menu. This will bring up a dialog like the one shown in Figure 21.14. In this dialog, provide a useful name that will help you remember where these Terminal settings will take you. Also, remember to set the save location to some place that you'll actually find useful.

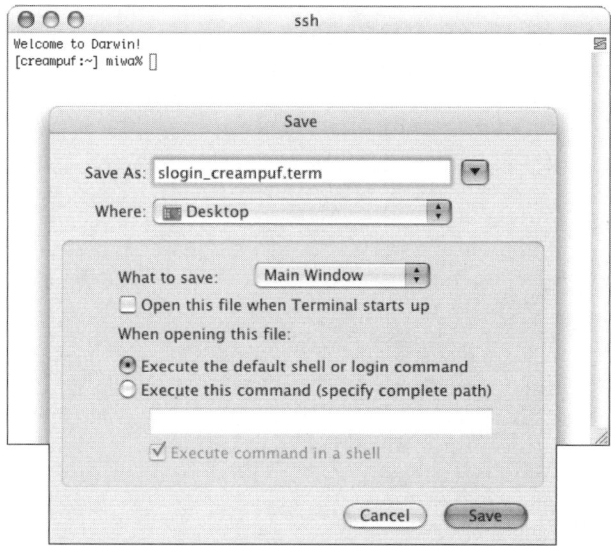

FIGURE 21.14 Saving a `Terminal.app` terminal session. This isn't saving the contents—it's saving what the terminal is doing.

And finally the nifty part. Figure 21.15 shows what `miwa`'s done with his SSH Agent–supplied identities, and with saved `Terminal.app` terminal sessions. The two icons shown in the Dock, one of which is labeled `slogin_ryoko.term`, is a saved terminal file for one of `miwa`'s IDs. The icon next to it is another saved `.term` file that `miwa` created for his `creampuf` ID. He's applied interesting icons to each to make them a bit more distinctive than the default little white rectangle icons they come with. Clicking on either will launch a Terminal session, using the command `miwa` set for it from the New Command menu item. That command will query the running SSH Agent, get the appropriate passphrase for `miwa` as necessary, and the connection to the remote server will be made with no further interaction needed on `miwa`'s part.

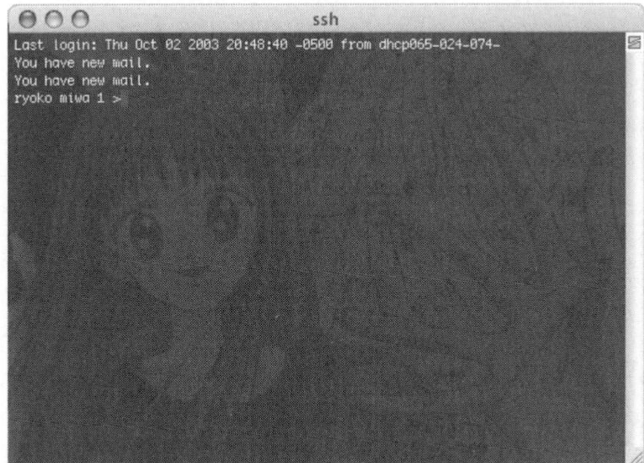

FIGURE 21.15 Saved `.term` files allow you to rerun their saved commands, in this case, saved `slogin` commands, which SSH Agent will allow to create secure connections with no further authentication required.

Single-click secure, encrypted connections to remote servers. What could be slicker than that?

SSH Clients for Windows, Traditional Mac OS, and Mac OS X

From other Unix machines with an SSH server installed, you should be able to use `ssh` or `slogin` to connect to your Mac OS X machine from a remote location. But you don't need a Unix machine to connect to your Mac OS X machine. Windows and traditional Mac OS clients are also available. This section includes a listing of popular client software, including a brief description of each client's features.

Windows

A number of Windows SSH clients are available. Among the available clients are

- Tera Term Pro with TTSSH—A free Terminal emulation program available at `http://hp.vector.co.jp/authors/VA002416/teraterm.html`. A free extension DLL called TTSSH is available for Tera Term at `http://www.zip.com.au/~roca/ttssh.html`. With the extension, Tera Term can be used as an SSH client. It supports only the SSH1 protocol. Additionally, it can handle public key authentication, tunneling, and X11 forwarding.

- PuTTY—A free Telnet and SSH client available at `http://www.chiark.greenend.org.uk/~sgtatham/putty/`. PuTTY supports both the SSH1 and SSH2 protocols, with SSH1 being the default protocol. It also supports public key authentication, tunneling, and X11 forwarding. Additionally, it includes `scp` (PSCP) and `sftp` (PSFTP) clients.
- F-Secure SSH—A commercial SSH client. It is available for Windows 95/98/Me/NT 4.0/2000/XP/2003. It supports both the SSH1 and SSH2 protocols. It also supports public key authentication, tunneling, and X11 forwarding. Additionally, it includes a built-in `sftp` client and command-line `ssh` tools. For more product information, see `http://www.wrq.com/products/reflection/ssh/`.
- SSH Secure Shell—SSH Communications Security has both a commercial and free SSH client for Windows 95/98/Me/NT 4.0/2000/XP. It supports both the SSH1 and SSH2 protocols. It also supports public key authentication, tunneling, and X11 forwarding. Additionally, it includes a built-in `sftp` client. For more product information, see `http://www.ssh.com/`. To download the freely available client, go to `ftp://ftp.ssh.com/pub/ssh/` and select the Windows client.
- SecureCRT—A commercial SSH client available from `http://www.vandyke.com/products/securecrt/`. It supports both the SSH1 and SSH2 protocols. It also supports public key authentication, tunneling, X11 forwarding, and `sftp`.

Macintosh 8/9

A few `ssh` clients are available for the traditional Mac OS. The clients that work in the traditional Mac OS probably also work in Mac OS X's classic mode. As a matter of fact, to tunnel connections in classic mode, you will need one of these clients with tunneling capabilities. Available clients include

- NiftyTelnet 1.1 SSH r3—A free Telnet and SSH client available at `http://www.lysator.liu.se/~jonasw/freeware/niftyssh/`. It supports only the SSH1 protocol. It also supports public key authentication and has a built-in `scp` function.
- MacSSH—A free client for SSH, Telnet, and various other protocols available at `http://www.macssh.com/`. For SSH, it supports only the SSH2 protocol. Additionally, it supports public key authentication, tunneling, and X11 forwarding.
- MacSFTP—A shareware `sftp` client available at `http://www.macssh.com/`. It supports both SSH1 and SSH2. You can download a 15-day trial. If you decide to keep it, the shareware cost is $25. It has an interface similar to Fetch's.

Mac OS X

Mac OS X, of course, has the command-line `ssh` tools available. However, if you are new to the command line, you might also be wondering whether any SSH GUI tools are available. As you might recall from Chapter 12, even `Terminal.app` provides some basic SSH GUI tools. For `sftp` and `scp` alternatives, you should also check whether your favorite FTP client includes or will include such support. Available clients include

- JellyfiSSH—A freeware product available from http://www.arenasoftware.com/grepsoft/. It provides a GUI login interface and bookmarking capabilities. After you've entered your login information, it brings up a Terminal window to the remote host, showing the command that was issued. If you are comfortable with using slogin or ssh to log in to a remote host, this application might not be useful to you. If you like the basic GUI login interface of the clients for traditional Mac OS, this application might be useful to you. If you want to learn how to use the ssh command-line client, this application might be useful to you because you can see how the command was issued.

- Terminal.app—As of Mac OS X 10.3, Terminal.app's Connect to Server option under the File menu offers a graphical interface to the ssh and sftp commands. Enter the information in the graphical interface, and a terminal opens up running the command. If you are comfortable with the basic command-line ssh and sftp, this interface might not interest you. Otherwise, you might find it useful for learning how to issue the commands.

- Fugu—A freeware product available from http://rsug.itd.umich.edu/software/fugu/. It is an scp/sftp/ssh tunneling client.

- SSH Tunnel Manager—A freeware product available from http://projects.tynsoe.org/en/stm/. As the name suggests, this is a graphical application that helps you set up and manage your SSH tunnels.

- MacSFTP—Also works in Mac OS X. This shareware sftp client is available at http://www.macssh.com/. It supports both the SSH1 and SSH2 protocols. You can download a 15-day trial. If you decide you like it, the shareware cost is $25. It has an interface similar to Fetch's.

- Gideon—A shareware sftp/ftp client available at http://www.gideonsoftworks.com/gideon.html. The shareware cost is $25, payable if you like it.

- RBrowser—An application available from http://www.rbrowser.com/. It provides a finder interface to ssh, scp, and sftp, and also supports tunneling. If you do not like the command line at all, this might be the application for you. The sftp feature works by dragging files from one "finder" to the other. This is a shareware product with two levels of licensing: a basic level that covers ftp and sftp features and a professional level that includes ftp, sftp, Unix, ssh, and ssh tunneling. Demo licenses are also available.

- SSH Agent—A graphical manager for ssh-agent. SSH Agent is freely available from http://www.phil.uu.nl/~xges/ssh/.

- SSHKeychain—A graphical manager for ssh-agent. This package is freely available from http://www.sshkeychain.org/. It also includes Apple Keychain support.

Accessing Mac OS X Remotely Using Apple Remote Desktop

One highly useful, but oddly unsung (except in the halls of system administrators) application for accessing and managing Macs remotely is the Apple Remote Desktop application, or ARD. ARD was born of a desire to provide a flexible way for administrators to manage (possibly many multiple) remote machines, in an environment where large portions of the interface require graphic interactions. The basic question was to find a way to share screens, keyboards and mice, so that an administrator sitting in her office could attach to a remote machine and interact with it as though she were sitting at its keyboard, viewing its monitor.

This question, and possible solutions to it, have been through several iterations over the years, but Apple seems finally to have settled on a solution that not only makes the Mac easy to administrate from a remote location, but also makes it easy to interoperate with the ubiquitous VNC shared-desktop solution that is available for Linux, Windows, and most other operating systems. With the release of ARD 2, Apple's solution is clean, elegant, interoperable, and provides many features that go beyond simple desktop sharing, and that makes ARD an indispensable tool in any administrator's arsenal. Apple's own documentation of ARD spans 116 pages, and might be considered light on detail in many places, so we can't hope to cover all ARD features in which you might be interested in this book. Instead, here we will hit the highlights that can help you decide whether ARD is for you, and if it is, try to cover some of the details that might help with remembering some of the less expected features.

Understanding the Features and Limitations of ARD

ARD comes in two simple-to-assemble pieces: the ARD client, which is installed by default on all Mac OS X Tiger (and Panther) workstations, and the administrative application, for which Apple charges the princely sum of $299 for 10 clients, or $499 for unlimited clients (`http://www.apple.com/remotedesktop/`). For the home user who simply wants a way to monitor or control a remote computer, these prices might seem steep, and a simple, freeware solution such as VNC (`http://www.realvnc.com/`) might be a more appealing option. For the administrator who needs to manage multiple machines, the additional features of ARD make it a must-have application that would be cheap at 10 times the price.

In addition to providing a way to share desktops and controls with a client computer (a task that can be easily accomplished with VNC), ARD allows administrators to observe an (almost) unlimited number of remote desktops simultaneously, or to completely take control of a remote machine and to lock the controls so that the person actually at the keyboard can only observe. Alternatively, the administrative user can also share her desktop out to the client computer to observe, for those instances where demonstrating something on a local machine is easier than doing it on theirs. Or, if it's a different remote user who can demonstrate the task best, you can select one remote user's screen, and share it to other remote users for viewing.

ARD also provides a number of nonobservation remote-control features that are, perhaps, even more important than the raw ability to interact with the remote computer graphically. These include functions such as sleeping, waking and restarting target computers; sending pop-up-window messages to remote computers; Locking the screen of remote computers; copying files to remote computers; running `pkg`/`mpkg` software installers on remote computers; running Unix shell commands and shell scripts on remote computers; specifying startup information on remote computers; collecting a wealth of system information on remote computers; and searching for files on remote computers; and many others. Although most of these might sound like things that you have learned how to do with a remote terminal session, the important feature here is that each of these actions can be performed on one remote computer or on any number of selected clients simultaneously. Even better, the actions can all be scheduled such that they happen (or repeat) at a particular time, so you don't even need to be there to press the button when they happen.

Need to reboot all of your machines at 10:00 p.m. because a server will be being rebooted then? Select them all, click the reboot button, and schedule the action for 10:00 p.m. Go to dinner and a movie, and check your ARD status at midnight when you get back. In the morning, you can impress your boss with your diligence for staying late and running all over the company hitting reboot buttons.

Just got a call that there are possibly malicious network probes coming from one of the lab machines you oversee, the machine's on the other side of campus, and it's raining? Either click the Observe button and take a look at what's going on, select the machine and shut it down, lock the screen, kick the current user off the machine, or whatever remedy you prefer. If there are multiple machines at the same location, select them all and lock them all down for good measure—if you have a physical intruder you don't want them just moving over to the next computer on the bench!

Need to install the latest iChat update on your client machines so that you can do a better job taking service calls over the network? Select the targets, click the Install Packages button, and toss in the iChat update. You can even roll your own `mpkg` installers using the Developer Tools PackageMaker application, allowing you to bundle up multiple `pkg` installs into a single sendable install action.

All in all, ARD provides features that could make it one of the best tools in an administrator's toolbox. It does, however, have some peculiar quirks, some annoying misfeatures, and one glaring omission that prevents it from being a one-stop-shop for administration goodness.

Among its quirks are the fact that it's oddly slower than standalone VNC clients, even though it seems to use VNC as a base transport, and that it has a peculiar sense of which keypresses should be interpreted as keyboard events to send to the remote machine and which are intended to go to the ARD application itself. For example, if a view of an ARD client is the frontmost window on your screen, and you press Command-Q, what do you expect to quit? So far, the actual behavior—quitting the frontmost application on the client computer, has not been the behavior that my fingers were expecting, although one could excuse this as a user-training issue. On the other hand, if you're viewing a client screen, and you press Command-Shift-3 to take a screenshot, do you expect a screenshot of the client screen, or of your screen, viewing the client screen? If you guessed that it'd take a screenshot of the client screen, you win the consistency-in-user-interface-design award, and lose the predicting-what-it-actually-does competition.

Chief among the misfeatures is the fact that ARD defaults to VNC screen ID zero, and provides no way for you to change this default. VNC was originally designed for the X Window System (refer to Chapter 17, "Using X Window System Applications"), and the X Window System display abstraction allows that there can be multiple displays attached to a single computer. As a matter of fact, it expects multiple displays, some of which may be local and some remote, and that any given user may not have permission to see some or all of the displays.

Therefore VNC incorporates the idea of screen IDs to allow the system to identify what screen and GUI a user is trying to connect to. On PCs, and Macs that aren't running an X Window session, ID zero is a fair bet for what ID VNC might grab for itself, but on a machine that's X Window–capable, such as a Linux box, or an Mac OS X machine running the X Window System, ID zero will rarely be available, and a user's VNC session will almost always be something other than zero. ARD currently provides no way to connect to these non-zero-ID displays, and so can effectively only be used with non–X Window System machines. Circumventing this limitation is possible at the client (by making VNC and X Window System run on nonstandard screen IDs, or by using a hokey VNC client that attaches to screen zero, rather than creating a new one for each user), but even using atypical VNC configurations that can attach screen zero, ARD will be incapable of connecting to any alternate VNC screens that may be available on the machine.

The glaring omission, which despite the fact that ARD is quite useful, limits it to being far less useful than it potentially could be, is the lack of any way to share the clipboard between machines. This is oversight is so fundamentally wrong, that one would be forced to the conclusion that the lack of functionality was either a bug, or a misunderstanding, except for the number of ARD users who are all unanimously cursing this problem. The only workaround we've stumbled on so far is to run iChat between your administrative machine and the remote machine as well, and use iChat as a copy/paste buffer for things you need to move. It feels rather stupid to sit there and have a conversation with yourself just to move URLs around between computers, but so far, it's the only solution we've found.

Activating Remote Desktop in Tiger

The ARD client module is activated by a simple check box in the Services pane of the Sharing Control Panel. Like other services on the services pane, check the check box, and ARD switches on, and connections are enabled. If you select the Show status in the menu bar check box that appears when select ARD, another status menu is added to the right of the menu bar. The icon for this looks like a pair of binoculars, and depending on other settings, provides a visual notification to the user that his machine is being watched or controlled.

To configure what remote ARD administrators can do, select ARD in the Sharing pane and then click the Access Privileges button that appears. Figure 21.16 shows the interface for configuring access privileges. On this sheet you can select what users are allowed to connect using ARD, and what they are allowed to do when connected.

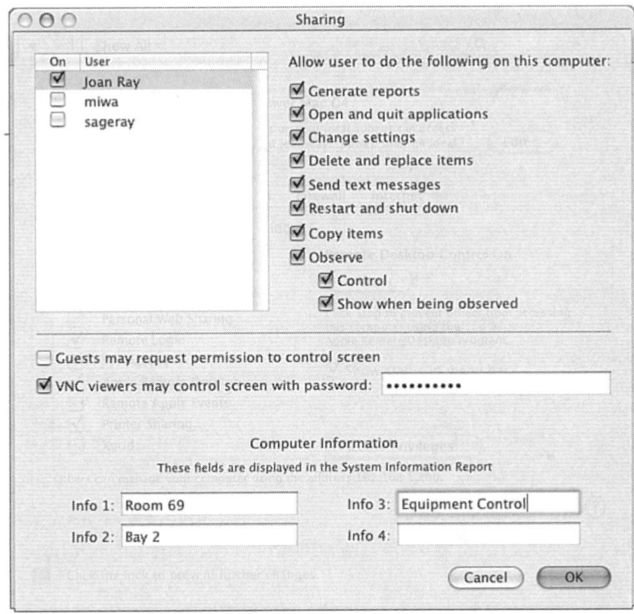

FIGURE 21.16 In the access privileges sheet for ARD, you can configure a number of privileges or limitations on the administrative user.

For each user on your system, you can enable and disable her ability to connect from a remote machine running the administration interface. Unlike desktop sharing applications like VNC, this setting does not enable a different login and session for each of these users, but rather, whether each (or any) are allowed to connect to and to view the desktop for *any user* who is currently logged in at the console. Against expectations (although completely logical in terms of how the interface is shared), the only setting/limitation that ARD takes from the account settings of the particular user that you select is the username and password. That is to say, you can have a user who is a severely limited managed user, with restrictions to the Simple Finder, and many Parental Controls engaged, and if that user connects using ARD while *you* are the user logged in at the console, the screen that user gets is yours, and access limitations to which that user is restricted are the ones configured for your user and the ones configured in the access privileges sheet in Figure 21.16.

The ARD administrative interface makes a nod to trying to ameliorate this disconnection of privileges and users, by allowing the ARD administration software to be configured to deny access to anyone who's not in the admin group on the computer. Unfortunately, Apple's default setup of making every computer owner into an admin-group member reduces this limitation to insignificance. Anyone who can boot a machine into a mode where they are the owner, and therefore an admin-group member (as in a default install of Mac OS X, perhaps booted off of an iPod), can tweak the settings on ARD to allow them complete control of a remote machine, even if they have only managed-access while physically at that remote machine.

> **CAUTION**
>
> To reduce the obvious risks involved, Apple recommends that special ARD-only users be set up on ARD client computers, and only these ARD-specific users given permission to access the machine remotely. This eliminates the problem of a low-privilege user being able to connect to the running session of a high-privilege user, but it is security that's entirely dependent on you configuring it properly, rather than something that Apple configures properly from the start.

Other privileges that can be configured (on a per-user basis, in terms of who can connect, although there is currently no provision in the ARD administrative interface to have multiple user configurations for a single machine), are as follows:

- Generate Reports—When enabled, the selected user can use the reports function of the ARD administrative tool to pull down rather detailed reports about the settings, contents, and status of your machine.
- Open and Quit Applications—When enabled, the selected user can launch applications through ARD. Note that this is a different meaning of *launch applications* than simply clicking on the application on a remote-controlled desktop. Even if this is disabled, a user with Control permission can still use the Finder to launch applications. Enabling the open/quit apps option allows the user to target this machine in the remote ARD interface for an application launch task. Using these tasks, a remote administrator can launch the same application on an entire room full of (ARD Client) Macs, simultaneously.
- Change Settings—Again, this doesn't limit what the user can do though a controlled session, but rather whether the user can tell the ARD administrative interface to change the ARD settings on this client computer, as part of a Change Settings Task.
- Delete and Replace Items—Whether the user is allowed to issue Copy, Install, and Empty Trash tasks from the ARD administrative interface. This must be enabled if you want to be able to upgrade client ARD versions automatically from within the ARD administrative interface.
- Send Text Messages—Whether an administrator, connected as this user, is allowed to send pop-up messages, or invoke the Chat function.
- Restart and Shut Down—Whether an administrator, connected as this user, is allowed to issue Sleep, Wake, Restart, and Shutdown commands. This must be enabled if you want to be able to upgrade client ARD versions automatically from within the ARD administrative interface.
- Copy Items—Whether an administrator, connected as this user, is allowed to target this computer with Copy Items and Install Package tasks. This must be enabled if you want to be able to upgrade client ARD versions automatically from within the

ARD administrative interface, or if you want to be able to change the client ARD settings from the ARD administrative interface Change Settings task.

- Observe—Whether an administrator is allowed to view the current desktop using this user's username and password. There are degrees of observation available. Selecting Observe alone allows the administrator to watch, but not otherwise interact with the current desktop session.
- Control—Whether an administrator, connected as this user, is allowed to control the current desktop session. A user with Control privileges can not only watch what's happening on the desktop, but can also take control of the mouse and keyboard, or lock the screen and lock out the current user. This must be enabled if you want to be able to upgrade client ARD versions automatically from within the ARD administrative interface.
- Show When Being Observed—Whether the ARD status menu icon should change *when this user connects*, to reflect that the machine is being observed or controlled. The use of this, like the configuration of the users, is counter-intuitive. You might imagine that if you're an admin-group user on the local machine, you'd want to know if someone was watching your machine using ARD, and that if you were configuring managed users, you might not want them to know they were being observed. Unfortunately, there appears to be no way to enact that control. If you try to use this check box in that fashion (and more than a few ARD admins have tried), what you'll do is configure your machine so that any time your admin-group user is watching the computer remotely, anybody who's at the console is immediately informed, and any time your limited-access managed user is watching, nobody will know.

In addition to per-user controls, you can configure several general ARD client settings:

- Guests May Request Permissions to Control Screen—When selected, the ARD client will allow remote administrative users to request control, even if they don't have a local user ID and password with which to connect. You can use this setting to allow, for example, help-desk people to connect momentarily to your machine to make a quick configuration change or to help find a well-hidden setting in a program with which you aren't familiar.
- VNC Viewers May Control Screen with Password—ARD seems to run over VNC (`http://www.realvnc.com/`) as a base transport system. This is convenient in two ways: It allows the administrative interface to view and control VNC client computers in addition to ARD client computers, and it also allows ARD clients to serve their screens out as VNC sessions to which a VNC viewer can connect remotely. This means that even if you don't have the ARD administrative software, you can still install a freeware VNC viewer, and (if you've selected this check box) take remote control of your machine. You won't have access to any of the ARD administrative interface niceties, but you will be able to view and interact with the current desktop session from remote.

There are also four user-configurable text-string settings that you can use to provide helpful identifying information in the reports, so that you aren't left trying to find the physical machine that's attached to a virtual desktop, armed only with an IP address.

TIP

Remember, ARD is stuck on VNC screen ID zero, so you'll need to point your client software at this ID to connect.

CAUTION

Be aware, if you enable VNC access, that the default VNC network transport is not secured in the same fashion as ARD, and that the password, as well as any interaction you do between the machines, can be sniffed off the network with relative ease. Apple claims that traffic between native ARD clients and the ARD administrative interface is encrypted with 128-bit AES, but we've seen very little documentation or discussion of this topic.

Controlling and Observing Remote Desktop Stations

The administrative interface component of ARD is simple, and with only a few exceptions, intuitive to use. Administrators are presented with either a list of configured machines, or semi-live screen views of a selection of machines. Selecting one or more machine in either interface will allow you to target them for ARD administrative tasks such as installing software or generating reports. Although the same administrative tasks are available from the menu bar in each view, the tasks that are available in the icon bar of the screen-views machine list, is very limited compared to the tasks that are available in the machine list view.

Figure 21.17 shows ARD viewing semi-live (updated about once every second or so) screens from three computers. The one in the upper left is a VNC session coming from a Linux box, whereas the other two are ARD clients in Tiger. In the Toolbar across the top of the screen are icons that let me configure the way the semi-live multi-screen view works and take control of any of the machines I'm viewing. At the left of the screen, the binoculars, concentric-circle target-like icon, thumb-tacked document, and lock icons, respectively allow me to observe (in closer to real-time) a selected machine, take control of a selected machine, send a pop-up message to any number of selected machine, and lock the screens on selected machines. At the top right of the screen are sliders that control the color size of the live previews, the refresh rate for the previews, and the color-representation quality on the previews. If I have enough live previews going that I can't see them all on the screen at the currently selected size, the left/right arrow buttons in the very top-left corner activate, and I can page between multiple pages of previewed screens.

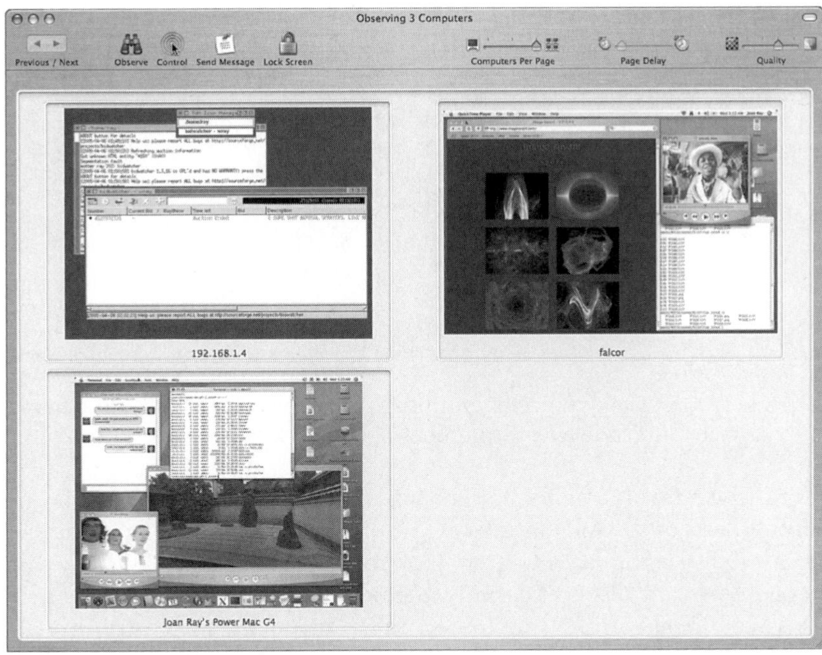

FIGURE 21.17 The multiscreen live view window (created by selecting multiple machines and clicking the View icon), lets you view the running desktop from multiple machines simultaneously.

Figure 21.18 shows ARD viewing the list-view of configured machines. This view doesn't provide the friendly live-preview feature, but it also consumes far less network bandwidth to produce, and it provides additional useful details regarding each machine. In this list you can see that I have one VNC client, two ARD clients to which I can connect, and one ARD client that's currently refusing access. Apple uses many graphical cues and icons to condense various status information into digestible bits—many more than can be documented here. The interested reader is directed to the ARD manual that comes as part of the help system for the software.

In addition to viewing screens and taking control, the Toolbar in this interface (by default) allows you to send your own screen to target computers; sleep, wake and restart target computers; send pop-up messages to target computers; lock the screen of target computers; copy items to target computers; install `pkg` or `mpkg` packages on target computers; execute Unix commands on target computers; configure target computer startup disks; get a system-overview report from target computers; and search all target computers for a particular file or files. The tasks that can be sent directly from the toolbar are configurable from a Configure item in the Window menu.

At the bottom of the window is a list of recent and pending tasks that have been executed by this administrative interface on the client computers. Several tasks have finished. One that's searching for a file is still working on generating a report, and one is queued up waiting for the file search to finish. These tasks can be saved for future re-use, or re-executed (possibly with minor modifications) as needed simply by double-clicking them, selecting the Duplicate Task option, and sending the duplicate off to be executed again.

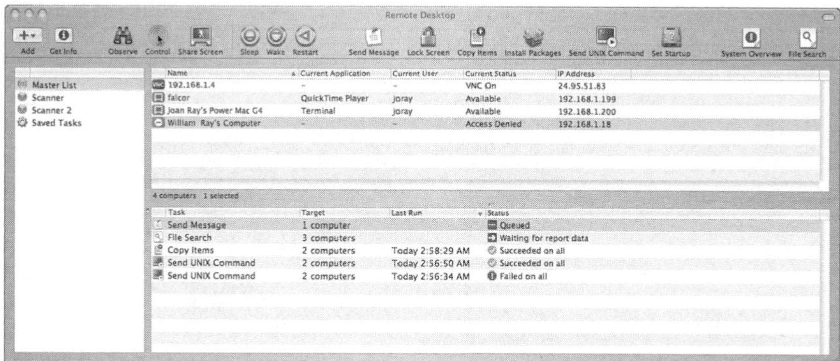

FIGURE 21.18 The List view of machines is used to view various identifying parameters for the machines, as well as to issue a larger number of one-click task assignments to clients.

At the left of the window is a panel that manages lists of things. This panel is one of the least intuitive aspects of the ARD interface. It is primarily devoted to managing lists of computers, but it also is the place to go to look for the list of saved Tasks. The lists of computers themselves are also not entirely identical in intent, creating a hierarchy of functions between them with no way to impose the hierarchy onto their display.

For example, you can only view and control machines that have been added to the Master List. You configure these machines by either dragging them out of the default scanner (if the default scanner can find them) in to the Master List, or by double-clicking them in the scanner. Either way you will be prompted for a name for the machine, and a username and password with which to connect. *This is the user and password against which the permissions configured in the Services/Remote Desktop/Access Privileges sheet on the client, are compared.* If the default scanner cannot find the computer, you need to create a new scanner, and give it enough information to find the computer you want (configuration of scanners is a complex topic, and interested readers are referred to the ARD manual for more information). This situation is confusing because the machine list produced by a scanner is almost identical to the machine list displayed for the Master List, and even interface features such as the Toolbar remain the same, but the behaviors and functions that are available when you select a computer are different.

Selections of machines that have been added to the Master List can have additional machine lists created to hold just them, conveniently allowing them to be selected and acted upon as a group. There's no good way to filter the machines on the Master List to select related machines that you might want. So, peculiarly, if you have lots of machines to work with, the most effective way to group them is to add them to the Master List, create a custom scanner that finds just the group you want, select them all from the Scanner, and create a custom list from that. Because they're already added to the Master List, they'll go into a custom list as a group, without further configuration effort.

Another point of confusion is that there is no way to configure multiple instances of the same machine in the Master List. Because you can configure multiple users with different permissions in the ARD client interface, it would make sense that you might want to be able to select among these in the administrative interface, perhaps using a user ID that has been assigned only nondestructive permissions for most day-to-day interactions with your clients, and reserving connections as an administrator with all privileges enabled for those times when there is more drastic work that needs done.

Alternatively, you might want to have two different users that have the Show When Being Observed option set differently, so that you can monitor your computers without detection when it's appropriate, and also have the option of letting users know that they're being observed, for normal operations. So far, this capability is missing. If you want to change the user you're using to connect in the ARD administrative interface, you need to Get Info on the configured computer in the Master List, edit the settings, and change the userID and password you're using to connect. You then need to close any open connections to the machine and re-open them. We hope Apple decides to change this in the near future because it's number 2 on our dumb omission list, right behind the lack of copy/paste functionality.

Double-clicking a machine in either the multimachine live view, or the List view of machines, opens a control window directly to that machine. Figure 21.19 shows a monitored client machine, as seen in an ARD administrator's window. The client's actually running a 21" monitor at 1600×1200, and my laptop is only capable of 1280×854, but ARD scales the remote display nicely, allowing it to run surprisingly well in a window on my laptop. Across the top of the window are buttons that configure the type of interaction I have with the remote machine. Clicking the leftmost one would allow me to take control of the machine (right now I'm just observing, although it's difficult to tell that the control button is deselected in a black-and-white printout on paper).

If I am controlling the machine, I have the options of locking out the user at the keyboard and controlling it exclusively, or of sharing control with the user at the keyboard. The second button at the top left of the window configures this behavior. The button with the four diagonally pointing arrows, configures whether ARD should scale the remote screen into my local window or deliver it at full size, and let me scroll around to get to the parts that don't fit in the window. I find the scaling option to be surprisingly useful for most situations, but if you're trying to help a remote user do pixel-perfect object placement in PhotoShop, there's no substitute for a real 1:1 look at what's happening on their machine.

Finally, at the right of the Toolbar is a quality slider that lets me control whether the remote screen is delivered to my administrative interface in full color, surprisingly good reduced color, grayscale, or dithered black and white (which will give you an idea of what the original Mac display looked like, although the GUI controls are obviously not well designed for living in this mode today). To keep the display interactive, while not putting too large a burden on the network, I've usually found it useful to use the grayscale option, or sometimes even the dither black and white setting. This improves the interactivity of the display considerably, at the cost of losing legibility of interface elements that depend on color or on shade. Depending on the task at hand, though, you might find more color to be more important. You can adjust this setting on the fly, so it's not a problem to turn up the quality to address an issue where color matters, and then turn it back down again to conserve bandwidth and improve speed.

FIGURE 21.19 Watching a client computer using ARD. From this interface I can view the client without interfering at all, or take complete control of the interface, as necessary.

A surprising limitation of the control view for a machine is that all the menu-based ARD task-assignment functionality is disabled while looking directly at a remote screen. For example, If you want to copy a file to the machine you're looking at, you have to put the screen aside, go back to the list or multiscreen machine view, select the machine again there, and then set up the file copy task. This again is a bizarre inconsistency on Apple's part, and it's one that we again hope will be fixed in the near future.

Summary

This chapter provided an overview of SSH and Apple Remote Desktop, two different ways to remotely access your machine. The SSH discussion included basic and advanced use for SSH2. Although we looked only at SSH2, the basics are the same for SSH1, if you should need to interact with an SSH1 server. Topics included making secure terminal connections, securely transferring files, tunneling connections, and enabling public key authentication.

In the ARD discussion, we looked at the features and limitations of ARD and how to activate and configure the client. Then we took a brief look at ARD in action, where we saw live views of multiple machines, list views of multiple machines, and even a control view of one client machine.

CHAPTER 22

Creating an FTP Server

IN THIS CHAPTER

- Activating the Mac OS X FTP Server: `tnftpd`
- Configuring `tnftpd` FTP Server Options
- Setting Up Anonymous FTP
- Setting Up ProFTPD as a Replacement for the Default `ftpd`
- Alternatives to FTP

Sometimes it's helpful to be able to transfer files between machines. If you're collaborating on a project, you and your collaborators might need to exchange files. Because mail spools frequently have file size limits, an FTP server can provide an alternative means to exchange files. If you've built a website on one machine but want to transfer it to your Mac OS X machine because you have a web server running on it, an FTP server can provide a way to do so. With little effort, your Mac OS X machine can run an FTP server to facilitate this activity. In this chapter, we look at the FTP server included in the Mac OS X distribution. Then we look at an alternative, highly configurable FTP server that you could install in place of the default FTP server. Finally, we take a brief look at alternatives that can be used in place of, or in conjunction with, an FTP server.

Activating the Mac OS X FTP Server: `tnftpd`

The Mac OS X distribution includes an FTP server called `tnftpd`, which is a port of the NetBSD FTP server. Because Apple is concerned about the security of your machine, this service is not turned on by default. Currently, you can FTP only from your Mac OS X machine to other FTP servers. After you've turned on the FTP service, you can FTP directly to your Mac OS X machine. Unfortunately, this service also makes your machine more vulnerable to outside attacks. Throughout the chapter, we provide suggestions for some simple precautions that you can take to protect your machine. Of course, the best protection is to not turn on the FTP server.

To activate the FTP server, check the FTP Access box under the Services tab of the Sharing pane. The FTP service starts via `launchd`.

Configuring `tnftpd` FTP Server Options

You've just turned on your FTP server. If you looked at the `/System/Library/LaunchDaemons/ftp.plist` file, you noticed that the server runs by default with the `-l` option (from the

```
<key>ProgramArguments</key>
        <array>
                <string>ftpd</string>
                <string>-l</string>
        </array>
```

section), which is the option that forces the logging of successful and unsuccessful FTP sessions.

Other options are available in the FTP server, and select options are detailed in the command documentation table, Table 22.1. To change FTP server options, add the appropriate strings in `/System/Library/LaunchDaemons/ftp.plist`, then start and stop the FTP server.

Note that whenever you turn the FTP service on or off via the System Preferences pane, any other configuration changes you have made to the service are retained instead of being reset. Nonetheless, it is a good idea to keep a copy of the file with your configuration changes, in case this default behavior ever changes.

TABLE 22.1 Command Documentation Table for `ftpd`

ftpd	Internet File Transfer Protocol server
`ftpd [-dHlqQrsuUwWX] [-a <anondir>] [-c <confdir>] [-C <user>] [-e <emailaddr>] [-h <hostname>] [-L <xferlogfile>] [-P <dataport>] [-V <version>]`	
`ftpd` is the Internet File Transfer Protocol process. It uses the TCP protocol and runs on the port specified as `ftp` in the `/etc/services` file.	
`-a <anondir>`	Defines `<anondir>` as the directory to `chroot` into for anonymous logins. Default is the home directory for the `ftp` user. This can also be specified with the `ftpd.conf chroot` directive.
`-c <confdir>`	Changes the root directory of the configuration files from `/etc` to `<confdir>`. This changes the directory for the following files: `/etc/ftpchroot`, `/etc/ftpusers`, `/etc/ftpwelcome`, `/etc/motd`, and the file specified by the `ftpd.conf limit` directive.
`-h <hostname>`	Explicitly sets the hostname to advertise as `<hostname>`. Default is the hostname associated with the IP address that `ftpd` is listening on. This capability (with or without `-h`), in conjunction with `-c <confdir>`, is useful when configuring virtual FTP servers, each listening on separate addresses as separate names.
`-H`	Equivalent to `-h <hostname>`.

TABLE 22.1 Continued

`-l`	Logs each successful and failed FTP session using syslog with a facility of `LOG_FTP`.
`-P <dataport>`	Uses `<dataport>` as the data port, overriding the default of using the port one less than the port `ftpd` is listening on.
`-q`	Enables the use of PID files for keeping track of the number of logged-in users per class. This is the default.
`-U`	Doesn't log each concurrent FTP session to `/var/run/utmp`. This is the default.
`-V <version>`	Uses `<version>` as the version to advertise in the login banner and in the output of `STAT` and `SYST` instead of the default version information. If *`version`* is `-` or empty, it doesn't display any version information.

Restricting Access

The FTP server uses three main configuration files for restricting access: `/etc/ftpusers`, `/etc/ftpchroot`, and `/etc/ftpd.conf`. By using these files, you can place restrictions on who can use FTP to access your machine—blocking certain users and allowing others. You can also configure limitations to the type and frequency of access granted by limiting the number of connections, and setting timeouts and other server-related limits on FTP server availability and capability.

An `/etc/ftpusers` file comes by default. This file contains the list of users who aren't allowed FTP access to the machine. Here's the default file:

```
brezup:sage Documents $ more /etc/ftpusers
# list of users disallowed any ftp access.
# read by ftpd(8).
Administrator
administrator
root
uucp
daemon
unknown
www
```

If you have additional users who shouldn't be granted FTP access, include them in this file. Also include any system logins that might not be listed by default in this file. Because the syntax for this file can be more complex, its documentation is included in Table 22.2.

TABLE 22.2 Documentation for `/etc/ftpusers`

`ftpusers`	`ftpd` access control files
`ftpchroot`	
`/etc/ftpusers`	

The `/etc/ftpusers` file provides user access control for `ftpd` by defining which users may login.

If the `/etc/ftpusers` file does not exist, all users are denied access.

The syntax of each line is

`<userglob>[:<groupglob>][@<host>] [<directive> [<class>]]`

These elements are

<userglob> is matched against the username, using `fnmatch` glob matching (for example, `f*`).

<groupglob> is matched against all the groups that the user is a member of, using `fnmatch` glob matching (for example, `*src`).

<host> is either a `CIDR` address (refer to `inet_net_pton`) to match against the remote address (for example, `1.2.3.4/24`), or an `fnmatch` glob to match against the remote hostname (for example, `*.netbsd.org`).

<directive> allows access to the user if set to `allow` or `yes`. Denies access to the user if set to `deny` or `no`, or if the directive is not present.

<class> defines the class to use in `ftpd.conf`.

If `<class>` isn't given, it defaults to one of the following:

`chroot` if there's a match in `/etc/ftpchroot` for the user.

`guest` if the username is `anonymous` or `ftp`.

`real` if neither of the preceding conditions is true.

No further comparisons are attempted after the first successful match. If no match is found, the user is granted access. This syntax is backward compatible with the old syntax.

If a user requests a guest login, the `ftpd` server checks to see that both `anonymous` and `ftp` have access. So, if you deny all users by default, you must add both `anonymous allow` and `ftp allow` to `/etc/ftpusers` in order to allow guest logins.

`/etc/ftpchroot`

The file `/etc/ftpchroot` is used to determine which users will have their session's root directory changed (using `chroot`), either to the directory specified in the `ftpd.conf chroot` directive (if set), or to the home directory of the user. If the file doesn't exist, the root directory change is not performed.

The FTP server also allows for `chroot`ed FTP access, which is a compromise between full access and anonymous-only access. With this compromise access, a user is granted FTP access to only his home directory. List any users who should have this type of access in the `/etc/ftpchroot` file.

The last major configuration file for the default `ftpd` is `/etc/ftpd.conf`. In this file, you can define classes and various types of restrictions for a given class. This FTP server is supposed to understand three classes of user: `REAL`, `CHROOT`, and `GUEST`. A `REAL` user has full access to your machine. A `CHROOT` user is restricted to his home directory or a directory otherwise specified in `/etc/ftpd.conf`. A `GUEST` user can connect to the machine for anonymous FTP only.

The basic form of a line in `ftpd.conf` is

```
<directive> <class> <argument>
```

Although there's no default /etc/ftpd.conf file, these are the defaults that the FTP server uses:

```
checkportcmd  all
classtype     chroot CHROOT
classtype     guest  GUEST
classtype     real   REAL
display       none
limit         all    -1      # unlimited connections
maxtimeout    all    7200    # 2 hours
modify        all
motd          all    motd
notify        none
passive       all
timeout       all    900     # 15 minutes
umask         all    027
upload        all
modify        guest  off
umask         guest  0707
```

Directives that appear later in the file override directives that appear earlier. This gives you the opportunity to define defaults as wildcards. In addition to the defaults you see listed in the preceding file, other available controls include ones for limiting the upload and download storage rates, maximum uploadable file size, and port ranges. The last control can be useful for setting up your FTP server to work while a firewall is also running on your machine. Table 22.3 details select directives for the /etc/ftpd.conf file.

TABLE 22.3 Documentation for /etc/ftpd.conf

ftpd.conf ftpd configuration file

The ftpd.conf file specifies various configuration options for ftpd that apply after a user has authenticated his connection.

ftpd.conf consists of a series of lines, each of which may contain a configuration directive, a comment, or a blank line. Directives that appear later in the file override settings by previous directives. This allows wildcard entries to define defaults and then have class-specific overrides.

A directive line has the format:

<command> *<class>* [*<arguments>*]

Each authenticated user is a member of a class, which is determined by ftpusers. *class* is used to determine which ftpd.conf entries apply to the user. The following special classes exist when parsing in entries:

all matches any class

none matches no class

Each class has a type, which may be one of the following:

GUEST Guests (as per the anonymous and ftp logins). A chroot is performed after login.

CHROOT chrooted users (as per ftpchroot). A chroot is performed after login.

REAL Normal users.

TABLE 22.3 Continued

The `ftpd` `STAT` command returns the class settings for the current user, unless the private directive is set for the class.	
`advertise` *<class>* `host`	Sets the address to advertise in the response to the `PASV` and `LPSV` commands to the address for host (which may be either a hostname or IP address).
`chroot` *<class>* `[`*<pathformat>*`]`	If *<pathformat>* is not given or *<class>* is none, uses the default behavior. Otherwise, *<pathformat>* is parsed to create a directory to create as the root directory with `chroot` into upon login. The default root directory is `CHROOT` The user's home directory. `GUEST` If `-a` *<anondir>* is given, uses *<anondir>*; otherwise, uses the home directory of the FTP user. `REAL` By default, no `chroot` is performed.
`classtype` *<class>* *<type>*	Sets the class type of *<class>* to *<type>*.
`conversion` *<class>* *<suffix>* `[`*<type>* *<disable>* *<command>*`]`	Defines an automatic in-line file conversion.
`homedir` *<class>* `[`*<pathformat>*`]`	If *<pathformat>* isn't given or *<class>* is none, uses the default behavior. Otherwise, *<pathformat>* is parsed to create a directory to change to on login, and to use as the home directory of the user for tilde expansion in pathnames, and so on.
`limit` *<class>* *<count>* `[`*<file>*`]`	Limits the maximum number of concurrent connections for *<class>* to *<count>*, with 0 meaning unlimited connections.
`maxfilesize` *<class>* *<size>*	Sets the maximum size of an uploaded file to size.
`maxtimeout` *<class>* *<time>*	Sets the maximum timeout period that a client may request, defaulting to two hours. This cannot be less than 30 seconds or the value for timeout. If *<class>* is none or time is not specified, sets to default of two hours.
`passive` *<class>* `[off]`	If *<class>* is none or off is given, prevents passive (`PASV`, `LPSV`, and `EPSV`) connections. Otherwise, enables them.
`portrange` *<class>* *<min>* *<max>*	Sets the range of port numbers that are used for the passive data port.
`rateget` *<class>* *<rate>*	Sets the maximum get (`RETR`) transfer rate throttle for *<class>* to rate bytes per second.
`rateput` *<class>* *<rate>*	Sets the maximum put (`STOR`) transfer rate throttle for *<class>* to *<rate>* bytes per second, which is parsed as per `rateget` rate.
`timeout` *<class>* *<time>*	Sets the inactivity timeout period.
`upload` *<class>* `[off]`	If *<class>* is none or `off` is given, disables the following commands: `APPE`, `STOR`, and `STOU`, as well as the modify commands: `CHMOD`, `DELE`, `MKD`, `RMD`, `RNFR`, and `UMASK`. Otherwise, enables them.

Logging

The FTP server logs connections to /var/log/ftp.log. Typical entries in the log look like this:

```
Dec 28 16:13:11 ryoohki ftpd[20298]: connection from rosalyn.biosci.ohio-state.edu
➥toryoohki.biosci.ohio-state.edu
Dec 28 16:13:22 ryoohki ftpd[20298]: FTP LOGIN FROM rosalyn.biosci.ohio-state.edu
➥as
joray (class: real, type: REAL)
Dec 28 16:13:30 ryoohki ftpd[20298]: Data traffic: 83085 bytes in 1 file
Dec 28 16:13:30 ryoohki ftpd[20298]: Total traffic: 84246 bytes in 2 transfers
Dec 28 18:04:17 ryoohki ftpd[20551]: connection from rosalyn.biosci.ohio-state.edu
➥to ryoohki.biosci.ohio-state.edu
Dec 28 18:04:22 ryoohki ftpd[20551]: ANONYMOUS FTP LOGIN FROM
➥rosalyn.biosci.ohio-state.edu, joray@ (class: guest, type: GUEST)
Dec 28 18:04:33 ryoohki ftpd[20551]: Data traffic: 1415 bytes in 1 file
Dec 28 18:04:33 ryoohki ftpd[20551]: Total traffic: 2228 bytes in 2 transfers
Jan 23 21:29:15 ryoohki ftpd[2776]: connection from ? to
➥ryoohki.biosci.ohio-state.edu
Jan 23 21:29:22 ryoohki ftpd[2776]: FTP LOGIN FROM ? as miwa
➥(class: chroot, type: CHROOT)
Jan 23 21:29:57 ryoohki ftpd[2776]: Data traffic: 2485381 bytes in 2 files
Jan 23 21:29:57 ryoohki ftpd[2776]: Total traffic: 2488561 bytes in 3 transfers
```

The ftp.log file shows who logged in, where the user logged in from, and what FTP class the user belongs to. In the case of an anonymous connection, the password used can identify the user. The file logs data size, the number of files transferred, the total amount of data, and the total number of files for a given session. Please note that some versions of this FTP server show the IP address for where the user logged in from, but this version shows ?.

Setting Up Anonymous FTP

As you've seen, setting up the FTP server to allow real users to have FTP access is not difficult. Unfortunately, it suffers from the basic design vulnerability of transmitting the user's information in clear text. In some instances, you can reduce this risk by setting up an anonymous FTP server instead.

Anonymous FTP servers allow users to connect, upload, and (potentially) download files without the use of a real-user user ID and password. Of course, this brings the risk that you will not know who is logging in to your system via the anonymous FTP service, and preventing unauthorized users from accessing the system is difficult if everyone is known only as "anonymous." But if anonymous users can't do anything damaging or see any data that's private while so connected, this might be a good trade-off for the security of not allowing real user connections and the problems this brings. Anonymous FTP servers also are useful for enabling users with no account on your machine to acquire or provide information, such as to download product literature, or upload suggestions or possible modifications to a project on which you're working. In other words, anonymous FTP servers provide an easy cross-platform way to conveniently distribute or receive files.

CAUTION

Remember, even if you set up an anonymous-only FTP server, there's nothing to prevent your real users from trying to enter their user IDs and passwords at the prompts.

Setting up the FTP server to allow anonymous FTP takes some work, however. Be warned that setting up anonymous FTP makes your machine vulnerable to more attacks. We recommend that you do not enable anonymous FTP unless you need it. However, we more strongly recommend against enabling unprotected FTP for real users.

Setting up anonymous FTP involves making an `ftp` user, whose home directory is where anonymous FTP users connect. Additionally, you copy the necessary system components to `ftp`'s account so that users can run `ls` properly. When a user requests a list of files via the FTP `ls` command, the command that is actually executed is a server-side binary program kept in a special directory for the FTP server's use, the home directory of the `ftp` user. When the FTP server is `chrooted`, it can't access `/bin/ls`; therefore, placing a copy of `ls` and any other system components that the FTP server needs in its special directory is normally an important step. However, starting with the Mac OS X 10.2 release, the system components don't seem to help for running `ls`. This isn't a problem with the default `ftpd` in the 10.3 or 10.4. Because it's difficult to predict how a new release of either system software or FTP server software will change things, we include the steps for the system components to install in case Apple modifies Mac OS X so that it is not using an `ftp` server with its own `ls`. Steps 4–10 listed in the following pages include the instructions for copying the appropriate system components and can be skipped with the current default `ftpd` available.

To set up an anonymous FTP site, do the following:

1. Create an `ftp` user in the NetInfo database. Follow the pattern of one of the generic users, such as user `unknown`. You might start by duplicating the `unknown` user and editing the duplicate user. Create your `ftp` user with the basic parameters shown in Table 22.4.

TABLE 22.4 Basic Parameters for an `ftp` User

Property	Value
`name`	`ftp`
`realname`	*<some generic reference to ftp>*
`uid`	*<some unused uid number>*
`passwd`	`*`
`home`	*<some suitable location>*
`shell`	`/dev/null`
`gid`	*<some unused gid number>*
`change`	`0`

Figure 22.1 shows the values we used for our `ftp` user.

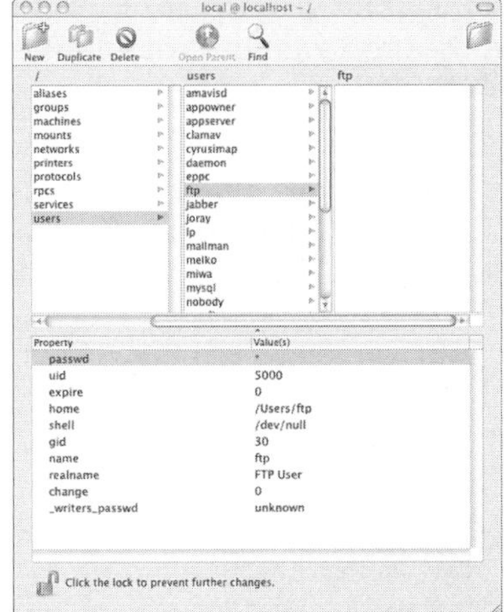

FIGURE 22.1 Here's how we chose to create our `ftp` user as shown in NetInfo Manager.

2. Create an `ftp` group in the NetInfo database. Make sure that you assign the same `gid` to the `ftp` group that you indicated for the `ftp` user.
3. Create a home directory for user `ftp`. Make sure that you create the directory that you specified in the NetInfo database (`/Users/ftp` in this example). The directory should be owned by `root` and have permissions `555`.
4. Create a `~ftp/bin/` directory, owned by `root` with permissions `555`.
5. Copy the system's `/bin/ls` to `~ftp/bin/`.
6. Create `~ftp/usr/lib/`. Each of those directories should be owned by `root` with permissions `555`.
7. Copy the system's `/usr/lib/dyld` to `~ftp/usr/lib/`. This is one of the files that helps `ls` function properly in this `chroot`ed environment.
8. Copy the system's `/usr/lib/libSystem.B.dylib` to `~ftp/usr/lib/`. This is another file that helps `ls` function properly in the `chroot`ed environment.
9. Create `~ftp/System/Library/Frameworks/System.framework/Versions/B/`. Each of the directories in this path should be owned by `root` with permissions `555`.
10. Copy the system's `/System/Library/Frameworks/System.framework/Versions/B/System` to `~ftp/System/Library/Frameworks/System.framework/Versions/B/`. This is another file that helps `ls` function properly in the `chroot`ed environment.
11. Create a `~ftp/pub/` directory in which files can be stored for download. Recommended ownership of this directory includes some user and group `ftp` or user `root`. Typical permissions for this directory are `755`.

12. If you also want to make a drop location where files could be uploaded, create `~ftp/incoming/`, owned by `root`. Recommended permissions include `753`, `733`, `1733`, `3773`, or `777`. You could also create `~ftp/incoming/` with permissions `751` and subdirectories that are used as the drop locations with any of the recommended drop-off permissions.

If you decide to allow anonymous FTP, make sure that you regularly check the anonymous FTP area and your logs for any unusual activity. In addition, regularly check Apple's website for any updates to Mac OS X that include `ftp` updates. Security holes are regularly found in `ftpd` and regularly fixed.

For your convenience, here's a listing of our `ftp` user's home directory:

```
brezup:sage Users $ ls -lRaF ftp
total 0
dr-xr-xr-x   7 root  admin  238 Jan 23 21:46 ./
drwxrwxr-t   9 root  admin  306 Dec 28 17:36 ../
dr-xr-xr-x   3 root  admin  102 Dec 28 17:51 System/
dr-xr-xr-x   3 root  admin  102 Dec 28 17:47 bin/
drwxr-x-wx   2 root  admin   68 Dec 28 17:52 incoming/
drwxr-xr-x   3 root  admin  102 Dec 28 18:03 pub/
dr-xr-xr-x   3 root  admin  102 Dec 28 17:48 usr/

ftp/System:
total 0
dr-xr-xr-x   3 root  admin  102 Dec 28 17:51 ./
dr-xr-xr-x   7 root  admin  238 Dec 28 17:51../
dr-xr-xr-x   3 root  admin  102 Dec 28 17:51 Library/

ftp/System/Library:
total 0
dr-xr-xr-x   3 root  admin  102 Dec 28 17:51 ./
dr-xr-xr-x   3 root  admin  102 Dec 28 17:51 ../
dr-xr-xr-x   3 root  admin  102 Dec 28 17:51 Frameworks/

ftp/System/Library/Frameworks:
total 0
dr-xr-xr-x   3 root  admin  102 Dec 28 17:51 ./
dr-xr-xr-x   3 root  admin  102 Dec 28 17:51 ../
dr-xr-xr-x   3 root  admin  102 Dec 28 17:51 System.framework/

ftp/System/Library/Frameworks/System.framework:
total 0
dr-xr-xr-x   3 root  admin  102 Dec 28 17:51 ./
dr-xr-xr-x   3 root  admin  102 Dec 28 17:51 ../
dr-xr-xr-x   3 root  admin  102 Dec 28 17:51 Versions/
```

```
ftp/System/Library/Frameworks/System.framework/Versions:
total 0
dr-xr-xr-x   3 root  admin  102 Dec 28 17:51 ./
dr-xr-xr-x   3 root  admin  102 Dec 28 17:51 ../
dr-xr-xr-x   3 root  admin  102 Dec 28 17:52 B/

ftp/System/Library/Frameworks/System.framework/Versions/B:
total 10312
dr-xr-xr-x   3 root  admin      102 Dec 28 17:52 ./
dr-xr-xr-x   3 root  admin      102 Dec 28 17:51 ../
-r-xr-xr-x   1 root  admin  5278668 Dec 28 17:52 System*

ftp/bin:
total 72
dr-xr-xr-x   3 root  admin    102 Dec 28 17:47 ./
dr-xr-xr-x   7 root  admin    238 Dec 28 17:47../
-r-xr-xr-x   1 root  admin  33112 Dec 28 17:47 ls*

ftp/incoming:
total 0
drwxr-x-wx   2 root  admin   68 Dec 28 17:52 ./
dr-xr-xr-x   7 root  admin  238 Dec 28 17:52 ../

ftp/pub:
total 8
drwxr-xr-x   3 root  admin   102 Dec 28 18:03 ./
dr-xr-xr-x   7 root  admin   238 Dec 28 18:03 ../

ftp/usr:
total 0
dr-xr-xr-x   3 root  admin  102 Dec 28 17:48 ./
dr-xr-xr-x   7 root  admin  238 Dec 28 17:48 ../
dr-xr-xr-x   4 root  admin  136 Dec 28 17:50 lib/

ftp/usr/lib:
total 13072
dr-xr-xr-x   4 root  admin      136 Dec 28 17:50 ./
dr-xr-xr-x   3 root  admin      102 Dec 28 17:48 ../
-r-xr-xr-x   1 root  admin  1412900 Dec 28 17:49 dyld*
-r-xr-xr-x   1 root  admin  5278668 Dec 28 17:50 libSystem.B.dylib*
```

For additional thoughts on anonymous FTP configuration, you might want to check these websites:

- CERT Coordination Center's Anonymous FTP Configuration Guidelines— `http://www.cert.org/tech_tips/anonymous_ftp_config.html`

- WU-FTPD Resource Center's Documents—http://www.landfield.com/wu-ftpd/
- AppleCare Service and Support—http://www.apple.com/support/

Setting Up ProFTPD as a Replacement for the Default `ftpd`

If you decide to activate anonymous FTP, especially anonymous FTP with an upload directory, consider replacing the default `ftpd` with a more modifiable `ftpd`. A popular, highly configurable replacement `ftpd` is ProFTPD, available at `http://www.proftpd.org/`. In addition to being highly configurable, it easily compiles under Mac OS X.

ProFTPD is intended to be a secure, highly configurable FTP server. It is modular in design, like the Apache web server, which is discussed in Chapter 23, "Creating a Web Server." Although it is intended to be a secure FTP server, ProFTPD is not exempt from security problems. It's still important to regularly monitor the anonymous FTP area, if you have one, as well as make sure that you have the latest version of ProFTPD, which is version 1.2.10 as of this writing.

ProFTPD is quite capable. We will look at only a handful of its capabilities, including the installation process, basic configuration, expanding its capabilities with modules, and interpreting its logs.

Installing ProFTPD

To replace the default `ftpd` with `proftpd`, first download, compile, and install `proftpd`. `proftpd` is one of the packages that follows this basic format for compilation and installation:

```
./configure
make
make install
```

By default, `proftpd` installs in `/usr/local` with `root` as the owner and `wheel` as the group. Being the highly configurable package that it is, you can these and many other parameters. To run `proftpd` as a different user who belongs to a different group, you will need to set the `install_user` and `install_group` variables.

With `proftpd`'s modular design, you specify at the `./configure` line any modules that you might want included. However, with its modular design, you can also easily modify which modules are included by recompiling `proftpd` whenever the need arises. The `proftpd` source does include a directory of contributed modules.

In a `bash` shell, your configure line might have a form like the following:

```
install_user=<user> install_group=<group>
➥./configure --with-modules=<module1>:<module2>
```

Table 22.5 provides information about some of the options you can configure for `proftpd`.

TABLE 22.5 Select Options to Configure for `proftpd`

Option	Description
`--prefix=<PATH>`	Specifies a prefix for the `proftpd` installation other than the default `/usr/local`.
`--with-modules=<list>`	Enables modules listed in the colon-separated module list.
`--enable-timeout-idle`	Sets the default timeout (in seconds) for idle connections (default = 600).
`--enable-timeout-no-transfer`	Sets the default timeout (in seconds) for no data transferred (default = 300).
`--enable-transfer-buffer-size`	Tunes the size (in bytes) of data transfer buffers (default = buffer size).

To distinctly separate the `proftpd` installation from the default `ftpd`, consider specifying paths in the various path parameters. In addition, you might consider running `./configure` with `--prefix=`*`<some-directory-for-proftpd>`* so that the `proftpd` binaries and man pages are all in one place. Next, run `make` and `make install`.

The most complicated part about replacing the default `ftpd` with `proftpd` is deciding how to run it. You can run it as a standalone FTP server, you can run it out of `launchd`, or you can it out of `xinetd` or `inetd`. Refer to Chapter 16, "Managing System Services and Configuration," for advice on the different ways to start up your new FTP server.

Table 22.6 includes some runtime options for `proftpd`. They are mostly useful for debugging purposes, but be sure to include any runtime options of interest to you in whatever startup method you choose. For most purposes, you probably will not need to specify any runtime options.

TABLE 22.6 Select Runtime Options Available in `proftpd`

`ftpd`	Internet File Transfer Protocol server
`ftpd [-h] [-n] [-q] [-d` *`<level>`*`] [-D` *`<definition>`*`] [-c` *`<config-file>`*`] [-p 0¦1] [-l] [-t] [-v] [-vv]`	
`ftpd` is the Internet File Transfer Protocol process. It uses the TCP protocol and runs on the port specified as `ftp` in `/etc/services`.	
`-h/--help`	Displays help.
`-n/--nodaemon`	Disables background daemon mode and sends all output to stderr.
`-q/--quiet`	Does not send output to stderr when running with `-n` / `--nodaemon`.
`-d` *`<level>`*	
`-debug` *`<level>`*	Sets debugging level (0–9, where 9 is the highest level)
`-c` *`<config-file>`*	
`--config` *`<config-file>`*	Specifies an alternative configuration file.
`-l/--list`	Lists compiled-in modules.
`-t/--configtest`	Tests the syntax of the configuration file.
`-v` *`<version>`*	Prints version number and exits.
`-vv`	Prints extended version information and exits.

Configuring ProFTPD Server Options

The ProFTPD server comes with a basic configuration file, located in a default installation in `/usr/local/etc`. To configure `proftpd`, you will have to edit this configuration file. As we have mentioned before, the FTP server is a powerful, flexible one. In this section we will look at the basic concept of configuration directives, applying access controls, setting up virtual hosts, adding transfer ratios, and creating guest user accounts.

Understanding ProFTPD Configuration Directives

The ProFTPD configuration file gets its inspiration from the Apache web server, whose configuration will be discussed in detail in Chapter 23.

ProFTPD has seven configuration contexts: main server configuration, `<Anonymous>`, `<Directory>`, `<Global>`, `<Limit>`, `<VirtualHost>` and `.ftpaccess`. The main server configuration, usually called *server config*, is everything that is not in the rest of the sections. The `<Anonymous>` context configures an anonymous FTP server. The `<Directory>` context is used for configuring specific directories. The `<Global>` context is where you specify configuration parameters that would apply to all of your virtual hosts without having to retype the same configuration directives for every virtual host. If a directive that is specified in the global section is also included in the server config or `<VirtualHost>` contexts, those specifications override the specifications in the `<Global>` section. The `<Limit>` context sets limits on specific FTP commands within a given context. The `<VirtualHost>` context is where virtual hosts are configured. Finally, `.ftpaccess` is a file that users can use in their own directories.

You can use a number of directives in configuring `proftpd`. Table 22.7 documents the directives used in the default configuration file as well as some interesting ones. Some directives can be used in multiple contexts. Not every variation of a directive type is shown in the table. For example, `Allow` is shown, but not `AllowUser`. For a complete listing of available directives, check `http://www.proftpd.org/docs/`.

TABLE 22.7 Select `proftpd` Directives

Directive	Purpose	Module
`ServerName`	Sets the name displayed to connecting users.	`mod_core`
`ServerType`	Sets the mode that the `proftpd` runs in.	`mod_core`
`DefaultServer`	Sets which server configuration is used as the default when an incoming connection is destined for an IP address which is not that of the primary host or any of the virtual hosts.	`mod_core`
`Port`	Sets the port for the control channel.	`mod_core`
`Umask`	Sets the default `umask`.	`mod_core`
`MaxInstances`	Sets the maximum number of child processes spawned.	`mod_core`
`User`	Sets the user the daemon runs as.	`mod_core`
`Group`	Sets the group the server normally runs as.	`mod_core`
`DefaultRoot`	Sets the default `chroot` directory.	`mod_auth`
`AllowOverwrite`	Allows files to be overwritten.	`mod_xfer`
`MaxClients`	Sets the number of users that can connect.	`mod_auth`

TABLE 22.7 Continued

Directive	Purpose	Module
DisplayLogin	Sets the file to display at login.	mod_core
DisplayFirstChdir	Sets the file to display when first entering a directory.	mod_core
Allow	Sets access control in the <Limit> context. Specifies which hosts and networks can access the server. Typically used in conjunction with Order and Deny.	mod_core
AnonRequirePassword	Requires anonymous logins to enter a valid password matches the password of the user that the anonymous daemon runs as. Can be used in conjunction with AuthUsingAlias to create guest accounts.	mod_auththat
AuthGroupFile	Specifies an alternate group file, having the same format as the /etc/group file.	mod_auth_file
AuthPAMConfig	Sets the PAM service name used in authentication. Default is ftp.	mod_auth_pam
AuthUserFile	Specifies an alternative password file, having the same format as the /etc/passwd file.	mod_auth_file
AuthUsingAlias	Specifies authentication via alias name instead of a mapped username. Can be used in conjunction with AnonRequirePassword to create guest accounts.	mod_auth
Bind	Binds the server or host to a particular IP address.	mod_core
Class	Controls class based access by classifying each Connecting IP address.	mod_core
Classes	Enables class-based access control.	mod_core
DefaultAddress	Sets the address for the main server to listen on.	mod_core
DefaultTransferMode	Sets the default file transfer mode.	mod_core
Deny	Sets access control in the <Limit> context. Specifies which hosts and/or networks are denied access to the server. Typically used in conjunction with Order and Deny.	mod_core
Directory	Sets up a block of configuration directories for the specified directory and its subdirectories.	mod_core
DirFakeUser	Hides the true owner of files in a directory. If turned on without specifying a username, displays all files as being owned by ftp.	mod_ls
ExtendedLog	Specifies custom log files.	mod_log
HideNoAccess	Hides directories that the current user has no access to in a directory listing.	mod_core
MasqueradeAddress	Sets the server address presented to clients.	mod_core
MaxConnectionRate	Sets the maximum rate at which new TCP connections are accepted. The number set is the number at which the restriction takes effect.	mod_core
MaxRetrieveFileSize	Restricts size of files that can be downloaded. Optional parameters include user, group, and class.	mod_xfer
MaxStoreFileSize	Restricts size of files that can be uploaded. Optional parameters include user, group, and class.	mod_xfer

TABLE 22.7 Continued

Directive	Purpose	Module
`Order`	Configures the order in which `Allow` and `Deny` directives are checked inside a `<Limit>` context.	`mod_core`
`PassivePorts`	Specifies the FTP data port range to be used.	`mod_core`
`PathAllowFilter`	Allows only new files that match the specified regular expression.	`mod_core`
`PathDenyFilter`	Denies new files that match the specified regular expression.	`mod_core`
`PersistentPasswd`	Sets whether ProFTPD holds files open during user/group lookups. Default is `on`. ProFTPD documentation recommends setting this to `off` for Mac OS X.	`mod_auth_unix`
`RequireVaildShell`	Sets whether or not to require that a user's shell be listed in `/etc/shells`. Default is `on`.	`mod_auth`
`ServerLog`	Disables the use of the `syslog` mechanism and redirects all logging output to the specified file. Can be used in server config, `<VirtualHost>`, and `<Global>` contexts.	`mod_log`
`SystemLog`	Disables the use of the `syslog` mechanism and redirects all logging output to the specified file. Can be used in server config context.	`mod_log`
`TransferLog`	Configures the full path to a `wu-ftpd`-style transfer log. Default is `/var/log/xferlog`.	`mod_core`
`TransferRate`	Sets the upload and download transfer rates.	`mod_xfer`
`UseFtpUsers`	Sets whether to block based on `/etc/ftpusers`. Option is `on` by default.	`mod_auth`
`UserAlias`	Aliases a username to a system user.	`mod_auth`
`UserDirRoot`	Sets the chroot directory to a subdirectory of the anonymous server.	`mod_auth`
`UserPassword`	Creates a password for a particular user that overrides a user's normal system password. Takes a hashed password argument that is clear text run through `crypt`. Can be useful when combined with `UserAlias` to provide multiple logins to an anonymous server.	`mod_auth`

The default `proftpd.conf` file has three contexts: the server config, `<Limit>`, and `<Anonymous>` contexts. Here is the server config context:

```
# This is a basic ProFTPD configuration file (rename it to
# 'proftpd.conf' for actual use.  It establishes a single server
# and a single anonymous login.  It assumes that you have a user/group
# "nobody" and "ftp" for normal operation and anon.
```

```
ServerName                      "ProFTPD Default Installation"
ServerType                      standalone
DefaultServer                   on

# Port 21 is the standard FTP port.
Port                            21

# Umask 022 is a good standard umask to prevent new dirs and files
# from being group and world writable.
Umask                           022

# To prevent DoS attacks, set the maximum number of child processes
# to 30.  If you need to allow more than 30 concurrent connections
# at once, simply increase this value.  Note that this ONLY works
# in standalone mode, in inetd mode you should use an inetd server
# that allows you to limit maximum number of processes per service
# (such as xinetd).
MaxInstances                    30

# Set the user and group under which the server will run.
User                            nobody
Group                           nogroup

# To cause every FTP user to be "jailed" (chrooted) into their home
# directory, uncomment this line.
#DefaultRoot ~

# Normally, we want files to be overwriteable.
AllowOverwrite          on
```

In the server config context, the `ServerName`, `ServerType`, `DefaultServer`, `Port`, `Umask`, `MaxInstances`, `User`, `Group`, `DefaultRoot` and `AllowOverrite` directives are included. One of the important directives in this section is the `ServerType` directive. This directive sets what mode `proftpd` runs in. By default, it is set to `standalone`. If you have a high traffic FTP server, this is the option you will want. Create a startup script to start the FTP server at boot time. It has been our experience that if you have any users with the `;basic;` authentication authority, they will not be able to log in to the standalone server. Otherwise, you might prefer to set that to `inetd`, which works for running `proftpd` from `inetd`, `xinetd`, or `launchd`. Users with `;ShadowHash;` or `;basic;` authentication authority can log in to the FTP server in this mode. By default, `proftpd` runs as user `nobody` in group `nogroup`. For Mac OS X, change that `nogroup` setting to `nobody`. You might want to consider creating a specific user and group for `proftpd` to run as. The `ServerName` is what is displayed after the ProFTPD version information when a user connects to your machine. You can put something more interesting there than the default.

Here is the main <Limit> context:

```
# Bar use of SITE CHMOD by default
<Limit SITE_CHMOD>
  DenyAll
</Limit>
```

The default configuration file's <Limit> context denies the `SITE_CHMOD` command to everyone. This does not allow users to `chmod` files on the FTP server. The <Limit> context, which can be used within other contexts, can be used for individual FTP commands, groups of FTP commands or on all commands. `SITE` commands are limited by prepending `SITE_` to the command. Limits on individual commands take precedence over limits on groups, which take precedence over limits on all commands. Table 22.8 shows what the <Limit> groups are and which commands belong to which groups.

Here is the <Anonymous> context:

```
# A basic anonymous configuration, no upload directories.  If you do not
# want anonymous users, simply delete this entire <Anonymous> section.
<Anonymous ~ftp>
  User                          ftp
  Group                         ftp

  # We want clients to be able to login with "anonymous" as well as "ftp"
  UserAlias                     anonymous ftp

  # Limit the maximum number of anonymous logins
  MaxClients                    10

  # We want 'welcome.msg' displayed at login, and '.message' displayed
  # in each newly chdired directory.
  DisplayLogin                  welcome.msg
  DisplayFirstChdir             .message

  # Limit WRITE everywhere in the anonymous chroot
  <Limit WRITE>
    DenyAll
  </Limit>
</Anonymous>
```

If you do not plan to run an anonymous FTP server, you can delete this context. The default configuration file includes a basic configuration for an anonymous FTP server that does not have any upload directories. It lists the anonymous user as user `ftp`, belonging to group `ftp`. The `anonymous` and `ftp` logins are aliased to that user. The maximum number of clients is set to 10, and it also includes settings for a welcome message and a message to be displayed for each directory. This section specifically denies the `WRITE` command group to all users using the <Limit> directive.

The default configuration file, however, does not quite work in Mac OS X. If your system has PAM installed, which Mac OS X does, proftpd assumes a default PAM authentication file located at /etc/pam.d/ftp. In Mac OS X, though, this file is /etc/pam.d/ftpd. To fix this problem, you can either copy /etc/pam.d/ftpd to /etc/pam.d/ftp or you can set the AuthPAMConfig directive to /etc/pam.d/ftpd.

Depending on the shell that you assigned to your ftp user, the default <Anonymous> context might not command groups> groups> command> work. If you assigned the ftp user a shell that is not in /etc/shells, anonymous FTP will not work. Either list that shell in /etc/shells or set the RequireValidShell directive to off.

TABLE 22.8 <Limit> Command Groups

<Limit> **Command Group**	**FTP Commands**
ALL	All FTP commands
DIRS	CDUP, CWD, LIST, MDTM, NLST, PWD, RNFR, STAT, XCUP, XCWD, XPWD
LOGIN	Logins
READ	RETR, SIZE
WRITE	APPE, DELE, MKD, RMD, RNTO, STOR, STOU, XMKD, XRMD

Applying Access Controls

Now that you have tested the basic functionality of the default proftpd.conf file, you probably want to expand the server's functionality. In this section we will look at some basic controls that you can apply.

To deny access to IP addresses that you have found to be troublesome, add a section like the following:

```
<Limit LOGIN>
  Order Allow, Deny
  Deny from 192.168.23., 192.168.1.4, .yourcompany.com
</Limit>
```

In the section, the order of the rules has been specified as Allow, Deny. This means that, by default, access is allowed from all hosts unless a specific deny statement exists. Then any host for which the deny statement is true, is denied access to the FTP server. In this example, then, access is allowed from all hosts, except to all users coming from the 192.168.23 subnet, the address 192.168.1.4 and the .yourcompany.com subnet.

NOTE

You could also choose to use TCP Wrappers for this type of control. Edit your /etc/xinetd.d/ftp file to list /usr/libexec/tcpd as the server, point the server_args to your proftpd, and add NAMEINARGS to flags.

Suppose that you wanted to allow only two users, `nermal` and `joray`, to connect to your FTP server. You could add a section like the following, which specifically allows `nermal` and `joray`, but denies access to all other users:

```
<Limit LOGIN>
  AllowUser nermal
  AllowUser joray
  DenyAll
</Limit>
```

If you wanted to then limit user `nermal` to coming from 192.168.1. subnet, you could add a section like the following:

```
<IfUser nermal>
  <Limit LOGIN>
      Order Deny, Allow
      Allow from 192.168.1.
  </Limit>
</IfUser>
```

Please note that the `<IfUser>`, `<IfClass>`, and `<IfGroup>` directives are available with `mod_ifsession`, which is not compiled in by default.

Suppose that you only wanted to have an anonymous FTP server, and not allow access to any of your users. You could do that by adding a section to the server config context that denies access to all:

```
<Limit LOGIN>
  DenyAll
</Limit>
```

Then in the `<Anonymous>` context, add a section that allows access to all:

```
<Limit LOGIN>
   AllowAll
</Limit>
```

As you are probably starting to see, the access restriction possibilities with ProFTPD are enormous. There are a variety of access restriction directives available. Some notable directives include `AllowUser`, `DenyUser`, `AllowGroup`, `DenyGroup`, `Class`, and `Directory`. With the `Class` directive, you can set up classes of hosts and apply restrictions based on the class. The `Directory` directive can be used to set up access restrictions to the specified directory and its subdirectories.

Setting Up Virtual Hosts

One of the reasons that you might have decided to replace the default `ftpd` with `proftpd` is to set up a virtual FTP server. In this section, we will take a brief look at setting up a basic virtual anonymous FTP server.

The <VirtualHost> context enables you to serve multiple FTP servers that don't relate to the main FTP server or main anonymous FTP server—all from the same machine. You will need an IP address and a domain name. Your network administrator or ISP can help you with those details.

Probably the easiest way to see how the virtual anonymous FTP server configuration works is to look at a modified version of the sample configuration that comes with ProFTPD.


```
#Virtual FTP server

<VirtualHost 192.168.1.201>
  ServerName                  "my.company.com's FTP server"
  Umask                       027

RequireValidShell off

ServerLog /var/log/ftp.mycompany.com
TransferLog /var/log/xferlog-ftp.mycompany.com

  <Limit LOGIN>
    DenyAll
  </Limit>

  <Anonymous /Users/virtual/mycompany.com>
    User                      ftp
    Group                     ftp
    UserAlias                 anonymous ftp

    <Limit LOGIN>
      AllowAll
    </Limit>

<Directory *>
      <Limit WRITE>
      DenyAll
    </Limit>
   </Directory>
    <Directory incoming>
      <Limit READ WRITE>
        DenyAll
      </Limit>
      <Limit STOR>
        AllowAll
      </Limit>
    </Directory>
  </Anonymous>
</VirtualHost>
```

The configuration for the virtual host looks a lot like the configuration for the main FTP server or main anonymous FTP server. The `<VirtualHost>` context takes either an IP address or a DNS name. In this example, we see that the virtual FTP server is running on 192.168.1.201. When someone `ftps` to this FTP server, it displays that it is my.company.com's FTP server, as set by the `ServerName` directive. The `ServerLog` and `TransferLog` directives have been used to specify alternative logs for the virtual FTP server. This makes it easier to track information regarding that FTP server. The next section denies login for all users.

The final section is the virtual FTP server's configuration for its anonymous FTP server. We see that its anonymous directory is running out of the `/Users/virtual/mycompany.com`. Like the standard anonymous FTP server, it runs as user `ftp` in group `ftp`. A user can log in as `anonymous` or `ftp` for login, and all logins are allowed. The last section configures directories. The `WRITE` command is denied to all directories by default. The incoming directory denies the `READ` and `WRITE` command groups by default, but does allow the `STOR` command that belongs to the `WRITE` command group.

If you are running a lot of virtual FTP servers, especially high traffic virtual FTP servers, you might want to run `proftpd` as a standalone server.

NOTE

To bind another IP address to your network card, you can just duplicate your interface in the Network Preferences pane and assign another IP address to the duplicate entry.

Alternatively, to bind another IP address to your network card (typically `en0` for most single network card systems), run this command at the command line:

```
sudo ifconfig en0 alias 192.168.1.201 255.255.255.255
```

Put this in a startup script. For more discussion on `ifconfig`, see Chapter 28, "Implementing Server Security and Advanced Network Configuration."

Adding Transfer Controls

ProFTPD has a variety of transfer controls available. Such control directives include `MaxConnectionRate`, `MaxRetrieveFileSize`, `MaxStoreFileSize` and `TransferRate`. The most complex of these directives is `TransferRate`, whose syntax is

```
TransferRate [<FTP commands>][<kilobytes-per-second>[:<free-bytes>]]

➥[user¦group¦class <expression>]
```

`TransferRate` is applied to a comma-separated list of FTP commands, selected from `APPE`, `RETR`, `STOR`, and `STOU`. The rate, in kilobytes/second, is the actual transfer rate used. The `<free bytes>` parameter sets the number of free bytes that can be transferred before the restriction is applied. This allows small files to be easily transferred, but throttles the transfer of larger files. The `TransferRate` directive can also be applied to a certain user, group, or class, with an `<expression>` that specifies what user, group, or class to which to restrict or not restrict bandwidth.

For example,

```
TransferRate RETR 1.5 user marvin
```

restricts user `marvin`'s rate to retrieve data from the FTP server to 1.5 KB/s.

The following statements restrict the append and store commands for all users to 8192 KB/s, and the retrieve command to 4096 KB/s:

```
TransferRate APPE,STOR 8192

TransferRate RETR 4096
```

Other transfer controls are available with the `mod_quotatab` module. This module also has driver modules `mod_quotatab_file`, `mod_quota_ldap`, and `mod_quota_sql`. You must install `mod_quotatab` and at least one of the driver modules. If you install `mod_quota_ldap`, you must also install either of the other two driver modules. If you install `mod_quota_sql`, you must also have installed `mod_sql`. In our examples, we have installed `mod_quotatab` and `mod_quotatab_file`.

To make use of `mod_quotatab`, you have to define two quota tables. One table keeps quota information for absolute file/byte limits for users, groups, and classes. The other table keeps a current tally of the file/bytes used by those users, groups, and classes. To keep track of the uploaded bytes/files limits, `mod_quotatab` uses the data from the `DELE`, `APPE`, `STOR`, and `STOU` commands issued; for downloaded bytes/files limits, `RETR`; for transferred bytes/files limits, `DELE`, `APPE`, `STOR`, `STOU`, and `RETR`. To create these tables for `mod_quota_file` and manipulate their data, the `ftpquota` utility, which is a Perl script, is provided. Table 22.9 contains command line documentation for `ftpquota`.

To create your tables, run commands of the following form:

```
ftpquota --create-table --type=limit ---table-path=<path-to-table>
ftpquota --create-table --type=tally --table-path=<path-to-table>
```

Next, populate the limit with your quota information. The tally table is automatically populated by `mod_quotatab`, although you can manually manipulate records in it.

In this example, we place limits on user `nermal`, who will have a limit of two upload files and two download files:

```
localhost: root# ftpquota --add-record --type=limit --name=nermal
➥--quota-type=user  --files-upload=2 --files-download=2
➥--table-path=/usr/local/etc/ftpquota.limittab
```

It is recommended that you place either file limits or byte limits, but not both. To see the contents of the table, run the following command:

```
localhost: root# ftpquota --show-records --type=limit
➥--table-path=/usr/local/etc/ftpquota.limittab
```

```
-------------------------------------------
  Name: nermal
  Quota Type: User
  Per Session: False
  Limit Type: Hard
    Uploaded bytes:     unlimited
    Downloaded bytes:   unlimited
    Transferred bytes:  unlimited
    Uploaded files:     2
    Downloaded files:   2
    Transferred files:  unlimited
```

We see that she can download and upload only two files, that a hard limit has been placed, and that the Per Session setting is currently set to `false`.

TABLE 22.9 `ftpquota` Command Documentation

`ftpquota`	Manipulates FTP quota tables
`ftpquota <operation-type> <table-type> <options>`	
Operation Types	
`--add-record`	Creates a new record with the specified limits. Requires the `-name` and `-quota-type` options.
`--create-table`	Creates table if not present. Default table locations are `./ftpquota.limittab` and `./ftpquota.tallytab`.
`--delete-record`	Deletes the specified record. Requires the `-name` and `-quota-type` options.
`--show-records`	Displays all the quota records in the table in a readable format.
`--update-record`	Updates a record with the specified quota limits.
Table Type	
`--type`	Specifies the table type to use as either `tally` or `limit`. Required option.
Quota-Limiting Options	
`--Bu` `--bytes-upload`	Specifies the limit of the number of bytes that may be uploaded. Defaults to `-1` (unlimited).
`--Bd` `--bytes-download`	Specifies the limit of the number of bytes that may be downloaded. Defaults to `-1` (unlimited).
`--Bx` `--bytes-xfer`	Specifies the limit of the number of bytes that may be transferred. Total includes uploads, downloads, and directory listings. Defaults to `-1` (unlimited).
`--Fu` `--files-upload`	Specifies the limit of the number of files that may be uploaded. Defaults to `-1` (unlimited).
`--Fd` `--files-download`	Specifies the limit of the number of files that may be downloaded. Defaults to `-1` (unlimited).
`--Fx` `--files-xfer`	Specifies the limit of the number of files that may be transferred, including uploads and downloads. Defaults to `-1` (unlimited).

TABLE 22.9 Continued

`-L` `--limit-type`	Specifies the type of limit, `hard` or `soft`, of the bytes limits. If `hard`, any uploaded files that push the bytes used counter past the limit will be automatically deleted; if `soft`, those extra bytes will be allowed, but future uploads will be denied.
`-N` `--name`	Specifies a name for the quota record. This name will be the user/login name, group name, or class name, depending on the quota type. Option is ignored if the quota type specified is `all`.
`-P` `--per-session`	Specifies that the quota limit is to be applied only to each session, rather than persisting across sessions. By default, quotas are persistent.
`-Q` `--quota-type`	Specifies a quota type for this record, where the type is which category of FTP users this quota applies to. The quota type must be one of the following: `user`, `group`, `class`, or `all`.
Miscellaneous Options	
`--help`	Displays help.
`--table-path`	Specifies the quota table location.
`--units`	Specifies whether to treats bytes as is, or in kilobytes, megabytes, or gigabytes. Allowable options are `B` or `byte`, `Kb` or `kilo`, `Mb` or `mega`, and `Gb` or `giga`. Defaults to `byte`.
`--verbose`	Toggles more verbose information about the tool as it works.

The `mod_quotatab` module provides these directives: `QuotaDirectoryTally`, `QuotaDisplayUnits`, `QuotaEngine`, `QuotaLimitTable`, `QuotaLock`, `QuotaLog`, `QuotaShowQuotas`, `QuotaTallyTable`. To use `mod_quotatab`, you will need to provide entries in the configuration file for at least `QuotaEngine`, `QuotaLimitTable`, and `QuotaTallyTable`.

We added these entries:

```
QuotaEngine on
QuotaLimitTable file:/usr/local/etc/ftpquota.limittab
QuotaTallyTable file:/usr/local/etc/ftpquota.tallytab
QuotaLog /var/log/proftpd-quota.log
```

To enable or disable `mod_quotatab`, `QuotaEngine` must be set to `on` or `off`, as appropriate. To disable `QuotaEngine`, simply set this directive to `off`, and then you don't have to worry about commenting out any other quota-related directives. The `QuotaLimitTable` and `QuotaTallyTable` directives tell `proftpd` where to look for the appropriate tables. The `QuotaLog` directive specifies an alternate log where quota activity can be logged.

After our user has uploaded and downloaded files, we see that the tally table information shows:

```
localhost: root# ftpquota --show-records --type=tally
➥--table-path=/usr/local/etc/ftpquota.tallytab
----------------------------------------
```

```
Name: nermal
Quota Type: User
  Uploaded bytes:     0.00
  Downloaded bytes:   0.00
  Transferred bytes:  0.00
  Uploaded files:     1
  Downloaded files:   1
  Transferred files:  0
```

The `nermal` user has uploaded and downloaded one file so far; only one more of each remains in her quotas. After she has reached a quota, she and her administrator will have to decide whether her quotas should be adjusted. Perhaps she should have higher limits; maybe per-session quotas would be more appropriate; perhaps her limits should be removed; or perhaps she is a trouble user, and no adjustment is appropriate.

The last type of transfer control that might be of interest is ratio control, available in `mod_ratio`. With this module, you can control upload and download ratios. This module includes quite a few directives, some involving the actual ratios and others involving error messages and such. The directives involving the ratios themselves are `AnonRatio`, `GroupRatio`, `HostRatio`, and `UserRatio`. To enable the module, you have to set the `Ratios` directive to `on`.

Each of these directives takes four parameters: file ratio, initial file credit, byte ratio, and initial byte credit. Setting a parameter to `0` disables that check. The default for each parameter is `0`.

The basic syntax for one of these directives is

```
<directive> <specific anon password/group/host/user> <file-ratio>
➥<initial-file-credit> <byte-credit> <initial-byte-credit>
```

The following sample sets up a restriction for users in group `test` to have a file ratio of 50:1, an initial credit of five files, a byte ratio of 5:1 and an initial byte credit of 100KB.

```
GroupRatio test 50 5 5 100000
```

Creating Guest User Accounts

In addition to allowing real users and anonymous users access to your FTP area, you might also be interested in allowing guest user access. You can restrict your real users' FTP access to their home directories, if you so choose. Whether you choose to do so is up to you. If you trust your users enough to give them full login access to your machine in the first place, you might also trust them with full FTP access. Anonymous users are users who have access to only the anonymous area of your machine, if you chose to create an anonymous FTP area. Guest users are users who have accounts on your machine but aren't granted full access to your machine. Although there are probably various ways to define a guest user, for our purposes, a guest user is a user who has an account on your machine, but who is not granted full access to your machine. Guest user accounts might be suitable for users who have websites on your machine and need FTP access only to occasionally update their websites.

A guest user account is a cross between a real user account and an anonymous FTP account. A guest user has a username and password but doesn't have shell access to his account. This enables him to use FTP to access files on the server via a user ID and password, but prevents him from being able to log in to the machine either through the network or at the console. Guest user accounts are useful if, for example, you need to set up a place where a group of collaborators can share sensitive information and data, but where you don't really want members of the group to be full users of your machine. If you set up a single guest user account for this group of users, all that group's users can access it with a user ID and password, and people without the user ID and password can't, so their information remains private. Because the users in the group don't have real shells, however, they can't log in to your machine and use any resources other than those available through the FTP server.

Guest user accounts are set up similarly to the anonymous FTP account. The users are restricted to their home directories only, as is the anonymous FTP account, and traditionally, their accounts contain the commands that they might need to run while accessing their accounts via FTP.

If you decide that you need guest user accounts, do the following to create a guest user:

1. Decide where the guest user's home directory should be. You could put your guest users in the same location as your regular users. You also could create a directory somewhere for guest users and place guest user directories in that location.

2. After you've decided where the guest account should reside, make a guest account. You could create your user in the Accounts pane in System Preferences. Your guest user, however, might not really have a need for all the directories that are made in a user account created in this way. You can decide what directories might be necessary. If you anticipate having many guest users, you could create a guest skeleton user as your basis for guest accounts.

3. The guest user should belong to some sort of guest group. Create a guest group with an unused GID number. Edit the guest user's account to belong to the guest group. The guest user's shell should be modified to some nonexistent shell. Make sure that the guest user's home directory and everything in it are owned by the guest user with the guest group.

4. Include the shell that you use for the guest in `/etc/shells`. You might want the contents of your fake guest user shell to be something like this:

   ```
   #! /bin/sh
   exit 1
   ```

5. Update the ownership information of the guest user's account to include the guest group GID indicated in the NetInfo database.

6. Copy the same system files used for the anonymous FTP user to the guest user's account. Specifically, make sure that the system files

   ```
   /bin/ls

   /usr/lib/dylib

   /usr/lib/libSystem.B.dylib

   /System/Library/Frameworks/System.framework/Versions/B/System
   ```

   are included in the guest user's home directory. In this example, for user `ralph`, the files would be placed in

   ```
   /Users/guests/ralph/bin/

   /Users/guests/ralph/usr/lib/

   /Users/guests/ralph/System/Library/Frameworks/System.framework/Versions/B/
   ```

   with the same permissions and ownerships that are used for an anonymous FTP account.

If you create a skeleton guest user account, these are files that would be useful to include in the skeleton guest user account. Note, however, that this step is not necessary for ProFTPD, but is shown in case the need should ever arise.

As you might expect, with ProFTPD's amazing flexibility, there are at least two ways that you could approach configuring ProFTPD to recognize your guest user as a guest user. The simplest way is to restrict your guest group users to their home directories by using the `DefaultRoot` directive. If you called your guest group `ftponly`, your statement would look like this:

```
DefaultRoot ~ ftponly
```

You could also treat the guest users more like anonymous users, and use an anonymous user configuration, like this modification of one of the sample configurations:

```
<Anonymous ~ralph>
  User ralph
  Group ftponly
  UserAlias artist ralph
  AuthAliasOnly on
  AnonRequirePassword on
# Deny write operations to all directories, underneath root-dir
# Default is to allow, so we don't need a <Limit> for read
# operations.
```

```
<Directory *>
  <Limit WRITE>
  DenyAll
</Limit>
</Directory>
# Deny all read/write operations in incoming. Because these are
# command-group limits, we can explicitly permit certain
# operations which will take precedence
# over our group limit.
<Directory incoming>
<Limit READ WRITE>
  DenyAll
</Limit>
# The only command allowed in incoming is STOR (transfer file
# from client to server)
<Limit STOR>
  AllowAll
</Limit>
</Directory>
</Anonymous>
```


This sample sets up a configuration for guest user ralph. This user can log in either as ralph or as artist, and is required to issue a password to log in. By default, the WRITE command group is denied to all of his directories. For his incoming directory, the READ and WRITE command groups are denied, but from the WRITE command group, the STOR command is allowed. With this configuration, user ralph can only upload to his incoming directory. The directory configurations can certainly be changed to suit whatever your guest user's needs are.

Expanding ProFTPD Capabilities with Modules

As you have seen throughout this part of the chapter, the default capabilities of ProFTPD can be expanded by installing modules. You can get news on the latest modules at http://www.proftpd.org/module_news.html. You can also find many modules at http://www.castaglia.org/proftpd/. The ProFTPD source distribution comes with a number of modules that aren't compiled in. However, there are other modules that do not come with the ProFTPD source.

Before you install a module, even one that comes with the source, read any pertinent READMEs and follow those instructions. For modules that are not included with the source, instructions frequently include first copying files to the contrib directory of the source tree, and then running configure with that module listed in the --with-modules option and recompiling.

If you wanted to recompile proftpd to contain additional modules we have mentioned, first make a backup of all of your proftpd binaries and your configuration file. Then re-run configure as you ran it originally, but also include the modules, and recompile and reinstall. For example, to compile in mod_ifsession, mod_ratio, mod_quotatab, and mod_quotatab_file, do this:

```
./configure --with-modules=mod_ifsession:mod_ratio:mod_quotatab:mod_quotatab_file
make
make install
```

Now your proftpd has even more capabilities!

Interpreting FTP Logs

While you are fine-tuning your ProFTPD configuration, undoubtedly something will not work as you hoped it would. That's when it becomes helpful to be able to interpret your FTP logs. As flexible as ProFTPD is, which FTP logs your system has will vary with your configuration.

By default, transfers are logged to /var/log/xferlog. Other logging is done via syslog, based on /etc/syslog.conf. You can bypass logging via syslog by using the SystemLog directive, which is what we did. These are the custom settings we put in place for our proftpd:

```
SystemLog /var/log/proftpd.log
QuotaLog /var/log/proftpd-quota.log
ServerLog /var/log/ftp.mycompany.com
TransferLog /var/log/xferlog-ftp.mycompany.com
```

In our /var/log/proftpd.log, we find statements such as these:

```
Jan 26 23:15:14 localhost proftpd[1069] localhost (192.168.1.13[192.168.1.13]):
➥FTP session opened.
Jan 26 23:15:21 localhost proftpd[1069] localhost (192.168.1.13[192.168.1.13]):
➥ANON anonymous: Login successful.
Jan 26 23:15:34 localhost proftpd[1069] localhost (192.168.1.13[192.168.1.13]):
➥FTP session closed.
Jan 30 14:21:44 localhost proftpd[232] localhost (192.168.1.17[192.168.1.17]):
➥FTP session opened.
Jan 30 14:21:48 localhost proftpd[232] localhost (192.168.1.17[192.168.1.17]):
➥USER nermal: Login successful.
Jan 30 14:21:58 localhost proftpd[232] localhost (192.168.1.17[192.168.1.17]):
➥FTP session closed.
Jan 30 14:33:42 localhost proftpd[243] localhost (192.168.1.4[192.168.1.4]):
➥FTP session opened.
Jan 30 14:33:47 localhost proftpd[243] localhost (192.168.1.4[192.168.1.4]):
➥USER nermal: Login successful.
Jan 30 14:33:47 localhost proftpd[243] localhost (192.168.1.4[192.168.1.4]):
➥USER nermal: Limit access denies login.
Jan 30 14:33:47 localhost proftpd[243] localhost (192.168.1.4[192.168.1.4]):
➥FTP session closed.
```

```
Jan 30 14:52:17 localhost proftpd[266] localhost (192.168.1.17[192.168.1.17]):
➥FTP session opened.
Jan 30 14:52:22 localhost proftpd[266] localhost (192.168.1.17[192.168.1.17]):
➥PAM(nermal): Authentication failure.
Jan 30 14:52:22 localhost proftpd[266] localhost (192.168.1.17[192.168.1.17]):
➥USER nermal (Login failed): Incorrect password.
Jan 30 14:52:23 localhost proftpd[266] localhost (192.168.1.17[192.168.1.17]):
➥FTP session closed.
Jan 31 22:03:15 localhost proftpd[18286] localhost (192.168.1.17[192.168.1.17]):
➥FTP session opened.
Jan 31 22:03:19 localhost proftpd[18286] localhost (192.168.1.17[192.168.1.17]):
➥USER ralph: Login successful.
Jan 31 22:03:25 localhost proftpd[18286] localhost (192.168.1.17[192.168.1.17]):
➥FTP session closed.
Jan 31 22:40:34 localhost proftpd[18388] localhost (192.168.1.17[192.168.1.17]):
➥FTP session opened.
Jan 31 22:40:37 localhost proftpd[18388] localhost (192.168.1.17[192.168.1.17]):
➥ANON ralph: Login successful.
Jan 31 22:40:55 localhost proftpd[18388] localhost (192.168.1.17[192.168.1.17]):
➥FTP session closed.
Feb 01 00:09:06 localhost proftpd[18665] localhost (192.168.1.17[192.168.1.17]):
➥FTP session opened.
Feb 01 00:09:11 localhost proftpd[18665] localhost (192.168.1.17[192.168.1.17]):
➥ANON artist: Login successful.
Feb 01 00:09:14 localhost proftpd[18665] localhost (192.168.1.17[192.168.1.17]):
➥FTP session closed
Feb 02 15:30:09 localhost proftpd[26333] localhost (sage[192.168.1.17]):
➥FTP session opened.
Feb 02 15:30:19 localhost proftpd[26333] localhost (sage[192.168.1.17]):
➥USER nermal: Login successful.
Feb 02 15:30:31 localhost proftpd[26333] localhost (sage[192.168.1.17]):
➥FTP session closed.
```

This log shows authentication information for a given session. From the typical line, we can find out the date and time of the activity, the process ID, the hostname of the connecting machine (if known), the connecting machine's IP address, and an action. If the user is a real user, the user is described as `USER`. If the user is an anonymous user, the description is `ANON`. If the user cannot log in, a reason is provided, such as `Authentication failure` or `Limit access denies login`. When our guest user `ralph`'s guest configuration was set using the `DefaultRoot` directive, the log describes him as a `USER`. When the `<Anonymous>` description was used instead for him, he is described as `ANON`. We can also see when he logs in as `ralph` and when he logs in as `artist`.

In our quota log, `/var/log/proftpd-quota.log`, we see entries such as these:

```
Jan 31 16:39:28 mod_quotatab/1.2.13[17863]: found limit entry for user 'nermal'
Jan 31 16:39:28 mod_quotatab/1.2.13[17863]: creating new tally entry to match
➥limit entry
```

```
Jan 31 16:39:28 mod_quotatab/1.2.13[17863]: new tally entry successfully created
Jan 31 16:40:27 mod_quotatab/1.2.13[17865]: found limit entry for user 'nermal'
Jan 31 16:40:27 mod_quotatab/1.2.13[17865]: found tally entry for user 'nermal'
Jan 31 16:52:43 mod_quotatab/1.2.13[17879]: found limit entry for user 'nermal'
Jan 31 16:52:43 mod_quotatab/1.2.13[17879]: found tally entry for user 'nermal'
Jan 31 16:53:01 mod_quotatab/1.2.13[17879]: STOR: quota reached: used 2 of 2
➥upload files
Jan 31 16:54:08 mod_quotatab/1.2.13[17879]: RETR: quota reached: used 2 of 2
➥download files
Jan 31 16:55:50 mod_quotatab/1.2.13[17879]: RETR denied: quota exceeded: used
➥2 of 2 download files
```

A typical entry in this log includes the date and time, process ID, and an action. We can see when the system found the limit information for user `nermal` and created her tally information. We can also see when the quotas for `nermal` were reached, and even that `nermal` must have attempted a download after having reached her download quota.

In our server log for the virtual FTP server for `ftp.mycompany.com`, `/var/log/ftp.mycompany.com`, we find entries similar to those in the main server log, `/var/log/proftpd.log`:

```
Jan 30 17:29:18 localhost proftpd[395] 192.168.1.201 (192.168.1.17[192.168.1.17]):
➥FTP session opened.
Jan 30 17:29:25 localhost proftpd[395] 192.168.1.201 (192.168.1.17[192.168.1.17]):
➥ANON anonymous: Login successful.
Jan 30 17:29:42 localhost proftpd[395] 192.168.1.201 (192.168.1.17[192.168.1.17]):
➥FTP session closed.
Jan 31 12:39:41 localhost proftpd[17756] ftp.mycompany.com
(192.168.1.17[192.168.1.17]):
➥FTP session opened.
Jan 31 12:39:46 localhost proftpd[17756] ftp.mycompany.com
(192.168.1.17[192.168.1.17]):
➥ANON anonymous: Login successful.
Jan 31 12:40:06 localhost proftpd[17756] ftp.mycompany.com
(192.168.1.17[192.168.1.17]):
➥FTP session closed.
Feb 02 15:52:29 localhost proftpd[26351] ftp.mycompany.com (sage[192.168.1.17]):
➥FTP session opened.
Feb 02 15:52:34 localhost proftpd[26351] ftp.mycompany.com (sage[192.168.1.17]):
➥ANON anonymous: Login successful.
Feb 02 15:52:38 localhost proftpd[26351] ftp.mycompany.com (sage[192.168.1.17]):
➥FTP session closed.
```

In the first section of entries, the server host does not know the name that belongs to the IP address that it is serving. By the second section of entries, it knows that `ftp.mycompany.com` is 192.168.1.201.

The most complicated of the FTP server logs is the transfer log, /var/log/xferlog. Its format follows the format of the xferlog that wu-ftpd creates. Each entry in the log consists of an entry in this format:

```
<current-time> <transfer-time> <remote-host> <file-size> <filename>
<transfer-type> <special-action-flag> <direction> <access-mode> <username>
<service-name> <authentication-method> <authenticated-user-id>
<completion-status>
```

At a casual glance, that format might seem a bit overwhelming. Let's look at some sample entries to better understand that format.

Here's an entry resulting from someone contacting the anonymous FTP server:

```
Wed Jan 26 23:31:04 2005 0 192.168.1.17 186880
➥/Users/ftp/incoming/train.wav b _ i a sage@ ftp 1 * c
```

Immediately apparent are the date and time when the transfer occurred. The next entry, the 0, indicates that the transfer time was only one second. The remote host was 192.168.1.17. If a name is known for the remote host, the name appears here instead. The file size was 186880 bytes. The file transferred was train.wav in the incoming area of the anonymous FTP server. The transfer was a binary transfer. No special action, such as compressing or tarring, was done. From the i, you can see that this was an incoming transfer; that is, an upload. From the a, you can see that this was an anonymous user. The string identifying the username in this case is sage@. That is the password that the user entered. The ftp indicates that the FTP service was used. The 1 indicates that RFC931 Authentication was used. The * indicates that an authenticated user ID is not available. The c indicates that the transfer completed.

Here are entries resulting from a real user contacting the FTP server:

```
Mon Jan 31 13:41:44 2005 0 192.168.1.17 753474
➥/Users/joray/Documents/terminal-split-2.tiff  b _ i r joray ftp 1 * c
Mon Jan 31 13:50:10 2005 490 192.168.1.17 753474
➥/Users/joray/Documents/terminal-split-2.tiff  b _ o r joray ftp 1 * c
```

These entries look much like the entry we saw for the anonymous transfer. In this example, r indicates that a real user made the transfer. In this case, the real user is joray. We learn from the o in the second entry that the transfer is an outgoing transfer; that is, a download. From these entries we see that joray uploads a file, and then downloads the same file, all from the same host. From the transfer times, we see that the upload only takes 0 seconds, but the download takes 490 seconds. This user probably has a low TransferRate set for the RETR command!

Here are some entries resulting from a guest user contacting the FTP server:

```
Mon Jan 31 22:08:40 2005 4 192.168.1.17 188970
➥/Users/guests/ralph/train.aif  b _ o r ralph ftp 1 * c
```

```
Mon Jan 31 22:24:37 2005 0 192.168.1.17 186880
➥/Users/guests/ralph/incoming/train.wav  b _ i a ralph ftp 1 * c
Wed Feb  2 16:30:27 2005 0 sage 2890 /Users/guests/ralph/incoming/unison-log
➥b _ i a artist ftp 1 * c
```

These entries also look much like entries we have seen before. Most notable about the guest user is how the guest user is labeled. Our guest user is labeled with an `r` when we use the `DefaultRoot` mechanism for defining the guest, and with an a when we use the `<Anonymous>` mechanism. In the last entry we see that our FTP server knows the remote host as `sage`, and that our guest user logs in using his alias, `artist`.

Finally, here is an entry from our virtual FTP server's xferlog, `/var/log/xferlog-ftp.mycompany.com`:

```
Mon Jan 31 12:40:04 2005 0 192.168.1.17 899
➥/Users/virtual/mycompany.com/incoming/miwa-key.pub
➥b _ i a miwa@ ftp 1 * c
```

The most interesting part about this entry is that the only clue we have that this is an entry for a transfer to the virtual FTP server is the upload directory.

If you are having problems with the FTP server, definitely check your logs. If you need even more information, particularly when you are trying to get it started, you might also consider running `proftpd` in standalone mode with debugging turned on. You can get a lot of information from your logs and debugging mode.

Alternatives to FTP

As we've mentioned, turning on the FTP server makes your machine more vulnerable to attacks from the outside. There are other, more secure options you could consider using as alternatives to FTP.

`scp` and `sftp`

As you already saw in Chapter 21, "Accessing and Controlling Tiger Remotely," two alternatives become available when you turn on the SSH server. You can transfer files either with secure copy (`scp`) or secure FTP (`sftp`). Transfers made using `scp` or `sftp` are encrypted, thereby providing an extra level of security. Specifically, the client creates a tunnel through SSH, using the standard port 22, and executes an `sftp-server` process on the server end, which sends data back through the encrypted channel. The `sftp` and `sftp-server` executables are part of the SSH package. Unlike SSH, the FTP protocol and servers we've covered earlier in this chapter transmit passwords in clear text, adding yet another vulnerability to FTP itself. This makes `scp` or `sftp` a strongly preferred option for users that can use them (appropriate clients are necessary on the client end).

With the SSH server turned on, you can transfer files to other machines running SSH servers. Likewise, those machines can transfer files to your machine by using `scp` or `sftp`. In addition, there exists a freely available (Classic) Mac OS client that has built-in `scp` capabilities. For PCs, there are clients with built-in `sftp` clients. Running SSH removes most needs for an FTP server for real users of your machine. It does not provide a useful substitute for providing data or data-exchange capabilities to anonymous users, or FTP-guest type users. For these purposes, FTP still rules the roost.

FTP and SSH

As you might recall, `proftpd` can be configured as an anonymous-only FTP server. If your real users are transferring files via `scp` or `sftp` but you still need to distribute files to anonymous users, you might then consider running an anonymous-only FTP server alongside your SSH server.

Regularly checking the anonymous FTP area for any irregularities and keeping your `proftpd` current remain important activities.

Tunneling FTP over SSH

If, for whatever reason, running the SSH server is not sufficient to meet your users' needs, you can tunnel FTP connections through `ssh` logins. This enables you to protect the command channel but can't easily protect the FTP data channel. If you're administering an FTP server, you can moderately increase your system security by using an FTP configuration that encourages users to tunnel their FTP connections into your machine.

As mentioned earlier, if you provide an open FTP port for your users to connect to, they'll be likely to try it, and likely to enter their user ID and password on the clear-text data channel to attempt login. You can bias your users against this behavior by exploiting `proftpd`'s capability for configuration and creating specialized FTP servers to handle real and anonymous users. By removing the `<Anonymous>` context that comes with the default `proftpd.conf` file, you can create a server that allows only real users to log in. To protect this server, you can restrict access to it to only connections originating from the server machine itself. This way, the data from the connections never visibly passes over the network, and any connections that come in over the network are rejected, preventing users from unintentionally disclosing their information. SSH can then be used to create tunnels between the users' client machines and the server so that their command channels are carried encrypted over the network to the server and unpacked on the server. Because the connection to the command channel looks to the FTP server as if it's coming from the server machine itself (where it's being unpacked), it is allowed. And because it came to the server over the encrypted SSH tunnel, it is protected against prying eyes. Here you'll learn how to configure a `proftpd` server for this use.

To make tunneling work on the server side, you have to wrap the FTP server to accept connections only from itself. The easiest way to set up the restriction is to use the `only_from` directive in `xinetd`. For machine 192.168.1.19, such an entry looks like:

```
only_from        = 127.0.0.1 192.168.1.19 localhost
```

Another easy way to set up the restriction is to use the TCP Wrappers program that comes with the Mac OS X distribution.

In an enhanced /etc/hosts.allow file, you would do this with the following syntax:

```
in.proftpd: <machine-IP> 127.0.0.1 localhost: allow
in.proftpd: deny
```

If you use TCP Wrappers, you must also indicate this in /etc/xinetd.d/ftp. Add NAMEINARGS to the flags, which tells xinetd that the server itself and its runtime options are listed in the server_args directive. The server directive then lists tcpd. Here is a sample /etc/xinetd.d/ftp file using TCP Wrappers:

```
service ftp
{
        disable = no
        socket_type     = stream
        wait            = no
        user            = root
        server          = /usr/libexec/tcpd
        server_args     = /usr/local/PROftpd/sbin/in.proftpd
        groups          = yes
        flags           = REUSE NAMEINARGS
}
```

Finally, have xinetd re-read its configuration file by running killall -HUP xinetd.

If you must also have an anonymous FTP server running, and even if you don't, it's a good idea to run the FTP server you're trying to make secure on noncanonical ports for FTP (such as 31 for ftp, 30 for ftp-data). If you're running an anonymous-only server, leave it running on the standard FTP ports (21 for ftp, 20 for ftp-data).

As you've seen, you don't need to edit anything to run an FTP server on the standard ports. All that's left, then, is to configure your real-user FTP server and install it on an alternative set of ports. Follow these steps:

1. For ease of administration, it's a good idea to have each FTP server installed in a distinctly separate location. For example, you could install your anonymous FTP server in /usr/local/ftp and your real users' FTP server in /usr/local/proftp.

2. Pick a set of unused port numbers. We like ports close to the standard FTP ports for convenience—31 and 30 are our favorites.

3. Edit the /etc/services file to include the alternative services. You could call them something like proftp and proftp-data. Whichever port number you assign to the proftp service is the one to which the clients wanting to connect need to tunnel.

4. Set the Port directive to whatever port you have picked for the command channel.

5. Finally, wrap the alternative FTP server to allow connections from only itself, but allow the anonymous FTP server access from all machines.

If you also decide to run Mac OS X's built-in firewall, `ipfw`, you must add statements to allow `ipfw` to grant access to the alternative FTP server. In addition, set the `PassivePorts` directive to a range of ports, such as 15001–19999. Then add a statement to the rules for `ipfw` to allow access to whatever range of ports you specified with passive ports. You might find that you have to keep tweaking your `ipfw` and anonymous and real FTP configurations until everything works in harmony. Be sure to check your logs as you're doing this. They're more informative than you might realize now.

Don't worry if the wrapping concept or `ipfw` seems confusing right now. Use of TCP Wrappers and `ipfw` is discussed in Chapter 28. These details are mentioned here so that you can quickly find a summary of the important information about running two FTP servers in one place. We recommend that, where possible, you use `scp` and `sftp` instead of running an FTP server.

Summary

This chapter looked at how to make the optional FTP server more secure. Although Mac OS X comes with an FTP server provided by Apple, we suggest that if you do want to provide FTP services, you run the more configurable ProFTPD. No matter which server you decide to run, restrict access to the server as much as possible, regularly check your logs, and keep the FTP server up to date. For the default FTP server, you can do this with the Mac OS X software updates or by compiling and installing the more recent versions by hand. For ProFTPD, you have to update manually.

You also saw alternative suggestions to using FTP. Most preferable is using `scp` or `sftp`. If you need an anonymous FTP server, have the regular users use `scp` and `sftp` while you provide an anonymous FTP server. However, you might also discover a need to have an FTP server available for your real users. In that case, consider configuring a real-users-only FTP server, wrapping it with TCP Wrappers, and teaching your users to tunnel connections to it over SSH.

You might have found some parts of the chapter confusing. However, as your needs evolve, so does your understanding. You can always return to this chapter to get a start on customizing your FTP needs.

CHAPTER 23

Creating a Web Server

IN THIS CHAPTER

- What Is Apache?
- Understanding Apache Administration
- Expanding Apache's Capabilities with Modules
- Interpreting Web Server Log Files

The early Macintosh was never synonymous with "powerful Internet server." Apple's early attempts to create server products never extended far beyond small Macintosh-only niches. As someone charged with pushing early adoption of Internet technologies and services, I typically found myself sitting in front of a Macintosh that was telnetted into a Linux machine.

For the past five years, Apple has made significant strides to position the Macintosh and Mac OS X as an enterprise-class server system. Xserve and Xraid have proven to be strong sellers in a market that hardly noticed Apple in the past. Likewise, the inclusion of powerful industry-standard server platforms has allowed the system to take on roles traditionally dominated by Windows servers.

One of the best examples of this is the Apache web server included in Tiger. Apache, an open source project similar to the Darwin core of Tiger, is a high-speed extensible server supported by thousands of developers around the world. This chapter introduces Apache, its capabilities, extensions, and basic administration.

What Is Apache?

Apache is an open source project developed by a worldwide group of volunteers known as The Apache Group (`http://www.apache.org`). It is available on dozens of operating systems, including Microsoft Windows. Apache's appeal comes from its flexibility and extensibility. The base server package excels at serving HTML, but to truly exploit the power of Apache, you can install a number of extension modules, including MP3 streaming servers, SSL security, Java Server Pages, and much more. With a total expenditure of $0, you can set up a secure e-commerce server that processes credit cards in real-time and delivers SQL database access.

Differences Between Classic Web Sharing and Apache

If you're looking for the features of the Mac OS 8/9 Personal web server, look elsewhere. The Apache server under Tiger does not offer the Finder mode, nor does it offer the SimpleText-to-HTML conversion of the early Mac OS operating systems. To place information online, you'll need to create HTML documents. This isn't difficult, but there is no direct upgrade path if you have a collection of SimpleText documents you've been serving to the Internet.

Although Mac OS 8/9 enabled you to use the primary address of your computer as the address for your website, Apache forces a URL based on your username. For example, if your computer's address is `http://192.168.0.1` and your username is `joeuser`, your website address would be `http://192.168.0.1/~joeuser`. This change is because of the multiuser capabilities of Tiger. Regardless of how many users are on the system, each can have his personal website online, simultaneously. To use this feature, users must place their web pages within the `Sites` folder of their home directory. If you want a single server without usernames, a master website can be created by placing documents in the `/Library/WebServer/Documents` folder.

> **TIP**
>
> If you are not connected directly to the Internet and want to view an Apache-served website on your local computer, you can refer to your local machine as `localhost`, `127.0.0.1`, or `<machine name>.local`—your Bonjour hostname.

Exploring the Advantages of a Fully Configured Apache Server

For many users, simply turning on Apache might be sufficient for their web serving needs. There is nothing wrong with working within the Apple default settings, but there are a number of advanced features that can be quickly unlocked just by tweaking a few lines. For example:

- Access Control—Easily password-protect portions of your site, or restrict resource access to specific hosts on or off of your local network.
- Virtual Hosts—Your computer can host multiple websites using multiple names. You could, for example, run your personal website from `www.myamazingwebpages.com` while a business-only site chugs along at `www.myamazinglyprofitablebusiness.com`.
- Load Limits—You can control the number of Apache processes available to service incoming requests just by changing a few numbers. Therefore, you can easily increase or decrease the resources Apache consumes.
- Web Applications—Apache supports web applications running from a number of development platforms; these capabilities are deactivated by default.

In addition to the base features of Apache, there are also add-ons that will transform your system into a web-serving powerhouse. Literally hundreds of Apache modules are available for download (`http://modules.apache.org/`), so we'll look at select few.

If you're not interested in these features, take a look at the other Apache modules available. It's best to install only the modules you really use. Additional modules can add overhead and potentially weaken the overall security of the server.

> **NOTE**
>
> I don't mean to imply that the modules included in this chapter are inherently dangerous. "Less is better" is always a good rule of thumb, whether you're talking about Apache modules or full-blown server applications.

Activating Apache

To activate Apache, open the System Preferences application (path: `/Applications/System Preferences`) and click the Sharing icon. You've seen the screen shown in Figure 23.1 before.

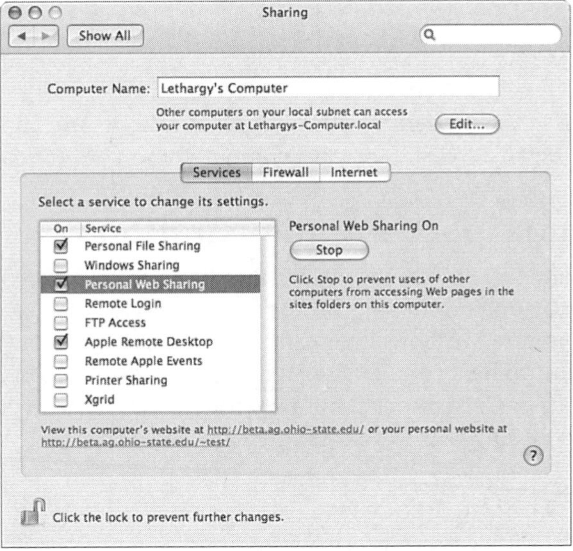

FIGURE 23.1 Use the Sharing Preference panel to activate Apache.

With the Services button selected, highlight the Personal Web Sharing line. Assuming that the screen reads Web Sharing Off, click the Start button to start Apache. After a few seconds, the server status should change to Personal Web Sharing On. Your web pages are now online at the URL located at the bottom of the pane.

The Sharing button does two things. First, it configures Tiger to start Apache when it boots. The `/etc/hostconfig` file is modified to read `WEBSERVER=-YES-`:

```
##
# /etc/hostconfig
##
# This file is maintained by the system control panels
##

# Network configuration
HOSTNAME=-AUTOMATIC-
ROUTER=-AUTOMATIC-

# Services
...
MAILSERVER=-AUTOMATIC-
NETINFOSERVER=-AUTOMATIC-
NFSLOCKS=-AUTOMATIC-
NISDOMAIN=-NO-
RPCSERVER=-AUTOMATIC-
TIMESYNC=-YES-
QTSSERVER=-NO-
WEBSERVER=-YES-
...
```

Second, it activates the Apache server with no need to reboot. You should immediately be able to bring up the default website for your computer and your user account.

Understanding Apache Administration

Apache is an extremely large piece of software that has hundreds of configuration options and possible setups. A number of books have been written about Apache. This section looks at the most common attributes that can be configured and how they affect your system. It is not meant to be a complete reference to Apache. Version 2.0 of Apache is available from `http://www.apache.org`, but it is not yet distributed with Tiger. The current shipping version, 1.3.33, is discussed here.

Controlling the Apache Process

You can start, stop, and restart Apache at any time using the `/usr/sbin/apachectl` utility. For example, to restart the server, type

```
brezup:jray jray $ sudo /usr/sbin/apachectl restart
```

> **TIP**
>
> The Start/Stop buttons and check box within the Sharing Preference panel can also be used to start and stop the Apache process.

Table 23.1 documents all the available `apachectl` options.

TABLE 23.1 The `apachectl` Administration Application Accepts These Commands

Options	Functions
`start`	Starts the Apache server.
`stop`	Stops the Apache server.
`restart`	Restarts Apache. This is equivalent to stopping and then starting the server. Current connections are closed.
`fullstatus`	Displays a full status of the server. This requires lynx to be installed.
`status`	Displays a summary of the server status. The lynx text browser is required.
`graceful`	Restarts the server gracefully. Current connections are not dropped.
`configtest`	Checks the configuration files for errors. Can be used regardless of the current server state.

An interface problem occurs with Apple's use of the Personal Web Sharing metaphor when it is applied to Apache. Each user has his own directory. When web sharing is turned on for one user, it is activated for everyone.

If the computer is a multiuser system and others have the administrative capability to control Apache, you cannot be certain whether web sharing is on or off. The only ways to guarantee that your files aren't being displayed on the Web is to manually disable viewing files using Apache configuration directives, remove the files from your `~/Sites` directory, or set their permissions so that they are readable by the owner only.

Apache Configuration File Locations

Apple has done an excellent job of making the Apache web server configuration manageable for machines with large numbers of personal websites. Instead of a single monolithic configuration, like the standard Linux or Windows installation, the server can be configured on two different levels:

Systemwide configuration—(path: `/etc/httpd/httpd.conf`) This is the master configuration file. It contains information about the system as a whole—what directories are accessible, what plug-ins are in use, and so on. Changes to the web server as a whole are included here.

User-directory configuration—(path: `/etc/httpd/users/<username>.conf`) When the Tiger Accounts System Preference panel creates a new account, it automatically adds a basic configuration file for that user within the `/etc/httpd/users` directory. This mini-configuration file determines the security for the web pages within a user's `Sites` folder.

By splitting up the configuration, the administrator can quickly adjust web permissions on a given account. To edit the user or system configuration, you must either log in (or `su`) as `root` or use `sudo`.

NOTE

Although the user configuration files are stored based on the user's name, they have no real connection to the actual user other than including the path to a personal `Sites` folder. These files can contain any Apache configuration option, including those that affect other users. The division by username is for ease of editing only.

Basic Apache Configuration Directives

Apache approaches configuration in a very object-oriented manner. The configuration files are XML-like, but not compliant, so don't attempt to edit them using the plist editor. Apache calls each configuration option a *directive*. The two types of configuration directives are

Global—Global directives affect the entire server, everything from setting a name for the web server to loading and activating modules.

Container-based—An Apache container is one of a number of objects that can hold web pages. For example, a directory is a container, a virtual host is a container, and an aliased location is also a container. If you don't know what these are, don't worry; we'll get there. For now, just realize that each container can be configured to limit who has access to what it contains, and what pages within it can do.

Global Options

The global options can fall anywhere within the server configuration file. If you're running a heavy-traffic website, you'll definitely want to change the defaults. By default, Apache starts only one server and keeps a maximum of five running at any given time. These numbers do not enable the server to quickly adapt to increased server load.

Table 23.2 documents the some of the most important configuration directives contained in the `/etc/httpd/httpd.conf` file. They are listed in the order in which you're likely to encounter them in the `httpd.conf` file.

NOTE

Several of the Apache directives refer to the number of server processes that should be started. These processes are subprocesses of the parent Apache process. When you use `apachectl` to control the server, you are controlling all the Apache processes.

TABLE 23.2 Global Apache Directives

Directive	Description
`ServerType<`*`standalone`*`¦`*`inetd`*`>`	The Server type determines how Apache starts. Standalone servers are the default. `inetd`-based servers use the `inetd` process to activate a server only when it is accessed. This is inefficient and not recommended for all but the lowest-traffic systems.

TABLE 23.2 Continued

Directive	Description
ServerRoot *<path>*	The base path of the Apache binary files.
PidFile *<path/filename>*	The path (and filename) of the file that should store Apache's process ID.
Timeout *<seconds>*	The number of seconds that Apache will wait for a response from a remote client. When the time period has expired, the connection will be closed.
KeepAlive *<On¦Off>*	Allows more than one request per connection. This is the default behavior of HTTP/1.1 browsers. Shutting this off might result in a higher server load and longer page load times for clients.
MaxKeepAliveRequests <#>	The maximum number of requests that can be made on a single connection.
KeepAliveTimeout	The number of seconds to wait between requests on a *<seconds>* single connection.
MinSpareServers <#>	Apache automatically regulates the number of running servers to keep up with incoming requests. This is the minimum number of servers kept running at any given time.
MaxSpareServers <#>	The maximum number of servers that will be kept running when there is no load. This is not a limit on the total number of server processes to start; it limits the number of unused processes that will be kept running to adapt to changes in load.
StartServers <#>	The number of servers to start when Apache is first launched.
MaxClients <#>	The MaxClients directive sets an upper limit on the number of servers that can be started at a given time. Keeping this number low can help prevent denial of service attacks from eating up all system resources. A heavy-volume server should rarely need more than 100.
MaxRequestsPerChild <#>	Some systems have memory leaks. A memory leak is a portion of the system software in which memory usage slowly grows in size. Apache recognizes that memory leaks might exist and automatically kills a server after it has processed a given number of requests, freeing up any memory it was using. The server process is then restarted, fresh and ready to go.
LoadModule *<modulename><modulepath>*	Loads an Apache module. Many modules will be installed automatically, so you rarely need to adjust anything.

TABLE 23.2 Continued

Directive	Description
`AddModule` *`<modulename.c>`*	Activates a loaded module.
`Port <#>`	The port number that the Apache server will use. The standard HTTP port is 80.
`User` *`<username>`*	The user ID under which Apache will run. Apache has the full access permissions of this user, so never, ever, EVER, set this to the `root` account. Tiger has the user `www` configured for the purpose of running Apache.
`Group` *`<groupname>`*	The group ID under which Apache will run. Like the `User` directive, this should never be set to a privileged value. If it is, any broken web applications could compromise your entire computer. You should use the `www` group for this purpose on Tiger.
`ServerAdmin _`*`<Email Address>`*	The email address of the web server operator.
`ServerName` *`<Server Name>`*	If your server has several different hostnames assigned, use the `ServerName` directive to set the one that will be returned to the client browser. This cannot be an arbitrary name; it *must* exist!
`DocumentRoot` *`<path to html files>`*	This defines the path to the main server HTML files. The Tiger default is `/Library/WebServer/Documents`.
`UserDir` *`<name of user's website directory>`*	The personal website directory within each user's home directory. As you already know, Mac OS X uses `Sites`; the default used in most Apache installs is `public_html`. Removing this directive will make individual users to unable to create websites.
`DirectoryIndex` *`<Default HTML file>`*	When a URL is specified by only a directory name, the web server attempts to display a default HTML file with this name.
`AccessFileName` *`<Access Filename>`*	The name of a file that, if encountered in a directory, will be read for additional configuration directives for that directory. Typically used to password-protect a directory. The default name is `htaccess`.
`DefaultType`	The default MIME type for outgoing documents. The `text/html` type should be used to serve HTML files.
`HostnameLookups` *`<On¦Off>`*	If activated, Apache stores the full hostname of each computer accessing the server rather than its IP address. This is not recommended for servers with more than a trivial load. Hostname

TABLE 23.2 Continued

Directive	Description
	lookups can greatly slow down response time and overall server performance.
`TypesConfig <mime-type configuration file>`	The path to a file that contains a list of MIME types and file extensions that should be served with that MIME type. For example, the type `text/html` is applied to files with the `.html` extension. The default MIME types are located at `/private/etc/httpd/mime.types`.
`LogLevel <level>`	One of eight different error log levels: `debug`, `info`, `notice`, `warn`, `error`, `crit`, `alert`, or `emerg`.
`LogFormat <Log Format><short name>`	Defines a custom log format and assigns it to a name. This will be discussed shortly.
`CustomLog <Logfilename><short name>`	Sets a log filename and assigns it to one of the `LogFormat` types.
`Alias <URL path><server pathname>`	Creates a URL path that aliases to a different directory on the server.
`ScriptAlias <URL path> <server pathname>`	Creates a URL path that aliases to a directory containing CGI applications on the server.
`Redirect <old URL> <new URL>`	Redirects (transfers) a client from one URL to another. Can be used to transfer between URLs on the same server or to transfer a client accessing a local web page to a remote site.
`AddType <MIME-type>_<extension(s)>`	Adds a MIME-type without editing the `mime.types` file.
`AddHandler server-parsed <file extension>`	Activates server-side includes for files with the specified extension. The default SSI extension is `.shtml`.
`AddHandler send-as-is <file extension>`	When activated, files with the defined extension are sent directly to the remote client as is.
`AddHandler imap-file<file extension>`	Sets the extension for server-side imagemap features. All modern web browsers use client-side image maps, but if you need compatibility with Netscape 1.0 browsers, you need to use server-side maps.
`ErrorHandler <error number> <Error Handler>`	Sets an error handler from any one of the standard HTML error messages. This will be discussed in greater detail shortly.
`Include <directory>`	Reads multiple configuration files from a directory. This is set to `/etc/httpd/users`.

This is only a partial list of commonly used global directives—for a complete list, visit Apache's website.

Container Options

The second type of Apache directives are container based. These directives control how Apache serves a certain group of files. Files are chosen based on pattern, location (URL), or directory and are denoted by a start and end tag in the Apache configuration file. For example, the /etc/httpd/users/ configuration files define a container consisting of each user's Sites directory. This is the configuration file created for my jray user account (in my case, that file would be /etc/httpd/users/jray.conf):

```
<Directory "/Users/jray/Sites/">
  Options Indexes MultiViews
  AllowOverride None
  Order allow,deny
  Allow from all
</Directory>
```

In this example, the directory /Users/jray/Sites is the container. Web pages within this container can use the Indexes and Multiviews options. The AllowOverride, Order, and Allow directives control who has access to the files within this container. This will be explained in more detail in the "Using Password Protection Features" section later.

Besides a directory container, there are other constructs that can also be added to the configuration file(s):

- Directory—Creates a directory-based container. All files within the named directory are part of the container.
- DirectoryMatch—Like Directory, but uses a regular expression to match directory names. Check out Chapter 18, "Using Scripting Languages," for an introduction to regular expressions.
- Files—Groups files based on their names. All files matching the specified name are included in the container. The filename should be given exactly, or you should use the ? and * wildcards to match a single unknown character or any number of unknown characters.
- FilesMatch—Similar to Files, but matches filenames based on a regular expression rather than an exact name.
- Location—The Location container is similar to Directory, but matches web content based on a URL, rather than a full-server directory.
- LocationMatch—If you've been following along, you'll probably guess correctly that LocationMatch is the same as Location, but matches the URL based on a regular expression.
- VirtualHost—The VirtualHost container defines a virtual server within the main server. For external clients, the virtual host appears identical to any other web server. To you, the system administrator, it is a directory on your server that gets its very own domain name. You'll see how this can be set up shortly.

Within the container objects, the administrator can add a number of directives to control access to the contents or what special features are available in that location. Table 23.3 includes the container directives you'll encounter most often. We're going to explicitly set up password protection and virtual hosting shortly because this can be a bit tricky just going on the directive definitions alone.

TABLE 23.3 Apache Container Directives

`Options <Option List>`	Sets the special capabilities of the server container. There are eight possible options; each can be preceded by an optional + or - to add or remove it.
`AllowOverride <All>¦<None>¦ <Directive Type>`	Chooses the server-defined directives that a local `.htaccess` file can override. The `.htaccess` file is used to apply directives outside of the main Apache server configuration and can be edited by any user with access to the directory. For that reason, it is important to allow only trusted users to override options. `None` disables all overrides; `All` allows all server directives to be overridden or specifies a combination of `AuthConfig`, `FileInfo`, `Indexes`, `Limit`, or `Options` to allow these directive types to be overridden.
`Order <Deny¦Allow>, <Deny¦Allow> ¦mutual-failure`	Controls the order in which security controls are evaluated—whether or not the list of allowed hosts (`Allow`) or denied hosts (`Deny`) is checked first.
`Allow from <allowed networks¦all>`	A list of IP addresses, networks and subnets, or domain names that can be *allowed* access to the resource.
`Deny from <allowed networks¦all>`	A list of IP addresses, networks and subnets, or domain names that should be denied access to the resource.
`AuthType <Basic¦Digest>`	Attaches HTTP authorization password protection to a directory.
`AuthName <text string>`	Identifies the password-protected resource to the end user.
`AuthUserFile _<userfile path>`	Sets a path to the userfile being used for basic authentication.
`AuthDigestFile <digest userfile path>`	Sets a path to the MD5 Digest password file used with Digest authentication.
`AuthGroupFile <groupfile path>`	Sets the path to a file containing group definitions for use with authentication.
`Require user¦group¦valid-user <user/group list>`	Allows only listed users, groups, or any valid user to access a directory. The users and groups are not Tiger users unless you're using `mod_auth_apple`, which will be discussed shortly. They are created with the `htpasswd` command.
`ErrorDocument <ErrorID><Document Path>`	Used to substitute a custom-error page in place of the default Apache pages. Use the standard HTTPD error codes (such as 404) and a path to the HTML page to display when the error occurs within the given resource.
`ServerAdmin`	The email address of the administrator of a virtual host.

TABLE 23.3 Continued

`DocumentRoot`	The root-level directory for a virtual host.
`ServerName`	The fully qualified domain name for a virtual host, such as `www.poisontooth.com`.

Common Apache Configuration Modifications

To get a handle on configuration, let's take a look at a few different directives in use. Remember that, because of their global nature, global directives can be used anywhere within the `/etc/httpd/httpd.conf` configuration file, whereas container-based directives must be used within a container as described earlier.

Creating URL Aliases (Global)

As you build a complex web server, you'll probably want to spread files out and organize them using different directories. This can lead to extremely long URLs, such as `/mydocuments/work/project1/summary/data/`. This URL is a bit bulky to be considered convenient if it were commonly accessed or publicly advertised.

Thankfully, you can shorten long URLs by creating an alias. Aliases work in a manner similar to the Tiger Finder aliases. A short name is given that, when accessed, will automatically retrieve files from another location. To alias the long data URL to something shorter, such as `/data/`, you would use the following command:

```
Alias /data/ /mydocuments/work/project1/summary/data
```

Aliases can be used to access files anywhere on the server, not just within the server document root. Obviously, the files in the alias directory need to be readable by the Apache process owner.

Redirecting from One URL to Another (Global)

Websites change. URLs change. For established websites, changing the location of a single page can be a nightmare for users—bookmarks break and advertised URLs fail. Although this might seem trivial to experienced web surfers, some users might not be persistent enough to figure out where the page has gone.

Many websites put a redirection page up in place of the missing page. This type of redirection relies on a browser tag to take the user to another URL after a set timeout period. This is effective for most modern browsers, but it takes several seconds between loading the original page and the redirection. In addition, a page needs to be created for each location that might be accessed by the client. This could be hundreds of pages!

A simpler, faster, neater way is to use the Redirect directive. Redirect forces the client browser to transfer to a different URL before the original page even opens. Entire URL structures can be redirected using a single command. The destination URL can even be on a remote server!

For example, if you've decided to move all the files under a URL called /ourcatalog/toys to a new server with the URL www.mynewstoreonline.com/toys, you could use

```
RedirectPermanent /ourcatalog/toys http://www.mynewstoreonline.com/toys
```

If a user attempted to access the URL /ourcatalog/toys/cooltoy1.html, he would immediately be transferred to http://www.mynewstoreonline.com/toys/cooltoy1.html.

Using redirects is more reliable and transparent for the end user. Avoid using HTML-based redirects, and rely on the Apache RedirectPermanent directive to hide changes in the structure of your website.

Increasing and Customizing Logging Capability (Global)

Apache on Tiger stores its log files in the directory /var/log/httpd. By default, there are two logs: access_log and error_log.

The access_log file contains a record of what remote computers have accessed Apache, what they asked for, and when they did it. For example:

```
140.254.85.2 - - [02/September/2003:16:49:47 -0400] "GET /extimage/images/
        26_thumb.jpg HTTP/1.1" 200 27012
140.254.85.2 - - [02/September/2003:16:49:47 -0400] "GET /extimage/images/
        27_thumb.jpg HTTP/1.1" 200 35793
140.254.85.2 - - [02/September/2003:16:49:47 -0400] "GET /extimage/images/
        28_thumb.jpg HTTP/1.1" 200 26141
140.254.85.2 - - [02/September/2003:16:49:47 -0400] "GET /extimage/images/
        30_thumb.jpg HTTP/1.1" 200 29316
140.254.85.2 - - [02/September/2003:16:49:47 -0400] "GET /extimage/images/
        29_thumb.jpg HTTP/1.1" 200 33626
```

This log excerpt shows five requests for .jpg images from the Apache server. Five fields are stored with each log entry:

- Remote Client—The machine accessing the Apache web server. In these examples, that client is 140.254.85.2.
- Date and Time—A time and date stamp for when the request was made. These five requests were made on September 2, 2003, at 4:49 p.m.
- Request String—The actual request that the remote machine made. Most requests begin with GET and are followed by the resource to retrieve, and then the version of the HTTP protocol to retrieve it with. The five requests in the example are for files within the /extimage/images/ directory of the server's documents folder.
- Response Code—Identifies how the remote server responded to the request. The code 200 shows that the request was successfully served. A 404, on the other hand, indicates that the request couldn't be satisfied because the resource wasn't found. The response codes for HTTP 1.1 are available from http://www.w3.org/Protocols/rfc2616/rfc2616-sec6.html.
- Response Size—The number of bytes sent to the remote client to satisfy the request.

NOTE

There are actually seven fields in this log format. The second and third fields contain a `-` that indicates a value could not be determined. It is unlikely that you'll see values here.

This style of access log is known as the *common* log format. Log formats are completely customizable using the global `LogFormat` directive. The common format is defined as

```
LogFormat "%h %l %u %t \"%r\" %>s %b" common
```

Each of the `%h` elements denotes an element to be stored in the log file. The `\"` is an escaped quote, meaning that a quote will also be stored in that location. You can build a log format using the following:

`%h`—Hostname of the requesting computer

`%a`—IP address of the remote computer

`%r`—Request string

`%t`—Time of request

`%T`—Amount of time taken to serve the request

`%b`—Bytes sent

`%U`—URL path requested

`%P`—Process ID of the child that served the request

`%>s`—The last status reported by the server.

`%{Referer}i`—The referring URL (the URL that contained the link to current page)

`%{User-Agent}i`—The string identifies the remote browser

TIP

This is only a partial listing. You can find a complete list of the Apache log elements at `http://httpd.apache.org/docs/mod/mod_log_config.html#logformat`.

You define a log format by using the `LogFormat` line, a string containing the format elements, and a name for the file. For example, to define a log called `mylog` that stores only the hostname of the remote client for each request, you would use

```
LogFormat "%h" mylog
```

Except for custom solutions, you'll be best served by one of Apache's default log formats. Although the `common` log is common, it probably isn't the best thing for doing extensive reporting. A better choice is Apache's `combined` log format. The `combined` log format includes `referer` and `user-agent` strings with each request. Most web analysis packages use the combined log style.

To activate a log format, use the CustomLog directive, followed by the pathname for the log and the log name. To activate the combined log format, uncomment the following line within the /etc/httpd/httpd.conf file:

```
CustomLog "/private/var/log/httpd/access_log" combined
```

Log files are an important part of any web server. They can provide important data on the popular pages of the server, errors that have occurred, and how much traffic your system is getting. We will look at an easy way to provide log analysis later in "Interpreting Web Server Log Files."

NOTE

The error_log is not shown here because it should contain only startup and shutdown messages. If a security violation or configuration error occurs, it is recorded to this file. In addition, programmers can find detailed information about program errors written to this location.

Using Password Protection Features

Password-protecting a directory is extremely simple. For example, suppose that a user wants to password-protect his entire public website for development purposes. The first step is to set up a username and password file that will contain the login information for those who are allowed to access the resource. This is accomplished using htpasswd. There are two steps to the process: First, create a new password file with a single user; second, add additional usernames/passwords to it.

To create a new file, use the syntax htpasswd -c *<pathname>* *<initial username>*. For example,

```
brezup:jray jray $ htpasswd -c /Users/jray/webpasswords jray
New password:
Re-type new password:
Adding password for user jray
```

A new password file (/Users/jray/webpasswords) is created, and the initial user jray is added.

Subsequent users can be added by calling htpasswd -b *<pathname><username>* *<password>*:

```
brezup:jray jray $ htpasswd -b /Users/jray/webpasswords testuser testpass
Adding password for user testuser
```

The password file now has two entries: the initial jray user, and testuser.

Next, create a directory container that encompasses the files that need to be protected. Because this example is protecting a personal website, the container already exists as a <username>.conf file in /etc/httpd/users:

```
<Directory "/Users/jray/Sites/">
  Options Indexes MultiViews ExecCGI
  AllowOverride None
  Order allow,deny
  Allow from all
</Directory>
```

> **NOTE**
>
> This file from this example has been modified slightly since the initial Tiger installation. The `options` directive includes `ExecCGI` to enable CGI development to take place.

To this directory container, add `AuthType`, `AuthName`, `AuthUserFile`, and `Require` directives. You must be `root` or using sudo to edit the file:

```
<Directory "/Users/jray/Sites/">
  AuthType Basic
  AuthName "John's Development Site"
  AuthUserFile /Users/jray/webpasswords
  Require valid-user
  Options Indexes MultiViews ExecCGI
  AllowOverride None
  Order allow,deny
  Allow from all
</Directory>
```

The `AuthUserFile` is set to the name of the password file created with `htpasswd`, whereas the `Require valid-user` directive allows any user in the password file to gain access to the protected resource. To activate the authentication, use `sudo /usr/sbin/apachectl restart`:

```
brezup:jray jray $ sudo /usr/sbin/apachectl restart
/usr/sbin/apachectl restart: httpd restarted
```

Attempting to access the `/Users/jray/Sites` directory (`~jray`) now opens an HTTP authentication dialog, as seen in Figure 23.2.

Authenticating Against User Accounts with `mod_auth_apple`

Using the basic Apache authentication is fine in many cases, but you might find yourself wanting to protect resources based on actual user accounts on your computer. Although it's simple enough to create a password file for each user, these passwords will not be updated as users update their Tiger passwords. The real solution is to provide an authentication mechanism by which resources could be protected by actual system accounts and system passwords. This is entirely possible courtesy of Apple's `mod_auth_apple` Apache module.

FIGURE 23.2 The directory is now password-protected.

Included with Tiger Server by default, Tiger client users can download and install `mod_auth_apple` with very little trouble. There are two components to the install: First, a missing header file `Security/checkpw.h` must be copied from the Darwin CVS repository or mirror, and then the source code for `mod_auth_apple` can be downloaded and installed.

The header file can be downloaded directly from Apple at `http://developer.apple.com/darwin/projects/darwin/darwinserver/`, but you'll need to register before downloading. Alternatively, download the header from `http://www.opendarwin.org/cgi-bin/cvsweb.cgi/src/Security/checkpw/`. After downloading, make a new directory `/usr/include/Security`, and copy the header file to the new location:

```
brezup:jray jray $ curl -O "http://www.opendarwin.org/cgi-bin/cvsweb.cgi/
➥~checkout~/src/Security/ checkpw/checkpw.h"
brezup:jray jray $ sudo mkdir /usr/include/Security
brezup:jray jray $ sudo mv checkpw.h /usr/include/Security/
```

Next, download the latest `mod_auth_apple` package from `http://developer.apple.com/darwin/projects/darwin/darwinserver/`, unarchive it, and then enter the source distribution directory. (Note: To download `mod_auth_apple`, you will need to create an Apple ID if you don't already have one.)

```
brezup:jray jray $ tar zxf mod_auth_apple-XS-10.3.tgz
brezup:jray jray $ cd mod_auth_apple
```

Be sure to check the Apple README file for installation instructions; they might change between versions. The instructions shown here are modified from Apple's directions so that the software configures automatically. Use `make` followed by `sudo apxs -i -a mod_auth_apple.so` to compile and install the module:

```
brezup:jray mod_auth_apple $ make
/usr/sbin/apxs -c -Wc,"-traditional-cpp -Wno-four-char-constants
 -F/System/Library/PrivateFrameworks -DUSE_CHKUSRNAMPASSWD"
 -Wl,"-bundle_loader /usr/sbin/httpd -framework Security"
```

```
 -o mod_auth_apple.so mod_auth_apple.c
gcc -DDARWIN -DUSE_HSREGEX -DUSE_EXPAT -I../lib/expat-lite
 -g -Os -pipe -DHARD_SERVER_LIMIT=2048 -DEAPI -DSHARED_MODULE
 -I/usr/include/httpd -traditional-cpp -Wno-four-char-constants
 -F/System/Library/PrivateFrameworks -DUSE_CHKUSRNAMPASSWD -c mod_auth_apple.c
...
brezup:jray mod_auth_apple $ sudo apxs -i -a mod_auth_apple.so
[activating module 'apple_auth' in /private/etc/httpd/httpd.conf]
cp mod_auth_apple.so /usr/libexec/httpd/mod_auth_apple.so
chmod 755 /usr/libexec/httpd/mod_auth_apple.so
cp /private/etc/httpd/httpd.conf /private/etc/httpd/httpd.conf.bak
cp /private/etc/httpd/httpd.conf.new /private/etc/httpd/httpd.conf
rm /private/etc/httpd/httpd.conf.new
```

The `mod_auth_apple` module is now compiled and installed. Using it is identical to the examples we've already seen for Basic authentication, except no password file is needed. For example, to protect my `Sites` directory so that only my account (`jray`) can access it, I would use the following in my `/etc/httpd/users/jray.conf` file:

```
<Directory "/Users/jray/Sites/">
  AuthType Basic
  AuthName "John's Development Site"
  Require user jray
  Options Indexes MultiViews ExecCGI
  AllowOverride None
  Order allow,deny
  Allow from all
</Directory>
```

To verify against any account on the machine, replace `Require user jray` with `Require valid-user`. Alternatively, to validate against a group, `Require group` *<groupname>* could be employed.

CAUTION

The authentication methods shown here uses Basic authentication, which passes clear-text information (usernames/passwords) over the network. A more secure form, called Digest authentication, is also available, which encrypts passwords before sending them. In addition, Apple offers a digest form of its authentication module that you can use to gain a bit of security. (See `http://httpd.apache.org/docs/howto/auth.html#digest` for more information on Digest authentication.)

Unfortunately, Digest authentication should not be considered truly secure because the encrypted password itself is sent as plaintext and could simply be provided to the remote server to authenticate. To *truly* be secure, you'll need SSL support, which is covered in the *Mac OS X Tiger Unleashed* supplement *Enabling Apache SSL Support*, downloadable at `http://www.macosxunleashed.com/downloads/apachessl.pdf`.

Restricting Access by Network

To create more stringent control over the users who can access a given resource, use `Allow` and `Deny` to set up networks that should or shouldn't have access to portions of your website. This is extremely useful for setting up intranet sites that should only be accessible by a given subnet. For example, assume that you want to restrict access to a resource from everyone except the subnet 192.168.0.x. The following rules define the access permissions:

```
Allow from 192.168.0.0/255.255.255.0
Deny from all
```


Because there isn't an ordering specified, what really happens with these rules is ambiguous. Is the connection allowed because of the allow statement? Or denied because all the connections are denied?

To solve the problem, insert the `Order` directive:

```
Order Deny,Allow
Allow from 192.168.0.0/255.255.255.0
Deny from all
```

With this ordering, an incoming connection is first compared to the deny list. Because all access is denied by default, any address matches this rule. However, the `Allow` directive is used for the final evaluation of the connection and will allow any connection from the network 192.168.0.0 with the subnet 255.255.255.0.

Using different orderings and different `Allow/Deny` lists, you can lock down a website to only those people who should have access, or disable troublesome hosts that misuse the site.

TIP

As with any change to the Apache configuration file, you must use `sudo /usr/sbin/apachectl` to restart the server.

An alternative to restarting is to add an `.htaccess` file to the directory you want to protect. This file can contain any of the standard directory container directives and will be automatically read when Apache attempts to read any file from the directory.

Creating Virtual Hosts

A virtual host is a unique container object, in that it can define an entirely separate web space unrelated to the main Apache website or user sites. For example, the three domains `poisontooth.com`, `vujevich.com`, and `shadesofinsanity.com` are all being served from a single computer. To the end user, these appear to be different and unique hosts. To Apache, however, they're just different directories on the same hard drive.

There are two types of virtual hosts—name-based and IP-based—as described in the following list:

Name-based—These hosts rely on the HTTP/1.1 protocol to work. A single IP address is used on the server, but there are multiple DNS name entries for that single address. When connecting to the server, the client browser sends a request for a web page, along with the name of the server it should come from. Apache uses that information to serve the correct page. This works for all but the oldest 2.0 revision browsers.

IP-based—These hosts rely on Apache's capability to listen to multiple IP addresses simultaneously. Each domain name is assigned to a different IP address. Apache can differentiate between the different incoming addresses and serve the appropriate documents for each. This works on any browser, but is costly in terms of the IP addresses that it consumes.

To set up a virtual host, you must first have an IP address and a domain name assigned for the host. If you're using name-based hosts, you will have a single IP address but multiple hostnames. Your ISP or network administrator should be able to help set up this information.

TIP

Tiger users who are attempting to configure IP-based virtual hosts will need to assign multiple IPs to an interface by duplicating their existing network interfaces within the Network System Preference pane.

Alternatively, additional IPs can be added from the command line by using `ifconfig <interface> alias <additional IP address> 255.255.255.255`. For most single-network-card systems, the interface will be `en0`. AirPort cards are usually identified with `en1`. For example:

```
sudo ifconfig en0 alias 192.168.0.200 255.255.255.255
```

This adds the IP address 192.168.0.200 as an additional address to the Tiger system. Aliases added in this manner will have to be included in a startup file such as `/etc/rc` to activate at boot.

There are only two differences in the Apache configuration of name-based and IP-based virtual hosts. Name-based hosts must include the `NameVirtualHost` directive, whereas IP-based hosts will need to use `Listen` to inform Apache of all the available addresses.

Let's take a look at two different ways to configure the virtual hosts `www.mycompany.com` and `www.yourcompany.com`. First, we'll use named-based hosting.

Assume that both `mycompany` and `yourcompany` domain names point to the IP address 192.168.0.100. To configure name-based virtual hosts, you could add the following directives to the end of the `/etc/httpd/httpd.conf` file:

```
NameVirtualHost 192.168.0.100

<VirtualHost 192.168.0.100>
    ServerName www.mycompany.com
    DocumentRoot /Users/jray/mycompany
    ServerAdmin president@mycompany.com
</VirtualHost>
```

```
<VirtualHost 192.168.0.100>
    ServerName www.yourcompany.com
    DocumentRoot /Users/jray/yourcompany
    ServerAdmin president@yourcompany.com
</VirtualHost>
```

The NameVirtualHost sets up the IP address that Apache will expect multiple domain name requests to come in on. The two VirtualHost directives define the basic properties of the two sites: what their real domain names are, where the HTML documents are loaded, and the email address for the person who runs the site.

Creating this same setup using IP-based hosts doesn't require much additional effort. For this sample configuration, assume that www.mycompany.com has the address 192.168.0.100 and that www.yourcompany.com uses 192.168.0.101. The configuration becomes

```
Listen 192.168.0.100
Listen 192.168.0.101

<VirtualHost 192.168.0.100>
    ServerName www.mycompany.com
    DocumentRoot /Users/jray/mycompany
    ServerAdmin president@mycompany.com
</VirtualHost>

<VirtualHost 192.168.0.101>
    ServerName www.yourcompany.com
    DocumentRoot /Users/jray/yourcompany
    ServerAdmin president@yourcompany.com
</VirtualHost>
```

This time, the Listen directive is used to tell Apache to watch for incoming web connections on both of the available IP addresses. The VirtualHost containers remain the same, except they now use different IP addresses for the two different sites.

Virtual hosting provides an important capability to the web server. Although available with a GUI configuration tool in Tiger Server, the Apache distribution included in the standard version of Tiger is every bit as powerful. It just takes a bit of manual editing to get things done!

Expanding Apache's Capabilities with Modules

One of the nicest features of Apache is its modular plug-in design. Developers can easily expand the capabilities of the Apache web server without forcing the end users to recompile their server software or make complex configuration changes. In this section, we'll be looking at a handful of modules—some included with Tiger, others that you'll need to download and compile. These are just a tiny sample of what is available for the world's most popular web server:

mod_dav—Enables the WebDAV protocol for cross-platform sharing of files via HTTP

mod_mp3—Creates a SHOUTcast-compatible streaming MP3 server

mod_bonjour—Advertises your Apache sites over the LAN using Apple's Bonjour technology

Mod_rewrite—Rewrites local URLs based on regular expressions and can proxy remote content through a given URL

NOTE

If you're interested in rebuilding Apache or enabling SSL support, you may be interested in the supplemental document *Enabling Apache SSL Support*, downloadable at `http://www.macosxunleashed.com/downloads/apachessl.pdf`

Sharing Files with WebDAV and `mod_dav`

Something that Apple hasn't advertised with Mac OS X is the integration of WebDAV as a native file-sharing format. If you're the proud owner of a .Mac account, you already use WebDAV to access your iDisk. WebDAV (Distributed Authoring and Versioning) is a relatively new protocol that operates on top of HTTP. What makes this attractive is the fact that it doesn't require additional `xinetd` or system daemons to be present, and works great through HTTP proxies.

WebDAV is entirely cross-platform, is integrated into the Windows operating system, and is supported natively in software such as Macromedia Dreamweaver MX. Using WebDAV, you can distribute authoring and editing websites across a number of different computers and operating systems—or just use it to share files. Best of all, WebDAV is easy to use and, because it operates through Apache, the same configuration directives you've already seen can apply directly to its setup.

Configuring `mod_dav`

Apple includes a precompiled version of WebDAV in Tiger. To enable it, open your `/etc/httpd/httpd.conf` file and look for the two (nonconsecutive) lines:

```
#LoadModule dav_module     libexec/httpd/libdav.so
#AddModule mod_dav.c
```

Uncomment both lines so that they read:

```
LoadModule dav_module     libexec/httpd/libdav.so
AddModule mod_dav.c
```

To finish the configuration and activation of WebDAV service on your Apache server, you need to create a directory that will hold WebDAV lockfiles and then turn on the service for a particular directory or location.

Use the `DAVLockDB` directive to set the directory and base filename for WebDAV's lockfiles. This should fall anywhere after the `LoadModule/AddModule` lines in the `/etc/httpd/httpd.conf` file:

```
DAVLockDB /var/tmp/davlock
```

This example specifies that the directory `/var/tmp` will be used to hold lockfiles and that `davlock` will be the base filename for the lockfiles. Be sure to include the base filename, not just a directory name. If the lockfile is not properly set, `mod_dav` will start, but won't operate correctly.

Now choose one of the directory or container objects that will support WebDAV service and add the `DAV On` directive:

```
<Directory "/Library/WebServer/Documents">
   DAV On
   Options Indexes FollowSymLinks MultiViews
   AllowOverride None
   Order allow,deny
   Allow from all
</Directory>
```


You should limit access to the DAV services using the same require directive in the standard Apache configuration. WebDAV relies on the HTTP protocol to authenticate users for editing. That means that you will need to create a password file using `htpasswd` just as we did earlier or use Apple's authentication module to limit access to user accounts on the computer. Unlike the previous example, however, a valid user will be required only when performing a modification to the file system. To create this sort of selective authentication, we'll use the `Limit` directive. For example, the following configuration file fragment defines an authentication scheme and limits it to the operations that WebDAV uses to add and update files.

```
AuthType Basic
AuthName "The Poisontooth Webserver"
AuthUserFile /Users/jray/webpasswords
<Limit PUT DELETE PROPPATCH MKCOL COPY MOVE LOCK UNLOCK>
     Require valid-user
</Limit>
```

To finish things up, just combine the authentication block with the resource that WebDAV support has been enabled (`DAV On`):

```
<Directory "/Library/WebServer/Documents">
   DAV On
   Options Indexes FollowSymLinks MultiViews
   AllowOverride None
   Order allow,deny
   Allow from all
   AuthType Basic
   AuthName "The Poisontooth Webserver"
   AuthUserFile /Users/jray/webpasswords
     <Limit PUT DELETE PROPPATCH MKCOL COPY MOVE LOCK UNLOCK>
       Require valid-user
     </Limit>
</Directory>
```

Line 1 sets up the directory to WebDAV-enable. This can be a directory that is already defined in the main Apache `http.conf` or one of the user configuration files.

Line 2 turns on DAV support, and lines 3–6 are standard directory security directives—not WebDAV related.

Lines 7–9 set up basic HTTP authentication. This will be used to authenticate potential WebDAV clients. Lines 10–12 limit the HTTP authentication to only those actions that would be triggered by a WedDAV client.

One small thing still needs to be adjusted before WebDAV can be used: the permissions on the directory that has WebDAV support enabled. Because WebDAV is nothing more than an extension to Apache, it has no more user rights than the Apache server process. This means that if Apache can't write to a resource (that is, it isn't owned by `www` or isn't set to world-writable), WebDAV won't be able to modify the resource either. To make a directory editable using DAV, you must use `chown` to modify the file and directory ownership. Type **`chown -R www:admin`** ***`<directory to DAV-enable>`*** and you're done!

Restart Apache (`sudo /usr/sbin/apachectl restart`) to begin using WebDAV.

Mounting WebDAV Shares

First, from within a Finder window, use the Go menu to choose Connect to Server (Command-K). The dialog box shown in Figure 23.3 will appear.

FIGURE 23.3 Use the Connect to Server menu item to connect to WebDAV-enabled servers.

Fill in the URL of the directory with DAV access in the Address field. This should be the web path to the resource, not the actual file path on the server. In the screenshot shown, the main root directory of the web server `http://www.shadesofinsanity.com/` has been enabled, so the URL given is just set to the main website URL. When satisfied that your settings are correct, click Connect. You will be prompted for a username and password for the resource. Use the username/password pair defined by your HTTP authentication configuration.

After a few seconds, the remote site should be mounted as if it were a local drive on your computer.

TIP

Although not entirely practical for high-volume sharing, WebDAV volumes work just like AppleShare or NFS volumes under Tiger. Unlike the implementation on certain other platforms, Tiger users can store and execute applications directly on WebDAV shares. In Mac OS X 10.2 and up, your iDisk is accessed entirely via the WebDAV protocol. This enables it to appear to be connected all the time. The end result is more convenient access for you and less of a load on Apple's servers.

Using WebDAV on Windows

Like Apple, Microsoft integrates WebDAV into the latest releases of their operating system. To access a WebDAV share on Windows XP, you must create a new Network Place.

Double-click My Network Places to open the Network Places window. Next, double-click Add Network Place to start the Add Network Place Wizard. If prompted, tell the Add Network Place Wizard to Choose Another Network Location, and then click Next. Windows will ask for the address of the network place, as shown in Figure 23.4.

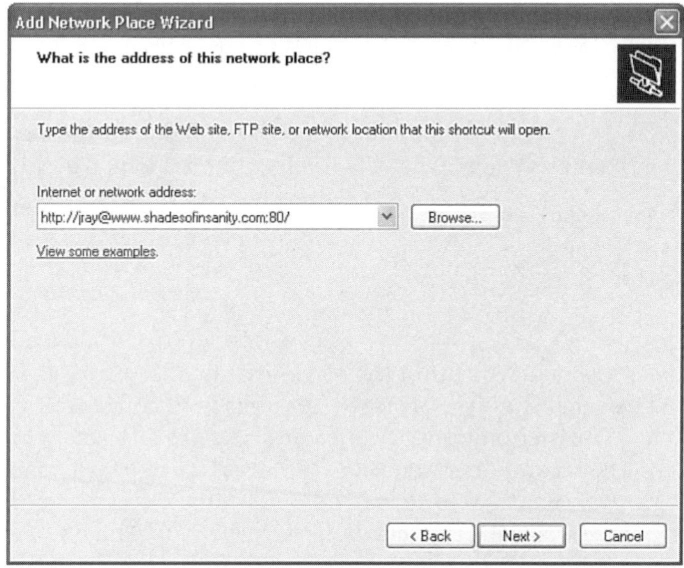

FIGURE 23.4 The Add Network Place Wizard will help set up a WebDAV resource in Windows.

Fill in the URL of the WebDAV resource, but in a slightly different format than you did on Tiger. On Windows XP, you must supply the URL with the username and port included; for example, `http://`*`<username>`*`@`*`<yourdomain.com>`*`:80/`*`<pathtoDAVshare>`*. After that has been entered, click Next. As with Tiger, you will be prompted for the username and password that were set using `htpasswd` or accessed by `mod_auth_apple`. Click Next to finish and mount the resource.

WebDAV support is an integral part of Mac OS X and Windows and can be used to unite a multiplatform environment for collaboration on websites and other projects. In a pinch, WebDAV can even serve as a file server for things other than web-related files.

Advertising Sites with `mod_bonjour`

Another module that Apple has included in Tiger (and neglected to tell anyone about) is its self-authored `mod_bonjour` module. `mod_bonjour` registers sites with Bonjour-enabled browsers (such as Safari) on your local network. Rather than bookmarking your local servers, the servers advertise their own bookmarks!

Unfortunately, Apple failed to provide a mechanism for disabling this—so if you happen to be running a private test server, there's a good chance your machine is advertising it via Bonjour to every other computer on your network. Let's take a look at how you can manually control `mod_bonjour` and what it does.

Configuring `mod_bonjour`

To disable the module completely, just comment out the appropriate `LoadModule` and `AddModule` lines from `/etc/httpd/httpd.conf`:

```
#LoadModule bonjour_apple_module libexec/httpd/mod_bonjour_apple.so
#AddModule mod_bonjour_apple.c
```

If, instead, you prefer to control which services are advertised, find the `mod_bonjour` directive block at the end of `httpd.conf`. The default block should look like this:

```
<IfModule mod_bonjour_apple.c>
RegisterUserSite all-users
RegisterDefaultSite
</IfModule>
```

There are two directives included within the block—the first, `RegisterUserSite all-users`, registers all personal sites (~*<username>*) for users with configuration files within `/etc/httpd/users`. To register only specific user sites, use `RegisterUserSite` *<username>* [*<username>* ...]. The second directive, `RegisterDefaultSite`, registers the default `/Library/Webserver/Documents` website via Bonjour. A final directive, `RegisterResource` *<resource name> <resource URI>*, enables you to register any URL on your server with an arbitrary resource name.

For example, to register my personal website (username `jray`) along with a URL `/bulletinboard/bbs.cgi`, I'd change the Bonjour directives in `/etc/httpd/httpd.conf` to read:

```
<IfModule mod_bonjour_apple.c>
RegisterUserSite jray
RegisterResource "My Local BBS" "/bulletinboard/bbs.cgi"
</IfModule>
```

After making the changes, restarting Apache puts them into effect immediately, removing the default site advertisement and adding my two custom Bonjour-enabled sites.

That's enough work for now. On to something a bit more entertaining—streaming audio from Apache!

Creating a Streaming MP3 Station with `mod_mp3`

If you've been using iTunes, you've probably got quite a collection of MP3 files built up on your drive. Rather than taking the MP3s with you wherever you go, you can create your own Internet radio station and broadcast music to your computer at work, home, or wherever your MP3s aren't. Apple briefly introduced this feature with iTunes 4.0, and then removed it because of pressure from the recording industry.

Using the Apache `mod_mp3` module, you bring this feature back in the form of a SHOUTcast-compatible streaming MP3 server. Of course, it goes without saying that anyone who listens to your streams has a legitimate copy of the music. Absolutely no sarcasm intended. None.

Installing `mod_mp3` only takes a few minutes of time. Download the latest release from `http://tangent.org/` and then unarchive and `cd` into the distribution directory. Now use `configure --with-apxs` to prepare the module:

```
brezup:jray jray $ cd mod_mp3-0.40
brezup:jray mod_mp3-0.40 $ ./configure --with-apxs
ARGS --with-apxs
checking for ghttp for yp.. could not find ghttp for yp support
checking for perl.. found
checking for apxs.. found
adding support for internal dispatch
Writing proto.h
Writing Makefile
...
```

Next, type **`make`** to compile:

```
brezup:jray mod_mp3-0.40 $ make
`/usr/sbin/apxs -q CC` -I`/usr/sbin/apxs -q INCLUDEDIR` `/usr/sbin/apxs -q
 CFLAGS` -DCONTENT_DISPOSITION -DSELECT_ENABLED  -c src/mod_mp3.c
 -DCONTENT_DISPOSITION -DSELECT_ENABLED  -o src/mod_mp3.o
`/usr/sbin/apxs -q CC` -I`/usr/sbin/apxs -q INCLUDEDIR` `/usr/sbin/apxs -q
 CFLAGS` -DCONTENT_DISPOSITION -DSELECT_ENABLED  -c src/directives.c
 -DCONTENT_DISPOSITION -DSELECT_ENABLED  -o src/directives.o
`/usr/sbin/apxs -q CC` -I`/usr/sbin/apxs -q INCLUDEDIR` `/usr/sbin/apxs -q
 CFLAGS` -DCONTENT_DISPOSITION -DSELECT_ENABLED  -c src/ice.c
 -DCONTENT_DISPOSITION -DSELECT_ENABLED  -o src/ice.o
`/usr/sbin/apxs -q CC` -I`/usr/sbin/apxs -q INCLUDEDIR` `/usr/sbin/apxs -q
 CFLAGS` -DCONTENT_DISPOSITION -DSELECT_ENABLED  -c src/load.c
 -DCONTENT_DISPOSITION -DSELECT_ENABLED  -o src/load.o
 ...
```

Finally, use **sudo make install** to add the module to /etc/httpd/httpd.conf:

```
brezup:jray mod_mp3-0.40 $ sudo make install
/usr/sbin/apxs -c -I`/usr/sbin/apxs -q INCLUDEDIR` src/mod_mp3.o
 src/directives.o src/ice.o src/load.o src/shout.o src/utility.o
 src/ogg.o src/common.o src/id3.o src/log.o src/internal_dispatch.o
 src/encode.o
cc -bundle -undefined suppress -flat_namespace -Wl,-bind_at_load -o
 src/mod_mp3.so src/mod_mp3.o src/directives.o src/ice.o src/load.o
 src/shout.o src/utility.o src/ogg.o src/common.o src/id3.o
 src/log.o src/internal_dispatch.o src/encode.o
/usr/sbin/apxs -i -a -n 'mp3' src/mod_mp3.so
...
+---------------------------------------------------------+
| All done.                                               |
| If you want to use the default mod_mp3 configure file   |
| go add:                                                 |
|                                                         |
| Include /private/etc/httpd/mp3.conf                     |
|                                                         |
| to your httpd.conf for apache.                          |
| If not, cat its content into your httpd.conf file.      |
|                                                         |
| Thanks for installing mod_mp3.                          |
+---------------------------------------------------------+
```

The MP3-streaming module is now installed and ready for use.

> **NOTE**
>
> Modules that are installed using the apxs utility, such as mod_mp3 are automatically placed in the appropriate location and have the appropriate LoadModule and AddModule directives added to the http.conf file.

Configuring mod_mp3

The mod_mp3 module is activated by setting up an Apache virtual host that will serve as the contact point for iTunes or any other streaming MP3 client. There are two ways to approach this: either by using a name-based or IP-based host, as you've already seen, or by using a virtual host running on a port address rather than the standard web server port 80. We'll use the latter approach.

A handful of directives are used to control the mod_mp3 streaming features. Several of these are documented in Table 23.4.

TABLE 23.4 These Directives Control `mod_mp3`'s Capability to Stream Music

Directive	Purpose
`MP3` *<file or pathname>*	Adds an MP3 file or directory containing MP3 files to the list of files to be served.
`MP3Engine <on¦off>`	Turns on the streaming engine.
`MP3CastName` *<stream collection.name>*	Sets a name for the streaming music.
`MP3Genre` *<stream genre>*	Sets a music genre for the stream.
`MP3Random <on¦off>`	Randomizes the order that MP3 files will be served.
`MP3Loop <on¦off>`	Loops through the music files indefinitely.
`MP3LimitPlayConnections`*<connection limit>*	The number of simultaneous streaming connections that will be supported.
`MP3ReloadRequest <on¦off>`	If turned on, `mod_mp3` will reload all files with each request. This is useful if you're adding to the available files during the broadcast.
`MP3Playlist` *<playlist file>*	Accepts the name of a file that contains a list of MP3 filenames.
`MP3Cache <on¦off>`	When on, the module will attempt to cache all MP3 files in memory. This can speed up the server, but will probably take up way too much memory if you have more than a handful of files.

Use these directives, coupled with a virtual host, to set up and start streaming. The following is a typical sample virtual host entry for the `/etc/httpd/httpd.conf` file:

```
1: Listen 8000
2: <VirtualHost music.poisontooth.com:8000>
3:   ServerName music.poisontooth.com
4:   MP3Engine On
5:   MP3CastName "Johns Tunes"
6:   MP3Genre "Hard Rock and 80s"
7:   MP3 /Users/jray/Music
8:   MP3Random On
9:   Timeout 1200
10: </VirtualHost>
```

Line 1 sets the port number for listening to incoming streaming requests. The default web port is 80, so if you're using the hostname for a website as well as streaming music, be sure to pick a different port.

Line 2 sets up the virtual host and port number for connections.

Line 4 turns on MP3 support.

Lines 5 and 6 set some identifying information for the streaming server.

Line 7 adds a directory containing MP3 files to the stream (you can add as many MP3 directives as you'd like).

Line 8 randomizes the playback order.

Line 9 sets a high timeout so that connections are properly serviced.

TIP

A sample `mod_mp3` configuration is installed under the filename `/etc/httpd/mp3.conf`. Feel free to use it rather than typing out all the directives by hand.

Restart Apache to turn on your new `mod_mp3`-streaming server: **`/usr/sbin/apachectl restart`**.

NOTE

Starting the Apache web server with `mod_mp3` and a reasonably sized MP3 collection can take several seconds. Don't worry if the system appears to stall momentarily.

To access your new MP3 server using iTunes, select Open Stream from the Advanced menu (Command-U) and enter the URL of your MP3 virtual host. The sample `mod_mp3` configuration used in this chapter would be referenced with the URL `http://music.poisontooth.com:8000`, as shown in Figure 23.5.

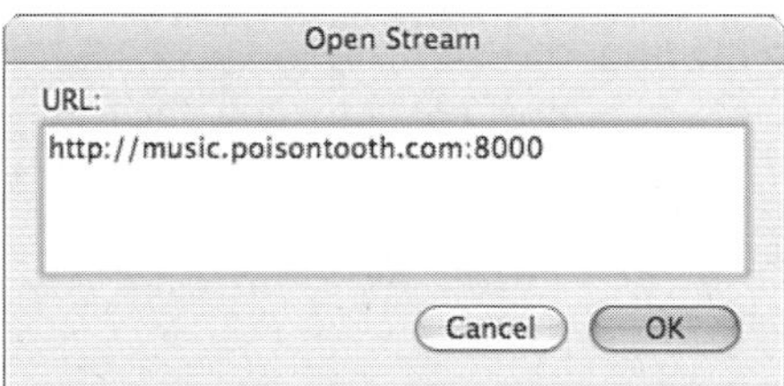

FIGURE 23.5 Open the Apache-served MP3 stream from within iTunes.

Alternatives

If you'd like to try another method of streaming MP3s, there are quite a few available (including Apple's own QuickTime Streaming Server available at `http://www.apple.com`). Here are a few you might be interested in checking out:

SHOUTcast—An official SHOUTcast server from nullsoft. Uses a command-line interface, but is fast and effective. `http://www.shoutcast.com/download/files.phtml`.

NetJuke—NetJuke provides a web interface (PHP-based) to your music collection. This very popular open source project is extremely flexible and, after is has been installed, offers a wonderful web-based interface that you can access anywhere. `http://www.netjuke.org/`.

LeanStream—A drag-and-drop approach to MP3 streaming, LeanStream is very easy to set up and use. Although not as configurable as other streaming servers, it can get your collection online in a flash. `http://www.melonsoft.com/products/leanstream`.

MP3 Sushi—An excellent Bonjour-enabled streaming server for Mac OS X. If you're not interested in tons of bells and whistles, but want a great interface to streaming music, this is it. `http://www.maliasoft.com/us/mp3sushi.html`.

Transparent Proxying with `mod_rewrite`

Apache and its associated modules can be configured to do some reasonably amazing things. As one more useful example, I offer up these two configuration lines that you can add to your `/etc/httpd/httpd.conf` file (after the `<Directory />` container is a good place):

```
RewriteEngine On
RewriteRule (.+\.pdf)\.html
http://view.samurajdata.se/ps.php?url=http://%{HTTP_HOST}$1 [P]
```

So, what does this code do? First, it activates the Apache `mod_rewrite` module, and then adds a rule to which Apache will compare every incoming request.

Assume that you have a PDF file on your site named `mydocument.pdf`. You want to serve the document online as HTML. You could convert it with a third-party piece of software or use an online PDF conversion service such as `http://view.samurajdata.se/`. This rule automates the process by looking for requests for `mydocument.pdf.html` (which doesn't exist). If it sees a matching request, it immediately sends the corresponding PDF file to the online conversion service, and then returns the results back to your browser—entirely transparently.

From the user's perspective, the file `mydocument.pdf.html` exists and is served from your web server.

The `mod_rewrite` module enables you to rewrite, redirect, and proxy remote servers through Apache using regular expressions. A complete guide to the many useful and varied features of this module is available at `http://httpd.apache.org/docs/misc/rewriteguide.html`.

Interpreting Web Server Log Files

An abundance of log analysis software is available for Unix operating systems (and thus Tiger). Log analysis is more of an art than a science. As you've seen by looking at the log file formats, you can determine the remote host, requested resource, and time of request from the log file. Unfortunately, many analysis packages try to go even further by providing information on how long visitors were at your page, or where (geographically) they are located. Neither of these pieces of information is tracked in the Apache logs.

Understanding Web Statistics

To determine how long someone has been at your site, the analysis software must look at all accesses and determine which are related, and the amount of time between them. This is entirely guesswork on the part of the server. Assume that a user opens her browser, views a page, walks away for 15 minutes, and then accidentally clicks on another page before closing her browser. If the software is set with a session timeout period greater than 15 minutes, it sees two separate hits on the page. The software assumes that the user spent at least 15 minutes reading both pages and registers that the browser spent 30 minutes on the site. In reality, only a minute or two was spent looking at the site content.

When determining geographic information, analysis software performs an even more amazing task—locating what city a user is coming from. To do this, the analysis utility looks up the domain of the client accessing the system. It retrieves the city and state that the domain was registered in. Unfortunately, this is almost completely worthless data.

For example, a WebTrends report on a local (Columbus, Ohio) e-commerce site showed that more than 95% of the remote requests are coming from Herndon, VA. In fact, an analysis of other (nonrelated) sites shows a similar amount of traffic from Virginia. The reason is simple—the RoadRunner cable model network. The `rr.com` domain is registered in Herndon, VA. There are thousands of users with RoadRunner-based access—no matter where they are actually coming from, the report displays Herndon, VA. That isn't very useful, is it?

The final web statistic fallacy is the number of hits a page receives. Many people are delighted when they find that they're getting a few thousand hits a day, but they don't realize what constitutes a hit. The Apache web server counts any information requested as a hit. If a web page has 10 tiny icons on it, it takes at least 11 hits to load the page (1 for the page, 10 for the icons). As pages become more graphically rich, it takes even more requests to load them. A 10,000-hit-per-day site might only be serving a few hundred pages per day!

Popular Web Statistics Tools

As long as you realize that log analysis data can be deceiving, it can still provide useful information. Here are a few popular web statistics packages available for Tiger:

- Analog—The world's most popular statistics software, Analog provides all the basics in a very simple layout. Analog doesn't create DTP-quality graphs or have the snazziest interface you've ever seen, but it's fast, does a good job, and it's free. `http://www.analog.cx/`.
- Sawmill—The Sawmill software provides complete statistics including search engine identification and a unique Calendar view for located information by month and date. Sawmill is a commercial package costing $99 and up. `http://www.sawmill.net/`.
- Summary—Summary is a great entry-level piece of software with advanced reporting features. Data can be exported directly to spreadsheet format for external graphing. Single-user licenses for Summary start at $59. `http://summary.net/download.html`
- AWStats—Advanced Web Statistics is a relative newcomer to the web stats arena, but brings with it extensive reporting and built-in graphing. A bit flashier than analog

and free for anyone's use, it is a good choice for budget-conscious web manager who wants to provide as complete and easy-to-read statistics as possible. `http://awstats.sourceforge.net`.

- Urchin—Urchin has, without a doubt, the most user-friendly and attractive interface of any of these offerings. Urchin is a great stats solution for websites with the resources to afford it. Urchin starts at $199 for an individual server license, but can operate in Lite mode for free. `http://www.urchin.com/download/`

Generating Statistics with AWStats

If you run a server, you'll want a stats solution implemented as soon as possible. Understanding what is happening on your server can help locate errors in your website, find potential hackers, and identify where you should focus your development efforts. To get your site up and running with a stats solution that will likely provide most of the features you'll ever need, let's take a look at how to setup AWStats on your system.

Installing AWStats

To begin, download the latest AWStats distribution from `http://awstats.sourceforge.net/#DOWNLOAD`, and unarchive it. Next, use `mv` to move the distribution directory to `/usr/local/awstats`.

Now, enter the directory `/usr/local/awstats/tools` and issue the command **`sudo perl awstats_configure.pl`**. This will walk you through a simple setup script, as follows:

```
----- AWStats awstats_configure 1.0 (build 1.3) (c) Laurent Destailleur -----
This tool will help you to configure AWStats to analyze statistics for
one web server. You can try to use it to let it do all that is possible
in AWStats setup, however following the step by step manual setup
documentation (docs/index.html) is often a better idea. Above all if:
- You are not an administrator user,
- You want to analyze downloaded log files without web server,
- You want to analyze mail or ftp log files instead of web log files,
- You need to analyze load balanced servers log files,
- You want to 'understand' all possible ways to use AWStats...
Read the AWStats documentation (docs/index.html).

-----> Running OS detected: Linux, BSD or Unix

-----> Check for web server install
  Found Web server Apache config file '/etc/httpd/httpd.conf'
```

If you've made the appropriate changes to use the combined log format, answer N to the next question to prevent AWStats from changing your configuration.

```
-----> Check and complete web server config file '/etc/httpd/httpd.conf'
Warning: You Apache config file contains directives to write 'common' log files
```

```
This means that some features can't work (os, browsers and keywords detection).
Do you want me to setup Apache to write 'combined' log files [y/N] ? N


  Add 'Alias /awstatsclasses "/usr/local/awstats/wwwroot/classes/"'
  Add 'Alias /awstatscss "/usr/local/awstats/wwwroot/css/"'
  Add 'Alias /awstatsicons "/usr/local/awstats/wwwroot/icon/"'
  Add 'ScriptAlias /awstats/ "/usr/local/awstats/wwwroot/cgi-bin/"'
  Add '<Directory>' directive
  AWStats directives added to Apache config file.

-----> Update model config file '/usr/local/awstats/wwwroot/cgi-
bin/awstats.model.conf'
  File awstats.model.conf updated.
```

Allow the setup tool to create the initial configuration file for you by answering Y to the following question. Provide a simple name for your site, such as `"MySite"`, used here, and then go with the default `/etc/awstats` directory to store the config files.

```
-----> Need to create a new config file ?
Do you want me to build a new AWStats config/profile
file (required if first install) [y/N] ? y

-----> Define config file name to create
What is the name of your web site or profile analysis ?
Example: www.mysite.com
Example: demo
Your web site, virtual server or profile name:
> MySite

-----> Define config file path
In which directory do you plan to store your config file(s) ?
Default: /etc/awstats
Directory path to store config file(s) (Enter for default):
>

-----> Create config file '/etc/awstats/awstats.MySite.conf'
 Config file /etc/awstats/awstats.MySite.conf created.

-----> Restart Web server with '/sbin/service httpd restart'
No such service httpd

-----> Add update process inside a scheduler
Sorry, configure.pl does not support automatic add to cron yet.
You can do it manually by adding the following command to your cron:
/usr/local/awstats/wwwroot/cgi-bin/awstats.pl -update -config=MySite
```

```
Or if you have several config files and prefer having only one command:
/usr/local/awstats/tools/awstats_updateall.pl now
Press ENTER to continue...


A SIMPLE config file has been created: /etc/awstats/awstats.MySite.conf
You should have a look inside to check and change manually main parameters.
You can then manually update your statistics for 'MySite' with command:
> perl awstats.pl -update -config=MySite
You can also read your statistics for 'MySite' with URL:
> http://localhost/awstats/awstats.pl?config=MySite

Press ENTER to finish...
```


Your installation is now complete, but before AWStats will actually run, you'll need to make a few changes to the configuration file and the `/usr/local/awstats` directory.

First, fix the permissions on `/usr/local/awstats` by typing **`chmod 755 /usr/local/awstats`**. This will allow Apache to execute the CGI application that has been installed.

Next, create a default data directory that is writeable by Apache:

```
brezup:jray jray $ sudo mkdir -p /var/lib/awstats
brezup:jray jray $ sudo chown www /var/lib/awstats
```

Finally, edit the configuration file created by the setup utility. The file should be located at `/etc/awstats/awstats.<your site config name>.conf` such as `awstats.MySite.conf` for the sample we've created here.

Search for the line beginning with `LogFile=`—this is should be set to the path of your Apache log, or, by default `/var/log/httpd/access_log`. Modify the line to read:

```
LogFile="/var/log/httpd/access_log"
```

Now, save the configuration file and restart Apache with `sudo /usr/sbin/apachectl restart`.

Running the Stats Analysis

Before you can view the results of AWStats, you must run the analysis on the current log data. To do this, first enter the AWStats `cgi-bin` directory: **`cd /usr/local/awstats/wwwroot/cgi-bin`**. Then execute AWStats with **`sudo ./awstats.pl -config=<your site config name> -update`**. For example, the site defined in `/etc/awstats/awstats.MySite.conf` is processed with

```
brezup:jray jray $ sudo ./awstats.pl -config=MySite -update
Update for config "/etc/awstats/awstats.MySite.conf"
With data in log file "/var/log/httpd/access_log"...
```

```
Phase 1 : First bypass old records, searching new record...
Searching new records from beginning of log file...
Jumped lines in file: 0
Parsed lines in file: 40
 Found 0 dropped records,
 Found 0 corrupted records,
 Found 0 old records,
 Found 40 new qualified records.
```

Your can now view your site statistics by pointing your web browser at `http://127.0.0.1/awstats/awstats.pl?config=`*`<your site config name>`*. A well-populated AWStats page is shown in Figure 23.6.

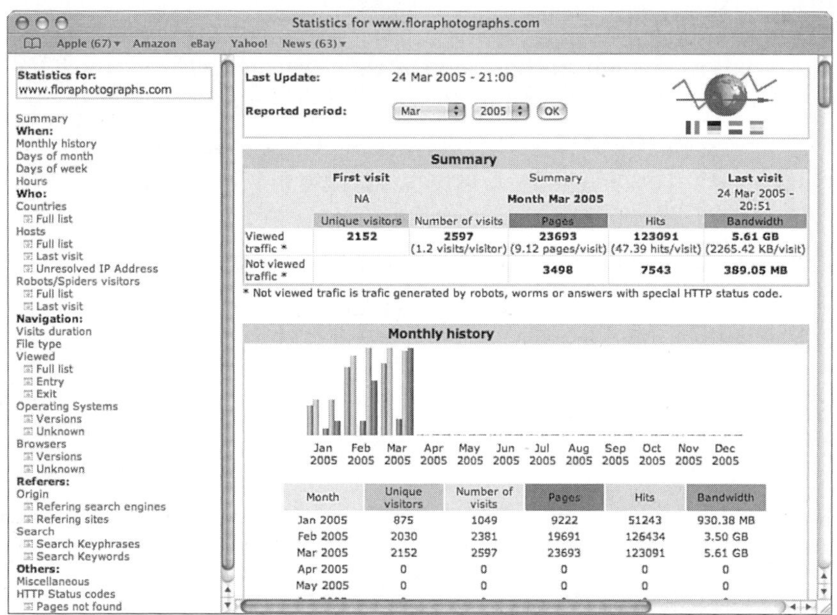

FIGURE 23.6 AWStats is a free tool for comprehensive web statistics.

> **TIP**
>
> You can automate the process of updating the stats by adding a line to `/etc/crontab`, such as
>
> ```
> 0     6     *     *     *     root cd /usr/local/awstats/wwwroot/
> ➥cgi-bin; ./awstats.pl -config=MySite -update
> ```
>
> This will re-run the analysis every morning at 6 a.m.

There are many tweaks and additional features of the AWStats package that you can make/enable within the configuration file. You might want to browse the official documentation at `http://awstats.sourceforge.net/docs/index.html` for more information.

Summary

Apache is an extremely configurable and a very powerful web server platform. The basic Apache software can be configured with network and user-level security and used to set up multiple virtual hosts on a single computer. If the basic software isn't enough, Apache can be expanded to include SSL support, MP3 streaming, and integrated file-sharing capabilities. The Apache module library continues to grow and add new features daily. As you might have guessed, Apache is a very large and capable server application. If you'd like to learn more, I suggest looking at an Apache-dedicated title, such as *Sams Apache Server Unleashed*, ISBN 0672318083. Apple's Personal Web Server is capable of publishing a few pages or your entire corporate website.

CHAPTER **24**

Developing Web Applications

IN THIS CHAPTER

A web server is only as good as its content. Creating a website that changes over time is an important step in keeping users interested. The Tiger BSD base provides access to many different programming and scripting languages, each of which can be used for creating dynamic web applications that run from within Apache.

This chapter serves as a beginner's guide to CGI (Common Gateway Interface) programming and introduces topics ranging from CGI security to Perl and PHP programming. As in many of the Unix chapters in *Mac OS X Tiger Unleashed*, it is important to remember that the information provided is appropriate for learning about the technology available in the operating system. If you're starting from scratch, you might want to look into additional references on web development.

Introduction to Web Programming

Writing an application for the Web is not as simple as writing an application or script that executes on a local machine. Web applications must obey the HTTP protocol, which, by design, is stateless and connectionless. This poses a problem for anything beyond simple programs that submit a form.

To understand the problem, consider the steps in running a normal piece of software from the Tiger desktop (this is a generic fictitious application):

1. Double-click the application to display the Welcome screen.
2. Provide basic input into the application screen by typing or clicking.

3. The application provides feedback based on your input.
4. Repeat steps 2 and 3 as necessary.
5. Choose Quit from the application menu.
6. The application saves your changes and preferences, and then exits.

To translate these operations into a web application, however, requires working around the limitations of the HTTP protocol.

Understanding the Stateless Nature of HTTP

When HTTP (Hypertext Transfer Protocol) was developed, the Web was never expected to become the consumer-driven mish-mash that it is today. HTTP was created to be simple and fast. When retrieving a web page, the client performs four actions. It first opens a connection to the remote server. The client then requests a resource from the server and sends form data, if necessary. Next, the client receives the results, and finally, it closes the connection.

This happens repeatedly for different page elements (or, depending on the browser and server, multiple requests can be made in one connection). When the browser has finished downloading data, that data is displayed on the user's screen. At this point in time, there is no connection between the client computer and the server. They have effectively forgotten each other's existence.

If the user clicks a link to visit another page on the server, the same process is repeated. The server has no advance knowledge of who the client is, even though they've just been talking. If you've seen the movie *Memento*, you'll understand this concept. The HTTP protocol suffers from a severe lack of short-term memory (statelessness).

Applying this new knowledge to the steps of using an application, the problems become obvious:

1. Double-click the application. This is the equivalent of clicking a link on a web page or entering a URL into a browser. Launching a web application is nothing more than browsing its URL. No problems so far.
2. It starts, displaying a welcome screen. An HTML welcome page is easily built with a link into the main application. Still no problems.
3. You provide basic input into the application screen by typing or clicking. The trouble begins. Data entered on an HTML form is sent all at once. Providing live feedback to data isn't possible, except for rudimentary JavaScript functionality. Clicking links transports the browser to other pages, effectively losing any information you've already entered.
4. The application provides feedback based on your input. The web application has access only to information provided as input in the form immediately preceding it. For example, assume that there are two forms in which a user inputs data, one right after the other. The first form submits to the second form. The second form, in turn,

submits its data to a page that calculates results based on the entries in both form pages. Only the data in the second form will be taken into account. The first form's information no longer exists after submitting the second.

5. Repeat steps 3 and 4 as necessary. During each repetition, the server is entirely unaware of what has come before. The application cannot build on previous input.
6. Choose Quit from the application menu. This is a tough one. Remember that the connection to the web server lasts only long enough to retrieve a single page and send form data. This means that the web application effectively quits after any step of execution. Web software must be developed with the knowledge that the user can quit his browser at any given point in time. Doing so must not pose either a functional or security risk to the original software.
7. The application saves your changes and preferences, and then exits. If a user quits in the middle of running an online application, there is no way for the software to know that this has occurred. It is up to the programmer to make sure that the website keeps track of a user's actions each time it is accessed.

So, how do you work around a protocol that was never designed to keep information between accesses? By employing session management techniques.

Maintaining State Through Session Management

A *session*, in web-speak, is the equivalent to the process of running an application from start to finish. The goal of session management is to help the web server remember information about a user and what that user has done in previous requests for the server. Using session management techniques, you can quickly create web applications that function like conventional desktop applications. Unfortunately, there is no perfect session management technique. There are several ways to approach the problem, but none offers a completely satisfying solution.

URL Variable Passing

URL variable passing is the simplest form of session management. To make a value available on any number of web pages, you can use the URL to pass information from page to page. For example, suppose that I had a variable, `name`, with the value of `johnray` that I wanted to be available even after clicking a link to another portion of the program. I could create links that looked like this:

```
http://www.acmewebsitecomp.com/webapp.cgi?name=johnray
http://www.acmewebsitecomp.com/reportapp.cgi?name=johnray
http://www.acmewebsitecomp.com/accountapp.cgi?name=johnray
```

Each of the three web applications would receive the variable name with the value `johnray` upon clicking the links. These applications could then pass the values along even further by appending the same information (`?name=johnray`) to links within themselves. Obviously, this would require the web applications to generate links dynamically, but it's a small price to pay for being able to reliably pass information from page to page.

This technique relies on the HTTP GET method. When a browser sends a GET request for a web resource, it can append additional data onto the request by adding it in the format:

```
?<variable>=<value>[&<variable>=<value>...]
```

The trouble with this approach is that to send large amounts of data between pages, you must construct extremely large URLs. Visually, this creates an ugly URL reference in the browser's URL field and could lead users to bookmark a URL that contains information about the current execution of the web application that might not be valid in subsequent executions—such as the date or other time-sensitive information.

In addition, users can easily modify the URL line of the browser to send back any information to the server that they want. If you've just created a shopping cart application that passes a user's total to a final billing page where it is charged against that user's credit card, it is unlikely that you want him to be able to adjust the price of the merchandise he's purchasing.

Form Variable Passing

Similar to passing variables within a URL (the GET method) is using the POST method of transferring data. Instead of passing data directly in the request for a page, data is sent *after* the initial page request and cannot be directly modified by the user.

With POST, developers can use hidden form fields to hold values before they are needed. Assume that you have two forms: the first collects a first and last name, and the second collects an email address and phone number. Submitting the first form opens the second form, which, when submitted, saves the data to a file.

Each form could save its data to a file independently, but this is problematic when considering applications in which all data must be present before it can be saved. Session management can be used to ensure that all data is present when the final form is submitted.

For example, assume that the first form looks something like this:

```
<form action="form2.cgi" method="post">
First Name: <input type="text" name="first"><br>
Last Name: <input type="text" name="last"><br>
<input type="submit">
</form>
```

This form submits two fields (first and last) to the form2.cgi. If the second form must collect an email address and phone number and submit them simultaneously with the first and last values, the form2.cgi could dynamically create a form that stored the original two fields in two hidden input fields:

```
<form action="savedata.cgi" method="post">
Email Address: <input type="text" name="email"><br>
Phone Number: <input type="text" name="phone"><br>
<input type="hidden" name="first" value="first-value">
<input type="hidden" name="last" value="last-value">
```

```
<input type="submit">
</form>
```

Submitting this form would make all the field data available to the subsequent page (`savedata.cgi`).

> **NOTE**
>
> These examples show how you might use different techniques to pass data between web pages. For them to be effective, you must be able to dynamically generate the URLs and forms that contain your data. We're getting to that—don't panic!

Unfortunately, the trouble with this approach is that only pages with forms can transfer data between one another. Form variable passing is usually used in conjunction with URL passing to cover all bases.

Data integrity is also an issue with this method because a savvy user could easily save an HTML form locally, edit the hidden field values, and then submit the data from the edited form.

> **NOTE**
>
> The URL and form variable passing methods are much more closely related than they appear. The technique of specifying variables and values within a URL is actually also a way of submitting a form called the `GET` method. When using the `GET` method, the values sent from a form are appended to the URL requested from the server. By doing this manually, we are simulating a form submission using `GET`.
>
> The `POST` method, shown in these examples, sends the variable/value data to the server after requesting a resource. It does not append information to the URL and can only be used to send data via an actual form submission. In some cases, these two methods are used together, but this is not a common coding practice.
>
> In general, `POST` is a cleaner code choice because it doesn't clutter your URL line. `GET`, however, creates URLs that can be bookmarked.

Cookies

Another way to pass information is to use a cookie. *Cookies* are variable/value pairs that are stored on a user's computer and can be retrieved by the remote web server. Many people are cautious about cookies because of the fear of information being stolen from the cookie without their knowledge. Cookies, however, can be a valuable tool for web developers and users alike.

From the developer's perspective, assigning a cookie is much like setting a variable. You can name the cookie and give it a value and an expiration day/time. That value then becomes globally available regardless of whether the user jumps to another page, retypes the URL, or starts over. Only if the cookie is reassigned or reaches its expiration does the value cease to exist. There is even a special type of cookie expiration that can limit a cookie's lifetime to the current browser session. In this case, the values are never stored on the client computer and are forgotten when the user exits the program. Using this special type of expiration, a programmer can create a web application that, after the user exits, leaves no remnants of the login information. This is as close to traditional programming-language variables as a web developer can hope to get.

From the user's perspective, cookies offer both security and ease-of-use advantages. If a web application stores a user's identifier in a cookie, that user can immediately be recognized when visiting a website. This is commonly used on sites such as Amazon.com to provide a personalized appearance. Because cookies can span multiple pages and applications, a single login can apply to many different portions of a website. Using URL or form variable passing, each link and form on a site must be constructed on the fly. No changes need to be made to the links when cookies are used. In the case of the former, the chance of programming error is much greater.

Cookies are saved to the local computer's drive and can be viewed in many popular browsers. Safari, for example, enables the user to examine stored cookies within the Security Preferences pane, shown in Figure 24.1.

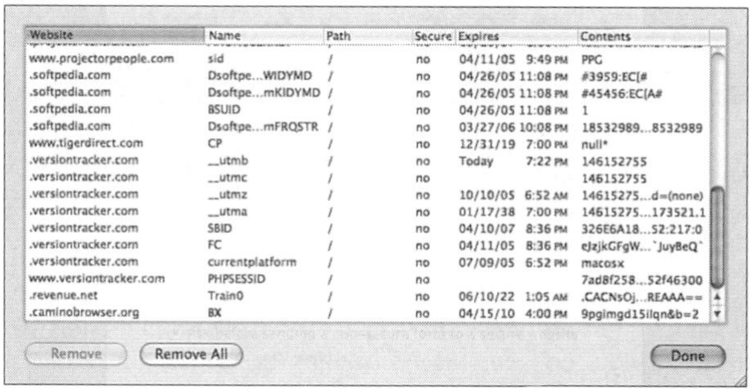

Website	Name	Path	Secure	Expires	Contents
www.projectorpeople.com	sid	/	no	04/11/05 9:49 PM	PPG
.softpedia.com	Dsoftpe...WIDYMD	/	no	04/26/05 11:08 PM	#3959:EC[#
.softpedia.com	Dsoftpe...mKIDYMD	/	no	04/26/05 11:08 PM	#45456:EC[A#
.softpedia.com	BSUID	/	no	04/26/05 11:08 PM	1
.softpedia.com	Dsoftpe...mFRQSTR	/	no	03/27/06 10:08 PM	18532989...8532989
www.tigerdirect.com	CP	/	no	12/31/19 7:00 PM	null*
.versiontracker.com	__utmb	/	no	Today 7:22 PM	146152755
.versiontracker.com	__utmc	/	no		146152755
.versiontracker.com	__utmz	/	no	10/10/05 6:52 AM	14615275...d=(none)
.versiontracker.com	__utma	/	no	01/17/38 7:00 PM	14615275...173521.1
.versiontracker.com	SBID	/	no	04/10/07 8:36 PM	326E6A18...52:217:0
.versiontracker.com	FC	/	no	04/11/05 8:36 PM	eJzjkGFgW...`JuyBeQ`
.versiontracker.com	currentplatform	/	no	07/09/05 6:52 PM	macosx
www.versiontracker.com	PHPSESSID	/	no		7ad8f258...52f46300
.revenue.net	Train0	/	no	06/10/22 1:05 AM	.CACNsOj...REAAA==
.caminobrowser.org	BX	/	no	04/15/10 4:00 PM	9pgimgd15ilqn&b=2

Remove | Remove All | Done

FIGURE 24.1 Popular browsers, such as Safari, enable the user to browse stored cookies.

COOKIES—ARE THEY EVIL?

Contrary to popular belief, cookies are not retrieved by a remote server; they are made available by the client browser. When a cookie is first set, it is given a path (URL) for which it is valid. If your browser comes across a request for a resource (HTML page, image, and so forth) that includes the path, the cookie is automatically sent to that server along with the request. Your browser will send cookies only to the paths where they belong, not to all websites you view.

The contents of a cookie are, indeed, determined by the remote server and can be set to any arbitrary string. They do not provide the capacity to upload binary files or executable applications. It's certainly possible that a cookie could hold a credit card number, but you would have had to enter that number into a web page before it could be stored in a cookie. I have never seen an e-commerce or banking site that worked in this manner, but it is possible that one might exist. If this were the case, other users on your system might be able to find the cookie and extract the sensitive information.

The most alarming use of cookies is the practice of allowing third parties to track browsing information and habits. Some popular websites allow cookies to be set by a common third-party host. Because the third-party host has access to the cookie as long as the main website allows it, information can be shared across a broad range of websites without your knowledge.

If you're concerned about using cookies on your system, the best advice is to inform your users about how cookies are being employed and make sure that they are comfortable with the information being stored. The dangers of cookies have been greatly exaggerated. Use of common sense and caution while programming with cookies will lead to applications that users will trust and enjoy.

Although it is possible to use other techniques for passing information, cookies are the fastest and easiest. Regardless of the technique used to maintain information two final elements are missing from the big picture—the session database and session ID. Together they form the Holy Grail of session management, session variables.

Session Variables

A *session variable* is a variable that can be set to any value, will be accessible by any portion of a web application, and will last only while the web application is being used. In principle, any of the techniques we've looked at so far can do this. Unfortunately, they all fall short when applied to a large system.

For example, imagine that you're passing variables using the URL method:

```
http://www.mywebsite.com/mywebapp.cgi?variable1=value&variable2=value
```

This works great for one or two variables, but extend it to a few thousand! Suddenly a two- or three-line URL seems short. There is a limit to the amount of data that can be contained within a URL, making this impossible for large amounts of information.

When using cookies or forms to pass data, you aren't necessarily limited by the size of the request string but by the overhead and complexity of the coding. For each variable that must be stored, a hidden field must be added to a form or a cookie sent back to the server. This process must be repeated on every page. This adds up, in terms of transmission time and processing.

Luckily, there is a solution that can be used with any of the approaches to variable passing—the use of a session database and a session ID.

The concept is simple—when a user comes to a website, his session starts. He is assigned a unique ID, called the *session ID*, by the remote web application. As the user interacts with the website, the web application passes the session ID from page to page. This process can be done using the URL, forms, or cookies. When the web application software wants to store a value, it stores it on the server, in a local database that is keyed to that particular session ID.

For programmers, this is a dream come true. They can store any information they want (including sensitive data), and it is never transmitted over the network. The only piece of data that is visible on the network wire is the session ID.

Because a single piece of information can keep track of an unlimited number of variables, the session management system can be written to pass the session ID using URL/form methods or a cookie. Either way is entirely feasible. To make things even easier, developers have included these capabilities in programming languages such as JSP and PHP. For example, in PHP, you can activate session management and store a variable for use on another web page using syntax like this:

```
<?php
        session_start();
        $_SESSION["x"] = $_SESSION["x"] + 1;
        print $_SESSION["x"];
?>
```

This example uses `session_start()` to create a new session ID, which is automatically stored in a cookie. Next, the variable `x` is incremented and stored again in the global `$_SESSION` array. Finally, the value of `x` is displayed. The result is a web page that displays an increasing count each time a user loads it.

NOTE

It is important to make the distinction that this is not the same as a web counter. A session ID is specific to a single user, as are all the variables registered with that session. If 50 users were accessing this script simultaneously, each would see a result independent of all the others.

More traditional languages (such as Perl or C) weren't created with web programming in mind. To implement session variables within Perl, you must create, manipulate, and manage session IDs and session databases. This has already been done so many times that a number of prebuilt solutions are available to work with, but none is as elegant as a language designed for the purposes of creating web applications.

Programming CGI Applications in Perl

Perl, which you were introduced to in Chapter 18, "Developing Applications and Widgets Using Scripting Languages," provides a quick and easy way to start developing your own web applications. Although not as elegant as PHP, Perl is an excellent starting point for learning about how web applications work. It is also a nearly universal cross-platform language with thousands of freely downloadable applications.

WHAT IS A CGI?

CGI stands for *Common Gateway Interface.* A CGI application is written to conform to a web server/application communication standard (the CGI). CGI applications pass and read their information to and from an underlying web server. The generic definition of CGI is just a standalone web application.

This chapter looks at two types of CGI applications: those programmed within a traditional language, such as Perl, and others based on embedded programming languages, such as PHP. The latter is not truly considered a CGI language because it uses a different mechanism for exchanging information with the web server, but the end result of each is a web application.

This section assumes that you either know a reasonable amount of Perl basics, or have diligently read the introduction to Perl scripts in Chapter 18.

Enabling CGI Support in Apache

For many web applications, you can create your CGIs in the Tiger folder `/Library/WebServer/CGI-Executables`. This location is already configured for CGI execution and can be accessed through the URL `http://localhost/cgi-bin/`*`<your cgi name>`*.

`CGI-Executables`, however, is a special directory that can only contain CGI files. The examples in this chapter use a CGI to display images in the same directory as the CGI and will fail when run from this location. In addition, `CGI-Executables` is a serverwide repository for CGI scripts. Because this is a learning exercise, it is more appropriate to use your own personal site folder `~/Sites` for development.

Because CGIs allow your web server to consume additional process resources and, when poorly written, can possibly lead to security holes, you must explicitly enable CGI support for your personal `Sites` before any web application can be run by Apache. To do this, first edit the `/etc/httpd/httpd.conf` file and search for the lines:


```
# To use CGI scripts:
#
#AddHandler cgi-script .cgi
```

Uncomment the `AddHandler` directive by removing the `#`. This tells Apache that files ending in `.cgi` should be treated as CGI applications.

```
AddHandler cgi-script .cgi
```

Next, you must also enable `ExecCGI` Option for the directory you are programming in. In the case of your personal `Sites` folder, just open the file `/etc/httpd/users/`*`<your username>`*`.conf` and edit to read as follows, replacing your username as appropriate:

```
<Directory "/Users/<your username>/Sites/">
    Options Indexes MultiViews ExecCGI
    AllowOverride None
    Order allow,deny
    Allow from all
</Directory>
```

Finally, save the file restart Apache with `sudo /usr/sbin/apachectl restart` or the System Preference pane. You're ready to go.

Outputting HTTP Headers

Let's start with the most basic CGI example possible: Hello World. Your initial reaction is probably to create a Perl script (`helloworld.cgi`) in your `Sites` directory along the lines of

```
#!/usr/bin/perl
print "Hello World! I have a Mac, shouldn't you?";
exit;
```

After enabling execution (`chmod +x helloworld.cgi`), try running the application from the command line (`./helloworld.cgi`) and then by accessing its URL through a web browser (`http://localhost/~<your username>/helloworld.cgi`). Although the command-line version runs fine, the browser reports an execution error message, as shown in Figure 24.2.

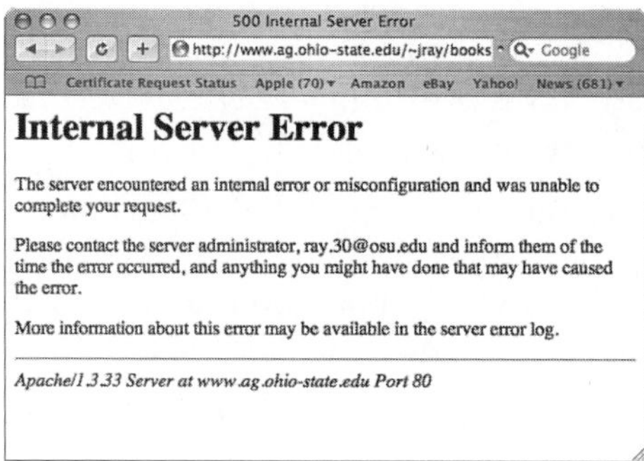

FIGURE 24.2 A simple Hello World isn't quite so simple.

So, what went wrong? Why is this program, which runs perfectly from a command prompt, broken when it tries to send its results over the Web? The answer lies in the way the web servers communicate their results back to a client browser.

For the simple Hello World application to work, it must produce the sort of output that a web browser expects. To the browser, it should send the same response as when a standard `.html` static web page is loaded. The easiest way to see that response is to generate one manually by using telnet to connect to a web server and request a page. For example, to retrieve the primary page from the local Tiger box, you would telnet to `localhost` (or `127.0.0.1`) on port 80, and then use `GET / HTTP/1.0` (followed by two carriage returns to complete the request) to retrieve the root level of the website:

```
% telnet localhost 80
Trying 127.0.0.1...
Connected to localhost.
Escape character is '^]'.
GET / HTTP/1.0

HTTP/1.0 200 OK
Date: Sun, 10 Apr 2005 03:39:06 GMT
Server: Apache/1.3.33 (Darwin)
Content-Location: index.html.en
Vary: negotiate,accept-language,accept-charset
TCN: choice
Last-Modified: Wed, 18 Jul 2001 23:44:21 GMT
ETag: "81b5e-5b0-3b561f55;3d3ba024"
Accept-Ranges: bytes
Content-Length: 1456
```

```
Connection: close
Content-Type: text/html
Content-Language: en
Expires: Sun, 28 Jul 2002 03:39:06 GMT
```

NOTE

This example does not include the text of the web page, just the headers that are sent from the server. If you attempt this on your own machine, you'll get similar results, along with the contents of the `index.html` file within your `/Library/WebServer/Documents` folder.

There are quite a few interesting lines in the group of headers that are returned, such as the language content and an expiration date (used to keep a page from being cached beyond a certain day and time). Only one of these headers, however, is required.

The `Content-Type` header tells the remote web browser what MIME type of file it is about to receive. When a user requests a JPEG image file, the server sends a header that reads

```
Content-Type: image/jpeg
```

Each type of file has a different MIME type (determined by the file `/private/etc/httpd/mime.types`). The server can decide what type of file it is about to serve based on the filename. Unfortunately, when working with CGIs, the web server cannot be certain what type of information is going to be sent back. In fact, a single CGI could easily send an image with one request and an HTML page with another.

To create a fully working CGI, the first thing that the web application must send is an appropriate MIME type. The initial version of `helloworld.cgi` did nothing but print out the Hello World message. The browser, however, was expecting a `Content-Type` header; when the header didn't appear, an error was generated. To correct the problem, the `Content-Type` header must be printed before any other output occurs:

```
#!/usr/bin/perl
print "Content-Type: text/html\n\n";
print "Hello World! I have a Mac, shouldn't you?";
exit;
```

After making the small change to the script, this smallest of web applications will happily run, as demonstrated in Figure 24.3.

NOTE

You can add any valid headers to the output that you want. The `Content-Type` header is the only one required. Each header needs to be printed with a single newline character at the end of each line. The final header must have two newline characters at the end.

These headers must come before any other output but not necessarily at the start of the program. As long as no parts of the page body are produced before a `Content-Type` header is sent, the headers can occur anywhere within the script.

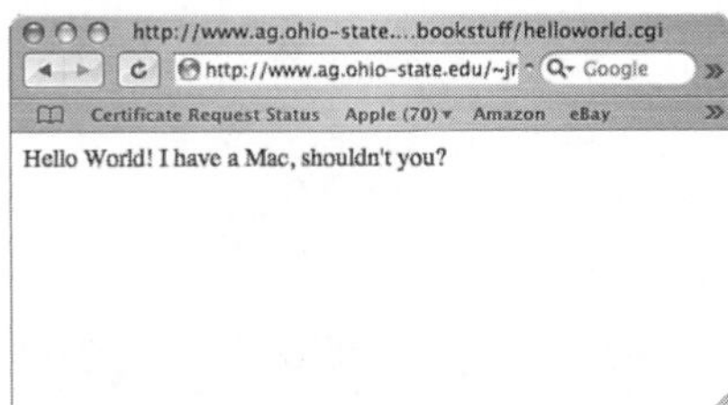

FIGURE 24.3 When the appropriate header is added to the CGI script, everything works as planned.

Generating HTML Output

Creating the output of a CGI is the second step of developing a web application. Unlike normal Perl scripts that produce plain text output, web applications produce HTML. This can take a while to get used to, but keep in mind that the goal is to produce a dynamic web page, not a plain text file.

When creating output from a CGI script, you can use any tags that you normally would in an HTML document. The trouble with doing this in Perl is that you have to escape all quotes when printing the HTML.

For example:

```
<table border="0" cellpadding="0" cellspacing="0">
```

When printed in Perl, this becomes

```
print "<table border=\"0\" cellpadding=\"0\" cellspacing=\"0\">";
```

When creating complicated output, this can get a bit tedious. It can also lead to programmers taking shortcuts and leaving out quotes around HTML tag attributes. The easiest way to display large amounts of complex HTML is to use Perl's alternative print method:

```
print <<ENDOFHTML;
  <table border="0" cellpadding="0" bgcolor="#FFDDDD" cellspacing="0">
  <tr><td align="right">This is more HTML</td></tr>
  </table>
ENDOFHTML
```

So, let's take a look at an example of CGI output in action. This is CGI output, so don't think that you won't be able to get information into your web application. We're going to get there; just be patient!

Let's start with something simple, such as creating a script that displays all the images and the associated filenames in a given folder.

To start the CGI, build a simple Perl script that lists all the JPEG (`.jpg`) files in a folder. Listing 24.1 shows such a script.

LISTING 24.1 When Building a CGI, It's Often Easiest to Start with Something That Runs from the Command Line

```
1: #!/usr/bin/perl
2:
3: $imagedir="imagefolder";
4: @imagelist=glob("$imagedir/*jpg");
5:
6: for ($x=0;$x<@imagelist;$x++) {
7:     $imagename=$imagelist[$x];
8:     print "Image $x = $imagename\n";
9: }
```

Line 3 sets the variable `$imagedir` to the directory that contains the images. In this case, I'm using `imagefolder` inside my `Sites` directory, which is also where this script is located. I have not specified the entire path because I'm only interested in the location of the images relative to the script.

> **NOTE**
>
> CGIs have access to only the files within "web space." You must use an image folder located in the same directory as your CGI, or you must dynamically build the URL for the images so that it matches a valid web URL.

Line 4 loads all the filenames within `$imagedir` that end in `.jpg` into the array `@imagelist`. The Perl `glob()` function takes a path and filename pattern as input and then returns any results that match.

Lines 6–9 loop through each element in the `@imagelist` array, temporarily storing them in the `$imagename` variable. Print a line that displays the image and its name.

When run, the CGI-in-the-making, which I've named `showimages.cgi`, produces the list we were hoping for:

```
% ./showimages.cgi
Image 0 = imagefolder/897.jpg
Image 1 = imagefolder/920.jpg
Image 2 = imagefolder/921.jpg
Image 3 = imagefolder/922.jpg
Image 4 = imagefolder/923.jpg
Image 5 = imagefolder/924.jpg
Image 6 = imagefolder/925.jpg
Image 7 = imagefolder/927.jpg
Image 8 = imagefolder/928.jpg
Image 9 = imagefolder/929.jpg
Image 10 = imagefolder/94.jpg
Image 11 = imagefolder/940.jpg
```

```
Image 12 = imagefolder/942.jpg
Image 13 = imagefolder/944.jpg
Image 14 = imagefolder/945.jpg
Image 15 = imagefolder/947.jpg
Image 16 = imagefolder/948.jpg
Image 17 = imagefolder/949.jpg
Image 18 = imagefolder/96.jpg
```

So, how can this be translated into a CGI that displays the actual images in a web browser? The first step, as mentioned earlier, is to produce a `Content-Type` header. Without this information, the browser has no idea what type of data it is receiving. At the same time, it's a good idea to translate any `\n` (newline) characters in the program into their XHTML equivalent: `<br/>`. Listing 24.2 shows the new CGI, which is capable of running in a browser.

LISTING 24.2 Adding a Content-Type and Fixing Line Breaks Is All You Need to Turn a Simple Command-Line Script into a CGI

```
#!/usr/bin/perl
print "Content-Type: text/html\n\n";
$imagedir="imagefolder";
@imagelist=glob("$imagedir/*jpg");

for ($x=0;$x<@imagelist;$x++) {
    $imagename=$imagelist[$x];
    print "Image $x = $imagename<br/>";
}
```

NOTE

The `\n` (newline) characters that come after the `Content-Type` header should not be translated to HTML breaks. The browser interprets data after the header lines and always expects the final (and in this case, only) header to be followed by two newlines.

Figure 24.4 shows the result of running the new CGI in a web browser.

Unfortunately, things still aren't quite where we want them. What good is a CGI that lists pictures but doesn't display them? To be able to show the pictures, the CGI must be modified so that the name is used within an `<img>` (image) tag rather than just displayed on the screen. Try adding a new line that uses an image, rather than the image name, as shown in Listing 24.3.

Image 0 = imagefolder/897.jpg
Image 1 = imagefolder/920.jpg
Image 2 = imagefolder/921.jpg
Image 3 = imagefolder/922.jpg
Image 4 = imagefolder/923.jpg
Image 5 = imagefolder/924.jpg
Image 6 = imagefolder/925.jpg
Image 7 = imagefolder/927.jpg
Image 8 = imagefolder/928.jpg
Image 9 = imagefolder/929.jpg
Image 10 = imagefolder/94.jpg
Image 11 = imagefolder/940.jpg
Image 12 = imagefolder/942.jpg
Image 13 = imagefolder/944.jpg
Image 14 = imagefolder/945.jpg
Image 15 = imagefolder/947.jpg
Image 16 = imagefolder/948.jpg
Image 17 = imagefolder/949.jpg
Image 18 = imagefolder/96.jpg

FIGURE 24.4 The command-line application now runs within a web browser.

LISTING 24.3 The Revised Code Displays an Image as Well as Its Name

```
1: #!/usr/bin/perl
2: print "Content-Type: text/html\n\n";
3: $imagedir="imagefolder";
4: @imagelist=glob("$imagedir/*jpg");
5:
6: for ($x=0;$x<@imagelist;$x++) {
7:     $imagename=$imagelist[$x];
8:     print "<img src=\"$imagename\" width=\"120\" height=\"90\"><br/>";
9:     print "Image $x = $imagename<br/>";
10: }
```

Line 8 performs the magic in the application. Using the same `$imagename` variable used to print an image's name (now in line 9), the variable is instead used to set an image source within an `<img>` tag. I've also added a width and height to the image tag to maintain some consistency in the display.

When viewed in a web browser, the result resembles Figure 24.5.

NOTE

When setting an image size within the image tag, be aware that it doesn't change the physical size of the images being sent to the browser. The amount of data transmitted is identical to what would be sent if the width and height tags were not included. To resize the image in real-time requires the use of additional software, such as the GD Perl module, downloadable from CPAN.org.

By now, you're starting to see the method to the madness. CGIs are just applications that write HTML as their output. The example we've been looking at is barely modified from the original command-line version, yet it includes full images for each file it finds. To fully realize the potential of a CGI, you must use HTML to its fullest. So far, the Perl script we've been developing is nothing but a simple port of the initial command-line utility.

With only a small amount of work, we can turn it into something far more useful. Listing 24.4 shows a more developed version of the application. Unlike the previous version of the CGI, this revision uses an HTML table to structure the layout of the images.

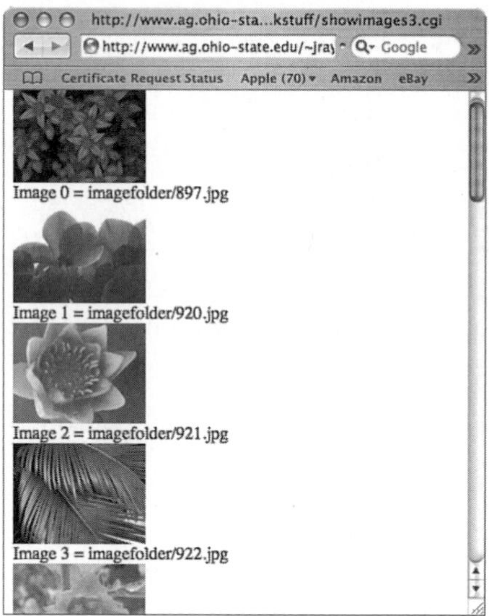

FIGURE 24.5 With the addition of the <img> tag, the images themselves can now be seen in the listing.

LISTING 24.4 With a Little Work, the CGI Can Take Advantage of HTML's Layout Capabilities

```
#!/usr/bin/perl
print "Content-Type: text/html\n\n";

$imagedir="imagefolder";
$columns=3;

@imagelist=glob("$imagedir/*jpg");

print "<table bgcolor=\"#FFFFFF\" border=\"1\" bordercolor=\"#000000\">";
while ($x<@imagelist) {
   print "<tr>";
   for ($y=0;$y<$columns;$y++) {
    $imagename=$imagelist[$x];
    if ($x<@imagelist) {
     $x++;
     print "<td align=\"center\">";
     print "<img src=\"$imagename\" width=\"120\" height=\"90\"><br/>";
     $imagename=~s/$imagedir\///;
     print "<font type=\"Arial\">$imagename</font>";
```

```
20:      print "</td>";
21:     }
22:    }
23:    print "</tr>";
24: }
25: print "</table>";
```

Line 5 sets a limit for the number of columns in the table (how many images will be displayed in a single line), whereas line 9 sets up the table structure using a table with a white (#FFFFFF) background and a black (#000000) border. In line 10, instead of using a for loop to go through each image, the counter $x is incremented when an image tag is output. The while loop continues as long as the counter is less than the total number of images.

Line 11 starts a new table row (<tr>). Lines 12–22 loop through the number of columns set for the table. For each column, increment the variable $x. If $x has not exceeded the total number of images available, output a table data cell (<td>) that contains the image and its name. Line 18 removes the path from the image filename. This is done using a simple Perl regular expression search and replace. After displaying all the data cells for a row, line 23 ends the table row (</tr>). Line 24 repeats lines 11–23 until all images have been displayed, and line 25 ends the table (</table>).

Figure 24.6 shows the output from the finalized CGI.

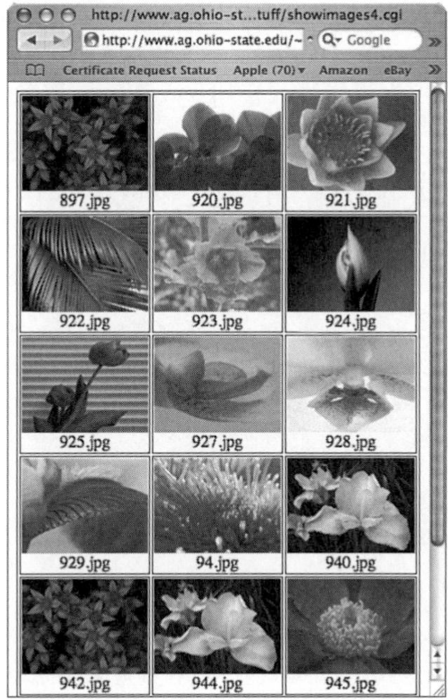

FIGURE 24.6 The final version of the CGI outputs the image directory in a nicely formatted table.

> **NOTE**
>
> The most common type of CGI/web application output is `text/html`. This doesn't mean that a web application can't output other types of data. If your script opens, reads, and outputs a JPEG file, it would use `Content-type: image/jpeg`. Any type of media that can be sent by a web server can also be sent from a CGI.

Using `CGI.pm` to Simplify CGI Development

This quick-and-dirty image viewer provides a reasonable start to CGI programming, but it is lacking in the one area that can be used to create truly dynamic and user-driven sites: user input. Getting input into a CGI can be a bit of a challenge if you're starting from scratch.

Thankfully, others have been here before, and Perl includes a module (`CGI.pm`) that handles most of the dirty work for you. Because we're going to be using only a few of the functions to handle incoming data, you might want to read `http://stein.cshl.org/WWW/software/CGI/` for full documentation. We will be using the software in *function* mode rather than *object-oriented* mode to avoid delving into the complexities of Perl's object-oriented model.

We'll introduce three functions:

- `use CGI qw(:standard)`—Makes the `CGI.pm` functions available to your Perl code.
- header(<*MIME-type*>)—Sends an appropriate `Content-type` header to the client browser. If no header is specified (that is, `header()`), the type `text/html` is assumed.
- param(<*variable name*>)—Returns the value of a submitted form variable.

Let's take a look at practical CGI input by altering the Hello World application we used previously so that it personalizes the message. If your name happens to be World, you might skip this exercise. Listing 24.5 shows the `helloworld.cgi` modified to display a person's name. I'll refer to this new version as `helloworld2.cgi`.

LISTING 24.5 Using the `CGI.pm` Module, Any Script Can Receive Input

```
1: #!/usr/bin/perl
2: use CGI qw(:standard);
3:
4: $myname=param('name');
5:
6: header;
7: print "Hello $myname! I have a Mac, shouldn't you?";
```

Although mostly apparent, the breakdown of the code is as follows:

Line 2 loads `CGI.pm`: the Perl CGI module. Line 4 sets the variable `$myname` to the submitted variable name. Line 6 sends the required content-type header, and line 7 prints a greeting containing the name submitted to the CGI in the `name` variable.

As you can see, the number of changes to the original application is small. This CGI should now correctly allow a name to be sent to it for use in a customized greeting. The problem remains, however, how do you go about actually sending the variable and value to the application?

Because the `parse()` function handles either `POST` or `GET` method transmission, there are two ways that this new CGI can be called. Using the URL to pass a variable is the easiest, so let's start there. Start a web browser and enter the URL for the new CGI, adding **`?name=John`** (or whatever is appropriate for you) to the end:

```
http://localhost/~<your username>/helloworld2.cgi?name=<your name>
```

My test system, for example, looks like this:

```
http://localhost/~john/helloworld2.cgi?name=John
```


Figure 24.7 shows the new personalized message.

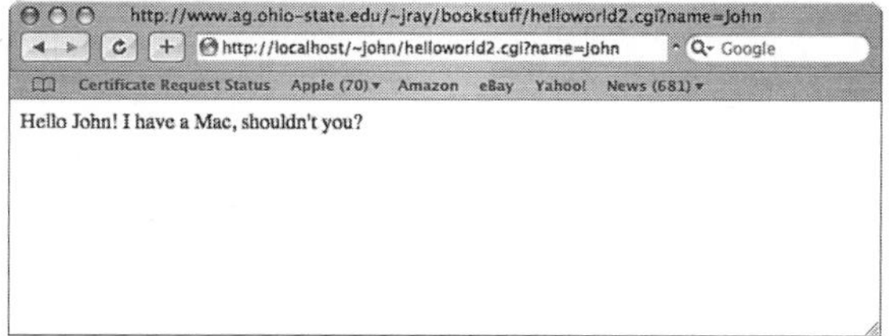

FIGURE 24.7 Providing an input method to a CGI enables interactivity.

To use the `POST` method to send information to the CGI, create an HTML form that submits its data to the web application. For `helloworld2.cgi`, the form needs nothing more than a name field and a submit button:

```
<form action="helloworld2.cgi" method="post">
Enter your name: <input type="text" name="name">
<input type="submit" name="submit">
</form>
```

Save the form code in a new HTML file (`hello.html`) in the same directory as the `helloworld2.cgi`. Open the new web page in your browser, type a name, and click Submit. You should see results identical to the earlier URL-based input shown in Figure 24.7.

NOTE

If you don't include the `method="post"` attribute for the form or use `method="get"`, submitting the form actually passes the name data through the URL.

As it stands, if you're using a separate HTML page to submit information to the CGI, two files comprise the entire project: `helloworld2.cgi` and `hello.html`. This isn't excessive, but it can be consolidated. Rather than `hello.html` containing the form, it can be added directly to `helloworld2.cgi`. Listing 24.6 consolidates the form and application into a single CGI file.

LISTING 24.6 A CGI Can Encapsulate HTML and Application Logic

```
1: #!/usr/bin/perl
2: use CGI qw(:standard);
3:
4: $myname=param('name');
5: header;
6:
7: if ($myname eq "") {
8:   print <<ENDOFHTML;
9:     <form action="helloworld2.cgi" method="post">
10:     Enter your name: <input type="text" name="name">
11:     <input type="submit" name="submit">
12:     </form>
13: ENDOFHTML
14:   exit;
15: }
16:
17: print "Hello $myname! I have a Mac, shouldn't you?";
```

Consolidating the code into the single CGI brings into play some of the session management techniques discussed earlier in the chapter. This revision of `helloworld2.cgi` has two states: prior to entering the name and after entering the name. To determine what the program should be doing, it checks the value of `$myname`—if a name hasn't been set, the HTML form should be displayed. If a name is defined, the Hello message is shown. A more detailed analysis of the changes follows:

Line 7 checks to see whether the `$myname` variable is empty. If it is, this is the first time the CGI has been executed—the user hasn't entered his name yet.

Lines 8–13 display the HTML form, and line 14 exits the CGI. This line is more important than it might appear. If it is not included, the CGI will continue to execute after displaying the HTML form; this will generate an empty hello message immediately following the form. Finally, line 17 displays the hello message with the user's name.

This demonstrates the fundamental workings of CGI applications. Although the example is only a two-step process, it could easily be extended to multiple steps by passing data from screen to screen. For an encore, let's add another form to the hello page that collects the user's age. After submitting this second form, a third page is shown with the user's name, age, and a few comments. Listing 24.7 shows the final version of this overly long Hello World application.

LISTING 24.7 The Extended Version of Hello World Now Includes Three Steps and Demonstrates CGI Input and Variable Passing

```
1: #!/usr/bin/perl
2: use CGI qw(:standard);
3:
4: $myname=param('name');
6: $myage=param('age');
7:
8: header;
9:
10: if ($myname eq "") {
11:   print <<ENDOFHTML;
12:     <form action="helloworld2.cgi" method="post">
13:     Enter your name: <input type="text" name="name">
14:     <input type="submit" name="submit">
15:     </form>
16: ENDOFHTML
17:   exit;
18: }
19:
20: if ($myage eq "") {
21:   print "Hello $myname!";
22:   print "</br>";
23:   print <<ENDOFHTML2;
24:     <form action="helloworld2.cgi" method="post">
25:     Enter your age: <input type="text" name="age"><br/>
26:     <input type="hidden" name="name" value="$myname">
27:     <input type="submit" name="submit">
28:     </form>
29: ENDOFHTML2
30:   exit;
31: }
32:
33: $dayage=$myage*365;
34: $hourage=$dayage*24;
35: $minage=$hourage*60;
36: print "Hello again $myname!<br\/>";
37: print "You have lived for $dayage days...<br\/>";
38: print ".. or $hourage hours...<br\/>";
39: print ".. or $minage minutes!<br\/>";
```

This final revision adds an additional form and output screen. Lines 20–31 display the standard hello message but also show a form where the user is prompted for his age. What makes this form unique is that it includes a hidden name field set to the original `$myname` value. This shows how information can be carried from page to page.

The final page, generated in lines 33–39, calculates a user's name in days, hours, and minutes. This demonstrates that the name has indeed been carried through each of the CGI screens.

As an exercise, you might want to try adding a search screen to the image catalog creator that was built earlier in the chapter. Suppose, for instance, that there are multiple image folders to view, a need for the number of columns to be adjusted, or even searching based on the image filename—these features can all be added easily to the application. Listing 24.8 is a two-step version of the image catalog application.

LISTING 24.8 This New Version of the Image Catalog CGI Now Offers Searching and Display Settings

```
#!/usr/bin/perl

use CGI qw(:standard);

$imagedir=param('imagedir');
$imagename=param('imagename');
$columns=param('columns');
$match=param('match');
if ($imagedir=~/\//) { $imagedir="imagefolder"; }
if ($imagename=~/\//) { $imagename=""; }

header;
if ($imagedir eq "") {
  print <<ENDOFHTML;
    <form action="showimages5.cgi" method="post">
Image dir: <input type="text" name="imagedir" value="imagefolder"><br/>
    Select the number of columns in the display: <select name="columns">
      <option>1</option>
      <option>2</option>
      <option>3</option>
      <option>4</option>
    </select><br/>
    Show images that match: <input type="text" name="match">
    <input type="submit" name="submit">
    </form>
ENDOFHTML
}

@imagelist=glob("$imagedir/*$match*jpg");

print "<table bgcolor=\"#FFFFFF\" border=\"1\" bordercolor=\"#000000\">";
while ($x<@imagelist) {
  print "<tr>";
  for ($y=0;$y<$columns;$y++) {
```

```
35:     $imagename=$imagelist[$x];
36:     if ($x<@imagelist) {
37      $x++;
38:      print "<td align=\"center\">";
39:      print "<img src=\"$imagename\" width=\"120\" height=\"90\"><br/>";
40:      $imagename=~s/$imagedir\///;
41:      print "<font type=\"Arial\">$imagename</font>";
42:      print "</td>";
43:     }
44:    }
45:   print "</tr>";
46: }
47: print "</table>";
```


The only modifications to the original image catalog are the addition of lines 3–27. The rest remains the same.

Line 3 loads the `CGI.pm` module.

Lines 5–8 store values for the columns to display, image directory to use, and a string to search for in the image names.

Lines 9–10 are very important. When processing user input, an application can never trust the incoming data. If the image catalog blindly accepted an arbitrary path, it could pose a serious security risk and give the user access to other parts of the filesystem. For that reason, any input that includes a `/` is disregarded. This eliminates the potential for the user to input any path information.

If an image directory has not been set (such as the application has not received the search criteria yet), lines 13–27 display a search form. This is a simple HTML form that includes elements for setting the image directory, number of columns, and a search string for the image name.

A modification to the original `glob`, this line 29 variation adds the `$match` string to the pattern, displaying only images that match the specified string.

By now, you should have a grasp of the basics of CGI programming, and how Perl can be used to create quick-and-dirty web applications.

Increasing Execution Speed with `mod_perl`

If you've decided on Perl for your Apache development environment, you might want to look into the `mod_perl` module. This add-on embeds a Perl interpreter to the Apache process, greatly speeding up CGI execution. If your site makes extensive use of large Perl applications, give it a try.

`mod_perl` can be enabled by following these steps:

1. Create a directory `/Library/WebServer/perl-bin/` to hold your `mod_perl`-based CGIs.

2. Uncomment the following lines in `/etc/httpd/httpd.conf` by removing the pound (#) signs:

   ```
   #LoadModule perl_module libexec/httpd/libperl.so
   ```

   and

   ```
   #AddModule mod_perl.c
   ```

3. Add the following lines to the end of your `/etc/httpd/httpd.conf` file:

   ```
   <IfModule mod_perl.c>
     Alias /perl-bin/ /Library/WebServer/perl-bin/
     <Location /perl-bin/>
       SetHandler perl-script
       PerlHandler Apache::Registry
       Options +ExecCGI
       PerlSendHeader On
     </Location>
   </IfModule>
   ```

4. Restart Apache using the Sharing System Preferences pane or `/usr/sbin/apachectl restart`.

5. Perl CGIs run from the new `/Library/WebServer/perl-bin` directory (via the URL `http://`*`<hostname or localhost>`*`/perl-bin/`*`<cgi name>`*) will be accelerated.

Although Perl is certainly capable of generating large-scale applications, many developers have had their heads turned by the popular PHP language. If you've grasped the basics of Perl, moving on to PHP will be no problem.

Developing Web Applications Using PHP

PHP (PHP Hypertext Preprocessor—it's recursive) is a relatively new language that integrates with the Apache web server. Whereas Perl is a general-purpose programming language, PHP provides web-specific functions that can speed up development time significantly.

One of the primary differences between Perl and PHP is how it is programmed. With Perl, the focus is on the application logic; integrating an interface is secondary. When using PHP, the logic is embedded into the HTML. Yes, there are means of writing embedded Perl, but the PHP language itself was designed to be used in this fashion from the start.

A PHP developer can use traditional web development tools, such as Macromedia Dreamweaver MX or Adobe GoLive, to create an interface and then attach logic. For example, in Perl, we used code like this to print a variable within some HTML:

```
print <<HTML;
    print "<tr>";
    print "<td align=\"center\">$myname</td>";
```

```
    print "</tr>";
HTML
```

The equivalent code in PHP looks like this:

```
<tr>
<td align="center"><?php print $myname; ?></td>
</tr>
```

As you can see, the application code is entirely isolated from the HTML. PHP code is contained with its own tags: `<?php` to start and `?>` to end. As Apache reads a PHP file, it executes the code in the PHP tags and then sends the final result to the waiting browser. The remote user cannot see these special tags in the HTML source—your application logic is safe from prying eyes. In addition to a clean programming model, PHP offers features such as built-in database access, advanced security, and real-time graphic generation.

Enabling the PHP Module in Apache

Your Tiger system comes with a fully functioning version of PHP installed. Activating it is simply a matter of changing a few lines in the /etc/httpd/httpd.conf file. Open the file, and look for the following lines:

```
#LoadModule php4_module     libexec/httpd/libphp4.so
#AddModule mod_php4.c
```

These lines are noncontiguous in the configuration file—they're shown together here to save space. Activate PHP by uncommenting each line (removing the #).

Restarting Apache with sudo /usr/sbin/apachectl restart will active your PHP module.

To fine-tune the PHP configuration, you'll need to install a PHP .ini file in /etc/php.ini. Apple has included the file /etc/php.ini.default on your system. Copy this file to /etc/php.ini, and then open it in your text editor of choice.

First, make sure that any system-specific settings are set. The default settings usually work perfectly fine. You might want to look at the resource settings, however, because they can be used to make sure that renegade scripts don't eat up the memory and CPU time on your system. Look in the php.ini for these lines:

```
;;;;;;;;;;;;;;;;;;;
; Resource Limits ;
;;;;;;;;;;;;;;;;;;;

max_execution_time = 30  ; Maximum execution time of each script, in seconds
memory_limit = 8M     ; Maximum amount of memory a script may consume (8MB)
```

By default, scripts can use up to 8MB of memory and take 30 seconds to execute. For many CGIs, these are rather liberal values. You can reduce them as you want; I've cut them in half on my system and haven't had any problems thus far.

Additionally, you should enable safe mode (`safe_mode = On`) on a public-use production server. This virtually eliminates the need to worry about environment variables being modified and misused:

```
; Safe Mode
safe_mode         =     On
```

This combination of settings enables you, the administrator, to prohibit environment variables from being modified unless they begin with one of the listed prefixes (`safe_mode_protected_env_vars`). You can also specify environment variables that, under no circumstances, should ever be allowed to change, regardless of the prefix settings. If there are certain functions you'd rather not be available to users, you can list these here as well (`disable_functions`).

Finally, to activate the changes, restart Apache again using the Sharing Preferences pane, or by typing `sudo /usr/sbin/apachectl restart` from the command line.

To verify that PHP is working, create a file (`test.php`) within one of your web directories (such as `Sites` within your home directory):

```
<?php
  phpinfo();
?>
```

Load this test page using a web browser. If the installation was successful, you should see a screen similar to Figure 24.8.

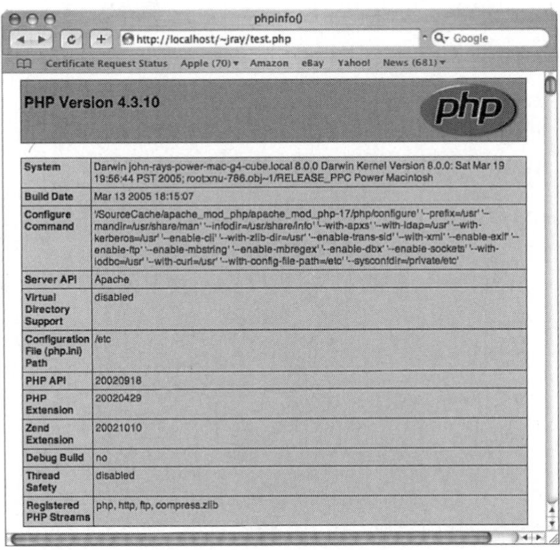

FIGURE 24.8 The `phpinfo()` function generates a screen of PHP installation information.

Understanding the PHP Syntax

The best introduction to programming PHP is a background in C or Perl. Check out Chapter 18 as a starter guide for the latter. PHP borrows heavily from Perl's free-form open scripting model and automatic data conversion. What truly makes PHP shine is the built-in web functions. Let's take a brief look at what you need to get started and then examine some of the unique features.

PHP programs are created as standard text files within any of your web-enabled directories. To execute the script, you must have the extension `.php`. This does not have a bearing on the HTML contents of the file. In fact, you can have an HTML file that contains no PHP code but ends in `.php`—it will still be served correctly, although with a slight performance penalty as the server checks the file for executable code.

PHP code itself is typically embedded within the `<?php` and `?>` brackets. Failing to place these tags around code results in the programming being interpreted as text within an HTML document. Even if you are working with a file that contains no HTML at all, you must still place all the PHP script within the brackets. There can be multiple PHP start and end tags in a single document.

If you've written JavaScript, this is similar to the behavior of the `<script>` and `</script>` tags that embed JavaScript code into a document. Regardless of how many PHP code segments are in your program, the code can be considered all part of one big global block. The variables defined in one section are available in another. For example:

```
<?php $myname="John"; ?>
This is some standard HTML in the middle...<hr><hr>
<?php print $myname; ?>
```

This code fragment assigns the value `John` to `$myname`, includes a bit of HTML, and finally prints the value of `$myname` (`John`). Even though `$myname` occurs within two separate PHP blocks, the value is still maintained.

NOTE

Perhaps not surprisingly, PHP can be embedded with the `<script>` and `</script>` tags. To use this format, just include PHP as the scripting language within the first tag: `<script language="php">`.

Each line of PHP code must end in a semicolon (`;`) to be correctly executed. Because of this requirement, extremely long lines of code can be broken across multiple lines to improve legibility.

Simple Data Types

Like Perl, PHP's data types are typecast from one to another internally. Although there is one primary data type, PHP is an object-oriented language and is used to create arbitrary object types with their own properties. Object-oriented programming is beyond the scope of this text, so only the basics are covered here. Don't worry; there's more than enough to start building complex web applications.

- `$<variable name>`—PHP defines a variable as an alphanumeric string prefaced by a `$`. Variable names cannot begin with a number. The variable can contain text, binary data, numbers, and so on. Type conversion happens automatically during program execution.
- `$<variable name>[<index>]`—Arrays offer more flexibility than Perl. An array can be defined during the course of program execution by adding an index to the end of a variable name. Unlike Perl, which differentiates between a standard array and associative arrays, an array index in PHP can be either a number or a string.

PHP variables are unique creatures and can be used in interesting ways. For example, the contents of a variable can be interpreted as variables themselves. Assume that you have a variable named `$peach`. Obviously, you can reference this variable by name (`$peach`). Now assume that a second variable, `$fruit`, contains the string `"peach"`. Using this second variable, you can reference the contents of the first variable through `$$fruit`. This works because `$$fruit` is functionally identical to typing `$"peach"`, which in turn is equivalent to `$peach`. This same technique can be applied to function calls to create a logic flow that changes itself based on variables in the program.

NOTE

Although not commonly used in simple applications, PHP does support passing variables by reference. As in C, you can pass a reference to a variable by placing an ampersand (&) in front: `&<$variable name>`.

Using Basic Variable Operators

The comparison and assignment operations work much like a simplified version of their Perl counterparts. The primary difference is that string comparisons are identical to numeric comparisons in syntax within PHP. Table 24.1 contains the common PHP operators.

TABLE 24.1 Common PHP Operators

Operator	Action	Description
==	Equals	Tests for equality
!=	Not equal	Tests for inequality
=	Assignment	Assigns the value on the right to the variable on the left
*	Multiplication	Multiplies two values together
/	Division	Divides two values
+	Addition	Adds two numbers together
-	Subtraction	Subtracts one number from another
.	Concatenation	Concatenates two strings together
&&	AND	Performs a logical AND on two values
||	OR	Performs a logical OR on two values

As previously mentioned, PHP automatically handles type conversions for you, making it possible to write code that looks like this:

```
<?php
$a="1";
$b="3";
$c=$a.$b;
$c=$c*2;
?>
```

Here, two strings, 1 and 3, are concatenated together and stored in `$c`. This new value is then multiplied by 2. Printing the result would display `26`, even though the only true number used in the calculation was 2 (during the multiplication).

There are a few shortcuts to the assignment as well. For example, incrementing or decrementing a number is common. Written in long form, adding 1 to the existing value of a variable `$a` looks like this:


```
$a=$a+1;
```

This can be shortened to

```
$a++;
```

The same applies to subtraction, using the minus (`-`) symbol.

Another shortcut applies to concatenating, adding, or subtracting to an existing value. For example, this line of code concatenates `$b` onto the end of `$a`:

```
$a=$a.$b;
```

The same thing can be written as

```
$a.=$b;
```

For addition and subtraction, just substitute the appropriate operator in place of the period (`.`). The basic syntax remains the same.

Adding Flow Control

Two types of control structures will be discussed here: linear flow operators and looping constructs. Linear flow operators can change the course of a program based on variables and other conditions. Looping constructs, on the other hand, can repeat sections of code based on similar criteria. Together they enable software to adapt to a particular task, instead of being hard-coded to work with one set of input.

`if-then-else` The most common linear flow control structure is the `if-then-else` statement. This can evaluate one or more conditions and act on them accordingly. The basic PHP `if-then` statement is structured like this:

```
if <condition> {
    <do something>;
}
```

This statement can be expanded to include an alternative course of action if the original condition is not met. This is considered an `if-then-else` statement:

```
if <condition> {
    <do something>;
} else {
    <do something else>;
}
```

One final variation of the statement exists that can evaluate multiple conditions within the single statement. This last variation is the `if-then-elsif` statement.

```
if <condition> {
    <do something>;
} elsif <another condition> {
    <do something else>;
} else {
    <do yet another thing>;
}
```

This example includes a single `elsif` line, but, depending on the needs of the programmer, this can be repeated as many times as necessary. A less verbose way to accomplish the same goal is to use the `switch` statement.

`switch` The `switch` statement takes a value as input and defines a set of possible outcomes that can occur, depending on that value. The best way to understand how this works is to look at an example:

```
switch ($x) {
    case 0:
        print "x=0";
        break;
    case 1:
        print "x=1";
        break;
    case 2:
        print "x=2";
        break;
    default:
        print "none of the above";
        break;
}
```

This piece of code examines the value of `$x`. If it is 0, PHP prints `x=0`. If `$x` equals 1, the code prints `x=1,...`, and so on. If `$x` doesn't match any of the listed values (`0`, `1`, `2`), it uses the default value and prints none of the values listed earlier.

The `switch` statement can be extended to include as many cases as needed. In addition, the cases do not have to be numeric. You can just as easily include strings:

```
switch ($name) {
    case 'John':
        print "John has a dog named Maddy";
        break;
    case 'Robyn':
        print "Robyn has a dog named Coco";
        break;
    case 'Jack':
        print "Jack has a bag of M&Ms";
        break;
    case default:
        print "I don't know you!";
        break;
}
```


The two portions of the `switch` statement that might require a bit more explanation are the `break` statement and the `default` case.

The `break` causes the `switch` statement to `exit`. If `break` is not executed, all code after the matching case is executed. If John is matched, all the `print` statements are executed until a break is encountered.

The default case is optional. It is executed only if none of the other cases is matched. It's usually a good idea to have a default case to keep untrapped errors from occurring.

`for` The `for` loop is the most commonly encountered loop in programming, regardless of the language. This loop executes a block of code until a condition is met. Each iteration of a `for-next` loop increments (or decrements) a counter variable. The loop is constructed using this syntax:

```
for (<initialization>;<execution condition>;<increment>) {
    <code block>
}
```

The *initialization* sets up the loop and initializes the counter variable to its default state. The *execution condition* is checked in each iteration of the loop; if it evaluates to false, the loop ends. Finally, the increment is a piece of code that defines an operation performed on the counter variable each time the loop is run. For example, the following loop counts from 0 to 9:

```
for ($count=0;$count<10;$count++) {
    print "Count = $count";
}
```

The counter, `$count`, is set to 0 when the loop starts. With each repetition, it is incremented by 1 (`$count++`). The loop exits when the counter reaches 10 (`$count<10`).

The format for the PHP for loop is identical to the Perl syntax.

`while` The `while` loop executes while a condition evaluates to true. Unlike a `for` loop, which usually ends based on a change in the counter, the `while` loop requires that something change within the code block that causes the condition to evaluate as false.

```
while (<execution condition>) {
    <code block>
}
```

The previous `for` example counted from 0 to 9. This same loop translated into a `while` loop looks like this:

```
$count=0;
while ($count<10) {
    print "Count = $count";
    $count++;
}
```

When you're using `while`/`do-while` loops, be sure that the execution condition eventually evaluates to false. It's easy to write infinite loops using this structure.

`do-while` Similar to the basic `while` loop, a `do-while` loop runs until a preset condition evaluates to false. The difference between the two loop styles is where the execution condition is checked. In a `while` loop, the condition is evaluated at the start of the loop. `do-while` loops, on the other hand, evaluate the condition at the end:

```
do {
    <code block>
} while (<execution condition>);
```

Again, let's translate the count from 0 to 9 into a `do-while` loop. As you can see, the difference is slight.

```
$count=0;
do {
    print "Count = $count";
    $count++;
} while ($count<10);
```

NOTE

Many languages have a similar loop structure known as a `do-until` loop. The only difference is that the `do-until` loop exits after a condition is met, not after it has become false.

Implementing Functions

Like any good programming language, PHP supports the notion of *functions*—independent pieces of code that can act on input and return a result. As you develop web applications, you'll find that a reasonable amount of code is reused each time. If applications are programmed as modularly as possible, you can create a library of commonly used functions to share among multiple applications and developers.

A function is set up using the `function` keyword; values are returned to the main program using `return`. For example:

```
function addnumbers($arg1,$arg2) {
    $result=$arg1+$arg2;
    return($result);
}
```

This function accepts two arguments (`$arg1` and `$arg2`), adds them together, and then returns the result to the main program. The `addnumbers` function could be called like this:

```
$theresult=&addnumbers(1,5);
```

In this example, the function is called with a preceding ampersand (`&`). This is optional but is required in code where the function's definition occurs after the function call is used in the code.

By default, all variables used in a function are automatically considered local to that function and cannot be accessed outside the function code. To make a variable's scope global, use the `global` keyword within a function:

```
global <variable name>;
```

A variable that is declared global can be accessed from the main program block as well as the declaring function.

Common Useful Functions

It's pointless to try to document all PHP's capabilities in this chapter. More than 1,500 functions are available in the PHP 4.3.x release. Table 24.2 provides a quick reference to some of the more interesting and useful functions. For those who are interested, when compiling this list I surveyed more than a dozen PHP scripts and noted the most frequently used operations as well as those needed for the examples in the chapter.

TABLE 24.2 With More Than 1,500 Available Functions, PHP Is Anything But Limited

Function	Purpose
addslashes(<*string*>)	Escapes special characters within strings (such as "") and returns the resulting string.
chop(<*string*>)	Removes trailing whitespace from a string and returns the result.
file(<*url*>)	Reads a file from a URL (local, FTP, web) and returns an array of each line in the file.

TABLE 24.2 Continued

Function	Purpose
`header(<string>)`	Outputs a header before processing any HTML output.
`join(<glue string>,<array>)`	Returns a single string containing all the elements of a given array joined together with the `glue string`. Same as `implode`.
`odbc_connect(<DSN>,<user>,<password>)`	Returns a link to an ODBC DSN on a given host.
`odbc_close(<link>)`	Given a database link, closes the connection.
`odbc_exec(<link>, <sql statement>)`	Sends an SQL statement to the ODBC DSN. Returns a pointer to the resulting data.
`odbc_fetch_array(<result>)`	Returns an array with the next available row of data from the resultset. The array is indexed by field name.
`odbc_num_rows(<result>)`	Returns the number of rows in a query result, or an error if the original query was invalid.
`preg_replace(<regex>, <replace string>,<string>)`	Searches a string for a Perl-style regular expression, replaces it with another, and returns the new string.
`print "<output>"`	Displays an output string. This is identical to the `echo` keyword.
`opendir(<directory name>)`	Opens a directory for reading and returns a file handle.
`readdir(<file handle>)`	Returns the next filename within a directory opened with `opendir`. Returns false if no more files are available.
`require(<filename>)`	Includes the contents of another file within the PHP code.
`session_start()`	Initializes a new session.
`session_destroy()`	Removes the active session.
`sort(<array>)`	Sorts an array.
`soundex(<string>)`	Returns a soundex value for a given string. This value is based on the sound of a string and can be used to compare two strings that sound similar but are spelled differently.
`split(<pattern>,<string>)`	Splits a string based on the characters in `<pattern>` and returns each of the results as the element in an array.
`stripslashes(<string>)`	Removes slashes from a string—the opposite of `addslashes`—and returns the result.
`strlen(<string>)`	Returns the length of a given string.

Visit `http://www.php.net/quickref.php` for a full list of the PHP functions.

PHP in Practice

In the Perl portion of this chapter, we created a simple image catalog. Let's see how that catalog can be rewritten in PHP. Listing 24.9 shows a PHP version of the Perl-image catalog.

LISTING 24.9 The Image Catalog, Rewritten in PHP

```
<?php if (!$_POST['imagedir']) { ?>
    <form action="showimages1.php" method="post">
Choose image dir: <input type="text" name="imagedir" value="imagefolder"><br>
    Select the number of columns in the display: <select name="columns">
      <option>1</option>
      <option>2</option>
      <option>3</option>
      <option>4</option>
    </select><br>
    Show images that match: <input type="text" name="match">
    <input type="submit" name="submit">
    </form>
<?php exit; } ?>

<table bgcolor="#FFFFFF" border="1" bordercolor="#000000">
<?php
$imagedir=$_POST['imagedir']; $columns=$_POST['columns'];
$handle=opendir("$imagedir");
while ($imagename = readdir($handle)) {
  if ($count==0 && $loop==0) { print "<tr>"; $loop=1; }
  if (preg_match("/.*$match.*\.jpg$/i",$imagename)) { ?>
    <td align=center>
    <img src="<?php print"$imagedir/$imagename"; ?>"
                width="120" height="90"><br>
    <font type="Arial"><?php print $imagename; ?></font>
    </td><?php
    $count++;
    if ($count==$columns) { print "</tr>"; $count=0; $loop=0; }
  }
}
if ($count!=0) { print "</tr>"; }
?>
</table>
```

The first two things you should notice looking at this code are that it is shorter than the Perl code and that the PHP is embedded in the HTML, rather than the HTML being embedded in the programming.

As the PHP application begins sending output, it automatically adds a `text/html` `Content-Type` header. In addition, no additional library or module, such as `CGI.pm`, is required. When a form posts information to a PHP program, the form variables are automatically translated into PHP variables with the `$_POST[]` or `$_GET[]` superglobal associative arrays. For example, an input field with the name address becomes accessible as `$_POST['address']` when submitted to a PHP script. A more generalized superglobal array—`$_REQUEST[]`—can be used to reference any variable that is available either from a `POST`, `GET`, or cookie. These shortcuts enable you to focus on the code rather than the specifics of HTTP.

A breakdown of the changes in the code follows:

Lines 1–13 check whether the variable `imagedir` has been posted from a form. If it hasn't, the user hasn't submitted a search request yet, and the search form should be displayed. Unlike Perl, which used `print` to show the form, PHP `if-then` tags can encompass HTML blocks. In this case, if the variable isn't defined, the HTML in the `if-then` is sent to the browser; otherwise, it is skipped.

Line 15 starts the HTML output table. In Line 17, the variables `$imagedir` and `$columns` are assigned to the values posted from the web form. Line 18 opens the image directory for reading. PHP, sadly, doesn't support a `glob` function, like Perl. While there are files in the opened directory, lines 19–29 parses them into `$imagename`.

If at the start of a row, send a `<tr>` tag. Line 20 must also set a flag (`$loop`) to indicate that the loop has started; this prevents multiple `<tr>` from being sent if the first few files read in the directory are not image files. Line 21 uses a Perl regular expression to match the filename to a file that ends in `.jpg` and includes the search string (`$match`).

Lines 22–25 display the table data cell for the image. Note that the image name is added to the HTML by embedded PHP `print` statements. Lines 26–27 increment the number of images displayed. If it is equal to the selected number of image columns, output a `</tr>`.

If the last file displayed occurred in the middle of a row, the program must add a final `</tr>` to close the row. This is done with line 30. Line 32 closes the output table.

For the most part, the programming syntax should closely resemble what you've seen in Perl. The lack of a `glob` function adds a few extra lines but doesn't prevent the PHP version from coming in 20% shorter.

Using Sessions in PHP

I've made such a big deal about sessions and how they make life easier; it's probably time to see one in use. Unfortunately, it's difficult to fabricate the use for a session in a reasonable amount of space. So, let's take a look at a simple case of sessions at work.

Imagine having a web page that remembers how many times you've visited it during your current browser session (since you last quit out of your web browser). This can't be done using a form because an action would be needed to submit the form each time you load the page. URL parameters can't be used because, likewise, the page would have to alter all the links it contains to include the number of visits using URL variable passing. With sessions, this is beyond simple. In fact, the following example keeps track of the cumulative number of visits to two distinct pages.

Create two web pages (one.php and two.php) that link to one another. In one.php, type the following:

```
<?php
        session_start();
        $_SESSION['x']++;
        $x=$_SESSION['x'];
        print "You've been to page one and two $x times";
?>
<br/>
<A HREF="two.php">Go to page two</a>
```

And in two.php, type this:

```
<?php
        session_start();
        $_SESSION['x']++;
        $x=$_SESSION['x'];
        print "You've been to page one and two $x times";
?>
<br/>
<a href="one.php">Go to page one</a>
```

Open either of the pages in your browser. Clicking the link to toggle between the two pages increments the counter, and the displayed number starts counting up. Although this is not a groundbreaking website, it demonstrates the capabilities of built-in session management. The two pages share a single counter session variable: x. The session_start() command starts a new PHP session if one doesn't already exist. The $_SESSION['x']++ registers the variable x with the current session and adds one to its current value.— Changing anything in the $_SESSION[] array effectively saves its value between pages. The $x=$_SESSION['x'] statement simply brings the session variable x into a normal local variable $x that is easier to work with.

The incrementing of x doesn't depend in any way on the links between one.php and two.php. You can reload one of the pages 30 times, and the counter will increment 30 times. You can even visit another website and then come back to either of the web pages, and the count is still present. The only way to lose the value of x is to drop the session—that is, close your web browser.

Accessing ODBC Data Sources in PHP

Finally, as an example of PHP's capability to work with databases, let's take a look at how easily code can be written to interact with an ODBC DSN (covered in detail in Chapter 19, "Serving and Connecting to Databases"). Because most database-driven

24

websites require a bit of setup, this example assumes that your Tiger installation is set up with a DSN called `myDSN` with a username `databaseuser` and password `databasepass`.

The database itself is named `employee` and contains a table `tblemployee` with at least the two fields `firstname` and `lastname`. You should easily be able to adapt this short script to work with any ODBC database you can design, or just use the sample database in Chapter 19. Listing 24.10 demonstrates PHP that retrieves and prints each person's name from `employee`.

LISTING 24.10 PHP/ODBC Example

```
1: <?php
2: $odbclink=odbc_connect("myDSN","databaseuser","databasepass");
3: $result=odbc_exec($odbclink,"select * from tblemployee");
4: $count=odbc_num_rows($result);
5: for ($x=0;$x<$count;$x++) {
6:    $record=odbc_fetch_array($result);
7:    $firstname=$record[FirstName];
8:    $lastname=$record[LastName];
9:    print "$lastname, $firstname<br/>";
10: }
11: odbc_close($odbclink);
12: ?>
```

Line 2 makes the initial connection to the ODBC DSN with the username/password pair `databaseuser/databasepass`. The variable `$odbclink` can be used to refer to the connection.

Line 3 queries the ODBC database `employee` by sending it the SQL query `select * from tblemployee`. A pointer to the resultset is returned to the variable `$result`.

Line 4 stores the total number of records in the result in the variable `$count`.

Lines 5–10 loop through the number of available records. Line 6 stores each row (one per loop) in the array `$record`. Lines 7 and 8 retrieve the `firstname` and `lastname` fields from the record, storing them in the `$firstname` and `$lastname` variables, respectively. Line 9, finally, outputs the name.

Line 11 closes the connection created in Line 2.

TIP

This example demonstrates how to pull information from a DSN, but the process for storing data is identical. The `odbc_exec` function can be used to send any SQL statement to the database server and retrieve the results. You could just as easily use an insert or update SQL command in place of the select shown here.

The virtues of PHP could be touted for pages, but, unfortunately, the room is not available. If you want more information on PHP development, look at any of these fine sites:

- PHP Homepage—`http://www.php.net/`
- PHP Builder—`http://www.phpbuilder.net/`
- `comp.lang.php`—PHP's official Usenet newsgroup

Additionally, Zend Technologies (`http://www.zend.org`) has released its Zend IDE for Mac OS X, which makes creating and debugging PHP applications much like working with traditional desktop applications.

Alternative Development Environments

Many alternative web development environments can run under Tiger, including Apple's own WebObjects. Personally, I have a thing for open source products, but depending on your needs, PHP or Perl might not be appropriate.

> **TIP**
>
> If you love Python (covered in Chapter 18), check out `http://www.modpython.org/` for information on an Apache module for creating an embedded Python server.

WebObjects, for example, is a Java-based development environment that includes RAD tools, distributed application logic and load handling, and a steep learning curve. WebObjects is used to deploy large-scale applications and requires a decent knowledge of the Tiger object model to begin programming. WebObjects comes with a reasonably high price tag outside the range of smaller groups. On the plus side, it is widely recognized as a superior web application server and has won numerous awards in the enterprise marketplace (`http://www.apple.com/webobjects/`).

Java Server Pages (JSP) is a fast-growing application development solution that leverages the cross-platform nature of Java. Like WebObjects, JSP requires knowledge of the Java programming language and has a similarly steep learning curve. A big advantage to JSP is that it is a supported server platform in software packages such as Macromedia's Dreamweaver MX—enabling graphical development of web applications. In addition, the JBoss (`http://www.jboss.org/`) application server is available as a custom install with the Tiger developer tools, enabling you to get started with JSP right away. See `http://developer.apple.com/internet/java/enterprisejava.html` for information on getting started with JBoss on Tiger.

Creating RSS Feeds

As you're probably aware, the version of Safari included in Tiger now supports RSS "channels." RSS (*Rich Site Summary*, *RDF Site Summary*, or *Really Simple Syndication* depending on who you ask and the time of day) provides a simple means of syndicating your website's content. If your site offers an RSS channel, any other website can display a summary of the content you have available. This is often employed on blogs and news sites but could be extended to just about any type of information that you might want to share: recipes, file uploads, and so on. The benefit of RSS is that it promotes content sharing rather than the content "borrowing" (stealing) that is prevalent. Sites can share information and offer customized RSS feeds to suite their users needs.

Although RSS is still in the early implementation stages for many sites, it has gained considerable momentum through acceptance by online news organizations and, sadly, advertisers. Integration into Safari and the popular cross-platform Firefox browser will further push its adoption by site owners around the world. If you aren't using RSS now, you should be. The good news, implementing RSS on a website is absolutely trivial, even if you just maintain a few static web pages.

Understanding the Components of an RSS Feed

If you're like many folks, you've heard the world extolling the benefits of XML for several years, but probably haven't seen many practical ways for you to use it personally. RSS is an application of XML that is easy to understand and demonstrates the power of the cross-platform markup language. To begin, let's take a look at Listing 24.11, an RSS feed published by NASA during the Ivan hurricane near the end of 2004.

LISTING 24.11 A Sample RSS File

```
<?xml version="1.0" encoding="UTF-8"?>
<rss version="2.0">
        <channel>
                <title>NASA Coverage of Hurricane Ivan</title>
                <link>http://www.nasa.gov/rss/ivan_at_nasa.rss</link>
                <description>How Hurricane Ivan was studied by NASA and
                               how it affected NASA facilities.</description>
                <language>en-us</language>
                <docs>http://blogs.law.harvard.edu/tech/rss</docs>
                <managingEditor>cenger@nasa.gov</managingEditor>
                <webMaster>brian.dunbar@nasa.gov</webMaster>
                <item>
                        <title>Hurricane Ivan's "CAT" Scan</title>
                        <link>/vision/earth/lookingatearth/IVAN_TRMM_9.15.html
                        </link>
                        <description>NASA looks inside the storm.</description>
                        <pubDate>09.15.04</pubDate>
                </item>
                <item>
                        <title>Ivan Inside Out</title>
                        <link>http://www.nasa.gov/vision/earth/lookingatearth
                               /Ivan_inside_out.html</link>
                        <description>Satellites look inside Ivan to find clues
```

```
            about its intensity as the storm approaches land.</description>
21:                 <pubDate>09.20.04</pubDate>
22:         </item>
23:         <item>
24:                 <title>Ivan's 'CAT' Scan</title>
25:                 <link>http://www.nasa.gov/vision/earth/lookingatearth/
                        IVAN_TRMM_9.15.html</link>
26:                 <description>NASA looks at Ivan's engine.</description>
27:                 <pubDate>09.20.04</pubDate>
28:         </item>
29:         <item>
30:                 <title>NASA Prepares for Hurricane Ivan</title>
31:                 <link>http://www.nasa.gov/home/hqnews/2004/sep/
                        HQ_04299_SSCprep_.html</link>
32:                 <description>Weather forecasts indicate some NASA
    centers and facilities could feel Ivan's terrible wrath.</description>
33:                 <pubDate>09.14.04</pubDate>
34:         </item>
35:         </channel>
36: </rss>
```


The start of all valid RSS files must declare the version of XML and RSS standards employed, as seen in lines 1–2. For virtually all feeds you'd be creating at this time, the proper values will be `"1.0"` and `"2.0"`, respectively. Next, a `<channel>` (line 3) tag marks the start of the information related to the content you are syndicating. A channel requires several mandatory metadata tags to be implemented in order to be considered valid. These tags are

`<title></title>`—The official name for the channel. This should be a clear, concise, and descriptive string (line 4).

`<link></link>`—A full URL to the website that the RSS channel corresponds to (line 5).

`<description></description>`—A brief description of what users can expect to find on a channel (line 6).

TIP

There is no hard-and-fast rule for how large attributes should be (such as the description, title, and so forth), but the implementation of RSS channels within many reader applications typically makes some assumptions when laying out the displays. For example, titles are short, descriptions are one or two sentences, and so on. Use common sense when creating your channels so that they display properly in RSS readers.

In addition to mandatory tags, there are several additional tags available to describe the channel. In the sample channel, for example, NASA has implemented the

<managingEditor>, <webMaster>, <docs>, and <language> tags (lines 7–10.) A list of the most useful optional tags is provided here:

<managingEditor>—The editor of the content provided by the channel.

<webMaster>—The individual in charge of the server providing the channel content.

<docs>—A URL that points to the RSS specification implemented in the channel, most likely "http://blogs.law.harvard.edu/tech/rss".

<language>—The language used for the channel content. A list of acceptable languages can be found at http://blogs.law.harvard.edu/tech/stories/storyReader$15.

<rating>—A PICS rating for the channel to help control access to the content. Details on PICS can be found at http://www.w3.org/PICS/.

<copyright>—A copyright notice for the channel.

<ttl>—The time a subscriber of an RSS channel can use the channel content without refreshing it.

<lastBuildDate>—The time of the last update to the channel.

After the basic channel properties are defined, the actual content must be provided. In the NASA feed, this is accomplished in lines 11–34, which defines each of four different stories within the <item></item> tags. Each item can be either a description and link to content or the entire content itself. The most common tags that can be used in each item definition are

<title>—The title of the article, story, or other content piece.

<link>—A URL that points to the specific piece of content.

<description>—In many cases, the description is treated as a document abstract. It should describe the content that is linked to. If desired, the description *can* be the content, in which case the title and link are not required.

<author>—An email address for an article's author.

<pubDate>—The publication date for the article.

After the articles have been defined, the RSS channel is closed with a </channel> and </rss> close tag. Based on the patterns set up in this sample, you should very easily be able to create your own RSS documents to include in your website.

RSS feeds are generally used to define content that changes frequently; manually keeping a document up-to-date can become a bit of a chore. To streamline the process, you can use an application such as Glass Onion Software's FeedMe (http://thenowhereman.com/hacks/) shown in Figure 24.9, to create and manage RSS feeds within a GUI environment.

Even with tools to help build RSS feeds, if your site publishes more than an article a day, you're likely to find yourself tiring of the process quickly. If your server provides access to PHP or another scripting language, you should definitely consider dynamically building the feed on the fly.

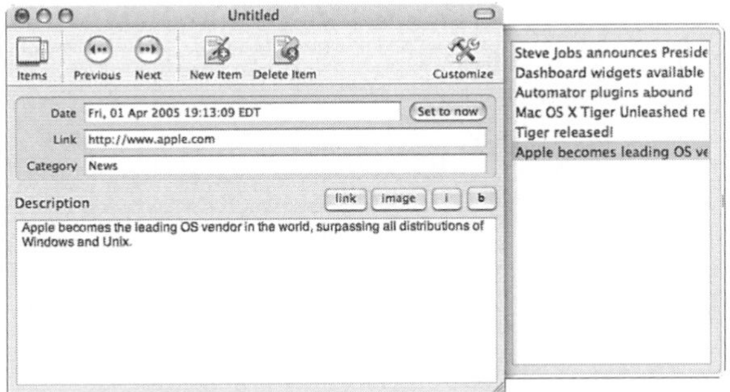

FIGURE 24.9 Onion Software's FeedMe can be used to manage RSS feeds within the Tiger GUI.

> **TIP**
>
> When creating an RSS feed, especially by hand, be sure to validate the code before putting it online. The site `http://feedvalidator.org/` provides free validation services and RSS banners that can be used to promote your standards-compliant RSS-enabled site.

Using PHP and FeedCreator to Build an RSS Feed

PHP can be used to create an RSS feed by dynamically generating the appropriate RSS tags instead of HTML. To make things even easier, the work has already been done for you. Free PHP libraries have been written that enable web developers such as you to build RSS channels without having to remember the document syntax and parse existing channels for inclusion in other websites. The library that we'll discuss here is FeedCreator, which you can download from `http://www.bitfolge.de/rsscreator-en.html`.

FeedCreator is a very simple to use PHP class that builds and saves valid RSS files, and, best of all, it's free. After downloading the source distribution, unzip it and review the contents. You should see two files: a license file, which you should take the time to read, and a PHP file called `feedcreator.class.php`. You will need to place this file in a location where it can be included by the PHP script you want to build the feed. You'll also need to make one change to the file before continuing: changing the default time zone.

To set the time zone in `feedcreator.class.php`, open the file in an editor and search for the line:

```
define("TIME_ZONE","+01:00");
```

Edit the number at the end of the line to reflect your time zone's offset from GMT, and then save your change. The file is now ready for use. One more change and you're ready to go. To keep from overwhelming your server by querying a data source repeated to build the RSS channel, FeedCreator will create an XML file with the contents of the feed and will attempt to use this cached version of the feed if the file is less than 60 minutes old. To create this file, FeedCreator requires a directory that your web server can write to.

Create a directory in your web space (such as ~/Sites/rsscache) and set "www" as either the owner or the group of that directory (that is, sudo chown www <*folder containing rss cache file*>).

Now you're ready to generate your RSS feed. To get you started, I've created a sample feed for a single story on the *Mac OS X Tiger Unleashed* support site. Review the code in Listing 24.12, and then we'll step through the lines to get a feel for what it does.

LISTING 24.12 FeedCreator Can Generate RSS 2.0 Files

```
 1: <?php
 2: include("feedcreator.class.php");
 3:
 4: $rss = new UniversalFeedCreator();
 5: $rss->useCached();
 6: $rss->title = "Tiger Unleashed News";
 7: $rss->description = "Updates and Errata for the Mac OS X Unleashed Series";
 8: $rss->link = "http://www.macosxunleashed.com/";
 9:
10: $item = new FeedItem();
11: $item->title = "Mac OS X Tiger Unleashed Released";
12: $item->link = "http://www.macosxunleashed.com/tigernews.html";
13: $item->description = "The Tiger Edition of Mac OS X Unleashed has hit the
                         stores.  Read about it now.";
14: $item->date = "Fri, 01 Apr 2005 12:59:23 -0500";
15: $item->author = "John Ray";
16: $rss->addItem($item);
17:
18: echo $rss->saveFeed("RSS2.0", "rsscache/myfeed.xml");
19:
20: ?>
```

Just looking at the listing you can probably very quickly identify the components that make up an RSS channel. The FeedCreator class is included in line 2; this gives us the features and functions needed to build the channel.

To start the channel, a new RSS object ($rss) is created, as demonstrated in line 4. Line 5 attempts to use a cached version of the feed if the cache is less than an hour old.

Lines 6–8 set up the three required components of describing an RSS channel: the title, description, and link. After the channel itself has been created, items are added.

Line 10 creates a new item ($item), whereas lines 11–15 set the title, link, description, date, and author, respectively. Finally, line 16 adds the item to the RSS channel ($rss).

On a real-world system, you would likely want to query a database or other data source and loop through lines 10–16 repeatedly for each story or article; you may use the same $item object for each iteration of the loop.

Finally, the RSS XML file is output and saved to the named file (`myfeed.xml`) in line 18. Note that the file is saved in the `rsscache` directory which *must* be writeable by the www user account.

> **NOTE**
>
> Line 18 also sets the version of RSS to use. RSS 2.0 is the latest and cleanest spec, and is what we've shown in this chapter. You can use older specs by specifying RSS0.91 or RSS1.0. There are additional syndication features and formats supported and described within the comments at the top of the `feedcreator.class.php`.

The output of this simple script should very closely resemble the following:

```
<?xml version="1.0" encoding="ISO-8859-1"?>
<!-- generator="FeedCreator 1.7.2" -->
<rss version="2.0">
    <channel>
        <title>Tiger Unleashed News</title>
        <description>Updates and Errata for the Mac OS X Unleashed Series
        </description>
        <link>http://www.macosxunleashed.com/</link>
        <lastBuildDate>Sat, 04 Dec 2004 13:00:27 -0500</lastBuildDate>
        <generator>FeedCreator 1.7.2</generator>
        <item>
            <title>Mac OS X Tiger Unleashed Released</title>
            <link>http://www.macosxunleashed.com/tigernews.html</link>
            <description>The Tiger Edition of Mac OS X Unleashed has hit the
                         stores.  Read about it now.</description>
            <author>John Ray</author>
            <pubDate>Fri, 01 Apr 2005 12:59:23 -0500</pubDate>
        </item>
    </channel>
</rss>
```

The benefits of automatically generating RSS feeds should be obvious: News of your latest publications can reach your content consumers without them needing to visit your website and without any additional work on your part. All done? Not just yet; there is still one more thing you need to do to publicize your feed.

Promoting Your RSS Feed in Safari RSS

As you've probably noticed, when you're browsing a web page in Safari and the page offers an RSS channel, a small blue RSS button appears in the URL, as shown in Figure 24.10. This enables you to quickly load and subscribe to the given feed. The page you were likely browsing, however, probably was an HTML page, so how did Safari know that an RSS feed was available?

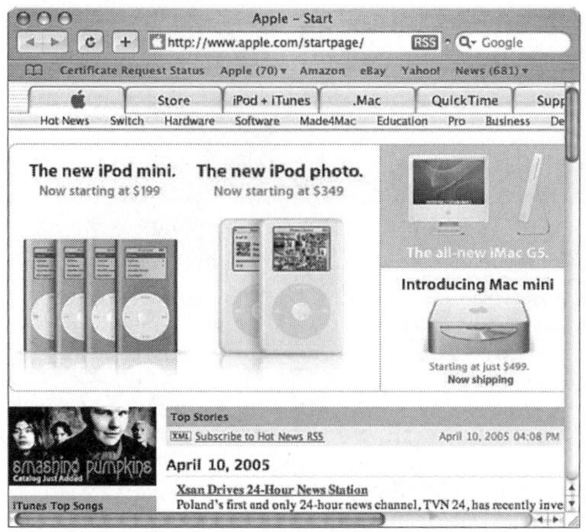

FIGURE 24.10 Safari identifies available RSS feeds.

The answer is a simple alternative content link in the `<head></head>` portion of the content page. For example:

```
<head>
        <meta http-equiv="Content-Type" content="text/html; charset=utf-8">
        <link rel="alternate" title="Mac OS X Tiger Unleashed RSS"
         href="http://www.macosxunleashed.com/rss.php" type="application/rss+xml">
        <title>Mac OS X Tiger Unleashed</title>
</head>
```

Here, the Mac OS X Tiger Unleashed RSS feed is promoted by adding the following tag:

```
<link rel="alternate" title="Mac OS X Tiger Unleashed RSS"
href="http://www.macosxunleashed.com/rss.php" type="application/rss+xml">
```

You can do the same for the pages of your site that offer RSS channels by inserting the appropriately formatted HTML tags into your documents.

Parsing RSS Feeds

Because you have the tools to create RSS feeds, it might also be useful to parse existing RSS feeds to include external content on your own website (called *aggregation.*) As with creating feeds, this is accomplished very easily by taking advantage existing PHP classes. MagpieRSS is one of the most popular, powerful, and easy-to-use PHP parsers. You can download the source code from `http://magpierss.sourceforge.net/`.

The MagpieRSS distribution will unarchive to a directory containing several files. You should place these in a location where they can be included from the PHP page where you want a feed displayed. Within the page itself, you will need to add a code block that displays the feed. For example, consider Listing 24.13.

LISTING 24.13 MagpieRSS Can Easily Parse and Render RSS Feeds

```
 1: <?php
 2:
 3: require('rss_fetch.inc');
 4: $rss = fetch_rss("http://extension.osu.edu/~news/rss.php");
 5:
 6: foreach ($rss->items as $item) {
 7:      $link = $item['link'];
 8:      $title = $item['title'];
 9:      $description = $item['description'];
10:      print "<b>$title</b><br/>";
11:      print "$description... ";
12:      print "<a href=\"$link\">[Read More]</a><br/>";
13:      print "<br/>";
14: }
15: ?>
```

This small piece of code generates page content similar to what you see in Figure 24.11.

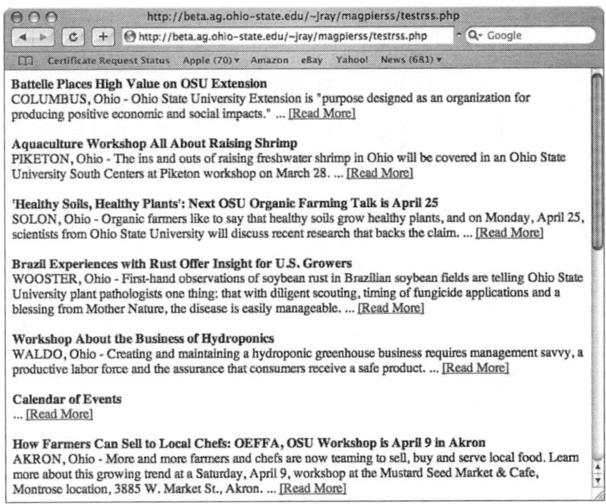

FIGURE 24.11 The MagpieRSS libraries can easily read and parse external RSS feeds for your website.

Of course you can customize the display to your liking. The code displayed here works as follows:

Line 3 includes the necessary MagpieRSS library (`rss_fetch.inc`). Next, line 4 creates an RSS object (`$rss`) based on the URL provided (if you'd like to test this on your system, the URL in this example is real).

The display is output in lines 6–14, which loops through each of the items in the RSS object. On each iteration of the loop, an associative array `$item` is assigned the values from the RSS channel. Each item attribute can be retrieved by indexing into the `$item` array using the attribute name— `$item['title']` for the title, `$item['author']` for the author, and so on.

Because the output is just HTML, you can customize the display in any manner you'd like. There is additional documentation and sample scripts available in the MagpieRSS Cookbook at `http://magpierss.sourceforge.net/cookbook.shtml`.

Summary

Professional web application development finally comes to the Macintosh platform. Perl offers a great starting language for programmers. A more web-centric development environment is PHP, which works by embedding development code into HTML, rather than embedding HTML into the code. Even if the Perl/PHP development solutions don't meet your needs, a number of other options are available for Tiger that can create enterprise-level websites and online applications.

Finally, no matter how you're developing your site, you should consider adding syndication support through RSS. By RSS-enabling your site, you can promote your content to a larger audience and enable your readers to work with your information in new and more flexible ways.

CHAPTER **25**

Darwin Streaming Server and QuickTime Broadcaster

IN THIS CHAPTER

- Introduction to Darwin Streaming Server
- Installing and Using Darwin Streaming Server
- Streaming Live Events with QuickTime Broadcaster
- Embedding QuickTime into Web Pages

In the last two chapters we've dealt with setting up a web server and then delivering dynamic web applications over it. This chapter will explore another type of content delivery that is becoming increasingly common on the Internet: streaming video and audio.

Apple presents live broadcasts of MacWorld, WWDC (Apple's Worldwide Developers Conference), and other events using the QuickTime Streaming Server and QuickTime Broadcaster products. You can use these same tools to stream your own AV presentations for business, education, and personal use. If you're so inclined, your Mac can even serve as a means of streaming your television or cable feed to the computers in your house.

Introduction to Darwin Streaming Server

Streaming media is an increasingly popular way to distribute information on the Internet. News releases, special company events, even your private home movie library—just about everyone has content that can be streamed, but very few want to make the perceived investment necessary to support streaming services. With Apple's Darwin Streaming Server (abbreviated here as *DSS*, it's the open source version of the official QuickTime Streaming Server [*QTSS*] available on Tiger Server), this investment is reduced to *any* modern operating system (the server runs on Windows, Linux, or Mac OS X), a Macintosh for broadcasting live events, and a means of getting video into your computer. If the explosion of iMovie HD and other video editing tools is any indication, many modern households already have the necessary infrastructure!

So, what exactly *is* streaming? In short, streamed video or audio does not require a user to download an entire file to view or listen to the content. Playback begins virtually instantly and the user has the ability to fast forward or rewind the content (unless it is a live stream!) just as he would a local file.

Using Darwin Streaming Server, you can stream prerecorded content, live events, and multiple media files arranged in a playlist—just like iTunes. Streams created using the MPEG-4 standard or based on audio MP3s can be viewed and listened to on a variety of platforms—not just QuickTime.

There are a number of different ways in which DSS can be set up and used. Large-scale installations would likely take advantage of the MBone *(Multicast Backbone)* or a multicast-enabled network. Multicasting takes advantage of a properly configured network's capability to broadcast a single transmission of packets to multiple machines. Multicasting reduces the total bandwidth needed for a large audience and greatly increases the number of clients that can be handled by a single server. Unfortunately, multicasting requires network setup that is beyond simply tweaking Tiger. For our purposes, we will look at a unicast configuration similar to that of Figure 25.1.

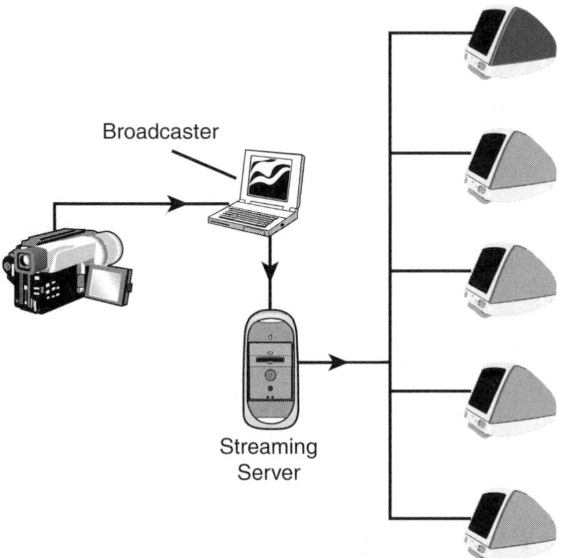

FIGURE 25.1 Our QTSS setup will use a single streaming server and QuickTime Broadcaster.

Unicasting, unlike multicasting, doesn't require any special network considerations. Instead of transmitting one stream to multiple clients, a unicast sends an individual stream to each viewing user. Although it consumes more bandwidth and limits the total number of simultaneous viewers, this approach is usually sufficient for modest deployments in which thousands of connections aren't likely. Unicasting is also much easier to configure, diagnose, and maintain.

NOTE

Because end users viewing a stream of prerecorded video can *scrub* through streamed prerecorded video (that is, choose exactly *where* in a stream they will be watching), it is impossible to serve multiple users with a single stream (multicast) This type of media streaming is always carried out through unicasting.

Two protocols are used for delivering QuickTime streams: RTP and RTSP.

RTSP—*Real-Time Streaming Protocol.* RTSP is used as the control protocol for streaming; it does not carry the stream itself, but rather the requests that a user has made during a stream: fast-forwarding, rewinding, pausing, and so forth.

RTP—*Real-Time Transport Protocol.* RTP handles the delivery of a stream. Based on UDP (*User Datagram Protocol*), it provides the fastest throughput possible while allowing for the stream to continue despite inevitable packet loss or errors. Unfortunately, RTP is often blocked by firewalls. To work around this problem, QTSS can tunnel RTP through the HTTP (*Hypertext Transfer Protocol*; the protocol of the Web) protocol, which is usually allowed through corporate and home firewalls.

The remainder of this chapter will first focus on getting Darwin Streaming Server up and running on your Tiger computer, followed by creating live streams using the Apple QuickTime Broadcaster tool. In short, everything you need to claim your place in the online world of media broadcasting!

Installing and Using Darwin Streaming Server

The first step to streaming is, obviously, installing the Darwin Streaming Server. DSS enables the streaming of prerecorded content and playlists—the backbone of all streaming services.

Installing DSS

To install Darwin Streaming Server, download the latest package from the Apple QuickTime Streaming Server page: `http://developer.apple.com/darwin/projects/streaming/`. An installer-packaged binary is available for Mac OS X, so just double-click and follow the onscreen directions.

When the installation has finished, Installer will launch your web browser to complete the setup. DSS is configured and administered through a web interface; the first step is creating an administrative username and password, as seen in Figure 25.2. These credentials are not tied, in any way, to a Tiger username or password.

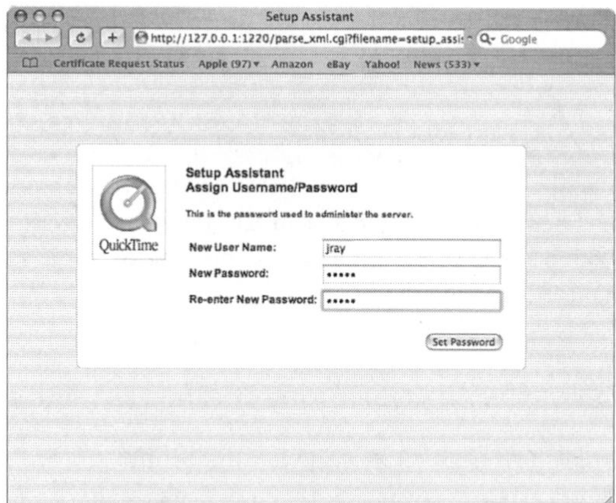

FIGURE 25.2 After installation has been completed, your web browser will be launched and setup will begin.

NOTE

If your browser is not launched automatically, open Safari (or another browser) and load the URL `http://127.0.0.1:1220/parse_xml.cgi?filename=setup_assistant2.html`. The administrative interface lives on port 1220 of your computer.

After entering a unique username and password, click Next. The web setup assistant will prompt for an MP3 broadcast password—this is a password required for broadcasting to another server, not an end user MP3 client, such as iTunes or Winamp. Again, choose a unique password and click Next.

Now you will be prompted whether to use SSL *(Secure Sockets Layer)* to encrypt the administrative control connection. If you're concerned about someone sniffing your password and reconfiguring your server to stream their illicit wares, enabling this is a good idea. To use SSL, however, you must also obtain a certificate signed by a CA *(Certificate Authority)* and install it as `/Library/QuickTimeStreaming/streamingadminserver.pem`. You can do this using the Certificate Assistant in Keychain Access (refer to Chapter 2, "Useful Tiger Widgets, Applications, and Utilities"), or by following the excellent instructions at `http://geeklog.afp548.com/article.php?story=20040722080720854`.

After you've made your selection, click Next to continue.

Next, the setup assistant will ask where your media files are stored; the default, `/Library/QuickTimeStreaming/Movies/`, should be sufficient (see Figure 25.3).

Finally, you will be asked whether streaming is enabled over port 80.

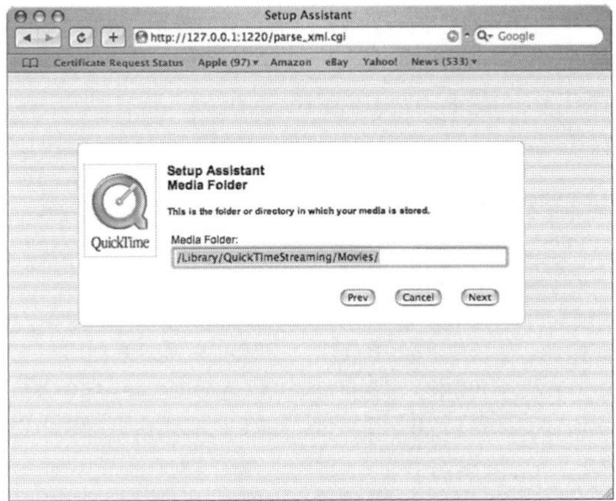

FIGURE 25.3 Choose where your media files are stored.

Although it might seem like a good idea to enable this by default, be aware that streaming over port 80 will not coexist with standard web services also running on port 80. If you need to run a web server on the same machine as your DSS, do *not* enable port 80 streaming in this step. Click Finish to complete the initial setup of Darwin Streaming Server.

TIP

You can always change these settings at any time in the future, so don't worry about making a mistake now.

Your browser should refresh to display the main administrative control page for DSS, as demonstrated in Figure 25.4. From here you can quickly view the vital statistics of your server: how long it has been running, how much traffic it has received, and how much processor time it is taking. You can reach this page at any time from the URL `http://127.0.0.1:1220/`.

Disabling DSS

DSS starts automatically each time you boot your computer. This is triggered by the `QuickTimeStreamingServer` StartupItem, located in `/System/Library/StartupItems/`. To disable DSS, either remove the StartupItem or edit `/etc/hostconfig`, looking for these two lines:

```
QTSSWEBADMIN=-YES-

QTSSRUNSERVER=-YES-
```

Setting both lines to `-NO-` will disable DSS and its web-based administrative interface.

Testing Your Darwin Streaming Server Installation

When you installed DSS, several sample files were included in the installation process. Assuming that you used the default media directory (`/Library/QuickTimeStreaming/Movies`), you should see something like this:

```
$ ls -al /Library/QuickTimeStreaming/Movies/
total 19880
drwxrwxr-x   7 qtss  admin      238 12 Dec 23:17 .
drwxrwxr-x  10 qtss  admin      340 12 Dec 23:17 ..
-rw-rw-r--   1 qtss  admin  1789985 18 Feb  2004 sample.mp3
-rw-rw-r--   1 qtss  admin  1090897 18 Feb  2004 sample_100kbit.mov
-rw-rw-r--   1 qtss  admin   947775 18 Feb  2004 sample_100kbit.mp4
-rw-rw-r--   1 qtss  admin  2990345 18 Feb  2004 sample_300kbit.mov
-rw-rw-r--   1 qtss  admin  3344372 18 Feb  2004 sample_300kbit.mp4
```

To test your server, open the QuickTime Player, and then choose File, Open URL in New Player. You will be prompted for a URL; enter a string formatted as `rtsp://`*`<your DSS name or IP>`*`/`*`<Media filename>`*, as shown in Figure 25.4.

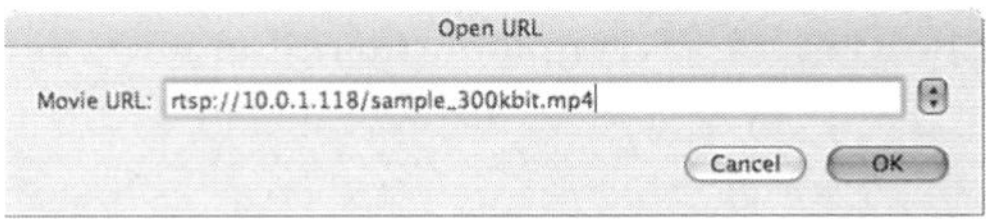

FIGURE 25.4 Enter the RTSP URL for a sample media file.

After a few seconds, the media clip should start streaming to your player. The sample videos included with DSS consist (at the time of this writing and quite awhile before that) of a repeating animation of the QuickTime logo—if that's what you see, you're in good shape.

TIP

If you do *not* see the video, make sure that the Tiger firewall is disabled and that you are not attempting to stream over port 80 while running Personal Web Sharing. I've found that a reboot is also required after installing the server even though it appears to be running correctly after the setup assistant has finished.

TIP

By default, only the `/Library/QuickTimeStreaming/Movies` directory is enabled for streaming. If you want to provide streaming services for users from their `~/Sites` directory, use the `createuserstreamingdir` *`<username>`* script provided in the `/Library/QuickTimeStreaming/Config/` directory. For example, to add a `Streaming` directory to my (`jray`) `Sites` directory, I could do the following:

```
$ sudo /Library/QuickTimeStreaming/Config/createuserstreamingdir jray
```

```
examining the home directory for ~jray
home directory path = /Users/jray
/Users/jray/Sites/Streaming is ready for streaming.
```

Preparing Media for Streaming

With Darwin Streaming Server installed, you're ready to begin publishing streaming videos. Unfortunately, you can't just add a file to the `/Library/QuickTimeStreaming/Movies` directory and expect DSS to serve it properly. Only movie files that have been *hinted* can be streamed. Hinting stores the necessary information in the movie file (called a *hint track*) so that DSS knows how to handle the interactions during streaming without needing to process the video itself.

NOTE

MP3 files do not require hinting to be streamed. All other `.mov` or MPEG-4 files must be hinted.

There are several ways you can hint your movie files. The first and easiest method is to use iMovie HD's Share feature: Select QuickTime, and then choose Web Streaming, as shown in Figure 25.5. Doing so will reduce the framerate and size of the video to what Apple considers acceptable—presumably for streaming from a .Mac account.

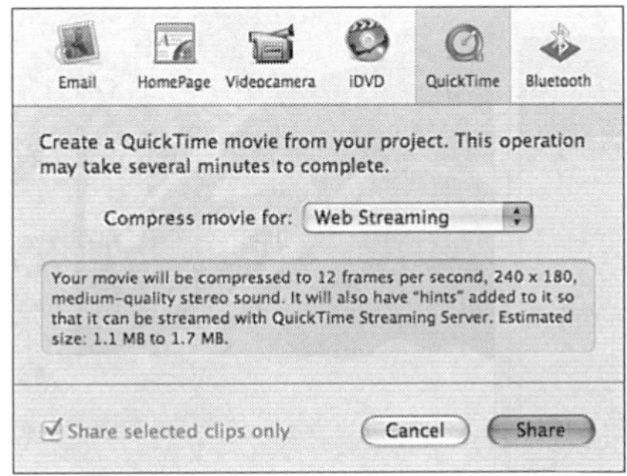

FIGURE 25.5 iMovie can quickly save a project in a stream-ready format.

The resultant hinted file can be saved to the streaming media directory and used immediately.

Exporting with the Default Codec

If you want more control over the export process, you can use either the Expert QuickTime Sharing option (File, Share, QuickTime) within iMovie HD, or use the Pro (registered) version of QuickTime Player to accomplish the same thing (File, Share).

When exporting manually in this manner, you should see an Export pop-up menu with the option Movie to Hinted Movie. Selecting this option and clicking Save, as demonstrated in Figure 25.6, will create a hinted movie without re-encoding the movie or changing any of its original characteristics.

FIGURE 25.6 You can quickly created a hinted version of an existing media file.

To optimize the hinted movie, click Options. The Hint Exporter Settings will be displayed, as shown in Figure 25.6. Unless you have very limited storage, be sure to enable the Optimize Hints for Server checkbox. This will result in a significantly larger movie file, but one that can be dealt with more efficiently by the server, enabling higher throughput and responsiveness.

From this dialog, you can also disable the audio or video tracks for the stream and configure several Track Hinter settings. The Hinter settings are used to force a packet size and duration for the resulting movie file. If you know the characteristics of your target network, you can change these values appropriately. The defaults, however (typically 1450 bytes and 100ms), should be sufficient for most clients connected via cable and xDSL or faster.

NOTE

The Track Hinter settings also enable you to change the RTP payload encoding (that is, how the video and audio tracks will be encoded). You can choose between the native encoder of the codec and a generic QuickTime encoder. Unless the codec documentation states otherwise, you should always use native encoding.

The trouble with exporting to a hinted file without re-encoding is that many movie files might not be appropriate for streaming. Assuming that the video is the product of an iMovie or an import from your video camera, it is likely in a straight DV (digital video) format and at a much higher resolution than what is appropriate for network streaming.

For the greatest compatibility, you should export the video to a format that is bandwidth friendly and compatible with as many playback devices and software products as possible: MPEG-4. MPEG-4 is an international standard created by the Motion Picture Experts

Group and supported natively by many popular audio/video frameworks on Windows, Linux, and (obviously), the Macintosh platform. Extensive information about MPEG-4 is available at `http://www.m4if.org/`.

TIP

Regardless of the codec used, a single media file is unlikely to satisfy all of your potential customers. QuickTime supports the use of *reference movies* to automatically choose between different movie files depending on connection speed and other criteria. You'll learn about this shortly in the "Adapting to the Client with Reference Movies" section, later in this chapter.

Exporting to MPEG-4

Although you can certainly choose any QuickTime codec you like for streaming, you'll probably want to research the codec to determine the quality versus bandwidth trade-offs, CPU usage, viable resolutions, and so on. The MPEG-4 codec, on the other hand, was designed with streaming in mind and provides immediate feedback on your quality choices and whether they will be feasible in your deployment environment.

To export to MPEG-4, use iMovie HD's QuickTime Sharing Expert settings, or with the movie opened in QuickTime Player, choose File, Export. When prompted for the Export format, choose Movie to MPEG-4. You can then choose from several predefined output options (ranging from modem to LAN) in the Use pop-up menu, shown in Figure 25.7, or click Options for more choices.

FIGURE 25.7 Several predefined settings are available.

The manually defined options provide a greater range of bandwidth control over the exported video. There are three areas within the Settings pane: Video, Audio, and Streaming.

Video—Select the framerate and bitrate (kbits/second) for the video track. Also choose between Improved and Basic video encoding for good quality or greatest compatibility, respectively. Also available is H.264 encoding—the new standard for the highest-quality streams.

Audio—Choose the bitrate (kbits/second) for the audio track and encoding quality settings.

Streaming—Enable hinting for the file by clicking the Enable Streaming button. Choose the Optimized for Server setting for best results with DSS. If you know the specifics of your client's network, you can also adjust the packet size and duration. The defaults should be appropriate for ethernet, cable, and most xDSL deployments.

As you adjust the MPEG-4 settings, you'll notice that the bottom portion of the window updates to reflect the results of your changes. By default, QuickTime will try to conform to the *ISMA* (*Internet Streaming Media Alliance*) specifications for compatibility. Changes to the settings that violate the compatibility will be shown in this status area.

Your best strategy when setting up the MPEG-4 encoder is to conform to the ISMA standards. The Basic video track settings conform to ISMA Profile 0, enabling the widest range of device playback and compatibility. The Improved video settings use ISMA Profile 1, which trades some compatibility for quality.

If you want to provide higher-quality video than allowed by Profile 1, you should disable ISMA compatibility by choosing MP4 from the pop-up menu at the top of the window. Adjust the audio and video bitrate (and, subsequently, quality) while paying close attention to the messages provided at the bottom of the pane. The status will update to show the connection type that your settings will work with. Figure 25.8, for example, shows the results of settings that will stream correctly over a T1 line *only*. Reducing the video and/or audio bitrates reduces the requirements for the receiver.

NOTE

Apple recommends not exceeding 75% of the bitrate of the client connection. The MPEG-4 settings are a bit more lenient, but a conservative approach to bandwidth utilization will yield the best results.

After choosing your settings, click Okay, and then choose Save to export your hinted stream-ready MPEG-4 file.

Adapting to the Client with Reference Movies

For streaming to be effective, a movie must be matched with a client's available bandwidth. To this point we've only looked at how single movies can be prepared for streaming. With a captive audience (a corporate Intranet or home network), this isn't a problem. When you have clients coming in over dial-in connections and different levels of broadband, using slow and fast CPUs, a single stream won't serve the audience effectively. Furthermore, although you can certainly create different stream-ready files for different users, asking them to choose which is appropriate for them is unreasonable.

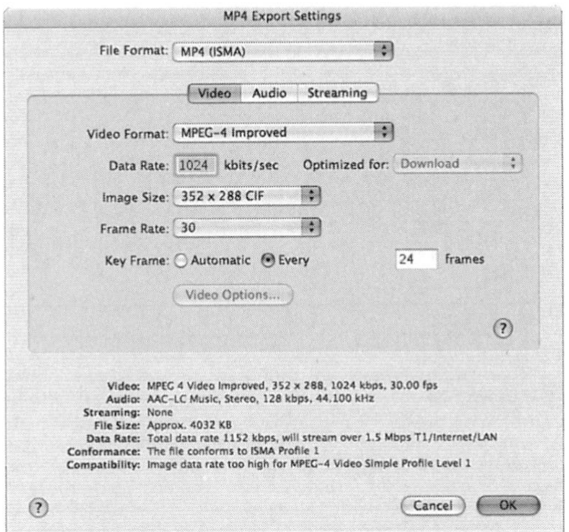

FIGURE 25.8 Choose the best bitrate for the connection type and quality you want to achieve.

In this situation, a *reference movie* can be created that uses factors such as connection speed, language, CPU Speed, and QuickTime version to determine automatically which stream is suited for a given client. Slower CPUs, for example, might be served a Sorenson-compressed `.mov` stream, whereas more capable modern machines would receive an MPEG-4.

The first step in creating a reference movie is to identify and export hinted files for all the combinations that you want to support based on the attributes of connection speed, language, CPU speed, and QuickTime version. You will also want to create a default movie that will be compatible with all players, regardless of the client attributes. After they've been created, these hinted movies should be saved in a common folder.

Your next step is to create the reference movie itself. Although this file ends in a `.mov` prefix, it is nothing more than a text file that lists media files and attributes. Even though it's possible to create the reference movie by hand, Apple offers a free tool—MakeRefMovie X—that can build the file with a simple drag-and-drop interface. Download the application from `http://developer.apple.com/quicktime/quicktimeintro/tools/index.html`.

To build the reference movie, start MakeRefMovie X. When prompted for a filename, choose the name of the `.mov` reference file that you want to create. From the client's perspective, this will be the file they are viewing; the server will deliver the correct file based on the selection criteria in the reference movie.

After you've named the file, the MakeXRef window will appear. Drag the media files you want to use into the window; they will be added to a resource listing, as shown in Figure 25.9.

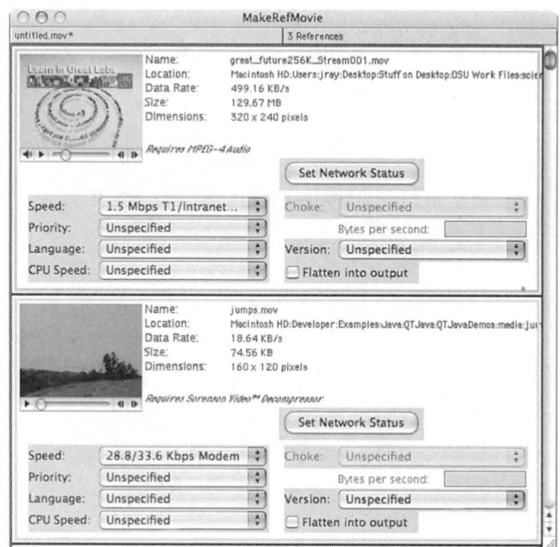

FIGURE 25.9 Add your media files to the reference movie.

For each file you've added, you can use the pop-up menus corresponding to that file's listing to set the viewing criteria. As mentioned previously, this includes network speed, language, CPU speed, and QuickTime version.

After you've chosen the files' attributes, you should also use the Priority pop-up menu to set your preferred movie order (first choice, second choice, and so on); this will serve as the final selection criteria if multiple movies match a given client's configuration.

Finally, choose your default movie (the movie that should be playable on any system configuration) by clicking the Flatten into Output button. Save your final reference movie by choosing File, Save. The resultant file should be stored in the same directory as the files it references and can be streamed like any other `.mov`—the difference being that it will adjust its output to accommodate the client's capabilities.

Applying Access Controls to Your Media

There is a level of security inherent within streaming video: Viewers cannot easily save the media coming from the streaming server. There *are* a few ways to get around this, but it is unlikely that a true 1:1 copy can be created.

Although this security keeps control of the content in your hands, it doesn't provide a mechanism to determine who can and can't access the content. To protect password-protect your files, you can use a very similar system to that of Apache and `htpasswd`, which is covered in Chapter 23, "Creating a Web Server."

Protection is applied on a per-directory basis. Access can be controlled based on user-names or groups of users, stored in the files

/Library/QuickTimeStreaming/Config/qtusers and /Library/QuickTimeStreaming/Config/qtgroups, respectively.

Password-Protecting a Directory

To password-protect a directory, simply create a plain text file named qtaccess in the directory with your media files. To protect the files with a simple username and password, add the following lines to the file:

```
AuthName "My Protected Media"
AuthUserFile /Library/QuickTimeStreaming/Config/qtusers
Require valid-user
```

The first line, AuthName, provides a message that will be displayed to the user requesting the media. The AuthUserFile keyword is used to identify the file that contains the usernames and passwords; in this case, I've used the default file /Library/QuickTimeStreaming/Config/qtusers. Finally, the last line, Require valid-user tells the system that any valid username and password may access the resources.

Before you can use your newly protected directory, you will need to create a new QuickTime user account. This is accomplished with the qtpasswd command. (If you've used Apache's protection features, you're probably experiencing déjà vu right about now.) For example, to add the user myuser with the password mypass to the default user file, you would use the following:

```
# sudo qtpasswd -p mypass myuser
Adding userName myuser
```

Now, attempting to access one of the password-protected files will display a login screen as shown in Figure 25.10.

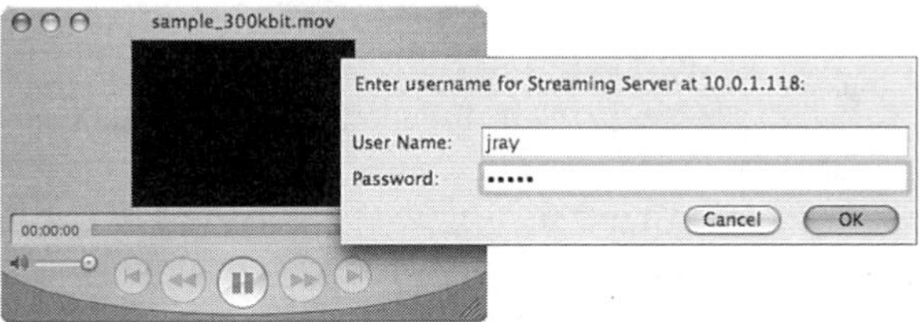

FIGURE 25.10 QuickTime will prompt for a username and password when a user tries to access a protected media file.

Managing Users and Groups

Managing many different users and the files they can access can be simplified by organizing users into groups. Just as Tiger has different groups for different capabilities, DSS can do the same. The qtpasswd command can manage users and groups easily. For example, to create a new group, training, and add the user myuser to the group, this command would be used:

```
# sudo qtpasswd -A training myuser
Adding user myuser to group training
```

Additional users can be added using `qtpasswd -A` *<groupname> <username>*.

TIP

If you ever forget or lose the DSS administrator password, you can create a new administrative user by adding a new user to the built-in `admin` group.

After the sample `training` group has been created, a `qtaccess` file similar to the following can be used to authenticate against the group:

```
AuthName "My Protected Media"
AuthUserFile /Library/QuickTimeStreaming/Config/qtusers
AuthGroupFile /Library/QuickTimeStreaming/Config/qtgroups
Require group training
```

Any user within the `training` group who provides a valid username and password will be allowed access to the media.

Unlike Apache's `htpasswd` utility, the QuickTime `qtpasswd` application provides much more management control over users and groups. Table 25.1 provides the most useful command-line switches for `qtpasswd`, using the syntax `qtpasswd` *<options> <username>*.

TABLE 25.1 Command-Line Switches for `qtpasswd`

Option	Description
`-F`	Don't ask for confirmation when deleting or overwriting information.
`-f` *<password file>*	Password file to use. If not specified, the default is used.
`-g` *<groups file>*	Group file to use. If not specified, the default is used.
`-p` *<password>*	Specify a password at the command-line rather than prompting for it.
`-d` *<username>*	Delete a username from the password file and all associated groups.
`-A` *<group>*	Add a username to a group. The group is added if necessary.
`-D` *<group>*	Delete a user from a group.
`-C` *<group>*	Create a new group. When using this option, you should *not* include the final username parameter.
`-R` *<group>*	Remove a group. When using this option, you should not include the final username parameter.

Additional `qtaccess` Options

You've seen that the media can be protected based on users and groups. The `qtaccess` file format offers a few additional options that can even further refine your authentication settings. These are described in Table 25.2.

TABLE 25.2 Additional Authentication Options for `qtaccess`

Option	Description
AuthName "<*message*>"	Choose a message that will be displayed in the authentication dialog.
AuthUserFile <*userfile path*>	The full path to the user file to use for authentication.
AuthGroupFile <*groupfile path*>	The full path to the group file to use for authentication.
require user <*username 1*>	Require one of the users specified on the line to log in. <*username 2*> ... <*username n*>
require group <*groupname 1*> <*groupname 2*> ... <*groupname n*>	Require a user in one of the groups specified to log in.
require any-user	Allow any user to access the resource without a username or password.
require valid-user	Allow any validated user to access the resources.
AuthScheme [basic¦digest]	Choose whether to use basic or digest authentication. Basic authentication is required for versions of QuickTime earlier than 5.0.

Working with DSS Playlists

When playing or viewing media files, there is often a logical progression that takes place through several files—all the songs in an album or all the sessions in a training workshop, for example. Rather than manually forcing the viewer to select each file sequentially or editing the files together, you can create a *playlist* that automatically joins the media. Playlists are also unique in that they are *live* streams of content. After a playlist has been created, it is started on your server. The content is in a continuous state of playback; when a user tunes in, she tunes in to the stream wherever it happens to be during playback.

Playlists are created by accessing the web interface of your streaming server (`http://`<*your server ip*>`:1220/`) and clicking the Playlists link along the left side of the web page. The Playlist management screen is displayed in Figure 25.11.

From here, you can create new MP3 playlists (for Shoutcast-compatible MP3 streams) and movie playlists, as well as edit and delete existing playlists.

Adding a Playlist

You must follow a few rules that when creating a playlist:

- MP3 files must be encoded identically.
- MP3 file playlists require streaming over port 80. If you are running Apache, this will not function correctly. You must stop Apache (Sharing Preference Pane) and enable port 80 streaming (click Port Settings in the DSS administrative website).
- Video files must use the same codec and encoding options.

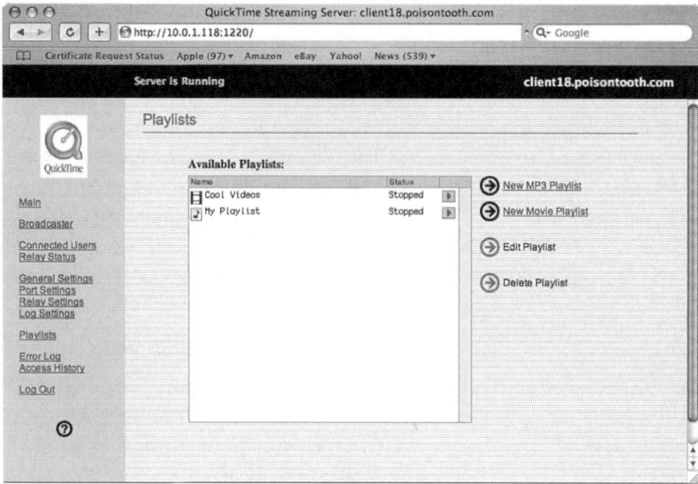

FIGURE 25.11 Use the Playlist link within the DSS administrative site to manage your playlists.

When your files meet these criteria, click the New MP3 Playlist or New Movie Playlist link along the right side of the web page. A playlist creation screen will be displayed, showing the MP3 or movie files contained in the `/Library/QuickTimeStreaming/Movies/` directory. The playlist creation screen is shown in Figure 25.12.

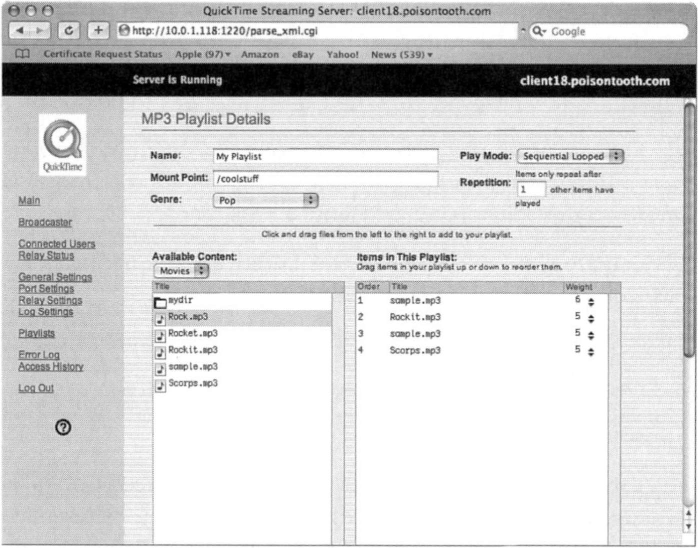

FIGURE 25.12 Create your playlists visually within the Playlists web page.

Complete the fields at the top of the page to identify and define how your playlist will function:

Name—The name of the stream. This should be a meaningful name that will be displayed to the end user. This should typically be the name of the streaming channel, such as "Ray's Streaming Garageband Songs."

Mount Point—The name by which the stream will be referenced. This should be a simple string that will be used in the URL to load the stream. For example, music published under the mount point `/mysongs` will be accessible from the URL `http://`*`<streaming server name>`*`/mysongs` within iTunes, whereas video with the mount point `/myvideos` will be made available to QuickTime Player at `rtsp://`*`<streaming server name>`*`/myvideos`.

Play Mode—Choose from the playback options Sequential Looped (one song after another, repeating after all have been played), Sequential (one song after another, ending the stream after all songs have been played), and Weighted Random (songs are chosen randomly from the playlist based on an assigned weight).

Repetition—Choose how many other files must have played before one can be repeated. This option, usefully only with the Weighted Random play mode, prevents DSS from playing one track over and over.

Genre—The musical classification for the stream (rock, alternative, classical, and so forth).

At the bottom of the page are two panes used to add and arrange content within your playlist. The list on the left displays the available media files that you can use as well as other folders within the main `Movies` directory. To move into a folder, double-click it or select it in the list and click the Open Folder arrow button at the bottom of the list. You can move to a previous folder level by using the pop-up menu at the top of the list.

To assign one or more files to your playlist, select them in the list on the left and drag them to the list on the right. After the files have been added to the playlist, the playback order (assuming that the Sequential Play mode has been selected) can be altered by dragging the items up and down within the list. Files can be removed by selecting them and clicking the Remove Item button at the bottom of the playlist.

As mentioned earlier, the Weighted Random play mode randomizes based on a file weight. Within the playback list, a weight value is shown to the right of every entry. To increase or decrease the weight, click the up arrow or down arrow to the immediate left of the value. Weights range from 1 to 10, with 10 receiving the most play time and 1 the least. Leaving the weight set to a constant value for each file indicates that no track should receive special playback priority.

To finish up your stream, enable logging using the check box Log This Playlist's Activity located at the bottom of the playlist page. Logs are stored in `/Library/QuickTimeStreaming/Logs/mp3_access.log` and `/Library/QuickTimeStreaming/Logs/StreamingServer.log` for MP3s and video, respectively, and within the playlist directories of `/Library/QuickTimeStreaming/Playlists/`. If you are creating an MP3 stream, you'll also be provided with a field from which to select the genre of audio you're streaming. This is used by the MP3 client for classification of the stream and should be set to whatever is appropriate for your broadcast. Click Save Changes to save the playlist.

NOTE

The Send This Playlist to a Broadcast Server option can be used in a multiserver setup to broadcast the stream to a second server for multicasting or unicasting. This chapter focuses on a single broadcasting system.

Starting and Stopping a Playlist

After a playlist has been created, it is stored, but isn't made available to QuickTime clients until the playlist has been *started*. Keep in mind that playlists are *live* streams. This means that they are always (assuming that they repeat!) playing some portion of the media you've set up—even if no client is connected. As such, they consume system resources and should be enabled only when you are expecting connections. Click the Playlists link on the right side of the DSS administrative website to manage your playlist streams.

As you can see in Figure 25.13, the status of each playlist (Stopped or Playing) is displayed to the right of the playlist name. By default, playlists are *not* started after they have been created.

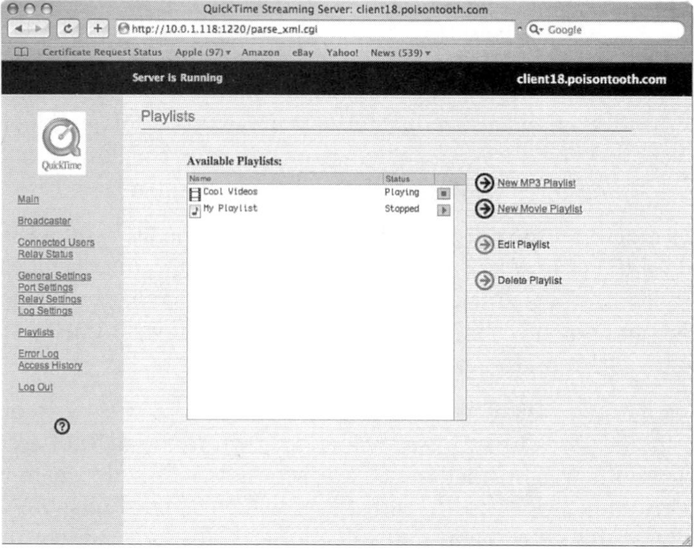

FIGURE 25.13 Use the playlist management screen to start and stop playlist streams.

To start or stop a playlist, use the Play and Stop buttons located directly to the right of their status within the playlist management screen. After a looping playlist has been started, it will not stop until you manually click the Stop button. Playlists will automatically start playing at system boot, if appropriate.

To edit or delete an existing playlist, select it in the list, and then click the Edit Playlist or Delete Playlist button as needed.

ON MOUNT POINTS AND SDP FILES

When setting up and starting a playlist, you are, in fact, creating a live stream—just as if you were capturing the media and sending it out in real-time (which you'll learn how to do in the next section). To do this, the server relies on the presence of an SDP *(Session Description Protocol)* file.

An SDP file describes the media being streamed and the requirements for receiving the stream. Although merely a text file, an SDP file is quite complex to build by hand and is usually created automatically—in this case, by the playlist manager. When you specify a mount point, its name is used to create the SDP file. Creating a video stream with the mount point of `coolvideos` will, for example, create an SDP file called `coolvideos.sdp` in the QuickTime streaming `Movies` directory.

Streaming Live Events with QuickTime Broadcaster

Much of the fun of streaming media comes from the ability to broadcast live media. DSS playlists, for example, enable you to create your own streaming music or video station and provide around-the-clock programming by continuously broadcasting a stream of predefined content. The drawback to what you've seen so far is that the media must already exist in order to be streamed.

To extend streaming to encompass live events, you need two additional components: Apple's QuickTime Broadcaster software (free) and a video input source.

Video input can come from any QuickTime-recognized video source such as an iSight, or a FireWire-equipped video camera. If you want to connect live analog video sources to your computer, products such as the Canopus ADVC110 (`http://www.canopus.us/US/products/advc110/pm_advc110.asp`) provide analog-to-DV connections. Budget-minded users might consider the InterView USB capture device that provides video input for well under $100 (`http://www.echofx.com/`).

After a video source has been established, download the QuickTime Broadcaster application from `http://www.apple.com/quicktime/download/broadcaster/`. Install the QuickTime Broadcaster package by double-clicking the `.pkg` file and following the onscreen instructions.

Running QuickTime Broadcaster and DSS from the Same Machine

There are two ways to work with QuickTime Broadcaster: either locally from the same machine as the QuickTime Streaming Server or from a remote machine the communicates directly with DSS. The benefit of running QuickTime Broadcaster directly on the DSS-enabled server is that the streaming server administration utilities are QuickTime Broadcaster–aware and can control the live stream directly through a web browser. Let's look at this approach first.

NOTE

If your machine has more than one audio and video input source, you must set the broadcast source manually within QuickTime Broadcaster (path: `/Applications/QuickTime Broadcaster.app`). See the "Running QuickTime Broadcaster Remotely" section later in this chapter for more information.

After the broadcasting application has been installed, you can create and launch a live stream using the Broadcaster link on the right side of the DSS administration web pages. After clicking the link the first time, you'll be asked whether you want to launch broadcaster, as shown in Figure 25.14.

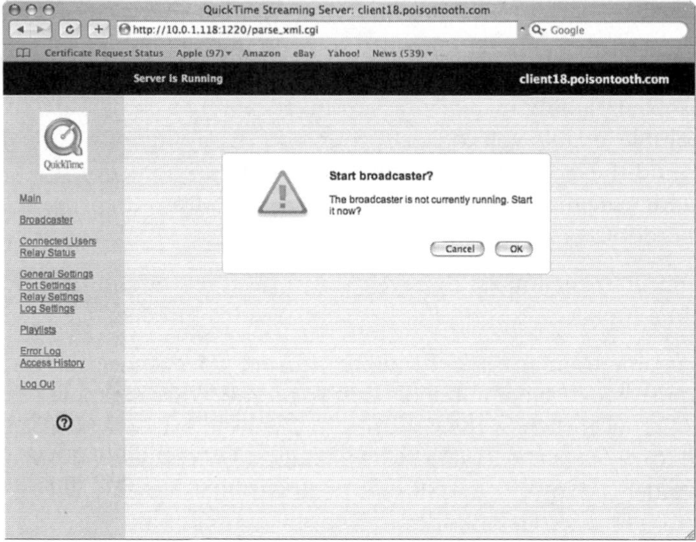

FIGURE 25.14 The DSS administration web pages can launch and control QuickTime Broadcaster.

Click OK to launch the broadcasting utility. After a few seconds, your screen should refresh to show the broadcast settings. If the settings do not appear, wait a few seconds and click OK again. I find that this is necessary about 50% of the time when using the current version of DSS and QuickTime Broadcaster. The settings screen is shown in Figure 25.15.

Use the audio and video pop-up menus to choose a preset encoding that best matches your clients network access—from modem to LAN, and the type of audio (music/speech) and video (high motion/low motion) you will be transmitting. If you want to disable the audio or video stream, uncheck the Enabled check box beside it.

Next, choose a mount point for the stream. Unlike the playlist setup, you should choose a name that includes the `.sdp` extension, such as `trainingsession.sdp`. Finally, provide a buffer delay, if any. This will force the client to buffer a certain number of seconds of video before it starts playing—this is effective smoothing over network hiccups during playback. Values of 5–15 seconds are not unreasonable.

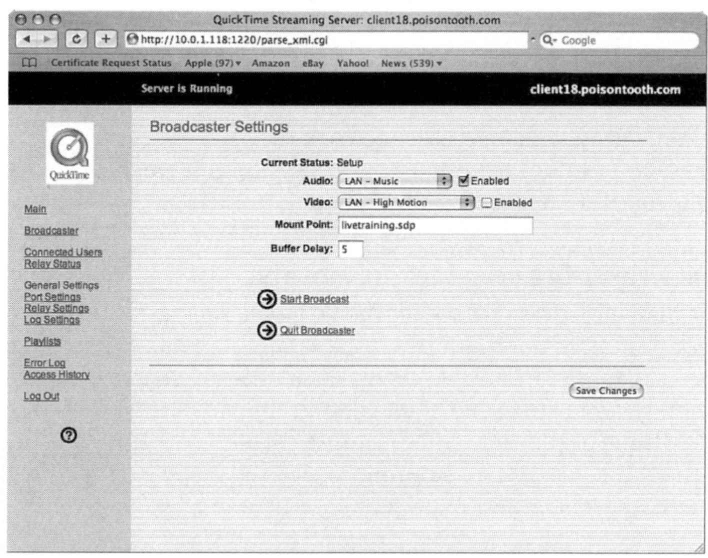

FIGURE 25.15 Customize the broadcast stream settings.

When your settings are complete, you can click the Start Broadcast button. After a few seconds, the screen will refresh to reflect the Broadcasting status, as demonstrated in Figure 25.16.

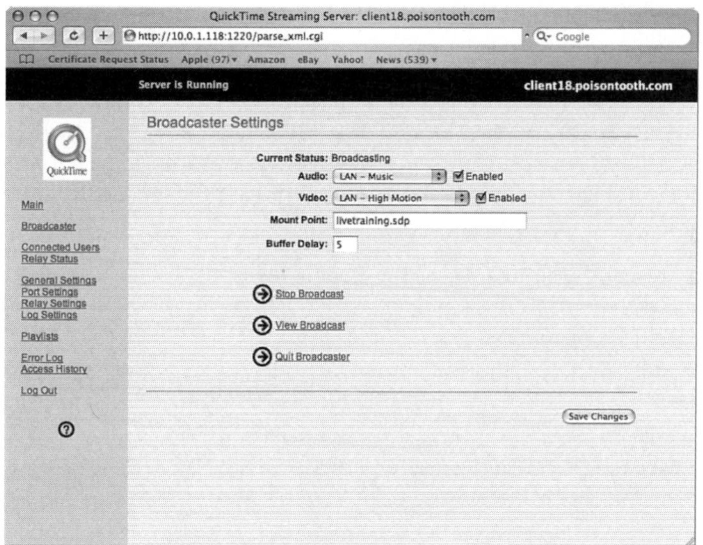

FIGURE 25.16 You are now broadcasting your video and/or audio streams live!

Your broadcast is now live and accessible via the mount point you specified. For example, when using the `trainingsession.sdp` mount point, the streaming URL would become `rtsp://<streaming server hostname>/trainingsession.sdp`.

To view the stream within your web browser, click the View Broadcast button below the broadcast settings. You can use the other buttons to stop the broadcast or Quit QuickTime Broadcaster altogether.

Running QuickTime Broadcaster Remotely

Managing QuickTime Broadcaster through the DSS web interface is nice, but it isn't always practical to run both applications on the same computer. When broadcasting a special event from a laptop or multiple events from different locations, it makes more sense to have a central streaming server and allow remote QuickTime Broadcaster applications to interact with it. To do this, you must first enable QuickTime Broadcaster to write its SDP file on the DSS server. When running locally, this happened automatically, but remote access requires the creation of a special username and password.

Granting Rights to QuickTime Broadcaster

To advertise a stream, QuickTime Broadcaster must have write access to the directory were the SDP file is located—typically `/Library/QuickTimeStreaming/Movies`. Earlier you learned how to create a `qtaccess` file to restrict user access to a directory. Now you're going to use that same file to provide additional user rights to a broadcaster user. To begin, create a new user, such as `broadcaster`, by using `qtpasswd`:

```
# sudo qtpasswd -p mypass broadcaster
Adding userName broadcaster
```

This adds the new user `broadcaster` with the password `mypass` to the `qtusers` file. You must now modify access to the `Movies` directory so that `broadcaster` has write permissions and everyone else can continue to retrieve movie streams and other files as normal. To do this, create a new `qtaccess` file in `/Library/QuickTimeStreaming/Movies/` with the following contents:

```
AuthUserFile /Library/QuickTimeStreaming/Config/qtusers
<Limit WRITE>
require user broadcaster
</Limit>
Require any-user
```

This modified `qtaccess` file provides write permissions to the `broadcaster` user while maintaining normal access for everyone else. You are now ready to create a remote broadcast.

Setting Up a Broadcast

To begin, open QuickTime Broadcaster (path: `/Applications/QuickTime Broadcaster.app`). When the application has launched, click the Show Details button in the lower-right corner to display all the available options, as shown in Figure 25.17.

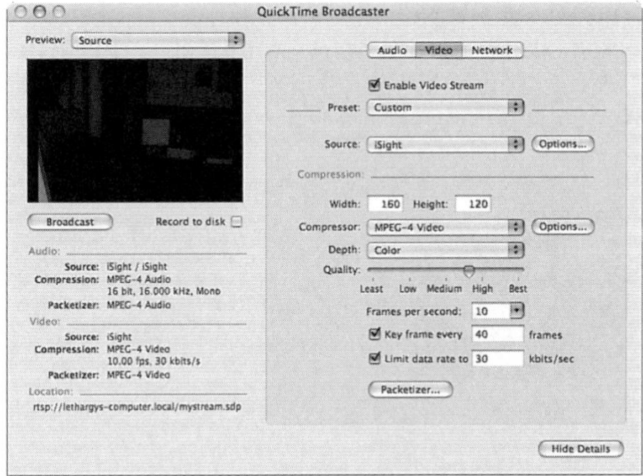

FIGURE 25.17 The QuickTime Broadcaster application provides full control over your broadcast stream.

To begin configuring QuickTime Broadcaster, review the settings within the Audio and Video portions panes, which re accessible from the buttons along the top right side of the window. Within these two areas, you can choose your audio and video sources, enable and disable their streams, and choose and adjust the codecs that will be used for the broadcast. These settings are virtually identical to the settings we looked at in the "Preparing Media for Streaming" section earlier in this chapter.

For greatest compatibility, using the MPEG-4 compressor for both audio and video is recommended. The Preset pop-up menu at the top of the Audio and Video panes will automatically configure MPEG-4 settings based on the type of audio (music/speech) or video (low/high motion) to be streamed and network access method of your clients. If you choose to change any of the settings, you can use the Save Preset option under the Preset pop-up menu to name and add your customized settings to the menu.

TIP

Your best bet for achieving the highest quality video is to start with the preset that best matches your broadcast environment, and then access the stream from a client computer to view the results. If the stream plays perfectly, increase the quality using the slider within the video pane, and view the stream again. Conversely, if there are obvious problems during playback, decrease the quality until the stream plays acceptably. Experiment with the audio and video quality to achieve the best possible stream for your transmission medium.

TIP

The top-left corner of the QuickTime Broadcaster window displays a preview of the source. You can use the Preview pop-up menu to toggle this to a compressed view of the source to get a better impression of what the final stream will look like.

After you've chosen your audio and video settings, you must configure QuickTime Broadcaster to talk to your streaming server. To do this, click the Network button to display the Network settings pane, shown in Figure 25.18. You should *always* use the Automatic Unicast (Announce) transmission type.

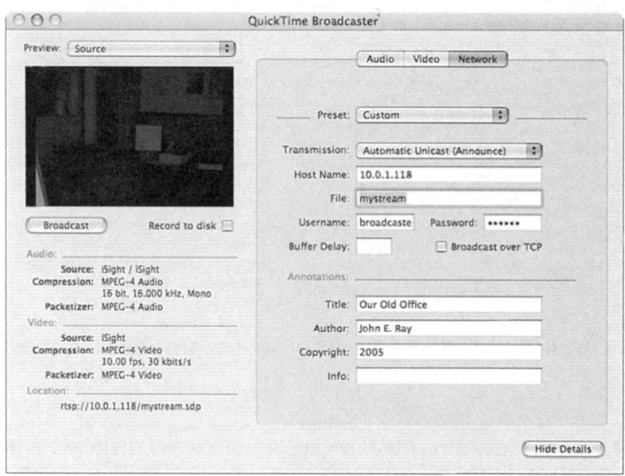

FIGURE 25.18 The Network settings pane is used to configure access to the streaming server.

Enter the information that describes your streaming server: hostname or IP *(Internet Protocol)* address, the file (or mount point) to advertise the stream, and the username and password to access the streaming server. For example, my streaming server is hosted on the IP address `10.0.1.118` and I'd like to use the file `mystream.sdp` as the mount point for the stream. The username and password are the same as what I set up earlier: `broadcaster` and `mypass`, respectively. You can also enter a stream buffer value in seconds; doing so will force the client to buffer *n* seconds of the stream before it starts playing, which should help to eliminate any network slowdown problems. A value of 5–15 seconds is reasonable and recommended. One final network setting is the option to stream over TCP *(Transmission Control Protocol)*; this can result in a higher-quality stream, but with a greater chance of network-induced jitter. After the broadcast has started, the stream will be accessible at `rtsp://10.0.1.118/mystream.sdp`.

Because network streams can be launched from virtually anywhere without a client necessarily knowing who created the stream or what it is, the bottom of the Network pane provides several fields that you can fill in to describe your content and its creator. This is purely optional, but completing it will help provide information to the end user and will serve to brand the content and clear up any potential copyright confusion.

Starting and Storing a Broadcast

You are now ready to begin broadcasting your live stream. Directly below the preview in the upper-left corner is the Broadcast button; clicking it will create the necessary SDP file on your remote DSS server and start broadcasting.

Before starting, however, you might want to archive the broadcast so that it can be streamed statically from your DSS at a later date. If the stream is not stored, there is no way to retrieve and view the broadcast again after it has completed.

To store a broadcast, first open the QuickTime Broadcaster preferences. Use the Recording settings to choose a path for the saved media file along with the name you want to use. Make sure that the Hint for Streaming Server checkbox is selected so that the resulting file will be ready for streaming. Click OK to save the preferences. Finally, enable the Record to Disk checkbox beside the Broadcast button.

You can now click the Broadcast button to begin streaming live video and/or audio to your server. Statistics of the broadcast (frames per second, bandwidth, and so forth) will be displayed directly below the preview video during the stream. Click the Stop button to end transmission. Your broadcasting station and server are now complete.

TIP

After you've configured everything to your liking, use File, Save Broadcast Settings to set the default state for QuickTime Broadcaster. You can also click the Hide Details button to simplify the display and provide an easy start/stop interface for creating future broadcasts.

Embedding QuickTime into Web Pages

To finish this chapter, let's quickly look at how you can embed streaming movies into a web page. Although you already know how to load them in QuickTime Player, chances are good that not all of your audience will know how. Providing access to content by simply visiting a web page is a far simpler approach to streaming to the masses.

For example, to embed a single movie named `mymovie.mov` with a height and width of 320×240, you could use the following:

```
<OBJECT CLASSID="clsid:02BF25D5-8C17-4B23-BC80-D3488ABDDC6B" WIDTH="320"
➥HEIGHT="256"
 CODEBASE="http://www.apple.com/qtactivex/qtplugin.cab">
 <PARAM name="SRC" VALUE="mymovie.mov">
 <PARAM name="AUTOPLAY" VALUE="true">
 <PARAM name="CONTROLLER" VALUE="true">
 <EMBED SRC="mymovie.mov" WIDTH="320" HEIGHT="256" AUTOPLAY="true"
 ➥CONTROLLER="true"
 ➥PLUGINSPAGE="http://www.apple.com/quicktime/download/">
 </EMBED>
</OBJECT>
```

As you look at this sample, you'll probably notice several unusual things about the code. First, the height is set to `256` instead of `240`. This is to provide 16 pixels for the display of the movie controller (activated by setting the `CONTROLLER="true"` attribute). Second, you'll notice that the code appears to provide the same information twice

(SRC="mymovie.mov" and name="SRC" VALUE="mymovie.mov", for example). This repetition is necessary to create an embedded movie that is compatible with both Netscape/Mozilla browsers (the EMBED tag portion) *and* the current releases of Internet Explorer on Mac OS X and Windows platforms (the OBJECT tag section). Lovely, isn't it?

Within the code, the CLASSID, CODEBASE, and PLUGINSPAGE attributes should never change. The additional attributes, such as SRC, AUTOPLAY, and CONTROLLER are used, respectively, to set the movie source, whether it should play automatically, and whether the movie controller should display as well. For each movie attribute, you must include it within the OBJECT *and* the EMBED tag. For example, the attribute CONTROLLER (if used) must appear as a line like this within the OBJECT tags:

```
<PARAM name="CONTROLLER" VALUE="[true¦false]">
```

and as an attribute within the EMBED tag:

```
<EMBED ... CONTROLLER="[true¦false]"... >
```

There are *many* attributes available for use when embedding a movie. The entire list is documented at http://www.apple.com/quicktime/authoring/embed2.html, but the most useful are provided in Table 25.3.

TABLE 25.3 Attributes for Controlling the Appearance and Function of an Embedded QuickTime Player

Attribute	Description
href="*<movie URL>*"	Provides a link to a movie that will be played when the SRC-specified movie is clicked. When using the href attribute, the SRC movie is usually created as a single-frame still image.
autoplay="[true¦false]"	When set to true, this attribute causes the player to automatically play the referenced SRC movie.
bgcolor="*<html color>*"	Sets a color to be used for the background of any space not taken up by an embedded movie.
controller="[true¦false]"	Used to toggle the display of the QuickTime controller. If the controller is displayed, you must add 16 pixels to the height of the movie.
height="*<height in pixels>*"	The height tag is a required attribute that specifies the height in pixels of the embedded movie display area.
width="*<width in pixels>*"	A required attribute the sets the width, in pixels, of the embedded movie display area.
loop="[true¦false¦palindrome]"	If set to true, this attribute causes a movie to loop continuously. When set to palindrome, the movie will play forward and backward, repeatedly.
playeveryframe="[true¦false]"	This attribute, when true, forces the player to display every frame of the referenced video, regardless of the speed issues this might cause.

TABLE 25.3 Continued

Attribute	Description
pluginspage="http://www.apple.com/quicktime/download/"	Sets the page to which browsers are directed if they do not have the QuickTime plug-in.
scale="[#¦tofit¦aspect]"	Scales the video output to the height and width tags (tofit), to the specified height and width while maintaining the aspect ratio (aspect), or, to a scaling value (2 for double size, and so on).
src="<*URL*>"	The URL for the source material to display. The source can be a movie file, SDP file, or a reference movie.
target="QUICKTIMEPLAYER"	If set, the movie will be launched in QuickTime Player rather than the browser.
volume="[0-100]"	Sets the initial volume for the movie playback, with 0 being mute and 100 being the loudest.

Summary

Streaming video is an increasingly popular form of content distribution. In this chapter, you learned how to set up and work with the Darwin Streaming Server (also known as *QuickTime Streaming Server*). DSS can stream static and video and audio files or live playlists. When coupled with the free QuickTime Broadcaster, DSS can provide live video streaming.

From web browsers to cell phones, QuickTime and the Darwin Streaming Server can easily (and certainly cost effectively) provide the capabilities that you need.

CHAPTER 26

Creating a Mail Server

IN THIS CHAPTER

The Unix operating system started the email phenomenon by running the servers that first brought mail to the electronic age. Tiger continues the tradition by bundling the full-featured server Postfix with every copy of Tiger. It can provide email services for a small workgroup or an entire corporation.

This chapter explores the steps needed to activate your dormant Postfix installation and implement basic security features. In addition, you'll learn how to install POP3 (*Post Office Protocol)* and IMAP *(Internet Message Access Protocol)* servers to deliver email to client computers across a network.

The Risks of Running a Mail Server

The first step in running a successful email server is determining that you actually *need* an email server. Unlike more basic services, such as Apache, email is a more intrusive process that enables complete strangers to store information on your computer. In addition, administration of an email server is an ongoing process. Monitoring and detecting problems is a must. Email has been around for more than 20 years, but it's still growing and evolving. Because it is one of the most highly utilized pieces of software on the Internet, it is also one of the most prone to attacks.

Mail server security is unlike basic server security because it occurs on two levels. First, you must protect the physical server software from being exploited. Remote users have found numerous holes in sendmail (included in earlier versions of Mac OS X) that enabled them to gain unauthorized access. Monitoring server logs for unexplained connections and abnormal mail transmissions is standard practice. This aspect of mail server security ought to seem familiar because it should be a common practice for other basic system services, such as FTP or HTTP.

The second security problem is mail server abuse. This doesn't necessarily equate to compromising the email server, but the results can be even more far-reaching. Email spam, for example, is the result of poorly implemented email security. In the case of spam, there are two possible problems. The first is that an authorized user is inappropriately using your email resources; the second is that an unauthorized user is taking advantage of an open relay on your mail server to do the work of distributing his or her spam.

In both cases, the result is the same. The second scenario is the most serious when considering the security of your network. It is much akin to hacking but without necessarily needing to exploit any program flaws on your system.

WHAT IS AN OPEN RELAY?

An *open relay* is an SMTP *(Simple Mail Transfer Protocol)* server that accepts and delivers mail for any user from any user. Mail servers should be configured to allow only certain clients to send email; otherwise, they can be used by anyone in the world to send spam or other harmful data.

For these reasons, you should seriously consider alternatives to running your own mail server. Users in need of controlling their own email accounts and the privacy of storing their own messages, or requiring complex mail relaying or automated processing are the best candidates for running their own server.

A properly configured server requires little maintenance and will perform well on Tiger. An improperly configured server, however, could be a disaster.

Activating the Built-in Tiger Postfix Mail Server

Many Unix and Unix-like distributions ship with sendmail as the primary message transfer agent *(MTA)*. Apple has instead chosen to shift Mac OS X to the Postfix server, often considered to be superior to the sendmail monstrosity. To quote the author of Postfix:

> Postfix attempts to be fast, easy to administer, and secure, while at the same time being sendmail compatible enough to not upset existing users. Thus, the outside has a sendmailish flavor, but the inside is completely different.

Many people are hesitant to move away from mainstream software such as sendmail, but Postfix has gained a following as one of the easiest and most stable Unix SMTP servers available. Better yet, it installs as a drop-in sendmail replacement, meaning that any other software or scripts that rely on sendmail (such as CGI scripts) can use it to function without additional modifications. Postfix supports Mac OS X, integrates with NetInfo, and is much easier to configure than sendmail.

Assuming that you've decided to create a mail server, the first step is to turn on the server application itself. Tiger includes the Postfix software, but it is not activated when the system first boots.

TIP

The assumption is made that the Tiger machine you're going to use as a mail server already has a registered hostname. If this is not the case, be sure to register with a domain name system *(DNS)* before continuing. In addition to the standard A record *(address record),* a mail server typically also registers an MX record *(message exchange record)* for the base-level domain. For example, although the server `postoffice.ag.ohio-state.edu` receives mail for accounts addressed directly to itself, there also is an MX record set up for `ag.osu.edu` that points to `postoffice.ag.ohio-state.edu`. This enables mail sent to an account at `ag.osu.edu` to be sent to the `postoffice.ag.ohio-state.edu` hostname transparently.

To configure Postfix startup, you'll need to add a new StartupItem to the system. First open the file `/etc/hostconfig` in your favorite text editor. Add a line that reads `MAILSERVER=-YES-`:

```
AFPSERVER=-NO-
MAILSERVER=-YES-
AUTHSERVER=-NO-
AUTOMOUNT=-YES-
CUPS=-AUTOMATIC-
...
```

Next, you'll need to restore the Postfix StartupItem files removed from Tiger. Create a new directory, `/System/Library/StartupItems/Postfix`. Add two files to this directory. The first, `Postfix`, should hold these contents:

```
#!/bin/sh

. /etc/rc.common

StartService ()
{
    if [ "${MAILSERVER:=-NO-}" = "-YES-" ]; then
            ConsoleMessage "Starting mail services"
            /usr/sbin/postfix start
    fi
}

StopService ()
{
        ConsoleMessage "Stopping Postfix mail services"
        /usr/sbin/postfix stop
}

RunService "$1"
```

The second file, `StartupParameters.plist`, should be edited to contain:

```
{
  Description    = "Postfix mail server";
  Provides       = ("SMTP");
  Requires       = ("Resolver");
  Uses           = ("Network Time", "NFS");
  Preference     = "None";
  Messages =
  {
    start = "Starting Postfix";
    stop  = "Stopping Postfix";
   };
}
```

Finally, in order for Tiger to recognize the StartupItem, you'll need to set the owner and group of the files to `root` and `wheel`, respectively with an absolute mode of 755:

```
brezup:jray jray $ sudo chown -R root:wheel /System/Library/StartupItems/Postfix
brezup:jray jray $ sudo chmod -R 755 /System/Library/StartupItems/Postfix
```

Configuring Basic Host Settings

When you reboot your Tiger computer, Postfix starts and runs under the user ID `postfix`. (You can also start it at any time by typing **`sudo /usr/sbin/postfix start`**.) Before you do, however, you still need to make a few more changes before the software will run correctly.

Edit the `/etc/postfix/main.cf` file now. To get up and running quickly, you need to tell Postfix what your server's hostname and domain are by using the `mydomain` and `myhostname` directives.

Look for the `myhostname` and `mydomain` lines, both of which are initially commented out with the # character. Uncomment both of the lines and change them to accurately reflect the state of your server and network. For example, my server is `mail.poisontooth.com` on the domain `poisontooth.com`. Thus, my `mail.cf` file contains the following (noncontiguous) lines:

```
myhostname = mail.poisontooth.com

mydomain = poisontooth.com
```

NOTE

After assignment, these setting variables (`myhostname`, `mydomain`) can be referenced with a dollar sign ($) in other configuration directives as discussed in the "Fine-tuning a Postfix Configuration" section later in this chapter.

Removing Apple's Limitations

Apple has intentionally included several lines at the end of the main.cf file that limit the capabilities of the Postfix server if it is activated. This is out of concern for security, but given that you've chosen to run a mail server, you should be willing to accept the obvious risks.

To remove the blocks, scroll to the end of the main.cf file and look for the lines which look similar to this:

```
# THE FOLLOWING DEFAULTS ARE SET BY APPLE
#
# bind to localhost only
#
#inet_interfaces = localhost

# turn off relaying for local subnet
#
#mynetworks_style = host

# mydomain_fallback: optional domain to use if mydomain is not set and
# myhostname is not fully qualified.  It is ignored if neither are true.
#
mydomain_fallback = localhost

# The mailbox_size_limit parameter controls the maximal size of a
# mailbox or maildir file (in fact, it limits the size of any file
# that is written to upon local delivery) The default is 50 MBytes.
# This limit must not be set smaller than the message size limit.
#
#mailbox_size_limit = 0
```

Comment out all the directives except for mydomain_fallback = localhost as shown in this example. If these lines are *not* commented out, Postfix will only run on the localhost interface, accept email only from itself, and have a mailbox size of zero—not a very effective server. Save main.cf after you've made your changes.

Verifying the Postfix Setup

Your Postfix servershould now be ready to run. To verify the configuration, run sudo /usr/sbin/postfix check to test for errors in your setup. Start the server itself by rebooting or typing **sudo /usr/sbin/postfix start**.

```
brezup:jray jray $ sudo /usr/sbin/postfix start
postfix/postfix-script: starting the Postfix mail system
```

Verify that Postfix is running by telneting to port 25 on your server computer. Use the QUIT SMTP command to exit:

26

```
brezup:jray jray $ telnet localhost 25
Trying 127.0.0.1...
Connected to localhost.poisontooth.com.
Escape character is '^]'.
220 client1.poisontooth.com ESMTP Postfix
QUIT
```

Assuming that your system responds similarly, everything has gone according to plan, and you're ready to fine-tune the Postfix system. For simple setups, this might be as far as you need to go. Postfix automatically configures itself to relay for only those machines on the same class subnet to which you're connected. All others are denied.

Congratulations. Your computer is now running an enterprise-class SMTP server.

Fine-tuning a Postfix Configuration

All the Postfix configuration we'll look at is done in the `/etc/postfix/main.cf`, and options within `main.cf` consist of lines in the form

```
<setting>=<value>[,<value>]
```

where *<setting>* is one of the Postfix directives, and *<value>* is a simple setting (such as a hostname, timeout value, and so on), a path to a hash file, such as `hash:/etc/aliases`, or, in the case of Mac OS X, a NetInfo path, such as `netinfo:/aliases`. In some cases, lists of values can be used, separated by commas.

A *hash file* is a binary lookup table that holds key and value pairs. There are two specific types of hash files you'll be interested in with Postfix: map files and alias files, generated with the `postmap` or `postalias` command, respectively.

Alias files contain *<key>* and *<value>* fields, separated by a colon (:) and whitespace, such as this example `/etc/postfix/aliases` file:

```
postmaster: root
operator: jray
admin: jray
```

All other hash files simply contain *<key>* and *<value>* fields separated by whitespace. The `postalias` command works exclusively on alias files, whereas `postmap` is used to generate all other hash files.

To use the Postfix utilities to generate hash files from the corresponding text file, type either **`postmap`** ***<text file>*** or **`postalias`** ***<alias text file>***. Within a few seconds, a binary hash will be created in the same location as the original file, with the extension `.db`.

Defining Local Domain Names

If your mail server has several different domain names that are capable of receiving mail, you must explicitly list them using the `mydestination` Postfix directive; otherwise, mail to any name other than your server's primary domain name will be rejected.

Add a line to the `main.cf` file with all the names for which your mail server should accept email. For example, I want to be able to accept email for `poisontooth.com`, `mail.poisontooth.com`, and `mail.shadesofinsanity.com`. Each of these hostnames' DNS entries points directly to the server. By default, the names `$myhostname` and `localhost.$mydomain` are used—so when adding new names, be sure to add the defaults back in as well.

To make sure that Postfix accepts email for all the names, my `mydestination` directive would look like this:

```
mydestination = $myhostname, localhost.$mydomain,
➥poisontooth.com, mail.poisontooth.com, mail.shadesofinsanity.com
```

Creating Account Aliases

Aliases provide simple mailing list functionality, enable users to receive email under multiple names, and forward messages to another email account. Aliases are added to the file `/etc/postfix/aliases`. The aliases file contains lines with the username that will receive email, followed by a colon, and then the email address (local or remote) that should get the message:

```
<email username>: <recipient email address>
```

For example:

```
webmaster: jray
jraywork: ray.30@osu.edu
root: jray, hlaufman
```

After editing, the aliases hash file must be rebuilt by running `newaliases` at the command line or `postalias /etc/postfix/aliases`. If the database is not rebuilt, Postfix will not notice the changes you've made.

In this simple aliases file, email addressed to `Webmaster` would be sent to the local user `jray`, whereas email addressed to `jraywork` would be forwarded to the account `ray.30@osu.edu`. Finally, any messages sent to `root` would be automatically sent to both `jray` and `hlaufman`—two local-user accounts.

To simplify and modularize aliases that direct email to multiple users, you can include files that list several email addresses. Consider a line such as

```
job-info: :include:/etc/mail/job.list
```

When this entry is added in the aliases file, it includes the list of email addresses in the file `/etc/postfix/job.list`. This is a convenient way to create a mailing list with little work.

Mac OS X's Postfix implementation offers an alternative way to add mail aliases: via the NetInfo database system. This results in a setup that isn't directly transferable to other Unix systems, but allows you to use the NetInfo Manager and `nicl` command-line utility to quickly add aliases.

To add aliases directly to the `/aliases` directory within the NetInfo database, you must first create a NetInfo directory with the name of the alias and then add a member's key with the appropriate alias information. Think of this as splitting the lines in the alias file on the first colon (:) character. The information to the left of the : is the NetInfo alias name, and the information to the right is the member name. For example, consider this line as it appears in `/etc/mail/aliases`:

```
jraywork: ray.30@osu.edu
```

This information could be added directly to NetInfo using

```
brezup:jray jray $ sudo nicl / -create /aliases/jraywork
brezup:jray jray $ sudo nicl / -append /aliases/jraywork members ray.30@osu.edu
```

The NetInfo GUI tools can be used to perform this action as well. Chapter 20, "Configuring Advanced System Features via NetInfo," discussed the use of the NetInfo Manager utility.

NOTE

Although the `/etc/postfix/aliases` file and NetInfo `/aliases` database can set up systemwide forward information for email addresses, individual users can do the same for their accounts by creating a `.forward` file in their home directory (path: `~/.forward`).

Within the `.forward` file, add a single line containing the email address to which email should be forwarded.

Protecting Postfix

When you changed the `myhostname` and `mydomain` directives to enable Postfix, you edited two out of hundreds of configuration options available for use in the `/etc/postfix/main.cf` file. Table 26.1 contains a number of settings that you might find useful.

TABLE 26.1 Common Postfix `main.cf` Settings

Setting	Description
`myhostname = `*<Postfix server name>*	Sets unqualified hostname for the machine running the mail server.
`mydomain = `*<Postfix server domain>*	The domain of the Postfix server.
`inet_interfaces = `*<all¦hostname¦ip,...>*	A list of the network interfaces on which Postfix is active. By default, it works on all active interfaces.
`mydestination = `*<domain name, ...>*	A list of domain names and hostnames for which Postfix accepts email. By default, Postfix accepts email for `$myhostname` and `$myhostname.localhost`. If your server accepts email for the entire domain, you should add `$mydomain` and `$myhostname.$mydomain`.

TABLE 26.1 Continued

Setting	Description
`mynetworks_style = <class¦subnet¦host>`	Sets how Postfix determines what portion of the local network it should trust for relaying. By default, the local `subnet` is trusted. To trust clients in the same class, use the `class` setting. Finally, to trust only the local computer, use `host`.
`mynetworks = <network/netmask,...>`	Used in lieu of `mynetwork_` style, `mynetworks` sets a list of network addresses that should be considered local clients. Specified in the format *network/netmask*, such as 10.0.1.1/24. This can also be set to a hash file or any of the supported Postfix table lookup methods, including a NetInfo path.
`relay_domains = <host¦domain¦file>`	A list of domains for which Postfix relays mail. The list can consist of host or domain names, files containing hostnames, or lookup tables (such as hash tables and NetInfo paths). These are in addition to the `mydestination` and `mynetworks` settings.
`local_recipient_maps = <user lookup tables>`	A list of lookup tables for usernames accepted as local for the mail server. By default, this is set to the local user accounts and any alias lookup tables that exist.
`alias_maps = <alias lookup tables>`	One or more lookup tables that contain the alias lists for the database. The defaults are `hash:/postfix/aliases` and `netinfo:/_aliases`. Remember, `postalias` is used to regenerate the alias hash file.
`home_mailbox = <mail box path>`	The path to the local mailbox files. Tiger users should use the default `/var/mail`.
`smtpd_banner = $myhostname <banner text>`	Sets banner text to be displayed when a host connects. RFC requirements state that the hostname must come at the start of the banner (`$myhostname`).
`local_destination_concurrency_limit =`	A limit on the number of local simultaneous `<limit integer>` deliveries that can be made to a single user. The default is `2`.
`default_destination_concurrency_limit =`	The number of simultaneous connections that `<limit integer>` Postfix makes to deliver mail. The default is 10. Keeping this number low can help protect against inappropriate use of your server if it is compromised. It is unlikely that your server will ever need to make 10 simultaneous connections to a single domain at a time.
`disable_vrfy_command = <yes¦no>`	Disables the `VRFY` SMTP command, which can be used by spammers to verify that an account exists on the server.

TABLE 26.1 Continued

Setting	Description
smtpd_recipient_limit = <*limit integer*>	The maximum number of recipients accepted per message. Keeping this limit low makes your server unusable for mass spam.
smtpd_timeout = <*timeout* s¦m¦h¦d¦w>	The timeout period to wait for a response from an SMTP client (in seconds, minutes, hours, days, or weeks).
strict_rfc821_envelopes = <yes¦no>	Sets a requirement for RFC821-compliant messages. If set to yes, MAIL FROM and RCPT TO addresses must be specified within <>.
smtpd_helo_required = <yes¦no>	Determines whether postfix requires the HELO or EHLO SMTP greeting at the start of a connection.
smtpd_client_restrictions = <*restrictions*>	Used to fine-tune the restrictions on the Postfix clients and can handle everything from real-time blacklisting to access control lists.
smtpd_helo_restrictions = <*restrictions*>	Used to fine-tune the restrictions on what machines are permitted within a HELO or EHLO greeting.
smtpd_sender_restrictions = <*restrictions*>	Used to fine-tune the restrictions on what machines are permitted within a MAIL FROM address.
smtpd_recipient_restrictions = <*restrictions*>	Used to fine-tune the restrictions on what machines are permitted within a RCPT TO address.

If you plan to operate a successful and secure mail server, you should learn how to control external access to Postfix. The smtpd <*object*>_restrictions directives provide a wide range of restrictions. These directives control access to the server and can be applied against client addresses, HELO/EHLO headers, and MAIL FROM/RCPT TO addresses.

Four different types of restrictions are considered here: client (smtpd_client_restrictions), helo (smtpd_helo_restrictions), sender (smtpd_sender_restrictions), and recipient (smtpd_recipient_restrictions). In addition to a standard access hash table (see /etc/postfix/access as an example), the restrictions also share some common additional restriction options, so rather than list them separately, Table 26.2 combines them.

TABLE 26.2 Common Options for Setting the smtpd Restrictions

Restriction	Description	Use In
reject_unknown_client	Reject the client if the hostname is unknown.	client, helo, sender, recipient_
reject_invalid_hostname	Reject the connection if the HELO/ELHO hostname is invalid.	helo, sender, recipient
reject_unknown_hostname	Reject the connection if the HELO/ELHO hostname does not have a matching DNS A or MX record.	helo, sender, recipient

TABLE 26.2 Continued

Restriction	Description	Use In
`reject_unknown_sender_domain`	Reject if the `HELO/ELHO` sender does not have a matching DNS A or MX record.	`sender_`
`reject_non_fqdn_sender`	Reject sender addresses that are not fully qualified.	`recipient, sender`
`reject_non_fqdn_recipient`	Reject recipient addresses that are not fully qualified.	`recipient`
`reject_rbl_client` *<RBL name>*	Rejects the connection, message, or so on, based on blacklisting DNS.	`client, helo, sender, recipient`

Let's take a look at a few examples of restrictions that can be made in your `main.cf` file.

Limiting Relaying

By default, Postfix only serves as a relay (only transmits messages) for your local subnet. This means that you can start the server without worrying about whether it will be used to send spam. As the administrator, you will, however, need to make choices on what relaying capabilities the server should have.

In a situation in which you need to relay for multiple domains or subnets, use the `relay_domains` directive to list the subnets that are allowed to transmit mail through your server. For example, assume that I want people in the subnet `192.168.10.0/24` along with those in the domain `mysaferelayusers.com` to be able to send messages via my Postfix installation. To enable this, I could add

```
relay_domains = 192.168.10.0/24, mysaferelayusers.com
```

to the `main.cf` file. If you want to break this out into a separate file, you can do so using a hash table or a simple text file with one network/domain listed per line:

```
relay_domains = $config_directory/my-safe-relay-domains
```

The file `/etc/postfix/my-safe-relay-domains` would be filled with any networks, clients, or domain names that should be allowed to use the server for relaying.

Applying Access Controls

Access controls determine who can connect to your Postfix SMTP server. Using the restriction directives, you can limit access based on the client address connection, `HELO` headers, and so on.

For example, assume that you have three possibilities for clients:

```
goodclient.mydomain.com
gooddomain.com
badbadbad.com
```

The first (goodclient.mydomain.com) is an individual host that should always be allowed; the second is a domain (gooddomain.com) that, likewise, should always be considered a valid client. The last domain (badbadbad.com) should be explicitly denied. Because these connections should be allowed or denied based on the client IP or hostname, the directive to use is smtpd_client_restrictions.

To add these controls to your server, create a new access map file, such as /etc/postfix/clientaccess, and then add these lines:

```
goodclient.mydomain.com  OK
gooddomain.com           OK
.gooddomain.com          OK
.badbadbad.com           REJECT Client not allowed
badbadbad.com            REJECT Client not allowed
```

The lines of the file are made up of a pattern (in this case, domain or client names) and an action. Domain names that begin with a period (.) match any subdomain within that domain. For restrictions that match against MAIL FROM addresses (such as smtpd_sender_restrictions), you can also provide full or partial email addresses to match and allow or reject individual senders.

In this example, two actions are used: REJECT [*rejection message*] and OK. As their names imply, the first rejects connections from the client and provides an optional error message, whereas the second allows the connection to be made. Documentation for other actions can be found in the file /etc/postfix/access.

After you've created the appropriate /etc/postfix/clientaccess file, compile it using postmap /etc/postfix/clientaccess. Finally, add the configuration line to main.cf that will impose the restriction:

```
smtpd_client_restrictions = hash:/etc/postfix/clientaccess
```

If you also want to block clients without a proper hostname, you could add the directive reject_unknown_client to the list of restrictions (refer to Table 26.2). The line for main.cf would become

```
smtpd_client_restrictions = hash:/etc/postfix/clientaccess, reject_unknown_client
```

Using Real-time Blacklisting

One of the first protection features to enable on any spam-sensitive Internet-connected Postfix server should be real-time blacklisting *(RBL)*. RBL services maintain a list of known open relay mail servers and spammers. If you enable RBL service on the mail server, it automatically checks each incoming message to determine whether it is from a known open relay or spammer. If it is, the message is returned as undeliverable.

To test for blacklisted addresses, a standard DNS lookup is performed on a specially constructed version of a hostname. For example, if you want to check the IP address 140.254.85.225 to see whether it is blacklisted, you would look up the special address

225.85.254.140.spam.dnsrbl.net. As you can probably tell, this is nothing but the IP address reversed with .spam.dnsrbl.net added to the end. If a lookup on the address *fails,* the address is not blacklisted:

```
brezup:jray jray $ host 225.85.254.140.spam.dnsrbl.net
Host 225.85.254.140.spam.dnsrbl.net not found: 3(NXDOMAIN)
```

To see an example of a successful (or blacklisted) lookup, use the IP address 127.0.0.2 or 2.0.0.127.spam.dnsrbl.net. This address, reserved for testing, should return a valid DNS lookup:

```
brezup:jray jray $ host 2.0.0.127.spam.dnsrbl.net
2.0.0.127.spam.dnsrbl.net is an alias for test.dnsrbl.net.spam.spam.dnsrbl.net.
test.dnsrbl.net.spam.spam.dnsrbl.net has address 127.0.0.4
```

Searching for RBL or RBL DNS is the easiest way to find the latest and greatest blacklisting servers that are currently active. Here are a few to try:

- spam.dnsrbl.net
- spamguard.leadmon.net
- korea.services.net
- xbl.spamhaus.org
- sbl.spamhaus.org

26

To enable RBL screening for client connections, simply use the reject_rbl_client *<RBL name>* restriction from Table 26.2. For example, to add an RBL filter using spam.dnsrbl.net to the client restrictions in the previous section, just change the line to the following:

```
smtpd_client_restrictions = hash:/etc/postfix/clientaccess, reject_unknown_client,
➥ reject_rbl_client spam.dnsrbl.net
```

Additional Information

For more information about Postfix and its operation and configuration, look into these resources:

- *Postfix,* by Richard Blum, Sams Publishing—The only printed reference specifically for Postfix, this book covers the use and configuration of the Postfix MTA in an easy-to-follow format.
- http://www.postfix.net—The Postfix home page provides links to the latest software release, FAQs, and supporting documentation.
- http://groups.google.com/groups?oi=djq&as_ugroup= mailing.postfix.users—An archive of the Postfix mailing list. (For information about subscribing to the list itself, see the Postfix home page.)

Adding Spam and Virus Protection

Modern mail servers can no longer just send and deliver mail. They must now also examine the content of a message to determine whether it poses a threat or nuisance to users. Without effective spam and virus filtering, valid email communications are likely to be overlooked in mailboxes filled with garbage.

Until recently, the only server-based solutions for spam and virus filtering were commercial packages that cost thousands of dollars. Today, two very popular open source applications are available that can quickly and easily add state-of-the-art protection to your Postfix MTA: ClamAV and SpamAssassin. ClamAV provides protection against all the latest viruses and features continuously updated virus definitions. SpamAssassin uses several techniques to identify and grade spam; it has become so popular that it forms the basis for several commercial systems, including the Barracuda Firewall.

The "glue" that attaches ClamAV and SpamAssassin to Postfix is amavisd-new. amavisd-new provides content filtering based on a plug-in architecture that recognizes both ClamAV and SpamAssassin and incorporates them into the mail transfer process. Surprisingly, this is quite straightforward to set up.

Installing SpamAssassin

SpamAssassin is installed as a Perl module (`Mail::SpamAssassin`) using the CPAN *(Comprehensive Perl Archive Network)* method introduced in Chapter 18, "Developing Applications and Widgets Using Scripting Languages." If you're familiar with the process, you know that it is highly automated—just follow this example. (If you haven't used CPAN before, you might be prompted to manually configure the system. Tell it `no` and let it automatically choose the best settings.)

```
brezup:jray jray $  sudo cpan

cpan shell -- CPAN exploration and modules installation (v1.7601)
ReadLine support available (try 'install Bundle::CPAN')

cpan> install Mail::SpamAssassin

CPAN: Storable loaded ok
LWP not available
CPAN: Net::FTP loaded ok
Running install for module Mail::SpamAssassin
Running make for F/FE/FELICITY/Mail-SpamAssassin-3.0.2.tar.gz
LWP not available
Fetching with Net::FTP:
...
```

You will be prompted to answer a few questions during the installation; for example:

```
What email address or URL should be used in the suspected-spam report
text for users who want more information on your filter installation?
(In particular, ISPs should change this to a local Postmaster contact)
default text: [the administrator of that system] jray@poisontooth.com
```

Unless the requested information is directly related to your mail server installation, simply go with the default response by pressing the Return key.

Eventually (after several minutes of tests, installation, and so forth), you should see this:

```
/usr/bin/make install  -- OK
```

SpamAssassin is now installed. The main configuration file is located in `/etc/mail/spamassassin`. You now have two choices: either install one or more of the SpamAssassin helper applications or go on to configuring SpamAssassin as-is.

SpamAssassin Helper Applications

SpamAssassin, by itself, is capable of using blacklists, header analysis, and learned content analysis to classify a message as *spam* or *ham* (not spam). It also can make use of a number of additional tools to further improve its accuracy.

At present, three products can be used by SpamAssassin: Razor (`http://razor.sourceforge.net/`), Pyzor (`http://pyzor.sourceforge.net/`), and the Distributed Checksum Clearinghouse (`http://www.rhyolite.com/anti-spam/dcc/`). These add-ons work by cataloging fingerprints of known spam. Incoming messages are fingerprinted and compared to a central database of spam. If a match is found, the message is known to be spam.

26

Because SpamAssassin understands these tools, the biggest challenge to using them is getting them on your system. Let's take a look at how to install Razor—the most popular tool of the bunch.

First, download both the agents and SDK packages from `http://razor.sourceforge.net/`. After they've been downloaded, unarchive them and enter the SDK directory:

```
brezup:jray jray $  curl -O http://voxel.dl.sourceforge.net/sourceforge/razor/
➥razor-agents-sdk-2.03.tar.gz
brezup:jray jray $  tar zxf razor-agents-sdk-2.03.tar.gz
brezup:jray jray $  cd razor-agents-sdk-2.03
```

Next, make and install the software with `perl Makefile.PL` followed by `sudo make install`:

```
brezup:jray jray $  perl Makefile.PL
Checking if your kit is complete...
Looks good
...
Writing Makefile for URI
Writing Makefile for razor-agents-sdk
```

```
brezup:jray jray $  sudo make install
cp lib/Digest/HMAC_MD5.pm ../blib/lib/Digest/HMAC_MD5.pm
cp lib/Digest/HMAC.pm ../blib/lib/Digest/HMAC.pm
cp lib/Digest/HMAC_SHA1.pm ../blib/lib/Digest/HMAC_SHA1.pm
Manifying ../blib/man3/Digest::HMAC_MD5.3pm
...
Installing /usr/local/man/man3/URI::ldap.3pm
Installing /usr/local/man/man3/URI::URL.3pm
Installing /usr/local/man/man3/URI::WithBase.3pm
...
```

Now, repeat the process for the second archive (`razor-agents`):

```
brezup:jray jray $  curl -O http://voxel.dl.sourceforge.net/sourceforge/razor/
➥razor-agents-2.67.tar.gz
brezup:jray jray $  tar zxf razor-agents-2.67.tar.gz
brezup:jray jray $  cd razor-agents-2.67
brezup:jray razor-agents-2.67 $ perl Makefile.PL
brezup:jray razor-agents-2.67 $ sudo make install
```

NOTE

If an error occurs during the compile, it is likely related to a version mismatch. You should download `Digest::SHA1` from `http://www.perl.com/CPAN/authors/id/G/GA/GAAS/Digest-SHA1-2.10.tar.gz`, unarchive it, and then use `perl Makefile.PL` and `sudo make install` to install the latest version of this component.

After the process for the second archive has finished, type **`sudo razor-client`** and Razor should create the appropriate links for the `razor-client` utility:

```
brezup:jray razor-agents-2.67 $  sudo razor-client
Creating symlink razor-client <== /usr/bin/razor-check
Creating symlink razor-client <== /usr/bin/razor-report
Creating symlink razor-client <== /usr/bin/razor-revoke
Creating symlink razor-client <== /usr/bin/razor-admin
```

Now you're ready to finish the Razor setup by creating a sitewide account that it can use. Because the `/etc/mail/spamassassin` directory already exists, you can use it as the home directory for Razor. Enter the following commands to create its working directory:

```
brezup:jray razor-agents-2.67 $  sudo razor-admin -home=/etc/mail/spamassassin/
➥.razor -discover
brezup:jray razor-agents-2.67 $  sudo razor-admin -home=/etc/mail/spamassassin/
➥.razor -create
brezup:jray razor-agents-2.67 $  sudo razor-admin -home=/etc/mail/spamassassin/
➥.razor -register
```

```
Register successful.  Identity stored in /etc/mail/spamassassin/.razor/
➥identity-ru-dl31jnY
```

Next, edit the /etc/mail/spamassassin/.razor/razor-agent.conf file and add the following line to the end of the file:

```
razorhome = /etc/mail/spamassassin/.razor/
```

After you've saved your file, Razor has been configured, registered, and ready to go. Your next step (unless you want to install another helper) is to make a few configuration changes to SpamAssassin.

Configuring SpamAssassin

SpamAssassin is configured sitewide by editing the file /etc/mail/spamassassin/local.cf. Individual users can have ~/.spamassassin/local.cf files with their own custom settings as well. To get SpamAssassin prepared for protecting your server, you have to edit the sitewide configuration file and change a few settings.

By default, /etc/mail/spamassassin/local.cf should look like this:

```
# This is the right place to customize your installation of SpamAssassin.
#
# See 'perldoc Mail::SpamAssassin::Conf' for details of what can be
# tweaked.
#
###########################################################################
#
# rewrite_header Subject *****SPAM*****
# report_safe 1
# trusted_networks 212.17.35.
# lock_method flock
```


Change the file to match the following sample. A full description of all of these options is available by typing **perldoc Mail::SpamAssassin::Conf**. The sample provided here should enable basic filtering through SpamAssassin's built-in mechanisms and Razor.

```
# This is the right place to customize your installation of SpamAssassin.
#
# See 'perldoc Mail::SpamAssassin::Conf' for details of what can be
# tweaked.
#
###########################################################################
#
always_add_headers 1
use_bayes 1
bayes_path /etc/mail/spamassassin/bayes
bayes_auto_learn 1
```

```
rbl_timeout 10
razor_timeout 20
razor_config /etc/mail/spamassassin/.razor/razor-agent.conf
required_score 9.0
```

Training SpamAssassin

As part of its heuristic approach to determining what is and isn't spam, SpamAssassin must be taught to recognize valid and invalid email. The easiest way to do this is to collect folders of spam and ham, and process them using the `sa-learn` tool. For example, assume that you've dumped messages into two directories for processing. You can load the spam into SpamAssassin with the following command:

```
sa-learn --spam -C /etc/mail/spamassassin --showdots --dir <spam path>
```

Similarly, a folder of ham can be processed with

```
sa-learn --ham -C /etc/mail/spamassassin --showdots --dir <ham path>
```

> **TIP**
>
> If your mail is stored in an `mbox` file rather than a bunch of files in a directory, use `--mbox` in the `sa-learn` command rather than `--dir` and SpamAssassin will process the messages correctly.
>
> You can use your Tiger mailboxes and messages directly by looking in the `~/Library/Mail` folder. Depending on your account type, your mailboxes might be stored in `.mbox` format or as a directory of individual message files stored under the account and mailbox name.

The key to *good* spam filtering is properly training SpamAssassin: Take the time to process as much mail of both the spam *and* ham varieties as possible. Eventually, the auto-learn feature (activated in our configuration file) will classify messages for you on its own, but to begin, you have to help out.

> **TIP**
>
> For a good collection of spam, visit `http://www.spamarchive.org/`. Spam Archive maintains a collection of user-submitted spam for analysis and testing.

Testing SpamAssassin

You should now be able to test SpamAssassin on a message to verify that it is working. To do this, pipe an existing message to the command `spamassassin -tD`. This will generate quite a bit of debug output, but should eventually give you some results on how SpamAssassin graded your message:

```
$ cat ~jray/Library/Mail/Mailboxes/INBOX.mbox | spamassassin -tD
...
Content analysis details:   (-0.4 points, 9.0 required)
```

```
 pts rule name              description
---- ---------------------- --------------------------------------------------
 0.4 SUBJ_ALL_CAPS          Subject is all capitals
-2.8 ALL_TRUSTED            Did not pass through any untrusted hosts
 2.0 PYZOR_CHECK            Listed in Pyzor (http://pyzor.sf.net/)
```

This particular message was ranked –0.4—not spam (and it wasn't). To be considered spam, a message must rate at least a `9.0` as configured in the `/etc/mail/spamassassin/local.cf` file.

Starting the SpamAssassin Daemon

SpamAssassin generally works by running a daemon process, `spamd`, and feeding it messages through a client—`spamc`. To finish your SpamAssassin installation, you should set `spamd` to launch at system startup by placing the following line in `/etc/rc` or a new StartupItem (refer to Chapter 16, "Managing System Services and Configuration," for more information or the StartupItem earlier in this chapter as an example):

```
/usr/bin/spamd -d -m 50 -H /etc/mail/spamassassin
```

Make sure that you've started `spamd` before continuing with the setup of `amavisd`.

Installing ClamAV

The second piece of our filtering puzzle is the ClamAV antivirus utility. Unlike SpamAssassin, ClamAV is a breeze to install. Download the latest source code from `http://www.clamav.net/`, unarchive it, and enter the distribution directory:

```
brezup:jray jray $  curl -O http://voxel.dl.sourceforge.net/sourceforge/clamav/
➥clamav-0.80.tar.gz
brezup:jray jray $  tar zxf clamav-0.80.tar.gz
brezup:jray jray $  cd clamav-0.80
```

Next, configure the compile with **`./configure --sysconfdir=/etc --with-user=amavisd --with-group=amavisd`**—this will prepare the software using the `amavisd` user that will be controlling ClamAV.

```
brezup:jray clamav-0.80 $ ./configure --sysconfdir=/etc --with-user=amavisd
➥--with-group=amavisd
checking build system type... powerpc-apple-darwin8.0.0b2
checking host system type... powerpc-apple-darwin8.0.0b2
checking target system type... powerpc-apple-darwin8.0.0b2
creating target.h - canonical system defines
checking for a BSD-compatible install... /usr/bin/install -c
checking whether build environment is sane... yes
checking for gawk... no
checking for mawk... no
...
```

Before compiling, you'll need to make a simple change to the source code. Within the distribution directory, edit the file `libclamav/zziplib/zzip-conf.h`. Look for the code block like this:

```
#ifdef TARGET_OS_FREEBSD
#include <sys/types.h>
#endif
```

Remove the `#ifdef` and `#endif` lines from the block, leaving only

```
#include <sys/types.h>
```

Save your changes and exit the editor.

> **NOTE**
>
> It's likely that this will be fixed sometime in the near future, so if you want to save some typing, try compiling without making the change—it just might work.

Now compile with `make` and subsequently install with `sudo make install`:

```
brezup:jray clamav-0.80 $ make
make  all-recursive
Making all in libclamav
if /bin/sh ../libtool --mode=compile gcc -DHAVE_CONFIG_H -I. -I. -I.. -I..
-I./zziplib -I./mspack  -I/usr/local/include  -g -O2 -MT scanners.lo -MD -MP
-MF ".deps/scanners.Tpo" -c -o scanners.lo scanners.c; \
then mv -f ".deps/scanners.Tpo" ".deps/scanners.Plo";
else rm -f ".deps/scanners.Tpo"; exit 1; fi
rm -f .libs/scanners.lo
...

brezup:jray clamav-0.80 $ sudo make install
Making install in libclamav
test -z "/usr/local/lib" || /bin/sh ../mkinstalldirs "/usr/local/lib"
 /bin/sh ../libtool --mode=install /usr/bin/install -c  'libclamav.la'
/usr/bin/install -c .libs/libclamav.lai /usr/local/lib/libclamav.la
/usr/bin/install -c .libs/libclamav.a /usr/local/lib/libclamav.a
ranlib /usr/local/lib/libclamav.a
...
```

We're ready to start setting up ClamAV.

Creating and Updating the Virus Definitions

Before you can test ClamAV, it has to be loaded with the latest virus definitions. The utility that manages this is called `freshclam` and should be installed in `/usr/local/bin`. Before `freshclam` can run, you must first make some changes to `/etc/freshclam.conf`.

First, comment out the line at the top that reads `Example` by placing a pound (#) sign in front of it, like this:

```
#Example
```

Next, search for the line

```
#DatabaseMirror db.XY.clamav.net
```

Uncomment this line, and then replace `XY` in the hostname with the appropriate county code for your location. (A list is available at `http://www.iana.org/cctld/cctld-whois.htm`.) A server in the United States, for example, would use this:

```
DatabaseMirror db.US.clamav.net
```

Now, update the ClamAV definitions by running `sudo /usr/local/bin/freshclam`:

```
brezup:jray jray $ sudo /usr/local/bin/freshclam
ClamAV update process started at Thu Dec 30 18:51:10 2004
SECURITY WARNING: NO SUPPORT FOR DIGITAL SIGNATURES
See the FAQ at http://www.clamav.net/faq.html for an explanation.
Downloading main.cvd [*]
main.cvd updated (version: 28, sigs: 26630, f-level: 3, builder: tomek)
Downloading daily.cvd [*]
daily.cvd updated (version: 646, sigs: 2329, f-level: 3, builder: tkojm)
Database updated (28959 signatures) from db.US.clamav.net (66.111.55.10).
```

26

Because you're obviously going to want to keep your virus definitions up to date, now is a good time to add an entry to `/etc/crontab` to run `freshclam` a few times each day. The ClamAV developers recommend adding a line something like this

```
<n> * * * * root /usr/local/bin/freshclam --quiet
```

where *<n>* is a number between 3 and 57 that isn't evenly divisible by ten. The ClamAV developers are apparently hoping to spread out traffic to their update servers as much as possible.

Testing ClamAV

You're finally ready to test ClamAV. Enter the source distribution directory again and type **`/usr/local/bin/clamscan test/*`**. You should see something like this:

```
brezup:jray clamav-0.80 $ /usr/local/bin/clamscan test/*
test/README: OK
test/clam-error.rar: RAR module failure
test/clam-error.rar: OK
test/clam.cab: ClamAV-Test-File FOUND
test/clam.exe: ClamAV-Test-File FOUND
test/clam.exe.bz2: ClamAV-Test-File FOUND
```

```
test/clam.rar: ClamAV-Test-File FOUND
test/clam.zip: ClamAV-Test-File FOUND
test/mbox/debugm.c: OK

----------- SCAN SUMMARY -----------
Known viruses: 28959
Scanned directories: 1
Scanned files: 8
Infected files: 5
Data scanned: 0.00 MB
I/O buffer size: 131072 bytes
Time: 1.907 sec (0 m 1 s)
```

You're now ready to finish the project and configure amavisd-new itself.

Installing amavisd-new

The final piece of software we need virus- and spam-protecting Postfix is amavisd-new. As much as I'd like to say this is a piece of cake, it isn't. There are a number of little steps that, if not followed closely, will bungle the whole thing. To start, you'll need to upgrade Berkeley DB, which is out of date on the shipping version of Tiger. Let's begin.

Updating Berkeley DB

Download the source distribution from `http://www.sleepycat.com` and unarchive it:

```
brezup:jray jray $ curl -O ftp://sleepycat1.inetu.net/releases/
➥db-4.3.27.NC.tar.gz
brezup:jray jray $ tar zxf db-4.3.27.NC.tar.gz
```

Next, `cd` into the `build_unix` directory within the distribution and execute `../dist/configure --prefix=/usr`:

```
brezup:jray jray $ cd db-4.3.27.NC/build_unix
brezup:jray build $ ../dist/configure --prefix=/usr
checking build system type... powerpc-apple-darwin8.0.0b2
checking host system type... powerpc-apple-darwin8.0.0b2
checking if building in the top-level or dist directories... no
checking if --disable-cryptography option specified... no
checking if --disable-hash option specified... no
checking if --disable-queue option specified... no
checking if --disable-replication option specified... no
checking if --disable-statistics option specified... no
checking if --disable-verify option specified... no
...
```

After the configure process has finished, compile with make:

```
brezup:jray build $ make
/bin/sh ./libtool --mode=compile cc -c -I. -I../dist/..
mkdir .libs
 cc -c -I. -I../dist/.. -O2 ../dist/../mutex/mut_tas.c -DPIC -o .libs/mut_tas.o
 cc -c -I. -I../dist/.. -O2 ../dist/../mutex/mut_tas.c -o mut_tas.o >/dev/null 2>&1
...
```

Finally, install with sudo make install:

```
brezup:jray build $ sudo make install
Installing DB include files: /usr/include ...
Installing DB library: /usr/lib ...
cp -p .libs/libdb-4.3.dylib /usr/lib/libdb-4.3.dylib
cp -p .libs/libdb-4.3.lai /usr/lib/libdb-4.3.la
cp -p .libs/libdb-4.3.a /usr/lib/libdb-4.3.a
...
```

You're now ready to install the dozen or so Perl modules that amavisd-new depends on.

Installing the amavisd-new Perl Dependencies

amavisd is, like SpamAssassin, Perl-based. In fact, amavisd is a simple Perl script that is copied to your computer. Unfortunately, you'll have to install a number of additional Perl modules before amavisd will run. To make life easier, cpan can automate much of the process. Enter the following commands at a command prompt:

26

```
brezup:jray jray $ sudo cpan
cpan> install Archive::Tar Archive::Zip Compress::Zlib Convert::TNEF
➥Convert::UUlib MIME::Base64 MIME::Parser Mail::Internet Net::Server Net::SMTP
➥Digest::MD5 IO::Stringy Time::HiRes Unix::Syslog BerkeleyDB
CPAN: Storable loaded ok
Going to read /Users/jray/.cpan/Metadata
  Database was generated on Thu, 30 Dec 2004 08:06:49 GMT
...
```

Perl will ask a number of questions during the installation, mostly about installing *additional* prerequisite modules. Accept the defaults and all should be well. This process will take quite some time, so be patient.

Now you're ready for amavisd-new.

Installing amavisd-new

Okay, you're not quite ready. First, you need to prepare some directories that the amavisd user can write to. Execute the following commands to create a working area within /etc/mail/amavisd and to set up /var/virusmails, which will contain quarantined virus-infected messages:

```
brezup:jray jray $ sudo mkdir -p /private/etc/mail/amavisd/db
brezup:jray jray $ sudo mkdir -p /private/etc/mail/amavisd/tmp
brezup:jray jray $ sudo mkdir -p /private/var/virusmails
brezup:jray jray $ sudo chown -R amavisd:amavisd /private/etc/mail/amavisd
brezup:jray jray $ sudo chown -R amavisd:amavisd /private/var/virusmails
brezup:jray jray $ sudo chmod 750 /private/var/virusmails
```

Now, download the amavisd-new distribution from `http://www.ijs.si/software/amavisd/`. Unarchive and enter the source directory:

```
brezup:jray jray $ tar zxf amavisd-new-2.2.1.tar.gz
brezup:jray jray $ cd amavisd-new-2.2.1
```

Because the software is distributed as a simple Perl script, your final installation step is to copy `amavisd` to `/usr/local/bin` and the `amavisd.conf` file to your `/etc` directory:

```
brezup:jray amavisd-new-2.2.1 $ sudo cp amavisd /usr/local/bin
brezup:jray amavisd-new-2.2.1 $ sudo cp amavisd.conf /etc
```

Finally (and we really mean it this time!), edit the `/etc/amavisd.conf` file, and look for lines (noncontiguous) similar to these:

```
$daemon_user  = 'amavisd';     # (no default;  customary: vscan or amavis)
$daemon_group = 'amavisd';     # (no default;  customary: vscan or amavis)

$mydomain = '<your mail domain name>';   # a convenient default for other settings

$MYHOME   = '/etc/mail/amavisd';   # a convenient default for other settings
$TEMPBASE = "$MYHOME/tmp";   # working directory, needs to be created manually
$QUARANTINEDIR = '/var/virusmails';
```

Edit the lines to reflect the values shown here, except for `$mydomain`, which should be set to your mail server domain name.

Congratulations, you've just completed the basic configuration of amavisd-new!

Testing amavisd-new

Aside from the settings you just tweaked, amavisd does a good job of finding and configuring itself. Both SpamAssassin and ClamAV should be automatically detected and used by the `amavisd` script.

To test this, execute **`amavisd debug`** as the user `amavisd`:

```
brezup:jray jray $ sudo -u amavisd /usr/local/bin/amavisd debug
Dec 30 20:09:27 pc-105.clonestem.loc /usr/local/bin/amavisd[17080]: starting.
/usr/local/bin/amavisd at pc-105.clonestem.loc amavisd-new-2.2.1 (20041222), Unicode aware
Dec 30 20:09:27 pc-105.clonestem.loc /usr/local/bin/amavisd[17080]:
```

```
user=83, EUID: 83 (83);  group=, EGID: 83 83 (83 83)
Dec 30 20:09:27 pc-105.clonestem.loc /usr/local/bin/amavisd[17080]:
Perl version                5.008004
...
Dec 30 20:09:28 pc-105.clonestem.loc /usr/local/bin/amavisd[17080]:
Found secondary av scanner ClamAV-clamscan at /usr/local/bin/clamscan
...
Dec 30 20:09:28 pc-105.clonestem.loc /usr/local/bin/amavisd[17080]:
SpamControl: initializing Mail::SpamAssassin
Dec 30 20:09:32 pc-105.clonestem.loc /usr/local/bin/amavisd[17080]:
SpamControl: done
...
```

As you can see, ClamAV is recognized as a secondary antivirus scanner, whereas SpamAssassin is identified for spam control.

There's only one more step left: tying amavisd-new to Postfix.

NOTE

If you experience MIME errors when attempting to run `amavisd debug`, download and reinstall `MIME-tools-5.417.tar.gz` from `http://www.cpan.org` following the Perl module installation instructions in Chapter 18.

Attaching amavisd-new to Postfix

To get the `amavisd` process communicating with Postfix, you should first configure `amavisd` to start at boot by placing it in `/etc/rc`, creating a new StartupItem (refer to Chapter 16), or placing it in the `/System/Library/StartupItems/Postfix` StartupItem. All you need to do to start `amavisd` is invoke it at the command line:

```
brezup:jray jray $ sudo /usr/local/bin/amavisd
```

After `amavisd` has been started, edit the Postfix file `/etc/postfix/master.cf`, and add the following lines (all of them!) to the end of the file:

```
smtp-amavis unix -      -       n       -       2       smtp
    -o smtp_data_done_timeout=1200
    -o smtp_send_xforward_command=yes
    -o disable_dns_lookups=yes

127.0.0.1:10025 inet n  -       n       -       -       smtpd
    -o content_filter=
    -o local_recipient_maps=
    -o relay_recipent_maps=
    -o smtpd_restriction_classes=
    -o smtpd_client_restrictions=
    -o smtpd_helo_restrictions=
```

```
    -o smtpd_sender_restrictions=
    -o smtpd_recipient_restrictions=permit_mynetworks,reject
    -o mynetworks=127.0.0.0/8
    -o strict_rfc821_envelopes=yes
    -o smtpd_error_sleep_time=0
    -o smtpd_soft_error_limit=1001
    -o smtpd_hard_error_limit=1000
    -o receive_override_options=no_header_body_checks
```

Save your changes, and then open `/etc/postfix/main.cf` and add this to the end of the file:

```
content_filter=smtp-amavis:[127.0.0.1]:10024
```

Reload the Postfix configuration by typing **`sudo postfix reload`**. You can verify that Postfix and amavisd-new are working correctly by telneting to ports 10025 and 10024 on your server. You should see a banner message from each.

Your server is now protected. To test it, send yourself a message. If everything is working as planned, you'll see a new header when you retrieve your email; something like this:

```
X-Virus-Scanned: amavisd-new at poisontooth.com
```

If a virus had been detected or the message graded as spam, it would be either quarantined in `/var/virusmails`, or bounced, respectively.

Fine-tuning amavisd-new Operation

To fine-tune your server, you'll want to read the amavisd-new documentation and edit the `/etc/amavisd.conf` file. For example, these lines control spam grading:

```
$sa_tag_level_deflt  = 2.0;  # add spam info headers if at, or above that level
$sa_tag2_level_deflt = 6.31; # add 'spam detected' headers at that level
$sa_kill_level_deflt = 6.31; # triggers spam evasive actions
$sa_dsn_cutoff_level = 10;   # spam level beyond which a DSN is not sent
```

By default, if a message receives a grade of `2`, spam headers are added to it. If it receives a score of 6.31 (their values, not mine), it will be bounced and not delivered. Finally, if the spam score is over 10, it will be discarded without a bounce.

You might also want to change the usernames that are used to generate bounced messages, just in case a valid email is bounced and the recipient needs to reply. Alternatively, just create these user accounts or aliases on your server so that messages sent to them can be delivered. Again, edit these lines in `/etc/amavisd.conf`:

```
$virus_admin               = "virusalert\@$mydomain";  # notifications recip.
$mailfrom_notify_admin     = "virusalert\@$mydomain";  # notifications sender
$mailfrom_notify_recip     = "virusalert\@$mydomain";  # notifications sender
$mailfrom_notify_spamadmin = "spam.police\@$mydomain"; # notifications sender
```

There are hundreds of options to explore in SpamAssassin, ClamAV, and amavisd-new. We recommend that you familiarize yourself with these products before deploying a production server. The setup presented here should be a good start, but spam filtering is an art; it will take training, tweaks, and attention to deploy an efficient and effective system.

Providing Remote Access to Email

Postfix makes up only part of the mail server picture. Although Postfix handles sending and receiving email on the server side, it does not have any provisions for the client software, such as Eudora or Outlook Express. To provide email for remote clients, Tiger needs an additional server components such as an IMAP server, a POP3 server, or a web-based email client—or a combination of any/all of these.

In this section, we will look at how to provide the end-user interface to the Postfix email server and also an easy-to-use technique to provide additional protection against unauthorized relaying.

Adding IMAP Support with University of Washington `imapd`

The UW `imapd` server is capable of handling both IMAP *(Internet Message Access Protocol)* and POP3 traffic, and it is already Mac OS X–aware, so it takes very little work to install. Even better, there is absolutely no configuration file for the software, so after it has been installed, it's ready to use.

> **NOTE**
>
> If you're wondering what POP3 and IMAP are, refer to Chapter 3, "Using the Tiger Internet Application Suite." These two mail delivery protocols are explained during the introduction to the Mail application.

A straightforward comparison between POP3 and IMAP can be found at the IMAP Connection: `http://www.imap.org/imap.vs.pop.brief.html`.

Installing UW `imapd`

Installing `imapd` is straightforward but requires a few additional modifications to be able to perform smoothly on your OS X computer. To start, fetch the current sources from `ftp://ftp.cac.washington.edu/imap/`. Unarchive the source and enter **`cd`** to move to the distribution directory:

```
brezup:jray jray $ curl -O ftp://ftp.cac.washington.edu/imap/imap.tar.Z
brezup:jray jray $ tar Zxf imap.tar.Z
brezup:jray jray $ cd imap-2004a/
```

Before compiling, an important change must be made to the file `src/osdep/unix/env_unix.c`. By default, the IMAP server attempts to create all mailboxes in the user's home directory. In fact, it assumes that any directory in the home directory is an IMAP folder; this results in potentially hundreds (or thousands) of folders being downloaded and displayed. To get around this, the env_unix.c file must be adjusted so that a directory other than the main home directory is used. This can be any directory, as long as it exists in every user's account. For our purposes, we'll use ~/Library/Mail/Mailboxes—just remember to create the directory name you choose in each account that will access the IMAP server.

Edit the src/osdep/unix/env_unix.c file to add the mailbox directory name you've chosen. Look for the line

```
static char *mailsubdir = NIL; /* mail subdirectory name */
```

Change the text to include the directory you've chosen. For example:

```
static char *mailsubdir = "Library/Mail/Mailboxes"; /* mail subdirectory name */
```

One final change is to make symbolically link /usr/include/pam to /usr/include/security so that the proper headers will be found during the compile:

```
brezup:jray imap-2004a $ ln -s /usr/include/pam /usr/include/security
```

The source code is now ready to compile by typing **make osx PASSWDTYPE=pam SSLTYPE=unix**. This builds a *partially* noncompliant IESG *(Internet Engineering Steering Group)* version of the software. This simply means that the software does *not* force the use of SSL encryption for transferring mail/passwords.

```
brezup:jray imap-2004a $ make osx PASSWDTYPE=pam SSLTYPE=unix
make sslunix
++++++++++++++++++++++++++++++++++++++++++++++++++++++++++++++++++
+ Building in PARTIAL compliance with RFC 3501 security
+ requirements:
+ Compliant:
++ TLS/SSL encryption is supported
+ Non-compliant:
++ Unencrypted plaintext passwords are permitted
+
+ In order to rectify this problem, you MUST build with:
++ SSLTYPE=unix.nopwd
++++++++++++++++++++++++++++++++++++++++++++++++++++++++++++++++++

Do you want to continue this build anyway? Type y or n please: y
Applying an process to sources...
tools/an "ln -s" src/c-client c-client
tools/an "ln -s" src/ansilib c-client
...
```

The compile process takes only a minute or two because the server application is really quite small. Unfortunately, installation of the compiled software is not automated, so you will have to copy the binary files (imapd and ipopd) to an appropriate directory.

A proper Unix location for user-installed interfaceless server binaries is /usr/local/libexec/, so that's where we'll pop our daemons. You'll have to create the libexec directory within /usr/local, and then copy the files imapd and ipop3d (created within the imapd and ipopd directories of the source distribution) to the new directory:

```
brezup:jray imap-2004a $ sudo mkdir /usr/local/libexec
brezup:jray imap-2004a $ sudo cp imapd/imapd /usr/local/libexec/
brezup:jray imap-2004a $ sudo cp ipopd/ipop3d /usr/local/libexec/
```

NOTE

Depending on what additional BSD software you've installed, you might already have the /usr/local/libexec directory on your system.

Configuring imapd Startup

Now that the binaries have been installed, you'll want to configure xinetd to automatically start the POP and IMAP servers when there is an incoming request. To do this, add two files (pop3.plist and imap.plist) to your /Library/LaunchDaemons directory.

The file /Library/LaunchDaemons/pop3.plist should read

```
<?xml version="1.0" encoding="UTF-8"?>
<!DOCTYPE plist PUBLIC "-//Apple Computer//DTD PLIST 1.0//EN"
➥"http://www.apple.com/DTDs/PropertyList-1.0.dtd">
<plist version="1.0">
<dict>
        <key>Label</key>
        <string>edu.washington.pop3</string>
        <key>Program</key>
        <string>/usr/local/libexec/ipop3d</string>
        <key>ProgramArguments</key>
        <array>
                <string>ipop3d</string>
        </array>
        <key>Sockets</key>
        <dict>
                <key>Listeners</key>
                <dict>
                        <key>SockServiceName</key>
                        <string>pop3</string>
                </dict>
        </dict>
        <key>inetdCompatibility</key>
        <dict>
                <key>Wait</key>
                <false/>
```

```
        </dict>
</dict>
</plist>
```

Similarly, the file /etc/xinetd.d/imap should read like this:

```
<?xml version="1.0" encoding="UTF-8"?>
<!DOCTYPE plist PUBLIC "-//Apple Computer//DTD PLIST 1.0//EN"
➥"http://www.apple.com/DTDs/PropertyList-1.0.dtd">
<plist version="1.0">
<dict>
        <key>Label</key>
        <string>edu.washington.imapd</string>
        <key>Program</key>
        <string>/usr/local/libexec/imapd</string>
        <key>ProgramArguments</key>
        <array>
                <string>imapd</string>
        </array>
        <key>Sockets</key>
        <dict>
                <key>Listeners</key>
                <dict>
                        <key>SockServiceName</key>
                        <string>imap</string>
                </dict>
        </dict>
        <key>inetdCompatibility</key>
        <dict>
                <key>Wait</key>
                <false/>
        </dict>
</dict>
</plist>
```

Reboot the computer or force the launchd process to load your new configuration files using launchctl load /Library/LaunchDaemons/pop3.plist and launchctl load /Library/LaunchDaemons/imap.plist. You're now *very* close to being able to use your new services, but one final step remains: enabling authentication.

Enabling PAM Authentication

To authenticate with your system, you must create the appropriate PAM *(Pluggable Authentication Module)* settings in /etc/pam.d. To do this, create two files /etc/pam.d/pop3 and /etc/pam.d/imap with the following contents:

```
auth       sufficient    pam_securityserver.so
auth       sufficient    pam_unix.so
auth       required      pam_deny.so
account    required      pam_permit.so
password   required      pam_deny.so
session    required      pam_permit.so
```

You can use the `/etc/pam.d/cups` file as a template if you like. After the files have been saved, the `imapd` and `ipop3d` servers will be able to authenticate with your Tiger system. You're now ready to test your server.

Testing the `imapd` Installation

Test to make sure that the services you want to run are running by telneting into port 110 (POP3) and port 143 (IMAP):

```
brezup:jray jray $ telnet localhost 110
Trying 127.0.0.1...
Connected to localhost.
+OK POP3 client1.poisontooth.com 2004.88 server ready
Escape character is '^]'.
Connection closed by foreign host.
```

and

```
brezup:jray jray $ telnet localhost 143
Trying 127.0.0.1...
Connected to localhost.
Escape character is '^]'.
* OK [CAPABILITY IMAP4REV1 LITERAL+ SASL-IR LOGIN-REFERRALS STARTTLS AUTH=LOGIN]
localhost IMAP4rev1 2004.352 at Wed, 29 Dec 2004 20:33:36 -0600 (CST)
```

Both services are running, just as we intended. As a rule, remember that less is more when it comes to servers. If you aren't going to use the IMAP or POP3 servers, don't activate them in your configuration.

The UW `imapd` server is now ready for use. You can connect to the machine to pick up email that has been received by the Postfix SMTP daemon.

> **TIP**
>
> The IMAP and POP3 servers are both installed and configured to use TCP Wrappers. TCP Wrappers, as you'll learn in Chapter 28, "Implementing Server Security and Advanced Network Configuration," can be used to limit access to any `inetd`-controlled services. It is recommended that you use TCP Wrappers to block mail services except for those domains that must have access—these servers offer hackers an excellent entry point for their activities.

Providing Relay Protection with POP Before SMTP

Common problems with mail servers are that many require you to enumerate the networks that can send email (which is difficult for mobile users) and don't include built-in support for SMTP authentication methods. As a result, SMTP servers are stuck with either having to act as an open relay in cases where they shouldn't or force restrictions on mobile users.

A clever way around this is to allow your IMAP/POP server software to approve connections to your SMTP server. Because both IMAP and POP require a username and password, these servers can authenticate a user and then pass on the authenticated IP address to the SMTP server, which can temporarily allow messages to be sent from that IP address. One easy solution that works with the Postfix and UW `imapd` software you've installed is `Pop-before-smtp` (`http://popbsmtp.sourceforge.net/`).

Written entirely in Perl, this utility watches your POP/IMAP server logs for a valid login and then authorizes that IP address to send email through Postfix for 30 minutes. Because this software requires no changes to the Postfix or `imapd` applications, you can install and use it with a minimum amount of configuration. If you're comfortable with installing Perl modules, you can jump right in at `http://popbsmtp.sourceforge.net/quickstart.shtml`. Otherwise, you might want to review Chapter 18, "Using Scripting Languages," first.

Providing Web-Based Email Access

Although `imap` and `pop` are certainly popular choices for getting email to your clients, providing a web interface is a virtual necessity nowadays. A web-based client enables users to check their email from any web-enabled computer without needing to set up any additional software. In this section, we'll look at how you can quickly set up SquirrelMail—a popular web-based IMAP client that works with PHP. As a prerequisite, you'll need PHP activated, as described in Chapter 24.

Installing SquirrelMail

To begin, download the latest SquirrelMail distribution from `http://squirrelmail.sourceforge.net/` and unarchive the code into a web-accessible directory, such as `/Library/Webserver/Documents`. You'll also want to remove the version number from the directory so that `squirrelmail` will be easier to access (for example, rename `squirrelmail-1.5.0` to `squirrelmail`).

Next, you'll need to prepare a data and attachments directory to store user information. Enter the following commands from within the main `squirrelmail` directory to prepare these storage locations:

```
brezup:jray squirrelmail $ sudo chown -R www:www  data
brezup:jray squirrelmail $ sudo mkdir /var/attachments
brezup:jray squirrelmail $ sudo chgrp -R www /var/attachments/
brezup:jray squirrelmail $ sudo chmod 730 /var/attachments
```

SquirrelMail now has everything it needs to run *except* a valid configuration file.

Configuring SquirrelMail

For SquirrelMail to operate, it needs to know what IMAP server it should communicate with, which SMTP server to use as a relay, and so on. SquirrelMail can even be personalized with organization logos and other custom settings. The configuration is handled by a menu-driven Perl process found in the `config` directory. To run, `cd` into `config` and type **`sudo ./conf.pl`**:

```
brezup:jray squirrelmail $ cd config
brezup:jray config $ sudo ./conf.pl
```

You should now see the main menu of the setup tool, similar to this:

```
SquirrelMail Configuration : Read: config.php (1.4.0)
---------------------------------------------------------
Main Menu --
1.  Organization Preferences
2.  Server Settings
3.  Folder Defaults
4.  General Options
5.  Themes
6.  Address Books (LDAP)
7.  Message of the Day (MOTD)
8.  Plugins
9.  Database
10. Language settings
11. Tweaks

D.  Set pre-defined settings for specific IMAP servers

C.  Turn color on
S   Save data
Q   Quit

Command >>
```

You can explore the settings and customize the system to your heart's content. The Organization Preferences option enables you to personalize the system for your group or company; the Folder Defaults option provides control over the default IMAP folders and what should happen to messages that have been deleted; the Themes option controls the look and feel, and so on. We are concerned with getting the system communicating with the IMAP server you've setup. To do this, press 2 and then press the Return key.

The menu should refresh to display server settings:

```
SquirrelMail Configuration : Read: config.php (1.4.0)
---------------------------------------------------------
Server Settings
```

```
General
-------
1.  Domain                 : poisontooth.com
2.  Invert Time            : false
3.  Sendmail or SMTP       : SMTP

A.  Update IMAP Settings   : localhost:143 (uw)
B.  Update SMTP Settings   : localhost:25

R   Return to Main Menu
C.  Turn color on
S   Save data
Q   Quit
```

Start by setting your domain. Press 1 and then press the Return key. When prompted, enter your server's domain name. The default settings for items 2 and 3 should be fine. Next, configure your IMAP server settings by pressing the A key and then the Return key. The menu will change slightly to show additional options:

```
SquirrelMail Configuration : Read: config.php (1.4.0)
---------------------------------------------------------
Server Settings

General
-------
1.  Domain                 : poisontooth.com
2.  Invert Time            : false
3.  Sendmail or SMTP       : SMTP

IMAP Settings
--------------
4.  IMAP Server            : localhost
5.  IMAP Port              : 143
6.  Authentication type    : login
7.  Secure IMAP (TLS)      : false
8.  Server software        : uw
9.  Delimiter              : detect

B.  Update SMTP Settings   : localhost:25
H.  Hide IMAP Server Settings

R   Return to Main Menu
C.  Turn color on
S   Save data
Q   Quit
```

Use numbers 4 and 8 to configure the hostname of your server (`localhost` or `127.0.0.1` if you're running SquirrelMail on the same machine as your IMAP server) and the server software itself (`uw` for the University of Washington IMAP daemon).

Use a similar process to update the SMTP settings: Press B to display the settings, and then update the SMTP hostname to reflect the system running Postfix.

When finished, press R to exit to the main menu.

One final change and you're finished. Press 4 to enter the General settings:

```
SquirrelMail Configuration : Read: config.php (1.4.0)
---------------------------------------------------------
General Options
1.  Data Directory              : ../data/
2.  Attachment Directory        : /var/attachments/
3.  Directory Hash Level        : 0
4.  Default Left Size           : 150
5.  Usernames in Lowercase      : false
6.  Allow use of priority       : true
7.  Hide SM attributions        : false
8.  Allow use of receipts       : true
9. Allow editing of identity   : true/true
10. Allow server thread sort    : false
11. Allow server-side sorting   : false
12. Allow server charset search : true
13. PHP session name            : SQMSESSID

R   Return to Main Menu
C.  Turn color on
S   Save data
Q   Quit

Command >>
```

Use the 2 option to set the attachments directory for SquirrelMail. This should be configured to `/var/attachments`, which was created earlier in the setup process. After making the change, press S to save your configuration, and then press Q to quit. SquirrelMail is now ready for use.

Accessing SquirrelMail

To use SquirrelMail, simply point your web browser at the URL where the `squirrelmail` directory was installed. You should see a basic login screen, as shown in Figure 26.1.

26

FIGURE 26.1 SquirrelMail should present a login screen for your IMAP server.

Enter your Tiger username and password and, after a few seconds the screen should refresh with a familiar email client display. Mailboxes and folders are shown on the left, a message list on the right, and the message content displayed when an entry in the list is clicked, as shown in Figure 26.2.

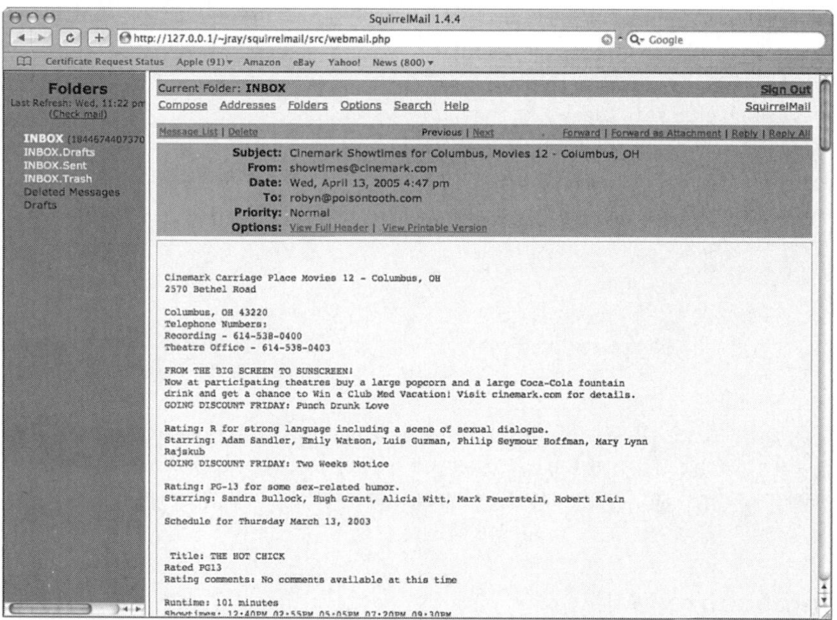

FIGURE 26.2 SquirrelMail works just like a traditional email client.

As you use SquirrelMail, you'll discover that it offers a very full IMAP experience. Folder management, attachments, searching, and many more features are all accessible from any web browser that can connect to your server.

You're now well on your way to having a mail server as capable as any commercial offering.

NOTE

One small problem that you might encounter is that by using the `/var/attachments` directory, you provide a more secure service to your users, but SquirrelMail cannot clean up abandoned attachments in this directory. To automatically clean things up, you might want to add a `crontab` entry such as `rm -f /var/attachments/*` that runs at a time when no one will be using the server. Chapter 12 contains more information on setting up `cron`-invoked processes.

Summary

Mail servers require disk space and a commitment from the administrator to monitor traffic and usage. An improperly configured mail server can be used to spread spam and viruses to remote clients around the world. Before setting up a server, you should first evaluate whether a local server is truly needed, and what alternative solutions are available.

Assuming that you decide to enable Postfix, most installations will want to install a server such as UW `imapd` to deliver messages to client applications such as Eudora, Outlook Express, and Mail. In addition, web clients can be added to create a mail solution that enables users to access email from anywhere there is web access.

CHAPTER 27

Working with Windows-Based Systems

IN THIS CHAPTER

- Understanding the Windows Protocols: SMB and CIFS
- Accessing and Sharing Windows Resources
- Using Tiger with MS Exchange
- Integrating Tiger into an Active Directory
- Samba

There's no denying it. There's no ignoring it. We live in a world dominated by Windows-based computers. Granted, this dominance will last only a few more years until the current generation of Unix-heads (Mac OS X users included!) takes over. In the meantime, despite the example set by the opposition, it's still a good idea to play nice with Windows computers.

This chapter introduces the software that will help your computer exchange files over a Windows network and take the place of a Windows server for file and print sharing. Best of all, you can do everything from within the familiar Aqua interface.

Understanding the Windows Protocols: SMB and CIFS

The Simple Message Block (SMB) protocol provides the basis for Windows file and print sharing. SMB provides support for file browsing and two levels of security:

- User—A user must authenticate with the SMB server during the initial connection. The supplied username and password determine what resources the user can access.
- Share—Share-level security operates on an individual shared resource. The resource has a single password. Anyone with access to the password can access the resource.

SMB is implemented on top of a transport protocol. Think of this as similar to the way that AppleTalk exists on top of LocalTalk (serial networking) and EtherTalk (ethernet-based networks).

The SMB protocol has gone through several phases in its existence. Early in life, it used NetBEUI as its transport protocol. NetBEUI is independent of TCP/IP and, as such, was only suited for local-area networks. Today, most SMB services run on top of NetBIOS (NetBT/NBT). NetBIOS is the equivalent of NetBEUI, but running on top of TCP/IP. This creates a routable file/print serving system that can be used across the Internet as well as in LAN situations.

Unfortunately, things aren't that clean and simple. The NetBEUI protocol used a simple broadcast protocol to enable browsing of local resources. When SMB moved to NetBIOS (and thus TCP/IP), finding remote resources became a bigger problem. Machines needed a new way to locate each other, besides sending broadcast packets. This was the only way to successfully handle spanning across multiple subnets.

The Windows Internet Naming Service *(WINS)* protocol was created to provide a central registration point for Windows computers. When coming online, a computer can register itself with a WINS server as well as look up other machines for creating a connection.

NOTE

Yes, WINS is a proprietary name resolution system that bears a resemblance to DNS *(domain name service).* Versions of Windows later than 98 and NT 4.0 support DNS resolution of remote computer names. Microsoft's latest attempt at a proprietary directory service is the Active Directory Service *(ADS).* ADS offers greater support for open standards, but continues to be based on a proprietary system.

The latest version of SMB is known as Common Internet File System *(CIFS)* and is backed by Microsoft as well as several third-party companies. CIFS is an open version of SMB with Internet-specific modifications. For the sake of remaining reasonably sane, you can assume that CIFS and SMB are synonymous.

TIP

The history of SMB, NetBEUI, NetBIOS, and how everything fits together is documented on the What Is SMB? page: `http://samba.anu.edu.au/cifs/docs/what-is-smb.html`.

Accessing and Sharing Windows Resources

Tiger provides integrated browsing of Windows shares directly in the Finder just like any other network volume. In addition, the system enables you to serve your files and printers to Windows clients—all within the Tiger GUI. These features are provided by the underlying Samba software suite, which we'll look at later in the chapter.

Browsing and Mounting Windows Shares

To browse available Windows shares, open the Network level in the Finder (Go, Network, or Shift-Command-K), as shown in Figure 27.1. Windows workgroups, domains, and computers will be mixed in with Appletalk Zones, and so on. Figure 27.1 shows a number of workgroups, including `Workgroup`, `West`, and `South`.

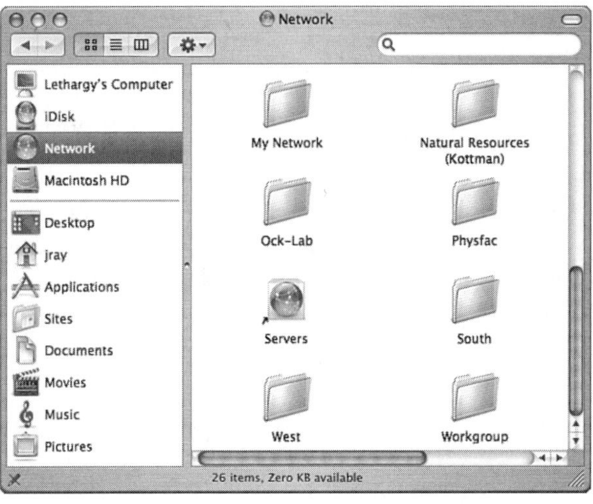

FIGURE 27.1 The Finder can browse Windows workgroups on your local network.

To connect to a server, double-click it within the Finder. You are prompted for login information, just like an Apple shared volume, as demonstrated in Figure 27.2. If you plan to connect to the volume in the future, you can choose to store the login information in your keychain. Mounted volumes behave just like any other network share.

SMB/CIFS File System Authentication

Enter the workgroup or domain and your user name and password to access the server "TIME-OUT."

Workgroup or Domain

POISONTOOTH

Name

JRAY

Password

Remember this password in my keychain

Cancel OK

FIGURE 27.2 Log on to the Windows share.

Mounting by Name and IP

It is often easier to mount a share by its IP address or hostname than by browsing—especially if the server is located on another subnet. Tiger supports connecting to Windows shares using the following naming conventions:

```
smb://<server name or ip>/[<volume>]
cifs://<server name or ip>/[<volume>]
```

To mount a volume by name, choose Go, Connect to Server (Command-K). Enter the connection string within the Server Address field and then click Connect. If a volume name is not supplied, you are presented with a list of available shares to choose from. The connection proceeds exactly as it would if you had browsed to the server directly.

Using smbtree

To browse the Windows network from the command line, use the smbtree command, which prints a hierarchical view of the available network resources. For example, to browse the publicly visible volumes on your network, use smbtree -N:

```
$ smbtree -N
WORKGROUP
        \\CLIENT19              Samba 2.2.3a (build 26)
        \\CLIENT19\ADMIN$              IPC Service (Samba 2.2.3a (build 26))
        \\CLIENT19\IPC$                IPC Service (Samba 2.2.3a (build 26))
        \\CLIENT18              Mac OS X
        \\CLIENT18\Test_on_10.0.       PT Laser
        \\CLIENT18\Darkness@clie       Darkness
        \\CLIENT18\ADMIN$              IPC Service (Mac OS X)
        \\CLIENT18\IPC$                IPC Service (Mac OS X)
POISONTOOTH
        \\PAINFUL               Painful
        \\PAINFUL\C$                  Default share
        \\PAINFUL\ADMIN$              Remote Admin
        \\PAINFUL\SharedDocs
        \\PAINFUL\IPC$                Remote IPC
        \\PAINFUL\Secret Stuff
    \\CARROT3               Mac OS X Server
        \\CARROT3\ADMIN$              IPC Service (Mac OS X Server)
        \\CARROT3\IPC$                IPC Service (Mac OS X Server)
        \\CARROT3\Groups              macosx
        \\CARROT3\www.cutelittl       macosx
        \\CARROT3\Websites            macosx
        \\CARROT3\Users               macosx
        \\CARROT3\Public              macosx
```

Here, the two workgroups, WORKGROUP and POISONTOOTH, are shown with two clients in each. Many of the shares shown here are default administrative shares that are normally invisible in Windows (those that end in $), so the list isn't exactly what you would see within the Mac browser.

You can modify the operation of smbtree to query using a username/password, or only display machines visible by responding to broadcast requests. Table 27.1 contains the most useful of the smbtree options.

TABLE 27.1 `smbtree` Command-Line Options

Option	Description
`-b`	Use broadcasts requests to query available network resources. Typically a master browser is queried. The master browser contains a browse list that servers register with. Using a broadcast query displays all machines that are online and responding directly.
`-D`	Display only workgroup/domain names on the network.
`-S`	Display only workgroup/domain and servers—not individual shares.
`-N`	Suppress the `smbtree` password prompt.
`-U=`*<username>*`%`*<password>*	Set a username and password.
`-k`	Attempt to authenticate with Kerberos for Active Directory lookups.

Mounting with `mount_smbfs`

To mount a network volume from the command line, use `mount_smbfs`. In its simplest form, the `mount_smbfs` syntax is `mount_smbfs "//`*<server name>*`/`*<share>*`"` *<mount point>*. Note that the slashes have changed direction from the output of `smbtree` and the direction typically used in Windows.

For example, to mount the volume `\\PAINFUL\Secret Stuff` in the directory `/tmp/mysmbmount`, use

```
brezup:jray jray $ mount_smbfs "//PAINFUL/Secret Stuff" /tmp/mysmbmount
Password: *******
```

A quick look at the output of the `mount` command displays that the mount succeeded (of course, looking in the `/tmp/mysmbmount` directory would do the same).

```
brezup:jray jray $ mount
/dev/disk0s11 on / (local, journaled)
devfs on /dev (local)
fdesc on /dev (union)
<volfs> on /.vol
/dev/disk0s9 on /Volumes/Laptop X2 (local, journaled)
automount -nsl [315] on /Network (automounted)
automount -fstab [320] on /automount/Servers (automounted)
automount -static [320] on /automount/static (automounted)
//JRAY@PAINFUL/SECRET STUFF on /tmp/thing (nodev, nosuid, by jray)
```

NOTE

When making the connection, `mount_smbfs` prompts for a password but not a username. By default it uses your login username for authentication. You can change this behavior using the `-U` command-line switch.

A common problem with using `mount_smbfs` in this fashion is the failure of server name resolution. If you experience any trouble finding the server, try specifying the fully qualified domain name or IP address in the connection string. Alternatively, you can provide a connection hostname using the `-I` command-line switch—such as `-I carrot3.poisontooth.com`. Table 27.2 contains a list of useful switches.

TABLE 27.2 Useful `mount_smbfs` Switches

Option	Description
`-I` *<hostname>*	Manually specify the name of the host that you are connecting to.
`-U` *<username>*	Set the username to be used when making the connection. Rather than use this option, you might want to modify the connection string to include the username and password, like this: `//`*<username>*`:`*<password>*`@`*<server name>*`/`*<share>*.
`-W` *<workgroup>*	Set the workgroup name you are connecting to.
`-N`	Do not prompt for a password.
`-u` *<uid>*	Set the user ID assigned to files on the mounted volume.
`-g` *<gid>*	Set the group ID assigned to files on the mounted volume.
`-h`	Print `mount_smbfs` help.

Interactive File Transfers with `smbclient`

If you prefer to interact with your SMB servers much as you would an FTP server, the `smbclient` utility (part of Samba), provides an interactive client that can query and transfer files to and from a server. Unlike `mount_smbfs`, `smbclient` doesn't mount the filesystem and can be run by any user.

To connect, use the syntax `smbclient -U` *<username>* `"//`*<servername>*`/`*<share name>*`"` *<password>*. For example, to connect to my local share `\\carrot3\Websites` with the username `admin` and password `mypass`, I'd use

```
brezup:jray jray $ smbclient -U admin "//carrot3/Websites" mypass
Domain=[POISONTOOTH] OS=[Unix] Server=[Samba 2.2.3a (build 26)]
smb: \>
```

When connected, `smbclient` presents the `smb: \>` prompt, indicating that you are located at the root level of the server (\) and it is ready to receive commands. If you've ever used command-line FTP, you'll feel at home here. For example, to list files, use `ls`:

```
smb: \> ls
  .                         D      0 Sat Jul 26 03:00:29 2003
  .                         D      0 Tue Jul  1 23:09:45 2003
  .DS_Store                   AH    15364 Sat Jul 26 03:00:29 2003
  .VolumeIcon.icns            H     46531 Sat Nov 10 00:46:21 2001
  calendar.poisontooth.com    D         0 Mon Feb 14 00:23:14 2005
  coco.shadesofinsanity.com   D         0 Mon Feb 14 22:38:52 2005
  html                        D         0 Wed Nov  7 21:39:54 2001
  icbins.poisontooth.com      D         0 Sun Nov 18 01:39:09 2001
```

```
 julie.vujevich.com          D     0 Mon Feb 14 14:37:48 2005
 Network Trash Folder        D     0 Mon Aug 26 14:23:01 2002
...
```

To enter a directory, use `cd`:

```
smb: \> cd www.macosxunleashed.com
smb: \www.macosxunleashed.com\>
```

To get/put files, use (surprise) `get` and `put`:

```
smb: \www.macosxunleashed.com\> put INSTALL.TXT
putting file INSTALL.TXT as \www.macosxunleashed.com\INSTALL.TXT (4.1 kb/s)
(average 4.1 kb/s)
```

The easiest way to learn the complete `smbclient` syntax is to use the `help` function to get a list of available interactive commands and then `help` *<command>* to get detailed help for a specific command. Table 27.3 contains the most important functions you'll need to manage your files.

TABLE 27.3 Interactive Commands for Use with `smbclient`

Command	Description
`ls`	List the files in the current directory of the server.
`cd` *<directory>*	Change to a different server directory.
`get` *<filename>*	Retrieve a file from the server.
`put` *<local filename>*	Send a local file to the server.
`mget` *<filename(s)>*	Transfer multiple files from the server.
`mput` *<filename(s)>*	Transfer multiple files to the server.
`prompt`	Toggle prompting on and off for unattended file transfer operation.
`del` *<filename>*	Delete the given filename from the server.
`mkdir` *<directory>*	Create a new directory on the server.
`rmdir` *<directory>*	Remove a directory from the server.
`exit`	Quit `smbclient`.

27

Using `smbutil` to Retrieve Server Information

Another command-line utility that you might want to keep your eye on is `smbutil`. Provided by Apple, this utility promises to provide several functions, such as login, logout, and printing on SMB servers. Unfortunately, at the time of this writing, `smbutil` doesn't actually seem to work as described by the Apple documentation. Three functions that are working, however, are `view`, `lookup`, and `status`. The first lists resources shared from a named host, the second translates NetBIOS names to IP addresses, and the third translates IPs to names. The basic syntax of `smbutil` is `smbutil` *<function> <name or ip>*.

For example, to display the shared resources on `painful`, use

```
brezup:jray jray $ smbutil view //painful
Password: ******
Share         Type    Comment
------------------------------
Secret Stuff disk
IPC$          pipe    Remote IPC
SharedDocs    disk
ADMIN$        disk    Remote Admin
C$            disk    Default share

5 shares listed from 5 available
```

> **TIP**
>
> Although this example uses just `//painful`, you can use the same connection string and *upper-case* options that were used in `mount_smbfs` to customize the connection.

To look up the IP address associated with `painful`, use the `lookup` function:

```
brezup:jray jray $ smbutil lookup painful
Got response from 10.0.1.107
IP address of painful: 10.0.1.107
```

Finally, to reverse the lookup, use the `view` function to find a NetBIOS name given the IP address:

```
brezup:jray jray $ smbutil status 10.0.1.107
Workgroup: POISONTOOTH
Server: PAINFUL
```

Presumably, the rest of `smbutil` will work as described in the man page at **some** point, but for now the command is only partially functional.

Sharing Files and Printers to Windows Systems

To share files and printers with a Windows system, open the Tiger preferences and click the Sharing pane. A single option—Windows Sharing—activates printer and folder sharing, as shown in Figure 27.3.

Before anyone can connect, however, you must enable the local accounts that will be given access to your system. Click the Enable Accounts button, and then click the On check box in front of each name that should be allowed to log in to Samba through SMB—you will be prompted for that user's password. To work correctly with Windows clients, Tiger must store the password in a different (and less secure) manner than the default. You can disable sharing for an account at any time by reversing these steps. Click Done when you have finished configuring the accounts.

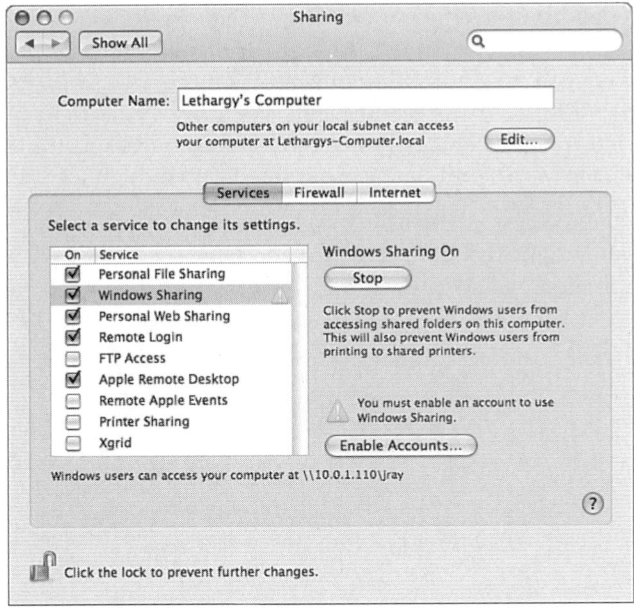

FIGURE 27.3 Activate file and printer sharing then choose the accounts you want to enable.

When Windows Sharing is active, a message appears at the bottom of the window with the connection string that Windows users can use to access your computer. For example, in Figure 27.3, the connection string is `\\client18.poisontooth.com\jray`. Windows machines should also be able to browse to your computer and connect to shares and printers.

You can verify that the shares are active using the `smbutil` command discussed previously:

```
brezup:jray jray $ smbutil view //client18.poisontooth.com
Password: *****
Share          Type     Comment
-------------------------------
IPC$           pipe     IPC Service (Mac OS X)
ADMIN$         pipe     IPC Service (Mac OS X)
Darkness@clie printer  Darkness
Test_on_10.0. printer  PT Laser
jray           disk     User Home Directories

5 shares listed from 5 available
```

In this example, the default `IPC$` and `ADMIN$` shares are visible, along with two printers and my home directory—`jray`.

Setting Your Workgroup and WINS Server

By default, Tiger registers your computer in the workgroup `WORKGROUP`. Although this might be amusing for you, it can be annoying for Windows users who expect to find a little order on their network. To fix the problem, you can use SWAT to edit the Samba configuration (which we'll see shortly), or use the Directory Access utility (`/Applications/Utilities/Directory Access`) to edit it through a GUI.

To change your workgroup, start the utility and authenticate, if necessary, by clicking the lock button. Next, highlight the SMB/CIFS line and click the Configure button. A dialog appears, as shown in Figure 27.4.

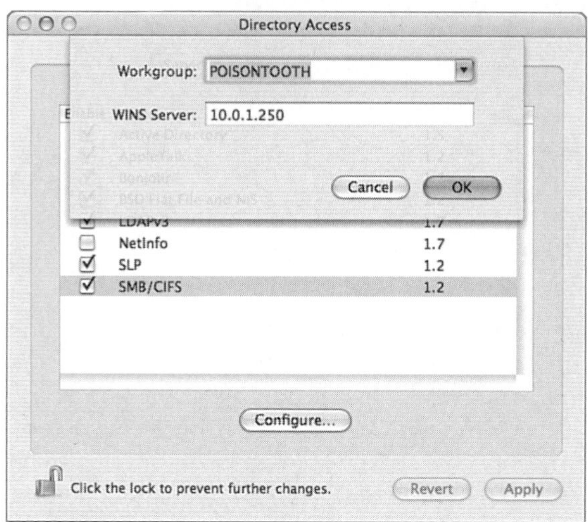

FIGURE 27.4 Set your workgroup and WINS server.

Enter the name of the workgroup that you want to join and specify a WINS server that Samba should register with, if desired. Click OK to save your changes.

NOTE

If you uncheck SMB/CIFS within the Directory Access utility, it disables browsing and SMB connections within the operating system.

Using Tiger with MS Exchange

Tiger offers rudimentary Exchange support in the form of Address Book synchronization and the capability to connect to an Exchange server via IMAP and Outlook Web Access. No, this does not mean that you'll be synchronizing calendars and scheduling with your Windows brethren. It does mean, however, that the Mail application can read email from an Exchange server, and Address Book can synchronize with your Exchange contacts.

Configuring Mail to Work with Exchange

To use Mail with Exchange, the Exchange server must be configured for IMAP *(Internet Message Access Protocol)* support. If the server also supports Outlook Web Access, the OWA server can be specified so that non-email–related information is filtered from the email. If OWA is **not** available, Mail still can access the account but might display extraneous information that, although useful in Outlook, has no purpose in Mac OS X. To add an Exchange IMAP account to Mail, follow the instructions in Chapter 3, "Using the Tiger Internet Application Suite," but, when choosing an account type, pick Exchange, as shown in Figure 27.5.

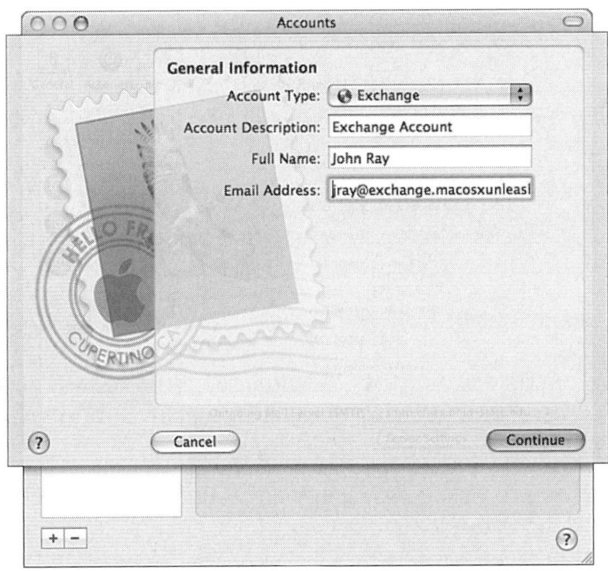

FIGURE 27.5 Configure your Mail application to access Exchange.

You will be prompted for the same information as IMAP, with the exception of the Outlook Web Access Server. Again, this is an optional field; talk to your network administrator to determine whether OWA is even available for your server. After the account has been configured, Mail operates identically to a standard IMAP account. Refer to Chapter 3 for more information.

Configuring Address Book to Work with Exchange

Address Book supports synchronization with Exchange's contact information by way of Outlook Web Access. To configure synchronization, start Address Book and open the General application preferences pane. Check the Synchronize with Exchange check box, and then click Configure. A dialog appears as shown in Figure 27.6.

FIGURE 27.6 Configure Address Book synchronization with Exchange.

Enter your Exchange username and password along with the address or hostname of your Outlook Web Access Server. If OWA is **not** available, synchronization will fail.

Click the Synchronize Every Hour check box to automatically synchronize hourly via iSync. If this is not checked, you can force a synchronization at any time using the iSync menu extra or by clicking Sync Now in iSync.

To disable synchronization, you must return to the General pane of the Address Book preferences. It cannot be removed from within iSync.

Integrating Tiger into an Active Directory

If your company is primarily Windows-based, it probably has or is moving to Microsoft's Active Directory. Active Directory *(AD)* is Microsoft's enterprise directory service. It provides centralized resource and user management for tens, hundreds, or thousands of users.

Tiger also supports directory services, such as NetInfo and LDAP, and can even integrate into an AD-based network without resorting to installing special software or compromising the way you use your computer. These features are part of the Apple Open Directory architecture. Open Directory allows Mac OS X computers to interact with directory servers, local files, and network resources to create distributed administration systems that can be used in a wide variety of settings.

A properly configured client is subject to the same login/password policies as a Windows client. Mac users can also have their home directory stored on a Windows server and accessed from anywhere on the AD network. Authenticated AD administrators will even have administrative access on Tiger.

New to Tiger are mobile AD users. When active, this feature caches the login credentials for users authenticating from the Active Directory and creates a local login for them. If the AD goes down or the machine is not communicating with the AD (such as the case of a laptop that moves around), users will still be able to log in to their accounts.

Configuring AD Support

To set up the connection, open the Directory Access utility (path: `/Applications/Utilities/Directory Access`). To use an AD server, you need the following information:

- The AD domain that you are joining
- The computer ID that has been assigned to your system
- A username and password with the proper permission to bind a machine to the AD
- The organizational unit *(OU)* that the computer you're binding will belong to

Collect this information from your Windows administrator before continuing.

Authenticate by clicking the lock button in the lower-left corner of the window. Highlight the Active Directory plug-in (make sure that it's checked) and then click Configure.

A dialog appears, and Directory Access prompts you for information about your AD server. Click the Show Advanced Options disclosure push button to display all the setting options, as shown in Figure 27.7.

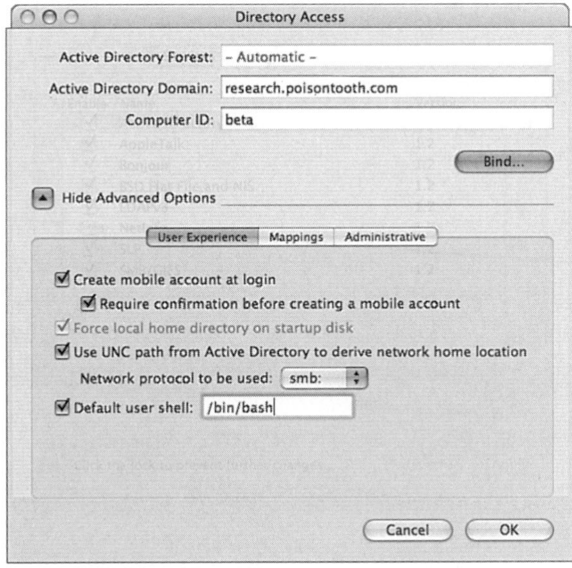

FIGURE 27.7 Enter the information necessary to connect to the Active Directory.

The first two pieces of information—your AD domain and computer ID—are required. The forest is identified automatically. The additional settings are optional but greatly affect how your machine operates within the Active Directory. Use the button bar at the bottom of the window to fine-tune your setup within the areas of User Experience, Mappings, and Administrative.

User Experience Options

The first setting group, User Experience, controls how the system will integrate Active Directory accounts into the Macintosh experience. Choose between the following settings based on how you want your system to handle home directories and the command-line interface *(CLI)* shell.

- Create Mobile Account at Login—When selected, Tiger will automatically create a local account for a user that authenticates via the AD. This allows the user to log in even if the AD cannot be reached—such as in the case of a mobile laptop or a flaky server setup. Use the Require Confirmation check box to prompt for each account before creating it.
- Force Local Home Directory on Startup Disk—Available if mobile accounts are *not* active. This feature will use a local folder in `/Users` for those logged in by way of the AD. The user will also have his network home directory automatically mounted, but it will not be used for system files (like `~/Library`).
- Use UNC Path from Active Directory to Derive Network Home Location—When selected, this option will use the standard AD universal naming convention path for the home directory. Choose the protocol the server will use to present the network home directory share. SMB is should be used unless the server has additional software installed to support Apple File Protocol *(AFP)*.
- Default User Shell—The shell that the system will default to when the user accesses the CLI via Terminal or through SSH login. A user can ultimately invoke any available shell, so this is really just a default setting.

Mapping Options

By default, Tiger automatically generates a UID/GID value for users that are logged in from the AD. Because these values don't necessarily correspond to what you might want, you can use the Mapping button to map user and group IDs to specific attributes within the active directory. Systems with Microsoft Services for Unix, for example, can use the SFU UID attribute to map directly to a Mac OS X UID.

This doesn't work out of the box, however. The AD schema must be updated to include the attributes that you will be mapping to. Assuming that your AD has these attributes in place, select the check box in front of the attribute you want to map and then enter the appropriate AD attribute.

Administrative Options

The final settings pane, Administrative, is used to control the default domain server and assign valid AD administrative groups.

- Prefer This Domain Server—If a preferred domain server is listed, Tiger attempts to use it by default. Otherwise, the AD is consulted and a nearby domain controller located.
- Allow Administration By—Choose the groups in the AD that are considered administrators by Tiger; `Domain Admins` and `Enterprise Admins` are the defaults.
- Allow Authentication from Any Domain in the Forest—If selected, users throughout the AD forest can log in. If unchecked, you will authenticate against the domain you've specified in the main directory access settings.

Binding/Unbinding with the Domain

After your options have been set, click the Bind button. Tiger prompts for a username, password, and search path to identify your computer OU in the Active Directory, as shown in Figure 27.8. This is an AD username and password with the appropriate permissions to add a machine to a domain; it is *not* your local Tiger admin account.

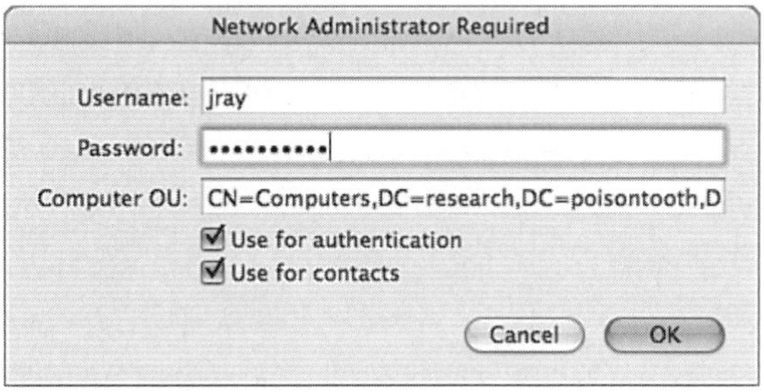

FIGURE 27.8 Bind with the Active Directory.

Choose how you will be using the binding by selecting Use for Authentication and/or Use for Contacts. Using the AD for authentication will allow AD users to log in to the Tiger system and potentially administrate it (refer to the previous section, "Administrative Options"). The Use for Contacts setting allows applications such as Address Book to query the AD for contact information. Finally, click OK to begin the binding process.

Tiger takes a few moments to complete the steps in connecting to the Active Directory. If any errors occur along the way, you will be given specific information to help correct the problem.

After the binding has been completed (and assuming that it was set up for authentication), users should be able to log in via the AD by clicking the Other user icon at the Tiger login screen and supplying the standard AD domain credentials instead of local login information.

To unbind from a domain, click the Unbind button within the Active Directory plug-in setup screen. You will be prompted for a username and password. Again, this is AD authentication information—not a local Tiger account. The supplied username and password must have permission to remove the computer from the AD. If you do not have permission or the unbind fails, click the Force Unbind button to forcibly disconnect from the AD.

TIP

Apple's support for Active Directory has progressed nicely in the past two (Panther/Tiger) releases of Mac OS X. For those seeking tighter integration, Thursby Software's ADmitMac might be the right choice (`http://www.thursby.com/products/admitmac.html`). ADmitMac provides better support for Windows technologies such as NTFS and DFS (Distributed File System). Thursby also offers AD administrative tools to provide basic Active Directory administration directly from Mac OS X.

Samba

Over the past few years, Windows-only shops have been slowly adding Unix and Unix-like systems to their server arsenal. The reason for this is a piece of software called Samba. Samba provides the Windows sharing services that you've already seen in Tiger, but is capable of much more than just sharing your home directory. It is also capable of replacing Windows NT and 200x servers on your network. Samba offers comparable performance, features, and a price that can't be beat (free, of course). To quote eWEEK:

> Samba is capable, flexible, mature, and fairly well-documented; runs on several Unix operating systems; offers web-based configuration and administration; and is free.
>
> Samba is now a viable option as a file and print server for many more Windows shops than before and earns an *eWEEK* Labs Analyst's Choice award for this remarkable technical accomplishment.
>
> To add this functionality, Samba Team developers (including those who are part of the Samba: The Next Generation project) had to reverse-engineer the proprietary protocols Microsoft Corp. uses to authenticate users and systems over the network, using, in many cases, nothing but a packet sniffer.

Samba offers web-based configuration and administration. Even if you've never used a Windows computer and don't know the first thing about Windows file sharing, you'll be able to get a basic server up and running in only a few minutes.

Samba supports several advanced features, including file and printer sharing, user and share security, WINS, and emulation of a Windows domain. Best of all, it runs natively on Mac OS X. Now Windows users can come to the Mac, rather than vice versa.

Samba is a large piece of software—approaching Apache in terms of complexity and number of configuration options. In this chapter, the focus is on setting up solid, general-purpose servers. High-end needs are best served by other sources, such as *Sams Teach Yourself Samba in 24 Hours* (ISBN: 0672316099). The Samba website is also a great source for information (`http://www.samba.org`).

NOTE

Apple has been reasonably good about including a new version of Samba with Mac OS X and keeping up with security patches. If you prefer to install from scratch and have about 30 minutes, you can easily compile and install Samba on your own. Download the latest Samba source from `http://www.samba.org/`.

Let's get down to business.

Activating the SWAT Web Interface

Although Samba can be activated and used with Apple's default configuration (stored in `/etc/smb.conf`), you'll be missing 99% of the functionality. Samba offers many advanced features that can be accessed only when you manually edit the setup. In its early days, Samba was configured entirely by hand by editing the `smb.conf` file. It worked, but wasn't really useful to anyone but the most die-hard Unix users. Today, however, configuration is handled entirely through a web-based GUI called SWAT.

CAUTION

Although Samba *can* be configured by hand (which you're welcome to do), it is recommended that SWAT be used at all times. Some small changes are easy enough to accomplish with a text editor, but the Samba configuration file is extremely sensitive to invalid settings.

If at any point in time you want to return to the original Mac OS X Samba configuration, just copy the file `/etc/smb.conf.template` over `/etc/smb.conf`, and all the changes you've made will be replaced.

27

SWAT is included with your system but not ready for use—you must configure how `launchd` will start SWAT. Edit the file `/System/Library/LaunchDaemons/swat.plist` to include `-a` as one of the program arguments. This will allow any local user to make changes to the Samba configuration via SWAT. Unfortunately, this is necessary as it is currently not possible to authenticate with the SWAT process. Notice, however, that the SWAT service is `Disabled` in the `plist` file. SWAT will not launch at boot and can be used only when an administrator explicitly starts it.

The resulting file should look like this:

```
<plist version="1.0">
<dict>
        <key>Disabled</key>
        <true/>
        <key>GID</key>
        <integer>0</integer>
        <key>Label</key>
        <string>org.samba.swat</string>
        <key>ProgramArguments</key>
```

```
        <array>
                <string>/usr/sbin/swat</string>
                <string>-a -d 10</string>
        </array>
        <key>Sockets</key>
        <dict>
                <key>Listeners</key>
                <dict>
                        <key>SockNodeName</key>
                        <string>localhost</string>
                        <key>SockServiceName</key>
                        <integer>901</integer>
                </dict>
        </dict>
        <key>inetdCompatibility</key>
        <dict>
                <key>Wait</key>
                <false/>
        </dict>
</dict>
</plist>
```

That's it; SWAT is ready to run. Type **`sudo /sbin/service swat start`** to begin using SWAT. When you've finished, you should stop SWAT by typing **`sudo /sbin/service swat stop`**.

> **NOTE**
>
> SWAT is not related, in any way, to the Apache process. Even if Apache is not activated, you'll still be able to use a web browser to configure the Samba server. The `launchd` process listens on port 901 for an incoming TCP connection, and then launches `/usr/sbin/swat` to service the request.

Configuring Samba Sharing

To configure Samba, start a web browser and point it at port 901 of the Samba server (`http://localhost:901`). Because authentication is disabled, you will have full access to the SWAT controls. Figure 27.9 shows the SWAT home screen.

The top of the SWAT display includes eight buttons to control the operation of the server:

- Home—Provides links to Samba documentation and supplemental material.
- Globals—Settings that affect the entire server, such as its name and security model.
- Shares—Shared file resources. If you used the sample configuration file that comes with the Apache distribution, a single home directory share already should be configured.

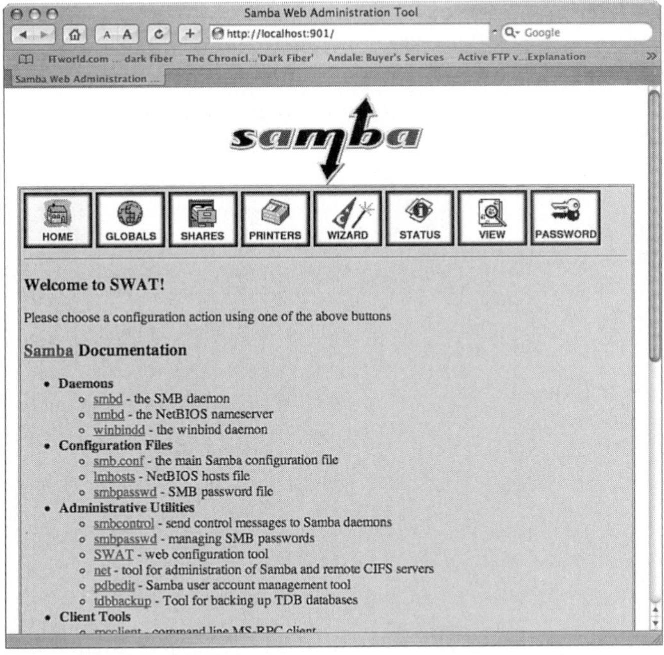

FIGURE 27.9 SWAT opens with a page providing easy access to Samba documentation.

- Printers—Shared printers. To share a printer, it must first be set up so that it can be accessed from Mac OS X. By default, all configured printers are shared.
- Wizard—A quick-start for configuring Samba to be a standalone server, domain controller, or domain member. Because Mac OS X already includes a standalone configuration with setup specific to Mac OS X, starting over isn't recommended.
- Status—Monitor and view the status of the server. If you're logged in as `root`, you can restart or stop the server process.
- View—View a copy of the text configuration file.
- Password—Set and edit Samba user passwords. Samba authenticates against Mac OS X passwords by default, so it is unlikely you'll need these settings.

Let's step through these configuration screens to see the options used in a typical sharing environment.

NOTE

Samba has so many configuration options that additional resources, such as *Sams Teach Yourself Samba in 24 Hours,* are recommended for complex configurations.

Globals

The Global Variables page, shown in Figure 27.10, is the starting point for setting up your Samba server. Many people jump the gun and immediately start setting up file shares. Failure to properly configure the global options might make it impossible to mount or browse shared resources.

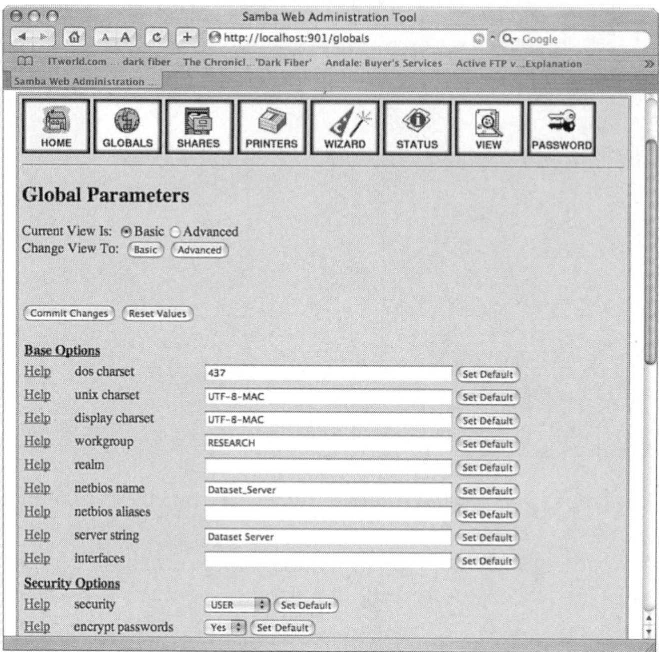

FIGURE 27.10 Global options set the operating parameters for the Samba server.

Two buttons can save server settings (Commit Changes) and reset changes (Reset Values). Choosing the Basic or Advanced button shows additional options—a number of which are listed in Table 27.4. If you don't see the setting you're looking for, move to the Advanced mode.

TABLE 27.4 Common Global Options and Their Purpose

Option	Purpose
`workgroup`	Sets the workgroup or domain that the server belongs to. Set this to the same value as the workgroup/domain of local Windows clients; otherwise, they cannot browse the server. This is the same value that can be set in the Directory Access application.
`netbios name`	The Windows (NetBIOS) name of the server.
`netbios aliases`	A list of additional NetBIOS names to which the Samba server responds.
`server string`	A string used to describe the server. This is entirely arbitrary.

TABLE 27.4 Continued

Option	Purpose
`interfaces`	The network interfaces that Samba broadcasts over. For example, Mac OS X's primary interface is `en0`. By default, all active interfaces are used. To limit the interfaces, enter the interface names to use or the network address followed by a subnet mask (that is, 192.168.0.0/255.255.255.0).
`password level`	The number of case-changes checked between the client login and the server password. Because client operating systems might transmit passwords in uppercase, they have to be altered to authenticate with the server. (Advanced)
`username level`	The same as the password level but alters the username in a similar manner. For example, if I have a Mac OS X username of `jray` and a Windows login of `JRAY`, I must set this value to 4 for it to be successfully permuted into the lowercase version. (Advanced)
`security`	The type of security model to use. User security bases access on a user login. Share password-protects individual shared resources. Domain and server security passes authentication duties to other Windows or Samba servers, respectively. You'll probably want user- or share-level security.
`encrypt passwords`	Sets encrypted password negotiation with the client. Encrypted passwords are required to access Samba from Windows 98 and later.
`guest account`	The local user that should be used for guest access and resource browsing. Mac OS X should use `unknown`.
`hosts allow`	A list of hostnames, IP addresses, IP addresses with subnet masks (`192.168.0.0/255.255.255.0`), or partial addresses (`192.168.0.`) that can access the server. The `except` keyword can create an exception to a rule. For example, `192.168.0.0/255.255.255.0 except 192.168.0.5` would allow any host in the `192.168.0.0` subnet, except `192.168.0.5`, to access the server. If left blank, all remote hosts can access the server.
`hosts deny`	Like `hosts allow` but used to list servers that should not have access to the server. Configure using the same method as `hosts allow`.
`log file`	The log file to store server accesses in. The `%m` in the default path appends the name of the remote machine to the log file name.
`max log size`	The maximum size in kilobytes that a log file should be allowed to reach before rolling over.
`domain logon`	Accept domain logins. This allows Windows clients to recognize the Samba server as a PDC (primary domain controller). (Advanced)
`preferred master`	If set to Yes, the Samba server attempts to force an election for master browser. Do not use on networks with multiple servers that want to be masters.
`local master`	Enables Samba to try to become the master browser for the local area network. If set to No, it does not attempt to assume this role.
`domain master`	Enables Samba's `nmbd` component to become a domain master browser that collects browse lists from remote subnets.

TABLE 27.4 Continued

Option	Purpose
`os level`	A number used to determine the ranking of Samba when a master browser is being elected on a Windows network. If Samba is the only server on the network, use the default 20. If NT/2000/XP machines are on the network and you want Samba to be the master browser, set this to a value greater than 32.
`dns proxy`	Attempts to resolve WINS queries through DNS if they cannot be resolved from locally registered machines.
`wins server`	A remote WINS server that Samba should register with.
`wins support`	Enables Samba's WINS service. Only a single machine should act as a WINS server on a given subnet.

The default settings should be sufficient for most small networks, with the exception of the base and security options (such as `hosts allow` and `hosts deny`). The best rule for Samba is that if you aren't sure what something does or whether you even need it, don't touch it.

Shares

The Share Parameters page sets up file shares that can be mounted on networked Windows-based computers. To create a new share, type a share name in the Create Share field and then click the Create Share button. To edit an existing share, choose its name from the pop-up list and then click Choose Share—or click Delete Share to remove it completely.

With the default Tiger Samba configuration file, a single `homes` share should already be available. `homes` is unique because it is equivalent to each user sharing his home directory. Figure 27.11 shows this share loaded.

The basic share parameters are listed in Table 27.5. A few advanced options are also included.

TABLE 27.5 File-Sharing Options and Values

Option	Purpose
`comment`	A comment to help identify the shared resource.
`path`	The pathname of the directory to share. Be aware that in user-level security, you must make sure that the corresponding Mac OS X user accounts have access to this directory. When using share-level security, a single-user account is used—usually the `guest` account. In that case, the next setting becomes very important.
`guest account`	The account used to access the share if the remote client is logged in as a guest. The default is unknown, but, if set to another username, the guest user will have the read/write permissions of that local user account. If you want to use share-level access control, you can set this value to the account whose permissions should be used when accessing the share.
`force user`	If entered, the `force user` username is used for all accesses (read/write) to the file share, regardless of the username used to log in. (Advanced)
`force group`	Similar to force user but forces a group rather than a user. (Advanced)
`read only`	When set to Yes, users cannot write to the share, regardless of the Mac OS X file permissions.

TABLE 27.5 Continued

Option	Purpose
`read list`	A list of users that should only have read-access to the volume, regardless of any other settings.
`write list`	A list of users that should have read/write access regardless of any other settings.
`create mask`	A set of permissions that newly created files will have. By default, the mask is set to 0744. (Advanced)
`guest ok`	If set to Yes, guests can log in to the server without a password.
`hosts allow`	A list of hostnames, IP addresses, IP addresses with subnet masks (`192.168.0.0/255.255.255.0`), or partial addresses (`192.168.0.`) that can access the share. The `except` keyword can create an exception to a rule. For example, `192.168.0.0/255.255.255.0 except 192.168.0.5` would allow any host in the `192.168.0.0` subnet, except `192.168.0.5`, to access the server. If left blank, all remote hosts can access the server.
`hosts deny`	Like `hosts allow` but used to list servers that should not have access to the server. Configure using the same method as allow.
`max connections`	Restricts the number of simultaneous users who can access the share. (Advanced)
`browseable`	When set to Yes, the share shows up in the Windows network browser. If no, the share still exists, but remote users cannot see its name.
`available`	If set to Yes, the share is made available over the network. Setting to No disables access to the share.

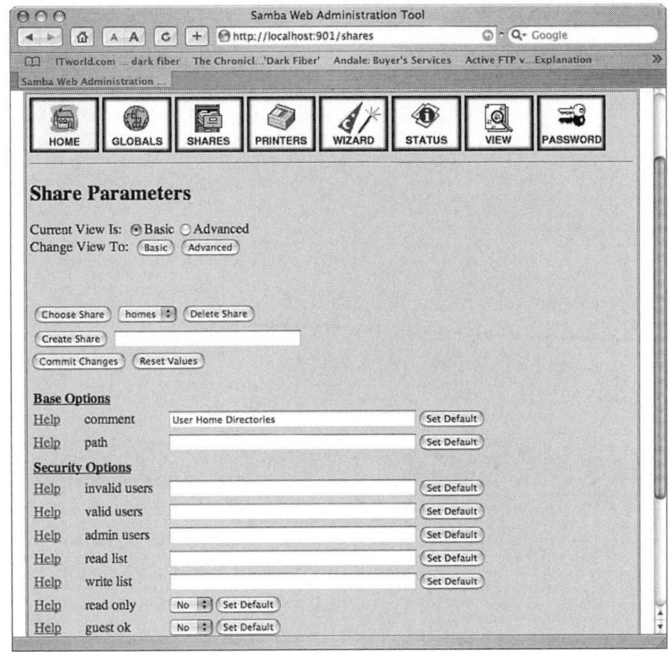

FIGURE 27.11 Use the Share Parameters page to set up your Windows SMB file shares.

The trickiest part of setting up a share is figuring out user access rights. Regardless of whether Samba is using user-level or share-level access, a Unix user must be mapped to the incoming connection.

The easiest security model is user level (the default), which requires Windows users to log in to their computers using the same username and password set up on the Mac OS X machine. When using user-level access, Windows users are mapped directly to Samba users. The Mac OS X file permissions apply directly to the permissions of the connected user.

Assume, for example, that the Mac OS X user `jray` has read/write permissions to the folder `/Stuff`, which is also set to be a Samba share. If `jray` logs in to a Windows computer using the same username as on Mac OS X, he can access the `Stuff` share and have read/write access. The SWAT Password page can be used to map Unix users to the passwords that they will use on the remote Windows client if the Windows password doesn't match their default OS X password.

NOTE

Apple's Samba implementation takes advantage of Open Directory for authentication. If, for example, a Tiger computer is bound to an active directory, AD users may authenticate with the Samba process using their windows credentials. Users that have authenticated with the domain that the Tiger machine is part of should also be able to automatically access shares to which they have permission without needing to supply an additional login or password.

Things are a bit different with share-level access. In such cases, a single password is needed to access the share for all users, and no matter who is logged in, a single account is used by Samba when interacting with the Mac OS X filesystem. To simplify share-level security, create a new Mac OS X user to use for logging in to your shares and then set the `guest` account for the share equal to the Mac OS X username. You should disable other login access (set the shell to `/dev/null`) if you **do** distribute a password among multiple people for the purpose of file sharing.

Wizard

The Samba Wizard options configure a Samba server to act as a standalone server, domain member, or domain controller. Use the radio buttons to choose your basic server settings, how WINS will be used (as either a client, server, or not at all), and whether home directories should be enabled. Click Commit to save the changes.

NOTE

Samba maintains the basic share settings and parameters configured before the wizard is used. The wizard feature tweaks a handful of global options to make the server more quickly adaptable to a given role.

Printers

Samba can act as a full print server for a Windows network. By default, all configured printers are shared through a share called `printers` that operates much like the `homes` share does for home directories. Refer to Chapter 6, "Printer, Fax, and Font Management," for information about setting up Mac OS X printers.

There are a few options for setting up printer sharing. You can go with the default of sharing every printer available through the `printers` share. You can also modify the settings of the `printers` share or any specific shared printer to control its use. A final option is to delete the `printers` share and configure each device manually. Because Mac OS X normally does most of the work for you automatically, this last option really just makes life more difficult. Shared printers can be configured using the options in Table 27.6.

TABLE 27.6 Printer Sharing Options

Option	Purpose
`comment`	A comment used to identify the printer share.
`path`	A directory where print spool files are saved before printing. The directory must be configured to be world-writable and have the sticky bit set.
`guest ok`	If set to Yes, guests may access the printer. This is not a wise idea on a publicly networked device.
`hosts allow`	A list of hostnames, IP addresses, IP addresses with subnet masks (`192.168.0.0/255.255.255.0`), or partial addresses (`192.168.0.`) that can access the share. The `except` keyword can create an exception to a rule. For example, `192.168.0.0/255.255.255.0 except 192.168.0.5` would allow any host in the `192.168.0.0` subnet, except `192.168.0.5`, to access the server. If left blank, all remote hosts can access the server.
`hosts deny`	Like `hosts allow` but used to list servers that should not have access to the server. Configure using the same method as `allow`.
`printable`	Allows authenticated clients to write to the print spool directory.
`printer name`	The CUPS *(Common Unix Printing System)* name for the printer; used if configuring the printer manually. You must switch to Advanced view to see this option. To view a list of the CUPS-recognized printers on your system, type **`lpstat -p`**. Any available printer can be shared.
`max print jobs`	The maximum number of print jobs that can be submitted to the print queue at one time.
`browseable`	When set to Yes, the printer shows up in the Windows network browser. If set to No, the printer share still exists but remote users cannot see its name.
`available`	If set to Yes, the printer is made available over the network. Setting to No disables access to the printer.

Enter the options needed to create the printer share and then click Commit Changes. Windows clients should be able to browse and print the device (with an appropriate driver) immediately.

NOTE

An alternative means of sharing printers with Windows clients is by way of the Mac OS X CUPS subsystem. This can be helpful for printing across subnets or where IP-based printing is the only acceptable solution. An excellent tutorial on using CUPS in this manner is provided at `http://stocksy.is-a-geek.com/information/pantherprint/pantherprintxp.php`. You should be able to disregard the information on fixing CUPS because it is (at the time of this writing) working correctly in Tiger.

Status

The SWAT Server Status page gives a quick overview of the server's current conditions, including active connections, shares, and files. Normally, the administrator can use this screen to restart the server or disable any active connections. Unfortunately, in Tiger, Apple has chosen to use `launchd` to start `smbd` and `nmbd` on demand—meaning that they will not show up as active in the display regardless of whether they truly are.

- Stop/Start/Restart `smbd`—Stops, starts, or restarts `smbd`—the Samba SMB file/print server. All active connections are terminated.
- Stop/Start/Restart `nmbd`—Stops, starts, or restarts `nmbd`—the Samba NetBIOS name server. Does not affect active connections.
- Stop/Start/Restart `winbindd`—Stops, starts, or restarts `winbindd`—A process that binds to a Windows domain to retrieve account information. Does not affect active connections.

The remaining two settings are still useful, regardless of how the daemon processes themselves are handled:

- Auto Refresh—Sets the SWAT status page to autorefresh based on the Refresh Interval field. This is useful for monitoring server activity.
- Kill—The Kill button (an X) appears to the right of every listed connection. Clicking the button immediately terminates the link.

NOTE

Terminating an active connection might result in data loss for the remote user. Although certainly a tempting prank, it isn't a nice thing to do.

View

View offers a glimpse at the configuration file behind SWAT's GUI. Sometimes it's easier to scan through a text file to locate a problem than to work with the web interface. The View page has two modes. The Normal view (default) shows the minimum configuration file needed to implement your settings.

Switching to the Full view displays all the settings, including default options, for the Samba configuration. Each option is explicitly listed, regardless of its necessity.

Password

The Password page is used to set up Samba passwords for existing Mac OS X users, or change remote user passwords if using domain-level security and a remote host for user authentication.

If you've enabled a Mac OS X user so that she can log in to her account from Windows, you've effectively already used this feature. Because Apple has tied Samba to the Mac OS X authentication system, there is no need to touch these settings; use the Tiger Sharing preferences pane instead.

If Samba uses domain-level security, another server (such as a Windows primary domain controller) is the source for all authentication information. To change a user's password on the remote server, use the Client/Server Password Management features of the password screen:

- User Name—The remote user to change.
- Old Password—The user's existing password.
- New Password—The new password to set on the remote server.
- Re-type New Password—The same as the New Password option; used to verify typing.
- Remote Machine—The remote server that contains the username/password mappings.

Click the Change Password button to send the password changes to the remote server.

Creating a Simple Samba Share by Hand

Now let's go through the process of accessing a shared volume from a Windows computer. This example uses Windows XP. By the time you read this, five or six new variations of Windows will probably be available, so I apologize if the instructions don't match up entirely.

First, set up the server defaults. For my machine, POINTY, I've created a bare global configuration. Rather than including a screenshot for the share, I'm including the configuration from the `/etc/smb.conf` file. Each resource has its own block in the `config` file. Within that block, the options we've covered are listed along with their associated value. This is the global configuration block for my simple Samba server:

```
[global]
    auth methods = guest opendirectory
    passdb backend = opendirectorysam guest
    guest account = unknown
    workgroup = POISONTOOTH
```

```
netbios name = POINTY
server string = Poisontooth SAMBA Server
encrypt passwords = Yes
preferred master = Yes
dns proxy = No
wins support = Yes
```

The workgroup, NetBIOS name, and server string are personalized for my server and local area network. I've also chosen to have the server act as a WINS server and register as the preferred master browser on the network. It's important to note that encrypted passwords are enabled; otherwise, newer Windows clients (such as Windows 2000/XP) wouldn't be able to connect.

Next, the file share. I've created a folder `/filestorage/mp3s` on my computer to hold my library of iTunes MP3 files. My user account (`jray`) owns the folder and has read/write permission to it. This simple share, named `MyMP3s`, is defined as

```
[MyMP3s]
    path = /filestorage/mp3
    read only = No
```

Now, with only a few clicks of the mouse (barring Windows lockups), I'll be happily listening to my iTunes music on a Windows computer.

Mounting a Samba Share in Windows

There are a number of different ways to mount a network drive under Windows. If your Windows XP computer is set up with the same workgroup name as the Samba server, double-click My Network Places and then View Workgroup Computers. The Samba server should appear using the NetBIOS name you specified in the Global configuration.

Right-clicking My Network Places (or My Computer) and choosing Map Network Drive from the pop-up menu is the fastest mounting method. The screen shown in Figure 27.12 is displayed.

Choose a drive letter to use for the mounted volume and then enter the share path in the Folder field. The share path is entered as `\\`***`<NetBIOS name>`***`\`***`<share name>`***. For the sample share I've set up, the path is `\\pointy\MyMP3s\`. Click the Reconnect at Logon button to automatically mount the shared resource when you log in to the Windows computer. The Tiger Folder, shared through Samba, becomes usable like any other network drive on Windows.

Monitoring Samba Connections with `smbstatus`

Although the SWAT interface is fully capable of telling you who is accessing your server, sometimes a web browser isn't convenient. In that case, the `smbstatus` utility provides information about the active connections and users. For example:

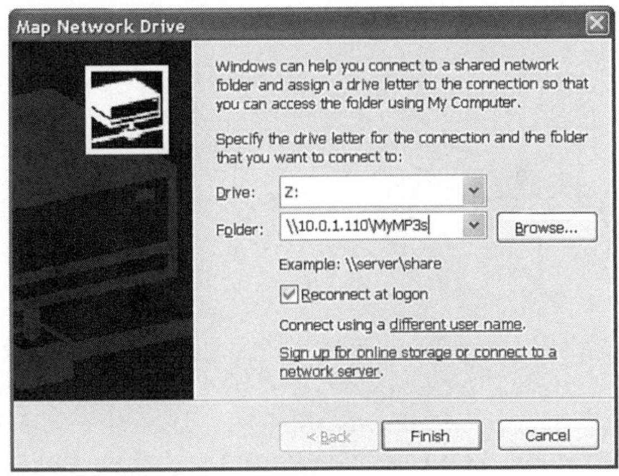

FIGURE 27.12 Map the shared folder in one simple step.

```
brezup:root root # smbstatus
NOTE: Service printers is flagged unavailable.

Samba version 3.0.0beta3
PID   Username   Group     Machine
-------------------------------------------------------------------
 951  jray      jray      client19   (10.0.1.119)
 965  jray      jray      painful    (10.0.1.107)

Service    pid   machine     Connected at
-------------------------------------------------------
IPC$       965  painful     Sat Mar 12 13:11:05 2005
jray       951  client19    Sat Mar 12 13:11:05 2005
jray       965  painful     Sat Mar 12 13:11:05 2005
No locked files
```

In this example, two client computers (`client19` and `painful`) are connected using the process IDs 951 and 965, respectively. The `painful` client is using the default `IPC$` and `jray` shares, whereas `client19` is just using `jray`. You can force a connection to close by killing the associated process ID.

Table 27.7 shows the most useful `smbstatus` options.

TABLE 27.7 `smbstatus` Options

Option	Purpose
`-b`	Summary of connected users.
`-d`	Detailed connection listing. This is the default mode.
`-L`	Lists locked files only.
`-p`	Lists the `smbd` process IDs and exit.
`-S`	Lists connected shares only.

TABLE 27.7 Continued

Option	Purpose
`-s <config file>`	Chooses the `smb.conf` file to use.
`-u <username>`	Displays only information relevant to a given username.
`-v`	Verbose output.

Summary

This chapter introduced the Windows SMB/CIFS file-sharing protocols and how they can be used on the Tiger platform. Mac OS X offers integration features with Windows, such as Active Directory binding, file and printer sharing, and basic Exchange server synchronization. For those wanting to share more than just their home directories, Tiger includes Samba 3.x. In a corporate environment, Apple's support of Windows technologies makes it possible to integrate and interoperate with Microsoft-centric networks.

PART VII

System and Server Health

IN THIS PART

CHAPTER **28**

Implementing Server Security and Advanced Network Configuration

IN THIS CHAPTER

- Managing Network Interfaces from the Command Line: `ifconfig`
- Performing Network Diagnostics: Network Utility
- Understanding the Importance of System Security
- Limiting Network Risks
- Detecting Attacks in Progress: Intrusion Detection
- Commonsense Preventive Measures

Managing Network Interfaces from the Command Line: `ifconfig`

You are already familiar with managing your network interfaces through the Network System Preferences pane, but if you need to, you can also manage your network interfaces from the command line, using the `ifconfig` utility.

Viewing Current Network Status

If you have ever changed your network location, and then found yourself unable to make a network connection, a convenient way to check your current network status is to use the `ifconfig` command. The `ifconfig` command displays and sets interface information on your system. The following is an example of running `ifconfig -a`, which lists all the interfaces on your machine:

```
brezup:sage sage $ ifconfig -a
lo0: flags=8049<UP,LOOPBACK,RUNNING,MULTICAST> mtu
16384
        inet 127.0.0.1 netmask 0xff000000
        inet6 ::1 prefixlen 128
        inet6 fe80::1 prefixlen 64 scopeid 0x1
gif0: flags=8010<POINTOPOINT,MULTICAST> mtu 1280
stf0: flags=0<> mtu 1280
en0: flags=8963<UP,BROADCAST,SMART,RUNNING,PROMISC,
SIMPLEX,MULTICAST> mtu 1500
        inet6 fe80::20d:93ff:fe49:f56 prefixlen 64
scopeid 0x4
```

```
        inet 140.254.104.243 netmask 0xfffffe00 broadcast 140.254.105.255
        ether 00:0d:93:49:0f:56
        media: autoselect (100baseTX <full-duplex>) status: active
        supported media: none autoselect 10baseT/UTP <half-duplex>
➥10baseT/UTP <full-duplex> 10baseT/UTP <full-duplex,hw-loopback>
➥ 100baseTX <half-duplex> 100baseTX <full-duplex> 100baseTX
➥<full-duplex,hw-loopback>
fw0: flags=8863<UP,BROADCAST,SMART,RUNNING,SIMPLEX,MULTICAST> mtu 2030
        lladdr 00:0d:93:ff:fe:49:0f:56
        media: autoselect <full-duplex> status: inactive
        supported media: autoselect <full-duplex>
```

Typically, the interface of interest would be `en0`, or for an AirPort card, `en1`. From this output, we see that interface `en0` has been assigned the IP address `140.254.104.243`, with a netmask of `0xfffffe00` (the hexadecimal for `255.255.254.0`). We see that its MAC address is 00:0d:93:49:0f:56, that the interface is active, that it autoselects what speed to use, and that it is currently running at 100BaseTX.

Configuring Network Interfaces

Not only can you use `ifconfig` to view the current network status of your machine, but you can also use it to configure your network interface.

You could, for example, change your machine's IP address using `ifconfig`. Here is the current IP address of interface en0:

```
creampuf:~ joray$ ifconfig en0
en0: flags=8863<UP,BROADCAST,SMART,RUNNING,SIMPLEX,MULTICAST> mtu 1500
        inet6 fe80::230:65ff:feca:f9a2 prefixlen 64 scopeid 0x2
        inet 192.168.1.200 netmask 0xffffff00 broadcast 192.168.1.255
        ether 00:30:65:ca:f9:a2
        media: autoselect (10baseT/UTP <half-duplex>) status: active
        supported media: none autoselect 10baseT/UTP <half-duplex> 10baseT/UTP
        ➥<full-duplex> 10baseT/UTP <full-duplex,hw-loopback> 100baseTX
        ➥<half-duplex> 100baseTX <full-duplex> 100baseTX
        ➥<full-duplex,hw-loopback> 1000baseTX <full-duplex> 1000baseTX
        ➥<full-duplex,hw-loopback> 1000baseTX <full-duplex,flow-control>
        ➥1000baseTX <full-duplex,flow-control,hw-loopback>
```

To change it to `192.168.1.201` with a netmask of `255.255.254.0`, do the following (from the console or you'll be a little surprised when your connection drops):

```
creampuf:~ joray$ sudo ifconfig  en0 192.168.1.201 netmask  255.255.254.0
```

Now `en0` has the new IP address and netmask as specified:

```
creampuf:~ joray$ ifconfig en0
en0: flags=8863<UP,BROADCAST,SMART,RUNNING,SIMPLEX,MULTICAST> mtu 1500
```

```
        inet6 fe80::230:65ff:feca:f9a2 prefixlen 64 scopeid 0x2
        inet 192.168.1.201 netmask 0xfffffe00 broadcast 192.168.1.255
        ether 00:30:65:ca:f9:a2
        media: autoselect (10baseT/UTP <half-duplex>) status: active
        supported media: none autoselect 10baseT/UTP <half-duplex> 10baseT/UTP <
full-duplex> 10baseT/UTP <full-duplex,hw-loopback> 100baseTX <half-duplex> 100ba
seTX <full-duplex> 100baseTX <full-duplex,hw-loopback> 1000baseTX <full-duplex>
1000baseTX <full-duplex,hw-loopback> 1000baseTX <full-duplex,flow-control> 1000b
aseTX <full-duplex,flow-control,hw-loopback>
```

If you want to change only the IP address without changing the netmask, run

```
creampuf:~ joray$ sudo ifconfig  en0 192.168.1.201
```

Select command documentation for `ifconfig` is included in Table 28.1. If you needed to move your IP address from one interface to the other, you might find `ifconfig down` and `ifconfig up` to be useful.

TABLE 28.1 Command Documentation Table for `ifconfig`

`ifconfig`	Configures network interface parameters
`ifconfig [-L] [-m]` *<interface>* `[create]` *<address_family>* `[`*<address*`[`*/prefixlength*`]`*>* `[`*<dest address>*`]] [`*<parameters>*`]`	
`ifconfig` *<interface>* `destroy`	
`ifconfig -a [-L] [-d] [-m] [-u] [`*<address_family>*`]`	
`ifconfig -l [-d] [-u] [`*<address_family>*`]`	
`ifconfig [-L] [-d] [-m] [-u]`	
`ifconfig` *<interface>* `vlan` *<vlan-tag>* `vlandev` *<iface>*	
`ifconfig` *<interface>* `-vlandev` *<iface>*	
`ifconfig` *<interface>* `bonddev` *<iface>*	
`ifconfig` *<interface>*`-bonddev` *<iface>*	
`ifconfig` assigns an address to a network interface and/or configures network interface parameters. It must be used at boot time to define the network address of each network interface. It may also be used at a later time to redefine an interface's network address or other operating parameters. Only the superuser can modify the configuration of a network interface.	
`-m`	If passed before an interface name, `ifconfig` displays all the supported media for the specified interface.
`-a`	Produces a full listing of all available interfaces.
`-l`	Produces a name-only listing of all available interfaces.
`-d`	Limits a listing to those interfaces that are down.
`-u`	Limits a listing to those interfaces that are up.
Available options for `ifconfig` are	
<address>	For the DARPA-Internet family, the address is either a hostname in the hostname database or a DARPA-Internet address expressed in the Internet standard dot notation.

28

TABLE 28.1 Continued

<address family>	Specifies the *<address family>*, which affects the interpretation of the remaining parameters. The address or protocol families currently supported are inet, iso, and ns.
<dest address>	Specifies the address of the correspondent on the other end of a point to point link.
<interface>	The *<interface>* parameter is a string of the form *<name of physical unit>*, such as `en0`.
The following parameters may be set with `ifconfig`:	
`add`	Another name for the alias parameter. Introduced for compatibility with BSD/OS.
`alias`	Establishes an additional network address for this interface.
`-alias`	Removes the network address specified.
`broadcast`	(inet only) Specifies the address to use to represent broadcasts to the network. The default broadcast address is the address with a host part of all 1s.
`delete`	Removes the network address specified. This is used if you incorrectly specified an alias or if it's no longer needed.
`down`	Marks an interface as down. When an interface is marked down, the system does not attempt to transmit messages through that interface. If possible, the interface is reset to disable reception as well. This doesn't automatically disable routes using the interface.
`tunnel` *<src-addr>* *<dest-addr>*	(IP tunnel devices only.) Configures the physical source and destination address for IP tunnel interfaces (gif(4)). The arguments *<src_addr>* and *<dest_addr>* are interpreted as the outer source/destination for the encapsulating IPv4/IPv6 header.
`deletetunnel`	Unconfigures the physical source and destination address for IP tunnel interfaces previously configured with `tunnel`.
`create`	Creates the specified network pseudo-device.
`destroy`	Destroys the specified network pseudo-device.
`mtu` *<n>*	Sets the maximum transmission unit of the interface to n; default is interface specific. The MTU is used to limit the size of packets that are transmitted on an interface. Not all interfaces support setting the MTU, and some interfaces have range restrictions.
`netmask` *<mask>*	(inet and ISO) Specifies how much of the address to reserve for subdividing networks into subnetworks. The mask includes the network part of the local address and the subnet part, which is taken from the host field of the address.
`up`	Marks an interface as `up`. Can be used to enable an interface after `ifconfig down` has been run. It happens automatically when setting the first address on an interface. If the interface was reset when previously marked down, the hardware is reinitialized.

Creating Interface Aliases

As you saw in Chapters 22 and 23, sometimes it can be helpful to have multiple IP addresses bound to the same interface. You can easily do this in the Network Preferences by duplicating your interface and editing the duplicate interface, but you can also use `ifconfig` to do this. The syntax is

```
ifconfig <interface> alias <additional IP address> 255.255.255.255
```

To add `192.168.1.201` as an additional IP address for `en0`, we do the following:

```
creampuf:~ joray$ sudo ifconfig  en0 alias 192.168.1.201 255.255.255.255
```

Now we can see that `en0` has two IP addresses:

```
creampuf:~ joray$ ifconfig en0
en0: flags=8863<UP,BROADCAST,SMART,RUNNING,SIMPLEX,MULTICAST> mtu 1500
        inet6 fe80::230:65ff:feca:f9a2 prefixlen 64 scopeid 0x2
        inet 192.168.1.200 netmask 0xffffff00 broadcast 192.168.1.255
        inet 192.168.1.201 netmask 0xffffff00 broadcast 255.255.255.255
        ether 00:30:65:ca:f9:a2
        media: autoselect (10baseT/UTP <half-duplex>) status: active
        supported media: none autoselect 10baseT/UTP <half-duplex> 10baseT/UTP
        ➥<full-duplex> 10baseT/UTP <full-duplex,hw-loopback> 100baseTX
        ➥<half-duplex> 100baseTX <full-duplex> 100baseTX <full-duplex,hw-loopback>
        ➥1000baseTX <full-duplex> 1000baseTX <full-duplex,hw-loopback> 1000baseTX
        ➥<full-duplex,flow-control> 1000baseTX
        ➥<full-duplex,flow-control,hw-loopback>
```

To make this change permanent, be sure to add that command to your startup scripts.

Performing Network Diagnostics: Network Utility

Unix-based operating systems are inherently networked operating systems from the original design, so they have a rather complete suite of network diagnostic software that comes with the basic operating system by default. We cover interaction with the command-line versions of these tools in several chapters to come. Apple has also provided a convenient GUI tool that functions as a front end to many of the diagnostics that the command-line tools can perform. Although it doesn't provide access to the complete range of options for each of the commands, the Network Utility application (path: `/Applications/Utilities/Network Utility`) is convenient for those who don't care to remember the syntax of command-line tools. The drawbacks are the need to navigate multiple windows to access the tool and the requirement for a graphical interface, whereas the command-line tools can be accessed to determine the health of your network from any machine with a network connection. The Network Utility application provides access to network diagnostics, which are described in the following sections:

- Info
- Netstat
- AppleTalk

- Ping
- Lookup
- Traceroute
- Whois
- Finger
- Port Scan

Info

The Interface Information (command-line command `ifconfig`) diagnostic gives you configuration information about your network interface. Shown in Figure 28.1, this diagnostic provides information regarding the traffic and error rate of the interface, as well as speed, hardware address, and vendor information.

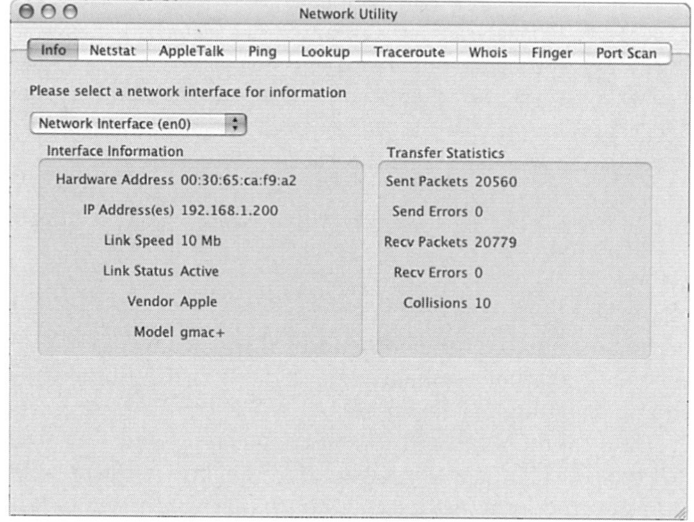

FIGURE 28.1 The Info pane of Network Utility provides information regarding the network interface and its performance.

Netstat

The Network Statistics (command-line command `netstat`) diagnostic gives you statistical information regarding your network. It can provide four types of network information—routing tables, by-protocol comprehensive statistics, multicast statistics, and current socket statistics. The information that's provided is extremely terse and dense, but with experience, it can prove invaluable in diagnosing network problems. Figure 28.2 shows the routing information display.

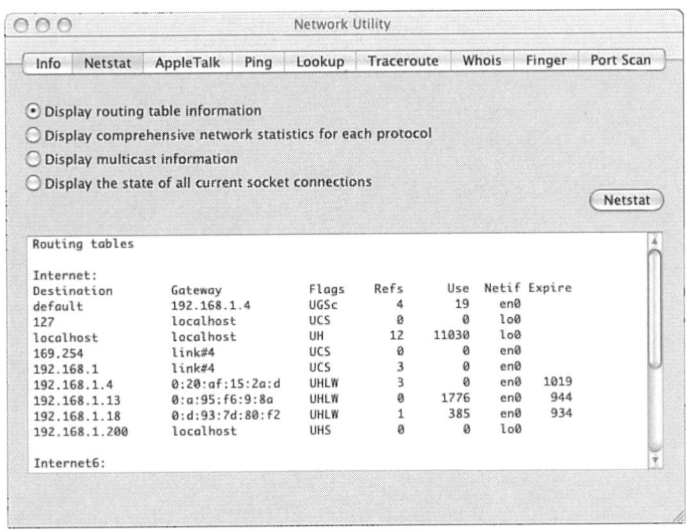

FIGURE 28.2 Click the Netstat button on the Netstat pane to look up connection information, but don't be surprised if you have to wait a while.

To get this information takes the GUI client some time, and you might have to wait for several minutes before the utility responds. The routing information specifies what your computer knows about how to get information to remote locations. The IPv4 information displayed in Figure 28.2 indicates that the machine knows how to send information to three machines (`192.168.1.4`, `192.168.1.13`, and `192.168.1.18`), directly to an entire C-class network (`192.168.1.`) by one route, directly to an automatically configured B-class network (`169.254.`, a network used by Rendezvous/Zeroconf), and to all other locations (`default`), by going through `192.168.1.4`, which is this machine's default router. The comprehensive network statistics display includes considerably more information than fits in the display in Figure 28.3. Included is a fairly complete listing of every type of network connection and traffic that your machine has engaged in, and any problems or abnormalities that have been observed with the data transmissions for that traffic.

The multicast information display provides information regarding multicast broadcast network information. If you are using your machine to stream QuickTime video or for other multicast applications, this display might provide useful information. Otherwise, expect it to remain essentially empty, as shown in Figure 28.4.

The socket connection section displays information on all current Internet and local (Unix) domain socket connections. The information displayed in this section is much larger than what is shown in Figure 28.5. The active Internet connections portion shows the local addresses and remote addresses involved in the connections as well as the state of the connection. Common states you'll see are established, closed, and listen. In the local (Unix) domain socket connections portion, the listing includes a connection type of stream or dgram, inode numbers, and occasionally a filename identifier.

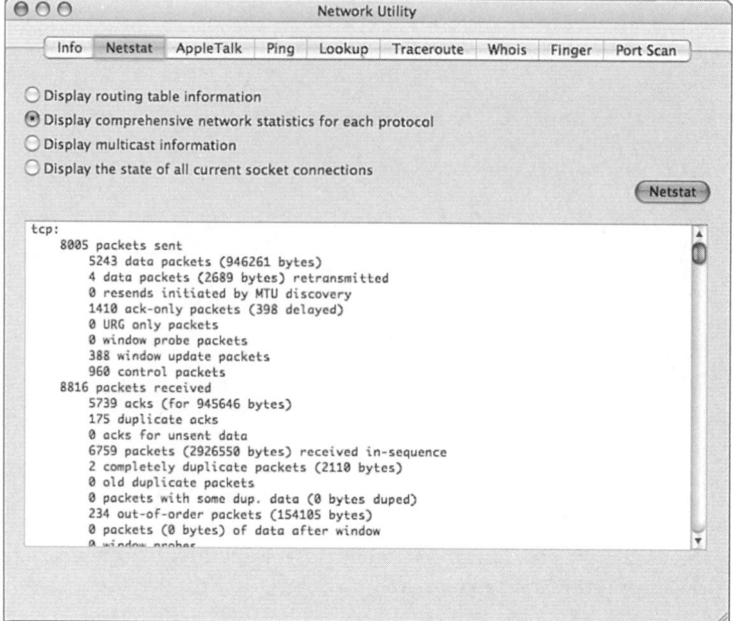

FIGURE 28.3 A portion of the comprehensive network statistics display of Network Utility.

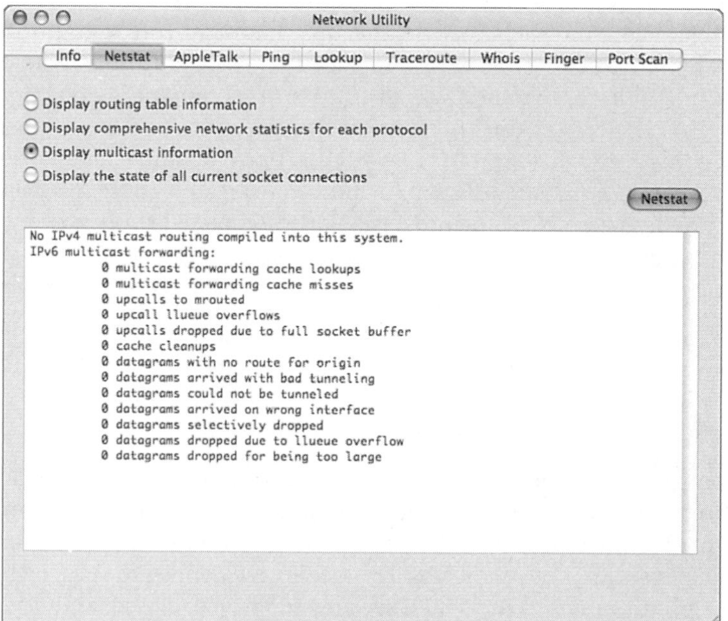

FIGURE 28.4 The multicast information display of Network Utility. If you do not use multicast services, expect this display to remain essentially empty.

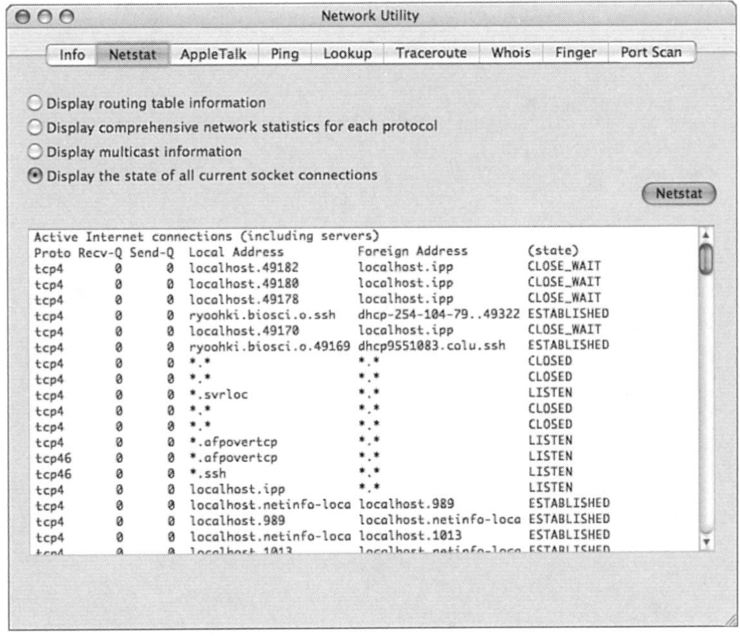

FIGURE 28.5 The active sockets connection information display of Network Utility.

AppleTalk

The AppleTalk (various command-line utilities) pane provides information on the AppleTalk network. Four types of information are available: AppleTalk statistics and error counts, saved PRAM AppleTalk information, available AppleTalk zones on the network, and information on a specific AppleTalk node. Of these four, the AppleTalk statistics and error counts display and the available AppleTalk zone information are probably the most interesting.

The AppleTalk statistics and error counts display, shown in Figure 28.6, can provide information on how healthy your AppleTalk network is at the given moment. If you have been having a lot of trouble and discover from this that many errors are occurring, let your network administrator know.

Figure 28.7 shows the AppleTalk zones display, which displays the available AppleTalk zones for your network. If you see many more zones than you ought to, let your network administrator know.

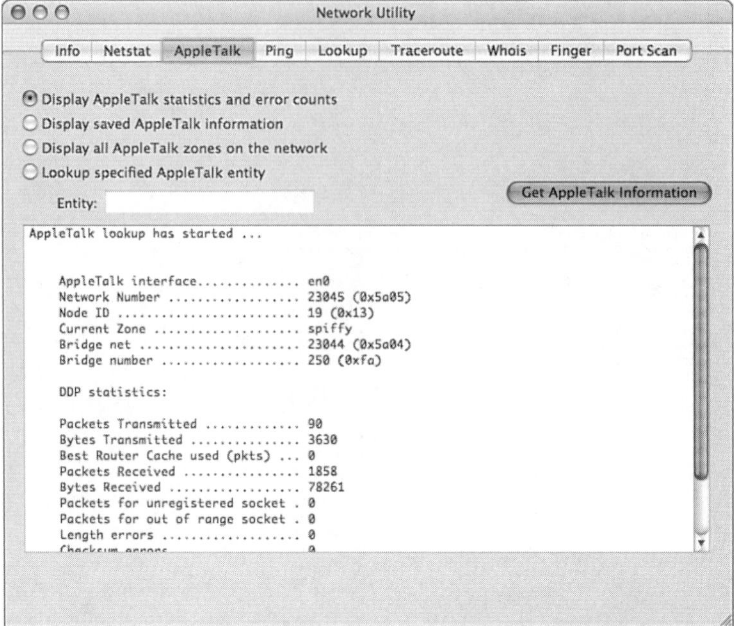

FIGURE 28.6 The AppleTalk statistics and error counts information display of Network Utility.

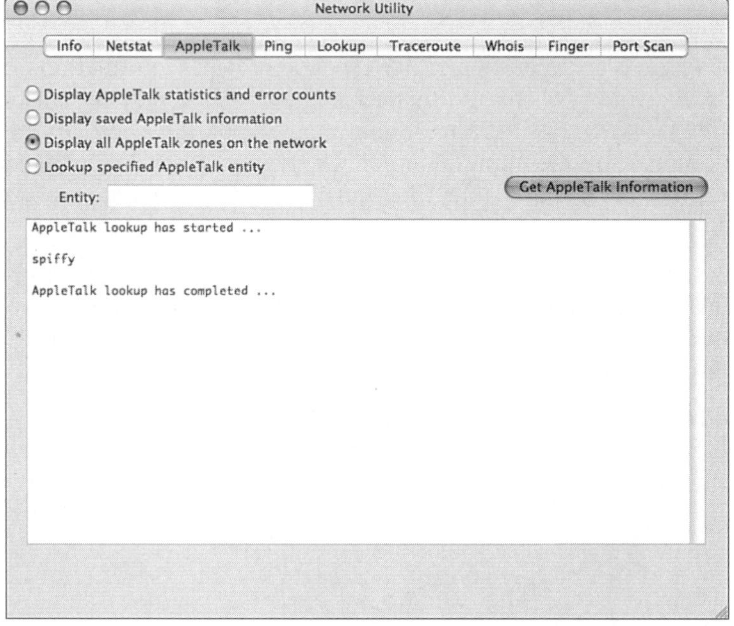

FIGURE 28.7 The AppleTalk zones information display of Network Utility.

Ping

The Ping pane provides network connection/traffic testing (command-line program `ping`), as shown in Figure 9.34. It enables you to ping a remote machine to determine whether it, and the network between your machine and it, are alive. The `ping` program injects packets destined for a remote machine into the network, destined for a mandatory service that echoes the ping back to the originating machine. Usually, 10 packets are injected into the network at one-second intervals; both the round-trip time and information regarding any packets that don't complete the trip are reported back. You have the option of continuously sending packets to the remote host, but unless you have permission and a good reason to do so, this is usually considered, at the minimum, to be rude. The `icmp_seq` value increases by one for every packet sent, so if you see a gap in the values displayed, you know that one (or more) packets did not complete their round-trips.

Also displayed is a TTL (Time To Live) value, which starts at 255 and decreases for every machine that reroutes the packet. Usually, all these values will be the same, but if network trouble causes packets to take alternative routes between the machines, differing TTL values might be reflected. To keep errant packets from circling the Internet forever, each packet is restricted to a finite number of machines—usually 255—that can touch it before it dies. Packets that get lost in routing loops and never make it to their destination quickly run out of TTL counts and are discarded. Finally, the time each packet took to traverse the network is displayed in milliseconds (thousandths of a second).

A number of modern firewalls optionally reject ping requests. Consequently, you might run into times when a ping request makes it seem like a host is unreachable when it really is not.

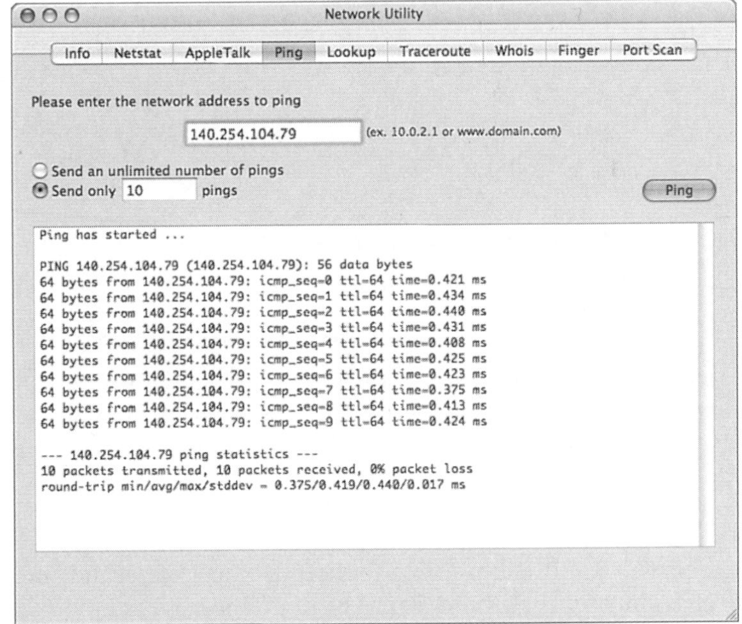

FIGURE 28.8 The Ping pane of Network Utility enables you to determine whether a remote host can be reached and how the network between the machines is performing.

Lookup

The Lookup (command-line command `nslookup` [deprecated] or `dig`) diagnostic enables you to query the DNS (Domain Name Service) information for a machine. This includes information that maps the fully qualified domain name (FQDN), such as `www.killernuts.org`, to an IP address, and considerable additional information as well. The default operation of the diagnostic is to look up IP addresses for an FQDN, as shown in Figure 28.9.

The diagnostic can also look up other types of information out of the DNS, such as what machine handles the email for a host and the canonical names (aliases) by which it might be known. Figure 28.10 shows the range of options for the lookup diagnostic.

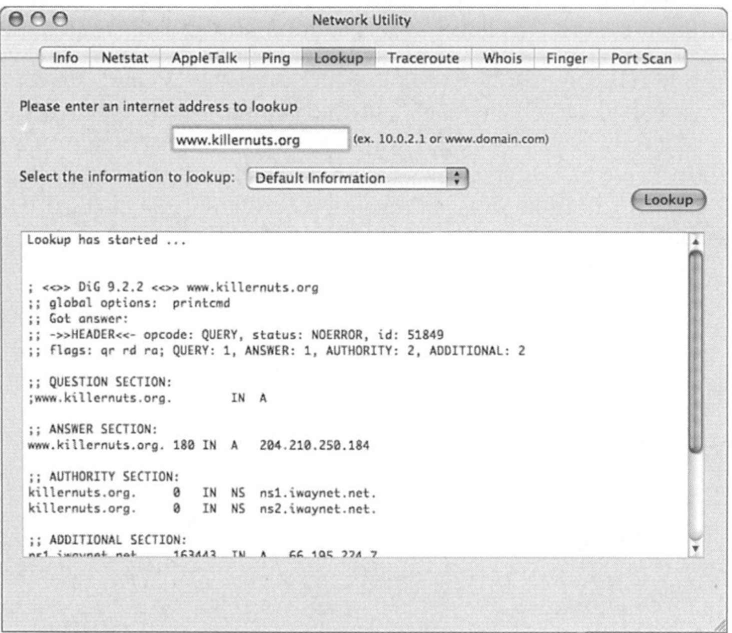

FIGURE 28.9 The results of a default search for `www.killernuts.org` with the Lookup tool of the Network Utility application.

The information that the Lookup tool can provide includes the following:

- Default Information—The default information returned by the DNS server in response to a query; typically, the IP address to hostname mapping, the Start of Authority (SOA) record holders for the domain name, and the authoritative DNS servers for the domain.
- Internet Address—The IP address associated with a host name.
- Canonical Name—An IP address can have both a proper name and potentially multiple alias names that point to it. The canonical name lookup provides information on the proper name that is equivalent to an alias.

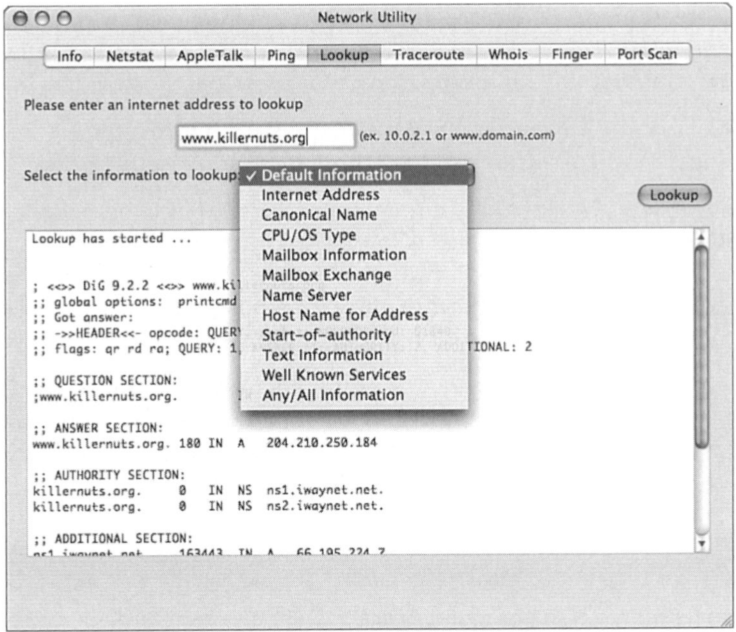

FIGURE 28.10 The Lookup type options for the Lookup tool of the Network Utility application set the amount of data that will be queried from the remote server.

- CPU/OS Type—Attempts to get operating system and CPU information for a remote host, but this is not a mandatory item for the host to provide to the world.
- Mailbox Information—Mailbox or mailing list information. There is no requirement that this information be maintained correctly on the DNS host, so the results of a query for this information should not be considered definitive.
- Mailbox Exchange—MX (Mail Exchanger) record information. It is frequently impractical to have every host in a domain manage its own incoming email. For this reason, a DNS record might specify that mail appearing to be destined for one particular host be routed instead to an alternative destination. This allows, for example, mail to `ray@calvin.biosci.ohio-state.edu`, `ray@suzie.biosci.ohio-state.edu`, and `ray@waashu.biosci.ohio-state.edu` to all be routed to, and received by, the mail server machine `ryoko.biosci.ohio-state.edu`.
- Name Server—Returns the list of authoritative name servers for a domain.
- Host Name for Address—Reverse lookup of an FQDN for a particular IP address.
- Start of Authority—A particular DNS server must be specified as the authoritative server for a particular IP-to-domain name mapping. An additional piece of information, known as the Start of Authority (SOA) record, specifies a host that is authoritative for other information, such as contact information for problems with the domain. Frequently these are the same, but it is possible that DNS information may be delegated to servers that do not have all the same information stored as the SOA

records—for example, when DNS information is maintained internally by a domain but a parent organization keeps administrative control. In this case, the SOA records should be consulted for all information other than IP-to-hostname mapping.

- Text Information—Any optionally registered textual information regarding the queried host. Few domains register anything interesting in this field.
- Well Known Services—Return information regarding well-known service types that the host might be providing. This is intended to give information regarding such things as whether the host is running FTP services, or HTTPD services, and so on. This is not a required piece of information for a host to provide to its DNS server, so few bother to provide correct or interesting information here.
- Any/All Information—Investigate and return all known information regarding the host. The actual information returned depends on the configuration of the server queried and the information it contains. Typically, a query for all information returns something similar to the default information.

Traceroute

The Traceroute (command-line program `traceroute`) diagnostic provides information on the route that a packet must travel between your machine and a remote machine. When the network is working properly, this information will usually be of little interest to you. If you can't reach a remote machine, however, it is sometimes useful to see this information so that you can tell whether the problem is with only a segment of the network, or if it's with the remote machine itself. Figure 28.11 shows the result of a successful Traceroute trace to the host `www.tcp.com`. Each line of the output indicates a machine through which the traffic to `www.tcp.com` had to be routed, and the time it took for that particular router to respond. The trace ends at the host `www.tcp.com`, indicating that the network is successful at transmitting data between the querying host and `www.tcp.com`.

Figure 28.12 shows the result of an attempt to trace the route to a host that is down, on the same subnet as `www.tcp.com`. The traffic in this case manages to make it almost all the way to its final destination, but cannot reach the requested final host. If we know that the host is not, in fact, the next machine along the network (that is, Traceroute fails somewhere between you and the target, rather than at the target), we can infer that the problem is actually a network problem. Therefore, the routing of traffic between your machine and the remote machine is currently defective.

If a transient failure were occurring in the Internet and the trace stopped well before reaching the target host's subnet, we could determine that problems reaching the host were because of something other than the host itself being down.

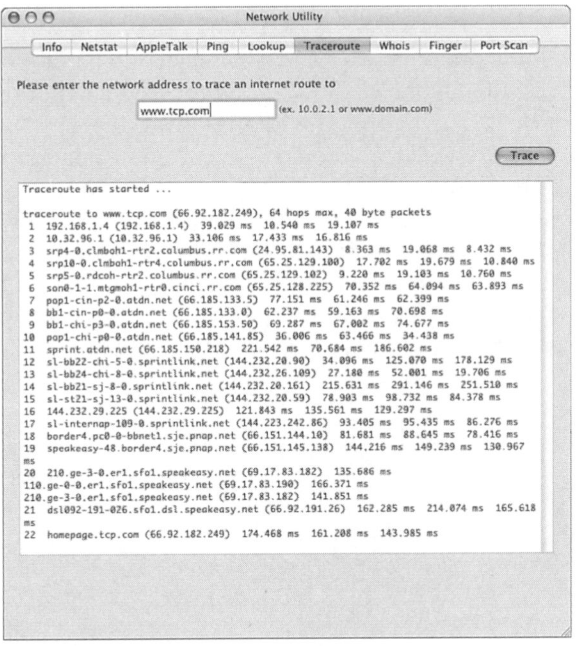

FIGURE 28.11 The Traceroute output includes diagnostic information regarding each router that the packet needed to traverse to reach the remote host.

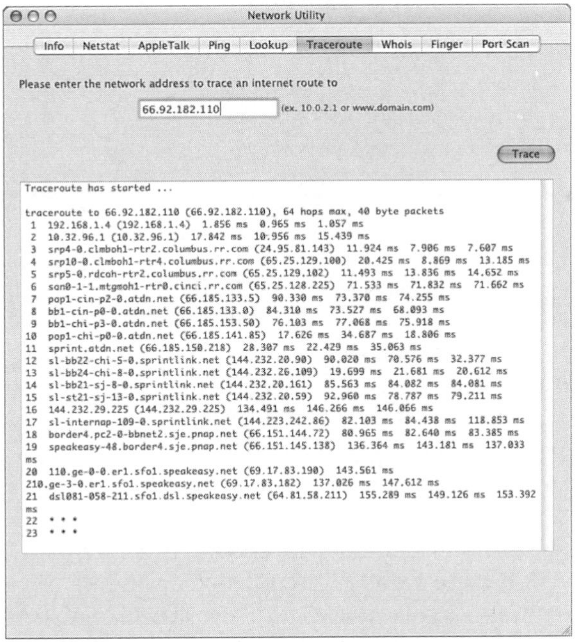

FIGURE 28.12 The output from Traceroute showing an unsuccessful attempt to reach a remote host on the same subnet as `www.tcp.com`.

Whois

The Whois (command-line program whois) program actually has a more flexible use than is presented by this tool. It is designed to talk to remote servers that provide a sort of phone directory function. Apple has pointed the Whois tool of the Network Utility application to a subset of whois servers that provide directory information regarding the ownership and management of hostnames and domains, but you can also specify a whois server that is not already on the list. Figure 28.13 shows the results of trying to use the Whois tool to look up itchysweater.com. The whois server selected, whois.internic.net, machine knows only that another server, whois.godaddy.com, should know the complete information for this host. Figure 28.14 shows a portion of the results of specifying whois.godaddy.com as the whois server and reissuing the whois query for itchysweater.com.

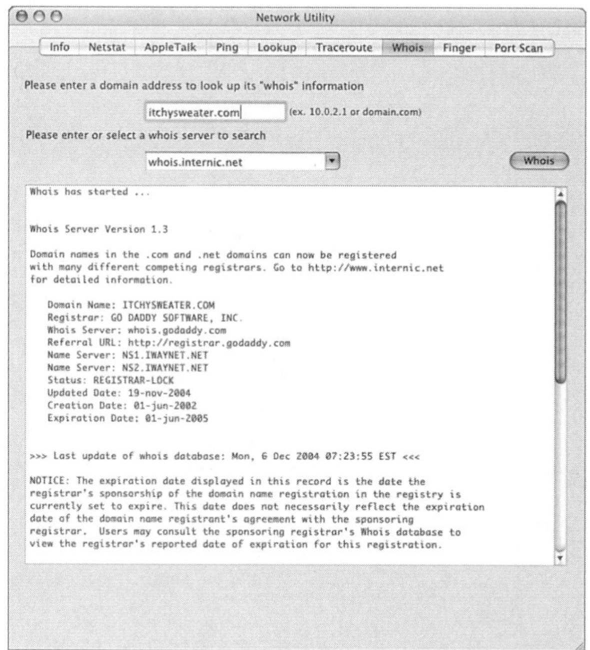

FIGURE 28.13 The output from whois for itchysweater.com at whois.internic.net.

You can also use the Whois tool from the Network Utility application to make other types of queries to whois servers. For example, if you point the whois server to osu.edu, you can find out everyone who has "ness" in their name by searching for ness in the domain address box. Figure 28.15 shows a portion of the results of this search. In this case, it's a listing of people and email addresses that the server knows about at the institution that match the query "ness". If there are a lot of results, you will receive partial output and a comment that the sizelimit has been exceeded. This particular Whois server also enables you to get more specific information regarding the people identified and gives instructions at the bottom of the listing of names. Other whois servers can be contacted similarly and can be used to obtain a range of types of information.

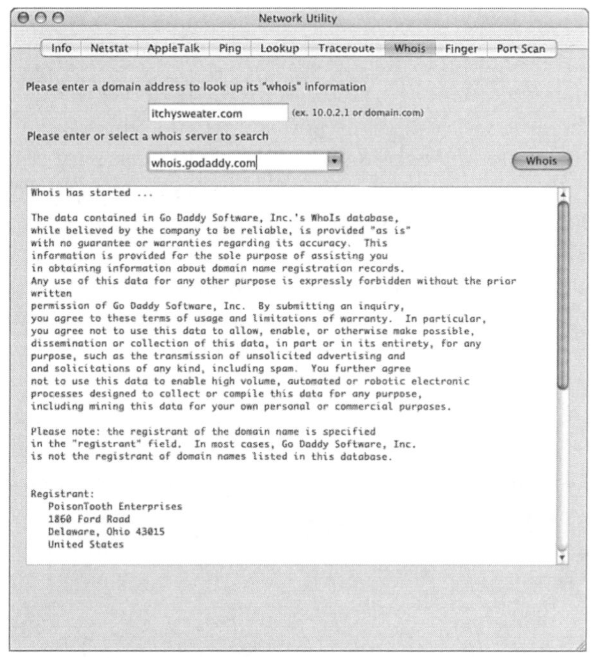

FIGURE 28.14 The output from whois for `itchysweater.com` at `whois.godaddy.com`. This server knows considerably more about the domain.

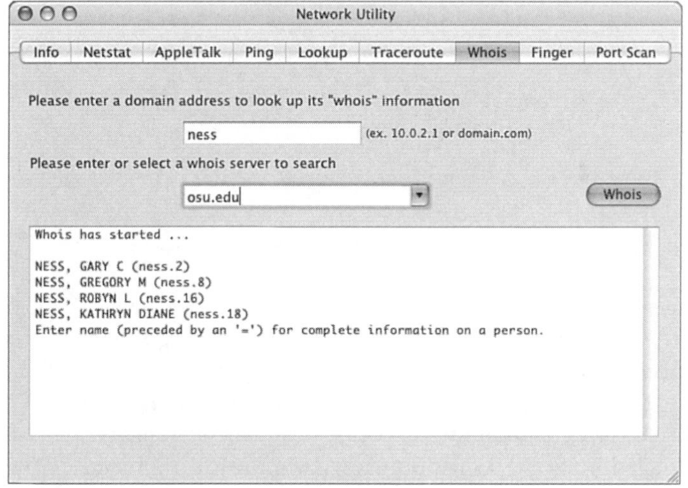

FIGURE 28.15 The output from a "misuse" of the Whois tool of the Network Utility application to query a `whois` server that doesn't provide domain name information.

Finger

The Finger (command-line program `finger`) tool of the Network Utility application gives you the ability to query the `finger` server of a host. This server, if enabled, provides information regarding who a user is (full name and so on) and when the user was most recently logged in. It is generally considered to be a minor security risk to run the `finger` server because it lets crackers know whether it's safe to break into a system. But, if you know of a machine that has the service enabled, you can use this tool to access it. Figure 28.16 shows the results of using the `finger` tool to finger `ray@rosalyn.biosci.ohio-state.edu`. Notice that the server returns information about all known users with `ray` in their names. Different `finger` servers return different information about users. This one is rather sparse, leaving out most of the users' personal information but still indicates whether the users are logged in.

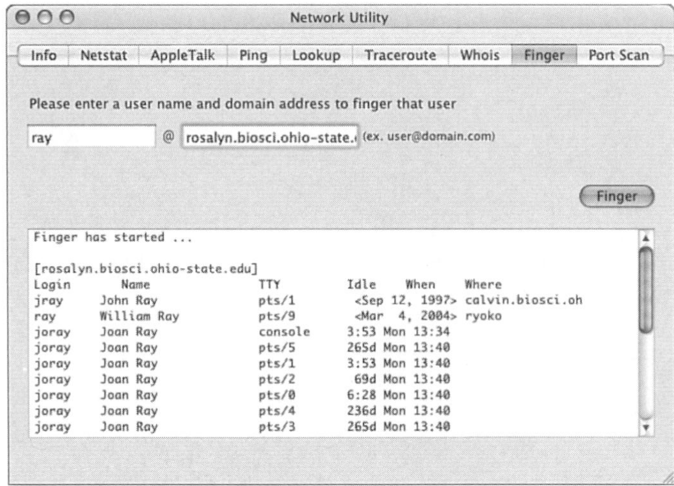

FIGURE 28.16 The output of a Finger tool lookup of `ray@rosalyn.biosci.ohio-state.edu`.

Port Scan

Port Scan (various command-line programs) examines a host for available opportunities to access it via the network. Conceptually, TCP/IP networking is accomplished by establishing connections between logical constructs, known as *ports*, created by the networking software of each machine. These ports can be thought of as analogous to a series of numbered sockets into which a network connection can be plugged. The network connection must be plugged into one socket on each communicating machine; hence, it has an originating port and a destination port. Some network services always exist at particular fixed ports and are connected to based on the knowledge that they exist at these known locations. Other applications attempt to generate a small level of security by opening a randomly numbered port and not advertising its presence. Connections then require that a connecting machine know where to look to find them. This isn't a particularly useful way of establishing security, but it does turn out to be a reasonably decent way for a cracker to hide the fact that he or she has broken into your machine. After the system has been compromised, many crackers will install a backdoor on an unknown port so that they can come and go undetected, instead of connecting to the normal known ports, and thereby incurring a noticeable connection to a known service.

The Port Scan tool of the Network Utility application causes your machine to examine all the ports on a remote machine and tell you which of them appear to have software listening to them. If the monitored ports don't correspond to known services, it's possible that there's been a network break-in. Figure 28.17 shows the Port Scan tool results for a machine running FTP and SSH. I can account all the ports shown in the results, but I did not have the patience to wait for the `portscan` to finish. There could be something else running that I don't know about. Additionally, it is considered to be excruciatingly bad form to `portscan` someone else's computer. This is exactly the methodology that crackers use to examine a machine for known vulnerabilities. We'd go so far as to say that it is a bit irresponsible of Apple to have put this tool in a user-level GUI application, and we recommend that you not use it, except on your own devices.

CAUTION

Think carefully before you use the Port Scan tool on a machine that you're not the owner or administrator of. Scanning a host without permission can be considered an attempted break-in and could result in legal action against you. Think carefully before you use it on one that you do own as well. Make a typo in your IP address, and it's probably someone else's machine that your Mac will be nosing through.

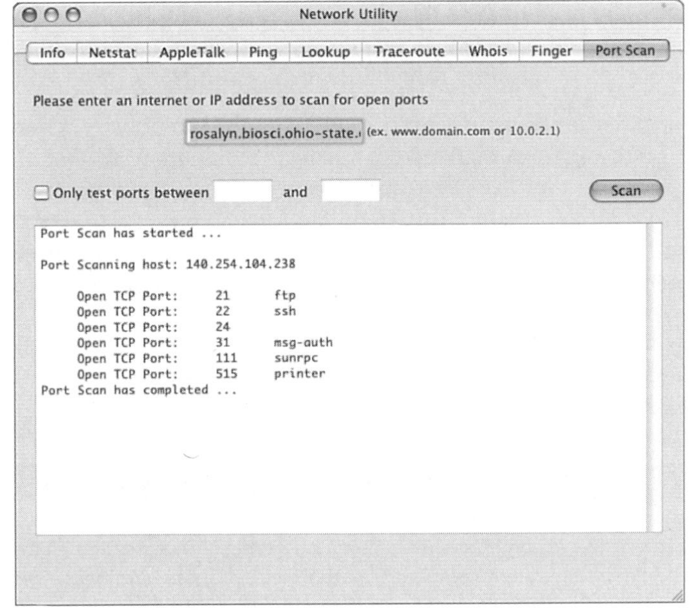

FIGURE 28.17 The output of the Port Scan tool of the Network Utility application.

Understanding the Importance of System Security

Before we can reasonably discuss ways to make your Mac OS X machine more secure, it's important to understand why you should care and what you're facing.

You might be wondering, "Why bother with security?" You've never cared about securing your Mac before. In fact, prior to Mac OS X, security has rarely been an issue for a Mac owner. However, as a Unix-based operating system, Mac OS X brings with it not only the advantages of a Unix operating system—it also brings the disadvantages. Unfortunately, one of those disadvantages is security, which has always been a problem for networked, multitasking operating systems. This is unsettling at the beginning, but the simple fact is that nothing can be done to make any network-connected Unix machine (Mac OS X or otherwise) completely secure. To paraphrase one system administrator's feeling about securing a Unix machine, "I'd pull the plug and the network, put the machine in a safe, fill the safe with concrete, lock it, and drop it in the middle of Hudson Bay—and even then I wouldn't be sure."

That take might be a little extreme, but you get the point. If your machine is on a network, and/or the hardware is physically accessible, it's vulnerable to something somehow. Your best efforts at security are only capable of increasing the effort, time, and creativity required for a cracker to access your hardware—you simply can't make it impossible.

Crackers target anything they can find on your computer or network. Your Mac OS X computer runs a variety of server processes that enable it to communicate with the outside world. A single programming flaw in one of these daemons could open administrative access to anyone. If a cracker can't find a way in directly, he can direct attacks on your network hardware or your ISP's hardware. Switches, routers, and other devices are also susceptible to attack. If your computer has blocked access to outside networks, the intruder might resort to IP spoofing to fake his real location.

The threat of computer break-ins is very real and a very real concern—even if you're doing everything right. For example, earlier versions of Sendmail (the mail server that used to be included with the Mac OS X installation) suffered from a bug that allowed remote crackers to send a specially formatted email to the server and force it to execute pieces of code with full administrator privileges. Imagine it: A person, anywhere in the world, could potentially take over control of your computer by sending it an email message. Even experienced administrators were at risk from this bug. Although Sendmail has since been patched, this is an excellent example of the type of attack that's possible. For more information about this particular exploit, check out `http://ciac.llnl.gov/ciac/bulletins/h-23.shtml`.

NOTE

Crackers, not hackers: There seems to be a popular misconception that the term *hacker* means someone who breaks into computers. This hasn't always been the case, and annoys the hackers out there who do not break into computers. To many hackers, the term *hacker* means a person who hacks on code to make it do new and different things—frequently with little regard to corporate-standard good programming, but also frequently with a Rube Goldberg–like, elegant-but-twisted logic.

Hackers, to those who don't break into computers, are some of the true programming wizards—the guys who can make a computer do almost anything. These are people you want on your side, and dirtying their good name by associating them with the average scum that try to break into your machine isn't a good way to accomplish this.

So, to keep the real hackers happy, we refer to the people who compromise your machine's security as *crackers* in this book. We hope you follow our lead in your interactions with the programmers around you.

You might still be wondering, "Why bother?" If the machine can't be made completely secure, why try? When your machine is brand new and not very customized, perhaps you can afford to have that attitude. Reinstalling the operating system is not all that traumatic at that stage. However, because you've made it to this chapter, you've seen Mac OS X from many angles and perhaps even implemented some customizations to your system. Hence, you might not feel like doing it all over again.

So, if you can't be *completely* secure, what can you do? You can be *reasonably* secure. Exactly how secure is reasonable differs from case to case, and depends on a wide range of factors. Later in this chapter, we discuss some of these factors and how to assess your needs. For now, understand that when designing security measures, there's a threshold beyond which expending extra effort does not produce a sufficient increase in security to make that effort worthwhile. You can liken this to the somewhat facetious advice given for how to protect yourself when hiking in bear country—"always hike with someone who runs slower than you do." Your goal in securing your system is to make your machine and your network less attractive than the next guy's system to the cracker. In this chapter, we look at some ways to accomplish that goal.

Types of Attackers

We divide the types of attackers you're likely to meet into three subsets. Although it might not seem obvious at first consideration, the variety that you're the most likely to meet—regardless of the type of data you're protecting—is frequently both the most and least dangerous.

The Motivated Cracker

The type of cracker you're probably least likely to meet is the dedicated and motivated professional or amateur cracker with a mission. This person might be an industrial spy trying to discover your company's trade secrets, a student trying to change his grade, or a hobbyist who simply finds your security measures a challenge.

CAUTION

Obscurity isn't to be relied on, but it sure doesn't hurt!

Many system administrators, and even OS vendors, have historically had a bad habit of attempting to implement security measures based only on the fact that people didn't know about the holes in them. This is a concept known as *security through obscurity*, and is generally considered a bad thing to rely on. On the other hand, obscurity in addition to other security measures certainly doesn't hurt. Keeping your system and security measures low profile is always a good idea. If you have a system with extra-tight security measures, telling people just how tight they are is the surest way to attract the person who delights in cracking systems "just because."

Rely neither on security through obscurity nor on the invincibility of your security measures. The best way to motivate a person to try to crack your system just because it's there is to let on that you think it can't be done.

The motivated cracker isn't likely to leave a large amount of evidence of his comings and goings. The types of this cracker vary between unlikely to do any significant damage (other than observing your data) to making insidious and difficult-to-detect modifications to the contents of your system.

To defeat this type of cracker, you must understand his motivation and either remove it or resign yourself to a constant battle to stay ahead. The only way to actually stop these people permanently is to track them down and pursue legal remedies against them.

The Casual Experimenter

The next type of attacker you're likely to meet is the casual experimenter. These individuals don't usually intend any significant harm and aren't usually very motivated to invade your system. They're frequently just a bit overcurious, and are trying out something that they stumbled across somewhere on the Internet. This doesn't mean that they're not dangerous—their lack of intent can't prevent simple typing mistakes that can be disastrous to a person with root access. Thankfully, these individuals aren't usually too difficult to defend against because they're usually not particularly sophisticated. They also don't tend to be worth investing much effort in tracking down legally.

The Script Kiddie

The most common type of cracker doesn't even deserve to be called a cracker. Historically, crackers have been frequently thought of as Robin Hood characters, with a sort of romantic fascination with their exploits. Not to minimize the impropriety of the legendary crackers' actions, but you can appreciate the creativity and tenacity of these individuals without approving of their actions. By the standards set by the crackers of old, the vast majority of today's crackers barely qualify as cracker-wannabe wannabes.

Today's prototypical cracker is a young adult with too much free time who found a cracking script on a Web site somewhere and is trying to use it to show his friends he's an "lEEt HaCkEr dOOd." In fact, these new crackers are called *script kiddies*.

These individuals are both a trivial and significant concern. If you keep your system up-to-date and pay attention to the latest cracking scripts and to the patches against them, you're almost invulnerable to actual intrusion at the hands of these people. They don't generally try anything more complicated than running a script they've borrowed from someone else. So, if you keep your system secure against these scripts, you're usually secure against cracker wannabes. That doesn't mean they're completely innocuous because they can still consume your network resources while trying to break into your system.

However, they can be very dangerous if you don't keep your system completely up-to-date because there are so darned many of them, and because they're basically glory hounds interested in nothing more than self-aggrandizement. To give you a perspective on the magnitude of their numbers, here at The Ohio State University, we see unsophisticated cracking attempts of this sort multiple times every week, directed at the thousands of machines on campus. A Linux machine, installed out of the box and not immediately secured against intrusion, stands a better than 50% chance of being cracked within 24 hours if it's attached to the network here. Fortunately, a Mac OS X machine installed out of the box is a bit more secure, but that doesn't mean it's invincible.

Also, because their basic goal is self-aggrandizement and also because they don't get that much glory for using someone else's script, these people are rarely content to break into a system, tread lightly, and leave without a trace. Instead, they're more likely to erase the contents of your hard drive, or replace your corporate web page with pornography so that they have some evidence to show their "lEEt HaCkEr dOOd" friends.

Securing your system against these attacks is simply a matter of watching every security discussion list and cracker site for signs of trouble and postings of new cracking scripts, and then applying every security patch as quickly as it becomes available. Simple, no? As satisfying as it might be to track them down and squash them like the insects they are, it's usually impractical. Ninety percent of these attacks come from users with transient accounts, and the best you'll usually do is chase them to a different account. If you do happen to catch one, please do let the Internet system administration community know—the newsgroup `alt.sysadmin.recovery` is a good venue—public lynchings are always well attended.

Types of Attacks

Next, let's look at what methods attackers might use to access your machine. This is especially important if your machine is connected to an unprotected network or if it serves as a firewall.

Software and Operating System Flaws

The most common type of attack you'll encounter is one that attempts to exploit flaws in application or operating system software. There's probably not much you can do about most software flaws other than hope that the providers find and fix the problems promptly. Although this is a problem from a security standpoint, the positive side is that if you're spending the time to watch the cracking web pages and the security mailing lists, you'll know about the problems as soon as the crackers do. With the information you get from these sources and your understanding of the special risks your site incurs, you can assess whether leaving that software on your machine is an acceptable risk until the vendor fixes it. Note that Apple does put out semi-regular security updates via Software Update.

You need to be aware that some of these flaws require prior access to your system to exploit, whereas others can be exploited from a remote site over the network. Don't make the mistake of assuming that because no one has actually logged in to your machine, you can't be or haven't been attacked.

Brute Force Attacks

Although not a particularly elegant form of attack, the brute force attack is one that you can only partially prevent. In its simplest form, this attack is a cracker attempting to log in to a system by sitting at a machine and iteratively typing attempts at passwords into the prompt. There's not much you can do to keep people from trying this sort of thing.

Keep an eye on the system logs, and you'll see the trivial attempts as they occur. However, there's typically much more danger from this sort of attack when a cracker manages to get your password file and can attempt to crack the passwords on his own machine at his leisure. To prevent this, some systems use a shadow password facility to keep the password file from being readable by a normal user. The early releases of Mac OS X did not include a shadow password facility, making it important to consider restricting the executable permission on NetInfo utilities, such as `nidump` and `niutil`, to `root` only. Starting around Mac OS X 10.2, a shadow password facility was implemented.

Denial of Service

Denial of service (DoS) attacks are generally destructive attempts rather than attempts to access your system. When the attacks come from a network of multiple machines, they're known as distributed denial of service attacks. Both types of attacks are targeted at preventing you and your users from using your machines instead of allowing an intruder access. Because this can be effectively accomplished without the aid of your system, there's little that you can do about many of these attacks. Because a denial of service attack rarely results in an actual security violation or illegitimate access of your system, your best defense is detection and elimination.

Although the specific methods employed in different varieties of denial of service attacks vary, they share a common feature: the exhausting of some service or resource that your machines require or provide. Why do people do this? Good question. You might expect this sort of behavior from a disgruntled ex-employee attacking a former employer or from a student who thinks it's a funny practical joke. Less expected are denial of service attacks that seem to happen as random vandalism just because the attacker can do it.

Certain denial of service attacks can be mitigated or prevented with software or hardware updates. In general, these updates tend to be installation of operating system patches to disallow certain types of connections or installation of filtering hardware to block certain types of network traffic. Denial of service attacks range from flooding users' email, to absorbing all your HTTP server connections, to running your printer out of paper, to flooding your network with ICMP ping packets. Unfortunately, there's little you can count on to be reliably effective other than constant vigilance and swift retribution.

CAUTION

Not all denial of service attacks are devoid of security risks. Some attacks are targeted at services that are known to break inelegantly and that sometimes allow privileged access when broken. Just because a denial of service attack looks relatively harmless, don't allow yourself to be complacent. It could be less harmless than it looks, or it could be a prelude to more unpleasant attacks.

Most attacks can generally be thwarted by taking the following precautions:

- Vigilance is your best defense against denial of service attacks. Watching your machine's load and network performance are the best ways to discover an attack in progress.
- Consider building a monitoring web page that collects this information from all your machines and provides you with a continuously updated representation of the state of the world.
- A gateway between your cluster and the outside world can be used to deny traffic from a problematic outside host. Unfortunately, this can't prevent an outside host from effectively denying your network services just by banging away at your gateway until your network bandwidth is consumed.
- Enlist the help of system administrators upstream from your site in tracking and blocking denial of service attacks as they occur. Because you can't effectively prevent users on the other side of the world from running flood-ping against your machines, you'll need to find someone between you and them who can help.

Physical Attacks

Many administrators in charge of system security overlook this area of obvious weakness in their security strategy. Computers don't need to be logged in for a person to access their data. A person unscrupulous enough to crack your machines is just as happy to simply yank a hard drive out of your machine to steal the data on it. These sorts of attacks are usually easy to detect, but can cause significant downtime while critical hardware is replaced.

Although distributed computing and distributed storage are popular in certain environments, if security is a goal, especially data security, you should severely restrict access to all hardware with mission-critical data.

By far the easiest physical attack on your hardware is the power switch or reset button combined with the capability to boot the machine into single-user mode without a password or to boot off of a device specified at startup, also without a password. When in single-user mode, an attacker can get a dump of your passwords, change your root password, and so on.

Limiting Network Risks

Although it might seem like there is nothing you can do to protect your machine, there are certain measures you can take to limit network risks. We will look at limiting per-service access with TCP Wrappers and using the built-in firewall, `ipfw`.

Limiting Per-Service Access with TCP Wrappers

A common way to restrict access to some TCP services is to use the TCP Wrappers program. TCP Wrappers is a package that monitors and filters requests for TCP (Transmission

Control Protocol) services. We don't look at the protocol in any detail here—that's a book subject in itself. Suffice it to say that the protocol has enough control information in it that we can use a package like TCP Wrappers to filter some of that traffic. TCP Wrappers can be used to restrict certain network services to individual computers or networks.

To make use of this program on some flavors of Unix, TCP Wrappers must be installed by the system administrator. This isn't a necessary step in Mac OS X because the TCP Wrappers program comes preinstalled on the system. You can use TCP Wrappers for services that you have running out of `inetd` or `xinetd`. The `/etc/inetd.conf` file in Mac OS X already assumes that you use TCP Wrappers, as evidenced by a line such as the following:

```
#ftp    stream  tcp     nowait  root    /usr/libexec/tcpd               ftpd -l
```

The `/usr/libexec/tcpd` portion of the previous line indicates that TCP Wrappers is used to call `ftpd`.

Although using TCP Wrappers with `inetd` is the default in Mac OS X, it isn't the default for using `xinetd`. That's because of the controls already available in `xinetd`. Recall that `xinetd` has the `only_from` and `no_access` directives, which can help you to restrict access to services. If you decide that you want to use TCP Wrappers for host access restrictions on a service controlled by `xinetd`, you need to add a flag, `NAMEINARGS`, to the service and further expand the `server_args` line to include the full path to the service. Replace the original path to the server with the path to `tcpd`. Here's an example for using TCP Wrappers for restricting access to the FTP service in `xinetd`:

```
service ftp
{
        disable         = no
        socket_type     = stream
        wait            = no
        user            = root
        server          = /usr/libexec/tcpd
        server_args     = /usr/libexec/ftpd -l
        groups          = yes
        flags           = REUSE NAMEINARGS
}
```

NOTE

To make use of TCP Wrappers with `xinetd`, `libwrap` support has to be compiled in. The `xinetd` that comes with Mac OS X has `libwrap` support. If you are using `xinetd`, check your logs and you will see a line indicating this:

```
Dec  5 13:42:08 localhost xinetd[370]: xinetd Version 2.3.11 started
➥with libwrap options compiled in.
```

If you decide to update your `xinetd`, and you're using TCP Wrappers or think that you might want to use it, be sure to compile in the `libwrap` option.

Configuring TCP Wrappers

The particularly difficult part about using TCP Wrappers is configuring it. In this section, we look at two ways you can configure TCP Wrappers in Mac OS X: the traditional method of using two control files and a newer method that uses only one control file.

Traditionally, TCP Wrappers has two control files: `/etc/hosts.allow` and `/etc/hosts.deny`. We look at the traditional method in more detail because it's the default setup for a machine when extended processing options aren't enabled. An understanding of the traditional method should carry over to the new method. Be sure to read the `hosts_access` and `hosts_options` man pages for detailed information.

Here's the format of the access control files:

```
daemon_list : client_list : option : option ...
```

Through `/etc/hosts.allow`, you can allow specific services for specific hosts.

Through `/etc/hosts.deny`, you can deny services to hosts and provide global exceptions.

The easiest way to think of and use these configuration files is to think of TCP Wrappers as putting up a big fence around all the services on your machine.

The specifications in `/etc/hosts.deny` tell the fence what services are on the outside of the fence and, therefore, aren't denied. The fence can appear to be around different sets of services for different clients. For example, an `/etc/hosts.deny` file might look like this:

```
ALL EXCEPT ftpd : 192.168.1. : banners /usr/libexec/banners
ALL : 140.254.12.100 140.254.12.135 : banners /usr/libexec/banners
ALL EXCEPT ftpd sshd : ALL : banners /usr/libexec/banners
```

This file says

- For the subdomain `192.168.1.`, deny all connections except connections to the FTP daemon, `ftpd`.
- For the specific machines `140.254.12.100` and `140.254.12.135` (maybe they're troublemakers), deny absolutely all connections.
- For all other IP addresses, deny everything except connections to `ftpd` and to the secure-shell daemon `sshd`.

28

The `banners /usr/libexec/banners` entry is an option that tells `tcpd` that if it denies a connection to a service based on this entry, try to find an explanation file in this location. Use this option if you need to provide an explanation as to why the service isn't available.

The specifications in `/etc/hosts.allow` make little gates through the fences erected by `/etc/hosts.deny` for specific host and service combinations. For example, an `/etc/hosts.allow` file might look like this:

```
ALL: 140.254.12.137 192.168.2. 192.168.3.
popd: 140.254.12.124 140.254.12.151 192.168.1.36
```

This file says

- Allow connections to any TCP service from the host `140.254.12.137` and all hosts in the `192.168.2.` and `192.168.3.` subdomains. (Perhaps the `192.168.2.` and `192.168.3.` subdomains are known highly secure networks, and we really trust `140.254.12.137` because it's so well run.)
- Allow connections to the `popd` service for three specific machines: `140.254.12.124`, `140.254.12.151`, and `192.168.1.36`.

If used in combination with the previous `/etc/hosts.deny` file, these allowances still stand. They override the denials in `/etc/hosts.deny`; even though the `192.168.1.` subdomain is denied all access except to `ftpd` by `/etc/hosts.deny`, the specific machine `192.168.1.36` has its own private gate that allows it access to the popd service as well.

NOTE

Services with a smile or without? There can be a bit of confusion as to the name of the service to put in an `/etc/hosts.allow` or `/etc/hosts.deny` file. If it's a service out of `inetd.conf`, the name to use generally is the service name from the leftmost column of the `inetd.conf` file, or of the `/etc/services` file (or corresponding NetInfo directory). If this doesn't work, try adding a d to the end of the service name (`ftp` → `ftpd`).

Other services use names that don't seem to be recorded officially anywhere. Other services that you encounter and decide to wrap with TCP Wrappers might require a bit of experimenting on your part. So far, my experience has been that their names are relatively easy to guess.

Now that you've seen how the traditional method of controlling TCP Wrappers works, let's take a brief look at a newer method that uses only the `/etc/hosts.allow` file. The newer method can be used on systems where extended option processing has been enabled. This is indeed the case with Mac OS X. Nevertheless, both methods work in Mac OS X.

In the single file, `/etc/hosts.allow`, you specify allow and deny rules all in the same file. With the `/etc/hosts.allow` only method, `tcpd` reads the file on a first-match-wins basis. Consequently, it's important that your allow rules appear before your deny rules.

For example, to restrict access to `ftpd` only to our host, `140.254.12.124`, we would use these rules:

```
ftpd: 140.254.12.124 127.0.0.1 localhost: ALLOW
ftpd: ALL: DENY
```

In the first line, we allow our host, `140.254.12.124`, access to `ftpd` using various addresses that it knows for itself. On the second line, we deny access to all other hosts. If we reversed these lines, even the host that we want to allow `ftpd` access to would be denied access.

After you've sufficiently tested that you have properly set up your allow and deny rules, there's nothing else you need to do to keep TCP Wrappers running. As you're testing your rules, check your logs carefully to see where, if at all, the behaviors are logged. You'll rarely see entries for tcpd itself in your logs, but you might see additional logging for a wrapped service under that service.

Wrapping Services to Allow Tunneling over SSH

As you saw earlier in the book, it's possible to tunnel connections over SSH. If you do decide to run the FTP service on your machine, you might be interested in restricting access to the service so that anyone who uses the service has to tunnel it through SSH. You saw in detail how to configure a Mac client running traditional Mac OS to do this, and you saw how to set up a tunnel in the command line in Mac OS X. We've not yet officially seen how to configure the Mac OS X machine to permit this.

The key to setting this up is restricting access to the desired service to your host by its IP address and as localhost addresses. Sometimes it can be helpful to include your machine by its name, too, but we haven't encountered this problem on a Mac OS X machine.

To restrict access to ftpd so that a user would have to tunnel her FTP connection, you could have an /etc/hosts.deny file like this:

```
ALL EXCEPT sshd: ALL
```

In this example, all services are denied except sshd.

In the /etc/hosts.allow file, add a line for your host that includes your host's IP address, 127.0.0.1 and localhost.

```
ftpd: 140.254.12.124 127.0.0.1 localhost
```

In this example, our host, 140.254.12.124, is the only host allowed access to ftpd.

In the /etc/hosts.allow only method

```
sshd: ALL: ALLOW
ftpd: 140.254.12.124 127.0.0.1 localhost: ALLOW
ftpd: ALL: DENY
```


Using BrickHouse as an Interface to the Built-in Firewall Package

As you've already seen, Mac OS X has basic tools available to help you secure your machine. In addition to the basic tools, Mac OS X comes with a firewall package called ipfw.

There are a few graphical packages available for configuring and using ipfw, the built-in firewall. There is a commercial package called Firewall Builder, which is available for a variety of platforms and supports a variety of firewalls, including ipfw, and looks like it should be a powerful product. Firewall Builder is available at http://www.fwbuilder.org/.

A freely available package, sunShield, should install itself as a System Preferences pane, and looks like it should be an intuitive package to use. Unfortunately, it does not install under Tiger as of this writing. You might check on it from time to time at http://www.sunProtectingFactory.com/sunShield/shield_news.html.

A fairly intuitive package is a shareware product called BrickHouse. The latest version is currently available at `http://brianhill.dyndns.org/BetaStuff/`. The developer's page is `http://personalpages.tds.net/~brian_hill/`.

There are also full-featured firewalls available, such as Intego NetBarrier, Norton Symantec Personal Firewall, and Firewalk X, but we are limiting our discussion to BrickHouse, which can be used to help configure the built-in firewall.

Even if you are just using an application such as BrickHouse, which configures `ipfw` for you, you cannot use the Firewall section of the Sharing preferences pane at the same time.

Preparation

Because you'll probably want to see some of the before-and-after effects of BrickHouse, we suggest that you take a quick look at a couple commands before you get started with the application.

Run this command:

```
brezup:root root # ipfw show
65535 49873 13969242 allow ip from any to any
```

What you just did was ask `ipfw` to show you the current firewall settings. As you probably guessed, `ipfw` on Mac OS X ships in an open state.

To correctly configure a firewall, you need to know the network interfaces being used on your system, especially if you are also hoping to use BrickHouse to help you set up your Mac OS X machine as a gateway for your home network. This process requires you to correctly identify the interface of your internal (private) network and main Internet connection. As we saw earlier, you can get this information from `ifconfig -a` or the Info section of Network Utility.

Because the firewall package can be tricky to work with, what you try to do in BrickHouse might make your machine completely unusable. This is no fault of BrickHouse, but you should be prepared to remove components that you might have BrickHouse install. Depending on your situation, this might be possible only in single-user mode. If you haven't yet put your machine in single-user mode, we suggest that you do so before you do anything in BrickHouse. If you tried single-user mode a while ago but have forgotten what you did, take this moment to try again. Press Command-S while rebooting to get into single-user mode. The last few lines that appear are as follows (the actual prompt might vary):

```
Singleuser boot - fsck not done
Root device is mounted read-only
If you want to make modifications to files,
run '/sbin/fsck -y' first and then '/sbin/mount -uw /'
localhost#
```

Using BrickHouse

After you have downloaded and installed BrickHouse, you're ready to start using it.

1. The Setup Assistant appears. Please note that you can also use the Setup Assistant at any time later by clicking on the Assistant button in the main BrickHouse window. The first part of the Setup Assistant is the External Network sheet, shown in Figure 28.18. Select your connection type and IP address assignment method (dynamic or static). Connection-type choices vary with what is available on your machine.

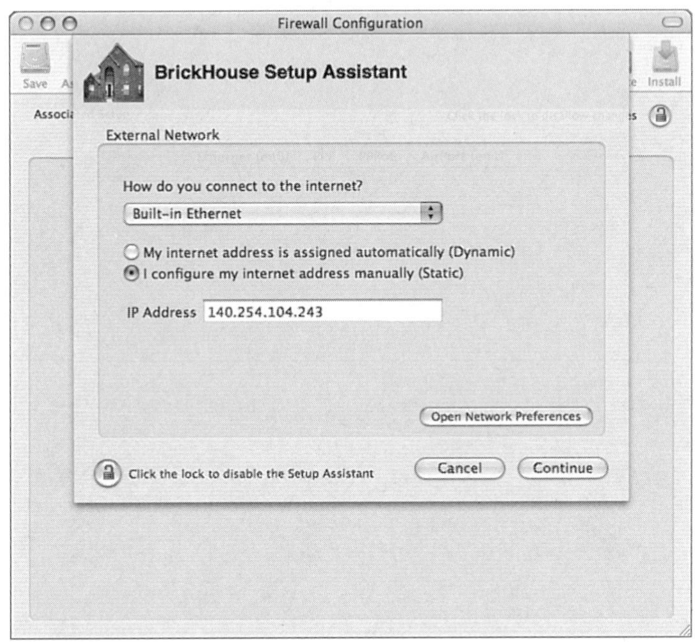

FIGURE 28.18 The BrickHouse Setup Assistant begins with your External Network settings.

2. The Public Services sheet, shown in Figure 28.19, is next. Check the boxes by the services that you want your machine to run. If you're not sure what a service is, select it, and a description appears at the bottom of the window. If you typically share your machine over an AppleTalk network, don't forget to check the appropriate AppleTalk services.

3. The next sheet to appear is the Firewall Setup Complete sheet, shown in Figure 28.20. To enable the configuration, click Apply Configuration. To install a startup script, click Install Startup Script. If you're interested in using your Mac OS X machine as a gateway for an internal network, click the Setup IP Sharing button. If you decide that you want to make changes to your configuration, you can make changes in the main window and apply a new configuration. Additionally, you can install or remove a startup script under the application's Options menu.

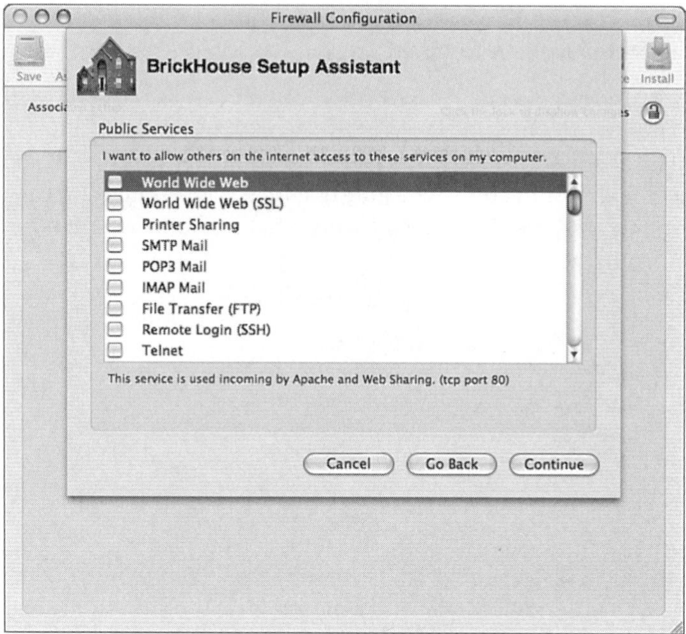

FIGURE 28.19 In the Public Services sheet, select the services you want your machine to run.

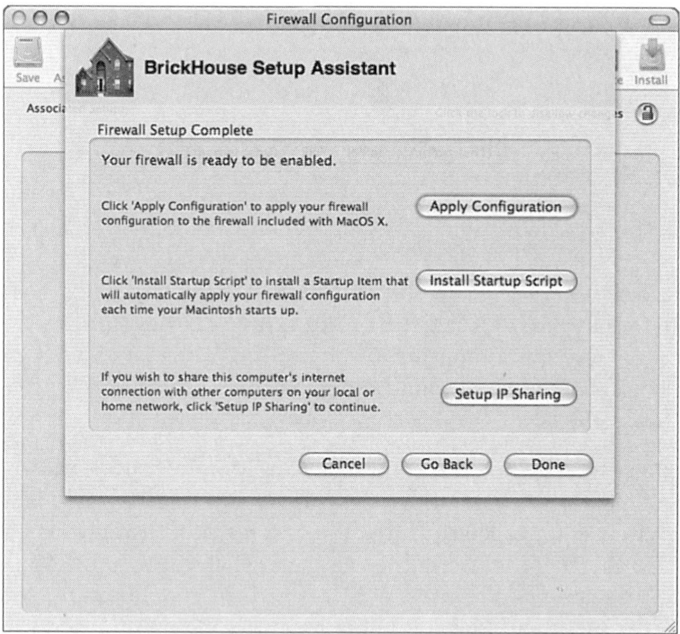

FIGURE 28.20 In the Firewall Setup Complete sheet, you can preliminarily finalize your setup or you can continue your setup by clicking on the Setup IP Sharing button to configure your machine to serve as a gateway for an internal network.

4. If you plan to set up your Mac OS X machine as a gateway for your internal network, the next sheet that appears is the IP Sharing sheet, shown in Figure 28.21. Here you select how your machine connects to the internal network and what internal IP address should be used for the machine. Connection choices vary with the machine.

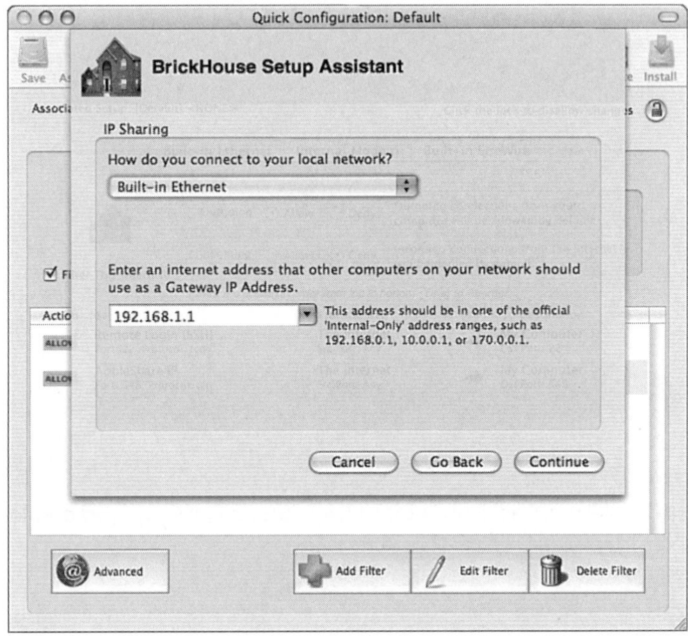

FIGURE 28.21 Make specifications about your local network in the IP Sharing sheet.

When you've completed this sheet, BrickHouse displays another sheet giving you instructions on starting IP sharing in BrickHouse. At this time, BrickHouse doesn't configure IP sharing to start at boot time.

You've just completed the initial BrickHouse setup. Now let's take the time to examine the rest of the BrickHouse interface. The default interface is the Quick Configuration, shown in Figure 28.22. The filters you selected during the setup process are shown under the tab for your interface.

The Advanced button opens a sheet, shown in Figure 28.23, that enables you to edit some additional settings involving rules for some select protocols, DHCP, and your domain name service. The bottom-right buttons enable you to add, edit, and delete filters. When you add a filter, you can choose among the same options you saw in the Setup Assistant, as well as Custom Service, which enables you to specify a port or port range. The interface for adding a filter is shown in Figure 28.24. You can rearrange the order of filter rules by dragging them around in the main window.

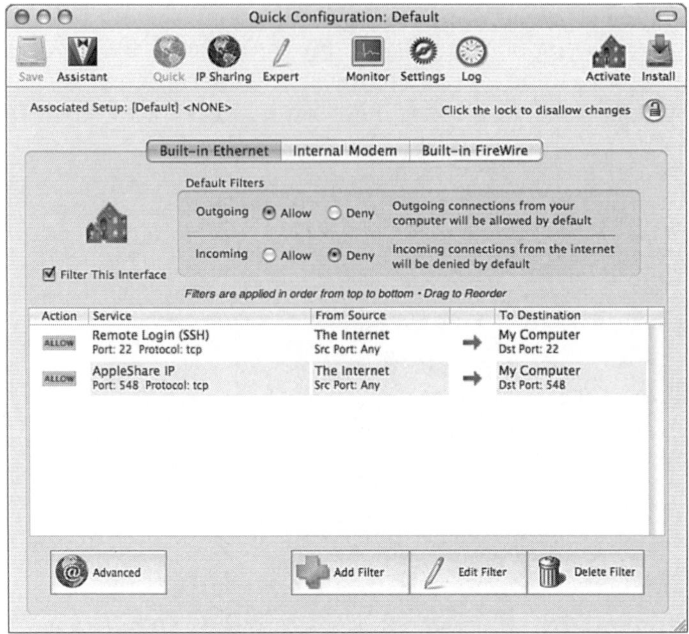

FIGURE 28.22 The default BrickHouse interface is the Quick Configuration interface.

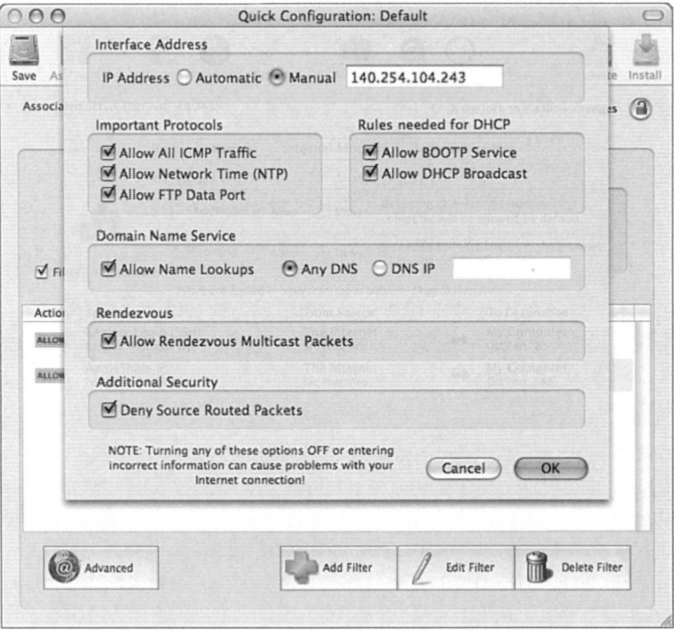

FIGURE 28.23 The Advanced button enables you to edit rules involving some select protocols, DHCP, and your domain name service.

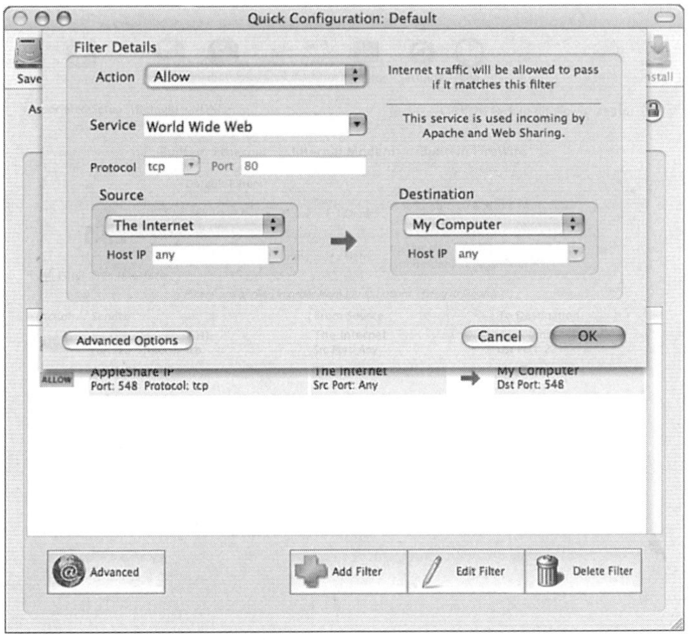

FIGURE 28.24 The Add Filter button opens this sheet, from which you can add another filter. Specify the action, service, protocol, port, source host, and destination host.

From the toolbar, you can access the Setup Assistant at any time by clicking the Assistant button. The Setup Assistant always starts from scratch. The IP Sharing button opens a sheet that enables you to further configure IP sharing. You can add, edit or delete a gateway, as well as add, edit or delete redirected services. The IP Sharing sheet is shown in Figure 28.25.

The Monitor button enables you to monitor the firewall. The Settings button enables you to manipulate settings files. You can duplicate, rename, delete, import, and export. By clicking the Log button, you can access the Daily Firewall Log window, from which you can enable logging. If you want logging to be enabled at startup, be sure to reinstall the startup script, which you can do by either clicking the Install button or under the Options menu. Even if you don't think you want to have logging all the time, you might find that having logging on at this stage helps you troubleshoot problems with the firewall configuration.

In addition to the default Quick Configuration mode is the Expert Configuration mode, accessible by clicking the Expert button. The Expert Configuration window, shown in Figure 28.26, is a split window that displays the rules that are being passed to `ipfw` as well as a configuration file for `natd`, which redirects packets to another machine if you configured your machine as a gateway. Not only can you edit in this window, but you can also check your syntax.

FIGURE 28.25 From the IP Sharing button you can further define your IP sharing settings.

FIGURE 28.26 In the Expert Configuration window, you can edit the firewall rules more precisely.

It's worthwhile to experiment with some filters that you might be most concerned about while you're still in the BrickHouse interface. With each set you want to try, just click the Activate button to apply those settings. The Quick Configuration mode is useful for adding basic filters, whereas the Expert Configuration mode enables you to tweak the configuration. When you have a set that you are happy with, don't forget to save the settings. If you're working in the Expert Configuration mode, you might also want to save the settings in a text file in a Terminal window just to be sure that you can easily find the file without the graphical interface. When you're relatively satisfied with the results, install the startup script if you want the firewall to start at startup.

If your Mac OS X machine is an NFS client, don't test to see whether the mounts still work in the graphical interface. If your mounts aren't working properly, you might hang your console when you check. If you check in the Terminal, you can continue testing until you're finally satisfied. For a Mac OS X machine that's an NFS client, you might ultimately find it necessary to add a line in the Expert mode that allows all traffic from your NFS server.

Finally, you should be aware of the options available under the Options menu: Allow Changes, Quick Configuration, Expert Configuration, Apply Settings, Install Startup Script, Clear All Rules, and Remove Startup Script. Only some of those options are available in the toolbar.

When you're satisfied with your firewall configuration, reboot your machine—especially if you had BrickHouse install a startup script for you. This tells you exactly what behavior to expect from the firewall starting from scratch. If something undesirable occurs, the potential cause for the behavior is fresh in your mind and more easily fixed.

Limiting Incoming and Outgoing Access with the BSD Firewall: `ipfw`

The easiest way to examine `ipfw` is to see how BrickHouse has manipulated it for you.

Run the first command that you ran before you started:

```
brezup:root root # ipfw show
01000  1598  388140 allow ip from any to any via lo*
01003     0       0 check-state
01004   414   45788 allow tcp from any to any established
01005     0       0 allow ip from any to any frag
01006     0       0 allow icmp from any to any icmptypes 0,3,4,11,12,13,14
02000    26    8124 allow udp from any 67-68 to any dst-port 67-68 via en0
02001     0       0 allow udp from any to 255.255.255.255 dst-port 67-68 via en0
65535 30394 5645940 allow ip from any to any
```

You should now have more output than you did previously. The open rule, which was the only rule before you started, is now the last rule. The Firewall Monitor in BrickHouse is a graphical view of `ipfw show`.

Next run `ifconfig -a`. If you configured your machine to be a gateway, you should now see information about your machine's interface to the internal and external networks. If you didn't configure your machine to be a gateway, you shouldn't see any changes.

If you had BrickHouse install a startup script, you now have a `/Library/StartupItems/Firewall` directory:

```
brezup:sage sage $ ls -l /Library/StartupItems/Firewall/
total 2352
-rwxr-xr-x   1 root  admin      496 Dec  6 15:33 Firewall
-rw-r--r--   1 root  admin      598 Dec  6 15:33 StartupParameters.plist
-rwxr-xr-x   1 root  admin  1195908 Dec  6 15:33 fwutil
```

Here's a sample startup script installed by BrickHouse to start the firewall and its logging facilities:

```
brezup:sage sage $ more /Library/StartupItems/Firewall/Firewall
#!/bin/sh
# Firewall Boot Script
# Generated by BrickHouse

#============================================================
# Activate Firewall Filters
#============================================================
/sbin/ipfw -q /etc/firewall.conf

#============================================================
# Enable IP Firewall Logging
#============================================================
/usr/sbin/sysctl -w net.inet.ip.fw.verbose=1
/usr/sbin/sysctl -w net.inet.ip.fw.verbose_limit=65535
```

As you can see from the startup script, BrickHouse installed a configuration file that it called `firewall.conf` in `/etc`. Look at the configuration file, especially if you didn't switch to the Expert Configuration mode in BrickHouse. The file is nicely commented. If you need to make additional changes to the ruleset, you can do so either in the BrickHouse interface or you can directly edit the `/etc/firewall.conf` file. Be sure to check the `ifpw` man page for specific details. The `ipfw` program reads the configuration file on a first-match-wins basis.

The general format of the lines BrickHouse created in the `/etc/firewall.conf` file is

```
add <rule_number> <action> <protocol> from <source> to
    <destination> [<options>] [via <interface>]
```

If you selected AppleShare as one of your services, you have entries that look approximately like this:

```
#################################################
## AppleShare IP
#################################################
add 2010 allow tcp from any to 140.254.104.243 548 setup keep-state in via en0
```

The first line is a rule that enables incoming TCP packets from any host to the host machine on port 548 via the interface en0. The setup rule option matches TCP packets with SYN bits, but no ACK bits. The keep-state rule option keeps the connection alive, even during idle sessions.

As mentioned in the previous section, if your Mac OS X machine is an NFS client, you might have to allow all incoming packets to the NFS server. You could do that with a rule like this:

```
ipfw add <rule_number> allow ip from <NFS_Server-IP> to <host_IP> via en0
```

The ip packet description means all packets. You can also use all. Select command documentation for ipfw is included in Table 28.2.

TABLE 28.2 Command Documentation Table for ipfw

ipfw	Controlling utility for IP firewall

```
ipfw
ipfw [-cq] add rule
    ipfw [-acdefnNStT] {list ¦ show} [<rule> ¦ <first>-<last> ...]
    ipfw [-f ¦ -q] flush
    ipfw [-q] {delete ¦ zero ¦ resetlog} [<set>] [<number> ...]
    ipfw enable {firewall ¦ one_pass ¦ debug ¦ verbose ¦ dyn_keepalive}
    ipfw disable {firewall ¦ one_pass ¦ debug ¦ verbose ¦ dyn_keepalive}

    ipfw set [disable <number> ...] [enable <number> ...]
    ipfw set move [rule] <number> to <number>
    ipfw set swap <number> <number>
    ipfw set show

    ipfw {pipe ¦ queue} <number> config <config-options>
    ipfw [-s [<field>]] {pipe ¦ queue} {delete ¦ list ¦ show} [<number> ...]

    ipfw [-cnNqS] [-p <preproc> [<preproc-flags>]] <pathname>
```

ipfw is the user interface for controlling the ipfirewall(4) and the dummynet(4) traffic shaper in FreeBSD.

Each incoming or outgoing packet is passed through the ipfw rules. If host is acting as a gateway, packets forwarded by the gateway are processed by ipfw twice. In case a host is acting as a bridge, packets forwarded by the bridge are processed by ipfw once.

A firewall configuration is made of a list of numbered rules, which is scanned for each packet until a match is found and the relevant action is performed. Depending on the action and certain system settings, packets can be reinjected into the firewall at the rule after the matching one for further processing. All rules apply to all interfaces, so it is the responsibility of the system administrator to write the ruleset in such a way as to minimize the number of checks.

A configuration always includes a DEFAULT rule (numbered 65535) which cannot be modified by the programmer and always matches packets. The action associated with the default rule can be either deny or allow depending on how the kernel is configured.

TABLE 28.2 Continued

If the ruleset includes one or more rules with the keep-state option, `ipfw` assumes a stateful behavior; that is, upon a match it will create dynamic rules matching the exact parameters (addresses and ports) of the matching packet.

These dynamic rules, which have a limited lifetime, are checked at the first occurrence of a check-state or keep-state rule, and are typically used to open the firewall on demand to legitimate traffic only.

All rules (including dynamic ones) have a few associated counters: a packet count, a byte count, a log count, and a timestamp indicating the time of the last match. Counters can be displayed or reset with `ipfw` commands.

Rules can be added with the `add` command; deleted individually with the `delete` command, and globally with the `flush` command; displayed, optionally with the content of the counters, using the `show` and `list` commands.

To manipulate rulesets, use `ipfw set`. Each rule belongs to one of 32 different sets, numbered from 0 to 31. Set 31 is reserved for the default rule. By default, rules are put in set 0.

To configure the traffic shaper, use `ifpw pipe` and `queue`. To temporarily disable the firewall, use `ipfw disable firewall`.

Available commands:

`add`	Adds a rule.
`delete`	Deletes the first rule with number *<number>*, if any.
`list`	Prints out the current rule set.
`show`	Equivalent to `ipfw -a list`.
`flush`	Removes all rules.

The following options are available:

`-a`	Shows counter values while listing. Also see `show`.
`-c`	When entering or showing rules, prints them in compact form, without the optional `"ip from any to any"` string when it does not provide any further meaning.
`-t`	Shows last match timestamp while listing.
`-N`	Tries to resolve addresses and service names in output.

To ease configuration, rules can be put into a file that is processed using `ipfw` as shown in the first synopsis line. An absolute pathname must be used. The file will be read line by line and applied as arguments to the `ipfw` utility.

Rule Format

The `ipfw` rule format is the following:

```
[prob <match_probability>] <action> [log [logamount <number>]] <proto> from <src> to
<dst> [<interface-spec>] [<options>]
```

Each incoming and outgoing packet is sent through the `ipfw` rules. In the case of a host acting as a gateway, packets forwarded by the host are processed twice: once when entering and once when leaving. Each packet can be filtered based on the following associated information:

Transmit and receive interface	(by name or address)
Direction	(incoming or outgoing)
Source and destination IP address	(possibly masked)
Protocol	(TCP, UDP, ICMP, and so on)
Source and destination port	(lists, ranges, or masks)

TABLE 28.2 Continued

TCP flags
IP fragment flag
IP options
ICMP types
User/group ID of the socket associated with the packet

Note that it might be dangerous to filter on source IP address or source TCP/UDP port because either or both could be spoofed.

The `ipfw` utility works by going through the rule list for each packet until a match is found. All rules have two associated counters: a packet count and a byte count. These are updated when a packet matches the rule.

Rules are ordered by line number from `1` to `65534`. Rules are tried in increasing order, with the first matching rule being the one that applies. Multiple rules may have the same number and are applied in the order they were added.

If a rule is added without a number, it's numbered `100` higher than the highest defined rule number unless the highest rule number is `65435` or greater—in which case, the new rules are given that same number.

One rule is always present: `65535 deny all from any to any`.

This rule, not to allow anything, is the default policy.

If the kernel option `IPFIREWALL_DEFAULT_TO_ACCEPT` has been enabled, the default rule is `65535 allow all from any to any`.

The previous rule is the default rule in Mac OS X.

`log [logamount number]`	If the kernel was compiled with `IPFIREWALL_VERBOSE`, when a packet matches a rule with the log keyword, a message will be logged to `syslogd`(8) with a `LOG_SECURITY` facility
`proto`	An IP protocol specified by number or name. (For a complete list, see `/etc/protocols`.) The `ip` or `all` keywords mean any protocol will match. `tcp`, `udp`, `icmp` are commonly used ones.
Available options for <*action*>:	
`allow`	Allows packets that match rule. The search terminates. Aliases are `pass`, `permit`, and `accept`.
`deny`	Discards packets that match rule. The search terminates. Alias is `drop`.
`check-state`	Checks the packet against the dynamic ruleset. If a match is found, the search terminates; otherwise we move to the next rule. If no `check-state` rule is found, the dynamic ruleset is checked at the first `keep-state` rule.
fwd <*ipaddr*> [,<*port*>]	Changes to the next hop on matching packets to <*ipaddr*>, which can be a dotted quad address or hostname. If <*ipaddr*> is not directly reachable, the route as found in the local routing table for that IP address is used instead.

TABLE 28.2 Continued

`pipe <pip-nr>`	Pass packet to a `dummynet(4)` pipe (for bandwidth limitation, delay, and so on. The search terminates; however, on exit from the pipe and if the `sysctl(8)` variable `net.inet.ip.fw.one_pass` is not set, the packet is passed again to the firewall code starting from the next rule.
`queue <queue-nr>`	Pass packet to a `dummynet(4)` queue (for bandwidth limitation using `WF2Q`).

`src` and `dst`:
`any ¦ me ¦ [not] <address/mask> [<ports>]`
Specifying `any` makes the rule match any IP number.
Specifying `me` makes the rule match any IP number configured on an interface in the system. This is a computationally semi-expensive check that should be used with care.
The sense of the match can be inverted by preceding an address with the `not` modifier, causing all other addresses to be matched instead. This does not affect the selection of port numbers.
With the TCP and UDP protocols, optional ports may be specified as
`{port¦port-port¦port:mask}[,port[,...]]`	

Some combinations of the following specifiers are allowed for `<interface-spec>`	
`in`	Only matches incoming packets.
`out`	Only matches outgoing packets.
`via ifX`	Packet must be going through interface `ifX`.
`via any`	Packet must be going through some interface.
`via ipno`	Packet must be going through the interface having IP address `ipno`.
The `via` keyword causes the interface to always be checked. If `recv` or `xmit` is used instead of `via`, only the receive or transmit interface (respectively) is checked. By specifying both, it is possible to match packets based on both receive and transmit interface, for example: `ipfw add 100 deny ip from any to any out recv en0 xmit en1` The `recv` interface can be tested on either incoming or outgoing packets, whereas the `xmit` interface can only be tested on outgoing packets. Options available for `<options>`:	
`keep-state[<method>]`	Upon a match, the firewall will create a dynamic rule whose default behavior is to matching bidirectional traffic between source and destination IP/port using the same protocol. The rule has a limited lifetime (controlled by a set of `sysctl(8)` variables), and the lifetime is refreshed every time a matching packet is found.
`ipoptions <spec>`	Matches if the IP header contains the comma-separated list of options specified in `<spec>`. The supported IP options are `ssrr` (strict source route), `lsrr` (loose source route), `rr` (record packet route), and `ts` (timestamp). The absence of a particular option can be denoted with a `!`.

TABLE 28.2 Continued

tcpoptions *<spec>*	Matches if the TCP header contains the comma-separated list of options specified in spec. The supported TCP options are mss (maximum segment size), window (TCP window advertisement), sack (selective ack), ts (rfc1323 timestamp) and cc (rfc1644 t/TCP connection count). The absence of a particular option can be denoted with a !.
established	TCP packets only. Matches packets that have the RST or ACK bits set.
setup	TCP packets only. Matches packets that have the SYN bit set but no ACK bit.
tcpflags *<spec>*	Matches if the TCP header contains the comma-separated list of flags specified in *<spec>*. The supported TCP flags are fin, syn, rst, psh, ack, and urg. The absence of a particular flag can be denoted by an !. A rule that contains a tcpflags specification can never match a fragmented packet that has a nonzero offset.

Important points to consider when designing your rules:

Remember that you filter packets both going in and out. Most connections need packets going in both directions.

Remember to test very carefully. It's a good idea to be at the console at the time.

Don't forget the loopback interface.

BrickHouse might also have installed a configuration file, /etc/natd.conf, for natd, which is used for IP Sharing. Here's a sample /etc/natd.conf created by BrickHouse:

```
interface en0
use_sockets yes
same_ports yes
```

This configuration file specifies the interface to be used. In addition, the use_sockets option is included as well as the same_ports option. The use_sockets option allocates a socket for the connection, and is useful for guaranteeing connections when ports conflict. The same_ports option specifies that natd should try to keep the same port number when altering outgoing packets. This also aids in guaranteeing the success of the connection.

Detecting Attacks in Progress: Intrusion Detection

Not only are there tools for limiting network access, but there are also tools for detecting an attack in progress. These tools are known as intrusion detection tools. We will look at Tripwire, PortSentry, and Snort.

Tripwire

Tripwire is a utility that monitors the integrity of important files or directories. It stores information in a database about files and directories that you've specified. You can then use Tripwire to check whether there have been any changes to your files. It checks the current state of the files against the information in its database.

There is an open source version of Tripwire available at `http://sourceforge.net/projects/tripwire/`. A patched version that runs on Mac OS X is available at `http://www.frenchfries.net/paul/tripwire/`. This is the version that we discuss. If you are interested in learning more about Tripwire, you might also check the commercial site, which unfortunately does not include a Mac OS X version, at `http://www.tripwire.com/`.

Remember that Tripwire can't detect any unauthorized changes that have already been made on your system. If you have any doubts about the system's current integrity, you can reinstall the operating system and then install Tripwire.

Download the patched version of Tripwire and compile it using the standard:

```
./configure
make
make install
```

Note that you will have to root privileges to install the package. During the installation process, you will be asked to create a site key and a local key by selecting good passphrases for each. The installation script recommends that your passphrase include uppercase and lowercase letters as well as numbers and punctuation, for a length of at least eight characters. Don't forget your site and local passphrases because you will need them to perform some tasks with Tripwire.

Tripwire comes with two main files: a configuration file and a policy file. Clear text versions of the files are included, but Tripwire itself uses binary versions of these files. The configuration file contains basic configuration information regarding the Tripwire software, whereas the policy file contains the information on how you want Tripwire to behave. The patched version of Tripwire installs these files in `/usr/local/etc`. The default `/usr/local/etc/twcfg.txt` file is shown next:

```
ROOT          =/usr/local/sbin
POLFILE       =/usr/local/etc/tw.pol
DBFILE        =/usr/local/lib/tripwire/$(HOSTNAME).twd
REPORTFILE    =/usr/local/lib/tripwire/report/$(HOSTNAME)-$(DATE).twr
SITEKEYFILE   =/usr/local/etc/site.key
LOCALKEYFILE  =/usr/local/etc/dogbone-local.key
EDITOR        =/usr/bin/vi
LATEPROMPTING =false
LOOSEDIRECTORYCHECKING =false
MAILNOVIOLATIONS =true
EMAILREPORTLEVEL =3
```

```
REPORTLEVEL      =3
MAILMETHOD       =SENDMAIL
SYSLOGREPORTING =false
MAILPROGRAM      =/usr/sbin/sendmail -oi -t
```

A couple of the more interesting items in this file are the `LOOSEDIRECTORYCHECKING` and `SYSLOGREPORTING` settings. Whenever a file is modified, Tripwire reports changes to the file and directory where the file is stored, creating redundant items in a report. To avoid the redundancy, the `LOOSEDIRECTORYCHECKING` variable is set to `false`. Also set to `false` by default is the `SYSLOGREPORTING` variable. This might be what you would like Tripwire to ultimately do, but as you are setting up Tripwire, you might find it useful to have its activities logged in the system log. With this variable turned on, Tripwire's activities are logged to `/var/log/system.log`. If there are any settings you would like to change here, change them. Then update the configuration file by running:

```
dogbone:/usr/local/etc root# /usr/local/sbin/twadmin --create-cfgfile
➥-S /usr/local/etc/site.key /usr/local/etc/twcfg.txt
Please enter your site passphrase:
Wrote configuration file: /usr/local/etc/tw.cfg
```

The clear text version of the policy file is `/usr/local/etc/twpol.txt`. This is quite an extensive document.

The clear text version of the policy file is `/usr/local/etc/twpol.txt`. This is quite an extensive document. The sample policy file provides details on the syntax of the file. You can specify directories or files for Tripwire to check and what kind of checking it should do in the `twpol.txt` file. The basic form of a line in the file is *<file>* *<flags>*. The sample `twpol.txt` file provides a rather detailed description about the available flags and modifiers to *<file>*, and the man page provides even more details. Basically, there are flags for a number of things to have Tripwire check, such as permissions, user ID, access time, modification time, and so on. Additionally, there are template definitions for certain combinations of the flags. You can use the template definitions for assigning how you want a file or directory to be checked, you can just assign flags, or you can assign a combination of the template with instructions to ignore something in the template or not to ignore something that's being ignored in the template. The default file contains entries that are more suitable to basic Mac OS X 10.3 or earlier installations. To start to get a feel for how to work with the `twpol.txt` file, you might run Tripwire with the default policy file and then update it. That will give you basic experience with updating the policy file. Then, if you like, you can experiment with making more sophisticated changes to the policy file.

Tripwire has four basic modes: database generation, integrity checking, database update, and test. Before you can use Tripwire, you have to generate, or initialize, the database. You do this by running

```
/usr/local/sbin/tripwire -init
```

or

```
/usr/local/sbin/tripwire -m i
```

Initializing the database with the current default `twpol.txt` files yields the following results:

```
dogbone:/usr/local/etc root# /usr/local/sbin/tripwire --init
Please enter your local passphrase:
Parsing policy file: /usr/local/etc/tw.pol
Generating the database...
*** Processing Unix File System ***
### Warning: File system error.
### Filename: /usr/local/etc/local.key
### No such file or directory
### Continuing...
### Warning: File system error.
### Filename: /private/var/db/prebindOnDemandBadFiles
### No such file or directory
### Continuing...
### Warning: File system error.
### Filename: /private/var/msgs/bounds
### No such file or directory
### Continuing...
### Warning: File system error.
### Filename: /private/var/spool/lock
### No such file or directory
### Continuing...
### Warning: File system error.
### Filename: /Applications (Mac OS 9)
### No such file or directory
### Continuing...
### Warning: File system error.
### Filename: /System Folder
### No such file or directory
### Continuing...
### Warning: File system error.
### Filename: /System Folder/Extensions
### No such file or directory
### Continuing...
### Warning: File system error.
### Filename: /System Folder/Clipboard
### No such file or directory
### Continuing...
### Warning: File system error.
### Filename: /private/var/spool/clientmqueue
```

```
### No such file or directory
### Continuing...
### Warning: File system error.
### Filename: /System Folder/Preferences
### No such file or directory
### Continuing...
### Warning: File system error.
### Filename: /System Folder/Apple Menu Items
### No such file or directory
### Continuing...
Wrote database file: /usr/local/lib/tripwire/dogbone.twd
The database was successfully generated.
```

Note that you have to enter your local passphrase to initialize the database. Also note that for my system, the default configuration checks a number of files that do not exist on my system. I can reduce the number of warnings by editing the `twpol.txt` file and updating the database. My system does not have any of the Classic environment files, and the default policy file does not have the right local key file listed to check. It checks for `/usr/local/etc/local.key`, rather than `/usr/local/etc/dogbone-local.key`.

```
After making changes to the twpol.txt file, the updated policy can be implemented
by running/usr/local/sbin/tripwire --update-policy -Z low /usr/local/etc/twpol.txt
```

or

```
/usr/local/sbin/tripwire -m p -Z low /usr/local/etc/twpol.txt
```

Do expect your Tripwire actions to take a bit of time to run. By default, Tripwire runs this in `high` security mode, which causes it to print a list of violations, but not update the database. The `low` security mode option also causes the updates to the database to be made automatically.

28

When you are satisfied with your basic configuration and policy files, run an integrity check by running

```
/usr/local/sbin/tripwire -check
```

or

```
/usr/local/sbin/tripwire -m c
```

Here is a sample integrity check that shows no changes of particular concern. This was run after changing the policy and machine location.

```
dogbone:/usr/local/etc root# /usr/local/sbin/tripwire --check
Parsing policy file: /usr/local/etc/tw.pol
```

```
*** Processing Unix File System ***
Performing integrity check...
Wrote report file: /usr/local/lib/tripwire/report/dogbone-20050425-084515.twr


Tripwire(R) 2.3.0 Integrity Check Report

Report generated by:          root
Report created on:            Mon Apr 25 20:45:15 2005
Database last updated on:     Sun Apr 24 23:49:42 2005

===============================================================================
Report Summary:
===============================================================================

Host name:                    dogbone
Host IP address:              Unknown IP
Host ID:                      None
Policy file used:             /usr/local/etc/tw.pol
Configuration file used:      /usr/local/etc/tw.cfg
Database file used:           /usr/local/lib/tripwire/dogbone.twd
Command line used:            /usr/local/sbin/tripwire --check

===============================================================================
Rule Summary:
===============================================================================

-------------------------------------------------------------------------------
  Section: Unix File System
-------------------------------------------------------------------------------

  Rule Name                       Severity Level    Added    Removed  Modified
  ---------                       --------------    -----    -------  --------
* Usr Local Files                 60                1        0        1
  Tripwire Binaries               100               0        0        0
* Tripwire Data Files             100               1        0        2
  OS Binaries and Libraries       100               0        0        0
* OS Boot and Configuration Files 100               1        0        2
* Variable System Files           60                0        0        4
  Variable System Files           100               0        0        0
  Running Services                60                0        0        0
  (/private/var/run)
  Mount Points                    60                0        0        0
  System Devices                  60                0        0        0
  (/dev)
```

```
  Home Directories                  60                 0        0        0
  (/Users)

Total objects scanned:  141251
Total violations found:  12

===============================================================================
Object Summary:
===============================================================================

-------------------------------------------------------------------------------
# Section: Unix File System
-------------------------------------------------------------------------------

-------------------------------------------------------------------------------
Rule Name: Tripwire Data Files (/usr/local/lib/tripwire)
Severity Level: 100
-------------------------------------------------------------------------------

Added:
"/usr/local/lib/tripwire/dogbone.twd.bak"

Modified:
"/usr/local/lib/tripwire"

-------------------------------------------------------------------------------
Rule Name: Usr Local Files (/usr/local/etc)
Severity Level: 60
-------------------------------------------------------------------------------

Added:
"/usr/local/etc/tw.pol.bak"

Modified:
"/usr/local/etc"

-------------------------------------------------------------------------------
Rule Name: Tripwire Data Files (/usr/local/etc/tw.pol)
Severity Level: 100
-------------------------------------------------------------------------------

Modified:
"/usr/local/etc/tw.pol"

-------------------------------------------------------------------------------
```

```
Rule Name: OS Boot and Configuration Files (/private/etc)
Severity Level: 100
-------------------------------------------------------------------------------

Added:
"/private/etc/appletalk.cfg"

Modified:
"/private/etc"
"/private/etc/printcap"

-------------------------------------------------------------------------------
Rule Name: Variable System Files (/private/var)
Severity Level: 60
-------------------------------------------------------------------------------

Modified:
"/private/var"
"/private/var/slp.regfile"

-------------------------------------------------------------------------------
Rule Name: Variable System Files (/private/var/tmp)
Severity Level: 60
-------------------------------------------------------------------------------

Modified:
"/private/var/tmp"

-------------------------------------------------------------------------------
Rule Name: Variable System Files (/private/var/spool/cups)
Severity Level: 60
-------------------------------------------------------------------------------

Modified:
"/private/var/spool/cups"

===============================================================================
Error Report:
===============================================================================

No Errors

-------------------------------------------------------------------------------
*** End of report ***
```

```
Tripwire 2.3 Portions copyright 2000 Tripwire, Inc. Tripwire is a registered
trademark of Tripwire, Inc. This software comes with ABSOLUTELY NO WARRANTY;
for details use --version. This is free software which may be redistributed
or modified only under certain conditions; see COPYING for details.
All rights reserved.
Integrity check complete.
```

Here is a sample integrity check that shows that an unexpected file modification:

```
dogbone:/usr/local/etc root# /usr/local/sbin/tripwire --check
Parsing policy file: /usr/local/etc/tw.pol
*** Processing Unix File System ***
Performing integrity check...
Wrote report file: /usr/local/lib/tripwire/report/dogbone-20050425-094933.twr


Tripwire(R) 2.3.0 Integrity Check Report

Report generated by:          root
Report created on:            Mon Apr 25 21:49:33 2005
Database last updated on:     Sun Apr 24 23:49:42 2005

===============================================================================
Report Summary:
===============================================================================

Host name:                    dogbone
Host IP address:              Unknown IP
Host ID:                      None
Policy file used:             /usr/local/etc/tw.pol
Configuration file used:      /usr/local/etc/tw.cfg
Database file used:           /usr/local/lib/tripwire/dogbone.twd
Command line used:            /usr/local/sbin/tripwire --check

===============================================================================
Rule Summary:
===============================================================================

-------------------------------------------------------------------------------
  Section: Unix File System
-------------------------------------------------------------------------------

  Rule Name                       Severity Level    Added    Removed  Modified
  ---------                       --------------    -----    -------  --------
* Usr Local Files                 60                1        0        1
  Tripwire Binaries               100               0        0        0
```

28

```
* Tripwire Data Files             100               1        0        3
* OS Binaries and Libraries       100               0        0        2
* OS Boot and Configuration Files 100               1        0        2
* Variable System Files           60                0        0        7
  Variable System Files           100               0        0        0
  Running Services                60                0        0        0
  (/private/var/run)
  Mount Points                    60                0        0        0
  System Devices                  60                0        0        0
  (/dev)
  Home Directories                60                0        0        0
  (/Users)

Total objects scanned:  141251
Total violations found:  18

===============================================================================
Object Summary:
===============================================================================

-------------------------------------------------------------------------------
# Section: Unix File System
-------------------------------------------------------------------------------

-------------------------------------------------------------------------------
Rule Name: Tripwire Data Files (/usr/local/lib/tripwire)
Severity Level: 100
-------------------------------------------------------------------------------

Added:
"/usr/local/lib/tripwire/dogbone.twd.bak"

Modified:
"/usr/local/lib/tripwire"

-------------------------------------------------------------------------------
Rule Name: Usr Local Files (/usr/local/etc)
Severity Level: 60
-------------------------------------------------------------------------------

Added:
"/usr/local/etc/tw.pol.bak"

Modified:
"/usr/local/etc"
```

```
---------------------------------------------------------------------------
Rule Name: Tripwire Data Files (/usr/local/etc/tw.pol)
Severity Level: 100
---------------------------------------------------------------------------

Modified:
"/usr/local/etc/tw.pol"

---------------------------------------------------------------------------
Rule Name: OS Boot and Configuration Files (/private/etc)
Severity Level: 100
---------------------------------------------------------------------------

Added:
"/private/etc/appletalk.cfg"

Modified:
"/private/etc"
"/private/etc/printcap"

---------------------------------------------------------------------------
Rule Name: Variable System Files (/private/var)
Severity Level: 60
---------------------------------------------------------------------------

Modified:
"/private/var"
"/private/var/root"
"/private/var/root/.viminfo"
"/private/var/slp.regfile"

---------------------------------------------------------------------------
Rule Name: Variable System Files (/private/var/db)
Severity Level: 60
---------------------------------------------------------------------------

Modified:
"/private/var/db/shadow/hash/7F79E4B7-8239-48F1-BE5C-C0E8DEE478B9.state"

---------------------------------------------------------------------------
Rule Name: OS Binaries and Libraries (/bin)
Severity Level: 100
---------------------------------------------------------------------------
```

```
Modified:
"/bin"
"/bin/ls"

-------------------------------------------------------------------------------
Rule Name: Tripwire Data Files (/usr/local/lib/tripwire/report)
Severity Level: 100
-------------------------------------------------------------------------------

Modified:
"/usr/local/lib/tripwire/report"

-------------------------------------------------------------------------------
Rule Name: Variable System Files (/private/var/tmp)
Severity Level: 60
-------------------------------------------------------------------------------

Modified:
"/private/var/tmp"

-------------------------------------------------------------------------------
Rule Name: Variable System Files (/private/var/spool/cups)
Severity Level: 60
-------------------------------------------------------------------------------

Modified:
"/private/var/spool/cups"

===============================================================================
Error Report:
===============================================================================

No Errors

-------------------------------------------------------------------------------
*** End of report ***

Tripwire 2.3 Portions copyright 2000 Tripwire,  Inc. Tripwire is a registered
trademark of Tripwire, Inc. This software comes with ABSOLUTELY NO WARRANTY;
for details use --version. This is free software which may be redistributed
or modified only under certain conditions; see COPYING for details.
All rights reserved.
Integrity check complete.
```

You'll have to run integrity checks regularly to start to get a feel for what types of modifications occur regularly on your system. In this report, notice that the `/bin/ls` file has been modified. That is a file that we would not ordinarily expect to be modified, except possibly as a result of a system update. If you weren't expecting this change, you should be suspicious.

To make Tripwire useful, you should run it regularly. The easiest way to do so is to run Tripwire in a daily `cron` job and have the results mailed to you. The Tripwire test mode allows you to test its email functionality. Even if you don't have the results emailed to you, you can always read the report it generated by running `twprint`.

If you enabled syslogging, expect entries like this to appear in `/var/log/system.log`:

```
Apr 24 22:47:32 dogbone tripwire[1137]: Database initialized:
➥/usr/local/lib/tripwire/dogbone.twd
Apr 24 23:23:13 dogbone tripwire[1205]: Integrity Check Complete:
➥/usr/local/lib/tripwire/dogbone.twd TWReport dogbone 20050424230146
➥V:16 S:100 A:1 R:10 C:5
Apr 25 00:15:01 dogbone tripwire[1292]: Policy Update Complete:
➥/usr/local/lib/tripwire/dogbone.twd
Apr 25 21:08:33 dogbone tripwire[1412]: Integrity Check Complete:
➥/usr/local/lib/tripwire/dogbone.twd TWReport dogbone 20050425084515
➥V:12 S:100 A:3 R:0 C:9
Apr 25 22:14:07 dogbone tripwire[1483]: Integrity Check Complete:
➥/usr/local/lib/tripwire/dogbone.twd TWReport dogbone 20050425094933
➥V:18 S:100 A:3 R:0 C:15
```

Be sure to read the all the man pages for Tripwire, especially those for `tripwire`, `twadmin`, `twconfig`, `twpolicy` and `twreport`.

Snort and HenWen

Snort, available from `http://www.snort.org/`, is a freely available package that has a packet sniffer mode and a network intrusion detection system mode. HenWen, available from `http://seiryu.home.comcast.net/henwen.html`, is a graphical interface to `snort`. HenWen also includes a slightly modified version of `snort` in its distribution. It's free for personal, education, and government users, but commercial users are asked to pay a shareware fee. Just as BrickHouse does for `ipfw`, HenWen provides an opportunity for you to learn how the `snort` configuration file works. The current version of HenWen, HenWen 2.0.4, runs on Mac OS X 10.2 or 10.3. As of this writing, it does not appear to work on 10.4, but given that the website does make an older version available for Mac OS X 10.1, we would expect the author to update the package sometime to support Tiger.

If you want to download and compile Snort yourself, it compiles and installs easily on Mac OS X. It follows the basic approach:

```
./configure
make
make install
```

By default, Snort installs in `/usr/local`. There are a number of compile-time options, including support for `openssl` and `mysql`. The `mysql` option can be useful for a number of reporting packages for Snort.

After you have Snort compiled, you might want to run it in packet-sniffing mode for a few seconds just to see how that looks and to verify that it runs. If you're interested in doing so, run `snort -v`. If you get no activity upon issuing this command, you might need to specify an interface. The `snort -v` output indicates which interface it is checking. Use `snort -v -i <interface>` to specify the interface. This prints TCP/IP packet headers to the screen. Here's an example of the very end of some output:

```
12/05-17:29:10.916730 147.229.16.120:1028 -> 224.2.127.254:9875
UDP TTL:48 TOS:0x0 ID:43660 IpLen:20 DgmLen:277
Len: 249
=+=+=+=+=+=+=+=+=+=+=+=+=+=+=+=+=+=+=+=+=+=+=+=+=+=+=+=+=+=+=+=+=+=+=+=+=+=+

12/05-17:29:11.015725 140.192.141.155:1029 -> 224.2.127.254:9875
UDP TTL:55 TOS:0x0 ID:13852 IpLen:20 DgmLen:315
Len: 287
=+=+=+=+=+=+=+=+=+=+=+=+=+=+=+=+=+=+=+=+=+=+=+=+=+=+=+=+=+=+=+=+=+=+=+=+=+=+

12/05-17:29:11.045173 131.151.10.7:1029 -> 224.2.127.254:9875
UDP TTL:52 TOS:0x0 ID:48504 IpLen:20 DgmLen:308
Len: 280
=+=+=+=+=+=+=+=+=+=+=+=+=+=+=+=+=+=+=+=+=+=+=+=+=+=+=+=+=+=+=+=+=+=+=+=+=+=+

12/05-17:29:11.049176 140.254.104.143:138 -> 140.254.105.255:138
UDP TTL:64 TOS:0x0 ID:25539 IpLen:20 DgmLen:218
Len: 190
=+=+=+=+=+=+=+=+=+=+=+=+=+=+=+=+=+=+=+=+=+=+=+=+=+=+=+=+=+=+=+=+=+=+=+=+=+=+

12/05-17:29:11.068150 193.190.113.20:37990 -> 224.2.127.254:9875
UDP TTL:240 TOS:0x0 ID:0 IpLen:20 DgmLen:669 DF
Len: 641
=+=+=+=+=+=+=+=+=+=+=+=+=+=+=+=+=+=+=+=+=+=+=+=+=+=+=+=+=+=+=+=+=+=+=+=+=+=+

12/05-17:29:11.077319 205.155.71.103:1026 -> 224.2.127.254:9875
UDP TTL:48 TOS:0x0 ID:32136 IpLen:20 DgmLen:336
Len: 308
=+=+=+=+=+=+=+=+=+=+=+=+=+=+=+=+=+=+=+=+=+=+=+=+=+=+=+=+=+=+=+=+=+=+=+=+=+=+

^C

===============================================================================
```

```
Snort received 269 packets
    Analyzed: 269(100.000%)
    Dropped: 0(0.000%)
===============================================================================
Breakdown by protocol:
    TCP: 84          (31.227%)
    UDP: 121         (44.981%)
   ICMP: 0           (0.000%)
    ARP: 7           (2.602%)
  EAPOL: 0           (0.000%)
   IPv6: 0           (0.000%)
    IPX: 3           (1.115%)
  OTHER: 18          (6.691%)
DISCARD: 0           (0.000%)
===============================================================================
Action Stats:
ALERTS: 0
LOGGED: 0
PASSED: 0
===============================================================================
Snort exiting
```

To run Snort in intrusion detection mode, however, you must edit the configuration file and run it as a daemon. The distribution comes with a default `snort.conf` file that you can edit. You should periodically get updates to the rules from `http://www.snort.org/dl/rules/`.

To be able to run Snort in intrusion detection mode, manually complete your installation as follows:

```
ryoohki:/Users/sage/builds/snort-2.3.0RC1 root# mkdir -p /usr/local/etc/snort/rules
ryoohki:/Users/sage/builds/snort-2.3.0RC1 root# cp rules/*
/usr/local/etc/snort/rules/
ryoohki:/Users/sage/builds/snort-2.3.0RC1 root# cp etc/* /usr/local/etc/snort/
ryoohki:/Users/sage/builds/snort-2.3.0RC1 root# chmod -R 600 /usr/local/etc/snort
ryoohki:/Users/sage/builds/snort-2.3.0RC1 root# mkdir /var/log/snort
```

In the configuration file, `snort.conf`, you configure network variables, preprocessor statements, output options, and Snort rules. The preprocessor statements determine how packets are handled before actually matching them against any rules. The output options determine how the Snort output is handled. Options include logging to a syslog or a database, such as MySQL. The rules are set up as separate files in a rules directory, like the services files for `xinetd`. It's easier to update the rules by storing them in a separate directory and having `include` statements in the configuration file for the rules rather than including them directly in the configuration file.

If you manually complete the installation as described earlier, the rules are copied to a separate rules directory located in `/usr/local/etc/snort/rules`, and `snort.conf`, like the `rules` directory, is also located in `/usr/local/etc/snort`. At the very least, the `snort.conf` file has to be edited to reflect this. Change the

```
var RULE_PATH ../rules
```

line to

```
var RULE_PATH rules
```

To run Snort in daemon mode, try a statement like this:

```
sort -D -c <path-to-snort.conf> -i <interface>
```

In this example, to run Snort on an AirPort interface, that would be

```
snort -D -c /usr/local/etc/snort/snort.conf -i en1
```

If you're satisfied with what Snort does, you might want to consider adding it to the startup scripts.

Assuming that an updated version of HenWen becomes available for Tiger, you might find it useful for familiarizing yourself with the configuration file. HenWen provides a graphical interface for setting up a basic `snort.conf` file and also comes with a detailed manual on setting up the configuration file. You can either use HenWen as its own package or for creating a base `snort.conf` file. By default, it creates a `snort.conf` file within its own hierarchy, but you can also choose to save a copy elsewhere. Additionally, you can have it start at boot.

Figure 31.14 shows the Network section of HenWen setup. This is HenWen's interface for setting up the network variables in the `snort.conf` file. The Preprocessors tab configures the preprocessors portion of the `snort.conf` file. The Output section configures the output options section of `snort.conf`. The Alerts section configures the rules portion; the Snort section, the snort decoder and detection engine; the Spoof Detector section, the arpspoof section of the preprocessors portion of `snort.conf`.

HenWen's `snort.conf` file and `rules` directory are located in `HenWen.app/Contents/Resources`. If you install HenWen, you can still periodically update the rules statements as you can with the regular Snort distribution.

Here's an example of what you might see in the Snort alert log:

```
[**] [1:1421:11] SNMP AgentX/tcp request [**]
[Classification: Attempted Information Leak] [Priority: 2]
12/05-20:52:04.206816 140.254.104.107:64331 -> 140.254.104.243:705
TCP TTL:43 TOS:0x0 ID:15400 IpLen:20 DgmLen:60 DF
******S* Seq: 0x52322FEA  Ack: 0x0  Win: 0xFFFF  TcpLen: 40
TCP Options (6) => MSS: 1460 NOP WS: 0 NOP NOP TS: 266875018 0
[Xref => http://cve.mitre.org/cgi-bin/cvename.cgi?name=2002-0013]
➥[Xref => http://cve.mitre.org/cgi-bin/cvename.cgi?
```

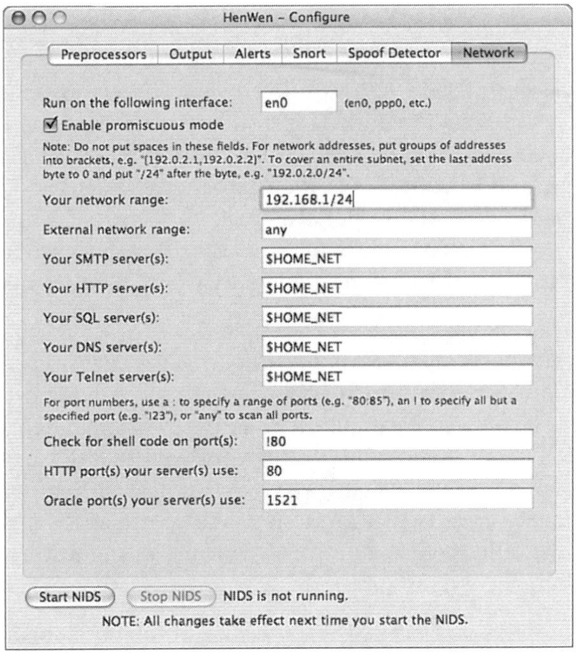

FIGURE 28.27 You can configure the network variables for `snort.conf` under the Network section in HenWen's interface.

```
name=2002-0012][Xref => http://www.securityfocus.com/bid/4132]
➥[Xref => http://www.securityfocus.com/bid/4089][Xref
=> http://www.securityfocus.com/bid/4088]

[**] [1:1418:11] SNMP request tcp [**]
[Classification: Attempted Information Leak] [Priority: 2]
12/05-20:52:05.507177 140.254.104.107:64671 -> 140.254.104.243:161
TCP TTL:43 TOS:0x0 ID:15740 IpLen:20 DgmLen:60 DF
******S* Seq: 0x1B600A5C  Ack: 0x0  Win: 0xFFFF  TcpLen: 40
TCP Options (6) => MSS: 1460 NOP WS: 0 NOP NOP TS: 266875020 0
[Xref => http://cve.mitre.org/cgi-bin/cvename.cgi?name=2002-0013]
➥[Xref => http://cve.mitre.org/cgi-bin/cvename.cgi?
name=2002-0012][Xref => http://www.securityfocus.com/bid/4132]
➥[Xref => http://www.securityfocus.com/bid/4089][Xref
=> http://www.securityfocus.com/bid/4088]

[**] [1:2189:3] BAD-TRAFFIC IP Proto 103 PIM [**]
[Classification: Detection of a non-standard protocol or event] [Priority: 2]
12/05-20:52:26.080257 140.254.104.1 -> 224.0.0.13
PIM TTL:1 TOS:0xC0 ID:5486 IpLen:20 DgmLen:54
[Xref => http://cve.mitre.org/cgi-bin/cvename.cgi?name=2003-0567]
➥[Xref => http://www.securityfocus.com/bid/8211]
```

PortSentry

PortSentry 1.2 is a utility available from http://sourceforge.net/projects/sentrytools/. It's part of the Sentry Tools suite, a suite of free host-based security and intrusion tools. Sentry Tools also include LogSentry, which helps you monitor your system logs and HostSentry, which detects anomalous login behavior. The project recently moved to SourceForge, and is in the process of updating its licenses. As a result, HostSentry and PortSentry 2.x are not yet available. PortSentry 1.0 for Mac OS X is also available from http://www.osxgnu.org/software/Security/portsentry/. Currently the Mac OS X port does not appear to install, but we expect that to change as Tiger becomes more prevalent.

PortSentry monitors connections to ports specified in the portsentry.conf file. If PortSentry detects a connection on one of those ports, you can choose to have it simply log the connection. You can also configure PortSentry to immediately block the connection. PortSentry adds a deny line for the host to your /etc/hosts.deny or /etc/hosts.allow, depending on which way you're using TCP Wrappers. It then blocks the connection via route or ipfw. You can also provide PortSentry with a list of hosts whose connections it should ignore. You must do some testing until you're completely satisfied with your PortSentry configuration.

PortSentry cleanly compiles on Mac OS X, so be sure to read the documentation carefully before you begin. The author clearly outlines the installation procedure in a step-by-step manner. Compiling with make generic works fine. By default, the package installs in /usr/local/psionic/portsentry.

The most important file you'll work with is portsentry.conf. The first part of the configuration file is the Port Configurations section. Here you specify which TCP and UDP ports are monitored. The author has provided three basic selections: anal, aware, and bare-bones. Of course, you can add any additional ports to whichever set you select.

Next is the Advanced Stealth Scan Detection Options section. Because these options apply only to Linux, you can ignore this section. PortSentry 2.0 is supposed to be able to detect stealth scans. That version is not available on SourceForge yet, but if you would like to try it, the source code for it is still available at http://www.macosxunleashed.com/downloads/portsentry-2.0b1.tar.gz. If you choose make bsd, in portsentry.h, in the section that starts with #ifdef BSD, comment out the line that reads #include <netinet/ip_ether.h> by placing // at the beginning of that line.

The section that follows is the Configuration Files section, where you specify the location of portsentry.ignore, portsentry.history, and portsentry.blocked. The portsentry.ignore file is where you specify which hosts' connections the program should ignore. The portsentry.history file is where PortSentry logs a history of the actions it has taken. The portsentry.blocked file is where PortSentry logs a history of its actions for the current session.

The next section is the Misc. Configurations Options section, which only has one configuration option. Here you set whether DNS lookups are done on attacking hosts. The default is off.

The next section is the Response Options section. In this section, you specify what the automatic response should be for TCP and UDP connections. In the Ignore Options subsection, you specify what level of `ignore` PortSentry should follow for TCP and UDP connections. You can have PortSentry block scans, not block them, or execute some external command. The Dropping Routes subsection is where you select what the blocking response should be. The program can be configured to block via `route` or via `ipfw`. I recommend using `ipfw` if you have it running. If you select `ipfw`, PortSentry, by default, adds a deny rule to `ipfw`. Of course, you can modify that rule. In the TCP Wrappers subsection, select the correct TCP Wrappers syntax for the way you are using it. An external command can be specified in the External Commands subsection. In the Scan Trigger Value subsection, you configure the number of port connects that are allowed before an alarm is given. In the Port Banner section, you can specify what text, if any, should be displayed when PortSentry is tripped.

After you have a basic `portsentry.conf` file, and you've installed the package, run the following to start PortSentry:

```
/usr/local/psionic/portsentry/portsentry -tcp
/usr/local/psionic/portsentry/portsentry -udp
```

Check `/var/log/system.log` for the PortSentry startup response. For each PortSentry, you'll see some initial startup lines, a line for each port it's monitoring, and a final line indicating that PortSentry is active and listening.

If PortSentry is set to immediately block a connection, here's the type of response you will see in the log:

```
Sep 11 01:11:51 localhost portsentry[1164]: attackalert: Host 192.168.1.200
➥has been blocked via wrappers with string: "ALL: 192.168.1.200"
Sep 11 01:11:51 localhost portsentry[1164]: attackalert: Host 192.168.1.200
➥has been blocked via dropped route using command: "/sbin/ipfw add
➥1 deny all from 192.168.1.200:255.255.255.255 to any"
Sep 11 01:11:51 localhost portsentry[1164]: attackalert: Connect from host:
➥192.168.1.200/192.168.1.200 to TCP port: 1
Sep 11 01:11:51 localhost portsentry[1164]: attackalert: Host: 192.168.1.200
➥is already blocked. Ignoring
```

Check your `/etc/hosts.deny` and run `ipfw show`. You'll see that it does add the offending host to the `/etc/hosts.deny` file and add an `ipfw` rule.

If PortSentry isn't set to block connections, here is a sample response in the log file:

```
Sep 11 01:03:52 localhost portsentry[1125]: attackalert: Connect
➥from host: 192.168.1.200/192.168.1.200 to TCP port: 21
Sep 11 01:03:52 localhost portsentry[1125]: attackalert: Ignoring
➥TCP response per configuration file setting.
```

Commonsense Preventive Measures

We've reached a good time to point out some commonsense preventive measures to provide basic security for your machine. They don't guarantee the safety of your machine, of course, but they provide good basic guidelines for you. These commonsense activities apply not only to Mac OS X, but also to any other operating system.

The commonsense preventive security measures that you should always keep in mind are

- Keep your operating system current. You can easily do this by setting Software Update to a regular update schedule. If you prefer not to have Software Update check for updates automatically, make sure that you check Apple's website regularly for any updates and subsequently run Software Update. This is perhaps the most important commonsense activity you can do.
- For Mac OS X, don't turn on any network services that you don't need. For other operating systems, this often means turning off services you don't need because many operating services tend to come with many network services turned on by default.
- Restrict access to the services you have to run. Using TCP Wrappers is one method for restricting access to some services.
- Replace insecure services with secure services. For many systems, this advice especially targets using `sshd` instead of `telnetd` because `sshd` typically has to be installed separately. For Mac OS X, enabling remote login in the Sharing pane automatically starts `sshd`, which is included in the Mac OS X distribution, rather than `telnetd`.
- Run services with the least privilege necessary for the job. Check the documentation for the service to see advice about this.

Limiting Access to Administrative Accounts: `sudo` and `/etc/sudoers`

Finally, an important commonsense measure you can take is to limit access to the abilities of the `root` account. The configuration with which Apple ships Mac OS X includes an `admin` group, any members of which can execute any command they want with `root` privileges. If you have multiple people with user accounts that you want to be able to perform various administrative functions, giving them all complete access to run any command as `root` is a serious security threat.

Your best option is to use the capabilities of the `sudo` command in the fashion it was originally intended: to provide limited access to specific privileged functions to specific users. Covering the complete syntax and configuration options for `sudo` is a topic best suited for an entire chapter, but we'll cover enough to get you started here.

`sudo`, and which users it will allow to execute which commands, is controlled by the file `/etc/sudoers`. This file is composed of a number of lines in Extended Backus-Naur Form (EBNF), which is a formalized way of writing definitions when the definitions are of the form "An A is a B or a C; Cs can be Ds or Es and Fs; and Es are types of fruit." That is, descriptions where left-side terms are equated to right-side definitions, and definitions may be other terms, ordered lists of terms, or terminal nodes. Terminal nodes are final, nonsubdividable entries. BNF and EBNF (the differences are beyond the scope of this book) are used, either directly or indirectly, in a number of computer configuration methods. BNF form definitions lend themselves to being used either as the direct content of a configuration file where the configuration must be a set of hierarchical definitions (such as who's allowed to run what commands), or the syntax of the configuration may be explained in terms of its BNF definition. (And, in fact, many computer languages, programs that can be thought of as very large configuration specifications, can be usefully defined in BNF.)

As an example of how BNF works, a simple first attempt at creating a BNF description for the English language might look something like this:

```
sentence  : ([subject] [verb] [object]), ([subject] [verb])
subject   : [phrase]
object    : (a [phrase])
phrase    : [noun], ([adjective] [noun])
verb      : hit, threw, chased
noun      : tommy, ball
adjective : red, big
```

If we consider things in parentheses to be ordered lists of terms, things separated by commas to indicate choices between multiple things, things in square braces to be terms, and things without square braces to be terminal nodes, we have a BNF definition that can be used to build potential English-language sentences. Using this BNF to construct valid sentences, we can come up with things such as

"tommy hit a ball"

"tommy hit a big ball"

"big tommy hit a red ball"

or

"tommy hit"

Although English makes a good example for explaining simple BNF grammars, it's much too complex a language to completely codify in BNF form. Because of this, the BNF grammar I've constructed also would allow sentences such as "ball threw" and "red ball chased a big tommy." Fortunately, the language required for most things such as constructing configuration files is not nearly as complex as English. For `/etc/sudoers`, the language required is simply a way of specifying users, the commands they are allowed to run, and the user IDs under which the commands are run when these users invoke `sudo`. In the case of `sudo`, the configuration file consists of individual configuration lines specifying aspects of the configuration. There can be as many configuration lines as you need to completely specify the users and permissions desired. `/etc/sudoers` contains two types of configuration lines: alias lines and user-specification lines.

The alias lines are used to build a hierarchical specification of users, user IDs, or commands. The user-spec lines are then used to combine these into useful definitions as to who is allowed to do what and how. The alias lines conform to `LINE`s created by the following EBNF—here I'm using commas to separate choices and square braces to indicate nonterminal terms. Parentheses again indicate an ordered grouping of terms, and angle braces denote textual explanations of a valid value. Single quotes surround characters that appear verbatim in a value, where those verbatim characters might be misunderstood as part of the EBNF itself. Exclamation point characters are used to negate a value.

```
LINE           : [User_Line], [Runas_Line], [Cmnd_Line]
User_Line      : (User_Alias     [NAME] = [User_List])
Runas_Line     : (Runas_Alias    [NAME] = [Runas_List])
Host_Line      : (Host_Alias     [NAME] = [Host_List])
Cmnd_Line      : (Cmnd_Alias     [NAME] = [Cmnd_List])
NAME           : <A NAME is a string containing upper-case letters, numbers,
                  and the underscore characters '_'.  A NAME must start with
                  an uppercase letter.>

User_List      : [User], ([User]',' [User_List])
User           : [UserType], ![UserType]
UserType       : <username>, %<groupname>, <NAME where NAME is a
                                           defined User_Alias>
```

A `User_List` is made up of one or more usernames, system groups (prefixed with `%`), and other `User_Alias` aliases. Each item can be prefixed with an `!` to negate the sense of the definition.

```
Runas_List     : [RunasUser], ([RunasUser]',' [Runas_List])
RunasUser      : [RunasType], ![RunasType]
RunasType      : <username>, #<userid>, %<group>, <NAME where NAME is a
                                                  defined Runas_Alias>
```

A `Runas_List` is similar to a `User_List` except that it can also contain numeric user IDs (prefixed with #) and instead of `User_Aliases`, it can contain `Runas_Aliases`.

```
Host_List      : [Host], ([Host]',' [Host_List])
Host           : [HostType], ![HostType]
HostType       : <hostname>, <ipaddress>, <network range>, <NAME where NAME is
                                                          a Host_Alias>
```

A `Host_List` is made up of one or more hostnames, IP addresses, network numbers, and other `Host_Alias` aliases. The `Host_Alias` directive is of only minor use if you're not building a cooperating group of machines. By allowing host specifications, the same `/etc/sudoers` file can be used on all machines of a cluster, yet have customized and specific actions on each. This allows much more convenient maintenance than if you needed to create and configure the file on each machine individually.

```
Cmnd_List       : [Cmnd], ([Cmnd]',' [Cmnd_List])
Cmnd            : [CmndType], ![CmndType]
CmndType        : [CommandName], <directory path>, <NAME where NAME is a
                                                    defined Cmnd_Alias>
CommandName     : <command path>, (<commandpath> <args>), (<commandpath> '""')
```

A `Cmnd_List` is a list of one or more `CommandNames`, directories, and other `Cmnd_Alias` aliases. A `CommandName` is a fully qualified file path that might include shell-style wildcards. A simple filename enables the user to run the command with any arguments she wants. However, you can also specify command-line arguments (including wildcards). Alternately, you can specify `""` to indicate that the command can be run only without command-line arguments. A `directory path` is a fully qualified path to a directory ending in a `/`. When you specify a directory in a `Cmnd_List`, the user can run any file within that directory (but not in any subdirectories therein). If a `Cmnd` has associated command-line arguments, the arguments given by the user on the command line must exactly match those in the `Cmnd` (or match the wildcards, if there are any). Note that the following characters must be escaped with a `\` if they're used in command arguments: "`,`", "`:`", "`=`", and "`\`."

TIP

In the actual file, a \ alone at the end of a line indicates that the line continues on to the next line unbroken.

After you've defined the various elements you need using the alias line syntax, you use these to define who may do what, using `ULINE`s in the following user-specification syntax:

```
ULINE           : ([User_list] [WhereWhat])
WhereWhat       : ([Host_List] = [Cmnd_Spec_List]),
                  ([Host_List] = [Cmnd_Spec_List] : [WhereWhat])
Cmnd_Spec_List : [Cmnd_Spec], ([Cmnd_Spec]',' [Cmnd_Spec_List])
Cmnd_Spec       : [Runas_Spec] [Passwd_Spec] [Cmnd]
Runas_Spec      : '(' [Runas_List] ')', ''
Passwd_Spec     : 'PASSWD:', 'NOPASSWD:', ''
```

28

A user-specification line consists of a `User_List` (constructed by the EBNF rules shown previously), for which this particular rule is true. This is followed by a `Host_List` defining the set of hosts on which the commands specified may be run. To this `Host_List` is assigned a `Cmnd_Spec_List` defining the commands that this user is allowed to run on the hosts that match the `Host_List`. There may be additional `[Host_List] = [Cmnd_Spec_List]` entries on the same line, separated from each other by colons. Each `Cmnd_Spec_List` is composed of previously defined `Cmnd` definitions (which, by convoluted logic, you'll note may be `Cmnd_Aliases` to lists of `Cmnds`). For each of these, the `Cmnd` may optionally be preceded by a `Runas_List` enclosed in parentheses or by the flags `PASSWD:` or `NOPASSWD:`. Inclusion of a `Runas_List` overrides the default `root` user ID as the commands run through `sudo` are executed. Inclusion of `NOPASSWD:` or `PASSWD:` allows overriding (or making explicit) the requirement for the user to enter a password to run commands in the Cmnd_Spec as the alternative user ID. Password checking can be turned on for some commands and off for others in the same ULINE by prefixing the respective group's Cmnd_Specs with PASSWD: and NOPASSWD: as appropriate.

All this might seem a bit complex, especially when you start looking at a definition such as that for a Cmnd, where a Cmnd may be the name of a defined Cmnd_Alias, which may be a Cmnd_List, which may be a Cmnd. But it's actually rather simple when you start following concrete examples through the EBNF grammar.

First, let's look at the /etc/sudoers file that comes with Mac OS X by default:

```
# sudoers file.
#
# This file MUST be edited with the 'visudo' command as root.
#
# See the sudoers man page for the details on how to write a sudoers file.
#
# Host alias specification
# User alias specification
# Cmnd alias specification
# Defaults specification
# User privilege specification
root    ALL=(ALL) ALL
%admin  ALL=(ALL) ALL
```

Not much to it, so it couldn't be too difficult to interpret, could it? Two lines of user specification. They both make rather copious use of the built-in ALL alias, which functions as "All valid values in this position." Parsing these lines is particularly easy. For the first ULINE, the User_List portion is simply root, so it's a line that specifies some things that root's allowed to do through sudo. The Host_List portion is ALL, so root's allowed to do the things listed anywhere. The optional Runas_Spec is ALL as well, so root's allowed to do (some as yet unspecified) things, as anyone through sudo. Finally, the Cmnd_Spec_List portion is again ALL, indicating that root is allowed to do anything, as anyone, anywhere, using the sudo command. This isn't particularly surprising. If root wanted to do something under an alternative user ID, even if it couldn't be done by specifying an alternative user ID to sudo, root can always su to anyone.

The second ULINE, which is quite similar to the first, is the one that's a bit disturbing for your day-to-day system security. Its User_List portion is specified by group name instead of by user ID, and it enables anyone in the group admin to have exactly the same complete access to the system as root. If you're the only user on your machine, this isn't a concern. But if your machine is a multiuser machine, having everyone who needs *any* administrative access getting *all* administrative access is a bad idea and a recipe for an eventual security disaster.

NOTE

The command `visudo` is used to edit the `/etc/sudoers` file. This command is functionally the `vi` editor, but it locks the `/etc/sudoers` file so that only one person can edit it at a time, and provides basic syntax checking to help eliminate parsing errors in the `/etc/sudoers` file.

Instead of this rather poor configuration, consider something that limits sub-administrator access to specific commands. Even with limited access, there might be ways for a person with malicious intent to find a way to do harm, but there's no sense in giving everyone the combination to the bank vault if what they need to do their job is only a key to the utility closet. Your needs will be as individual as your system, but you should be able to build a much more competent administrative hierarchy for `sudo` by studying the following example and adapting it to your needs.

Let's consider an `/etc/sudoers` file that contains the following definitions (lines that start with # are comments):

```
# User alias specification
User_Alias      FULLTIMERS  = john, will, joan
User_Alias      PARTTIMERS  = adam, robyn, jack
User_Alias      WEBMASTERS  = sandy, rich
User_Alias      PROGRAMMERS = dave, bob
User_Alias      SECRETARIES = karen, nancy, dan
```

Here, the file defines five named groups of users: `FULLTIMERS`, `PARTTIMERS`, `WEBMASTERS`, `PROGRAMMERS`, and `SECRETARIES`. You might imagine that these separate full-time administrative staff from part-time staff, and webmaster-type administrators (who probably aren't experienced Unix administrators, but who need some `root`-like functions to do things such as stop and start the web server) from programmers and secretaries. Programmers might have some reason to have limited special privileges, such as installing software, and our secretaries can do some general maintenance without needing an administrator around.

28

```
# Runas alias specification
Runas_Alias     OP = root
Runas_Alias     DB = mysql
Runas_Alias     SW = software
```

Three aliases are constructed to specific users to allow the commands to be run with their user IDs:

```
# Host alias specification
Host_Alias      SPARC   = soyokaze, rosalyn, ryoko, rodan :\
                SGI     = waashu, oni, halo :\
                ALPHA   = godzilla :\
                LINUX   = mother, venice, hedora
Host_Alias      CUNETS  = 140.254.12.0
```

```
Host_Alias      SERVERS = ftp, mail, www
Host_Alias      CDROM   = waashu, ryoko, soyokaze
```

The first Host_Alias line uses the : separator to define several aliases simultaneously for a number of different machines by name. The next line (remember that \ in the file itself causes the next physical line to be read as a continuation of this one) specifies a network range. They are all machines in the 140.254.12. C-class network; there's an additional netmask parameter available if you're building truly complex configurations—see the sudoers man page for more information. Next, an alias for some server machines is constructed, and finally an alias for some machines that have CD-ROMs. Note that membership in one Host_Alias doesn't preclude membership in others. All the machines that have CD-ROMs are also members of their respective hardware-type alias groups.

```
# Cmnd alias specification
Cmnd_Alias      DUMPS    = /usr/bin/mt, /usr/sbin/dump, /usr/sbin/rdump,\
                           /usr/sbin/restore, /usr/sbin/rrestore
Cmnd_Alias      KILL     = /usr/bin/kill
Cmnd_Alias      INSTALL  = /usr/bin/make install
Cmnd_Alias      PRINTING = /usr/sbin/lpc, /usr/bin/lprm
Cmnd_Alias      SHUTDOWN = /usr/sbin/shutdown
Cmnd_Alias      HALT     = /usr/sbin/halt, /usr/sbin/fasthalt
Cmnd_Alias      REBOOT   = /usr/sbin/reboot, /usr/sbin/fastboot
Cmnd_Alias      SHELLS   = /usr/bin/sh, /usr/bin/csh, /usr/bin/ksh, \
                           /usr/local/bin/tcsh, /usr/bin/rsh, \
                           /usr/local/bin/zsh
Cmnd_Alias      SU       = /usr/bin/su
```

Now we have some Cmnd_Alias lines configured with a few useful groups of commands. The DUMPS Cmnd_Alias includes commands you'd need to run to do dump/restore-type backups. PRINTING includes control programs for lpr/lpd access to CUPS. SHELLS includes those applications that can also function as user login shells. The others are fairly self-explanatory.

Making use of all these definitions is now rather easy: Simply construct ULINE entries that tie them together to explain who can do what and where it can be done. Perhaps we want to allow our full-time staff complete access to any machine as root, whereas our part-time staff should be able to run various commands as root, but we don't want them to be able to start up a root shell:

```
FULLTIMERS      ALL = (OP) ALL
PARTTIMERS      ALL = (OP) ALL, !SU, !SHELLS
```

CAUTION

The negated SU and SHELL entries here should be considered to be mostly informative, rather than a strict preventative measure. If the PARTTIMERS really wanted shell access, they could easily get it by invoking a command shell out of some application that they're allowed to run.

We have an additional administrative user (scott) who's only responsible for backup and restore functions on the server machines:

```
scott           SERVERS = (OP) DUMPS
```

We want the secretaries to be able to kill off printer jobs that are causing problems. We'd also like them to be able to use the CD-ROM burner to write a user's files to CD-R without needing them to be able to su to that user ID to access the files, so the secretaries need hdiutil and ditto:

```
SECRETARIES     ALL = (OP) PRINTING, /usr/bin/hdiutil, \
                                     /usr/bin/ditto
```

We also have a few people who fiddle with and compile software, who we trust enough to install it as under the auspices of our software user, but to whom we don't want to give full access to the software user's account:

```
PROGRAMMERS     ALL = (SW) INSTALL
```

On the Linux boxes, we'd like scott to be able to do shutdown and reboot type administrative tasks:

```
scott           LINUX = (OP) SHUTDOWN, HALT, REBOOT
```

User dave needs to have access to kill hung processes on his desktop machine:

```
dave            192.168.1.18 = (OP) KILL
```

The webmasters need to have permission to run any command on the web server (a machine named www), with a generic webmaster user ID (which won't necessarily be able to do much). They also need to be able to restart the web server as root because it's run by the system startup scripts and the parent server is owned by root:

```
WEBMASTERS      www = (webmaster) ALL, \
                      (OP) /System/Library/StartupItems/Apache/Apache start,\
                      (OP) /System/Library/StartupItems/Apache/Apache stop, \
                      (OP) /System/Library/StartupItems/Apache/Apache restart
```

28

Because we've been having a bit of trouble with the power in the room where the SGI workstations live, we're going to let any user run sync on them as root. This way, if any user happens to be around when the power goes out, she might be able to sync the drives before the uninterruptible power supplies die. We're not even going to require a password for this because it would be hard to hurt the machines by syncing the drives:

```
ALL             SGI = (OP) NOPASSWD: /bin/sync
```

This is nowhere near a complete iteration of what can be configured using sudo and /etc/sudoers, or even a complete itemization of what can be built using the simple alias lines constructed in the first part of the example. It should, however, be enough to demonstrate how you can compartmentalize your administrative needs into separate tasks and users who can perform them. This compartmentalization, combined with a judicious use of reassigning directory and application ownerships, will enable you to vastly increase your machine's day-to-day security because it removes much of the need and/or temptation to run as the `root` user. If you believe your cluster configuration would benefit from greater richness in what can be permitted and limited via `sudo`, please see the `sudoers` man page—the discussion here only brushes the surface.

CAUTION

The examples given here are somewhat contrived to show the possible uses, and aren't specifically an indication of good thinking when it comes to security practices. A user who wants to abuse the system could probably find ways to circumvent the limitations placed on their access, and gain complete root access to the machine though a number of these rules. If you're going to allow users `sudo` access to run some commands with root privileges, you must be either very certain that your users are trustworthy or very careful when you pick which commands they're allowed to run.

For example, imagine that the `WEBMASTER` users own the executable file that's the Apache web server, and they want to usurp root powers. All they would need to do is replace `apache` with a shell script of their own devising and issue a root-privileged `apache` restart to have whatever commands they choose run as root.

When you design your `/etc/sudoers` rules, you need to consider this type of subterfuge and plan your permissions accordingly.

Summary

In this chapter we looked at advanced network configuration and utilities as well as security issues. On the advanced network side, we saw how `ifconfig` could be used to assign an IP address to your machine, or more interesting, bind another IP address to it, for such purposes as virtual host web serving. We also took an in-depth look at Network Utility, which provides a suite of diagnostic tools for a Mac user to test his connections.

Network security has never been as important on the Macintosh as it is with Mac OS X, which provides a wider variety of network services than any previous release. Luckily, Mac OS X includes a variety of tools that can fend off attacks before they occur—without the need for additional software.

Many users find that their network security issues can be simply addressed by applying TCP wrappers to their critical services and shutting down those protocols that aren't being used. Advanced users can use `ipfw`, or graphical tools that interface with `ipfw`, such as BrickHouse, to provide low-level control over the flow of network traffic to and from the Mac OS X computer. In addition, administrators might want to take proactive measures by employing an intrusion detection tool such as Tripwire or Snort. These applications can detect an attack and react to it—potentially saving your system, data, and peace of mind.

CHAPTER 29

Maintaining a Healthy System

IN THIS CHAPTER

- Keeping Software Updated
- Performing System Backups
- Monitoring Tiger System Operation
- Built-in Diagnostic and Repair Tools
- Third-Party Disk and Virus Tools

Although we'd like to believe that you'll never need to deal with a "sick" machine, things don't always (often?) go as planned. In this, the final chapter of *Mac OS X Tiger Unleashed*, we'll deal with a few of the more mundane tasks involved in keeping a healthy Tiger. Here you'll find information on how to maintain your system and what products are available to aid your efforts.

Keeping Software Updated

An important part of maintaining a functioning and secure system is staying on top of the operating system updates. With a BSD core, Tiger needs more frequent attention than the Classic Mac operating system. Critical security utilities such as SSH are revised regularly and, unless updated, might open your system to outside attack. Updates in mid-2004 fixed holes in Safari and Help Viewer that could potentially allow malicious scripts to run without warning on your system. Although it might be tempting to let Tiger coast for a few months and perform all the updates at once, doing so is not wise. A machine with a full-time Internet connection is vulnerable from the moment that a new software exploit is found and very likely will be compromised.

For example, consider my home cable-connected computer, which logs each connection attempt made:

```
12/27/2004 03:38:28 Host:
www.allstat.com/216.168.220.18 Port: 137 UDP Blocked
12/27/2004 03:51:47 Host: 211.109.221.80/211.109.221.80
Port: 27374 TCP Blocked
12/27/2004 04:22:09 Host: 71dial170.xnet/213.233.71.170
Port: 27374 TCP Blocked
```

```
12/27/2004 07:46:43 Host: 92dial132.xnet/213.233.92.132 Port: 27374 TCP Blocked
12/27/2004 08:03:51 Host: 65.103.240.60/65.103.240.60 Port: 1433 TCP Blocked
12/27/2004 08:10:57 Host: pc172.jeleniag/217.96.243.172 Port: 22 TCP Blocked
12/27/2004 09:49:30 Host: rrcs-central-24-12/24.123.46.10 Port: 515 TCP Blocked
12/27/2004 10:35:34 Host: 64dial26.xnet.ro/213.233.64.26 Port: 27374 TCP Blocked
12/27/2004 12:53:05 Host: 211.137.136.118/211.137.136.118 Port: 111 TCP Blocked
12/27/2004 14:15:47 Host: 6535208hfc65.tampa/65.35.208.65 Port: 137 UDP Blocked
12/27/2004 15:00:20 Host: Sherbrooke-HSE/65.93.184.161 Port: 27374 TCP Blocked
12/27/2004 19:01:57 Host: 210.0.179.119/210.0.179.119 Port: 21 TCP Blocked
12/27/2004 19:51:48 Host: 67-92-203-151/67.92.203.151 Port: 1433 TCP Blocked
12/27/2004 20:26:33 Host: AC83C299.ipt.aol/172.131.194.153 Port: 23 TCP Blocked
12/27/2004 21:05:20 Host: 66.84.150.13/66.84.150.13 Port: 1433 TCP Blocked
12/27/2004 23:19:13 Host: 195.113.153.9/195.113.153.9 Port: 21 TCP Blocked
12/27/2004 23:32:48 Host: 61-220-153-179/61.220.153.179 Port: 1433 TCP Blocked
```

In the course of one day, there are more than 15 connection attempts. Some are innocuous—simple probes for Internet sharing services such as Kazaa—whereas others are attempts to connect to well-known services, such as telnet, SSH, and FTP, presumably for the purpose of exploitation. On a production computer with a real Internet connection running real services, you might experience hundreds of inappropriate connection attempts a day, and unless you want to spend your time reinstalling Tiger, you should keep your system updated and prepared to handle the threat.

Checking for Updates

Tiger automates the process of upgrading software through the use of the Software Update System preferences pane (path: `/Applications/System Preferences`), shown in Figure 29.1.

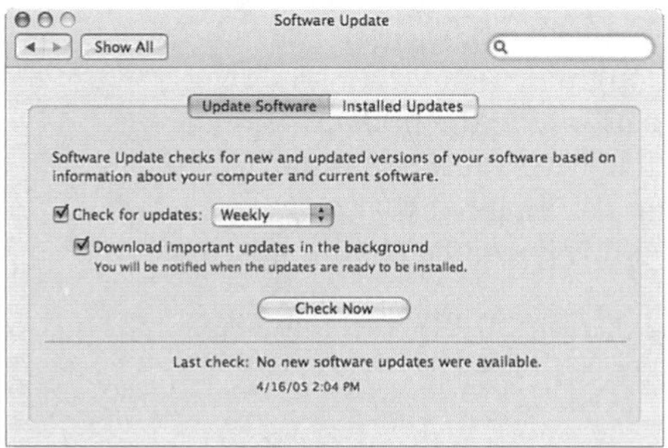

FIGURE 29.1 The Software Update pane controls automatic system updates.

Use the check box to choose whether to run the software update application automatically or invoke it manually. If you've chosen an automatic install, use the pop-up menu to select a schedule (Daily, Weekly, Monthly) for the update library to be queried. If you want the system to automatically download updates in the background so that they can be installed faster, click Download Important Updates in the Background.

NOTE

The Tiger software update mechanism does not automatically install any updates. An administrative user must confirm the update process before it will be carried out.

To force the system to look for updates immediately, click the Check Now button or choose Software Update from the Apple menu at any time. Your computer contacts Apple and detects available software packages.

If updates are found, a system update application is launched, as shown in Figure 29.2.

FIGURE 29.2 Check the items that you want to install.

Downloading Updates

Click the check box in front of each package that you want to install. Packages that will require a reboot are denoted by a small arrow icon in their listing. (All updates to the base operating system require a reboot before becoming active.) When you've finished selecting packages, click Install to start the updates. You will be prompted for an administrator password before continuing.

During each installation, the system displays a status bar for the update. If a component hasn't already been downloaded in the background, it could take quite awhile for the system to download and install; you might want to take a break during this process.

For some software packages, you might see a license agreement during the installation. In addition, the installation is likely to pause for a long period of time while it optimizes your installed packages. This is completely normal, albeit slightly annoying. Just wait patiently even if the update seems to be taking an unusually long time.

NOTE

For those who want to put the update on a CD or file server, Apple offers normal file downloads for all the available system updates. To download an update file to your desktop through the Software Update application, select the item in the update list; then choose Update, Download Only or Install and Keep Package from the menu. The former will download the updates without installing them; the latter will download the update packages *and* install them on the local computer.

TIP

In the event of an installation failure, Apple suggests manually forcing an update, and then reselecting and reinstalling the failed upgrade. I've found that downloading the update package to the desktop and installing manually often works.

Disabling Unnecessary Updates

If there are updates that don't apply to your system, select them and choose Update, Ignore Update from the menu (or press Delete). This prevents Software Update from attempting to install them in the future.

To *show* updates that you've previously made inactive, choose Software Update, Reset Ignored Updates.

NOTE

When you choose to ignore an update, the system will ignore the update *and* any future versions of the same type of update. If you choose to ignore an iPod update, for example, all iPod updates will be ignored.

Reviewing Installed Files

Many users, for good reason, want to keep track of what software has been installed on their system. Opening the Software Update preferences pane and clicking the Installed Updates button displays a log of installed updates. Figure 29.3 shows this listing.

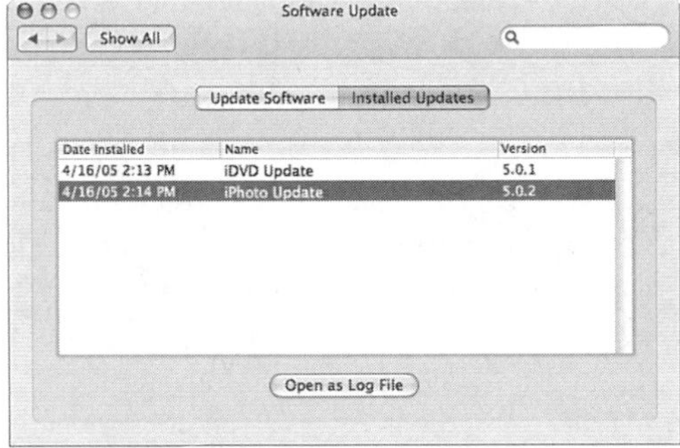

FIGURE 29.3 The Software Update pane displays a list of installed update packages.

In some cases, packages that are partially installed might be listed even though they weren't completely installed. To make Mac OS X forget about an update so that it can be reinstalled, open the directory `/Library/Receipts`. This folder contains receipt files for all software installed using Apple's built-in Installer program. The receipts are named based on the updated package; for example, Security Update July 2003 has the receipt file `SecurityUpd2003-07-14.pkg`.

Throwing out a receipt file will usually effectively convince Mac OS X that the update was never installed.

Listing the Bill of Materials with `lsbom`

The receipt files, in addition to keeping track of which packages have been installed, also contain a *bill of materials (BOM)*. The BOM tracks every file that was updated or installed. Users can access the BOM using the command-line `lsbom` command. You'll need to dig deep into the receipt files, accessing a directory with this pattern: `<receipt package>.pkg/Contents/Resources/<receipt package>.bom`. For example, to view the BOM for the Tiger Seed Update 8A323A receipt file:

```
brezup:jray jray $ sudo lsbom /Library/Receipts/TigerSeedUpdate8A323A.pkg/
➥Contents/Archive.bom
.       41775   0/80
./System        40755   0/0
./System/Library        40755   0/0
./System/Library/CoreServices   40755   0/0
./System/Library/CoreServices/SystemVersion.plist 100644  0/0  506  921025735
./System/Library/Frameworks     40755   0/0
./System/Library/Frameworks/ApplicationServices.framework       40755   0/0
./System/Library/Frameworks/ApplicationServices.framework/Versions      40755   0/0
./System/Library/Frameworks/ApplicationServices.framework/Versions/A    40755   0/0
...
```

The `lsbom` command can limit its output to only specific types of files contained in the BOM, such as directories or files, by using flags such as `-d` and `-f`, respectively. The Apple `lsbom` documentation, contained in Table 29.1, displays many of the available options and filters for viewing BOMs as documented in the man page.

29

TABLE 29.1 Command Documentation Table for `lsbom`

Option	Description
`-b`	List block devices
`-c`	List character devices
`-d`	List directories
`-f`	List files
`-l`	List symbolic links
`-m`	Print modified times (for plain files only)
`-s`	Print only the path of each file
`-x`	Suppress modes for directories and symlinks

TABLE 29.1 Continued

Option	Description
`-arch`	`-archVal` when displaying plain files that represent fat `mach-o` binaries; print the size and checksum of the file contents for the specified `archVal` (either `"ppc"` or `"i386"`)
`-p` *<param>*	Print only some of the results (each option can only be used once):
`c`	32-bit checksum
`f`	Filename
`F`	Filename with quotes (that is, `"/usr/bin/lsbom"`)
`g`	Group ID
`G`	Group name
`m`	File mode (permissions)
`M`	Symbolic file mode (that is, `"dr-xr-xr-x"`)
`s`	File size
`S`	Formatted size
`t`	Mod time
`T`	Formatted mod time
`u`	User ID
`U`	Username
`/`	User ID/group ID
`?`	Username/group name

BOM files can be useful in determining what has changed on your system. If you've modified the location of system software or configuration files, a system update might modify or move these files. Viewing the BOM can tell you exactly what happened during a system update.

Updating from the Command Line

In Tiger, all the functionality of the Software Update utility can be accessed through the command-line program `softwareupdate`. Invoking `sudo softwareupdate -l` produces a list of the available updates:

```
brezup:jray jray $ softwareupdate -l

Software Update Tool
Copyright 2002-2004 Apple

Software Update found the following new or updated software:
   * 4082
        Hard Disk Update (1.0), 840K [recommended]
```

Each package is listed with a number (called a *label*) by which you can refer to the update and a flag as to whether the update is recommended.

To install an update, simply invoke softwareupdate -i followed by the label for each update. You can specify as many updates on a single line as you want, and each will be downloaded and installed in turn:

```
softwareupdate -i <update label> <update label> ...
```

For example:

```
brezup:jray jray $ sudo softwareupdate  -i 4082

Software Update Tool
Copyright 2002-2004 Apple


Downloading Hard Disk Update
Downloading Hard Disk Update     0..10..20..30..40..50..60..70..80..90..100
Expanding Hard Disk Update
Installing Hard Disk Update      0..10..20..30..40..50..60..70..80..90..100
Done.
```

If an update requires a system restart to become active, you will be prompted to reboot after the installation has completed. You can reboot from the command line by typing **sudo /sbin/reboot**.

> **NOTE**
>
> Failing to reboot after installing an update that requires a restart might result in unusual and unpredictable system behavior.

As we mentioned, softwareupdate can perform all the same functions as the GUI equivalent—in fact, it is *more* flexible than the GUI. The basic syntax for softwareupdate is always softwareupdate *<options>* [*<label>* ...] . Table 29.2 contains a list of the available arguments and their use.

TABLE 29.2 The softwareupdate Utility Can Perform All Your Update Tasks from the Command Line

Option	Description
-l	List all available updates.
-d	Download the updates.
-i *<label>* ...	Install the named updates.
-i -a	Install *all* the available appropriate updates.
-i -r	Install only the recommended updates—usually security and serious bug fixes.
-i -u *<url>* ...	Install updates from a URL. Unless you are distributing updates via Tiger Server, you won't need this.
--ignore *<label>*	Ignore the named update (current and future versions). Configured on a per-user basis.

TABLE 29.2 Continued

Option	Description
`--reset-ignored`	Reset the ignored updates so that they appear when updates are listed. Configured on a per-user basis.
`--schedule [on¦off]`	Turn automatic update checking on and off. Configured on a per-user basis.

Performing System Backups

As much as all of us hate to do it, keeping a backup of your important applications and data is a crucial part of maintaining a Tiger system. Backups generally fall into two categories: full and incremental. A full backup is an exact duplicate of everything within your filesystem (or a branch thereof, such as `/Users` or `/usr/local`). From a full backup, you can quickly restore the state of all the backed-up files as they existed at the time the backup was made. Full backups are time-consuming (all files must be copied each time the backup is run) and cannot efficiently be used to store multiple versions of files over an extended period of time. If, for example, you want to have a copy of each day's updates to your file server for the period of a year, you would need to make 365 full copies of each of the files—this could quickly add up in terms of storage media. Full backups are usually reserved for mostly static information that can be copied and stored.

An incremental backup, on the other hand, is used to archive filesystems that aren't static. You start with a single full backup and then periodically back up the files that have changed since the full backup took place. Incremental backups can take place at multiple levels, with each level backing up only the files that have changed since the preceding level was backed up.

This section of the chapter looks at software available for backing up files and volumes.

Tiger GUI Backup Utilities

For most people, backing up the contents of the `/Users/<username>` home directories will suffice for protecting personal information. This, of course, doesn't help much with applications and Unix system services that have been installed, nor does it cover additional accounts for other family members or friends.

We'll take a look at what tools are available, and what they're appropriate for. Finally, we'll review several command-line tools that can be employed to back up both Carbon/Classic applications and generic data files.

Retrospect

Retrospect is the most well-known and accepted backup solution for the Mac, featuring the capability to back up and restore Windows, Red Hat, and Macintosh systems, store backups on Internet FTP servers, and more. Figure 29.4 shows Retrospect Backup.

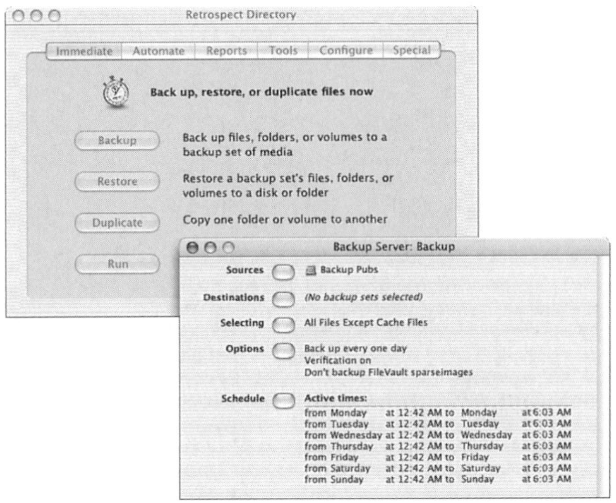

FIGURE 29.4 Retrospect 6.0 is a complete backup solution for Tiger and other popular platforms.

Retrospect works based on a client/server model. After the Retrospect client has been installed on the systems to backup, a Retrospect Server administrator can locate the client computers, select the files and volumes to back up, and store them on a variety of media including CDRW, DVD, DAT, and Internet storage sites. Backups can be scripted for automatic execution, or run at any time with the click of a mouse. Restoring files from a backup is a simple point-and-click operation that automatically copies files from the source media back to the client.

Mixed-platform networks will be happy to find that Retrospect clients are available for older Mac systems as well as Windows. Unfortunately, Retrospect has a history of annoying "gotchas" that can affect users with advanced setups. I strongly urge that you read the Dantz forums to figure out whether there are any known issues with your setup.

Retrospect 6.0 comes in several different versions, ranging from a single-desktop backup solution to workgroup and server editions. Find out more about Retrospect from `http://www.dantz.com/`.

29

TOLIS Group's BRU

Another enterprise-ready backup solution is BRU. Like Retrospect, BRU can work on a client/server model and comes in a variety of versions from single machine to server editions. BRU covers a much larger range of client platforms—from Windows NT 4.0, Server 2003, and XP to just about every Unix and Linux distribution available.

BRU has been a popular backup solution for Unix systems for quite some time, and should be definitely be considered for deploying a disaster recovery system. The entire application is scriptable and can be run from the command line. To appeal to traditional Mac users, TOLIS has also introduced a GUI for BRU, as shown in Figure 29.5. At present, the GUI isn't quite as well developed as that of Retrospect, but given the stability and performance of the platform as a whole, this might not be an issue for you. Visit `http://www.tolisgroup.com/` for more information.

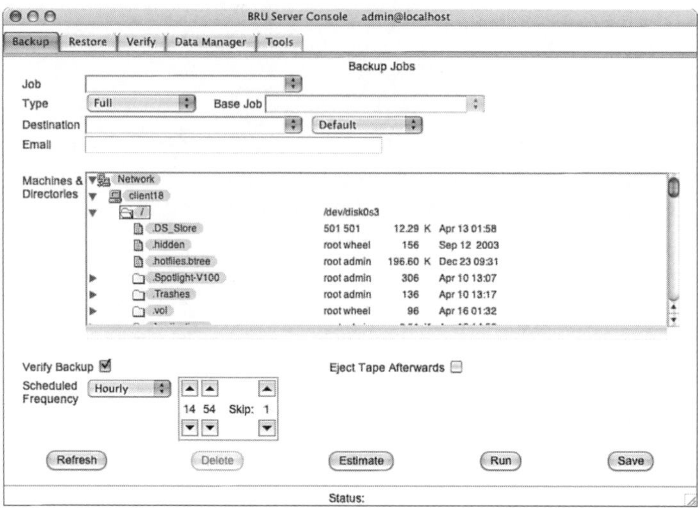

FIGURE 29.5 BRU can be controlled through the command-line interface or a native Tiger GUI.

Apple's Backup

For the home user who just wants to make sure that his critical data is backed up to CD, DVD, or iDisk, Apple's aptly named Backup could be the right answer. Shown in Figure 29.6, Backup is a simple piece of software that is capable of selecting common file types (such as Microsoft Word documents), system information (such as Safari preferences), or arbitrary files and folders and backing them up to your Mac's optical drive or .Mac iDisk. Backup does not currently offer a command-line interface, incremental backups, or a way of performing unattended backups.

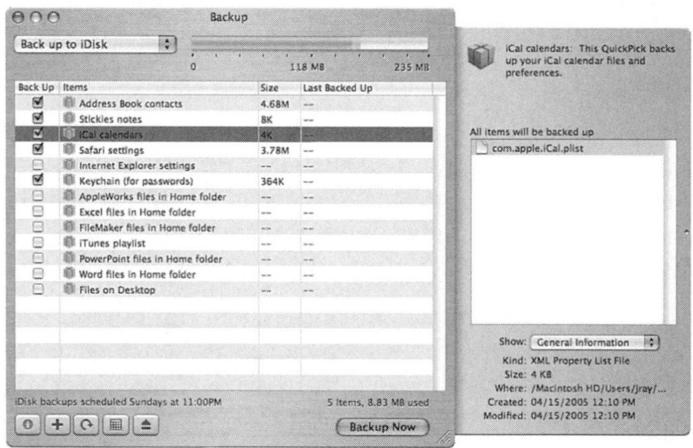

FIGURE 29.6 Apple's Backup is a simple tool for backing up data files.

Unfortunately, besides the entry-level capabilities, there's another catch to the software: Backup is exclusive those with a .Mac membership. This means that to download and use the tool, you'll need to pay the $100 entrance fee (`http://www.mac.com/`).

NOTE

On a positive note, .Mac membership also buys you a copy of Virex virus scanning software, along with the mac.com email, iDisk, and iSync capabilities. For Mac users who aren't running servers or using Unix tools, this might be a wise investment. For others, however, the money might be better spent on a third-party backup solution.

Data Backup X

Data Backup X from ProSoft Engineering (`http://www.prosoftengineering.com/products/data_backup.php`) is a complete personal backup system that picks up where Apple's tool left off. It offers advanced features such as scheduling, compression, mirroring, synchronization, incremental backups, and an "evolutive" mode that preserves different versions of files as they change across backups. For personal workstations, Data Backup X is hard to beat. If you can afford the $50 expense, Data Backup X is one of the most feature-filled personal backup software currently available.

Synk

The Synk application is an open source Cocoa-based utility that provides synchronization and backup services between folders and volumes. Synk allows the creation of AppleScript Run documents that can be used to launch a specific backup configuration with a simple double-click from the desktop. When used to synchronize storage locations, Synk even offers the capability to archive files that would normally be replaced or deleted during a synchronization process. Download Synk from `http://www.decimus.net/synk/`.

Carbon Copy Cloner

An entirely different backup approach is to mirror your system and data disks exactly. With Tiger, this is a simple process of using the `ditto` command, which we'll look at in the section "Using Command-Line Backup Tools." Although this feature is built into the operating system, a number of graphic utilities have sprung up around it to provide a more Mac-like experience.

The most popular of these utilities is Carbon Copy Cloner (`http://www.bombich.com/software/ccc.html`). Written in AppleScript Studio, Carbon Copy Cloner adds a user-friendly interface to the `ditto` command (as shown in Figure 29.7), and enables quick, easy, and even scheduled drive mirroring. Copied volumes are bootable and are created with all file permissions and ACLs intact.

NOTE

Carbon Copy Cloner can also prepare ASR-ready (Apple System Restore) disk images. ASR, a command-line utility that you'll learn about shortly, can restore entire volumes over a network.

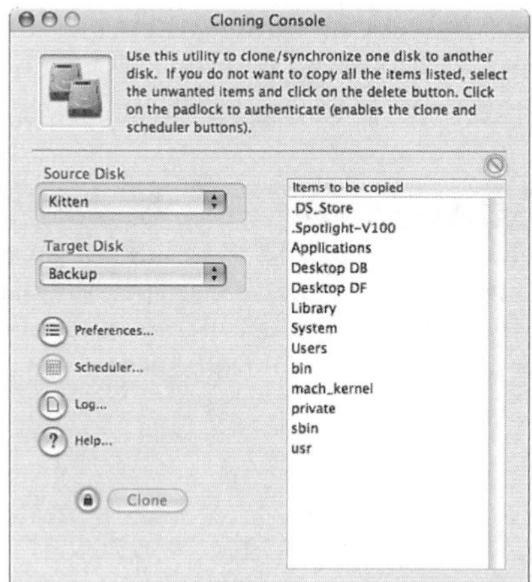

FIGURE 29.7 Carbon Copy Cloner uses the `ditto` command to create duplicates of your system volumes.

Although not an efficient solution for those who just want to back up changed data files, Carbon Copy Cloner, along with an external FireWire drive, makes a fantastic complete-system backup for servers and other machines with complex configurations.

TIP

Carbon Copy Cloner (or `ditto`) can be used to replicate an existing partition onto a different partition or volume. This is a no-cost way to resize a partition. If you resize partitions frequently, however, VolumeWorks from SubRosaSoft (`http://www.subrosasoft.com/thestore/product_info.php?products_id=431`) is the only way to go.

Using Command-Line Backup Tools

Traditional Mac users are obviously the target audience of most of the GUI backup software. Unfortunately, this has led to a plethora of tools that can only be controlled or configured if you are sitting in front of your computer. Remote command-line administration of Retrospect, for example, is virtually impossible.

The Unix side of Tiger provides some command-line backup tools that you've seen earlier (`tar`/`cp`), but aside from basic HFS+ compatibility in Tiger, they aren't necessarily the best tools for the job. Let's take a look at a few other utilities that are a bit more capable.

Mirroring Files and Folders: `ditto`

The `ditto` function (for those who don't remember the addictively good-smelling purple copies from grade school that share the name) creates a duplicate of a file or folder structure on your system. `ditto` is capable of dealing with the HFS+ filesystem and can quickly and easily replicate entire bootable system volumes.

The basic syntax of ditto is

```
ditto [-<options>] <source file/folder> <destination file/folder>
```

ditto can be used to copy multiple files or folders to a folder, or a single file to another file. In the former case, the destination directory will be created if it doesn't already exist.

By default, ditto preserves all the resource fork and extended attributes/metadata of the files it is copying—making it safe to copy files with resource forks and other Mac OS–specific information.

Using ditto For example, to verbosely copy the entire /Applications folder (and subfolders) to another location, /Volume/NewDisk, I'd use

```
brezup:jray jray $ sudo ditto -V /Applications /Volumes/NewDisk

>>> Copying /Applications
copying file Applications/.DS_Store .. 15364 bytes
copying file Applications/.localized .. 0 bytes
copying file Applications/Acrobat Reader 7.0/Info-macos.plist .. 3043 bytes
copying file Applications/Acrobat Reader 7.0//ACELiteCarbonLib .. 417634 bytes
copying file Applications/Acrobat Reader 7.0/Acrobat Reader
 5.0 .. 4285090 bytes
...
```

and so on.

The ditto command can also be used to create a zipped archive (/tmp/myhomedirectory.zip) of my home directory (/Users/jray) using the -c and -k options (archive and zip, respectively):

```
brezup:jray jray $ ditto -c -k -V /Users/jray /tmp/myhomedirectory.zip

>>> Copying /Users/jray
copying file ./.bash_history ... 1375 bytes
copying file ./.CFUserTextEncoding ... 3 bytes
copying file ./.DS_Store ... 6148 bytes
copying file ./.lpoptions ... 17 bytes
copying file ./Desktop/.DS_Store ... 6148 bytes
copying file ./Desktop/.localized ... 0 bytes
```

29

This archive can then be restored with -x (extract) and -k (zip), reversing the process.

```
brezup:jray jray $ ditto -x -k -V /tmp/myfile.zip /tmp/MyHome
>>> Copying /tmp/myfile.zip
copying file .bash_history ... 1375 bytes
copying file .CFUserTextEncoding ... 3 bytes
copying file .DS_Store ... 6148 bytes
copying file ._.DS_Store ... 82 bytes
```

```
copying file .lpoptions ... 17 bytes
copying file Desktop/.DS_Store ... 6148 bytes
copying file Desktop/._.DS_Store ... 82 bytes
...
```

Another interesting use for `ditto` is to copy only files that are contained within a given BOM (bill of materials). Using the `-bom` option followed by a valid BOM file limits the files copied to those contained within a given BOM file. For more information on BOM files, read about the `lsbom` command, earlier in this chapter. Table 29.3 provides Apple's options for `ditto`.

TABLE 29.3 Command Documentation Table for `ditto`

Option	Description
`-v`	Print a line of output for each source directory copied.
`-V`	Print a line of output for every file, symbolic link, and device copied.
`-X`	Do not descend into directories on a different device.
`-c`	Create a CPIO archive at the destination path.
`-z`	Create compressed (zipped) CPIO archives.
`-k`	Create PKZip (.zip) archives rather than CPIO archives.
`-x`	The first source is an archive to decompress.
`--keepParent`	Keep the parent directory as part of the archive.
`--arch` *<arch>*	Thin multi-architecture binaries (also known as *fat binaries*) to the specified architecture. If multiple `-arch` options are specified, the resulting destination file will be multi-architectural, containing each of the specified architectures (if they are present in the source file). `arch` should be specified as `"ppc"`, `"i386"`, and so on.
`--bom` *<bom>*	If this option is given, only files, links, devices, and directories that are present in the specified BOM file are copied.
`--rsrc`	Preserve resource forks and HFS metadata. `ditto` stores this data in AppleDouble files on filesystems that do not support resource forks. This is the default behavior in Tiger.
`--norsrc`	Do not preserve resource forks or HFS metadata.
`--extattr`	Preserve POSIX extended attributes. This is the default Tiger behavior.
`--noextattr`	Do not preserve extended attributes.
`--sequesterRsrc`	Preserve resource forks and metadata in the `__MACOSX` subdirectory when creating PKZip archives. PKZip will automatically detect these resources when decompressing.

Synchronizing Files: `rsync`

Having a backup of critical files is the best way to avert disaster. But restoring a backup can be time-consuming and creating an exact mirror on a day-to-day basis is often impractical. In many cases, the best solution is to synchronize files between two or more machines as changes are made. Starting in Tiger, Apple has included an HFS+-compatible `rsync`, an open source utility designed to make folder synchronization fast, scriptable, and painless.

rsync can operate locally to synchronize files between directories on a single machine, or can work over a network. An especially nice feature of the software is its capability to use several different transport mechanisms for network transfers. The rsync utility, for example, can operate as a server and be used to host rsync-accessible directories on remote machines. But if setting up an additional dedicated server process isn't desirable, you don't have to. An alternative (and often overlooked) method of providing rsync access is through a remote shell such as SSH. If your machines are running SSH, they are ready to use rsync immediately, without any additional software or configuration.

Using rsync The basic rsync syntax is simple: rsync [options] *<source>* *<destination>*. For example, to synchronize the contents of the folder /Users/jray/source with /Users/jray/destination, I would use the following:

```
brezup:jray jray $ rsync -va source/ destination
rsync: building file list...
rsync: 6 files to consider.
./
Icon
apache_pb.gif
index.html
macosxlogo.gif
web_share.gif
wrote 25079 bytes read 100 bytes 50358.00 bytes/sec
total size is 24711 speedup is 0.98
```

In this example, the -v (verbose) and -a (archive) options are included so that rsync displays files being copied and includes all attributes (permissions, owner, and so on) of the original files. Running the command again produces slightly different output because rsync doesn't need to recopy the files:

```
brezup:jray jray $ rsync -va source/ destination
rsync: building file list...
rsync: 6 files to consider.
wrote 172 bytes read 20 bytes 128.00 bytes/sec
total size is 24711 speedup is 128.70
```

Here, no files were copied because the directories are already in sync.

29

NOTE

Trailing slashes mean something to rsync. If a path is given with a trailing slash, it refers to the contents of the named directory. If the slash is excluded, it means the directory itself.

Although synchronizing local directories might be useful, the true power of rsync is revealed when it is used over a remote network connection. To do this, all that is needed is a running SSH daemon on the remote side and an account with access to the directory you want to sync. If you've ever used scp, you'll recognize the syntax for an SSH-tunneled rsync immediately; for example, assume that I want to synchronize the directory /Users/jray/Tools located on a remote server www.poisontooth.com with a local directory Tools—and, at the same time, compress the data as it is sent:

```
brezup:jray jray $ rsync -vaze ssh jray@www.poisontooth.com:/Users/jray/
➥Tools/ Tools
jray@www.poisontooth.com's password: ******
receiving file list .. done
./
htdigsearch/
adduser
authuser.pl
backupdisdain.pl
cgiinput.pl
deluser
footer.html
...
runindex.pl
setupconfig.pl
ticker.tar
wrote 448 bytes read 216031 bytes 18824.26 bytes/sec
total size is 1262138 speedup is 5.83
```

This example introduces the use of -e ssh to specify that ssh should be used as the remote shell that rsync connects through and -z, which compresses data in real-time to increase the transfer rate. A number of additional switches can be used with rsync to change its behavior. Table 29.4 documents many of the useful options.

TABLE 29.4 Useful rsync Options

Option	Description
-v	Use verbose output.
-a	Recursively copy files, preserving as much information as possible.
-c	Calculate a checksum before sending and after receiving to verify file integrity.
-b	Create a backup of existing files. Any file that would be replaced is renamed with a ~ (tilde) extension.
--suffix=<*string*>	Set the string used as a suffix when using the -b option. By default, the suffix is ~ (tilde).
-u	Skip any files that are already newer (have a more recent date stamp) at the destination.
-n	Perform a dry run of the operation, displaying what would be copied but without making any changes.
--existing	Do not copy any files that don't already exist on the destination.
--delete	Delete files on the destination that are not in the source.
--max-delete=<#>	Set the maximum number of files that can be deleted (to avoid disaster).
--delete-after	Delete files only after they have been successfully transferred.
--exclude=<*pattern*>	Exclude files from the operation based on a pattern, such as *.dmg.

TABLE 29.4 Continued

Option	Description
`--include=<pattern>`	Do not exclude files that match the given pattern (used in conjunction with `--exclude`).
`-z`	Compress transferred data.
`-p`	Transfer file permissions. Implied by `-a`.
`-o`	Transfer file ownership (must be root). Implied by `-a`.
`-g`	Transfer file group membership. Implied by `-a`.
`-t`	Transfer file modification times. Implied by `-a`.

Make sure to read through the `rsync` man page for additional information on command use. The `include` and `exclude` options can be used to generate complex file selection rule-sets beyond simple wildcards. Also, if you want to run a dedicated `rsync` server rather than use an SSH, you can view a tutorial on the setup of an `rsync` daemon at `http://www.macosxhints.com/article.php?story=20021023063424701`.

File Synchronization with Perl: `psync`

A fast and easy-to-install alternative to `rsync` is `psync`, a Perl script based on the `MacOSX::File` module, which handles reading and writing data to and from the HFS+ filesystem. `psync` does not require any special server daemons to be running; it simply works across whatever local or remote volumes you have mounted on your system. The `psync` home page is located at `http://www.dan.co.jp/cases/macosx/psync.html`.

To install `psync`, all that is required is installation of the `MacOSX::File` module—`psync` is included. To install the module, use the same CPAN *(Comprehensive Perl Archive Network)* steps covered in Chapter 18, "Using the Perl and Python Scripting Languages."

First, invoke the interaction Perl CPAN shell:

```
brezup:jray jray $ sudo cpan

cpan shell -- CPAN exploration and modules installation (v1.70)
ReadLine support enabled
```

Next, use **`install MacOSX::File`** to download, compile, and install the required Perl module. (Note: You must have the current developer tools installed for this to be successful.)

```
cpan> install MacOSX::File

CPAN: Net::FTP loaded ok
Fetching with Net::FTP:
Scanning cache /Users/jray/.cpan/build for sizes
MacOSX-File-0.66
MacOSX-File-0.66/bin
MacOSX-File-0.66/bin/pcpmac
MacOSX-File-0.66/bin/pgetfinfo
```

```
...
MacOSX-File-0.66/t/spec.t

 CPAN.pm: Going to build D/DA/DANKOGAI/MacOSX-File-0.66.tar.gz

Checking if your kit is complete...
Looks good
Writing Makefile for MacOSX::File::Catalog
Writing Makefile for MacOSX::File::Copy
Writing Makefile for MacOSX::File::Info
Writing Makefile for MacOSX::File::Spec
Writing Makefile for MacOSX::File
...
Installing /usr/local/bin/pgetfinfo
Installing /usr/local/bin/pmvmac
Installing /usr/local/bin/psetfinfo
Installing /usr/local/bin/psync
Writing /Library/Perl/darwin/auto/MacOSX/File/.packlist
Appending installation info to /System/Library/Perl/darwin/perllocal.pod
 /usr/bin/make install -- OK
```

Using psync The psync syntax is `psync [options] <source> <destination>`. For example, to copy my `Sites` directory (`/Users/jray/Sites`) to `/Volume/backup`, I'd use `psync /Users/jray/Sites /Volumes/backup`. All file attributes are retained during the copy, including permissions and HFS+ resource forks.

```
brezup:jray jray $ sudo psync /Users/jray/Sites /Volumes/backup
Scanning Destination Directory /Volumes/backup ...
     0:.
65 items found.
Scanning Source Item /Users/jray/Sites ...
     0:..
178 items found.
    0 items to delete,
   68 items unchanged,
   117 items to copy.
copying items ...
+f /Users/jray/Sites/imagefolder/Classic Aqua Blue.jpg
+f /Users/jray/Sites/imagefolder/Classic Aqua Graphite.jpg
...
f /Users/jray/Sites/joestuff/feed.sql
+d /Users/jray/Sites/joestuff/files
+f /Users/jray/Sites/joestuff/files/1/left.htm
+f /Users/jray/Sites/webdav.key
fixing directory attributes ...
00777,jray,staff /Volumes/backup/joestuff/images
```

```
00777,jray,staff /Volumes/backup/joestuff/files/6
00777,jray,staff /Volumes/backup/joestuff/files/5
...
```

Subsequent executions of psync to synchronize the same directory do not result in any files being copied:

```
brezup:jray jray $ sudo psync /Users/jray/Sites /Volumes/backup
Scanning Destination Directory /Volumes/backup ...
     0:..
178 items found.
Scanning Source Item /Users/jray/Sites ...
     0:..
178 items found.
    0 items to delete,
   185 items unchanged,
    0 items to copy.
copying items ...
fixing directory attributes ...
```

psync can create incremental backups across Samba, NFS, and AppleTalk volumes in addition to other HFS volumes. If you're backing up to a remote filesystem, use the -r option to store permission information in the file .psync.db on the remote system. If psync finds a .psync.db file in the source volume, it uses the file to restore the permissions to the destination. Although -r is usually the only psync option you'll need, several more options that you might find somewhat useful are documented in Table 29.5.

TABLE 29.5 psync Options

Option	Description
-r	Remote backup/restore mode. Uses the .psync.db file for storing ownership and permission information for copied files.
-d	Delete files from the destination that no longer exist on the source.
-f	Force all files to be copied—even those that haven't changed.
-n	Run as a simulation, showing what would be copied or deleted, but do not carry out any of the actions.
-v<*1-3*>	Set the verbosity of the output (from 1 [the least] to 3 [the most]).
-q	Quiet—silence all output.

psync can be combined with a cron to create an effective (and free) incremental backup solution.

TIP

If you want to add a GUI front end to psync, psyncX can be downloaded from http://sourceforge.net/projects/psyncx/.

29

Creating and Restoring Disk Images: `hdiutil` and `asr`

Apple has built a useful backup and restore tool into Mac OS X, but, to date, its use is a bit confusing. Specially prepared disk images that are created from a volume or folder can be used to restore a drive to a known state. The images can even be hosted on web servers and restored from a remote server. Chapter 5, "Configuring Tiger Hardware Support and Preferences," discusses how Disk Utility can be used to create and restore images from the GUI. Because we're mentioning it here, you might guess that these actions can also be performed from the command line. You'd be right.

To create a disk image from the command line, you can use the tool `hdiutil`. `hdiutil` provides access to all operations that can be performed on disk images and has been mentioned throughout the book. For our purposes, we're interested in using the following syntax: `hdiutil create -format UDRO -srcfolder` *`<source directory> <destination disk image>`*. This will create a read-only disk image based on the source folder you specify. Be sure to save the image to a different directory or volume from what you are using as the source! For example, to create an image of my Tiger home directory, I could use this:

```
brezup:jray jray $ hdiutil create -format UDRO -srcfolder /Users/jray
➥/tmp/myhome.dmg
Initializing...
Creating...
Initialized /dev/rdisk1s2 as a 215 MB HFS Plus volume with a 8192k journal
Copying...
........................................................
```

After the image has been created it must be scanned to generate the appropriate checksum information to use with Apple Software Restore. To do this, we have to change gears and use the `asr` command-line interface utility with the syntax `asr -imagescan` *`<image to prepare>`*. For example:

```
brezup:jray jray $ asr -imagescan /tmp/myhome.dmg
Checksumming partition of size 62 blocks...done
Block checksum: ....10....20....30....40....50....60....70....80....90....100
asr: successfully scanned image "/tmp/myhome.dmg"
```

After `asr` has completed its run, the image file is ready for use as a restore image directly within the Disk Utility application or with the `asr` utility itself. To restore a disk image to a volume with `asr`, use the command `asr -source` *`<path or http URL to prepared restore image>`* `-target` *`<Path to target volume>`* `-erase`. This simple command will prepare the target volume to match the source image and will automatically bless any appropriate folders found on the source.

TIP

ASR can also be used to do simple volume to volume cloning like this: `sudo asr -source` *`<path to source volume>`* `-target` *`<path to destination volume>`* `-erase`.

Incremental Backups with `dump`/`restore`

For years, Unix systems have relied on the functionality of the `dump` and `restore` commands for performing tape backups. Although Tiger includes these utilities, they are of limited value unless you are using the UFS filesystem. Since the initial release of Mac OS X five years ago, we have covered these tools in *Mac OS X Unleashed* with the hope that they would eventually work well with HFS+ and tape drives. Unfortunately this has yet to happen, so, for now, we will be making the existing documentation available at `http://www.macosxunleashed.com/downloads/dumprestore.pdf`.

TIP

Even if you don't plan on using `dump` or `restore`, you might want to download this additional text for information about the planning process for incremental backups.

Monitoring Tiger System Operation

Beneath the shiny blue Aqua buttons and metallic skin of the Finder, there are dozens of processes and supporting subprocesses that manage your computer. If a problem that affects system operation occurs, chances are there is some sort of audit trail that can lead you to the culprit.

In this section, we will look at how you can monitor the inner workings of your operating system and computer—from developing a baseline for a properly functioning machine to viewing logs and customizing the configuration of the system logging daemon itself.

Creating an Overview of Your System: System Profiler

The Apple System Profiler (path: `/Applications/Utilities/System Profiler`) is a tool for browsing the hierarchy of components in your computer, connected to your computer, and installed on your computer. This information can be useful in developing a baseline profile that can be compared against a profile of a "sick" system.

To clarify, consider that most computers just "work"—or we'd be writing 28 chapters on system troubleshooting and 1 chapter on operation. After a user has configured a working system and is happy with how it operates, a *baseline* is developed. This baseline includes all the functional parameters for the machine: hardware configuration, software installations, and so forth. If the machine stops working correctly at sometime in the future, it is very likely that something has changed. A comparison of the original baseline to the current configuration can help determine *what* has changed and give the user an idea of what must be done to fix the problem. System Profiler can create and save full profiles of virtually every system setting in Tiger, giving you the flexibility to analyze working versus nonworking machines without relying on what a user might or might not have installed or changed on the system.

System Profiler collects information about your computer when initially launched. Information is divided into four major categories (labeled Contents): Hardware, Software,

Network, and Logs. The categories are listed in a pane on the left side of the window. In the initial display, Hardware is highlighted, providing an overview of your system hardware, as shown in Figure 29.8.

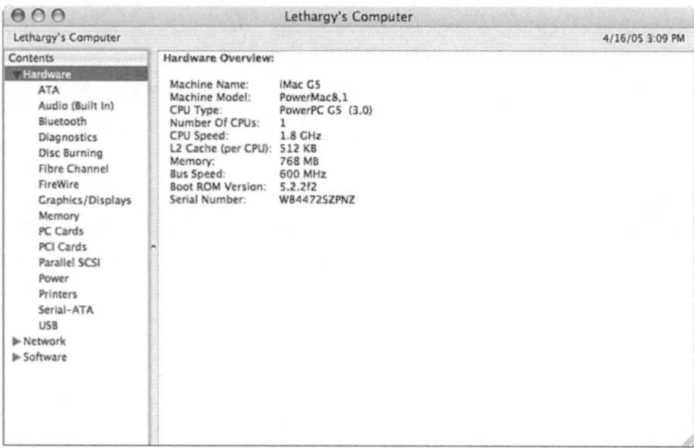

FIGURE 29.8 System Profiler collects and displays your system's hardware configuration.

Each of the categories can be expanded or collapsed by clicking the disclosure arrow in front of the topic. Disclosure arrows are used extensively throughout the application, so be sure to click around—you'll be surprised at the total amount of available information.

NOTE

The View menu offers the capability to switch between three levels of reported information (Mini, Basic, and Full). The information in this section assumes that Full (Command-3) has been selected.

Hardware

The Hardware category, displayed in Figure 29.8, contains a summary of the base computer. By expanding Hardware to show each of the subtopics, you can find everything from the serial and sales order number assigned when your machine was first built to the vendor IDs of devices plugged in to your USB bus.

For example, to see the internal disks and ATA *(Advanced Technology Attachment)* storage devices, click the ATA hardware category. The content area of the screen refreshes with a list of devices at the top and a detail view of the selected device at the bottom. Figure 29.9 shows an example of this screen.

If you're unfamiliar with the standard Macintosh bus types, this list might provide some insight:

- USB—*Universal Serial Bus.* In its initial implementation (version 1), USB is a slow (12Mbps) bus used for connecting external peripherals such as low-speed storage, scanners, printers, cameras, mice, and keyboards. USB 2.0, now included on new Macs, supports much faster speeds and can be much like FireWire.

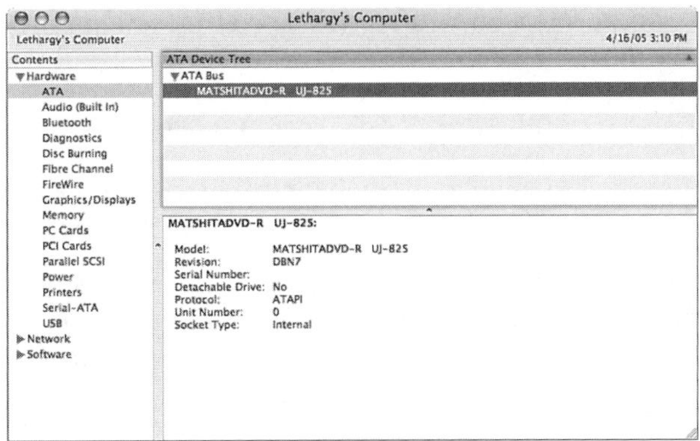

FIGURE 29.9 View details of a given piece of hardware.

- FireWire—An Apple-developed bus technology that supports speeds of 400Mbps and 800Mbps, hot-swappable devices such as high-speed storage, and digital-video cameras. The FireWire bus is also known by its IEEE name, *1394,* and as Sony's *iLink*.
- PCI—*Peripheral Component Interconnect*. The PCI bus was developed by Intel (yes, that Intel) and is the standard for connecting internal video cards, sound cards, and so on.
- ATA—*Integrated Drive Electronics*. The IDE standard was developed by Western Digital and is used for internal CD-ROM and disk storage.
- Parallel SCSI—*Small Computer System Interface.* A fast bus for high-speed storage devices, typically used on server-class computers.
- Serial ATA—The current high-speed ATA standard for drives shipped in new Apple computers. This is another PC standard that Apple has successfully adopted.

Software

Selecting the Software profile category displays information about your Tiger system configuration, including version, kernel, boot volume, and active user. You can use the three categories within Software to display extended information about installed components of the operating system.

- Applications—The Applications selection scans your drive to display all the installed applications (the BSD subsystem is not taken into account). You can view version, creator, and modification dates in the upper pane. Selecting an entry in the list displays details, including location, in the bottom pane.
- Extensions—Extensions, like frameworks, provide functionality to the operating system. Unlike frameworks, they work directly with the hardware to enable the operating system to access devices such as network cards, sound cards, and other components. Mac users are familiar with extensions. In Mac OS 8 and 9, extensions

had similar capabilities but often made the operating system unstable. In Mac OS X, the Classic extension is replaced by a `.kext` (kernel extension). These plug-ins for the Mach kernel cannot be installed by unprivileged users and are no longer appropriate for creating cool (but crash-causing) additions to the system.

- Fonts—Identifies the available fonts that are installed in your Tiger distribution, along with each font's full name, creator, and family/style information.
- Frameworks—A *framework* is a collection of shared object libraries. Instead of each application reimplementing code, the operating system can provide commonly used functions in the form of a shared library. There are dozens of frameworks in the base installation of Tiger—ranging from AppleShare to Speech Recognition.
- Logs—The Logs category enables you to view recent activity in a number of Tiger logfiles. This functionality is replicated in a number of locations, such as the Console utility (which you'll learn about shortly), so its inclusion here is a bit curious.
- Preference Panes—Displays the System Preference panes that are installed on your machine along with their visibility status.
- Startup Items—Provides an overview of all the Tiger StartupItems, the order in which they are started, and the services they provide.

Network

The Network category provides an overview of your installed network configurations, their interface IDs, and IP addresses (if any), as shown in Figure 29.10. Selecting a configuration displays additional information including MAC *(Media Access Control)* address and subnet mask in the lower details pane.

Within the network category are several subcategories for an even greater depth of information:

- AirPort Card—Provides specific information about any AirPort (original or extreme) hardware that is installed.
- Firewall—Provides a view of the `ipfw` firewall status and rulesets.
- Locations—Lists any defined network locations and the parameters for their use.
- Modems—Displays information about any built-in modem, the standards it uses, and basic manufacturer/driver information.
- Volumes—Identifies active network volumes and the protocols they are using.

Exporting System Profiler Information

When diagnosing a system problem, it is often useful to have all the configuration information with you. If you aren't sitting in front of the problem computer or need someone else to diagnose a problem remotely, you'll have to get information out of System Profiler and into another machine.

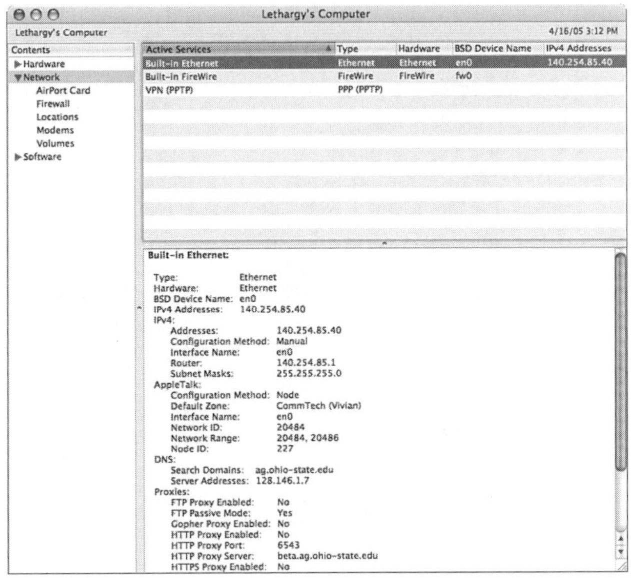

FIGURE 29.10 The Network category gives you a quick overview of your network status.

To do this, use File, Save As to save in either plain text, RTF, or XML formats. The advantage of an XML-based System Profiler document is that it can be opened on another Tiger system and viewed as if it were the local computer.

> **NOTE**
>
> Tiger's System Profiler adds an option under the File menu for sending the contents of a profile to Apple. There should never be a need to do this unless you're requesting computer support from Apple.

Running System Profiler from the Command Line

In the event that you need to perform a remote diagnosis, System Profiler can even be run from the command line with `system_profiler`. For example, to generate a mini report (rather than a basic report or a full report), I could use `system_profiler -detailLevel mini`:

```
brezup:jray jray $ system_profiler -detailLevel mini
Hardware:

    Hardware Overview:

      Machine Name: Power Mac G4 Cube
      Machine Model: PowerMac5,1
      CPU Type: PowerPC G4  (2.9)
      Number Of CPUs: 1
```

```
        CPU Speed: 500 MHz
        L2 Cache (per CPU): 1 MB
        Memory: 768 MB
        Bus Speed: 100 MHz
        Boot ROM Version: 4.1.9f1
...
```

Likewise I could use the `basic` or `full` keyword to generate more verbose output.

To limit the display to a certain type of data, the `-listDataTypes` option can be useful. This option lists all the types of information that can be displayed, which, in turn can be specified on the command line as an option to `software_update`. For example, `SPNetworkDataType` is a known data type that displays network information:

```
brezup:jray jray $ system_profiler SPNetworkDataType
Network:

    Internal Modem:

        Type: PPP (PPPSerial)
        Hardware: Modem
        BSD Device Name: modem
        Has IP Assigned: No
        IPv4:
            Configuration Method: PPP
        IPv6:
            Configuration Method: Automatic
        Proxies:
            Proxy Configuration Method: Manual
            ExcludeSimpleHostnames: 0
            FTP Passive Mode: Yes
            Auto Discovery Enabled: No
...
```

Finally, you can also export the System Profiler data directly into an XML file compatible with the GUI application by using the `-xml` option and redirecting the output to a file with the extension `.spx`:

```
brezup:jray jray $ system_profiler -xml -detailLevel full > systemreport.spx
```

A summary of the `system_profiler` options and their use is provided in Table 29.6.

TABLE 29.6 System Profiler Can Be Easily Controlled from the Command Line

Option	Description
`-listDataTypes`	List all the available data types for the purpose of limiting information.
`<data type> ... <data type> ...`	When data types are specified on the command line, the report output is constrained to those elements.

TABLE 29.6 Continued

Option	Description
`-xml`	Output the results in a System Profiler–compatible XML file. (The `.spx` extension must be used.)
`-detailLevel [`*`mini`*`¦`*`basic`*`¦`*`full`*`]`	Choose the level of detail in the output report.

Understanding Tiger Logfiles and Apple System Logger

Almost every server process on your computer generates a logfile. What is logged, and when, is up to the software writing to the log. A centralized process, called *`syslogd`*, manages the incoming log data from other applications and directs it to the system console, files, or remote `syslogd` servers. In previous versions of Mac OS X, `syslogd` was directly based on the BSD version of the server. In Tiger, `syslogd` is now known as the *Apple System Logger (ASL)* and provides support for many additional features that, unfortunately, aren't well documented at this time.

Many applications send data to `syslog`, some to `syslog` *and* local logfiles, others only to local files. Apple's goal in introducing ASL is to provide a better logging facility that can be used by Unix applications as well as native Mac OS X programs. We're still a long way from keeping everything in one place. Our first priority will be to get you familiarized with the primary Tiger logfiles as they are initially configured on your computer.

Tiger, like other Unix systems, uses `/var/log/` as its primary repository for logfiles. Apple has also chosen to create `/Library/Logs`, and `~/Library/Logs` for a handful of other Apple-specific logfiles and `/Library/Receipts` for logs of installed software.

NOTE

Logfiles, by their nature, log things. In doing so, they use up drive space. It is common practice to use a separate partition for `/var/logs` (or reconfigure system processes to log to a different drive) so that an attacker can't fill up a volume with logfile entries, thus disrupting processes that are attempting to store critical data on the same drive.

So, what *is* stored on your system? Table 29.7 lists the common default Tiger logfiles, their location, and what they contain.

29

TABLE 29.7 Tiger Default Log Locations

Logfile	Description
`/var/log/asl.log`	Apple's new ASL system log location in Tiger. This is almost identical to `/var/log/system.log` but uses a new, more readable format for storing information.
`/var/log/cups`	The cups directory contains `access_log`, `error_log`, and `page_log`–providing information on access to the CUPS web interface, errors encountered by the CUPS process, and a print job log, respectively.

TABLE 29.7 Continued

Logfile	Description
`/var/log/crashreporter.log`	Identifies application crashes and the location where crash information was saved.
`/var/log/fax`	This directory contains logs of the Tiger fax system usage.
`/var/log/ftp.log`	Logs login/logout information from the Tiger FTP server `lukemftpd`.
`/var/log/httpd`	The `httpd` directory contains a web server `access_log` with each Apache request, and an `error_log` containing errors reported by the server process.
`/var/log/ipfw.log`	A log of firewall activity. This log will only accumulate data when your firewall is active.
`/var/log/lastlog`	Similar to `/var/log/wtmp`; this log identifies the last time a user logged in (binary logfile).
`/var/log/lookupd.log`	Historically, the location for errors from the `lookupd` process. `lookupd`, however, does not use this file in Tiger, and it should remain empty (unless configured otherwise in NetInfo) on your system. Instead, `lookupd` logs to `syslog`, which places `lookupd` messages in `/var/log/netinfo.log`.
`/var/log/lpr.log`	Logs print requests made via `lpr`.
`/var/log/mail.log`	Contains Postfix errors and message delivery logs.
`/var/log/netinfo.log`	Includes messages logged from the `netinfod`—the central repository for `user/group/host` information on your computer. Also contains error messages logged by `lookupd`.
`/var/log/samba`	The `samba` log directory contains the `log.smbd` and `log.nmbd` files, which contain access and error messages from the Samba file server, and the Samba NetBIOS name server, respectively.
`/var/log/secure.log`	Logs authorization failures, such as failed FTP logins.
`/var/log/system.log`	Contains operating system notices, authorization failures, errors, and other logging goodness get stored in the main Mac OS X `system.log`. This logfile might be phased out in favor of `/var/log/asl.log` in Tiger.
`/Library/Logs/DirectoryService`	The Apple Directory service logs (`DirectoryService.server.log` and `DirectoryService.error.log`) log messages and errors related to Apple's directory service architecture—BSD files, NetInfo, LDAP, and so on.
`/Library/Logs/CrashReporter`	Consists of detailed logs containing application-specific crash information for use in troubleshooting software instability.

TABLE 29.7 Continued

Logfile	Description
/Library/Logs/AppleFileService	AppleFileServiceAccess.log and AppleFileServiceError.log record logins and errors in the built-in AppleShare server. The access log is not enabled by default.
/Library/Logs/Software Update.log	Logs all automatic updates performed via the Software Update preference panel.
/var/log/wtmp	Contains a history of user logins/logouts and system restarts. This is a binary logfile and is viewable with the last and ac commands.
/var/log/windowserver.log	Stores information related to the operation of the windowserver process that manages the GUI.
/var/run/utmp	Stores the currently logged-in users.

Looking at this list, you might be wondering, "Why are logs for multiple services showing up in a single logfile?" or "Why are multiple logfiles used for a single service?"

Remember that many processes log their output via a centralized process called `syslog`. Messages that are sent to `syslog` can be stored in multiple locations and directed to different logfiles depending on their *level*—a 32-bit value that contains an encoded facility and level. As you add new Unix software to your computer, you'll find that many applications *can* and *do* log via `syslog`—and the only real way to know *what* is going *where* is to understand how `syslog` works, and how you can configure it, which we'll cover in the next section.

WHY ARE THERE LOGFILES WITH THE EXTENSION .#.GZ AND NO RECORDS OLDER THAN A WEEK?

Many of the Tiger logfiles are rotated on a daily, weekly, or monthly basis by the files `/etc/daily`, `/etc/weekly`, and `/etc/monthly`, respectively. To view the contents of a file that has been rotated out of use, you need to unzip it (`gunzip <filename>`) first.

In some cases, you might want to disable the rotation altogether or change it so that it operates at a different interval. You can do this by either commenting out or simply moving the appropriate portions of the daily, weekly, and monthly files. This code (in `/etc/daily`), for example, rotates the `/var/log/system.log` files:

```
cd /var/log
for i in system.log; do
    if [ -f "${i}" ]; then
        printf %s " ${i}"
        if [ -x /usr/bin/gzip ]; then gzext=".gz"; else gzext=""; fi
        if [ -f "${i}.6${gzext}" ];
           then mv -f "${i}.6${gzext}" "${i}.7${gzext}"; fi
        if [ -f "${i}.5${gzext}" ];
           then mv -f "${i}.5${gzext}" "${i}.6${gzext}"; fi
        if [ -f "${i}.4${gzext}" ];
```

```
                then mv -f "${i}.4${gzext}" "${i}.5${gzext}"; fi
            if [ -f "${i}.3${gzext}" ];
                then mv -f "${i}.3${gzext}" "${i}.4${gzext}"; fi
            if [ -f "${i}.2${gzext}" ];
                then mv -f "${i}.2${gzext}" "${i}.3${gzext}"; fi
            if [ -f "${i}.1${gzext}" ];
                then mv -f "${i}.1${gzext}" "${i}.2${gzext}"; fi
            if [ -f "${i}.0${gzext}" ];
                then mv -f "${i}.0${gzext}" "${i}.1${gzext}"; fi
            if [ -f "${i}" ]; then
                    touch "${i}.$$" && chmod 640 "${i}.$$" &&
                            chown root:admin "${i}.$$"
                    mv -f "${i}" "${i}.0" && mv "${i}.$$" "${i}" &&
                    if [ -x /usr/bin/gzip ]; then
                      gzip -9 "${i}.0"; fi
            fi
        fi
done
```

To change the rotation, simply move these lines to a script that is executed at a different interval or comment them out.

Using `syslogd`

The ASL daemon can be a bit confusing for users coming from other platforms or migrating from earlier versions of the Macintosh. The first point to understand is that `syslogd` is *not* generating the messages that are showing up in your logfiles. It provides a logging system that other software can take advantage of, rather than that software having to write its own files—similar to the Event Viewer in Microsoft Windows. ASL can redirect incoming log information to remote `syslogd` servers, the console, logged-in users, and, of course, files—providing far more flexibility to developers than if each had to develop logging functions independently. The second point is that `syslogd`-generated files are often configured to be "message-centric" rather than "application-centric," meaning that logs contain a similar type of message (failed logins, perhaps) from multiple different daemons, rather than multiple messages from a single daemon.

NOTE

In centralizing the system's logging, ASL also presents a single point for disrupting critical log messages for attackers. As you'll see shortly, `syslog` could easily be configured to dump high-level messages to `/dev/null`.

Understanding Facilities and Levels

To configure syslogd, you first need to understand the vocabulary of the logging system. There are four terms used by syslog, its documentation, and our discussion that you must understand before proceeding:

- Facility—An identifier for the portion of the system that is sending the log entry to syslog, such as the kernel, mail, or FTP processes.
- Level—A ranking of the importance of the incoming log message, from simply informational notifications to emergency warnings.
- Selector—A combination of one or more facilities and levels that are matched against log messages coming into syslog. If the selector matches the level and facility of the message, syslog executes an action.
- Action—A syslog action determines what happens to an incoming log message if it matches a selector in the configuration file. Actions can write to files and devices, forward the messages to remote log servers, and notify logged-in users.

Levels and facilities are *not* arbitrary values that the user determines; the syslog daemon defines them. Table 29.8 provides the documentation for the available facilities as found in man 3 syslog.

TABLE 29.8 Syslog Logging Facilities

User-Level Name	Direct Name	Logging Purpose
kern	LOG_KERN	Kernel messages
user	LOG_USER	User-level messages
mail	LOG_MAIL	Mail system
daemon	LOG_DAEMON	System daemons
auth	LOG_AUTH	Security/authorization messages
syslog	LOG_SYSLOG	Internal syslog messages
lpr	LOG_LPR	Line printer subsystem
news	LOG_NEWS	Network news subsystem
uucp	LOG_UUCP	UUCP subsystem
cron	LOG_CRON	Clock daemon
authpriv	LOG_AUTHPRIV	Security/authorization messages (private)
ftp	LOG_FTP	FTP daemon
netinfo	LOG_NETINFO	NetInfo daemon
remoteauth	LOG_REMOTEAUTH	Remote authentication/authorization
mark	LOG_MARK	Logs an info message every 20 minutes

What facility a program uses to log is determined not by syslogd but by the application itself. You should check the documentation of your software to determine what facilities are used, and how to change them if you want to do so.

Note that there are *user-level* facility names and *direct* facility names. You'll use the short user-level names when configuring syslogd actions for each facility, but will likely need to use the direct name (which maps to an internal constant) when configuring which facility individual daemons are logging to.

Like there are different facilities, there are also a number of predefined levels that can be sent to `syslogd` with a log message. Levels indicate the nature of the incoming message, and are found in `man 3 syslog`. Table 29.9 documents the `syslogd` levels ranked from most to least serious.

TABLE 29.9 `Syslogd` Levels

User-Level Name	Direct Name	Level Meaning
`emerg` or `panic`	`LOG_EMERG`	System is unusable
`alert`	`LOG_ALERT`	Action must be taken immediately
`crit`	`LOG_CRIT`	Critical conditions
`err` or `error`	`LOG_ERR`	Error conditions
`warn` or `warning`	`LOG_WARNING`	Warning conditions
`notice`	`LOG_NOTICE`	Normal but significant condition
`info`	`LOG_INFO`	Informational
`debug`	`LOG_DEBUG`	Debug-level messages
`none`	`INTERN_NOPRI`	No priority

Fine-tuning `/etc/syslog.conf`

The `syslogd` process is configured via `/etc/syslog.conf`—a simple text file that matches selectors (facilities and levels) with an action to perform.

A selector is written as `<facility>.<level>`, where the values are taken from Tables 29.8 and 29.9. An asterisk (`*`) can be substituted for the facility and/or level to match any facility (except `mark`) or level.

> **NOTE**
>
> The level in a selector is the *base* level for a match. All levels equal to (or greater than) the base level are matched.

Actions are can consist of any of the following:

- A path to a logfile (for example, `/var/log/ftp.log`)
- A remote syslog server specified with the syntax `@<hostname or ip>` (for example, @192.168.0.100)
- A device (for example, `/dev/console`)
- A comma-separated list of usernames (for notifying users logged in via terminal sessions) or an asterisk (`*`) to notify everyone

For example, to log all messages logged to the `ftp` facility at the level of `error` or higher to the file `/var/log/ftperror.log`, you would use a line like this:

```
ftp.error                                   /var/log/ftperror.log
```

CAUTION

The selector and action must be separated by a *tab*. If spaces are used, the entry will not work.

If you want multiple selectors to log to the same file, you can use multiple `/etc/syslogd.conf` lines, or add multiple selectors to a single line by separating them with semicolons. For example, to log *all* authentication information to the console, you could write:

```
authpriv.*;remoteauth.*              /dev/console
```

The asterisk can also be applied to the facility in a selector to select *all* facilities at a particular level. This can be combined with the `none` level to exclude certain facilities from the selector. For example, you could use the following line to log all errors *except* those coming from the mail facility:

```
*.err;mail.none                 /var/log/allerrorsexceptmail.log
```

A final shortcut is to write multiple facilities that share the same selector as a comma-separated list with only the last facility also containing a level, such as `ftp,mail,netinfo.error`, which is the same as writing `ftp.error;mail.error;netinfo.error`.

The default Tiger `syslogd.conf` file should look very similar to this:

```
*.err;kern.*;auth.notice;authpriv,remoteauth.none;mail.crit
➥/dev/console
*.notice;*.info;authpriv,remoteauth,ftp.none;kern.debug;mail.crit
➥/var/log/system.log

# Send messages normally sent to the console also to the serial port.
# To stop messages from being sent out the serial port, comment out this line.
#*.err;kern.*;auth.notice;authpriv,remoteauth.none;mail.crit /dev/tty.serial

# The authpriv log file should be restricted access; these
# messages shouldn't go to terminals or publicly-readable
# files.
authpriv.*;remoteauth.crit                          /var/log/secure.log

lpr.info                                            /var/log/lpr.log
mail.*                                              /var/log/mail.log
ftp.*                                               /var/log/ftp.log
```

```
netinfo.err                                          /var/log/netinfo.log
install.*                                            /var/log/install.log
local0.*                                             /var/log/ipfw.log
*.emerg                                              *
```

As you can see, many of the logfiles mentioned earlier are created via `syslog`, and the `system.log` file and `console` contain selectors that will capture messages from all available facilities. This causes in some of the redundancy you might see when viewing the logs.

NOTE

Any changes to `/etc/syslogd.conf` can be put into effect immediately by sending the `-HUP` signal to the `syslogd` process (`killall -HUP syslogd`).

TIP

Apple does *not* include the output of TCP Wrappers in any of the default logs. If you use TCP Wrappers (which logs to the `syslog` facility), you might consider adding this line to `/etc/syslog.conf`:

```
syslog.err                                 /var/log/secure.log
```

Creating a Network `syslogd` Server

Creating a centralized network ASL server can help get you keep an eye on all your systems without having to directly watch dozens of different machines and files. To do this you must add either `-udp_in 1` or `-u` as an argument to `syslogd`.

This change has to be added directly to the file where `syslogd` is invoked. In the case of Tiger, this is `/System/Library/LaunchDaemons/com.apple.syslogd.plist`. The line

```
<string>/usr/sbin/syslogd</string>
```

should be modified to read

```
<string>/usr/sbin/syslogd -udp_in 1</string>
```

Client machines can now be configured to send `syslog` messages to the centralized server. The default Tiger `/etc/syslog.conf` could be rewritten to send its logs to a log server at `192.168.0.100` like this:

```
*.err;kern.*;auth.notice;authpriv,remoteauth.none;mail.crit
➥/dev/console
*.notice;*.info;authpriv,remoteauth,ftp.none;kern.debug;mail.crit
➥@192.168.0.100

# Send messages normally sent to the console also to the serial port.
# To stop messages from being sent out the serial port, comment out this line.
```

```
#*.err;kern.*;auth.notice;authpriv,remoteauth.none;mail.crit
➥/dev/tty.serial

# The authpriv log file should be restricted access; these
# messages shouldn't go to terminals or publicly-readable
# files.
authpriv.*;remoteauth.crit                      @192.168.0.100

lpr.info                                        @192.168.0.100
mail.*                                          @192.168.0.100
ftp.*                                           @192.168.0.100
netinfo.err                                     @192.168.0.100
install.*                                       @192.168.0.100
local0.*                                        @192.168.0.100

*.emerg                                     *
```

Thankfully, `syslog`-written logs contain the hostname of the machine generating the message. Logs follow the format:

<time stamp> <host generating message> <process name> <log message>

This enables an administrator to quickly `grep` through the contents of a combined logfile for a specific machine's messages.

Whether you choose to create a centralized server for a network for simply monitor the activity on your personal computer, a knowledge of `syslogd` will help make it easier.

NOTE

Unfortunately, knowing how to use `syslogd` isn't going to help you read and analyze your logs. The messages that are written to the logging daemon are arbitrary; they're determined by the program that sends them. The facility and level are also arbitrary, which can lead to log messages that you don't necessarily feel are appropriately classified, but the author did.

29

Monitoring Console and Log Output: Console

The Tiger GUI hides a tremendous amount of operation information from the user. You've seen that this information is often sent to a number of logfiles. In some cases, however, it is not stored in a file, but sent to a device called the *console* (`/dev/console`). On some Unix systems, the console actually *is* a separate device, such as a VT100 terminal display. On Mac OS X, it exists as a virtual device and is responsible for reporting information as it arrives.

The Console application (path: `/Applications/Utilities/Console`) enables you to watch console-directed error and status messages as they appear. If your computer appears to be stalled or is acting in an unusual manner, Console might be producing information that can help debug the problem. Figure 29.11 shows the Console application.

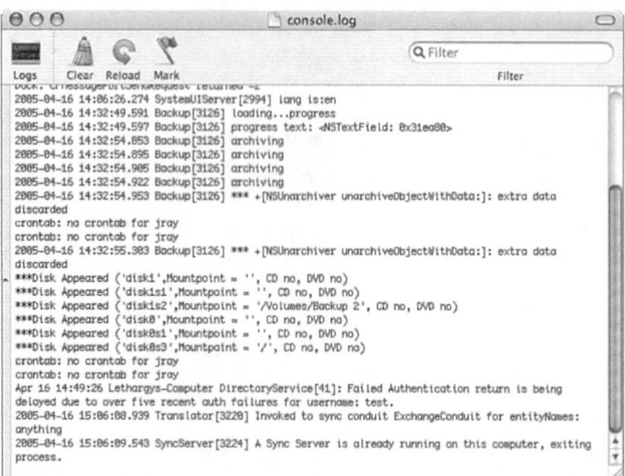

FIGURE 29.11 The Console application shows internal system error and status messages as they appear.

Even on a properly working Tiger system, Console displays error and warning messages related to day-to-day application use. This shouldn't be taken as an indication of a problem, but rather as a demonstration of how closely you can trace your system's operation.

Managing the Log View

To filter the Log view, use the filter field in the upper-right corner to enter a string that each line must match to be displayed. For example, to display information from the Safari web browser, you would type **`Safari`**.

To clear the filter, either remove the string or click the X icon at the end of the field.

You can also use the toolbar icons to mark the log, which enters a time stamp into the log display, or to clear the display entirely. This does *not* modify the actual logfiles, just the information display. To reload the full log at any time, click the Reload button, or use File, Reload (Command-R).

> **TIP**
>
> Additional functions (such as a full Find pane) can be added to the toolbar using View, Customize Toolbar.

Viewing Other Logfiles

The Tiger system maintains a great deal of log information in addition to what is sent directly to the console. Logs are stored in three key locations: your home directory (`~/Library/Logs`), the system log directory (`/Library/Logs`), and the BSD log directory (`/var/log`).

The Console application can display the contents of any of the logfiles we've discussed in this chapter (or any other). To view an arbitrary logfile, choose File, Open from the menu, and then drill down through the filesystem until you locate the file you want.

An alternative way to locate logfiles is to click the Logs button in the toolbar or choose View, Show Log List from the menu. This opens a pane on the left side of the window with lists of logs in each of the three primary locations, as shown in Figure 29.12.

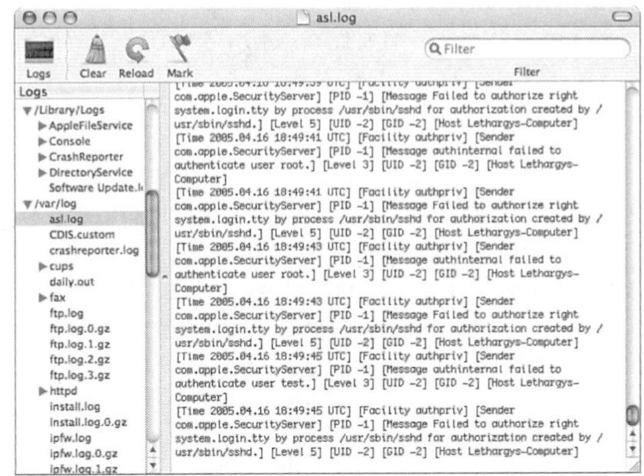

FIGURE 29.12 Browse other logs on your system.

Use the disclosure arrows to browse to the logfile that you want to view, and then select its name to display the file's contents. You can also choose File, Open Quickly to select one of the recognized logfiles for display.

> **TIP**
>
> If you choose a zipped (`.gz`) logfile, the Console application will automatically decompress it for viewing.

To save a copy of the entire log you are viewing, or a portion of it, choose File, Save a Copy As or File, Save Selection As (Option-Command-S), respectively.

Getting Notified When a Log Changes

Use the Console application preferences to set how (and if) you will be notified when a logfile window changes. Click Bounce Icon When Log Is Updated to cause the Dock icon to bounce when there are incoming messages.

If you'd prefer to immediately view the log itself, clicking the Bring Updated Log Window to Front check box causes the application to appear and display the new information. The Send Back slider is used to set the length of the delay before the Console application hides itself.

> **TIP**
>
> The new Tiger ASL utility `syslog` can also be used for viewing as well as managing log files. `syslog` provides direct access to the ASL logs and can watch (`-w`), filter (`-k`), or even clean out (`-p`) the logs.

Built-in Diagnostic and Repair Tools

With a complex operating system like Tiger, things can sometimes go wrong, and the user is left with little recourse for solving the problem. Thankfully, operations such as repairing damaged operating system installations, resetting the root password, and fixing damaged disks can all be performed even if your machine is not properly booting into the operating system.

Verbose Boot

Mac OS 8 and 9, although they hid much of the system operation from the user, gave a clearer picture of what was going on during a system boot. When Tiger starts, dozens of support processes and drivers are loaded at the same time. If something fails, it is left to the imagination of the user to guess exactly what has gone wrong. In many cases, a user might not even be aware that there are problems with the system configuration because the boot process hides behind a simple GUI startup screen.

To view exactly what is happening as the system boots, you can hold down Command-V at power-on to force a verbose startup. The verbose boot displays all status and error messages while the computer starts. This can be a bit startling to many Mac users because instead of the usual blue or gray background present during startup, the screen will be black and filled with text. Windows and Linux users will feel right at home.

The verbose startup messages are similar to those contained in `/var/log/system.log`. For example:

```
Jun 29 17:30:30 localhost mach_kernel: .Display_RADEON: i2cPower 1
Jun 29 17:30:30 localhost mach_kernel: .Display_RADEON:
➥user ranges num:1 start:9c008000 size:640080
Jun 29 17:30:30 localhost mach_kernel: .Display_RADEON:
➥using (1600x1024@0Hz,32 bpp)
Jun 29 17:30:30 localhost mach_kernel: AirPortDriver:
➥Ethernet address 00:30:65:11:37:15
Jun 29 17:30:30 localhost mach_kernel: ether_ifattach called for en
Jun 29 17:30:30 localhost mach_kernel: kmod_create:
➥com.apple.nke.ppp (id 58), 6 pages loaded at 0xc20, header size 0x1000
Jun 29 17:30:30 localhost mach_kernel: kmod_create:
➥ com.apple.nke.SharedIP (id 59), 5 pages loaded at 0x0, header size 0x0
Jun 29 17:30:30 localhost mach_kernel: kmod_create:
➥IPFirewall (id 60), 5 pages loaded at 0xc292000, header size 0x1000
Jun 29 17:30:30 localhost mach_kernel: ipfw_load
Jun 29 17:30:30 localhost mach_kernel:
➥IP packet filtering initialized, divert enabled, rule-based forwarding
➥enabled, default to accept, logging disabled
Jun 29 17:30:31 localhost sharity[161]: [0] Sharity daemon version 2.4 started
Jun 29 17:30:39 localhost ntpdate[204]:
➥ntpdate 4.0.95 Sat Feb 17 02:38:39 PST 2001 (1)
Jun 29 17:30:43 localhost ntpdate[204]:
```

```
➥no server suitable for synchronization found
Jun 29 17:30:43 localhost ntpd[206]:
➥ntpd 4.0.95 Thu Apr 26 13:40:11 PDT 2001 (1)
Jun 29 17:30:43 localhost ntpd[206]: precision = 7 usec
Jun 29 17:30:43 localhost ntpd[206]:
➥frequency initialized 0.000 from /var/run/ntp.drift
Jun 29 17:30:43 localhost ntpd[206]: server 128.146.1.7 minpoll 12 maxpoll 17
```

This small sample of the verbose output shows the Apple Radeon driver loading, followed by the AirPort software, Classic SharedIP driver, firewall, Sharity, and `ntp` *(network time protocol)* software.

Interestingly enough, in capturing this example, I ascertained what I had suspected for several weeks: The `ntpdate` utility, which is responsible for automatically contacting a remote time server for synchronization, has been failing:

```
Jun 29 17:30:39 localhost ntpdate[204]:
➥ntpdate 4.0.95 Sat Feb 17 02:38:39 PST 2001 (1)
Jun 29 17:30:43 localhost ntpdate[204]:
➥no server suitable for synchronization found
```

Similar feedback is provided for almost all the services on the computer, from low-level device drivers to Apache and Postfix. If your computer hangs during boot, you can use the Verbose startup mode to determine exactly where the sequence has gone amiss.

TIP

If you want to boot into Verbose mode at every startup, you can (as root) use the command `nvram boot-args="-v"` to set the boot arguments to always include the verbose boot flag. You can disable this by unsetting the flag with `nvram boot-args=""`.

TIP

You can use the `dmesg` command on a booted system to show the current contents of the system message buffer at any time, including error messages.

Getting Access to Your Drive on a Damaged System

The original Mac OS versions (7/8/9) allowed you to disable extensions by holding down the Shift key while booting your computer. This simplified the process of debugging by providing a way in to your computer so that you could figure out what software had been installed that was messing things up and then remove it.

Performing a Safe Boot

In Mac OS X, the "Classic" Extensions Off mode has been replaced with Safe Boot mode. In Safe Boot mode, only the components necessary to get your Mac booted and running are loaded. Additional software, even networking, is disabled.

When you're running in Safe Boot mode, you can manually remove any software you've added and perform most basic repair tasks from within the GUI. To start your computer in Safe Boot mode, hold down the Shift key while starting up, until the Tiger startup screen appears with the words `Safe Boot`. You can then release the Shift key and allow your Mac to finish booting.

NOTE

You might notice that startup takes longer than usual when in Safe Boot mode. This is because Safe Boot forces your Mac to run the disk check and repair processes on the system volume during startup.

Entering Single-User Mode

Another modification to the startup process is booting into Single-User mode. Holding down Command-S starts Tiger in Single-User mode, enabling an administrator to directly access the system through a command-line interface. This is a last-resort method of booting your computer that should be used only if absolutely necessary.

Single-User mode boots in a text-only fashion, just like the Verbose startup mode. The process finishes by dropping the user to a shell:

```
Singleuser boot -- fsck not done
Root device is mounted read-only
If you want to make modifications to files,
run '/sbin/fsck -yk' first and them '/sbin/mount -uw /'
localhost#
```

CAUTION

Be aware that the Single-User mode command prompt carries with it full root access. This is not a place for playing games or learning Unix.

Repairing Filesystems: `fsck`

Using the `fsck` command, you can repair local filesystems from the command line. To fix a damaged filesystem, type **`fsck -fy`** at the single-user prompt. This is equivalent to running the First Aid Disk Utility:

```
brezup:root jray # fsck -fy
** /dev/rdisk0s9
** Root file system
** Checking HFS Plus volume
** Checking Extents Overflow file.
** Checking Catalog file.
** Checking multi-linked files.
** Checking Catalog heirarchy.
** Checking volume bitmap.
```

```
** Checking volume information.
** The volume Shakey appears to be OK.
```

If an error occurs during this process, you might have to tell the system that it is okay to perform repairs. Table 29.10 lists additional command-line arguments for `fsck`.

TABLE 29.10 `fsck` Command-Line Options

Option	Purpose
`-d`	Debugging mode. Displays the commands that `fsck` will execute without actually carrying them out.
`-f`	Forces a check of the filesystems, even if they are considered clean.
`-l` *<max parallel processes>*	Sets the number of scans that `fsck` will run in parallel. Usually defaults to one scan per disk.
`-n`	Assumes that the answer to all interactive questions is no.
`-p`	Preens (cleans) the filesystems marked as dirty.
`-y`	Answers yes to all interactive questions.

TIP

If you just want to run a disk repair, the easiest way to do it is to start in Safe Boot mode, which forces a repair automatically.

Alternatively, you can boot from the Tiger installation disk and then choose Disk Utility from the Utilities menu. Chapter 4 discusses the use of Disk Utility for repairing volumes.

When booted into Single-User mode, the filesystem is mounted as read-only as a precaution. If you've installed a new daemon or script that is stalling the system at startup, it would be useful to be able to edit files from within single-user mode. To mount the filesystem with write permissions, use `/sbin/mount -uw /`.

Again, be aware that changes made while in Single-User mode are made as the root user.

TIP

Starting in Tiger, you can boot from the System Install CD and choose Terminal from the Utilities menu to have command-line interface access to volumes that might not be booting correctly.

Logging In to the Console

If your problem lies not with the boot process, but with logging in, you might want to try a standard boot followed by a non-GUI login. To do this, you must have username and password fields enabled in the login window. If you do, allow the system to boot to a standard login window; then type **`>console`** as your username and click the Login button.

Your screen goes black, and you see a prompt similar to

```
Darwin/BSD (brezup.poisontooth.com) (console)

login:
```

Type your username and password to log in and use the system via the console. Logging out of the console restarts the window manager and takes you back to a GUI login screen.

Mounting a Disk Using Target Disk Mode

A final option if your machine isn't booting at all is to use a second computer and attempt to access your drive through Target Disk mode. When a computer is placed into Target Disk mode, it can be connected via FireWire to another machine and will present its drive just like any other removable disk, enabling you to run repairs on the drive or at least copy critical information from the volume.

To start a computer in Target Disk mode, simply hold down the T key while turning on the machine. After a few seconds, a FireWire symbol will appear onscreen and the machine will be ready to be connected to another Macintosh computer for diagnostics, repair, or recovery.

Identifying Software Conflicts

When dealing with stalled startups, take the same approach as with extensions and control panels under Mac OS 8 and 9: Remove the last item to load before the system failure and then reboot.

Assuming that you haven't found what is crashing the machine in your `system.log` or by running a verbose boot, disable any new software that runs with root privileges or drivers for add-on devices. After you've gained access to your system (either through Safe Boot mode, Single User mode, or Console login), search the list of usual suspects to find newly installed files.

As you already know, both the `/Library/Startupitems` and `/System/Library/Startupitems` directories contain the services that are started at boot time. If software in your auto-launch Login Items list is causing the problem, it's stored in `~/Library/Preferences/loginwindow.plist`. `/Library/Components` and `/System/Library/Extensions` provide two more common hiding places for installed drivers and kernel extensions.

In addition, the `/etc/hostconfig` and `/private/var/db/SystemConfiguration/_preferences.xml` files hold information on your machine's network configuration and boot parameters. Although editing these files isn't a guaranteed cure for any problem, it's a good place to start.

Testing Kernel Extensions

If you suspect an extension is causing a problem but aren't sure, you can use the capability of Tiger to dynamically load and unload kernel extensions to test your hypothesis.

To list the currently loaded extensions, use the utility kextstat with the argument -k to hide kernel components (which you wouldn't want to touch):

```
brezup:jray jray $ kextstat -k
Index Refs Address    Size       Wired      Name (Version) <Linked Against>
   16   11 0x402000   0xa000     0x9000     com.apple.iokit.IOPCIFamily (1.6)
   17    0 0x40c000   0x8000     0x7000     com.apple.driver.AppleCore99PE
   18    1 0x854000   0x4000     0x3000     com.apple.driver.IOPlatformFunction
   20    0 0x49d000   0x7000     0x6000     com.apple.driver.AppleI2C (3.4.5d2)
   21    2 0x43f000   0x3d000    0x3c000    com.apple.iokit.IOHIDFamily (1.4)
   23    0 0x984000   0x3000     0x2000     com.apple.driver.AppleCore99NVRAM (1.1)
   24    0 0x918000   0x9000     0x8000     com.apple.driver.AppleMacRiscPCI
   25    1 0x84f000   0x5000     0x4000     com.apple.iokit.IOKeyLargo (1.6.0d4)
   26    0 0x858000   0x7000     0x6000     com.apple.driver.AppleKeyLargo
...
   79    1 0x594000   0x291000   0x290000   com.apple.NVDAResman (3.3.8) <78 76 16>
   80    0 0x9a6000   0x82000    0x81000    com.apple.nvidia.nv10hal (3.3.8)
   81    0 0x85f000   0x33000    0x32000    com.apple.GeForce (3.3.8) <79 78 76 16>
```

A normal system should have roughly 60–90 extensions loaded.

Each line contains the name of the extension and information about where it is loaded in memory. The fields you'll be most interested in are the Name field (such as com.apple.GeForce) and the Ref field. The Name field contains the name by which the system refers to the loaded extension and is what you will need to use to unload it. The Ref field contains the number of active references to that extension. If other components are using an extension, it cannot be unloaded. For example, the com.apple.NVDAResman extension has a reference count of 1, (which I happen to know is because it is being used by the com.apple.GeForce extension), so it cannot be unloaded without first unloading com.apple.GeForce.

Unloading an Extension: kextunload

To unload a kernel extension, you must be root (or use sudo) and issue the command **kextunload -b <*extension name*>**. For example, in the kextstat listing we looked at previously, to unload the com.apple.NVDAResman extension, you would type:

```
brezup:jray jray $ sudo kextunload -b com.apple.NVDAResman
unload id com.apple.NVDAResman failed (result code 0xe00002c2)
```

This is syntactically correct, but the unload failed because of the reference count. To unload the extension, you must first unload com.apple.GeForce and then com.apple.NVDAResman:

```
brezup:jray jray $ sudo kextunload -b com.apple.GeForce
unload id com.apple.GeForce succeeded (any personalities also unloaded)
brezup:jray jray $ sudo kextunload -b com.apple.NVDAResman
unload id com.apple.NVDAResman succeeded (any personalities also unloaded)
```

TIP

You can also unload a kernel extension based on its filesystem name by simply typing **kextunload** *<full path to extension>*.

Loading an Extension: `kextload`

Loading an extension is virtually identical to unloading but uses the command `kextload` instead: **kextload** *<path to extension>*. For example, to reload the GeForce extension, you would type

```
brezup:jray jray $ sudo kextload /System/Library/Extensions/GeForce.kext
kextload: /System/Library/Extensions/GeForce.kext loaded successfully
```

Reinstalling the Operating System

Most Windows users are familiar with the word *reinstall*. I've listened in on many support calls, only to hear the technician give up and tell the end user to reinstall. Unfortunately, Mac OS X users might find themselves doing the same thing. The difference, however, is that reinstalling Tiger does not replace your system accounts, information, or configuration.

I have found on numerous occasions that rerunning the Installer is the fastest and easiest way to return to a viable system. There are, however, a few drawbacks—most notably, the system updates are replaced by the original version of the operating system. After running the Tiger Installer to recover a damaged system, be sure to open the `/Library/Receipts` folder, throw away any receipt files stored by system updates, and then manually force a software update to reinstall the latest versions of system updates and other support software.

Another anomaly is that if you've moved or removed any of the system-installed applications, they will be restored during the install process.

Restoring the Administrator Password

If an administrator password is forgotten or misplaced, Apple has provided a facility for restoring a password. Boot your computer from the Tiger install media (hold down the C key while turning on your computer with the media in the CD-ROM/DVD drive). When the Installer application starts, choose Reset Password from the Utilities menu. Figure 29.13 shows the interface to the Password Reset facility.

Detected bootable volumes are listed along the top of the window. Click the main boot drive to load the password database for that volume.

Next, use the pop-up menu to choose the user account that you want to reset. Fill in the new password in both of the password fields provided. Finally, click Save to store the new password.

FIGURE 29.13 Use the boot media and Password Reset application to ease your forgetful head.

This really isn't useful for much beyond resetting the administrator password. As long as there is access to the administrator account from the command line, you can easily use `passwd <username>` to reset the named user's password:

```
brezup:jray jray % sudo passwd jackd
Changing password for jackd.
New password:
Retype new password:
```

TIP

It is not possible to recover a password that has been forgotten—it is only possible to reset it. Tiger passwords are encrypted and can only be decrypted using the user's own password. If you're setting up a large-scale network with dozens of accounts, it's a good idea to develop a default password policy. Several organizations that I've worked for base the user's passwords on a combination of their initials and the last four digits of the user's Social Security number. This enables the administrators to reset passwords to a safe default value that the user can remember.

Third-Party Disk and Virus Tools

Although Tiger provides a number of tools for recovering from system trouble, there are certain issues that the supplied tools cannot deal with. If you've been using a Mac for a few years and have ever run the Apple Disk Repair tools, you've almost certainly run across an instance of the repair process stating `Disk Repair cannot fix this problem.` The usual reaction (immediately following the "Oh, poop!") is, "Well, what can solve the problem?"

Likewise, when it comes to viruses, Tiger provides virtually no protection. Only members of .Mac get virus protection with their systems. The rest of us either take our chances or are forced to install additional software to get any level of protection.

Let's take a look at some of the disk and virus tools you might want to consider purchasing for your system.

Choosing Disk Repair Tools

Several commercial utilities are available that can aid you in keeping your system running smoothly and error free, and can repair problems should they occur. Even if you never experience a disk error, it's a good idea to keep one or two of these packages around:

- Drive 10 by Micromat Inc. (`http://www.micromat.com/`)—Offers extensive disk diagnostic utilities ranging from power supply tests and buffer validation to disk optimization. Unfortunately, it is lacking several of the more generalized system diagnostics of its big brother, TechTool Pro.
- TechTool Pro by Micromat Inc. (`http://www.micromat.com/`)—The undisputed king of diagnostics. It can locate problems with almost any hardware component, from memory to CPU failures. It also includes extensive drive repair and optimization facilities. A version of TechTool Pro is included as part of Apple's AppleCare package.
- DiskWarrior by Alsoft (`http://www.alsoft.com/DiskWarrior/index.html`)—An award-winning piece of software that takes a different approach to repairing disk problems. Rather than fixing damaged drive information, it rebuilds the data from scratch, often offering superior results to traditional utilities such as Norton Utilities.
- Virtual Lab by Binary Biz (`http://www.binarybiz.com/vlab/mac.php`)—The software you need if you've lost files from disk problems or carelessness. It is fast, thorough, and intuitive. You can even download a free trial capable of retrieving 1MB of data directly from its website. Its purpose is to *retrieve* data, not fix your drive, so make sure that this is what you need before you buy.
- Data Rescue X by Prosoft Engineering (`http://www.prosoftengineering.com/products/data_rescue.php`)—Another tool, like Virtual Lab, that provides data recovery features for damaged drives. Unlike Virtual Lab, Data Rescue's focus is on recovering from failing disks, not undeleting files. For that, the company has a separate product.
- Data Recycler by Prosoft Engineering (`http://www.prosoftengineering.com/products/data_recycler.php`)—Although not the only product capable of undeleting files on Mac OS X, it is currently the only one capable of doing it *well*. Data Recycler maintains separate storage for holding deleted files and offering safe recovery if you find yourself in an "oops" situation. Undeletes are virtually instantaneous and do not require scanning your drive.
- Norton Utilities by Symantec, Inc., (`http://www.symantec.com/product/index_macintosh.html`)—The oldest and best-known Macintosh repair software available. Norton Utilities focuses entirely on drive repair, optimization, and data loss prevention.

Protecting Against Viruses

If you're a sensible web surfer and download code from reputable sources (that is, NOT BitTorrent or shady Hotline/Carracho sites), there is currently little risk of getting a Macintosh virus. Of course, the Macintosh isn't impervious to viruses and eventually we will be hit hard. As such, it is important to have the tools on hand to detect and remove infected files if they are found. Because Tiger offers superb integration with Windows networks, you'll also want virus protection to help protect your Windows brethren from the latest and greatest Microsoft Office viruses. The Macintosh version of Office is quite capable of infecting files, which can subsequently cause harm if opened on the Windows platform.

Consider keeping a virus protection package installed and up-to-date on your system:

- Virex by McAfee by way of Apple (`http://www.mac.com/`)—As part of the .Mac membership, Apple offers an enhanced version of McAfee/NAI's Virex utility. Virex 7.5 provides virus protection for your Macintosh as well as any Windows files stored on it. Because Tiger offers superb integration with Windows networks, any user who shares files in a cross-platform environment will find this a valuable preventative tool. Virex provides command-line virus scanning capabilities in `/usr/local/vscanx`.

- Norton AntiVirus by Symantec, Inc., (`http://www.symantec.com/nav/nav_mac/index.html`)—Norton AntiVirus is an easy-to-use alternative to Virex that offers the same basic features in a cost-effective and user-friendly package. If you're accustomed to the Norton Utilities package, this might be the right virus solution for your system.

- clamXav, (`http://www.markallan.co.uk/clamXav/`)—In Chapter 26, "Creating a Mail Server," we discussed installing the open source ClamAV package for virus scanning. Mark Allan has taken this same software and wrapped it in an attractive GUI (pictured in Figure 29.14) that you can use to scan files and folders on your machine. clamXav is currently available free of charge, but a donation is appreciated.

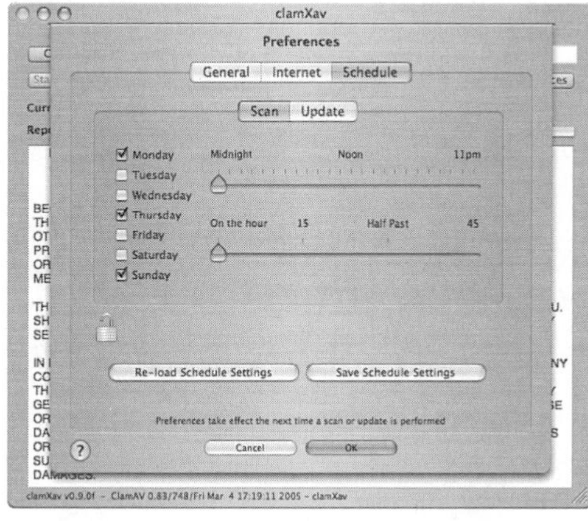

FIGURE 29.14 clamXav wraps the powerful free ClamAV package in an attractive (and free!) GUI.

Summary

Tiger provides many tools and logs to help you diagnose, correct, and prevent system problems. Third-party support has done a great job of filling in the holes left by Apple. This chapter demonstrated the use of Single-User and Verbose boot modes, introduced tools for backing up your system, and identified products that go beyond the capabilities of Disk Utility.

Eventually, Mac OS X will probably mature into a system that can be documented entirely without ever seeing a command line (unless you want to!). For now, we hope that this book provides a balanced view of what you can do through the GUI and via the command line. Best of luck!

Sincerely,

John Ray (`jray@macosxunleashed.com`)

Will Ray (`wray@macosxunleashed.com`)

Index

Symbols and Numbers

A

B

C

D

E

F

G

H

I

J - K

L

M

N

O

P

Q - R

S

T

U

V

W

X - Y - Z